(8/37/B1283)

(1931.)

£20

Theol

THE MESSIAH JESUS AND
JOHN THE BAPTIST

PRESUMED PORTRAIT OF FLAVIUS JOSEPHUS

FIRST CENTURY ROMAN MARBLE HEAD OF JEWISH TYPE, FOUND IN ROME, FORMERLY IN POSSESSION
OF THE PRINCELY FAMILY BORGHESE, NOW IN THE NY CARLSBERG GLYPTOTEK, COPENHAGEN
(SEE ALSO FRONT VIEW, PL. III)

THE MESSIAH JESUS
AND JOHN THE BAPTIST

ACCORDING TO

FLAVIUS JOSEPHUS'
RECENTLY REDISCOVERED
'CAPTURE OF JERUSALEM'
AND THE OTHER JEWISH AND CHRISTIAN SOURCES

BY

ROBERT EISLER, Ph.D.

WITH FORTY PLATES, INCLUDING REPRODUCTIONS OF THE INEDITED
RUSSIAN, RUMANIAN, AND HEBREW MSS. AND KINDRED DOCUMENTS

ENGLISH EDITION BY
ALEXANDER HAGGERTY KRAPPE, Ph.D.

METHUEN & CO. LTD.
36 ESSEX STREET W.C.
LONDON

First Published in 1931

PRINTED IN GREAT BRITAIN

TRANSLATOR'S PREFACE

THE book which is now presented for the first time in English dress is the outcome of six years' unceasing labour on the part of the author. A complete departure, in more ways than one, from the customary treatises on this extremely important and fascinating subject, it should interest wider circles of an English-speaking public than could easily read Dr. Eisler's German original. This is the explanation of this translation and at the same time its excuse.

The task itself was suggested to me by the author in the winter of 1928-9, which I had the pleasure of spending in Paris. As I had the double advantage of following Dr. Eisler's lecture course at the Sorbonne and of asking and receiving his counsel in places where the intricacy of his German constructions, or some note filled with more Hebrew lore than I could muster, seemed to require it, the translation advanced rapidly and was completed before the beginning of July.

It gives me pleasure, in concluding, to acknowledge the quite considerable assistance I derived from the late Dr. H. St. John Thackeray's new edition of the *Jewish War* (in the 'Loeb Classical Library'), and from the same author's rough draft of a translation into English of a large portion of the second volume of Dr. Eisler's German edition. I am equally obliged to the library authorities both of the Bibliothèque Nationale and the University of Paris, who have readily and generously granted me access to their treasures. Any one working, as I have been for years, under intolerable library conditions will grasp the true meaning of this appreciation.

To Dr. Eisler, finally, I would offer my hearty thanks for the trouble he has taken in going over both MS. and proofs. To him is due all the honour of the work, coupled, it is true, with the responsibility for the theories therein advanced.

A. H. K.

PARIS, *June* 1929

AUTHOR'S PREFACE

THE present work is fundamentally different in method, scope, and outlook from any 'Life of Christ' or any other book dealing with Christian origins, or any 'History of the Jewish People in the Time of Jesus,' that I know of. For it claims to show :—

First. That there once existed a rich fund of historical tradition about the Messiah Jesus both among the Jews and the non-Christian Greeks and Romans.

Second. That this precious material was deliberately destroyed, or falsified, by a system of rigid censorship officially authorized ever since the time of Constantine I. and reinstituted in the reigns of Theodosius II. and Valentinian III. (477 A.D.).

Third. That, in spite of the tireless efforts of ecclesiastical revisers, enough has been preserved in certain out-of-the-way corners of the world, among Jews and heretics as well as in quotations occurring in Christian polemic and apologetic literature, to allow us to reconstruct with sufficient clarity and plausibility, and even with a certain amount of picturesque detail, the fundamental features of Jesus' personality and his mission, particularly as they appeared to his enemies.

Fourth. That through a careful comparison of this mercilessly cold, detached, and unsympathetic pen-portrait of the man Jesus with the naïvely idealizing presentation of the *Kyrios Christos* by the writers of the early and later Christian Church, it is possible to come quite close to the historical truth about the Naṣōraean prophet-king and about his elder relative, the schismatic high priest of the Jews, Joḥanan 'the Hidden One,' better known as the Baptist.

It is thus my claim that a history of Christian origins—more exactly, of the Naṣōraean Messianist movement—can be written which will chronologically coincide with the history of the Jews and the Romans from 4 B.C. to A.D. 135—that is, from the first appearance of Joḥanan to the downfall of Bar-Kokhᵉba.

In face of the prevalent historical scepticism [1] and the Neo-Marcionite subjectivism of certain critics, who claim for themselves the right to disregard any evidence in the Gospels which conflicts with their own preconceived picture of Jesus,[2] the present work represents a radical departure. *For I claim no such right.* I refuse to reject from among the documentary materials this or that statement as 'unworthy' of Jesus' personality and his mission. On the contrary, I humbly and honestly accept whatever I find in the sources, duly weighing the evidence when there is conflict or contradiction, unless indeed the trustworthiness of a given source is disproved by facts quite independent of any judgment of values.

' As it is now,' said Max Müller, ' it is always open to us to say, whenever we read of anything that is incredible or unworthy of Christ, *as we conceive him*,[3] that it came from his disciples, who confessedly had often failed to understand him, or that it was added by those who handed down the tradition before it was written down.[4] . . . The true interests of the Christian religion are better served by showing how much time and how many opportunities there were for human misunderstandings to creep into the Gospel story.'

It seems to me that it is not the business of the historian, quite unconcerned as he is with questions of apologetics, to discredit, on what after all are apologetic grounds, sources fully as good or fully as bad as any ordinary source bearing on profane history. Everywhere tendencies can be detected to a certain extent and therefore must be discounted in a certain measure. The nature of the material being the same, the methods of utilizing it should logically be the same.

If one were timidly to disregard all sources which show a certain tendency one way or other, it would mean a negation of all history-writing; and if the maxim be adopted that the scientific accuracy

---

[1] The best example is the *Jesus* of Prof. Rudolf Bultmann, published in Berlin in 1925.

[2] Few modern authors will admit this as frankly as honest Max Müller in his time, who said (*Chips from a German Workshop : On the Proper Use of Holy Scriptures*), after praising as a blessing the fact that Jesus left no written record of his teaching : ' Because, whenever the spirit of truth within us protests against certain statements in the Gospels as unworthy of the high character of the founders of this religion, we can claim the same liberty which even the ancients claimed with regard to the fables told of their gods, namely, that nothing could be true that was unworthy of the gods.'　　　　　[3] Italics mine.

[4] This is—*avant la lettre*—the whole of the new ' formgeschichtliche Methode ' !

of a historian's work is in direct proportion to the depth of his scepticism, we should inevitably end with the neo-Pyrrhonist doctrine that we cannot know anything at all about the past of humanity.

I am fully aware of the fact that every single bit of evidence presented in the following pages can be frittered away and made to crumble into dust by the simple application of certain widely practised methods of criticism and exegesis. Let me say that I am not at all ignorant of these methods. Alas! I have tried again and again these two-edged, over-sharpened tools, only to find them ineffective in the end. Any student who, through sheer inability to synthetize the mass of his evidence, prefers to carry analysis to the length of hair-splitting, and who will go on for ever weighing undecidedly all the possibilities that might come under consideration, will be thoroughly antagonized by the present book, without presumably deriving much profit from it. That I cannot help. I have been working and writing for those who are as convinced as I am myself that no explanation of a single fact is satisfactory which cannot be made to fit into some plausible consecutive scheme enabling us to account for the totality of facts and phenomena—for those who feel that we cannot go on for ever with our traditional histories of New Testament times, into which a life of Jesus cannot be made to fit, and with lives and characteristics of Jesus which cannot be made to fit into the contemporary history of Jews and Romans. To those readers I hope that the new sources, analysed and utilized in this volume, will come as a relief and a genuine intellectual satisfaction.

I sincerely believe that nothing in this book can possibly give offence to a true Christian—that is, a true believer in the deeply rooted messianic hopes of humanity. Yet it may cause somewhat of a startling shock to those whom Bernard Shaw has pertinently called Christian idolaters, defenders of an idolatrous or iconolatrous worship of the Christ—to people, that is, who are only concerned with the traditional pictures and statues of Jesus and the pretty stories attached to him.[1]

' If you speak or write of Jesus as a real live person or even as a still active God, such worshippers are more horrified than Don Juan was when the statue stepped from its pedestal and came to supper with him. You may deny the divinity of Jesus, you may doubt

[1] Preface to *Androcles and the Lion*.

whether he ever existed, you may reject Christianity for Judaism, Mohametism, Shintoism, or Fire Worship, and the iconolaters, placidly contemptuous, will only classify you as a freethinker or a heathen. But if you venture to wonder *how Christ . . . looked* or *what size he stood* [1] in his shoes . . . or even if you tell any part of his story in the vivid terms of modern colloquial slang, you will produce an extraordinary dismay and horror among the iconolaters. You will have made the picture come out of its frame, the statue descend from its pedestal, the story become real, with all the incalculable consequences that may flow from this terrifying miracle. It is at such moments that you realize that the iconolaters have never for a moment conceived Jesus as a real person, who meant what he said, as a fact, as a force like electricity, only needing the invention of suitable political machinery to be applied to the affairs of mankind with revolutionary effect. Thus it is not disbelief that is dangerous in our society; it is belief. The moment it strikes you (as it may any day) that Jesus is not the lifeless, harmless image he has hitherto been to you, but a rallying centre for revolutionary influence, which all established States and Churches fight, you must look to yourselves, for you have brought the image to life, and the mob may not be able to stand that horror.'

As to 'colloquial slang,' the reader will, I hope, find nothing of the sort either in the German original or in the English translation. Yet I have not refrained from applying, wherever it seemed required, the terminology of modern political ideology and sociology, in order to make it quite clear to the reader that the social and political problems of those times are fundamentally identical with those of the present epoch, notwithstanding the differences which, after all, separate that period and civilization from our own. It is this which, I fear, will shock more profoundly than the unveiling of the quaint contemporary pen-portrait of the Naṣōraean Messiah all those who want to convert, and have in part succeeded in converting, churches and chapels into a world-wide organization for the effective repression of the very tendencies for which the Jewish prophet-king suffered and died.

It has been suggested, and will doubtless be suggested again, that this work is itself inspired by a revolutionary Messianist tendency. To this accusation I can only say that I wish it were true. I wish I could honestly plead guilty to being moved in the depths of my conscience by the most powerful religious impulses of my race. Yet for the sake of plain truth I must own that in the unravelling of the mysterious history of this movement I was actuated almost exclusively by a boundless curiosity and a

[1] Italics mine. See below, p. 427[20]

passionate desire to get at the real truth of this maze of documents, authentic and spurious, falsified in part or altogether forged.

The main difficulty of the presentation lay in the fact that a discussion of the events cannot be separated from a discussion of the sources. A large and expensive volume dealing exclusively with the literary and philological problems raised by the discovery of the Slavonic, the Rumanian, and the less expurgated Hebrew versions of Josephus, could not be published in this poverty-stricken after-war period, because nobody but half a dozen specialists would read it. Still less thinkable was a simple, straightforward history of the messianic uprising and the origins of the Christian Church on the basis of the new sources, but without a thoroughgoing critical analysis of the documents. Such a volume would inevitably be mistaken for one of those *biographies romancées* which are turned out in our days by the dozen.

An even greater difficulty was presented by the natural desire of both author and publisher to reach both the scholar and the so-called general reader. To justify my theses as far as possible before the forum of the learned critics, I had to include much documentary material which may possibly not interest any one but specialists. Still, to ensure that this book should not attain the unwieldy proportions of the German original, I had to omit practically all of the critical discussion devoted to the previous literature on the subject.[1] The logical argument, it is hoped, has not suffered thereby. Yet if any objections should present themselves to the learned reader, he is requested to look into the German original before starting an argument which has possibly already been definitely disposed of there.

To the general reader, who would probably prefer a less cumbersome book, I venture to offer a few suggestions which may perhaps be resented as superfluous by expert skippers, but may be of some value to those who still follow the time-honoured and certainly praiseworthy custom of beginning a book at the beginning. Such readers might not unprofitably begin by looking at Pl. vi. and Pl. vii. They will see there without any difficulty the *demonstratio ad oculos* of my general thesis regarding the ruthless censorship applied to all sources discussing Christianity and its

---

[1] I regret even more the forced omission of a systematic exposition of the Oriental origins and the Jewish development of political Messianism, a subject I hope to deal with in the form of a separate volume some time in the future.

founder from a non-Christian point of view. If they will then turn to p. 594, App. IV., they will find the proof that all anti-Christian literature was hunted down systematically from the fourth century on. Having thus caught a glimpse of this process of deletion of words, phrases, and whole sections, and duly noted on Pl. VIII. and Pl. XI. that our chief authority, Flavius Josephus, did not fare any better under the hands of the ecclesiastical censors, the reader may be prepared to admit that the standard texts of the *Jewish War* and the *Antiquities* may after all not contain everything that Josephus meant to convey to his Jewish and Gentile readers. Having got thus far, he may now be ready for a look at the newly reconstructed texts on pp. 62 and 466 ff., and for an unprejudiced reading of the striking statements printed in these chapters.

As likely as not, he will then ask on whose authority he is expected to accept as sound historical facts such surprising and, for many readers, shocking statements. The answer to that question is given in the chapters about Flavius Josephus, his life and work.[1] Very probably, after reading the man's edifying biography, the reader will not care to trust him[2] without further checks and verifications. Yet by turning to the Introduction (pp. 9 ff.) he will find that the general view which he takes of Jesus Christ is shared by all ancient non-Christian authors of whose writings we still have a few fragments. He will see, moreover, on pp. 201 ff. that Flavius Josephus—unworthy indeed of any trust whenever his own interests come into play—throughout his work used first-hand evidence, that is, contemporary official documents. Having been so often told that there never were any legal documents about the trial of Jesus, the reader may be surprised to learn (on pp. 13 ff.) that detailed records of this famous case must have existed, and in fact did subsist down to A.D. 311, when they were broadcast in hundreds of copies by the imperial chancery of Rome. By what silly-clever forgeries these genuine *Acts of Pilate* have been discredited after A.D. 312 for more than 1500 years, I have endeavoured to show on pp. 17 ff. If by this time the reader has become

---

[1] Below, pp. 22-35.

[2] These words were already in type when Dr. Burton Scott Easton wrote at the end of a fair and courteous review of the German edition of this book in the *Anglican Theological Review* of 1930: 'Dr. Eisler's estimate of Josephus' truthfulness and objectivity is as low as is conceivably possible. . . . What conceivable right has Dr. Eisler, then, to use his anti-Christian evidence . . . as . . . infallible ? ' My answer to this legitimate question has been given by anticipation in the lines which follow.

more interested in all the forgeries, simple and complicated, resorted to by apologetic ingenuity in order to convert the writings of the unbelieving Jew Josephus into a huge edifying *Testimonium Flavianum* for the essential truth of the Athanasian creed, let him now turn to pp. 425 ff., where he will find in parallel columns the genuine pen-portrait derived from the official ' hue-and-cry' of the Messiah Jesus, and the idealizing corrections applied to this startling text by the Christian revisers. If he still doubts the authenticity of the description printed on the left side of p. 427, let him turn to p. 416 f. and satisfy himself how exactly this *signalement* tallies with certain hitherto enigmatic passages in the Gospels and with a number of patristic witnesses on the shortness and uncomeliness of Jesus' ' servile body,' spoken of by Paul. Thus introduced, though as in a mirror darkly, yet almost face to face, to this great prophet and king of the Jews, the reader will now be eager to turn to the history of the world-shattering movement in which he was destined to play such a dominant part.

No doubt he had best begin, as do Josephus and the Gospels, with the ' Forerunner.'[1] Yet any reader shunning as yet the more arduous task of reading the consecutive historical narrative is invited to read the concluding chapter on pp. 562 ff., where I have tried to present, as concisely as possible, the main outlines of this most startling history. If eager for the details, the reader may now turn to the story of Joḥanan the Hidden One or the Baptist, the revolutionary and schismatic high priest[2] of the year 4 B.C., who outlived Jesus by fourteen years ; he may read on to the story of the three messiah kings, Judas, Simon, and Athronga, who answered his call; and finally he may follow the career of the Baptist's erstwhile disciple, the Naṣōraean Jesus,[3] who died on the cross for the liberation of his people from the Roman yoke, the rulers of this world, in the night from the 15th to the 16th of April of the year A.D. 21.

I am aware that a good many of my readers, accustomed to the traditional accounts, will consider the thesis here proposed as a gigantic paradox. This cannot very well be helped. I am simply and honestly concerned with what appears to me to be the essential truth for which we have been searching ever since the beginnings of Unitarianism in the sixteenth century and rationalistic Deism in the eighteenth. The ' thoroughgoing eschatological' exegesis

---

[1] Below, pp. 223 ff.   [2] Below, pp. 259 ff.   [3] Below, pp. 312 ff.

of the Gospels has led us up to the threshold of the gate which was finally thrown open to Western scholarship by Alexander Berendts of Dorpat as early as 1906. For twenty years no one has cared to walk into this hitherto unexplored field, where a good deal still remains to be done.

I should like to conclude with a word of sincere gratitude to all those who have so generously given me their material and scholarly help, without which I could not have undertaken and after many years of hard work carried through such an arduous task. First and foremost my unstinted thanks are due to Mrs. Alice Chalmers and Dr. James Loeb, who defrayed the huge cost of several thousand photostats of the various MSS. ; to the former President of the Russian Academy of Sciences, Prof. Sergius von Oldenbourg, for procuring the necessary permits from his Government ; to Prof. Beneševič for superintending the photographer's work and for much useful information ; to Prof. Vasilij N. Istrin of the Russian Academy for various apographa from Slavonic Josephus MSS. ; to Prof. André Mazon and his pupils MM. Antoine Martel and Boris Unbegaun of the Paris Institut des Études Slaves ; to Proff. Nikolas van Wyck and Berndt von Arnim of Leyden, and Prof. N. Bubnov of Kiev, now of Ljubiana, for their kind help in editing and analysing the Old Russian texts ; to the Most Rev. Ḥakham Dr. Moses Gaster for the kind communication of transcripts and for a translation of the inedited Rumanian Josephus fragments, discovered by him, in his MS. 89 ; to the Right Rev. Grand Rabbin de France, Israél Lévy, who directed my attention to the Paris Josippon MSS., and specially obliged me by copying for me a number of pages from the codex Edmond de Rothschild No. 24 ; to Messeigneurs Giovanni Mercati, Eugène Tisserant, and Giovanni Galbiati of the Vatican Library and of the Bibliotheca Ambrosiana for kind information and for permission to reproduce various MSS. ; to Prof. Charles Boreux of the Louvre and Prof. E. Rostagno of the Laurentiana in Florence for two important illustrations ; to His Excellency Baron von Oppenheim for the photograph of the Ṣlebi types ; to the late Dr. H. St. John Thackeray, who in the most painstaking and conscientious manner translated about 900 printed pages of the German original; to Dr. A. Haggerty Krappe, who completed, revised, and to a large extent completely rewrote this first draft, condensing it into its present shape. It is needless to add that neither is to be held responsible in any way for any of my theories, hypotheses, or valuations. To my great pleasure, Dr. Thackeray was able to accept certain essential results of my analysis, as the reader will see for himself by studying his admirable new book, *Josephus, the Man and the Historian*, New York, 1929. Dr. Krappe should not be held altogether responsible for the final literary form of the work. His already difficult task has been rendered even more arduous by my repeated additions to the text. Mr. Theodor Gaster has much obliged me by his kind help in reading the proofs and adding the last polish to the style of the translation.

And now, " καὶ ἡμεῖς τρέχωμεν τὸν προκείμενον ἡμῖν ἀγῶνα " (*Heb.* xii. 1), which means, I believe, if translated from the stately and altogether admirable language of King James's Bible into a plain and more prosaic modern English, something like—

Let us run the gauntlet and be flogged along the line.

ROBERT EISLER

PARIS, 1930

'Ea, ut potero explicabo, nec tamen quasi Pythius Apollo, certa ut sint et fixa, quae dixero: sed ut homunculus unus e multis, probabilia conjectura sequens. Ultra enim quo progrediar, quam ut veri similia, non habeo. Certa dicent ii, qui et percipi ea posse dicunt et se sapientes esse profitentur.'

CICERO, *Tuscul. quaest.* i. 8.

TABLE OF CONTENTS

b

X

XI

XII

b 2

XIII

XIV

XV

XIX

XX

LIST OF ILLUSTRATIONS

LIST OF ILLUSTRATIONS

THE MESSIAH JESUS

'Nonnulli enim paganorum, ut noverint Christum . . . suspecti, ne forte a Christianis ista conficta sint, malunt credere codicibus Iudaeorum.' AUGUSTIN, *Sermo* cccxl, 4.

1

THE PRIMARY IMPORTANCE OF THE NON-CHRISTIAN SOURCES OF CHRISTIAN ORIGINS

'Neque enim in angulo quidquam horum gestum est.'—Act. Ap. xxvi. 26.

THE present work is the first attempt to write a history of Christian origins on the basis of non-Christian or rather anti-Christian sources, and to point out the peculiar light in which the memorable events at the root of the Christian religion appeared to its adversaries. Lack of historical documents more than any other factor has so far stood in the way of such an attempt. As late as 1896 the German theologian Harnack could say with a good deal of truth that 'all non-Christian testimonies about Jesus and the origin of Christianity might be written on a single quarto page.' Such, indeed, was the situation when in 1906 Alexander Berendts published parts of the Slavonic version of Josephus, a text which is the chief source drawn on for the present attempt at analysis and reconstruction. Yet even so one may well question how it came about that so portentous a series of events has left but so few traces in contemporary Jewish and Pagan literature, that no non-Christian literary text of any importance should give at least some details. One must ask, furthermore, Could it be that such events as are recorded in the Gospels have passed so completely unnoticed by the Roman government and its officials as to justify the reply put by Anatole France in the mouth of the aged Pilate : ' Jésus de Nazareth ? Je ne me rappelle pas.' Is it conceivable that a man should be proclaimed king of the Jews by the people at Jerusalem and crucified for political reasons by a Roman governor, without any report being sent to the Emperor giving an account of all these transactions ? If, however, such a report must have been sent, why is there hardly an echo of it in any Roman historian ?

Explanations of this apparent paradox have indeed not been wanting. Thus the German scholar Johannes Weiss [1] wrote : ' To the official world the execution of a carpenter of Nazareth was the most insignificant event of Roman history during those decades ; it disappeared completely among the innumerable *supplicia* inflicted by the Roman provincial administration. It would be a most miraculous accident had it been mentioned in any official

---

[1] *Jesus von Nazareth, Mythus oder Geschichte*, Tübingen, 1910, p. 92.

report.' Such a presentation of the facts, however, is quite misleading. For it was no ordinary carpenter executed for some crime of no relation to the security of the Empire. On the contrary, the execution in question was a political act of the first importance, as were the events leading up to it ; for that carpenter had been hailed as the Liberator of Israel, as a saviour-king, and at a time, too, when the capital was filled with pilgrims from all over the known world. Nor is there any reason to suppose that the Roman governor was not aware of his own act ; the inscription of the cross, ' Jesus Nazoraeus Rex Judaeorum,' that is an epigraphical document of the first importance, in fact the earliest of all non-Christian and anti-Christian documents, leaves no doubt whatever as to the political character of the events. This document, the clearest expression of Roman official opinion of the case, must be the starting-point for any correct presentation of the evidence. In the prosecution leading to the catastrophe the political nature of the charge alone mattered ; for the Roman officials consistently declined to meddle with Jewish religious quarrels,[1] and any neglect of the political aspect of the case must therefore be regarded as a grave methodological error. According to the rules imposed upon the Roman bureaucracy,[2] a political event of this character must therefore have been the subject of a full report to the Emperor ; Pilate could not possibly have failed to send one to Rome, were it only in the interest of his own safety. If, then, as Tertullian[3] takes for granted, a report of the case existed in the public records, how is it that the dramatic story is not repeated by a single contemporary historian ?

The common modern answer to this puzzling question, as advanced by certain radical critics, is to deny outright the truth of the Gospel narrative. If we are to believe them, there are no trustworthy non-Christian witnesses to the life and passion of Jesus, for the simple reason that no human being answering to the description of that exalted personage ever lived. The whole story, including even the inscription on the cross, is—according to them—but a pious legend, a rationalising adaptation of the old and widespread myth of the suffering, dying, and resuscitated god.

This theory is first met with in the eighteenth century, when it arose as a natural consequence of Descartes' principle *de omnibus dubitandum*, here applied for the first time to the foundations of positive religion, and as a result of the first crude application of the comparative method to the wealth of ancient mythology and astral lore. The dangers of this method of excessive scepticism were

---

[1] *Acts* xviii. 14-15 : ' Gallio said unto the Jews, If it were a matter of wrong, or wicked lewdness, O ye Jews, reason would that I should bear with you : But if it be a question of words and names, and of your law, look ye to it ; for I will be no judge of such matters.' Gallio was a brother of the philosopher Seneca.
[2] App. I. pp. 591 f. and Pl. I.   [3] See below, p. 11 note 2.

promptly seen by Jean-Jacques Rousseau, who in his *Émile* thought it necessary to throw out the following warning : ' Should we say that the Gospel story is the outcome of fanciful invention ? My friend, it is not thus that people invent. The facts about Socrates, which nobody questions, are less solidly attested than those concerning Jesus Christ. Indeed, this is but to push the difficulty further back without solving it. It would be more inconceivable that several persons, to wit, four, should have combined to fabricate this book than that one should have furnished the subject of it. Jewish authors would never have discovered this tone nor these ethics, and the Gospel bears marks of truth so great, so striking, so perfectly inimitable, that their inventor would be more astonishing than the hero. Yet, for all that, this same Gospel is full of incredible things, things repugnant to reason which it is impossible for any intelligent person to understand or to admit.'

Voltaire, like so many other critics, was convinced that the famous passage about Jesus in the eighteenth book of Josephus' *Antiquities* (discussed below, pp. 36-62) was a Christian forgery. Yet, after emphasising the fact that neither Justus of Tiberias nor Philo the Jew mentions the Galilaean Messiah, he adds : [1] ' Are we to conclude from this that Jesus never existed, as some have ventured to conclude from the Pentateuch story that there never was a Moses ? Certainly not. Since after the death of Jesus *people wrote not only for but also against him*, it is clear that he did exist.'

The sage of Ferney, when he wrote these lines, had just seen ' certain disciples of Lord Bolingbroke, men of more ingenuity than learning, who denied the existence of Jesus because the story of the Magi and the star and the Massacre of the Innocents was, they said, the height of extravagance. The contradiction existing between the two genealogies of Jesus as given by Matthew and Luke respectively was one of the reasons alleged by those young people in support of their conviction that Jesus never lived ; but they drew a very false conclusion. Our countryman Houel here in France had a most ridiculous genealogy drawn up for himself ; certain Irishmen have written of him and Jeansin that they had a *spiritus familiaris* which always gave them the aces when they played cards. Hundreds of extravagant tales have been told of them. Yet that does not prevent their having really existed ; those who lost their money in gambling with them were well satisfied about that. What nonsense has not been said about the Duke of Buckingham ? None the less, he lived in the reigns of the kings James I. and Charles. Apollonius of Tyana certainly never resuscitated any one, Pythagoras had no golden leg ; yet Apollonius and Pythagoras were real men.'

[1] *Dieu et les hommes*, 'Œuvres,' ed. Garnier, Paris, 1879, tome xxviii. p. 195. § 9.

These arguments of the great rationalist and sceptic are quite to the point. No amount of improbability in a given story can prove, taken by itself, that the hero is himself a creation of mythological fancy. Dieteric of Bern, though celebrated as a slayer of dragons in mediaeval German sagas, is none the less no other than the famous king Theodoric the Goth, who most certainly resided at Verona, ruled over Italy, struck money, built churches, and gave a lot of trouble to the contemporary Byzantine rulers. The fact that Berenice's Hair can still be pointed out among the constellations of the nightly sky does not disprove that this gracious queen lived a very earthly life at Alexandria in Egypt. The coins and other documents representing Queen Cleopatra as the goddess Isis nursing the infant god Horus, and her claims to divine rights, are no argument against her historicity. Examples of this obvious truth might be multiplied, since Oriental history in particular teems with royalties exalted to divine rank and heavenly splendours. Even if one were to grant, for the sake of argument, the mythological fancies of Dupuis and Volney and their modern followers,[1] according to which the Gospel story is but the reworking of older Oriental symbolism carried out in the interests of the nascent Church, this would not in the least invalidate the historicity of the *man* Jesus, of whom Tacitus[2] expressly states that he was crucified under Pontius Pilatus. One would then simply have to admit that his life was misrepresented by his followers to suit their particular aim. Such a possibility—and as a possibility it must certainly be admitted—makes it all the more desirable to secure, so far as that may still be possible, non-Christian and even anti-Christian (that is, purely secular) source material.

As to the ' mythological theory,' one may admit, of course, that a figure such as the Christ of the Gospels *may* have been created by a poet, though even then one would have to acknowledge also that Mark or whatever other author was at the basis of the first Gospel was one of the greatest poets that ever lived. But it would be incomprehensible that avowed opponents of the new religion should have overlooked this weakest spot of its history and should have done a fictitious person not at all to their liking the gratuitous honour of treating him as a man of flesh and blood. As a matter of fact, not even the most hostile antagonists of Christianity ever levelled against its founder the reproach that he never existed at all, though otherwise they were certainly not very sparing in terms of opprobrium. Nor does the vast literature of Christian apologetics show the faintest trace of such an assertion ever

---

[1] W. B. Smith, John M. Robertson, Arthur Drews, Paul-Louis Couchoud, Georg Brandes. A full bibliography of this literature is given by Robert Stahl at the end of the French translation of Arthur Drews' *Le Mythe de Jésus*, Paris, 1926.   [2] See below, p. 9 n. 1.

having been advanced on the part of the enemies of Christianity. Indeed, doubts of the historicity of Jesus were absolutely unknown until the eighteenth century. What divided Christians and non-Christians was not the question whether or no Jesus existed, but the vastly more pertinent and essentially different question whether or no the obscure Galilaean carpenter, executed by a Roman governor as king of the Jews, was really a superhuman being who had overcome death—the longed-for saviour of mankind, foretold by the prophets, the only-begotten son of God Himself.

This is the point which is of paramount importance for the present analysis. As yet we have no Pagan documents, such as papyri or inscriptions concerning Jesus and his immediate following, or any other literary sources of Pagan origin which have not passed through the hands of Christian copyists, and which are therefore, theoretically at least, proof against the suspicion of having been tampered with in the interest of Christian apologetics. Since, however, no one before the eighteenth century denied the historicity of Jesus, it is absurd to suppose that a Christian scribe of the first centuries of our era, foreseeing by a clairvoyance rarely equalled the doubts of eighteenth- and nineteenth-century sceptics, should have purposely inserted the earliest of the vicious attacks on Christ and the Christian religion which is found in the *Annals* of Tacitus. What is true of Tacitus and his famous passage is, of course, equally true of other Pagan *testimonia* of antiquity—such as Lucian, Celsus, Hierocles—and still more so of Josephus. If it is gravely asserted that the famous passage of the *Antiquities* was inserted *in toto* by Christians merely in order to establish the historicity of Jesus, the obvious answer is that in that case the forgers would have been wasting their time and labour for the very good reason that no such proof was necessary, no one having until then doubted the historicity of Jesus.

Let us now envisage our central problem. Suppose we had to reconstruct the history of Theodoric the Goth from the Middle High German poems and the Norse saga which have him for a hero. The only available method would be that of rationalistic interpretation, the same by which Euhemerus attempted to prove that Zeus had been a real prehistoric king of flesh and blood. How the Theodoric so reconstructed would look, and in particular how much he would resemble the historical personage whom we meet in the pages of Cassiodorus, Boethius, Ennodius, and the *Gesta Theodorici*, can be easily surmised.

It is not different with the problem in hand. Since whatever is handed down about supernatural beings cannot be history, but mythology, saga, or legend, it follows that no amount of rationalising Euhemerism will ever recover an historic account of Jesus the

man from Gospels the obvious tendency of which is to present
him as the Superhuman Christ, the son of God.[1]   Such an account
can only be obtained if we base our investigations, in the first
instance, on that modest quarto page of non-Christian *testimonia*,
whose whole aim is to speak of him as a man in express
denial of the Gospel claims ; adding then, in the second instance,
any such features in the Christian tradition as will be found consistent with the picture thus recovered.   If this method be followed,
it will at once appear that the common opinion, according to
which those *testimonia* do not yield anything of great importance,
is not at all well founded.

Among the rabbinical testimonies to Jesus (which have been
discussed frequently enough) [2] there is indeed a certain number
which have no reference at all to the founder of Christianity, but to
namesakes of his, belonging to different periods.[3]   Yet there is at
least one of extraordinary importance.   According to this document, a certain Jacob of the hamlet of Sekhanjah states that in his
youth he had heard from the mouth of his teacher, *Ješu han-noṣri*,
i.e. the Naṣōraean, a sharp attack on the temple of Jerusalem
suggesting that it appeared to him totally defiled by an unworthy
venal priesthood.[4]   The phraseology of this attack is in very close
agreement with the tone adopted by Jesus in the same connexion,
according to the synoptical Gospels.[5]   It can be shown, moreover,
that the quotation cannot very well have been invented by the
Christians, for the simple reason that they would not have derived
any conceivable benefit from it, and moreover never quote it.   Nor
can it be a Jewish invention, for, as we shall see later on (p. 593),
our Jewish authorities for this passage did not fully understand it.
What gives it such decisive weight in the discussion of the historicity problem is the fact that Jacob of Kephar Sekhanjah quoted
it to R. 'Eli'ezer b. Hyrkanos—a witness to the destruction of the
temple in A.D. 70—in connexion with an embarrassing problem
concocted by himself.   R. 'Eli'ezer, then an old man, told it to
R. 'Aqiba in the year A.D. 110.   The transmission of the testimony
of *an eye-witness who saw and heard Jesus* is then known in its exact
filiation, comprising no more than two generations.   The trans-
mitters are well-known historical personages who deserve absolute
confidence in such matters, since their unrelenting hostility towards
the Christian sect is obvious from the context of the passage.   The
conclusion is therefore justified that a man called *Ješu han-noṣri*,

---

[1] See Albert Schweitzer, *The Quest of the Historical Jesus* (²), London, 1911,
p. 314, quoting and approving of words of Albert Kalthoff.
[2] The English reader may now consult, beside the well-known book of R.
Travers Herford, especially Joseph Klausner, *Jesus of Nazareth*, tr. by Canon
H. Danby, London, 1924.
[3] See App. II. p. 592.   [4] See App. III.
[5] See below, p. 484 n. 8.

hated by the rabbis as an agitator and an heretic, did live and interpreted the law in an unorthodox spirit, and that certain sayings of
his, in close agreement with passages of the same tendency in the
Gospels, were current for some time both among his adherents and
among his opponents, and maintained themselves with a tenacity
which is typical of Jewish oral tradition. The Gospels themselves, it will be recalled, contain a nucleus of such bits of oral
tradition put in writing many years later ; and the Talmud, similarly, is just such a collection of the *obiter dicta* of certain rabbis,
put together and arranged a considerable time after their death.

There follows, in the order of the chronology, the testimony of
Tacitus,[1] who refers to the Christians as to a gang of men hated by
the whole world, not only on account of their *exitiabilis superstitio*
but also because of their shameful actions (*flagitia*),[2] so that they
were suspected and some confessed themselves guilty of having
started the fire of Rome in the reign of Nero.   For Tacitus, who
as governor of Asia Minor had had plenty of chances to question
Christians in court, the ' Christus,' after whom the mob calls
them ' Chrestiani,' is nothing but the founder of this band of
criminals, who to him are the enemies not only of Rome but of all
mankind, presumably because they long and pray for the Day of
Judgment and the end of the world and because they appear inclined to hasten the coming of that catastrophe.[3]   The experienced
magistrate, to whom the archives of the State were easily accessible, does not even hint at the possibility that that ' Christus '
never existed and that he was but a clever invention of those
anxious to attribute a part of their guilt to a man long since judged
and dead.

A short time later the younger Pliny,[4] on the basis of an official
interrogation of Christians, reports that they were in the habit of
singing hymns to that ' Christus' *quasi deo*, ' as though he were a
god.'   He is therefore very far from considering that alleged god
as anything but a man who owed such unmerited honours only
to the *prava et immodica superstitio* of his adherents.

Neither Tacitus nor Pliny allows us to know on account of what
particular crime that ill-famed *Christus* or *Chrestus* had been
executed.   On the other hand, Celsus and Lucian [5] supplement

---

[1] Tac., *Ann.* xv. 44 : ' *igitur primum correpti, qui fatebantur, deinde indicio
eorum multitudo ingens haud proinde in crimine incendii quam odio humani generis
convicti sunt* ' (*coniuncti, Cod. Flor.* ; accepted by Gronovius [see Walter *in loc.*]
and Ed. Meyer; but see Reitzenstein, *Hell. Mysterien-relig.*, Leipzig, 1927, p. 114).

[2] Pliny mentions *flagitia cohaerentia nomini*, crimes essentially connected with
the Christian denomination.   Further details may have been expurgated.   As the
comparison with Tertullian, *Apolog.* ii., and Eusebius, *H.E.* iii. 33, shows, the
text of Trajan's reply to Pliny has certainly been tampered with.

[3] Minuc. Felix, ii. 1 : ' . . . *toto orbi et ipsi mundo . . . minantur incendium,
ruinam moliuntur.*'

[4] *Epist.*, xcvi.   [5] *De Peregrini Morte*, ch. xii.

those statements by expressly designating Jesus as a γόης and μάγος, i.e. a sorcerer, and—what is even worse in Roman eyes—as a στάσεως ἀρχηγέτης, i.e. the fomenter of a rebellion, both indeed capital crimes according to Roman law.

The same accusation appears even more distinctly in the statements of the famous persecutor of Christians, Sossianus Hierocles,[1] who was in succession governor of Phoenicia, Arabia Libanitis, Bithynia, and prefect of Egypt,[2] during the reign of Diocletian, thus in a way a successor of Pilate. He states that Jesus was overcome by the Jews after committing highway robberies (*latrocinia*) at the head of a band of 900 men. Ever since Lactantius, scholars have only seen an absurdity in this assertion, forgetting that the terms ' *latro* ' and ' *latrocinium* ' are *termini technici* of ancient sociology and political science, that Josephus, for example, constantly uses them with reference to the Jewish patriots in the war of rebellion ; forgetting, furthermore, that the Gospels themselves use this terminology when speaking of the companions of Jesus on the cross, condemned on the strength of the same accusation.[3] They also forget that the oldest of them (*Mark* xv. 7) does not hesitate to speak of ' *the* revolution ' (ἐν τῇ στάσει) when referring to the tumultuous incidents connected with the triumphal entry of Jesus into Jerusalem.[4] Yet one might have read in St. Augustine [5] that the kingdoms (*regna*), leaving aside the question of ' right or wrong ' (*dempta iustitia*), are but ' *magna latrocinia*.' Just as Rome was founded by a band of robbers collected by Romulus, so, according to the saint, a *latrocinium*, if powerful enough (*addita impunitate*), will develop into a kingdom, and the *latronum dux* will then style himself a ' *rex*.' All this means nothing but the banal truth that success will justify high treason, at least in the eyes of those who—in our days—would call Sir Roger Casement a traitor, but George Washington an ardent patriot and a statesman, the ' father of his country.' ' *Latrocinia facere*,' in the phraseology of Sossianus, is the same thing as to ' commit high treason,' ' start a rebellion,' and his accusation is the exact equivalent of the indictment before the tribunal of Pontius Pilate, repeated, according to Roman legal usage, in the inscription on the cross, the reality of which only the worst hypercriticism [6] can doubt. The executed victim had been condemned as a ' *rex*

---

[1] Lactantius, *Div. instit.*, v. 3, 4. See below, p. 363 n. 2.

[2] *Corpus Inscript. Lat.*, iii. 133-6661.

[3] *Luke* xxiii. 40. See below, p. 11.

[4] In the parallel passage in *Luke* (xxiii. 19), the meaning of the sentence is intentionally obscured by speaking of ' some riot ' (ἐν στάσει τινί) as if it were ' some trifling riot in the town.'

[5] *Civ. Dei*, iv. 4, 1, p. 150, Dombart.

[6] See Edgar Salin, *Civ. Dei*, Tübingen, 1926, p. 22, cp. p. 34, against Wilh. Bousset, *Kyrios Christos*, p. 26. Bousset himself has not repeated his doubts in the 2nd edition of his book.

Judaeorum,' a king of the Jews, on whom this dignity had been conferred by the *acclamatio* of the people when he had entered Jerusalem. In exactly the same way did the Caesar receive his imperial dignity by the *acclamatio* of the Roman army. Such a king, proclaimed against the will of Caesar, and hence no tolerated vassal-king, no '*rex socius et amicus populi Romani,*' was, for the Roman administration, a '*latronum dux,*' an ἀρχιλῃστής, and his adherents, of whom two suffered for the same crime (ἐν τῷ αὐτῷ κρίματι συσταυρωμένοι),[1] were *latrones,* that is, rebels.

It is this conception of the non-Christian world which strikes any attentive reader of the few passages that could be collected on Harnack's little quarto page. To the Jews, Jesus was indeed an heretic and an agitator of the lower orders ; to the Pagans he was a magician who through sham miracles and with subversive words had incited the people to rebellion and as leader of a gang of desperate men had attempted to seize the royal crown of Judaea, as others had done before and after him.

If this be so, one must next ask why it is that such a *mundi casus* [2] should not have left a more voluminous echo in the non-Christian sources. It will not do any more to minimise the importance of the case ; nor is it admissible to accuse the Roman provincial administration of habitually putting to death a number of its subjects as part of the day's work.[3] To generalise mass executions which were resorted to in extreme cases, and to declare such executions the common and ordinary thing in normal times of peace or comparative peace, would be a grave historical error. The true solution of the enigma must be sought elsewhere.

Granting that the non-Christian writers referred to Jesus—as well they might—as to a wizard, a demagogue, and a rebel, it stands to reason that such statements were necessarily highly offensive to Christian readers, who naturally regarded them as outright blasphemies. Under these circumstances any such passage would simply have had to disappear : witness the substitution, in the Talmud, of the expression '*peloni,*' i.e. ' a certain one,' for the name of Jesus, where this name occurred in the original text ; [4] witness also the treatment of Lucian's reference to Christ [5] at the hands of the Christian scribes, whose indignation is still visible on the margin of some of the extant MSS. The writings of Celsus and of Sossianus Hierocles have been preserved in fragments only, thanks to the verbal quotations of their attacks in the detailed answers of the Church fathers Origen, Eusebius, and Lactantius. In the same way the anti-Christian works of Porphyry, which were

---

[1] *Luke* xxiii. 40. [2] Tertullian, *Apolog.,* xxi.
[3] Cp. the words of Johannes Weiss above, p. 3 n. 1.
[4] See e.g. Strack-Billerbeck, i. p. 38.
[5] *Peregr. Proteus,* chaps. xi. and xiii. and the *scholia.*

drawn on by Sossianus Hierocles, fell a victim to ecclesiastical censure, for as early as the time of Constantine the State had given the Church the discretionary power to suppress all anti-Christian literature.[1]

Since the law of Diocletian concerning books ' *improbatae lecturae* '—a term denoting originally magical books, astrological tables to determine the death date of an emperor, etc., applied by him so as to cover even the holy scriptures of the Christians—had been turned by Constantine and later on by Theodosius and Valentinian [2] against the Pagan and Jewish owners of books hostile to Christianity, anybody possessing writings in which Jesus the Christ was referred to as a 'magician,' an 'agitator,' a 'demagogue,' etc., exposed himself to severe, even capital, penalty. The least that might happen to him was the destruction of the MS., which might be (and often was) of no mean value. The natural consequence of such a state of affairs may still be gauged from the ' new edition ' (νέα ἔκδοσις) of the anti-Christian writings of Eunapius after the death of Julian, quoted by Photius.[3] As we learn from the patriarch, the most violent anti-Christian passages had disappeared from it, and the emendation had been done so clumsily that often enough the logical connexion had been completely destroyed.

As a matter of fact, the wholesale erasing and blotting out of all anti-Christian passages in Jewish and Pagan writings—witness the illustrations on our plates [4]—is the only, and at the same time the best, explanation of the apparent scarcity of such documents. This fact explains, among others, the disappearance of the book of Antonius Julianus, *De Judaeis*, and the rest of the literature occasioned by the Jewish War (still mentioned in Josephus' introduction), and the curious silence observed about Jesus—much to the astonishment of Photius—in Jewish books on the same subject, such as that of Justus of Tiberias. Only a person naïve enough to believe that the Christians might have found in Jewish and Pagan writings of this type statements flattering to the founder of their religion or to his disciples, or facts otherwise of an edifying nature, can be astonished at the almost complete disappearance of anti-Christian books. It is one of the many ironies of history that

---

[1] See App. IV. p. 594.   [2] See App. IV. p. 594.
[3] *Bibliotheca*, cod. lxxvii. towards the end.

[4] In a review of the German edition of this book (*Röm. Quartalschrift*, xxxvii., 1929), p. 179, Prof. Leo Wohleb calls the author's attention to the fact that in the archetype of the principal MS. of the Historia Augusta, Codex P (Palatinus 899 of the Vatican Library), nineteen complete sentences and clauses have been deleted (E. Hohl, *Beitr. zur Textgeschichte d. H.A.*, *Klio*, xiii., 1913, pp. 389 *sqq.*). It is no more due to pure chance that Dio Cassius' report of the conflagration at Rome and the ensuing persecution of the Christians by Nero (the parallel version to Tacitus' famous paragraph, quoted *supra*, p. 9 n. 1) is known to us only through exceedingly scrappy Byzantine extracts. See also below, p. 65 n. 2.

PLATE I

A LEAF FROM THE DIARY OF A ROMAN OFFICIAL IN EGYPT

RENDERING ACCOUNT FOR THE SMALLEST DETAILS OF HIS OFFICIAL ACTIVITY

(PAPYRUS PARISIENSIS 69 IN THE LOUVRE)

precisely this material would now be of the greatest value in defending the Church against the charge of having arbitrarily invented a founder of its religion, who never existed at all. What is astonishing is that even as much as a quarto page of such anti-Christian source material should have escaped the universal destruction, a fact which is no doubt due partly to the stupidity of absent-minded, mechanical copyists, partly to the negligence of certain censors, and partly to the reverence for the great monuments of old as shown by men like Synesius of Cyrene who, though outwardly Christians, remained at heart so-called Pagans, or rather (as they preferred to style themselves) ' philosophers.'

THE PROBLEM OF THE 'ACTA PILATI' AND THE CHRONOLOGY OF THE PASSION

The same considerations which account for the complete disappearance of most of the anti-Christian literary sources about the Nasōraean Messiah are sufficient to explain also the loss of all official documents referring to the trial and passion of Jesus.

At a very early time doubts expressed against the trustworthiness of Christian historical material and the tradition of the Church led to an insistent demand for the production of official documents. The letter of Ignatius to the Philadelphians shows, for example, how irritated the clergy felt at the taunts of certain recalcitrant Jews, who frankly told them that they would refuse to believe the Gospel narrative so long as they could not find the story also in the archives.[1]

The alleged insignificance of the case of Jesus of Nazareth,[2] even if it were true, would never satisfactorily explain this silence of all official sources. We know better from the Egyptian papyri, the so-called ' Pagan acts of martyrs,' the habits and usages of the Roman bureaucracy, which kept a running index of even the smallest incidents of their official life as they came up. Such notices were collected so as to form the official diary (*commentarii*) of the governor, copies of which were kept in provincial and central archives, whilst extracts were regularly sent to the Emperor in Rome. Furthermore, the governors themselves would have duplicates of certain acts placarded for public cognizance,[3] and in cases which were of a nature to interest larger circles extracts of the official judicial proceedings were made and distributed by the partisans of the accused or condemned,[4] a method which in those

---

[1] ἐν τοῖς ἀρχείοις. *Ignatii Epistula ad Philadelphenos*, viii. 2. On the variant reading ἐν τοῖς ἀρχαίοις, see App. V.

[2] See above, p. 3, the words quoted from Anatole France and Johannes Weiss.

[3] See App. I., Pl. I.

[4] O. Schulthess, *Wochenschrift für klass. Philologie*, xvi., 1899, 1055 f. A. Neppi Modona, *Protocolli giudiziarii o romanzo storico?* Raccolta in onore di Gio. Lumbroso, pp. 407-38. See App. VI.

days had to replace the modern newspaper with its regular accounts of sensational 'cases.' The so-called *acta sincera*, i.e. the genuine acts of Christian martyrs, are nothing but the edifying reworkings of just such pamphlets, based on the original protocols as composed by the official *notarii* or *exceptores*. Such excerpts could be made with perfect legality whenever the authorities granted the *facultas inspiciendi et describendi commentarios*,[1] i.e. permitted an examination of the court acts. If that permission was refused, recourse was had to bribery of the state police officials, the so-called *speculatores*. As a matter of fact, such *acta sincera* are not lacking in the case of a number of infinitely less important trials in connexion with certain early Christian martyrs. For example, 200 *denarii* are stated to have been the exact cost to the Christians of a copy of the acts of Tarachus, Probus, and Andronicus.[2]

Under these circumstances we understand perfectly how Justinus [3] and Tertullian [4] can take it for granted that such records about the trial of Jesus were to be found in the state archives. Further, in the *acta* of the three martyrs just quoted the governor tells one of the accused : ' Non scis, quem invocas, Christum *hominem*, quem reum fuisse factum sub custodia Ponti Pilati et punitum constat cuius extant acta passionis.' This significant phrase may well be derived from the genuine official *acta* of these martyrs, who suffered under Diocletian.

At all events, no capital cases in the Roman State were ever tried without due documentary records being kept,[5] any more than such a disorderly procedure would be permissible in our time in any of the modern civilized countries. Once read in court and approved by the judge, such documents could not be altered after the close of the affair, and the officials were compelled by law to deposit one copy in the archive of the governor or whoever else had the supreme authority in a given region.[6] Pilate could no more execute a freeborn man, not to speak of an important leader of a popular movement, without a protocol of the case being duly written and put on file, than a British judge could do such a thing in India to-day. To assume the contrary and to suspect the Roman governor of neglecting the proper judicial procedure in such an affair betrays only a gross ignorance of the obligatory steps in the Roman administrative and judicial machine.

Granting this, as we may without the slightest hesitation, and

---

[1] Max Memelsdorff, *De archivis imperatorum*, Diss. Hall., 1890, p. 50, n.5.
[2] See App. vi.   [3] *Apolog.*, xxxv. and xlviii.   [4] *Apolog.*, xxi.
[5] E. Le Blant, Suppl. to Ruinart's *Acta Sincera*, Paris, 1882, p. 16. Rambaud, *Le droit criminel romain dans les Actes des martyrs*, Lyon, 1885. P. Monceaux, *Revue Archéol.*, iiie série, t. xxxviii., 1901, pp. 240-71.
[6] Cf. Apuleius, floridorum libri iv. 9, 30 f., p. 11, ed. Helm : '*proconsulis autem tabella sententia est, quae semel lecta neque augeri littera una neque autem minui potest, sed utcumque recitata est, ita provinciae instrumento refertur.*'

considering furthermore the comparative ease with which copies of such documents could be procured and circulated in abridged form, it is certainly a remarkable fact that the accounts of the trial of Jesus in the Gospels are *not* based on anything like an extract from the acts of the trial. They resemble in no way the *acta martyrum sincera* with their abundant correct detail about the legal procedure, beginning with the date of the trial and ending with the correct formula of the judgment pronounced. On the contrary, they are full of legal impossibilities which have for ever puzzled all the numerous specialists dealing with this tragical case. Similarly, the *Acta Pilati* and the report of Pilate to Tiberius mentioned by Justinus and Tertullian are obvious forgeries, for no genuine acts or reports could contain anything like the details for which they are quoted. Rather do they resemble certain mediaeval legends of martyrs, freely invented and almost without any basic truth.

It is certainly curious, then, to see that the Christians never took the trouble to procure for their own libraries these documents, which should have been most precious to them—in other words, that they failed to do for Jesus what they commonly did, and at great expense, for various martyrs of the early Church. And yet there can be no doubt whatever that the genuine *Acta Pilati* were kept in the files of the Emperor's correspondence in Rome, among the *commentarii principis* (above, p. 13). Still more peculiar : in the latter part of the first century—just about the time when Mark wrote his Gospel in Rome—two members of the reigning dynasty, Flavius Clemens and Domitilla, had been converted to the Christian faith, and through them, if not through a humble *servus librarius* of the *procurator ab epistulis*—one of those Christians 'that are of Caesar's household'[1]—a copy of the genuine *Acta Pilati* could easily have been obtained from the *tabularium principis*. Why, one asks, was no effort ever made in this direction ? Was it really, as many would have it, because no such acts could ever have existed, since no such trial ever took place under Pilate ?

We can only say that precisely the contrary is true, for we have definite proofs of the existence of genuine *Acta Pilati*. The reason why the Christians did not choose to avail themselves of this document was simply that these *Acta* contained κατὰ τοῦ Χριστοῦ βλασφημίας,[2] that is, material highly offensive to them and hence of no use for missionary purposes. That such must necessarily have been the case will be fairly obvious from the following considerations. Those *Acta* must have contained the justification of the capital sentence passed on Jesus—his guilt, that

---

[1] *Epistle of St. Paul to the Philippians*, iv. 22.
[2] Eusebius, *Hist. eccl.*, ix. 5, 7.

is, or what in Roman eyes constituted his guilt. Such a document could obviously be of use only to all anti-Christian polemists, who on this basis could attempt to prove that Jesus had indeed been a magician, a demagogue and what not, and its publication could only be extremely embarrassing to the Christians, who of course considered the documents in question as full of blasphemies against the founder of their religion. Indeed, it is pertinent to ask, What else could we expect to find in the protocols of a trial obviously intended to establish that Jesus was *not* a prophet or son of God, but a mere man, a wizard, and a pretender to the throne of David and to the crown of the world-ruler ? Would not witnesses have been summoned to determine whether Jesus was of royal blood, a ' son of David,' or a mere impostor of humble origin, claiming to belong to a still extant family[1] which, no doubt, took great pains to disclaim any such relationship ?

As a matter of fact, as we know from Eusebius,[2] this is the reason why the *Acta* in question were published by the Roman government, at the order of the Emperor Maximinus Daïa, in A.D. 311,[3] when they were broadcast in a vast number of copies and listed among the prescribed readings for all schools of the Empire. Naturally enough, these *Acta Pilati*—dated, in contradiction to the conjectural traditional chronology of the Church, from the fourth consulate of Tiberius, that is, A.D. 21—must have appeared to the Christians as a collection of the worst blasphemies. It is humanly understandable that the Church, thus driven into a corner by the publication of this exposure, should have used the first opportunity to destroy the obnoxious documents root and branch. Still, a number of years had yet to pass before the Christians were granted such an opportunity. For the time being they had no other means than that of accusing their opponents of having forged genuine documents, and this bold assertion of theirs one of them tried to make others believe by a clever falsification of the chronology of Josephus.

Let us turn again to Eusebius, the first to discuss this problem. He sets out to prove that the *Acta* published by Maximinus must have been forgeries because they put the trial and execution of Jesus in the fourth consulate of Tiberius, the *seventh* year of his reign (A.D. August 21-22), whilst on the other hand, according to Josephus, Pilate did not enter Judaea until the *twelfth* year of Tiberius (=A.D. 26).

It is to be noted first that the historian does not appear to be perfectly sure of his authority, for he adds the clause : εἴγε τῷ Ἰωσήπῳ μάρτυρι χρήσασθαι δέον, that is, ' if [*or* provided that] one may call in Josephus as a witness.' Further, if, for the sake of

---

[1] See below, p. 322 n. 1.   [2] *Op. cit.*, i. 9, 2-10.
[3] As to the date, cf. H. M. Gwatkin, *Encyclop. of Religion and Ethics*, ix. 748b.

PLATE II

PORTRAIT OF EMPEROR MAXIMIN DAÏA

WHO PUBLISHED, IN A.D. 311, THE GENUINE ACTS OF PILATE
CONCERNING THE TRIAL OF JESUS

ENLARGED FROM A CAST OF A CONTEMPORARY MEDAL IN THE
CABINET DES MEDAILLES, PARIS

argument, we grant that the *Acta* in question may have been forgeries, it is utterly unlikely that the Roman chancellery, which had, at the least, access to the writings of Josephus, the court historiographer of the Flavians, whose works were in every public library, should have been so negligent as to choose a date which is in open contradiction to the statements of Josephus. Further, at the time of Maximinus Daïa the Gospels were of course easily accessible to anybody, and if the imperial chancellery had not possessed the genuine *Acta Pilati*, and had been obliged to produce false ones, it would certainly have used one of the dates based by the Church on *Luke* iii. 1, that is, A.D. 29, 32, or 33, but never the year A.D. 21, which no doubt surprised all Christians.

Lastly, one wonders why, if the *Acta* of Maximinus *were* false, Eusebius made no effort of his own to counter them by more exact researches undertaken by himself in the imperial archives. Indeed, when the peace between Church and State had at last been concluded, it was quite common that the Christians undertook just such researches in the archives of the various governors. For example, Apollonius, as quoted by Eusebius,[1] refers to the acts of the provincial archive of Asia to show that a certain Alexander had been tried before the Roman governor as a common criminal and not on account of his Christian confession, and Eusebius [2] himself quotes excerpts of such official records. As late as the sixth century it was still possible to consult judicial minutes dating from the reign of the Emperor Valens [3]—that is, documents two centuries old—with the same facility as if they had been written the day before. Moreover, Eusebius does not even say, as well he might have said, that the *Acta* published by Maximinus were forgeries because no report of the trial existed among the various genuine documents kept in the archives—because, let us say, the reports of Pilate and the *commentarii* of Tiberius were lost, etc. Indeed, he is careful not to venture such an assertion, because among the higher officials of the palace there were surely still enough opponents of Christianity and partisans of the old religion who could easily have refuted such a statement, and would moreover not have tolerated a falsification of the *divinae litterae* of the great Tiberius.

The Christian apologists could then do nothing else than fabricate a chronological argument by converting—a trifling change indeed!—the figure sixteen (I5) for the number of years of Pilate's administration (*Ant.*, xviii. 4. 1, § 89) into ten (I), and the corresponding number Δ (four years) for his predecessor Gratus (*Ant.*, xviii. 2. 2, § 35) into IA (eleven years), thus making Pilate's administration begin in A.D. 26 instead of in A.D. 19. There is indeed

---

[1] *Hist. eccl.*, v. 18.   [2] *Ibid.*, vii. 11.
[3] Lydus, *De magistrat. pop. Rom.*, iii. 29.

conclusive proof of such a brazen attack on the text to which a whole phrase about the high priest Caiaphas has fallen a victim in the crucial chapter (xviii. 2. 2, § 35).

St. Jerome in his commentary on Matthew states that he read in his Josephus about the high priest Caiaphas having bought his office, and that for one year only, by bribing King Herod Antipas.[1] A corresponding statement is wanting in the standard Greek text, and St. Jerome has been most frivolously accused of having invented it. As a matter of fact, the wording of Josephus cannot be intact in this place. The whole matter of the high-priestly office, and the manner in which it was bought and sold, clearly show what has happened to the text. The governor Gratus, the first of the officials of Judaea appointed by Tiberius in A.D. 15, just after the death of Augustus, came to Palestine toward the end of the year at the earliest, and during his term removed and appointed four high priests. Now, attention has been called[2] to the rabbinic tradition according to which the term of each priest was limited to one year by the Roman governor Valerius Gratus,[3] a custom which has parallels in other Roman provinces at this particular period. Josephus himself expressly states of two of the high priests appointed by Gratus that they held office for just one year, and even of the third there is nothing in the text[4] warranting that his term of office was longer.[5] Now, the logical conclusion from the fact that Gratus appointed altogether only four high priests, each for an annual term of office, seems to be that he himself held the governorship only for the four years A.D. 15, 16, 17, 18 ; for it is hardly likely that it took him seven years to invent such a profitable method, the less so because he can in no wise be regarded as its originator.[6] In the fourth Gospel (xi. 49) Caiaphas himself is spoken of as the 'high priest of the year.' Evidently a one-year term of office had become the rule since Gratus, and Caiaphas' long term, lasting throughout the administration of Pilate, is to be explained

[1] Ed. Vallarsi, vii. 223 : ' refert Josephus istum Caiapham unius tanti anni pontificatum ab Herode pretio redemisse.'
[2] Klausner-Danby, Jesus of Nazareth, London, 1925, p. 163 n. 1.
[3] See below, p. 599, the statement of the Rumanian Josephus that Valerius was recalled because he had been bribed by Ishmael to confer upon him the high-priestly dignity. This statement is not found anywhere in the Greek Josephus or in any other ancient author. Since it cannot very well have been invented by the Russian, Polish, or Rumanian translator, it must be derived from a passage in the Greek Josephus which was blotted out by the censor in the standard text.
[4] Ant., xviii. § 34 : "καὶ τοῦτον μετ' οὐ πολὺ [after a short term] μεταστήσας."
[5] This has been noticed by Hans von Soden in Cheyne's Encycl. Bibl., 171 : ' Valerius Gratus gave the post in succession to three men, none of whom held it, however, more than one year.' Schürer, Geschichte (4), ii. 271 (Engl. trans., Edinburgh, 1910, ii. 1, p. 198d), also places these four high priests in those years : Ishmael b. Phiabi 15-16, 'Ele'azar b. Anan 16-17, Simon b. Kamith 17-18, and Caiaphas 18-19.
[6] It had been planned by Lysias at the time of Antiochus v., Eupator (2 Macc., xi. 1-3, "πρατὴν . . . τὴν ἀρχιεροσύνην κατ' ἔτος ποιεῖν").

on the basis of a personal understanding he had with the latter, which means, that he paid him annually a bribe as high as or higher than that which any of his rival candidates could afford. Since Josephus reports the removal of Caiaphas through Vitellius as late as *Ant.* xviii. § 95, it follows that this high priest did indeed, as Jerome states after Josephus, buy his office from year to year by paying Herod (above, p. 18 n. 1) and, obviously, also the Roman governor, who had the right of veto. He was finally drawn into the ruin of his protector Pilate and removed at the same time as the latter. But since the whole passage about Caiaphas' tenure of office in *Ant.* xviii. § 35 left no doubt as to the sixteen-year term of Pilate's administration, it had to disappear entirely or in part [1] before the Christian censor.

This censor, fortunately, did not know the date of still another episode which, inserted as it is in the economy of Josephus' narrative, fully corroborates the above conclusion. Our writer puts the story of Mundus and Paulina (*Ant.* xviii. 3. 4-5), which we know from Tacitus [2] took place in A.D. 19, in the chapter dealing with the administration of Pilate in Judaea, although according to the standard text this administration did not begin until A.D. 26—a fact which has led various scholars to assume that this episode too is a late interpolation. But the apparent contradiction at once disappears if we assume that Pilate did indeed come to Palestine in the fall [3] of A.D. 18. The year A.D. 21 as the date of the passion, the date given for the trial of Jesus in the *Acta* published by Maximinus Daïa, would then fall entirely within the administration of Pilate. Nor is there any ground for doubting such a long term of office as the resulting seventeen years of Pilate. For we know from Josephus himself Tiberius' pertinent quotation of the Aesopian fable of the blood-sucking flies and his habit of leaving his servants as long as possible in office. Since, on the other hand, we are able to determine the date of the Passover of A.D. 21 (16th of April), it should now at last be possible to indicate with preciseness the day of the passion. To this problem we shall return in the second part of this work.

For the present we are mainly concerned with the important result that we have finally obtained a definite *terminus post quem* for tangible Christian forgeries and deletions in Josephus' text; the *terminus ante quem* being the moment when the Emperor Constantine gave power to the Church bodily to destroy anti-

---

[1] As in other cases (below, p. 54 l. 26 f.), St. Jerome's copy was less extensively expurgated than the standard text.

[2] *Ann.*, ii. 85 : ' *actum de sacris Aegyptiis et Judaicis pellendis.*'

[3] The season is indicated by the words μεθιδρύσας στρατιὰν χειμαδιούσαν| in *Ant.*, xviii. § 55. Immediately upon his arrival Pilate led the troops into their winter quarters in Jerusalem. He was quite inexperienced when he made the mistake about the medallions on the legionary standards (below, pp. 314 ff.).

Christian writings, and when it was therefore no more necessary
to counter the publication of Caesar Maximinus by elaborate
forgeries, since it could now be confiscated and burned by the
public executioner.

CONCLUSIONS

The historicity of Jesus as a heretic teacher of Jewish law is
established beyond doubt by the testimony of his disciple Jacob
of Kephar Sekhanjah—a man unknown to Christian sources—
transmitted through the rabbis 'Eli'ezer b. Hyrkanos and 'Aqiba
(A.D. 110), both of the latter witnesses being decidedly hostile to
Christianity. The execution of one ' Christus ' by the Roman
governor Pilate under Tiberius, as a criminal and founder of a band
of conspirators hostile to the whole human race, is established
thanks to the testimony of Tacitus.

The nature of the Roman charges against Jesus is clear, first
from Pilate's inscription on the cross, second from the attacks of
Celsus and Sossianus Hierocles. Jesus was considered a rebel king
proclaimed by the Jews—that is, legally, a robber chief, a leader
of bandits armed against the safety of the Roman empire. His
ascendency over his following was attributed to the performing of
sham miracles by magical arts, as well as to a sophistic, *i.e.* dema-
gogical, power of oratory. The remains of anti-Christian literature
prove that the opponents of Christianity described him as a
fomenter of rebellion (στάσεως ἀρχηγέτης), a sorcerer (γόης), a
demagogue (σοφιστής), a rebel and a robber chief (ἀρχιληστής).

The scarcity of anti-Christian sources about Jesus is accounted
for by the fact that Christian copyists would be reluctant to
reproduce what they considered blasphemous charges, and that
Christian censors had power, ever since the fourth century,
to destroy and consequently also to expurgate books of anti-
Christian tendencies.

The same considerations account for the total loss of the genuine
official documents regarding the trial of Jesus, about the former
existence of which, however, there can be no reasonable doubt.
From a passage in the text of Eusebius it may be inferred that they
were still accessible in A.D. 311, when they were published by the
Emperor Maximinus Daïa. The controversy about the chronology
as given by them according to Eusebius, in contradiction to the
Greek standard text of Josephus, yields an altogether unexpected
result, to wit, the true date of the passion at Easter of A.D. 21, and
the true date of Pilate's arrival in Palestine in the late fall of A.D. 18
(above, p. 19 n. 3). It also follows that the text of Josephus was
tampered with by Christian forgers in the matter of the chronology
of the governors Gratus and Pilate. The sole reason for this

forgery was to obtain a valid argument against the genuineness of the *Acta* published by Maximinus[1] in A.D. 311. A further consequence, of course, is a general presumption that the text of the Jewish historian Flavius Josephus has certainly not been handed down to us in its original integrity, but has suffered from the interference of Christian scribes and revisers.

[1] Cf. Eusebius, *Hist. eccl.*, i. 11. 9 (Dr. Kirsopp Lake's trans. in the Loeb Library, vol. cliii., 1926, p. 83) : ' When a writer sprung from the Hebrews themselves handed on in his own writing these details concerning John the Baptist and our Saviour, what alternative is there but to convict of shamelessness those who have concocted the Reports (ὑπομνήματα = *Acta*) about them ? '.

II

FLAVIUS JOSEPHUS

I T would be difficult to exaggerate the depth of our ignorance
in matters of Christian origins and contemporary Jewish
history had we nothing to go by but the Roman and Jewish
sources analysed in the preceding chapter. If it is at all possible
to write a coherent account of the period and the political struggle
going on between Jews and Romans, we have to thank the peculiar
circumstances which induced a certain Joseph bar Mattathia
Kahana of Jerusalem to relate, in a number of consecutive books,
the history of the origins and antecedents of that conflict, events
in which he had himself played a rather inglorious rôle. To understand fully the problems discussed in the present work, a summary
of the life and work of this writer will prove, if not necessary, at
least rather desirable. Nor have I seen any objection to anticipating some of the results of the following inquiry, the less so
because the currently known facts about Josephus may be found
in a number of well-known handbooks and reference works.[1]

This Joseph, later on called Flavius Josephus, claimed to
belong to an old priestly family and to be descended, through his
mother, from the royal stock of the Hasmonaeans. If this were
true, the blood of the Maccabees would have flowed in the veins of
this unworthy scion of a heroic race. He himself refers to genealogical documents in the archives of Jerusalem which, at the time
of his writing, had already been committed to the flames. At all
events, his opponents had a less exalted opinion of his ancestors.
Born in Jerusalem in A.D. 37-38, in the reign of Caligula—that is,
just one year after Pontius Pilate had been recalled from Judaea—
he boasts of his precocious talents. He had received, of course,
the religious and secular education of the Jews of that period, and
it is quite possible that the boy showed unmistakable signs of intelligence at an early age—as did many others of his nation in
ancient and recent times. We may well believe that he was, as he
says, occasionally given tests in the form of subtle questions on

[1] The English reader will find them most conveniently in the articles on
'Josephus' by Benedictus Niese in the *Encycl. of Religion and Ethics*, by Prof. v.
Dobschütz in Hastings' *Dictionary of the Apostolic Church*, and by Dr. H. St. John
Thackeray in the extra volume of Hastings' *Dictionary of the Bible*. The excellent
introduction to Dr. Thackeray's edition of Josephus in the Loeb Classical
Library, and his recent Hilda Stich Strook Lectures on Josephus, published by
the Jewish Institute of Religion, New York, 1929, on 'Josephus the Man and the
Historian,' may also be consulted.

points of the Law by high priests and learned scribes who came as guests to his father's house.

Another piece of boasting is his statement that some time in his youth (during what would now be one's university years) he studied the peculiar tenets of what he styles the three Jewish philosophical schools, the Pharisees, the Sadducees, and the Essenes. Since the first two were certainly not philosophical schools comparable to the Stoics and Epicureans of the Roman and Greek world, as he would have us believe, but rival parties of the priests and scribes, each with its own politico-religious programme, it looks as though in his early career he had wavered between the two opposite factions or forsaken the one to join the other. As for the third 'school,' the famous Essenes, it was in reality an ascetic brotherhood living under a system of communism, silent obedience and absolute submission to its superior, not unlike certain mediaeval orders of chivalry, and perhaps resembling somewhat the modern Mahomedan order of the Sanūsī in North Africa; at all events, probably a much less pacifist and mystical organization than Philo of Alexandria and Josephus himself would have their readers believe.[1] It is not at all improbable that Justus of Tiberias, against whose attacks Josephus defended himself when he wrote his *Life*, had dropped a few rather disparaging remarks on the latter's short-lived affiliation with this brotherhood, the oath of initiation of which may have been designed to guard more dangerous secrets than the powerful names of certain angels.

Having thus gained a first-hand knowledge of Sadducees, Pharisees, and Essenes, Josephus admits that he went out into the desert, the gathering-place of all the unruly spirits and outlaws in arms against the Romans and the Herodian dynasty. There he lived with a certain ' Banous '—not a proper name but a word meaning ' baptizer,' ' bather,' or ' baptist '[2]—another mysterious personage

---

[1] He has to admit that they carried arms when travelling 'because of the highwaymen'! (*B.J.*, ii. § 125), and that one of them headed the revolution against the Romans in the district of Thamna (*loc. cit.*, i. § 567, below, p. 257 n. 4). On the Sanūsī cp. D. S. Margoliouth, *Encycl. of Relig. and Eth.*, vol. xi. p. 194 ff.

[2] Cp. Jastrow's *Dictionary of the Targumim*, where *banna'ah* will be found as the equivalent for Greek βαλανεύς, ' bather,' ' frequenter of baths ' (*Targum Esther*, ii. 6, 12), and *bannej, bannaj* as equivalent of *balneum*, βαλανεῖον (Shabb. 33b, 41a, Meg. 16a). The *banna'im* of the much-discussed passage Mikw. ix. 6 (clothes of the *banna'im* considered as particularly clean) have been ingeniously and convincingly explained by Sachs (*Beitr.*, ii. 199) as the clothes of the *hemerobaptistae* (*tobělēj shaḥrith*). *Bannai(a)* does indeed occur as a proper name of various rabbis, but that is simply a parallel to the frequency of ' Baader ' as a proper name in German, such names being merely derived from a man's profession or peculiar habits. Names like *Bun* or *Buna*, probably abbreviated from *Abun* and *Abuna*, and *Buni* or *Bunai* (S. A. Cook's *Glossary* and Jacob Levy's *Nhb. Wb.* s. vv.), cannot be identified with *Banous*. The Greek secretary who translated Josephus' Hebrew or Aramean draft into Greek (see below, pp. 130 ff.) mistook the word— which the author may have used intentionally instead of *'ṭobel*, ' baptist '—the word used in the lines quoted below, p. 99 nn. 1 and 2—for a proper name.

whom he endeavours to deck with the innocent colours of a harmless leaf-wearing and fruit-eating hermit, but who may have shown a far less pacific aspect in the lost pamphlet of Justus of Tiberias designed to expose his former comrade-in-arms. At all events, his Maccabee ancestors, when they were on the war-path against the Seleucids, seem to have lived this same ascetic vegetarian life ' among the beasts ' in the hills and in the desert,[1] the life, that is, of the hemerobaptist zealots.

Josephus next affiliated himself with the Pharisees. At the age of twenty-six he journeyed to Rome to obtain by straight or devious means the release of some priests who had been arrested by the governor Felix and sent to Rome for trial before the Emperor, very distinguished ($\kappa\alpha\lambda o\kappa\alpha\gamma\alpha\theta oi$) and pious men ' living on figs and nuts ' on their sea voyage and throughout the time of their captivity, hardly in order to avoid eating the unclean meat of the heathen—bread, fish, and eggs would have been permissible in this case—but because they followed the vegetarian diet of Josephus' baptist teacher in the wilderness. Yet, in spite of, or perhaps because of, this exemplary piety,[2] they were obviously under some suspicion of political disaffection in the eyes of Felix, who did not of course care a straw for their religious beliefs or disbeliefs.

Having suffered shipwreck, Josephus ' outstripped, through God's providence ' and his own recklessness, all the other victims in a swimming race towards a rescuing Cyrenaean ship, and was landed in Puteoli. With the help of Haliturus, a famous actor of Jewish descent, he wormed himself into the presence of Poppaea, the wife of Nero, a Jewish or at least Judaizing lady of great influence with her imperial husband. From her he obtained not only the release of his imprisoned vegetarian friends, but in addition ' great gifts,' a fact which goes far to suggest that the young Jew was not deficient in good looks and courtly manners and well acquainted with the great art of flattering those who might be useful to him. On his return to Palestine, in A.D. 66, he found the revolution against Rome fully on its way and his compatriots quite unwilling to be held back by his impressive traveller's yarns about the power and wealth of the Romans. Yet his pessimistic views about the possible chances of the war for liberty recommended him to the peace-loving moderate party of the high priests, so that they saw fit to attach him to a diplomatic mission which they sent to Galilee under the direction of two distinguished priests, to keep that unruly province quiet.

---

[1] 2 *Macc.* v. 27: 'But Judah the Maccabean, with nine other men or thereabout, withdrew [into the desert [$\dot{\alpha}\nu\alpha\chi\omega\rho\dot\eta\sigma\alpha s$ $\epsilon\dot{\iota}s$ $\tau\dot\eta\nu$ $\ddot\epsilon\rho\eta\mu o\nu$] and lived in the hills after the manner of beasts [$\theta\eta\rho\dot\iota\omega\nu$ $\tau\rho\dot o\pi o\nu$] with his company, feeding on a vegetarian diet [$\tau\dot\eta\nu$ $\chi o\rho\tau\dot\omega\delta\eta$ $\tau\rho o\phi\dot\eta\nu$ $\sigma\iota\tau o\dot\upsilon\mu\epsilon\nu o\iota$ $\delta\iota\epsilon\tau\dot\epsilon\lambda o\upsilon\nu$], so as not to defile himself like the other people.'

[2] See below, pp. 236 n. 7, 237, and 541 n. 7.

With the help of considerable sums taken from the treasury of the temple they were further to collect troops for the support of the hierarchy as against the rebels, who were well armed, thanks to the booty they obtained at the initial defeat of Cestius.   This trust vested in him by the Jerusalemitan hierarchy and by the two ambassadors he most shamefully misused.   Noticing that in Galilee public opinion was overwhelmingly hostile to the Romans and to the hierarchy, and that the ambassadors would never succeed in carrying out their orders, he promptly negotiated with the revolutionaries, took an active part in the establishment of a Galilaean counter-Sanhedrin, and even proceeded to the collecting of troops as a sort of bodyguard for himself.   It is not true that, as he states, he himself was the commander-in-chief of the whole of the Galilaean force and that he had ' chosen ' the Sanhedrin in question. What is certain, however, is that the ambitious young man did his best to foment the rebellion, partly with the co-operation, partly against the will, of numerous local rivals; that he misused his position to enrich himself by engaging in war-profiteering of the most doubtful character—e.g. scandalous speculations in Galilaean, ritually pure oil; and, worst of all, that to all appearances he remained in touch with the Romans.   He attempted to counteract the just suspicions entertained against him by the authorities at Jerusalem by sending them a report concerning the political situation, a report which was to form the nucleus of his later works.   At the first encounters of his troops with the Romans the former were miserably beaten, thanks largely to the military incompetency and cowardice of this ambitious bureaucrat.   Although he consistently represents himself as the commander of his troops, it has now become clear through the comparison of the earliest draft of his history with the later editions that his position was somewhere between that of an army-chaplain and that of an army-clerk, resembling somewhat the rôle of the revolutionary commissaries of the French armies during the Great Revolution.

On the arrival of Vespasian and his army he withdrew with the Galilaean main force into Tiberias, then to Jotapata, a mountain stronghold which defended itself, or—according to our ' hero '—was defended by him, for six weeks against the besieging Romans. On the taking of the town, through a breach in the wall, Josephus and some other leaders hid in a cistern.   His brave comrades, who had made up their minds to kill one another rather than to survive the downfall of their nation, he cheated in the casting of the lots,[1] and then surrendered to a Roman officer, an old acquaintance of his, as he puts it.   How he had come to make such useful acquaintances in the enemy's camp he is careful not to tell, but he

---

[1] See App., p. 654 of vol. iii. of Dr. Thackeray's *Josephus*.   Below, p. 199.

obviously wants his readers to infer that he had made them during his stay in Rome.

From now on his progress was rapid.   He won the favour of the Roman commander-in-chief, Flavius Vespasianus, by pretending to have had an inspired prophetic dream foretelling the impending rise of the general to the imperial throne and proclaiming Vespasian the divinely chosen world-ruler mentioned by the Jewish prophets.   In reality, the ' god-sent inspiration ' of this ' dream ' was most probably derived from more earthly sources. For a number of men in the general headquarters, among them a wealthy and ambitious Alexandrian Jew, Tiberius Alexander, a nephew of the philosopher Philo and himself completely Romanized, were anxious to push the undecided and cautious Vespasian on to the road of political adventure and to engineer his future glory.   However that may be, Vespasian accepted the prophecy as one of the ' *omina imperii* ' of his house, and for ever after kept the man whom he affected to regard as the divine instrument near himself and his son Titus throughout the Jewish campaign, and later on at his private house in Rome, as one of his clients and paid propagandists.   During the war Josephus was not ashamed of serving as an interpreter and of taking upon himself the odious task of questioning Jewish prisoners for the Roman intelligence department.   Nor did he refuse to translate into his native tongue and to read to the defenders of the besieged city the proclamations of general headquarters.   In the discharge of this noble office the traitor was nearly killed by a well-aimed stone flung at his head. Our sincere thanks are due to a kind fate which spared him for a greater purpose.

Either on his own initiative or at the suggestion of the Roman ally of the Jewish king Agrippa II., or that of Tiberius Alexander, the Jewish chief of Titus' general staff, Josephus conceived the plan of writing a history of the Jewish rebellion on the basis of his own notes and the *Acta* of general headquarters.   He succeeded in persuading Vespasian and Titus of the usefulness of such a work, if it attempted to describe the rebellion not as an affair of the whole Jewish people but as an uprising of the extremists, the zealots, or as we should say nowadays the have-nots, against the Romanophile *élite*, the noble and the wealthy of their own people.   Such a presentation of events could not but have calming effects upon the prominent Jews of the Diaspora and in Mesopotamia.

To reach these populations, he was to write his work first in Aramaic and then have it translated into Greek by the proper men, to be found either among the *servi literati* of the imperial staff or among the *Graeculi esurientes* always on the look-out for work of that kind.   To facilitate this, the Emperor placed at his disposal whatever official material there existed on the subject.   For the treatment of the events leading up to the rebellion he utilized the history of Nicolaus of Damascus, which carried him down to the death of Herod the Great. He does not seem, however, to have drawn on the Greek original of the work, but—according to certain indications—on a Semitic translation, or rather a Pharisaean reworking from a point of view hostile to the Romans and the Herodian dynasty, altogether easier to read for his poor Greek scholarship than the original text. For the period following he utilized the reports of the governors, which he probably found in the *commentarii* of the Julian and Claudian emperors in the *tabularium principis* in the imperial palace. It is equally possible, however, that even before his second voyage to Rome he was given access to the archives of the governors of Judaea, at Caesarea. For the history of John the Baptist he drew on indigenous Naṣōraean material,[1] dating back, no doubt, to the period of his youth when he had himself lived in the desert as the follower of a ' Baptist.' Of much the same provenance is still another source of his, a compilation on the interpretation of dreams by the various prophets and seers of his nation.[2]

From the preface of Josephus' work it may be inferred that it was originally meant for the triumph of Titus, with which event the table of contents in the procemium comes to a close. The copies destined for a Roman public and presented to Vespasian, Titus, and their generals bore a title betraying completely the Roman viewpoint of the author and his work—to wit, *The Jewish War*. On the other hand, the copies meant for sale among his co-religionists bore the title *On the Capture of Jerusalem*, less apt to offend Jewish national susceptibilities. His first draft, completed in A.D. 72, of the weaknesses of which he must have been aware, he constantly improved by correcting mistakes, deleting passages which had proved distasteful to influential readers, and by adding new material. Finally, at a certain period during the reign of Domitian, he had the whole matter rewritten in better Greek by a more competent collaborator. Throughout his literary activity he was most anxious to whitewash himself and to attribute the blame for everything to the insurgents, whom after Roman official custom he styles ' bandits ' or ' robbers,' and whose leaders he designates as ' mountebanks ' (γόητες) and ' demagogues ' (πλάνοι or σοφισταί). Such measures on his part were all the more necessary because he appears to have been accused repeatedly on the score of his former activity among the rebels. The weaver Jonathan, one of the leaders of the uprising of the Jews of Cyrene, and later on the pedagogue of his own son—who may have been one of his literary collaborators—are two of his accusers of whom we have a certain amount of knowledge, thanks to his own reference to them. Yet

---

[1] Below, p. 226 l. 36. [2] Below, p. 226 ll. 37 ff.

.most damaging must have appeared to him the work of his old opponent and rival, Justus of Tiberias. To refute the accusations there brought forward against him, he compiled a most insincere and unreliable autobiography. His last literary effort—60,000 στίχοι of penny-a-lining, as he is careful to point out in the dedication to his publisher—was the *Jewish Antiquities*, a vast compilation about the history of the Jews from Adam until the outbreak of the war against the Roman empire, completed in the thirteenth year of Domitian (A.D. 93-94). Incidentally, the work contains much material by way of additions and corrections to the *Jewish War*, i.e. data which had been placed at his disposal by the readers of his first work. Among the most generous of these contributors must be reckoned King Agrippa II., who got into the habit of sending him letters with additions to and corrections on each of the subsequent instalments, more than five dozen of them altogether. Further, whilst in the *War* there is no trace of his knowledge of Christian sources, in the *Antiquities* we seem to observe a polemical allusion [1] to a work known already to the Samaritan Thallus,[2] which was a compilation of passages from the Prophets supposed to have found their fulfilment in the life of Jesus. These *testimonia*—which have been fully discussed by Dr. Rendel Harris [3] —are ascribed by Papias, probably correctly, to the tax-gatherer Matthew, the follower of the Naṣōraean Messiah. No doubt Josephus' literary activity, in which his *servi litterati* did most of the real work, must have paid him reasonably well, for in the year 14 of Domitian's reign he published a new edition of the *War*, preceded by the *Antiquities* and provided with a continuation bringing events up to the time of his writing, altogether in twenty-four books.[4] He even had shorter editions published in very elegant Atticizing Greek by a specially good συνεργός, of which there remain to us only the so-called *epitomē* of the *Antiquities*. An *epitomē* of the *Polemos* which Ludovicus Capellus (died 1722) gave to Jacob Usher has not yet turned up, although it probably survives in some English private library. Jerome [5] mentions an edition of the *Antiquities* dating from the fourteenth year of Domitian, i.e. A.D. 94-95. The extant text of the book is a reworking made after the death of Agrippa II. Posterior to the first edition of the *Antiquities* is a little treatise called *Contra Apionem* ever since the time of St. Jerome. Whether he ever carried out his project of

---

[1] See below, p. 55, on the phrase about the myriad of miracles of Jesus foretold by the divine prophets.

[2] See below, p. 298 n. 5.

[3] *Testimonies*, i. and ii., Cambridge, 1916, 1920.

[4] This is known through a statement of the mediaeval chronicler Jeraḥm'el ben Shelomo, who seems to have drawn on a lost preface of the Hebrew version of Josephus. See below, pp. 83 ff., on the quotations from this lost work, found in the Byzantine chronographers.   [5] *De vir. ill.*, xiii.

PLATE III

FRONT VIEW OF PRESUMED JOSEPHUS HEAD

NOTE THE INTENTIONAL ASSIMILATION OF THE FACE OF THE FLAVIAN COURTIER TO THE TYPE OF
EMPEROR TITUS' WELL-KNOWN COLOSSAL BUST IN THE NAPLES MUSEUM

elucidating the philosophic reasons underlying the Mosaic Law to the sceptic Gentiles, we do not know. Such a work may well have served as groundwork to the *Mosaicarum et Romanorum legum collatio* of Isaac Hilarius-Gaudentius, the Latin translator of Josephus' book on the *Jewish War*.

He was married at least three times, divorced his first wife, the mother of three sons, who had followed him into exile, and espoused a Jewish girl belonging to one of the wealthiest families of the Cretan Diaspora.

As a client and a parasite of the Emperor, Josephus enjoyed the revenues of landed estates in Palestine ruthlessly taken away from the rightful owners by virtue of Roman martial law and custom. His name was put on the pension list of the slush fund, endowed by the Flavian emperors for venal writers and orators. Following the well-known custom, he adopted the family name of his protector. His writings were officially approved by the imperial signature of Titus and put in the public libraries. According to Eusebius [1] and St. Jerome,[2] he was honoured with a statue erected somewhere in Rome. If this statement were exact, Josephus would not have failed to mention the fact in his autobiography. The statue might have been dedicated to his memory after his death. Since by that time the last of his imperial patrons had preceded him to Elysium, we might presume that his publisher Epaphroditus, in the interest of the sale of Josephus' collected works, headed a subscription of his grateful readers for the erection of this well-deserved monument. More likely, however, the portrait-statue mentioned by Eusebius and St. Jerome was ordered by the conceited historian himself during his lifetime, in defiance of the laws of his pious ancestors forbidding those 'graven images' which enabled the heathen to immortalize the transient shape of their perishable bodies. This must have been the case if—as I feel convinced—the inedited first-century Roman marble bust [3] of

---

[1] *Hist. eccl.*, iii. 9. 2, p. 226 of Dr. Kirsopp Lake's translation.

[2] *De vir. ill.*, xiii.

[3] *Ny Carlsberg Glyptotek* in Copenhagen, Cat. No. 646, bought by Helbig in Rome from Princess Piombino, *née* Borghese. It had stood for a long time in Prince Borghese's study. I owe the photographs to the courtesy of Prof. Frederik Poulsen. The only other Roman statue with a Jewish-looking face among the seven or eight hundred extant Greek and Roman portraits is that of the so-called 'Drusus' of the Naples Museum, which was discovered in the meat-market hall (*macellum*) of Pompeii, together with a statue thought to be Livia, on the strength of an inscription found near it. Since young Herod Agrippa (III.) was killed in 79 A.D. through the eruption of Mt. Vesuvius (Josephus, *Ant.*, xx. 144), this might very well be a votive statue of the son of Felix and fair Drusilla. No other Jewish-looking face is found in the comprehensive collections of portraits brought together by Arndt-Bruckmann and Poulsen. Owing to the severe prohibition of portrait-sculpture by Jewish law, it must indeed be very exceptional to find a portrait-statue or bust of a Jew. See my paper, 'Deux sculptures représentant des Juifs de l'Antiquité Classique,' in M. Jean Babelon's *Aréthuse* (January 1930).

a typical Jew [1] (see our frontispiece) is nothing but the head [2] of this otherwise lost statue. Even if we discount the natural tendency of an artist to flatter a vain client by making him look more youthful, this portrait—if it be indeed that of Josephus, born A.D. 36-37 — cannot be attributed to a later date than A.D. 76-80. It would therefore be at the very time when he had the satisfaction of publishing the second edition of the *Jewish War* that the author, intoxicated by this success, might have yielded to the temptation of having his statue made by one of the skilful Greek artists who frequented the antechambers of the imperial palace in order to obtain commissions, were it only from the freedmen and opulent clients surrounding the imperial majesties —maybe by a rival of that unknown sculptor who wrought the portrait of the learned freedman, M. Mettius Epaphroditus of Chaeronea, the grammarian, book-collector, and bookseller of Herculean stature and strength of body,[3] the κράτιστος ἀνδρῶν, as Josephus jestingly calls him, who acted, according to the identification of Prof. Laqueur of Giessen, as publisher of the *Antiquities*, the *Life*, the *Contra Apionem*, and of the last edition of Josephus' complete works, collected under the title of *Jewish Histories*.

In so far as it is at all permissible to speak of the world-wide popularity of a work of literature, the Jewish history of this Flavius Josephus did have such a success. The Christians appear to have read him from the very beginning; witness the utilization of his work by the *Acts of the Apostles* which is now admitted by most specialists.[4] Hand in hand with this utilization went a process of adulteration of the text, especially in regard to the passages bearing on the lives of John the Baptist and Jesus himself. The fact that

---

[1] The hooked nose is rather thick at the lower end, and therefore very different from the aquiline nose which is often found among Romans. The forehead strongly convex just above the brows, but the upper part plainly retreating and hidden under the curly hair; the expression of the eyes sad, restless, and watchful; the rather sulky mouth; above all, the slightly protruding lower lip, the slight beard forming a kind of down, the untrimmed side-locks (*Lev.* xix. 27)— all these features are not those of a Roman, although the person in question plainly wished to look as like the Emperor Titus as possible (witness the latter's well-known and often-reproduced colossal bust in the Naples Museum). As a result of this tendency, the front view of the head shows indeed the likeness of a '*Flavius*,' while the profiles are just as unmistakably those of *Joseph bar Mattathia Kahana*. The whole head is handsome enough to be that of the young scapegrace who knew how to please the Empress Poppaea and—twenty years later—the Empress Domitia (*Life*, § 429). See front view of bust (our Pl. III.).

[2] The reproduction shows clearly that a part of the left shoulder has been restored in modern marble. It can be easily seen, by the outline of this restoration and of another piece on the right side, that the head was part of a statue the left shoulder of which was covered by the end of the toga, and that it had originally been wedged into the torso of a statue.

[3] See Pl. IV.

[4] F. C. Burkitt, *Gospel History and its Transmission*, pp. 106 ff. Holtzmann (1873), Hausrath, Keim, Clemen; cf. Krenkel, *Josephus und Lukas*, Leipzig, 1894, and Paul W. Schmiedel in Cheyne's *Encycl. Bibl.*, 5056, where further references are given.

PLATE IV

M. METTIUS EPAPHRODITUS, THE PUBLISHER OF JOSEPHUS, WORKS

INSCRIBED HALF LIFE-SIZE STATUE ON THE STAIRCASE OF VILLA ALTIERI, ROME.   THE IDENTIFICATION
IS DUE TO PROFESSOR RICHARD LAQUEUR OF GIESSEN

Origen knew a genuine text of Josephus only proves that this excellent philologist still had such a copy in his library ; it does not prove at all that the process of alteration itself began at a later date. A Christian interpolation, for example, influenced the Jewish Christian Hegesippus as early as A.D. 180 in his dating the death of James the Just.[1] Omissions and deletions of whole passages were as common as the interpolations. Fortunately, the process did not go on uniformly in the various MSS., and there is still a possibility of discerning the wording of the original text through the variant readings and old quotations. A regular new edition, definitely expurgated, was produced by the Greek Church as late as the eleventh century, in order to counteract the ever-growing power of various Judaizing heretic sects,[2] whose Unitarianism drew its main strength from the writings of Josephus.

In antiquity Josephus was translated twice into Latin, first by a converted Jew, whose name Isaac had been Latinized into Hilarius or Gaudentius,[3] about A.D. 370, and again on the suggestion of Cassiodorus, hence probably by some monks of Vivarium (Squillace). Anterior to the sixth century is a Syriac translation, of which the sixth book of the *War* was actually incorporated in the canons of the Syrian and Armenian Churches.

The Mesopotamian Jews of Aramaic speech have to all appearances never read the Semitic version of the *War*.[4] The Latin version of Hilarius-Gaudentius was destined for the Jews of the West, who had forgotten their Greek like the rest of the Occident, and whom he hoped to convert. With the same aim of religious propaganda in view, another converted Jew, living in one of the Jewish settlements on the Illyrian coast of the Adriatic a few centuries later, translated the Latin version into Hebrew, this Christianized *Josippon* being erroneously ascribed to the high priest Joseph ben Gorion, a contemporary of our Joseph bar Mattathia. A reworking of this *Josippon*, with the help of a Greek MS. of Josephus' last edition of the *Polemos*—the one of A.D. 94-95, in twenty-four books —was undertaken by Illyrian or Italian Jews some time in the ninth century. Naturally enough, they omitted the Christian interpolations and alterations as much as was in their power, yet could not hope to be altogether successful in this task, the result being that even in this reworking numerous traces of the underlying Christian version are still found. Most of the passages hostile to Christianity and its founder which were added from the Greek original to this reworking were discovered by the censor and duly suppressed in most copies. What is left of these passages—

---

[1] See App. VII.　　　　　　　　　[2] See below, p. 169.
[3] See Joseph Wittig, *Kirchengesch. Abhandl.*, hg. v. Max Sdralek, vol. v., Breslau, 1906, p. 47.　　　　[4] See below, p. 98 ll. 37 f.

little enough, to be sure—has been utilized critically for the first time in the present work.[1]

The *Josippon* was translated into Arabic by a Yemenite Jew residing in Sicily. It is probably this Arabic version [2] which was translated into Ethiopic,[3] for the use either of the Ethiopian Christians or of the Jewish Falashas.

The Hebrew *Josippon* was known to the Jews in Angevine England, and attracted there the attention even of a learned abbot of St. Frideswide's near Oxford.[4] The sixteenth century saw the production of a Yiddish [5] and of a Judeo-Spanish translation, the latter destined for the women of the Jewish faith driven out of Spain. For the men, who read Hebrew, of course, Hebrew-printed editions followed upon the Mantua *editio princeps* of the *Josippon*. I note the following editions : one from Constantinople (1510), one from Venice (1544), Cracow (1589), Frankfurt-a.-M.(1689), Amsterdam (1723, 1739), Leghorn (1794), Zolkiew (1808), Vilna (1812), Szitomir (1851), Lemberg (1855), Warsaw (1871), Berditschev (1896-1913). Even in Calcutta this work was printed in 1841, for the benefit of the Indian Jews. Primarily destined for Christian scholarship were the editions of Worms (1529), Basle (1541, 1559), Paris (1575), Gotha (1707, 1710), and Oxford (1706).

An English translation by P. Morvyng of a mediaeval extract from the *Josippon* dates from 1561,[6] a French translation (by a Christian named Belleforest) from 1569.

An Armenian translation made from the Greek text is supposed to have perished during the Tatar invasions. A new one, with the help of the Latin translation of Rufinus, was made in the seventeenth century.

Josephus' first draft, dating from A.D. 72, was read in Bulgaria as late as the twelfth century. Between 1250 and 1260 it was translated, somewhere in Lithuania, from the Greek into the Old Russian, from a MS. annotated in the Byzantine empire during the period of the Latin empire. The translation was the work of a Judaizing sect of heretics who hoped thereby to win over King Mindauvas of Lithuania.[7] The MSS. utilized came from the circle of the sect of the so-called Josephinists, scattered over Asia Minor,

---

[1] See below, pp. 96 ff.

[2] It was printed repeatedly as late as the nineteenth century in the Orient (Algiers and Beyruth). Two MSS., Arab. No. 1906 and de Slane No. 287, are in the Paris National Library.

[3] Unedited MSS. in London, Berlin, and Frankfurt-a.-M. Cf. Goldschmidt, *Die abessinischen Handschriften der Staatsbibliothek zu Frankfurt a. M.*, 1897, pp. 5-9. Wright, Catal. of Ethiop. MSS. in the Brit. Mus., No. ccclxxviii. The Ethiopic title is *Zena Aihud*.

[4] See below, p. 93.

[5] The oldest Yiddish translation (by the converted Jew Michael Adam), printed at Zürich in 1548. Later editions : Prague, 1607 ; Fürth, 1767, 1771 ; Warsaw, 1875.

[6] See below, p. 604, App. xi.   [7] See below, p. 148, last lines.

Thrace, and Macedonia. This explains the curious fact that they somehow escaped the orthodox censor and contain most invaluable passages concerning John the Baptist and Jesus. Though not entirely free from Christian additions,[1] they yet represent most faithfully the original text of Josephus' first draft.

Through this translation the old Ebionite Jewish Christianity, regarding Jesus not as a god but merely as a prophet, was transplanted to Slavonic soil. There it spread rapidly, thanks largely to the general approval it was bound to meet with in the circles of pseudo-converts to Christianity descended from the numerous Russian proselytes to Judaism made under the old Jewish empire of the Khazars. After dominating all Russia, the movement was finally broken by the ruthless despotism of Ivan III. Vasiljevitch, who had at first favoured it. Fugitives took some of the precious MSS. with them to Lithuania and Poland, where they laid the foundations of that Unitarianism which was later to invade Western Europe.[2] There the Old Russian Josephus was translated into Polish.[3]

In the sixteenth century the movement was transplanted to Transylvania, where the sect continued to live an independent life as late as 1793. This fact explains the translation from Polish into Rumanian of the text under discussion. Of this translation only the fragments about John the Baptist and Jesus have been preserved.[4] The invasion of South Slavonic territory by the Unitarian movement was no doubt responsible for the Servian translation made in 1585, of which a MS. is preserved in the Chilandari Lavra of Mt. Athos, another in one of the Fruška Gora monasteries of Syrmia.[5]

In Russia the Judaizing sect never died out. Even the Hebrew *Josippon* was accordingly translated into Russian, no doubt for the benefit of Russian 'Sabbathizers' (*subbotniki*), a work of which a MS. is in the Royal Library of Copenhagen, another in Moscow,[6] another in Leningrad.[7] The Orthodox Church did not persecute further the Judaizing Josephus MSS., but was satisfied with certain Christian additions and interpolations. The learned

[1] See below, pp. 224 ff. and pp. 385 ff.
[2] The movement is closely connected with the names of the Piedmontese physician Giorgio Blandrata, who went to Poland in 1558, and of the humanist Fausto Socino of Siena, who went there in 1579. It proudly records a number of martyrs, first among them Katharina Vogel, who was burned to death in Cracov.
[3] No trace of a MS. of this version has been found so far.
[4] See App. VIII.
[5] This MS. has been pointed out to me by my Bulgarian colleague, Professor N. Ivanov.
[6] Musée Historique, Synod. No. 745. Specimen pages of it are reproduced by Sol. Zeitlin, *Jew. Qu. Rev.*, 1929, vol. xx., between pp. 10-11 and 26-27, without the library signature and under the misleading title 'Slavonic Josephus.'
[7] Public Library, No. 262. Specimen pages reproduced by Zeitlin, *loc. cit.*, before p. 1 and after p. 6.

C

Archbishop Makarios himself (1542-1563) saw no objection to adding it to his *Četji Minei*, a collection of edifying works suitable for public readings. Thus it was that the Russian Orthodox Church possessed only this Old Russian Josephus translation of the Judaists, until as late as 1804 Michaelov Samuelovič made a Modern Russian translation after a Latin version of the Greek standard text which was printed by the Imperial Academy of Sciences. This Modern Russian translation was the basis of the Georgian translation made by the priest David Inanashwili.

There is no need to emphasize the great popularity of both Latin translations throughout the Middle Ages. There are, as Prof. Ussani kindly tells me, literally hundreds of MSS. of the Latin Josephus to be found in all European libraries. Magnificently illuminated copies—the finest of them in the Paris National Library [1]—prove that the wily courtier of the Flavian emperors remained in favour with the princes and rulers of this world throughout the Middle Ages. Almost contemporaneously with the first printed edition of the *Josippon*, at Mantua, there appeared the *editio princeps* of the Latin Josephus, at the shop of Johann Schüssler at Augsburg. But even after this the work was printed many a time, until the appearance of the *editio princeps* of the Greek standard text.[2] By far the most interesting of these reprints is the Basle edition of 1524, published by Frobenius. In 1551 the Swiss theologian and philologist Sebastian Chateillon, a follower of Calvin, added the Latin Josephus to his Latin edition of the Bible.

The first printed Greek edition dates from 1544. It was the work of the humanist Arnold Peraxylos Arlen,[3] and appeared at Basle, in the print-shop of Frobenius and Episcopius. The edition was pirated in Geneva in 1611, and again in 1634. But there is also quite a number of later learned editions.[4]

The first English translations were made from the Greek, and are the work of Thomas Lodge (London, 1640) and Roger Le Strange (London, 1716). Both were excelled by that of the Unitarian William Whiston (Dublin, 1738-41), who in 1710 had lost

---

[1] See *e.g.* Cod. Lat. 8959, saec. xii., of the Paris National Library. The best illustrated MSS. of Josephus' works are those of the fifteenth-century French translation (by Guillaume Coquillard, 1463); the one with Jean Fouquet's celebrated miniatures (published by Comte Durieu, Paris, 1908), cod. fr. 247, Bibl. Nat.; another one (Arsenal, 5082-3) once owned by the great book-lover, the Bastard Antoine de Bourgogne. See also Bibl. Nat., codd. fr. 248-9, 405-6, 11-16, and 404.

[2] See App. ix.

[3] Christian Gottlieb Jöcher, *Allgemeines Gelehrten-Lexikon*, iii. (Leipzig 1751), coll. 1375: ' Peraxylus ist der Nahme, welchen sich Arnoldus Arlenius, ein gelehrter Mann aus Brabant, gegeben. Derselbe lebte im 16. Saeculo, war in der griechischen Sprache wohl erfahren, gab den Josephus nach einem vortrefflichen MS. griechisch heraus,' etc., ' und starb um 1561 zu Basel.' [Translator's note.]

[4] See App. x.

his chair in Cambridge in consequence of his religious convictions. This edition, reprinted time and again, proved to be a most popular one ; witness the numerous reprints in the course of the eighteenth and nineteenth centuries, notwithstanding the fact that it was by no means the last attempt to translate our author into English.[1] Even eighteenth-century America published a Josephus translation, pirated from the English version of George Henry Maynard, illustrated by Edward Kingston (London, C. Cooke, 1789).[2] The excellent translation into French, begun by the late Th. Reinach, has now been completed by Mr. Salomon Reinach.

It may well be said that few works outside the Bible itself have exercised such a powerful and far-reaching influence as the writings of this wretched renegade. Certainly, no ancient writer can even be said to approach him in this peculiar popularity. To say nothing of the vast number of translations into languages utterly unknown to the *orbis Romanus*, it has been the subject of innumerable commentaries and discussions ; nor is it to be supposed that this tremendous interest will wane in the near future. Neither can he be said to have missed popularity among his own people, the people whose cause he so ingloriously betrayed, and who, after more than two thousand years of disappointment and exile, still dream of the Land of Promise, the land they are not likely to find anywhere until the fulfilment of the world-old dream and hope of a true *Civitas Dei*—the whole earth, that is, united in one great spiritual union, with all national and religious hatreds vanished never to return.

Habent sua fata libelli. Yet in spite of the many vicissitudes of Josephus' work, vicissitudes which we have followed in all their bewildering intricacy, the ' mirror dark ' and scratched though it is, still shows events long past but whose reflexions cast their strange glamour even on our own age. Above all, though not making him appear to us ' face to face,' yet it allows us to see the contours, dimly perhaps yet distinctly, of the great ' king who never reigned,' the Servant of the Lord who has yet left on mankind an imprint compared with which those of all the great world-conquerors and world-destroyers both before and after him must be regarded as trivial and insignificant.

---

[1] See App. x.   [2] The work appeared in New York in 1792.

III

THE CONTROVERSY OVER THE SO-CALLED 'TESTIMONY TO JESUS CHRIST' IN THE 'JEWISH ANTIQUITIES' OF JOSEPHUS

'The false pen of the scribes hath made of it falsehood.'

JER. viii. 8.

JOSEPHUS ACCEPTED AS AN 'INSPIRED' WITNESS

FOR fully 1200 years the Church could boast of the sure and undisputed possession of an extremely remarkable testimony, *pretiosissima et vix aestimabilis gemma*, as the old Viennese court librarian Petrus Lambeccius called it, a testimony rendered by an outsider to the truth of the historical foundations, not only of its faith, but even of its dogma, its creed. The Jewish historian Flavius Josephus, a man born just a few years after the traditional date of the death of Christ, seemed to affirm in the eighteenth book of his *Jewish Antiquities* that 'Jesus called the Christ' did so many and such great miracles that one might hesitate to regard him as a man at all ; that he taught the truth ; that this true teaching of his was received with joy by multitudes both of Jews and Gentiles ; that this Jesus was really the Christ, that is, the Messiah, expected by the Jews, for the thousands of wonderful things which he did and suffered exactly corresponded with what the inspired prophets had foretold of the expected redeemer of their people ; that he was crucified by Pilate on the indictment of the Jewish leaders, but on the third day reappeared alive to his disciples, who consequently did not waver in their allegiance to him, the result being the survival, at the time of the witness Josephus, of the new race called Christians after the founder of their sect.

Throughout the eleven long centuries which separate the edict of toleration of Milan (312) from the disruption of the Occidental Church with the Protestant Reform—in other words, the time lying between the *Historia ecclesiastica* of Eusebius and that of Cardinal Baronius—not a doubt was cast on the authenticity of Josephus' precious *Testimonium*, which was constantly quoted and turned to good account by all Church historians. The obviously paradoxical fact that an unbelieving Jew should have acknowledged Jesus to have been the true Christ foretold by the prophets was attributed to the peculiar and miraculous power of the Redeemer, which had forced as it were even a recalcitrant infidel to yield to its spell and extracted a blessing from this second Balaam who must have set out to curse.   The important fact that he did not himself believe in Jesus as the Christ did not impair the value of his testimony in the eyes of the Church.   On the contrary, it was strengthened by the fact that even an unbeliever and an adversary of the faith had reluctantly to confess to its truth. ' And therein the eternal power of Jesus Christ was manifested, that the princes of the synagogue, who handed him over to death, acknowledged him to be God ' ;   these are the words of Isaac, a converted Jew, writing about 370, known to the Christians under the name of Gaudentius or Hilarius, as found in the Latin para-phrase of the *Halōsis* or ' Capture of Jerusalem ' [1] of Josephus, commonly attributed to one ' Egesippus.' [2]   Nor does the opinion of Cardinal Baronius [3] sensibly differ from this view.   In 1588 he writes : ' But certainly I believe that in so far as he confesses Christ, acknowledging him to be the son of God, he was compelled and constrained to do so solely by the power of God.'

Six years after the appearance of the first printed edition of Josephus' works (Basle, 1544), Sebastian Chateillon, the Protestant professor of theology at Basle, incorporated the *Jewish War* in his Latin edition of the Bible, unconsciously following the lead of the Eastern churches, the Syrian and Armenian, which had included Josephus' writings in the canon of the Scriptures, and of those Greek *catenae* in which the Jewish historian is quoted in the same breath with the Greek church fathers.   Even in the seventeenth century there were still learned theologians who frankly pro-nounced Josephus to have been divinely inspired.   As every reader of the *Jewish War* knows, Josephus himself was impudent enough to claim divine authority for his ' revelations,' not, of course, for the testimony to ' Jesus who was called the Messiah,' but for the shameless lie to which he owed the saving of his life and which was the basis of his whole ignoble existence as a client of the Flavian house, the brazen assertion, that is, that Vespasian was the world-ruler and world-redeemer foretold in *Gen.* xlix. 10 (below, p. 557).   It is to the belief of the Church in the miraculous inspira-tion of this second Balaam that we owe the preservation not only of the *Testimonium Flavianum* but perhaps of the writings of Josephus as a whole.

The miracle itself is all the more remarkable since it must have happened a considerable time after the death of this second Balaam.

---

[1] See below, p. 119 n. 1.
[2] ii. 12, ed. Ussani, p. 164, l. 11 ss. (*Corp. Script. Eccl. Lat.*, vol. lxvi.).
[3] *Ann. eccl.*, i. (Rome, 1588), ad ann. xxxiv.

For whilst Eusebius (died *c.* 340) quotes this 'precious testimony' thrice,[1] Origen (died *c.* 254), 'the greatest and most conscientious scholar of the ancient Church,' makes it quite clear, in two different passages,[2] that in *his* text of the *Antiquities* Josephus did *not* represent Jesus as the Christ. From these passages Eduard Norden,[3] among others, has inferred that, in his version of Josephus, Origen had found nothing whatever concerning Christ. But this hypothesis lacks a sound basis, for it is quite impossible that so scholarly and conscientious a writer as Origen appears to have been should have based his explicit statement on Josephus' rejection of the Christ as the Messiah on nothing more positive than the silence of the Romanized Jew concerning Jesus' life and work, or simply on Josephus' use of the somewhat ambiguous expression 'called the Christ,' a phrase which, besides, occurs also in the Gospel of Matthew (i. 16), whom nobody, because of these words, has ever accused of disbelief in the Messianic dignity of Jesus.

What the two passages of Origen do show is that whatever Origen read in his Josephus edition cannot have been the extant text of that famous passage with its orthodox Christian wording, but quite a different text, hostile to Jesus and the Christians and quite in keeping with the deserter's cynical assertion that it was really in the Emperor Vespasian that the expectations of the Jews found their fulfilment. This amounts to saying that there is no proof of the existence of the famous testimony before the time when Christianity as a state religion was able to suppress all writings hostile to its founder or its teachings, a power officially conferred upon it by an edict of Constantine and re-enacted by the Emperors Theodosius and Valentinian after the brief Pagan revival under Julian.[4]

Naturally, a party possessing the power to destroy obnoxious books will *ipso facto* be in a position to enforce minor omissions and alterations [5] in works in which only individual passages were felt to be objectionable. It is equally clear that owners of valuable MSS., whether private individuals, book-vendors, or officials in libraries and synagogues, should have preferred the excision of a few lines or certain alterations to the alternative of seeing their treasures devoured by the flames. Add to this the loss involved in the destruction of a whole Josephus in MS., and the laws imposing capital punishment on the concealed possession of writings hostile to Christianity,[6] and the natural consequence will be obvious to every one. As a matter of fact, not a single Greek, Latin, Slavonic, or other Josephus text has come down to us which has not passed through the hands of Christian scribes and Christian

---

[1] Below, p. 59 ll. 13 f. [2] App. XII.
[3] *N. Jahrb. f. d. klass. Altert.*, xxxi. (1913), p. 649, § 9.
[4] App. IV. [5] See Pls. VII. and XIV. [6] App. IV.

owners.   The numerous glosses and marginal notes, abounding in every single MS.,[1] fully bear out this statement.

First Doubts on the Authenticity of the 'Testimonium Flavianum'

The genuineness of the 'precious jewel' has been admitted only in circles wholly dominated by the Church.   The beautiful ' testimony' has somehow never made an impression on the Jews, although they, too, certainly knew it well.   When mediaeval Christian scholars taunted them with the argument that the Jewish historian Josephus, whose works they possessed and held in high honour, had freely admitted that Jesus *was* the Messiah, they stubbornly replied (as we may gather from certain pages of Giraldus Cambrensis [2]) that this testimony was not found in their own Hebrew MSS. of the author.   The Christians would then retort that the Jews had erased the passage from their MSS., and such MSS. showing manifest erasures were indeed not wanting (below, pp. 93, 97 ff.), and were repeatedly pointed out to the Jews to show that it was *they* who were in error.

Of course, with these mutual accusations that the one party, the Christians, had interpolated the passage, and that the other, the Jews, had erased it, the argument could not advance very much.   With the revival of learning the cultivated Jews were indeed not slow in putting up another and far more sweeping argument.   The learned Isaac Abravanel [3] (1437-1508) in his commentary on Daniel drily and curtly observes : ' If Josephus wrote this, we accept it not from him, for he has written much, but not all is true.'   Thus he doubts the genuineness of the *Testimonium*, but considers the whole matter of secondary importance in view of the well-known character of the writer, a commonsense view which can be warmly recommended to such blind believers among the Christians as may still think that anything can be gained for their cause by a statement made by so characterless an individual as was Flavius Josephus, who, Jew though he was, did not feel ashamed to proclaim Vespasian the Messiah of his people.[4]   Were the passage as it stands genuine beyond the shadow of a doubt, one could only draw the conclusion that the clever sycophant had

---

[1] App. XIII.

[2] *Giraldi Cambrensis opera*, vol. viii., ed. George F. Warner, London, 1891 (*Rer. Brit. med. aevi scriptores*), p. 64 f.

[3] Fonte x. palma vii. of the Pesaro edition of 1512 of his commentaries to the later prophets.

[4] Cf. Saint Alfonso Liguori, *De Fidei Veritate*, ii. 11 (*Opp. Dogm.*, i., Rome, 1903, p. 195) : ' *Ceterum Hebraeo nimium honorem tribuerunt nonnulli protestantes, ut Car. Daubuz et Ernst Grabe, qui tantopere desudarunt, ut hunc textum re vera Josephi esse assererent : non indiget Ecclesia inimicorum suorum testificatione.*'

introduced it at a moment when it appeared to him that Christians such as Flavius Clemens and his wife Domitilla might after all gain some power at court—enough, at all events, to be useful to him or to hinder his career.[1]   That would take away from the passage all independent value which otherwise it might possess.   For it stands to reason that Josephus would then have been wily enough to draw on the right sources, i.e. the oldest Gospel narratives.[2] Nor would the conversion of such a person as Josephus unquestionably was redound to the particular glory of any religion.   At any rate, this much is clear : if the ' testimony ' were proved to be authentic it could only be the work of a Christian, and it would matter very little, for our argument, whether that Christian were Josephus or Eusebius, and as a consequence it would have only the smallest value for the historicity of Jesus.

THE AWAKENING OF CRITICISM IN THE AGE OF HUMANISM

'. . . praeclarum ad Christiani dogmatis confirmationem testimonium . . . si non anxia hominum nimis curiosorum et otiosa sedulitas paene illud labefactasset.'

P. D. HUET, Bishop of Avranches (1679).

The first Christian scholar who boldly declared the *Testimonium* a forgery was the Protestant jurist and philologist Hubert van Giffen (Giphanius), a native of Buren in the duchy of Gelders. Born in 1534, he held a law degree from the University of Orleans, where he founded a library for the use of Teutonic students. Later he was professor at Strassburg, Altdorf, and Ingolstadt, embraced Catholicism, and died at the court of Rudolph II. of Hapsburg, in Prague, in 1604.   His view on the famous Josephus passage [3] does not seem to appear anywhere in his printed works. It is probable that for the sake of his own safety he was satisfied with expressing it only in his letters and lectures.

The oldest *printed* attack on the *Testimonium* is from the pen of the Lutheran theologian Lucas Osiander, who was born at Nuremberg in 1535, and who in his later life filled quite a number of Protestant ecclesiastical posts.   Though anything but a Judaeophile, he was accused in certain circles of having Jewish ancestors.   He frankly regarded the Josephus passage as spurious in its entirety.[4]

---

[1] A similar view has indeed been advanced recently by Prof. Laqueur of Giessen.

[2] ' Mark ' is at all events prior to ' Matthew,' who is about contemporary with Josephus' *Antiquities*.

[3] Sebast. Lepusculus ap. Goldast, *Centum epist. Philol.*, Frankfurt-a.-M., 1619, p. 250.

[4] *Epitomes eccl. cent.*, xvi. cent., i., lib. ii. c. 7 (Tübingen, 1592).

Osiander was followed by Professor Sebastian Schnell (Snellius) of Altdorf.   His arguments, as well as the replies which they called forth from contemporary scholars who came to the rescue of Josephus, have been preserved in MS. letters which in those days circulated from hand to hand and played very much the same rôle as our modern scientific journals and were occasionally printed. They have been published by Christian Arnold.[1]   It is natural enough that the critics of the passage were chiefly philologists, and its defenders theologians.   In these discussions practically all of the possible arguments *pro* and *con* used by modern scholars are anticipated in one form or another.

    The first of the scholars who pointed out—as Eduard Norden [2] has but recently done again—that the *Testimonium* interrupts the logical structure of the narrative, and must therefore be regarded as an interpolation, was not the famous French Calvinist Tannéguy Lefèvre, mentioned by Norden, but a certain Portuguese rabbi (*Rabbi Lusitanus*) who drew upon himself the wrath of the Protestant divine Johannes Müller of Hamburg, because the learned Sephardi seems to have been on good terms with Benedict de Castro, the Jewish physician of Queen Christina of Sweden, and to have had through this compatriot a chance to present his views to her Majesty during her stay in Hamburg.

    The *Rabbi Lusitanus* is probably identical with the well-known Jewish physician and philosopher Abraham Zacuto Lusitano, born in Lisbon in 1575, a student of the Universities of Coimbra and Salamanca, a doctor of Siguenza, who for thirty-nine years lived as a pseudo-converted Jew (Maraño) in Portugal, until he could escape to free Amsterdam in 1625.   He died on New Year's Day of 1642, having returned, in Holland, to the faith of his fathers. The MS., seen by Johannes Müller, was the public disputation which he had in Middelburg with the Jesuit Nicolas Abram (1589-1655), a very learned theologian and philologist, author of a commentary on the Gospel of St. John, a Cicero commentary, and a Vergil edition.   What should be stressed here is the Portuguese Jew's argument that the *Testimonium* interrupts the logical sequence of the text and must therefore be considered an interpolation.   The same rabbi, according to Pastor Johannes Müller, states : ' . . . Josephus telleth first / how Pilate hath given cause for rebellion / whereupon the text should continue to say / how about the same time still another tumult happened unto the Jews : but because in between them is told the history of Jesus / the text doeth not hang together / the other tumult pointeth to the first.'

[1] *Epistulae hist. et philol. de Flavi Josephi testimonio*, etc., Nürnberg, 1661.
[2] *N. Jahrb. f. d. klass. Altert.*, xxxi. (1913), pp. 648 ff.

Tannéguy Lefèvre, Eduard Norden, and Others

The French Huguenot Tannéguy Lefèvre (Tanaquil Faber), who does not mention Zacuto Lusitano and can hardly have known his work, circulating in MS. form only, argues in quite a similar strain : ' To speak in plain Latin, this interpolation [παρεγχείρημα] could not have been more ineptly inserted anywhere else.' The matter calls for some elucidation. In the portion of the text containing *inter alia* the *Testimonium* there is a mention of 'two calamities' (θόρυβοι). Having finished with the first, Josephus adds these words : ' And so the riot [στάσις] ceased.' The second, described in chapter v., he connects with the first, saying : ' And about the same time another calamity [ἕτερόν τι δεινόν] disturbed the Jews,' etc. Eichstädt (1814) and Niese (1893-94), without knowing their predecessors of another age, have repeated verbatim this line of argument. Prof. Norden quotes Lefèvre with approval, adding that this argument should have sufficed to dispose of the whole question.

We may then say that we are facing an argument which seems to have lost nothing of its force in the course of centuries, and to have taken with Norden's attractive and skilful presentation a new lease of life. A more detailed discussion is therefore unavoidable. Prof. Norden rightly stressed the fact that Josephus 'found in his source a representation of Pilate's governorship as a series of tumults' (θόρυβοι). To illustrate :—

First ' tumult ' (§§ 55-59) : the incident of the Emperor's standards. Pilate threatens the Jews with dire punishments if they do not desist from their turbulence (θορυβεῖν) and depart to their homes.

Second ' tumult ' (§§ 60-62) : uprising of the Jews because Pilate spent temple money on the construction of an aqueduct. After a brutal charge of the soldiery the riot is quelled.

(Follows the *Testimonium* concerning Jesus (§ 63 *sq.*).)

Third 'tumult ' (§§ 65-84). The section opens with the words : ' Now about the same time another calamity disturbed the Jews'; but, strangely enough, it contains neither a 'tumult' nor a sedition, but the society scandal of Mundus and Paulina in Rome, an episode which, as Norden admits, has nothing to do with the Jews. They only appear in the following story, a trick played by a Jewish impostor upon Fulvia, a Roman lady and a convert to Judaism. This incident leads to the expulsion of the Jews from Rome by order of Tiberius. In both cases the victim brings the facts before the Emperor for trial (*cognitio*). The petitions and the imperial decisions were therefore found in the official diaries (*commentarii*) of Tiberius, whence Josephus must have obtained his knowledge.[1]

Fourth ' tumult ' (§§ 85-87). It is introduced with the words : ' The Samaritan tribe, too, was not exempt from disturbances.' It includes the bloody repression by Pilate of the uprising caused by a Samaritan pseudo-prophet. Josephus adds: ' When the disturbance was put down, the subsequent complaints of the Samaritans led to Pilate's dismissal.'

Prof. Norden justly observes that the account of the appearance and crucifixion of Jesus, characterized in the text as a wise and wonder-working rabbi and founder of a new sect, does not fit at all into this series of national calamities. The interruption of the logical sequence is evident. The *Testimonium* is indeed the only section of the passage in which the words ' riot,' ' rioting,' etc., do not appear. Prof. Norden further points out the connexion between the closing words of § 62, ' And so the sedition [στάσις] was quelled,' and the opening words of § 65, ' Now about the same time another calamity disturbed the Jews ' ; for the sedition (στάσις) is the first calamity (δεινόν), to which the account of a second calamity is appended. The German scholar quotes three parallel passages from Books iv. and v. of the *Antiquities*,[2] and adds the following observation : ' In the phraseology of Book v., πάλιν (=again) corresponds to ἕτερον (=another) in Book xviii. The decisive point is the combination of events in series which finds its formal expression in the use of conjunctions. Nothing of this sort is found in the *Testimonium* lines, which stand there unconnected, isolated, like a typical interpolation.'

It is difficult, at a first perusal, to deny the force of these remarks. Yet on second thought they carry far less weight than one might at first be inclined to suppose. It is perfectly true, of course, that the section in its extant form does not fit into the enumerations of ' tumults.' But in a narrative observing a purely chronological order of sequence and written in the ordinary style of annalists it should be possible to insert here and there some miscellaneous notes among the ' disturbances ' which form the nucleus of the story. Whether, as Prof. Norden believes, Josephus is here dependent upon an annalist such as Cluvius Rufus, or, as I

---

[1] See below, p. 204.

[2] iv. 59.

"τὴν μέντοι στάσιν οὐδ' οὕτως συνέβη παύσασθαι, πολλῷ δὲ μᾶλλον αὔξειν καὶ φύεσθαι, χαλεπωτέραν τ' ἐλάμβανε τῆς ἐπὶ τὸ χεῖρον προκοπῆς αἰτίαν, ὑφ' ἧς οὐδέποτε λήξειν τὸ δεινὸν ἦν εἰκός."

v. 135.

" στάσις αὐτοὺς πάλιν καταλαμβάνει δεινὴ . . . ἐκ τοιαύτης αἰτίας."

xviii. 62-65.

"καὶ οὕτω παύεται ἡ στάσις καὶ ὑπὸ τοὺς αὐτοὺς χρόνους ἕτερόν τι δεινὸν ἐθορύβει τοὺς Ἰουδαίους."

hope to show later on, whether he had access to the official notes of the imperial chancellery (*commentarii*), his source no doubt, and very naturally, contained all sorts of facts out of which he chose what appeared to him most important or most appropriate. Bearing this in mind, we must admit the possibility of some minor affair or even a mere anecdote having slipped in with the mass of more serious political events. Prof. Leo Wohleb,[1] for example, has adduced quite a number of instances in the text of Josephus where obviously foreign matter has been inserted, more or less awkwardly, by the compiler, whose artistic preconceptions were evidently not of the highest order, and who is, moreover, at times fully conscious of adding details which are not essential to the story he is telling.[2]

Prof. Norden's arguments of a purely formal and stylistic character are not so easy to combat. Even the peacefully novelistic narrative of Paulina and Mundus, which has repeatedly been attacked as an interpolation, does contain the verb form ἐθορύβει, and hence unquestionably belongs to the series of ' troubles ' with which the reader is by now familiar. It is all the more surprising (since the use of a simple catchword such as ' tumult ' was perfectly sufficient, in the eyes of our not too exacting author, to establish a logical connexion) that he should not at least have attempted to link by such a simple device the *Testimonium* passage with the rest of his narrative. Tumultuous scenes were certainly not wanting in the history of nascent Christianity, and a supposition that Josephus intentionally refrained from using his favourite term in this connexion attributes to him a feeling of delicacy which he was very far from possessing. The observation of Prof. Norden about the absence of such words as στάσις, θόρυβος, etc., in the *Testimonium* is therefore of the greatest importance. But when the German scholar proposes to get rid of the difficulty by eliminating the passage in question as a simple interpolation, he falls into a methodological error. For it stands to reason that in the case of a mere stringing together of episodes in chronological order such as we witness in Josephus it will always be an easy matter to cut out this, that, or the other adventure without destroying in the least the logical sequence of the narrative. The problem must be tackled from an altogether different angle.

Supposing for a moment that Josephus *did* use his favourite catchwords also in the *Testimonium* passage, we can understand that any Christian would have objected to such a presentation of the facts. He would have brooked with difficulty the association of the founder of his religion with riots and seditions. Prof.

---

[1] *Röm. Quartalschrift*, xxxv., 1917, p. 157 f., about *Ant.*, xiii. 5, 9.

[2] Cp. *Ant.*, xii. 2. 2, § 59, on certain parerga " τῆς ἱστορίας οὐκ ἀπαιτούσης τὴν ἀπαγγελίαν " ('the story not absolutely requiring their retelling'); similarly, *Ant.*, xvii. § 354, " οὐκ ἀλλότρια νομίσας αὐτὰ τῶδε τῷ λόγῳ " (' I have not considered this as matter unconnected with the subject ').

Norden's error lies in his assumption that the extant text of the *Testimonium* is genuine in the sense that it never existed in a different form and that it can thus be used as a basis for 'critical' examinations and analyses of style.   Since his essay was directed against scholars, such as Prof. F. C. Burkitt and Prof. A. v. Harnack, who wanted to save the *Testimonium* in its entirety, Prof. Norden had no special reason to discuss the view of those who take a middle path and consider the famous passage neither entirely genuine nor on the other hand wholly an interpolation.   Among the defenders of such a view was the celebrated German historian Leopold v. Ranke, and it would, then, not be quite fair to dismiss it as summarily as Norden does in his essay.

The view itself, let us say, does by no means belong to the realm of lofty speculations of a purely metaphysical nature.   In the first place, Origen did not have the extant text in his version of Josephus, but quite a different one, from which he concluded that Josephus refused to acknowledge Jesus as the Messiah.   In the second place, the brief and abrupt mention of Jesus as ὁ λεγόμενος Χριστός (*Ant.*, xx. 9. 1, § 200), acknowledged to be genuine by Norden himself, presupposes a foregoing and more detailed discussion of this personage.   As it stands, the passage would have puzzled the Hellenistic reading public of Josephus, and even the Jewish readers would have expected to learn more about this so-called Messiah. If the objection be met with the answer that at the time of the publication of the *Antiquities* almost every one must have known about Jesus the Christ, so that Josephus could spare himself the trouble of a detailed story, we can only say that in that case it would be unthinkable that in his history a personage of such importance should not have loomed larger.   Nor would his brief allusion have saved him from the reproach of having omitted from his work a fairly important political fact, or rather a series of facts. Moreover, the Christians, who would, logically, have been the party to object to such an omission, as a matter of fact never reproach him for his silence but always and only for his unbelief in Christ.

It is well to add, also, that there is no conceivable reason why Josephus should intentionally have passed over in silence the life and death of the founder of Christianity.   Such a silence on his part (and still more the *Testimonium* in its extant form) would on the contrary have exposed him to an accusation of sympathy for this particular Messiah; and if we remember the cases of Flavius Clemens and Flavia Domitilla, two members of the imperial dynasty who had to pay for their Christian leanings with death or banishment, it will be clear that such an accusation might have cost him his favour with his imperial masters.   Josephus as we know him was far too self-seeking to run the slightest risk for any cause, let alone that of a despised and persecuted sect.

A last objection might be found in the careless manner in which Josephus compiled his materials. One might suppose, for example, that he copied literally from his source the above-quoted reference to Jesus, forgetting that he had not mentioned him before in his own work. Yet this objection does not hold, since Origen, as he expressly says, read in Book xviii. of the *Antiquities* a statement of Josephus concerning Jesus from which he inferred that Josephus ' disbelieved in Jesus as Christ.' Origen cannot very well have drawn this inference from the phrase ' who was called Christ ' (*Ant.*, xx.), since the very same phrase occurs also in *Matthew* i. 16, where there can of course be no question of such disbelief. Even granting that the allusion is due to mere carelessness on the part of our author, one would yet have to admit that his source did give a fuller account of Jesus, a conclusion which would make that testimony even more valuable, bringing it closer to the time of the events.

In going over the literature connected with the exegesis of the *Testimonium*, one is struck by the fact that a number of scholars saw in it only a decidedly Christian colouring, whilst others, equally competent, believed that they could discern a peculiarly ironical and even satirical tone. It is indeed likely that both are right— in other words, that the extant text is neither entirely genuine nor entirely interpolated, neither the work of Josephus alone nor entirely proceeding from the pen of some Christian forger. There seems to exist, rather, a nucleus hostile to Christ and his doctrines but covered with layers of Christian reworkings, so much so that the true meaning of the author can just be dimly discerned underneath the growth of Christian alterations and modifications of the original text.

This view is by no means an arbitrary conjecture, but it is largely supported by the MS. material as interpreted by Henri Weil and Théodore Reinach.[1] I can here give only a few examples.

Several MSS. of Eusebius' *Historia ecclesiastica* (i. 11. 7) have after the name of Jesus the disparaging particle τις, corresponding to the Latin *quidam*, ' a certain Jesus.' The phrase is thoroughly in keeping with Josephus' stylistic habit ; he speaks, in fact, in much the same way of the two pseudo-Messiahs who appeared on the stage shortly after the death of Herod the Great. He likewise refers to Menaḥem, a son of the rebel Judas of Gaulan, as ' a certain Menaḥem,' and that although he mentions his glorious father in the same breath. This mode of expression does not, then, imply mere obscurity on the part of the personage in question, but simply Josephus' dislike of and contempt for the men whose names are thus introduced. This phraseology, moreover, was adopted by the spurious *Acts of Pilate*, directly dependent upon Josephus, as

[1] See the bibliography below, p. 58.

will be shown in a subsequent chapter. There the governor is made to write to the Emperor, ' They have delivered to me a certain man called Jesus,' a phrase indeed in the strictest accordance with Roman official style. For Tacitus, who did not of course use Josephus, as some have thought, but who, like Josephus, drew on official sources, likewise refers to the Jewish pretender Simon as ' Simo quidam ' (*Hist.*, v. 9). More important still, the phrase ἀνήρ τις, corresponding exactly to the ποιμήν τις used of the messiah Athronga, occurs in the *Halōsis* of Josephus, and is there applied to no other than Jesus himself.

A second equally important reading is found in the *Demonstratio evangelica* (iii. 5) of Eusebius, where the phrase ' who worship ' (σεβομένων) replaces ' who receive ' (δεχομένων), the sentence being, ' a teacher of men who receive the truth with pleasure.' Since the expression is normally used in Josephus *in malam partem*, a Christian copyist who had noticed this altered the passage, though none too skilfully. In the same way and acting on the same principle, another Christian copyist had deleted the derogatory τις in the connexion just mentioned in the previous section.

What we hope to have established, then, is the existence of alterations and modifications of the text since the time of Eusebius. From the fact that the latter himself does not quote a standard text it follows further that no such text existed in the fourth century, and that even before that time the famous passage was constantly subject to emendations and corrections. This result is in full harmony with the fact that Origen had before him a thoroughly ' unorthodox ' *Testimonium* which must have been altogether different from the one drawn on by Eusebius. The text tradition consequently proves that a genuine Josephus text hostile to Christ has been reworked by Christians. It does not prove at all that the passage is *in toto* a brazen interpolation ; for there exist no MSS. of the *Antiquities* lacking altogether in the celebrated passage, xviii. 3. 3. Nor is there any ground for supposing that such ever existed.

An hypothesis postulating that the *Testimonium* was composed by a Christian and interpolated in the Josephus text can in no wise explain the unmistakably derogatory expression ' a certain Jesus ' in the quotation of the passage by Eusebius. On the other hand, one can understand that such objectionable phrases might, for some time at least, escape the notice of the copyists. Another important consideration to bear in mind in this connexion is the chronology of Josephus, who puts the execution of John the Baptist after the first public appearance of Jesus, a chronology quite different from that of the Gospels.[1] One fails to see why

---

[1] See below, p. 302.

a Christian author—who must of course be presumed to be familiar with the writings of the New Testament—had he interpolated the *Testimonium*, should have done so in contradiction to the chronology of the Gospels.

The opposite theory, that the extant text comes from the pen of Josephus, in the first place does not explain the friendly and sympathetic tone used in speaking of Jesus, and in the second place does not account for the enigmatic indifference with which the author narrates without a word of approval or disapproval an event which, according to his own words, implies a horrible judicial murder committed by his Roman friends with the connivance of the foremost of his own compatriots, men of his own social class, whilst in the case of the deaths of John the Baptist and James the Just he is at pains to pronounce himself most unequivocally. Above all, the complete absence of all motivation cannot but strike the reader, who remembers, of course, that in the case of the execution of John the Baptist Josephus not only mentions the fear of Herod Antipas of a rebellion caused by his preaching, but mentions also the disapproval of the act by public opinion.   James the Just and his companions were stoned as violators of the law by the Sadducees, whose judicial severity and harshness are frequently censored by Josephus the Pharisee.   In addition, we read 'many of the most respected and law-abiding citizens sharply protested ' against these proceedings to the new governor.   Nothing of the kind appears in the *Testimonium*, not a word of the reasons for Jesus' death, though motives were certainly easy to find—violation of the Sabbath or the purity laws, or the more general reproach of ' innovations ' so hateful to Josephus.   We read not a word to suggest that the people feared Divine retribution for the murder of a righteous man, not a word of blame for the cruelty of Pilate or the Sadducaean informers, no explanation at all, though lack of sufficient motivation cannot possibly be counted among the weak spots of his narrative.   In short, we have here no trace of that play of lively human emotions and passions which forms the usual charm of Josephus' way of representing his facts, and which does certainly not lack in the dramatic.

' Crucified under Pilate, risen on the third day, honoured as the Messiah by the Church.'   That is what we are told here, with a serene indifference and apathy quite intelligible in the drawling recital of a familiar—even all too familiar—confession of faith, in a theological ' testimonium,' that is (and it is not by accident that the passage has obtained that name), but wholly inconceivable in an historian who is anything but tedious and dispassionate.   Still, here he would seem to relate a miracle unparalleled in the annals of mankind—the resurrection of one crucified and the continued recognition of the victim, notwithstanding his shameful death, as the promised anointed Saviour-King of the Jews.   And yet he tells this staggering tragedy, the execution of the innocent wonder-working sage through malicious denunciation and tyrannical cruelty, without betraying by a single word his own opinion of these unheard-of events.   Such an attitude defies all explanation ; it is neither probable nor even possible.   There remains at the end but the single hypothesis, confirmed by patristic evidence, that Josephus was not spared the indignities which Christian copyists did not hesitate to inflict upon the Christian fathers—nay, even upon the very Gospels themselves.   They falsified what he had written, suppressing things which he wished to say and making him say things which he would never have dreamt of saying, they being altogether foreign to his own mode of thinking.

The Remnants of the Genuine Testimony of Josephus on Jesus in the ' Jewish Antiquities '

In the preceding section the view has been advanced, supported by new arguments, that beneath the clearly manipulated *Testimonium Flavianum* the outlines of a genuine statement of Josephus concerning Jesus have been preserved.   Such a view has been deprecated in the eyes of many by Schürer's [1] observation that any critic seeking to remove from the account of Jesus as given by Josephus' extant text such touches as can only have been added by a Christian hand, will be left with practically nothing of importance.   Schürer's procedure, however, is far too clumsy, and might properly be compared with the attempt of an inexperienced amateur who seeks to clean an old portrait but by an all too ready use of his alkalines only brings to light the naked canvas.   For it must be borne in mind (and it has been proved repeatedly [2]) that almost every word and phrase of the extant text corresponds most closely to the vocabulary and stylistic habits of Josephus.   Hence it is that advocates of the interpolation theory have been forced to admit that the forger was intimately acquainted with the author's style and must have made a careful study of it.   Such skill on the part of a forger is indeed not altogether impossible ; the less so if we suppose him to have been a copyist who, after having copied more than seventeen books of the *Antiquities*, must necessarily have become sufficiently impregnated with his author's phraseology to patch together without undue effort those seven lines of the *Testimonium*.   For those, however, who believe in a falsification of an original text the conclusion will be evident that the

---

[1] Vol. i. p. 148 of the English edition, Edinburgh, 1910.

[2] Cp., besides Prof. Wohleb's paper quoted above, p. 44 n. 1, another by van Liempt (*Mnemosyne*, lv., 1927).   Most of the material has first been collected by Daubuze, in the eighteenth century (bibliography below, p. 58).

D

forgery was carried out with a good deal of care and that the restoration of the original text through conjecture must proceed with a minimum of alterations—a principle which devolves, moreover, from the well-known axiom according to which in the discussion of the genuineness of an historical document the burden of proof lies with the party impugning that genuineness.

The resources available for this purpose may be divided into two groups. First, there are the relevant parallel passages. Josephus' style—or rather the style of the *servi literati* he employed—is characterized by a certain monotony, and the reproaches he levels against political opponents are always of the same type. In the second place, a number of verbal resemblances or analogies to certain typical statements of Josephus may be found in the apocryphal *Acta Pilati*, which, as has been indicated before and will be more fully demonstrated below, drew on the narrative of Josephus.

A critical analysis of the *Testimonium*, taking one word after the other, accompanied by a comparison with the parallels just mentioned, will result in a number of observations in complete harmony with the main conclusions arrived at in a previous chapter.

The first word of the *Testimonium*, γίνεται, ' there arose,' has always been a difficulty. In Cedrenus we find it changed to ἦν, a variant corresponding to the *Egesippus* reading, ' *fuit* autem eisdem temporibus.' The same *fuit* (instead of γίνεται) recurs in the Latin translation attributed to Rufinus and in the literal quotation of the *Testimonium* by St. Jerome.

There are excellent reasons for this correction, for Josephus never uses the word γίνεται, when he wants to introduce a new, hitherto not mentioned person into his narrative, in order to convey the meaning that this man ' lived ' or ' flourished ' at that particular time. In all these cases he is careful to say ἦν δὲ κατὰ τοῦτον τὸν χρόνον, ' at that time there was a man, called N. N.' [1] The verb γίνεται does, however, occur quite frequently in Josephus, particularly at the beginning of paragraphs ; but the subject of the sentence is then almost without exception a word such as θόρυβος (tumult), or στάσις (rebellion),[2] or ταραχή (trouble), or some

---

[1] *Ant.*, viii. 7. 6, § 203 : "κατὰ δὲ τὸν αὐτὸν καιρὸν ἦν τις οἰκῶν ἐν Μωδαὶ . . ὄνομα Ματταθίας . . ", e.g. *Ant.*, ix. § 239 : " ἦν δέ τις κατὰ τοῦτον τὸν καιρὸν προφήτης, Νάουμος ὄνομα," or xv. § 373 : " ἦν δέ τις τῶν Ἐσσηνῶν Μανάημος ὄνομα . . " ; vi. § 45 : " ἦν δέ τις ἐκ τῆς Βενιαμίτιδος φυλῆς ἀνήρ, Κεὶς ὄνομα," or vi. § 295 : "ἦν δέ τις τῶν Σιφηνῶν ἐκ πόλεως Ἐμμᾶν πλούσιος . ." ; viii. § 236 : " ἦν δέ τις ἐν τῇ πόλει πρεσβύτης πονηρὸς ψευδοπροφήτης " ; viii. § 326 : " ἦν δέ γυνή " ; xvi. § 220 : " ἦν μὲν γὰρ ὁ τῆς Ἀραβίας βασιλεὺς Ὀβάδας . . " ; xvii. § 149 : " ἦν Ἰούδας ὁ Σαριφαῖος καὶ Ματαθίας ὁ Μαργαλώτου Ἰουδαίων λογιώτατοι . ." ; xviii. § 273 : " ἦν δὲ καὶ Σίμων δοῦλος μὲν Ἡρώδου τοῦ βασιλέως ἀλλως δὲ ἀνὴρ εὐπρεπής . . ."

[2] *B. Bell. J.*, i. 4. 7, § 99 : "γίνεται δὲ αὐτῷ πάλιν ἀρχὴ θορύβου Ἀντίοχος . ." : *ibid.*, i. 4. 2, § 85 : " γίνεται δ' αὐτῷ καὶ πρὸς τὸν Λάθουρον συμβολή " ; i. 12. 1, § 236 ; " πάλιν στάσις ἐν Ἱεροσολύμοις γίνεται Ἕλικος . . ἐπαναστάντος Φασαήλῳ " ; i. 33. 2, § 648:

such term.   Thus it is highly probable that the original text read:
" γίνεται δὲ . . κατὰ τοῦτον τὸν χρόνον ⟨ἀρχὴ θορύβου⟩ . . ." ; or
" γίνεται κατὰ τοῦτον τὸν χρόνον δὲ Ἰησοῦς τις ⟨ἀρχὴ θορύβου⟩" ; or
" ⟨στάσεως παραίτιος⟩ " ; and that a Christian copyist omitted, or
a Christian censor deleted, the objectionable words, making Jesus
himself the immediate subject of the verb γίνεται.   The remark of
Celsus concerning Jesus preserved by Origen (cp. *Celsum*, viii. 14),
" ὅσπερ ἐστὶν αὐτοῖς στάσεως ἀρχηγέτης καὶ ὠνόμασάν γε τοῦτον υἱὸν
θεοῦ," may very well have been borrowed verbatim from the lost
passage of Josephus.   The phrase, " γίνεται δὲ κατὰ τοῦτον τὸν χρόνον
Ἰησοῦς τις σοφὸς ἀνήρ," is at all events quite impossible from what
we know of the author's style and phraseology.   For it could
mean ' at that time a certain Jesus was born, a wise man '
(a chronological impossibility), or even ' at that time a certain
Jesus became a wise man ' (which is, of course, nonsense).   The
reader will notice that the proposed restoration of the words ἀρχὴ
θορύβου completely disposes of Zacuto Lusitano's, Tannéguy
Lefèvre's, and Prof. Norden's argument that the whole *Testimonium* is a fraudulent insertion because it does not contain the
words θόρυβος, στάσις, ταραχή, nor another similar expression.   As
a matter of fact, the use of the verb γίνεται goes far to prove that
the word was used, but was deleted by a Christian reviser.

The expression σοφὸς ἀνήρ, ' a wise man,' does not present a
stylistic difficulty.   The epithet in question is a word of the highest
praise in Hellenistic Greek, and is applied by Josephus in two cases
only—to the wise old King Solomon and to the prophet Daniel ;
and this very fact makes it practically impossible that Josephus
should have used it when speaking of ' a certain Jesus,' a carpenter's son unlearned in the scriptures.[1]   The epithet which he
does use when speaking of the various leaders of the opposition who
were so distasteful to him is not σοφός, but σοφιστής,[2] and it is
indeed probable that σοφιστής was the original reading in the
present passage, the more so because Justinus[3] implies that
certain of his contemporaries did call Jesus a sophist.

Of common application to Jesus, by writers hostile to Christianity, were the terms γόης and μάγος, and in the Lucian MSS.[4] the

"γίνεται δ᾽ ἐν ταῖς συμφοραῖς αὐτοῦ καὶ δημοτικὴ ἐπανάστασις· δύο ἦσαν σοφισταί . .
Ἰούδας καὶ Ματθίας" ; i. 8. 6, § 171 : " μετ᾽ οὐ πολύ γε μὴν αὐτοῖς ἀρχὴ γίνεται θορύβων
Ἀριστόβουλος . ." ; i. 10. 10, § 216 : " καὶ ἐν τούτῳ γίνεται περὶ Ἀραμείαν ταραχὴ Ῥωμαίων
καὶ πόλεμος ἐμφύλιος " ; iv. 3. 13, § 208 : " γίνεται δὲ τούτοις πᾶσιν ὀλέθρου παραίτιος
Ἰωάννης." *Ant.*, xviii. 9. 1, § 310 : " γίνεται δὲ συμφορὰ δεινή " ; xix. 9. 2, § 366 : " . .
οἱ καὶ τοῖς ἐπιοῦσι χρόνοις τῶν μεγίστων Ἰουδαίοις ἐγένοντο συμφορῶν ἀρχή " ; xx. 2. 6, § 51 :
" γίνεται δὲ αὐτῆς ἡ ἄφιξις δεινή " ; xx. 6. 1, § 118 : " γίνεται δὲ Σαμαρείταις πρὸς Ἰουδαίους
ἔχθρα " ; xx. 8. 7, § 173 : " γίνεται δὲ Ἰουδαίων στάσις . . ", κτλ.
[1] μὴ μεμαθηκὼς τὰ γράμματα, *John* vii. 11, even in Christian tradition !
[2] *B.J.*, ii., § 118 (Judas the Galilaean) : σοφιστὴν ἰδίας αἱρέσεως. *Ibid.*, i., § 648
(Judas and Mattathias, the rabbis rebelling against Herod the Great), σοφισταί.
[3] *Apolog.*, i. 14. 11.   Similarly Lucian, *Peregr. Proteus*, ch. xiii.
[4] See above, p. 9 n. 5 ; p. 11 n. 5.

Christian copyists changed τὸν μάγον ἐκεῖνον, ' that sorcerer,' into τὸν μέγαν ἐκεῖνον, ' that great one.' Such different meanings may be produced by the simple change of two letters! It is at least possible that in the original Josephus' text the words καὶ γόης were added to the epithet σοφιστής, and a passage in the *Demonstratio Evangelica* of Eusebius [1] would seem to bear out this conjecture.

The most difficult piece of the whole section is the phrase εἴγε ἄνδρα λέγειν χρὴ αὐτόν. The use of εἴγε is typical of Josephus; it can be translated by ' provided that,' ' if,' or even ' since.' A good illustration of this obscure passage is furnished by a parallel in the so-called *Letter of Lentulus*, a Christian forgery, reading : ' Apparuit temporibus istis . . . homo magnae virtutis, si fas est hominem dicere . . . quem eius discipuli vocant filium dei.' Another useful parallel is furnished by a phrase of Clement of Alexandria, who, speaking of the various Orpheuses, refers to them as ' men who are not men but impostors ' (ἄνδρες τινὲς οὐκ ἄνδρες, ἀπατηλοί)—that is, men who claim to be supermen but are in reality impostors. One who is ' no man ' may be as well an unhuman monster as a superman, and the passage in Josephus is therefore quite well possible in the mouth of an enemy of Jesus. The most important parallel, however, is furnished by the spurious ' Acts of Pilate ' : [2] "οἴμοι, γλυκύτατε Ἰησοῦ, ἐξ ἀνθρώπων φίλε ἐξαισιώτατε· εἰ χρὴ μὲν καὶ ἄνθρωπον ὀνομάζειν σε τὸν οἷα οὐδέποτε πεποίηκεν ἄνθρωπος θαύματα ἐργασάμενον." These lines are obviously borrowed from Josephus by the unintelligent Christian forger of these ' Acts of Pilate.' No Christian would have chosen the epithet ἐξαισιώτατε, as applied to Jesus, on his own account. The passage may therefore be tentatively used to restore the original wording of the Josephus text. The word ἀνήρ, which does not correspond to the Latin *homo* but to *vir*, and which is not the contrary to θεός, ' god,' but to γυνή, ' woman,' may have been chosen in this particular passage to avoid the repetition of ἄνθρωπος, simply because in all probability the original text was as long as that of the *Letter of Lentulus* or the lines just quoted from the *Acta Pilati*, and must have read somewhat like this : ' if one may call a man [ἄνδρα] the most monstrous [ἐξαισιώτατος] of men (ἀνθρώπων), whom his disciples call a son of God,' etc. Nor is the Greek word here translated by ' monstrous ' (ἐξαίσιος) at all rare in Josephus. On the contrary, he speaks, for example, of βοαῖς ἐξαισίοις (vehement shouting), and the term is always used *in malam partem*. The forger of the ' Acts of Pilate ' ignorantly took over a term used first in a sense hostile to Jesus, no doubt because he found it in Josephus and had lost all feeling for the niceties of the Greek language. The phrase ' whom his disciples call a son of God ' likewise is far too cool, too

---

[1] iii. 6 ; *P.G.*, 222, 224 : " πρὸς τοὺς οἰομένους γόητα γεγονέναι τὸν Χριστὸν τοῦ Θεοῦ."
[2] rec. B., *Evang. apocrypha*, ed. Tischendorf, 1876, p. 314.

objective, to admit of an assumption that it was coined by an enthusiastic Christian. The obvious conclusion, then, is that the extant text of the *Testimonium* is the result of a drastic reduction of a text which formerly was far longer and anything but favourable to Jesus.

The expression παράδοξα ἔργα occurs elsewhere in Josephus ; but it need not always express supernatural deeds. In one passage of the *Antiquities*[1] he uses it to designate works of art of a novel and surprising design, though in another the words refer to the marvellous acts of a prophet.[2] It follows that in our context Josephus may well have said something of this sort, to explain, of course, the reputation Jesus had with his adherents. On the other hand, the word ποιητής is certainly objectionable, because in Josephus it always means ' poet,' whilst in the meaning of ' doer ' or ' perpetrator ' it is frequent in Christian writers. It is therefore certainly a Christian interpolation, necessitated by the reduction of the preceding phrase. What is left, παραδόξων ἔργων διδάσκαλος, corresponds to the common term ' wonder-rabbi,' still used, but nowadays always *in malam partem*. The word διδάσκαλὸς is common in Josephus, both where he speaks of a ' teacher ' of good and useful knowledge and also where he means a man who sets bad examples of wickedness and deceit.

The phrase ἀνθρώπων τῶν ἡδονῇ δεχομένων is not without significant parallels. For example, in the story of the false Alexander the Jews of Puteoli and Crete ' accept ' likewise ἡδονῇ, ' with delight,' the words of the impostor. A similar use of the word occurs in the description of the rebellion of Judas the Galilaean. The word ἡδονή in Josephus generally denotes, according to Stoic use, a low and base sort of pleasure, the pleasure of an easily incitable mob, and suchlike.

The word τἀληθῆ cannot of course have been used by Josephus of the teachings of Jesus, as was in fact pointed out by the late Théodore Reinach, for that would imply that Josephus endorsed the teachings of Jesus about the Sabbath, about man not being defiled by unclean food, about non-resistance, etc. In fact, it has long ago been conjectured that τἀληθῆ is simply a correction of τἀήθη, meaning ' the unusual.'[3] The text then read, ' people who accept with pleasure the unusual,' (all) that is unusual, because it is un-

---

[1] xii. § 63. [2] ix. § 182.

[3] Prof. H. Windisch of Kiel has called this, in a review of the German edition (*Theolog. Rundschau*, N.F. i., Heft 4, p. 281), an ' unnecessary' correction. But surely an author who calls the teaching of Jesus ' the truth ' could not be anything but a believing Christian. So this conjecture of Heinichen's is absolutely necessary, if the *Testimonium* is not to be thrown out altogether. Indeed, Dom H. Leclerq in the new article ' Josèphe' in Cabrol's *Dict. of Christ. Archaeol.*, vii. (1927) c. 26, 79, would rather accept Henri Weil's conjecture τὰ καινά than let ταληθή stand. The corruption δι' ἀλήθειαν for δι' ἀήθειαν occurs in Cod. Paris., 1676, of Plutarch's *Cato minor*, c. 59, 35 = iv. 94, 8.

usual; that is a phrase of the type one has to expect from the pen of a Josephus, hostile as he was to any innovator (νεωτερίζων) and opponent of the Pharisees in particular and the upper classes in general.

There follows the phrase καὶ πολλοὺς μὲν Ἰουδαίους πολλοὺς δὲ καὶ τοῦ Ἑλληνικοῦ ἐπηγάγετο, which is quite unobjectionable and has a good parallel, *Ant.*, xvii. § 327 : 'Ἰουδαίοις ὁπόσοις εἰς ὁμιλίαν ἀφίκετο, ἐπηγάγετο εἰς πίστιν,' where the subject of the sentence is the impostor, pretending to be King Alexander, the son of the Hasmonaean Queen Mariamne.

But it would seem as though in the original text there preceded at least a short outline of his doctrines, just as in connexion with Josephus' other *bêtes noires*, Judas the Galilaean, Ṣadoq, the sophists Matthew Margalothon and Judas Sariphaeus, etc., we are given such a sample. Nor did he have the slightest reason to pass them over in silence ; on the contrary, it was in the interest of his work of apologetics to justify the denunciation of Jesus by his co-nationals and the people of his own class. The whole passage no doubt fell before the hand of Christian copyists and revisers.

There comes next the famous confession ὁ Χριστὸς οὗτος ἦν, which has given rise to so much controversy. A close examination of the context can only confirm the old conjecture of Richard Montague, bishop of Norwich (1577-1641), to wit, that the phrase is a Christian gloss. Yet what follows makes it necessary that Josephus here mentioned the title of ' Christ ' given to Jesus, and the sentence reporting the denunciation requires that Jesus had been introduced before as the Messiah. St. Jerome still read in his Josephus copy something corresponding to the Latin ' et Christus esse credebatur,' to which Josephus had probably added something like ' by the mob ' (ὑπὸ τῶν ὄχλων, ὑπὸ τοῦ πλείστου ὄχλου). Even so the phrase is too short and abrupt, and some-thing else was probably deleted by the Christian scribe or reviser. Josephus must have given some sort of explanation, for the benefit of his Hellenic readers, of what the Jews meant by the ' Messiah '— he may, in fact, have mentioned here that the true Messiah was the Emperor Vespasian ; and, lastly, he must have somehow ex-plained why Jesus was denounced to the Roman authorities. It is in this place that he must have given the details about the θόρυβος or the στάσις alluded to in the restored introductory sentence which Dr. Norden missed in this paragraph, and which must have appeared most objectionable to the Christians. For the fact that his entry into Jerusalem was not altogether peaceful is fully corroborated by certain incidents reported in the Gospels.[1] In other words, we must assume a considerable gap, caused by Christian deletions.

[1] See below, pp. 472 ff.

The following sentence is perfectly correct : 'And when, on the indictment of the principal men among us, Pilate had sentenced him to the cross,' etc.   It is to be noted that the phrase σταυρῷ ἐπιτετιμηκότος Πιλάτου corresponds exactly to the Latin ' per Pontium Pilatum supplicio affectus' of the well-known Tacitus passage.   It is obviously a literal translation of a piece of Roman judicial phraseology.

On the other hand, the phrase οὐκ ἐπαύσαντο is certainly not complete in itself; and in view of the events connected with the names of Stephen and Paul, it is no bold conjecture to assume that what dropped out was an infinitive such as θορυβεῖν or a participle such as νεωτερίζοντες.

In the phrase οἱ τὸ πρῶτον ἀγαπήσαντες the verb ἀγαπᾶν has been attacked as un-Josephan, since with our author it hardly ever means ' to love,' but only ' to be content with some one or something.'   The critics unfortunately overlooked the important parallel in B.J., i. 8. 6, § 171, where the subject of the sentence is Aristobulus.[1]   Of course, Josephus did not wish to say that Aristobulus was 'loved ' (a rather difficult matter in any case), but simply that he was ' liked,' ' admired,' or something of the kind.

There follows the famous testimonium for the resurrection, which is stylistically correct enough but which cannot possibly have come from the pen of Josephus, at least in such a form.   Of course, he is careful to say ἐφάνη γὰρ αὐτοῖς, that is, ' he appeared to them,' i.e. to people belonging, according to Josephus, to the lowest of the low, people without education and critical sense.   In other terms, even the present wording leaves no doubt that for Josephus it was merely a question of a purely subjective phenomenon.   To this must be added that, since the text is by no means free from alterations, the original may have had instead of ἐφάνη the infinitive φανῆναι, completed by the verb ἔδοξε, 'they imagined he had appeared to them,' etc., a conjecture first advanced by G. A. Müller in 1895 and fully confirmed eleven years later by the Slavonic version (below, p. 539).   With such a reading of the text his mention of the prophetic passages likewise becomes clear.   The words are written in a spirit of polemic against the collection of prophetic testimonia current among the Christians and attributed by Papias to the evangelist Matthew—a book which has been brought but recently to the attention of the learned world by a number of English scholars, foremost among them Dr. Rendel Harris.

The phrase τρίτην ἔχων ἡμέραν[2] has been said by Dr. Norden (op. cit., 646) to be a ἅπαξ λεγόμενον with Josephus, but Prof. van Liempt has drawn my attention to Ant., vii. § 1, αὐτοῦ δύο ἡμέρας ἔχοντος ἐν τῇ Σικελίᾳ, and Ant., iii. § 290, τοῦ μὲν ἄρρενος ὅσον

---

[1] B.J., i. § 171: "τοὺς δ' ἀγαπῶντας αὐτὸν πάλαι."
[2] Cp. Jo., xi. 17: " εὗρον αὐτὸν τέσσαρας ἤδη ἡμέρας ἔχοντα ἐν τῷ μνημείῳ."

τριακοστὴν εἶχεν ἡμέραν γενόμενον. These parallels,[1] together with the Latin version *post triduum mortis* of the so-called Egesippus, seem to suggest that the original text was τρίτην ἔχων ἡμέραν (θανάτου), 'having been dead for three days,' and that the word θανάτου, 'death,' was deleted by a reviser because of the legend —elaborately developed in the 'Acts of Pilate'—that Jesus Christ was not dead during those three days, but was occupied with the *descensus ad inferos* and the liberation of the pious patriarchs from She'ol (see, however, below p. 62 note 1).

There remains the final sentence, εἰσέτι τε νῦν τῶν Χριστιανῶν ἀπὸ τοῦδε ὠνομασμένων οὐκ ἐπέλιπε τὸ φῦλον. The redundant accumulation of particles which has been criticized as entirely un-Josephan is simply due to the habit of later scribes. ἔτι νῦν, καὶ νῦν, νῦν ἔτι, καὶ νῦν ἔτι, ἔτι καὶ νῦν, are frequent in Josephus. What is noteworthy is the use of the word φῦλον, meaning not only 'people' or 'tribe' in the ethnical acceptation of the word, but also in a pejorative sense, as in English we speak of the 'tribe of the politicians' or the 'tribe of the lawyers.'[2] The fact itself that φῦλον here does not designate an ethnical unit, but the 'Christians,' makes it clear that the author did not mean to use a term of affection.

To this must be added the fact that the phrase οὐκ ἐπέλιπε certainly does not imply a wish on the part of the author for their continued growth.[3] For if we say of a party that 'it has not died out yet,' we imply a certain pious wish—a silent hope or, eventually, a certain apprehension that it may some time do so after all.

The chief conclusion of the foregoing analysis is the important fact that, though falsified by Christian scribes, the genuine and original text of the passage is not definitely lost, but may still be discerned, like the original writing of a palimpsest. It need hardly be added that the reconstructed text must be in complete harmony with the general vocabulary and phraseology of Josephus, and that it must be free from the various inconsistencies which have for centuries been objected against the genuineness of the *Testimonium*.

For the convenience of the reader and as a sort of summary of the results attained by our critical analysis, a hypothetical reconstruction of what may very well have been the original text, accompanied by an English translation, is printed below, together with a critical edition of the traditional or 'received' text with

[1] Prof. van Liempt compares also Alciphron, *Epist.*, iii. 21, p. 49 (Meinecke, Leipzig, 1853), "Ὁ μὲν ἀνὴρ ἀπόδημός ἐστι μοι τρίτην ταύτην ἡμέραν ἔχων ἐν ἄστει," and Epictet., ii. 15. 5, "ἤδη τρίτην ἡμέραν ἔχοντος αὐτοῦ τῆς ἀποχῆς."
[2] Samuel Butler would even call them 'too wise a nation T'expose their trade to disputation.' Ben Jonson styled physicians 'a subtle nation.'
[3] Therefore the Christian translator 'Egesippus' (ii. 12. 1, p. 164, l. 1 ff., Ussani) has altered the whole phrase and said instead : '*ex quo coepit congregatio Christianorum et in omne hominum penetravit genus, nec ulla natio Romani orbis remansit quae cultus eius expers relinqueretur.*'

just such a translation. A comparison of the two texts either in the original Greek or in the translation will, it is hoped, enable the reader to judge for himself the merits of the method followed.

What may be achieved by the systematic application of the well-known methods of comparative analysis of Josephus' style and vocabulary will be clearly seen. No attempt has been made to conceal or even to minimise the purely hypothetical character of the reconstructed text.[1] This much may, however, be claimed for this new attempt at such a restoration, in contrast especially to the previous attempts of G. A. Müller and the late Théodore Reinach, that it stands on a much broader basis. Thanks largely to the co-operation of Dr. Thackeray and Dr. van Liempt, it is indeed probable that no parallel of any importance in the whole work of Josephus has been overlooked or neglected.

The reader will do well, moreover, to remember that hitherto not one of the critics has taken into consideration the existing evidence on the treatment of Jewish literature, in so far as it dealt with Jesus Christ and Christianity in general, at the hands of the Christian censors. Late as the extant tangible traces of such passages may seem, both in MSS. and prints, the legal basis for such official expurgations and the pressing need for them on the part of cautious owners of such MSS. can be shown to have existed ever since Constantine the Great and the Emperors Theodosius and Valentinianus.[2]

Under these circumstances it may be well for the reader to compare the distribution of dots (indicating irrecoverable deletions) and of words in small print (indicating possible restorations of words wholly or partly corrected by the censor) over the page constituting our *textus restitutus*, with the reproduction of a censored text from a Jewish anti-Christian work on our Pl. VI.

No one, I think, can fail to observe the close analogy in the aspect of Pl. VI. and p. 61. In both texts whole passages consisting of several lines have been obliterated ; in both the corrections are frequently confined to single words or even parts of words,

---

[1] Prof. H. Windisch, *loc. cit.*, p. 281 : ' It is incredible that a historian may delude himself into believing that we could, with the means at our disposal, recover the lost original text.' This, however, is not at all the opinion of those who have made the *modus dicendi* and the *copia verborum* of Josephus the object of special study. The attempted reconstruction is in no way more difficult or more uncertain than the average restorations of badly damaged inscriptions or papyri. I am doing for the *Testimonium Flavianum* what Furtwaengler did for the Aegina sculptures when he freed them from the awkward restorations of Thorwaldsen and attempted to recover the original compositions. Neither is there any ' combinatory magic ' (M. Dibelius) about it, nor do I cherish any illusions about the result. I know that *parts* of the original are irrecoverably lost. The restoration offered on p. 61 is accepted as ' a highly plausible conclusion' by Burton Scott Easton in the *Anglican Theolog. Review* (1930). A. D. Nock (*Class. Review*, Dec. 1929) says : ' It has the merit of doing justice to the facts observed by Burkitt and by Norden alike. It may be right: σώζει τὰ φαινόμενα.'

[2] See below, Appendix IV.

changes designed to convert an objectionable into a harmless statement. The reproduction of an uncensored copy of the respective page of Jacob ben Asher's *'Arba' Turim* side by side with the reproduction of the censored text, as shown in Pl. VI., would show differences of exactly the same kind as the two texts of the *Testimonium* printed on pp. 59 f. and 61 respectively.

Considered quite objectively, this seems to be a new, weighty, and very concrete argument and far beyond the realm of mere hypothesis, an argument never before taken into account in this connexion and which may yet very well turn the balance in favour of the solution here proposed of this extremely vexed problem.

TESTIMONIUM JOSEPHI DE JESU CHRISTO. TEXTUS RECEPTUS
CUM APPARATU CRITICO

Vide : Andreae Bosii, *Exercitationem in periocham Josephi de Jesu Christo*, Jena, 1673, c. 2, § 45.
Caroli Daubuzii, *appendicem in Havercampii editionis*, vol. ii. p. 191.
Bened. Niese, *Josephi Flavii opera*, vol. iv., Berol., 1890, p. 151$_3$.
Théodore Reinach, *Revue des Études Juives*, 1897, p. 3.
Johannes Aufhauser, *Antike Jesuszeugnisse*, Kleine Texte für Vorlesungen und Übungen, hrsg. von H. Lietzmann, Nr. 126, Bonn, 1913, p. 10 f. (2. Auflage 1925).
Kurt Linck, *De antiquissimis veterum quae ad Jesum Nazarenum spectant testimoniis*, p. 3. *Religionsgeschichtliche Versuche und Vorarbeiten*, hrsg. von Richard Wünsch u. Ludwig Deubner, Bd. xiv., Heft 1, p. 3, Giessen, 1913-14.
Leo Wohleb, Das Testimonium Flavianum, *Röm. Quartalschrift*, xxxv., 1927, p. 155.

Codices, qui xviii. librum *Antiquitatum* continent, hi sunt :

A, Ambr. F 128 *sup.* s. fere xi. membr. (*vide* Pl. VI.) ;
M, Med. plut. 69 cod. 10 s. fere xv. chart. ;
W, Vat. gr. n. 984 membr. rescriptus anno 1354.

Praeter codices manuscriptos nonnullis locis etiam alii fontes adhibendi erunt nempe hi :

E. h. e. epitoma *Antiquitatum*,[1] cuius maxime est adhibendus cod. Busbekianus olim Constantinopolitanus, qui invenitur in bibliotheca olim Caesarea Vindobonensi inter historicos Graecos no. 22 ; ad nonnullos locos sanandos praeterea consulendus est cod. Laur. plut. 69, 23.

Lat. h. e. versio Latina, quae dicitur Rufini, *vide* Nieseanae editionis praef. vol. i. p. xxvii *sqq.*, et p. lix *sqq.*

Egesippus h. e. versio Latina, quae S. Ambrosii Mediolanensis opus primum esse creditur sed potius Isaaco, alias Hilario aut Gaudentio, qui dicitur Ambrosiaster (*supra*, p. 15$_{1.2}$), tribuenda est,

---

[1] *Vide* Niese, praef. vol. iv. p. iii *sq.*

quam denuo edidit Vincentius Ussani, *Corpus Scriptorum Ecclesiasticorum Latinorum*, vol. lxvi., Vindobonae MCMXXX., lib. ii., c. 12, pp. 163 s., lin. 24-1.

S. Hieronymi versio latina, *De Vir. Ill.*, 13.

Zonaras, chron. i. 478, qui epitomam supralaudatam (E) adhibuit.[1]

Exc. h. e. Excerpta, quae ex Josepho Constantinus Porphyrogenitus in titulos *de virtutibus et vitiis et de legationibus* recepit,[2] quorumque hodie adeuntur praecipue Excerpta codicis Peiresciani nunc Turonensis, et codicis Ursiniani nunc Vaticani gr. 1418.[3]

Suidas, *s.v.* Ἰώσηπος, ed. G. Bernhardy, Halis et Brunsvigae, 1853, T. i., p. 2, 1041.

Eusebius, *Hist. eccl.*, i. 11. 7 ; *Dem. evang.*, iii. 5. 105 ; *Theoph.* 5. 44 ; *vide* Ed. Schwartz, GCS, 9. 3, p. clxxxvi s.

B. h. e. Belli Judaici nonnulli codd., qui idem illud testimonium continent : M,[4] V,[5] Rost.,[6] T,[7] Neapolitanus,[8] Coislinianus [9] ; nec non et alia, quae infra laudantur, testimonia Malalae, Cedreni Isidori Pelusiotae, Sozomeni, Mich. Glycae, etc.

Iam sequantur verba, quae hodie *Ant. Jud.*, xviii. 3. 3, § 63 *sq.* leguntur :

Γίνεται δὲ[10] κατὰ τοῦτον[11] τὸν χρόνον[12] Ἰησοῦς,[13] σοφὸς ἀνήρ,[14] εἴγε αὐτὸν ἄνδρα λέγειν χρή.[15] Ἦν γὰρ παραδόξων ἔργων ποιητής, διδάσκαλος[16] ἀνθρώπων τῶν ἡδονῇ τἀληθῆ δεχομένων,[17] καὶ

---

[1] K. Krumbacher, *Gesch. byz. Lit.* (²), 370 *sq.*, 372.
[2] *Vide* Niese, praef. vol. i. p. xxix, lxi *sq.* ; iii. p. xlii.
[3] *Ibid.*, vol. iii. p. xiv.   [4] *Ibid.*, vol. vi. pp. vii, xxxi, lxx.
[5] *Ibid.*, pp. ix, xxxvi, lxxi.   [6] *Ibid.*, pp. xvii, xlix, lxxi.
[7] *Ibid.*, pp. xvii, xlii, lxxi.   [8] *Ibid.*, p. xiv.   [9] *Ibid.*, p. xvii.
[10] δὴ E ; ἦν pro γίνεται, Cedrenus, *Hist. comp.*, p. 345 ed. Bonn. ' Egesippus ' et auctor versionis latinae, quae Rufino tribuitur, et Hieronymus, ' fuit autem eisdem temporibus . . .'
[11] κατ᾽ ἐκεῖνον, Eus., *Dem.* ; ' illo in tempore,' Egesippus.
[12] Cedrenus, *loc. cit.*, "κατὰ τὸν καιρὸν τοῦτον." *Idem*, Isidor. Pelus., lib. iv. ep. 225, Cod. Vat. gr. 650. Versio latina dicta Rufini : ' eisdem temporibus '= ὑπὸ τοὺς αὐτοὺς χρόνους, ut scribit Josephus ἀρχ. xviii. 3. 4, § 65 : ' istis temporibus,' epist. Lentuli (*infra*, p. vi, c. 2)="κατὰ τούσδε τοὺς χρόνους," h. e. ' nunc.'
[13] Ἰησοῦς τις, Eusebii, *Hist. eccl.*, cod. Paris, 1430 s. xi praep. codd., quidam.
[14] ἀνὴρ σοφός, Niceph., *Callisti hist. eccl. libri*, Migne Patr. Gr. 145, 747='vir sapiens,' quod praebent S. Hieronymus et Ambrosiaster (Rufinus : ' sapiens vir '). ἄνθρωπον ἀγαθὸν καὶ δίκαιον, Malalas, *loc. cit.* (cf. *infra*, p. iv, c. 7, de S. Joanne Bapt., qui a Christiano ' Antiquitatum Iudaicorum ' correctore ἀνὴρ ἀγαθός, a Josepho ipso autem ἀνὴρ ἄγριος appellatus est), et Philippus Sidetes, Bratke *T. u. U.*, N.F. iv. 3, 1897, p. 36₈₋₁₁.
[15] χρὴ ἄνδρα αὐτὸν λέγειν, transpos. Exc. ; αὐτὸν λέγειν ἄνδρα χρή, transpos. B. Jo. Malalas Chronogr., lib. 10, p. 319, ed. Oxon. : " εἴπερ ἄρα τὸν τοιοῦτον ἄνθρωπον δεῖ λέγειν καὶ μὴ θεόν." Verba "εἴγε ἄνδρα αὐτὸν λέγειν χρή" in codice ante octavum saeculum exarato, qui penes J. Vossium fuit, latine expressa non erant, ut ipse attestatur. *Vide* Ittigii in Havercampii editionis, vol. ii., suppl. p. 91, verba : ' quin etiam innuit Vossius sic alia quoque quae consuluit exemplaria adhibere.' Daubuz, *loc. cit.*, p. 192.
[16] διδάσκαλον λόγων ἀληθῶν, Hermias Sozomenos, *Hist. eccl.*, lib. i., c. i., p. 8 ed. Bonn. ἀληθείας, Sozom., *loc. cit.*
[17] τἀληθῆ σεβομένων, Eus., *Dem.* ; ἡδονῇ σὺν, suprascr. M2 a.

πολλοὺς μὲν Ἰουδαίους,¹ πολλοὺς δὲ καὶ² τοῦ³ Ἑλληνικοῦ⁴
ἐπηγάγετο.⁵

Ὁ Χριστὸς οὗτος ἦν.⁶ Καὶ αὐτὸν ἐνδείξει⁷ τῶν πρώτων
ἀνδρῶν παρ' ἡμῖν⁸ σταυρῷ ἐπιτετιμηκότος Πιλάτου οὐκ⁹
ἐπαύσαντο¹⁰ οἱ τὸ¹¹ πρῶτον¹² ἀγαπήσαντες. Ἐφάνη γὰρ αὐτοῖς
τρίτην ἔχων ἡμέραν πάλιν¹³ ζῶν τῶν θείων προφητῶν ταῦτά τε¹⁴
καὶ ἄλλα μυρία περὶ αὐτοῦ θαυμάσια¹⁵ εἰρηκότων. Εἰς ἔτι τε¹⁶
νῦν τῶν Χριστιανῶν ἀπὸ τοῦδε¹⁷ ὠνομασμένων¹⁸ οὐκ ἐπέλιπε¹⁹
τὸ φῦλον.

ANGLICE :

' Now about this time there arose Jesus, a wise man, if indeed he
may be called a man. For he was a doer of marvellous acts, a teacher
of such men as receive the truth with delight. And he won over to
himself many Jews and many also of the Greek nation. He was the
Christ. And when, on the indictment of the principal men among us,
Pilate had sentenced him to the cross, still those who before had loved
him did not cease [to do so]. For he appeared to them on [lit.
' having '] the third day alive again, as the divinely-inspired prophets had told—these and ten thousand other wonderful things—
concerning him. And until now the race of Christians, so named from
him, is not extinct.'

---

¹ τῶν Ἰουδαίων B ; Eus. praep. ; *Judeorum* Lat. ; τοῦ Ἰουδαϊκοῦ, Eus., *Dem.*
² καὶ om. Exc.
³ ἀπὸ τοῦ B ; Eus. praep. et fórtasse versionis Latinae exemplar, in qua
' *ex gentibus*.'
⁴ τοῦ Ἑλληνικοῦ exc. ; τοὺς Ἑλληνικούς corr. A.
⁵ ἀπηγάγετο, Euseb., *Hist. eccl.*, codd.—aliter ignoti—apud Th. Reinachium et
C. A. Muellerum laudati ; ἠγάγετο Χριστός ; Cedrenus, *loc. cit.*
⁶ A Cedreno, *loc. cit.*, hoc Josephi testimonium allegante omissa sunt ὁ Χριστὸς
οὗτος ἦν. Eadem verba desunt in S. Ambrosii vel Ambrosiastri versione latina
(Ps. Egesippi, lib. ii. c. 12), necnon in antiquissima sine loci et temporis nota
editione versionis latinae, quae Rufini sub nomine fertur (*Bibl. Nat., Paris.*,
Reserve H 287). Vide Daubuz, *loc. cit.*, p. 192. De S. Hieronymi lectione,
' et credebatur esse Christus,' *vide supra*, p. 54.
⁷ S. Hieronym. (*De Viris illustr.*, 13, ' invidia nostrorum principum ') in codice
suo " φθόνῳ " pro " ἐνδείξει " invenit.
⁸ τῶν παρ' ἡμῖν ἀρχόντων, Eus., *Dem.*   ⁹ Ante οὐκ in marg. σεβάζειν add. M 2.
¹⁰ ἐξεπαύσαντο, Eus. praep. codd. plurimi ; ἐπαύσαντο κηρύσσοντες περὶ αὐτοῦ,
Cedren. ; " πίστεως οὐκ ἐπαύσαντο " invenit S. Hieronymus (' perseveraverunt
in fide '). Vide *B. J.*, i. § 94, " ἐπαύσαντο πίστεως."
¹¹ οἴγε, W Exc.   ¹² πρῶτον αὐτὸν, M E.
¹³ ἔχων, om. Eus., *Dem* ; πάλιν, om. Sozom., *loc. cit.* ; Mich. Glyc. *Ann.*, iii. p. 436,
Bonn, Egesippus, Hieronymus, Cassiodorus, *Hist. trip.*, i. 2. Vide Ussani,
infra, p. 62 n. 1.
¹⁴ τε, om. W Exc.   ¹⁵ περὶ αὐτοῦ θαυμάσια, om. Eus., *Dem.*
¹⁶ Εἰς ἔτι τε, E B Eus. praep. ; εἰς τε, A W Exc. ; εἰσέτι καὶ, σέτι, i. ras. m. 2, τε
suprascr. M 2 ; ὅθεν εἰσέτι, Eus., *Dem.* ; " εἰς τε νῦν," Suid. ; " εἰς δὲ τὸ νῦν," Isid. Pelus.,
lib. iv., epist. 225, Cod. Vatic. ; ἰδὲ τοίνυν, idem, ed. Paris ; " οὐκέτι νῦν," Sermo
Macarii, Acta Sanctorum, Maii tom., p. 149.
¹⁷ " ἀπὸ τοῦδε τῶν Χριστιανῶν," transposuit Eus., *Dem.*, τῶν, ὦν, i. ras. corr. A.
¹⁸ ὠνομασμένων, M 2. E. Exc. B. Eus. praep., om. Eus., *Dem.* ; ὠνομασμένον, corr.
Niese.
¹⁹ ἐπέλειπε, Exc. ; ἐξέλιπε, Isid. Pelus., *loc. cit.*

FLAVII JOSEPHI 'ANTIQUITATES JUDICAE,' XVIII., 3. 3.

TEXTUS RESTITUTUS

ΓΙΝΕΤΑΙ[1] ΔΕ ΚΑΤΑ ΤΟΥΤΟΝ ΤΟΝ ΧΡΟΝΟΝ[2] ἀρχὴ νέων
θορύβων[3] ΙΗΣΟΥΣ ΤΙΣ[4] ΣΟΦιστὴΣ[5] ΑΝΗΡ,[6] ΕΙΓΕ[7] ΑΝΔΡΑ
ΛΕΓΕΙΝ ΧΡΗ ΑΥΤΟΝ,[8] τὸν ἐξ ἀνθρώπων ἐξαισιώτατον,[9] ὃν οἱ
μαθηταὶ υἱὸν θεοῦ ὀνομάζουσιν,[10] τὸν οἷα οὐδέποτε ἐπεποιήκει
ἄνθρωπος θαύματα ἐργασάμενον[11] . . . . . . [12] ΗΝ ΓΑΡ ΠΑΡΑΔΟΞΩΝ
ΕΡΓΩΝ[13] ΔΙΔΑΣΚΑΛΟΣ,[14] ΑΝΘΡΩΠΩΝ ΤΩΝ ΗΔΟΝΗΙ Τ'
ΑΗΘΗ[15] ΔΕΧΟΜΕΝΩΝ[16] . . . . . . [17] ΚΑΙ ΠΟΛΛΟΥΣ ΜΕΝ[18]
ΙΟΥΔΑΙΟΥΣ, ΠΟΛΛΟΥΣ ΔΕ[18] ΚΑΙ ΤΟΥ ἙΛΛΗΝΙΚΟΥ[19]
ΑΠΗΓΑΓΕΤΟ[20] καὶ (ὑπὸ τούτων)[21] Ο ΧΡΙΣΤΟΣ εἶναι ἐνομίζετο[22]

. . . .

ΚΑΙ ΑΥΤΟΝ[23] ΕΝΔΕΙΞΕΙ[24] ΤΩΝ ΠΡΩΤΩΝ ΑΝΔΡΩΝ[25] ΠΑΡ'
ΗΜΙΝ[26] ΣΤΑΥΡΩΙ ΕΠΙΤΕΤΙΜΗΚΟΤΟΣ[27] ΠΙΛΑΤΟΥ ΟΥΚ
ΕΠΑΥΣΑΝΤΟ θορυβεῖν[28] ΟΙ ΤΟ ΠΡΩΤΟΝ ΑΓΑΠΗΣΑΝΤΕΣ[29].
ΦΑΝΗναι[30] ΓΑΡ ΑΥΤΟΙΣ[31] ἔδοξε[32] ΤΡΙΤΗΝ ΗΜΕΡΑΝ
ΕΧΩΝ[33] [θανάτου ΠΑΛΙΝ][34] ΖΩΝ, ΤΩΝ ΘΕΙΩΝ ΠΡΟΦΗΤΩΝ[35]
ΤΑΥΤΑ ΤΕ ΚΑΙ ΑΛΛΑ ΜΥΡΙΑ ΠΕΡΙ ΑΥΤΟΥ ΘΑΥΜΑΣΙΑ[36]
ΕΙΡΗΚΟΤΩΝ[37].   ΕΙΣ ΕΤΙ ΚΑΙ ΝΥΝ[38] ΤΩΝ ΧΡΙΣΤΙΑΝΩΝ
ΑΠΟ ΤΟΥΔΕ ΩΝΟΜΑΣΜΕΝΩΝ[39] ΟΥΚ ΕΠΕΛΙΠΕ[40] ΤΟ
ΦΥΛΟΝ[41]. XVIII, 3. 4: . . . . [42] ΚΑΙ ΥΠΟ ΤΟΥΣ
ΑΥΤΟΥΣ ΧΡΟΝΟΥΣ ΕΤΕΡΟΝ ΤΙ ΔΕΙΝΟΝ ΕΘΟΡΥΒΕΙ[43]
ΤΟΥΣ ΙΟΥΔΑΙΟΥΣ.

---

[1] Cf. *supra*, p. 50 not. 1 et 2.   [2] Cf. *supra*, p. 51.   [3] Cf. *supra*, p. 50 not. 2.
[4] Cf. *supra*, pp. 46 f. et 50 not. 1.   [5] Cf. *supra*, p. 51 not. 2.
[6] Cf. *supra*, p. 52.   [7] Cf. *supra*, p. 52.   [8] Cf. *supra*, pp. 51 f.
[9] Cf. *supra*, p. 52 not. 2.   [10] Cf. *supra*, p. 52 lin. 13.
[11-12] Hic aliquid deletum esse videtur ; cf. *supra*, p. 54 § 3.
[13] Cf. *supra*, p. 53 not. 1 et 2.   [14] Cf. *supra*, p. 53.   [15] Cf. *supra*, p. 53 not. 3.
[16] Cf. *supra*, p. 53.   [17] Cf. *supra*, p. 54 § 3.
[18] Cf. van Liempt, *l.c.*, p. 111₅.   [19] Cf. *B. J.*, ii. § 268.
[20] Cf. *supra*, p. 60 not. 5.   [21] Cf. *supra*, p. 54 lin. 28.
[22] Cf. *supra*, p. 54, lineam 27 ss.   [23] Cf. *Antiqq.*, xviii. § 314 ; xx. § 74.
[24] Cf. *Antiqq.*, xix. § 133 ; xiii. § 306.   [25] Cf. van Liempt, p. 112.
[26] Cf. *Antiqq.*, xx. §§ 2, 198.   [27] Cf. *Antiqq.*, xviii. §§ 68, 255, 262, 294.
[28] Cf. *supra*, p. 60 not. 10.   [29] Cf. *supra*, p. 55 not. 1.
[30] Cf. *supra*, p. 55 l. 30 f.
[31] Cf. Celsus, ii. 70 : "τοῖς ἑαυτοῦ θιασώταις κρύβδην παρεφαίνετο."
[32] Cf. *supra*, p. 55 l. 30.   [33] Cf. *supra*, p. 55, ultima linea.
[34] Cf. *supra*, p. 56 l. 4 ; 60 not. 13.   [35] Cf. *Antiqq.*, viii. § 234 ; x. § 35.
[36] Cf. *supra*, p. 60 not. 15.   [37] Cf. *supra*, p. 28 not. 1 ; p. 55, l. 37 ff.
[38] Cf. *supra*, p. 56.   [39] Cf. *B. J.*, v. § 162.
[40] Cf. *supra*, p. 56 not. 3.   [41] Cf. *supra*, p. 56 not. 2.
[42] Deest forsitan aliquid in principio capitis xviii., 3, 4 ; cf. *infra*, App. xv., not. 1.   [43] Cf. *supra*, p. 42 lineas 35 ss.

ANGLICE :

Restored Text	Traditional Text
Now about this time arose (an occasion for new disturbances) a certain Jesus, a wizard of a man, if indeed he may be called a man (who was the most monstrous of all men, whom his disciples call a son of God, as having done wonders such as no man hath ever yet done). . . . He was in fact a teacher of astonishing tricks to such men as accept the abnormal with delight.	Now about this time arose Jesus, a wise man, if indeed he may be called a man. For he was a doer of marvellous acts, a teacher of such men as receive the truth with delight.
And he seduced many Jews and many also of the Greek nation, and (was regarded by them as) the Messiah.	And he won over to himself many Jews and many also of the Greek nation. He was the Christ.
And when, on the indictment of the principal men among us, Pilate had sentenced him to the cross, still those who before had admired him did not cease (to rave). For it seemed to them that having been dead [1] for three days, he had appeared to them alive again,[1] as the divinely-inspired prophets had foretold— these and ten thousand other wonderful things—concerning him. And even now the race of those who are called ' Messianists ' after him is not extinct.	And when, on the indictment of the principal men among us, Pilate had sentenced him to the cross, still those who before had loved him did not cease (to do so). For he appeared to them on (lit. ' having ') the third day alive again, as the divinely-inspired prophets had told—these and ten thousand other wonderful things —concerning him. And until now the race of Christians, so named from him, is not extinct.

[1] According to a recent publication of Prof. Vincente Ussani (*Casinensia*, Montecassino, 1929, pp. 612-14) which reached me after this chapter was in type and had been put into pages, the word ' again ' is a later addition to the text of Josephus, unknown to the so-called Egesippus, to St. Jerome and other Latin as well as Greek witnesses (see above, p. 60 n. 13). This precious find makes me think that even as '*iterum*' ('again,' πάλιν in the Greek MSS.) the word θανάτου=*mortis* after *triduum*, above, p. 56 l. 2, was added by a corrector to an original intentionally vague, ' For after three days he had appeared to them alive,' in order to make Josephus attest that Jesus had *died* and *risen again* from death, whereas the real wording of Josephus left it an open question whether the condemned Messiah had died on the cross or had somehow escaped and reappeared alive and free. Anyhow, here is a new proof that the text has been tampered with by Christian scribes.

IV

THE ALLEGED SILENCE OF JOSEPHUS' 'JEWISH WAR' ABOUT JESUS

AS is well known, Josephus does not mention Jesus at all in the Greek text of his earlier work, the *Jewish War*, written some twenty years before the *Jewish Antiquities*. This fact remains a very troublesome problem in any enquiry into Christian origins, even if the partial authenticity of the *Testimonium* be admitted. For if we were to suppose that Josephus knew nothing about Jesus in the years immediately following the capture of Jerusalem, whilst twenty years later he thought it necessary to insert a whole chapter on this ' sophist,' [1] the partisans of the non-historicity theory might well argue that during that interval Josephus had become acquainted with the Gospel of Mark, composed, probably, near the Flavian court shortly after A.D. 75,[2] or even with Matthew, written some time during the reign of Domitian.[3] Such an argument, it is true, would at best be but an ingenious conjecture and devoid of all textual basis, there being no point of contact between either of the two Gospels on the one hand and the *Testimonium* on the other. Even so, the very fact that Josephus could ignore at first the ' disturbance ' caused by the appearance of Jesus, and then repair this seeming omission in a later and more detailed account of the same period, could not but give a certain support to the opinion of those inclined to minimize the political significance of the events connected with Jesus' name. For it is to be noted that such an omission and subsequent addition is by no means without parallel in the work of Josephus. For example, in the *War* he knows nothing about the messianic career of Menaḥem, the son of Judas of Galilee (A.D. 66), for the very simple reason that at the critical time he was prudently hiding in a secret back-chamber of the temple precinct, and it was only after the publication of his book that his readers drew his attention to the interesting incident he had missed. It is at first sight not at all unthinkable that similarly he should have known nothing of

[1] See above, p. 51 note 2, and p. 61 note 5.
[2] The *terminus post quem* is given by the Christian legend of the torn veil exposed to the public in Rome since A.D. 75. See below, p. 147 n. 1.
[3] The date may be inferred from the story of the penny in the fish's mouth. See my *Orpheus*, London (Watkins), 1921, p. 93.

John the Baptist, likewise passed over in silence in the *War*, and
of Jesus, and that what he reports about these men in his *Antiquities* should have been wholly derived from subsequent information.   Yet it must be admitted that such an omission would none
the less diminish the political importance of the events connected
with John and Jesus in the eyes of the modern historian.   It
would justify in a certain measure the opinions of scholars such as
Ernest Renan [1] and Maurice Goguel,[2] who held that the Gospels
magnified out of all proportion a series of facts which had passed
almost unnoticed by the contemporaries.   The cries of '*Osanna,
Son of David, King of the Jews,*' are thus supposed, according to
this view, to have been drowned in the general noise of an excited
Oriental crowd of pilgrims.   The overturning of the tables of the
money-changers is regarded as a single trivial incident among the
many petty cases of local brawling and personal bickerings so
common at the time of the great pilgrimages.

It is unnecessary to point out to any one conversant with mass
psychology and with the Oriental mentality how utterly impossible
such an interpretation is in fact.   Could any one think of a
similar event happening in modern India and remaining unknown
to an indifferent outside world in England or Europe generally ?
Nor is it conceivable, should another such incident occur, say, in
modern Egypt, that a native Arab historian writing a history
of the Nationalist movement some fifty years afterwards should
pass over in silence such an occurrence as altogether too trivial.
Nor, again, is it permissible to adduce, with Prof. Dibelius of
Heidelberg,[3] the lowly social strata in which Jesus and his Galilaean
fishermen moved as the reason why the events in question are
supposed to have been ignored by the contemporary historians.
Indeed, every student of political history knows that no ruling
class can afford to ignore these strata in a subject country;
and should he be naïve enough to believe that, any high official of
a European foreign or colonial office will teach him better.   Nor
does anything in Josephus' work justify such an assumption.
On the contrary, the weaver Jonathan of Cyrene and his indigent
followers, as also Theudas the Samaritan and the Egyptian
messiah appearing under Festus, all of them belonged to the very
riff-raff of ancient society, to say nothing of the slave Simon mentioned by Tacitus [4] as the would-be successor of Herod the Great.
It would seem certain, therefore, that no amount of belittling of
the events narrated in the Gospels will satisfactorily account for
Josephus' apparent strange silence about both John the Baptist
and Jesus in his earlier work.

---

[1] *Vie de Jésus*, 13th ed., Paris, 1867, p. 388.
[2] *Revue de l'histoire des religions*, 1926, p. 42.
[3] *Theologische Blätter*, vi. (1927), cc. 213 *sqq.*   [4] See above, p. 47 line 7.

One might think, of course, that Josephus might have had a personal motive for withholding these particular facts. It has been suggested that he did not care, for apologetic reasons, to mention the messianist hopes of his people. But, if that be true, why does he speak without the slightest reserve of Theudas, of Judas of Galilee, and of all the other messiahs, keeping a diplomatic silence only in the case of Jesus ? All these explanations really explain nothing, and the true solution must be sought in an entirely different direction.

In the first place, it is well to note that the striking difference between Tacitus, who knows and mentions [1] the execution of Jesus by Pilate,[2] and Josephus, who, though obviously drawing on the same sources, seems to ignore that event, represents by no means an isolated case. An exact parallel is found in the equally puzzling fact that Josephus in his *Antiquities* and Philo Judaeus together mention four other uprisings in the administration of Pilate, whilst Tacitus,[3] writing on the same period, merely remarks '*sub Tiberio quies* ' (i.e. *in Judaea*). One might feel tempted to explain the divergence by supposing that Tacitus did not think the incidents mentioned by Josephus and Philo important enough to figure in his work. Yet in the same passage Tacitus adds that the Jews rose in arms (*arma potius sumpsere*) against Caligula when this mad emperor insisted on placing his statue in the interior of the Jewish sanctuary in Jerusalem. On the other hand, Josephus knows of no such violent resistance to the projects of the imperial megalomaniac. He seems to know only of piteous mass-delegations to the sensible governor of Syria, Petronius ; of peaceful petitions backed by men and women of all ranks and ages ; and, as the nearest approach to anything that could be called active opposition, of a threatened general strike of the Jewish peasant-farmers ; but there is not a word about armed resistance and a threatened uprising, prevented only by the timely assassination of the tyrant in far-away Rome. Here, then, it is Tacitus who appears to magnify a peaceful and strictly constitutional protest into a revolutionary movement.

---

[1] *Hist.*, v. 9.

[2] In view of the fact that Tacitus mentions Jesus in connection with the accusation against the Christians of having set Rome on fire, it is very curious to remember that the standard text of Josephus does not contain a single word about the burning of the capital of the world, although it happened while he himself was in Rome (Corssen, *Zeitschr. f. neutest. Wiss.*, xv., 1914, p. 139). The simplest explanation of this startling fact would be to suppose that Josephus did devote a chapter to the great catastrophe, which must have been a terrible blow to the Jews of Rome, but that it was deleted because it spoke of the Christians and the founder of their religion in the same way as Tacitus, only with many more objectionable details. The phrase ' all these subjects being so hackneyed, I propose to pass over,' etc., in *B.J.*, ii. § 251, is probably inserted as a bridge over a vast lacuna caused by the censor's deletions. Cp. above, p. 12 n. 4, on the mutilated report of Dio Cassius.　　　　　　　　　　　　　　　　[3] *Loc. cit.*

E

Thus it is obviously impossible to explain the divergence between Tacitus and Josephus, both using the same source, by any presumed tendency on the part of the former; for in one case he would be accused of having toned down the narrative of his source until nothing is left of its historical contents, and in another, a few lines further, of having exaggerated a report of his authority so as to convert a series of peaceful proceedings into an armed rebellion.

Applying this analogy to our central problem, the silence of Josephus about Jesus the Naṣōraean, I venture to submit the following explanation. Supposing, as suppose we must, that Josephus *did* give proper space to the events connected with the life and death of the founder of the Christian religion, and supposing also, as well we might, that the chapter in question was no less hostile to Jesus than the parallel passages are to Theudas, Judas of Galilee, and the Samaritan and Egyptian messiahs, would it be conceivable that this passage could have escaped the hands of the ecclesiastical censors at a time when Christianity was powerful enough to exercise such a censorship? The answer to the question is obvious. No ecclesiastical authority would have allowed the circulation of a book which treated the founder of its religion as a ' robber chief ' commanding a handful of rebels against the established society, as a 'magician ' who through sham miracles and 'signs of liberation ' [1] worked upon the imagination of the multitude, just as the sorcerers mentioned elsewhere in the pages of Josephus. No Christian scribe would copy such passages, insulting to the founder of the Christian religion. Nor are we left to conjecture alone, for parallels are indeed not wanting. In precisely this manner an obviously insulting passage in Lucian [2] has been deleted, and after the death of the Emperor Julian Apostata the most striking attacks against Christianity were suppressed in the ' new edition ' of Eunapius. [3] A passing glance at Pl. VII. will easily convince the reader of how little a Christian censor thought of destroying a whole chapter concerning Christianity in a Jewish book simply because it appeared to him ' blasphemous.'

If this explanation be accepted, for the present, as a working hypothesis, what else is needed to explain the silence of Josephus on the subject of the crucifixion, of which Tacitus certainly knew? What else is needed to explain also the strange silence of Tacitus on the troubles happening in Judaea in the reign of Tiberius? Who can exclude offhand the possibility that after the now enigmatically short words of the historian, ' *sub Tiberio quies*,' some such words as ' *brevis turbata*,' etc., may have been destroyed, and

---

[1] *B.J.*, ii. § 259.
[2] *Peregr. Prot.*, ch. xiii. The gap was first noticed in Gesner's edition.
[3] See above, p. 12 n. 3.

רשד ובן ציני כמו כמו שנבאר למטה ולדעת זרה
זרע האשה אינה נאות להולדה זה כתב בס׳
בח׳ במאמר יז׳ ויש מחכמי הרפואות חולקין
עליו ואומרו כי חסר הולד הוא כדם האשה
וזורע הזכר יחד ׳ ואומרו כי הבשר והדבר
האדומים חן מן הדם ׳ ועל כן יכרת ועוד
יחליף ׳ והעור והעצמות הם מזרע הזכר ועל
כן לא יחליפו אך כשיתקבץ שם ליחה אחרת
מדובקת ודביק שני החלקים יחד ׳ ויש
אחרים שאומרו ואבן זהר מכללם כי משני
הזרעים יחד יהיה החמר הולד והדם שכרחם
הוא מזונו ולזה כשיפסוק עת נדחת לא תוכל
להתעבר כי לא נמצא מזן לולד ואף על פי
שהחסר לא נעדר בעת ההוא כי עדיין היא
מזרעת כמו האדם אבל הסוון נפסק ׳
ראייה אחרת כי הדם הוא חמזן
שהתעבר לא יצא מכנחה הדם ההו
שם למזון העובר וגם יצא משם דרך
לישדים ויתבשל שם וישוב חלב שהוא
היונק אחר יצא את מבטן אמו ׳ ואבן
חולק על זה הדעת וסותר אותו שא
הדבר כן אי אפשר לנקבה שתתעבר
הוצאת זרעה והוא כמה פעם אחת ו
הנשים אסרו כי לפעמים מתעברר
תענוג. ובל א הוצאת זרע וחתע ענו
הזרע אם כן זה הדעת בטד ל ו
אריסטוטלום ׳ גם כתב ארים
בסף בח בח ׳ ובזרע הזכר כחלקי
אריסטוטלום יש מקרתם אנ
כהפרש חמעמיד הג בינ
החלב כלל אנ ונא עם
ציני כתב כי הוא מציר ח
עור הם הרוחות הטבעיים ו
רשד אומר כי הוא נתב כל
המציור הולד ביום הראשון
השלמת הצורה ׳ אך נאל יכלם
הזכר הוא מן חחסר והביא ראייר מאשר
שהפילה ביום ששי ונמצאו קרוסים על חזר
נמצא שחסר הולד גם הוא מזרע רש ג ל

שמתערב יחד עם דם האשה ׳ וזו אינו ראיית
כלל כי אפשר שאותם הקרוסות אשר היו
שם ביום הראשון והזרע מן הזכר הוא אשר היו
קיים מפני שלא נתך עד השלמת הצורה מלה
כי אם מעט מעט ׳ אך לדעת זה צריך ׳ לתת
טעם מפני מה הבשר מחליף והעור והעצמו
אינם מתחליפים והלא חומר אחד לחם ׳ עוד
צריך לברר לרעת זה מפני מה מקצ האברים
לבנים ומקצתם אדומים נתלה ה
לבלם וחוא הדם ציר יהבכ
ויש על הביני ו חי ר וחת ו ו
חלב כ ע ז הב ב א ו

שמתקב ני
בפיתיה וו מן כתב אוקר אצל וצא
מהגוף כלי כעת תנועת המש ג ל ויתרורה
בבצים

PAGE לה (=35) OF GERSHOM BEN SHELOMOH'S SEPHER SHA'AR HASH-SHAMAIM
('DOOR OF HEAVEN') PRINTED IN VENICE 1547 (COLUMBIA UNIVERSITY LIBRARY)

SHOWING THE OBLITERATION OF LARGE PARTS OF THE TEXT BY THE CENSOR
BY RECKLESS SPREADING OF INK OVER THE PRINTED PAGE

(SEE P. 56, LINE 32)

PLATE VII

that the original text had a reading something like this : ' under Tiberius a period of quiet (was interrupted through Pontius Pilatus' recklessness, who carried the standards of his troops with the portrait medallions of the Emperor, etc. . . . and by a man rising in protest against this violation of the law of the Jews, pretending to be a descendant of their old kings,' etc.) ?

Had Tacitus thus represented Jesus as the fomenter of all the troubles which occurred in Judaea under Tiberius, would the Christian copyists have transcribed the passage and would the Christian censor have tolerated it and let it pass ?

The same possibility may account for the remarkable fact that Josephus' present text knows nothing of an armed uprising of the Jews against Caligula's command to set up his statue in the temple.[1] This is what he says : ' Gaius . . . sent Petronius with an army to Jerusalem to instal in the sanctuary statues of himself. . . . § 186 : Petronius accordingly with three legions . . . left Antioch on the march for Judaea. § 187 : Among the Jews some had no belief in the rumours of war, others believed but saw no means of defence ; alarm, however, soon became universal, the army having reached Ptolemais.' Is it probable, in view of what happened on other occasions, that this time none of the Jews thought of desperate armed resistance against what they considered the supreme outrage on their national religion ? Or is it not more probable that the original text of Josephus (just like the parallel passage in Tacitus) contained the tripartite phrase : ' Among the Jews, some had no belief in the rumours of war, others believed but saw no means of defence (still others armed themselves and took to the mountains, saying . . .) ' ? If such a phrase has been excised by the censor, this could be explained only by the assumption that Josephus somehow attributed this armed uprising to the Christians, even as Tacitus, for example, says that ' the pernicious superstition,' quelled for a brief space of time through the crucifixion of the Christ under Pilate, ' soon broke out again.' Since we read in St. Jerome [2] that the prophecy about the ' abomination of desolation ' in Daniel [3] may be understood as referring either to the image of the Emperor Tiberius which Pilate set up in the temple or to the statue of Gaius which that emperor wanted to place in the sanctuary, and since on the other hand the apocalyptic prophecies of Jesus [4] admonish his disciples to take to the mountains as soon as the ' abomination of desolation ' is set up in the sanctuary, why should not Josephus have attributed to the influence of the pro-

---

[1] See, on the contrary, the Latin version of ' *Egesippus*,' ii. 5. 5, p. 140 f., ed. Ussani : ' *mortuo Tiberio Gaius successit, qui dominum se ac deum videri atque appellari volens causas dedit* JUDAEIS GRAVISSIMAE SEDITIONIS . . .'
[2] In *Matt.* xxiv. (opp. ed. Vallarsi, vii. 194).   [3] xii. 11.
[4] *Mark* xiii. 14-20 ; *Matt.* xxiv. 15-22.

phecies of Jesus and to the agitation of his disciples the action of those who in Tacitus' words 'took to armed resistance' against Caligula ? Such a passage, had it existed, would assuredly not have been tolerated by a Christian censor or copied by Christian scribes.

So far, let us repeat, these conjectures would seem nothing but a very bold hypothesis : all the same, they would seem infinitely more plausible, even without further support, than the extremely questionable hypothesis of the non-historicity of Jesus͵ or the little more probable assumption of the essential insignificance of the Gospel events, or Josephus' unknown private reasons which are held responsible for his passing over in silence what he knew about Jesus, whilst he does not appear to impose upon himself the slightest reserve when he comes to speak of the other messiahs of that troublesome period.

However that may be—and it is only fair to admit that we cannot arrive at any higher degree of probability on this point without the utilization of further material hitherto neglected, which will be analysed in the following chapters [1]—it is certainly a noteworthy fact that Josephus' silence about Jesus in the *Jewish War* was felt to be a defect at quite an early period, with the result that attempts were made to remedy this state of affairs by a bold insertion of the *Testimonium* into the *War*. The reason for this procedure, which we shall analyse presently on the basis of the reproduction given in Pl. VI., is easy to see. Of course, for the Ἱστορίαι, the *Collected Works* of Josephus, his silence about Jesus in the *War* was of no importance, since the *Testimonium* passage in the *Antiquities* fully supplied the need of Christian readers. But it was quite different for the separate editions of the *War*, the popularity of which is attested by a considerable number of MSS. Here the pious would very certainly miss a reference to the Naṣōraean Messiah, and the obvious remedy was simply to insert in some appropriate place in the *War* the passages concerning the Baptist and Jesus as found in the *Antiquities*. In one group of MSS. this insertion was done in a very mechanical manner, the passages in question being put either at the beginning or at the end of the MS.[2] In the Codex Vossianus, now in the University Library of Leyden, on the other hand, we have the *Testimonium* at the end of the second book of the *War*, followed by a number of curious supplementary lines subsequently deleted (see Pl. VI.), and unidentified by Niese. The whole insertion is not the work of the scribe but an addition written by a second hand, from which

---

[1] See below, pp. 383 ff.

[2] Codd. Marc., 383 (saec. xi.-xii.) ; Vatic. gr., 148 (saec. xi.) ; Neapol. Mus., iii. B 17 (saec. xiv.) ; Philippicus (saec. xii.) ; Havniensis bibl. reg. major vet. fundi, No. 1519 (saec. xiv.) ; Coislin., 131 (saec. xiv.).

PLATE VIII

THE 'TESTIMONIUM' OUT OF 'ANTIQUITIES' INSERTED INTO THE 'WAR'

AND FURTHER FALSIFIED BY AN ADDITION FROM A BOOK BY BISHOP HIPPOLYTOS OF ROME

CODEX VOSSIANUS GRAEC. 72 OLIM PETAVIANUS OF THE UNIVERSITY LIBRARY, LEYDEN

(SEE P. 59, NOTE 5; P. 68, NOTE 5; P. 72, NOTE 1)

it follows that the original scribe had purposely left a blank for such an insertion. Of the curious fact that the space thus provided was far too large for the insertion of the usual *Testimonium Flavianum* I can offer no other explanation than that the scribe found a passage of just this length in his original, blotted out by some censor in the brutal way which can be seen on fig. VII. Yet it is quite impossible that the deleted passage in question could have contained anything resembling the text filled in by the second scribe, to wit, the *Testimonium*, for in that case there would have been no reason for the interference of a Christian censor. Nor could it have contained anything about Jesus at all. For since the beginning of Pilate's governorship is not mentioned before § 169, that is, at the beginning of the fifth line from the bottom of fig. VI., it follows that the space preceding line eighteen, that is, preceding the sentence reporting the beginning of Tiberius' principate, must have dealt with some event or events falling into the last years of the reign of Augustus, whose death (A.D. 15) is mentioned at the top of § 168—more exactly, something fitting in between the death of Salome (A.D. 9-12) and the death of Augustus.

A closer comparison of the two texts, the *Antiquities* and the *War*, will furnish the clue. In *Ant.*, xviii. 31, the death of Salome is mentioned as occurring in the governorship of Marcus Ambibulus (or Ambivius), the successor of Coponius. Now, oddly enough, in the Greek *War* no Roman governor is mentioned between Coponius (ii. § 117) and Pilate (ii. § 169), an omission which cannot but arouse our suspicion if we remember, as pointed out above (p. 17 f.), the tampering on the part of the Christians with this very chapter of the *Antiquities*. The object of these alterations, it will be recalled, was to falsify the true chronology of events so as to conceal the true date of the Passion. As a consequence the paragraphs dealing with Pilate's predecessors [1] had likewise to be ' doctored,' or, if this seemed too difficult, deleted outright, in the *Jewish War*. A comparison of the two texts will easily show what has been suppressed in the extant text of the *War*.

B.J., ii. 8. 1, § 117	*Ant.*, xviii. § 29
The territory of Archelaus was now (A.D. 6) reduced to a province, and Coponius, a Roman of the equestrian order, was sent out as governor, entrusted by Augustus with full powers even over life and death. . . .	When Coponius followed in Judaea, who as I said (§ 20) came out together with Quirinius, the following thing happened. . . .

---

[1] They have survived in the Rumanian version of Josephus' *War*. See below, p. 70 n. 1.

§ 167

When the monarchy of Archelaus was converted into a province, Philip and Herod Antipas continued to govern their tetrarchies ; . . . as for Salome, she at her death bequeathed her tetrarchy to Julia, the wife of Augustus, together with Jamnia and the palmgroves of Phasaelis.

> BLANK OF SEVERAL §§ IN
> CODEX VOSSIANUS

§ 168

On the death of Augustus, who had directed the State for fifty-seven years . . . the empire of the Romans passed to Tiberius, son of Julia.

§ 169

Pilate, being sent by Tiberius as governor of Judaea.

§ 31

After a short time, Coponius goes back to Rome, his successor in office being Marcus Ambibulus,

under whose administration Salome, King Herod's sister, died and left Jamnia and the whole toparchy to Julia, that is, the plain of Phasaelis and Archelais, where there is a large culture of palm-trees with the best dates growing on them.

After him follows Annius Rufus, under whose administration Caesar (Augustus) died, the second Emperor of Rome, who had reigned

for fifty-seven years, etc. The

successor of Caesar is Tiberius . . . by him the fifth governor, Valerius Gratus, successor to Annius Rufus, is sent to Judaea.

Gratus, having done this (above, p. $18_{3.5}$), goes back to Rome, having been eleven years in Judaea ; Pontius Pilate, his successor, arrives.

Were it not for the curious blank in the Codex Vossianus, one might be led to think that Josephus had at first been ignorant of the names and accomplishments of Marcus Ambibulus, Annius Rufus, and Valerius Gratus, and only in his later work had corrected this trifling omission. Yet in the light of this very blank it is much more probable that the passage thus deleted contained Josephus' account of the three administrations in question. Such a passage, giving a short summary of the chief transactions of the three governors,[1] something like what we find in *Ant.*, xviii. 34 *sq.*, would very well fill the blank. It had to be deleted to make possible the chronological falsification referred to above. Even so, it is to be noted that the extant text of the *War* does not give an impression as though a period of ten years had elapsed between the accession of Tiberius and the nomination of Pilate. On the contrary, one is led to think that Pilate was the first governor

---

[1] The story of Valerius changing the high priests for a consideration, and being recalled because of this abuse, has survived in the Rumanian version of the *War*. See below, p. 599 ll. 1-3.

appointed by Tiberius, coming to Judaea immediately after the death of Augustus.

As for the guess of the second scribe in filling the blank, it is plausible enough that he assumed the gap in question to have been caused by an expurgation of the *Testimonium*. He simply concluded that the obliteration in his original was the work of some mischievous Jew, a former owner of the MS. As a matter of fact, we shall see below (pp. 93 *sqq.*) that it was precisely this explanation which Robert of Cricklade, Giraldus Cambrensis, and Cardinal Baronius gave for the absence of the corresponding lines in the Hebrew version of Josephus. His readiness to insert the *Testimonium* in just this place merely proves that he took the crucial expression γίνεται in the sense of ' at that time was *born* [1] Jesus, a wise man,' etc. A statement to the effect that the Messiah was born in the reign of Augustus would have seemed to him to be in perfect harmony with the chronology in *Luke* ii. 1 *sqq.* Since the six lines of the *Testimonium* were, however, too short to fill the blank left by the first scribe, the reviser saw fit to add the following lines : [2]

> ' All the righteous and the unrighteous will be led before the divine Logos ; for to him has the Father given the judgment. And, fulfilling the will of the Father, he whom we call the Christ will appear as judge. For not even over you, ye Greeks, Minus and Rhadamanthys will be judges, but he whom God the Father has glorified. About him we have spoken elsewhere with more detail, to those who are seeking the truth. He will administer to each one the right judgment of the Father, and prepare what will be just to each according to his deeds. And when he giveth judgment all men, angels, and demons will be present and exclaim with one voice, saying : Just is thy decision. And the resounding of this voice will bring what is just to each party : to those who have acted well it will justly convey everlasting delight ; to the lovers of evil, however, eternal punishment. And for those an inextinguishable and never-ending fire is waiting, and a fiery worm, who will not destroy the body but out of an unperishing body pain will erupt and never leave them.'

As will be remembered, both the late Théodore Reinach and Dr.

---

[1] See above, p. 51 ll. 12 f.

[2] Niese, ed. maj., vol. vi. p. 57 : " πάντες γὰρ δίκαιοί τε καὶ ἄδικοι ἐνώπιον τοῦ θεοῦ λόγου ἀχθήσονται· τούτῳ γὰρ ὁ πατὴρ τὴν κρίσιν δέδωκε. καὶ αὐτὸς βουλὴν πατρὸς ἐπιτελῶν κριτὴς παραγίνεται ὃν Χριστὸν προσαγορεύομεν. οὐδὲ γὰρ Μίνως καὶ Ῥαδάμανθυς κριταὶ καθ' ὑμᾶς "Ελληνες, ἀλλ' ὃν ὁ θεὸς καὶ πατὴρ ἐδόξασε. περὶ οὗ ἐν ἑτέροις λεπτομερέστερον διεληλύθαμεν, πρὸς τοὺς ζητοῦντας τὴν ἀλήθειαν. οὗτος τὴν πατρὸς ἑκάστῳ δικαιοκρισίαν ποιούμενος, πᾶσι κατὰ τὰ ἔργα παρασκευάσει τὸ δίκαιον. οὗ κρίσει παραστάντες, πάντες ἄνθρωποί τε καὶ ἄγγελοι καὶ δαίμονες μίαν ἀποφθέγξονται φωνὴν οὕτως λέγοντες· δικαία σοῦ ἡ κρίσις. ἧς φωνῆς τὸ ἀνταπόδομα ἐπ' ἀμφοτέροις ἐπάγει τὸ δίκαιον· τοῖς μὲν εὖ πράξασι, δικαίως τὴν ἀίδιον ἀπόλαυσιν παρασχόντος, τοῖς δὲ τῶν φαύλων ἐρασταῖς, τὴν αἰώνιον κόλασιν ἀπονείμαντος καὶ τούτοις μὲν τὸ πῦρ ἄσβεστον διαμένει καὶ ἀτελεύτητον, σκώληξ δέ τις ἐμπυρὸς μὴ τελευτῶν μηδὲ σῶμα διαφθείρων ἀναπαύστου δ' ὀδύνη ἐκ σώματος ἐκβράσσων παραμένει."

E. Norden have found ' almost the whole ' apostolic creed in the famous *Testimonium*. This latest addition, then, makes Josephus testify not only to the messianic dignity of Jesus, but furthermore to the truth of the belief that in the future he will ' come again with glory to judge the living and the dead,' which is rather more than could reasonably be expected from an historian such as Josephus was, and from a Jew to boot.

As a matter of fact, this last interpolation was too much of a good thing even for a certain Byzantine scribe, who crossed out the paragraph in question and added the following amusing comment on the right-hand margin [1] (Pl. VIII.) :

> ' The reader should know that this matter is rightly expurgated by us, since we neither find it in other copies nor is it quoted by any one of the doctors of the Church of Christ. Neither is it quoted by the later historian copying the *Halōsis*. Nevertheless, (the same) is found in the eighteenth book of the *Antiquities*.' [2]

This simply proves that the second scribe of the Leyden MS. merely copied the queer addition from an interpolation he found in the *Antiquities*.

Niese had confessed his inability to locate the source of this extraneous matter. Linck [3] appears to have been the first to notice that it is a paragraph taken from the treatise ' On the Essence of the Universe ' (περὶ τῆς τοῦ παντὸς οὐσίας), wrongly ascribed to Josephus by John Philoponos [4] (A.D. 475-540), John of Damascus [5] (c. 700-754), and John Zonaras (died after 1118), and printed in Havercamp's *Josephus*. [6]

The true author of this treatise is beyond any doubt the schismatic Bishop Hippolytus of Rome (the adversary of Pope Callistus), who died some time about A.D. 235. [7] This fact was known to the learned Photius, [8] who had correctly noticed the author's self-quotation in *Philosophoumena*, x. 32. The title is mentioned in the list of Hippolytus' works on the throne of his statue in the Lateran Museum. The attribution of such an obviously Christian

---

[1] " ἰστέον ὅτι τοιοῦτον ὠβέλισται δικαίως παρ' ἡμῶν· ἐπεὶ μηδὲ ἐν ἑτέροις ἀντιγράφοις τοῦτο εὕρομεν, ἀλλ' οὐδέ τις τῶν τῆς ἐκκλησίας τοῦ χριστοῦ διδασκάλων τούτων ἐπεμνήσθη. οὔτε μὴν ὑπὸ τῶν ἐσύστερον ἱστορικῶν ἀνδρῶν (ἀπογραφο) μένων ' (cod. -μόνων) ἄ(λ)ω(σιν) εἴρηται. ἀλλὰ καὶ (ταὐτὸ) ἐν τῷ ιηῳ λόγῳ τῆ(ς) (ἀρ)χαιολο(γίας) εὑρίσκετ(αι)."

[2] This last statement is confirmed by a gloss to *Ant.*, xviii. 3. 3, in the Codex Laurentianus plut. 69, cod. 23. The author of this note read the lines in question after the end of bk. xx. of some MSS. of the *Antiquities*.

[3] *Loc. cit.* (above, p. 58 l. 22), p. 181 n. 3.

[4] *De opificio mundi*, ed. Reichardt, 1897, lib. iii. cap. xvi. (*Script. sacri et profani*, fasc. i.).

[5] *Sacra Paral.*, opp. ed., Le Quien, ii. 789 *sqq.* ; Holl, *Kirchenväter aus den Sacra Paral.*, 1893, pp. 137-143.

[6] Vol. ii. (2), p. 146 *sq.*

[7] Cf. A. Siouville's translation of the *Philosophoumena*, Paris (Rieder), 1928, p. 38.

[8] *Bibl. cod.*, xlvii.

treatise to Josephus, on the face of its title, since Josephus at the end of his *Antiquities* promised to write a book on ' God and His Essence ' (περὶ θεοῦ καὶ τῆς οὐσίας αὐτοῦ), was preceded by the equally arbitrary attribution to the shady client of the Flavians of a most virtuous treatise on the exemplary sufferings of seven Maccabee martyrs, variously called ' On Autonomous Reason ' (περὶ αὐτοκράτορος λογισμοῦ) or the ' Fourth Book of Maccabees,' even as a separate edition of the sixth book of Josephus' *Jewish War* was circulated under the title of ' Fifth Book of Maccabees,' both these apocryphal works being adopted into the New Testamental canon of the Syrian and Armenian churches.

There can be no reasonable doubt that the motive for all this was merely the pious wish to whitewash the Jewish historian Josephus—who badly needed it—since his evidence on Christian origins was felt to be too precious to be invalidated by any strictures on the character of this ' truth-loving ' witness.[1]

The climax of this posthumous career of the old scoundrel was reached with his identification with Joseph of Arimathea ; [2] but there is no need to follow him further on his curiously devious road to respectability. Yet the story, with its multiple falsifications of documents, has its humorous aspect, and is moreover apt to give a timely warning against the confidence with which the extant text of Josephus is generally treated by unwary scholars, who are as far from suspecting the vicissitudes it has undergone in the course of the centuries as they are ready to accuse any one attempting to restore the original wording of a corrupt sentence of 'tampering with the text.'

---

[1] Isidor Pelusiotes, bk. iv., epistle 75 (*P.G.*, lxxviii., 1320), and others.

[2] Writing in the *Catholic Encycl.* (vi. 720, art. ' Grail '), Prof. Arthur F. I. Remy makes the following acknowledgment respecting the *Gospel of Nicodemus*, aliter *Acts of Pilate*, and the *Vindicta Salvatoris*: ' Furthermore, Joseph [of Arimathea] was confused with the Jewish historian Josephus, whose liberation by Titus is recounted by Suetonius.' It is an open question whether this Joseph of Arimathea (a place not yet identified) is not merely a corruption of Josephus bar Mattathia, in which case that saintly personage would be a most curious early metamorphosis of the old sinner.

V

THE EXTANT NON-GREEK VERSIONS OF JOSEPHUS

IF the results of the foregoing chapters are to be more than a mere hypothesis, it will be necessary to marshal into line every scrap of corroborative evidence that may be available, since a single new fact is always more valuable than a dozen of the most ingenious and most carefully drawn-up conjectures. For this purpose a renewed scrutiny of the known material will be the first logical step.

It has been said before at greater length that we possess an astounding number of Josephus translations in many languages and dialects. Some of the Eastern churches [1] have even seen fit to include our author in the canon of Holy Scriptures, and with the Bible he shared the fate of being translated into a number of Oriental languages. [2] Now, just as those Bible versions and translations are currently used in Biblical text criticism, so the different versions of Josephus should prove of the greatest value for the restoration of a text so obviously corrupt and mutilated in many places. Strange to say, this necessary though difficult work has practically not been begun heretofore. Let us look a little into the history of the Josephus text.

From the preface of Josephus' first work we learn that the first draft of the *Jewish War* was not in Greek. On the contrary, the first Greek version had been preceded by another ' in the tongue of the fathers ' (τῇ πατρίῳ γλώσσῃ). Whether by this expression he means Hebrew, the old sacred language of the Jews, or Aramaic, the everyday language of the non-Greek Orient of his time, remains to be seen. This version was written for the benefit of the ' barbarians,' i.e. non-Greeks and non-Romans—more precisely, the Parthians, the Babylonians, the border tribes of Arabia, the Jews beyond the Euphrates, and the Judaizing natives of the petty Assyrian kingdom of Adiabene. [3] All these people spoke Aramaic, which was also the official language of the Parthian empire. [4] Thus it follows that if Josephus wanted to have a reading public, and if his imperial patrons wanted his books to have a particular effect

---

[1] See above, p. 31 ll. 21 f.   [2] See above, p. 32 nn. 2 and 3.
[3] *B.J.*, prooem., §§ 3 and 6.
[4] Ed. Meyer, *Gesch. a. Altertums.*, iii. (1901), pp. 47 ff.

upon those Eastern populations, the version in question must have been Aramaic.

Of the Greek version, which must have followed shortly after the Semitic one, we have two different editions—one full of minor mistakes and barbarisms (the so-called ' worse MSS.'), and another revised and polished (Niese's so-called ' better MSS.'). The original Semitic version seems to be entirely and definitely lost. Heyman Kottek's hypothesis, according to which it survives in part in the shape of the Syrian translation, has been disproved by Th. Nöldeke ;[1] and Sebastian Münster's still more improbable idea that it is identical with the Hebrew version, the so-called *Josippon* (below, pp. 93 ff.), was exploded, centuries ago, by none other than the great Joseph Scaliger [2] himself.

The existence of this new Syrian translation calls for some explanation. The Babylonian Jews undoubtedly rejected the traitor's propagandist writings with the utmost contempt.[3] Among the other Orientals of Aramaic speech the class of lettered individuals who would have had any interest in such a work was but small. Throughout the Roman empire, including Italy, Josephus was read in Greek, so far as he was read at all among non-Jews (the absurd idea that he could have been read by an aristocrat of refined literary taste such as Tacitus has been justly ridiculed by Norden and others). Thus it is no wonder that the first Semitic version, composed by the author himself, should have disappeared without leaving any trace.

When toward the end of the Empire fewer and fewer of its Western inhabitants came to know Greek, a Latin translation was felt to be a desideratum. It was at this period that a converted Jew, whose Hebrew name Isaac he variously Latinized as Hilarius or Gaudentius, undertook to translate Josephus into Latin (about A.D. 370). His is not a translation in the modern sense of the term, but a seemingly independent history of ' the downfall of Jerusalem,' which Josephus quotes only occasionally, though as a matter of fact it has no other source. In addition it is distinguished by a decided proselytizing, Jew-baiting tendency. The name 'Egesippus' which is prefixed to the work in a number of MSS., and commonly used to designate it nowadays, has been shown by Prof. Ussani to be due to the fact that the author has incorporated in his story a fragment of the *Hypomnēmata* of the Christian traveller Hegesippus (about A.D. 180) on the exploits of the apostles Peter and Paul. Later on, ignorant copyists concluded that the whole compilation was by one ' Egesippus.' [4] The resemblance of

---

[1] See Niese, ed. maj., vol. vi. p. 21. See below p. 76 n. 3.
[2] *Elenchus Trihaeres. contra Nicol. Serarium*, 1605, cap. iv.
[3] See below, p. 98 ll. 37 ff.
[4] In the same way the anonymous *Philosophoumena* of Hippolytos have formerly been attributed to Origen, because of marginal glosses such as ' Origenes,'

the names ' Egesippus ' and Josephus (in the vulgar Greek pronunciation *Josipos*) no doubt facilitated the error and gave it permanence.

In the fifth century the Roman senator Cassiodorus knew a fairly literal Latin version of the *War* commonly attributed to Rufinus, a contemporary and rival of St. Jerome (fourth century), and encouraged the production of a Latin translation of the *Antiquities* by the monks of his monastery Squillace. A critical edition of it is yet to be published.

The above-mentioned Syrian translation of the sixth book of the *Jewish War* has been preserved under the title of ' Fifth Book of the Maccabees '[1] in a MS. of the Ambrosiana (Milan), accessible in a photo-lithographic copy made by A. M. Ceriani (Milan, 1876-1883), and in a literal rendering into German by Kotteck.[2] It is not at all improbable that all the seven books of the *War* once existed in a Syrian translation. Th. Nöldeke[3] definitely proved that it is derived from the Greek text of Josephus.

A Hebrew translation commonly called *Josippon* exists in seven MSS. and many printed editions. *Josippon* may mean the ' large Josephus ' or the ' little Josephus,' and therefore either designate an edition supplementing the material of the *Jewish War* by additions from parallel passages in the *Antiquities* and other sources—and this the Hebrew version does in fact—or it may apply to an epitome of the *War*, a shortened ' little Josephus.' Indeed, we have such an one too, from the pen of R. Abraham ibn Daûd, a Spanish-Jewish Aristotelian of the twelfth century (printed by Sebastian Münster at Worms in 1529). A critical edition of the *Josippon* is planned by Dr. Greyzel of the New York Jewish Theological Seminary. It is written in a relatively pure Biblical Hebrew such as was again cultivated by the Jews of the so-called Carolingian renaissance of classical scholarship. The spelling of the proper names and the range of the geographical interest evinced would show that the vulgate text was written down in a place where Italian was the spoken language. From a peculiar passage (below, p. 78 n. 1) it may be concluded that the version was made on the east coast of the Adriatic.

There are unmistakable traces showing that the Latin version has used, strange to say, not the standard version of Rufinus, but the older one with its crude proselytizing tendencies. One would

---

' doctrines of Origenes,' in some of the MSS. Another example is the so-called *Liturgy of St. Chrysostomus*, to which this title has been attached in a twelfth-century MS. because two prayers contained in it bear the ascription : " Χρυσοστόμου." See Lietzmann, *Messe u. Herrenmahl*, Bonn, 1926, p. 2.

[1] See above, p. 73.

[2] *Das 6. Buch des Bell. Jud., n.d.v. Ceriani ed. Peshittahs. übers. u. krit. bearb.*, Berlin, 1886.

[3] *Lit. Zentralblatt*, 1886, 881-4.

like to conclude that the *Josippon* antedates the translation attributed to Rufinus, and that it goes back to the beginning of the
fourth century, when the Western Jews began to lose their former
knowledge of Greek. The features of the extant *Josippon* which
would point to a later date could be explained by the obvious fact
that *our 'Josippon'* is an edifying ninth-century compilation of
which the fourth-century Latin translation of Josephus might be
but the nucleus. A more powerful objection to such a theory is
the fact that the Jews of the Diaspora did not speak either Hebrew
or Aramaic any more than they do now. The Semitic tongues
were used only in the synagogue service and in Talmudic learned
discussions. Even for homiletic purposes the vernacular of the
homeland (Greek in the empire, Arabic in the Moslem countries)
was preferred. What was then the need of a Hebrew *Josippon* in
fourth-century Italy?

Whatever motive may have prompted the unknown translator
to undertake the work, the latter itself looms large enough to merit
a fuller discussion. The MSS. as well as the now quite rare prints
of the *editio princeps* attribute the work to one Joseph ben Gorion,
a personage named by Josephus in his *War* (ii. § 583) as one of the
dictators nominated at the beginning of the revolution against Rome
by the Jews of Jerusalem. There can, of course, be no question
about the character of the compilation, which is certainly anything
but a translation in the modern sense of the term. It clearly
belongs to the type of the Latin and Byzantine chronographers
flourishing about the same period, though it draws in the main on
Josephus and quotes him quite frequently. The incredible chronology of the compilation—for example, it makes Julius Caesar the
direct successor of Ptolemy Philadelphus—admits of no other
explanation than that the unknown compiler was ignorant of the
events leading up to the Jewish War, and had himself to paste
together as best he could various materials culled from different
sources.

The chief basis of the compilation was, as has been pointed out
above, the Latin *Egesippus*. The author's knowledge of Greek
was of the scantiest,[1] though in a number of places the *Josippon*
text stands closer to the Greek Josephus than to the *Egesippus*.
In view of these facts, good knowledge of Latin and Hebrew and a
mere smattering of Greek, one might be tempted to see in the
author an Italian Jew. A better clue is furnished by the impudent
assertion that the Hebrew exemplar of the Septuagint had been
brought to Alexandria from Illyria, where there lived many Jewish
families in those days. This bold statement was obviously de-

---

[1] He believes, e.g., that 'world-empire' is called in Greek *imperaousia*—a
blunder which finds a partial explanation by a possible acquaintance with St.
Augustine's 'imperiosa civitas' (e.g. *Civ. Dei*, p. 366[19], Dombart).

signed to flatter the Jews settled at Salona, Valona, Durazzo, and other communities of the Illyrian coast.[1]

In Book vi., 30, p. 667 *sqq.*, the coronation of Vespasian is described with details which at once suggest that the imperial coronation of one of the German kings of the Saxon dynasty (936-1024) has served as a model. This chapter is missing, however, in some of the MSS., and may well be a later embellishment of the original text. The oldest mention of the *Josippon* is said to be found in the Italian poet R. 'Ele'azar of Cagliari, who seems to have flourished prior to the ninth century. Yet the statement itself has still to be substantiated.

Like a typical chronography, the compilation begins with Adam, explains the ethnical genealogy table of *Genesis* x., and then passes over to the oldest parts of Roman history and to the story of the Tower of Babel. Then begins the Jewish history, which is followed down to the time of Darius and Esther. With a bold leap the author passes on to Alexander the Great, barely touches upon the history of the Diadochs, only incidentally mentioning Rome. Then follow the Syrian wars, the history of the Maccabees and of the Herodian dynasty, down to the destruction of the third temple, with very brief interruptions having reference to Roman history.

The various MSS. and editions differ considerably, some of them containing, among other materials, a Hebrew summary of the Alexander Romance of Pseudo-Callisthenes. The language of this insertion shows incipient Arabic influences, a feature quite unknown to the other MSS. One can see how subsequent scribes naïvely added to this favourite and popular work whatever piece of additional historic information they were able to obtain. This is, of course, no peculiar feature of the *Josippon* ; the *Egesippus* does precisely the same sort of thing.

Toward the middle of the eleventh century the *Josippon* was translated into Arabic, probably in Sicily, for the benefit, no doubt, of Jews living there or in one of the Mahometan countries of the Western Mediterranean, by one Zakharia ibn Sa'id al Yemeni al Israili, a Jew of South Arabia. This translation, of which we have at least two modern printed editions (above, p. 32 n. 2), is first mentioned by an Arabic author of Spain, Ibn Ḥazm, who died in A.D. 1063.[2]

Whether it was this Arabic translation or the Hebrew original

---

[1] We know of a number of forgeries designed to show that certain Jewish diaspora settlements existed before the crucifixion, and that their inhabitants could therefore not be held responsible for this judicial murder.

[2] *Ny Kongelig Samling*, 147b, folio f. 548-75. The Hebrew exemplar of this version exists in the Bodleian (Cod. Huntingdon, 345). Photostats of both MSS. and a typewritten German translation by the Rev. Dr. Heinrich Guttmann, Rabbi of Bingen a. Rh., are available in the Institut des Études Slaves in Paris.

which was translated into Ethiopic, and whether this version was intended for the Abyssinian Jews, the so-called Falashas, or for the Christians of Habesh, I cannot say, since so far no one has taken the trouble to study the MSS., though they are easy of access in the Berlin and Frankfurt libraries. A Russian translation of the *Josippon* exists in a sixteenth-century MS. of the Royal Library in Copenhagen, in a MS. of Moscow, and in a MS. of the Leningrad Public Library.[1]

An Armenian Josephus, translated in 1666 by one *vardapet* Stephanus of Lwow in Galicia, according to the late F. C. Conybeare, from the Latin of Rufinus but with variants from other sources, was printed in Eschmiadzin in 1787. A MS. of an earlier Armenian version of Josephus has been rumoured to have been discovered by F. C. Conybeare in 1915 in the library of the Armenians on the island of St. Lazaro near Venice. But thorough-going explorations made on the spot by Prof. Frederick Macler of Paris, facilitated by the generous help of Dr. James Loeb, have not confirmed this report, which is probably due to a misunderstanding.

According to information I received from Prof. Beneševič of the Leningrad State Library, and subsequently from Prof. Cornelis Kekelidze of Tiflis University, there is a Georgian (Grusinian) version of Josephus, derived through a modern Russian version from Havercamp's Latin translation, and therefore of no independent value.

The most important of all hitherto known versions is a translation of Josephus' earliest work into a Northern dialect of Old Russian, which was first brought to the attention of the learned world by Alexander N. Popov in 1866. The work in question exists in sixteen MSS. A seventeenth, formerly at Wilna, was unfortunately burned in 1918-19. They are found in several Russian libraries (Leningrad, Moscow, Kasan, etc.). A critical edition of the text is being prepared by Prof. Vasilij N. Istrin. In the meantime, photographs of the whole of one of the best MSS., the codex Cyrillo-Bjelosersky 62/1303 in Leningrad, which I owe to the liberality of Dr. James Loeb, are available to students at the Institut des Études Slaves in Paris.[2] A German translation of the first four books, with ample notes illustrating the divergences from the Greek text, was prepared on the basis of copies of the most important MSS. by the late Prof. Alexander Johannes Berendts of Dorpat (fig. VIII.) and published after his untimely death in 1912 by

---

[1] See above, p. 33 n. 7.
[2] Dr. James Loeb has generously given another copy of our photographs to the library of the Jewish Theological Seminary of America in New York. On the other hand, the above-mentioned Russian MSS. have been recently photographed for Dr. Solomon Zeitlin of the Dropsie College of Philadelphia.

his colleague and executor, the late Prof. Konrad Grass of Dorpat, in 1924-27. The extraordinary importance of the Old Russian version consists in the fact that it reproduces its original with such mechanical accuracy as to be almost unintelligible before it is put back into Greek through an equally mechanical retroversion, and that the Greek text which it reproduces is *in hundreds of sections* widely different from the Greek standard version.

The most important of all these variants are several passages of altogether about seven octavo pages in length, and dealing with the history of John the Baptist, Jesus, and the earliest disciples of Christ. To these passages nothing whatever corresponds in the standard Greek text, though slight traces of a similar tradition remain clearly visible in the so-called *Egesippus*. These chapters have been separately translated into German and discussed by Berendts, and are easily accessible in an exact English translation in vol. iii. of Dr. Thackeray's Josephus edition for the Loeb Classical Library. A MS. still in the possession of Dr. Moses Gaster, No. 89 of his famous collection (now largely in the library of the British Museum), proves that the Old Russian version of Josephus, or at least the fragments dealing with Christian origins, were translated from Russian into Polish, and again, some time in the seventeenth century, into Rumanian. With the kind permission of Dr. Gaster I publish in Appendix VIII. for the first time the contents of this remarkable MS. It offers a most interesting confirmation of the above-mentioned hypothesis, to wit, that the Christian so-called *Acta Pilati* were intended to offset the effect of Josephus' statements about Christ and of the genuine *Acts of Pilate* published by the Emperor Maximinus Daïa. It is in fact a compilation which combines the Jesus passages of the Russian Josephus with the so-called *Acta Pilati*, and the fragments of the Russian Josephus dealing with the Baptist with the contents of a fifth-century *Life of John the Forerunner* written in Emesa. The manifest object of this compilation is to defend as far as possible the orthodox tradition about John the Baptist and Jesus against the widely different conclusions which an unwary reader might draw from a reading of Josephus alone.

THE VARIANT READINGS OF THE GREEK ORIGINAL AND ITS VARIOUS DERIVATIVES, AND THEIR IMPORTANCE FOR THE RESTORATION OF THE ARCHETYPE

The different versions enumerated (above, p. 75 ff.) and passed in review deviate, in a number of cases, from the standard text of the ordinary Greek editions. It goes without saying that these

variant readings are of supreme importance in the present connexion. At first sight one will be inclined to attribute such variant
readings either to the arbitrary action of the translator or to the
no less arbitrary action of an interpolator, copyist, or reader, who
inserted a gloss, a clause, or a whole paragraph of his own. But the
possibility must not be overlooked that the translator may have
been working on MS. material differing from the extant MSS.,
because Josephus or one of his collaborators or one of the copyists
of his publisher had altered the wording of his original draft in a
subsequent edition. Further, the possibility cannot be denied
that the absence of a given paragraph from the Greek standard
text may be due to the fact that the passage in question was
blotted out or erased by a censor or omitted by some scribe after
the intact original text had been translated, or after a number of
copies had been made, one of which, or its derivatives, fell into the
hands of the translator. Finally, the author himself may have
suppressed a certain paragraph in a subsequent edition of his book ;
the Greek standard texts may go back to this revised edition, whilst
the translator worked on a copy of the original edition.

Conversely, if a clause of the Greek standard text is wanting in
one of the derivatives, it may have been suppressed by the translator because he did not like its contents, or because he was anxious
to shorten his work, or because accidentally he skipped it. It may
have been omitted by some copyist for any one of the same three
reasons, or by some censor or a reader with the censorial instinct, or
by one afraid of the ecclesiastical censor who erased or deleted the
passage he objected to. The result would, of course, have been
that it could not be repeated in all derivatives from that particular
MS. Or it may be that the passage in question was wanting in
the Greek MS. on which the translator worked, because it had been
damaged by accident or by the hand of the censor, or because it
was a copy of the earlier edition of the work which did not yet
contain this later addition from the author's own hand. Or,
finally, it may also be that the passage in question is an interpolation of the Greek MS. which was not made until after the translation had, directly or indirectly, been derived from it.

From these statements it would follow that a careful comparison
of the different versions with the Greek MS. material may serve to
detect and to nullify the work of the various glossators and interpolators, and to offset the damage done by the censor as well as by
lazy and careless copyists. For it is clear that unless the interpolations and omissions affect the archetype itself they will not
appear in all MSS., let alone in all translations. A measure of
censorship taken, let us say, by the Byzantine Greek Orthodox
Church will not necessarily affect the territory of the autocephalic
churches of the Slavs. Quite aside from such considerations, the

F

different versions may shed a good deal of light on the evolution of the archetype, because it is *a priori* unlikely that the different translators working in widely separated countries actually had identical MS. material to work on.

It is well also to bear in mind that, contrary to modern usage, where an author has to wait for his second edition to make any changes in his book, by adding, suppressing, or merely altering a passage, the ancient author might at any moment alter the text of the copy which served as an archetype in the publisher's scriptorium, where a ' dictator ' read aloud the model text for one or several dozens of scribes, a fact which has only recently been realized in its full meaning.   Thus different MSS. or classes of MSS. may not simply represent the natural reading variants due to the carelessness of the scribes, but different stages in the evolution of the work itself, corresponding to the different editions of modern books.   The existence of several such ' editions ' for ancient authors has lately been proved for Cicero, for Thucydides, for Eusebius' *Historia ecclesiastica*, for Polybius, and also for Flavius Josephus.

Prof. Laqueur [1] of Giessen has shown long ago that the extant *Jewish War* does not represent the first edition of that work, but a later rewriting subsequent to the publication of the *Antiquities*. The differences between the two classes of MSS. already referred to are beyond doubt the result of the constant pains the author took to improve his style, no less than the diplomatic presentation of his materials.   There is, of course, no ground for the supposition that any one of the extant MSS. represents the very first or even the very last of the editions which Josephus himself saw through the *scriptorium* of his publisher Epaphroditus.   On the contrary, there are certain features in the extant MSS. tending to show that the process of ' improvement ' and ' revision ' did not stop with the author's exit from the scene.   On the other hand, it is equally certain that even the worst of Niese's ' inferior ' MSS. does not represent the earliest edition of the work.

From Josephus' own statements we know that a Semitic edition preceded the Greek one, and that in the thirteenth year of the reign of Domitian he proposed to rewrite the *War* and in that connexion to bring the history of the Jews down to that date.   No extant MS. of the *War* has the slightest trace of such an appendix, and it is most tantalizing for us not to know how he tackled such delicate subjects as Domitian's attitude toward the Jews, the vexatory exactions of the poll duty, the *Judaici fisci calumnia*, etc., at least during the lifetime of the third, the most touchy and suspicious, of his imperial patrons.   Curiously enough, the Byzantine Jews appear to have known this second edition of the *War*, since there

---

[1] *Der jüdische Historiker Flavius Josephus*, Giessen, 1920.

is an unmistakable allusion to it in the extracts of the *Josippon*
made by the eleventh-century chronicler Jeraḥm'el b. Shelomo,[1]
who speaks of twenty-four books of Josephus beginning with Adam
and extending to the fourteenth year of Domitian. This hitherto
overlooked statement shows that—a most natural thing to do—
he combined for this new edition a revised text of the twenty books
of his *Jewish Antiquities* with the partly overlapping five books of
the *Jewish War* into a colossal work of twenty-four books in all,
probably called ' Jewish histories.'

The existence of such an edition in the Byzantine empire
explains also the occurrence of a considerable number of Josephus
fragments in certain Byzantine chronographers hitherto regarded
as spurious since they have defied all identification.[2] The German
scholar H. Gelzer [3] considered them a forgery and the work of
Panodorus of Alexandria ; yet there exists no conceivable reason
why precisely the passages in question, of no importance for any
particular creed or tendency, should have been forged. The mere
fact that the one or the other of these fragments occurs also in the
literature of the *midrashîm* only indicates that Josephus either drew
on this literature or on one of its sources, a fact not at all surprising
considering the *haggadic* character of his compilation.[2] Nor is there
any reason to suppose that Panodorus (end of the fourth century),
Georgius Syncellus (*c.* 800), Georgius Monachus (tenth century),
and Cedrenus (eleventh century) should all have attributed the
fragments in question to Josephus if they had not actually found
them in his work.

In quoting the fragments in question I follow the order in which
they must have occurred in the lost text of Josephus.

1. ' The sabbath was called a day of rest, and being the model of
the thousand-year week and of the destruction of sinners, as Josephus
testifies and the *Leptogenesis*.' [3]

As will be seen, this passage occurred in Josephus' account of the
Creation, and no doubt toward the end of the narrative. It is significant to see Josephus expect the coming of the Messiah after a
lapse of 6000 years, counting from the Creation. It is clear at once
that he on good purpose chooses such a late date ; it was to take
away all political significance from this eschatological dream and to
calm the minds of those who longed for that fateful coming.

[1] Ad. Neubauer, *Mediaeval Jewish Chronicles*, i., Oxford, 1887, p. 190 B (from
Cod. Bodl. MS., d. 11).
[2] The N.T. scholar will recall the exactly analogous case of the so-called
' Agrapha '—unidentifiable quotations from the scriptures—discussed and
collected by Alfr. Resch (Leipzig, 1906).
[3] Cedren, p. 9, line 20, ed. Bonn : ". . σάββατον ὡς καταπαύσιμος προσηγορεύθη καὶ
ὦν τύπος τῆς ἑβδομῆς χιλιοετηρίδος καὶ τῆς τῶν ἁμαρτώλων συντελείας, ὡς Ἰώσηπος μαρτυρεῖ
καὶ ἡ λεπτὴ Γένεσις . . ."

2. ' The animals, both the quadrupeds and the reptiles, according to Josephus and the *Leptogenesis*, had, before the fall, the same language as the first human couple.' [1]

The fragment evidently belongs to the description of Paradise, where men and animals had the same language.

3. ' And his tomb was in the land of the Jerusalemites, as a certain Jewish tradition goes, according to Josephus.' [2]

Adam, that is, had been buried near Jerusalem, a fiction common to both Jews and Christians.

4. ' In his fourteenth year Abraham came to know the God of the universe and began to worship him, but the idols of his father he broke and burnt them together with the house. Together with them his brother Harran perished in the flames when he tried to smother the fire. And he also admonished his father to abandon the cult and the manufacture of idols, as Josephus says.' [3]

The well-known episode of Abraham's burning the idols in his father's house. The additional touch that Abraham's brother Harran perished on that occasion is in contradiction to the *Halōsis*,[4] or rather to its source.

5. ' Rebecca having baked cakes, as Josephus relates, gave them to Jacob and sent him to Isaac with other presents.' [5]

Taken from the story of Jacob and Esau and the deception practised on the old Isaac. The mention of the cakes is not found in the Old Testament, but does occur in the apocryphal *Leptogenesis*. Josephus evidently fused various accounts.

6. ' He got these blessings from the patriarch Abraham before (his death), as Josephus confirms, and the story is true.' [6]

Taken from the *Book of Jubilees*. The passage is in contradiction with the *Antiquities*, where Abraham dies before the birth of the twins.

---

[1] Syncell., p. 14, 4ff. Cp. Simeon Logeth., p. 23 v⁰=Sync., p. 18: "... τὰ θηρία, καὶ τὰ τετράποδα καὶ τὰ ἑρπετά, φήσιν ὁ Ἰώσηπος, καὶ ἡ λεπτὴ Γένεσις ὁμόφωνα εἶναι πρὸ τῆς παραβάσεως τοῖς πρωτοπλαστοῖς."

[2] Georgius Monachus, ed. de Boor, i. p. 43.   Cedren, i. p. 18₁₁.₁₈.

"καὶ μνῆμα αὐτῷ κατὰ τὴν Ἰεροσολύμων γεγονέναι γῆν Ἑβραϊκή τις ἱστορεῖ παράδοσις, ὥς φησιν Ἰώσηππος."

"ἡ δὲ ταφὴ αὐτοῦ κατὰ τὴν Ἰεροσολύμων γεγονέναι γῆν ὡς Ἰώσηπος ἱστορεῖ."

[3] Syncell., p. 184₂.₆: "τῷ ιδ ἔτει αὐτοῦ ὁ Ἀβραὰμ ἐπιγνοὺς τὸν τῶν ὅλων θεὸν προσκύνει, τὰ δὲ εἴδωλα τοῦ πατρὸς συντρίψας κατέκαυσε σὺν τῷ οἴκῳ. συγκατεκαύθη δὲ αὐτοῖς καὶ Ἀρρὰν ὁ ἀδελφὸς σβέσαι τὸ πῦρ σπουδάζων, ἐνουθέτει δὲ καὶ τὸν πατέρα ἑαυτοῦ ἀποστῆναι τῆς εἰδωλολατρείας καὶ εἰδωλοποιίας, ὥς φησιν ὁ Ἰώσηπος."

[4] See Dr. Thackeray's *Josephus*, vol. iii., app. p. 642, frg. No. 6.

[5] Syncell., p. 197, line 1, ed. Bonn : "κολλυρίδας ποιήσασα Ῥεβέκκα, ὥς φησιν Ἰώσηππος, ἔδωκε τῷ Ἰακὼβ καὶ εἰσήγαγε μεθ' ἑτέρων δώρων πρὸς Ἰσαάκ."

[6] *Ibid.*, "προεῖχε δὲ αὐτὰς (τὰς εὐλογίας) παρὰ τοῦ πατριάρχου Ἀβραάμ, ὡς Ἰώσηπος βεβαιοῦται, καὶ πιστὸς ὁ λόγος."

7. ' Josephus relates how Jacob before the beginning of his sixty-third year had not touched a woman, and boasted of this to his mother Rebecca.'

It is impossible to place this curious fragment.[1]

8. ' In the 153rd year of Isaac, Jacob went up to him from Mesopotamia, and Isaac looking up and seeing the sons of Jacob, blessed Levi as archpriest and Judah as king and ruler.' [2]

From the *Book of Jubilees*, cap. xxxi., the blessing bestowed by Isaac on Levi and Judah.

9. ' Rebecca asked Isaac in his old age to admonish Esau and Jacob to love each other. He did so, and foretold them that if Esau should rise against Jacob he would fall into his brother's hands.' [3]

From the *Book of Jubilees*, cap. xxv., admonition of Rebecca to her sons to abstain from their quarrels. Immediately after this follows the fragment :

10. ' After the death of Isaac, Esau, moved by his sons and gathering together their tribes, went to war against Jacob and his sons. Jacob, however, shut the gates of his tower and called out to Esau to remember the warnings of their parents. But as he did not listen but became insolent and abused Jacob, the latter, forced by Judah, bent his bow, struck the right side of Esau and overthrew him. When he had died the sons of Jacob opened the gates and slew most (of the sons of Esau). This is written in the *Leptogenesis*.' [4]

From the *Book of Jubilees*, containing the last struggle of the hostile twins and Esau's death at the hands of Jacob. The Hebrew word βάρις for the ' tower ' of Hebron is commonly used by Josephus for the castle of the temple at Jerusalem. It occurs also in the Septuagint.

No. 11.[5]

Taken from the story of Moses, but too long to be reprinted here.

---

[1] Syncell., p. 197, line 12ff. : " 'Ιώσηππός φησιν ὅτι ὁ 'Ιακὼβ ἐτῶν ὑπάρχων ξ̄η̄ οὐκ ἔγνω ὅλως γυναῖκα ὡς αὐτὸς ἐξεῖπε τῇ μητρὶ 'Ρεβέκκα.''

[2] *Ibid.*, p. 202₁₉-203₁₄: 'Ιωσήππου: " Τῷ ρ̄ν̄γ̄ ἔτει τοῦ 'Ισαὰκ ἐπανῆλθεν 'Ιακὼβ πρὸς αὐτὸν ἀπὸ Μεσοποταμίας καὶ ἀναβλέψας 'Ισαὰκ καὶ ἰδὼν τοὺς υἱοὺς 'Ιακὼβ ηὐλόγησε τὸν Λευὶ ὡς ἀρχιερέα καὶ τὸν 'Ιούδαν ὡς βασιλέα καὶ ἄρχοντα." *Ibid.*, p. 207₂₀ᶠ·: " καὶ ὅτι ὁ 'Ισαὰκ ἀναβλέψας ὅτι ὁ 'Ιακὼβ ἐκ Μεσοποταμίας ἐπανῆλθε καὶ ἰδὼν τὸν Λευὶ καὶ τὸν 'Ιούδαν εὐλόγησε τὸν μὲν ὡς ἱερέα, τὸν δὲ ὡς βασιλέα καθ' ἃ φησιν 'Ιώσηππος."

[3] " ἡ 'Ρεβέκκα ᾔτησε τὸν 'Ισαὰκ ἐν τῷ γήρᾳ παραινέσαι τῷ 'Ησαῦ καὶ τῷ 'Ιακὼβ ἀγαπᾶν ἀλλήλους. καὶ παραινέσας αὐτοῖς προεῖπεν, ὅτι ἐὰν ἐπαναστῇ τῷ 'Ιακὼβ ὁ 'Ησαῦ εἰς χεῖρας αὐτοῦ πεσεῖται."

[4] " μετὰ οὖν τὸ τελευτῆσαι τοῦ 'Ισαὰκ κινηθεὶς ὑπὸ τῶν υἱῶν 'Ησαῦ καὶ ἀθροίσας ἔθνη ἦλθεν κατὰ τοῦ 'Ιακὼβ καὶ τῶν υἱῶν αὐτοῦ εἰς πόλεμον. 'Ιακὼβ δὲ ἀποκλείσας τὰς πυλὰς τῆς βάρεως παρεκάλει τοῦ 'Ησαῦ μνησθῆναι τῶν γονιῶν ἐντολῶν. τοῦ δὲ μὴ ἀνεχομένου, ἀλλ' ὑβρίζοντος καὶ ὀνειδίζοντος βιασθεὶς 'Ιακὼβ ὑπὸ τοῦ 'Ιούδα ἐνέτεινε τόξον καὶ πλήξας κατὰ τοῦ δεξίου τὸν 'Ησαῦ κατέβαλε. τοῦ δὲ θανόντος ἀνοίξαντες τὰς πύλας οἱ υἱοὶ 'Ιακὼβ ἄνειλον τοὺς πλείστους. Ταῦτα ἐν λεπτῇ Γενέσει φέρεται." This occurs also in Gaster's *Jerahmeel* (London, R.A.S., 1899), xxxv. 1, and in Comestor, *Genesis*, ch. xli.

[5] Syncell., p. 225, line 20-228₁₀.

It is largely in agreement with Josephus' narrative (*Ant.*, ii. 9-10). Only the forms of the proper names betray the utilization of an additional source. For example, in the *Antiquities* the name of the Egyptian princess is Thermonthis; here it is given as ' Thermonthis, also called Pharia,' the second name being most probably her father's name.[1] The original name of Melchias, translated ' king,' and given to Moses, betrays an apologetic source, the designation of Moses as a Meluḥi, i.e. a man from Meluḥa, i.e. the Sinai Peninsula, in an Egyptian, anti-Semitic source, being objectionable to the Jews. The mention of Justus (of Tiberias) in the fragment may possibly indicate that Josephus drew on his rival for certain bits of information. But it is equally possible that it was Justus who plundered Josephus, and that the Byzantine chronographer drew on Sextus Julius Africanus, who in his turn is known to have utilized Justus. The question is fortunately of no importance for our problem. What needs emphasis is the certainty that the chronographers drew in the last analysis on the lost edition of Josephus, and that the fragments are therefore genuine. The fact that they cannot be found in the extant *Antiquities* is, then, no argument against their essential genuineness.

LOST PASSAGES OF JOSEPHUS IN THE OLDEST LATIN VERSION

The so-called ' Egesippus ' contains some substantial expansions of the geographical character sketches of Palestinian landscape. They offer a very good illustration of the difficulties besetting the task of determining which of the various causes passed in review are at the bottom of each variant reading :

Josephus, *B.J.*, iii. 33, §§ 44 *sq.*	*Hegesippus*, iii. 6.
'. . . But Peraea, though far more extensive (than Galilee), is for the most part desert and rugged and too wild to bring tender fruits to maturity. However, there are also tracts of finer soil, productive of every kind of crop ; and the plains are covered with a variety of trees, olive, vine, and palm being principally cultivated. The country is watered by torrents descending from the mountains and by springs which never dry up and provide suffi-	' But Peraea, though more extensive, is for the most part desert and rugged . . . ignorant of the softening influence of the plough and slow to tame the wilder fruits. But here again a portion of it is soft for tilling, fertile for use, pleasing to the eye, mild to work, useful for grafting fruit, productive of every kind ; so that its fields have their border of trees and others of lovely beauty in their midst, which often screen the crops from excessive sun or cold. And above all,

---

[1] *p͗ R͑*, 'he of Re͑,' is a man's name. The female form would be *t͗ R͑ =* Θάρια. Perhaps Θ was misread for Φ.

cient moisture when the torrents dwindle in the dog-days.'

the country is clad with olive or interlaced with vines or adorned with palms. Ineffably charming is it when, swayed by the breeze, the rows of palm-trees rustle, and sweeter than their sound the odours of the dates are wafted abroad. Nor is it wonderful at all that all that gracious greenness is there, when the country is bathed and watered by those pleasant-winding streams which descend from the mountain ridges above and abound in those snow-cool springs. (No wonder) the land is jealously held in affection. . . .'

Josephus, *B.J.*, iii. §§ 49 *sq.*

' For both (Judaea and Samaria) consist of hills and plains, yield a light and fertile soil for agriculture, are well wooded, and abound in fruits, both wild and cultivated ; both owe their productiveness to the entire absence of dry deserts and to a rainfall for the most part abundant.

Hegesippus, iii. 6.

' For both (countries) consist of hill and plain in diverse districts : the whole is neither an expanse of plain nor everywhere cleft by the mountain rocks, but it has the charm of both these conditions. The soil is friable and soft for agriculture and therefore beneficial for crops ; and for fertility (well-nigh) second to none, certainly for the maturity of its fruits it surpasses all. For while elsewhere the crops are still being sown, there they are being reaped. The species and nature of the crops are moreover unrivalled anywhere. The water is sweet, pleasant to the eye and agreeable to the taste. And thus, thanks to the (favour of the) elements the Jews regard this as the land flowing with milk and honey that was promised to their fathers by God, *when he covenanted to give them the privilege of resurrection, and the righteous deity would have conferred both (boons) upon them had they kept the faith, but from their faithless souls were snatched away the one here by the yoke of captivity, the other there by the chain of sin.*

' All the running water has a singularly sweet taste :

and owing to the abundance of excellent grass the cattle yield more milk than in other districts. But the surest testimony to the virtues and thriving condition of the two countries is their dense population.'

' The region is well wooded and therefore rich in flocks, and it has milk in abundance ; nowhere, in fact, are the udders of the flocks so swollen with milk. The fruits both wild and cultivated exceed in quantity those of all regions. Both Judaea and Samaria have a dense population.'

How is the modern critic to account for the surplus text in *Egesippus* as compared with the Greek original ? The passages in the latter are sober enough to have been derived, according to the conjecture of Prof. Wilhelm Weber of Halle, from the official reports of the Roman *mensores* who had to explore the country, the theatre of future operations, to inform the general headquarters of the possibilities there were of supporting the troops on the products of the land. Yet the additions of *Egesippus* are the typical patriotic idealizations of the 'land of promise,' overflowing with obvious sentimentality. Who, then, was responsible for it ? A converted Jew like Isaac-Gaudentius, living in beautiful Italy and who had never seen Palestine, who was moreover exclusively interested in proselytizing for the Church ? Not very likely, one may say. On the other hand, it would be natural enough that the old traitor Josephus, hard-boiled though he was, should thus have given vent to his longing for his lost home-country. The lyric expansions of the military geographer's topographical and economic report no doubt came from the pen of the old Josephus himself, to whom Palestine was after all the land of his childhood and youth.

If I feel a certain hesitation in definitely attributing these expansions to the lost *last* edition of the *War*, the reason is that the corresponding parts of the Russian version have not yet been made accessible. Thus Josephus' homesickness may after all have been most intensely felt in the *first* years of his captivity. It is therefore just possible that these lyric additions belong to the first draft of his work, which was subsequently translated into Russian, and that he deleted them in a later edition because they called forth the gibes of his Roman readers, who knew what the 'land of promise' was like. What it is of importance to note in connexion with the above quotations is the fact that a plus in any of the versions may be either the work of the translator (witness the theological argument printed in italics) or of the author of the original work, i.e. Josephus.

Nor is the present writer's mode of procedure and critical method in any way new ; on the contrary, it is merely an application of methods commonly used in Old Testamental criticism. The above-mentioned passage has, moreover, nothing to do with

Christian origins, and it is a fitting starting-point for our discussion precisely because it can be quite dispassionately discussed and because it matters little whether we believe that Josephus himself or one of his translators expatiated so touchingly on the charms of Palestine.

We come now to another passage which will be found to be of some bearing on the central problem, the famous *Testimonium*. Although the *Egesippus* follows in general the narrative of the *Jewish War*, in the chapter dealing with the reign of Tiberius he inserts the scandalous story of Paulina and Mundus, which Josephus tells only in his *Antiquities* (xviii. 3. 4). Now, it has been observed repeatedly that in its present context the episode has no connexion whatever with what precedes and follows—in fact, has nothing to do with the history of the Jews. Hence it has been regarded as an interpolation by a number of critics. It is true, Josephus himself admits having introduced occasionally certain 'paddings'; [1] yet even in their worst form they are never entirely disconnected from the main topic. Naturally enough, the critics have been discussing this particular problem since the age of the first humanists, one might almost say, and the true solution has in fact been found not once but quite a number of times. As far as I can make out, the Dutch scholar John Cloppenburgh (1597-1642) was the first to see that if Josephus in his *Antiquities* (xviii. 3. 3) really spoke of Jesus he can only have tried to throw ridicule on him and the Christian dogma of the virgin-birth, [2] after the manner of the ill-famed *Toldoth Jeshu* (below, p. 107 n. 1; p. 111 l. 38). The most effective way in which to do this was to relate in this connexion a Boccaccian tale as a proof of the essential truth of Ovid's well-known verse:

> '. . . *Multi*
> *Nomine divorum thalamos iniere pudicos.*'

Over and above this, our author appears to have had a peculiar taste for stories of this type. For example, in *Ant.*, v. 8. 3, where he paraphrases the story of the annunciation of Samson's birth, [3] he without any scriptural authority makes the wife tell her husband about the visit of a tall and beautiful angel, whereupon, naturally enough, the husband evinces clear signs of jealousy and entertains a not uncertain suspicion against his better half. To get her out of this difficult position and to oblige the husband, Jahveh consents to a repetition of the miracle and sends the messenger a second time on his errand. This silly, albeit rather humorous, addition to the

---

[1] See above, p. 44 n. 2.
[2] The last and one of the best and most convincing presentations of this thesis is Clyde Pharr's paper, 'The Testimony of Josephus to Christianity,' *American Journal of Philology*, xlviii., 1927, pp. 137-147.
[3] *Judges* xiii. 7.

sacred text goes a long way toward indicating Josephus' attitude as regards stories about virgin mothers and miraculous births. If our author quoted the scandal in the Roman temple of Isis in support of his own explanation of the birth story in *Luke*, his words, ' In the Roman sanctuary of Isis, too, events happened not differing from those shameful deeds,' must have been the genuine beginning of the paragraph following immediately after his chapter on Jesus, and have served to tack it on to the preceding lost gibes at the Christian legend. On the contrary, the now preceding words, ' and at the same time something else terribly upset the Jews,' must have stood before the present § 81, 'There was a Jewish exile,' etc., which introduces another pertinent anecdote : to wit, how a Jewish swindler persuaded a noble Roman matron to send gold and purple to Jerusalem and then appropriated the precious gifts for the benefit of his own purse, and how Tiberius, on hearing the complaint of her husband, drove the whole Jewish community out of Rome, etc. Since the gold and purple curtain of the sanctuary —or rather its two curtains [1]—were renewed every year, and since, therefore, the material for these tapestries must have been provided for in the regular temple-budget, the impostor could hardly persuade the God-fearing Roman proselyte lady—unless she was uncommonly badly informed about Jewish ritual customs—that *her* contribution was wanted for this annual pious work. On the other hand, the severe repression by the Emperor of the whole Roman Jewry is inexplicable if this petty case of embezzling had no political background. If, however, we remember the famous lines of the prophet Zechariah (vi. 9-12) about the men of the Babylonian captivity who had sent silver and gold to make a crown for Zerubabel, the messianic ' branch ' of the root of David, it seems probable that the Jewish swindler persuaded the Lady Fulvia to follow this classical example and to send purple and gold to Jerusalem *for the royal cloak and the crown of the Messianic king Jesus*, mentioned in the preceding chapter (*Antiq.*, xviii. 3. 3). What would otherwise have been a petty swindle becomes, under this supposition, a case of high treason against the Emperor, and we can well understand his sentence of banishment from the metropolis of the Roman Empire against the whole apocalyptically excited Jewry of his capital.

In view of this plausible explanation [2]—indeed the only one to account for the presence of these scandalous stories in this part of the *Antiquities*—it is a most remarkable fact that the shocking analogy between Paulina's adventures and the corresponding passage in

---

[1] See below, p. 146 n. 1.

[2] I am glad to say that it has been approved by M. Salomon Reinach in his review of the German edition of this book in the *Revue des Études Juives*, 1929, p. 127 (reprinted in his *Amalthée*, vol. ii., 1930, p. 320 f. ; cp. *ibid.*, p. 347).

the so-called Infancy Gospel in *Luke* is much more patent in the Latin version of the Christian *Egesippus* than in the standard Greek version of the Jew Josephus. The two texts have been compared in detail by Dr. Otto Weinreich [1] in his well-known study of this story type. For the convenience of the English reader an English translation of them is given in Appendix XV.

The most characteristic divergency is the dialogue between the seducer and the victim, found only in *Egesippus*. The dramatization of the story is patent even to the most casual reader, and the correct explanation was given, as far back as the eighteenth century, by the Frenchman Jean Clerq. A secondary source, that is, has been utilized to enliven the original account of Josephus, and this source is the little farce *Anubis as Paramour* by the Roman aristocrat Lentulus, which is first mentioned by Tertullian. The identification of this Lentulus rests on an uncertain basis ; but he must have been pretty nearly contemporaneous with the interesting adventure which furnished the plot of his little work, because such comedies are most appreciated by the public when they still have the added attraction of actuality. The comedy, then, supplied the dialogue of the *Egesippus* version. Now, as we have said before, it is precisely in this *Egesippus* text that we find the most shocking parallels to the account of the Annunciation in *Luke* :

' beata Paulina concubitu . . . dei Anubis '	' ave Maria, gratia plena, dominus tecum
' de se quoque et illa deum esse generandum persuadet mulieri '	
' promit exempla quod et Iovem *summum deorum* Alcmena susceperit et Leda . . . et plurimae aliae, quae ediderint deos partu.'	' ecce concipies et paries filium et vocabitur filius *altissimi.'*

No Christian such as St. Ambrose (who has sometimes been held to be the author of the *Egesippus* version), and still less a freshly converted Jew, intent upon converting others, would have deliberately introduced such blasphemous allusions into a text if it did not previously contain anything of the kind. Nor is it likely that a Christian deliberately set to work to search for such material in the libretto of a *mimus* itself 300 years old, especially if we remember the horror the Church had of this type of literature. On the other hand, it is easy to imagine the delight of a Josephus when he came across the *Anubis moechus* (which may have been still popular in his own time, or which he may have found in the library of Epaphroditus) and saw how effectively he could embellish the

---

[1] *Der Trug des Nectanebos*, Leipzig, 1911, p. 24.

old story with a little drama. It is therefore likely enough that Josephus himself is responsible for the amplified text. At all events, it is utterly unlikely that a St. Ambrose or an Isaac-Hilarius should have indulged in such coarse indelicacies.

If this be granted—and I see no alternative—the conclusion is important not only for the dating of the ' gospel of infancy ' prefixed to *Luke*, but also because it shows Josephus to have been the first of the long series of polemists, from the Jew of Celsus and the *Toldoth Jeshu* down to Anatole France, who took neither the orthodox nor even the artistic view of that naïve and touching Christian legend.

VI

THE PASSAGES ABOUT JOHN THE BAPTIST AND JESUS IN THE HEBREW 'JOSIPPON'

THE *Josippon* is commonly believed by modern historians not to contain any mention of Jesus whatever, a view which is contradicted by two remarkable statements duly recorded in Fabricius-Harles' *Bibliotheca Graeca*, repeated many a time since and variously interpreted. One comes from the pen of Cardinal Baronius,[1] who states that in a Roman MS. of the *Josippon* he found the *Testimonium* passage erased, much to his indignation at this impudence on the part of the Hebrews. This statement was ironically doubted by Isaac Casaubonus,[2] the French Huguenot humanist, who suggested that the venerable cardinal had simply been the victim of a practical joker. Pierre Daniel Huet,[3] Bishop of Avranches, on the authority of Hackspan, adds that the MS. in question could be found in the Vatican Library, and Count Windischgrätz went so far as to say that he had been shown the MS. in the papal city. All these assertions must be accepted with a good deal of caution, since it is certain that none of the four copies now at the Vatican was there at the time of Baronius, who, moreover, does not say at all that the MS. in question was in the possession of the Papal Library. On the contrary, it would be quite reasonable to conclude from his account that it was the private property of some Jew, and the MSS. shown to Hackspan and Count Windischgrätz may in fact have belonged to one of the keepers or perhaps to the contemporary Prefect of the Library. The second statement comes from the well-known Giraldus Cambrensis, who says that Robert Canutus, also called Robert of Cricklade, Prior of St. Frideswide (a Benedictine monastery near Oxford), and Chancellor of Oxford University in 1159, a scholar conversant with Hebrew, had found the *Testimonium* intact in two copies of the Hebrew *Josippon* which formed part of a MS. collection he had acquired from Jews living in various English towns. He goes on to say that in another copy in his possession a freshly erased blank occupied the space of the *Testi-*

---

[1] *Ann. Eccles.*, i., Antwerp, 1597, ad a. 34, c. 226, p. 215B.
[2] *De Reb. sacr. et Eccl. diss.*, xvi., Geneva, 1657, p. 677.
[3] *Demonstr. evang.* (⁵), Leipzig, p. 57.

monium. In the remaining copies he had consulted, the passage was simply non-existent, no doubt because they were derived from some archetype from which the text in question had already disappeared. The statement of Giraldus is corroborated, so far as the occurrence of the *Testimonium* passage in the Hebrew *Josippon* is concerned, by the eleventh-century Jewish chronicler quoted once before (above, p. 83 n. 1), Jerahm'el b. Shelomo, who says, referring to Josephus, whom he identifies, of course, with Joseph b. Gorion (above, p. 31) :

> ' And he also speaks of Johanan and of Shime'on son of Johanan,[1] nicknamed Kepha', born in the village Beth-Saida, and of Jacob, son of Joseph, the brother of (Ješu) [2] the crucified one on the father's side. For Joseph, the husband of (Marjam),[2] the daughter of Hannah, the daughter of Jehojaqim, the mother of (Ješu) [2] the crucified one, before he was engaged to Marjam,[3] had a wife, her name was Marjam bath Hannah, and she was a sister of Marjam the mother of (Ješu) [2] the crucified one. And she bore Jacob to Joseph and died, and he took as his bride Marjam the sister of (Marjam).[1] And there was lapidated (Jacobus) [1] in Jerusalem by the Pharisees. And also of Matthew the Evangelist, whose name was Levi; this Levi with the surname Matthia wrote the book *Aven Gilion* [4] in the Hebrew tongue for the Hebrews. And also of Sha'ul, surnamed Pa'ul, that is Paulus, he wrote, who is of the tribe Benjamin. And also he wrote of Bar Nabas of Kipris, who is Joseph the Levite, and of the disciples (read : of his disciple) Johanan surnamed Markos the Evangelist. And of Judah and of Lukos (*sic*) the healer and Markos, the disciples of Shime'on Kepha. And Johanan son of Zebadjah the Evangelist, who wrote the book of secrets (*sefer ha-razim*) on the island of Padmos (*sic*), and died forty-eight (read : four-and-eighty) years old in the days of Trajan.'

It is needless to say that this quotation could only be derived from a Christian source,[5] for no one but a Christian, anxious to safeguard the late dogma of the perpetual virginity of Mary, could have found enough interest in this type of genealogical hair-splitting. Furthermore, none but a Christian could have repeated the fanciful statement of Irenæus' [6] 'presbyters' that John the Evangelist, who was in reality beheaded in A.D. 44 in the reign of Agrippa I.,[6] died in hoary old age under Trajan. Finally, the term used for Christ, ' the crucified one,' is not used by Jewish writers, who call him 'the hanged one.'

---

[1] A genealogy peculiar to the fourth gospel (i. 42, xxi. 15) and the 'Gospel of the Hebrews.'

[2] The name is erased in the Bodleian MS.

[3] Not erased this time ! *N.B.*: The negligent and inconsequent procedure of the censor.

[4] Jewish distortion of the word ' evangelion.'

[5] St. Jerome, *De Viris illustr.*, chs. iv., vii., viii., xiii., has very similar passages.

[6] ii. 22, 5 ; iii. 3, 4.

PLATE IX

את הבחור לא הרג כי אמר המלך
קיסר כי אהבתו בעזרה בו וייראו
גבר בליו וידיחהו למרחוק
בל כן כתבנו את הנבלה אשר
בעשה ברומה בימי תבידיאוו קיסר
ובימיו כעבור גבלות כמלה הרבה
ובימים ההם מת ארכילאוס
בן אורורדוס וימלוך אנטיפס אחיו
תחתיו ריסרב את שמו אורורדו וגם
הוא הרשיע לעשות מכל אשר היו
לפניו ולא עזב תועבה אשר לא
עשה וימלוך יא שנה והוא לקח
אשת פליפוס אחיו בעודנו חי וגם
היה לה בנים מאחיו ריקחה לו
לאשה ויהרוג רבים מחכמי ישראל
וגם הרע הרג את יוחנן של אשר א
אמר לו אסור לך לקחת את אשת א
פיליפוס ויהרגהו   הוא יוחנן
אשר עשה טבילה

ריגלה אותו תבידיאוס קיסר מלך
רומה את אורודוס לארץ ספרד וי
רימת טס   וימלוך אגריפס בן
אריסתובולוס בן אורודוס הגדול ו
וימלוך כג סנה ובימיו מת תביד
תבידיאוס קיסר   וימלוך תחתיו
ג'וס אשר הרשיע לעשות מכל אשר
היו לפניו הוא ג'וס אשר קרא עצמ
בעמר אלהים   וייצו לבנות לו
מזבחות בכל הארץ ולהזכיר שמ
אלהים ולהסביע בשמו כל אדם כ

כבשס אלהיס ויאותו לו כל הגוים
לבנית לו מזבחות ויסבבו בשמו
ריניכירו אותו באלהיס רק היהודים
לא אבו שמוע לו   ריתנרריך
למלחמות ויאמרו כמותה יחד ולא
נשמע ולא נעבוד לו   בימיס
ההס היו מלחמו וקטטות ביהודה
בין הפרושיס ובין פרייכי שמכר ה
הברטיס אחדי בן יוסף וכו'
ובעוד אשר עשה רעות גדולות בי
בישריל עד אשר ניתחו אותו העדר
בימיס ההס שלחו אנטי מיכרים
שליח אל ג'וס מלך רומה   ושמר
אפירן וגם היהודים שלחו סמר כן
שליח אל ג'וס מלך מלכים   ושמר
פולו איט חכס אשר עשה ספריס ה
הרבה זה פולו   ריבן אפירן לבני
ג'וס מלך רומה ויאמר כל הגוים
יוכירו שמך אלהיס ויבגו לך מזב
מזבחות על סמך   ויסבבו בשמך
כבשס אלהיס   רק אלה היהודים
לבדיס לא יבנו לך מזבחות ולא יו
יוכירו שמך אלהיס   ולא יסבבו
בשמך   ריבן פולו ריאמ אמנס כי
לא כבנה מזבח רק ל' יהי ישריאל
ולא נוכיר שס אלהיס אחדיס בלתי
שס ה' יהינו ולא נסבב בשס אחר
זולתי בשמו הגדול והנכ'ם ולא כ
כזבח לאלהי בלתי ל' לבדו טרס
נמסור נפשותינו למות   כי אין

We know, moreover, through a quotation in the mediaeval *Golden Legend*,[1] exactly what this Josephus, interpolated according to St. Jerome's *De viris illustribus*, said about 'Jacob, son of Joseph, the brother of Jesus the crucified one' :

'Friday after the death of the Lord—as says *Josephus* and Jerome in the book on famous men [2]—James made a vow that he would not eat until he saw the Lord risen again from the dead. On the day of the resurrection—when James had not tasted food unto that very day—the Lord appeared to him and said to those about him, " Place a table and bread " (upon it) ; then he took the bread, blessed it and gave it to James the Just, saying, " Rise up, brother, and eat, for the Son of Man has risen from the dead." '

A MS. of the *Josippon* containing such obviously Christian material would necessarily also reproduce the *Testimonium*. If Jerahm'el b. Shelomo says nothing about it, the reason is that his copy no longer contained it, obviously owing to recent erasure by the hand of a Jewish owner. To explain the presence of the other Christian material two different hypotheses are possible. The most simple is to suppose the whole passage to be an interpolation made by converted Jews acting as censors. We know [3] that in the age of the printing-press this office of censorship was performed by baptized Jews, who were authorized to search private and synagogue libraries for ' blasphemous,' i.e. anti-Christian, literature, and to expurgate it at the expense of the owners. Nor were things done much differently in the Middle Ages. In an edict dated the 19th of August 1263, King Jayme I. of Aragon prescribes that the Jews should either expurgate their own books or have them censored by the Jewish apostate Paulus de Burgos. Still, we have no proof that censors ever inserted long passages into Hebrew books, and it is therefore much more probable that these interpolations were made by converted Jews for proselytizing purposes, and even the *Testimonium* passage in Robert of Cricklade's copies of

---

[1] Jacobus de Voragine, *Legenda aurea*, lxvii.: ' *In Parasceue autem, mortuo domino, sicut dicit Josephus et Hieronymus in libro de viris illustribus, Jacobus votum vovit, se non comesturum, donec videret dominum a mortuis surrexisse. In ipsa autem die resurrectionis, cum usque in diem illam Jacobus non gustasset cibum, eidem dominus apparuit, ac eis, qui cum eo erant, dixit : Ponite mensam et panem : deinde panem accipiens benedixit et dedit Jacobo Justo dicens : Surge, frater mi, comede : quia filius hominis a mortuis resurrexit.*'

[2] Opp. ed. Martianay, t. iv.[b], p. 102 : ' *Evangelium quoque, quod appellatur secundum Hebraeos, et a me nuper in Graecum Latinumque sermonem translatum est, quo et Origenes saepe utitur, post resurrectionem Salvatoris refert : Dominus autem cum dedisset sindonem servo sacerdotis ivit ad Jacobum et apparuit ei. Iuraverat enim Jacobus se non comesturum panem ab illa hora, qua biberat calicem Domini, donec videret eum resurgentem a dormientibus* (v. l. : *mortuis*). *Rursusque post paullum : Afferte, ait Dominus, mensam et panem. Statimque additur : Tulit panem et benedixit ac fregit et dedit Jacobo Justo, et dixit ei : Frater mi, comede panem tuum, quia resurrexit Filius hominis a dormientibus* (v. l.: *mortuis*).'

[3] See Joseph Jacobs' article ' Censorship of Jewish Books,' in the *Jewish Encyclopedia*.

the *Josippon* had probably no other origin. Yet there is still another possibility to explain this feature. Ever since Scaliger and Casaubonus it has been pointed out that the *Josippon* in a number of details shows a close dependence on the *Egesippus*, the proselytizing tendency of which is manifest on every page of the compilation. It is probable that the lost archetype of the *Josippon* was nothing but a Hebrew translation of the *Egesippus*, undertaken by a Jewish apostate for the purpose of converting his former co-religionaries,[1] just as the *Egesippus* has been composed for an identical purpose by the baptized Jew Hilarius-Gaudentius, alias Isaac.[2] Just as this Isaac interpolated the passages about Peter and Paul from the writings of the Christian traveller Hegesippus, later copyists of Isaac's version used by the Hebrew translator may have added from St. Jerome's *De viris illustribus* the material just passed in review. The Jews, who naturally found the *Josippon* quite interesting otherwise, on discovering the *Testimonium*, for which they must have felt a particular aversion, simply erased it. The strongly anti-Christian tendency of certain other passages in the extant *Josippon* has so far not been noticed because most of the common editions of this popular book are so thoroughly expurgated by the censor as to create an impression of neutrality, i.e. that it does not mention Jesus and his followers at all. The true spirit of the work may be gauged from the exceedingly rare *editio princeps*, printed by R. Abraham Conat at Mantua prior to 1470. The crucial passage in this rare book reads as follows : [3]

> ' In those days [4] there were wars
> and quarrels in Judaea between the
> Pharisees and
> the " robbers of our people " who followed [5]
> the son of Joseph, etc.' [6] | BLANK | [7]
> [8] ' . . . 'Ele'azar, who committed great
> crimes in Israel
> until the Pharisees overpowered him.'

One might, of course, doubt the identity of the ' son of Joseph ' just mentioned with Jesus, the more so because the name Joseph itself is extremely common. Yet a comparison of this text with

---

[1] See above, p. 31.   [2] See above, p. 58, last lines.
[3] The passage is found on fol. 89 of the unpaginated book. See Pl. IX., left column, lines 6-11.
[4] I.e. the principate of Caligula.
[5] Lit. ' inclined after ' ; cf. *Acts* v. 36 : Θευδᾶς ᾧ προσεκλίθη ἀνδρῶν ἀριθμός.
[6] The reader will notice the Aramaic abbreviation וכו' immediately before the blank in line 5 in the left column of Pl. VII.
[7] On a similar blank indicating an expurgated passage in the *Historia Augusta* (above, p. 12 n. 4), see Hohl, *Klio*, xiii., 1913, p. 391 n. 4.
[8] There must have followed something like ' chief among them.'

PLATE X

THE PARIS MS. OF R. JUDAH LEON B. MOSHEH MOSCONI'S *RECENSIO* OF THE 'JOSIPPON'
WITH THE PASSAGES ON JOHN THE BAPTIST AND JESUS (COD. HEBR. 1280 F° 123 R° AND V° (15TH CENTURY). BIBLIOTHÈQUE NATIONALE

(SEE P. 97, NOTE 1)

another, found in a Josippon MS. in the Bibliothèque Nationale[1] and reproduced on Pl. x., will speedily dispel such doubts. Here the passage in question runs as follows :

> ' In those days there was much party strife [2]
> and great disputes in Judaea
> between the Pharisees
> and the "robbers" in Israel
> who followed Jeshu'ah
> ben Pandera the Naṣōraean,
> who did great miracles in Israel until
> the Pharisees overpowered him
> and hanged him upon a pole.'

The text shows quite clearly that in the archetype of this redaction the hand of the censor had deleted the name of the chief of the ' robbers,' namely, 'Ele'azar. The reader or copyist was thus no longer able to see that the two fragments belonged to two different sentences, the less so because the gap was evidently not greater than it is in the *editio princeps*. He therefore concluded that what had dropped out was simply the objectionable patronymic of Jesus, ' ben Pandera,' and the ordinary surname, ' *han-noṣri*.' He contracted the two sentences, and thus Jesus became the subject of a predicate formerly referring to 'Ele'azar. Once this was done, the censor could not tolerate any more the expression ' crimes ' (originally referring to 'Ele'azar), and replaced it by ' miracles.' The mention of the pole (or tree) proves, of course, that the archetype of this redaction no longer contained anything about the crucifixion under Pilate, and the copyist thus had to mention it in a different context, notwithstanding the risk of creating a false impression, to the effect that Jesus had been executed in the reign of Caligula, during which the misdeeds of 'Ele'azar were perpetrated.

Another fifteenth-century copy of the same archetype, viz. the *Josippon* with the preface of R. Judah Leon b. Mosheh Mosconi (born in Macedonia in 1328), telling how he compared five different MSS. to establish his text, was until lately in the Museo Borgiano of the Congregatio de Propaganda Fide in Rome, and is at present in the Vatican Library. Here the expurgation of the crucial passage is even more radical, and nothing remains of the text but the words, ' In those days there was great party strife with great disputes in Judaea between the Pharisees and the " robbers in Israel." ' The sentence following, ' who followed Jesus, son of

---

[1] MS. Hebr. 1280, fol. 123vᵒ, written by Juda b. Shelomo of Camerino degli Saraceni for the physician Raphael Cohen of Lunel in Manfredonia in the realm of Naples, in A.D. 1472. The archetype was written in the latter half of the thirteenth century for R. Judah b. Mosheh Mosconi. See our Pl. x.

[2] *maḥᵃlaqōth*.

Pandera the Naṣōrean,' etc., has been carefully blotted out.[1]
Whereas the expurgation in the printed edition of Mantua could
be established only indirectly through the mutilation of the two
sentences, the significant blank, and the Aramaic abbreviation for
' and so forth,' in this MS. the censor can be seen at his work of
deletion. A comparison of the three texts—that is, the Mantua
edition, the Paris and the Vatican MSS.—will clearly show how a
passage on the ' bandits ' following Jesus in the reign of Caligula
and on their chief 'Ele'azar has been gradually mutilated so as to
make the names of 'Ele'azar and Jesus disappear first of all from
the context, and finally have no trace left of the whole story in the
MSS. derived from these, and, naturally, in the subsequent printed
editions of the standard text of the Hebrew *Josippon*.

The same set of facts likewise explains the silence of the *Josippon* on the public appearance and death of Jesus, as it explains
the corresponding silence of the Greek standard text of the *Jewish
War*. Christian censors mercilessly deleting objectionable passages,
and Jewish readers deleting in their turn the (to them) obnoxious
Testimonium in its Christian form, are jointly responsible for
this wholesale disappearance of the crucial passages bearing on
Christian origins.

Nor is it impossible to determine with any degree of accuracy
the period when the passage on Jesus was deleted from the
chapter dealing with Pilate's administration. The passage in
question was missing as early as the twelfth century when R. Abraham ibn Daûd of Granada composed his epitome of the *Josippon*
(Pl. XII.). For either he or a scribe, astonished at the silence of the
work on Jesus, inserted the words ' in those days Jesus the Naṣōraean was captured,' [2] but he put it in the chapter dealing with
Pompey, just before the passage corresponding to *Ant.*, xiv. 1. 3,
so that it would seem that Jesus was arrested in 63 B.C. : this
strange blunder is explained by a confusion of Jesus the Naṣōraean
with another Jesus, a disciple of R. Jehoshu'ah b. Perahja.[3]

Such a blunder would, of course, have been impossible had the
Jews of that period still possessed a statement of Josephus concerning the life and death of Jesus the Naṣōraean. The very fact
that such mistakes occurred in the Talmud shows that the Aramaic
version of Josephus' *War* no longer existed at the time of the com-

---

[1] See our Pl. xi. The reader can easily verify that the expurgated text was
identical with the untouched words reproduced in our Pl. x., if he will bear in mind
that there is only one Hebrew letter, the ל, extending above the line. The little
pinnacles crowning the black spot in Pl. xi. show the place where a ל was obliterated by the censor.

[2] ' *baiamim hahem nithphas Jeshu han-nosri.*'

[3] On this earlier Jesus the reader will find some information in R. Travers
Herford, *Christianity in Talmud and Midrash*, London, 1903, p. 50 *sqq.* This con-
fusion led into error my old friend Mr. G. R. S. Mead when he wrote his book
Did Jesus live 180 B.C. ? See below, App. 11.

PLATE XI

THE PASSAGE ON JESUS DELETED IN THE VATICAN MS. OF R. JUDAH LEON B. MOSHEH
MOSCONI'S 'JOSIPPON'

COD. BORGIANUS HEBR. I F° 128 V° (15TH CENTURY)

(SEE P. 90 NOTE I)

position of the Talmud.   It is worth mentioning, also, that in the
eleventh century, when the Moslem writer Ali ben Aḥmad Abn
Muhammed ibn Ḥasm reports of *Jusuf ibn Qorion*, that is, Josephus, that he speaks favourably of John and his baptism but ' says
nothing more of the history of Jesus Christ, the son of Mary, on
whom be peace,' this statement finds its explanation in corresponding passages occurring in the Vatican [1] and Paris [2] MSS.   At all
events, the deletion of the passages bearing on Jesus (aside from
the Christian *Testimonium*) must have happened before the
eleventh century.

Fortunately, the destructive work of the censors was not uniform or uniformly thorough, and could not be so.   Thus in the
fifteenth century R. Abraham b. Mordekhai Farissol [3] (1451-1526)
still found, as he himself states, the words ' *bajamim hahem*,' that
is, ' in those days,' and referring to the life of Jesus, in the *Josippon*
chapter concerning Pilate.   He rightly concludes that Jesus must
have lived in the reign of Tiberius, to which those words refer.   It
is in the nature of things that individual owners managed to conceal their copies from the censors, and that some censors were more
negligent than others, or could even be bribed.   Even the employment of various censors on the same job by the Church [4] was no
absolute guarantee.   In the case of printed editions, where the
censorship was exercised before the book went to press, the work
was, of course, much more effective.

The six lines in the printed edition of Abraham Conat (quoted
above, p. 96) owe their existence to just such negligence or corruption on the part of the official censors.   The publisher, we may
suppose, attached high hopes to just these lines, which were doubtless meant to stimulate the sales.   The event does not appear to
have justified his optimism.   For it is certainly no accident that
the edition in question is extremely rare.   Evidently it was
hunted down and ruthlessly destroyed so far as was in the power
of the ecclesiastical authorities.   Nor were things much different

---

[1] Hebr. 438, fo 95, ro, line 15: ' this was Joḥanan who made a baptism before
all who baptized according to the words of Jesus.'

[2] Hebr. 1280 (see Pl. x.) : ' this was R(abbi) Jehoḥanan who baptized before
all those who baptized [for the remission of sins] according to the order of the
words of those who confirm in the law of Jeshu'ah son of Joseph son of Pandera the
Naṣōraean.'   The bracketed words, ' for the remission of sins,' in the same connexion
are only found in the Arabic version of the *Josippon*.   It is significant that the
Christian censors uniformly blotted them out ; they naturally objected to any
statement giving such undue credit to the mere forerunner.

[3] *Magen 'Abraham*, ch. lxx. (MS. of the Rabbinic Seminary in Budapest, quoted
by Sam. Krauss, *Das Leben Jesu nach jüdischen Quellen*, Berlin, 1902, p. 242, and
300 n. 9, who could make no sense of this important witness, having only a very
slight acquaintance with the state of the problem of the *Josippon* paragraphs
on Jesus).   This book was written after 1473.

[4] See Pl. XIII. and below, p. 107 n. 3.   The signatures of the various censors
are still visible in many copies of Hebrew books.

in the Turkish empire. As is well known, Isa ibn Maryam is considered a great prophet even by the Moslems, and any patriarch
complaining of Jewish ' blasphemies ' was therefore bound to find
a willing ear among Turkish officialdom. Furthermore, a Stambul
publisher of Jewish books had necessarily to consider the export
market in Christian Europe, and the peril to which the possession
of such copies would expose any travelling Jew after crossing the
boundary of a Christian country.

Having thus dealt at some length with the vicissitudes of the
Josippon and the vexed clause about Jesus, we may now proceed
to analyse what by a fortunate combination of circumstances has
been left to us, with a view to extracting whatever historical data
may be obtained in this way.

The essential and hitherto entirely unknown fact is that the
Jewish *Josippon* refers to the followers of Jesus as ' bandits of our
nation ' (*p^eriṣe 'amenu*), a transparent allusion (in the usual
rabbinical way) to the prophecy of *Daniel* xi. 14 : ' and in those
days many shall stand up against the king of the South, also the
children of the bandits among thy people [*p^eriṣej 'amekha*] shall
rebel in order to realize the vision, but they shall stumble.' Such
an allusion was easy to understand by any reader learned in the
Scriptures, who would then be quick to take the hint and to
identify the ' king of the South ' with the ' Edomite ' ruler, and
to rejoice at the prophesied failure of those ' bandits,' ' eager to
realize the Messianic vision.' This quotation from *Daniel* xi. 14
is quite in the style of the *Josippon*, in which this and similar allusions abound. As a matter of fact, the term λῃσταί,
' bandits,' habitually used by Josephus to designate the nationalist
revolutionary and anti-Roman party among the Jews, in the
Josippon is regularly rendered by *pariṣim*, ' bandits,' ' marauders.'
If the same term, then, is applied to the followers of Jesus, it
shows for once that the Jews, not content with expurgating a
proselytizing text of the *Josippon*, proceeded more aggressively
when they saw a chance and came right out with the assertion that the followers of Jesus belonged to the *pariṣim*, the
revolutionary, anti-Roman party of the *kananajim* (zealots) and
barjonim (extremists).[1] This statement receives a certain amount
of confirmation from the fact that at least one, possibly two,
of Jesus' followers were known as *qannaja*, ' the zealot,' and at
least one, possibly two, as *barjona*, ' the extremist,' or even
r'aš barjonim, ' leader of extremists.'[1] If the passages in
question came from the text of Josephus—as we shall try to prove
—they can only have been derived from uncensored copies of
Josephus' MSS., such as fell later into the hands of the Russian
translator. It seems evident that, to revise the *Josippon* ' han-

[1] See below, p. 103 n. 3 ; p. 252 n. 3.

PLATE XII

IOSIPPVS

obediebat Romanis. Misit itaq̃ fortissi/
mus ille epistolā ad Hartā regē Arabiæ
dicens: Recede a Ierusalē, & si nolueris,
scias q̃ ruperis fędus tuū cū seniorib⁹ Ro
manis, & totus exercitus Romanoꝝ con
tra terrā tuā castrametabit̃. Cū Hartam
epistolā legisset recessit a Ierusalē, sed &
Hyrcanus & Antipater recesserūt cum
confusione & ignominia. Porro Aristo
bolus cōgregauit residuū Israelē p̃sequu
tusq̃ est post eos, & p̃cussit gentē Arabię
& filios Israel qui adiuuabāt Hyrcanum
plaga ualde magna: reuersusq̃ est cū lęti
cia in Ierusalē. In illis diebus cōprehen
sus est Iesus Nazarenus. Post hæc uenit
Pampius in Damascum: cui Aristobo/
lus misit unam uitem auream, ingenioso
formatam opere. Radices eius Pampini,
folia, botri & uuæ, quæ fuerūt in ea, erāt
aurum mundum. Pondus eius fuerunt
quingentæ libræ auri. De qua Pampius
magno lætatus est gaudio, misitque eam
Romam seniori, qui Romæ gubernacu
la tenebat. Trecenti uerò uiginti consi
liarij sui omnes mirati sunt artem & in/
genium illius qui fecit eam, gauisiq̃ sunt
de ea

Hic fuit a/
lius Iesus a
saluatore,
multis eū
preueniēs
annis. immo
idē, fuit sed
fallunt in Iu/
chronologia.

היה נשבע לרומי . וישלח הגבור ספר
לחרתם מלך ערב לאביר עלת מעל ירד
ירושלם אם לא רע כי הפרת בריתך עם
זקני רומי ובל היל רומיים על ארצך חו
הנים ובקרא הרתם את הספר נסע מעל
ירושלם וגב חורקנוס ואנטיפטר נסעו ב
בבשת ובכלמה ויאכות ארסתבלוס את
שארית ישראל וירדות אחריהם ויך בגוי
ערב ובבני ישראל העוזרים את חורקנוס
מכת גדולת מאד . וישב ירושלם ב
בשמחה : בימים ההם נתפש ישו
הנצרי : ואחר בן בא פמפיוס אל דמ
רמשק וישלח לו ארסתבלוס גפן זהב א
אחת מעשה חושב כולה שרשית ושר
ושריצית ועליה ואשבלות ענבים שהיו
בח זהב טהור משקלם תק ליטרין זהב :
וישמח בת פמפיו' שמחה גדולה ושלחת
לרומי לזקן המנחיג את רומי ושלש מי
מאיה ועשורים יועציו תמהו כולם מה
מחכמה החושב שעשה אותו ושמחו
כא

יוכח

FOLIO 82 OF SEBASTIANUS LEPUSCULUS' JOSIPPUS, *DE BELLO JUDAICO, DEINDE DECEM*
JUDAEORUM CAPTIVITATES, ETC. *BASILEAE, APUD HENRICUM PETRI MDLIX*

IN THE MARGIN, A PRINTED REFERENCE TO THE PASSAGE ON JESUS, DISCUSSED ON P. 982 BY LEPUSCULUS : HIC
FUIT ALIUS JESUS A SALVATORE, MULTIS EUM PRAEVENIENS ANNIS ' (' THIS WAS ANOTHER JESUS, DIFFERENT
FROM THE SAVIOUR, PRECEDING HIM BY MANY YEARS '). BELOW THIS GLOSS IS AN AUTOGRAPHIC NOTE BY
FATHER CASIMIR OUDIN : ' IMMO IDEM FUIT, SED FALLUNT (SC. JUDAEI) IN CHRONOLOGIA ' (' ON THE CONTRARY,
IT IS THE SAME [JESUS] BUT [THE JEWS] ARE MISTAKEN ABOUT HIS CHRONOLOGY ')

(SEE P. 98, LINE 27)

nosri,' the Christian proselytizing translation of the Latin *Egesippus,*
a Jew from the Byzantine provinces of Italy who could read Greek
and write Hebrew must have turned to a copy of the Greek original
which had come down to him through an unbroken line of Jewish
owners and had thus escaped Christian censorship. Unfortunately for us, his labour was vain, for the essential part of the
passages in question has been finally blotted out by the pen of
the Christian *reveditori.* The phrase deleted must have told the
reader what the object of the ' wars ' and ' quarrels ' between the
' bandits straying after Jesus ' and the Pharisees (above, p. 96 n. 5)
were about.

A conjecture as to the contents of the lost passage is, fortunately, not altogether impossible. We know from Origen [1] that
Daniel's prophecy about the ' abomination of desolation ' was
believed to have been realized first when Pilate brought the
Emperor's image on the legionary standards into the sanctuary of
Jerusalem, and again when the Emperor Gaius wanted to set up his
statue in the temple.[2] Now, we know from Josephus' Greek work
that the Jewish authorities and the reasonable and honest governor
Petronius opposed a passive procrastination to the caprice of
the imperial madman. But the messianists of the time, waiting
for the Second Coming, must have recalled the words of Jesus : [3]
' When ye see the abomination of desolation spoken of by Daniel
the prophet stand where it ought not, then let them that are in
Judaea flee to the mountains.' They must have interpreted
Caligula's order as the foretold sign of the imminence of the Second
Coming, and would therefore quite naturally exhort their compatriots to betake themselves to the hills, there to await the return
of Jesus in glory and, as suggested in the Hebrew text, ' to
stand up against the king of the South,' that is, their king Agrippa,
the Idumaean Southerner, and to ' arise in order to realize the
vision.' We know from the Greek text of Josephus [4] that the Jews
refused to till the soil and to sow corn during this critical period,
this agricultural strike making Petronius anticipate a famine
throughout the land. It would, of course, have greatly aggravated
the difficulties had a really considerable part of the population
taken to the mountains and begun to live there on what are
euphemistically called ' the resources of the land,' that is, to use
Josephus' blunt words, as ' robbers.' It is very understandable
that the Pharisees should have done all they could to counteract
this eschatological propaganda for a new Maccabean exodus. That
it came to violent quarrels, to blows and even to genuine wars,
between the messianist activists and the Pharisee opportunists is

---

[1] Comm. in *Matt.* xxii. 15ff. (tom. xvii., ch. xxv.).
[2] See St. Jerome, above, p. 67 n. 2.
[3] *Mark* xiii. 14 ; *Matt.* xxiv. 15.   [4] *B.J.*, ii. p. 200 f.

not at all surprising, since Josephus [1] says of the latter that they were 'overbearing and easily roused to fighting.'

But the censor's ink must have blotted out more than a phrase about mere internecine war and strife between the Pharisees and the messianist followers of Jesus. We have noted above [2] that according to Tacitus the Jews resorted to arms at the approach of the troops of Petronius to Jerusalem, to prevent the placing of the statue in the temple. Though the Greek Josephus says nothing of all this, the censored text of the *Josippon* [3] states : ' and there arose wars because of this,' or ' they were aroused to wars.' Only the Mosconi MS. in Paris (cp. Pl. VIII., line 7) has ' and they raised wars against them,' in order to put the responsibility for the outbreak of hostilities on the Romans.

Even from these scanty remains in the *Josippon* it is easy to see that the Greek original must have had a passage corresponding to the statement of Tacitus about the armed resistance of the Jews under Caligula. Since the six lines, expunged later on, of the Mantua edition of the *Josippon* [4] attribute the responsibility therefor to the followers of Jesus, it is clear that on this account the passage in question has been blotted out in the Greek and, though less completely, also in the Hebrew text.

But the most interesting historical detail found in that portion of the Mantua edition occurs in the phrase following the blank : '. . . 'Ele'azar, who committed great crimes in Israel until the Pharisees overpowered him.' If we want to know who this 'Ele'azar was, we have only to turn over the said folio 89 of Abraham Conat's edition, to find on the verso (left column, line 17) the statement : ' Felix sent 'Ele'azar the robber (*hap-pariṣ*) to Rome,' a sentence which, by the way, proves definitely that *pariṣîm* is indeed the exact equivalent of Josephus' λῃσταί, ' robbers.' Felix is simply the well-known Roman governor, and the robber 'Ele'azar is 'Ele'azar son of Deinaios, the ' robber chief ' (ἀρχιλῃστής), mentioned both in the Greek text of Josephus and in the Latin *Egesippus* as having been arrested and sent to Rome in chains by the governor Antonius Felix (A.D. 52-80), ' after he had harassed the country for twenty years.' This 'Ele'azar son of Dinai is quite well known also to the Mishnah,[5] where he is mentioned as a famous ' murderer,' and to the Midrash,[6] which knows him as the leader of one of the unfortunate generations who tried to force the messianic redemption of Israel before the time of God's own good

---

[1] *Ant.*, xvii. § 41.   [2] P. 65.
[3] See also above, p. 67 n. 1, about the *gravissima seditio* of the Jews in *Egesippus*.
[4] See above, p. 96 n. 3.
[5] *Sota*, ix. 9 ; *Babl.*, 47a ; *Jerush.*, 23b. Cp. *Tosephta Sota*, ch. xiv., ed. Zuckermandel, p. 320₁₆.
[6] *Midrash Siphrē* to *Deut.* 205 (ed. Friedmann, 111b) ; *Jalqut, sect. shofᵊtim*, § 923 ; Varsow, col. 632 ; *Midrash to Canticles*, ii. 7 (99a)₈

will. Both these statements agree perfectly with what Josephus says about him as a 'robber chief,' i.e. a nationalist revolutionary leader of the Jews. The ' twenty years ' during which he ' harassed the country,' until Felix rounded him up and sent him to Rome for trial, are quite compatible with the statement of the Hebrew *Josippon* that he ' committed many misdeeds ' in the days when Caius Caligula wanted to place his statue in the temple (A.D. 40). The hitherto enigmatic words of Tacitus (*Ann.*, xv. 44) to the effect that the Messianic ' superstition,' temporarily suppressed through the crucifixion of the Christ under Pilate, ' soon broke out again' (*rursus erumpebat*), is now explained through the mutilated sentence of the *Josippon*, the partial erasure of which can only be understood if this 'Ele'azar was originally described as one of those who 'strayed after the son of Joseph,' that is, if the *Josippon* and its source described 'Ele'azar as a Christian rising against Rome because he expected the immediate Second Coming of the Christ.

Nor does the name of 'Ele'azar seem to be quite unknown in Christian tradition. In the so-called pseudo-Clementines,[1] early apocryphal writings based on lost *Acts of Peter*, there is a list of sixteen or thirteen followers of Peter, among them, at the end, Aἰνείας καὶ Λάζαρος οἱ ἱερεῖς, in the Latin version *Phineas, Lazarus*, etc., so that evidently either Aἰνείας or *Phineas*, or both, are corruptions of one and the same name. 'Ele'azar being regularly written לעזר, *L'azar*, in the Palestinian Talmud, and the famous New Testament ' Lazarus ' being a witness to the fact that this abbreviation was the popular pronunciation of the name in Palestine, there is no difficulty in identifying Λάζαρος ὁ ἱερεύς, ' 'Ele-'azar the priest,' *'Ele'azar hak-kohen*, with the 'Ele'azar mentioned as one of the followers of Jesus during the reign of Caligula.

It may, of course, be objected that the name of 'Ele'azar is itself far too common to make such an identification a very safe thing, at least so long as we have no father's name to go by. Still, in this case it seems extremely tempting, from a palaeographic point of view, to submit *Dineas=Deineias* as the true original of the two evidently corrupt forms *Aineias* and *Phineas*, since Λ and *A* are as easily confused as Latin *P* and *D*, *H* and *E*, in capital script. If this conjecture be accepted, it would seem as though both father and son, two men of priestly race, had been followers of Peter,[2] the *barjona* or ' extremist '[3] among the disciples of Jesus.

---

[1] *Hom.*, ii. 1, P.G., 78b (45) ; *Recogn.*, ii. 1 (P.G., i. 1247 *sq.* below).

[2] The case would be entirely parallel to the fact—not noticed hitherto by any modern scholar—that Theudas, the pseudo-messiah of the time of Cuspius Fadus and the Emperor Claudius, was ' an acquaintance ' (γνώριμος) of Paul (Clem. Alex., *Strom.* vii. 17 : ' Valentine (the gnostic) was a disciple (ἀκηκοέναι) of Theudas, γνώριμος δ' οὗτος ἐγεγόνει Παύλου ').

[3] On this meaning of the name, cp. below, p. 252 n. 3.

However that may be—and it goes without saying that I attach no importance to this conjecture—there is certainly a strange distortion of Josephus' text in this connexion visible in the *Josippon*, which is obviously connected with the erasure of the line referring to 'Ele'azar, which survives only in the *editio princeps* of Mantua. Instead of speaking of the devastations of the robber chief 'Ele'azar, as does Josephus in the original, the *Josippon* says : ' In this space of twenty years *Agrippa* (ii.) did not desist from robbery and spoliation, so that he caused much slaughter and enormous loss of life all over Syria.   In Judaea, too, he strewed the land with many corpses, until Felix was made commander of the Roman army, who sent a strong host against him and butchered his bandits, captured Agrippa himself and sent him to Rome in chains.   And although Felix had sent 'Ele'azar the robber to Rome, the country was not cleansed from blood, for the Jews butchered each other, moved by fratricidal hatred.'   At first sight one would suppose a simple mistake of the copyist, writing *Agrippa* instead of *'Ele'azar* the robber.   This, however, is impossible, because the whole paragraph about Agrippa ii. is made to refer to these twenty years and to the alleged revolutionary fight of Agrippa ii. against the Romans, a fight which is, of course, entirely unhistorical.   The paragraph begins, quite unmistakably, with the words, ' As long as this Agrippa, son of Agrippa (i.), lived and reigned, wars between the people of Israel and the Romans never ceased until the captivity of the Jews who were led up to Rome.   This is the second captivity, when the second temple was devastated in the twentieth year of Agrippa on the ninth day of the fifth month which is called Abh.'   How crudely the compiler went to work may be seen from the date, ' twentieth year of Agrippa ii.,' which he gives for the destruction of the temple.   This cannot, of course, be based on Josephus ; for Agrippa became king of Chalcis in A.D. 48, of Trachonitis in A.D. 53, and never in all his life was king of Judaea. These ' twenty years ' are simply transposed from the history of the ' robber ' 'Ele'azar to the history of Agrippa ii., ' the philo-Roman and philo-Caesarian,' as he is called on his coins, who never had the slightest difficulty with the Romans.   The obvious object of this strange transposition was to get rid of 'Ele'azar the robber altogether, an elimination which is now perfectly clear because we know the six partially expurgated lines of the Mantua edition.   It must have been the work of a Christian copyist, perhaps of the author of what the Oxford MS. of Jerahm'el calls the *Josippon hannoṣri*, (the ' Christian *Josippon* ').   On the other hand, the meagre phrase about the capture of 'Ele'azar the robber by Felix must be due to the Jewish scribe who completed and corrected the Christian *Josippon*, as well as he could, by comparing the most important passages of a Greek Josephus.

The example just mentioned is, however, but one of the many deviations existing between the *Josippon* and the standard text of Josephus. The former does not mention a single one of the many Jewish rebel chiefs conquered by the Romans after a more or less bitter struggle before the final uprising of the Jews in A.D. 66. Judas the Galilaean and his sons, Theudas, and all the rest, are conspicuous only by their absence. What Josephus has been accused of unjustly, namely, that he attempted to conceal from the Romans as much as possible what he must have known about the messianic movement among the Jews,[1] that the *Josippon* does, or, better, the falsified Josephus' MS. which served as its model. The entire guilt of the Jewish rebellion is here attributed to—*the Herodian dynasty*. Herod the Great is said to have rebelled against Augustus and to have been led to Rome in chains.[2] Throughout this part of the narrative the place of the rebels, the fighters for national independence, is taken by the hired mercenaries of the Herodian kings. It is only in strict accordance with this whole set of absurd fancies that at the end Vespasian should capture Agrippa II. after the fall of Jerusalem, should drag him to Rome, and have him beheaded by the sword.[3]

This queer falsification of history appears to have taken place gradually. The *Josippon* MS. seen by Jerahm'el,[4] for example, still knew the names of a few rebel leaders, Judas the Galilaean among them, though the shepherd *Athrongas* had already become *Agrippa*. Naturally, no one after the first century had the slightest interest in deliberately using the Herodians as scapegoats. The whole tendency is rather to be regarded as the natural consequence of the misgivings which Jewish Christians and converted Jews generally must have felt on beholding the striking parallelism between Jesus and the various rebel leaders mentioned by Josephus as having arisen just about the same critical period which saw the origins of Christianity and of their belief that Herod the Great was the foretold Antichrist.

Still more curious, though of course perfectly understandable, is the fact that this type of redaction was again altered in an anti-Christian sense by a Jew who had better information at his disposal, no doubt, in the form of a good Greek Josephus MS. Thus it happens that side by side with the presentation of Herod as a rebel we find him the favourite of Augustus and appointed king by him. Of the 'rebel' Agrippa I. we hear in the same way that he was highly honoured by the Emperor Claudius; and Agrippa II., his alleged rôle of 'robber' notwithstanding, actually makes the

---

[1] Above, p. 65, first *a linea*.
[2] *Josippon*, lib. i., c. xxv. p. 163.
[3] *Ibid.*, lib. vi., c. xx. *sq.*, pp. 666 and 673a.
[4] Fol. 151, lines 19 *sqq.*, of *Cod. Oxon.*, 2797 (Neubauer-Cowley, ii., col. 208).

famous speech in which he advises the Jews not to resist the
Romans, in view of the latter's invincibility. His execution at the
order of Vespasian is explained by the invention of calumnies
listened to by the Emperor, though of course they deserved no
credence whatever.

This Jewish reworker very naturally represented the part
played by the Christians quite differently from the proselytizing,
Jew-baiting text he had before him. For him the adherents of
Jesus were ' bandits,' and 'Ele'azar the ' robber ' was a follower of
Jesus. What remains of his account of the struggle between the
Pharisees, described as a fighting body, in accordance with Josephus [1] and the Galilaean adherents of Jesus, agrees remarkably well
with the general phraseology of Josephus and with the contro-
versies between the Galilaean messianists and the Pharisees, well
attested from the Gospels and the Mishnah.[2]

It is quite understandable that the Christian translator or
censor should have insisted upon the expurgation, and even the
total deletion, of a passage in which a man referred to as a robber
chief by Josephus is rightly or wrongly reckoned among the number
of Jesus' followers, and of another paragraph where the same man
is accused of having waged a guerilla war of the most sanguinary
description for twenty years against the Romans—the more so
because these statements are thrown into a particularly strong
relief by a peculiar feature of the Hebrew version which seems so
far to have eluded the attention of modern critics.

We have pointed out before that the printed editions of the
Josippon (how far the statement applies to the MSS. we shall see
after the publication of Dr. Greyzel's critical edition) show no trace
of most of the revolutionary messianic movements of the age. The
object of this careful editing of the original Josephus is not difficult
to guess. The redactor simply wished to concentrate the responsibility for all the uprisings of the ' bandits of his nation,' which led
to the conflict with the Romans and the destruction of the national
sanctuary, on the one group of messianists still in existence in the
Middle Ages and which was still regarded by the Jews as a group
of Jewish sectarians and heretics, though at the same time as the
worst enemies of the Jews and their oppressors, to wit, the Christians. No doubt, in the lost paragraph about Jesus in the chapter
on Pilate's governorship the same redactor wished to represent
him as the fomenter of all the trouble caused by the *pariṣîm* or
' bandits ' of Israel. There can be no doubt about the fact that,
since the Christians of the apostolic generation were spoken of in

---

[1] *Ant.*, xvii. § 41, εἰς τὸ πολεμεῖν ἐπηρμένοι; cp. *Sext. Julius Africanus*, Κέστοι,
ch. iii. (H. Gelzer, *S. J. Africanus*, Leipzig, 1898, i. p. 265), after Justus of Tiberias,
about the stratagems employed by the Phariseans fighting against the Romans.
[2] *Jad.*, iv. 8.

PLATE XIII

THE PASSAGE ON JESUS IN MOSES MAIMONIDES' *HILKHOTH MELAKHIM* (1145-1204), CH. II

DELETED BY THE CENSOR, REWRITTEN IN THE MARGIN OF THE BOOK BY THE OWNER AND REDESTROYED BY A SUBSEQUENT CENSOR

(SEE P. 99, NOTE 4; P. 107, NOTE 3)

such unflattering terms, the Master and Inspirer must have fallen under a similar condemnation in a preceding chapter. Indeed, that lost account of Jesus must have been similar in tone and contents to the well-known passages in the Talmud in which Jesus is characterized as a sorcerer who used magic to seduce Israel from the way of the Law—similar, above all, to the ill-famed mediaeval *Toldoth Jeshu*,[1] in which Jesus is said to have been in command of more than 2000 armed bandits, who had fought real battles with his adversaries, when he was finally made a prisoner on the Mount of Olives.

In the curtailed text of the *Josippon*, with its suppression of all rebellions before Jesus but with its accounts of all rebellions following, among them especially that of 'Ele'azar *hap-pariṣ* under Caligula, the long series of 'bandit chiefs' leading up to the great revolt in the reign of Nero must have appeared as descending in a straight line from Jesus the arch-revolutionary and fomenter of the whole unfortunate war against Rome, the ultimate cause of Israel's ruin.

The anti-Christian tendency of the Jewish *Josippon* as opposed to the proselytizing *Josippon han-noṣri* is then fairly clear, I hope. Small wonder that we possess it only in a badly mutilated shape.

Yet an attentive study of the *Josippon* texts reveals still more. Jewish readers, when stumbling upon blackened and erased passages, would try to fill in the gaps, often by honest and conscientious though not altogether philologically sound conjectures, and this in spite of the fine of a hundred pieces of gold attached to such an offence. In the Mosconi recension, for example, we have been able to show (above, p. 97) that the name of 'Ele'azar has been replaced by Jesus' familiar by-name, 'the Naṣōraean,' *han-noṣri*. The Jewish scribe appears to have concluded from the last letter of the name of 'Ele'azar, the *r*, still dimly visible in spite of the general obliteration of the name, that this letter had really been left over from Jesus' usual surname, *han-noṣri*.

A more difficult problem had to be faced by the Jewish scribe of the two other MSS. of the *Josippon*.[2] He seems to have found nothing less than an erasure of the larger part of two pages; and although he could probably discern a word here and there of the original text, he still made bold to reconstruct [3] the whole by drawing extensively on his imagination. It is unnecessary to dwell on his complete ignorance in historical matters displayed in the resulting fanciful tale, on the fantastic invention of a visit paid to Caligula by Jesus and of the execution of the 'three bandits' under

---

[1] See Sam. Krauss, *Leben Jesu nach jüd. Quellen*, Berlin, 1902.

[2] *Cod. Rothschild*, No. 24 (Paris), and *Vatic. Ebr.*, 408. See Pl. XIV.

[3] Cf. Pl. XIII., where the owner has tried to restore in the margin what the censor had recklessly destroyed in the text—only to see the work of his pen blotted out again by another reviser.

Claudius,[1] or on the silly tale they are relating to Caligula. Aside from a few authentic words, the value of this obviously spurious passage consists in proving the loss of more than merely a few lines. Its considerable length shows that in the original *Josippon* the history of Christian origins must have loomed rather large. No doubt it was given as much space here as in the Slavonic version, which will be discussed further on.

Those critics who would wish to attribute the extremely valuable Slavonic chapters on Jesus to the clever efforts of mediaeval Jewish interpolators should first compare them with the following ineptitudes :

' At that time arose the " robbers of our nation " and presumed to do each one what seemed right in his own eyes and to " walk in the way of evil " and to " change their way," and when they were called to account before the judges of the Sanhedrin of those days the robbers went to the Roman governors who were in Judaea and said to them : " Lo, because we have abandoned their law and have rallied ourselves to the law of Caesar, these are trying to kill us." And since they[2] swore by the life of Caesar, the governors of Caesar saved them (from the judge). And there went forth many of the " robbers of our nation," and many strayed away from the people of the Lord, and they went over to Edom and changed their law and " wandered in the wilderness where there is no way,"[3] and made unto themselves continually signs and miracles through their sorceries, and the wise men of Israel were unable to cope with them (for they were protected by Gaius Caesar). And there came some of the sons of the city of Edom, robbers, and the robbers went into the hiding-places of Edom, and many fell away. And those robbers grew rich from the wealth which the king gave them. And in those days walked about Jesus and with his companions went to Gaius Caesar, and they said : " Arrived is an angel of God,[4] even as the prophets have foretold about him unto this day for a long time, and he said to the inhabitants of Jerusalem to take unto them thy command and to call thy name god. But they have not listened to him and have endeavoured to kill him." And Gaius said : " Where is he ? ", and they called him, and he came into his presence. And he said to the emperor : " God hath sent me to anoint thee as a god on earth and to build for thee an altar as unto a god and call thy name over it." And Gaius loved him and honoured him. And Gaius Caesar sent the image of his own soulless body[5] to Jerusalem and sent them word : " Lo, here is the image of my likeness ; adore it, bow before it, and build before its face an altar, because thus has commanded your god, and your feasts and your rejoicings shall you observe, and

---

[1] The dating of the crucifixion in the reign of Caligula, or even later, is obviously but a development of the sentence found in the Mosconi MS. discussed above, p. 97.
[2] The ' robbers of our nation.'   [3] *Ps.* cvii. 40 ; *Job* xii. 24.
[4] With this cp. below, p. 384 l. 4 f. in the Slavonic *Josephus* : ' I will not call him an angel.'
[5] *gol*e*mō.*

PLATE XIV

THE LONG PASSAGE ON JESUS, THE 'BANDITS' AND EMPEROR GAIUS CALIGULA

COD. VATICAN EBR. 408 F° 94 V° AND 95 V° (TRANSL. ON PP. 108 FF.)

(SEE P. 107, NOTE 2)

you shall let the image enter into Jerusalem." And it came to pass that when it was brought the inhabitants of Jerusalem barred the gate of the city and did not allow the image to enter. And King Agrippa sent wise men of Israel to Rome, Joshuah and Jehudah and ten of his companions, and they went to Rome into the presence of Gaius Caesar, and Caesar said to them : " Lo, thus says your God, who has sent me to be a god, and the whole earth accepts me as a god ; but you, why do you deliberate ? Tell me your desire." And Joshuah replied and his colleagues, and they said : " Known be it to thee, O king, that we will not listen to thee, to this command, and it is not seemly to obey thy decision and to call by the name of god other gods than our Lord alone, and the name of our Lord God, and we will not build an altar but the altar of God, to the name which is hallowed and exalted." But the " bandits of our nation " spoke words to the Lord our God which must not be related, and they altered the interpretation of the law.

' And in those days the men of Egypt sent an ambassador to Gaius, the king of kings, whose name was Apion ; and the Jews likewise sent an ambassador to Gaius, king of kings, whose name was Philo, who was a wise man and author of a large number of books. And Apion began to speak in the presence of Gaius, King of Rome, saying : " All the nations call thy name ' god ' ; only those Jews do not build altars for thee, do not call thy name ' god ' and do not swear by thy name." And Philo began and said : " Truly we do not build altars but to the Lord our God, and we swear by no other name but by the name of the Lord, the great and terrible, and we do not sacrifice to other gods but to the Lord alone. We are ready to lose our lives rather than yield and listen to your words." Then the emperor's wrath was raised and he ordered his army to start and to march against Herod and to devastate the Holy Land. But the bandits of (Ješu)—may his name and memory be blotted out !—settled at his right side, and likewise many of our nation who strayed after them. But Claudius fought against it [1] before the emperor, for he was a prince. And Gaius was angry against him and dismissed him with dishonour from his presence and ordered him out of the room. But Philo said to the Jews who waited for him in the hall of the palace : " Mend your ways and turn whole-heartedly to the Lord, for the time is one of hardship." And the Jews said each to his brother : " Let no one of us anoint himself to-day, for it is a time of hardship for Israel, for Gaius, King of Rome, is very angry. But there is a remedy for this, to wit, to turn to our stronghold, to the Lord our God, who was the stronghold of our fathers. Let us fast and call a prayer-meeting in the land of our enemies." And the Jews observed a fast and called a three days' prayer-meeting in the country of Rome, and called upon the Lord their God with fasting and praying. And it happened on the third day that the Lord turned the spirit of his soldiers against Gaius, so that they attacked him with drawn swords and cut him to pieces, so that his body could not be buried, but the dogs ate his flesh. Thus God took his revenge for the Jews

---

[1] Viz., against the sending of an army to devastate Palestine.

against Gaius. But after him ruled Claudius, and he dismissed Joshuah and his colleagues with great honour after he had given them a banquet and they had sat in his presence. And he honoured them and delivered into their hands the bandits. And Claudius took three bandits, who had escaped, and executed them, throwing their corpses to the dogs, so that they should not be stolen by those " straying about by night " who strayed after them. And Joshuah and his colleagues returned to Jerusalem and brought the remainder of the bandits before the Sanhedrin. And Jehudah [Ishkharioth] [1] arose before the Sanhedrin on behalf of King Herod, for the king spoke, asking : " What is the judgment of the men who have raised against me Gaius Caesar ? " And he bade them to be hanged on a tree. And they hanged them by order of the king, but not with the approval of the whole nation ; for there were people who said : " They are such as have been in the band but have repented and returned." But the rulers and elders and the majority of the people rejoiced at the sight of them ; for they had tried to raise against them wars with the Romans, and many strayed after them in secret.'

The reason why I venture to insert, if not the original text,[2] which the initiate among my readers may easily decipher for themselves on Pl. xv., at least an English translation of this worthless interpolation, is the opportunity it affords to the critics of the Slavonic texts discussed below to judge for themselves what can be expected in the way of historical knowledge from mediaeval Jewish forgers, and what cannot.

As has been said before, some of the sentences in the interpolated passage make quite good sense if isolated from their context. They are, moreover, in perfect harmony with the conclusions we have drawn from the allusion to *Daniel* xi. 14.

In the *Antiquities* (xx. 8. 6 ; cf. *War*, ii. 13. 4), Josephus, speaking of the governor Felix who captured 'Ele'azar b. Dinai, observes : ' but the sorcerers and impostors persuaded the masses to follow them into the desert. They promised to show them wonders and signs . . . and many who allowed themselves to be persuaded paid the penalty of their folly, for Felix made a punitive expedition against those who had been led out of the country.' As for the life of such outlaws in the caves and mountain strongholds of Edom, it is well attested for the time of the Seleucids,[3] for the age of Herod I.,[4] and for the insurrection quelled by Varus.[5] Nothing, then, is more natural than that the messianists should have

---

[1] Obvious interpolation of a scribe who thought of the considerable rôle played by Judas Ishkharioth in the *Toldoth Jeshu*. Of course, the aforesaid Jehuda (ben Tabbai), one of the two alleged ambassadors—Jehoshu'ah (ben Perahja) and Jehuda (ben Tabbai)—is meant by the original author of the story.

[2] It is printed *in extenso*, with all variants and a full commentary, in the German edition of this book.

[3] 1 *Macc.* i. 53 ; ii. 31 ; xxxvi. 41 ; 2 *Macc.* vi. 11 ; x. 6.

[4] *B.J.*, i. §§ 310 *sqq.* ; *Ant.*, xiv. §§ 241 *sqq.*

[5] *Assumptio Mosis*, ix. 6.

taken ' to the hiding-places of Edom ' when the Emperor Gaius threatened to desecrate the sanctuary. The ' bandits of Edom,' who joined them, are exact parallels to the Idumaean radicals who gathered in Jerusalem[1] in A.D. 67, and who are commonly referred to as ' robbers ' by our author.

It is, then, just possible that the following words belong to the original text :

'in those days there were wars and quarrels in Judaea between the Pharisees and the " robbers of our nation " who strayed after Jesus, son of Joseph. And there went out some of those robbers and wandered in the wilderness where there is no way, and made unto themselves signs and miracles through their sorceries. And there came some of the sons of the city of Edom, robbers (too), and they (all) went into the hiding-places of Edom and seduced many (saying) : " in the days (of . . .) Jesus came to . . . (us) . . . Arrived has the angel (messenger) of God foretold by the prophets throughout the ages, and he has said . . . but they listened not to him, but sought how they might kill him. Now, however, let us

. . . .
. . . .
. . . .(The chief of these bandits) was 'Ele'azar, who committed great crimes in Israel, until the Pharisees got the better of him.'

The discovery of the above-quoted passages on Jesus in the *editio princeps* and in certain MSS. of *Josippon* yields another important result, to wit, that the extant versions of the mediaeval *Toldoth Jeshu* are in a large measure dependent upon the anti-Christian edition of the *Josippon*. This comes out quite clearly at the very opening of chapter i. in a Vienna and in an Oxford MS. of this ill-famed pamphlet :

' During the second temple *in the days of Tiberius Caesar and in the days of Herod the Second, King of Israel, who was an evildoer, as may be seen in " Josippon,"* in those days came forward a man from the seed of David, and his name was Joseph Pandareus, and he had a wife and her name was Mirjam, and this man was God-fearing, and he was a pupil of R. Shime'on b. Shetaḥ, etc. But the neighbour of the said Joseph was an evildoer by name Joḥanan the Wicked, a transgressor and adulterer, and Mary was a beauteous woman,' etc.

The last four lines of this text contain an obvious anachronism, since R. Simon Setacides lived in the reign of the Hasmonaean king Jannai and not under Herod ; they cannot, therefore, be derived from the genuine *Josippon*. But the italicized lines are an almost literal quotation from that work, all the more valuable since they come from the now lost passage on Jesus in the chapter concerning Tiberius which is quoted by R. Abraham Farissol.

[1] *B.J.*, iv. 4 *sqq.*

A second passage of interest in this connexion is found in another chapter of certain *Toldoth Jeshu* MSS.:[1] 'Jesus went into Upper Galilee. The wise men gathered together, went to the queen[2] and said to her: "Our Lady, he practises magic and seduces men." Therefore she sent horsemen against him . . . who tried to lead him away, but the men of Upper Galilee would not suffer it and made war.'

The last lines of this fanciful story are simply derived from the 'war' between the Pharisees and the followers of Jesus, as mentioned in the *Josippon*. A late reader could not imagine the Pharisee rabbis warring effectively against the 'robbers of the nation' and finally overpowering ''Ele'azar the robber.' So they substituted different vowels and read *parašîm*, 'horsemen,' for the *pərušîm* of the original text. This altered text was adopted by nearly every one of all extant *Toldoth Jeshu* versions. In the early redactions of the work, as quoted by ninth-century Christian writers such as Hrabanus Maurus and Agobard of Lyons, not the slightest trace of such violent armed conflicts is found, and the inevitable conclusion is that these episodes go back to no other source than the Hebrew version of Josephus, the *Josippon*, itself not anterior to the ninth century. If it could be proved that this in turn goes back to a lost paragraph of the Greek Josephus, we should possess an erratic block of most important historical information.

[1] Krauss, pp. 42-54.
[2] The widow of King Alexander Jannai, contemporary with R. Simon Setacides—both evident anachronisms in a history of Jesus.

VII

THE CONTROVERSY ON THE VALUE OF
THE SLAVONIC VERSION

' The stone which the builders refused is become the head stone
of the corner.'—*Ps.* cxviii. 22.

HARDLY one of the numerous scholars who have dealt
with the problems presented by the *Testimonium Flavianum* has taken the trouble to study the corresponding
portions of the Slavonic version of the *War*, not so much because
it was unknown or little known in Western and Central Europe as
rather because a number of hasty and superficial reviews [1] of the
first German translation of the fragments in question had given
an impression that the texts preserved in Russia were of no value
whatever.

The first Western scholar to mention the Slavonic version of the
War was N. Bonwetsch [2] as early as 1893. The important fact
that this Old Russian translation contains statements concerning
John the Baptist and Jesus, missing in the Greek standard text of
Josephus, was first pointed out by Andrej N. Popov (1866), the
discoverer and editor of the Slavonic *Book of Enoch*, who also published a part of the passages in question.[3] Further samples, from
another MS., were published by Ismail Sreznjevski.[4] Both publications were in Russian only.

Western Europe became acquainted with these materials
through the work of Alexander Berendts, professor of ecclesiastical
history at the Baltic University of Dorpat.[5] Yet his revelation
of the momentous chapters on John the Baptist and Jesus in a
Slavonic Josephus text was by no means hailed with that eager
enthusiasm which the author may have expected to arouse. Aside

---

[1] See the bibliography below, p. 624.

[2] *Die christlich vornicänische Literatur in slavischen Handschriften*, Appendix in
Harnack-Preuschen, *Geschichte der altchristlichen Literatur bis Eusebius*, i. 917.

[3] *Obzor chronografov russkoj redakcii (vypusk pervyj)*, Moscow, 1866, pp. 130,
134, 139 (in Russian). See Popov's portrait, on our Pl. xva.

[4] Nos. lxxxiv. and lxxxv. of his *Svěděnija i zamětki o maloizvěstnych i
neizvěstnych pamiatnikach*, suppl. to vol. xx., No. 4 of the *Sbornik otděstenija
russkago jazyka i slovesnosti*, 1879, p. 143 *sqq.* (in Russian). See Sreznjevski's
portrait, on our Pl. xvb.

[5] Gebhardt-Harnack,*Texte und Untersuchungen zur Geschichte der altchristlichen
Literatur*, xiv., No. 1, Leipzig, 1906. See Berendts' portrait on our Pl. xvia.

H

from the inevitable reaction to anything new, German liberal theologians would naturally feel inclined to adopt a severely critical
attitude against any publication hailing from Dorpat, then a
stronghold of Lutheran fundamentalism, which so unmistakably
bore the signs of a credulous readiness to accept any document at
its face value.

It must be admitted that the new source is indeed most apt to
arouse the scepticism of any serious historian ; for does it not contain such a late legend as the story of Jesus' miraculous healing of
Pilate's wife ? does it not tell how Pilate, because of this exploit,
dismissed the ' wonder-worker ' whom he had just arrested for
very good reasons, and how the Jewish scribes, moved by envy
against Jesus, bribed the governor with a gift of thirty talents
of silver ? Incredible as it may seem, Berendts accepted such
nonsense almost unreservedly as so many genuine statements of
Josephus. For one thing, his publication must be called hasty
and premature, since he had not taken time to study the MS.
material of the whole work. As it was, at the moment of his first
publication he had not yet all the decisive evidence which he could
have marshalled against his critics. When two years later [1] he
published a striking example of a momentous divergency between
the Russian and the Greek text, in the story concerning the false
Alexander, a divergency which could not possibly be attributed to
a Christian forger, it was too late. No one in Germany took the
slightest notice of this article. A subsequent one, showing that
the chapter of Hippolytus of Rome about the Essenes uses a text
of Josephus more akin to the Russian version than to the Greek
standard text, was politely returned by the editor of the *Zeitschrift
für neutestamentliche Wissenschaft*. All the later results of Berendts' persistent researches had to be printed in an obscure Baltic
Protestant church review which is almost unobtainable anywhere
outside Russia. The author died, sadly disappointed, in 1912—not,
however, without having laid, through his disinterested painstaking research work, a foundation on which other scholars, less
prejudiced than his critics, might yet build.

In fairness to these critics of his it must be admitted that he
lacked the critical acumen to do for the Slavic Josephus passages
what the late Théodore Reinach had done, with so much good sense
and sagacity, for the Greek text of *Antiquities*, xviii. 3. 3, namely,
to sift the obviously Christian additions from the original text with
its violent anti-Christian tendency.

In spite of these shortcomings of the Baltic pioneer, it is impossible to lay too much stress on the debt owed him by Western
scholarship, since he most unselfishly sacrificed twelve years of his
life to the difficult task of transcribing the various MSS., translat-

[1] *Z.N.T.W.*, ix. (1908), p. 47 *sqq.*

PLATE XV

(b) ISMAIL IVANOVIČ SREZNJEWSKI

FIRST EDITOR OF A NUMBER OF OTHER FRAGMENTS FROM THE
OLD RUSSIAN JOSEPHUS (1879)

(a) ANDREJ NIKOLAJEVIČ POPOV

DISCOVERER OF THE SLAVONIC 'BOOK OF ENOCH', AND OF THE
OLD RUSSIAN JOSEPHUS (1866)

(SEE P 113, NOTE 3)

ing and minutely comparing them with the Greek text, etc., without receiving any reward whatever. A debt of honour is also due, let us add, to the late Konrad Grass, a colleague of Berendts, to whose unfailing devotion we owe the posthumous publication of the *magnum opus* of Berendts, the annotated German translation of the first four books of the Slavonic Josephus' *O plenenie Jerusolima*, i.e. 'On the Capture of Jerusalem.' He, too, died, in November 1927, before he could enjoy the result of his painstaking work and witness the final justification of his late friend's incessant labours. (See our Pl. xvib.)

The materials utilized in the following pages consist, apart from the translation of Berendts and Grass, of an investigation undertaken by Prof. Vasilij N. Istrin on the Old Russian Josephus version. Of this text a number of specimens had been printed by Andrej N. Popov,[1] by Ismail Sreznjevski,[2] and by the late Prince Obolenski.[3] Prof. Istrin's essay, accompanied by numerous samples of the text,[4] has confirmed on a far larger basis Berendts' observation concerning the utilization of a Greek model by the Slavonic translator. A critical edition of the whole Old Russian text is being prepared by the same scholar, who had the kindness to place at my disposal a number of careful copies of the most important passages at variance with the Greek standard text of the *Jewish War*, and a copy of the chapter on Jesus of the Russian text in the possession of the former Clerical Academy of Moscow but emanating from the Volokolamski Convent. It so happened that Berendts, too, had completely copied this MS., the readings of which are thus doubly assured. Konrad Grass supplied complete copies (the work of Berendts) of all the chapters dealing with Christian origins. In the examination of the materials I was greatly helped by Prof. André Mazon of the Sorbonne, and by his pupils, M. Antoine Martel, fellow of the Fondation Thiers, and M. Boris Unbegaun, librarian of the Paris Institute of Slavonic Studies ; further, by occasional suggestions of Prof. N. van Wyck of Leyden, Prof. N. Bubnov of Kiev (now at Ljubljana), and Prof. Berndt von Arnim of Leyden. The great number of photostats used for these analyses have been contributed through the munificence of Mrs. Alice Chalmers in London and Dr. James Loeb in Murnau. There is no need to emphasize once more my feelings of sincere gratitude for such kind and generous cooperation, without which the present work could not have been carried through.

[1] See above, p. 113 n. 3.
[2] See above, p. 113 n. 4.
[3] *Der Chronograph von Perejaslawl Suzdalski*, in *Jahrb. d. k. Moskauer Ges. f. Gesch. u. Altert. Russlands*, ix. (1851).
[4] Festschr. f. Ljapunov, *Učenje Zapiski* of the Municipal University of Odessa, sect. sc. hum. et soc., ii., 1921, pp. 27-40.

The publication of Alexander Berendts' momentous discovery aroused a certain amount of interest in European countries, and was the centre of a considerable number of critical discussions in the various learned periodicals. The disposition of the present book made it desirable to confine myself to adding a mere bibliography of this literature.[1]   Yet I should like to draw attention to the fact that every single argument of these authors has been most carefully considered, and every previous objection to the authenticity of the Russian text refuted in all details, in the German edition of this book.[2]

For the general information of the English reader it may suffice to state that Berendts' critics were prone to prove the spuriousness of his texts by pointing out the numerous contradictions between them and the Greek original.   They forgot, alas! that Josephus was such a superficial and shallow compiler that even the Greek texts we possess from his pen are full of similar and even worse contradictions, a number of which, highly amusing in themselves, are treated fully in a subsequent chapter.

THE MS. TRANSMISSION OF THE SLAVONIC 'CAPTURE OF JERUSALEM'

The Slavonic translation of the *Jewish War*, or, to be more exact, of the Greek treatise περὶ ἁλώσεως Ἰερουσαλήμ, is written in Old Russian, more particularly in the dialect of Kiev—a language slightly different from Old Slavonic, i.e. the Old Bulgarian of the Church—and has come down in sixteen MSS.   There exists, moreover, a Servian translation from the Russian in a MS. of the Chilandari Lavra of Mt. Athos, dating from A.D. 1585, and in another copy in one of the monasteries of the Fruška Gora in Syrmia ; and there are a number of fragments in Rumanian on the life of John the Baptist and Jesus, translated, according to the express statement of the scribe, from the Polish, in a MS. of Dr. Moses Gaster's library in London.   These facts make it more than likely that there never was a South Slavonic Josephus, and that the translation is the work of a Northern Slav.

In view of the importance of the whole problem, a careful examination of the MS. material is indispensable.   The Old Russian MSS. may be divided into two different classes, as follows :—

---

[1] See App. xxv.
[2] Dr. W. Emery Barnes, *The Journal of Theol. Stud.*, 1928, p. 68, is quite justified in saying that the German edition of this book 'is heavily overladen with the discussion of scholars from the sixteenth century downwards.'   Still, this inventory of all previous discussions had to be drawn up once, were it only to prevent critics from repeating again and again arguments put forward and refuted long ago, by reference to positive facts formerly ignored or overlooked since.

PLATE XVI

(b) KONRAD GRASS
1870—1927

BERENDT'S COLLEAGUE, FRIEND AND EDITOR OF HIS POST-
HUMOUS TRANSLATION OF THE SLAVONIC JOSEPHUS

(SEE P. 115, LINES 1 FF.)

(a) ALEXANDER JOHANNES BERENDTS
1863—1912

WHO INTRODUCED THE SLAVONIC JOSEPHUS TO THE KNOW-
LEDGE OF WESTERN SCHOLARSHIP

(SEE P 113, NOTE 5)

Class A

1. Cod. Moscow Academy 651 (=cod. 227 of the Volokolamski Monastery), 16th cent., now in the Academy Library, *Sergiev Possade*).
2. Cod. of the Floriščev Hermitage 93/110 (date unknown to me), now probably in possession of the Commission of Scientific Archivists in the city of Vladimir (Kljazma).
3. Cod. Kasan (Clerical Academy 444/322), 16th cent.
4. Cod. Kasan (Clerical Academy 445/325), almost identical with No. 3, 16th cent.
5 and 6. (Copies of 4.) Cod. Kasan 446/323 and 447/324, 16th cent.
7. Cod. Moscow Synodal Library 770, 16th-17th cent.
8. Cod. Barsov No. 633, in the Moscow Musée Historique, unknown to Berendts ; according to information kindly supplied by the director, Mr. N. Popov, an *apographon* of the same exemplar as No. 7.
9. Cod. Moscow Synodal Library 991 (=Cod. Uspenski, a complete Četji-Minei (monthly lectionary) of the Metropolitan Makarius (1542-1563), the Josephus occupying foll. 771-890 in the February volume).
10. Cod. Moscow Synodal Library 178 (=cod. of the Czar, of the same Četji-Minei, January vol., foll. 797-917).
11. Cod. Moscow Synodal Library 182, a work of the same class, July vol., foll. 856-953. Nos. 7-11 are now in the Moscow Musée Historique.
12-13. Three MSS. from the Kyrillo-Běloserski Monastery, now in the Leningrad Public Library, in Berendts' time in the library of the former Petersburg Clerical Academy, viz. 63/1302 (15th cent.), 64/1303 (16th cent.), 65/1304 (15th or 16th cent.).[1] These have not been copied by Berendts, but have been photographed for me through the kindness of Dr. James Loeb in Murnau.

All the Moscow MSS. have now been photographed for Prof. Sol. Zeitlin of Dropsie College, Philadelphia, Pa.

---

[1] A fourth MS. of Leningrad—*Petrogradskaya Duchovnaia Acad.*, No. 262— pointed out to me by Prof. Beneševič and duly catalogued in the German edition of this book, has since been found by Prof. Sol. Zeitlin to contain a Russian version of the Hebrew *Josippon* and not the Slavonic *Josephus* (specimen photographs reproduced in *Jew. Quart. Rev.*, N.S. xix., 1929, pp. 1, 6-7). The MS. Synod No. 745, now in the Historic Museum of Moscow, which Zeitlin reproduces —without any signature!—on pp. 10-11 and 26-27, is not a Slavonic *Josephus* either but is a Christianized *Josippon*. I do not know whether the MS. reproduced by Zeitlin as ' Leningrad No. 343 ' on pp. 30-31 *loc. cit.* is or is not identical with any of the enumerated MSS. studied by Berendts.

Class B

This class consists of the MSS. of the so-called Russian chronographers, containing the Old Russian text of Josephus in the same translation as it appears in the above-mentioned MSS., but cut up and inserted between portions of the Chronicles of John Malalas, Georgius Hamartolus, and others, in one case (No. 16) annexed to the historical books of the Bible.

14. Cod. misc. 279/658 of the Central Archives of the Foreign Office, Moscow (15th cent.).[1] The text of Josephus is interspersed throughout the Chronicle of Malalas, to which is appended the so-called Chronographer of Perejaslavl Suzdalski, extending to the year 1214. According to a note in the MS., unfortunately not reproduced by Berendts, it is a copy of another MS. begun in the year 1261. We are told by Jagić that in the year 1882 Theodor Mommsen wished to have this MS. sent to Berlin, but was unable to obtain it because an unnamed Russian was said to be engaged upon an edition of it. Nothing has ever been heard of his work. Had Mommsen obtained the codex we should probably have had a scientific edition of the Old Slavonic version of Malalas forty years ago, and it would no doubt have exercised a decisive influence on the whole development of our knowledge of Christian origins. For a critical edition of the Old Russian Josephus, produced under Mommsen's eagle eye, with a detailed investigation of the state of the tradition, the investigations, and the like, would have been available at the right moment for Niese's great edition of the Greek *Polemos*.

15. Closely related to 15 was cod. 109/147 of the Vilna Public (now University) Library. This MS. was not used by Berendts. Through the kind services of Prof. O. von Halecki of the University of Warsaw and of Dr. K. Chodynicki, professor at the University of Vilna, I had hoped to have it sent for me to Paris; unfortunately, the inquiries undertaken by these gentlemen have shown that it was carried off by the Russians in their retreat of 1915. Prof. Beneševič of Leningrad has since kindly ascertained for me the sad truth, that it perished in a fire during the troubles of 1919. The Josephus portions in it were interspersed between passages from Malalas, Georgius Hamartolus, the Gospels, and various apocrypha.

16. Lastly, in the library formerly belonging to Count Uvarov, which is now in the Musée Historique in Moscow, there is

---

[1] Now in the Zentroarchiv, Moscow, Vagankov Pereolouk.

a half-uncial MS. (cod. 3/18) of the 15th century, in which Josephus occupies foll. 409-533, as an appendix to the historical books of the Bible.

Now that we know through Jerahm'el ben Shelomo (above, p. 83 n. 1)—what Berendts and the Russian scholars ignored—that Josephus published a second edition in twenty-four books, beginning with Adam and reaching to the fourteenth year of Domitian, it remains to be seen whether these MSS. are really late Byzantine compilations, or whether they are not by any chance translations of the lost twenty-four books of Josephus, perhaps overworked and christianized, on which the Byzantine chroniclers might themselves be dependent.

THE TITLE OF THE OLD RUSSIAN JOSEPHUS

As Prof. Laqueur has shown, the very title chosen by Josephus for his work, *The Jewish War*, clearly indicates his own position within the Roman camp. The Romans, not the Carthaginians, speak of the ' bellum Punicum ' ; Caesar, not Vercingetorix, of the ' bellum Gallicum.' The matter is exactly the same as if an Englishman referred to the South African War, not as the ' Boer War ' but as the ' English War.' Now, the fact that Berendts had chosen the title of ' Josephus' *Jewish War* ' for his Russian version might itself have induced the critics to doubt the validity of his assumption that the work in question ever was a redaction destined for the Oriental Jews. As a matter of fact, Berendts had no MS. basis whatever for his title. Neither the chronographers nor the first book of the work, with its first part missing, give a title on the frontispiece. The first MS. title is found at the beginning of the second book. It says nothing about a ' Jewish War,' but reads, ' Second Book of Josephus on the Conquest of Jerusalem,' similar in this to the eleventh-century Codex Vaticanus (V) of the Greek text, which is inscribed Ἰωσήπου περὶ ἁλώσεως λόγος δεύτερος. In both cases even the surname ' Flavius ' of the imperial client is absent. It is clear that there are good reasons why the various Greek MSS. as well as the ancient quotations show such different titles as the ' Jewish War ' or the ' Jewish War against the Romans,' or the ' Capture of Jerusalem.'[1] Josephus, it is true, had become used to quoting his book as the ' Jewish War,' according to the

---

[1] Origen, *Selecta in Threnos*, opp. iii. 348, De la Rue, xiii. 211 : " Ἰώσηπος γὰρ ἐν τοῖς περὶ ἁλώσεως." St. Jerome, *Comm. in Jesaiam*, c. 64, s. fine (opp. ed. Vallarsi, iv. 766) : ' quae Josephus Judaïcae scriptor historiae septem explicat voluminibus, quibus imposuit titulum Captivitatis Judaïcae id est περὶ ἁλώσεως ' (Vallarsi, ii. 343). Id., *De vir. illustr.*, c. 13 (Vallarsi, ii. 851). *Chronicon paschale*, ed. Dindorf, i. 463: " Ἰώσηπος ἱστορεῖ ἐν τῷ πέμπτῳ λόγῳ τῆς Ἁλώσεως." Isidor. Pelus., lib iv. epist. 225, P.G. 78, 1320: " Ἰωσήπου . . . Ἰουδαίου . . . περὶ τῆς Ἁλώσεως ἱστορία." See also the quotation by Suidas, below, p. 120 n. 2.

point of view of his Roman readers. Still, most MSS. have the title
περὶ ἁλώσεως,[1] without the addition of the word 'Jerusalem'
found in the Slavonic texts.

Yet in this abridged form no Roman or Greek reader would
have understood what was meant. Ἰωσήπου περὶ ἁλώσεως might
mean 'Josephus on his own captivity,' a title corresponding to the
Latin *Historia Josephi captivi*, which does occur in several MSS. of
the *Egesippus*.[2] When St. Jerome speaks of the '*titulus Captivitatis Judaicae id est* περὶ ἁλώσεως,' he, as well as the MSS. of the
Egesippus referred to before, must have thought of the Aramaic
expression *galutha*, Hebrew *golah*, 'exile,' in a vaguer sense an
equivalent of 'captivity,' which is used in an identical manner.
As a matter of fact, *sefer hag-golah*, or *sifra de galutha*, would have
been fitting titles for the book of Josephus, and the ambiguity
arising from them, in that the captivity of the author might be
implied, would have been considered as a clever artifice of style in
any Semitic dialect. It may be that he chose this title when he
had no other project than to write his own justification, i.e. to
explain why he himself preferred captivity to an honourable death,
and I personally think such a view extremely likely. Later on,
when the scope of the work grew, he probably changed the title
to the form still extant in the Russian version by adding 'of Jerusalem.' His Roman editions were given the title of *Jewish War*,
necessarily as distasteful to his compatriots as his Latin cognomen
'Flavius.' Hence, when he prepared his final edition, after the
publication of his *Antiquities*, for which he needed Jewish readers
and Jewish sympathies, he preferred to change the title again into
Φλαυίου Ἰωσήπου Ἑβραίου ἱστορία Ἰουδαϊκοῦ πολέμου πρὸς
Ῥωμαίους, a form still preserved in the *Codex Parisinus*, and with
its awkward mixing of two incompatible points of view an excellent
proof of how little Josephus, even at the end of his literary career,
had entered into the spirit of the Greek language.

The Remains of the Genuine Preface to the 'Halōsis'

It was not to be supposed from the beginning that a work of
the type of this translation of Josephus into Old Russian was
done independently by two people twice in succession. On the
contrary, a single translator may safely be assumed. This translator evidently started his work on a Greek text the first part of
which had come down to him in very poor shape. Later on he

---

[1] Niese, ed. maior, vol. i., proleg. p. vi ; vol. vi. p. 3.
[2] E.g. *Codex Vatic. Palat.*, 170 (ninth century). See also below, p. 482, the
quotation from Suidas, s.v. Ἰησοῦς: " εὕρομεν οὖν Ἰώσηπον τὸν συγγραφέα τῆς Ἁλώσεως
Ἱεροσολύμων φανερῶς λέγοντα ἐν τοῖς τῆς αἰχμαλωσίας αὐτοῦ ὑπομνήμασιν. . . ."

managed to find a better MS. and thus to complete his work. For it is to be noted that the MSS. of class *A* begin with chapter xxv. of the first book in the middle of the text, so that no other explanation is possible.

There is further a gap between ii. 18, § 505, and iii. 2, § 28, owing to a missing leaf, and the scribe does not even appear to have been aware of the fact. For he jumped from the end of § 505 in Book ii. 18 (ὑπέστρεψεν εἰς τὴν Πτολεμαίδα), and without punctuation, into the middle of § 27 of Book iii. 2. In English translation the passage in question then reads as follows :

'. . . he turned back to Ptolemais // and in entering there he saved himself from the fire ///, and on the third day he came out and made himself heard by his people, thereby filling them with unexpected joy at having got back the general for the fight to come.
'Third Book of Josephus on the Capture of Jerusalem. Of Vespasian. Vespasian took over the chief command in Asia,' etc.

At the place marked /// there commences the verso of fol. 108 ; at the place marked // (not at all noticeable in the MS.) there is the leap from the second to the third book, not noticed by the scribe, evidently because a number of pages had fallen out. Only in the following paragraph there follows the title, ' Third Book of Josephus,' etc., of course put in at a later date, which ought to stand at the place marked //. The translator then connected mechanically the end of the missing story of the escape of the Peraïte Niger with the narrative of the return of Cestius Gallus to Ptolemais, and added the title, taken from the running title on the top of the page, after the first paragraph of a recto page of his model. It is clearly a case of a damaged exemplar, from which fact no further conclusions can be drawn for the original text of the *Halōsis*.

Much the same thing obtains for §§ 45-71 of the third book, missing in all the MSS. of group *A*, a gap likewise caused by loss of pages. It is to be regretted that Berendts failed to supplement his MS. with the help of the MS. of the Moscow Principal Archive, since, for the reasons discussed above,[1] it would have been useful to compare the Slavonic version of Josephus' description of Palestine with the corresponding passages in the Greek *Polemos*.

The Slavonic MSS. of class *A* are headed by an introduction which, in spite of its confused form, was recognized by Berendts as part of a preface preceding the original *Halōsis* of Josephus. The text is full of the author's favourite attacks on the Zealots, whom he accuses, rightly or wrongly, of being responsible for the national catastrophe. It contains furthermore Josephus' self-defence against attacks made on him, and not without foundation, by those very Zealots ; while in the Greek *War* he engages in

---

[1] Cf. p. 88 l. 31.

polemics not against his Jewish adversaries but against certain
Greek writers who have distorted the facts for the purpose of
flattering the Romans. The confused form of this introduction
finds its explanation in the fact that in the book whole pages were
lost, for it is well known that in a bound codex of this type very
often only the first and second pages remain, thanks to their
closer attachment to the cover, whilst the following pages are as a
rule the first to become detached. The first and second pages
naturally contained title and preface. The cause responsible for
the loss of the parts discussed above had for a consequence the
damaging of the said first and second pages. To make up for this,
a reader seems to have added below or above the damaged parts
—from another copy—portions of the text which had become more
or less illegible. A later copyist must have inserted those passages,
sometimes in the wrong place, thereby causing the textual confusion referred to. A rearrangement of the text is, then, not only
permissible but necessary if we want to get some order into this
chaos and arrive at a logical and coherent text. By a comparison
of the extant and the rearranged texts, placed side by side, the
reader may convince himself that no undue liberty has been taken
with the former.

Preface as translated by Berendts from the MSS.

' There precedes [1] a story of the
Herods and
the history of the kings, well-
known matters,
and of that which comes after,
the lesser deeds of each prince
and dynast,
because in much (?) in the midst
of Archelaus and
Herod, of Antipater and Alexander, the son-in-law
of Archelaus, and of Pheroras
and of Salome
and of all the rest unceasingly (?),
vain pride kept itself, daring to
resist the majesty of truth and
to put up the opposite and
greater ones.
Such will be caught in their own
nets,
as will be said in the following

Suggested restoration of the Preface.

' The story of the Herodeans and
(of the Conquest of Jerusalem)
is preceded by the history of the
kings, matters of common
knowledge.
What follows (I will tell in full
detail) :
the (greater and) lesser deeds of
each prince and dynast
. . . .
of Archelaus Herod, of Antipater
and Alexander, the son-in-law
of Archelaus, and Pheroras
and of Salome and the rest. . . .
. . . .
(By internal dissension the
country suffered terrible
things),
because in many of the grandees
there maintained itself a vain
pride, as they dared to resist

[1] I follow in the main the *Cod. Mosqu. Acad.*, No. 651, fol. 1 recto. A full list
of variants will be found in the German edition, i. p. 244 *sq.*

(sequel)	the majesty (Christian interpol.: *the Truth*)
where the order will show the proper time. For the godless Zealots were constantly egged on to slander, both by stinking aspersions and by inventing words of discontent, which is filled with deadly poison. And in such tumults Archelaus was angry at his son-in-law Alexander, then Herod was angry at Pheroras and Salome on account of the quantity of their wickedness. And after that Pheroras was accused by Herod of a crime. . . .	and to put up the opposite. Suchlike will be caught in their own nets, as will be told in the sequel, where the proper order (of the narrative) will indicate the true time (of each event).[1] For the Zealots of godlessness [2] are constantly egged on to slander, both by stinking aspersions and words of discontent, inventing what is filled with deadly poison.

The concluding sentence, ' and in such tumults . . . crime,' is the unsatisfactory attempt of the translator to construct a bridge between preface and text. He evidently knew nothing of the original preface, and had to rely entirely on what he still found in the damaged first pages. Yet there can be no doubt that what preceded was precisely the original preface to the *Halōsis*, replaced later on, in the edition addressed to a circle of Graeco-Roman readers, by the extant *procemium*.

THE VARIOUS ENDINGS OF THE OLD RUSSIAN JOSEPHUS MSS.

From the final event recorded in an historical document it is generally possible to determine the date of publication, at least the so-called ' terminus post quem.' The MSS. of group *A* (above, p. 117) form no exception to this rule. The Greek *War* and the Slavonic chronographer's version begin with a mention of the schism between the two factions of the Jerusalem hierocracy and of the high priest Onias, the founder of the temple of Heliopolis. One of the Old Russian MSS.[3] ends accordingly with Vespasian's order to destroy the temple of Heliopolis. This appears to be the only

---

[1] The chronology was indeed of the first importance to the old scoundrel, who had weighty reasons for concealing as much as possible the influence which his own doubtful actions had on the outbreak of the revolution.

[2] Cf. *B.J.*, iv. § 161 ; vii. §§ 268-270. The contrary term, ' zealots of good works,' *Tim.* ii. 14 ; 1 *Peter* iii. 13 ; ' of virtue,' Philo, *de praem.* 11.

[3] *Cod. Syn. Mosq.* 991, f⁰ 878 v⁰. Berendts-Grass, p. 16.

reason why Josephus goes back to an event of the age of the Hasmonaeans in spite of his having announced in the preface that he is not going to repeat what may be read in the books of Maccabees. As is well known, Josephus himself belonged to the class of Jerusalemite priests who regarded with utmost horror the rival sanctuary of Heliopolis.[1] He also seems to have laboured under the pious illusion that the time between the foundation and the destruction of the temple of Heliopolis amounted to exactly 343— i.e. seven times seven times seven—years.[2] If one remembers his conviction that the ultimate captivity was caused through the dissension among the Jews under Aristobulus and Hyrcanus, which made it possible for Pompeius to intervene and to take Jerusalem, it is clear that he regarded the destruction of both temples as the just punishment of God for the transgression of the Deuteronomic law prohibiting the setting up of a rival sanctuary. Hence the curious idea to begin his narrative with the foundation of the temple of Heliopolis and to end it with its destruction.

Yet he cannot have formed this plan before A.D. 73, the date when the temple of Heliopolis was actually desecrated. In fact, such a scheme was still foreign to him when he composed the extant Greek prologue—which contains a table of contents ending with the triumph of Titus—and the preface which has been preserved in the Old Russian translation. The codex of the Moscow Ecclesiastical Academy 651 (227) has the standard epilogue after vii. 10. 1, § 419, which means that the destruction of the temple of Heliopolis was not even mentioned at this stage of the work. There was therefore not the slightest reason why in such an edition Josephus should have spoken, at the beginning, of the foundation of that temple. Nor was there then any reason for Josephus mentioning events going back to the time of Antiochus Epiphanēs. It stands to reason, then, that originally Josephus began his work with the rivalry of Hyrcanus and Aristobulus, which marks also the beginning of the Herodian dynasty, that is, with chapter vi. of the standard edition. The peculiar rhetorical ring of the introduction to this chapter would certainly bear out such an assumption. It was doubtless logical to begin the narrative with the origins of the dynasty which was still reigning when the catastrophe occurred. Only after the destruction of the temple of Heliopolis did he conceive the idea of rearranging his work in the sense indicated. This important fact settles the date of the Greek original of the codex of the Moscow Ecclesiastical Academy as being posterior to the fall of Masada (April of A.D. 73), after the Alexandrian tumults and the massacre of the Jews at Thebes, yet prior to the imperial decree concerning the temple of Heliopolis.

The chief result of the foregoing considerations is the following

---

[1] *Ant.*, xiii. 3. 1-2.　　　　[2] *B.J.*, vii. § 436.

development of Josephus' work, which grew under his hands, as it were:

1. His first project began with the rivalry of Hyrcanus and Aristobulus and ended with the triumph of Titus, described, no doubt, according to the official programme which had been placed at his disposal before the event. It is probable that the book was given in this form to Titus and some generals of the headquarters before Jerusalem shortly after the triumph (end of June of A.D. 71).

2. Josephus went on completing his work with the help of the official reports placed at his disposal by the imperial administration. The pieces added at the end of the seventh book are: the conquest of Machaerus by Lucilius Bassus (chap. vi.), the deposition of the King of Commagene in A.D. 72 (chap. vii.), the conquest of Masada in A.D. 73 (chaps. viii. and ix.), and the tumults of Alexandria and Thebes (chap. x.). This redaction is at the base of the codex of the Moscow Ecclesiastical Academy. A MS. of the same class was also utilized by Isaac-Hilarius for the so-called 'Egesippus.'

3. Josephus heard the news of Vespasian's decree concerning the levelling of the temple of Heliopolis. He believed he could now discern the Divine plan and meaning of the general punishment inflicted upon the Jews, and proceeded to fit his work into such a historico-philosophical scheme. He added chapters i. to v. of the first book, without, however, changing the preface.

4. The destruction of the temple of Heliopolis could not be carried out immediately, because it was too difficult to tear down the megalithic structure of the tower-like building. The consequence was a somewhat drawn-out correspondence between the governor of Egypt and the imperial chancellery. From this correspondence Josephus gathered his information as to the shape and the cult utensils of that sanctuary, information which he duly utilized for his next redaction.[1]

5. The last addition concerned the events of Cyrene, where a poor weaver, in Josephus' eyes a misguided fanatic, had started a revolutionary exodus into the desert, at the head of a band of paupers. The wealthy Jews, for obvious reasons not favourably disposed toward such an attempt at 'rebedouinizing' Israel (below, p. 362 n. 4), duly informed the Roman governor, Catullus, who had the pious pilgrims overtaken and cut down by his cavalry. This did not help the wealthy Jews very much, since the clever governor, coveting the booty of rich confiscations and wishing to curry favour at Rome, managed to involve a number of them in the scandal.

It is highly significant that this § 446 is the point to which the narrative of Josephus extends in the form presented by the so-called chronographer's text, i.e. in the MS. in the archives of the

---

[1] B.J., vii. 427; cp. i. § 33.

Moscow Foreign Office (No. 15). Nothing could more precisely mark the date of composition of the archetype of the Josephus MS. utilized by the Russian translator for a second edition of his work, in order to supply the initial lacuna in his first imperfect edition, than the passage which in the Greek edition of the *War* immediately follows the point where the Russian text closes. There we read (§§ 447-451) :

> ' Moreover, to prevent any Jews elsewhere from exposing his iniquity, he extended his lies further afield, and prevailed on Jonathan and some others who had been arrested along with him to bring a charge of sedition against the most reputable Jews both in Alexandria and in Rome. Among those thus insidiously incriminated was Josephus, the author of this history. The upshot, however, of the scheme did not answer to Catullus' expectations. For he came to Rome, bringing Jonathan and his associates in chains, in the belief that the false accusations brought up before him and at his instance would be the end of the enquiry. But Vespasian, having his suspicions of the affair, investigated the facts ; and discovering that the charge preferred against these men was unjust, he on the intercession of Titus acquitted them, and inflicted on Jonathan the punishment that he had deserved. He was first tortured and then burnt alive. Catullus on that occasion, owing to the lenity of the emperors, suffered nothing worse than a reprimand. . . .'

When Josephus produced the edition preserved in the writings of the Russian chronographers, it is possible that he was not yet fully aware of the storm which was brewing over his head ; or it may be that he simply did not think it advisable to make any mention of the affair. One can readily conceive that he was told nothing about his accusation until after the investigation. There was doubtless an element of truth in the allegations of Jonathan, for, as Josephus himself admits, great hopes had been placed by the insurgents upon a rising of the western diaspora, and letters and money must certainly have passed on that occasion. Jonathan himself was probably an emissary of the type of those Syrian travelling agitators who had aroused the suspicion of the Emperor Claudius,[1] so much so that he forbade their being received and sheltered in Alexandria. Since Josephus can be shown in his earlier days to have fomented the revolt in Galilee, it is quite possible that Jonathan was in possession of incriminating documents. Josephus, however, had succeeded in lulling the emperors into the belief that whatever he had schemed then he had done in his official capacity as a general under the Jewish government of Jerusalem, and he had of course obtained full pardon for his actions

---

[1] H. Idris Bell, *Jews and Christians in Egypt*, London, 1924, p. 25. "μηδὲ ἐπάγεσθαι μηδὲ προσείεσθαι καταπλέοντας ἀπὸ Συρίας . . . καθάπερ ἐξεγείροντάς τινα νόσον κοινὴν τῆς οἰκουμένης."

in open war. Thus it is clear why an exposure of the type attempted by Catullus and his former accomplices had to fall to the ground if he could prove that the incriminating actions belonged to the period of his life preceding his capture by the Romans at Jotapata in A.D. 66.[1]

To sum up : the Old Russian version was based on two different MSS., representing two different redactions of the author's seven books ' on the capture of Jerusalem.' The unknown translator began his work with a badly mutilated MS. of the edition completed before Josephus learned the news of the fall of the Heliopolitan sanctuary. On further search he discovered more perfect MSS. As far as may be judged from the statements of Berendts,[2] in the course of time he managed to obtain at least two more MSS., distinguishable by their different endings. The Old Russian Josephus, which is at all events [3] prior to 1260, was circulated by its author in different editions, alike in this to the Greek Josephus and to many mediaeval histories.[4] So far as our present knowledge permits us to judge, none of the Russian MSS. contains the final paragraphs about the accusation brought against Josephus by Catullus and Jonathan. This proves that the Greek originals of the Russian must have been older than the oldest form of the Greek text, which was not published until after that affair. The interval which may have elapsed between the various editions must remain a matter of doubt. If Josephus hastened to inform the universe of his little affair and his glorious acquittal, as well he might, the complete edition may have seen the light as early as A.D. 73 ; for the judicial enquiry itself certainly did not last more than a few months at the very most.

On the other hand, it is well to bear in mind also the following facts. The standard edition of the *War* contains quite late additions, as for example the paragraph, vii. 158, on the *templum Pacis*, inaugurated in A.D. 75, and it is therefore possible that the chapter on his affair with the Cyrenaean Jews is just such a belated addition, perhaps composed about A.D. 81, when at the beginning of the reign of Domitian he had again been accused of high treason.[5] For it was then in his interest to give the Romans the impression that the whole matter was essentially a *res iudicata*, a thing of the past. That such was the case is proved by the fact that the dedication of the temple of Peace is actually found in the Old Russian translation. The Greek original was then an edition posterior to A.D. 75, yet it did not contain the affair of Catullus. We may then safely conclude that the latter was indeed added in the reign of Domitian on

---

[1] This is the reason why he is so particular about the ' chronology of events ' (see the preface above, p. 123 n. 1).
[2] Berendts-Grass, *loc. cit.*   [3] See below, p. 148.
[4] E.g. Ekkehard of Aura.
[5] *Vita*, § 429.

the occasion of the second accusation of the author. The *Halōsis* dates, therefore, from the reigns of Vespasian and Titus, whilst the *Polemos* did not appear until the time of Domitian. This result concerning the general working method of Josephus is fully corroborated by prior investigations of Prof. Laqueur [1] regarding two different editions of the *Antiquities* distinguishable by their different endings.

THE DATE OF THE GREEK ORIGINAL OF THE SLAVONIC TEXT

Having thus endeavoured to shed some light on the importance of the Russian versions for the study of Josephus' work, we must now enter upon the important question of the Greek original from which this translation is derived. A very good point of attack is furnished by a curious passage in the thirty-first chapter of the first book. Here the *Halōsis* reads as follows :

'And thereafter he (i.e. Antipater, living in Rome) gave large presents to the Roman authorities, and he induced them to write letters in praise of himself to Herod. And after the *Italians*, who are called *Latins*, had received the presents, they wrote such praise of Antipater as cannot be expressed. . . . *For such are the Latins : they run to accept presents and break their oath for the sake of presents. And they see no sin in calumny, saying, "With words have we spoken, but we have not killed (any one) ourselves," those accursed wretches thinking that he is a murderer who kills with the hand, but that calumny and denunciation and fomenting against one's neighbour are not murder. Had they known the law of God, they would have been shown long since what a murderer is. But they are aliens and our doctrine touches them not.* Therefore did they lie against the two sons of Herod, who were then being educated in Rome, Archelaus (and) Philip, and wrote so that he should kill them. But Herod, who had fortified his mind against external things and as a consequence of the first interrogatory, did not attach much credit to the Roman letters.'

What strikes the reader in this passage is the severe and general condemnation of the Romans and the allegation of their ignorance of the Mosaic law as the only cause of their moral perversion. The party exclaimed against is evidently that of the Roman grandees, whose venality is insisted upon. Yet at the same time they are referred to as ' Latins ' or even ' Italians,' though there can be no talk about non-Roman Italians and still less of Romanized provincials. For the scene of the story is the capital, and in a parallel passage which immediately follows the Romans alone occur :

'And he (Antipater) was delighted and made a sumptuous dinner for his travelling companions and for the Romans, who through

---

[1] *Der jüdische Historiker Flavius Josephus*, Giessen, 1920, p. 5.

flattery had received from him 300 talents. *For they are insatiable in receiving*; but if to-day any one gives them more, to-morrow they want (still) more. And as the sea cannot be filled, nor hell satisfied, nor woman's passion, even so are the Romans insatiable in receiving. In truth they are Solomon's leeches,[1] people who give their body and soul for a reward. Nay, they are ready to give their limbs and their brothers and children, some by converting natural boldness and audacity into manliness, others by being as greedy after gold as the ravens on a corpse. Many also for some such thing are prepared to surrender cities, as also their generals (and their clothing). We must describe them in the sequel ; but for the present we (will) relate the matter in hand.'

To begin with, we may say with full assurance that expressions such as ' Italians ' and ' Latins ' as a designation for the Romans are unknown in Josephus. We are therefore evidently dealing with the corrections of a Byzantine copyist anxious to distinguish the Byzantines, who still called themselves Ῥωμαῖοι, from the Western Romans. Such an antagonism is indeed quite possible, in the Byzantine empire, from the time of the schism between the Pope of Rome and the Patriarch of Constantinople. But a hatred against Italians as such is improbable between 733—when Sicily and the south of Italy were placed under the crozier of the Byzantine Patriarch—and 1138, when Naples was finally lost to the Normans. ' Thus the whole expression rather points to the period of the most bitter hatred of all Greeks for the Venetians, Genoese, and the other 'Italians' who possessed most of the Greek islands ; that is to say, it most probably dates from the time of the Latin empire (1204-61). Now, it is noteworthy that the year 1261-62, when the scribes of the Moscow Archival codex and of the Vilna MS. began their work, was also the year when the Palaeologi returned to Constantinople after the downfall of the Latin empire. It is therefore probable that the Greek original was written about half a century previously by a Byzantine cleric in Constantinople or somewhere in Asia Minor, for this would explain perfectly the substitution of the terms ' Italians ' and ' Latins ' for ' Romans ' in the invective of Josephus.

But the problem does not end there. The invective itself cannot be the work of the Old Russian translator, who had obviously no reason for hating Romans—Latins or Italians. Moreover, the Jewish provenience of the passage in question is perfectly clear. So the only two persons who can have been responsible for it are either the hypothetical Jewish interpolator proposed by Dr. R. Seeberg and Johannes Frey, or Josephus himself. If the passage is genuine, it goes without saying that it cannot have stood in a Greek book destined for Vespasian and Titus.

---

[1] An allusion to *Prov. Sol.*, xxx. 15, characteristic of the familiarity of the author and his presumptive public with the Old Testament.

Furthermore, it is evident that the original of the Russian text was Greek, as is proved by the substitution of ' Italians ' and ' Latins ' for ' Romans ' by a Byzantine clerk, by a number of Greek words taken over literally by the Russian,[1] and, above all, by the easy retroversion of certain difficult passages,[2] ill understood by the translator.　But it is altogether improbable that a Byzantine author of the thirteenth century, possessing the *Polemos* in its standard form, should have translated a defective Semitic *Halōsis* into Greek.　In the first place, only a baptized Jew would have had the prerequisite linguistic equipment; in the second place, this man (who would most certainly have left a name behind him) would have to have had the most pronounced purely philologico-critical interests to undertake such a task, a thing quite inconceivable in the Middle Ages.　In the third place, the Semitic Josephus, if the Byzantines still knew him as late as the thirteenth century, would still be known, if only through allusions and quotations.　As a matter of fact, the Jews of Illyria [3] had to translate the second edition of the *Polemos* and the *Antiquities* back from Greek and Latin into Hebrew in the ninth century.

A translation of the Semitic Josephus into Greek was perfectly useless from the moment when Josephus himself had edited his work in an improved and revised Greek edition—that is, as early as the summer of A.D. 71 or, at the very latest, in the summer of 73. Even if it be supposed that this Semitic edition contained material of interest for the Greek Church, it would have been sufficient to translate just those, and no one would have dreamt of performing such a task for the whole work.　One might further assume that the opponents of Josephus would in due time have called the attention of the Roman authorities, especially in the reign of Domitian, to those compromising passages, and it is likely enough that they did so.　The pedagogue of Josephus' son, i.e. an educated Greek slave who may originally have been one of his secretaries, may well have brought forward just such an accusation.[4]　But for such a purpose the Semitic copy would have perfectly sufficed if the two passages themselves were translated into Greek.　Yet even such an accusation would not necessarily prove fatal.　The wily parasite would simply have declared that the passages in question had been interpolated by his enemies,[5] who had bribed his secretaries.　As a matter of fact, the existence of the invectives is explained entirely by Josephus' well-known carelessness in revising the copies made by his *servi librarii*, of which the reader has by this time had enough

---

[1] E.g. *igemon, metropolja, archierei, skinopigja, katapetasma, aramatji*.　In ii. § 361 Berendts-Grass, p. 308₄, ἀδοξεῖτε is not translated but transcribed *adoxite* in the Russian version, etc.

[2] See below, p. 516.　Some of the proper names are quoted in their Greek form, e.g. below, p. 137 l. 23, Ananos not Ḥanan, etc.

[3] See above, p. 78 n. 1.　　　　[4] *Vita*, § 429.　　　　[5] Cp. *Vita*, § 337.

examples. As a result of this lack of proper ' proof-reading,' as we should say nowadays, parts of the original draft or even of the source matter utilized by his clerks, which ought to have been deleted according to his intentions, survived in a group of MSS.

This carelessness is certainly due in the main to Josephus' own extremely defective knowledge of the Greek language, a reproach which was in fact thrown in his teeth by Justus of Tiberias. He was unable to speak Greek correctly,[1] to say nothing of writing it. It is true that, nowadays, the intellectual Jew of the second or third generation, completely assimilated to his environment, has no particular difficulty in acquiring mastery over a foreign language, and we have no reason to suppose that the same facility was denied to their remote ancestors. On the contrary, the examples of a Justus of Tiberias and a Philo fully corroborate this experience. It is quite different with the eastern pupils of the Orthodox *Ḥeder* and *Talmud-Thorah* schools, who learn the gentile idiom only as grown-ups and never manage to acquire a faultless pronunciation, to say nothing of a correct and elegant style of composition, in the foreign language. It follows from what we know of Josephus' life that he clearly belonged to the second category. He certainly never attempted to compose in Greek, since it was far easier for him to write the draft in Semitic and have it translated by his collaborators. Add to this his own confession that he must leave the reader of his *War* to judge how his narrative has been translated,[2] a sentence which clearly reveals that a history of the *Jewish War* or of the *Capture of Jerusalem* written in the author's native tongue in his own scriptorium had been translated into Greek, not by Josephus but by his secretaries, though in his preface he boasts of having executed the translation himself.

TRACES OF THE SEMITIC ORIGINAL IN THE OLD RUSSIAN TRANSLATION

If the MSS. at the basis of the *Halōsis* belonged to one of the Greek editions carefully revised by the author, it would indeed be difficult, if not impossible, to prove traces of a Semitic version in the Old Russian translation. Fortunately, the Greek MSS. utilized by the Slav are derived from a very rudimentary Greek translation of a Semitic text, with the result that quite a number of more or less gross errors have gone over into the Slavonic text and are still clearly discernible.

---

[1] *Ant.*, i. 7 ; xx. 263.
[2] *B.J.*, vii. 454 f. : ' Here we close the history which we promised to relate with perfect accuracy. . . . How it has been translated (ἡρμήνευται, cp. *Antiqq.*, i. § 75, " ἐκ τῶν Ἑβραικῶν μεθερμηνευμένην γραμμάτων διάταξιν ") my readers must be left to judge.'

For example, we find there the form *Kondas* for ΒΟΝΔΑ, based on the easy confusion of כ and ב.[1] If instead of Ptolemy *Lathurus* we read *Thathurus*,[2] the error is not explainable on the basis of a Greek text, where Λ and θ are never confused, but is easy to understand in a Semitic text, where the confusion of ל and ח is quite common. In the Slavonic text the Greek Γίσχαλα has become *Nog-chal*,[3] due to a confusion of initial נ with ג, an error equally common, and of a special form of the שׁ resembling an F with a Greek Γ.

Mutilations of proper names, largely due to wrong syllable division, are frequent in the Slavonic text. Thus *Noaros* has become *Unor*.[4] The initial *U* is of course the Semitic ו=' and,' erroneously added to the name. The error, be it noted, occurs also in a number of still extant Greek MSS. The same mistake occurs in connexion with the name 'Ele'azar', which in the Slavonic version has become *Velezarja*.[5] Similarly *Dor* (Δῶρα) in the Slavonic becomes *Udorus*.[6] When the Greek ΓΑΒΑΩ or ΓΑΒΑΩΝ has become *Agawaof*,[7] we have in the initial *A* simply the Semitic article, erroneously taken for part of the name. The reading 'against Jechono' for a Greek ἐπὶ Ἰεριχοῦντος cannot be explained from the Greek at all, because one would have to suppose the dropping out of five different letters, which is highly improbable. But it is most plausible to assume that the Greek secretary of Josephus read יחונו for ירחו in the original and therefore transcribed ΙΕΧΩΝΩ.[8]

The queer form *Sekostus* for *Sextus*[9] finds its explanation in the fact that the Hebrew alphabet lacks the letter *x* and therefore writes *qs*. The transcription Σέκοστος for Σέξτος in the corresponding place of the Greek *Polemos* is due to the same cause.

In § 383 of Book ii. the Arabs of Transjordania flee on an island, *na ostrow*, where they are compelled to surrender to Herod 'for want of water.' Aside from the fact that there are no islands in that region, one cannot imagine an army on an island suffering from lack of water. In the Greek text the Arabs flee εἰς τὸ χαρά-κωμα, within the palisades, which is the correct translation of a Hebrew בצרה ,בצר, בצרון. The Greek translator of this rough draft evidently did not know the Hebrew word *boṣrah*, and concluded that the Arabs fled to a place named *Boctrooy*. Even as the translators of the Septuagint did in such cases, the Greek secretary of Josephus merely transcribed the difficult words. The Slav reading then *Ba Boctrooy*, trying to make some sense of the word, converted it then probably into *na ostrow*, 'on to an island,' as we have seen.

---

[1] i. 4, § 90.
[2] Slav. *Fafurus*, i. § 86.
[3] ii. § 621.
[4] ii. § 481.
[5] ii. § 236.
[6] i. § 156.
[7] ii. 19, § 544.
[8] ii. § 323.
[9] iii. § 325.

The Slavonic text has preserved the Semitic form *Bethzur*, against Βηθσουρών in the Greek.[1]   Only in the reading of a Semitic script lacking the vowels could *Babylon* have been read for *Byblos*.[2]

The Old Russian version shows furthermore a considerable number of Semitisms, which Josephus carefully removed from his later definitive editions.   I mention ' men of war ' =Greek ἄνδρες συσστρατιῶται, a literal translation from the Hebrew *'anshēj milḥamah*.[3]   These examples might be increased considerably, without apparent utility.

It may even be possible to determine, on the basis of the Old Russian version, whether it was Hebrew or Aramaic that Josephus in the Greek preface calls his ' ancestral language ' (πάτριος γλῶσσα). In the *Halōsis*[4] we find the word *maglawijem'*, which is nothing but the Hebrew *maglabhejhem*, ' their whips,' corresponding to the μάστιξιν in the corresponding passage of the *Vita*,[5] meaning ' with their whips.'   (The Aramaic form would be *maglabhahon*.) Unfortunately, the matter becomes more complicated by the fact that the word *maglabh* is also a Saracen loan-word in Byzantine Greek, and that the ending *-em'* is the suffix of the Slavonic *instrumentalis*.   But to assume from this that the Slav arrived at the form of his text independently from any model, one would have to postulate the existence of a Slavonic * *maglawij*, which word is not to be found at least in the existing dictionaries of the Slavonic tongues.   But it is altogether unthinkable that the word μαγγλαβίοις should have taken the place of the μάστιξιν of the common MSS. of the Greek work, for the Saracen loan-word obviously cannot have come into being before the ninth century. Nor would any one at this late age have taken the trouble to translate the Semitic original (if it still existed) into Greek, since the Greek text was then readily available throughout the Byzantine empire in numerous MSS.   The chances are, then, that the original draft of the *Halōsis* was written in Hebrew, though it is well not to conclude too much from this one word, since it is found in a report of Josephus addressed to the regents in Jerusalem, and it is possible that in an official document of this type the priest's son Josephus should have used Hebrew.   The use of the Hebrew and not the Aramaic definite article in connexion with certain place names,[6] and the striking frequency of sentences beginning with the word ' and,' [7] would thus no doubt be best explained.

Since, however, the work in question was a piece of political

---

[1] i. § 41.   [2] i. § 422.   [3] ii. § 612.
[4] Berendts-Grass, p. 277. 11.   [5] § 147.   [6] Cf. above, p. 132.
[7] Cp. C. F. Burney, *The Aramaic Origin of the Fourth Gospel*, Oxford, 1922, p. 50, on the frequency of sentences opening without a connective particle as an essential characteristic of Aramaic syntax, contrasting with the Hebrew preference for sentences beginning with ' And ' (which has often to be rendered ' Then,' ' Now,' ' So,' ' Yea ').

propaganda designed to reach not only the Eastern Jews of Mesopotamia but also the heathen Parthians, Arabians, Assyrians of Adiabene, and Armenians, it is indeed highly probable that Josephus used for the definite text of his Oriental edition the Aramaic language, which, as is well known, was the official language of the Parthian empire and the *koinē* of those regions.

THE ORIENTAL EDITION OF THE 'HALŌSIS.' THE AUTHOR'S SEMITIC DRAFT AND THE ROUGH GREEK VERSION OF HIS ASSISTANTS

From the author's preface one might infer that the Semitic draft of the Greek *War* which he mentions is in fact identical with the Oriental edition intended for the 'upper barbarians.' But, as early as 1886, Th. Nöldeke thought such an identity of the Oriental and the Occidental editions, coming from a man of Josephus' character, very unlikely. Granting the truth of this observation, and the possibility that Josephus might have thought the Romans would never find out exactly what he wrote in his own language for the Jews of the Orient, it is yet a far cry to assuming that in the Oriental edition he left intentionally the two venomous invectives against the Romans. Moreover, it is clear that this Oriental edition, written in Rome, was intended to be a work of Roman propaganda ; for it was with such a political aim in view that the Romans had given him access to their archives and secret documents. Furthermore, Agrippa's speech, with the 'fortune of the Romans' and their invincibility for a keynote,[1] is clearly a piece of political propaganda designed to 'pacify' the Orient, such as was badly needed because of the general political situation of the Eastern provinces and the Parthian menace.[2] The detailed description of the Jewish War, with the even more detailed account of the disasters which befell the Jews after its close, was evidently meant to inspire the Eastern barbarians with a holy fear, and Vespasian certainly did not accidentally pick out for this task the man who had been one of the leaders of the Jewish rebellion. This observation, the general result of Prof. Laqueur's prior enquiries, is fully confirmed by the *Halōsis*. The Greek *Polemos* expressly mentions the princes Monobazos and Kenedaios, relations of the King of Adiabene, and a certain Silas of Babylon, allies of the Jews, who through their personal bravery had a good share in the victory over Cestius Gallus.[3] The whole passage, the historicity of which need not be doubted at all, is missing

---

[1] *B.J.*, ii. 345 ff., especially 373.
[2] Cf. Pliny's *Paneg. in Traj.*, ch. xiv. : 'ferociam superbiamque Parthorum ex proximo auditus magno terrore cohibere.'
[3] *B.J.*, ii. 19. 2, § 520 *sq.*

in the *Halōsis*. Nor do we find there, in the great speech of Agrippa, the mention of the Parthian hostages brought to Rome by Tiridates in A.D. 66 and the other Parthian hostages living in Italy, some princes of the Parthian royal dynasty and sons of King Monobazes of Adiabene.[1] No doubt Josephus omitted these passages because they were offensive to the Parthians, and, more important still, because he did not wish to give the Parthians the impression that the Roman Jews were looking for their aid. The military situation in Britain and Germany, anything but favourable to the Romans in the critical year of 69-70, probably induced him also to omit from the *Halōsis* Agrippa's mention of the complete pacification of these nations by the Roman arms.

Coming now to the question of the invectives against the Romans, one might perhaps think that they were inserted on purpose to conceal the official character of the work of propaganda. Still, this is unlikely, for the Parthian administration of Mesopotamia and the neighbouring districts was certainly not more honest and more unselfish than the Roman administration in Judaea and elsewhere. It is therefore more probable that the definitive Oriental edition did not contain those passages at all, but that these are peculiar to the first draft which was reworked for the definitive Semitic edition and on the other hand translated into Greek by his secretaries,[2] and that it was this Greek draft which Josephus constantly improved and revised. Since he was pressed for time—his work was to be ready for the triumph of Titus—it is likely that he just managed to look over the copies destined for the monarchs and the more important among the generals. For the rest of the edition he had to rely on the honesty of his secretaries, and either from carelessness or in order to play him a prank they copied those two passages against his directions. No doubt he noticed the matter soon enough and took his measures, for none of the MSS. of the *War* shows the slightest trace of them. The date of the deletion of the passages cannot be very well determined, since the Russian translator used the second edition of the *Halōsis* only for chapters i. to xxv., because they were missing in the old edition to which he had access. Thus chapter xxxi. was translated only after the older edition.

JOSEPHUS AND THE SEMITIC TRANSLATION OF NICOLAUS OF DAMASCUS

There remains the problem of determining how the invectives against the Romans got into Josephus' draft, and especially into

---

[1] Dio. Cass., 63. 1-7. Sueton., *Nero*, ch. 13. Plin., *N.H.*, xxx. 16.
[2] See above, p. 130 f.

that portion of his work which he copies from Nicolaus of Damascus, the intimate friend of Augustus himself.

As Dr. Hölscher already intimated—and the Slavonic text fully confirms his observations—Josephus did not utilize Nicolaus directly but through the medium of a Jewish author far more hostile to Herod than Nicolaus had been, and who occasionally joins issue with the Damascene historian. The simplest explanation of this fact would be to assume that there existed a free Hebrew or Aramaic translation of Nicolaus which Josephus drew on in preference to the Greek original. The invectives against the Romans could come only from the pen of such a violent anti-Roman, and Josephus' secretaries included them in their translation either from carelessness or from malice, though, as has been said before, our author managed to discover them in most MSS. and promptly deleted them before they could do him harm with his patrons.

The same Jewish translator or reworker of Nicolaus may be responsible for a chapter about a secret discussion between different priests of Jerusalem, a passage found in the nineteenth section of the first book of the Slavonic *Halōsis* but absent from the Greek *Polemos*. The §§ 364-9 are missing in the Slavonic text. Dealing with Herod's expedition against the Arabs, they were probably inserted at a later date and from a secondary source. This source can be easily determined, thanks to Josephus' own statement in the parallel passage of the *Antiquities* (xv. 5. 1-5) : ' The account we here give was that contained in the memoirs of King Herod.' The long speech of Herod recorded by Nicolaus (§§ 373-9) has no other source. When, for reasons presently to be discussed, Josephus thought fit to delete the discussion of the priests about the messianic hopes of the Jews, he filled the gap by the more detailed description of the Arabic campaign in Herod's memoirs used by Nicolaus, of which the heir of Herod, Agrippa ii., no doubt possessed a copy. It is, of course, equally possible that everything he took from those memoirs he borrowed through the medium of Nicolaus. He may at first have abridged the story of the Arabic expedition, just because as a priest and a priest's son he was interested in the theme of the messiah and also in the murder of the scribes engaged in the discussion ; and when he saw himself obliged after all to omit that interesting passage, he may simply have gone back to Nicolaus in order to give what remained of the details concerning the Arabic campaign. The discussion is sufficiently important for the history of Jewish messianism to make a literal translation with commentary well worth our while :

' But Herod spent little (time) in Jerusalem and marched against the Arabs. At that (lit. " the ") time the priests mourned and grieved one to another in secret. They durst not do it openly for fear of Herod and his friends.

'For (one Jonathan) [1] spake : " The law [2] bids us have no foreigner for king. Yet we wait for the Anointed one,[3] the meek,[4] of David's line. But of Herod we know that he is an Arabian,[5] uncircumcised. The Anointed will be called meek,[4] but this (is) he who has filled our whole land with blood. Under the Anointed it was ordained that the lame should walk [6] and the blind should see [7] and the poor become rich.[8] But under this man the hale have become lame, the sighted are blinded, the rich have become beggars. What is this? Or how? Have the Prophets lied ? The Prophets [9] have written that there shall not want a ruler from Judah until he come unto whom it is delivered ; for him do the Gentiles hope.[10] But is this man the hope for the Gentiles ? For we hate his misdeeds. Will the Gentiles perchance set their hopes upon him ?

'Woe unto us, because God has forsaken us, and we are forgotten of him! [11] And he will give us over to desolation and to destruction.[12] Not as under Nebuchadnezzar and Antiochus (is it). For then were the Prophets teachers unto the people, and the prophecies concerning the captivity and concerning the return. And now neither is there any one whom one could ask [13] nor any one with whom one might find comfort.

'But Ananos the priest answered and spake to them : " I know all books.[14] When Herod fought before the city,[15] I had never a thought that God would permit him to rule over us. But now I understand that our desolation is nigh. And consider the prophecy of Daniel.[16] For he writes that after the return the city of Jerusalem shall stand for seventy year-weeks, which are 490 years, and after these years shall it be desolate. And when they had counted the remaining years (they) were thirty and four. But Jonathan answered and spake : " The numbers of the years are even as we have said.

---

[1] The name has dropped out, but can easily be restored from the context.

[2] *Deut.* xvii. 15. Cp. Bab. Talm., *Baba bathra*, 3b-4a, about Herod finding out the rabbis who invoked *Deut.* xvii. 15 against him, and having them all executed except R. Baba ben Butah.

[3] The Messiah.

[4] *Zach.* ix. 9; *Ps.* cxxxi. 1 : " μνήσθητι, κύριε, τοῦ Δαυὶδ καὶ . . . τῆς πραότητος αὐτοῦ " (the M.T. of *Ps.* cxxxii. has other vowel-points, therefore A.V. 'remember . . . David and all his *afflictions* ' instead of ' his meekness ').

[5] In Christian tradition he figures, on the contrary, as an uncircumcised Philistine hailing from Ascalon (Eusebius, *H.E.*, i. 7. 11, cf. i. 6. 2-3).

[6] *Is.* xxxv. 6, 7.   [7] *Ibid.*, v. 5.

[8] *Is.* lxi. 1. The prophet says only that the poor will get good news. But for our author there is nothing but wealth which could be ' good news ' to the poor.

[9] *Videl.*, the prophet Moses as the alleged author of the book of *Genesis* (xlix. 10), and Ezekiel, who speaks (xxi. 26 f.) of 'the crown and the diadem ' and of the time ' until he come, whose right it is ; and I will give it him.'

[10] *Genes.* xlix. 10.   [11] *Is.* xlix. 14.

[12] *Ezek.* vi. 14 ; xxxiii. 28 f.

[13] *Ps.* lxxiv. 9 ; *Dan.* ix. 24.

[14] A Semitism : *kethubim* in Hebrew (Aram. *kethuboth*)=' the scriptures,' i.e. the sacred books.

[15] *B.J.*, i. § 343 ff.—that is, in the chapter preceding this conversation.

[16] ix. 24 ff.

But the Holy of Holies,[1] where is he ?   For this Herod he (sc. the prophet) cannot call the Holy One,[2] (him) the bloodthirsty and the impure."

' But one of them, by name Levi, wishing to outwit them, spake to them with stammering speech, not from the Scriptures but in fancied speech.   But they being learned in the Scriptures began to search for the time when " the Holy One "[2] would come.   But the speeches of Levi they execrated, saying, " Putty[3] is in thy mouth but a bone in thy head."   They said this to him because they meant that he had been breaking fast all day and that his head had become heavy from drink, like a bone.   But he, seized with shame, fled to Herod and informed him of the speeches of the priests which they had spoken against him.   But Herod sent by night and slew them all,[4] keeping it secret from the people, lest they should be roused.   Then he appointed others.

' And when it was morning the whole land quaked.'

In the Greek *Polemos*, and no doubt also in Nicolaus of Damascus, the earthquake of § 370 was recounted without any special motivation; in the *Halōsis* it appears the direct punishment of God, intent upon avenging his priests.   The priests have been killed at night, and in the morning the earth quakes, incidentally killing 6000 victims entirely innocent of the crime.   Instead of the phrase ' when it was morning,' the Greek has the sober statement ' at the beginning of spring,' i.e. at the time when the army was again about to take the field ; but in the words ' a God-sent catastrophe ' we can still recognize a trace of the Pharisaic doctrine of immediate Divine retribution so characteristic of the Jewish reworker of Nicolaus, from whom Josephus had taken it over directly.

The time of this episode was no doubt well fixed already in the source of Josephus.   It is the year 32 B.C., and the earthquake is certainly not later than 31 B.C.   The priests then expect the destruction of Jerusalem and the coming of the messiah in thirty-four years, that is, A.D. 2.   Since the history of Nicolaus of Damascus appears to have extended as far as the confirmation of Archelaus as the successor of Herod by Augustus, that is, 4 B.C., the free translation of the work from the Greek into some Semitic idiom may have taken place shortly after the war of Varus, and may be the work of some pessimistic Pharisee who had the apocalyptic turn of mind.   The messiah in question, who was the

---

[1] *Dan.* ix. 24 : ' seventy weeks are determined . . . to anoint the Most Holy ' (lit. the Holy of Holies, *qodesh qadashim*), i.e. the high priest (1 *Chron.* xiii. 13 : Aaron separated as *qodesh qadashim*).

[2] The Holy One of God, with reference to *Ps.* cvi. 16, ' Aaron, the saint of the Lord.'

[3] Russ. *ukha*, ' soup,' makes no sense.   I suppose Hebr. *marqah*, ' putty,' has been mistaken for *maraq*, ' soup,' by the Greek translator.

[4] Cf. above, p. 137 n. 2.

hope of all enemies of the Herodian dynasty, can have been no other than Judas the Galilaean, the only one of the three pretenders to that honour who had escaped from the slaughter of 4 B.C. with his life, and who held himself concealed somewhere in the hills or in the desert.

The prophecy cannot have been invented after A.D. 2, which year had conclusively shown that it was essentially erroneous. But Josephus, who had seen the destruction of the city in A.D. 70 and who pretended to see the *shilo* foretold in *Gen.* xlix. 10 in Vespasian, may have relished the episode, if only to show how even the wise had been in error. If the whole section were the work of a Christian interpolator, he would certainly have turned the chronology so that it would have pointed either to the official year of Jesus' birth [1] or to the year of his first appearance in public, that is, according to *Luke* iii. 1, A.D. 29, or, lastly, to the year of the crucifixion, that is, either A.D. 30 or 32.   Nor would there have been any special difficulty. All that was necessary to juggle the figures correctly would have been to take the year 458 B.C. as the year of the ' return,' based on a passage in *Ezra* (vii. 8).   Finally, had the interpolator done his work after A.D. 70 he would certainly not have failed to point somehow to that catastrophe as being the ' desolation ' foretold by Daniel. The only justifiable conclusion is therefore that the discussion between the priests is a genuine chapter of Josephus' *Halōsis*, and that the source from which it is derived was written some years before 2 B.C.

It is of course perfectly transparent why Josephus in his later edition of the *Polemos* omitted the whole passage with its mention of a connexion of the messianic hopes with the name of Herod. It would not have been very flattering for Vespasian, whom Josephus finally proposed as the real messiah, to be mentioned in the same breath with a petty king of Judaea, who had, to boot, the sinister reputation of a merciless tyrant. Moreover, the discussion between the priests would have shown the Romans only too well how perfectly un-Jewish his own application of the Old Testamental prophecies to the person of Vespasian was, and what a

---

[1] If it *were* true that in a MS. of the Moscow Musée Historique, quoted and reproduced by Prof. Sol. Zeitlin (without any number or other indication), *Jew. Quart. Rev.*, N.S. xix., 1929, p. 26 f, this dialogue is placed in the year of the siege of Jerusalem (37 A.D.), so that the ' thirty-four years ' still left before the impending ' destruction of the city ' and the appearance of the ' Holy One ' might be explained as pointing to the burning of the temple porticoes during the war of Varus (4 B.C.) and to the birth of Jesus in the last year of Herod the Great (4 B.C.), this rearrangement would be an obviously Christian chronological falsification, a parallel to the similar fraud discussed above, p. 17 ff.   But not a word of what Zeitlin pretends to have read on the page ' 792b ' reproduced on his Pl. IV., *not a word of this dialogue is found either on this or on any other page of this MS.* (Synod. p. 745), for the very simple reason that it is a *Josippon* and not a *Josephus*!   Even the page number is wrongly quoted, for the page is clearly a *recto* (*a*) and not a *verso* !

bold lie he had after all started when he spoke of a Divine inspiration in this connexion. Worse still, every argument advanced by the priests to show that Herod could not be the messiah, since he was neither meek nor a benefactor, would have applied with equal force to Vespasian, who, if anything, had treated the Jews even more harshly than Herod had ever done.

Nor can there be any question of the passage being a late interpolation. As early as the fourth century all remembrance of the once propounded messiahship of Herod the Great [1] had vanished. The interpolation would then have to be far older. Nor can it be a Christian interpolation. Among the Christians, Herod, as I have said before,[2] had the reputation of being of Philistine descent. It was only by the Jews that he had always been called an Arab and an uncircumcised gentile.

The Manifestly Christian Interpolations in the Slavonic Josephus, and their Date

The Russian ' Chronographer of the year 1512,' quoted by Berendts [3] and since printed,[4] has a remarkable and hitherto neglected quotation from Josephus. This is what he says :

> ' This Josephus, although what he wrote does not testify to his having completely accepted the faith in Christ, is still praiseworthy in his writings, because he has said the truth about the capture of Jerusalem, to wit, that this catastrophe happened to the Jews *because of the Christ* and according to the prophecy of Christ. Therefore he himself left Jerusalem and went over to the Romans and Titus. With him went to Titus also Mannaeus, the brother's son (*bratanič* = ἀδελφιδοῦς) of Lazarus, whom Jesus, as he (Josephus) says, had raised from the dead after he had become putrid.'

Nothing corresponding to this quotation is to be found in the Greek standard editions. Yet the good faith of the Russian writer cannot well be doubted, because one part of what he says is found in the Slavonic version of Josephus, whilst the rest is confirmed by a hitherto equally unidentifiable quotation of the Bulgarian bishop Theophylactos of Ochrida, and another much earlier

---

[1] Epiphanius, *Adv. Haeres. haer.*, xx.; *P.G.*, 41, 269. Catena 400 ed. Cramer to *Matt.* xxii. 15. Tertullian, app. to *De praescr. adv. haer.*, 45 : ' Herodiani, qui Herodem Christum esse credebant.' Jerome in *Matt.* xxii. 15 : ' quidam Latinorum ridicule Herodianos putant, qui Herodem Christum esse credebant.'

[2] Above, p. 137 n. 5.

[3] Gebhardt u. Harnack, *Texte und Untersuchungen*, xiv. 1. p. 13 f.

[4] *Polnoje sobranije russkich lětopisei*, vol. xxii. sect. 1 (St. Petersburg, 1911, p. 249), reproduced (in Russian characters) vol. i. p. 429 of the German edition of the present book.

occurring in the so-called *Chronicon Paschale*, a late fourth- or a fifth-century adaptation of Eusebius. The Old Russian Josephus says in Book v. § 467 : ' In these days Mannaeus, a brother's son of Lazarus, *whom Jesus raised out of his grave after he had become putrid*, fled to Titus,' etc. On the other hand, we read in Theophylactos of Ochrida : [1] ' as Josephus testifies, this happened to the Jews because of the death of Jesus.' The *Chronicon Paschale* (i. 463) says : ' Josephus relates in the fifth book of the *Capture* that the captivity of the Jews occurred in the third year of Vespasian, that is, forty years after their daring against Jesus. In that time, he also says, James the brother of the Lord, and bishop of Jerusalem, was precipitated from the height and stoned to death by them.' There is nothing in the Greek standard text corresponding to the details of the quotation, but it is easy to see that the words quoted explain the praise bestowed by the Russian chronographer upon Josephus for having justly described the ruin of the Jewish nation as a consequence of what was done to Jesus. This approval given to Josephus is precisely the contrary of what Origen said on the basis of what *he* read in *his* Josephus text :

> ' Although not believing in Jesus as the Christ, Josephus, when searching for the true cause of the fall of Jerusalem, *ought* to have said that *the persecution of Jesus* was the cause of its ruin, because the people had killed the prophesied Messiah ; yet as if against his will and not far from the truth he says that this befell the Jews in revenge for James the Just, who was the brother of Jesus the so-called Christ, because they killed him, although he was a perfectly just man.'

It is now very easy to see what happened to the text of Josephus. The Church was, and for that matter still is, repeating that the past and present miseries of the Jews are the Divine retribution for the crucifixion of Jesus. Origen would have liked to find an explicit confirmation of this doctrine in Josephus ; but the great philologist is conscientious enough to tell us that Josephus says nothing of the kind, though that writer mentions, unintentionally as it were, ' almost against his will,' [3] the popular opinion that Jerusalem was destroyed for what had been done to the brother of Jesus—a passage which does not exist in the Greek standard text, evidently because it was removed as a direct consequence of the point of criticism started by Origen. Later scribes had none of the scruples of Origen, and simply inserted into the text of Josephus what they sincerely believed he *ought* to have written. The *Ege-*

---

[1] *Comm. in John*, xiii. p. 762, ed. Paris, 1631 ; p. 695, ed. Venice, 1685 ; *P.G.*, cxxiv., c. 165 C. The author was born in Euboea, and lived under the emperors Michael Ducas and Alexios Comnenos (1081-1118).

[2] c. Cels., i. 47, ed. Koetschau, *Griech. Christl. Schriftst.*, Berlin, 1899, i. p. 96.

[3] Cf. above, p. 37.

sippus text [1] as well as the Chronicle of Malalas [2] follows the common current. A copyist of the *War*, not to remain behind in his zeal, made a bold insertion in Book v. § 568 *sq.*, speaking of the frenzy of those 'reprobates' and of the Divine punishment of their sins :

'I believe that had the Romans delayed to punish these reprobates, either the earth would have opened and swallowed up the city, or it would have been swept away by a flood or have tasted anew the thunderbolts of the land of Sodom. For it produced a generation far more godless than the victims of those visitations, seeing that these men's frenzy involved the whole people in their ruin. But why need I severally recount the calamities ? Why indeed, when Mannaeus, son of Lazarus (ὁ Λαζάρου), sought refuge with Titus,' etc. [3]

So he inserted after 'these men's frenzy involved the whole people in their ruin' the two sentences read by the Alexandrian author of the *Chronicon Paschale* : [4] ' In the third year of Vespasian occurred the capture,' etc. ' In that year James . . .' This date, 'the *third* year of Vespasian,' is in obvious contradiction to Josephus, who, in the same work, [5] correctly calls the year of the destruction the *second* year of Vespasian. The reason for this shifting of the date of Jerusalem's fall is obvious : the Christian writer believes with *Luke* iii. 1 that the ministry of Jesus began in 29, the fifteenth year of Tiberius, and lasted for two years, the passover of the crucifixion being the third during this period. This brings the passion to the year A.D. 31 ; and if the destruction of Jerusalem is to happen after the classical period of forty years, it had to be shifted to A.D. 71. On the other hand, the death of James the Just in reality occurred, according to Josephus' well-documented account, in A.D. 62, i.e. eight years before the fall of the city. Because to the interpolator God's mills seemed to grind too slowly in this particularly atrocious case, he said a little vaguely that James died 'at the time' of the fall of the city. These words were paraphrased by the early Judeo-Christian traveller and historian of Christian origins, Hegesippus [6] —the genuine Hegesippus!—still more diplomatically: *'and immediately* after this [*scil.* the murder of James] Vespasian destroyed the city.' This proves incidentally that these callous forgeries were perpetrated before Hegesippus' time, who wrote about A.D. 180, that is, at the latest about the middle of the second century of our era. Similarly, Eusebius [7] speaks of the passion of James and the ' *im-*

---

[1] ii. 5, p. 139, Ussani : '. . . Christum dominum cruci suffixerit . . . Ex illo itaque Judaeorum res proditae, ex illo exitium genti temploque maturatum excidium.'

[2] x. 31, p. 247 of the Bonn edition : 'Josephus the Hebrew philosopher said also that *ever since the Jews have crucified Jesus*, sorrow (ὀδύνη) has not ceased in the Jewish country.'

[3] Thackeray's trans., iii. p. 375.　　　　[4] See above, p. 141.

[5] *B.J.*, vi. 4. 8, § 269 ; vi. 10. 1, § 435.

[6] Ap. Eusebium, *H.E.*, ii. 23. 18.

[7] *H.E.*, iii. 11. 1.

mediately following fall of Jerusalem,' thus placing the death of Jesus' brother eight years later than it really occurred ; for all this there is no other authority than the above-quoted spurious lines in the text of Josephus.

The most impudent interpolation in that mare's nest of forgeries is the one by which Josephus is made to bear witness on the greatest of the miracles of Jesus, the raising of Lazarus from the dead. Going over the Slavic text, we note right away the queer expression ' brother's son,' an expression which has no parallel in the extant Greek text, which refers to Mannaeus as the son of Lazarus. One asks, of course, why the interpolator converts the son into a nephew. On consulting the Hebrew *Josippon* one promptly discovers that the Mannaeus in question or his equivalent [1] is there called ' the son of Seruq.' Since there is no reason whatever to doubt this reading, obviously *bona fide*, it becomes clear that the interpolator had to make Mannaeus the nephew of Lazarus, because the original had already provided a father for the young man. So there was not even a casual mention of that name in this connexion as an inducement to drag in Lazarus at all. The whole history of the forgery runs then something like this : The original reading was ' Mannaeus, the son of Seruq.' The forger changed ' Seruq ' to Lazarus to wedge in a testimony for the miracle. Naturally, this could not be done in all copies, and in a number of them the original reading remained. A subsequent corrector became aware of this, and to do away with the contradiction he made Lazarus Mannaeus' uncle. The interpolation of the testimony was so outright silly that even Isaac and the Latin translator of the age of Cassiodorus rejected it, though they allowed the phrase ' Mannaeus, the son of Lazarus ' to stand because they no longer knew the original patronymic ' son of Seruq.'

From what has been said above about Origen's criticism of Josephus and the subsequent alteration of the text by the Church, it follows that the Greek original accessible to the great philologist must have read something like this : *Ant.*, xx. § 200, ' Ananias . . . convened an assembly of judges and dragged before it the brother of Jesus the so-called Messiah [   ],[2] Jacob by name, and some others, accusing them of breaking the law, and handed them over to be stoned.   [   ] [3] (The people, when searching (later on) for the cause of the fall of Jerusalem and of the destruction

---

[1] In Hebrew, ' *Menahem.*'   According to Philippus Sidetes, Papias mentioned ' the miraculous resurrection of Manaimos' mother ' (de Boor, *T.U.*, v. ii. 170).

[2] Something is probably missing here, since Josephus is accustomed to insert a reference harking back to the first mention of a name when reintroducing a person for the second time (cp. *Ant.*, xv. § 3, xx. § 102 ; *B.J.*, ii. § 56, § 433, etc.). Some words about Jesus which sounded blasphemous to Christian ears—e.g. τοῦ ἀρχιλῃστοῦ σταυρωθέντος ὑπὸ Πιλάτου, or the like—may have been deleted by the censor.

[3] Here, too, something may be missing.   See below, p. 546 ll. 15 ff.

of the temple, believed that this suffering happened to our nation through the wrath of God, because of what those men dared to do.) Those, however, who were considered the most worthy and most exact about the observance of the law in the city were loth to put up with this. And they sent to the king,' etc. The words here enclosed in brackets were deleted in consequence of Origen's criticism, the motivation being now thought to have been Jesus' death exclusively. Probably at the same time the corresponding passage about James the Just, quoted above, p. 141, was interpolated into the *Jewish War*, where a suitable place for it was easily found. The genuineness of the words read by Origen cannot well be doubted because they do not even reflect Josephus' own opinion, any more than his words about the defeat of Herod Antipas by the Arabs, regarded by the same type of public opinion as a punishment for the death of John the Baptist. Being only a belief of the people, they are not at all in contradiction to *Ant.*, xx. 8. 5, § 166, where Josephus himself explains the downfall and burning of the city as the Divine chastisement for the misdeeds of the Sicarians, especially for the murder of the high priest Jonathan.

Another clumsy interpolation in the Old Russian text, in spite of its spurious character, throws some unexpected light on two quotations by the patriarch Photius of Constantinople (ninth century) and Eusebius of Caesarea respectively. They both refer to Josephus as testifying to the truth of the legend about the massacre of the children of Bethlehem. This is what Photius says : [1] ' this Herod is the son of Antipater the Idumaean and the Arabian (queen) named Kypros, under whom Christ . . . was born, against whom Herod raged and sinned against the Lord, and became the murderer of many infants.' All this as a quotation from Josephus. At first sight one might believe the words about the slaughter of the innocents to be merely an addition by Photius. That supposition falls when we turn to Eusebius : [2]

> (Mention is made of Herod's murder of his own family) ' . . . for the shadows in their story, which Josephus has narrated at length in the history of Herod, are darker than any in tragic drama. But it is well to hear *from the words of that writer* how, from the moment of the plot against our Saviour and the other innocents, a scourge sent from God seized him and drove him to death.'

Because of this quotation Eusebius has been accused ever since the days of Tannéguy Lefèvre of having fabricated the *Testimonium Flavianum de carnificina puerorum Bethlehemi*. The same accusation would have to be levelled against the Armenian historian Moses of Khorni [3] (eighth century), who says about Herod I. that

---

[1] *Bibl.*, cod. 238 (written before 858).
[2] *H.E.*, i. 8. 14 f. Dr. Kirsopp Lake's transl. in the *Loeb Class. Libr.*, p. 67.
[3] Transl. by Langlois in Carol. Muller's *H.G.V.*, ii. p. 326.

he was ' weighed down by sufferings as a retribution for his criminal
behaviour against Christ, *as Josephus testifies.*' What all these
witnesses quote Josephus for, though of course absent from the
Greek text, is found verbatim in the Old Russian version, which as
a matter of fact corresponds to the quotation of Photius fairly
closely.   In i. 21. 1, § 401, mention is made—just as in Photius'
quotation—of the magnificent rebuilding of the Jewish temple;
then follows a list of his other buildings, then a panegyric of
Herod's qualities as a rider, hunter, and army leader, terminating
with the statement that he was hardly ever vanquished in battle—
if at all, only by the disobedience of his subordinate officers.   Then
the text goes on to say, with an abrupt break in the line of thought:
' and for another reason, mentioned before, because *of his search
for Christ and because of the massacre of the children.*[1]   And they
(=the Bethlehemites) cursed him (saying) : may he himself have
no children.'

Then follows the well-known account of Herod's own domestic
misfortunes.   What is meant by the words ' mentioned before '
may be seen if we read on to i. 33. 5, § 656.   There the terrible description of Herod's mortal venereal disease and consequent gan-
grene of his private parts closes with the following edifying remark : [2] ' for the eye of God looked invisibly upon his sins.   He
had indeed defiled his dominion with bloodshed and with illicit
intercourse with foreign women.[3]   *And because he had made others
childless*, therefore killed he also his children with his (own) hands;
and because he spared not his body in wantonness, therefore contracted he so foul a disease.'   The genuine words of the text,
' because he had made others childless,' do not of course in the
least refer to the legendary massacre of Bethlehem, but to the story
of the eighty young students of religious law whom Herod had
burned in a furnace for having destroyed the golden eagle over the
porch of the temple, a chapter directly preceding the description
of his final disease.

It is clear, then, that a Christian forger, or maybe a *bona fide*
Christian reader, annotating his own copy for his private use, is
responsible for the interpolated line on the massacre of Bethlehem
in the various copies of Josephus' *Capture of Jerusalem* read by
Eusebius, Moses of Khorni, Photius, and the unknown Russian
translator.

A third no less obviously Christian interpolation [4] is quoted
by the Russian chronographer of 1512 immediately before the

---

[1] *o izbinij mladenecij* =τεκνοκτονίας ἕνεκα.   Josephus does speak of τεκνοκτονία
with reference to Herod, *B.J.*, i. § 543 : ' none supposed that Herod would carry
cruelty to the length of murdering his children,' μέχρι τεκνοκτονίας.

[2] Thackeray's transl., iii. p. 643.

[3] The usual Pharisee doctrine about the punishment fitting the crime.

[4] For further examples of the same kind, see App. xv.

K

words reproduced above, in support of still another of the great
miracles of the New Testament, the rending of the veil of the
temple at the death of Jesus. This addition is entirely unknown
to the Western Greek MSS. of Josephus; but the Slavonic branch
has it after §§ 212-14, where Josephus describes the Holy of Holies
of the temple :

' It had golden doors fifty-five cubits high and sixteen wide. . . .
Before these hung a veil of equal length, of Babylonian tapestry,
with embroidery of blue, and fine linen of scarlet also and purple,
wrought with marvellous skill. Nor was this mixture of materials
without its mystic meaning : it typified the universe. For the
scarlet seemed emblematical of fire, the fine linen of the earth, the
blue of the air, and the purple of the sea, the comparison in two cases
being suggested by their colour, and in that of the fine linen and
purple by their origin, as the one is produced by the earth and the
other by the sea. On this tapestry was portrayed the whole aspect
of the sky, but without the animal outlines of the constellations.

**' This curtain was before this generation entire, because the
people were pious ; but now it was grievous to see, for it was
suddenly rent from the top to the bottom, when they through
bribery delivered to death the benefactor of men and him who
from his actions was no man.**

' And of many other fearful signs might one tell, which happened
then. And it was said that he, after being killed and laid in the
grave, was not found. Some indeed profess that he had risen, others
that he was stolen away by his friends. But for my part I know not
which speak more correctly. For one that is dead cannot rise of
himself, though he may do so with the help of the prayer of another
righteous man, unless he be an angel or another of the heavenly
powers, or unless God himself appears as a man and accomplishes
what he will and walks with men and falls and lies down and rises
again as he pleases. But others said that it was impossible to steal
him away, because they had set watches around his tomb, thirty
Romans and a thousand Jews.

**' Such (is the story told) of that curtain. There are also (ob-
jections) against this reason for its rending.'**

It is easy to prove that the paragraphs printed in different type
are a forgery. Josephus could not possibly have said that the veil
in question was torn in his days and had been so ever since the
death of Jesus, because the veil of the Jewish sanctuary was renewed every year. A second reserve curtain was always hung up
behind it, in case it should have to be removed in the course of the
year because of some Levitical impurity touching it by accident.[1]
Had the miracle really happened, the damaged texture would have
been removed, not only in the year of the passion, but on the very
day when it was rent asunder.

[1] See the Tannaitic testimonies collected by Heinr. Laible in Strack-Billerbeck's
Comm., vol. iii., Munich, 1926, p. 733 f.

We know, moreover, how this particular legend originated. The last of the temple curtains was carried away to Rome by Titus with the rest of his spoils, and kept in the treasure-room of the imperial palace,[1] where it could be seen by interested sightseers. Now, this last curtain of the temple had really been rent and was seen in this state by various Jewish visitors;[2] small wonder, since it must have been torn from the door of the temple by the rough hands of Roman soldiery or even rescued from under the ruins. Jewish legend attributed the rending to the impatience of Titus to enter the Holy of Holies and to desecrate it. The emperor was even said to have cut his way through the curtain with his sword.[2]

It is obvious that the Christian legend about the rent curtain must have grown up in Rome after A.D. 75, when the spoils of Jerusalem were first exhibited in public in the temple of Peace. It is, like its Jewish parallel, an aetiological myth evolved, maybe, under the influence of a pertinent prophecy in the Testaments of the Patriarchs,[3] and understood afterwards in a symbolic way.[4]

THE OLD RUSSIAN TRANSLATION OF JOSEPHUS AND THE LITHUANIAN CHRONOGRAPHER OF 1261. THE SCEPTICAL INTERPOLATION ON THE RESURRECTION OF JESUS

Of far greater and indeed fundamental importance for the criticism of the whole matter is the question, to which hitherto not even an approximate answer has been found : *Where, when, under what circumstances and with what object was the Slavonic translation of the ' Halōsis' composed ?*

Everything bearing on this question to be extracted from the peculiarities of the MSS. has been diligently collected by Berendts. It is extremely little. None of the codices is older than the fifteenth or sixteenth century ; but the text followed by the Metropolitan Makarios in his Četji-Minei (a lectionary for the various months of the church year) contains an entry according to which this Josephus MS. was written in Constantinople by a monk named John in the year 6907 of the Byzantine world era = A.D. 1399, was copied in Novgorod in 6976 = 1468, and was finally re-copied in A.D. 1711 and 1714. Since Russian merchants and clergymen can be shown to have been at Byzantium in consider-

---

[1] Josephus, *B.J.*, vii. § 162.
[2] Strack-Billerbeck, *loc. cit.*, vol. i. p. 1044 ; cf. 946 f.
[3] *Levi*, ch. 10 : ' a time will come when the wickedness of the Levites will grow to such a point that the curtain of the temple will split asunder and not hide them any more. And then you will be sent into captivity.' *Benj.*, ix. : ' the curtain of the temple will be split and the spirit of God descend (from the mountain of Jerusalem) to the Gentiles.'
[4] See Eisler, *Weltenmantel*, Munich, 1910, p. 252 n. 5.

able numbers as early as the eleventh century, this statement is
quite trustworthy ; and indeed one would be readily inclined to
assign the genesis of this translation to Byzantium and to this
period, were it not for the character of the language, which
Sreznĕvski has identified as Old Northern Slavonic, as distinct
from the Old Bulgarian ecclesiastical language, which a tenth-
century translator would have employed.

Moreover, a note in the Moscow MS. of the Chronographer of
Perejaslavl (a work containing a compilation of extracts from
the Slavonic Josephus, the Slavonic Malalas, etc., with a continuation down to the year 1214, derived from the Chronographer of
Perejaslavl) states that the copy of this MS. was begun in the year
1261 ; according to Prof. Istrin this work was written in Lithuania,
in which country the second important MS. of this type, the codex
of Vilna, had in fact been preserved down to 1916.

Prof. Istrin rightly recognized that the author of the compilation contained in the Moscow and Vilna codices aimed at writing
a history of the Jewish people, and that he began this work in
Lithuania about the year 1261. Now, since the whole MS. is
written in a uniform style, and since the laborious translation of
the entire *Halōsis* (of which only quite a few brief and—as shown
by the example of a Russian codex recently found by Prof.
Benešević [1]—easily detachable sections could have had any direct
interest for Christian readers) betrays an interest in Jewish history
quite uncommon at this period and in these surroundings, it is
surely needless to seek for an author of this Lithuanian ' Chronographer of 1262 ' other than the patient translator of Josephus
himself. How indefatigable that translator was in constantly
accumulating fresh Josephus MSS., to supplement his first complete
edition, has been shown above (p. 127). In the course of this
search for MSS. he finally hit upon a Greek ἐκλογή, containing
the compilation of Georgius Monachus, Malalas, etc., and Josephus,
which he rendered into Old Russian, rejoicing at this increase of
his materials. A gloss mentioned above (p. 129), which can only
have been added to the Greek *Halōsis* during the period of the
Latin kingdom by a Byzantine scribe (1204-1261), shows that the
original used by the Slavonic translator was still in Byzantium
in the first half of the thirteenth century. This fully accords with
the conclusion that the translation was executed between the
years 1250 and 1260.

That seems to me the simplest explanation of the matter. The
Lithuanians were still half heathens ; their king, Mindowe
(murdered in 1263), had only just gone over to Catholicism (1251),
while his son Vojšelk attached himself to the Greek Church. Among
such a people the number of learned persons acquainted with

[1] Софійск, No. 1428.

Greek and Russian [1] possessing an interest in Jewish history so unusual and unparalleled in all mediaeval Europe, and capable of producing such extensive translations, must have been extremely small. Orthodox Jews cannot be thought of, because, among other reasons, they would not have failed to omit from their Greek copies the Christian interpolations, which to them were so objectionable, or at any rate the undoubtedly Christian chapter-headings. Apart from that, even if Byzantine Jews knew Josephus, there is no apparent reason why they or Slavonic Jews, who had learned Greek at Constantinople, should have translated him into Old Russian.

It was, however, just the extraordinary nature of these facts which put me—following up a hint of the learned Russian lawyer Dr. H. Sljosberg in the discussion after my lecture before the Société des Études Juives in Paris—upon what I regard as the only track leading to a satisfactory solution of all these difficulties.

I had previously been led to a correct understanding of the tendency of the whole Slavonic translation by a more thorough study of a passage recognizable at the first glance as a Christian interpolation. I refer to the seventh of the ' additions ' in Berendts' first publication, discussed above, p. 146, i.e. the story of the rent veil of the temple.

For the convenience of the reader the passage is here repeated :

> ' This curtain was before this generation entire, because the people were pious ; but now it was grievous to see, for it was suddenly rent from the top to the bottom, when they through bribery delivered to death the benefactor of men and him who from his actions was no man.
>
> ' And of many other fearful signs might one tell, which happened then. And it was said that he, after being killed and after being laid [2] in the grave, was not found. Some maintain [3] that he had risen, others that he was stolen away by his friends. But for my part I know not which speak more correctly ! For a dead man cannot rise of himself, though he may do so with the help of the prayer of another righteous man, unless he be an angel or another of the heavenly powers, or unless God himself appears [4] as a man and accomplishes what he will and walks with men and falls and lies down and rises again, as pleases his will. But others said that it was impossible to steal him away, because they set watchmen around his tomb, thirty Romans and a thousand Jews.
>
> ' Such (is the story told) of that curtain. (But) there are also (objections) against this reason for its rending.'

[1] The literary language of Lithuania used in the documents of the court chancery was the dialect of Kiev.

[2] *Cod. Arch.* : ' that he was killed, and after being laid.'

[3] Or ' pretend.' *tvorechu*, equivalent to Greek ποιοῦσιν, the word used for the production of ' poetic ' fiction.

[4] *Cod. Arch.* : ' has appeared.'

By indentation and variation of type I indicate that here we have what is doubtless an 'interpolation within an interpolation.' That is evident from the position of the summary statement, ' Such (is the story told) of that curtain,' etc., which must originally have stood immediately after the sentence actually referring to the curtain, and not after the narrative of the 'many other fearful signs.' Accordingly, everything between is an interpolation by a second hand, probably *the latest of all Christian interpolations in the whole work.*[1]

The interpolation of the first hand concerning the curtain already presupposes the passage about Jesus discussed below (pp. 383 ff.) *in the form in which it stands to-day*, as altered by Christian omissions and Christian interpolations. If, for instance, the curtain passage, for no obvious reason, avoids the name of Jesus, it does so intentionally, because the proper name, in consequence of the reasons discussed later, is wanting also in the Jesus passage. Similarly, the periphrases ' the Benefactor' and 'the man who from his actions (i.e. his divine works) was no man ' are clear references to the significant words, which are shown to be Christian marginal notes, ' (Pilate) saw . . . he was a benefactor, not a malefactor,' and, higher up, ' his works, however, were godlike. . . . Therefore it is not possible for me to call him a man.' Lastly, the phrase ' when they *through bribery* delivered (him) to death ' refers back to what is undoubtedly a Christian insertion (see below) in the section on the Roman judicial proceedings against Jesus.

The passage concerning the rending of the veil of the temple comes, therefore, either from the hand which is responsible for the Christian omissions and interpolations in the section about Jesus and Pilate, or from some still later reader or copyist.

On the contrary, the interpolation of the *second* hand, which from what has been said must be of even later date, has a tendency totally distinct from that of all other Christian insertions so far discussed, including the interpolation about the curtain. Whereas these without exception emanate from believing, indeed from orthodox, Christians, here unquestionably a doubter speaks. M. Goguel,[2] it is true, maintains that ' we do not see how, concerning this text, one can speak of scepticism on account of the resurrection.' But I fail to see how the sceptical character of a man who says of believers that they '*pretend* that he had risen ' can possibly be disputed. The glossator, in fact, proceeds expressly to emphasize his complete scepticism. ' I know not,' he says, ' which speak more correctly, those who pretend that he had risen, or the others who pretend that he was stolen away by his

---

[1] I had arrived at this conclusion before I knew that Dr. Gaster's MS. of the Rumanian version actually omits these sentences.

[2] *Revue de l'Histoire des Religions*, 1926, p. 40.

friends.' If the assertion that Jesus is risen appears to him merely as some *mala fide*, fictitious ' pretensions,' then the expression ' I know not which speak more correctly ' is more than sceptical : it is ironical, and means ' I know not which speak less falsely.' An unbiased reader can surely be in no uncertainty as to the sense of these words. Whoever speaks thus, clearly doubts both statements, the testimony to the resurrection no less than the allegation of opponents, reported by Matthew,[1] that the body was carried away. The third possibility he admits is clearly expressed at the beginning of the interpolation. The fact that the body of Jesus was not found in the grave he by no means regards as the one certain and historically established point, but as a mere rumour. ' It *was said* that after his death and deposition in the grave he was not found,' ' and of many other fearful signs which happened then might one *tell*.' It is therefore for him quite questionable whether even these ' tales ' are true.

As regards the resurrection, he with subtle dialectic bases his doubt on reasoned grounds and challenges certain quite definite doctrines. In the first place—and this point has hitherto been entirely overlooked—he controverts Marcion.[2] ' For a dead man cannot rise of himself.' Orthodox Christians had in fact never asserted so much of Jesus, but had taught with Paul [3] that God himself through his miraculous power raised him from the dead. Marcion, however, to suit his view of the relation between God the Father and God the Son, which approximated to modalism, so altered and abridged the text in Galatians as to extract from it the statement that Jesus raised *himself* from the dead. Similarly, in *Rom.* vi. 9 he replaced the passive ἐγερθείς, ' being raised,' by the active ἀναστάς, ' rose '; while inversely, in 2 *Cor.* iv. 10, for ' the dying of Jesus ' he substituted the incredible ' dying of God.' It is this conception of Marcion which the unknown glossator roundly rejects.

On the other hand, and this is very remarkable, he readily admits that a (righteous) dead man can be raised ' with the help of the prayer of another righteous man.' Origen in his time had made the objection to Celsus that a Jew who believed in the Bible must recognize as possible what is told ' in the third and fourth books of Reigns ' concerning the resurrections wrought through the prayer of the prophets Elijah and Elisha.[4] Thus far the sceptical glossator of Josephus actually went. He is therefore no

---

[1] xxvii. 64 ; xxviii. 13, 15.

[2] *Gal.* i. 1 : ' through Jesus Christ (and God the Father) who raised him from the dead.' Marcion struck out the bracketed words and instead of ' him ' (αὐτὸν) read ' himself ' (αὐτόν). Cf. Origen ap. Jerome, *Comm.*, in loc., ' Sciendum quoque in Marcionis Apostolico non esse scriptum (et per Deum patrem), volentis exponere Christum non a Deo patre sed per semet ipsum suscitatum.'

[3] 1 *Cor.* vi. 14.

[4] *Contra Celsum*, ii. 57.

' Epicurean,' [1] but *goes just so far as the Old Testament evidence extends*, i.e. *takes up precisely the Jewish standpoint*. The writer's intention would, however, be entirely missed if one declined to see that, while admitting this possibility as such, he attributes no historical importance to it in the case of Jesus. Why he does not is not stated in his terse gloss, for obvious reasons. No Christian authority ever taught that Jesus was raised from the dead through the prayer of James the Just or of any of his disciples; this hypothesis, therefore, alike for Christians and for their critics, never came into consideration.

The next possible case of a ' resurrection ' which he considers is one where ' an angel or another of the heavenly powers ' is concerned. That which ' a dead man ' cannot do might very well be achieved by an angel, archangel, seraph, cherub, etc., only seemingly dead. That such is the explanation of the marvellous phenomenon is in fact the doctrine of certain early Gnostics and also of the Paulicians of Asia Minor, whose errors are combated in a polemical work of an otherwise unknown Hegumenos (i.e. abbot) Peter, and later by Photios, Patriarch of Constantinople, and others, upon whom the Bogomils [2] are dependent. According to these docetic and Marcionite heretics, who may be assigned certainly to the seventh and eighth centuries and possibly to the sixth, Jesus was no man, but an angel sent down by a good God for the enlightenment of mankind, under an obligation to let himself— seemingly—be born of a woman, maltreated by sinners, put to death by crucifixion and buried, after which he might rise again and return to heaven.

But this possibility, too, is only mentioned because it has already been refuted in the earlier passage about Christ (below, p. 384), on which this whole interpolation is so plainly dependent, and where it is expressly stated that Jesus ' in view of his ordinary nature ' cannot be called an angel. There remains, therefore, for the sceptic but one final possibility, that ' God himself has appeared as a man and falls and lies down and rises again, as pleases his will.' This final possibility, as Schürer [3] first rightly recognized, is the Christology of the co-called Monarchianists, Patripassianists, or Theopaschitae : it is the view of people such as Noetus, Epigonus, Cleomenes, Marcellus, Photinus, Praxeas, Sabellius, and many others. But neither Schürer nor Couchoud [4] has seen that the sceptical glossator, far from being a Patripassianist or Modalist himself, *rejects* these views *a limine*, precisely as he rejects those previously

---

[1] *Contra Celsum*, ii. 60.

[2] Bogomil, the Slavonic equivalent of Theophilos, founder of a Gnostic sect in the tenth century in Bulgaria. Bury's *Gibbon*, vi. 122 [translator's note].

[3] *Theolog. Lit.-Zeit.*, 1906, p. 256.

[4] *Revue de l'Histoire des Religions*, 1926, p. 54.

mentioned.   Here Frey's statement [1] is undoubtedly right : ' The idea that God himself has suffered that fate appears to the writer so inconceivable that he thinks he has but to mention it in order to rule out any application of this possibility to the case of Jesus.' Were the sceptic not rejecting this possibility just as decisively and bluntly as all that had gone before, there would have been no need for him to proceed to dispose of the possibility, likewise rejected, of the stealing of the body.   Yet he goes straight on : ' But others say that it was not possible to steal him away.'   He must therefore have already tacitly reached the conclusion : ' Since God himself cannot have been treated or suffered thus, the Benefactor also cannot have been God himself.   Was then the body stolen ?   But others say that it cannot have been stolen, because thousands of Jews and Romans watched the tomb.'   *So the question cannot be decided at all*, and the end is that nothing is known in the matter, as from the very beginning we find nothing but ' *on dit*,' 'they say,' ' others say,' 'might one tell'—in short, mere rumour and report.

The position is therefore quite peculiar.   The writer, from the highly remarkable conjunction of Marcionite and Sabellian doctrines controverted by him, can hardly be older than the end of the fourth century, and from the mention of a Paulician error hardly older than the sixth, while if he is drawing upon literary tradition he may be of a still later date.   This learned glossator not only possesses an exact knowledge of the Christologies of different heretics, but elaborately follows traditions contained in canonical and apocryphal Gospels which can be quite definitely fixed.   In the original interpolation on the curtain of the temple one may still be uncertain whether *Mark* xv. 38 or *Matt.* xxvii. 51 served as his model, because both narratives present the words ' torn from top to bottom ' of the Slavonic.   But the dependence of the second interpolator on the narrative in *Matthew* is patent.   Only in *Matt.* xxvii. is v. 51 (describing the rending of the curtain) followed by ' many other fearful signs which happened then,' viz. ' the earth did quake, the rocks were rent, the tombs were opened,' etc.   Only in *Matt.* xxvii. 64, xxviii. 13-15 is the discovery of the empty tomb followed by the assertion of opponents that the body had been stolen, along with the legend of the watching of the tomb, designed to refute the charge.   The actual statements of this section are therefore simply taken over in order from the Gospel of Matthew, while the words ' 30 [v.l. 1000] Romans and 1000 [v.l. 30] Jews,' appended to the clause ' set watchmen around his tomb,' come from the apocryphal *Acts of Pilate* or the *Gospel of Peter*. The glossator thus betrays the most accurate knowledge of the orthodox and heretical views on the resurrection, but rejects them all, partly as impossible, partly as uncertain, resting only on

[1] *Der slav. Josephusbericht*, etc., Dorpat, 1908, p. 190.

'hearsay' from beginning to end, and adheres to his Jewish Old Testament standpoint.

An interpolation such as this is certainly not to be explained as an extremely clever forgery, intent upon putting nothing into the mouth of Josephus which a Jew could not have written. The supposed forger of the secondary interpolation, on this hypothesis so extremely careful, and yet in every line betraying his knowledge of Christian sources—a forger whose like there is not throughout the rest of the work—must have pursued this interesting game quite for its own sake. For as a Christian *testimonium veritatis* the section is obviously valueless, because it leaves 'as its final impression only doubt and uncertainty' (Frey), accounts for the resurrection on the basis of a fiction, indeed regards the discovery of the empty tomb not as a fact but as hearsay, and even leaves open the possibility of the stealing of the body (since the watching of the tomb is only vouched for by an 'others said'), and finally appears to deny not only the equality of Jesus with God the Father but even the divinity of 'the Benefactor.' With what object could *a Christian* interpolate this agnostic-sceptical passage into one which in its original form could be put to good use from the Christian standpoint, purporting to come from Josephus and to confirm the miracle of the rent curtain ?

Frey is here quite right in excluding the assumption of a Christian forgery, whether highly artificial or wholly inappropriate. He has also correctly seen that the author's standpoint is purely Jewish. The latter regards as possible whatever is consonant with the Old Testament miracles of Elijah and Elisha in raising the dead ; he is therefore no 'Epicurean' sceptic. But the idea of an incarnation, of a suffering and dying God, is for him quite impossible ; he even avoids the expression 'if God die' as blasphemous, and speaks only of a 'lying down' of God. He does not believe in the resurrection of Jesus, which he pronounces 'imaginary' or 'pretended'; the very story of the empty tomb remains for him doubtful.

Here, then, speaks one who found Josephus already interpolated by a Christian hand, one who knew the Gospel of Matthew, the Gospel of Peter, and the Christian *Acts of Pilate*, but yet maintained an entirely Jewish standpoint. Where and when can such a person have written his ideas on the margin of a MS. of Josephus that had been or was found in Christian possession ?

To this question, in my opinion, only one answer is possible. The answer will at the same time afford a surprisingly simple explanation of that remarkably strong interest in Jewish history, discussed above, which is indispensably required to account for the existence alike of a Slavonic translation of Josephus and of the 'Chronographer of 1262.'

THE JUDAIZING HERESY IN RUSSIA

It is precisely in Russia, and in the fifteenth century, that is to say, at the very period when all extant MSS. of the old Roman Josephus were written, that we have evidence of a *powerful Judaizing movement* — the so-called *Židovstvujuščaja jeres* — which penetrated into the highest clerical ranks and even into the family of the Grand Duke of Moscow, and brought the Pravo-Slavic or Orthodox Russian Church to the verge of ruin.

Of the beginnings of this movement nothing is known. Anatole Leroy-Beaulieu [1] conjectures that the ' Sabbatarians ' (Russ. *Subbotniki*) are, like the Maraños of Spain and Portugal, descended from Jews compulsorily converted to a sham Christianity. These people, under the direction of Jewish Rabbis, continue to this day, especially in Southern Russia and the Caucasus, and after severe persecutions under the Tsars at last enjoy as much religious freedom as other denominations ; the late Konrad Grass estimated that before the War (1914) some 400,000 Russian peasants were secret adherents of the Jewish faith.

Leroy-Beaulieu's theory has indeed great intrinsic probability. For it is well known that under the rule of the Khazars, a South Russian people of West Turkish origin, and their Khagans, Judaism was the state religion of the realm. That realm embraced the whole district from the Caspian to the Black Sea, from the Don to the Volga, indeed for a time from the Dnieper to the Urals, extending southwards to the Caucasus and occasionally beyond, and northwards to the lower valley of the Oka and Moskva. Judaism had held this position since the eighth century, when, after a previous conversion of the people to Christianity, the Khagan Bulan—probably from political motives, to ensure the spiritual independence of his state, which lay between the Christian Byzantium and the Islamic kingdom of the Abbasids—under the influence of Jewish exiles from Constantinople went over to the Mosaic religion. Within this empire in the time of Masudi (ninth century), Mahometans, Christians, and heathen lived peaceably side by side along with the Jews. Kiev for a time belonged to it, as well as the later principalities of Moscow and Perejaslavl Suzdalski. When the Russians under Prince Svjatoslav overthrew the dominion of the Khazars in the year 967 or 968, the position of the Jews and Jewish Khazars in the country must have been precisely similar to that of the Spanish Jews after the fall of Granada. Mass movements into the Greek Church must natur-

---

[1] *L'Empire des Tsars*, Paris, 1889, iii. 515-18.

ally have resulted in a sham Christianity,[1] which could conceal itself much more easily than the Maraño religion in Catholic Spain, because the Old Russian Church itself, perhaps under the influence of Jewish converts, strictly observed the so-called Noachian prohibitions of consuming blood and 'animals strangled' or 'torn,' which were regarded by rabbis also as binding upon 'proselytes of the gate.'

On the 'Judaizing heresy' at its flourishing period, dating from the last third of the fifteenth century, we possess detailed information in the contemporary work of Abbot Josif Volotzki of Volokolamsk († 1516), entitled 'Prosvjetitel' = 'Illuminator' or 'Revealer,' i.e. of the Judaizing heresy.[2]   According to him, the great and decisive crisis arose from the rich merchant republic of Novgorod, at that time seething with political, religious, and social unrest.   Because through it, by the Neva and the Volkov, flowed Russia's trade with the Baltic and so with the Hanseatic towns and Western Europe, Russian historians like Ilovajski have sought to find some connection between the Russian Church crisis at the end of the fifteenth century and the German Reformation, a view which both chronologically and from the standpoint of doctrinal history is completely mistaken.

Novgorod, which had always been a breeding-ground for heretical movements, and had already been seriously disquieted by the so-called Strigolniki of Karp, found itself at that time in a position of extreme difficulty.   The plague years of 1465-7 had almost crippled its trade with the West, while a deep-seated opposition between the rich patrician merchants and the lower classes, who were badly hit by the stagnation of trade, had seriously weakened the city's defensive strength.   To meet the threat to its independence as a free state from the Grand Duke of Moscow, Ivan III. Vasiljevič, the council sought political support from Casimir IV. of Lithuania and Poland.   Casimir on his side, with shrewd calculation, favoured the Catholicizing efforts of Gregory the Metropolitan Bishop of Kiev, a supporter of reunion of the Eastern and Western Churches, and had brought over a considerable number of Russian nobles to recognize at once the overlordship of Lithuania and the spiritual primacy of Kiev.   A section of clergy and laity of Novgorod, clinging tenaciously to the independence and strict observance of the rules of the Greek Church, viewed with the greatest disinclination these overtures to Lithuania, dictated by

---

[1] A 'circumcised' monk, Adrian (Andreas) of Kiev, is generally named as the first heretic in Russian Church history.   He is said to have fought hard against the worship of images and to have attacked the Russian clergy as idolatrous, thus betraying typical Jewish-Christian tendencies.

[2] The exact title of the book is 'The unworthy monk Joseph's story of the newly risen sect of Novgorod heretics and apostates,' etc.   Many printed editions, notably that of Kasan, 1852 and 1888.

PLATE XVII

TSAR IVAN III VASSILIEVIC
PROTECTOR AND PERSECUTOR OF THE JUDAIZING HERESY OF RUSSIA
WOODCUT AFTER A CONTEMPORARY PORTRAIT SUPPLIED TO ANDRÉ THEVET BY A GREEK RESIDENT OF
GALATA

politics, and were assiduously supported by the partisans of Moscow.   Ivan himself in a letter to Jonas, Archbishop of Novgorod, bluntly pronounced Gregory of Kiev a heretic, and admonished Jonas to hold fast the Pravo-Slavic faith.   When the Novgorodians openly broke with Moscow and received from the hand of Casimir a sovereign who, though a Lithuanian, was of the Greek Orthodox Church, namely, Michael Olelkovič (8th November 1470), a number of Lithuanian Jews followed in his train, probably as financial agents of the Lithuanian court.   Their names were Osif, Shmoilo, Skaryei, Moisei, and Chanush, their leader being a certain Skharia (=Zacharias) of Kiev.   He is described as a Karaïte [1] and an adept in astrology,[2] necromancy, and the magic arts, laudatory epithets from which we may perhaps infer that he was simply a physician practising his profession after the fashion of the age.   That he was a Karaïte is not improbable, since Witold, Grand Duke of Lithuania, had in the fourteenth century carried off a number of Karaïtes from the Crimea [3] and settled them in Troki near Vilna : moreover, it is well known that, while the Karaïtes regarded Pauline Christianity as an unpardonable apostasy from Judaism, many of them held Jesus himself to be a pious, just, and God-favoured man—a point of view exactly in accordance with the doctrines of this Skharia set forth below.

According to the full and credible statement of Josif of Volokolamsk, he taught his disciples that the belief in a triune God was vain ; that there was but one God ; that Jesus was not the Son of God nor the Messiah, but only a prophet like Moses, and therefore could not have risen from the dead; and that the Messiah had not yet appeared, but would come at the end of time, and even then not as Son of God *according to his essence*, but only *according to his works*, like Moses and the prophets of old.   Consequently, until then the Law of Moses was binding; the Sabbath and the food laws must continue to be observed, circumcision be practised, and the veneration of icons and saints shunned as idolatrous.   The writings of the New Testament were full of errors and incredible statements ; the Lord's Supper was only an allegorical form of the Passover rite, which should be kept according to the Jewish calendar; the Wednesday and Friday fasts were useless ; and so on.

Astonishing as it sounds, the testimony of his opponents leaves no room for doubt that these doctrines of Zacharias met with extraordinary favour among a section of the higher ecclesiastics of Novgorod.   He succeeded in converting to his views Gabriel, the

---

[1] The Karaïtes were Jewish ' protestants,' who rejected the oral Rabbinic tradition, and regarded the Old Testament as the only source of revelation.

[2] Perhaps because the Karaïtes insisted on an astronomically calculated calendar.

[3] They had ventured into that district in the time of the Khazars, and can be traced there from the thirteenth century onwards.

protopope of the church of Hagia Sophia in Novgorod, the proto-popes Alexis and Dionys, Gregory Michailovič Tučin, son of a Novgorod patrician, and many other clerics of Novgorod and Pshkov. We ask ourselves whether we have not from the outset to reckon with some political intrigue of Ivan III. of Moscow, striving to produce a cleavage, the deepest and widest possible, between the people and clergy of Novgorod, with perhaps the whole of Russia on the one hand, and the Catholicizing, pro-union metro-politans of Kiev along with the Lithuanian-Polish kingdom on the other. The fact remains that the new archbishop Theophilus, the successor of Jonas, who died two days before the arrival of Michael Olelkovič, was working for Moscow and took no action against the Judaists ; also that Ivan III. during a visit in 1480 to Nov-gorod, which had meanwhile fallen completely under his sway, treated the Judaizing protopopes Dionys and Alexei with great respect, and indeed subsequently took them with him to Moscow, where he appointed them archimandrites of the churches of the ' Anastasis ' and the ' archangel Michael.' Here they started upon a lively and apparently quite unimpeded propaganda movement, favoured by the fact that the court, in consequence of an incident at the solemn dedication of a church, was on very bad terms with Gerontios, Metropolitan of Moscow (1472-89). Among their converts the most important were Feodor Kurytzin, who as private secretary to the Tsar enjoyed his unbounded confidence ; Zosima, the archimandrite of the Simeon monastery in Moscow ; and a certain monk named Škhariah.

Even Helen, the emperor's daughter-in-law, and her son Dmitri, the heir to the throne, were won over to the Judaistic cause ; the Tsar himself tacitly but emphatically favoured it. When the Metropolitan Gerontios, disliked at court, died on the 28th of May 1489, the seat remained vacant for eighteen months— a symptom of the protracted intrigues and counter-intrigues which preceded the nomination of a successor ; finally, *Zosima the Juda-ist was appointed Metropolitan of Moscow*. The same year, it is true, saw the death of Alexis, described by Josif of Volokolamsk as the real ' boar of hell ' and ' devastator of the garden of Christ '; still, after the occupation of the metropolitan see of Moscow by a Judaist, after the conversion of the Tsar's chancellor Kurytzin and Dmitri, heir to the throne, the sectarians might well hope for a brilliant victory, the more so because the Tsar Ivan III. appeared to welcome everything which impeded the pro-union efforts of Kiev and thereby counteracted the political influence of the Catholic king of Lithuania and Poland.

It goes without saying that the Greek Orthodox clergy did not quietly look on at this cynically calculated toleration of such a movement by the *Gossudar* of all Russia, who was a queer charof Jesus than the Unitarian-Judaistic doctrine of the heretics described above.

Just as the opponents of the Judaists had Nicolas of Lyra translated into Russian as a counterblast to the Jewish heresy (p. 155), so must the Jews on their side have translated Josephus into Slavonic for the sake of their religious propaganda. That this happened in Lithuania of all places and at the time when the Catholic and the Orthodox Greek Church were competing for the soul of the heathen King Mindowe is now readily intelligible. As the case of the heretic monk Adrian shows (p. 156 n. 1), there were crypto-Jews even among the 'white' monastic clergy of the Orthodox Church. In provinces like Lithuania, where Christianity was not yet the dominant religion, they may have been in closer contact than elsewhere with their unbaptized brethren, and have nursed daring hopes of bringing back Christianity to Judaism on a Unitarian basis, or at least of convincing the Lithuanian Grand Dukes of the advantages of the Mosaic religion, by the same means of public religious discussion as had once served—at least according to a pious legend—to convert Bulan, Khagan of the Khazars, to Judaism. The use made of the so-called ' Chronographer of Perejaslavl Suzdalski,' whose history extends to the year 1214, shows that the translator or translators of Josephus had associates, assisting in the work, even in Suzdal, the northernmost extremity of the old province of the Vjatitches, once tributary to the empire of the Khazars.

All particulars of the MS. tradition accord excellently with the result so far reached. The codex of Vilna (p. 118, No. 15), *written*, according to Istrin, *in Lithuania*, lay until 1916 in the very district from which Prince Michael Olelkovič came to Novgorod with the five Lithuanian Jews and with Zacharias the Karaïte of Kiev, and to which the two Moscow merchants afterwards repaired to get themselves secretly circumcised—clearly, therefore, the starting-point of the whole movement. Zacharias must have been connected with the Karaïtes of Troki near Vilna. The copy of the Josephus MS. used by the Metropolitan Makarios was written in Novgorod (p. 147), i.e. at the place where Zacharias, as early as 1468, had converted to Judaism the protopopes Alexei and Dionys, Gabriel and the patrician Tučin, three years before he himself entered it with Olelkovič. This proves either that this was not the Karaïte's first visit to Novgorod, or that he had previously sent out the propaganda literature of his sect through fellow-members journeying on business to the great merchant city on the Volkov. The highly remarkable fact that the MS. copied at Novgorod in 1468 had itself been written in 1399 at Constantinople can be easily explained by the assumption that the Karaïte Zacharias was in touch with the flourishing Karaïte community in Constantinople.

The MS. 654 of the Moscow Clerical Academy (p. 117), which Berendts chose as a basis for his translation, comes from the monastery of Volokolamsk, whose abbot Josif was the most active opponent of the 'Jewish heresy' (p. 160), and expressly mentions the evidence of Josephus in the second chapter of his book ' Pros-vjetitel.' It will not be over-hazardous to conjecture that in it we have the very copy made for the use of the famous anti-Judaizing controversialist, Josif Volotzki of Volokolamsk. The Josephus MS. 445 of Kasan contains at the top of a blank leaf the note, ' This book is a gift of Ivan Vassilievič, Tsar, ruler and Grand Duke of All Russia '—that is to say, the great protector and subsequently executioner of Feodor Kurytzin and the other Juda-ists ! One would like to know *to whom* the Grand Prince presented this remarkable book, where, in those portraits of the demoniacal Herod, his quarrelsome wives and rebellious sons, he must have seen, as in a spectral mirror of history, himself, his wives Mary and Zoe-Sophia, his daughter-in-law Helen, and his treacherous heirs Basilios and Demetrios. Like the almost identical Codex Kasan 444, with the two codices copied from it, 445 and 446, it comes *from the Soloveitzki monastery on that barren island in the White Sea* which, used to this day by the Russian Government as an ill-famed dumping-ground for ' political offenders,' served the Tsars so long as a place of exile for heretics, until the monastery, in consequence of these numerous deportations, fell into the hands of the exiled Raskolniki, was recovered after repeated military expeditions against a stubborn resistance, and on the 22nd of January 1676 had to be demolished. The four MSS. must have belonged to as many Judaizing clerics condemned to confinement in distant monasteries. More detailed investigation of the extant records and authorities on the judicial procedure against heretics in the year 1504, to which I have so far not had access, would perhaps enable us to identify the particular monastery to which the Juda-ists who escaped death were banished. But even now one may conjecture that the three MSS. of the St. Kyrillos monastery at Bjelo Osero, as well as the four from the Soloveitzki monastery, were once the property of interned Judaists.

On the other hand, the Rumanian MS. of the Very Rev. Dr. Moses Gaster (p. 116), translated from Polish, is clearly, if one may judge from its main contents (Christian *Acts of Pilate*, etc.), a col-lection of materials made by an Orthodox controversialist to combat the Judaists. This indicates that the movement sup-pressed in Russia must have spread to Poland and ultimately to Moldavia and Valachia (p. 597 ll. 20 ff.).

The Sect of the Josephinists in Northern Italy and Provence, and the Heresy of 'Josephus Epaphroditus' in Asia Minor

The close parallel existing between the sceptical gloss concerning the resurrection and the views of the Russian Judaists discussed above, at first led me to a belief that it, too, was a late interpolation of purely Slavonic origin and of the same nature as the Slavonic explanations of ancient place-names and names of ancient peoples.[1] I am indebted to M. Paul Alphandéry for calling my attention to the fact that the gloss may go back to the Byzantine original of the Slavonic translator. This important fact in turn permits us to trace the origins of the Judaizing heresy a few centuries further back in the history of the Greek Church. M. Alphandéry also was not slow in suspecting a connexion between the Russian phenomenon and the sect of the Josephinists[2] which sprang up in Northern Italy and Provence some time in the thirteenth century—that is, at approximately the same period which saw the Slavonic Josephus translation in Lithuania. The term (*Josepini, Josephini, Josephistae*) first occurs in a decree of Pope Lucius III. and the Council of Verona (1184), in a bull of Gregory IX. of 1231, and in charters of the Emperor Frederick II. (1239), always in the fixed formula ' circumcisos, passaginos, Josephinos,' from which one may infer that it is a question of Judaists practising circumcision. The term *passaginos*, of doubtful meaning, most probably indicates ' vagabonds,' ' vaganti,' corresponding to the *strojniki*, the ' straying' apostles of the Bulgarian Bogomils—that is, people who leave their settled homes and take up a wanderer's life from religious conviction, just as Leo Tolstoi did at the end of his life.

Of the terms *Josepini* or *Josephistae* there exists only a very ancient and doubtless erroneous explanation. A treatise attributed to the inquisitor Rainier Sacconi, who died in 1258, derives the word from the *matrimonium spirituale* still called 'Joseph's marriage.' Were the treatise really the work of Sacconi, himself a converted Catharist, the explanation would deserve some attention. Yet the treatise is absolutely spurious, a work of the fourteenth century, and altogether untrustworthy. It is furthermore quite impossible that the Judaizing sect should have adopted the ascetic doctrines of the Marcionites and Manichaeans, the American ' Shakers' of more modern days. Dr. Amman,[3] however, pointed out that the sect in question is most probably derived from

---

[1] See below, p. 216 ll. 15-20.
[2] Bibliography in L. J. Newman, *Jewish Influence on Christian Reform Movements*, New York, 1926, p. 300 *sqq.*
[3] Art. ' Joséphistes' in the *Dictionnaire de Théologie Cath.*, t. viii. c. 1547.

a seventh-century sect of Asia Minor, usually counted among the Paulicians, and which the Byzantine heresiologists of the ninth, tenth, and eleventh centuries attribute to a founder named Josephus Epaphroditus, ' whose very existence is doubted by some,' as the Greek text has it.   If one recalls that to some Jewish Talmudists the Gospels themselves took on the shape of a mythical heretic called ' Euangelion,' a hypothetical founder of the Christian ' sect,' one cannot but suspect in this enigmatical Josephus Epaphroditus the names of our old acquaintances Flavius Josephus and his publisher Epaphroditus.[1]   The Pseudo-Photius and Petrus Siculus are indeed the first who speak of a ' spurious Josephus ' ('Ιώσηπος νόθος), evidently with reference to the discrepancies they noticed between the Josephus of the heretics and the canonical Josephus of the Byzantine Church.

If these alleged ' spurious ' writings of Josephus could originate a new sect in a community which had already embraced an adoptionist Christology, the point at issue can naturally only have been statements about Jesus in the unabbreviated text whether of the *Halōsis* or of the *Antiquities*. Since in the extant MSS. the name of Epaphroditus in the form of a dedication occurs only in the *Antiquities* and not in the *War*, the allusion to one Josephus Epaphroditus is a valuable hint to the effect that the text of the *Antiquities*, too, must have contained a statement about Jesus which appeared objectionable to the Orthodox on dogmatic grounds.

It is interesting to see just how far this text could and must have helped to shape the sect's conception of Christ.   The Paulicians, as is well known, assumed that Jesus was one of God's angels sent to earth under the obligation to suffer vicarious death.   This conception coincides with the Jewish explanation of the Messiah as an angel (*ben 'elohîm*), a ' son of God ' in the Old Testament sense, an explanation found as early as the debate between Justin and R. Trypho.   It is clearly with reference to this early Judeo-Christian doctrine that the Slavonic text thinks it necessary to refute the theory that Jesus of Nazareth was an angel.   Paulicians, taking for a basis of their doctrine the accounts of Jesus as found in Flavius Josephus, must have denied that Jesus was an angel, and the Paulician adherents of the hypothetical 'Josephus Epaphroditus ' would then simply be a special sect which had adopted the writings of Josephus (or some of them) into their canon, a procedure which is by no means unique in the annals of the Christian churches.[2]

The spread of the sect is explained in part by the transplanting of Paulicians from the Taurus to Constantinople and Thrace in the reign of the Emperors Constantine Copronymus (741-75) and

---

[1] See above, p. 30 n. 3.
[2] See e.g. above, p. 119, on the Uvarov MS.   Cp. also above, p. 31 l. 22.

John Tzimiskes (970) ; further by the primitive apostolic practice of itinerant preaching adopted by these heretics.[1]   Thus they spring up in Northern Italy and Provence on the one hand and in Lithuania on the other.   There and in Constantinople they spread their Josephus in the Old Slavonic language.   With the Paulicians they have in common their hostility to the organized clergy, the monks, and image-worship.   Their resumption of the practice of circumcision connects them with the Russian Judaists and with the same practice in the Armenian Church.

THE ' ORTHODOX ' AND THE ' SPURIOUS ' JOSEPHUS

We are now in a position to follow up the history of the MS. tradition of our author in the Greek world.   Origen, as we saw, knew a Josephus who did not acknowledge in any way the messiah-ship of Jesus, and he was therefore rather astonished to find in the same book a fairly neutral attitude toward the lapidated James the Just.   Eusebius knows and quotes *Ant.* xviii. 3. 3 in a form recognizing in Jesus the messiah, a version which has altered in the most remarkable manner the original statements absolutely hostile to Jesus.   He knows the chronological falsification of the dates of Pilate's administration and of the date of the miracle concerning the exit of the *Shekinah* from the temple in the *War* (vi. 5. 3),[2] and, lastly, the interpolation of the slaughter of the innocents, absent from the standard Greek text but still found in the Slavonic version, in Photius, and in Moses of Khorene.[3]   We also saw that these chronological falsifications were occasioned by the publication of the genuine *Acta Pilati* at the order of the Emperor Maximinus Daïa in A.D. 311.[4]   The reworking of most of the MSS. found in public and private libraries was facilitated by the censorship estab-lished in the reign of Constantine and still more enforced under Theodosius and Valentinian in A.D. 449.   There actually exists no Josephus MS., Greek, Latin, Aramaic, Hebrew, or Arabic, which does not show clear traces of Christian interpolations and deletions.

The writings of Josephus thus falsified were given the honour of being adopted into the canons of several Eastern churches, chiefly because the author now was supposed to furnish an im-

---

[1] Petrus Siculus, p. 36 ed. Gieseler : one of their apostles says that he ' travelled from east to west, from south to north, till his knees began to shake.'

[2] Eusebius, *Chron.*, ap. Sync., p. 324 f. (cf. Jerome, *Ep. Paulae et Eutocii ad Marcellam*, opp. ed. Vallarsi, vol. i. p. 202).   Both quote from Josephus the story about the mysterious voice from the inner sanctum, 'let us emigrate from here,' as happening *at the time of the crucifixion*, while the standard texts say that that sign happened a short time before the fall of the city in A.D. 70.   Cp. above, p. 141 ff., on a similar falsification, perpetrated before A.D. 180, of the date of the murder of James the Just.   [3] Above, p. 144 n. 3.   [4] Above, p. 16 n. 3.

partial testimony, though grudgingly given, not on Christ's existence (which no one ever doubted in those days) but on his messiahship. Josephus was even made to prove the historicity of the massacre of the innocents, of the destruction of Jerusalem as a punishment for the death of Christ, of the rending of the temple curtain, and even of the resuscitation of Lazarus, and all that as early as the end of the second century of our era. The account in the *Antiquities* was so condensed and worked over that it seemed to confirm almost the entire apostolic creed. The fact that the account in the *War* and the *Halōsis*, less reworked than the other, rather emphasized the human traits of the historical Jesus did not in itself meet with objection on the part of the Church, until it was noticed with horror that Josephus had remained a most dangerous weapon in the hands of Judaizing Unitarians—witness the rise of the sect of Josephinists. In spite of all deletions and interpolations Josephus was still at variance with the accounts of the Gospels, especially in his mention of a rebellion planned by the adherents of Christ. Aside from this, Josephus revealed a certain revolutionary past of Christianity, now become a highly respectable state religion, which could not but fill the clergy with alarm, the more so because the rebellions of the Paulicians and the Bogomil preachers of the ' kingdom of the poor ' had just revealed that dangerous social doctrines were still slumbering in the hidden recesses of the Church.

Such a state of affairs led to the complete deletion of all passages dealing with Jesus, whilst the MSS. in the hands of the heretics and therefore inaccessible to the ecclesiastical censor were simply denounced as ' falsified.' The deletion of the Jesus passages had as a natural consequence the omission also of the statements regarding his disciples and John the Baptist. Nor is it difficult to determine the period of these changes in the Josephus text. Neither Petrus Hegumenus nor Photius (died in 891) knows anything of a spurious Josephus—who does not appear before the writings of the Pseudo-Photius, himself dependent upon Euthymius of Zygabene (died after 1111), and of Petrus Siculus. This result is fully corroborated by the quotation in the works of the patriarch Photius of the passage concerning the slaughter of the innocents, a passage missing in the extant MSS. of Josephus. The revision of the *War* to which it owes its present form is therefore in fact posterior to Photius, so that, for example, the Russian library of Kiev, the first Russian bishopric, founded at the time of Photius, if it possessed the *Halōsis* (as is extremely likely), can have possessed only an unexpurgated copy.

Since none of the extant expurgated MSS. is older than the eleventh century, and since the Bulgarian bishop Theophylactos of Ochrida, a contemporary of the first emperor of the Comnene dynasty, still quotes from the interpolated *Halōsis*,[1] it is very probable indeed that precisely at that time (end of the eleventh century) the Greek Church ordered the radical revision of Josephus, as a check upon the heretics, and denounced all MSS. containing the older and genuine version as ' spurious,' in this way trying to cut the ground from under the feet of the Josephinist sect and the other Judaizing heresies.

[1] See above, p. 141 n. 1.

VIII

PASSAGES IN THE SLAVONIC JOSEPHUS WHICH CAN-NOT BE ACCOUNTED FOR AS CHRISTIAN FORGERIES

THE existence of a number of Christian interpolations in the Slavonic text of Josephus may, then, be taken for granted. Yet I should confidently challenge any one to try to interpret in that simple way the following paragraphs. The passages in question, absent from the Greek standard text as well as from the Latin translations, cannot for a moment be considered Christian in meaning or sentiment. As a matter of fact, they have nothing whatever to do with the history or pre-history of Christianity. They are reprinted here from Dr. Thackeray's version of Berendts' German translation, revised after the Russian text first published in the German edition of this book from MS. copies kindly supplied by Prof. Vasilij N. Istrin of Leningrad.

Antipater before Caesar.

Standard Greek text, B.J., i. 10. 2-3, §§ 197 sqq.

Slavonic version, Berendts-Grass, p. 871.

'At these words Antipater stripped off his clothes and exposed his numerous scars. His loyalty to Caesar needed, he said, no words from him; his body cried it aloud, were he to hold his peace. But the audacity of Antigonus astounded him. The son of the enemy of the Romans, son of a fugitive from Rome, one who inherited from his father a passion for revolution and sedition, presuming to accuse others in the presence of the Roman general and looking for favours when he ought to be thankful to be alive. Indeed (said Antipater), his present ambition for power was not due to indigence; he wanted it in order to sow sedition among the Jews and to employ his resources

in order to sow dissension between the Jews and the Romans and to rise

170

against those who had provided them.

against him who had given (him) the power. Mithridates, however, testified before Caesar to Antipater's valour.

'After hearing both speakers, Caesar pronounced Hyrcanus to be the more deserving claimant to the high-priesthood, and left Antipater free choice of office. The latter, replying that it rested with him who conferred the honour to fix the measure of the honour, was then appointed viceroy of all Judaea. He was further authorised to rebuild the ruined walls of the metropolis. Orders were sent by Caesar to Rome for these honours to be graven in the Capitol, as a memorial of his own justice and of Antipater's valour.'

'Caesar, however, having heard both speeches and seen the wounds of his body which he had received in the war, honoured him with a high Roman dignity,

and remitted the tax to his country.[1] The high-priestly dignity he confirmed to Hyrcanus for his sake. But Hyrcanus he honoured with the higher rank.'

Explanation of Roman Customs for Jewish Readers.

Greek *B.J.*, i. § 285.

'The meeting (of the Senate) was dissolved and Antony and Caesar left the senate-house with Herod between them, preceded by the consuls and the other magistrates, as they went to offer sacrifice and to lay up the decree in the Capitol.

Berendts-Grass, p. 107.

'After the senators had dispersed, Caesar and Antony with Herod between them went into the palace;[2] the Roman priests,[3] however, the princes, and the consuls to the Capitol to a sacrifice and to make a record concerning the kingdom of Herod.

'For thus is their custom: if Caesar gives a dignity[4] to some-

---

[1] This is probably untrue, and Josephus had to delete the statement in the revised edition of his work. It is unthinkable that the Slavonic translator should have added this passage. Nothing could be more indifferent to him than the question whether thirteen centuries before his age the Jews were or were not taxed by the Romans.

[2] What or whose palace? The author imagines that even in those republican times there was an imperial palace of Caesar's in Rome.

[3] No mention of them in the Greek text and no need for them in reality, because the magistrates could very well throw some incense or pour out a libation on the altar of Jupiter Capitolinus without priestly assistance. But the Jewish priestly author cannot imagine a sacrifice without its being performed by the priests or a procession of state, without their playing the main part in the show. The reader will observe that the priests are given precedence before the 'princes and consuls' by our *Joseph hak-kohen*!

[4] The author has not understood his source (Nicolaus of Damascus), which states clearly that the Senate, on the suggestion of Antony, made Herod king. For him 'Caesar' is even at that time—before the battle of Actium and in the lifetime of Antony!—the omnipotent Roman emperor, making and unmaking kings!

On this, the first day of his reign, Herod was given a banquet by Antony.'

body, it is not valid until he (!) writes it down on the Capitol. When it is proclaimed, a royal sacrifice[1] is offered, and through it it (the kingdom) will become valid. On the first day of (his) kingdom Antony offered a banquet for him.'

Herod's Dream.

Greek *B.J.*, i. § 328.

' But while Herod was at Daphne, near Antioch, he had a dream.

distinctly warning him of his brother's death, and springing in horror from his bed was met by the messengers bringing news of the catastrophe. After brief lamentation for his loss, he deferred further mourning for another season and set out in haste to meet his foes.'

' But when Herod was in Antioch he saw a dream which revealed to him in advance his brother's death. Now the dream was in this wise. There were four ears of corn : the first was dry through frost, but the second stood upright, while wolves fell upon the third and cut it down and dragged it behind them. But the interpretation of it was in this wise. The first ear was Phasael, whom poison had dried up ; the second ear was himself, inasmuch as he was unscathed ; while the third was his brother Joseph, whom warriors cut down and dragged away without burial. And his soul was stirred within him ; at once terror seized him, and he went forth from the bedchamber about midnight like one possessed. For the soul, which had understood sooner than the spirit, was afraid (and forthwith there came to him the melancholy tidings).'

While the reader of the Greek version is led to believe that in a dream Herod had seen his brother die, rose in nocturnal fright from his bed, and immediately got confirmation of the bad news, the Slavonic version has all the details of a dream allegory which needs interpretation, and reminds the reader forcibly of the famous dream about ears of corn in the story of the Old Testament

[1] This 'royal offering' is derived from the priestly law in *Ezekiel* xlvi. 4! Roman ceremonial knows nothing of it. The sentence is not even consistent in itself : of course, a regal offering is not required for every kind of dignity conferred upon a man. But for Josephus, of course, no office could be held legally by its incumbent unless he had properly sacrificed with due priestly assistance.

Joseph, the namesake of our Josephus, who elsewhere [1] takes great pride in his priestly craft of interpreting dreams and loses no opportunity to relate prophetic dreams and their successful interpretation by Essenes and other specialists.   For a Western, Hellenized reader the story is infinitely more dramatic if the stilted and not very plausible allegory is left out ; but it is easy to imagine the pleasure of a reader or a writer steeped in Biblical lore when he read or described this symbolical picture and its ' wise ' interpretation.

Phasael and Hyrcanus trapped by the Parthians.

Greek *B.J.*, i. 253-270.

Berendts-Grass, p. 101 *sq.*

' When the feast called Pentecost came round, the whole neighbourhood of the temple and the entire city were crowded with countryfolk, for the most part in arms.

Phasael defended the walls ; Herod, with a small force, the palace.

With this he descended upon the enemy's disordered ranks in the suburb, killed *large numbers* of them, put the rest to flight, and shut *them* up, some in the city, others in the temple, others in the entrenched camp outside the walls. Thereupon Antigonus petitioned for the admission of Pacorus as mediator.

Phasael consented, and received into the city and offered hospitality to the Parthian, who, with five hundred horsemen, had come ostensibly to put an end to strife—in reality to support Antigonus.

With this object, Pacorus insidiously induced Phasael to go on an embassy to Barzapharnes with a view to the cessation of hostilities. : So, notwithstanding the strong dissuasion of Herod, who urged his brother to kill the schemer and not to abandon himself to his schemes, barbarians being (he said) by nature perfidious,

' But since the feast had begun which is called Pentecost, all the people had assembled, partly in arms, partly simply (as civilians).

And at that time Herod took the rest of the troops with him and suddenly broke forth out of the court.   And he killed *twenty thousand* of the people.   But the rest shut themselves up in the Temple.

—

And therefore Antigonus—with Pacorus—entreated him to make peace.

Phasael, having concluded the peace with them and prepared a sumptuous banquet, invited them with their troops, and, having honoured them, dismissed them with gifts.

Pacorus, however, in his wiliness tried to get Phasael and Hyrcanus.   And having prepared a banquet, he invited them.

Herod, however, sent to Phasael a warning to be wary of Pacorus and not to trust himself into the hands of those lusting for his death, neither to put faith in barbarians even if they sware oaths.

[1] *B.J.*, iii. 352.

Phasael left the city, accompanied by Hyrcanus.

To allay suspicion, Pacorus left with Herod some of the cavalry called by the Parthians "freemen"; with the remainder he escorted Phasael on his way.

On their arrival in Galilee they found the inhabitants in revolt and up in arms. The satrap, with whom they had an audience, was a very crafty individual who disguised his plot under a show of benevolence : he gave them presents, and then laid an ambush to catch them on their departure. They discovered the conspiracy at a maritime town, where they halted, named Ekdippa. There they heard of the promise of the thousand talents, and that the five hundred women whom Antigonus had devoted to the Parthians included most of their own ; that the barbarians invariably kept a watch upon them at night ; and that they would long since have been arrested, had not the conspirators been waiting till Herod was caught at Jerusalem, fearing that the news of their capture would put him on his guard. This was now no mere idle gossip ; for already they could see the sentries posted in the distance. Phasael, however, notwithstanding the urgent exhortations to flee made to him by a certain Ophellius, who had learnt the whole plan of the conspiracy from Saramalla, the wealthiest Syrian of his time,

Phasael, however, trusting in his good right and straightforwardness and in the oath, took Hyrcanus with him and went without any precaution.

And [1] while they went to the banquet they [2]

---

[1] Obviously standing for ' but ' !   Cp. C. F. Burney, *The Aramaic Origin of the Fourth Gospel*, Oxford, 1922, p. 66 : ' a striking Semitic usage may be seen in the employment of καί to link *contrasted* statements, where in English we should naturally employ " and yet " or " but." '

[2] Here something seems to have dropped out.   The brothers must *at least* have noticed *some signs* of treachery, when it was too late.   Supply, perhaps, ' they were surrounded by a detachment of cavalry.'   It is quite possible, however, that the omission of such a logically necessary clause is due to the negligence of Josephus himself, whose first draft was properly corrected afterwards by one of his ' collaborators.'

could not bring himself to desert Hyrcanus. Instead he went to the satrap and frankly reproached him for the plot, and in particular for acting as he had done from mercenary motives ; undertaking, for his part, to give him a larger sum for his life than Antigonus had promised for a kingdom. To this the Parthian made a wily reply, clearing himself of suspicion by protestations and oaths, and went off to join Pacorus. Immediately after, certain Parthians who had been left behind, with orders to do so, arrested Phasael and Hyrcanus, the prisoners cursing them bitterly for their perjury and breach of faith.

were both full of repentance and cursed his [1] infidelity !

. . . .

In Jerusalem, meanwhile, the Parthians gave themselves up to pillage, breaking into the houses of the fugitives and into the palace ; refraining only from the funds of Hyrcanus, which, however, amounted to no more than three hundred talents. Elsewhere they found less than they had expected; for Herod, long since suspecting the barbarians of perfidy, had taken the precaution of removing the most precious of his treasures to Idumaea, and each of his friends had done likewise. After the pillage, the insolence of the Parthians proceeded to extremes. They let loose on the whole country the horrors of implacable war, laid the city of Marisa in ruins, and, not content with raising Antigonus to the throne, delivered up to him Phasael and Hyrcanus, in chains, for torture. Hyrcanus threw himself at the feet of Antigonus, who with his own teeth lacerated his suppliant's ears, in order to disqualify him for ever,

And Antigonus jumped up and with his teeth bit away both ears of Hyrcanus, when he in an unmanly way begged for his life.

[1] viz. Pacorus'.

under any change of circumstances, from resuming the high - priest-hood; since freedom from physical defect is essential to the holder of that office. Phasael, on the other hand, courageously forestalled the king's malice by dashing his head upon a rock, being deprived of the use of hands or steel. Thus show-ing himself to be a true brother of Herod, and Hyrcanus the most ignoble of men, he died a hero's death—an end in keeping with his life's career.'

But Antigonus did that to him, so that, although being alive later on, he should not become high priest.

For the law enjoins that the high priest must not have any bodily defects. Phasael, however, who had much rebuked Pacorus because of his hard-heartedness, insidiousness, and avarice, died in consequence of this, without hav-ing said anything low-spirited.'

In this case the two versions differ as to the way in which the two men were trapped by the Persians. The Slavonic version seems to imply that they were taken prisoners in Jerusalem by Pacorus—in the city where Herod is present with his army. The Greek version has a much more detailed and plausible story about their arrest in Galilee. The more detailed story may have been inserted into a shorter, less exact account, or the full account may have been curtailed by an awkward hand. As there can be no doubt about the fact that something has dropped out of the Slavonic text in the middle of the clause—between our notes 1 and 2 on p. 174—and since there is no clear motive for deleting the episode of Phasael and Hyrcanus' journey to Galilee, it seems evident that either Josephus by misadventure skipped a paragraph in his source—an error which was properly rectified in the revised edition of his first draft—or that by accident a leaf had dropped out of the MS. which the Russian translator used for his work, or that, finally, the author of the Slavonic translation had jumped a paragraph of his exemplar without noticing the mistake.

Accusations of Herod against the Wife of Pheroras.

Greek B.J., i. § 571.

Berendts-Grass, p. 194 sq.

' The king assembled a council of his friends and relations and accused the wretched woman of numerous misdeeds, among others of insulting his own daughters, of subsidizing the Pharisees to oppose him . . .

' And he said, Thou hast given to the Pharisees great gifts against me and prepared all kinds of magic as well for (my) food as for (my) vestments as for (my) shoes and also for my carriage. Remember, Pheroras, what a death happened ⟡

to Pesia the prince when I wanted
to eat of thy food and—because
God had protected me—did not
partake of it and sent Pesia. Because he tasted (of it), his eyes
protruded out of his head and his
limbs fell asunder, joint after joint,
and howling he gave up his ghost
on the third day. Once, however,
when I touched the bridle (of my
carriage) my hand dried up after
this. If at that time a Syrian
snake-killer [1] had not turned up
who cut open a living horse and
put my hand into it, (she) would
have killed me through a mysterious and miraculous death. And
I tortured my stable-boy and he
put the blame upon her.

and of alienating his brother after
bewitching him with drugs.

' And with all that, she has put
over thee such an enmity against
me that thou hast forgotten God
as well as nature and brotherhood
and the burning love and the
dignity and the honour which my
painstaking and this head have
given thee. And now thou art
inimical against me and searchest

In conclusion he addressed Pheroras and told him

death for me. Since Pheroras did
not dare to utter a word in reply
and violently trembled because of

that he must choose one or the
other, either his brother or his
wife.'

his wife, Herod said : I give thee
two possibilities, take one. Either
abandon me and keep the woman,
or hold me as a brother but dismiss this woman.'

This passage calls for some comment. The first question is,
Who is this ' prince ' or ' commander ' *Pesia* of the Slavonic text,
whom Herod sends in his place to partake of the food prepared for
him at his brother's and his sister-in-law's house, and who is being
so miserably poisoned ? From the context it follows that he must
have been a distinguished member of the court, most probably a
relation of the king. Now, the Hebrew *Josippon* [2] calls Herod's
brother *Phasailu*—once,[3] however, *Phasiah*. This may be an

---

[1] The Russian has ' a snake-footed Syrian,' which is rank nonsense. ὀφιοκτόνος
was misread as ὀφιόπους.
[2] v. 3, p. 364, Breithaupt ; v. 7, p. 378, Br. ; v. 8, pp. 382, 384, 386, 387, Br.
[3] iv. 17, p. 315, Br.

M

ordinary form of endearment—as *Vassja* is used in Russian for
Vasilij (=Basilios)—but more likely it is the result of the euphem-
istic use of -*'el*, ' God ' (*ilu* might be the Idumaean pronunciation)
for -*jah* (=Jahveh), so that *Phasa'el* and *Phasajah* would stand in
the same relationship to one another as *Nathanjah* and *Nathanael*.
The Russian form *Pesia*, with P instead of a form with Φ, shows that
the name was originally written in Semitic characters, where פ
represents either Π or Φ. Now, if ' Pesia the prince ' is none but
Herod's brother Phasael, it is quite fitting that he should take
Herod's place at a banquet, and the poison story would agree with
the interpretation of Herod's dream.[1] But it is absolutely incon-
sistent with the previous paragraph, where Phasael is said, in the
Slavonic text, to have died a brave death at the hands of Antigonus, after having been captured treacherously by the Parthian
commander, whilst the corresponding Greek text even adds the
detail that he dashed his head against a stone. The contradiction
between this dramatic story and the interpretation of Herod's
dream is in a certain measure removed through Josephus' inserting
immediately after: ' according to another account, Phasael recovered
from his self-inflicted wound, and a physician sent by Antigonus,
and ostensibly attending to him, injected noxious drugs into the
wound and so killed him.' This addition, quite unnecessary in
the present Greek text since it says nothing about the interpretation of Herod's dream, would harmonize the story with the dream
but would be incompatible with Herod's accusations against the
wife of Pheroras, since she could not very well be made responsible
for the death of Phasael (*Phasia, Pesia*) at the hands of Antigonus'
physician. The whole muddle is obviously the result of Josephus
having negligently compiled various incompatible sources. At the
bottom is no doubt the fact that there were three princes named
Phasael in Herod's family—to wit, his brother, who probably died
a captive of Antigonus ;[2] this man's son by one of his wives, named
Pallas ; and Herod's own son Phasael. Either the second or the
third may have been sent to the fatal banquet to be poisoned there.
Josephus' source, probably some compilation of prophetic dreams,
confused the latter victim with the king's unfortunate brother.
Josephus noticed the contradiction and tried to remedy the ensuing confusion by adding the harmonizing sentence according to
which, as some say, Herod's brother died of poison after having
fractured his skull. Finding this expedient insufficient, he cancelled the story of Phasael's death at the fatal banquet, and finally,
when he had found out from the observations of his patron

---

[1] ' The first ear was Phasael, whom poison had dried up,' above, p. 172 l. 22.
[2] According to Sextus Julius Africanus (fragm. xvii. 1)—who probably draws
in Justus of Tiberias—Phasael was slain in the fray, while Herod fled for his life
from the Parthians.

Agrippa that there was an obvious confusion of two different Phasaels in the dream story, he deleted even that.

It is thus possible to account for the absence from the Greek standard text of both the dream and the banquet on the assumption that the text translated into Russian is an earlier draft of the Greek version. With the best will in the world I cannot imagine the reverse development—that is, the possibility of a moderately consistent text of Josephus having been thrown into this hopeless confusion through the awkwardness of some later interpolator adding, one cannot imagine why, these conflicting details. It is also well to bear in mind that Josephus may have had reasons of his own for saying as little as possible about poisoned food, bewitched raiment, poisoned horse and carriage harness, etc., in an edition destined to edify the Roman court. For was not one of the belles of this same Herodian family the mistress of the Emperor Titus, Josephus' gracious patron ?

Antipater's Comparison of himself with Heracles fighting the Hydra.

Greek *B.J.*, i. § 588.	Berendts-Grass, p. 200, 11-16.
' Then were these hydra heads	' But there are growing up against me and my children the heads of the Hydra. Just as Heracles sought to cut off the hundred heads of that beast with the sword, and when he had not yet reached the last head the heads again grew up, until he called Iolaus to his aid, and as Heracles hewed, Iolaus burned out with a firebrand the places that appeared through the gash, and thereby the growth of the heads of that beast was stayed,
the sons of Aristobulus and Alexander shooting up.'	even so have I cut off Aristobulus and Alexander but have gained no profit therefrom. For there are those who stand in their place, their sons, but I have no Iolaus to help me. And I know not how I should fulfil my desire.'

As is well known, in this book Josephus is largely indebted to Nicolaus of Damascus. It is out of the question that a rhetorically educated Greek like Nicolaus should interrupt a dramatic speech by such a silly elaboration of a myth known to every Greek schoolboy. Obviously, the paragraph in question is destined for Jewish readers unfamiliar with the heathen story. It is possible that

Josephus himself felt the need for his elucidation, but it is more probable—and we have tried to prove this in a previous chapter [1] —that he found it in a Semitic adaptation of the Greek historian, which he used in preference to the Greek original. Nothing is easier to explain than the deletion of these lines in his definite Greek edition.

A considerable number of similar divergencies might be adduced. Nor are they peculiar to the initial books. A few more examples culled from Book iv. will convince the reader of the contrary. A curious piece of information, found nowhere else in ancient literature, occurs in the Slavonic Josephus' account of the battle of Bedriacum between the troops of the rival emperors Otho and Vitellius.

Greek *B.J.*, iv. § 547.	Berendts-Grass, p. 495.
' In the battle fought at Bedriacum in Gaul against Valens and Caecina, the generals of Vitellius, on the first day Otho had the advantage, but on the second the troops of Vitellius.'	' On the first day Otho was victor, but on the second Vitellius. For he had during the night strewn (the ground with) three-pronged irons.[2] And in the morning, after they had drawn up in order of battle, when Vitellius feigned flight Otho pursued after them with his troops. And they reached the place on which the irons were strewn. Then were the horses lamed, and it was impossible either for the horses or for the men to extricate themselves. And the soldiers of Vitellius, who had turned back, slew all who lay (there). But Otho saw what had befallen (and) killed himself.'

Dio Cassius, Plutarch, Suetonius, and Tacitus know nothing of such a stratagem deciding the battle of Bedriacum ; yet the story may well have been true,[3] and may have been found by Josephus in one of the dispatches which Vespasian received concerning the encounter and duly entered in his correspondence books, which he placed at Josephus' disposal.[4] Yet it was certainly all the more tactless and awkward to give credit for strategic ability to Vespasian's obese and incompetent enemy, Vitellius not even having been present at

---

[1] Above, p. 136.
[2] The so-called *tribuli*. See Daremberg-Saglio's *Dictionnaire des Antiq.*, s.v.
[3] See Sal. Reinach in the *Comptes rendus de l'Académie des Inscript.*, 15th February 1929, p. 42. Reprinted in *Amalthée*, vol. ii., Paris, 1930, pp. 336-341.
[4] Below, p. 202.

the battle. A correction of the *faux pas* by a timely and diplomatic deletion of the offending paragraph was therefore inevitable. Any one trying to explain this passage as a late interpolation would have to attribute it to a partisan of Vitellius, who was dead and buried and deserted by all his followers long before Josephus even wrote his book. The absurdity of the supposition that in the thirteenth century Russians knew anything about a Roman implement of war which even to-day is known to only a small number of specialists, is of course obvious.

After all, what I venture to postulate are simply divergencies between different editions of the *War*, divergencies of the type which has been admitted all along to exist between the *War* and the corresponding portions of the *Antiquities*; and it is my contention that the Slavonic translation goes back to an earlier redaction of the *War* than the MSS. of the Greek standard texts. The interpolation theory, therefore, had better not be resorted to before all other explanations have been tried in vain. Nor can this claim be regarded as in any way excessive. On the contrary, it is a general principle admitted by all historians that an historical document must be accepted on trust unless proved untrustworthy, and that the burden of this proof lies on those who contest its value. From this viewpoint the case under debate is most simple. The Slavonic document purports to be a translation of the work of a definite author, Josephus. It is not the task of the discoverer or editor of the work to prove that the statement is true. If any proof is required, it is rather to the effect that the statement is false and that the work is really the product of another author or other authors, and the burden of this proof rests obviously on those who make such an allegation.

It is only fair to say that attempts at such a proof have not been entirely wanting. Critics have observed, for example, that the Slavonic text represents the tetrarch Herodes Philippus as corrupt, avaricious, and violent, in strict contradiction with *Ant.*, xviii. 4. 6, where he is described as a particularly gracious, just, and righteous ruler. Hence the application of a theory of interpolation to the Slavonic text, although it is difficult to see who should have had any interest in thus blackening the character of Philippus. What the critics did not notice was of course the frequency with which similar contradictions in character-drawing are met with in the pages of Josephus, partly the inevitable consequence of his uncritical and mechanical method of compiling various sources, and partly due also to his insincere subservience to various interests. As the Dutch scholar Samuel Naber, the editor of the Teubner edition of Josephus, puts it: 'No one ever knows *utrum laudet an oderit quorum hominum ingenia depinxerit.*' A few examples of the many which might be quoted must suffice.

In one passage [1] the high priest Ḥanan is called a very reasonable man who would have saved the city had he not fallen a victim to the insidious persecutions of the revolutionaries. In the famous passage about the death of James the Just, where Josephus draws on an anti-Sadducaean document, the same dignitary is called an uncommonly lawless and reckless man, a member of the Sadducee party, who are more cruel than any other Jews when sitting in judgment. At the end of the *Antiquities* Josephus records a long list of the misdeeds of the last high priests, [2] obviously from a series of complaints against those dignitaries addressed to the Roman authorities and copied from their commentaries by Josephus. These extracts are so indiscriminately compiled that the author's own dear friend, Jesus ben Gamala, [3] is represented as a most mean scoundrel. [4] Had such things been pointed out to Josephus, he would most probably have attributed them proudly to his own impartiality and scrupulous truthfulness. As a matter of fact, often enough he did not take the trouble to form a personal opinion of men and events, at least when his own interests were not directly concerned. For example, in *Ant.*, xx. § 235, the removal of the high priest Onias is characterized as a sacrilegious crime; in xii. §§ 384 *sq.*, as just retribution for the man's own misdeeds.

Nor have the critics who so unreasonably used the discrepancy between the characterization of Herodes Philippus in the Slavonic text on the one hand, and Josephus' earlier work on the other, taken into consideration the important fact that at least twenty years must have elapsed between the one and the other publication, and that Josephus had received sixty-two letters from King Herod Agrippa II., containing additions and corrections, which means that he had been bribed by the favours of the Herodian dynast into presenting the transactions of that fatal period in a light which was at least not openly hostile to the interests of that family. No wonder, then (and this fact was likewise unknown to the critics), that in the Rumanian version of the chapter in question [5] all expressions which throw an unfavourable light on Herodes Philippus are absent from the text. No later editor or censor had any interest in sparing the Herodian family, which had died out at the end of the first century of our era. Yet nothing is more certain than that Josephus himself wished to please Agrippa II. by first amending and finally entirely deleting a chapter which he had carelessly copied from an anti-Herodian source.

---

[1] *B.J.*, iv. 3. 7, §§ 319-22.
[2] xx., §§ 180 *sq.*, 198 *sq.*, 205-7, 213b-214.
[3] *Vita*, § 204 : ' Jesus, son of Gamala—an intimate friend of mine.'
[4] *Ant.*, xx. 213.   [5] Below, pp. 229 n. 2 and 599 f. No. 9.

IX

THE CONTRADICTIONS BETWEEN THE DIFFERENT ACCOUNTS GIVEN BY JOSEPHUS OF HIS OWN ACTIVITY IN GALILEE

THE most conclusive refutation of the theory that the larger part of the major divergencies between the Greek and the Slavonic text might be attributed to interpolations, deletions, omissions, and corrections by a late Jewish or Christian editor, or to arbitrary alterations on the part of the Slavonic translator, and the best proof of my contention that—with the exception of a number of well-defined Christian alterations—they are all to be explained by the fact that the Slav simply worked on an earlier edition of Josephus' history of the Jewish revolt against the Romans, will be found in the comparison of the passages relating to Josephus' own life and actions in both versions. If in these cases the divergencies can be explained as the result of Josephus' continual attempts to whitewash and to defend himself against the various accusations of his enemies, it will become obvious that these divergencies cannot be due to the Slavonic translator or to any Jewish or Christian reworker of the Greek text, since it is inconceivable that any early or late mediaeval reviser should have tried to blacken indirectly, through the cleverest additions and omissions, the character of Josephus.

As has been shown by Prof. Laqueur,[1] certain parts of the *Polemos*, especially §§ 603-8 of the second book, can have been written only on the occasion of a reworking of the whole compilation. Where I venture to differ from his conclusions is only in his assumption of a very late date for these insertions, which he would attribute wholly to the second edition of the *War* announced at the end of the *Antiquities*.[2] It is unfortunately impossible to determine, on the basis of the Old Russian translation, whether the paragraphs in question formed part of the archetype behind the class *A* of Slavonic MSS. It so happens that these paragraphs would fall into the gap which has been pointed out above.[3] Yet the §§ 604-8 do occur in the archetype of the so-called chrono-

---

[1] *Der jüdische Historiker Josephus Flavius*, Giessen, 1920, pp. 76 ff.

[2] Laqueur did not know the passage of Jerahmel (above, p. 83 n. 1) about this second edition in twenty-four books, published in A.D. 94.

[3] P. 121, fifth *a linea*.

grapher's version, which mentions the inauguration of the temple
of Peace and must therefore be posterior to A.D. 75. If those paragraphs were indeed not older than A.D. 93-4, this fact itself would
be of considerable importance for the correct dating of that version.
The reasons adduced by Prof. Laqueur for his late dating of those
paragraphs are not cogent, his arguments being based on a misinterpretation of Josephus' speech in § 605.[1] Aside from this one
question of detail, I can only share the conclusions and inferences of the German scholar. The Slavonic *Halōsis* now affords
a third source, beside the *Polemos* and the author's autobiography,
and it is interesting to disentangle the tissue of lies spun by Josephus in his own defence.

As was seen by Prof. Laqueur, the nucleus of the *Vita* is merely
an expansion of a report written by Josephus prior to his captivity
(A.D. 66) for the benefit of the Government of Jerusalem. It is
therefore in the main older than his presentation of the same
materials in the *Halōsis* (first edition, A.D. 72) and the *Polemos*.
Through a comparison of his subsequent statements about the same
facts, Laqueur has been able to show that he consciously misrepresented his own position in Galilee when he asserted that he
had been sent there by the Government of Jerusalem as a general
and commander-in-chief. The boldness of his lies can be easily
seen from a comparison of the three different versions which are
now accessible to the students.

In the *Polemos* [2] he expressly states that he would rather have
died than betray his ' position of trust.' In the Slavonic *Halōsis* [3]
the ' position of trust ' has been replaced by a mere ' power vested
in him,' which may mean his perfectly illegal power which he had
managed to acquire in Galilee with the help of the insurgents, the
so-called ' robbers.' In this version he still calls his adherents
' the people,' whilst in the later *Polemos*—in fact, in all his later
writings—he takes the viewpoint of the patrician and attributes all
the evil to the mob. It is further of interest to note that in the
Vita [4] he admits having received his commission from the " κοινόν,"
the ' commons' of Jerusalem, a popular, probably revolutionary,
body far less conservative than the Sanhedrin. In the *Polemos*
he represents himself as one of the eight generals sent out by the
' dictators ' at Jerusalem ; but the Slavonic *Halōsis* proves that
at the time of the first edition of his work he did not even know the
ordre de bataille of the war, nor does he mention there the important fact that the high command in Jerusalem had passed from
the high priest to the revolutionary leader of the zealots, 'Ele'azar
b. Shime'on—for the sole purpose, of course, of making it appear as
if he owed his office to the legitimate power. In the *Vita* [5] he was

---

[1] The details are explained in vol. i. p. 262 of the German edition of this book.
[2] iii. 136.   [3] Ber.-Grass, p. 370.   [4] § 393.   [5] § 28.

afterwards compelled, by the exposures of Justus of Tiberias, to confess the truth by restoring the crucial passage of his old report:

' After the defeat of Cestius, the leading men in Jerusalem, observing that the brigands and revolutionaries were well provided with arms, feared lest, being without weapons themselves, they might be left at the mercy of their adversaries, as in fact actually happened. Being informed, moreover, that the whole of Galilee had not yet revolted from Rome, and that a portion of it was still tranquil, they despatched me with two other priests, Jo'azar and Judas, very distinguished men, to induce the disaffected to lay down their arms and to impress upon them the desirability of reserving these for the leading men of the nation. The latter—such was the policy determined on—were to have their weapons constantly in readiness for future contingencies, but should wait and see what action the Romans would take.'

According to § 80 of the *Life*, Josephus was at that time about thirty years old, and was therefore much too young for the office of an ambassador, which, as the Greek term $\pi\rho\acute{\epsilon}\sigma\beta\upsilon\varsigma$ or $\pi\rho\epsilon\sigma\beta\epsilon\upsilon\tau\acute{\eta}\varsigma$ implies, was as a rule entrusted only to elderly worthy people. He was therefore clearly only an official, a secretary in attendance on Jo'azar and Judas, but clever enough in his position to pursue his own schemes, to make himself gradually independent of his superiors, and to get them to return empty-handed to Jerusalem, while he contrived to create for himself a position of considerable power in Galilee. A careful comparison of the relevant passages in the *War* [1] and in the *Life* [2] shows that this same pair were the leaders of a second embassy subsequently sent out from Jerusalem to render Josephus innocuous.

What Josephus was to do in Galilee and what he actually did comes out clearly in the *Halōsis*. The alleged commission of the embassy to disarm the insurgents in Galilee was utterly impracticable, as Josephus himself admits.[3] The envoys had of course received quite different instructions—to wit, with the help of tithes which they were to collect,[4] to recruit an armed force in Galilee and to conduct it to the high priest in Jerusalem, so that he might not be left defenceless against 'Ele'azar b. Shime'on and his troops. They further were to strengthen the power of the peaceful population and to recruit soldiers to hold the ' brigands,' i.e. the anti-Roman zealots, in check. In this way the ' dictators ' in Jerusalem, who had no army but disposed of the treasury of the Temple, hoped to keep the country at peace with Rome and themselves in power. The temper of the Galilaean population and the relative strength of the parties were obviously not quite what the leaders of the embassy and those who had commissioned them had

---

[1] ii. 627 (cf. *Halōsis*, Ber.-Grass, p. 349).   [2] § 196 *sqq.*
[3] *Vita*, § 77.   [4] *Ibid.*, §§ 63, 80.

expected, and Josephus was cunning enough to turn this circumstance to good purpose for his own plans.

From his three contradictory accounts [1] it is not difficult to discover the truth, which for Josephus is gravely incriminating. During the negotiations the real deputies appear to have left him too free a hand, with the result that he transacted business on his own account with both the ' brigands ' and the peaceable and propertied notables of Galilee. He finally succeeded in duping his superiors and sending them home without having achieved anything of what they had been sent out for. He himself, however, induced the ' wisest ' of the Galilaeans to form an autonomous administration through a Sanhedrin of their own, consisting of seventy Galilaeans, and with the money accruing from the tithes due to the priests of Jerusalem to take the ' brigands ' into their own pay. Such an action of the thirty-year-old Josephus was clearly high treason and rebellion against the high priests of the metropolis. Naturally, he seeks to disguise these hard-and-fast facts by ' doctoring up ' his account in the *Life* and presenting that, ' under the guise of friendliness,' he had dragged with him about the country ' some seventy ' (not *precisely* seventy, the exact number of a Sanhedrin !) of the Galilaean notables ' as hostages.' In the *Halōsis* he would represent these seventy members no longer as ' hostages ' but as a purely judicial assembly, a supreme *beth-din* for the trial of cases of more than local importance. The people who in the *Halōsis* are called the ' wisest ' (i.e. wise enough to enter into Josephus' schemes), in the *War* become ' persons of mature years and the greatest discretion,' to create an impression that he had brought together the notables, the elderly local magnates, whereas in reality it was ' the people,' that is, small *homines novi* eager for adventure, upon whom he relied. With the help of these people and with the armed support of the insurgents won over by him, he blackmailed the well-to-do, and on special ' court days ' of his revolutionary tribunal exacted large fines for non-payment of tithes, opposition to the new authorities, and the like. Thus he got the means to pay the ' brigands ' and the special bodyguard which was to protect his own precious person.

Nor was he in any way the commander-in-chief of the troops thus recruited and paid. For in the *Halōsis* [2] he lets escape the truth that they had another commander-in-chief ; he himself, of course, did not have the faintest notion of the elements of strategy, in spite of his assertions to the contrary. He even has to admit that he did not manage to arm his troops adequately and that he did not have the time to drill his men, important facts which

---

[1] *Halōsis*, ii. § 569 *sq*., p. 388, Ber.-Grass ; *Polemos*, ii. 569 ; *Vita*, § 78 *sq*.
[2] § 576.

explain the easy victory of the Roman troops, inferior in numbers though they were to the army of patriots. The final paragraph (584) is clearly intended to parry the accusation that he merely plundered the country with his armed rabble.

JOSEPHUS AS FORTRESS-BUILDER

The most instructive of the discrepancies between the *Life*, the *Halōsis*, and the *War* are afforded by the sections dealing with the fortifications of the country. There the vain braggart who pretends to be descended through his mother[1] from the Hasmonaeans clearly seeks to claim for himself the laurels of a second Simon Maccabaeus. In the *Life* (§ 188), i.e. in the old official report, he maintains that he fortified not only Tarichaea and Tiberias but also Sepphoris. In the *War*, in the middle of a list not altogether consistent with another given elsewhere, he admits that ' only the Sepphorites were permitted by him to build their walls themselves, because he had found them well off for money [2] and eager for war. In the case of the other fortifications he not only gave the orders but personally assisted in the work.' What this great Vauban really did may be seen from the case of Gamala, whose fortifications he insists that he strengthened, both according to the *Halōsis* and the *War*. In the *Life* (§ 186) he says that the people of Gamala had written to ask him for troops and workmen to repair the town walls, and that he had refused neither request. Evidently he ascribes to himself the fortification of all places with which he had corresponded on such matters or to which he occasionally granted some men out of ' his ' army. The *War* mentions a second place which was fortified by the orders, though not at the cost, of Josephus—to wit, Gischala, whose walls were built by John, a native of that place and a leader of a rebel volunteer corps. The story how this man raised the money for this patriotic purpose may now be read, with admiration, in three separate forms, all in Josephus.

Vita, x. §§ 43-5.	*Halōsis*, §§ 585-8 ; Berendts-Grass, p. 340 *sqq.*	*Polemos*, ii. 21, §§ 585-592.
' Such was the position of affairs at Tiberias ; at Gischala the situation was as fol-	' After that there rose against Josephus a man named John, son of Levi, a wily impostor,	' While Josephus was thus directing affairs in Galilee, there appeared upon the scene an in-

[1] *Vita*, § 2.
[2] *Vita*, § 38, shows that the royal exchequer (βασιλικὴ τράπεζα) of Agrippa was situated in Sepphoris !

lows. John, son of
Levi, observing

distinguished and more
treacherous than all
others, strong in lies but
for that reason not fam-
ous. And for a long time
his poverty kept him
from wickedness. His
tongue fed on lies, but
his cleverness procured
credence for his lies.
He adorned himself
with fraud better than
with a garland, and as
chief of hypocrites he
did well. Therefore
he not only cheated
strangers but also
(people) among his
nearest and dearest.
Bloodthirsty for pos-
session's sake, he was
the more eager for war.
For this purpose he
gathered around him
people of his type, re-
bellious souls and
bodies and thinking
nothing of death.

triguer, a native of
Gischala, named John,
son of Levi, the most
unscrupulous and
crafty of all who have
ever gained notoriety
by such infamous
means. Poor at the
opening of his career,
his penury had for long
thwarted his malicious
designs; * a ready liar
and clever in obtaining
credit for his lies, he
made a merit of deceit
and practised it upon
his most intimate
friends; while affect-
ing humanity, the pro-
spect of lucre made him
the most bloodthirsty
of men; always full of
high ambitions, his
hopes were fed on the
basest of knaveries.
For he was a brigand
who at the outset prac-
tised his trade alone,
but afterwards found
for his daring deeds ac-
complices, whose num-
bers, small at first,
grew with his success.
He was, moreover,
careful never to take
into partnership any
one likely to fall an
easy prey to an assail-
ant, but selected good,
strapping fellows, with
stout hearts and mili-
tary experience. He
ended by mustering a
band of four hundred
men, for the most part
fugitives from the
region of Tyre and the
villages in that neigh-
bourhood. With their
help he plundered the
whole of Galilee and
harried the masses,
whose minds were al-

— Since the phrase after the second asterisk is a repetition of the sentence
preceding the first one, it is clear that the character sketch between *—* is a later
insertion.

ready distracted by the impending war.

* He was already aspiring to the command, and had yet higher ambitions, but was checked by impecuniosity.

that some of the citizens were highly elated by the revolt from Rome, tried to restrain them and urged them to maintain their allegiance. (45) His earnest efforts, however, proved unavailing ; for the inhabitants of the neighbouring states, Gadara, Gabara, Sogane, and Tyre, mustered a large force, stormed and took Gischala, burnt and razed it to the ground, and returned to their homes. Incensed at this outrage, John armed all his followers, made a determined attack on the aforesaid peoples, and defeated them. He then rebuilt Gischala on a grander scale than before, and fortified it with walls as a security for the future.¹

But when he saw that Josephus liked his adroitness,

Perceiving that Josephus was delighted at his energy, John first

§§ 70-76.

From Tiberias I went with my colleagues to Gischala to meet John, whose attitude I desired to ascertain. I soon discovered that he was eager for revolution and ambitious of obtaining command ; (71) for he requested me to authorise him to lay hands

¹ In this account, then, there is no connexion as yet between the plundering of the grain stores, the oil transaction, and the building of the fortifications.

on the imperial corn stored in the villages of Upper Galilee, professing a desire to expend the proceeds on the repair of the walls of his native town. (74) Detecting his ultimate design and present intentions, I refused his request; as the authority entrusted to me by the Jerusalem authorities extended to that district, I intended to reserve the corn either for the Romans or for my own use. Unsuccessful with me, he turned to my colleagues, who were blind to coming events and quite ready to receive money. These he bribed to vote that all the corn stored in his province should be delivered to him. Unsupported and outvoted by the other two, I held my peace.

This knavish trick John followed up with a second. He stated that the Jewish inhabitants of Caesarea Philippi, having, by the king's order, been shut up by Modius, his viceroy, and having no pure oil for their personal use, had sent a request to him to see that they were supplied with this commodity, lest they should be driven to violate their legal ordinances by resort to Grecian oil.[1] John's motive in making this assertion was not piety, but profiteering of the most barefaced description;

he asked him to be entrusted with the construction of the city walls. And it (i.e. this work) yielded him considerable revenue. For this reason, on account of the money, he took it up.

And after that he came again to Joseph and said to him: " The Jews living in Syria beware of buying oil from gentiles. Command me to bring them (oil), and to sell it to them."

induced him to entrust him with the rebuilding of the walls of his native town, an undertaking in which he made a large profit at the expense of the wealthy citizens.

He next contrived to play a very crafty trick: with the avowed object of protecting all the Jews of Syria from the use of oil not supplied by their own countrymen, he sought and obtained permission to deliver it to them at the frontier.

[1] Foreign oil was forbidden, according to one Talmudic authority, as likely to be tainted by unclean vessels (Thackeray).

for he knew that at Caesarea two pints were sold for one drachm, whereas at Gischala eighty pints could be had for four drachms. So he sent off all the oil in the place, having ostensibly obtained my authority to do so. My permission I gave reluctantly, from fear of being stoned by the mob if I withheld it. Thus, having gained my consent, John by his sharp practice made an enormous profit.'

And he commanded him. And buying four *amphorae* for one drachm, he sold them there for ten drachms. But no other was permitted to buy up in this way.

And thereby he collected a large quantity of gold, turning it immediately against him who had given him such power.'

He then bought up that commodity, paying Tyrian coin of the value of four Attic drachms for four *amphorae*, and proceeded to sell half an *amphora* at the same price. As Galilee is a special home of the olive and the crop had been plentiful, John, enjoying a monopoly, by sending large quantities to districts in want of it, amassed an immense sum of money, which he forthwith employed against the man who had brought him his gains.'

From the wording in the *Halōsis*, cancelled in the *War*, 'and he (Josephus) bade him do so,' it is clear that both of these worthies had a share in the transaction. One may well ask oneself whether Josephus was not the instigator of the whole dirty business. Anyhow, too many people must have known about it to allow Josephus a diplomatic silence. In the *War* the whole matter has been visibly toned down, and in the reworking of the *Life* John is frankly said to have extorted Josephus' permission with threats. As Prof. Laqueur recognized, §§ 43-5 of the *Life* (portions of the oldest part, of course) still show Josephus and John on good terms. Josephus' later rage, which shows itself in the unfavourable characterization of John in the *War*, a characterization borrowed from the picture of Catiline in Sallust,[1] is easily explained by the fact that in the scandalous transaction John got the whole booty and Josephus nothing.

At all events, the three instances of Sepphoris, Gamala, and Gischala sufficiently show what was behind Josephus' claim and what his fortifications looked like. Nor is one surprised to find the astonishingly long list of fortified places missing in the *Halōsis*. He added them to his later work, no doubt to explain the disappearance of certain sums which he had taken 'into his safekeeping.'

JOSEPHUS AS TRUSTEE

The *Life* (§§ 69 *sqq.*) contains one highly edifying narrative of facts which Josephus could not well conceal, because his enemy

1 This has been first noticed by Dr. Thackeray.

Justus of Tiberias had been present. The story is preceded by an insidious attack on the leaders of his embassy, who, he says, had decided to return ' home ' [1] with the money which they had collected from the tithes. Then he continues :

' But on my request they consented to stay until we had put matters in order. I accordingly set out with them from headquarters at Sepphoris and came to a village called Bethamaus, four furlongs distant from Tiberias, and from there sent to the council and principal men of that town, requesting them to come to me. They came, Justus being one of the number. I told them that I and my associates had been commissioned by the Sanhedrin of Jerusalem to press for the demolition of the palace erected by Herod the tetrarch, containing representations of living creatures—such style of architecture being forbidden by the Law—and I requested their permission to proceed at once with the work. Capella and the other leaders for a long while refused this, but were finally overruled by us and assented. We were, however, anticipated by Jesus, son of Sapphias, the ringleader, as already stated, of a party of sailors and riff-raff. Helped by some Galilaeans, he set the whole palace on fire, expecting to obtain from it large spoils, as he saw that the roof was partly of gold. There was much looting, contrary to our intention. . . . On hearing of these proceedings I was extremely indignant, and went down to Tiberias and devoted my energies to recovering from the looters as much as I could of the palace furniture, namely, some candelabra of Corinthian bronze, regal tables, and a large mass of uncoined silver. I decided to keep all I had rescued in trust for the king, and accordingly sent ten of the principal councillors, with Capella, son of Antyllus, and left the property in their charge, with instructions to deliver it to none but myself.'

It is hardly necessary to add that the Sanhedrin at Jerusalem had other things to do at that time than to meddle with the palace of Agrippa II. because it contained a few telamones, caryatides, sphinxes, or suchlike architectural designs. Josephus simply lied. Acting on his own motion, he first incited the Galilaeans to destroy and plunder the palace, and was then deeply offended because Jesus ben Sapphias, the leader of the harbour mob, had been quick enough to secure for himself a large part of the spoils. During the looting, of course, Josephus was ' not on the spot ' : he only appeared to ' save what could be saved.' What was collected he professes to have handed over to precisely those councillors, including Capella, who had opposed the destruction of the palace. The truth behind the story, no doubt, is that those councillors attempted to save something for King Agrippa. What is certain is that whatever fell into the author's hands went the same way

---

[1] Videl., to Jerusalem, where they were indeed in duty bound to go. But the word is meant to suggest that they intended to carry the money to their own houses.

as the spoils he admits elsewhere to have sent to his relations in Jerusalem (*Life*, § 81).

Quite as diverting—if not more so—is the episode of the highwaymen of Dabherat, again available in three versions. Here Prof. Laqueur has been able, even without knowing the text of the *Halōsis*, to disentangle a large portion of this tissue of lies and brazen falsehoods.

Vita, §§ 126-48.	*Halōsis*, ii. §§ 595 *sqq.*; Berendts-Grass, p. 343.	*Polemos*, ii. §§ 595-8.
' Some adventurous young men of Dabarittha lay in wait for the wife of Ptolemy, the king's overseer. She was travelling in great state, protected by an escort of cavalry, from territory subject to the royal jurisdiction into the region of Roman dominion, when, as she was crossing the Great Plain, they suddenly fell upon the cavalcade, compelled the lady to flee, and plundered all her baggage. They then came to me at Tarichaea with four mules laden with apparel and other articles, besides a large pile of silver and five hundred pieces of gold. My own desire was to keep these spoils for Ptolemy, seeing that he was a compatriot and we are forbidden by our laws to rob even an enemy ; to the bearers I said that the goods must be reserved for sale and the proceeds devoted to the repair of the walls of Jerusalem.	' And when at that time Ptolemy, the governor of Agrippa, passed by, coming from Debarittha, with royal property, the guards fell upon him in the Great Plain and took away all treasures and of costly garments 2000 and of silver vessels a thousand and of great golden vessels 600. And not daring to conceal what they had robbed, they brought the whole to Joseph at Tarichaea. But the latter reproached them for having laid a violent hand on royal treasures, and deposited the whole with Aeneas, the most influential among the inhabitants of the town, having in mind to send it to the Temple when an occasion would present itself.	' About this time some young men of the village of Dabarittha, units of the guard posted in the Great Plain, laid an ambush for Ptolemy, the overseer of Agrippa and Berenice, and robbed him of all the baggage which he was conveying, including a large number of rich vestments, a quantity of silver goblets, and six hundred pieces of gold. Being unable to dispose secretly of such booty, they brought the whole to Josephus, then at Tarichaea. He censured them for this act of violence to servants of the king, and committed the goods to the keeping of Annaeus, the most important citizen of Tarichaea, intending to return them to their legitimate owners when an opportunity presented itself.

Indignant at not receiving their expected share of the spoils, the young men went to the villages around Tiberias, declaring that I intended to betray their country to the Romans. My assertion about keeping the outcome of their raid for the repair of the walls of the capital was, they said, a mere blind ; I had really decided to restore it to its owner. So far, indeed, they correctly interpreted my intention ; for, when they left me, I sent for two of the leaders, Dassion and Jannaeus, son of Levi, who were special friends of the king, and ordered them to take the stolen goods and dispatch them to him, threatening them with capital punishment if they reported the matter to any one.

A rumour had now spread throughout Galilee that I was intending to betray the country to the Romans. . . .

By this act of his he drew upon himself a great calamity. For those robbers, full of rage because they had not obtained a share in the booty, and understanding well Josephus' intention of sending the fruit of their labour to the king,

at night ran into the villages, announcing that on account of these things he was a traitor.'

This action brought him into the greatest peril. For the plunderers, indignant at receiving no portion of the spoil, and divining the intention of Josephus to present the king and queen with the fruits of their labours,

ran round the villages by night, denouncing Josephus to all as a traitor.'

A brief commentary on the passages just cited and their true import for a correct grasp of the character of the man Josephus will prove helpful to the reader.

In the *Vita* the robbery is committed by a few anonymous νεανίσκοι θρασεῖς, which Prof. Laqueur interprets to mean 'courageous young fellows.' In the *Polemos* they are νεανίσκοι τινὲς τῶν ἐν τῷ μεγάλῳ πεδίῳ καθεζομένων φυλάκων ; and in the *Halōsis* they are the ' guards of the great plain,' i.e. the plain of Esdraelon—that is to say, members of the garrison, and not simply some volunteers. In the oldest account the victim is the wife of the royal administrator Ptolemy, accompanied by a small escort. The exploit, then, was decidedly secondary. The whole booty consisted of the burden of four mules with considerable baggage, and the valuables carried by a noble lady who evidently did not feel comfortable in the territory controlled by the rebels and was anxious to go over to the districts occupied by the Romans. The *Halōsis* grotesquely exaggerates the incident, making of it a matter of political importance. The victim is the royal administrator himself, and the booty the property of King Agrippa II.

In the *Polemos*, Ptolemy is an official not only of the king but also of the queen, Berenice—evidently to explain thus the large number of costly garments. For in the *Halōsis* the four mules' burdens have become 2000 garments, more than sufficient to supply a monster circus show. One can imagine what a caravan would have been necessary for the transporting of the garments, to say nothing of the silver and gold vessels mentioned in addition.

Even more instructive is a comparison of the texts relating the good intentions of Josephus in regard to the booty delivered to him. In the *Vita* he wants to sell it and to use the money for the strengthening of the city walls of Jerusalem. Though away in Galilee, this great Jewish Vauban thinks even of the fortification of far-off Jerusalem. In the *Halōsis* he declares more diplomatically that he intended to send the treasure to Jerusalem, to the Temple, on a suitable occasion. That might mean that he wished to deliver it to the treasury of the Temple and the hierarchy, or else that he merely wanted it to be kept in the Temple for the rightful owner, i.e. Agrippa. In reality the gold pieces were to go to Jerusalem to be handed over to the kinsmen of our great patriot, and no doubt ultimately went that way. The precious objects, which he could of course no more get rid of than could the robbers, he cleverly gave in trust, according to the *Vita*, to Dassion and Jannaios; according to the *Halōsis* and the *Polemos*, only to Aineias (=Jannai); according to the *Vita*, with the injunction to return them discreetly to the king. Thus, if the package did not arrive safely, the blame would clearly lie with either one or both. The disinterested Josephus, of course, did not even think of appropriating anything for himself.

Very important is the mention of a rumour according to which he was in communication with the Romans, a mention occasioned, no doubt, by some more or less definite accusation by Justus of Tiberias. That the rumour was not without foundation is proved by at least three facts—to wit, the very good treatment accorded to him by the Romans after he had gone over to them; the admission of Josephus in *Polemos*, iii. 8. 2, that he was in communication with the tribune Nikanor, his 'old acquaintance'; and the extraordinary ease with which he managed to keep in touch with Jerusalem, though himself in Galilee, through Samaria,[1] all the time occupied by the Romans. The letters he gave his armed henchmen, and which were addressed to his 'friends in Samaria,' can

---

[1] *Vita*, §§ 286 *sq.*

hardly have been directed to any one else than Roman intelligence officers (*speculatores*). It is quite clear, moreover, that the party of the high priests at Jerusalem, averse as they were to an open break with Rome, must have kept in touch with the Romans as long as it was at all possible, and Josephus' Roman connexions no doubt date from the period of his first diplomatic mission to Galilee. However that may be, the numerous contradictions between the three reports [1] about the consequences of the affair with the highwaymen of Dabarittha are evident. In one account all his guardsmen forsake him except four; in another there is only one left to him. In one all his ' friends ' bid him flee; in another his last stand-by, Simon, will persuade him to commit suicide. In one he tears his garment, according to Jewish custom; in another he puts on a black garment in sign of mourning, as the pagans do, to stir his opponents to pity. The treasure he left with Jannai or with both Jannai and Dassion he still has, according to ii. § 602, in his own house, and is willing to give it up for general pillage (ii. § 607). That same treasure, delivered to his friends to be kept for the king, is then to be used for the fortifications of Tarichaea and ' all other cities.' In one account it was a detachment of ten people that was enticed into Josephus' house, there to be drubbed by his slaves; in another it was only a single man (*Vita*, § 147), ' the boldest of them all,' etc.

In short, it is the typical spectacle of the swindler giving three different accounts to the police, to the prosecuting attorney, and at the trial.

JOSEPHUS AS A TACTICIAN

Among the passages representing later efforts on the part of our author to defend himself against his opponents' attacks, must be reckoned one in the third book of the *War* (§§ 129-31), which is significantly absent from the Slavonic version. The Greek text relates how Vespasian drew out his army to frighten the Jews, while he made preparations for the siege of the fortified places. The sight of the Roman army did indeed not fail in its purpose. Then follow the taking of Gabara, one of the three chief cities of Galilee, completely forsaken by its garrison; the destruction of the city; and the devastation of the outlying districts. Next we read: ' Josephus' arrival at Tiberias, which he had chosen for his place of refuge, filled the city with alarm, for the Tiberians felt that he would never have fled had he not abandoned all hope of success in the contest.' The original narrative (absent in the Slavonic) thus passed over in silence the fact that the great ' general ' Josephus, instead of protecting Gabara, had abandoned it to

---

[1] *Halōsis*, Ber.-Gr., p. 347, and *Polemos*, ii. 600 *sq.* ; *Vita*, § 145 ss.

Vespasian. One can only surmise what Justus of Tiberias in *his* narrative of the war may have said about this glorious episode.

The lame excuse offered by Josephus is found in §§ 129-31. The ' general ' endeavours to shift the blame on to his troops. This is what he says :

> ' The troops which under the command of Josephus were camping not far from Sepphoris, discovering that the war was upon them, and that at any moment they might be attacked by the Romans, dispersed and fled, not only before any engagement, but before they had even seen the foe. Josephus was left with a few companions ; he saw that he had not sufficient forces to await the enemy, that the Jews were crestfallen, and that the majority of them, if they could gain the enemy's confidence, would gladly capitulate. Already he had fears for the ultimate issue of the war ; for the moment he decided to remove as far as possible from risk of a battle, and accordingly with the remainder of his troops took refuge in Tiberias.'

In place of these edifying words we find in the *Halōsis* a shorter and more confused account :

> ' And when the Galilaeans had seen them (the Romans), they were all terrified, and many began to feel remorse. Those round Josephus, before (having) a glimpse (of the enemy), fled and dispersed with Josephus to Tiberias.'

From the whole arrangement of the text it follows that our author originally intended to suppress the unsuccessful attack on Sepphoris, which had gone over to the Romans, and all that happened at Garis. The postscripts (*B.J.*, iii. §§ 59 *sqq.* and 129-31) contain the most unavoidable and most necessary admissions which he saw himself forced to make. In the *Life* (§ 397) he still speaks of a ' stubborn resistance ' near Garis ; in the postscript to the *War* (iii. § 130) he admits that his men deserted him at Garis before any engagement and even before having caught a glimpse of the enemy. It is clear that the ' general ' (and in this he does not stand alone in history) ascribes the successes to himself, whilst the troops must shoulder the responsibility for the defeats. He also passes over in silence the encounter at Tarichaea, mentioned in the *Life* (§ 74), which was certainly no victory either, since it forced him to beat a retreat to Jotapata, a retreat which thus remains unexplained in the *War*.

A considerable number of sections absent from the *Halōsis* in the story of the siege of Jotapata are clearly later rhetorical embellishments. Conversely, palpable exaggerations of the earlier version are toned down in the *War*, though even what remains is ludicrous enough. For example, two men of Ruma,[1] who in the

---

[1] One of them and his fabulous exploits are mentioned also in the Talmud *Gittin*, 57a.

Halōsis 'annihilated the whole of the tenth legion,'[1] are in the
Polemos content with ' routing all whom they encountered ' (iii.
§ 233). A list of such divergencies would be highly amusing, but
I cannot quote them all within the available space. One truly
marvellous detail, however, may be mentioned. In the *Halōsis*
(iii. § 271), Josephus, at a critical moment of the siege, has molten
lead poured upon the besiegers, whereby 'many were burnt' and
general confusion was created. If one remembers that a single
quart of lead weighs more than twenty-two pounds, that no lead
is found in Palestine and must therefore have been proportionately
dear, and, lastly, that Jotapata can have had neither leaden water-
pipes laid on to the houses nor leaden gutters, it is inconceivable
that even ten quarts of lead could have been collected in the whole
town. Accordingly, in the *War*, Josephus has altered this fanciful
idea of ' molten lead ' into ' boiling oil.' This age-old stratagem
of all ancient siege defences he then claims as his own invention,
just as in a preceding passage (§ 172 *sq.*) he speaks of the ox-hide
screens to ward off missiles as a discovery of his own. On the
principle propounded in his preface that the prestige of the Roman
generals can only be enhanced by recognition of their opponents'
valour, he proceeds, in his later edition, to enlarge on the wonderful
effects of this ' invention ' of his (§ 274 : ' for the oil instantane-
ously penetrated beneath their armour from head to foot,' etc.),
and adds as a second stratagem the pouring of boiled fenugreek
over the scaling-ladders to make them slippery. He represents the
repulse of the assault by all these alleged expedients as a battle of
his own, and appends the precise date (the 20th of Daesius). For
the purpose of the later edition he has clearly perused the emperor's
journal, and, combining its precise data with the master-stroke of
his first draft, to wit, the boiled fenugreek, and with some descrip-
tive touches about the terrible effects of the seething oil, formed a
new chapter.

JOSEPHUS' CAPTURE

One of the most repulsive parts of the whole *Historia Josephi
captivi* is the eighth chapter of the third book—the story of how,
after the capture of Jotapata, he held himself concealed, with other
comrades-in-arms and notables of the town, in a cistern, and how
he managed his desertion to the enemy's ranks with great cleverness against the desperate resistance of his companions in misfortune. Even more disgusting is his comedy of a God-inspired
prophet in favour of Vespasian, all the more so if we remember

---

[1] This would hardly strike Josephus' Jewish readers as an overstatement,
since they were accustomed to recite from the Scriptures (*Deut.* xxxii. 36) :
' Behold, one of us pursueth a thousand of the heathen and two of us make ten
thousand to flee.'

that, to him, the priest and son of a priest, such things must have appeared as little less than blasphemy. The whole passage is well worth quoting.

' But as Nicanor ' (the Roman tribune known to him—how and since when, he is careful not to say) ' was urgently pressing his proposals and Josephus overheard the threats of the hostile crowd, there came back into his mind those nightly dreams in which God had foretold to him the impending fate of the Jews and the destinies of the Roman sovereigns. Being an interpreter of dreams and skilled in divining the meaning of ambiguous utterances of the Deity, a priest himself and a descendant of priests, he was not ignorant of the prophecies in the sacred books. At that hour he was inspired to read their meaning, and, recalling the dreadful images of his recent dreams, he offered up a silent prayer to God. " Since it pleases thee," so it ran, " who didst create the Jewish nation, to break thy work, since fortune has wholly passed to the Romans, and since thou hast chosen my spirit to announce the things that are to come, I willingly surrender to the Romans and consent to live ; but I take thee to witness that I go, not as a traitor, but as thy minister." With these words he was about to surrender to Nicanor.'

But his companions, who had resolved upon death, would not let him go, and said to him, ' If you meet death willingly, you shall die as general [1] of the Jews; if unwillingly, you fall a traitor.' ' With these words they pointed their swords at him and threatened to kill him if he surrendered to the Romans. Josephus, fearing an assault, yet holding that it would be a betrayal of God's command should he die before delivering his message, proceeded in this emergency to reason with them.' Failing to move them, he pretends to acquiesce in their plan, but advises them to draw lots to determine in what order they are to kill themselves : ' Let him who draws the first lot fall by the hand of him who comes next.'

At this point, however, the texts significantly diverge. In the Greek we have the unctuous statement : ' But he (should one say by fortune or by the providence of God) was left alone with one other ; and anxious neither to be condemned by the lot nor, should he be left to the last, to stain his hand with the blood of a fellow-countryman, he persuaded this man also, under a pledge, to remain alive.' In the Slavonic, on the other hand, he admits with cynical candour to having assisted the luck of the lot : ' he cunningly counted the numbers [2] and so misled them all.' This juggling with the lots, in such circumstances, evidently was not sufficiently admired by the more decent of his readers, since he

---

[1] About this doubtful generalship, see above, p. 186 n. 2.

[2] The process hinted at is evidently the rabbinic *taḥbula* explained by Abraham ibn Ezra (M. Steinschneider, ' Abraham ibn Ezra,' *Gesch. d. mathem. Wiss. i.* 12. *Jahrh.*, p. 123 *sq.*, § 20, 4).

found himself compelled, in his later edition, to retract his original compromising candour.

The underlying 'philosophy' of the good man can be gauged from another significant correction in the first book. In § 140, speaking of Aristobulus, he says that he had promised great presents and his submission ; but he did not promise the carrying out thereof—which important circumstance sufficed to make him break his promise. Here again the clever casuistry implied by this noble priest and priest's son does not seem to have been appreciated by a number of his readers, and accordingly in the Greek *Polemos* we merely read the simpler admission that Aristobulus broke his promise.

X

THE DOCUMENTARY BASES OF THE ADDITIONS TO THE GREEK 'POLEMOS.' THE IMPERIAL 'COMMENTARIES' AS A SOURCE OF JOSEPHUS

EVER since Isaac Abravanel (1437-1508)—long before the Slavonic version acquainted the learned world with something very near the earliest draft of Josephus' Jewish history—the truthfulness of this remarkable author has been seriously doubted by all those who had more thoroughly studied his various books. Thus it will not surprise any one to find Josephus finally discredited through the comparisons made possible by the Slavonic version. An author of this type would certainly not deserve our attention were it not for two reasons: the first being the lamentable fact that for the most important events of the period treated by him we have no other source at all; the second, more important, reason being the fact that we can show now—more thoroughly than ever before—that Josephus, however untrustworthy he may be himself, has had access to, and has made extensive use of, first-hand official source-material, chiefly the diaries and correspondence copybooks of the Roman Caesars in the archives of the imperial palace.

An instructive case of this kind occurs in *B.J.*, iii. 10. 9 (§§ 522-31), this whole section being missing in the Slavonic version. The facts are the following. Vespasian surrounds the town of Tarichaea, and has rafts constructed to start in pursuit of the fugitives who had escaped on the lake. This ended that part of the narrative in the Greek original of the Slavonic text, for what follows in the latter is a rather sentimental description of the lake of Gennesareth. But in the Greek *Polemos* there follows a detailed account of the naval victory of Vespasian's flotilla over the small craft of the Tarichaean fugitives. The fact evidently is that the account followed by Josephus in his first redaction had centred about Titus, whilst the second source was designed to extol the merits of Vespasian. Probably Josephus, who had for some time followed the official 'commentaries' of Titus, had noticed later on that the journal of the campaign at this particular juncture indicated an engagement of greater magnitude subsequent to the arrival on the scene of the commander-in-chief. As a docile courtier he naturally took the hint and hastened to make good his first oversight. There can be no question that we are dealing here with additions to the Greek original and not with abridgments on the part of the Slavonic translator.

Another interesting case is furnished by the second book, §§ 15-19, 21-23, 40-66, 68-72, 73-74, all omitted in the Slavonic text, ' yet in such a manner that without a knowledge of the Greek text one would not suspect the slightest gap.' [1] The portions in question contain a good account of the disturbances in Judaea caused by Sabinus, the agent of Augustus, and quelled with great bloodshed by Varus. The Greek original of the Slavonic version, i.e. the older redaction of Josephus, knew nothing about the causes of the rebellion and the avarice and lack of tact of Sabinus. Our author merely says that the Jews did not want to live under Roman rule,[2] whilst a few lines previously [3] he had stated precisely the contrary—that is, the Jews did not so much object to the Romans as to their tyrants of the Herodian dynasty—and whilst a few lines further on he reports the arrival of fifty Jewish notables at Rome, petitioning Augustus to send them a Roman governor and speaking with abuse of their own king.[4] It is clear that Josephus at first did not know anything about the real causes of the rebellion ; as soon as he learned more details he set to work and rewrote his account. As sources he utilized, on his own confession,[5] the official reports of Sabinus and Varus, mutually contradictory though they are. No doubt he obtained these documents, the original letters of the two officials, in the imperial house archives,[6] both Vespasian and Titus having given special orders [7] to place the relevant material at the disposal of their court historiographer. Josephus must have been all the more glad to obtain this material because at precisely this point the history of Nicolaus of Damascus, whom he had followed all along, broke off. It is well known to students of the Roman methods of political administration that letters addressed to the emperor and drafts of the replies were pasted together by the imperial secretary (scriniarius ab epistulis) [8] in large rolls and preserved in round wooden boxes.[9] Pliny,[10] a younger contemporary of Josephus, writes to Trajan enquiring after the authentic originals of edicts of Augustus, Vespasian, and Titus, and the emperor replies [11] that the edicts of Domitian in-

---

[1] Berendts in Ber.-Grass, p. 240₈. What is wanting here is not to be found either in the Latin Egesippus, in the Hebrew Josippon, or in the Arab Jusifus.
[2] Ber.-Grass, p. 240, § 39. [3] Ibid., § 22, p. 235.
[4] Ibid., p. 241, § 80 (altered in the Greek text).
[5] B.J., ii. §§ 22, 25, 39. [6] See below, pp. 613 f. App. xvi.
[7] The regular ' potestas inspiciendi describendique commentarios principis ' (Max Memelsdorff, De archivis imperatorum, Diss. Hall, 1890, p. 50 n. 5).
[8] C.I.L., x. 527=Dessau, 1671.
[9] The ' scrinia ' (Plin., N.H., xvi. 229 ; Jo. Lyd., De mag., iii. 35).
[10] Ad Trajanum, lxv. 3. [11] lxvi. 1.

dicated had been found. In the same way the petitions addressed to the emperors were filed by the *scriniarius a libellis* or *custos a libellis*. Further, protocols of transactions at audiences (*admissiones*) granted by the emperors, and, in particular, transactions with embassies, would be drawn up by the secretary *ab epistulis* and duly filed. Copious extracts from such records referring to the reign of Hadrian have been transmitted to us by the grammarian Dositheos.[1] It goes without saying that the material in question was of the utmost value for every historian of the period, a fact which was well known and duly acted upon. For example, a letter of the younger Pliny [2] addressed to Cn. Octavius Titinius Capito, the *procurator ab epistulis* under Domitian,[3] Nerva, and Trajan, requests a selection of the proper materials for a basis of the history which he has been asked to write. Josephus' quoting of the petition handed to the emperor by the representative of Herod Antipas,[4] the testament of Herod the Great presented by Archelaus,[5] the speeches in the negotiations of Augustus with the Herodians,[6] a letter of Varus, and finally several letters of both Varus and Sabinus, makes it perfectly clear, I should think, that he utilized precisely such official sources. If, on the other hand— and Dr. G. Hölscher has tried to prove it—the history of Nicolaus of Damascus went as far as the installation of Archelaus by Augustus, the essential correctness of the above observations is in no way diminished. For Nicolaus, the friend of Augustus and living moreover in Rome, had as easy access to those same documents in the correspondence-files of the emperors (*commentarii principis*) as Josephus was to have later on, under the Flavian dynasty. It is even probable that Josephus got the first hint on the usefulness of such material from his greater predecessor, and that he merely followed in his wake.

Upon a closer examination of the portion lying between the end of Nicolaus' work and the beginning of his own notes, not much prior to A.D. 66-7, one cannot help being struck by the obviously official nature of the material. The history of the false Alexander, culminating in an account of the audience of the pretender with the emperor, carefully prepared by one Celadus, obviously the imperial private secretary; the complaints of both Jews and Samaritans against Archelaus; the latter's banishment to Vienna (in Gaul); and the confiscation of his private fortune—all

---

1 *Divi Hadriani sententiae et epistulae*, ed. Boecking (*Corp. Jur. Anteiustin.*, i. 210 ff., §§ 2, 4, 5, 7, 8, 10-14.
2 *Ep.*, v. 8, 12. 3 *C.I.L.*, 798.
4 *B.J.*, ii. § 23. 5 *Ibid.*, ii. 26.
6 According to *Hal.*, ii. § 25, Tiberius, according to *B.J.*, ii. § 25, the young Caligula, assisting for the first time at such a sitting, was present as assessor. Where else but in the document itself could Josephus find such absolutely unessential details mentioned with scrupulous exactitude ?

doubtless go back to extracts culled from the *commentarii principis*. The dream episodes connected with this history have, of course, a different source, which will be discussed later on in the chapter on John the Baptist. Then follows the account of the transformation of Archelaus' territory into a Roman province, on the basis of an imperial decree, as may be concluded from the *obiter dictum* that Coponius obtained power over life and death (*ius vitae necisque*), and thus even on this point was quite independent of the governor of Syria, a statement which has no bearing whatever on what Josephus tells us in these chapters. The subsequent mention of the uprising of the Jews who refused to pay the tribute appears to have no other source than either the *commentarii principis* or else the reports of the Roman administrative and financial authorities located in the so-called *Aerarium Saturni*. What Josephus has next to say about the three Jewish 'philosophical schools' is probably his own property, except the long chapter on the Essenes, which he probably copied from a lost book of Philo ' on active life or on the Essenes,' acquired, it may be, during his brief stay in Alexandria.[1] Then follows the testament of Salome in favour of Livia, the wife of Augustus, a copy of which must have existed in the imperial chancellery. The tumults in Pilate's administration no doubt go back to the governor's reports to Tiberius, later incorporated in the *acta et commentarii Tiberii Caesaris*—the only literature that the Emperor Domitian, the third of Josephus' patrons, ever read.[2] The transactions reported of the last years of Tiberius and the short reign of Caligula show the same official stamp.

Thus in § 5 we meet with the complaint of Agrippa, the son of Aristobulus, against the tetrarch Herod, as presented to Tiberius. There follow short excerpts of a denunciation, before Tiberius, of a slave of Caligula concerning a treasonable utterance of Agrippa (I.) on the occasion of a banquet at Caligula's house. The exact date of Tiberius's death is given according to the *commentarii* of this emperor. There follow the liberation of Agrippa by Caligula, according to an official entry; the document naming Agrippa tetrarch in place of the deceased Philip, taken from the *commentarii* of Caligula; again, statements drawn from the protocols regarding an audience of the tetrarch Herod and his wife Herodias with Caligula; his petition to be granted the title of king; the accusation of Agrippa against Herod, submitted by him personally, and the banishment of Herod; the appointment of Agrippa to be administrator of Herod's tetrarchy. Chapter x. is based upon the official reports of Petronius to Caligula and the latter's replies. The

---

[1] *Vita*, § 75.
[2] Sueton., *Vita Domitiani*, xx.: ' praeter commentarios et acta Tiberii Caesaris nihil lectitabat.' Cf. Sueton., *Tiberius*, lxi. 1.

statement of Petronius to the effect that he received the official letter about the death of Caligula exactly twenty-seven days before the last official letter of that emperor, in consequence of severe tempests at sea, can come only from an official letter of the governor to Claudius, i.e. from the *commentarii* of Claudius. The absolutely exact date of Caligula's death at the beginning of chapter xi. can be derived only from the official record of the *commentarii*. What follow are excerpts from the *acta senatus*, derived, like the whole chapter, from notes of Agrippa II. given by the latter to Josephus so that he might discreetly stress the merits of Agrippa's father with Claudius. In § 5 we have a document concerning the grant by Claudius to Agrippa, not only in excerpt, but even its duplicate in the form of a proclamation addressed to the people and another to the senate, to which must be added the placing of a bronze tablet in the state archive in the Capitol. § 217 is wanting in the *Halōsis*, which means that Josephus, at a later date, appended to the excerpts he received from Agrippa II., and which concern Agrippa I., those concerning the grant of the kingdom of Chalcis to Herod, the brother of Agrippa. The transactions between Claudius and Agrippa have a decidedly official source, as may be judged from the numerous quotations of official acts. In the section dealing with the attempted construction of the wall by Agrippa I., a work which was never completed, Josephus mentions his source neither in the *Halōsis* nor in the *War*, and for a very good reason. From the parallel account in the *Antiquities*,[1] it follows that Claudius, warned by the governor of Syria, C. Vibius Marsus, had prohibited the continuation of the work by a very brusque decree. Evidently the king was not free from the suspicion of wanting, on a favourable occasion, to break loose from the Romans, and such a fact would fit in badly with Josephus' favourite thesis concerning the absolute loyalty of the Jewish princes and notables and the sole guilt of the common people and its 'tyrants,' i.e. the Zealots. Only in the second edition of the *Antiquities* and after the death of Agrippa II. did he dare to let the cat out of the bag. Yet there is no reason to doubt that he had known the facts from the beginning, thanks to the documents at his disposal.

The Errors of Josephus on the Birth and Parentage of his Patron, Agrippa II.

It is characteristic of the dependence of Josephus upon the extracts from documents he happened to have, and his extremely scanty knowledge concerning the events of his early childhood,

[1] xix. 7. 2.

that the *Halōsis* (ii. § 220) asserts that King Agrippa I. died without leaving a son, whilst a few pages later (§ 247) he says, in accordance with the statements of the Greek *Polemos*, that Claudius gave the territory not included in the Roman province to Agrippa the son of Agrippa. Such a flagrant contradiction would be unthinkable if the work had been done with even a reasonable amount of care. All he had to say in the first of the two passages was simply that Agrippa I. died without leaving a *grown-up* son. Inconsistencies such as the one just quoted (and their number might be multiplied) simply show that Josephus relied entirely, for this period, on documents and extracts from documents which were placed at his disposal or which he had had made for himself. As a matter of fact, the blunder just referred to may have been the consequence of a misinterpretation of some document with an intentionally vague wording, as if it read, for example, ' since King Herod Agrippa has left no son who might succeed him in his tetrarchy.' Josephus, having no other information on the subject, would then infer that it meant Agrippa's having died childless, when it meant only that he had left a minor son to whom the government could not very well be entrusted.

The blunder is all the more flagrant because the Agrippa in question (whose existence is thus denied in the first passage) was none other than Josephus' own patron. But if the reader should feel tempted to conjecture that Josephus could not very well have committed such a blunder, here is another, coming not from the Slavonic text but from the Greek *Polemos*, i.e. the *revised* version. Agrippa, in the year A.D. 73, was in reality forty-six years old. If, as Josephus states in the second of the passages just referred to, he was at the death of his father only a ' very small child,' a ' baby ' ($\pi\alpha\nu\tau\acute{\alpha}\pi\alpha\sigma\iota\nu$ $\nu\acute{\eta}\pi\iota\sigma\varsigma$), he could have been in A.D. 73 only thirty years old at the most. A look at the face of his royal patron should have sufficed to correct the statement; yet when even in such a matter our author commits an error of such magnitude, one may well believe that he did worse in statements which could not be checked quite so easily. As a matter of fact, the blunder admits of an explanation, though not of an excuse. Agrippa II. had first been given by Claudius the kingdom of Chalcis, and only later on Judaea. Since his predecessor in Chalcis, Herod the brother of Agrippa I., had a grandson called Agrippa, Josephus may well have inferred that M. Julius Agrippa II. was this grandson of Herod and thus grand-nephew of King Agrippa I. There is still another possibility. We are told in the *Polemos* (ii. § 220) that Agrippa I. ' left issue by his wife Cypros three daughters, Berenice, Mariamne, and Drusilla, and one son, Agrippa. Since the last was a minor, Claudius again reduced the kingdom to a province and

sent Cuspius Fadus as governor,' etc.   An ignorant collaborator, or
even Josephus himself, might very well have referred the words
' and a son by the same ' (υἱὸν δὲ ἐκ τῆς αὐτῆς, in the Aramaic
original *uminnah bar ḥad*), not, as he should have done, to Cypros
the wife of Agrippa, but to his daughter Drusilla, whose name immediately preceded.   Agrippa II. would then really have been a
grandson of Agrippa I.   But, as is well known, in Hebrew and
Aramaic the same word (*ben* or *bar*) may mean either ' son ' or
' grandson,' just as the word *'abh* may be either ' father ' or
' grandfather.'   This false interpretation may in addition have been
supported by the fact that, at the time of Josephus' writing, such
a grandson of Agrippa I., a son of Drusilla,[1] was still alive ; it was
Agrippa, son of the governor Felix and of Drusilla, who perished
in the eruption of Mt. Vesuvius in A.D. 79.   Our author may therefore have thought his patron Agrippa II. either the grand-nephew
or the grandson of Agrippa I. ; but the matter certainly does not
speak well for his store of knowledge or for the efforts made by
him to secure exact information.[2]   It is these very mistakes and
their insufficient correction in the earliest copies of his works
which show that he did not compose his history of the Roman
governors of Judaea (A.D. 44-66) from memory or after oral tradition, but that on the contrary he used extracts from documents and
followed them so mechanically and closely that to his whole compilation one may apply the Roman lawyer's slogan, ' Quod non
est in actis, non est in mundo.'

So much for the facts.   In the matter of the judgments, they
are, of course, his own ; but this only makes matters worse, for
one can surmise how he may have distorted his sources in the
service of his ' cause,' to make them say what they never meant, or
ruthlessly to suppress their true meaning when it did not suit him.[3]
This result, I might add, is in absolute harmony with the conclusions of Prof. Laqueur,[4] who after an analysis of the *Antiquities*
proved that the documents there quoted were actually collected
by Josephus himself or by his collaborators, and that he did not
take them over from a previous writer.   He lived in Rome ; the

---

[1] A pedigree of the Herodian family is found in most editions of Josephus, e.g.
in Dr. Thackeray's translation, in Cheyne's *Encycl. Bibl.*, c. 2041 *sq.*, and in all
similar works.

[2] Those who—because of this blunder—want to attribute the whole important
chapter which contains the precious lines about the 'helpers of the wonder-worker'
Jesus to a late ignorant interpolator, would do well to remember that no less a
historian than Tacitus (*Ann.*, xii. 33) confused Herod of Chalcis and Agrippa I.
(see Ed. Meyer, *Ursprung und Anfänge d. Christentums*, vol. iii., Stutt., 1923, p. 43).
I have not heard of any competent critic, because of this gross error, attributing the
chapter in question to the pen of a mediaeval copyist !

[3] Th. Zielinski, *Rev. de l'Univ. de Bruxelles*, 1926-7, p. 4 *sq.*, has shown what
use Josephus has made of the imperial documents about the conflict between Jews
and Greeks in Alexandria.

[4] *Loc. cit.*, pp. 223-8, notably p. 226 *sq.*

material lay at his door, as it were; and he used it as extensively as he could.[1]

The Documentary Basis of the Josephan Narrative of Events from A.D. 44 to 46

Precisely the same method may be recognized in the second book of the *Polemos*. In the documents connected with the governors Cuspius Fadus and Tiberius Alexander, Josephus found distinct references to the political cases of certain ' helpers ' of an apparently unnamed 'wonder-worker,' previously condemned and crucified under Pilate. The adherents in question had been transported for judgment, partly to the emperor, partly, first, to the governor of Syria, and had been sent on to Rome by the latter. If the persons in question had not been judged by the Roman authorities, who kept regular records of such proceedings, Josephus would have remained entirely ignorant of these matters. Indeed, he does not say a word about the proceedings of King Agrippa I. against the Jewish messianists, and he has no notion that James and his brother John had been executed by him,[2] whilst Petrus Kepha had been arrested but had managed to escape. Of the hypercritics who considered the whole section a Christian interpolation, none has even put to himself the question why it is that the same Christian interpolators did not insert also the story of the execution of the two brothers and of Peter's arrest.

The documentary basis is equally transparent for the administration of Ventidius Cumanus, as even a superficial reading of the text will show. We have there, first, the complaints of the Samaritan notables and of the Jews, led by the high priest Jonathan b. Ḥanan, against Ventidius Cumanus before Numidius Quadratus, the governor of Syria, in *oratio recta* in the *Halōsis*. There follow the death sentences pronounced by Quadratus on the ringleaders at Caesarea. § 242 is missing in the Slavonic version, evidently because it represents a later addition on the part of Josephus. The complaints against Cumanus and the tribune Celer (§§ 243 *sq.*), the hearing of the case before Claudius (§§ 245-6), duly entered in a protocol and filed with the rest in the imperial archives—all this fully shows the author's working method. The Greek text alone has it that King Agrippa was present at the hearing and took up the cause of the Jews. This is

---

[1] Dr. Thackeray (*Josephus the Man and the Historian*, New York, 1929, pp. 71 f., 72 n. 63; *Journ. Theolog. Studies*, 1929, vol. xxx., No. 120, p. 369 n. 2) has even been able to trace in the verbally quoted documents the style of one of the author's able assistants who translated them. The underlying Latin occasionally shines through, e.g. in the use of the *dativus* (=Lat. *ablativus*) *absolutus* in place of the genitive, *Ant.*, xiv. §§ 228 ff.

[2] See below, p. 542 n. 7.

evidently an insertion made by the author at Agrippa's request. The section ends with the banishment of Cumanus and the death sentence on Celer. Yet we do not learn the precise nature of the latter's guilt. As a matter of fact, he is probably the soldier mentioned in § 224 as having wantonly insulted the Jews in the temple precincts with a coarse joke customary with the mob in Rome,[1] and thereby caused the uprising. One is inclined to ask whether Josephus himself had failed to see the connexion, or whether he hesitated to relate that the shameful death inflicted upon the wretched man was the punishment for an offence which in Roman eyes would not appear so odious. It is noteworthy that the sentence itself, in the Greek text, represents a judicial impossibility, and is evidently an exaggeration on the part of our author, intent upon driving home his conception of the *iustitia principis*. In the Slavonic version it seems perfectly regular and as it were coming directly from the documents. The section ends with the precise date of Claudius' death—that is, it was taken from the final clause of the *commentarii* of Claudius.

The reign of Nero sets in with a few moralizing phrases of no particular weight. Then follow a series of facts, obviously of a purely documentary provenance—for example, the conferring of Armenia upon Aristobulus the son of Herod, and of four Peraean and Galilaean districts upon Agrippa II. (missing in the Slavonic version). There comes next the punishment of some insurgents (whom Josephus as usual calls 'robbers') whose leader had been sent by Felix to Rome with a few accomplices. The Slavonic version does not know as yet that this 'leader' was none other than the famous 'Ele'azar ben Dinai.[2] On the other hand, this version tells with perfect frankness that 'the lesser folk' (i.e. those from whom nothing could be extorted) were crucified, whilst the notables were dismissed after countless confiscations. In the Greek text this passage was deleted, for the imperial tribunal could not of course be laid open to such transparent charges. There follow statements concerning the uprisings of the *Sicarii* (§§ 254-6), on the basis of the reports of Felix and not from the recollections of the author, who at that time was about fourteen or fifteen years of age. The Slavonic text does not yet know the Roman term 'sicarians,' though we know from the Mishnah that it was not uncommon among the Jews. The passage ends with the murder of the high priest Jonathan, again according to the report of Felix; for the suspicion of the Jews, or Josephus' own opinion as expressed in the *Antiquities*, to wit, that the governor had instigated the *Sicarii* to such a crime, is not once referred to.

There follow next the tumults of the pseudo-visionaries and their fantastic plan to start a new exodus into the desert, again ac-

---

[1] ' curtis Judaeis oppedere,' Horace, *Sat.*, i. 9. 70.   [2] See above, p. 102 f.

O

cording to the reports of Felix, and the story of the Jewish-Egyptian impostor—probably Simon Magus, educated in Alexandria—who planned a surprise attack on Jerusalem and was beaten back with much bloodshed by Felix. In the *Polemos* a little more sympathy is shown for those people, and matters are represented as though Felix had attacked a band of peaceful pilgrims. For this purpose the connexion of the ' pilgrims ' with the ' impostor,' still visible in the Slavonic text, was completely abandoned in the Greek *Polemos*. Yet the Roman character of the source, though occasionally coloured by Josephus' Jewish sympathies, appears most clearly in § 264, where the uprising is referred to as the outbreak of a ' fever,' just as in Claudius' decree to the Greeks and Jews of Alexandria.[1]

It is no less characteristic that the late *Antiquities* stands alone in attributing to the 'impostor' the attempt at a repetition of the miracle of Jericho. In his first redactions of this affair Josephus used the official report of Felix, who would have been the last to put such an interpretation upon the desperate horn-blowing which he could hear resounding from the Mount of Olives, let alone reporting such (for Romans) utterly incredible nonsense to Rome, even had he known of the eschatological background of the crazy affair. On the other hand, Josephus would not have omitted such a picturesque touch, had he had any knowledge of it—witness the corresponding passage in the *Antiquities*; but the fact is that he learned such details only much later from his distinguished patrons and readers, who were naturally eager to furnish him with more and more interesting material about the wanton madness of the rebellious rabble.

In the treatment of the rivalry between Jews and Syrians at Caesarea the Slavonic text[2] repeats the allegations of both parties in *oratio recta*, a sure sign that again documents were drawn upon. We know from § 270 that both parties had sent ' notables ' to the Emperor Nero to have the matter decided by him. The decision of the emperor was in favour of the Hellenized Syrians ; but it goes without saying that this did not bring matters to a close—on the contrary, the fight continued, and with it the official documents and Josephus' extracts. But in the midst of these petty bickerings, common enough in all Hellenic cities of the East, Josephus in his early redaction, preserved in the Slavonic text, inserted the following section :

' And the twelfth year of the principate of Nero, the seventeenth of Agrippa, saw ' (Slav. ' received ': Greek προσελάμβανεν) ' the beginning of the war. Its initial occasion was slight, but it grew to such proportions as make it impossible to describe the magnitude of the calamity.'

---

[1] Above, p. 126 n. 1.   [2] Ber.-Grass, p. 289, §§ 226 *sqq.*

The short § 271 about the accession of the governor Porcius Festus, and all the rest of chapter xiv. 1, 2, 3 of the Greek *War*, are missing in the Slavonic version.   Showing as it does the bitterest hostility to the governors Lucceius Albinus and Gessius Florus, it has obviously no Roman documentary basis; Josephus was by now old enough—twenty-two years—to have distinct recollections of his own.[1]   The inference is obvious.   Josephus intentionally ante-dates the beginning of the war in order to minimize the fatal con-sequences of his own ambiguous activity in Galilee.   The existence of the Slavonic text based on an early Greek redaction, where this measure of precaution has not yet been adopted, leaves no doubt whatever on the subject.   Since his procedure was after all some-what too obvious, he tried to obscure it in the later editions by the insertion of a little more material from his source.

In the years extending from A.D. 60 to 64 Josephus was some-how officially connected with the Sanhedrin, probably in the capacity of a clerk, as may be surmised from his pathetic outcry when he calls the chancelleries of Jerusalem—burnt down by the rebels—the ' sinews of the state.' [2]   Thus the method of utilizing archives must have been familiar to him from his early youth, and with it also the bureaucratic method of letting secretaries ($\sigma\upsilon\nu\epsilon\rho\gamma o\iota$) do the real work for their superiors.   As a young Pharisaean priest with good family connexions he certainly found it easy to ' make his way.'   Hence his post as secretary to the fatal embassy, de-scribed in a previous chapter.[3]

For the years of his absence in Italy (A.D. 64 to the spring of 66) he could draw on the recollections of the young Berenice, the mistress of Titus, and on her letter of complaint against Florus, together with Florus' defence, both of course found in the Roman archives.   Finally, we shall presently see that he drew also on the archives of King Agrippa II., a well-arranged collection brought together and administered after the model of the Ptolemaean archives at Alexandria, of which Josephus' enemy, Justus of Tiberias, had been in charge for a time.[4]

THE GREAT DIATRIBE OF KING AGRIPPA II.

Among the documents in Agrippa II.'s library must have been the draft of his great speech supposed to have been delivered in A.D. 66 before the Jewish ambassadors, and advising most strongly against a war with Rome.   But in its extant form the speech cannot have been made in 66, since it has long been noticed that

---

[1] Cf., e.g., § 321, the important supplicatory procession of the priests, which he clearly describes as an eye-witness.

[2] *B.J.*, ii. 17. 6, § 428.   [3] Cp. above, p. 185 f.   [4] Josephus, *Vita*, §§ 355 f.

it is in contradiction to the military situation of that year and would rather fit a time after A.D. 75.[1] Yet since the Slavonic text does not speak of eight legions in Germany, one of the chief contradictions would fall. As a matter of fact, a number of details in the *Halōsis* clearly point to the year 66, and it is to be suspected that Josephus reworked it after 75. For example, the *Halōsis* does not mention the two legions keeping Illyria quiet, and it is certain that precisely about 66 the V[a] Macedonica and the IV[a] Scythica were used in Syria and had been sent there from Moesia. The *Halōsis* says nothing, either, about the fleet in the Black Sea, possibly because that fleet was in A.D. 66 used for the transportation of troops between Alexandria and Alexandretta. It is true that Prof. Laqueur and others have thought the whole speech a free invention of Josephus, who wished to utilize in some manner whatever information had been placed at his disposal about the distribution of troops in the Roman empire. Yet, what speaks against such an hypothesis is the phrase (in § 365), 'that the Greeks are nobler of descent than anything else under the sun.' Josephus was, after all, too much of a Jew to write such a thing, the more so because he had no particular reason to flatter the Greeks, whilst Agrippa II., completely Hellenized as he was, merely expressed his own feelings on the subject. The phrase, however, comes most probably from the pen of the Greek secretaries of Agrippa's office. The corrections found in the MSS. M, L, and A[2] are, of course, the work of Josephus himself, who was afraid of offending the Romans. It is interesting to note the original wording preserved in the Slavonic version, and to see from it how little either Agrippa or Josephus cared to spare Jewish nationalist sensibilities.

The list concerning the distribution of troops in the empire, taken from some *breviarium totius imperii*, was, of course, easily accessible to Agrippa in his quality of *rex socius* and commander of an auxiliary contingent. We shall show below that Josephus gave the full text of the speech only in his definitive edition of the *Polemos*. In the *Halōsis* there is but a very diplomatically curtailed outline. The latter version passes over in silence the two Egyptian legions stationed in Alexandria. As a matter of fact, Titus had led them to Palestine as early as the spring of 66. If, further, in § 383 the North African legion is not mentioned, we find the explanation in the statement of Josephus (*B.J.*, ii. 18. 8) that—to the misfortune of the Jews—there were at that time 5000 men of Lybian troops at Alexandria, evidently sent there to take the place of the legions led to Palestine by Titus. To sum up :

---

[1] Ritterling, *De legione Romanorum X[a] gemina*, Diss. Lips., 1885, f. 32 *sqq* and others.

[2] ' the Greeks who think they are nobler ' (M, L) ; A has ' who think . . . and who are ' !—the last words being due, of course, to a Greek copyist.

not only are the much-discussed contradictions absent in the *Halōsis*; the latter has even a number of positive statements which fit most excellently the situation as it existed in A.D. 66. The speech is therefore really to be regarded as a contemporaneous document coming from the chancellery of Agrippa. This does not mean, of course, that the king ever delivered it in actual fact. As Prof. Laqueur pointed out, after this masterpiece of rhetoric the second discourse of the monarch (§§ 403 *sq.*) appears rather flat and even superfluous. This second speech was indeed, in a previous redaction, the only one, so that § 403 originally followed directly upon § 344. But the monarch was not satisfied with those two short phrases, and sent the historian a very nice draft which he would no doubt have read off in style had not the poor taste of his listeners, their noise and stone-throwing, prevented him. Yet it is doubtful whether Agrippa even delivered his short speech. For the sequence of events in §§ 405 and 406 of the Slavonic text is quite unintelligible.

§§ 405-408.

Slavonic *Halōsis*.	Greek *Polemos*.
' The people obeyed these words	'Acting on this advice, the people went up to the Temple, with the king and Berenice, and began the reconstruction of the porticoes, while the magistrates and the members of the council dispersed to the various villages and levied the tribute. The arrears, amounting to forty talents, were rapidly collected. Thus for the moment Agrippa dispelled the menace of war. Subsequently, he endeavoured to induce the people to submit to Florus until a successor was sent by Caesar to replace him. But this exasperated the Jews, who heaped abuse upon the king and formally proclaimed his banishment from the city; some of the insurgents even ventured to throw stones at him. The king, seeing that the passions of the revolutionaries were now beyond control, and indignant at the insults which he had received, sent the magistrates and principal citizens to Florus at Caesarea, in
and after separating, one party built the halls,	
but the others, going into the villages,	
collected quickly the remainder of the tax, forty talents.	
But Agrippa commanded the people to obey Florus, until the emperor should send another in his place. But those, indignant, reviled the king,	
and hitting him with stones, they drove him from the city.	

	order that he might appoint some of their number to collect the tribute in the country ; he then withdrew to his own dominions.
' And others collected and went to the town of Masada.'	'And now some of the most ardent promoters of hostilities banded together and made an assault on a fortress called Masada.'

According to the narrative of this redaction it would be necessary to suppose Agrippa to have remained standing on the bridge while the destroyed halls were being rebuilt and the tribute in arrears collected.   Then, after an initial success, he would have committed the *faux pas* of defending Florus and thus provoking a popular outburst.   To make this nonsense less palpable, the Greek secretary has striven honestly to conceal its essential absurdity by proper insertions.   Yet the whole awkward representation is merely the consequence of Josephus' insertion of the two speeches one after the other.   Originally the first sentence of § 343 was followed directly by § 406, and the whole section read as follows :

§ 342. ' And the people pressed for an embassy to be sent to Nero to denounce Florus, saying : " If we keep silence on so great a fight and do not promptly denounce this man as the originator of the wrong, the blame for the battle will be laid upon us."

§ 343. But to Agrippa it did not appear expedient to write and denounce Florus.

§ 406. (And he) commanded the people to be obedient to Florus until the emperor should send another in his place.'

The whole passage gives an excellent idea of how Josephus, to suit his patrons, inserted additions and left his Greek secretary in charge of the polishing of the style and the arranging of the subject-matter of his patchwork.

What is left of chapter xvii. is based on Josephus' own impressions, though postscripts of matter given him by his readers are not wanting.   In the Slavonic version (§ 421) Agrippa is said to have dispatched 3000 horsemen under the command of a certain Darius.   In the *Polemos* we find added the name of the supreme commander, Philip, son of Jaqim.   Evidently that noble general of the Transjordanian cavalry had felt slighted at the omission of his name in the first redaction.   On his complaint Josephus hastened to correct his mistake.

Another addition of vastly greater importance is found in §§ 429 and 431-4.   It concerns the rôle played by Menaḥem, the son of Judas the Galilaean, and his fights with 'Ele'azar, the son of the high priest, who in that version is alone responsible for the rebellion.   It is clear that these omissions cannot possibly be regarded as abridgments on the part of the Slavonic translator (as even Berendts was inclined to believe). The mediaeval Russian had no interest whatever in reducing a chapter in such a manner that the part of a certain personage, highly indifferent to him, in certain cases appeared altogether blurred. But it is quite conceivable that an eye-witness such as Josephus—who was hiding in an inner chamber of the Temple during the tragic episode of Menaḥem's ephemeral kingship [1]—did not perceive at first certain events, and that he therefore felt called upon to add them later on, according to the statements of others. Any one trying to chronicle the events of 1914-18, even on a sector of the front where he was present himself, would have the same experience.

Matters are not much different for chapter xviii., likewise based on Josephus' reminiscences. Only § 7, dealing with the events at Alexandria, has a documentary basis, to wit, the report of the commanding officer of the city, Tiberius Alexander, to the emperor. § 6, dealing with the treason of No'ar from the point of view of King Agrippa ii., obviously utilizes materials placed at the author's disposal by his royal patron Agrippa ii. In the description of the defeat of Cestius, official documents, the reports of Florus and Cestius, are mingled with the author's reminiscences of the impressions made by these events upon the Jews. The reproach levelled against Cestius in *Halōsis*, § 531, that he might have nipped the rebellion in the bud by a timely assault on Jerusalem, a reproach characteristic of the Romanophile Jew, i.e. Josephus himself, is repeated in the *Polemos* (§ 532), with the addition that Florus had bribed the commanders of the cavalry into voting against such a measure. Josephus would certainly never have dared to report such matters of a Roman governor without some support for them in the documents of the imperial archives.

From chapter xx. 4 on, Josephus utilizes the draft of an old report sent by him to Jerusalem from Galilee, as has been amply shown by Prof. Laqueur. With the beginning of the third book the analysis of the sources was successfully effected by Prof. Wilhelm Weber of the University of Halle in his well-known work, *Josephus und Vespasian*.[2] The chief result is the fact that Josephus really utilizes to a great extent, beside his own former report, the *commentarii* (ὑπομνήματα) (that is, the official campaign diaries) of Titus and Vespasian. This is true for the first redaction of his work as well as for the second and definitive one. Dr. Weber has pointed out the complete inability of the civilian author to follow and to describe in such an admirably lucid and comprehensive way the complicated military operations on the Roman side. What he did was to draw on the well-arranged and skilfully synthetized army reports assembled by the staff-officers at general headquarters,

---

[1] *Vita*, § 21. 　　　　　　　[2] Stuttgart, 1921.

As for the events within the besieged city, he eventually got them from deserters whom he had to interrogate in the service of the Roman intelligence department, as the vainglorious traitor admits without shame or scruple.[1]

Conclusions

We may, then, claim to have proved, in the foregoing chapters, that the numerous important and intrinsic differences between the Slavonic version of Josephus' *Capture of Jerusalem* (*Halōsis*) and the Greek standard text of the *Jewish War* cannot by any means be attributed, exclusively or even for the larger part, to the activity of the mediaeval translator, a Judaizing heretic working on a Greek original somewhere in Lithuania between 1250 and 1260. We can attribute to him at the utmost the sceptical interpolation into the passage concerning the miraculous rending of the veil, which is still missing in the Rumanian version, and certain minor glosses explaining geographical and ethnological names, such as are found in the following passages: ii. § 269 *sq.*,[2] 'the Dacians, who are called Bulgarians,' or *ibid.* § 363,[3] 'the Istros, which is the Danube,' or vii. § 244, where the Greek *War* mentions the Alanoi, whilst the Slavonic text adds, 'the Ossetian (*jasjskyj*) people, which is well known to be descended from the Pečeneg tribe, living between the Tauros and the Maeotian lake.'

All the rest of his work can be regarded as a faithful, painstaking translation of so mechanical and literal a type that in many cases it is unintelligible without an equally mechanical retroversion into Greek. So far from shortening or omitting anything, it is on the contrary perfectly plain that the translator has taken the greatest trouble to fill up accidental gaps in his Greek MS. by drawing on additional, more complete MSS., which he carefully compared, adding conscientiously to the successive copies of his version whatever paragraph or single line he could find in those more complete MSS. Wherever he did not understand a Greek word, rendered unintelligible by some copyist's error, he carefully transcribed it letter for letter, although he might easily have glided over the difficulty by a vague phrase or some bold guess.

The total retranslation of this Slavonic text into Greek is not only possible, but is even a fairly easy task for a scholar moderately conversant with both the Greek and the Slavonic language and style. The dictionaries of Sreznĕvski and Miklosič indicate the usual equations between Greek and Slavonic words as far as they are found in the extant versions of the current biblical and patristic literature. On the other hand, Dr. Thackeray's forthcoming *Lexicon Josephinum* catalogues the *copia verborum* and

---

[1] C. Ap., i. 48 f.   [2] Ber.-Grass, p. 310.   [3] *Ibid.*, p. 309.

modus dicendi of Josephus' Greek secretaries, thereby making it possible to judge which one of several Greek words, suggested as an equivalent for a given Russian expression by Sreznĕvski's and Miklosič's collections, is likely to have been used by Josephus. By using these three works of reference for a judicious retranslation we shall be able to obtain a Greek history of *The Fall of Jerusalem*, and of the events leading up to it, which is in many respects not identical with the standard text of the *Jewish War*. The differences between the two versions are in part due to the obvious chronological priority of the original at the base of the Slavonic text, in part to the author's consideration for a different circle of readers. For whilst the standard version of the *Jewish War* was adapted to the viewpoint of a Graeco-Roman public, the first draft was intended for Josephus' own co-religionists.

There is yet more. Just as a number of mistakes and untranslated Greek words prove that the Slavonic translator worked on a Greek original, so a number of other mistakes and transcribed words show that there was a Semitic original behind that first Greek draft, a conclusion fully corroborated by Josephus' own statement in the preface to his *Jewish War*.

Both the Greek standard text of the *War* and the *Antiquities*, and the lost Greek original of the Slavonic *Halōsis*, have suffered from interpolations and deletions at the hands of various Christian scribes and ecclesiastical revisers. These forgeries, always clumsy in the extreme, are clearly recognizable by their manifest apologetic tendencies. The interpolations can be easily discarded, whilst the deletions can be sometimes overcome through the testimony of early quotations, imitations of or allusions to the expurgated passages in question.

In no case does any one of these Christian apologetic interpolations add anything new to what we learn from the most generally known Christian sources, in particular the Gospels; while, on the contrary, such differences between the Greek and the Slavonic text as cannot possibly be attributed to the hand of a Christian interpolator frequently contain the strangest and most valuable bits of information, of a type that could not be furnished by any other source but a contemporary witness of the events in question. Cases in point are, for example, the curious detail of Vitellius using *tribuli* against Otho's cavalry in the battle of Bedriacum, or the statement that the Essenes were eager to study the religious and mystic literatures of other nations [1] (which so strikingly confirms the modern observations about foreign, especially Pythagorean, influences which underlie the special tenets of this religious order).

It would be contrary to the elementary rules of sound method were we to attribute such valuable statements to some unknown

---

[1] *Halōsis*, ii. § 136.

interpolator, instead of accepting them as coming from Josephus himself, and on no other ground than their absence from the later work, a fact attributable in each case to very good reasons. The different date of both works and the different public to which they are addressed fully account for such differences and contradictions as have been pointed out by critics. On the same ground exception might be taken to statements occurring in the *Antiquities* but absent from the *War*, or to open contradictions existing between these two works ; yet in this case critics have not hesitated, justly and logically, to attribute such divergencies to deletions and corrections by the author himself.

What holds good for the numerous passages analysed in the foregoing chapters, passages which are quite indifferent from the Christian point of view, must of course apply with equal force to the passages of the Slavonic text dealing with the messianic movement, more particularly with the two greatest protagonists of that movement, namely John the Baptist and Jesus. These chapters, too, are likely to show clear traces of Christian interpolations and expurgations of an apologetic tendency, and the possibility must be admitted that they also suffered interpolations and deletions from non-Christian—that is, primarily Jewish—hands, of much the same type as could be found in the Hebrew *Josippon*. Yet it would be contrary to all sound method to reject them wholesale and without any attempt at a separation of the wheat from the chaff, on the sole ground that they do not occur in the Greek standard text of the *War*. From what we know and have been able to point out in the matter of ecclesiastical censorship, it is much more likely that long passages of anti-Christian character and tendency should have been deleted in copies under the more or less direct control of the Orthodox Church, whilst they were tolerated in copies treasured by Jews or Judaizing heretics, than that they should have been interpolated by *unknown* forgers.

For these reasons it would seem evident to the present writer that the text in question has not received so far the proper attention and critical analysis of competent scholars. Quite aside from the righting of the great wrong done to Alexander Berendts, students of the history of primitive Christianity may demand at last the thoroughgoing investigation of a unique source which, if it can be proved to be a part of the genuine *Capture of Jerusalem* by Josephus Flavius, must be considered as antedating the earliest of the Synoptic Gospels. Even if the passages could not be traced further back than to an individual of Josephus' own time and general character and outlook, they would still constitute interesting and valuable documents. If, however, as I think I have proved, Josephus drew his entire information on the subject from the official commentaries of Tiberius, the favourite reading of

Domitian, his accounts about Jesus are of necessity nothing more and nothing less than extracts from the official reports of Pilate.

Under these circumstances it ought to be well worth the author's and the reader's while to start anew on an unbiased analysis of these crucial chapters, too light-heartedly dismissed by critics only imperfectly acquainted with Josephus' character and working methods.

THE GENUINE STATEMENTS OF JOSEPHUS ABOUT JOHN THE BAPTIST

'From the days of John the Baptist until now the kingdom of Heaven suffereth violence, and men of violence take it by force.' MATT. xi. 12.

XI

The Appearance of the 'Wild Man'; his Promise and his Baptism

IMMEDIATELY after the narrative of the pseudo-Alexander,[1] introduced with no other connecting link save the temporal adverb 'then,' stereotyped by Biblical use—in other words, in the artless manner so typical of Josephus when he passes from one source to another—there follows in the Slavonic version the story of the Jordan Baptizer. It is significant that Josephus did not know his name when writing the *Halōsis*;[2] we may infer that it did not occur in his source—unless we should prefer to suppose that it was cancelled for fear of the censor, just as we shall see in a subsequent chapter [3] that for this very reason the name of Jesus was deleted in a number of MSS.—for a mediaeval forger would certainly have spoken without any reticence of 'John the Baptist' or 'John the Forerunner.' The mention of 'Joannes Prodromos,' found in the chapter headings of all the Slavonic MSS., had no place in the original text; even Berendts ranks it among the notes which have as little claim to belong to the text of Josephus as have the rubrics to individual chapters and the variously composed tables of contents (*didascaliae*) of individual books found in some MSS. of the Greek *Polemos* and the *Antiquities*. It was left to the tendentious criticism of Prof. Paul W. Schmiedel [4] of Zürich to find a proof of the Christian origin of the succeeding chapter in the use of the word *prodromos* by the various late authors of these rubrics.

I quote the passage verbatim, including the last sentence of the preceding section, so as to show clearly the primitive manner of linking up the various portions of the narrative.

Slavonic *Halōsis* (Berendts-Grass, p. 247).[5]	*Polemos*, ii. 110.
'But Caesar laughed when he looked at him, and ordered him	'Caesar laughed at these words and enrolled the pseudo-Alex-

---

[1] *B.J.*, ed. Niese, ii. 101-110.
[2] See below, p. 229₁.
[3] Below, p. 548 n. 2.
[4] *Neue Züricher Zeitung*, 22nd Aug. 1926, No. 1346.
[5] See our Plates XVI. *a* and *b*.

to live henceforward [1] among his galley-slaves.

ander, because of his athletic looks, among the oarsmen of his galleys ; his inspiring genius he ordered to execution.

But the Melians, because they had borne him in procession on their hands and honoured him with regal honours, were executed *en masse*.

The Melians he considered sufficiently punished for their folly by their lavish extravagance.

Now [2] at that time there walked among the Jews a man in wondrous garb, for he had stuck on to his body animals' hair wherever it was not covered by his own. But in countenance he was like a savage. This man came to the Jews and allured them to freedom, [3] saying, "God hath sent me to show you the way of the law, [4] by which ye shall be freed from many tyrants. [5] And no mortal shall rule over you, but only the Highest [6] who hath sent me." And when the people heard that, they were glad. [7]

(And there went to him all Judaea and the region around Jerusalem.) [8]

And [9] he did nothing else to them, save that he dipped them in the stream of the Jordan and let

---

[1] The Slavonic word reproduces the Greek μένειν.

[2] The following lines are given in Dr. Thackeray's translation, revised by myself for the appendix to his *Josephus*, vol. iii. p. 644 *sq*.

[3] Cf. the inscription ' to freedom ' (*l⁰ ḥeruth*) on Jewish revolutionary coins. Cf. fig. 24, p. 60, in Th. Reinach, *Les Monnaies Juives*, Paris, 1888, reproduced below, p. 245.

[4] =' the way to justice,' in the Baptist's sermon, *Matt.* xxi. 23=*Apoc. Pet.*, xxii. 28, ' *derekh ṣedaqah*,' *Prov.* xvi. 31.

[5] As a close parallel, cf. Florus, ii. 7, 4 : ' Syrus quidam nomine Eunus . . . *ad libertatem* . . . servos quasi numinum imperio *concitavit*.'

[6] No exact parallel to this absolute use of "Υψιστος =*'El 'Eliōn* (without θεός) occurs in the Greek text of Josephus, except *Ant.*, xvi. § 163, 'Υρκανοῦ ἀρχιερέως θεοῦ ὑψίστου, in an edict of Augustus (Thackeray).

[7] Probably corrected from ἤρθησαν, ' they were excited.' See below, p. 246 nn. 2-4.

[8] Christian interpolation. The sentence is not to be found in the Rumanian version of Josephus, cod. Gaster, No. 89. This and the close parallelism with *Matt.* iii. 5 : ' then went out unto him [i.e. to John] Jerusalem and all Judaea and all the region round about Jordan ' ; *Mark* i. 5 : ' And there went out unto him all the country of Judaea and all they of Jerusalem,' as well as the ignorance displayed by the author, who does not see the tautology implied in ' all Judaea ' and the ' region about Jerusalem,' stamp it as a very late addition. By its omission one gains a perfectly satisfactory context.

[9] =' but.' Semitic *vav adversativum* ! Cp. above, p. 133 n. 7. The author's ironic meaning is quite clear : ' Big words, small deeds.'

PLATE XVIII

PLATE XIX

THE APPEARANCE OF THE 'WILD MAN' (JOHN THE BAPTIST)
UNDER ARCHELAUS ACCORDING TO THE SLAVONIC JOSEPHUS
COD. KYRILLO-BJELOS. 63/1302 F° 50 V° AND 51 R° IN THE LENINGRAD PUBLIC LIBRARY
(SEE P. 224-6)

them go, warning them that they should renounce evil deeds. So would they be given a king who would free them and subject all who are insubordinate, but he himself would be subjected to none. At his words some mocked, but others put faith in him.

And when he was brought to Archelaus [1] and the learned doctors of the law had assembled, they asked him who he was and where he had been until then. And he answered and said, "I am a man;[2] as such [3] has the spirit of God called me, and I live on bulrushes [4] and roots and wood-shavings." [5] But when they threatened to torture him if he did not desist from these words and deeds, he said : " It is meet rather for *you* to desist from your shameful works and to submit to the Lord your God."

And Simon,   by birth an Essene,[6]
a scribe, arose in wrath and said : "We read the divine books every day. But thou, only now come forth like a wild beast from the wood, durst thou teach us and lead the multitudes astray with thy accursed speeches ? "

And he flung himself forward to rend his body. But he said in reproach to them : "I will not reveal to you the secret which is among you,[7] because you desired it not. For this cause has unspeakable

Polemos, ii. 111.

---

[1] Ethnarch from 4 B.C. to A.D. 6, a date much earlier than the one assigned by *Luke* (iii. 1) to the first appearance of John. Needless to add that a Christian forger would have adhered to the traditional chronology.

[2] So most MSS. Only the one unfortunately followed by Berendts : ' I am pure ' (*čist* misread for *člk=čelověk*).

[3] *jim'že=ὅν* ; one MS., *i zde*, ' and hither ' ; Berendts with the other MSS. reads ' because.'

[4] Cf. Suidas, s.v. *meleagri*, ' he fed them on *meleager* roots and on the heart (=marrow) of bulrushes.'

[5] For an explanation of this malicious pun, cf. below, p. 237.

[6] In reality ' a Sadducee ' (see below, p. 227 n. 1). It is the Sadducees who are ' rude and cruel in the exercise of justice ' (*B.J.*, ii. 166). There is obviously a confusion, hardly due to Josephus himself, of this Simon and the Essene interpreter of dreams of the same name mentioned a few lines further on and in *Antiq.*, xvii. 346.

[7] On this ' secret,' cf. *Luke* xvii. 21, *Matt.* xiii. 11.

P

misfortune befallen you and for your own doing." And when he had thus spoken, he went away to the other side of the Jordan. And since no man durst hinder him, he did as he had done before. Archelaus, however, ever since he had taken possession of his ethnarchy, mindful of the enmity of the Jews, harassed them with intolerable oppression, likewise also the Samaritans.'

But Archelaus, having taken possession of his ethnarchy, did not forget old feuds, but treated not only the Jews but also the Samaritans with brutality.'

This section is followed (§ 112 *sqq*.) by matter also found in the Greek, to wit, Archelaus' dream of the oxen and the ears of corn, its interpretation by Simon the Essene, and its fulfilment through the banishment of the ethnarch. There follows the dream of Glaphyra his wife, and its fulfilment (§§ 114-116), the appointment of Coponius as governor (§ 117), and the appearance of Judas of Galilee as founder of a fourth Jewish party. The mention of his 'special sect' (ἰδία αἴρεσις) affords occasion for the insertion of the celebrated passage on the three sects of the Pharisees, the Sadducees, and the Essenes (§§ 119-166). The description of the last-named sect, with its ample details, is probably derived from a lost work of Philo, acquired by Josephus during his stay at Alexandria ; what he adds, from his own knowledge, on the Pharisees and Sadducees is little enough. There follows a reference to the removal of Archelaus told previously, and a notice on the Palestinian cities founded by the tetrarchs, the death of Augustus, and the accession of Tiberius. Then follows, without any transition worth the name, the second passage on the Baptist, comprising the prophetic dream of Philip and its fulfilment, the illegal marriage of the tetrarch's brother Herod, the ' wild man's ' reprimand and his death, along with a summary of the principles governing the Baptist's life and preaching. The ' doubling ' noticed in the two accounts of the Baptist is due to the use of two different sources, the one evidently a biographical account composed by one of John's disciples, the other a compilation of prophetic dreams and their interpretation and speedy fulfilment, the latter no doubt of Essene origin, as may be judged from the prominent rôle given therein to the Essene sect. It is perhaps not too much to assume that Josephus became acquainted with the former during or in consequence of his stay with the ' Banus,' whilst his acquaintance with the latter is due to his erstwhile flirtation with the Essenes.

THE 'WILD MAN' AS INTERPRETER OF DREAMS AND CENSOR OF ROYAL MORALS. HIS DEATH

I add to this second passage the narratives of dreams which precede it.

Slavonic *Halōsis*, Berendts-Grass, p. 249.	Greek *Polemos*, bk. ii. § 111 *sqq.*, Niese.
'But Archelaus, ever since he had taken possession of his ethnarchy, mindful of the enmity of the Jews, harassed them with intolerable oppression, likewise also the Samaritans.	'Archelaus, having taken possession of his ethnarchy, did not forget old feuds, but treated not only the Jews but also the Samaritans with brutality. Both parties sent deputies to Caesar to denounce him, and in the ninth year of his rule he was banished to Vienna, a town in Gaul, and his property confiscated to the imperial treasury.
And in the ninth year of his rule	
	§ 112.
	It is said that, before he received his summons from Caesar, he had this dream : he thought he saw nine tall and full-grown ears of corn on which oxen were browsing.
he saw a dream, namely that there were nine ears of corn in the field, full-grown and tall, and oxen came and cropped them, grubbing them up by the roots.	
And he called for the Chaldaeans, the interpreters of dreams, (and) asked them what this sign (meant). And when one said this and another that, a Sadducee [1] named Symos spoke thus : " The ears of corn are years, but the oxen a change in the state of affairs. And it is *not* [2] allotted to you to reign according to the number of the ears of corn. And after enduring various changes and tribu-	He sent for the soothsayers and some Chaldaeans and asked them their opinion of its meaning. Various interpretations being given, a certain Simon, an Essene [1] by affiliation,[3] said that in his view the ears of corn denoted years and the oxen a revolution, because in ploughing they turn over the soil ; he would therefore reign for as many years as there were ears of corn, and then, after a

---

[1] Obviously the Greek text is right in calling this Simon an Essene. On the confusion, cf. above, p. 225 n. 6.

[2] The *not* is due to some reviser anxious to bring this dream into harmony with the true chronology.

[3] τὸ γένος. If this be translated ' by birth,' the man would belong to the variety of Essenes who did not refrain from marriage (*B.J.*, ii. 161).

lations, you will die." And forthwith, five days after the dream,
Caesar summoned him to his trial.

For the Jews and Samaritans
had previously sent to Caesar to
complain of his violence. When
Caesar had investigated (the case)[1]
he banished him to the Gallic town
of Vienna. And his riches were
brought to Caesar's palace.

And thereafter (there was) his
wife Glaphyra—the daughter of
Archelaus, king of Cappadocia,
who had previously been the wife
of Alexander the son of Herod,
whom (his) father put to death, as
we have related—and Juba the
Libyan king had taken her.[2] And
when he died she returned to her
father's house. And when this
Archelaus, the ethnarch, saw her,
he fell so passionately in love that
he forsook his wife Mariamne and
took her. And then she saw a
dream, to wit, Alexander, who
came with a threat and spoke
(thus): "I have borne thy defiling
(me) when after my death thou
marriedst the Luvian [3] king. But
now, since thou hast returned to
my house, shameless woman, and
attached thyself to a third husband, to my brother, I will not
brook the outrage but shall take
thee to me, whether thou wilt or
no." And after she had seen the
dream, she lingered for two days
and died. . . .'

chequered experience of revolutionary changes, would die. Five
days after hearing this, Archelaus
was summoned to his trial.

I think mention may also fitly
be made of the dream of his wife
Glaphyra. Daughter of Archelaus,
king of Cappadocia, she had for
her first husband Alexander, the
brother of Archelaus of whom we
have been speaking, and son of
King Herod, who put him to death,
as we have already related.[2] After
his death she married Juba, king
of Libya, on whose decease she
returned home and lived in widow-
hood with her father. There
Archelaus, the ethnarch, saw her
and fell so passionately in love
with her that he instantly divorced
his wife Mariamne and married
her. So she came back to Judaea,
where, not long after her arrival,
she imagined that Alexander stood
beside her and said : ' Thy Libyan
marriage might have sufficed thee,
but, not content with that, thou
now returnest to my hearth, having taken to thyself a third husband, and him, audacious woman,
my own brother. But I will
not brook this outrage and shall
reclaim thee, whether thou wilt
or no.' After relating this
dream she survived barely two
days.'

[1] These words, occurring only in the Slavonic text, are the equivalent of a quotation by Josephus of the *commentarii principis* (see above, p. 203 ll. 26 f.). Had Caesar not investigated the case, Josephus would not have found the sentence in the acts.

[2] Note the clumsy style of the earlier text and compare it with the polished later version.

[3] *Ljuvijski*. Note the correspondence of the Slavonic form with the Biblical *Lubhiim* as against the Greek *Libyes*.

Slavonic *Halōsis* (following after
      B.J., ii. 168).

' While Philip was in power, he
saw a dream, in which an eagle
plucked out both his eyes. And
he called all his wise men together.
When some had explained the
dream in this manner and some in
that, there came to him suddenly
without being called that man of
whom we have written above,[1]
how he went about (clothed) in
animals' hair and cleansed the
people in the waters of the Jordan.
And he spoke : " Hear the word of
the Lord : the dream which thou
hast seen : the eagle is thy venality,[2] for that bird is brutal and
rapacious.[3] And this sin[4] will
take away thine eyes, which are
thy dominion and thy wife." [5]
And when he had thus spoken,
Philip expired before the evening,[6]
and his dominion was given to
Agrippa.[7]
      And his wife[8] was taken by
Herod his brother. Because of
her all law-abiding people abhorred
him, but they durst not accuse
him to his face.[9] But only that
man, whom we have called a wild

---

[1] See p. 224 and p. 223 n. 2.
[2] Cod. Pogodin, 1440 : ' thy power.'   A correction having for aim the elimination of this stricture on the character of Philip ; cf. above, p. 182₅.
[3] This type of zoological symbolism is first found in the letter of Aristeas,
§§ 145-8. On its origin, cf. my book *Orphisch-dionysische Mysterien-Gedanken
in der christlichen Antike*, Leipzig-Berlin, 1925, pp. 71 *sqq.*, 76, 115 n. 1.
[4] Cod. Pogodin, 1440 : ' thy acquisitiveness.'
[5] Rumanian Josephus : ' The dream that thou hast seen heralds thy death,
for the eagle is a bird of prey and has destroyed thine eyes.'   Another change in
the same direction as the variant quoted above, n. 2.
[6] Philip the Tetrarch died in A.D. 33-34 (*Ant.*, xviii. 106). It follows that
according to Josephus the Baptist died after A.D. 34, a fact in striking accordance
with his mention in *Ant.*, xviii. 116—that is, long after Jesus (xviii. 63) and after
the death of Philip (xviii. 106).
[7] Agrippa I. was appointed king by Caligula on his accession to the principate
in A.D. 37.
[8] Slav MSS., ' his wife Herodias.'   The name is wanting in the Hebrew and
Arabic *Josippon* as well as in the Rumanian Josephus (below, p. 600, No. 15)
dependent upon a Russian text.   It is no doubt a late addition and a borrowing
from *Mark* vi. 17.
[9] The Hebrew *Josippon* (Cod. Vat. Ebr., 408, *c.* A.D. 1444) adds a line of
protest against the assertion that the other rabbis did not dare to speak their
mind on this scandal.

man, came to him in wrath and
spoke : " Because thou hast taken
thy brother's wife, thou transgressor of the law,[1] even as thy
brother has died a merciless death,
so also shalt thou be cut off by the
heavenly sickle.[2] For the divine
decree will not be silenced, but
will destroy thee through sore
afflictions in other lands ; [3] because thou art not raising up seed
to thy brother, but satisfying
fleshly lusts and committing adultery, since he has left [4] children."
But Herod, when he heard (that),
was wroth and ordered him to be
beaten and driven away. But he,
wheresoever he found Herod, never
ceased to accuse him, until Herod
grew furious and ordered him to
be slain.

Now his nature was strange and
his ways were not human. For
even as a fleshless spirit, so lived
this man. His mouth knew no
bread, nor even at the passover
feast did he taste of the unleavened bread, saying : " in remembrance of God who redeemed the
people from bondage is this given
to eat,[5] and for the flight only,
since the journey was in haste." [6]
But wine and strong drink he
would not so much as allow to be
brought nigh him. And he loathed

---

[1] *Deut.* xxvii. 23 : ' Cursed be he that lieth with his sister-in-law ' (*ḥathanah*.
LXX., " μετὰ τῆς ἀδελφῆς τῆς γυναικὸς αὐτοῦ." A.V., ' mother-in-law '). The rigoristic
explanation wanted to understand *ḥathanah* in the widest sense, including the
brother's wife.

[2] This is the constellation *falx* ; cf. Firm. Mat. and Manilius, v. 2. 2 ; also the
sickle of the archangel Gabriel, *Talmud Sanh.*, 95b. No mediaeval forger could
have invented such a detail.

[3] Antipas was banished by Caligula to Lugdunum in Gaul in A.D. 39 (*Ant.*,
xviii. 252).

[4] Slav MSS. : ' four children.' The Hebrew *Josippon* has ' quamvis habuerit
liberos ' ; the *Egesippus*, ' habentem semen de germano ipsius ' ; cf. Tert., *Adv.
Marc.*, iv. 34, ' habentem filiam ex illa.' ' Four ' is therefore obviously a late
gloss of a reader who included with the daughter of Herodias the three children
of Philip's wife Salome by her second marriage with Aristobulus.

[5] Text transposed. The Slavonic has ' nay, even to the passover feast he
tasted not . . . saying : In remembrance of God who released . . . is (this)
given,' etc.

Cf. *Exodus* xii. 11 : ' ye shall eat it in haste.'

(to eat of) any animal. And
every act of injustice he exposed.
And wood-shavings served for his
needs.'[1]

Reflecting on this passage, taken in connexion both with the
other accounts of dreams and with the previous section on the
Baptist, an unprejudiced reader cannot fail to note the perfect
homogeneity of the narrative and its derivation from some special
source trying to extol the skill of Essenes and kindred ascetes as
interpreters of dreams and soothsayers. Josephus, who boasts of
his own ability in the interpretation of dreams,[2] must have had
just such a source at his disposal. From these considerations it
would seem almost inconceivable how Berendts could say ' a first
glance gives the unfavourable impression . . . that the whole
story of Philip's dream is a formal imitation of that of Archelaus.'
As if it were not the case with all prophetic dreams throughout the
literature of the world that they display and from their very nature
must display a certain similarity of form! As well might one say
that Joseph's dream of the sheaves in *Gen.* xxxvii. is a spurious
interpolation, modelled on his dream of the stars.

Instead of dwelling on such fancies, let us turn to the invaluable details of this tradition, since they throw a surprising light on
circumstances hitherto unexplainable and in any case lying quite
outside the range of a mediaeval Christian forger.

Naṣōraeans and Rekhabites

It may appear strange that Josephus does not know the
Baptist's name and speaks of him only as the ' wild man ' ('*ish
sadeh*). But the explanation is surprisingly simple ; it is given by
the Baptist's elusive answer, as quoted by the historian, to the
question as to who he is : *čelověk esmi*, ' I am a man, and as such
(hither) has the spirit of God called me.' The Baptist therefore
replied, '*Enosh 'ani*, or, in Aramaic, '*Enash 'ana*, ' I am 'Enosh,'
i.e. simply ' man,' just as Jesus called himself *Bar nasha*,[3] the ' Son
of Man,' or simply ' the man.'

This explains at last how the Mandaeans, i.e. the Naṣōraeans
of Mesopotamia,[4] arrived at their peculiar doctrine, namely, that

---

[1] For an explanation of this mischievous statement, cf. below, p. 237 f.
[2] *B.J.*, iii. 352.
[3] Cf. the Mandaean *Bar-'Anosh*='Adam, Ginza, ed. Lidzbarski, p. 118 n. 14.
[4] For a bibliography, cf. W. Brandt, art. 'Mandaeans' in Hastings' *Encycl.*, viii.
(1915), p. 384b, § 15 ; *Mandäische Religion*, Leipzig, 1889, p. 155 *sq.* ; R. Reitzenstein, 'Das mandäische Buch des Herrn der Grösse,' *Sitz.-Ber. d. Heidelberg. Akad.*,
1919, Abt. xii. p. 11 *sqq.*, 22 *sqq.* The texts in German translation in Lidzbarski,
Das Johannesbuch der Mandäer, Giessen, 1915, c. 76, pp. 243 ; *Mandäische Lit-
urgien*, Berlin, 1920, 10 *sqq.*, 25 *sqq.* ; Ginza, *Der Schatz oder das grosse Buch der
Mandäer*, Göttingen, 1925, pp. 29, 32, 47, 35 ; cf. also H. H. Schaeder, *Stud. d.
Bibl. Warburg*, vii., Leipzig, 1926, p. 308 n. 2.

'Enosh reappeared in Jerusalem *at the same time* as *'Ishu Mshiḥa,* Jesus Christ. The latter they are wont to call the ' liar ' or ' impostor ' [1] because he posed as a worker of miracles whom, however, 'Enosh unmasked. This 'Enosh worked numerous prodigies of healing, preached the true religion, made 360 or 366 disciples in Jerusalem, and then returned to ' Life,' his ' Father,' who bade him destroy Jerusalem, a task which in the form of a white eagle [2] he actually accomplished. In all these transactions 'Enosh appears in a cloud, wherein he dwells or conceals himself and wherefrom at need he makes for himself the semblance of a body, walking thus on earth in human form.[3] It has long since been recognized that this cloud has its origin in Daniel's version, ' there came with (or ' on ') the clouds of heaven one like unto a son of man.' [4]

From all this it would appear that there must have existed a fierce rivalry between the disciples of the Baptist and those of Jesus who belonged to this particular circle. The inference might long ago have been drawn from the passage in the Fourth Gospel on the Baptist as the ' forerunner ' of the Messiah, inasmuch as the ' wild man ' throughout regards himself not as the forerunner of some one greater, but as the ' reborn 'Enosh ' foretold in Daniel's vision, i.e. as the Messiah. At any rate, he was so regarded by his disciples.[5]

The conclusion, thus assured, that the Mandaic figure of the *'Uthra* or 'angel' Enosh [6] goes back to a designation applied by the Jordan Baptist to himself, strikingly confirms the correctness of Lidzbarski's recent identification of the name *Naṣōraia*, by which the Mandaeans called themselves, with the Ναζωραῖος or Ναζωραῖοι used in the New Testament of Jesus and the early Christians, as also with the Jewish designation of Christians as *noṣᵉrîm*. Lidzbarski interprets *naṣōraia* to mean *observantes* =' keepers of secrets,' guardians of special usages [7] or doctrines. In the instructive

---

[1] Ginza, r.p. 49 *sqq.*, ed. Lidzbarski.

[2] Brandt, *op. et loc. cit.* Cf. the ' white falcon ' in *Bundahishn*, xix. 23. The eagle no doubt symbolises here the Roman legions (cf. *Ezra* iv. 11).

[3] Ginza, ed. Lidzbarski, p. 29, § 199 *sq.*

[4] *bar 'enash, Dan.* vii. 13.

[5] Ps.-Clem.,*Recogn.*,ed.Gersdorf (1838), i. 60 : 'et ecce unus ex discipulisJoannis adfirmabat Christum Joannem fuisse et non Jesum ; in tantum inquit, ut et ipse Jesus omnibus hominibus et prophetis maiorem esse pronuntiavit Joannem.' *Ibid.,* i. 54 : ' ex discipulis Joannis, qui videbantur esse magni, magistrum suum veluti Christum praedicarunt.' Ephraem Syr., *Ev. expos.*, ed. Moesinger, 288 : ' et discipuli Joannis de Joanne gloriantur et dicunt eum esse Christo maiorem qui ipse id testatus est dicens: non est major,' etc. *Luke* iii. 15 : ". . . διαλογιζομένων πάντων ἐν ταῖς καρδίαις αὐτῶν περὶ τοῦ Ἰωάννου, μήποτε αὐτὸς εἴη ὁ Χριστός."

[6] The Baptist as an ' angel ' is not unknown to the Christian fathers ; cf. Tertullian, *Scorp.*, viii. 161, ed. Vienna; *Adv.Jud.*,ii. 725, Oehler; Origen, *InJoann.*, ii. (25, 31) ; Chrysostom, *Hom.*, 68 (on which Nestle, *Z.N.T.W.*, viii., 1907, p. 238). Byzantine art often represents the Baptist as an angel with wings. See Pl. XIX.

[7] *naṣar da'ath,* ' preserve knowledge,' *Prov.* xxii. 12 (LXX., φυλάσσειν) ; *naṣar bᵉrith,* ' observe the covenant,' *Deut.* xxxiii. 9, (LXX., διατερεῖν) ; *Ps.* xxv. 10,

literature on the subject both he and Prof. Zimmern[1] have over-looked some highly important evidence which I think makes the correctness of this interpretation quite certain. In the first place, it was known to the ancient Church, and is actually found in the *Onomastica Sacra*[2] of Jerome (or Origen), along with two others which have obviously no reference to *noṣᵉrim*, Ναζωραῖοι, but to *nazirîm*, Ναζιραῖοι, Νασαραῖοι. An Ethiopic onomasticon in the Bibliothèque Nationale in Paris has the explanation, 'Nazaraei sanctificati[3] sive floridi[4] aut *observantes* aut coronati coronis.'[5] Prof. Zimmern's demonstration that this word ' keep ' (*observare*) refers to the keeping or guarding of secrets[6] finds an excellent parallel in Paul's designation of Christians as οἰκονόμοι μυστηρίων θεοῦ, ' stewards of the mysteries of God.'[7] The mysteries there referred to are naturally 'the mysteries of the kingdom of heaven'[8] —when it is to come, what are the signs of its approach, who will ' inherit' it, etc. The 'mystery of the Gospel'[9] is another—the secret, that is, of the good news concerning it for the blessed elect : in fine, just the ' mystery of Christ,'[10] the ' messiah-secret,' i.e. who is to be the Elect One, what he will do and suffer, etc.

Again, Lidzbarski's original suggestion that what the *noṣᵉrîm* ' observe ' must have been special rites of purification, baptism in particular, finds a striking confirmation in the liturgic language of the Church. In a beatitude in the *Acts of Paul and Thekla*[11] read : ' Blessed are they who keep the baptism.' Similarly Origen :[12] ' And blessed is he who hath part in the first resurrection, who kept (τηρήσας) the baptism of the Holy Spirit.' Since baptism, with reference to the baptizer's act of ' sealing ' with the sign of the cross,[13] came to be called simply ' seal ' (σφραγίς), we

---

noṣᵉrēj bᵉrith, ' such as keep his covenant ' ; *Ps.* lxxviii. 7, ' observe his command-ment ' ; *Ps.* cv. 45, ' observe his statutes ' ; *Ps.* cxix. 45, ' keep thy law ' ; *Prov.* xxviii. 7. Similarly, *Matt.* xix. 17 : " τὰς ἐντολὰς τηρεῖν" ; *Mark* vii. 9, " τηρεῖν τὴν παράδοσιν" ; *John* viii. 51, " τηρεῖν τὸν λόγον" ; *Acts* xv. 5, " τηρεῖν τὸν νόμον."

[1] *Z.D.M.G.*, lxxiv. (1920), pp. 429-38 ; lxvi., pp. 45 ff.

[2] Aeth., l. fol. I et 2 (saec. xvii.), ed. Wutz, *Onomastica Sacra*, ii., Leipzig, 1915 (Harnack-Schmidt, *T.U.*, iii., R. xi., vol. xli. 2, p. 1021).

[3] This cannot be separated, of course, from Ναζαραῖοι=*nazirîm*.

[4] Derived from Hebr. *neṣer*=shoot, Arab. *naḍara*=to shine, to spring forth (of verdure).

[5] *Nezer*=turban, diadem. In the Mandaic *Book of John*, § 20, the Baptist has three diadems and a crown of immense value—i.e. the three crowns of the king, the high priest, and the prophet, the triple *tiara* still now worn by the Roman pontiff.

[6] Bab. *mudu naṣir piriŝti ilani*, ' the *initiate*, the *knowing*, who keeps the secret of the gods,' corresponds exactly to *mandājā*=γνωστικός, ' he who has the *manda*,' Aram. *madda*, the ' knowledge ' (Nöldeke, *Mand. Gramm.*, § 75), *naṣōraia*, ' who keeps this knowledge.'

[7] 1 *Cor.* iv. 1.

[8] *Matt.* xiii. 11, with parallels.   Cf. *Daniel* xii. 10, below, p. 331 n. 4.

[9] *Eph.* vi. 19.   [10] *Col.* iv. 3.

[11] Lipsius, *Act. Apost. Apocr.*, i. 239.

[12] *Comm. in Jerem.*, ii. 3.

[13] On the meaning of this sign, see below, p. 255 n. 4.

also find the expression 'to keep the (baptismal) seal' (sc. safe from injury), which is specially significant, because the Mandaeans also seal the baptized with the '*pure sign of Johana.*'

Under these circumstances it is not surprising to find that another fragment of an onomasticon, not noticed by Wutz, and preserved by the lexicographer Hesychios,[1] offers us, beside the usual interpretation of the word *nazir* (=Nazirite), precisely the equation Ναζιραῖος = βαπτιστής. This explanation doubtless refers to *noṣᵉrî*, Ναζωραῖος, and it attests that the equation of these ideas, obvious in the case of the Mandaean *Ṣubbas* and *Mughtasilas* (='Baptists' or 'Naṣōraeans'), holds also for the pre-Christian Palestinian Νασαραῖοι of Epiphanius,[2] i.e. the disciples of the Baptist or John.

Lastly, there is a highly remarkable rabbinic gloss on 1 *Chron.* iv. 25, a passage concerning 'the potters (*joṣᵉrim*, LXX. κεραμεῖς) who dwell in the plantations and enclosures beside the king ; in the work of his service dwell they there.' Those workmen of the royal potteries[3] are mentioned in the books of *Chronicles*, along with the carpenters (*ḥarashîm*) of the valley of carpenters and other craftsmen of the tribe, in the pedigree of the Rekhabites and Qenites, which has been transmitted in a very corrupt form and will be treated by the author at length elsewhere.[4] On these workmen the Talmud[5] writes : 'These potters are the descendants of Jonadab son of Rekhab, who keep (*nṣr*) the oath of their Father, viz. to drink no wine, to lay out no vineyard or other plantation, nor to till the soil, nor to build houses to dwell in them.'[6]

It appears, then, that the so-called Rekhabites, the 'caravanners' or 'wayfaring people,' i.e. the various itinerant craftsmen, were also known as *noṣᵉrîm*, and that this 'keeping' and 'guarding' of secrets[7] and special usages referred in the first instance to the preservation of technical or magical 'knowledge,' i.e. the craftsman's secrets and tricks of his trade, such as the special usages, customs, and taboos still in vogue to-day among the modern gipsies of the desert, the so-called *Ṣleb* or 'crossed ones.'[8]

---

[1] "Ναζιραῖος· ὁ θεῷ κεχαρισμένος καὶ ἀφιερώμενος (=*nazir*) βαπτιστὴς καὶ ἱερεύς." βαπτισταί as a name for the disciples of John is found in Justin, *Dial. c. Tryph.*, 80.
[2] *Haeres.*, xxix. p. 327, ed. Holl.
[3] These royal manufactures account for the frequently found stamp למלך. 'for the king.' *P.S.B.A.*, 1910, p. 143 *sq.* Macalister, *P.E.F.Q.S.T.*, 1903, p. 245 *sq.*
[4] *Le Monde Oriental*, 1929, p. 101.
[5] *Baba bathra*, 91b.
[6] *Jerem.* xxxv. 8 *sqq.*
[7] Anthropologists will remember that such tribes will cultivate a special secret language, such as the *shelta* or 'tinkers' talk.'
[8] The name is derived from the fact that this class of itinerant craftsmen wore on their foreheads the mark †, the famous 'sign of Qain' (=the smith). See our Pl. xviii. and my paper, 'Das Qainszeichen und die Qeniter,' *Le Monde Oriental*, ed. by Prof. Nyberg, Upsala, 1929, pp. 48-112. The cross-mark of the Ṣleb is known to the rabbis of the third century (see below, p. 343 n. 6).

A number of facts are thereby at once explained. There is first the striking fact, never to my knowledge understood, that the Mesopotamian *mandaia* or γνωστικοί, the *naṣōraia* or ' keepers ' of secrets, are without exception craftsmen, in particular *carpenters*, boat-builders, smiths, locksmiths, gold- and silver-smiths, and eventually shopkeepers,[1] all of which professions are found in the pedigrees of Rekhabites and Qenites. Again, these people abstain from wine [2]—a prohibition the more striking because the vine, as the tree of life, plays a great part in Mandaic writings—and, during the consecration of priests, dwell in reed-tents.[3] Lastly, we find in the angelology of the Mandaeans the remarkable interpretation of Ptaḥ-il,[4] i.e. the old Egyptian or Canaanite god of smithies and metal-engravers, as the creator of heaven and earth as well as of mankind.

THE BAPTIST'S FOOD AND CLOTHING

The Baptist's abstinence, according to the Slavonic Josephus, from wine and all strong drink would on this hypothesis need no further explanation, such being the well-known cult-law of the Rekhabites. His strict abstinence from bread would be perfectly in harmony with the prohibition against tilling the soil, attested by the passage in Jeremiah already quoted, for those ' wayfaring people ' who strictly adhere to the Bedouin life of the desert. The Rekhabite prohibition of all cultivation of plants [5] explains why the ' Banus,' the hermit and baptist with whom Josephus himself lived in his early days, fed only on ' such things as grow of themselves.' [6]

According to Jewish traditions, obviously of Rekhabite origin and curiously reappearing in the tradition of Islam, the forbidden fruit of Paradise is either the grape or the wheat-plant, an interpretation which imparts a convincingly logical meaning to *Gen.* ii. and iii., seeking to explain the endless ploughing of the toiling *fellaḥin*, and how cultivation of the soil ' in the sweat of the brow' came into a world where man originally enjoyed the blessed life of the *nauaḥle*, the owners of palm-tree gardens in the oases.

---

[1] Cf. W. Brandt, *op. cit.*, p. 380a, § 1, and E. S. Drower in *The Quest*, xvi. 80 *sq*.
[2] Lidzbarski, *Mand. Lit.*, Einleitung, p. xix. *The Quest, loc. cit.*, p. 89.
[3] They thus avoid dwelling in permanent buildings.
[4] Cf. E. Peterson, *Z.N.T.W.*, 1926, p. 247, and my *Kenitische Weihinschriften*, Freiburg-i.-Br., 1919, p. 103 *sqq*.
[5] Cf. R. H. Kennett in Hastings' *Encycl. of Rel. and Ethics*, x. (1918), p. 603a. According to Qenite tradition in *Gen.* iv. 5, God refuses to accept a sacrifice from the produce of agriculture. The Qenite ought not to till the soil and become a ' serf of the earth ' (*'obed 'adamah*).
[6] Jos., *Vita*, ii., ed. Niese.

The stern preacher in the wilderness teaches a complete
'return'[1] to the original diet ordained by God for men *before* the
fall, as it is written: 'Behold, I have given you every herb yielding
seed which is upon the face of the earth, and every tree in the
which is the fruit of a tree yielding seed; be that your meat.'[2]
The preacher, who regards himself as the reborn antediluvian
'Enosh, in whose time men began to call upon the name of Jahweh
(*Gen.* iv. 26), durst not avail himself of the permission to eat meat
granted by God to men[3] on account of their hardness of heart, and
after the generation of the flood in their wickedness had arbitrarily
given themselves up to the abomination of devouring living beings,
and even to cannibalism.[4] The caller in the solitude, who announces that the kingdom of heaven is at hand, feeds on the herbs
and roots of the desert, just as, according to rabbinic doctrine,[5] the
Israel believing in the Messiah will, in the final days of tribulation,
live in the wilderness and reedy wastes upon salt weeds and the
roots of the broom plant.

The express statement of the Slavonic Josephus, that the
Baptist abhorred all animal food, flatly contradicts the Gospel
tradition of his feeding on locusts,[6] but agrees perfectly with an
almost unanimous tradition of the Greek Church, according to
which John restricted himself on principle to a vegetable diet,[7] the
ἀκρίδες of the gospels being explained as 'points' or shoots of
some plants.[8]

I am myself much more inclined to believe that the word
ἀκρόδρυα = 'tree-fruits' was maliciously distorted into ἀκρίδας
by the hand of an enemy of the Baptist's sect, desirous of making
the Baptist appear as one feeding on vermin, naturally loathsome
to Gentile Christians of the educated classes. As a matter of fact,

---

[1] *shubhu*, of which 'Repent ye' (μετανοεῖτε) in *Matt.* iii. 2 is an inexact
rendering.
[2] *Gen.* i. 29, P.   [3] *Gen.* ix. 3, P.
[4] *Book of Jubilees*, v. 2 sqq.
[5] *Midr. shir*, r. vi. 10 (124b; Strack-Billerbeck, ii. 284 *sq.*, 4a): 'R. 'Aqiba
said: Forty years is the duration of the days of the Messiah, just as the Israelites
spent forty years in the desert, and he (i.e. the Messiah) makes them go forth into
the desert to live on salt herbs and broom roots' (*Job* xxx. 4). *Pesiqta*, 49b:
'Whither does the Messiah lead them? Some say into the desert of Judah; others,
into the desert of Sichon and 'Og.' 'Wherefore, lo, I shall persuade them and
lead them into the desert' (*Hos.* ii. 16). 'He who believes in him (i.e. the Messiah)
eats salt herbs and broom roots' (*Job* xxx. 4).
[6] Mr. Th. Gaster has pointed out to me the curious fact that there is a Babylonian word *ḥarubu*, 'locust,' 'grasshopper' (Muss-Arnold, i. 336a, b). That the
word—which is beyond any doubt Semitic and simply means the 'devastator'—
is not found in our Hebrew and Aramean dictionaries may be due to the merest
chance. If the word *ḥarub*, 'locust,' existed in Hebrew or Aramean, the confusion of
ḥarubîm, 'locust,' with *ḥarubîm*, 'carob-pods,' would need no further explanation.
[7] See App. XVII., pp. 614 ff. His pupils are aimed at by Paul, *Rom.* xiv. 2,
cp. 21.
[8] Isidor. Pelus., *Epistles*, i. 132, cf. i. 5; *Euthym. Zygab.*, P.G. cxxix, 160;
Pantaleo diac., P.G. ii. C. c. 1245.

long before the discovery of the Slavonic text, such a scribal variant, though generally assumed to be a mere slip of the pen, has been supposed to account for the enigmatic ' locusts.'   The same or a very similar inimical hand was, if my theory be right, also responsible for the restrictive gloss, unknown to the disciples of John,[1] ' yet the least in the kingdom of heaven[2] is greater than he,' appended to the words in which Jesus exalts the Baptist above all born of woman.[3]   However this may be, the assumption of some such malicious distortion of the original text appears to me indispensable for the understanding of the Slavonic Josephus, where the ' wood-shavings ' of our MSS. are clearly quite impossible, since a man eating sawdust or the like would die of peritonitis within a few days.   I first thought that a Hebrew *perîj ha 'es* = ' tree-fruit ' had been mischievously distorted into *peruṣ ha 'es* = ' broken-off piece of wood.'   There are other possible explanations, but the most attractive is the one suggested by Prof. Wohleb, namely, that in place of (τροφὴ) καρπῶν ξυλίνων =' (food) of wood-fruits,' that is, ' wild fruits ' or ' tree-fruits,' exactly corresponding to the Semitic *perîj ha 'eṣ*, the Greek copy of the Slavonic translator had (τροφὴ) καρφῶν ξυλίνων =' food of chips of wood.' Small though the difference may seem between καρπῶν and καρφῶν, and ingenious as is this conjecture, a purely accidental interchange of π and φ is impossible.   Here, as in the case of the Evangelist's ἀκρίδας for ἀκρόδρυα, we have one of those caustic punning witticisms for which Jews notoriously have a special weakness.   A *calembour* of this type, on the rabbinic principle ' Read not . . . but . . .,' might quite well have been made by Josephus himself when copying his Naṣōraean authority on the Baptist, though as a pupil of a ' Banus '[4] he must have known well enough what was the Baptist's customary food not to fall into an accidental error on such matters.   Anyhow, the assertion of Josephus that John ate chips of wood is on a par with the malicious statement that he ' stuck over his body ' the hair of beasts wherever it was not covered by his own.

As was pointed out above, there can be no doubt about the mischievous intention of this description.   What the Baptist himself meant by his peculiar garb will be clear if we recall the import of his food-regulations discussed above.   He regarded himself as the reborn 'Enosh, as son of Sheth and grandson of Adam, who was the first to do penance for his sins by baptism

---

[1] Mandaean *Book of John*, ed. Lidzbarski, p. 95, l. 13 : 'Jahjah preaches in the nights and says, " Is there any one greater than I am ? " '
[2] See below, p. 415 n. 7, on this appellation applying to Jesus.
[3] *Matt.* xi. 11.
[4] See p. 23 n. 2, also above, p. 24, on his journey to Rome on behalf of certain priests, observing a vegetarian diet.

in the Jordan.[1] The preacher of repentance therefore appropriately wears the penitential robe of raw skin ('*ōr*), bestowed
by God upon the first human couple after the fall, in place of the
robes of light ('*ōr*) which covered their nakedness in Paradise,
which they forfeited by their sin, and which, according to Naṣōraean
doctrine, would be restored to those admitted to bliss.[2] It is
remarkable, moreover, that Josephus, just like Matthew and
Mark, speaks not of animals' skins, but expressly of animals'
hair (τρίχες). That is of course essential, because fabrics of
camel's hair are made from the hairs of the living beast, which
have either fallen out or been plucked out without any injury
being inflicted upon the animal. A skin, on the other hand, can
come only from a dead beast, slaughtered or come to a natural
end. Now, the rabbinic comments [3] on the God-given ' coats
of skins ' [4] clearly show that some interpreters strove to exclude
the idea that for the making of these garments God killed any of
the animals then still in a state of innocence. The explanation
given interprets, therefore, 'skin-clothes,' 'hide-clothes' as clothes
' which closely fit man's skin,' or that they were made ' of milk-
white wool,' of shaggy fleeces, or indeed of the hair of camels and
hares. Syrian Christians [5] go yet further, explaining these God-
given coverings of our first parents as clothes of bark, made from
the ' skin ('*ōr*) of trees ; only the blessed Moses called the bark
"skin," because in trees it takes the place of the skin.' This was
obviously the view held by the baptist with whom Josephus was
personally acquainted, the ' Banus ' who took his ' clothing from
trees.' That may equally well mean ' paradise ' clothes like the
coats of fig-leaves, or a mantle literally of bast or of rushes, such as
is worn to this day by the keepers of vineyards on night duty
in the neighbourhood of Vienna as a protection against damp
and cold.

The coat of skin over the bare body, with the ' leather girdle,'
is, moreover, no other than the primitive Edomite garb of the
Rekhabites, still worn by the *Sleb* mentioned above (p. 234 n. 8)
and pictured on Pl. xx.

Three different views on the true meaning of the Baptist's

---

[1] Cf. the *Life of Adam and Eve* and the so-called *Apocalypse of Moses* (more
correctly 'of Sheth,' *Short Dict. of Christ. Biogr.*, i. 39 *sqq.*). Since we know that the
Baptist called himself 'Enosh, the latter may now be easily recognized as one of
the basic writings of the Naṣōraeans. The penitential baptism of Adam in the
Jordan is mentioned in the tract. In Budge's *Coptic Apocalypse* the story occurs
in a compilation entitled ' Secrets of St. John ' ; see his pp. 244 *sq.* According to
a kind hint of Mr. Th. Gaster, the same legend is found in the Midrash Gan-Eden.

[2] *Midr. Beresh. r.*, 20 ; cf. also my *Orphisch-dionysische Mysteriengedanken*,
p. 305.

[3] *Gen. r.*, 4, 20 (14a), Strack-Billerbeck, i. p. 97.

[4] *Gen.* iii. 21.

[5] *Cave of Treasure*, p. 7, ed. Bezold. Solomon of Basra, *Book of the Bee*, p. 24,
ed. Budge.

PLATE XX

THE SLEB, A TRIBE OF WANDERING CRAFTSMEN OF SYRIA AND ARABIA, SO-CALLED FROM THE MARK OF THE CROSS (SALĪB) ON THEIR FOREHEADS

DESCENDANTS OF THE REKHABITES AND QENITES OF THE OLD TESTAMENT

(SEE P. 238, LINES 34 F.)

garb may, then, be quite clearly distinguished. The emphasis laid by Josephus and the Evangelists on the fact that he went about clothed in animals' *hair*, not animals' *skins*, can have had its origin only in a special tradition of the Naṣōraean Baptists common to the Christian witnesses and to Josephus. If they laid this stress on the mantle of *hair*, we may be sure that the girdle was of the same material, like those which according to Dr. Musil [1] are still made to-day. The ' leathern girdle about his loins ' in *Matthew* and *Mark*—Dr. Klostermann rightly notes that the phrase is a verbal quotation from 2 *Kings* i. 8—as well as the ' camel's skin ' [2] in the MSS. *D* and *a* in *Mark*, serve to support the interpretation of John as 'Elijah. That interpretation goes back to Jesus or his disciples, is quite unknown to Josephus, and according to one piece of Christian evidence,[3] which is above suspicion because flatly contradictory to the ordinary view of the Church, was decisively rejected by the Baptist himself.

According to the tradition of the Baptist's circle, their founder wore this peculiar hair garb because he was 'Enosh, and ' hair-clothes ' were given by God to the Adamites. The Baptist's garb, then, according to this view, is the garb of 'Enosh. The leather girdle and the coat of skin of the Christian sources is the garb of 'Elijah. If the source of Josephus prefers to represent John as a ' hairy saint,' [4] i.e. as a man completely covered by matted hair and wild beard, it is not because 'Elijah is described in 2 *Kings* i. 8 as a ' hairy man,' but because a legend of which by mere chance only a modern Greek version [5] has come down to us states that Adam and Eve were as shaggy as bears.

The third view, quite clearly expressed in Josephus, is the assertion that the ' wild man ' had hair ' stuck ' upon his body. It is evidently the personal opinion of the scoffer to the effect that the Baptist was simply an impostor. Of the 'Elijah conception Josephus knew nothing ; else he would not have failed to call John a ' false prophet,' which term he uses for the Egyptian messiah of the Mount of Olives, and he would certainly have explained the strange garb as that foreseen by *Zech.* xiii. 4 referring to lying prophets : ' neither shall they wear a hairy mantle to

---

[1] *Arabia Petraea*, iii. 262 : ' Aside from milk, the camel provides hair which falls out in spring and is collected or softly pulled out each morning by the girls and women. This camel's hair is used by the women for the making of carpets, saddle-bags, ropes, girdles, and cloaks.'

[2] " δέρρις καμήλου."

[3] *John* i. 21 ; cf. 25 : ' Art thou Elijah ? And he said, I am not.'

[4] Cf. on this subject the excellent monograph of Dr. Charles Allyn Williams, *Oriental Affinities of the Legend of the Hairy Anchorite*, Urbana, Ill., 1925-6 (*University of Illinois Studies in Language and Literature*, x. 13 *sqq.* and xi. 57-138 ; cf. *Nieuw theologisch Tijdschrift*, 1928, p. 282 *sqq.*).

[5] *Z.N.T.W.*, 1928, p. 308.

deceive.' Josephus' own explanation of this peculiar mode of dress is quite different.

The Greeks and Romans, as is well known, believed the mountain forests to be peopled by shaggy, half-bestial, demoniac creatures, *la gente selvatica* of Italian folklore, satyrs, little Pan-gods, sileni, fauni, silvani, etc., The widespread tale of the captured demon is of course well known, as are the prophecies he is supposed to have uttered to regain his freedom.[1] Just so the Semitic peasants and nomads regarded the desert as haunted by ' hairy ' (*śe'irim*) demons (*shedim*), the Arabian *jinn* (*ahl al 'ard*), or by ' he-goats ' or ' calves '[2] or other spectres in animal form.[3] A person sticking hair on his body, and thus desiring to be taken for a completely hairy being, who partakes of no ordinary human food, leads a ' non-human existence like a bodiless ghost,'[4] and ' comes out of the bush like a beast,' wishes to be regarded as nothing else than an (*'ish*) *śa'ir*, a hairy or wild man,[5] or a *shed* in animal form, and it is precisely as such a lycanthropic scarecrow that the 'wild man' is here represented. His refusal to give his name, and his reply 'A man!' to the question ' Who are you ? '— a reply unintelligible alike to Josephus and to the questioners— perfectly accords with world-wide legends of wild men, with the motive well known from the story of Odysseus and Polyphemus (οὔτις) mixed in.

THE VARIOUS NAMES OF THE BAPTIST

The Baptist's habit of calling himself simply '(the) man' (above, p. 225 n. 2) is probably the cause alike of the total ignorance of his true name displayed by Josephus and of the twofold tradition concerning this name as presupposed by the Gospel of the Infancy prefixed to Luke's narrative.[6] According to this account, he would at his circumcision have been given his father's name and been called Zechariah ben Zechariah ; only, his mother wished him to be named John, although ' none of her kindred bore this name.' Similarly we read in the Mandaean *Book of John* :[7]

' The Jews assembled and came to Aba Saba[8] Zakria and spoke to him : " O Aba Saba Zakria, thou must have a son. Tell us now what

---

[1] Cf. A. H. Krappe, *Le Rire du Prophète* in *Studies in English Philology*. A miscellany in honour of Frederick Klaeber, Minneapolis, 1929, pp. 340-61.

[2] Cf. also 2 *Chron.* xi. 15.

[3] Cf. Wellhausen, *Reste arabischen Heidentums*, [1] 135 *sq.*, [2] 151 *sq.* ; and my *Orphisch-dionysische Mysteriengedanken*, p. 260 n. 2.

[4] Slav. *doh' besploten'* = πνεῦμα ἀσώματον.

[5] Cf. Philostr., *Vita Apoll. Tyan.*, vi. 27.

[6] *Luke* i. 59 : ' They came to circumcise the child, and they would have called him Zachariah after the name of his father.'

[7] Ed. Lidzbarski, p. 115.

[8] =' Old Father.'

name we should give him. Should we give him the name of ' Wisdom-tracker,'[1] that he may teach the book in Jerusalem? Or should we give him the name Zathan Estuna,[2] in order that the Jews may swear by him? . . ." When Enishbai (=Elizabeth) heard this she cried out and said : " Of all these names by which you call him will I give him none, but I will give him the name Jahiah-Johana, which Life itself has given him." '

The Mandaeans themselves have two different names for the Baptist side by side, Jahiah[3] and Johana, which they use simultaneously in a kind of poetical *parallelismus membrorum*.[4] In the Quran, which draws upon the traditions of the Arabian Jews and *Nasran*[5] (i.e. the primitive Nasōraeans), the Baptist is called only Jahiah. Brandt's explanation[6] of the use of this name by the Mandaeans as due to Arabic influence was far too rash an assumption. As early as the end of the eighteenth century C. F. Dupuis put forth the conjecture, since revived by Drews, that the Baptist's name Ἰωάννης may be no other than that of the strange Babylonian god of revelation who emerges from the water, according to the account of Berossus, to wit, Ὠάννης,[7] Ἰάννης,[8] or Ἰωάννης.[9] Such a possibility is quite conceivable. For not only does the form *Joannes*, attested by Chaeremon[9] in the time of Nero, exactly coincide with the New Testamental name for the Baptist, but according to the view expressed in the *Fourth Book of Esdras* (xii. 25 ; xiii. 51 *sq.*) the Messiah is thought of as concealed in the deepest ocean, from which he is to emerge in the end. Similarly, according to Berossus, under the first dynasty of the antediluvian kings of Babylon, the Ὠάννης, (J)ōannes, being the first of a series of such antediluvian ' sages,' emerged from the sea to teach the people all manner of wisdom, including politics and law.

Again, the remarkable feature of a total abstention from food and drink, attributed to the Babylonian (J)o(a)nnes,[10] is in striking

---

[1] Aram. 'Wisdom-*Jaqif*.' This and *estuna*, 'pillar,' seem to be malicious allusions to James and John the sons of Zebedee, the ' pillars ' of the earliest Christian church.

[2] *Estuna*='pillar.' *Zathan* is unexplained. I think it is the name ' Zeithan ' =' olive ' mentioned in 1 *Chron.* vii. 10.

[3] This word is not at all an Arabic form of Johanan, but the name Jᵉhijah (1 *Chron.* xv. 24)='Jahweh lives.' The vocalization of the first syllable is the archaic (Arabic) one of the Qenites, as in *Jahweh* (=' he falls ') itself.

[4] The recurrent chapter-title in the Mandaean *Book of John* runs : ' Jahijah called forth in the night, Johana in the evenings of the nights '—whatever that may mean.

[5] The Arabian *Jusifûs* (above, p. 32 n. 2), § 90, says of the Baptist : ' Some call him Jahja, the *nasran* call him Johanan as-Sabî.'

[6] Hastings' *Encycl. Rel. and Ethics*, 391, § 40.

[7] Alex. Polyhist. ap. Syncell., ed. Dind., p. 51.

[8] Hippolyt., ref. v. 7, p. 80, ed. Wendland.

[9] Chairemon, ed. Sathas, *Bull. corr. Hell.*, 1877, p. 129.

[10] Schnabel, *Berossos*, p. 253 ; Eusebius, *Chron.*, ed. Karst, p. 7=Syncell., ed. Dind., p. 51.

Q

agreement with the hyperbolical expression, ' John came neither eating nor drinking ' ;[1] as also is the comparison of John as a ' beast ' in the Slavonic Josephus (above, p. 225) with the similar designation ($\zeta\hat{\omega}o\nu$) for the Babylonian (J)ōannes in Berossus. It is therefore by no means an impossible supposition that the name Ἰωάννης was first given to the Baptist, emerging, as it were, with his doctrine from the waters of the Jordan, by certain Naṣōraeans who thereby intended to identify him with the Babylonian revelation-god. If the Noṣ^erîm were originally ' itinerant ' tradesmen, travelling to and fro between Transjordania and Mesopotamia, in the manner of the present-day Ṣleb, such an influence of Babylonian mythological ideas would not seem too far-fetched. It might equally be referred, however, to the Babylonian Jews, settled by Herod the Great in the region of the Ḥauran mountains.[2]

It is quite possible, then, that the Baptist's real name was Jaḥijah bar Zekharjah, and that 'Enosh, Zekharjah bar Zekharjah, Joḥanan bar Zekharjah, Jōannes, etc., were the various aliases he assumed to conceal his identity from his persecutors.

If such was the case, there would be an easy explanation of the strange fact that the rabbinic tradition (which knows and mentions Jeshu han-noṣri, the Naṣōraean, and the hemerobaptists) does not seem to know an individual called Joḥanan ham-maṭ^ebil, that is, 'John the Baptist.'

The apparent difficulty just mentioned would at once disappear if confirmation were forthcoming for a conjecture put forward in 1910 by Dr. Kaufmann Kohler, namely, that the Baptist is no other than the wonder-worker Ḥanan han-neḥ^eba mentioned in the Babylonian Talmud, i.e.[3] (Jo)ḥanan or Johannes, ' the hidden ' or ' the hiding one.' This nickname would fit exceedingly well the man who lived in the brushwood of the Jordan valley 'like a beast in the forest,' the John who was persecuted by the Herodians, who passed for the prophet Elijah still lingering in concealment, and, according to our hypothesis, under cover of various assumed names eluded search ; it is the more appropriate in that Ḥanan han-neḥ^eba is said precisely to have hidden himself ' on account of religious persecution.' The nickname ' the hidden one ' may on the one hand connote ' the hermit ' who hides in the solitude of inaccessible regions, whilst on the other it is also the typical title of the ' hidden ' Messiah,[4] the 'Adakas ' or ' hidden man ' (' hidden Adam ') of the Mandaeans.[5]

[1] Matt. xi. 18.   [2] Jos., Ant., xvii. 23 sqq. ; Vita, §§ 47, 54, 177, 183.
[3] Ta'anith, 23b.
[4] On the Messiah as first ' hidden ' (neḥ^eba) and then ' revealed ' (niglah, ἐπιφανής), cf. Targ. Jonath. to Micah iv. 8 ; Midrash, Ps. xxi., § 1, f°. 89a. Cf. John viii. 59 and xii. 36 on Jesus, who ' hid himself ' (ἀπεκρύβη) from his followers.
[5] Cf. v. Gall, Βασιλεία Θεοῦ, Heidelberg, 1926, p. 162. Reitzenstein, Hell. Mysterienrel., Leipzig, 1927, p. 13 f.

This quite simple hypothesis would, moreover, furnish the easiest solution of another old riddle. For in that case it is no other than this 'hidden one' who is intended by that 'righteous man' (i.e. that ṣaddiq), Elkesai, Elxai or Elchasai (i.e. in Arabic 'the hidden one' [1]), whom the Baptist communities on the northern frontiers of Arabia, where it extends to the Dead Sea and the Euphrates, have honoured for centuries as the founder of their religion. Thus the Mandaean Naṣōraeans and the Elkesaites would represent only two different groups of disciples of John developing along Gnostic lines, that is, in the direction of the teachings of Simon Magus and Dositheos.[2]

Conversely, the rite of purifying men through immersion in the water of a miraculous spring, gushing forth at the end of times,[3] as it was taught by John, would be perfectly suited to a rain-maker such as Ḥanan the Hidden.[4] The Mandaean tradition of the cloud of 'Enosh [5] would also fit very well the figure of Ḥanan the Rain-maker ; for from a tale of the *Arabian Nights* proved by the late W. Bousset to be of Jewish origin,[6] the type of the holy man with a cloud that accompanies him wherever he goes, at least so long as he continues in spotless piety,[7] is well known. The Mandaean conversion of John's shaggy coat into a vesture of water-clouds [8] at all events recalls the use of a woollen fleece, intended to imitate the fleecy 'lambkin' clouds, in the analogous rain-charm of Gideon.[9] It is also well to recall those Thessalians who ascended Mt. Pelion clad in lambs' fleeces (κώδια) to pray for rain.[10]

The grandfather of Ḥanan the Hidden, Ḥoni the Circle-drawer (*hamm*ᵉ *agel*), appears in Josephus [11] as a martyr for his piety and rectitude. While Aristobulus II. was being besieged on the Temple Mount by Hyrcanus and the Arabian King Aretas (*c.* 65 B.C.), this man, who had '*hidden himself*' on the approach of the civil war, was at the request of the besiegers fetched to curse the besieged, and on his refusing to do this was stoned to death. The grand-

---

[1] The Arabic definite article '*al* ('*el*, '*il*) is first found in the inscription of Nemara in the Louvre. See the bibliography of this monument in D. Nielsen, *Handb. d. altarab. Altertumsk.*, i. 49 n. 2. It dates from the fourth century of our era. There is no reason whatever why the Arabian article should not have existed three centuries before that time.

[2] See App. XVIII.

[3] See below, p. 272 n. 2, on *Zech.* xiii. 10.

[4] For a translation of his legend with the Hebrew original, cf. *Z.N.T.W.*, xii. (1911), p. 290.

[5] Cf. the Life of the Baptist by Serapion, ed. Mingana, *Bull. John Rylands Libr.*, xi. (1927), p. 449, and *Ginza* r., trsl. by Lidzbarski, p. 29, § 199 *sq.*, line 25 *sqq.*

[6] *Arch. f. Rel. Wiss.*, xxi. (1922), pp. 11-12 ; *Nachr. d. Gött. Ges. d. Wiss., phil.-hist. Kl.*, 1916, p. 484.

[7] Williams, *op. cit.*, pp. 37 n. 2, and 476.

[8] *Ginza*, r. ed. Lidzbarski, p. 29 : 'Enosh 'Uthra goes to Jerusalem in a raiment of watery clouds.

[9] *Judges* vi. 36 *sqq.*   [10] Dicaearch., c. 60.

[11] *Ant.*, xiv. 22-4, where he is called Onias.

father thus shows the same inclination for a life of solitude and concealment as the grandson. The hermit's ascetic practices seem to have been hereditary in this family of *Ṣadiqqîm*. The Onias stoned in the time of Aristobulus had two other grandsons beside Ḥanan the Hidden (his daughter's son)—one named Abba Hilquia,[1] and the other, like his grandfather, Ḥoni; the latter continued the practice of circle-drawing and praying for rain, and lived till shortly before A.D. 70.[2] The chronological difficulties objected by W. Brandt to Kaufmann Kohler only exist if the dates in Luke's *Gospel of Infancy* are adhered to, and if Jesus and the Baptist are regarded as of approximately the same age. If, however, following the special Mandaean or Naṣōraean tradition,[3] we presume that the latter had been baptizing for many years when Jesus presented himself at the Jordan,[4] and, following the Slavonic Josephus, which again goes back to traditions of the Baptist's circle,[5] we hold that the Baptist had been brought up for trial under Archelaus, all is in excellent order. He must, then, have been an old man in the time of Jesus, between fifty-five and sixty-five years of age, as he is in fact generally represented in early Christian art.[6]

The chronological thesis of the *Gospel of Infancy*, limiting as it does the difference in age between John and Jesus to a period of six months only, is clearly connected with the astral symbolism of the famous passage: ' He must increase, but I must decrease.'[7] It is furthermore intended to exclude the idea of Jesus the Naṣōraean being a pupil of the Baptist. But apart from these spurious and tendentious dates, the traditions there recorded concerning the Baptist's parents may quite well be historical. The daughter of the elder Ḥoni *ham-mᵉagel* may really have been called Elizabeth,[8] and her husband, unmentioned in the Talmud, may indeed have been a certain Zechariah of the priestly course of 'Abijah. The statement that Elizabeth belonged to the house of Aaron agrees well with the tradition that Ḥoni traced his descent back

---

1 Cf. b. Ta'an., fol. 23a.
2 Jer. Ta'an., iii., fol. 66b.
3 *Ginza*, p. 191 *sq.* For an English translation, cf. G. R. S. Mead, *The Quest*, xviii. (1926), p. 58.
4 According to a Life of the Baptist by a monk Paphnutius (*Patrol. Or.*, iv. p. 523). John had baptized for twenty-five years when he administered baptism to Jesus.
5 See above, p. 23 n. 2 and p. 27 n. 1.
6 Cf. our fig. XIX., and Salomon Reinach, *Cultes, Mythes, Religions*, iii. 22; cf. C. Torr in *Revue Archéolog.*, 1902, i. 14 *sqq.*, and 1903, ii. 125.
7 *John* iii. 30.
8 According to the Syriac commentary of Isho'dad (cf. Nestle, *Expos. Times*, xvii. 140), Elizabeth's father was named '*Anon*. This form may come from a Greek source substituting ″Ανων for Ḥanan. Cf. Αυναυ for Ḥanan or Ḥanon in 1 *Chron.* xi. 43; *Jer.* xlii. (35) 4; 1 *Esdr.* ii. 46; *Neh.* vii. 49; and 1 *Chron.* xix. 14.

to Moses.[1] Even the Rekhabite character of the Baptist's life discussed above (p. 235 ff.) is quite reconcilable with priestly parentage, since, according to rabbinic tradition,[2] Rekhabites married the daughters of priests and their grandsons ministered as priests in the Temple. In any case, it is a curious coincidence that we are told of this Elizabeth (at once the daughter of the Onias-Ḥoni who according to Josephus 'hid himself,' and the mother of that Ḥanan or Joḥanan who is called in the Talmud han-Neḥ'ba, 'the hidden one') that she also without apparent reason 'hid herself for five months' before the birth of John.[3]

The most transparent allusions to Ḥanan 'the hidden one' are found in the Protevangelium of St. James,[4] where Elizabeth heard that 'they sought for John . . . went up into the hill country and looked about her, where she should hide him, and there was no hiding-place . . . and the mountain clave asunder . . . Now Herod sought for John and sent officers to Zechariah saying: "Where hast thou hidden thy son?"' The same motive occurs also in an ancient legend published by A. Berendts from Russian MSS.[5]

On the whole, then, Kohler's suggested identification of the Talmudic 'hidden' or 'hiding' Ḥanan with the Baptist Joḥanan, as portrayed in Josephus, and in Christian as well as Mandaean tradition, appears to be highly probable.

THE BAPTIST'S CALL TO LIBERTY

In the same way as the Greek paragraph about Jesus in the Antiquities,[6] so the account there given of the Baptist shows clear

---

[1] In the Mandaean 'Book of Jahjah,' § 18 (Engl. transl. by Mead, The Gnostic John the Baptizer, London, 1924, p. 39), the descent of Zechariah, the father of the Baptist, and consequently the genealogy of John himself, are equally traced back to Moses.

[2] Jalqut on Jerem. xxxv. 12.   [3] Luke i. 24.

[4] Chap. xxii. sq.; cf. M. R. James, The Apocryphal New Testament, Oxford, 1924, p. 48.

[5] Cf. his Zacharias Apokryphen, Dorpat, 1895, p. 75. Cf., further, the Emesan Vita (below, p. 254 n. 1), and the so-called Barbarus Scaligeri (Th. Mommsen, Mon. Germ. auct. antiq., ix. 91), the Latin translation of an Alexandrian chronicle. Further, Cedren, ed. Bekker, i. 328, and E. Petersen in Z.N.T.W., xxvii. (1928), p. 86 n. 4, in all of which texts we find the story of John's hiding. The mountain-cave to which the angel led him is pictured in the famous 'Madonna in the Grotto,' by Leonardo da Vinci, who seems to have identified it with the cave in which the Virgin gave birth to Jesus, according to the Proto-evangel of James, xviii. 1 (Engl. transl. by M. R. James, Apocr. N.T., Oxford, 1924, p. 46).

[6] See above, p. 61 f.

traces of improvements, interpolations, and omissions at the hand of Christian copyists. This will be obvious to any one reading with an open mind the following passage of the extant text : [1]

> 'Some of the Jews, however, regarded the destruction of Herod's army as the work of God, who thus exacted a *very just* retribution for John, surnamed the Baptist. For Herod slew him, a *good* man, who bade the Jews cultivate virtue, practise justice toward each other and piety toward God, and to come together through baptism ; for thus immersion would appear acceptable to God, if practised, not as an expiation for certain offences, but for a purification of the body, after the soul had already been previously cleansed by right-eousness. And when the *others* (τῶν ἄλλων) banded together (συστρεφομένων) — for they were highly *delighted* (ἥσθησαν) [2] to listen to his words — Herod feared that the powerful influence which he exercised over men's minds might lead to some act of revolt ; for they seemed ready to do anything upon his advice. Herod therefore considered it far better to forestall him by putting him to death, before any revolution arose through him, than to rue his delay when plunged in the turmoil of an insurrection. And so, through Herod's suspicion, John was sent in chains to Machaerus, the fortress already mentioned, and there slain. Now *the* Jews believed that the destruc-tion of Herod's army was the penalty inflicted upon him to avenge John, God being wroth against Herod.'

The authenticity of the whole passage has sometimes been disputed, though not so often as that of the *Testimonium* con-cerning Jesus. Emil Schürer rightly observed : [3] 'Suspicion is awakened in particular by the favourable estimate of John, who could have been regarded with sympathy by Josephus only in certain respects, to wit, as an ascetic and a preacher of morality, but not as the prophet of the coming Messiah stirring up the people.' To obviate this criticism, Niese put in his text ἥσθησαν ἐπὶ πλεῖστον, 'they were overjoyed,' instead of ἤρθησαν ἐπὶ πλεῖστον, 'they were aroused to the highest degree of excite-ment,' in spite of the fact that all the three MSS. of Josephus (*A*, *M*, and *W*) and of the epitome [4] have the correct wording. There is nothing in the words of the Baptist, as quoted by Josephus, which could fill his audience with exultation. On the other hand, the excitement he is said to have produced must have been mentioned, else there would be no reason for Herod's alarm.[5] ἥσθησαν, 'they were delighted,' is therefore a demonstrably Christian correction.

---

[1] *Ant.*, xviii. 5. 2, § 116 *sqq.*
[2] Thus Niese, with some MSS. of Eusebius and against some MSS. of this church father and all MSS. of Josephus, who wrote ἤρθησαν, ' they were excited.'
[3] *G.J.V.*, i. 4. 438 n. 2 ; cf. Jean Juster, *Les Juifs dans l'empire Romain*, Paris, 1914, ii. 131, note.
[4] See above, p. 28 ll. 29 ff.
[5] Cf. M. Goguel, *Jean Baptiste*, Paris, 1928, p. 16.

A highly significant piece of evidence to the effect that even the *Halōsis* could not escape the Christian revision so often pointed out in the foregoing pages, is afforded by the fact that in the copy used by the Russian translator ἤρθησαν must also have been corrected to ἤσθησαν ; for the Old Russian version reads ' when the people heard that, *they were glad.*' In the *Halōsis* the ' joy ' of the people is not so devoid of any object as in the *Antiquities,* for the censor of the former work had not deemed it necessary to suppress the Baptist's call for liberty, and the promise that through following the path of justice the Jews would be freed from their ' many tyrants.'[1] The reason for this leniency was that John appeared to recommend a ' legal way ' to freedom, ' the path of the law '[2] as opposed to an attempt at insurrection.   What he decided to suppress by the clever change of a single letter (ρ > σ) was the effect of the Baptist's call in stirring up the people to political activity.[3]

Other alterations may reasonably be traced to the same hand which sacrificed the word ἤρθησαν, 'they were roused (to revolt'). Even before the Slavonic *Halōsis* was known, one might have seen that the passage must originally have contained some more solid grounds for Herod's alarm.   Immediately before the words ' for they were roused,' the censor overlooked the highly significant expression ' when they banded together ' (συστρεφομένων), allowing it to stand.   But the subject of the phrase, ' the others,'[4] cannot be in order, because those who banded together were actually the Jews summoned by him to baptism and not any ' other ' people, much less ' *the* others,' which, given the connexion, could only mean ' the heathen,' a manifest absurdity.   Here again, then, we have a Christian alteration, mitigating the *seditious* effect of John's preaching, and instead of τῶν ἄλλων we should rather read τῶν πολλῶν, ' and when the masses banded together, for they were roused to the greatest revolt by the words which they heard.'   This text was still read by the author of the Latin version of the *Antiquities* produced at the instance of Cassiodorus, where τῶν πολλῶν (or possibly even παμπολλῶν[5]) is rendered by *perplurima multitudo.*

In place of the reading presented by the Cod. Ambrosianus printed in Niese's text,[6] Samuel Naber rightly adopted the simple ἐπὶ στάσει τινί on the evidence of the Medicean and Vatican

---

[1] See above, p. 224₅.   [2] See above, p. 224 n. 4.

[3] It is to be noted that he dealt in the same manner with the section about Jesus, allowing the plan of marching into the city and massacring the Roman garrison to stand and striking out only the actual execution of the Zealots' proposal.   See below, pp. 464 ff.

[4] τῶν ἄλλων ; see above, p. 246.

[5] This word does not occur, however, in *Ant.*, xvii.-xix. (Thackeray).

[6] " μὴ ἐπὶ ἀποστάσει τινὶ φέροι."

codices and the epitome. Most probably ἀποστάσει is a Christian correction, to make Herod's alarm appear as based on fear of a *religious* apostasy from orthodox Judaism and not of a political insurrectionary movement (στάσις).

If nothing was preached to the Jews beyond ' virtue ' and a baptism in water, and if their excitement or joy consisted merely in some kind of religious or spiritual ecstasy of the type observed after a camp meeting of a Texas Baptist community, the persecution madness of an insane tyrant would be required to put to death such an innocent preacher of morals. Nor can Josephus well be supposed to have contemplated drawing such a malicious caricature of Herod Antipas in a book written in the lifetime of his patron Herod Agrippa II., still less of depicting as a ' *good* man ' one who had stirred up the masses to the highest pitch of excitement.

In reality, a comparison with the extant Slavonic version of the *Halōsis* shows at a glance that the friendly estimate of the Baptist suspected by Schürer does not go back to Josephus at all. On the contrary, the section dealing with John has been falsified by Christian copyists in the approved manner.

The pathetic words of assent, ' and very justly ' (καὶ μάλα δικαίως), are the exclamation of a Christian reader standing wholly on the side of the ' forerunner ' of Jesus, and not siding at all with Josephus, who ridicules the Baptist's appearance and dress. In the last sentence of the section, ' But to the Jews ' (τοῖς δὲ Ἰουδαίοις), implying that *the* Jews as a body expected chastisement to be inflicted for the murder of the Baptist, is another Christian alteration of τισὶ δὲ Ἰουδαίοις, as appears from a comparison with the introductory words, ' But *some* of the Jews.' Where the *Halōsis* has ' a wild man ' (ἄγριος ἀνήρ), we read in the *Antiquities* ' a good man ' (ἀγαθὸς ἀνήρ),[1] a reading effected by the alteration of only two letters, and manifestly of the same tendency as the alteration of ἤρθησαν into ἤσθησαν. After ἄγριον ἄνδρα something must have been struck out : that description clearly requires amplification, such as is found in the *Halōsis*. Guided by the Slavonic rendering of the passage in question, and the notable parallel in the description of Sabinus the Syrian in the Greek *War*,[2] one may supplement the text somewhat as follows :

' For Herod killed him, a *wild* man (with a shaggy body and clothed in animals' hair, who incited) the Jews (to liberty and) bade them cultivate valour,[3] practise justice toward each other and piety toward God, and to band together through baptism.'

---

[1] Cf. above, p. 51 n. 2, the alteration of σοφιστὴς ἀνήρ in σοφὸς ἀνήρ in the passage on Jesus.

[2] B.J., vi. 1. 6, § 55 (see below, p. 392) : ' his skin was black, his body shrunk and shaggy.'

[3] ἀρετή does not mean ' virtue ' in a speech inciting men to strive for liberty !

Even in the sentence about the meaning of baptism a Christian copyist, unwilling to admit that John's baptism was efficacious for the forgiveness of sins, has clearly had a hand. W. Brandt [1] found it strange that by this sentence attributed to the Baptist the purification instituted by him is entirely robbed of its religious efficacy and reduced to an ordinary ablution for the sake of bodily cleanliness. That this is a falsification of the real state of affairs is obvious, but it can be proved by the evidence of one of the non-Greek versions that Josephus is completely innocent of this particular distortion of the facts, in which as a Jew he could have taken no interest whatever. For the Arabic *Jusifûs* expressly states of John the Baptist : ' This man baptized the Jews for the forgiveness of sins,' which is the exact reverse of what stands in our Greek text. The Arabic *Jusifûs* goes back to the Hebrew *Josippon*, which frequently accords with the Latin *Egesippus*. Now, this version also says of John, ' baptismum propter purificationem *animi* et corporis instituerat, cujus causa necis *libertas* . . .' Fortunately, it is easy to see how the Christian copyist went to work to distort the sentence to the disadvantage of John's baptism ; in the adversative clauses linked by $\mu\grave{\eta}$ $\grave{\epsilon}\pi\acute{\iota}$ . . . $\mathring{a}\lambda\lambda'$ $\mathring{\epsilon}\phi'$, 'not for . . . but for,' he simply transposed the members. Originally the passage must have run : ' For baptism would only appear acceptable to God if practised, not for the purification of the body, but for the expiation of sins ($\tau\hat{\omega}\nu$, not $\tau\iota\nu\hat{\omega}\nu$ [2] $\mathring{a}\mu\alpha\rho\tau\acute{a}\delta\omega\nu$), after the soul had been thoroughly cleansed by righteousness.'

Only in this form does John's doctrine of baptism agree with that of the Therapeutae in Philo,[3] 'having purged bodies and souls, the one with the waters of the bath, the other by the floods of the laws and of right discipline ' ; with that of Silvanus in the first epistle of *Peter*,[4] and the command in the Clementine *Homilies* (xi. 28), ' Cleanse the heart from ill by divine instruction and wash the body in the bath, letting purity follow after goodness ' ; and, lastly, with the oracle of the Jewish Sibyl.[5] Only in this form —and this is what the Christian corrector would take amiss—does it appear as the basis, such as the history of religion requires, of the Christian baptism of repentance for the remission of sins,[6] practised, not indeed by Jesus,[7] but doubtless by the disciples of John who went over to him, namely, Andrew and his brother Simon Peter bar-

---

[1] *Z.A.W.T.*, extra vol. xviii. p. 80. Cf. also Goguel, *op. cit.*, p. 19.
[2] The restriction would imply that some sins—only those against the purity laws—could be washed away.
[3] *De plantatione Noe*, p. 327, ed. Mangey, i. 354.
[4] iii. 21 : ' . . . baptism doth . . . save us, not as the putting away of the filth of the flesh, but through a questioning of one's good conscience toward God ' ("$\sigma\upsilon\nu\epsilon\iota\delta\acute{\epsilon}\sigma\epsilon\omega\varsigma$ $\mathring{a}\gamma\alpha\theta\hat{\eta}\varsigma$ $\mathring{\epsilon}\pi\epsilon\rho\acute{\omega}\tau\eta\mu\alpha$ $\epsilon\mathring{\iota}\varsigma$ $\theta\epsilon\acute{o}\nu$ ").
[5] *Orac. Sib.*, iv. 164 *sqq.*
[6] *Mark* i. 4 ; *Luke* iii. 3 ; *Acts* ii. 8.
[7] *John* iv. 2.

jona, or the ' anonymous disciple,' [1] and afterwards became the rite of initiation into the Christian church. The Hebrew *Josippon*, dependent on the second edition of the *War* combined with the additional matter in the *Antiquities*,[2] says in so many words of Johanan : ' It was he who instituted baptism.' [3] Only if the account in the *Antiquities* is taken in the above sense and supplemented in the way suggested above,[4] on the model of the parallel narrative in the *Halōsis*, by a mention of John's call to liberty, only then does it agree with the statement in *Matthew* that John announced the impending establishing of the ' kingdom of God.' [5]

The invaluable account in the *Halōsis*, derived from information coming from the Baptist's own following,[6] at last enables us to understand how John conceived of and preached the 'kingdom of God ' and what is that ' way of the law ' by which he wished to lead Israel to ' liberate it from its many tyrants.' [7]

The opinion defended by Frey,[8] that the Baptist advocated a ' legal way ' to freedom as opposed to ' illegal ' attempts to gain independence by armed rebellion, is open to grave doubt. True, his admonition to the Jews to renounce evil deeds shows that he propounded the well-known rabbinical doctrine [9] to the effect that God in his mercy will send Israel the Messiah as soon as it is converted, does penance, and completely fulfils the law. His release by Archelaus after his first arrest and trial presupposes the fact that his preaching at least admitted of a quietist interpretation. On the other hand, this arrest would itself be unintelligible had his speeches not had some provocative effect upon the masses.

It is further worth noting that the phrase ' the way of the law' must have had reference to some quite definite passage in the law and its interpretation. Else one would have difficulty in understanding the angry retort of the learned scribe Simon :

' We read the books of God daily ; but thou, only now come forth like a beast from the forest, durst thou teach us and lead the multitudes astray with thy accursed speeches ?'

The text underlying this sermon of liberty leading the multitudes

---

[1] *John* i. 35, 40, 41.　　　　　　　[2] See above, p. 83 ll. 7 ff.

[3] Such parentheses, explaining who a certain person was or what he did, are found, e.g., in *Ant.*, xv. § 4 (' this Pollion had predicted at the time when Herod was tried,' etc.) ; xx. § 102 (' the sons of Judas the Galilaean—of him who had incited the people to revolt against the Romans in the days of the census of Quirinius ') ; *B.J.*, ii. § 433 ('Judas, surnamed the Galilaean—that redoubtable doctor, who in old days under Quirinius,' etc.) ; *B.J.*, vii. § 253, etc.

[4] See above, p. 248 last lines.　　　　[5] *Matt.* iii. 2.

[6] See above, p. 27 n. 1 ; p. 23 n. 2.　　[7] See above, p. 224₅.

[8] See below, p. 257 n. 10.

[9] Cf. the passages collected in Strack-Billerbeck's commentary on *Matt.* xi. 12, i. 599, and 162 *sqq.* on *Matt.* iv. 12.

astray can indeed be no other than the well-known Deuteronomic
' royalty law ' : [1]

> ' When thou art come unto the land which Jahweh thy God giveth
> thee, and shalt possess it and shalt dwell therein, and shalt say, I
> will set a king over me, like as all the nations that are round about
> me ; thou shalt in any wise set him king over thee, whom Jahweh
> thy God shall choose : *one from among thy brethren shalt thou set king
> over thee* : thou mayest not put a *foreigner* (*'ish nakhri*) *over thee,
> who is not thy brother.*'

It is this law which caused King Agrippa I., when in accordance
with the old custom [2] he was reciting the *Book of Deuteronomy* on
the feast of tabernacles in A.D. 41, to ' burst into tears ' at the
words, ' thou mayest not put a foreigner over thee, who is not thy
brother ' ; [3] whereupon the scribes of the Pharisees, pampered by
him in every way, were moved to comfort him by exclaiming :
' Be not distressed, Agrippa, thou art our brother, thou art our
brother.' [4] This touching display of sentiment, enacted before an
immense public, shows how the Herodian family sought to re-
concile their constitutional position with the Jewish law. What
attitude their opponents took up can be easily seen. The chief
objection raised was the fact that the ancestor of the royal house
was *not* an Edomite. Antipater, they said, had been a native of
Ascalon ; [5] he was consequently a Philistine, an ἀλλόφυλος or a
gôj par excellence. Moreover, *Deut.* xxiii. 8, 9 at best permitted
the descendants of Edomite proselytes to belong to the community
of Israel ; but from this it by no means followed that a converted
foreigner could be king over Israel. As for the rule of the Roman
emperors over the Holy Land, it could certainly not be made to
appear legitimate by such an evasion of the spirit of the law.

The ' way of the *torah* ' leading to ' liberation from many
tyrants,' as inculcated by John, demanded then of the people a
complete fulfilment of the law alike in its moral and in its political
aspect. From the moral point of view it required ' perfect justice
toward men and piety toward God ' ; [6] in the political sphere
obedience to the law concerning the Israelitish monarchy, i.e. the
installation of a native king chosen by God, non-recognition of
foreign rule,[7] refusal of the oath of allegiance,[8] and perhaps also

---

[1] xvii. 14 *sq.* See above, p. 137 n. 2. [2] *Deut.* xxxi. 10 *sqq.*
[3] *Mishnah Sotah*, vii. 8.
[4] Referring, of course, to *Deut.* xxiii. 8 *sq.* : ' Thou shalt not abhor an Edomite,
for he is thy brother.'
[5] Sextus Julius Africanus, *Epistle to Aristides,* ap. Euseb., *Hist. eccl.,* i. 7.
13 *sq.*; *Chron.,* ed. Karst, p. 209.
[6] Cf. the oath of the Essenes in *B.J.,* ii. § 139 : ' first that he will practise piety
toward the Deity, next that he will observe justice toward men.'
[7] Cf. *B.J.,* iii. § 259, where the Jews in the cave of Jotapata prefer suicide to
violation of the law by submitting to foreign rule.
[8] This is what the more radical Pharisees had done under Herod the Great.

a refusal to pay taxes to foreigners such as was required of the Jews by Judas the Galilaean.

THE BAPTIST AND JUDAS OF GALILEE

In spite of the well-known looseness with which Josephus strings together the extracts from his various sources—in this case a document hailing from the Baptist's circle and an official report of the governor Coponius—the political principles of the Baptist are clearly seen to be similar to, if not identical with, those of Judas of Galilee. On the latter the *Halōsis* [1] has the following brief remarks, immediately after the first mention of John :

> 'In his time (i.e. the administration of Coponius) there was a man of Galilee who upbraided the Jews because, though of the seed of Abraham, they were now doing menial service and paying taxes to the Romans, and because they had accepted mortal masters after forsaking one who was immortal. The name of this man was Judas, and he found a way to live in the outside (*sic*) and one not corresponding (to that) of others. (§ 119) There is, you must know, among the Jews a threefold order of life in conformity with the law. One (school) has the name of Pharisees, the second that of Sadducees, the third, which is more Puritan than the other two, that of the Essenes.'

Here the remarkable phrase ' to live in the outside ' only becomes intelligible through retranslation into the language of the rabbis. In the Talmud [2] we hear of a nephew of R. Johanan b. Zakkai, named 'Abba Sikara, i.e. the ' sicar,' who is there mentioned as ' head of the *Barjonîm* of Jerusalem ' and as having, during the siege of the city by the Romans, managed the escape of a rabbi from the town in a coffin. These *Barjonîm* (sing. Hebr. *barjon*, Aram. *barjona*) are mentioned elsewhere quite a number of times. The expression *barjon*, Syr. *baraja*, Arab. *barj^{un}*, is derived from Sum. *bar* ='outside,' 'free space,' 'desert,' and bears the same relation to Hebr. *bar*, 'the outside,' 'the open land,' [3] as does '*eljôn*, 'the Highest,' to '*al*, 'above,' '*in excelsis*.' The *Barjonîm* are accordingly those who ' stand outside,' the *externi*, or indeed, according to the formation of the word (which is almost equivalent to a superlative), those 'who stand furthest out,' the ' extremists.' This expression, in the mouth of opponents, easily

---

[1] ii. 118. [2] *Giṭṭin*, 56a.

[3] Gesenius-Buhl, [15], 113a, s.v. *bar*, iv.: Arab. *barr*, 'flat country,' *terra firma*; bibl. Hebr. *bar*, 'the ground,' *Ps.* ii. 12 ; 'the open country,' *Job* xxxix. 9 ; bibl. Aram. *bar*, i. ; Jew. Aram. *bara*; Syr. *bara*, ' the open country '; Egyptian Aram. *bara*, ' outside,' *hinaus*. Sachau, *Aram. Papyri und Ostraka*, 1911, p. 56, line 15.

takes on the sinister sense of ' outsider,' ' outcast,' ' outlaw,' indicating those who evade the oppression of foreign rule by taking flight into inaccessible mountains, woods, and deserts.[1] Josephus would indicate, then, that Judas of Galilee was the founder of the party of the *Barjonîm*, those who live an outlaw's life in the desert, and that this party, along with Sadducees, Pharisees, and Essenes, was the fourth αἵρεσις among the Jews.

This evidence is of great importance for the New Testament history of the time, because, according to *Matthew* (xvi. 17), in the fateful hour of the revealing of his Messiahship at Caesarea Philippi, Jesus addresses Simon Peter as Simon *barjona*. The Gospel of the *Hebrews*, as well as that of *John* (i. 42), is either ignorant of or wishes to ignore the compromising meaning of this name, and would accordingly take it as a patronymic ' son of Jonas ' or ' son of Joḥanan.' Such an interpretation cannot, in the light of such names as *Barabbas*, *Bartholomai*, *Barjesus*, and *Barnabas*, be proved to be an error. Yet it is a natural suggestion to interpret the name on the analogy of the noteworthy title Simon the Canaanaean or Simon the Zealot, or Judas the Zealot,[2] that is, as a party name. ' Simon *barjona* ' is probably no other than ' Simon the extremist,' the ' outcast,' an adherent of the radical Zealot, Judas of Galilee. It is a well-known fact that even as this meaning was intentionally obscured by later copyists by the simple device of dividing the word and reading *Bar Jonah* or *Bar Joḥanan*, some MSS.—notably א—write Κανανίτης, i.e. Cana'anite, or ' man of Cana,' instead of Καναναῖος, the Zealot, because it did not please a later generation that one, or even two, of Jesus' disciples should have belonged to the party of the Zealots or Jewish nationalist fanatics.

In the Greek *War* [3] we are expressly told that this Judas incited the Galilaeans to revolt (from Roman rule), and the same statement appears in the *Antiquities*.[4] The son and successor of the Zealot leader Hezekiah, defeated and slain by Herod the Great,[5] was the soul of the opposition to the census of Quirinius,[6] in A.D. 6 or 7, and at his death left sons behind him who in the rebellion of 66 distinguished themselves as leaders in the struggle for independence.

Josephus may be right in attributing the ' invention of the way of living in the outside' to Judas of Galilee, and considering him the founder of the party of the Barjonîm. But there is good

---

[1] See above, p. 24 n. 1, on Judas Maccabaeus taking to the mountains and living there ' on grass,' ' after the manner of the beasts,' to avoid pollution.

[2] Mentioned in some MSS. of the *Vetus Latina*. On the possibility of two apostles being each called 'the Zealot,' see Rendel Harris, *The Twelve Apostles*, Cambridge, 1927, p. 34.

[3] *B.J.*, ii. 8. 1, § 118.   [4] xx. 5. 2, § 102.   [5] *B.J.*, ii. 4. 1, § 56.

[6] *B.J.*, ii. 17. 8, § 433 ; *Ant.*, xviii. 1. 1.

evidence to the effect that John's disciples credited their own master with the counsel to ' leave the towns.' A life of John the Baptist,[1] purporting to have been written by a disciple of John called Mark,[2] evidently worked over, to a large extent, by an unknown fifth-century Syrian author, since it gives an account of the discovery of the head of St. John in Emesa in the year 453 A.D., contains a sermon of the Baptist advising his disciples ' to leave the towns,'[3] to ' depart out of the towns '—an obvious parallel to 2 Cor. vi. 17, where Paul, quoting the prophet Isaiah (lii. 11), admonishes the faithful : ' come out from among them and be ye separate.'[4] The order ' get out from the towns ' will immediately remind the reader of the catchword, ' and there went out unto him all . . . they of Jerusalem,'[5] and of ' the multitude that went out to be baptized '[6] by John, in the Synoptic gospels. As a matter of fact, the Ps.-Clementines[7] say in so many words that the disciples of the Baptist—under the leadership of his successors,[8] Simon Magus and Dositheos—did carry through what Roman political theory would call a ' secessio plebis ' : ' Believing themselves more righteous than the others,' these so-called ' righteous ones ' or Ṣadoqites ' segregated themselves from the contact of the people.' Through a fortunate discovery of Dr. Schechter's[9] in the geniza of the old Synagogue in Fostat (1896), we possess the ' Book of the New Covenant ' of those Dosithean Ṣadoqites[10] who worshipped John the Baptist as the ' righteous teacher ' (joreh ṣedeq)[11] of the

---

[1] Extant in five MSS. in Vienna, Geneva, and Paris. Ed. in Patrol. Or., iv., fasc. 5, p. 527. The Rumanian MS. Cod. Gaster contains a combination of this ' Life of John ' with the above-quoted chapters on the Baptist in the Slavonic Josephus.

[2] There is no trace of an attempt to identify this Mark with the evangelist, and there is thus no reason to doubt that Mark was the name of the unknown author of that Life of John the Baptist.

[3] " τῶν πόλεων ἐξέλθατε."

[4] " ἐξέλθατε ἐκ μέσου αὐτῶν καὶ ἀφορίσθητε."

[5] Mark i. 5: " καὶ ἐξεπορεύοντο πρὸς αὐτὸν . . . οἱ Ἱεροσολυμῖται πάντες "; cp. Matt. iii. 5.

[6] Luke ii. 8: " ἔλεγεν οὖν τοῖς ἐκπορευομένοις ὄχλοις . . ."

[7] Recogn., i. 54 : " erat ergo primum schisma eorum qui dicebantur Sadducaei, initio Joannis iam paene temporibus sumpto. Hique ut caeteris iustiores segregare se coeperunt a populi coetu. . . . Auctor vero sententiae huius primus Dositheus, secundus Simon fuit . . . ex discipulis Joannis, qui (sibi) videbantur esse magni, segregarunt se ex populo et magistrum suum veluti Christum praedicarunt.'

[8] Ps.-Clem., Hom., ii. 23.

[9] Documents of Jewish Sectarians, vol. i. ; Fragments of a Zadokite Work, Cambridge, 1910.

[10] Dr. Schechter found this name mentioned by the Karaïte Qirqisani (died 937 A.D.) as that of a sect in possession of a ' book of Ṣadoq,' and later on united with the sect of the Dositheans. But he had overlooked the statement of the Ps.-Clementines quoted in our note 7.

[11] This explanation has been found independent of the decisive testimony of the Ps.-Clementines—above, note 7—by the late Rev. Dr. George Margoliouth of the British Museum (Athenaeum, Nov. 26, 1910 ; Expositor, Dec.-March 1912 ; Bibl. Sacra, July 1912, pp. 421 ff.).

Last Days, and—a short time before the capture of Jerusalem [1]—
left Judaea to transfer their 'camps' to the country round about
Damascus, so as to be 'separate from the men of perdition'[2] and
'from all impurity.'[3] These secessionist covenanters, who wore
the sign of the cross, the † mentioned in *Ezekiel* ix. 4, on their
foreheads,[4] and called themselves the 'house of separation'[5] (*beth
peleg*), the 'secession' (*p⁰lugta*)[6] or 'schism,' must have existed
as early as the war of Varus (4 B.C.), i.e. at the time of the first
appearance of John the Baptist,[7] since 'those pestiferous men who
think themselves just ones,' who consider the rest of Israel like
heathen and say to them, 'Do not touch me, lest thou shouldst
pollute me,'[8] those 'hide themselves so as not to be recognized,'[9] those 'who think themselves princes,'[10] are violently
attacked in the *Assumption of Moses*, which was certainly composed at that critical moment.[11] All this leaves hardly any doubt
about the identity of the *barjonim* or 'outsiders' of the Talmud,
and of those whom either John the Baptist or Judas the Galilaean
taught 'a way to live in the outside' in order to escape from the
yoke of the foreigners into the desert after the manner of their
Maccabaean ancestors, and to remain faithful to the law of God.

The passionate libertarian 'activism' of this Judas, the ruling
principle of political struggle for independence, is thus paraphrased by Josephus :[12]

'The Deity does not co-operate in restoring liberty otherwise
than by influencing man's decision, and God will be much more ready
to assist us if we do not shirk the toil entailed by the great cause
which we have at heart.'

---

[1] Josephus, *B.J.*, ii. § 279 : 'It so happened that the cities were deserted, and
many had to leave the customs of their fathers and to take refuge in the districts
of the heathen.' *Ant.*, xx. § 255 : 'the unfortunate Jews . . . were forced to
leave their own customs and to expatriate themselves, thinking it better to dwell
among the heathen.'

[2] Damascus-Book, vi. 15.

[3] *Ibid.*, vii. 3 ; cp. xix. 20 about those 'who have not separated themselves
from the mass.'

[4] *Ibid.*, xix. 12 (only those will be saved whose foreheads are marked with
the sign mentioned by *Ezekiel* ix. 4). See above, p. 233 n. 13 ; p. 234 n. 8.

[5] *Ibid.*, xx. 22 (*beth Peleg*), with reference to *Gen.* x. 25.

[6] Mandean *Book of Jahjah*, xx. 7³⁻⁴, the *p⁰lugta* (=schism, above, p. 254 n. 7,
secessio) is marked with the 'royal seal' (*hatma de malka*).

[7] See above, p. 225 n. 1.   [8] *Ass. Mosis*, vii. 10. 4, below, p. 258 n. 5.

[9] Below, p. 258 n. 4 ; above, p. 242 ff.

[10] See above, p. 254 n. 7, about those '*qui sibi magni videbantur*.' In the
Damascus-Book, where (vi. 2) the chosen ones of Israel identify themselves with
the 'Sadoqites,' the privileged servants of the sanctuary (*Ezek.* xliv. 15), it is also
said (viii. 6) that the repentant ones of Israel who have emigrated out of the land
of Judah to the country of Damascus are those whom God has called 'princes'
digging the well of the Law in *Num.* xxi. 18.

[11] See Schürer, *G.J.V.*⁴, iii. p. 299 (Engl. transl., II. III., p. 79), who followed
Ewald, Wieseler, Drummond, Deane, Thomson, de Faye, Charles, Clemen,
Burkitt, and others.

[12] *Ant.*, xviii. 5.

That is a typical Sadducaean idea, for the thinkers of that school most decidedly rejected idle resignation to fate as destined by the supposed will of God : [1]

> ' The Sadducees abolish fate, maintaining that there is no such thing, that the issues of human life are not dependent upon it, and that all things fall within our own control ; so that it is we who are responsible for our blessings and bring our misfortunes upon ourselves through our own lack of resolution.'

That sounds, and in the rendering of Josephus, who hates the Sadducees, is intended to sound, like daring atheism. But it simply implies the recognition of the full moral responsibility of the brave and determined man resorting to action after mature consideration, the man who in *acting* feels himself as much in God's hands as does the quietist in waiting ; on the one hand he holds God's will not to be unalterable,[2] while on the other it is only in the completed events of the past that His intention can be surely recognized.

Present evils such as servitude, exile, and the like, are inflicted as terrestrial punishments for sin ; transcendental retribution they ignore.[3] But if a man is conscious of his faults and repents and with energetic determination seeks the right way, then it is God's will to assist the courageous toiler on the road to success. God has given man a free will, so that he may choose between good and evil ; [4] mere thoughtless drifting and irresolution are the source of all evils.

Even the Pharisees do not contest this doctrine in its main essentials, but merely limit it to some extent : [5] ' The Pharisees assert that some, but not all, events are the work of fate, and some are under our own control . . . they attribute everything to fate and God ; yet they admit that the act rightly or otherwise rests for the most part with men, though in every case fate co-operates.' Even from this standpoint it is inconceivable that a war of liberation such as the Maccabaean rising would have been regarded as a wicked interference with God's decree. The only divergence from Sadducaean opinion is that on the basis of considerations developed in the *Book of Job* they simply committed the issue to God's inscrutable decision. The Maccabees were victors in a just war of liberation ; Ḥizqiah, the father of Judas of Galilee, was, like Bar Kokhᵉba at a later date, defeated. That in no way in-

---

[1] *Ant.*, xiii. 5. 9, § 173.
[2] Philo (*Quod deus sit immutabilis* ; *de Cherub.*, 111 B, 142 M ; *Leg. Alleg.*, 49 C, 53 M) has derived this notion from Parmenides and from Platonic doctrines. The Pharisee Josephus, *c. Ap.*, ii. § 167, seems to base his notion of God's immutability on *Exod.* iii. 14 and *Mal.* iii. 6.
[3] *B.J.*, ii. § 165 ; *Halōsis*, trans. Ber.-Grass, p. 264 n. 1.
[4] *B.J.* and *Halōsis*, ii. § 164.
[5] *Ant.*, xiii. 5. 9, § 172 ; *B.J.*, ii. 8. 14, § 162 *sq.* Cf. *Ps. Sol.*, ix. 7.

validates the justice of their cause. Even he who is defeated in a righteous contest fulfils God's will ; his fate may be interpreted as a sin-offering for past guilt, his own or another's.

God expects magnanimous men to give themselves up to no passive resignation ; he loves Israel, who 'wrestles with his God' ;[1] nay, more, he loves to let himself be conquered.[2] The Essene pacifists,[3] if they really *were* pacifists[4] and not a congregation similar to the modern Moslem *Sanūsiyyah*, stand alone in preaching the doctrine of detachment from politics and quiet resignation towards 'the powers' ordained by the grace of God,[5] an attitude adopted later on by Paul and his disciple Silvanus,[6] clearly in opposition to the teaching of Judas of Galilee and his sons. The same quietism may also be traced in certain rabbinical doctrines of 'redemption through penitence and sitting still,' disapproving the 'pressing for the end ' of the world.[7]

Of course, there were also people of the stamp of Josephus who sought to conceal their cowardice under the garb of pious submission to God's will. The base thoughts of such persons are unblushingly expressed by the historian in his shameful speech to the besieged in Jerusalem :[8]

'In short, there is no instance of our forefathers having triumphed by armed force or failed of success without arms when they committed their cause to God ; if they sat still, they conquered, as it pleased their Judge ; if they fought, they were invariably defeated. . . . Thus[9] invariably has our nation been forbidden the use of arms ; resorting to arms invariably led to defeat. For it is, I suppose, the duty of the occupants of holy ground to leave everything to the arbitrament of God and to scorn the aid of human hands, if they can but conciliate the Arbiter above.'

The assumption of Frey[10] that the Baptist, who 'incited to freedom,' indicated a 'way to deliverance from many tyrants' and

---

[1] *Gen.* xxxii. 28.
[2] *Pesaḥ.* 119c ; Bacher, *Agada d. babyl. Amoräer*, i. 411.
[3] *B.J.*, ii. § 135 : " εἰρήνης ὑπουργοί " ; *Halōsis*, p. 256, 5 : ' servants of peace.'
[4] See above, p. 23 n. 1.
[5] *B.J.* and *Halōsis*, ii. § 140 ; cf. *Dan.* ii. 37 ; *Soph. Sal.*, vi. 1 ; *Henokh*, 465 ; *Apoc. Bar.*, 829 ; *Berakh.*, 58a, 40 ; 'even the guardian of a public well is chosen by God,' a saying from which this guardian of wells could conclude that he must not be replaced by another man even in case of misconduct. The servile argument that the powers that be must be respected, no matter how flagrant their malfeasance, because they exist by the grace, or at least by the tolerance, of God, forgets to take into account the significant fact that governments have also been overthrown by the will of God (*Dan.* ii. 21), and that men are more often used as instruments of God's will than are the powers of nature (cf. 2 *Kings* xviii. 7). A useful summary of ' monarchomachian ' theology will be found in a Heidelberg thesis by Rud. Michael Treumann (Leipzig, 1895).
[6] *Rom.* xiii. 1-7 ; 1 *Pet.* ii. 13 *sqq.*
[7] Strack-Billerbeck, i. 599.
[8] *B.J.*, v. § 390 *sq.*   [9] *B.J.*, v. § 399 *sq.*
[10] *Der slavische Josephusbericht*, Dorpat, 1908, p. 36.

R

promised the coming of a king who would liberate the Jews and defeat all the obstreperous, at the same time preached against a popular rising and in favour of a mere waiting for a miracle of God, is intrinsically rather improbable. Quite true, in the time of Archelaus, i.e. at the time of John, Judas, and the war of Varus, there did exist a quietist party, to which, for example, the author of the *Assumption of Moses* belonged. That party looked, indeed, for the impending end of the world ; its members wished to bring about the Divine redemption by a flight from the world into a cave, by fasts and their own martyrdom ; at the same time they no more sought the kingdom of God on earth, but in the starry heavens, and expected the people of Israel to be 'wafted away on eagles' wings ' to this ' kingdom of heaven,' whence they would exultantly look down upon their enemies below.[1] This party, however, was most strenuously opposed to the ' homines pestilentiosi qui se esse justos docent';[2] in other words, to the followers of 'the man of proved rectitude,'[3] who (being purified by baptism) regarded the rest of Israel as heathen and addressed them thus :

> ' Touch me not lest thou shouldst pollute me. . . . But in truth they are deceivers . . . who devour the goods of the poor but feign sympathy with them . . . *people who conceal themselves lest they should be recognised* [4] . . . and regard themselves as princes.' [5]

The views of these quietists have found an echo in the Mandaean writings in which the Baptist is adjured : [6]

> ' Cast not rebels into the Jordan, else no one will be able to resist its force ';[7]

and in which that heavenly paradise of the pious and peaceable fugitives from the world, that πεδίον 'Αληθείας [8] for the righteous who are ' wafted away,' [9] the ἐπουράνιος βασιλεία,[10] the ἐπουράνιος πατρίς,[11] has become an essential element in the hopes for a hereafter entertained by these ' quiet in the land.' [12]

The followers of the Baptist are *not*, however, to be sought among those persons who hoped for redemption by ' repentance and sitting still.' The clearest proof of this is the much-debated

[1] *Ass. Mos.*, 9 *sq.*   [2] *Ass. Mos.*, vii. 3 ; cf. above, p. 254 n. 7.
[3] This is how the Baptist is described in the Mandaean *Ginza r.* Lidz., p. 195₇.
[4] Cf. above, p. 242 f., on Ḥanan the 'hidden one.'
[5] *Ass. Mos.*, vii. 10, 4 *sqq.*; see above, p. 255 n. 8.
[6] Mand. *Book of John*, transl. Lidzbarski, p. 17, l. 20.
[7] Cp. with this the strange answer of the Baptist, ' fieri non potest, *ut rapinam assumam*,' to the request of Jesus, ' accede, baptiza me ' (Severi Alexandri, *De ritibus baptismi liber*, p. 25 ; A. Resch, *Agrapha*², Leipzig, 1906, p. 73).
[8] *IVth Ezra* v. 1.   The ' field of truth ' is mentioned by the magus Gobryas in Ps.-Plato, *Axiochos*, 371a.   Plutarch, *De def. or.*, 22 f., p. 422 B, D ; cp. Plato, *Phaedr.*, 4 28c.
[9] ' mᵉshunnē kushṭa,' ' those transported into truth.'   *Ibid.*, p. xviii ; 45 n. 2 ; 116 n. 6 ; 194 n. 3 ; *Ginza*, p. 30 n. 11.
[10] 2 *Tim.* iv. 8.   [11] *Hebr.* xi. 16.   [12] *Ps.* xxxv. 20.

saying of Jesus about the 'storming' of the kingdom of heaven, which 'from the days of the Baptist until now has been forcibly seized by men of violence.' [1] This utterance has hitherto occasioned grave misgivings on chronological grounds. If, as is implied in the *Gospel of Infancy*,[2] Jesus was only six months younger than the Baptist; if, moreover, according to the express statement in *Luke* iii. 11, the Baptist's active live only began in the fifteenth year of the Emperor Tiberius (August A.D. 28-29),— then Jesus, who according to the chronology presupposed in the synoptic Gospels did not long outlive the Baptist, could never have used such words as 'from the days of John the Baptist *until now.*' If, however, according to the evidence of the source used in the *Halôsis* of Josephus, and derived from the circle of the Baptist's own disciples, John made his appearance as early as the time of Archelaus (4 B.C.-A.D. 6), then, as will be shown below, the whole saying admits of a very simple and plausible explanation.

THE BAPTIST ELECTED HIGH PRIEST BY THE INSURGENTS

Immediately after the death of Herod the Great his cruelly oppressed people in Jerusalem rose in armed revolt against his successor. Herod in weak moments had regarded himself as the world-ruler chosen by destiny; [3] to the pious, however, he was but the tyrant 'expected by the heathen,' and the Antichrist who immediately before the end of time would remove 'the sceptre from Judah.' When Archelaus tried to celebrate his accession to the throne by a royal address to his subjects, he was overwhelmed by outcries. Amidst roars of lamentation for Matthias and the other martyrs, whom Herod had burnt at the stake for the destruction of the golden eagle on the temple door, clamorous demands were made for a reduction of the prevailing imposts and a reimbursement of previous taxes, for the abolition of oppressive market duties, the liberation of political prisoners, and, above all, for the removal of the hated high priest, Jo'azar b. Boethus, appointed by Herod, ' because he was impious and unsatisfactory, and not frankly outspoken in matters concerning God.' [4] They claimed that ' they had a right to choose a man of greater piety and purer morals.' [5]

This hitherto unheard-of demand of the people to *elect* the high priest, the ' height of madness,' according to Josephus,[6] was never again abandoned by the revolutionary party, and was actually carried into execution by the followers of John of Gischala in the besieged city in A.D. 67.[7]

---

[1] *Matt.* xi. 12 ; *Luke* xvi. 16.   [2] *Luke* i. 26, 37; cp. above, p. 244[7].
[3] See above, p. 140 n. 1.
[4] *Halôsis*, ii. 1. 7 ; transl. Ber.-Grass, p. 233.
[5] *B.J.*, *ibid.*   [6] *B.J.*, iv. 3. 6, § 147.   [7] *Ibid.*, iv. 3. 8.

That is the reason why the Romans from the time of the banishment of Archelaus to the recall of Pilate (A.D. 6-36) kept the high priest's royal robe under their own lock and key, so as to be in a position to prevent at any time the investiture with this symbol of world-rule [1] of a high priest elected by the people of whom they did not approve.[2]

Since it is now established on the evidence of the Slavonic Josephus that the Baptist made his appearance under Archelaus, a conjecture as to the particular person whom the insurgents of that period demanded to have for a high priest is strongly suggested by a remarkable detail in the Hebrew [3] and the Arabic [4] *Jusifûs*, which no one so far has even attempted to explain. There Joḥanan b. Zechariah, whom Herod Antipas put to death— that is to say, the Baptist—is designated not only as a 'great master' (*rabban*),[5] but actually as a high priest (*kohen gadol*). Since there is no apparent reason why the narrative of Josephus should have been amplified at a later date by a midrashic statement of so remarkable a character, and nowhere else attested, I can only account for this tradition by supposing that something of the kind originally stood in the Greek Josephus, the lost amplified second edition of the *War*, on an epitome of which the Hebrew *Josippon* is based, and that it was afterwards struck out, along with the sentence about the seditious effect of the Baptist's preaching.

At that time, under the influence of the *Epistle to the Hebrews*,[6] people had long been wont to discover the promised high priest of the last times,[7] the *kohen le'olam*, not in John but in Jesus. But for the period immediately after the fall of Herod there is

---

[1] Cf. my *Weltenmantel und Himmelszelt*, München, 1910, p. 25 n. 4.

[2] *Ant.*, xviii. 4. 3 ; xv. 2. 4.

[3] Ed. of Venice, 1544, p. צב (*i.e.* 92), right column, l. 18 from the bottom ; ed. Breithaupt, Gotha, 1707, v. 45, p. 529; Gotha, 1710, p. 533 n. 4. The words *kohen gadol* are missing in the *editio princeps*, Mantua, 1470; in Münster's edition (Bâle, 1543) ; in the New York MS. derived from R. Gershom's copy; in the Paris MS. of Mosconi's recension ; and in the two Vatican MSS., Ebr. Urbin. 52 and Ebr. 408 : all this being strong evidence that the passage was deleted by the Christian censor whenever it was possible to do so.

[4] Wellhausen, *Der arabische Josephus*, Berlin, 1897, § 90.

[5] This title is not found except in the *Josippon* MS. of the New York Jewish Theological Seminary, and it may be due to a scribe's confusion of the Baptist with the later Rabban Joḥanan ben Zakkai (Sol. Zeitlin, *Jew. Quart. Rev.*, N.S., xix., 1929, p. 39 n. 81).

[6] iii. 1 ; vii. 5.

[7] *Test. Levi*, 18 : ' In the seventh week priests will come, idol-worshippers . . . greedy . . . impious—and after the Lord will have punished them He will awaken a new priest for the priesthood, and to him all words of the Lord will be revealed, and he will hold a court of truth on earth . . . like a king . . . and there will be peace all over the earth. The heavens will open, and from the temple of glory there will come upon him sanctity with a fatherly voice . . . and the glory of the Most High will be pronounced upon him, and the spirit of understanding and of sanctity will rest upon him . . . and he will have no successor in all eternity.'

(so far as we may judge from our source, that is, Josephus) scarcely another figure who comes at all into consideration for such a popular high priest. At all events, it would be inadmissible to consider 'Ele'azar, the brother of the unworthy Jo'azar, whom Archelaus finally installed, as such a candidate put forward by the rebellious people.

Moreover, the proclamation of the Baptist for this dignity is in complete harmony with his own ' call to freedom ' :

' a mortal shall not reign over you, but the Most High, *who has sent me.*'

This clearly means that he considered himself the *vicarius* of God sent down to rule this true and renewed theocracy, precisely as did the dynasty of the Hasmonaeans. With this dignity of a temporary *vicarius* of the Most High his further promises of the speedy appearance of a real king, a liberator and ruler of the nations, are quite in keeping. Hence his references, in the Synoptics, to the ' coming one ' (ὁ ἐρχόμενος, *habba'*), who is stronger than he, and whose shoe he, the *shilo,* as he says with a play on words,[1] is unworthy to draw off.

In fact, the fulfilment of the Deuteronomic law concerning the national kingdom discussed above, i.e. the appointment of a king *whom God has chosen,* requires a procedure such as is presupposed in the election, installation, and anointing of Saul and David by Samuel the seer (*ro^e*), prophet (*nabî*), and priest. Not to the chosen king himself, who need be no ' prophet ' and visionary, does God reveal His will, but to the specially favoured prophet who then announces as the herald of God the will of the Lord to the people. When the unfortunate attempt to re-establish the kingdom after the exile was made in the time of Zerubabel, the son of David, chosen by Jahweh to be the leader of the world,[2] there stood beside this piteous royal puppet the high priest Jeshu'a, to whom the Lord had announced the speedy coming of his ' servant,' of the ' branch ' of the root of David. Again, at a later date, beside the messianic prince Simon *bar Kokh^eba,* according to the evidence of the coins, there stood at the head of the people one

---

[1] See the very curious etymology in the excerpts from Origen (cf. Wutz, *Onomastica Sacra,* ii. 747) : ' Silo, avulsio vel excalceatio,' and, in the supplement (p. 1055) : ' Silo, excalceatio,' evidently from נשל,' to take off shoes ' ; cf. שלל. The same derivation with reference to *Job* xvii. 8, ישל, and *Deut.* vii. 1, xix. 5, נשל in Samuel b. Chofni Gaon (died in 1034) in his *Genesis* commentary, xlix. 10, ed. Petersburg, 1886, p. 138 ; cf. Poznanski, *Schiloh,* Leipzig, 1904, i. 5. The etymology of the Origen excerpts is probably a remainder of some good old commentary on *Mark* i. 7 or *Luke* iii. 16. The Greek author of the *Gospel of Matthew* no longer understood the true meaning of his source. That text must have had the false reading נשא = ' to carry,' for נשל = ' to take off,' and the wordplay was thus naturally lost.

[2] *Hagg.,* iii. 20 *sqq.*

'Ele'azar the priest.   Similarly, the Baptist appears to have been regarded as the last high priest chosen for the messianic period to anoint the liberator king of Israel and ruler of the world.   Such indeed is virtually the teaching of a rabbinic tradition : [1]

> ' To that generation (in Egypt) thou didst send redemption through *two redeemers*, as it is said : " He sent Moses his servant and Aaron whom he had chosen." [2]   And also to this generation (in the messianic age) he sendeth two, corresponding to those (other two). " Send out thy light and thy truth." [3]   " Thy light," that is, the prophet 'Elijah of the house of Aaron, of whom it is written, [4] " the seven lamps shall throw their light in front of the lamp-stand." And " thy truth," that is, Messiah ben David, as it is said, [5] " Jahweh hath sworn unto David (in) truth, he will not turn from it."   And likewise it is said, [6] " Behold my servant whom I uphold." ' [7]

THE BAPTIST'S ' FIELD SERMON '

Aware that he still lacked the necessary confirmation as the successor of King Herod the Great by Augustus, Archelaus natur-ally enough sought to appease the excited masses, yet was unable to prevent the outbreak of open rebellion on the part of the pilgrims who streamed into the temple on the feast of the Passover of 4 B.C.   To follow the account of the *Halōsis* : [8]

> ' And he sent the commander of his troops and entreated them to desist from these wicked proceedings.   When this (officer) came into the temple, they pelted him with stones, before he had even uttered a word, because they wished to provoke a war.   And when the feast of unleavened bread, called Passover, began at the time (when) a multitude of sacrifices is offered to God, countless numbers of the people came from the whole country to worship ; and the insurgents *stood in the temple unnoticed* and suddenly leapt up. And all were thrown into confusion.   And Archelaus sent in (troops) to arrest the leaders of the insurgents.   Thereupon the whole multitude flung themselves upon them ; and many of the (troops) sent they thrashed with clubs, while the commander escaped with difficulty, streaming with blood.   And then, as if they had done nothing wrong, they proceeded to the sacrifice.   But when Archelaus saw that they would not be quieted without bloodshed, he sent against them all his troops, the infantry across the city [9] and the cavalry across the plain.   These fell upon the men engaged in offer-ing their sacrifices and slew 30,000 (of them). [10]   And their feast was turned into mourning, according to the saying (in Scripture). [11]

---

[1] *Midrash Ps.* xliii. § 1 ;   Strack-Billerbeck, i. 87.
[2] *Ps.* cv. 26.   [3] *Ps.* xliii. 3.   [4] *Numb.* viii. 2.
[5] *Ps.* cxxxii. 11.   [6] *Mal.* iii. 23.   [7] *Is.* xlii. 1.
[8] ii. 8 *sqq.*   Ber.-Grass, p. 233.
[9] Thus the Greek text.   The Slavonic has ' across the plain ' in both cases, which is an obvious error.
[10] *B.J.* : 3000 ; so *Egesippus.*   [11] *Amos* viii. 10 ; *Job* ii. 6.

But the rest of the multitude dispersed into the mountains and woods.[1] The heralds of Archelaus followed them proclaiming that every one of them might go to his home, now that they had abandoned the festival.'

The rebels, however, had no intention of giving up the contest, the less so because their attack was also directed against the Romans, who at that moment, under the governorship of Sabinus, were cordially detested. ' While he (Augustus) was still considering (whether he should appoint Archelaus king) '—so we read in the *Halōsis* (ii. 39)—' a letter was brought from Varus, the governor of Syria, announcing that the Jews were up in arms, because they did not wish to be under Roman rule '; this at a time when one of the Jews had just explained in Rome that ' the people wished to live in independence (i.e. without the Herodian kings) under the administration of Roman governors.' So far the account in the *Halōsis*. In the *War* [2] Josephus has utilized further information sent by Sabinus and Varus to Augustus, so that the course of events can be reconstructed in greater detail :

> ' On the arrival of Pentecost it was not the customary ritual so much as indignation which drew the people in crowds to the capital. A vast multitude flocked in from Galilee, from Idumaea, from Jericho, and from Peraea beyond the Jordan, but it was the native population of Judaea itself which, both in numbers and in ardour, was pre-eminent. Dividing into three bands, they formed three camps, one on the north of the temple, another on the south, adjoining the hippodrome, and the third near Herod's palace, on the west. Thus investing the Romans on all sides, they held them under siege.'

There followed the frightful battle in which the gorgeous porticoes of Herod's temple perished in the flames ; [3] the besieging of Sabinus in Antonia ; the desertion to the insurgents of the bulk of Herod's troops, with the exception of the Sebastenians of Samaria ; the rising against the Romans of Herod's veterans in Idumaea ; and the insurrections in Galilee and Transjordania. Three different leaders simultaneously appear, each claiming to be the liberator-king whose advent had been promised by John. In Galilee there was Judah b. Ḥezekiah the Gaulanite ; [4] in Peraea a former slave of Herod named Simon, a man whose audacity Josephus expressly attributes to his tall and handsome figure, aspired to the throne. The same claim was made by a shepherd, likewise of powerful stature and extraordinary strength, with the queer name of

---

[1] The *Halōsis* frequently mentions woods where there are only bare rocks to-day (cf., e.g., ii. § 511 ; Ber.-Grass, p. 329).

[2] *B.J.*, ii. 3. 1, § 42 *sqq.*

[3] *Ass. Mos.*, vi. 9 : ' A part of the temple they will burn with fire.'

[4] See above, p. 253 nn. 3-6.

Athrongas or Athrongaeus,[1] i.e. the *ethrog* or citrus fruit, the apple from Adam's tree in Paradise.[2] But whereas Simon and Athrongas were got rid of by Gratus, Ptolemaeus, and Archelaus,[3] Judah the Gaulanite must have maintained his hold in the mountains or deserts, even after the crushing of the revolt by Varus and the crucifixion of thousands of the insurgents ; after the banishment of Archelaus he appears again under the administration of Coponius as a leader of rebels.[4]

This time it was the census of Quirinius, governor of Syria (A.D. 6-7), which caused the flames of rebellion to break out afresh. The date when Judah fell and his followers were dispersed cannot be precisely fixed, but his work was carried on by his sons and the so-called Zealots or *Qan'anāia*. ' It is to their machinations that we must ascribe the continuous smouldering of the fire of revolution under the ashes, until finally, sixty years later, it burst forth in a mighty flame ' (Schürer).[5]

Nothing, then, could be clearer than that the saying of Jesus, ' From the days of the Baptist until to-day the kingdom of heaven is being stormed and men of violence take it by force,'[6] refers to the insurrections of the reign of Archelaus, undertaken to establish a national kingdom by the grace of God, i.e. a messianic theocracy. The ' men of violence ' (βιασταί) are the champions of the guerilla war of independence[7] against the Romans, dwelling as ' outsiders,' ' outcasts ' (*barjonîm*), in the mountains and deserts, and called by their opponents λῃσταί, *latrones*, bandits or plunderers.[8] The famous encomium upon the Baptist[9] as the greatest of all men yet born, because before his time Moses and the prophets had only *spoken* and prophesied of the kingdom of God, whereas he had been the first to attempt a realization of the idea, to ' prepare the way,' surely implies that Jesus attributed to the Baptist the authorship of the Zealotic activist movement for independence. Josephus, on the other hand—or, better, the report of Coponius to the emperor—regarded the Galilaean as the originator of a fourth party. The apparent contradiction is easily explained on the supposition that the Zealots of Judah and the Naṣōraeans of the Baptist, as the result of inevitable

---

[1] Names of this type are not uncommon ; cf. *Rimmon* (='pomegranate '), *Zethan* (='olive '), above, p. 241 n. 2. The symbolism of the Christ considered as the fruit of the ' tree of Life ' has been transferred from Athrongas to Jesus, to whom we find it applied in Christian art and poetry.

[2] *Midr. Gen. r.*, sect. xvi. 16a.

[3] *B.J.*, ii. 4. 2 and 3.   [4] *B.J.*, ii. 8. 1.

[5] i[4]. p. 487, Engl. transl., div. 1., vol. ii., p. 81.

[6] For the political meaning of ἁρπάζουσιν, cf. *John* vi. 15 : '' ἁρπάζουσιν αὐτὸν ἵνα ποιήσωσιν αὐτὸν βασιλέα,'' and Josephus, *B.J.*, ii. § 264 : '' ἁρπάζεται εἰς τὴν ἀρχὴν Κλαύδιος.''

[7] Thus Klausner and Danby, *Jesus of Nazareth*, London, 1924, p. 206 n. 46.

[8] See above, p. 10,   [9] *Matt.* xi. 11-13.

differences of opinion, early parted company, and that after the breach the followers of Judah disclaimed their dependence on the Baptist's teaching. We know that precisely the same phenomenon of a parting of the ways took place afterwards between the disciples of Jesus and those of John, both disclaimers being clearly contrary to all historical probability.

That the Baptist actually did preach during and in consequence of the risings in Peraea and the Jordan district in the time of Archelaus may, moreover, be seen quite clearly from the summary report of John's teachings as contained in *Luke*.[1] The words in question must have been a sort of field sermon delivered before the march into battle. Here is the traditional translation of the crucial passage :

' And soldiers (or warriors) also asked him, saying, " And what must *we* do ? " ' etc.

But in this translation no regard is had to the fact that the Greek word is not στρατιῶται, ' soldiers,' but στρατευόμενοι, i.e. ' persons on the warpath,' or ' going to war,' or ' engaged in war.'[2] If the Baptist in the reign of Archelaus preached to persons ' going to war,' it is, in view of the contents of his sermon as reported by Josephus, perfectly inconceivable that he preached to the troops of Varus, Archelaus, or the generals Gratus or Ptolemaeus. But it is perfectly understandable that he should have addressed the revolutionary champions of liberty who had flocked to him from Judaea, and especially from the neighbourhood of Jerusalem, to take refuge in the wild thickets and marshes in the Jordan valley.[3]

The contents of his address, ' Do violence to no man (μηδένα διασείσητε), extort from no man by intimidation, make no (predatory) raids upon houses (μηδένα συκοφαντήσητε), be content with your rations,' closely correspond to the exhortation to military discipline which Josephus claims to have delivered himself to the volunteers and insurgents, the so-called ' robbers ' (λῃσταί), whom he recruited in Galilee. Thus reads the *Halōsis* :[4]

' And he collected a hundred thousand young men, armed them and taught them the art of warfare. . . . And he said to them, " If you thirst for victory, abstain from the ordinary crimes, theft, robbery, and rapine. And do not defraud your countrymen ; count it no advantage to yourselves to injure another. For the war will

---

[1] iii. 14.
[2] Cf. 1 *Cor.* ix. 7 : " τίς στρατεύεται ἰδίοις ὀψωνίοις ποτέ," ' who ever caters for himself during a campaign ? ' (A.V. ' who goeth a warfare any time at his own charges ? ').
[3] *Mark* i. 5. Cf. 1 *Macc.* ix. 45.
[4] ii. §§ 576 and 581 ; Ber.-Grass, p. 339 *sq.* The corresponding part of the *War* is in indirect address and rather condensed.

have better success if the warriors have a good name and [1] *their souls are conscious of having purified themselves from every offence.*[2] If, however, they are condemned by their evil deeds, then will God be their enemy and the aliens (will) have an easy victory.'' '

The agreement in contents between the Baptist's exhortation to the στρατευόμενοι and this address of Josephus to his recruits cannot, I think, be missed. The words about the *purification of souls from every offence* as a condition essential to success bear so close a resemblance to Josephus' words discussed above [3] about the purifying effect of John's baptism, that one would be tempted to suspect some after-effect of the Baptist's preaching upon Zealot circles. Perhaps Josephus had heard these or very similar words from the mouth of his baptist teacher, ' Banus.' [4] But it is well to admit the possibility of a mere coincidence, since the idea of a lustration before marching into battle, regarded as a judgment of God, is fairly obvious.[5]

The banality of the whole sermon, traditionally regarded as a sort of homiletic exposition of the duties incumbent on the various walks of life, disappears at once if considered as a simple address delivered on a very definite occasion to the combatants for freedom. In this difficult situation, with no regular military supplies, they ask the Baptist as their *kohen mashuah milḥamah*, their ' priest dedicated to warfare ' [6] or ' army chaplain ': ' What should *we* do ? ' And he replies that they should as far as possible, as comrades-in-arms, help each other out. ' Let him who has two under-garments give to him that hath none, and he that hath provisions,[7] let him do likewise.' As a general summons to an unlimited surrender of every superfluity beyond the barest needs, this sermon is as hard to understand as it is simple and easy to explain when regarded as an injunction to meet an immediate necessity.

Last come the publicans, the *mokᵉsin* or tax-gatherers, asking for their instructions and getting them. The reason why they have to enquire is the fact that the rebels had demanded of Archelaus the abolition of the oppressive taxes and duties, and

---

[1] The italicized words are wanting in the Greek *War*.

[2] Cp. Ps.-Philo, *Bibl. Ant.*—a midrash composed by the zealots around the revolutionary high priest Phineas and Prince Kenedaios of Adiabene between 66 and 70 A.D.—ch. xxv. (transl. M. R. James, p. 147) : ' God said to them : If you go up with a pure heart, fight ! but if your heart is defiled, go not ! ''

[3] See above, p. 249.   [4] See above, p. 23 n. 2.

[5] *Joel*. iv. 9 : '' ἁγιάσετε πόλεμον,'' *hithqadesh milḥamah*. *Jerem*. vi. 4 ; *Josh*. iii. 5 : *qiddesh milḥamah*. *Mic*. iii. 5.

[6] *Sota*, viii. 1 (42a) : ' the priest ordained for war through unction with the sacred oil or by putting on the eight high-priestly garments. For he made an address to the army marching out.'

[7] Cf. 1 *Sam*. xvii. 17, 2 *Sam*. xvii. 28, on the rather primitive provisioning of an army in war through voluntary contributions of the kinsmen of the soldiering men.

that therefore the insurgents might have been expected to do away with them. Hence their question and his answer. Given the present emergency and the necessity for finding the finances necessary for the war of liberation and the maintenance of troops, the Baptist rules, very naturally, that the taxes should be exacted, but no more than the prescribed amount, that is, without the illegal supertaxation which the publicans and tax-collectors in the service of Herod or the Romans had hitherto claimed for themselves. Thus, notwithstanding the continuance of the levy, the people would still obtain considerable relief.

Here again we get a simple and yet sufficient and plausible explanation of instructions in practical politics meant for a particular emergency, but which, if regarded as prophetic *torah* and general moral advice, must needs appear highly trivial—too trivial, indeed, to be solemnly proclaimed as a new moral code.

THE POLITICAL SIGNIFICANCE OF JOHN'S BAPTISM

' And he shall . . . turn the disobedient to the wisdom of the just; to make ready a people prepared for the Lord.'

LUKE i. 17.

The foregoing remarks strongly suggest that the baptism in the Jordan by the preacher of liberty should be regarded as a special lustration rite preceding the march to war, and, as on the Day of Atonement, took the form of a purification of souls from every offence through a public confession of sins.[1] In the same spirit the Israelites of old, at Mizpah, before the decisive battle against the Philistines, ' drew water and poured it out before Jahweh and fasted and confessed, We have sinned against Jahweh.'[2] The two great ' confessions of sins ' of the whole people in *Daniel*[3] and *Nehemiah*[4] may illustrate the probable words and prayers of the persons 'confessing their sins' at the Jordan baptism.[5]

Dr. Pettazzoni[6] has shown by a long array of instances that the oral acknowledgment of sins is regularly accompanied by a symbolical, originally magical, act of casting off a burden or removing a defilement. That explains why the word *jadah*, ' cast,' is used, in the Hiphil form *hodah*, to express the verbal action ' to confess.'[7] One such symbolic act, representing man's guilt and his release from it, is the drawing and pouring out of water at Mizpah. Other similar acts are the shaking out of sins over running water or over the fishes in the stream, a rite still practised

[1] Called *widduj* ; *Joma* iii. 8, iv. 2, vi. 2.
[2] I *Sam.* vii. 6.   [3] ix. 4-19.   [4] ix. 2 *sq.*, 6-57.
[5] *Mark* i. 5 ; *Matt.* iii. 6.
[6] *Annales de l'histoire du Christianisme*, 1928, Paris-Amsterdam, i. 96 *sqq.*
[7] Lagarde, *Orientalia*, ii. 22.

by orthodox Jews on New Year's Day, and some years ago proved
to be of Babylonian origin.[1] The practice, called ἄφεσις ἁμαρτιῶν,
'remissio peccatorum,' 'sending off of sins,' is known to the Jews
as *thash᷎lih̬*, 'thou wilt wash down,' or 'send down,' from the
passage in Micah [2] used in the penitents' prayer on that occasion :

> 'yea, thou wilt wash away all our sins into the depths of the sea.
> Thou wilt fulfil . . . the promises of mercy to Abraham, which thou
> hast sworn unto our fathers from the days of old.'

The passage is also used with reference to baptism in patristic
tradition.[3] Since already in the *Didachē* running water appears
to be no longer essential for Christian baptism, the train of thought
must originally have referred to baptism in the Jordan and go back
to the preaching of the Baptist. The introduction to John's
sermon [4] runs :

> 'Ye offspring of vipers, who has warned you to flee from the
> wrath to come ? . . . Think not to say within yourselves, We have
> Abraham for our father, for I say unto you, that God is able of these
> stones to raise up (new) children unto Abraham ' (*sc.* if you are
> submerged).

This introduction becomes at once intelligible if the Baptist linked
his sermon on to the speech of Micah [5] just mentioned, in which the
terror of the heathen (who are compared to serpents) at the impending judgment is contrasted with the confident hope of the
children of Abraham in the forgiveness of their sins.

In any case, the most remarkable feature in this sermon to 'the
multitudes' is the fact that the preacher refuses to recognize the
crowds [6] who stream to him for baptism and purification as children of Abraham, i.e. as Israelites or Jews, but vilifies them as
' sons of vipers ' [7] and requires them to undergo a bath of purification like *heathen* proselytes.

---

[1] See my *Orpheus*, London, 1921 (Watkins), p. 141. Cf. *ibid.*, pl. xlviii.

[2] vii. 19 *sq.*

[3] Cf., e.g., Rupertus Tuitiensis in Migne, *P.L.*, clxviii. 525.

[4] *Matt.* iii. 7-9 ; *Luke* iii. 7 *sq.*

[5] vii. 15-20 : ' As in the days of thy coming forth out of the land of Egypt
let him (thy people) see marvellous things. The nations shall see and be ashamed
of all (their trust in all) their might . . . their ears shall be deaf. They shall lick
the dust like *the serpent*, like crawling things of the earth . . . and shall be afraid
because of thee. Who is a God like unto thee, that *forgiveth the iniquity* and *passeth
by the transgression* of the remnant of his heritage, that retaineth not his anger for
ever, because he delighteth in mercy ? He will turn again and have compassion
upon us . . . yea, thou wilt *cast all our sins into the depths of the sea*. Thou wilt
show the truth to Jacob and *the mercy to Abraham*, which thou hast sworn unto our
fathers from the days of old.'

[6] *Luke* iii. 7 ; *Matt.* iii. 7 : ' Pharisees ' and ' Sadducees ' are an attempt to
restrict the injurious words to the scribes.

[7] In ch. ix. 20 of the Damascus document quoted above, p. 254 n. 9, the militant
disciples of the Baptist explain the ' dragon's poison ' and the ' cruel venom of
asps ' in *Deut.* xxxii. 33 as denoting ' the kings of the heathen ' and ' the chief of
the kings of Javan '—that is, the Roman emperor.

The explanation of this astonishing demand, and consequently of what is really the central problem of John's baptism, is furnished by a most valuable statement of Josephus [1] on the followers of 'Ele'azar, a descendant of that Judas of Galilee whose doctrines, as has been shown above,[2] were in closest agreement with those of the Baptist. These irreconcilable combatants for the liberty of the Jewish people declared that those who submitted to Roman rule were apostates from their race and *in no way different from the heathen*. One sees at once that this is a logical deduction drawn from the Deuteronomic 'royalty law,' the observance and enforcement of which forms the ' way of the law,' practised by the Baptist and after him by Judah the Gaulanite.[3]

The recognition of the non-Jewish royal house of the Herods, and still more that of the Roman overlords, constitute an apostasy from the kingdom of God and of the divinely selected future national king—nay, the unpardonable apostasy which, so long as the culprits do not repent, excludes them from the community of the descendants of Abraham. According to this doctrine, one cannot be both a Jew and a servant of heathen masters, a subject of the theocracy and a slave of Caesar, the enemy of God and lord of this world. Only he who repents of the sins which the people committed by their submission to Herod, Pompey, Caesar, and Augustus, he who is 'converted' and confesses (casts off) his sins, can be readopted as a son of the kingdom of heaven. Since all Israel has through its defection to Herod sunk into heathenism, the renovated Israel which believes in a Messiah—in other words, waits for a national king—will consist wholly of newly reclaimed converts, dying to heathenism through the baptism [4] of proselytes and rising regenerated from the water.[5] Only now the expression used by Josephus [6] becomes intelligible, βαπτισμῷ συνιέναι, ' to congregate,' ' be united' through baptism—to the new συναγωγή of a new people of Israel. As God has smitten his apostate faithless people on account of their sins and delivered them to their enemies, so now when they again return to him and acknowledge his name he will hearken to them, forgive them their sins, and restore to them the land which he gave to their fathers. This ' confession of the name of God,' that is, of God as the true ruler and lord of the world, and of his Messiah, i.e. the national king, and at the same time the repudiation and abjuration of any allegiance to the false and un-

---

[1] *B.J.*, vii. 8. 1, § 253 *sqq.* [2] See p. 252 ff. [3] See above, p. 250 n. 7.
[4] Cf. *Col.* ii. 12 : " ἐν τῇ ἀπεκδύσει τοῦ σώματος . . . συνταφέντες ἐν τῷ βαπτισμῷ."
Tit., iii. 5 : " λουτρὸν παλιγγενεσίας."
[5] According to Jewish doctrine the proselyte through baptism by immersion becomes like a newborn child in the literal sense, so that he can no longer inherit from his heathen relations nor commit incest with them. Cf.W. Brandt, *Z.A.T.W.*, suppl. xviii. 56-62.
[6] *Ant.*, xviii. § 117, above, p. 246.

godly lord of this world, is what is meant by the expression
βαπτίζεσθαι ἐν ὀνόματι κυρίου in John's baptism. The disciples
of Jesus, later on, demand the additional confession of faith
that their master, Jesus, and not any other of the various
claimants, is that Messiah, the true king-liberator, chosen by God.
Through this solemn declaration of allegiance to the kingship of
God and his viceroy, preceding or accompanying the baptismal
immersion, the whole rite acquired a significance quite analogous
to that of the ordinary soldier's oath in the Roman army, an oath
taken in the name of the emperor [1] by the commanders, immediately before marching out. Through this oath only, the soldier's
service becomes a *solemnis et sacrata militia*, and we know that the
Jews, too, had peculiar rites for the sanctification of war.[2] This
analogy explains why baptism is so often called, in the terminology
of the Roman Church, a *sacramentum*, a Latin word meaning
primarily and essentially the soldier's oath of allegiance.[3]
Indeed, the baptismal confession *is* the soldier's oath in the *militia
Christi*, the army of the fighters for the Messiah.[4] As early as the
second century, in the ninety-sixth epistle of Pliny to the Emperor
Trajan, we hear about the Christians stating: 'seque sacra-
mento . . . obstringere, ne furta, ne latrocinia, ne adulteria com-
mitterent, ne fidem fallerent, ne depositum appellati abnegarent.'
Even the formula of this early Christian *sacramentum* may well be
understood as a soldier's oath, pledging himself not to rob, nor to
plunder, nor to rape, nor to break faith, nor to deny when called
to account for property received in trust. The new Israel, regenerated through the baptism of John into a ' new covenant ' with
the national God, is primarily a militia of the coming Messiah, an
army of the Christ, the future anointed national king who is their
war-lord and army commander [5] and to whose service [6] their
soldiers' lives are devoted.

---

[1] Tac., *Ann.*, i. 8, xv. 16 ; *Hist.*, i. 55, iv. 31 ; Pliny, *Ep.*, x. 60 ; Tertull.,
Apost., 16.

[2] Cf. above, p. 266 n. 5. The covenanters of Damascus are ' mustered ' even
as soldiers (xvii. 2), and they have to take an ' oath of the covenant ' (xix. 8).

[3] Cf. Livy, x. 38, on the *sacramentum* taken by the Samnite army before
marching to war. Justin, xx. 4, calls the oath of the members of the Pythagorean
order a *sacramentum* (=συνωμοσία ; *Apol.*, ap. Jambl., 260).

[4] This important evidence is time and again neglected by commentators such
as the Rev. Alban Blakiston, who declares (*John Baptist and his relation to Jesus*,
London, 1912, p. 220 *sq.*) : ' The baptism of John . . . bound its recipients to no
sort of discipleship and it initiated them into no sort of religious community,' etc.

[5] Cf. Ignat., *Ad Polyc.*, vi. 2 : ' please your war-lord from whom you get your
pay, so that none of you should be found a deserter. Let baptism be
your armour. . . .'

[6] The symbolism is derived from *Job* vii. 1 : ' Militia (*saba*) est vita hominis
super terram et sicut dies mercenarii dies eius.'

BAPTISM AS A PLEDGE OF SALVATION IN THE DAYS OF THE LAST JUDGMENT

The foregoing enquiries have made it clear that the baptism of John was basically the baptism of Jewish ritual prescribed to all proselytes, and which the prophet and chosen high priest with inexorable rigour imposed upon Jews who, by their failure to observe the Deuteronomic 'royalty law,' had apostatized from God and from their nation. This baptism, then, was in the first instance an outward sign that they earnestly desired liberty, that is, the 'kingdom of God,' independence of foreign despots, and victory in the holy war. Yet it is no less certain that in the Baptist's eyes it was also a way of escape from the 'wrath to come,' that is, from the last judgment. It was truly a 'washing for salvation,' an 'eschatological sacrament in view of the final judgment.' [1]

Such an institution cannot well be understood unless one bears in mind not only the pertinent predictions of the prophets but also the prevailing universal conviction of the immediate proximity of the 'kingdom of God' [2] and the immediately impending destruction of 'the present world.' This conviction, quite unintelligible on the basis of the chronology hitherto accepted, had at that time been brought about by the discussions concerning the Shilo 'for whom the gentiles wait,' by the calculation of the 'year-weeks' of Daniel's prophecy,[3] and finally by the death of Herod the Great. The explanation of this baptism in the waters of Jordan must therefore be sought in the relevant prophecies concerning the Last Days.

It was pointed out long ago that the waters of the Jordan and the Jarmuk are, in the eyes of Jewish rabbis,[4] particularly unsuitable for a religious bath of purification, since they are a mixture of 'dead' (i.e. marshy or stagnant) water and 'living' spring water. Now, John was essentially a man intent upon the 'fulfilment of all righteousness,' and cannot therefore be supposed to have displayed the antinomian indifference to Pharisaic scruples peculiar to the later Christians.[5] Nor can he have been content merely to accommodate himself to accidental circumstances.

Now, a passage in *Ezekiel* [6] foretells that in the last days a

---

[1] Albert Schweitzer, *G.L.J.F.*[3], Tübingen, 1921, p. 424 (Engl. trans. by W. Montgomery, *The Quest of the Historical Jesus*, London, 1911, p. 377).

[2] *Matt.* iii. 2 : 'Turn back, for the kingdom of heaven has drawn near.'

[3] See above, p. 137 n. 16.

[4] *Parah*, viii. 10 ; cf. W. Brandt, suppl. xviii. 2 to *Z.A.T.W.*, pp. 80 *sqq.* and 47 *sq.*

[5] According to *Acts* viii. 36 *sqq.*, the Christians baptized in any puddle by the wayside. *Didachē*, cap. vii., declares any water whatsoever suitable for baptism.

[6] xlviii. 1-9. Cf. *Isaiah* i. 16-20.

spring will issue from under the threshold of the temple at Jerusalem, the overflow of which will run down into the deep hollow
of the lower course of the Jordan and the Dead Sea, and sweeten
the brackish or salt water in that region. ' Every living creature
which swarmeth, whithersoever the river cometh, shall live. . . .
And by the river, upon the bank thereof, on this side and on that,
shall grow every tree for meat, whose leaf shall not wither, neither
shall the fruit thereof fail.' It is at once evident that the Baptist
connected this passage with another prophecy of Ezekiel,[1] long
since recognized as fundamental for his doctrine, and that in this
invisible temple spring flowing down to the Jordan, and removing
its disabilities, he discovered the ' pure water ' which God had
promised to pour out upon Israel to purge the people from the
filth of idolatry and to ' give them a new spirit.' Here, too, was
the ' fountain ' which, according to the prophet Zechariah,[2] will
be opened up to the house of David and to the inhabitants of
Jerusalem for purification from all defilement and sin. From
Ezekiel's promise of the *fruit-bearing* trees which are to thrive
on the banks of Jordan in place of the brushwood now standing
there, the Baptist derives his warning to the multitudes flocking
together to receive baptism, ' to bring forth good fruits of repentance.' The same metaphor, employed alike by Christians[3] and
Mandaeans,[4] of the newly ' planted ' believers thus originates in
the Baptist's allegory: every 'tree which bears no fruit ' will be cut
down and cast into the fire. 'Bring forth, therefore, fruit worthy
of repentance.'[5]

The figure of the fall of the barren trees[6] on the day of judgment is likewise borrowed from the language of the Old Testament
prophets. In *Isaiah*[7] we read that

' there shall come a day of Jahweh upon all that is proud and
haughty and upon all that is lifted up, and upon all the oaks of Bashan ';
and again :[8]

' Behold, the Lord, Jahweh of hosts, loppeth the boughs with
terror : and the high of stature are felled and the lofty are brought
low. The thickets of the forest are cut down with iron, and Lebanon
shall fall by a mighty one. But there shall come forth a shoot
from the stock of Jesse, and a twig from his roots shall bear
fruit . . .' etc.

In *Ezekiel*[9]

' the mighty one of the nations fells the lofty cedar of Lebanon and
deals with it according to its wickedness.'

---

[1] xxxvi. 16, 25 *sq.*, 31.　　　　[2] xiii. 1.　　　　[3] 1 *Cor.* iii. 6 ; 1 *Tim.* iii. 6, etc.
[4] See index to Lidzbarski's *Mand. Liturgies*, p. 292, s.v. ' Pflanzung.'
[5] *Matt.* iii. 8 should follow v. 10.
[6] It was also taken over by Jesus ; cf. *Matt.* vii. 18.
[7] ii. 12 *sq.*　　　　　　　[8] x. 33, xi. 1.　　　　　　　[9] xxxi. 12.

The axe itself which the Lord will wield at the judgment comes from *Psalm* xxxv. 3, where Jahweh brandishes the spear and battle-axe against his enemies. The ' Scythian ' word [1] here employed, *s*gor*, *σαγαρίς*, Lat. *securis,* shows that the Psalmist has transferred to Jahweh the tree-splitting lightning-stroke of the double axe of the heathen thunder-gods.

The allegorical interpretation of the trees [2] which in Ezekiel's vision grow on the banks of Jordan allows us to see how the Baptist, too, understood metaphorically the messianic stream welling up from under the threshold of the temple, the *ὕδωρ ἀφέσεως* of the Septuagint.[3] Like the prophet Ezekiel, the fourth evangelist,[4] and the author of the *First Epistle of Peter*,[5] he, too, read in his *Isaiah* [6] the word of Jahweh concerning the foundation-stone of the temple :

> ' Behold I lay in Zion (a living stone), a tried stone, a precious threshold stone as foundation. (Out of its hollow shall flow streams of living water ;) he that believeth in me shall not perish.'

The water streaming out from beneath the threshold must there-fore have seemed to him symbolical of a living faith in Jahweh or of the cleansing righteousness of *Amos*.[7]

To understand how far the washing in Jordan could have appeared to the Baptist as a pledge of salvation in the last judg-ment, we must go back again to Ezekiel's prophecy.[8] The water of the messianic spring, which at first merely trickles through the walls, rapidly increases in volume, first ankle-deep, then knee-deep,[9] then reaching to the loins, until finally it becomes a stream which none can wade through, which must be crossed by swim-ming. As is shown by the *Odes of Solomon*,[10] these words inevit-ably call up a picture of a flood gradually covering the whole earth. That such was the prophet's meaning can hardly be doubted ; for according to ancient pre-Israelitish folklore [11] the whole rock on the Temple Mount of Jerusalem, the foundation-stone (*'eben shethijah*) of the world, shuts the entry to the cosmic water-cavern of the abyss, to the primaeval flood beneath the earth. And thus the world was constantly threatened by a flood, held back only with difficulty through the talismanic power of the name of God, when this stone was moved at the time of David's

---

[1] See *Herodot.*, i. 215.
[2] Cp. *Ps.* i. 2, 3 ; *Jerem.* xvii. 7, 8 ; *Is.* lxi. 3 ; *Ep. Barn.* xi.
[3] *Ezek.* xlvii. 4, for *majîm birkaîm,* ' knee-deep water.'
[4] *John* vii. 38.   [5] ii. 4.
[6] xxviii. 16. On the reconstructed text of this verse, cf. my *Orpheus*, London, 1921, p. 148 f.
[7] v. 24.   [8] xlvii. 1-12.   [9] See above, n. 3.
[10] vi. 7 *sqq.* : ' a brook has gone out and grown into a stream long and broad which has inundated everything and brought it to the temple.'
[11] Dr. Moses Gaster in *Folklore*, vol. ii. p. 204.

S

excavations for the temple of Solomon. Consequently, and with
a simple word-play, this foundation-stone (*'eben shethijah*) was
regarded also as a ' stone of drinking ' (*'eben shethijah*), the idea
being readily suggested that out of it there would at some future
time burst forth ' streams of living water,' watering, as in David's
time—nay, flooding—the whole world.

Such a flood in the final messianic age must naturally have
appeared as a ' deluge of judgment ' in the light of the pertinent
prophetic utterances. ' With an overrunning flood ' will Jahweh
' make a full end of those who resist him.'[1] ' Only a remnant
in Israel shall return : a consumption is determined, a flood of
righteousness. For a consumption, and that determined, shall
the Lord, Jahweh Sabaoth, make throughout all the land.'[2]
' Because you have said . . . when the overflowing scourge shall
pass through, it shall not come unto us . . . the hail shall sweep
away the refuge of lies, and the waters shall overflow the hiding-[3]
place. And your covenant with death shall be disannulled and
your agreement with Sheol shall not stand ; when the overflowing
scourge passeth along, ye shall be crushed by it ; as often as it
passeth along, it shall take you away.'[4]

In the *Book of Enoch*[5] the final judgment is viewed as a repetition of Noah's flood, which is spoken of as the ' first end of the
world.' To the Baptist, who regarded himself as a reincarnation
of the 'Enosh, in whose day men first ' began to call upon the name
of the Lord,' the judgment flood must rather have appeared as a
repetition of that first partial deluge[6] which, according to Jewish
Hagadah,[7] in the time of the first 'Enosh, the grandson of Adam,
destroyed a great part of the earth and swept away the reprobate
' generation of 'Enosh.'

Just as Paul interpreted the passage of Israel through the
Red Sea as a baptism in the sea,[8] through which the chosen people
waded as through a ' flood of salvation,' whilst their enemies were
drowned ; or again, as his disciple Silvanus[9] taught, that baptism
is the counterpart of the Noachian flood by which the righteous
were once saved,—even so still earlier must the Baptist have
expounded the immersion and metaphorical drowning of the

---

[1] *Nahum* i. 8.   [2] *Isaiah* x. 22 *sq.*
[3] I.e. the holy rock on Mt. Zion.
[4] *Isaiah* xxviii. 15 *sqq.*   [5] xci. 5-10 ; xciii. 4.
[6] This flood in the days of 'Enosh is in fact adduced by the rabbis (*Pal. Sheq.*,
vi. 50a, 3), in a commentary on Ezekiel's vision of the stream issuing from the
sanctuary and flooding the whole world, to explain a difficult expression in xlvii.
8 : ' They flow into the sea of the waters "that have broken forth" : that is, the
great sea (the ocean). Why is it called *ḥamuṣaim* ? (as if it were a dual), "the
two that have broken forth " : once in the age of 'Enosh, and once in the age of
the dispersion.'
[7] *Bereshith rabba*, 23.
[8] 1 *Cor.* x. 1 *sq.* See Joach. Jeremias, *Z.N.T.W.*, xxviii., 1929, pp. 314 ff.
[9] 1 *Pet.* iii. 20 *sq.*

apostate Jews in the Jordan as a salutary anticipation of the destruction in the final deluge. He who now submits to purification in the waters of Jordan escapes ' the wrath to come ' : penitential conversion (*shubha*, Aram. *thubᵊ*) is the ark (*thebah*) which will rescue Israel from the flood of divine displeasure.[1] ' As were the days of Noe, so will be the days of the new Enosh,' [2] the ' Son of Man.'

THE MESSIANIC BAPTISM WITH WIND AND FIRE

After what has been said, the sequence of thought in the Baptist's preaching will in its main essentials be intelligible. The message—his secret not to be revealed to unworthy ears [3]— is wholly built upon the imagery of the ancient prophets :

' Ye offspring of vipers, who hath warned *you* how to escape from the wrath to come ?   Think not to say, We have Abraham for father : for I say unto you that God is able of these stones to raise up children unto Abraham. Even now is the axe laid to the root of the trees : every tree that bringeth not forth good fruit is hewn down and cast into the fire.   Bring forth, therefore, meet fruits of repentance.   I baptize you with water, but he that cometh after me, whose shoes I am not worthy to draw off, he will baptize you with wind and with fire.   His fan is already in his hand and he will sweep his threshing-floor, and gather the wheat into his garner, but the chaff he will burn up with unquenchable fire.'

In the same first psalm, in which the Baptist found the comparison of the righteous to a fruit-bearing tree planted by the water-courses, he read the reverse picture : [4]

' Not so the wicked : they are like the chaff which the wind driveth away.   Therefore the wicked shall not stand in the judgment.'

As is well known, in the Orient the separation of the chaff from the wheat is effected by the wind, against which the as yet unseparated grains and chaff are cast by the winnowing fan.   The second purification, therefore, which the Baptist predicts for the time of ' the coming one,' following upon the baptism by water, is a baptism with *wind* (*ruaḥ*=πνεύματι), not at all a baptism ' with the holy spirit.'   That the word ἁγίῳ must be an interpolation by a Christian hand into the text of the original Naṣōraean Baptist source, a document upon which both Matthew and Luke have drawn, might long since have been recognized had the correct conclusion been drawn from the statement in the *Acts of the Apostles* [5] which says in so many words that those who had been

---

[1] Samaritan tradition (Merx, suppl. xvii. to *Z.A.T.W.*, 1909, p. 82).
[2] *Matt.* xxiv. 37=*Luke* xvii. 26=Q.
[3] Above, p. 225 n. 7.   [4] *Ps.* i. 4 *sq.*   [5] xix. 2-4.

baptized with John's baptism were wholly ignorant of the idea of the ' holy spirit.'

In the book of *Isaiah* [1] the Baptist could find the prophecy of that terrible day on which the Lord would ' purge the blood-guilt of Jerusalem from her midst by the wind of judgment (*ruaḥ mishpaṭ*) and the wind of burning (*ruaḥ ba'er*),' and the prediction [2] ' Thou shalt fan them and the wind shall carry them away and the whirlwind shall scatter them.' It is with reference to this God-sent ' storm of judgment ' which will separate the chaff from the wheat that the Baptist speaks of the coming messianic king as of a winnower whose fan is already in his hand. The same prophet Isaiah [3] speaks of the day when the Lord will ' thresh (wheat) from the ear of the river (Euphrates) unto the river of Egypt ; and ye shall be gathered one by one, O ye children of Israel.' Once again in *Isaiah* [4] the people of Israel is addressed as ' O thou my threshed son (=wheat) of my threshing-floor.' The wheat which is gathered into the granary is accordingly Israel regenerated in baptism : the chaff winnowed away by the wind of judgment under the fan of the Messiah is the sinful people accounted as heathens because they have submitted to the yoke of the Romans and the Idumaean dynasty.

The last item mentioned, the burning of the chaff in unquenchable fire, is simply Malachi's prediction [5] of a purification by a world-conflagration on the Day of Doom, which will consume the malefactors like the stubble after the harvest, and will ' refine ' [6] the remnant of the people after the manner of the fire of the smelter and the chemist.[7] Such a ' fire-flood ' or ' baptism of fire ' is also expected in the prophecies of Jesus concerning the end of the world,[8] by Paul [9] and by the author of the *Second Epistle of Peter*.[10] In this last-named passage a different final catastrophe is foreseen for each age. God cannot threaten a second deluge because, according to *Gen.* ix. 14 *sq.*, he has promised no more to annihilate all flesh upon the earth by a flood [11] and to send no more floods to destroy the earth. The final judgment must therefore take the form of a conflagration.[12] But since the promise in question might be interpreted in a more restricted sense as a pledge never again in the future to exterminate *all* flesh and never to destroy the earth itself, it would not be surprising if the Baptist and Jesus himself expected a flood both of fire and of water on the

---

[1] iv. 4 ; cf. lvii. 13. [2] xli. 16. [3] xxvii. 12.
[4] xxi. 10. [5] iv. 1 ; cf. *Hab.* iii. 19. [6] *Mal.* iii. 2.
[7] The comparison is of course taken from the daily life of the wandering Rekhabite smiths. It is the common property of the prophets; cf. *Isaiah* i. 25, xlviii. 10, also my book *Das Geld*, München, 1924, p. 132 ; *Monatsschr. f. Gesch. u. Wiss. d. Judentums*, lix. (1925), p. 369 n. 1-4.
[8] *Luke* xvii. 26. [9] 2 *Thess.* i. 7. [10] ii. 6 *sq.* [11] *Isaiah* liv. 9.
[12] Ṣebaḥ. 111a, Strack-Billerbeck, ii. 354a ; *Isaiah* lxvi. 16.

day of judgment, just as of old the judgment on the 'generation of the flood' was succeeded by the judgment on the 'generation of Sodom.'

From this train of ideas one might conclude that the purification of the world or of mankind by the ' wind of judgment,' the ' baptism with wind,' represents not only a world catastrophe impending in the last days but one which occurred in the past. That this is actually so is well attested by a series of Midrashic traditions. In the third book of the *Sibylline Oracles* (101 *sqq.*) the author, an Egyptian Jew, writing under Ptolemy VII., Physcon, mentions the building of the tower of Babel, and adds: ' But forthwith the Immortal laid great constraint upon *the winds*, and thereupon the blasts hurled the great tower from its height and aroused strife in mortals against each other. But when the tower had fallen and the tongues of men had been distorted into all manner of languages, forthwith the whole earth was filled with mortals whose kingdoms were divided.' Again, in the *Book of Jubilees*,[1] a Pharisaic work composed most probably in Palestine in the last century before our era, the tower of Babel is overthrown by 'a mighty wind.' Josephus [2] tells how the generation of Nimrod decided to build a great tower to secure themselves by its height against the wrath of God in the event of another flood ; but God by the division of tongues created disunion among them. He goes on to quote a Sibylline utterance, distinct both in its phraseology and in its polytheistic character from the extant oracle, and no doubt derived from the so-called Chaldaean Sibyl of Berossus :

' Now this tower and the confusion of tongues are also mentioned by the Sibyl in these terms : " When all men spake the same language, some of them built a very lofty tower thinking thereby to ascend to heaven. But *the gods* sent winds and overturned the tower and gave a special language to each." '

According to Rabbinic tradition,[3] the tower was built in despite of God and the warnings of Abraham : the builders blasphemously said that, heaven reeling once every 1656 years (the year of the flood according to the reckoning in the *Seder 'olam rabba*), the result being that the upper waters pour down upon the earth, the firmament must be supported by a tower so that no further flood might be possible ; but the tower was blown to pieces by mighty winds.

The Syrian Church [4] is also acquainted with this story :

' There was once a deluge through wind, and the people reserved for this were slain by a terrific north wind, and the righteous

---

[1] x. 26.   [2] *Ant.*, i. 4. 2 *sq.*
[3] Ginzberg in *Jewish Encycl.*, ii. 398 *sq.*
[4] *Apology of Ps.-Melito*, ed. Otto, *Corp. Apol.*, ix. 432.

only remained alive to tell the tale. At another time came the water-flood and drowned all living creatures, and the righteous only remained alive in the ark by the will of God. So, too, at the end of time there will be a flood of fire, which will burn up the earth with all its mountains . . . but the righteous will be saved, even as those like them survived the water-flood.'

The Syrians [1] teach that the flood of wind annihilated the generation of the tower-builders ; only Abraham was saved because he at God's command had previously left the country.

There can be no doubt, then, that the Baptist supplemented this ancient conception of a return of the days of Noah and of Lot in the last days, a conception which in *Luke* is attributed to Jesus, by a mention of a return of the flood of wind such as occurred in the days of Abraham, a catastrophe to take place between the two other calamities. He doubtless interpreted in the same manner the prophecy of Zechariah [2] concerning a tripartition of mankind through divine judgment :

‘ And it shall come to pass, saith the Lord, that in all the land two parts thereof shall be cut off and die, but the third shall be left therein. And I will bring the third part through the fire, and will refine them as silver is refined, and will try them as gold is tried. They shall call on my name and I will hear them : I will say, This is my people ; and they shall say, Jahweh is my God.'

According to this prophecy the Baptist may have imagined that one-third will perish in the water, another in the storm, whilst the last third will be refined in the fire.

The Baptist clearly has in his mind this threefold trial ($\pi\epsilon\iota\rho\alpha\sigma$-$\mu\acute{o}s$) awaiting the just and the unjust ; but whilst the ordeal of passing through water, wind, and fire annihilates the wicked, the just will remain unscathed, just as the Red Sea let the chosen people pass but engulfed their enemies.

‘ And then shall all pass through the devouring fire and the unquenchable flame ; and the righteous shall all be saved, but the godless after them shall perish ’ :

so says the Sibyl.[3] Or, as we read in the *Odes of Solomon* : [4]

‘ Great rivers are the power of the Lord, and they carry headlong those who despise him, and entangle their paths, and they sweep away their fords, and catch their bodies and destroy their lives (or ‘ souls ’). For they are swifter than lightning and more fleet, and those who cross them in faith are not moved, and those who walk on them without blemish shall not be afraid. For the sign upon them [5] is that of the Lord, and the sign is the way of those who cross in the name of the Lord.'

---

[1] *Book of the Bee*, ed. Budge, p. 40 *sq.*   [2] xiii. 8 *sqq.*   [3] ii. 252 *sq.*
[4] xxxix. 1-6.   I use the translation of Dr. Rendel Harris.
[5] Cp. Ps. Sal., xv. 6.   See above, p. 234 n. 8 ; below, p. 356 n. 8.

Just as John's baptism in water is at once a lenient and a protective anticipation of the water-flood of judgment, so will the liberator-king who is to follow him grant to the elect a purification by ' wind ' and ' fire.' Whether the Baptist held that an actual rite of baptism with wind and with fire, a fanning or swinging and fumigating of sinners, and a passage of the elect through all three elements, were necessary, had better be left open. But it is worth noting that Josephus twice [1] speaks of a purifying fire (καθάρσιον πῦρ) which God through the Romans will pour out over Jerusalem.

Certain it is that Jesus did not refer this prediction to himself and never instituted such a baptism, a fact noted as strange as early as Origen.[2] The primitive Christian community saw its fulfilment in the ecstatic speaking with tongues of the disciples assembled at Pentecost, and described this experience as an outpouring of πνεῦμα, i.e. the breath of God, and of fire, i.e. of the fiery word of God,[3] on the Apostles ; they further looked upon it as a restoration of the primitive universal comprehension which was supposed to have existed between the diverse nations before the building of the fateful tower.[4] To them also it was a repetition of the wonders attending the revelation of the law on Mt. Sinai, which filled the hearers with the fear of a flood of fire.[5] The Church saw the fulfilment of the Baptist's prophecy of a messianic ' baptism with the Holy Ghost ' (to use the short formula found in Mark, corresponding to the prophecy of Ezekiel [6]) in the pneumatic gifts of grace exhibited in the neophytes. The introduction of a special eschatological rite of a baptism by spirit and fire was put in the mouth of the risen Jesus only by certain Gnostics by whom such mysteries were actually practised.[7]

It need hardly be added that the Baptist did not reach this highly complicated conception of three successive world catastrophes by flood, wind, and fire (κατακλυσμός, ἀνέμων συστροφή, ἐκπύρωσις) by piecing together, in the fashion of a mosaic, the prophetical passages quoted above. It should rather be connected with the idea, widespread in the East and partially also adopted by the Greeks, of a great ' world-year.' According to the *apokatastasis* doctrine of Berossus, which was taken over by the Stoics and probably taught still earlier by Aristotle in his lost *Protreptikos*, the ' great year ' of the world had two solstices. At the height of the world-summer, when all the planets stand in Cancer, this overheating produces the world-conflagration (ἐκπύρωσις) ; when in the world-winter they all stand in Capricorn, the result is a κατα-

[1] *B.J.*, ii. § 110 ; *Ant.*, xx. § 166.
[2] *Hom.* xxiv. on Luke, *Patrol. Or.*, xiii. 961.
[3] *Jer.* xxiii. 29.
[4] See above, p. 277.
[5] *mabbul shel 'esh* Ṣebaḥîm, 116a.
[6] Above, p. 272 l. 15.
[7] See my paper on ' The Three Baptisms in the Gnostic *Pistis Sophia*,' *The Quest*, 1924.

κλυσμός, a world-flood. But, since the Greeks, like the Egyptians, divided the year into three seasons, spring, summer, and winter, and interpreted these seasons by a cyclic ' overbearing ' (ἐπικράτεια) of the three elements, air, fire, and water, there must have been a Hellenistic theory postulating three world-cata-strophes, by water, wind, and fire, corresponding to the rainfall of winter, the equinoctial storms of spring, and the glow of the summer sun ; such a theory as is actually found in Indian tradition.[1] Under the influence of such ideas, of astrological origin, the Baptist must have regarded ' the woes of the Messiah ' as a *catastrophic year*, whose winter would induce a world-flood, its spring a catastrophic tempest, and its summer a world-conflagration. That in his case we can establish such an influence, however weak, of astrological ideas need not surprise any one.

For the point has previously been raised that in his mention of the heavenly sickle he may have referred to a constellation. The same suggestion probably holds good also for the allusion to the ' fan,' said to be already in the hand of him who is to come after him, if Schiaparelli is right in his identification of a Hebrew constellation called the ' winnowing-shovel ' (*mizrē*) in the *Book of Job* (xxxvii. 9) ; it may also, perhaps, apply to the axe or double-axe (*segor*) already laid to the root of the trees. For according to an old gloss [2] the ancients thought they could recognize in the con-stellation of Orion [3] the image of a double-axe (σκεπάρνη), more strictly speaking a pickaxe, such as would be used for the up-rooting of a useless tree. So one may well suppose that John did actually accompany the fearful words ' the axe ' and ' the fan of God ' with those threatening heavenward-pointing gesti-culations which Christian art loves to portray in its represen-tations of the Baptist, and that he received his inspiration from ' nightly visions ' while contemplating the starry heavens, like the author of the visions in *Daniel* concerning the astral beasts and the four world-kingdoms,[4] or like the seer to whom we owe the Johannine apocalypse.

The Descent of the Spirit and the Voice from Heaven at the Baptism of John in the Primitive Naṣōraean Tradition

Precisely at what time Jesus received baptism from John is a question requiring separate treatment.[5] The historicity of

---

[1] L. de la Vallée Poussin, *Encycl. Religion and Ethics*, i. 188 *sq.*
[2] *Etym. Gudianum*, 1581 n. 1.

[3] *   *   *.

[4] See vol. ii. pp. 660 ff. Germ. ed.
[5] See below, p. 293.

the baptism itself cannot well be doubted, because at an early date Christians had grave objections to the tradition as attested by *Matthew* [1] and the *Gospel of the Hebrews*.[2] On the other hand, we have to reckon seriously with the possibility that the vision at the outset of his public career and the temptation by the devil had originally, i.e. in the primitive Naṣōraean source utilized by the Synoptists, nothing whatever to do with Jesus, and were only transferred to him by means of interpolations on the part of the Christian evangelist.

As a matter of fact, in all three Synoptists the simple omission of some words immediately appended to the Baptist's preaching produces a statement which is not only no less but is indeed even more intelligible than the traditional text. Take for instance *Luke* iii. 21 *sq.* :

'Now it came to pass, when all the people were baptized, that

Jesus also having been baptized and praying,

the heaven was opened, and the Holy Spirit descended in a bodily form, as a dove, upon him, and a voice came out of heaven, ' Thou art [3] my beloved son : in thee I am well pleased.'

If the line which is here set in the margin is an interpolation, then the words ' upon him ' (ἐπ' αὐτόν) refer to ' all the people ' (ἅπαντα τὸν λαόν), and the old debated question what meaning should be attached to the words of *Isaiah* xlii. 1, quoted by the heavenly voice, is answered in quite an unexpected fashion. The opening words of the *Songs of the Servant of Jahweh* run :

' Behold my servant (LXX. ὁ παῖς μου) whom I uphold, my chosen in whom my soul delighteth : I have put my spirit upon him.'

These words, which Matthew (xii. 18) quotes from Isaiah, and with the correct translation ὁ παῖς μου, were at a very early date regarded as referring to *the people of Israel*. The Septuagint text has '*Jacob* my servant, I will help him ; *Israel* my chosen,' etc. Now, since it has been shown [4] that the intention of John's baptism was to purify the children of Abraham who had fallen away from God into servitude to the heathen, and to resuscitate a regenerate Israel, the reference of the *Bath Qōl* to the newly baptized people is perfectly in keeping. The voice from heaven greets them as they emerge, newborn like proselytes, from the water, with the words of the prophet Isaiah : ' Behold (Jacob) my servant . . .

---

[1] iii. 14 *sq.*
[3] Var. : ' this is.'
[2] Fragment 3.
[4] See above, p. 268 ff.

(Israel) my favourite, in whom my soul delighteth : I have put my spirit upon him ' ; and in fact the spirit of God descends upon them (ἐπ' αὐτόν, the people collectively), as they had been promised just before, ' He shall baptize you in (*or* with) spirit.' The breath of God glides down in the shape of a dove, because in a well-known midrash to *Gen.* i. 1 the spirit of God brooding over the waters is likened to a brooding dove, since the dove is for the Haggadists [1] a symbol of God-fearing Israel, and at the same time recalls the salvation of Noah and his sons from the flood, the prototype of the baptism of John, designed to save the new Israel of the elect from the final flood at the judgment.

It is evident, then, that the words ' my son ' (υἱός μου, instead of παῖς μου) and ' thou art ' [2] got into the quotation from *Isaiah* xlii. 1, only in consequence of contamination with a quotation from a passage of quite a different character, *Ps.* ii. 7 : ' Thou art my son, this day have I begotten thee.' The latter verse appears, indeed, in quite a number of MSS.

The two distinct passages obviously have very different meanings. The Isaiah passage certainly does not indicate an adoption of the new Israel as ' God's son,' but merely the election of God's servant to suffering. On the other hand, the passage in the famous royal psalm (ii. 7), also quoted in the *Epistle to the Hebrews* (i. 5), doubtless denotes an adoption to filial rank through υἱοθεσία, i.e. through a symbolic ritual act of regeneration. This passage has been connected by the rabbis, artificially enough, with *Is.* xlii. 1, and similarly applied to the people of Israel. Thus the *Midrash Tehillim* (on *Ps.* ii. 7, § 9) runs : ' I will tell of the decree, Jahweh said unto me, Thou art my son.' This is written in a decree of the Torah, in a decree of the Prophets, and in a decree of the Hagiographa. It is written in a decree of the Torah, ' My firstborn son is Israel ' ; [3] and it is written in a decree of the Prophets, ' Behold my servant shall deal wisely ' ; [4] and below [5] it is written, ' Behold my servant whom I uphold, my chosen in whom my soul delighteth.' [6] Thus this passage, too, may originally have referred to the adoption of ' the Israel of God ' regenerated by baptism.

In any case, the reference in *Ps.* ii. 7 to the individual who in verse 2 is called the Lord's ' anointed ' is so obvious, and must at all times have been so clearly felt, that quite naturally in *Mark* and *Matthew*, after the tentative omission of the clauses referring to the baptism of Jesus, we are left with a personal reference of the heavenly voice to the Baptist himself and not to the ' new Israel,' such as may be extracted from *Luke*.

---

[1] *Midr. Cant.*, i. 15 (93b), and other passages in Strack-Billerbeck, i. 123 f.
[2] Some MSS. have ' this is.'
[3] *Ex.* iv. 22. [4] *Isaiah* lii. 13. [5] Read ' above.' [6] *Isaiah* xlii. 1.

Mark i. 9 *sqq.* runs :

'And it came to pass in those days that

Jesus came from Nazareth of Galilee and was baptized of John in the Jordan ; and straightway coming up out of the water

he saw the heavens rent asunder, and the spirit as a dove descending upon him ; [1] and a voice came out of the heavens, Thou art my beloved son, in thee I am well pleased. And straightway the spirit driveth him forth into the wilderness.[2] And he was in the wilderness forty days tempted of Satan ; and he was with the wild beasts,[3] and the angels ministered unto him.' [4]

One cannot but be struck by the aptness with which the clause 'and he was with the wild beasts,' ' lived with the beasts,' [5] applies to the Baptist who lived the life of an anchorite, the 'Enosh in the primaeval conditions of Paradise, the man who in the Naṣōraean source used by Josephus [6] is addressed by his opponents with the words : ' Thou but now come forth from the bush like a beast.' Because he, like primaeval man in Paradise, abstains from all animal food, and like the Babylonian En-gidu ' eats herbs ' at the watering-place with the beasts of the wilderness, therefore he lives with them in primitive paradisaical or messianic peace. As a matter of fact, this motive in connexion with the figure of John has been preserved in Byzantine-Russian art. The Russian *icon* represented on Pl. XXI., dating from the beginning of the seventeenth century, shows the Baptist as a youthful hermit among the gazelles of the desert, and on his knees quenching his thirst in the waters of the Jordan.[7] But aptly as this detail applies to the Baptist, who 'ate nothing and drank nothing,' it has little meaning when transferred to Jesus, who laid no stress whatever on abstinence in the matter of food or drink, and was therefore derisively called by his adversaries a ' gluttonous man ' and a ' wine-bibber.' [8]

[1] See above, p. 281.   [2] Cf. *Matt.* iv.
[2-4] In *Matt.* all this follows after the temptation.
[5] Cf. Jos., *Ant.*, xv. § 346, and 2 *Macc.* v. 27 (above, p. 24 n. I).
[6] Above, p. 250 n. 6.
[7] The Russian *icons* of this type are ultimately derived from some Life of the Baptist similar to the *Vita et Passio Sti. Johanni* of Emesa (above, p. 254 n. I). The Arabic Life of John says : ' instead of a desert full of wild beasts he will walk in a desert full of angels.'
[8] *Matt.* xi. 19 ; *Luke* vii. 34.

Since it is improbable that the insertion concerning Jesus has ousted anything corresponding to the Lucan 'when all the people had been baptized' (the interpolation might very well have followed these words, if it had ever stood after ' In those days '), the possibility must be taken into consideration that in the Naṣōraean text, the source of Mark, the spirit of God descended ' upon him,' i.e. upon the Baptist himself, and that consequently the voice from heaven addressed him personally with the words of the Psalmist, ' Thou art my son.' That, too, would be quite appropriate. For the rabbis were accustomed to see in ' the Lord's anointed ' of *Ps.* ii. 2 a reference to the high priest of Aaron's line regarded as the anointed by God's grace.[1] The *Testament of Levi,* certainly a pre-Christian work, foretells [2] that over the high priest of the last days, who is compared to a king, ' the heavens shall open, and from the temple of glory shall sanctification come upon him with the Father's voice ; and the glory of the Most High shall be uttered over him.' That passage, in particular the words about ' the Father's voice ' and the descent of sanctification, must have the same meaning as in that Naṣōraean source is expressed by ' the spirit descending upon him,' i.e. upon *John the high priest,* and by the *Bath Qōl,* ' Thou art my son ' or ' he in whom I am well pleased.' This source accordingly did not allude here to the royal consecration of Messiah b. David, as depicted in the extant texts of the Synoptic Gospels, but to the heavenly confirmation of the Baptist's election by the people as High priest, and to the divine favour in exalting Ḥanan ' the Hidden ' to be a royal ' high priest for ever after the order of Melchizedek.'

The same observations apply to Matthew's narrative. Here verses 13-15, including the Baptist's refusal and his appeasement by Jesus, a passage unknown to all other witnesses, are a parti-cularly clear case of interpolation. Omit them and the narrative passes directly from the last words of the Baptist's sermon to the miraculous apparition : [3]

' But when he (John) saw many of the Pharisees and Sadducees [4] coming to his baptism, he said unto them, " Ye offspring of vipers," etc. . . . " but the chaff he will burn with unquenchable fire." And lo, the heavens were opened and he saw the spirit of God descending

---

[1] *Midr. Tehillin,* ii. § 3 (13a) ; Strack-Billerbeck, iii. 304 : ' Against Jahweh and his anointed ' (*Ps.* ii. 2). This refers to Qorah, who murmured against Aharon on account of the priesthood, though Aharon was the anointed of Jahweh. Moses said unto him : ' If my brother 'Aaron had taken upon himself the priest-hood, you would rightly murmur. But since God has given it to him, to whom belongs the greatness and the kingdom and the strength, whoever is against 'Aaron is against God.' That is what is written, ' against Jahweh and against his anointed.' Cf. above, p. 138 n. 2.

[2] xviii. 5.   [3] iii. 7.

[4] Another correction for ' people.' Cf. above, p. 268 n. 6.

PLATE XXI

RUSSIAN *ICON* BY NAZARIJ SAVIN IN THE OSTRUKHOV MUSEUM, MOSCOW

IN THE BACKGROUND THE YOUNG JOHN THE BAPTIST ' IN THE DESERT AMONG THE BEASTS ' AND ' ANGELS MINISTERING TO HIM.'   MARC. I, 13   REFERRING NOT TO JESUS, BUT TO THE BAPTIST !   IN THE LOWER LEFT CORNER AN ANGEL LEADING YOUNG JOHN INTO THE DESERT, ACCORDING TO THE RUSSIAN APOCRYPHAL ZACHARIAS LEGENDS.   THE MAIN FIGURE REPRESENTS THE FORERUNNER IN THE ACT OF BAPTIZING THE INFANT JESUS—ACCORDING TO MANDEAN, I.E., NAṢORAEAN TRADITION.   THE INFANT IS IMMERSED IN A EUCHARISTIC CUP, A QUEER IDEA BASED ON THE USE OF THE BAPTIST'S WORDS : ' SEE, THIS IS THE LAMB OF GOD '' IN THE *Prothesis*-RITUAL OF THE GREEK MASS-CEREMONIAL

(SEE P. 283, LINE 31)

as a dove and coming upon him (self) ; and lo, a voice out of the heavens saying, " This is my beloved son, in whom I am well pleased " (iv. 1). Then was he led up into the wilderness by the spirit to be tempted of the devil.'

Viewed from the standpoint of John's disciples, Jesus was but one of the multitude coming for baptism and receiving the blessing of the Spirit. The tentative omission of the lines relating to his baptism from the assumed narrative of the Naṣōraean source is confirmed in a most striking manner by a more detailed investigation of the three temptations in the wilderness to which, in the primitive account freed from Christian interpolations, the Baptist himself and not the newly baptized Jesus must have been exposed. Just as the life in the wilderness 'with the wild beasts' is much more appropriate to the Baptist than to Jesus, so one now sees that the description of the enticements of the devil belongs to a life of the Baptist and not to a life of Jesus. He who has but now been chosen 'son of God' and yet refuses to employ the miraculous power bestowed upon him by the Spirit for the turning of stones into bread and the appeasement of physical hunger, is the fasting, Rekhabite Baptist John, who ate no bread, not even unleavened bread at Passover.[1]

He it is who quotes [2] the famous passage of *Deut.* viii. 3, and must so have interpreted it, ' For not by bread does man live in his loneliness (*or* his seclusion, *l*ᵉ*bhado*) : [3] not by the *maṣṣa* but by every *muṣā*, every word that proceedeth out of the mouth of God, doth man live.' To Jesus, who ate his bread untroubled by scruples, and who, according to the Gospels, showed no aversion whatever to repeating Moses' miracle of the manna and satisfying thousands by the miraculous multiplication of the loaves, this story is not in the least appropriate.

The same considerations apply to the devil's tempting offer of world-dominion, the actual privilege of the Messiah.   The Baptist, even in the Naṣōraean source, speaks with humility of one greater than he, of the 'Shilo' of *Gen.* xlix. 10, to whom 'the peoples' of the earth shall show 'obedience.' He regards not himself as the Messiah, the king of the world anointed by God, but merely as one chosen and confirmed by God as *kohen lᵉōlam*, the high priest of the final age, who some day, by God's orders, may be accounted worthy to reveal the messianic king to the people and to anoint him.   Yet the Baptist, after his vision and after hearing the *Bath Qōl*, the voice from heaven, might well have to combat the temptation to set himself up as the *Christos Kosmokrator*, as the Macca-

---

[1] *Matt.* xi. 18 ; cf. above, p. 230 nn. 5 and 6.   [2] *Matt.* iv. 4 ; *Luke* iv. 4.
[3] Needless to say, the correct grammatical translation would be ' not by bread alone.'   But grammatical rules have never prevented an allegorist from twisting his text so as to fit the requirements of the moment.

baeans before him had disregarded the claims of the house of David and assumed the title not only of High Priest but of King as well. The people had elected him their High Priest and, according to the evidence of Herod, were prepared to follow him everywhere.[1] For him, at least at the time when Archelaus was not yet confirmed in office and was craving the favour of Augustus, the temptation was strong to ' fall down before the Satan ' who swayed the Roman world-empire—in other words, to petition the Romans for confirmation in the high-priestly office, and, having been enthroned as Jewish high priest by the favour of Rome, to do as Herod the Great had done before, that is, in an assured position and with apparent power behind him, to spin idle spiders'-webs for the realization of Jewish dreams of world-dominion. That idea he rejected in loyalty to the Deuteronomic law, which forbade the Jews any recognition of a foreign ruler. Jesus, on the other hand, never rejected the central messianic idea, i.e. the thought of being, by God's grace, the future world-ruler and of proving his claim to the title by his teaching and suffering ; on the contrary, that and no other was the idea to which he sacrificed his whole life. The temptation to rule as a king of the Jews by the favour of Caesar, who for the pious Jews is Satan, only presented itself to Jesus in the childish legends of later apocryphal Gospels,[2] never in reality. It is impossible that the legend in *Matthew* and *Luke* on the devil's offer of world-dominion should be derived from those quite secondary inventions.

The temptation to leap from the pinnacle of the temple into Jerusalem is based on a literal interpretation of the vision in *Daniel* (vii. 13) of the coming of the 'man' who 'sinks down' or 'falls down'[3] with the clouds of heaven. A doubter or mocker might naturally object that a Messiah ' of flesh and blood ' could not fall from heaven and yet remain alive. If this objection were met by an appeal to the almighty power of God, with whom all things are possible, it might be retorted : Well, if he is so firmly convinced that he is God's elect and destined, like Elijah, to travel to heaven on a fiery chariot and from there to sink down again on the clouds of heaven, let him put his belief to the test and risk the far more modest leap from the top of the temple into the abyss and see whether, in virtue of his firm faith, angels will bear him softly down on their hands.[4]

Offhand, such a train of thought is highly probable in one who,

---

[1] Jos., *Ant.*, xviii. § 118 ; cf. above, p. 246.
[2] The so-called Gospel of Gamaliel, M. R. James, *op. cit.*, p. 148 *sqq.*
[3] *athē havah.*
[4] Cf. the legend of the catastrophic downfall of Simon Magus (below, p. 287 n. 1), derived from the story of the unfortunate Icarian experiment of a poor *Graeculus esuriens* before Nero (Juvenal, *Sat.* iii. 78 ss. ; Dio Chrysost., *Or.* xxi. 9 ; Sueton., *Nero*, 12).

like John, was of priestly descent and had, so to speak, passed his early youth in the temple, and upon whose memory was deeply graven the thought of that glance from the top of the battlements, producing giddiness and a vague impulse to fling oneself into the town below, which is mentioned by the priest Josephus.[1] It is far less appropriate in Jesus, to whom Jerusalem and the temple were so unfamiliar that he went to ' look round upon all things,' [2] like a pilgrim visiting the holy city for the first time, when he made his way there in the last week of his life.

There is, then, I think, a high probability that the visions both at the baptism and at the temptation are alike derived from a Naṣōraean *Life and Passion of the Baptist*, and therefore were originally told, not of Jesus, but of John. Only when the verse, 'Now after that John was delivered up, Jesus came into Galilee,' [3] following the narrative of the temptations, is reached, do the Synoptists abandon the Naṣōraean source narrating John's history up to his arrest, and begin the record of the tradition which emanates from the circle of Jesus' own disciples in Galilee.

---

[1] *Ant.*, xv. § 412. Simon Magus, the successor of John the Baptist in the leadership of his disciples (Ps.-Clementine hom. ii. 23 ; *Patrol. Gr.*, ii. 92) claims to be able to do what his master would not attempt (Ps.-Clemens, *Recogn.*, ii. 9, Engl. by Dr. Thomas Smith, *Ante-Nicene Christian Library*, vol. iii. p. 198) : ' If I should throw myself headlong from a lofty mountain, I should be borne unhurt to the earth as if I were held up.'

[2] *Mark* xi. 11.   [3] *Mark* i. 14 ; *Matt.* iv. 12.

XII

THE CHRONOLOGY OF THE BAPTIST

THE YEAR OF THE BAPTIST'S DEATH ACCORDING TO THE SOURCES OF JOSEPHUS—A.D. 35

IT will be evident to every observant reader that the source relating to the Baptist's life and death utilized by Josephus in the *Antiquities* [1] was quite distinct and of a different character from that drawn upon in the *Halōsis*.[2] The latter, by the stress laid upon the ostensibly successful interpretation of dreams, by its admiration of the Baptist still clearly discernible underneath the malicious touches added by Josephus, as also by the suppression of the personal name of the 'Hidden One,' unknown at that time even to Josephus, betrays itself at first glance as a glorification ($\dot{a}\rho\epsilon\tau a\lambda o\gamma\acute{\iota}a$), or an account of the martyrdom of the Baptist, emanating from the circle of those who wished to 'keep' his 'secret'—in other words, from the Naṣōraeans or Baptists.[3] Just like the synoptic tradition, dependent on a similar source, it attributes his execution to the wrath of Herod Antipas aroused by the Baptist's reproaches for his illegal marriage. It knows nothing, or at least says nothing, of his detention in Machaerus. The other source mentions the Baptist under his real name John, bases his arrest and removal on Herod's fear of a threatening insurrection, and attaches weight to the popular opinion that the loss of the battle against Aretas was God's punishment of the tetrarch for the murder of the preacher of repentance.

The Naṣōraean source used in the *Halōsis* may have been obtained by Josephus from his alleged teacher, the hemerobaptist 'Banus.' It must have been a popular work of the same kind as the one utilized by Matthew and Luke and, later on, by the Emesan Life of the Baptist and the Zaccharias Apocrypha edited by Berendts. As there existed different 'Gospels' of Jesus, there must have been more than one such work on John,[4] echoes of

---

[1] See above, p. 246.   [2] See above, pp. 224-31.   [3] See above, p. 234 n. 1.
[4] Prof. Dan. Völter, *Theol. Tijdschr.*, xxx., 1896, pp. 244 ff. ; *Die ev. Erzähl. v. d. Geburt u. Kindheit Jesu*, Strassburg, 1911, pp. 11 ff. ; Harnack, *Neue Untersuch. z. Apostelgesch.*, 1911, pp. 108 f. ; Norden, *Geburt des Kindes*, Leipzig, 1924, pp. 88 note 1 and 102 ff. ; Klostermann, *Das Lukasev.*[2], Tübingen, 1929, p. 5, have traced the influence of such a source in the initial chapters of Luke. But we see now that these traditions are not derived from a ' Lost Book of the Nativity of John,' as Hugh J. Schonfield has tried to show in a book bearing this title (Edinburgh, Clark, 1929), but from a lost *Vita et Passio Sti. Johannis Baptistae*,

which are heard in the just-mentioned Christian and Mandaean writings.

Of quite a different origin is the account of the Baptist found in the *Antiquities*. In the *War* [1]—not in the *Halōsis*, where only the Naṣōraean source is used—Josephus attributes the banishment of Herod Antipas to accusations brought against him by the friend and boon-companion of Caligula, Agrippa, the new king of Judaea. In the *Antiquities* he is still better informed. Now only does he know that Agrippa did not for this purpose journey to Rome, as he still had stated in the *War*, no doubt after a cursory perusal of an unsatisfactory extract, but that he sent to Caesar one of his freedmen named Fortunatus with a bill of indictment against Antipas. It reached the court at Baiae at the moment of the arrival of the accused. Knowing the way in which the Herodian family were on such occasions in the habit of bringing just or capricious charges against one another,[2] we cannot doubt that Agrippa depicted the murder of the Baptist to the emperor in the light in which it was regarded by popular opinion and by his Pharisaic friends, namely, as a judicial murder committed by the suspicious tyrant, a deed which had met with just retribution from God. The justification of the act by the fear of a popular rising and the characteristic principle of preventive justice, 'precaution is better than regret,' [3] is clearly taken from the tetrarch's self-defence. Agrippa's letter and the protocol of the trial of Antipas were naturally preserved in the *commentarii principis* of Caligula, where they were consulted by Josephus or his collaborators ; this is apparent from the detailed knowledge shown of the contents of the ἐπιστολαί, the name of the bearer, the time of his arrival, the place where Caesar held the trial, etc. Consequently, just as with the narrative of the martyrdom of James the Just, the brother of 'Jesus who was called Christ,' derived from the letters of expostulation from the Pharisees to the governor Albinus and his report to the emperor, we are dealing here with documentary evidence of primary importance.

All the more significant is the fact, not noticed by Berendts, Frey, and their critics, that the two perfectly independent sources

---

of which the Emesene Life of the Baptist, his Life by Serapion of Alexandria, are Christian imitations. *Mark* i. 2-13 ; *Matt.* iii. 1-10, 16b-17, iv. 1-11 ; *Luke* iii. 2b-14, 15b-18, 21a, 22, iv. 1b-13 ; *Matt.* xi. 2, 3, 4, 7-17, 19b ; *Luke* vii. 18-20, 22a, 24-32, 35b ; *Mark* vi. 17-29 ; *Matt.* xiv. 3-12, are all derived from this or a similar source, just as are the chapters concerning the Baptist in Josephus analysed above, pp. 224 ff.

[1] ii. 9. 6, § 160.

[2] *Halōsis*, ii. 29 : ' The people has become indignant on account of your impiety. You have sent warriors and massacred a great multitude in the temple. . . . Over the victims they were themselves used as victims. And you have committed a murder such as not even barbarians have committed.'

[3] See above, p. 246.

T

of Josephus are in complete agreement with each other on the *date* assigned to the Baptist's death. Here their chronology is most sharply opposed to that of the Synoptists, a fact which, in my opinion, finally disposes of the theory that the passage on the Baptist was inserted by a Christian interpolator. In the story of the interpretation of dreams quoted above,[1] Philip the tetrarch died on the evening of the day on which the Baptist had interpreted to him his dream about an eagle. Incidentally we may note that the interpretation is not very prophetic ; for if a man dies he loses not merely his wife and his dominion, but his life and *all* his belongings, and it is not the eagle (that is, his greed) which robs him of wife and dominion, but death. The interpretation being so obviously inadequate, we may be sure that we have here no mere *vaticinatio ex eventu*. It is quite possible that the tetrarch, now at least fifty-four years old and probably even much older, was really so alarmed by the evil prophecy of this uncanny 'wild man' that he had a stroke of apoplexy and died 'before evening' on the same day. In any case, according to the tradition of the Baptist's circle, which Josephus took over and accordingly approved, the Baptist outlived Philip the tetrarch. Now, we know from the *Antiquities* [2] that Philip died in the spring or summer of A.D. 34. Since we possess only a late edition of that work, published after the death of Agrippa II., we are dealing with a book which a member of the Herodian family had read in an older form and, where necessary, carefully corrected.[3]

Thus, apart from other evidence, this story of Philip's dream is quite irreconcilable with the Gospel tradition that Jesus did not make his first public appearance until after the Baptist's arrest, and outlived him. This contradiction remains unaffected in whichever of the various years adopted by the Christian fathers, A.D. 29, 32, or 33, we may put the crucifixion.

But the year of the Baptist's death presupposed in the Naṣōraean source of the *Halōsis* may be much more precisely fixed. For after the death of Philip, the Baptist further proceeded to predict for Herod Antipas ' a merciless death . . . through sore tribulations in other lands,' a prophecy which is ' fulfilled ' by the banishment of Herod and Herodias to Lugdunum. In this case the verification of the prediction rests entirely upon the words 'in other lands,' words which the narrator of the story may have introduced into the Baptist's speech after the actual banishment of Antipas. Thus this simple story, too, may have an historical nucleus. It is highly significant that the Naṣōraean source of Josephus—which cannot therefore come from a contemporary— believes that Herod Antipas was deposed and banished by *Tiberius*, i.e. before 16th March 37. From the statement that Herod made

---

[1] See above, p. 229. [2] xviii. 4. 6. [3] See above, p. 182 ll. 27 ff.

his journey to the Emperor Tiberius 'a short time' after the murder of the Baptist, and taking into consideration the cessation of navigation in the Mediterranean between the autumn and spring equinoxes, we conclude that this narrative dated the Baptist's death at the latest not after the close of A.D. 36.

Let us now compare with this the statement of Josephus in the *Antiquities*, i.e. the fixed points obtainable from Agrippa's letter of indictment and the defence of Antipas before Caius Caligula. It is maintained by Agrippa (or by the Pharisees behind him) that the defeat of Antipas in the campaign of A.D. 36 against the Arabian king Aretas was the punishment inflicted by God for his execution of the Baptist. The execution must therefore have taken place before the spring of 36. · Conversely, Herod justifies his act by his apprehension of a revolt. That he should have entertained such an apprehension is most credible in A.D. 35, in which year, immediately to the south of Galilee, in the district of Samaria, through which lay the shortest route to Jerusalem, the Samaritan false messiah, probably Simon Magus, collected his bands, eager for revolt, in Tirathana at the foot of Mt. Garizim, intending to march them up the mountain to rebuild the old tent of the covenant on the summit. Accordingly, the statements of both sources indicate with a high degree of probability that the Baptist was arrested and executed in A.D. 35, after he had wearied Antipas for many years with his repeated predictions of punishment and by his messianic preaching of baptism and liberty had aroused the suspicions even of politicians who knew nothing of his activity in the time of Archelaus and the war of Varus (4 B.C.).

These dates, having been obtained only indirectly from Josephus and his sources, are open to no suspicion of bias of any kind whatever. The irreconcilable opposition between them and the ordinary chronology, based on a series of New Testament passages, need surprise no one ; for it has long been known that even Luke [1] assigns to the appearance of Theudas a date, before the rising of Judas of Galilee in the days of the census, quite different from that given by Josephus, who, dependent on Roman documents, is certainly right in stating that Theudas was crushed by Cuspius Fadus about A.D. 45. Equally notorious is the fact that all apologetic endeavours have so far failed to absolve Luke from the reproach of having placed the census under Quirinius the governor of Syria (A.D. 6-7) in the days of Herod the Great, i.e. before 4 B.C.

In reality, however, the chronological statements in Luke's Gospel admit of a quite different explanation from that which, under the spell of conventional harmonistic views, has hitherto been assumed.

Even critical scholars like Schürer have felt justified in com-

[1] *Acts* v. 36.

bining the date suggested by the passage in *Matt.* ii. 1, ' Now Jesus was born . . . in the days of Herod the king,' with the statement of a totally different character in *Luke* i. 5, although it has long been established that Luke was ignorant of the whole narrative in *Matt.* i.-ii. That text was probably drawn from a pseudepigraphic 'book of the generations of Jesus' emanating from the circle of the δεσπόσυνοι and attributed to James the Just.[1] Luke, on the other hand, has made use of other *Toldoth Jeshu*, produced in the same circle, in which an announcement to the shepherds replaced the adoration of the magi.[2] In my opinion it is quite unnecessary to interpret the passage of *Luke* i. 5, ἐγένετο ἐν ταῖς ἡμέραις Ἡρῴδου βασιλέως τῆς Ἰουδαίας ἱερεύς τις ὀνόματι Ζαχαρίας κτλ., as if the author meant that Elizabeth's pregnancy and the birth of the Baptist narrated in the sequel fell *within* the reign of Herod the Great. ἐγένετο bears its usual sense : Zaccharias ' flourished,' ' lived,' in the days of Herod, and (i. 7) when he and his wife were now well advanced in years, toward the end of their lives, they through God's mercy had a son.

But if, with this interpretation, *Luke* i. 5, 7 does not, like *Matt.* ii. 1, fix the birth of the Baptist and that of Jesus within the limits of Herod the Great's life, we are left with no reason for assuming an error in *Luke* ii. 1-15 on the date of the census under Quirinius. Luke may quite well have placed the birth of Jesus, and therefore also that of the Baptist, in the correct year of the census, namely A.D. 6 or 7.

If he proceeds, in iii. 1, to place the beginning of John's baptism of repentance in the fifteenth year of Tiberius (A.D. 28-9), thus making the Baptist enter on his active life between the ages of twenty-one and twenty-three, this creates no objection from the standpoint either of the narrator or of an intrinsic probability. Nor is there any inconsistency between this and the further statement (iii. 23) drawn from the family tree of Jesus attributed to James the Just, which his relations carried about with them on their far-flung journeyings,[3] that Jesus at the beginning of his activity (ἀρχόμενος) was thirty years old. This is clearly intended to establish an analogy between Jesus and King David, who is

---

[1] See App. XIII., below, pp. 606 ff.

[2] H. Jeanmaire, *Revue archéologique*, 1924, xix. 255, was the first to see that this legend manifestly refers to the year 40 B.C., the year of the Parthian invasion, when Persian kings and magi really were in Palestine and tried to enthrone a national king of the Jews, a creature of their own, instead of the Roman *protégé* Herod. Obviously Christian legend tried to show that the three Parthian chiefs, the two Pacoruses—the king's son and the homonymous cupbearer—and Barzapharnes (*B.J.*, i. §§ 248 f.), or their magi, recognized the infant Jesus as the legitimate king of the Jews according to their knowledge of star lore. The hitherto enigmatic prophet Πάρχωρ (Clem. Alex., *Strom.*, vi. 6, 53) is obviously the mage-king Pacorus—Πάχχωρ.

[3] Sextus Julius Africanus ; see above, n. 1.

said (2 Sam. v. 4) to have begun his reign at the same age.[1] For Luke neither says that he was thirty years old at the time of his baptism (βαπτιζόμενος), nor that he began his active ministry immediately after his baptism. On the contrary, the remarkable way in which the statement about the Baptist's imprisonment is proleptically inserted in iii. 19 may very well lead one to suppose John to have baptized in the Jordan for several years before his arrest by Herod Antipas, and that Jesus until then, i.e. until he, 'full of the Holy Spirit, returned from the Jordan' (iv. 1), and his own activity began, had remained with John as his associate. In that case a period of from seven to ten years might be supposed to have elapsed between the baptism of Jesus, regarded as about six months younger than John, and the ' beginning ' of his own proclamation, while the year of his passion, the same year in which he made his first public appearance, might quite well have been Pilate's last year of office (A.D. 35-6). This it is indeed represented to have been in the Latin version of Josephus, the so-called *Egesippus*, where the crucifixion of Jesus *follows* the uprising of the Samaritan Messiah, which occurred in A.D. 35. If the Baptist was arrested and put to death in the year before the battle with Aretas (A.D. 36), i.e. at the beginning of 35, then everything in *Luke* is in agreement with the view upheld by *Mark* i. 14a and *Matthew* iv. 12—in other words, with the common synoptic tradition that Jesus began his active ministry only after the Baptist's imprisonment, as his successor and not as his rival and apostate disciple, and was crucified after the Baptist's death.[2]

We thus reach the surprising result that the chronology advocated by Theodor Keim, solely on the basis of the statements in the *Antiquities* concerning the Baptist's death and the battle with Aretas, is actually quite reconcilable with the statements of Luke, by which Schürer [3] imagined that it would be confuted.

The resultant gain for apologetic purposes is, to be sure, quite negligible. For if, in accordance with this interpretation, Luke has correctly dated the census of Quirinius and the Baptist's death, he has, as stated above, adopted as the date of the birth of Jesus a year (A.D. 6) no more reconcilable with *Matt.* ii. 1 than it (or the previous year, in which he places the Baptist's birth) is reconcilable with the *Halōsis* of Josephus, according to which the ' wild man ' was already preaching in the reign of Archelaus [4] (4 B.C.-A.D. 6) and was brought up to him for trial. Moreover, the date which, on the above theory, Luke adopted as that of the passion (A.D. 35-6) is

---

[1] Similarly, Joseph became viceroy of Egypt at thirty (*Gen.* xli. 46). Thus for the Messiah ben David as well as for the Messiah ben Joseph thirty years is the proper age.
[2] If Jesus had been born in A.D. 6, he would then have suffered in his twenty-ninth year (ὡσεὶ ἐτῶν τριάκοντα).
[3] i.⁴, p. 443₃₄. Engl. trans., div. i. vol. ii. p. 30.   [4] Cf. *Matt.* ii. 22, iii. 1.

wholly irreconcilable with the one adopted by the majority of the Church fathers, who place the crucifixion in the fifteenth year of Tiberius (A.D. 29), a date which also appears to have been in the mind of the fourth Evangelist.[1] If, then, Luke dated the birth of Jesus and of the Baptist in the time of the census of Quirinius (A.D. 6), he can only have done so to make the Christ, who, in the genealogy of the δεσπόσυνοι, taught and died at the age of about thirty, outlive the Baptist, put to death, according to the Naṣō-raean tradition, only after the death of Philip (A.D. 34) and after the marriage of his supposed widow with Herod Antipas. The assertion that Jesus outlived the Baptist had proved indispensable in the controversy with the disciples of John,[2] and attempts were made to establish it on an even firmer basis by various interpola-tions into the text of the Synoptic Gospels. Luke has therefore taken great pains to adjust the date of the passion of Jesus to the late date of the Baptist's death, as it could be computed on the basis of the Philippus episode, told in his Naṣōraean source, with-out, however, paying the slightest regard to the tradition current among Baptists concerning the activity of their founder under Archelaus. Consequently the Life of the Baptist was known to him, not in the form in which it came to Josephus, but in some Christian reworking, in which all these incidents dating back to the time of the war of Varus had been discarded or detached from their true historical setting. This intermediate source may quite well have been the document known to have been used elsewhere both by Matthew and Luke, the so-called Q.

The Date of John's Baptism in the Gospel of Luke

It is remarkable that the precise statement in *Luke* iii. 1 about the Baptist making his first public appearance in the fifteenth year of Tiberius (A.D. 29) is meant by that author, not to fix the date of the crucifixion, but rather to mark the date of the baptism of Jesus, which was the occasion or means of his spiritual new birth as son of God and messianic king.[3] The Third Gospel thus lays the main stress on this date of the miraculous birth of the Messiah, and fixes alike the year of the conception and that of the adoption of Jesus by the *Bath Qōl* at the baptism in the Jordan, leaving at the same time the year of the crucifixion undecided. The reason for this omission may perhaps be that the author is dealing only with the dates of the birth and royal consecration, i.e. the accession to the throne of a king whose rule does not end with his death and re-moval from this world, but is eternal. But perhaps there was a

---

[1] *John* ii. 20 : forty-six years have passed since the beginning of the con-struction of Herod's temple (15 B.C.).
[2] Cf. below, first lines of p. 307.   [3] *Luke* iii. 22, quoting *Ps.* ii. 7.

further reason why Luke was unwilling to contradict expressly the opinion, then already prevalent, that the crucifixion took place in the fifteenth year of Tiberius.   Both dates are obviously computed artificially and without any historical foundation.   The dating of the birth of Jesus in the year of the census has already been explained.[1]   By a calculation backwards from the last possible passover, occurring before the departure of Pilate (A.D. 36) but after the death of Philip (A.D. 34) and the execution of the Baptist (A.D. 35), this date was arrived at on the basis of the statement that Jesus at the beginning of his messianic reign was about (ὡσεί) thirty years old.

The year 35 or 36 for the crucifixion and the year 6 for the birth are, however, intrinsically improbable dates, because they would bring Jesus much too close to Paul, whose conversion on the road to Damascus must have happened in one of the years between A.D. 28 and 35, the earlier date being preferable for various reasons.[2]

As for the year A.D. 29, that is, the fifteenth year of Tiberius, it is clear that this can only be a date arrived at by purely chronological considerations.   As is well known, the ancient Church unanimously assumed that the day of the παρασκευή, on which Jesus was crucified, was the παρασκευή of the Sabbath, that is, the προσάβαττον, 'erebh shabbath, our Friday, though there was some hesitation as to whether the day in question was the 14th or the 15th of the lunar month Nisan.   The Pagan Christians in their turn evidently attempted to determine this date according to the Roman calendar.   Quite naturally they hit upon viii. Kal. Aprilis (=25th March), the day of the spring equinox after the reform of the calendar by Caesar.   For the Jews of the Diaspora, as proved by Philo,[3] translated Pesaḥ by διαβατήρια, i.e. 'pass-over,' and connected it with the 'passing' of the sun through the equator.   To this must be added the well-known fact that the day of the spring equinox was identified with the day of the creation of the world—a belief which has left its trace in the first canto of Dante's divine poem—and the temptation was strong to put the piacular death of the Messiah and the beginning of the new messianic aeon on the same day.[4]   Thus the whole matter resolved

---

[1] See above, p. 292.   [2] Von Soden, in Cheyne's Encycl. Bibl., 814.
[3] Vita Mosis, iii. 686 ; Anatolius in Euseb., Hist. eccl., vii. 32. 16-19.
[4] Mr. Th. Gaster kindly reminds me that in the cult of Attis the vernal equinox (24th of March) was the ' day of blood,' when the image of Attis—the effigy of a young man tied to the stem of a felled tree (J. G. Frazer, Adonis, Attis, Osiris, London, 1907, p. 222₅)—was lamented, and that on the 25th of March the resurrection of the god was celebrated. Sir James (loc. cit., p. 227₃) has shown that the Christian term ' Dominica Gaudia ' for the resurrection-day of Christ is derived from the name of these ' Hilaria' of Attis. The date of the death of Attis has certainly had a decisive influence upon the identification of the day of the crucifixion with the spring equinox.

itself into the problem to find a year, within the reign of Tiberius and the administration of Pilate, in which the 25th of March fell on a Friday.

This problem itself was not difficult, since there existed, at the latest since the time of Augustus, Roman calendars which considered also the Jewish-Alexandrian planetary week.[1] A research in old calendars of this kind, or even a simple computation by cycles, would enable any one to see that the 25th of March of A.D. 29, i.e. of the fifteenth year of Tiberius, fell on a Friday. Nor can there be any doubt that similar cycles, equally useful to Jews and to Christians, were in vogue long before their official adoption by the Church—nay, probably even before the rise of Christianity itself.[2] It is certainly no accident that the Easter cycle of eighty-four years obtained by Cardinal Noris from a purely Pagan calendar, the consular *fasti* of the chronographer of 354, shows the 25th of March of A.D. 29 to have been a Friday, a fact which surprised the chronologist Ideler in the first quarter of the 19th century. In fact, the day was not the fourteenth or fifteenth day of the lunar month, but the seventeenth ; yet no great importance can be attached to this slight divergence, since both Jews and Jewish Christians knew that the Sanhedrin would, when the atmosphere was cloudy and the new moon not clearly visible, postpone the announcement to the following day. Such a thing might happen on two months in succession, and as a result the seventeenth day might easily be counted in some years as the fifteenth and hence as the regular day of the Passover.

To find a year in which the 25th of March was both a Friday and exactly the fifteenth day of the lunar cycle, one would have been obliged to go back as far as A.D. 18, when Gratus was still governor of Palestine and not Pilate.[3] Between A.D. 29 and the last year of Pilate's administration (A.D. 35-6) no such year can be found. As a matter of fact, the chronographer of 354 significantly states : '*Gemino et Gemino Sat. xxiii.*,' that is, in this year the New Year's Day (*Saturnalia*) falls on the twenty-third day of the new moon ; and it adds : ' His consulibus dominus Jesus Christus passus est die Veneris luna xiiii.' This is also the reason why Hippolytus arranged his Easter cycle, beginning in A.D. 222 and comprising 112 years, so that there is a full moon on Friday, 25th March of A.D. 29.

---

[1] Cf. Roscher's *Lexikon*, iii. 2. 2537 *sq.* ; F. Boll in Pauly-Wissowa's *R.E.*, vii. 2573.

[2] Convenient pocket editions of Petosiris' astrological calendar were carried about by Roman ladies, according to Juvenal, vi. 574. The whole question is treated in full detail in vol. ii. p. 134 *sq.* of the German edition of this book.

[3] See above, pp. 17 f.

PHLEGON OF THRALLES AND THALLUS THE SAMARITAN ON THE ECLIPSE AT THE CRUCIFIXION

The fifteenth year of Tiberius must have recommended itself to the early Christian chronologists by still another series of considerations. As is well known, Luke is the only evangelist to give this date and also to mention the darkness (σκότος) occurring at the death of Jesus as an universal phenomenon extending over the whole earth, and hence to refer to it as an eclipse of the sun, as though such a phenomenon were at all possible on or near the full moon.

Now, Eusebius[1] has pointed out with a good deal of satisfaction that according to the chronicler Phlegon of Thralles,[2] a freedman of Hadrian, there actually was an eclipse of the sun accompanied by an earthquake[3] in the 202nd Olympiad, a phenomenon which the historian is not slow in identifying with the one happening at the death of Jesus. Eusebius, in his citation of Phlegon, quotes the year as the 4th of the 202nd Olympiad, and uses this date in support of his own assumption that the year of the passion was the nineteenth of Tiberius, i.e. A.D. 33, an assumption based on his belief that Jesus' public career lasted four years,[4] and on a corresponding interpretation of the festivals mentioned in *John*.

But as early as the seventeenth century the great astronomer Kepler,[5] and after him his less famous colleague Wurm,[6] calculated with the utmost precision that in the 202nd Olympiad there occurred only one great eclipse of the sun visible in the Levant, and that its date was 24th November of A.D. 29, that is, the fifteenth year of Tiberius, the same year in which, according to the Roman calendar, the full moon and the spring equinox fell on a Friday. When, therefore, a reader who was not a professional astronomer found a mention of this eclipse and earthquake in some annalist[7] of the type of Phlegon, unaccompanied by an indication of the month and the day, he would naturally identify the phenomenon with the one given in *Luke*, and this identification would in turn confirm his view that the year of the passion was A.D. 29.

What documents did this Phlegon utilize? Eusebius[8] mentions one—the important one in this connexion—in the enumeration

---

[1] *Chronicon* (a. d. Armen. v. Karst, *G.C.S.*, xx. p. 213) ; cf. Migne, *Patrol. Gr.*, xix. 535.
[2] *Fragm. Hist. Gr.*, ed. C. Müller, iii. 607a.
[3] Cf. *Matt.* xxvii. 51.   [4] *Hist. eccl.*, i. 10.
[5] *Eclog. chron.*, p. 615.
[6] Cf. Bengel's *Archiv f. Theol.*, ii. 2 (1818), pp. 1-78, 261-313.
[7] The special astrological compilations of eclipses and earthquakes do not come into consideration, since in them the zodiacal sign is added in which the phenomenon occurs, so that any one could infer the month of the event.
[8] *Chron.*, ed. Schoene, i. 265 ; Karst (1911), p. 125.

of his own sources when he says: 'e Thalli tribus libris, in quibus ab Ilio capto usque ad ccvii. olympiadem collegit.' This Thallus has long since been identified [1] as Thallos [2] the Samaritan freedman of Tiberius who two years before the death of the emperor had helped the bankrupt Herodian prince Agrippa with a considerable loan, and who may very well have survived his former master by fifteen or twenty years. In his chronicle, as we know from Sext. Julius Africanus,[3] he identified the darkness of the crucifixion with the well-known astronomical eclipse of A.D. 29. As for the source of Thallus, one might think of the influence of Christian tradition. Yet since neither Matthew nor Mark shows the slightest trace of the year A.D. 29 as the year of the passion, it is not very likely that there existed as yet any definite tradition on the subject, and it is therefore highly probable that Thallus, writing in the reign of Claudius, after A.D. 52, was himself the originator of this chronology. The Samaritan's ignorance of the Jewish method of determining the day of the new moon, and his equally great ignorance of matters astronomical in general, did not of course allow him to see the difficulties of his proposed identification, with which he merely wanted to explain 'rationally' the alleged miracle of the Christians.

At all events, it is a fact worth noting that as early as the reign of Claudius—that is, half a century before Tacitus—a Hellenized Samaritan writing at or very near the imperial court mentioned the crucifixion of Jesus and at the same time attempted to explain in a rational way the alleged prodigies observed on that occasion.[4] It is certainly strange that this document has never been utilized in the debate concerning the historicity of Jesus, since it is of course evident that a man like Thallus would never have taken the trouble to correct and criticize a miraculous story existing only in oral tradition. On the contrary, he must have known a written source dealing with the crucifixion and its attendant phenomena. Nor is it difficult to guess that this source was the collection of Old Testament prophecies (λόγια) attributed to Matthew, a collection the existence of which has been made exceedingly probable by quite a number of scholars.[5]

---

[1] *Fragm. Hist. Gr.*, iii. 517a ; Schürer, *G.J.V.*, iii. 495 ; cf. 66 *sq.*

[2] Through a regrettable accident the initial Θ of his name has fallen out in the Greek standard text of Josephus, ed. Niese (*Ant.*, xviii. § 167). But since ἄλλος Σαμαρεύς is impossible in this connexion, the old restoration of Θάλλος, a name occurring in inscriptions as that of several people belonging to the imperial household of that period, is obviously inevitable.

[3] Ap. Syncell., i. 610, ed. Dindorf.

[4] I note with pleasure that Prof. M. Goguel agrees with these results of mine ; cf. *Évangile et Liberté*, xliii., No. 51, 191₁₂, 1928, p. 204 ; *Revue de l'Histoire des Religions*, xcviii., 1928, pp. 1 ff.

[5] F. C. Burkitt, *The Gospel History and its Transmission*, Cambridge, 1906, p. 126 ; Carus Selwyn, *The Oracles of the New Testament*, 1911 ; cf. Salomon Reinach, *Revue archéologique*, 1912, p. 451 ; Rendel Harris, *Testimonies*, Cambridge, 1916-20.

It has been recognized long since that the darkness covering the whole earth and lasting from the sixth to the ninth hour[1] owes its origin to the prophecies of Amos,[2] of Zephaniah,[3] of Zechariah,[4] of Joel,[5] of Ezekiel,[6] and of Isaiah.[7] It is fairly clear that the λόγια of Matthew in their endeavour to prove the messiahship of Jesus must have mentioned some or all of these prophecies and their fulfilment on the day of the crucifixion. It is equally clear that Thallus, as an opponent of Christianity, could not miss such a splendid opportunity of showing that the alleged miraculous phenomenon was a perfectly natural event, to wit, the total eclipse of A.D. 29.[8] Nor is it astonishing that the Christians soon adopted the identification of their opponent, evidently considering a well-attested eclipse of the sun precisely on the day of the crucifixion as a sufficiently great miracle. At all events, Luke himself cannot very well be responsible for the introduction of these features in the history of Jesus, since in his story, as pointed out above, the year A.D. 29 is not at all the year of the passion but that of the baptism of Jesus. Originally the year in question must have occurred in a gospel narrative which assumed that Jesus' public career lasted just one year, so that both his baptism and his passion occurred in the fifteenth year of Tiberius.

What is certain is that none of the dates computed for the passion has any historical foundation. The eighty-four-year cycle of the consular *fasti* could not be of any real use, since the Jews not only did not apply it for the intercalation of their thirteenth month, but were altogether ignorant of it. The Jewish cycle restored by M. Daniel Sidersky[9] conclusively proves that between A.D. 29 and 33 there did not exist any Friday of Nisan coinciding with the full moon and with 25th March of the Roman calendar. In 29 the Easter full moon fell on Monday, 19th April; in 32 on Monday, 15th April; and in 33 on Friday, 4th April.

THE DAY OF THE CRUCIFIXION

A careful analysis of the texts clearly shows that the oldest tradition in all probability knew nothing of the fact that the crucifixion of Jesus should have taken place on a Friday.[10] The

---

[1] *Matt.* xxvii. 45 ; *Mark* xv. 33.   [2] viii. 9.   [3] i. 15.
[4] xiii. 6.   [5] ii. 10 ; iii. 15.
[6] xxxii. 7.   [7] xiii. 10 ; xxiv. 22.
[8] Incidentally, this is a good proof that Jews and Samaritans at the Roman court did not hesitate to speak of Jesus, or more exactly, against him and the claims of his followers.
[9] *Études sur l'origine astronomique de la chronologie juive*, in *Mém. Acad. Inscr. et B.L.*, xi. 2, Paris, 1911, p. 38.
[10] This is also the conclusion of Eduard Meyer, *Ursprung und Anfänge des Christentums*, i. 170.

only fixed fact was the celebration by Jesus and his disciples of the last supper shortly before his arrest, on the eve of the Passover.[1] But there must have existed, besides, a different tradition according to which Jesus was also crucified on the day before the Passover, the παρασκευὴ τοῦ πάσχα.[2]

The explanation of this divergency is far more simple than many critics have thought. For if, according to Jewish custom, the day is supposed to begin with the sunset and to end with the sunset, and if it is furthermore borne in mind that the Passover meal took place after the first star had become visible, it cannot reasonably be said by a Jew that the arrest of Jesus took place on the day *before* the Passover. But if one uses as a basis the Graeco-Roman custom of reckoning the day either from morning to morning or from midnight to midnight, a method which was of course in the minds of all Pagan Christians, it is clear that Jesus celebrated the last supper and was arrested on the eve of the Passover. And if, finally, still another tradition insisted that he was crucified too on the eve of the Passover, this would merely prove that the execution took place with the lightning speed peculiar to the military character of the whole transaction—the governor being anxious to have done with the matter before the masses crowding the city on the day of the festival had time to think of liberating their unfortunate king.[3]

The extant versions, putting the execution on the morning of the following day, owe their origin to the legend of the cock's crow during the alleged judicial procedure before the high priest, an episode preceding the trial by Pilate, and to the exaggeration [4] with which the perfectly informal, short preliminary interrogation before the scribes assembled at the high priest's palace on the Mount of Olives is reported. Once this informal and quite unessential incident had been converted, by anti-Jewish tendencies, into a regular trial before the Sanhedrin, it was also remembered that this body could not condemn any one to capital punishment during the night,[5] and the episode was 'doubled,' and a regular session of the Sanhedrin in the morning of the following day was

---

[1] This, too, has been questioned by Eduard Meyer, *op. cit.*, p. 173 *sqq.*, but on insufficient grounds. See my papers on the Last Supper in the *Z.N.T.W.*, 1925 and 1926. Even if Marmorstein's and Lietzmann's objections (*ibid.*) were justified—which they are not—nobody has been able to oppose anything to my explanation of the cup and the 'vine of David.'

[2] *John* xix. 14; cf. also the *Baraitha Talmud Sanhedr.*, 43b; Strack-Billerbeck, ii. 843 E (bottom of the page).

[3] *Mark* xiv. 2; *Matt.* xxvi. 4: 'not on the feast-day, lest there be an uproar among the people.'

[4] On the anti-Jewish and pro-Roman tendency of these changes, cf. below, p. 385 ll. 33 f.

[5] *Tosefta* to *Sanh.*, vii. 1; Philo, *De migr. Abr.*, § 16 M, i. 450. The Jews had no reason whatever to deviate from their law and to shoulder the responsibility of the case. All they had to do was to hand it over to the Romans.

added to the story. Of course, the probability of the tale did not increase thereby, since no such sessions could take place on a Sabbath or other Jewish holiday.[1]

As a matter of fact, the crucial passage in *Mark* shows the particle εὐθύς followed by an obviously interpolated πρωί, after which the εὐθύς was deleted in a number of MSS. It is therefore fairly obvious that immediately after the short preliminary trial at the house of the high priest Jesus was taken in fetters to Pilate the same night. The court-martial before the governor was of the utmost shortness, since the accused openly confessed that he was the 'king of the Jews.'[2] He was then led away under a military guard, in the midst of the tumult of the mob, of which one party clamoured for the liberation of one Jesus Barabbas, likewise arrested by the Romans,[3] whilst the other demanded the crucifixion of Jesus. There follows the scourging of the unfortunate king and the march to the place of the execution, in which a Cyrenaean Jew who was just approaching the city, and had evidently taken the Passover supper in one of the villages around Jerusalem, was forced to carry the cross. The hour of the crucifixion given by Mark[4] appears at the first glance as a late interpolation. The two other gospels would certainly have taken over this important detail had they found it in their copies of *Mark*.

Perhaps on account of the festival, during which the corpse was not supposed to remain hanging on the cross, perhaps as a measure of prudence, to avoid exciting still more the fanatic crowd through an open violation of their festival, perhaps also to obviate any attempt on the part of the mob to take down the crucified victims while they were still alive, at all events it is indeed likely that the Jewish authorities requested Pilate to shorten the torments of the condemned and to take down their bodies.

The notion that the day of the crucifixion was not only an eve of the Passover but an eve of a Sabbath, i.e. a Friday, arose only in the course of the development of the resurrection story.[5] According to an old Jewish superstition,[6] it is a good omen to die on the eve of a Sabbath. Since the kingdom of the Messiah was at an early age compared to the final Sabbath,[7] it was natural to suppose

---

[1] This fact has been wrongly doubted by Eduard Meyer, *op. cit.*, p. 173 *sqq.*; cf. also J. Klausner, *Jesus of Nazareth*, p. 329 n. 32.

[2] *Mark* xv. 2. As to the much-debated meaning of οὐ λέγεις—which may be ambiguous in Greek (cf. Euripides, *Hippol.*, 352), while Aram. אמרת is a straightforward ' yes ' !—see Strack-Billerbeck, i. 990.

[3] On the details of this episode, see below, pp. 437 ff.

[4] xv. 25 : ' and it was the third hour and they crucified him.' This after the previous verse has already said ' and they crucify him.'

[5] In *Mark* xv. 42 the relative clause is obviously an explanatory gloss.

[6] Kethuboth, 103b ; Aboth di R. Nathan, 25 ; Strack-Billerbeck, i. 1043, on Matt. xxvii. 50.

[7] Iren., v. 28. 3 ; *Didascalia*, xxvi. p. 137 ; Hippolytus' *Comm. on Dan.*, iv. 23 ; *Epistle of Barnabas*, ch. xv. ; *Sanhedr.*, 97a.

the day of Jesus' death to have been the eve as it were of that final Sabbath. As a consequence, the day of the resurrection became the Sunday of the planetary week,[1] the day of the *Sol invictus*, the ' sun of justice.' It is at bottom the same cosmic symbolism which is also responsible for the dating of the crucifixion on 25th March,[2] when the sun passes the big X [3] formed by the ecliptic and the equator, and for the fixing of Jesus' birthday on 25th December, the *dies natalis solis invicti*. At all events, there is not the slightest reason to suppose that any Christian witness remembered the week-day of an event of which even the year was soon forgotten.[4]

This means, of course, the disappearance of the last fixed point for a determination of the year of the passion from what we read in the Gospels about the crucifixion having taken place on a Friday or the resurrection on a Sunday.

The Origin of the Statement that Jesus outlived the Baptist

The foregoing enquiries have reduced our main problem of the chronology of early Christianity to the two following alternatives.

If we are to trust the Christian tradition that Jesus outlived the Baptist, or began his preaching only after the Baptist's imprisonment, the crucifixion must be placed in the year 35 or 36, in accordance with Luke's conception of the course of affairs. In this case the sequence of events under Pilate's administration in the *Antiquities* of Josephus, where the debated section (xviii. 3. 3) implies that Jesus appeared at the beginning of A.D. 19,[5] must rest upon a confusion of dates in the extracts made by Josephus from his documents, if not upon an actual falsification—this being the reason why the Latin edition of the *Halōsis*, the *Egesippus*, or the original Greek text behind it, possibly affected by Christian interpolations, has inserted the mention of Jesus immediately after the story of the massacre of the Samaritans in A.D. 35.[6] Again, the *Acts of Pilate*, published by the Emperor Maximinus Daïa [7] and bearing the date ' *Tiberio iv° cons.*,' i.e. A.D. 21, must then, contrary to all historical probability, be regarded, with Eusebius, as wrongly dated and consequently spurious. In that case it would remain quite unexplained how the imperial chancery could have hit upon a date so early and so completely at variance with the traditional Christian chronology.

---

[1] *Mark* xvi. 9 ; *Matt.* xxviii. 1 ; *Luke* xxiv. 1 ; *John* xx. 4.

[2] See above, p. 295.

[3] It is described also in Plato's *Timaeus*, and is the mystic cross (σταυρός) of the Gnostics. Cf. Justin, *Apol.*, i. 60 ; Iren., *Ep.*, i. 34, v. 18. 3 ; *Act. Petri Vercell.*, 8 *sq.* ; Bousset, *Z.N.T.W.*, xiv. (1913), pp. 273-85.

[4] The week-day of any important event is soon forgotten. How many remember even now the week-day of the armistice of 1918 ?

[5] See above, p. 19.   [6] See above, p. 293.   [7] See above, p. 16 nn. 2, 3.

If, on the other hand, the statements on which the chronological order of the martyrdoms of the Baptist and of Jesus is ordinarily based lack sufficient authority for such far-reaching conclusions, the way is clear for a new chronology based solely on Josephus and the documentary materials utilized by him. In estimating the value of the fixed data in question as presented in the Gospels, it is well to remember that the statements making John and Jesus of approximately the same age proved at the outset [1] to be a tendentious invention and historically untenable. We have found the statements of Josephus or of his Naṣōraean source on the appearance of John in the reign of Archelaus uncommonly instructive and illuminating ; Luke's dating of Jesus' baptism in the Jordan in the fifteenth year of Tiberius, on the contrary, renders impossible all understanding of the historical sequence of events. If the Christian sources did either not exactly know, or deliberately falsified, the chronological order of the births of Jesus and the Baptist, this certainly does not predispose the critic in favour of their notions on the sequence of their deaths.

The only reason for pronouncing another and a more favourable verdict upon the tradition of the synoptists would be the fact that we seem to deal not only with their own statements, which may or may not be accepted, but also with the utterances of Jesus or of Herod Antipas quoted by them and evidently pointing to the same result.

As for the direct statements of Mark and Matthew,

' Now after that John was delivered up, Jesus came into Galilee ' (*Mark* i. 14),	' Now when he heard that John was delivered up, he withdrew into Galilee ' (*Matt.* iv. 12),

the underlying primitive tradition need not have referred to the arrest of the Baptist by Herod Antipas ; the occasion might quite well have been his first arrest by order of Archelaus on his first appearance, which is best placed in the period immediately after Herod's death and before the journey of Archelaus to Rome (A.D. 4). Only the desire of Archelaus, owing to his uncertain position as unconfirmed heir to the throne, not to exasperate unnecessarily his subjects, can account for the release of their leader, the accused Baptist, on this occasion. Had Archelaus got him into his hands 'after he had received the ethnarchy from Augustus ' and begun 'to harass the Jews with intolerable oppression,' [2] the Baptist would not have come off so easily. Even after the rising at the Passover this enforced mildness on the part of the ethnarch is no longer imaginable. This incident must consequently have occurred between the death of Herod and the Passover of 4 B.C. The passages of Mark and Matthew quoted above might, therefore,

---

[1] Above, p. 244₇. [2] *Halōsis*, § 111.

have meant originally, 'Now after the Baptist was *betrayed*'—
i.e. after the 'secret' of the 'Hidden One's' preaching of liberty
had come to the ears of Archelaus and the Baptist had been
arrested and brought before him, in 4 B.C.—'Jesus betook himself
to Galilee.'

But so early a date for the first appearance of Jesus in Galilee
would be in flat contradiction with the time and occasion of the
opening of his public ministry to be inferred from Josephus.[1]
Moreover, the versets in question,[2] as has previously been shown,[3]
mark the point of transition from the Nasōraean source hitherto
drawn on to the tradition of his own circle of Galilaean disciples.
It is highly improbable that these lines should refer to anything
except the closing chapter in the life of the Baptist, namely, his
final 'delivery' into the power of his enemies.   Up to this point
the Christian narrator follows his first source, an account of the
life and passion of the Baptist.   He has fastened upon this because
he had somehow to find a place for the baptism of Jesus and his
rather short contact with John.   The fact itself was so well
attested by the disciples of John who had gone over to Jesus that
it could not very well be omitted, though, apart from Jesus' speech
about the Baptist,[4] clearly nothing was known of that particular
period of his life to which he owed his surname of 'the Nasōraean.'[5]
But in so artless a composition the juxtaposition of passages taken
from different sources might easily be mistaken for a sequence of
events, so that the speeches of Jesus in Galilee after the close
of the Baptist's life would appear to begin with John's arrest.
Furthermore, the verset in *Luke's Gospel* (iii. 20), which in the
interests of his peculiar chronology discussed above [6] has been
interposed so awkwardly and all the more strikingly in the midst
of his account of John's baptism, makes it perfectly clear that
Jesus begins his ministry in Galilee after the final arrest of the
Baptist by Herod Antipas, i.e. that the ' delivering up ' of the
Baptist in *Mark* and *Matthew* means his consignment to death.

The early death of John is further presupposed in the saying
attributed to Herod Antipas by Mark and Matthew, that Jesus
was but the Baptist risen again from the dead.   But a careful
comparison of the relevant passages [7] at once shows that *Luke* ix. 7,
and an array of MSS. in *Mark* vi. 14, quote the saying only as a
popular opinion and not as a statement of Herod's.   *Luke* ix. 9,
indeed, makes the tetrarch reject this popular belief as impossible.

Only *Matt.* xiv. 1 *sq.* puts the saying expressly in the mouth
of Herod, but in terms which originally appear to have made
no reference to the Baptist's resurrection: ' This is John the

---

[1] See above, p. 225 n. 1.   [2] *Mark* i. 14; *Matt.* iv. 12.   [3] See above, p. 287₃.
[4] See above, p. 259 n. 1.   [5] See above, p. 234.   [6] pp. 293 ff.
[7] *Mark* vi. 14-16 ; *Matt.* xiv. 1 *sq.* ; *Luke* ix. 7-9.

Baptist.' That might mean that he seemed to see in Jesus that baptizing hermit, emerged from the thickets of the Jordan valley, a person by that time already veiled in myth and superstitious legends, known to appear under the most various names. As Origen [1] strikingly suggested, Jesus must have borne some likeness to the Baptist, at least in certain externals of dress, which recalled the much talked-of appearance of John ; in other words, he must have worn the distinctive garb of the Naṣōraeans or Rekhabites.[2]

But the texts of Mark and Matthew, as they stand, present a further difficulty. ' He is arisen from the dead, and *therefore* do these powers work in him.' The idea that one who is risen from the dead thereby becomes forthwith capable of miraculous acts of power is unsupported. A dead man thus returning to life, a ' twice-born,' may on that account know more of the next world than ordinary mortals ; but such knowledge by no means enables him to work miracles. Neither the almost inexhaustible old Wetstein nor Strack and Billerbeck can offer parallels in illustration : the fact is that there are none. But the text is in a state of confusion. If a prophet rises from the dead, then, because he was and is a prophet, the miraculous powers of the spirit work in him. The words '(he) is risen from the dead and therefore do the powers work in him ' simply stand in a wrong position. After ' it is Elijah ' they are as impossible as in their present place, for Elijah did not die and therefore cannot have risen from the dead. But they can well be said of one of the prophets, such as, for instance, Jonah, the preacher of penitence, whom Elijah had once before raised from the dead and who is variously identified with the son of the widow of Sarepta. Again, the clause relating to this subject, ἔλεγον ὅτι προφήτης ὡς εἷς τῶν προφήτων, is not in order. Notwithstanding Blass, this ὡς εἷς should not be explained as =ὥς τις καὶ ἄλλος, but ὡς εἷς τῶν προφήτων is an old stylistic correction of ὅτι προφήτης, which has come into the text along with the corrected phrase because a copyist failed to observe the corrector's dots indicating deletion. Lastly, the words ' for his name had become known ' are not in the right place. If the name of Jesus had become known (φανερόν) through the acts of his disciples [3] all these guesses as to the identity of this newly arisen miracleworker would have been meaningless. The explanatory clause, misplaced because originally written between the lines, refers to the fact that the name of the Baptist, long kept secret, had meanwhile become known, whereas the name of Jesus was still unknown. The inserted clause must have suppressed, or rendered illegible, the words which originally followed, 'And King Herod heard ' ; for

---

[1] *Comm. in Joann.*, vi. 30.
[2] See above, p. 238 and Pl. xx.
[3] *Mark* vi. 12 *sq.*

U

the section absolutely requires a link with what precedes, a mention
of the personal preaching and activity of Jesus, such as is actually
found in the parallel verset, *Matt.* xi. 1, clearly dependent upon a
still unimpaired text of Mark. At least the text must have contained something like ' heard of the works of Jesus.' [1] Luke's [2]
' heard of all that was done ' does not reproduce the sentence
properly. The whole section will therefore run as follows :

> (*Mark* vi. 12) 'And they went out and preached that men should
> repent. (13) And they cast out many devils and anointed with oil
> many that were sick, and healed them, (14) and Herod heard (it). And
> they (people) said, It is John the Baptizer, for his name had become
> known. (15) But others said, It is Elijah. And others said that a
> prophet [3] is risen from the dead, and therefore do the(se) powers
> work in him.'

I agree with G. Wohlenberg in reading Herod's words in the
following verse (*Mark* vi. 16) as an ironical question, 'John whom
I beheaded, is he risen ? ' This corresponds in sense to the parallel
passage, *Luke* ix. 9, 'John have I beheaded (therefore it cannot be
he) : but who is this of whom I hear such things ? '

In *Luke* this remark of Herod's appears very odd, because
hitherto he has only mentioned the Baptist's imprisonment (iii. 20),
and yet here he has not thought it in the least worth while to append
an explanation of the words, such as is added in *Mark* vi. 17 *sqq.*
and *Matthew.*

Moreover, even the arrest of John is mentioned in *Luke* iii. 20,
in a sentence which is not in the author's usual style, or is at any
rate strangely halting. Every unprejudiced reader will see that
the second ' Herod ' is quite superfluous and disturbing : it is in
fact omitted in a considerable number of MSS. That, however, is
a mere glozing over of the awkwardness of the phrase ; it does not
explain the striking fact of the genuine *lectio difficilior.* Rather,
the sentence originally ended before the second ' Herod ' : ' With
many other exhortations, therefore, preached he good tidings unto
the people : but Herod the tetrarch (was) reproved by him for
Herodias his brother's wife and for all the evil things which he had
done. Herod added this above all, that he shut up John in
prison.' With this division of sentences, not only is the grammatical difficulty removed, but it is at once apparent that the
sentence which awkwardly breaks the chronological order of the
narrative is a later interpolation.

Its purpose can be easily seen. If the people were of opinion
that Jesus was John, then John's disciples, who declared their
master to be the Messiah, could assert without anybody being able

---

[1] Cf. *Matt.* xi. 2.   [2] ix. 7.
[3] Old correction : ' that one of the prophets.'

to contradict them that all those great miracles attributed to Jesus by the Gospels had, according to the testimony of the people or of Herod, in reality been wrought by John. This obvious possibility could only be shown to be excluded by finding counter-evidence to the effect that John lay helpless and inactive in prison while Jesus was performing all those mighty deeds. To this end the verset in *Luke* iii. 20 and the words in *Matt.* xi. 2, ' in the prison ' (of which the parallel passage, *Luke* vii. 18, shows no knowledge), were interpolated, no regard being had to the difficulty thereby imported into the narrative, viz. that a person incarcerated as a potential rebel leader cannot receive or send out messengers, unless this strange proceeding is explained by collusion of the gaoler or a similar individual cause.

But since, according to the Naṣōraean Life of the Baptist used by Josephus, John had already been arrested and again freed under Archelaus, it was not enough merely to establish the fact that he had been put in prison before Jesus began to display his miracles. The Baptist's final arrest and execution by Herod had also to be placed before the first public appearance of Jesus, to cut away the ground at the outset from all objections which the disciples of John might base on the doubly attested statement that Jesus was placed by contemporaries on a par with the Baptist.

We may recall how certain Gospels maintained that it was not Jesus who was crucified, but Simon of Cyrene, the bearer of the cross, who suffered in his place : that Jesus escaped and from afar beheld the crucifixion with a smile,[1] and that there was therefore no need for him to rise from the dead to show himself on many occasions to his disciples after his supposed crucifixion and burial. If one recalls such absurd fancies, it is clear that with far greater probability it might be concluded from Jesus being mistaken for John in *Mark* vi. 14, viii. 28, *Matt.* xiv. 2, and *Luke* ix. 7, that the disciples had mistaken the surviving John for the supposed risen Jesus. Such arguments could only be precluded by furnishing evidence that John suffered a martyr's death *before* Jesus. For no other purpose was the short speech of Herod first inserted into *Luke* ix. 9, and the detailed narrative of the Baptist's martyrdom later on taken over from his Naṣōraean *Vita et Passio* and incorporated in *Mark* vi. 16 *sqq.* and *Matt.* xiv. 2 *sqq.* Luke, in any case, did not read this impressive story in his copy of Mark.

Moreover, it has never been satisfactorily explained why the imprisonment and beheading of the Baptist finds no place in the Fourth Gospel. The explanation of this surely remarkable fact is simply to be found in the chronology of the events, now elucidated by Josephus ; a narrative which closed with the death and resurrection of Jesus had no occasion at all to mention the Baptist's

---

[1] Lipsius, *Apocr. Acts of the Apostles*, Leipzig, 1883, i. 95 *sq.*, 204, 427.

execution, which did not occur till later. If the author of the Fourth Gospel had known any traditions about the Baptist's end occurring before the crucifixion of Jesus, one could not understand why he should have failed to make use of evidence the importance of which, in the conflict with John's disciples, would certainly have been clear to any intelligent follower of Jesus.

THE ALLEGED SAYING OF JESUS ON THE SUFFERINGS OF ELIJAH 'ACCORDING TO THE SCRIPTURE'

There remains only to investigate the authenticity of the saying concerning the Baptist's fate put in the mouth of Jesus by Mark and Matthew. It is there appended to the remarkable story of the transfiguration discussed below.[1]

Mark ix. 9-13.

'(9) And as they were coming down from the mountain, he charged them that they should tell no man what things they had seen, save when the Son of man should have risen again from the dead. (10) And they kept the saying, questioning among themselves what the rising again from the dead should mean.

'(11) And they asked him saying, Why say the scribes that Elijah must first come ? (12) And he said unto them, Elijah indeed cometh first and restoreth all things : and how is it written of the Son of man, that he should suffer many things and be set at naught ? (13) But I say unto you that Elijah is come, and they have done unto him whatsoever they listed, even as it is written of him.'

Matt. xvii. 9-13.

'(9) And as they were coming down from the mountain, Jesus commanded them saying, Tell the vision to no man until the Son of man be risen from the dead.

'(10) And his disciples asked him saying, Why then say the scribes that Elijah must first come ? (11) And he answered and said, Elijah indeed cometh and shall restore all things.

'(12) I say unto you, that Elijah is come already, *and they knew him not,* but did unto him whatsoever they listed. Even so shall the Son of man also suffer of them. (13) Then understood the disciples that he spake unto them of John the Baptist.'

The conversation is extremely remarkable. Jesus forbids his disciples to communicate to any one the vision they have had of his association with Moses and Elijah, or some other secret—if it

[1] See pp. 371 ff.

be assumed that the conversation in question had originally no connexion with the vision—until the 'Son of man,' the *bar nasha* of Daniel's vision,[1] should have risen from the dead. Not knowing how to explain the saying, the thought occurs to them that perhaps the prophet Elijah will raise the Messiah, who has given his life as an offering for sin, at the time of his predicted coming and the accompanying *apokatastasis*, the general restoration of the world to its former state. In other words, the silence enjoined by the Master is thought to hold good until the general resurrection day, when the kingdom of God will come 'with power,' [2] and the second coming of the Redeemer in glory.

According to this view, the narrative of the 'metamorphosis' in the Gospel would amount to a betrayal of one of the ' secrets of the kingdom ' and a criminal breach of the command to silence imposed by Jesus. The Christians therefore sought to justify themselves against this reproach [3] by appealing to a saying of Jesus that Elijah had come already. By this mention of the prophet, as Matthew correctly explains, the disciples doubtless understood that Jesus, as on an earlier occasion, referred to the Baptist ; moreover, they saw at work in the resurrection of Jesus after the crucifixion the beginnings of the restoration which he was to accomplish. The injunction to silence was thought no longer to hold, since the 'Son of man' is already risen from the dead, though even then malevolent persons might choose to assert that, whether resident in heaven or in the grave, he is at any rate not living again with, or come back from the dead to, his disciples. To meet such attacks of opponents, who mockingly declared that the disciples with this publication of their story would have had to wait for the second *parousia*, before which Elijah was to come,[4] an appeal was made to the saying of Jesus that Elijah *had* already come in the form of the Baptist : the visions of their risen master were thus to be considered as equivalent to the beginning of the final resurrection.

From this it is apparent that the scene in question represents the clothing in historical form of discussions dating from the time of the earliest polemic against the Gospel message of a Redeemer who *had* already appeared and, notwithstanding his suffering and death, *had* victoriously risen.

For this purpose the words of Jesus, 'But I say unto you, Elijah *is* come, as it is written of him,' would have perfectly sufficed, even if the text had not originally contained the further

---

[1] On this cryptic name of the Messiah ben David, see below, p. 560 n. 3.

[2] *Mark* ix. 1.

[3] It may have been brought forward at a time when the narrative in the original *Mark* or the *Logia* of Matthew ended with *Mark* ix. 8 (*Matt.* xvii. 8). Luke found and transmitted the tradition in this form (ix. 36).

[4] Justin, *Apol.*, 49.

words about the Baptist's martyrdom, to which exception must now be taken on chronological grounds. The former words are quite in keeping with the mind of Jesus, and were doubtless really once spoken by him ; but the passage of Scripture to which he alludes, and which has always been sought for in vain, need not have referred to any sufferings of Elijah but might simply have been the familiar prophecy of Malachi. Just as Matthew has appended to Mark's text the words 'and they knew him not,' so might this glossator, from his knowledge, subsequently acquired, of the imprisonment and beheading of the Baptist, have appended to the traditional words of Jesus 'and they have done unto him whatsoever they listed.'

The inquiry may, however, be carried a stage further. The words in *Mark*, 'as it is written of him,' are omitted in *Matthew*, clearly because no passage about the suffering of Elijah could be found in Scripture. Even the most recent commentators have failed to adduce any text of the kind.

Nevertheless, as, thanks to the kindness of Dr. Rendel Harris, I was able to point out some years ago, there really is something pertinent ' written ' concerning Elijah. It is found in a non-Christian, purely Jewish work, extant in Latin [1] and Hebrew.[2] It consists of a Midrash to the so-called Octateuch, known as the *Biblical Antiquities of Philo*,[2] though, of course, not from the pen of the Alexandrian philosopher. Here we learn (§ 48) that according to Haggadic tradition the third in the series of high priests, the zealot Phineas (or Phinees), did not die but was carried away to Mt. Horeb, to return in the form of the prophet Elijah, then once more to ascend to heaven, and finally, at the end of the ages, to descend to earth and now for the first time to suffer death. Nothing indeed is said of a violent death, but from the words 'taste what is death ' a reader might easily infer that a martyrdom of the 'true witness' was intended. If, then, the Baptist was the Elijah of the prophecy, he too must suffer the predicted fate. There can be no doubt, then, that in *Mark* ix. 13, ' and they have done unto him whatsoever they listed, even as it is written of him,' there is a reference to this remarkable apocryphal work.

Now, it can be proved that the Midrash in question was not composed before the capture of Jerusalem by the Romans. For it predicts that the temple will be destroyed on the 17th Tammuz, thus placing the destruction on the date which to this day the Jews observe as a fast-day in memory of the storming of the city. The destruction of the temple took place on the 9th Ab, a day likewise hallowed by an annual fast. The confusion between the

[1] English translation by Dr. M. R. James, S.P.C.K., 1917.
[2] English translation by Dr. Moses Gaster, Oriental Translation Fund, new series, vol. iv., 1899.

two memorial days suggests a Jew living in a period not too close to the events and writing not before A.D. 70,[1] perhaps a little later. A reputed saying of Jesus alluding to this apocryphon as ' holy Scripture ' cannot of course be genuine. Nor is it admissible to suppose Jesus to have quoted from an older Midrash ; for the whole fiction underlying the myth of the reborn Phineḥas can have been invented only in the interest of a person called Phineas and claiming to be the messianic high priest and Elijah *redivivus*. This person, again, cannot have been any one else but that Phineḥas[2] the son of Samuel of Aphthia whom the Zealots elected in A.D. 66 by lots to be their high priest, ' dressing their victim up for his assumed part as on the stage.'[3] It is hardly conceivable that the reputed saying of Jesus can have been inserted into Mark's Gospel very soon after the destruction of Jerusalem. In support of the ordinary assumption that Jesus outlived John and of the ordinary chronology of Gospel history, it certainly cannot be adduced henceforth. Thus the way is at last cleared for a frank recognition of the really illuminating sequence of events as presupposed in the narrative of Josephus.

[1] James, *op. cit.*, p. 30 *sq.*
[2] His name is variously written Φάννι, Φάννιας, etc., in the MSS., but the true form has been fixed by Schürer, *G.V.J.*[4], i. 618$_{53}$ (Engl. trans., ii. 1, p. 202 n. 561).
[3] *B.J.*, iv. 155. The otherwise unexplained panegyric in chapters xxv.-xxviii., which Pseudo-Philo devotes to a saviour-hero Kenaz, of whom nothing but the name is known to the canonic scriptures, is obviously intended to flatter the young prince Kenedaios (Aram. *d* = Heb. *z* !) of Adiabene, and to celebrate his exploits in the battle against Cestius-Gallus.

XIII

THE APPEARANCE OF JESUS IN THE NARRATIVE OF JOSEPHUS

PILATE AND THE ROMAN STANDARDS. THE 'ABOMINATION OF DESOLATION' OF DANIEL'S PROPHECY

THE thoughtless way in which Josephus has strung together his transcripts and excerpts culled from various sources to make up his history could hardly be better illustrated than by the opening of Book ii. § 169 of the *Halōsis*. He has just reached the end of one source, the Naṣōraean Life of the Baptist relating the removal and banishment of Herod Antipas, an event falling into the reign of Caligula (A.D. 39), though in the source it was attributed to the orders of Tiberius and hence placed in the year 36 or the beginning of 37. Nevertheless, the compiler here recklessly appends the coming of Pilate to Judaea (A.D. 19, or 26 according to the falsified text), without betraying the slightest consciousness of any retrogression in the sequence of events. He simply proceeds :

'And after this there was sent to Judaea by Tiberius a governor, who secretly brought into Jerusalem by night the (*or* an) image of the emperor which is called *semaia*.'

The Naṣōraean source, in consequence of the popular custom of referring to the emperors of the first dynasty as simply 'Caesar,' did not rightly know under which of the Caesars Herod Antipas was banished, and happened to fix upon Tiberius. The error was no worse than that of some Christians who supposed Jesus to have been crucified under Claudius or Nero ; [1] but it misled Josephus, who assumed from the last words of his source that he was still in the reign of Tiberius, in which particular year he neither knew nor cared. His extracts on the incidents falling within Pilate's term of office were, through his own carelessness, or rather through that of his scribes and collaborators, likewise undated. He had therefore no exact idea of the duration of Pilate's governorship. The gravest of these errors is corrected in the *War* (ii. 178 *sqq.*), where we are told the story of Agrippa I., his imprisonment by Tiberius, and his liberation and elevation to the throne by Gaius after the

---

[1] Dom J. Chapman in *Journ. Theol. Stud.*, viii. (1907), p. 590 *sqq.*

death of Tiberius, and where the struggle of Herod Antipas for the crown arises from jealousy of his wife Herodias provoked by Agrippa's new dignity. Thereby the removal and banishment of Antipas are dated with approximate accuracy, but we are brought no nearer to a precise chronology of events under Pilate. Only in the still more recent edition, the eighteenth book of the *Jewish Antiquities*, with further extracts from a source freely used also by Tacitus, carefully studied by Domitian, and easily accessible to Josephus, to wit, the memoirs of Tiberius, do we obtain somewhat fuller data for fixing the chronology. In that particular context two facts of particular importance are the two metropolitan scandals concerning the matrons Paulina and Fulvia, dated by Tacitus in A.D. 19, but mentioned by Josephus in the chapter devoted to Pilate's administration, immediately after the paragraph relating the appearance of Jesus.

If we may assume that Josephus in his latest edition, taking due account of all criticisms that had reached him from his readers, arranged his extracts in the proper order as they stood in the *Acta et commentarii Tiberii*, Pilate must have entered on his office toward the end [1] of A.D.18, and as a new official, unacquainted with Jewish susceptibilities, at once made that unfortunate blunder with the imperial standards. Shortly afterwards, i.e. early in A.D. 19, there followed the appearance of Jesus ' who was called Christ,' or at least Pilate then heard of him for the first time and sent his first report to the emperor. Since, according to the *Acts of Pilate* published by the Emperor Maximinus Daïa, the trial of Jesus occurred in the spring of A.D. 21, we should have for his public ministry and preaching of the kingdom a period of rather more than two years, i.e. a chronology approximating to that of the Fourth Gospel with its references to several pilgrimages of Jesus to Jerusalem for the feasts. On the other hand, the chronology of the synoptists, compressing his ministry into one year, might be explained by the fact that the festivals in memory of the important events of his life, however their dates were fixed, had naturally to be arranged within an annual cycle, the later church year, from the day of the conception to its anniversary, the day of the passion.

That in *Ant.*, xviii. 3. 3, a section, as we can no longer doubt, mangled by a Christian hand, Josephus mentions the crucifixion though falling in A.D. 21—in other words, that he carries to its close a narrative opening in the year 19, before reverting, in the next section, to the Mundus-Paulina episode of the year 19—is quite in keeping with his usual procedure in the paragraphs analysed above.[2]

---

[1] According to *Ant.*, xviii. § 55, he leads his troops into their winter quarters in Jerusalem immediately after his arrival.
[2] See p. 312.

But what to my mind above all confirms the correctness of the dates thus obtained is the fact that they suggest a very simple explanation of Jesus' decision to make his first public appearance, and to preach in the synagogues [1] of Galilee, ' The kingdom of God is at hand: repent and believe in the glad tidings,' [2] exactly at that time and not a few years earlier or later. Josephus, so far as we can judge from the contents, does not appear to have seen the connexion between the incident of the standards and the appearance of the ' so-called Christ,' for the simple reason that such a connexion was not evident to the Romans, and that Josephus, as will appear immediately, is throughout dependent upon Roman official sources.

Pilate's foolish act of provocation is mentioned also by Philo, [3] in connexion with the complaint against the governor's conduct lodged by the Jews with the Emperor Caligula and supported by Agrippa. Here we are expressly told that Pilate set up or ' dedicated ' ($\dot{a}va\theta\epsilon\hat{\imath}vai$) the standards with the image of the emperor in the temple, whereas Josephus, in the *Halōsis* passage quoted above, merely speaks of the introduction and setting up in the city of a single *semaia*.

These variant readings are surely not accidental, as will be seen by a careful comparison of the passage in Philo with the three parallel statements in Josephus :

Halōsis, ii. 169.	*Polemos*, ii. 169.	*Ant.*, xviii. 55 *sq.*
' And after that there was sent to Judaea by Tiberius a governor who secretly brought into Jerusalem by night the (*or* an) image of the emperor which is called *semaia*. And he set it up in the city.'	' Pilate, being sent by Tiberius as governor to Judaea, stealthily introduced into Jerusalem by night and under cover the effigies of Caesar which are called standards ($\sigma\eta\mu a\hat{\imath}ai$)'.	' Now Pilate, the governor of Judaea, having marched an army from Caesarea into its new winter quarters in Jerusalem, conceived the idea of defying Jewish ordinances by introducing into the city the emperor's busts which were attached to the standards. . . . Pilate was the first governor . . . to bring these images into Jerusalem and to erect them there.'

As may be seen at once, the two parties to the dispute have represented differently what actually took place. The Jews in their

---

[1] *Luke* iv. 14 *sq.*   [2] *Mark* i. 15.
[3] Cf. Euseb., *Dem. evang.*, viii. p. 403 : ' The same is asserted by Philo, who says that Pilate by night " set up the imperial standards in the temple " ($\dot{\epsilon}v\ \tau\hat{\wp}\ i\epsilon\rho\hat{\wp}$ $\dot{a}va\theta\epsilon\hat{\imath}vai$).' Similarly Origen, *Comm. in Matt.*, t. xvii. c. 25 : " $\dot{a}v\delta\rho\iota\dot{a}v\tau a\ K a\iota\sigma a\rho os$ $\dot{a}va\theta\epsilon\hat{\imath}vai\ \dot{\epsilon}v\ \tau\hat{\wp}\ i\epsilon\rho\hat{\wp}.$"

expostulation had obviously exaggerated and spoken so loosely of an ' image of the emperor ' that others, like Origen and St. Jerome, might well think of a statue (ἀνδρίας) of the sovereign and of its solemn erection (ἀναθεῖναι) in the temple. In reality, the objects in question were those small medallions in relief with portrait-heads (προτομαί) of the emperor, affixed to the standards and exchangeable (see Plate XXII.). Pilate's action, then, was no solemn erection of these portrait medallions but the ordinary planting (ἱδρύειν) of the standards (signa constituere, figere) which the standard-bearer stuck into the ground. Again, the variation between singular and plural, the discrepancy between Philo and Josephus (Halōsis)—one speaking of the standards being brought into the temple, the other of a single semaia brought into the city—clearly reflect the contention of the respective parties over the details of the case.

Although the text of the Antiquities does not tell us the strength of the force (στρατία =exercitus) led into winter quarters in Jerusalem by Pilate, it is self-evident that they carried with them more than one standard. On the other hand, it is improbable, not to say impossible, that the whole garrison was quartered on the temple mount, i.e. in the castle of Antonia, where as a rule only a single cohort lay.[1] At least the cavalry contingent of this cohort, a cohors equitata, must have been quartered elsewhere in the lower town, probably in Herod's palace ; we must also, of course, allow for garrisons for the principal towers on the city walls, etc., all in possession of their own standards.

The majority of these ensigns (σημαῖαι) was therefore undoubtedly in the city and not in the temple. The single semaia mentioned in the Halōsis on which the controversy must have mainly turned was that of the one cohort in the Antonia. The Jews clearly regarded the castle as part of the sacred precincts, which in their view embraced the whole of the temple mount. The Romans, on the other hand, reckoned as sacred the temple with the walled courts surrounding it, and consequently maintained that this standard also had only been planted ' in the city.' The Jews, moreover, held that the whole of Jerusalem was holy ground, el quds, as the Arabs still call it ; for which reason before Pilate's time the troops had been accustomed to leave behind in Caesarea their standards, including the eagles with their thunderbolts of Jupiter Capitolinus and the imperial medallions,.

The unbounded excitement of the Jews at a proceeding which they regarded as an outrage on their religion, a defiance of their God, and a desecration of their sanctuary, is impressively depicted by Josephus, and in very similar language in all three accounts. I quote the hitherto unknown version of the story in the Halōsis, and

[1] B.J., v. 5. 8.

would draw attention to the abrupt way in which Pilate's name, not mentioned in the introductory lines on the new governor (p. 314 above), now crops up in the middle of the narrative, a clear indication either of the casual method by which the excerpts made for the first edition of the work were simply tacked together without any revision, or—according to our previous discussion—of the fact that some preceding paragraph has been deleted by the Christian censor.[1]

'And when morning came, the Jews saw (it, viz. the *semaia*) and raised (lit. fell into) a great uproar. And they were in consternation at the sight, because their law had been trampled under foot, for it ordains that there shall be no image within the city. And the people of the neighbouring country, on hearing what had happened, all with zeal rushed in and hastened to Caesarea and begged Pilate to remove the *semaia* from Jerusalem and to permit them to maintain the customs of their fathers. And when Pilate continued to decline their request, they fell on their faces and remained motionless for five days and nights. And after that Pilate took his seat on the throne in the great hippodrome and summoned the people, as though he intended to answer them. And he commanded the soldiers suddenly to surround the Jews in arms. And when they saw the unexpected sight of three bodies of troops surrounding them,[2] they were sore afraid. And Pilate said to them menacingly : " I shall cut you all down, if you will not admit Caesar's image," and he commanded the soldiers to draw their swords. But the Jews all with one consent fell down and, extending their necks, exclaimed that they were ready like sheep for the slaughter rather than transgress[3] the law. And Pilate, marvelling at their fear of God and (their) purity,[4] ordered the *semaia* to be taken out of Jerusalem.'

Still more instructive is a passage of Jerome :[5] "τὸ βδέλυγμα τῆς ἐρεμώσεως potest . . . accipi . . . *de imagine Caesaris, quam Pilatus posuit in templo.*" From this we learn that Jerome, or his rabbinical advisers who helped him to translate the Bible, were still aware that contemporary Jews saw in Pilate's outrage the fulfilment of Daniel's prophecy of the ' abomination of desolation,' to which impressive reference is made in the apocalyptic speech put into the mouth of Jesus.[6] According to *Dan.* xii. 11, this desecration of the sanctuary by the Romans[7] was to usher in the last times, extending over 1290 days or about three and a half years—in other words, roughly the period which Eusebius[8] on the basis of

---

[1] See above, p. 70.
[2] Greek : ' finding themselves in a ring of troops, three deep.'
[3] Slav., with change to *oratio recta*, ' rather than we will transgress.'
[4] Greek "τὸ τῆς δεισιδαιμονίας ἄκρατον." ἄκρατον = ' unmixed,' ' unmitigated,' was mistaken by the Slav as meaning ' pure.'
[5] On *Matt.* xxiv. 15, ed. Vallarsi, vii. 194.
[6] *Mark* xiii. 14-20 ; *Matt.* xxiv. 15-22.
[7] *Dan.* xi. 31.
[8] *Hist. eccl.*, i. 10.

PLATE XXII

ROMAN LEGIONARY STANDARD
WITH EXCHANGEABLE PORTRAIT-MEDALLION OF THE EMPEROR
COLLECTION OF E. J. SELTMAN, CAMBRIDGE

statements in the Fourth Gospel wished to assign to the public ministry of Jesus. At the end of this period the expiatory death of the Messiah (*jikareth mashiaḥ*) was to be looked for, and the devastation of the holy city in the messianic war which would continue ' unto the end.' The war would conclude with the annihilation of the prince of this world, the adversary of God, and of the godless in general, by a flood.[1] The prophecy in *Daniel*, directed against the eagle idol of Baal Shamîn,[2] i.e. of the Olympian Zeus of the Seleucides on the altar of the burnt-offering in Jerusalem, would now be taken to refer to the eagle on the standard of the legion and the medallion attached to it bearing the emperor's image. The desecration of ' the sanctuary, even the fortress,' [3] would be applied to the planting of the standards in the castle of Antonia on the temple mount ; the ' violation of the covenant ' to Pilate's preventing the Jews from ' maintaining the customs of their fathers.' Even the ' one week ' during which this oppression would continue [4] could appear to correspond well enough to the ' five days and nights ' of the supplication before Pilate, along with the day of his session in the hippodrome, in the narrative of Josephus. The apocalypse put into the mouth of Jesus [5] shows that many of his contemporaries expected the destructive flood to follow immediately the desecration of the sanctuary :

> ' When therefore ye see the abomination of desolation, which was spoken of by Daniel the prophet, standing in a holy place . . . then let them that are in Judaea flee unto the mountains : let him that is on the housetop not go down to take out the things that are in his house. . . . But woe unto them that are with child and to them that give suck in those days.' [6]

Of course, when as in the days of the prophet Jonah the flood of judgment did not come, the difficulty was got over by interpreting the oracle as pointing to a ' flood of war.' [7]

As the prophecy now stands, we cannot say with absolute certainty whether it really goes back to the time of Jesus and the offence caused by Pilate's standards, or whether it is not rather a prophecy of the world-judgment dating from the days of Caligula when that emperor desired the ' abomination of his image ' to be set up in the temple,[8] when the discreet Petronius hesitated as long as possible to carry out this mad order, until at the last moment the emperor's death averted the desecration of the sanctuary.

---

[1] See above, pp. 273 f.
[2] The ' abomination of desolation ' (*shiquz mᵉshomem*) is an alteration of *Ba'al beshamaim*, ' lord in heaven ' ; cf. Cheyne in *Encycl. Bibl.*, i. 21.
[3] *Dan.* xi. 31.　　　　　　　　　　[4] *Dan.* ix. 27.
[5] *Mark* xiii. 14 *sqq.* ; *Matt.* xxiv. 15 *sqq.*
[6] *Matt.* xxiv. 15 *sqq.* ; cf. *Mark* xiii. 14 *sqq.*
[7] Thus the δεσπόσυνοι, that is, Jesus' relatives according to Euseb., *Chron.*, trans. Karst, *G.C.S.*, xx. 209.　　　　[8] Jos., *Halōsis*, ii. 185.

But this does not imply that pious people in the time of Jesus
and Pilate, having heard of the desecration of the temple by the
standard of the cohort, did not really urge an immediate flight into
the mountains—not so much from any fear of the final flood, but
simply to seek refuge in the wilderness from Roman domination,
like those determined champions of liberty who since the war of
Varus had been living after the manner of the early Maccabees as
brigands in the mountains.   When Caligula gave orders for the
erection of his statue, the Jews retorted with the menace of an
agricultural strike, refusing to till or sow the ground, thus trying
to bring famine upon both the population and the garrison.   The
activist movement cannot, of course, have gone very far in this
first instance during the single week in which Pilate kept up his
attitude of defiance.   Still, it may safely be assumed that in those
days also, beside those Jews who ' like sheep ' ready for the
slaughter lay for five days in the dust before the governor, there
were not wanting others, more headstrong, of those ' brigands '
and ' zealots ' so hateful to Josephus, who immediately upon hearing of the blasphemous act took to the mountains, there to expect
the imminent judgment of God.

In any case, the words of the apocalypse in question,

' If therefore they shall say unto you, Behold, he is in the wilderness, go not forth,' [1]

are only intelligible in the light of those constantly recurring
attacks of Josephus against the champions of independence who
repaired to the hill-country,[2] the caves of Ḥauran,[3] or the wilderness [4] to escape intolerable oppression, and against those ' seducers
of the people ' who in the wilderness preached a return to desert
and Bedouin life already proclaimed by Hosea,[5] a new exodus for
the sake of liberty and independence.   Rabbinical traditions [6]
expressly interpret the forty-five surplus days before the end in
Daniel's prophecy as the time when the Messiah will lead into
the wilderness those who believe in him, but will immediately again
' hide himself ' from Israel : [7]

' From the time that . . . the " abomination of desolation " shall
be set up, there shall be 1290 days.   Blessed is he that waiteth and
cometh to the 1335 days.[8]   What is meant here by the surplus ?

---

[1] *Matt.* xxiv. 26.
[2] Cf. 1 *Macc.* ii. 28 : ' he (i.e. Judas the Maccabaean) and his sons fled into
the mountains . . . then there came down many searching for justice and right,
in order to dwell there in the desert.'
[3] *B.J.*, and *Hal.*, i. §§ 304-14.
[4] Cf. *Ps. Sal.*, xvii. 18 *sqq.* : ' the Ḥasidaean communities flee into the desert,
because king, judges, and people are polluted by sin.'
[5] ii. 14, 15 : ' I will allure her into the wilderness . . . as in the day when she
came up out of the land of Egypt.'
[6] Strack-Billerbeck, ii. 285.   [7] *Ibid.*   [8] *Dan.* xii. 11 *sq.*

These are the forty-five days when the Messiah after his manifestation shall again hide himself from them.   And whither does he lead them ? Some say, into the wilderness of Judah, and others say, into the wilderness of Sihon and Og :[1] " therefore, behold, I will allure her and bring her into the wilderness."[2]   He who believes in him will eat salt-wort[3] and roots of broom : he who believes not in him goes to the peoples of the world, and they kill him.'

Such a prediction might readily be referred to that portion of the people which resorted to Pilate to protest against the desecration of the temple, but were so maltreated by the soldiers that ' many perished from the blows.'[4]

It may be assumed, then, with a certain amount of probability that in the time of this uproar under Pilate, as on other occasions, the radical patriots withdrew into the wilderness.   Judas of Galilee was then doubtless dead, but Joḥanan the Baptist, the ' hidden one,'[5] was still to be found in the wild lowlands by the Jordan, and surely not slow in preaching to the crowds flocking to him on the ' abomination of desolation ' and the final flood now quite nigh at hand.   This is the situation which would best explain the Gospel story telling how Jesus gave his address in praise of the Baptist to the crowds which had flocked together in the Jordan valley to demand the redeeming baptism.   It explains also his praise of the 'violent men' who since the days of Archelaus (4 B.C.) have tried to ' take the kingdom of heaven by storm.'   It is probable that Jesus did not himself receive baptism until then, that is, in A.D. 19 and not in 4 B.C.   That would agree with the Mandaean traditions according to which John had for a whole generation administered the rite of baptism before Jesus came to him to receive it for himself.   For an assumption to the contrary—that is, to the effect that Jesus had joined the circle of the Baptist as early as the time of Varus and thus lived with the Baptist until the time of his first public appearance—we have only the support of the chronology of Luke, which, at least since the verset iii. 20 was inserted into this Gospel, seems to presuppose such a sojourn of Jesus for a number of years in the Jordan valley.   But in view of the artificial construction of this chronology discussed above,[6] I do not think that much importance can be attached to it.   On the contrary, the passing contact of these two preachers of the kingdom of God, who were spiritually not much alike, a contact such as is clearly intimated by the Gospels, would probably come closest to the historical reality, and Jesus no doubt soon after his baptism separated from John and his followers.

If he regarded himself as the promised Messiah, without any

---

[1] Bashan (Transjordania).   [2] *Hos.* ii. 14.
[3] Botan. ' orache.'   [4] *B.J.*, ii. 177.
[5] See above, p. 242.   [6] Cf. above, pp. 244, 303.

hope of being able definitely to convince his compatriots of his
Divine vocation, there was no place for him in the circle of the
patiently waiting disciples of the man who, after all the disappointments, after the downfall of Simon, Athrongas, and Judas of Galilee,
was still waiting for the 'greater one' to come and to bring liberty
to the enslaved and deeply stirred people.

THE CARPENTER AS MESSIAH BEN DAVID

How did Jesus become conscious of a Divine call as the anointed
king and liberator of his people ? The question can no longer be
answered in the conventional way by a reference to the vision of
the Spirit and the voice from heaven at his baptism, once the strong
probability is realized that those phenomena have been transferred, in a purely literary way, from the Baptist to Jesus. This
hypothesis notwithstanding, it is of course conceivable that some
ecstatic experience like the vision in question, or like that of Paul
on the road to Damascus, may have awakened the first consciousness of his own messiahship, and this experience may well be
imagined as happening in connexion with the sacred act of baptism,
convulsing his whole being to its depths. It may, indeed, have
been connected with that solemn sacrifice of the old life and regeneration as a royal 'son of God.'

Yet the fact—which is indeed the best proof of the perfect
sincerity of Jesus and cannot be lightly set aside—still remains that
he never either publicly or privately claimed to have had a vision
of God or some audition of a heavenly call, although that would
have been the one answer most likely to convince the Jews who so
often asked him about his ' authority ' for saying or doing such
unusual things. There is therefore nothing whatever to indicate
that he ever was a visionary or an ecstatic. The opinion of his
kinsfolk and fellow-citizens,[1] inclined to consider him as out of his
mind,[2] is simply due to their ignorance of his spiritual development. The Gospels mention it only as an example of the total
lack of understanding of his mission among his next of kin. The
passage in *Luke* x. 17 is the story not of a vision but rather of an
' omen,' a celestial phenomenon [3] really seen and interpreted in an
apocalyptic sense.

Recognition of these facts enhances the significance of a most
plausible theory of Dr. Albert Schweitzer.[4] He conjectures that

---

[1] *Mark* iii. 21 ; *John* x. 20.

[2] The ' psychiatric ' literature about Jesus is essentially worthless ; cf. A.
Schweitzer, *op. cit.*, p. 362 *sqq.* (not mentioned in the second Engl. ed. of 1911).

[3] In *John* xii. 29, 31 it is a thunderstroke ($\beta\rho\text{ov}\tau\acute{\eta}$) which heralds the falling
of the ' Lord of this world.' This goes well with the lightning ($\dot{a}\sigma\tau\rho\alpha\pi\acute{\eta}$) in Luke
x. 17.

[4] *Gesch. d. Leben-Jesu-Forschung*[3], p. 393 *sqq.*, Engl. transl., 2nd ed., London,
1911, p. 393.

the contention met with at a very early date, that Jesus was descended from some member of the Davidic line returned with Zerubabel from exile, has a sound historical basis and may well be at the bottom of the messianic claims of Jesus to kingship over the Jews.

It is indeed remarkable that so early a writer as Paul emphasizes the descent of Jesus from the old royal house.[1] ' How could he have ventured,' says Dr. Schweitzer, ' two or three decades after the death of Jesus, to make such an assertion if it had not the concurrence of those who knew the facts about his genealogy ? ' It is now actually established that the relatives of Jesus, the so-called δεσπόσυνοι, opposed the claims of the Naṣōraean Messiah to those of the Ascalonite (i.e. Philistine) usurper, Herod the Great,[2] supporting their contention by a Davidic pedigree of Jesus. If, then, Paul, 'who is elsewhere completely indifferent to the details of the earthly existence of Jesus,'[3] in one of his letters, written within the lifetime of James the Just, speaks of Jesus as a descendant of David, it necessarily follows, in my opinion, that ' Jesus' brother '[4] regarded himself and his family as of David's line. Paul, then, merely recognized this claim. Thus it was not only the nephews and grandnephews, starting from their villages of Kokhᵉba and Naṣareth to wander through the world as itinerant craftsmen, but James the Just himself, who asserted his claim to this pedigree. Nor can we suspect of *mala fides* a man whose strict rectitude is attested even by an opponent like Josephus, whatever we may think of the pedigree itself.

There are two arguments commonly adduced to disprove the Davidic descent of Jesus. In the first place, it is generally assumed that in the famous question, ' David himself calleth him Lord : how then is he his son ? '[5] Jesus questioned the justice of the common Jewish expectation that the Messiah would be a descendant of David, because he was not one himself, or because at least his descent from the old pre-exilic royal house was insufficiently established. But Dr. Schweitzer has rightly observed that the words may have borne a totally different meaning ; modern theologians have not taken into consideration the possibility that it may have been the speaker's consciousness of his own descent that prompted the question. Dr. Schweitzer, to be sure, does not

---

[1] *Rom.* i. 3 ; cf. 2 *Tim.* ii. 8. I am, of course, fully aware of the fact that there are critics who consider even the *Epistle to the Romans* as partly interpolated, while 2 *Tim.* is entirely rejected by a great number of scholars.

[2] See below, p. 606 ns. 3, 4, App. XIII.

[3] Schweitzer, *loc. cit.*

[4] On the title ' brother to the king,' severally attested in Oriental inscriptions for the vizier or viceroy, cf. Lucien Cerfaux, ' Le titre Kyrios et la dignité royale de Jésus,' *Revue des Sciences philosophiques et théologiques*, xii. (1923), fasc. ii.-iv., p. 141 n. 2.

[5] *Mark* xii. 35-37, and parallels.

X

touch the real problem, viz. what answer Jesus expected or would have given himself—perhaps because, like the old source itself, he thought that the answer might be left to the reader. To me it seems evident that Jesus intended to interpret *Ps.* cx. 1 by reference to another well-known *Psalm* (ii. 7), in which God says to the chosen king, 'Thou art my son, this day have I begotten thee.' He meant that it was not enough to be merely a son of David 'after the flesh'; the true Messiah must be called and chosen by God as his Anointed, adopted or newly begotten as his son; such a 'son of God' would then be the God-given 'Lord' and master of King David as of all other men. The speaker's meaning was simply: 'The Messiah *is* a *ben David* and must be so; yet not every descendant of David is the Messiah, else there would be many messiahs, but it is only the elect "son of God" who by his mercy will be the liberator.' The deciding factor is not genealogical descent alone, or indeed the right of primogeniture, which, of course, belonged not to Jesus but to the *zaken*, the oldest living member of the still flourishing clan of David,[1] but Divine calling, just as God through Samuel had called David and not the eldest of Jesse's sons to be king. The enigmatic question about the son of David asked in the temple appears, therefore, to be, like so many sayings of Jesus, but a stray fragment of a longer rabbinical disputation. It affords no argument against, but on the contrary it may be explained as supporting, the contention that Jesus actually laid claim to Davidic, i.e. royal, descent.

A second reason for hesitation in imputing to Jesus such lofty claims may be found in the well-attested fact that he belonged to the class of carpenters, to those Qenite and Rekhabite 'wayfaring people' from the 'valley of the carpenters.'[2] But this fact

---

[1] The clan of David was doubtless still living in Jerusalem, though, of course, devoid of all political importance, since it is never mentioned in connexion with the political struggles of the period. According to the *Mishna Ta'an.* iv. 5 (Schürer, ii.[4], 316 n. 59, Engl. trans., vol. ii. 1. p. 252 n. 112), they used to bring their offering of firewood to the altar of the temple on the 20th of Tammuz. Since thus, like a few other clans, their impost fell due on a special day, and not, like that of the rest of the people, on the 15th of Ab, the reason for this arrangement evidently was that they still owned so much real estate that the delivery of their wood required a good deal of time. A sept of the clan, as we know from other sources, had remained in Babylon; cf. Isr. Lévy, *Revue des Études juives*, xxxi. 211. Old Hillel, likewise of Davidic descent, was so poor that he had to earn his living as a wood-cutter. Thus it need not cause surprise that among the poorer members of the tribe there also was a carpenter. Flavius Josephus, however, had good reasons for not emphasizing unduly the royal descent of Jesus, or of any other member of the Davidic clan, and thereby invalidating his own interpretation of *Gen.* xlix. 10 proclaiming Vespasian as the Messiah. That the latter had no illusions on the subject is shown by his proscription of Davidides, as reported by Hegesippus in Euseb., *Hist. eccl.*, iii. 12; cf. also Eduard Meyer, *Ursprung u. Anf. d. Christentums*, i. 73 n. 2.

[2] 1 *Chron.* iv. 14 read: '*ubᵉnēj qa(j)n ze(h) 'abhi gēj ḥarashîm*,' '. . . and the sons of Qain (=smith), the ancestor of the valley of carpenters, for they are carpenters.'

in no way excludes a descent, more or less established, from some one of those obscure members of the Davidic clan of the post-exilic period who are named at the end of the genealogy. The Qainite genealogies show that it was well known that it was just among those homeless vagabonds that one might expect to find fugitives and ' sons of Jared,' persons who had ' come down¹ in the world.' It was proverbial that even women of noble birth, deserted or divorced by their husbands, sought shelter with these roving folk : 'As people are wont to say, "A descendant of princes and sovereigns, she associated with carpenters." ' ²   But there were doubtless also men of noble birth among the Rekhabites. According to the Jahvist's genealogy of the Qainites,³ Qain the ' smith ' or smelter of metal begat Ḥanukḥ, i.e. the ' initiate,' and he 'Irad the ' fugitive,' i.e. the ejected ⁴ and hunted one who goes about with the nomads and fugitives.⁵ In the parallel genealogy of the Priestly Document (Gen. v. 12 sqq.), Qenan ⁶ the 'smith' begets Mahal-le'El the ' circumciser for God,' or ' operator,' the itinerant surgeon for man and beast, carrying on the same trade as to-day,⁷ and he Jared, the man who has ' come down ' in the world.⁸

If the genealogy of Jesus in Luke iii. 37 is expressly carried back to this 'Jared son of Mahal-le'El, son of Qainan,' member of the tribe of the Qainites or itinerant craftsmen, we should compare with this the rabbinical tradition ⁹ that the Messiah 'will not come from the great sons of Jacob, but from his fallen children (habbanîm hajjarudîm) : God says, To the humblest and smallest of the sons of Jacob will I bring the sinful kingdom (i.e. the Roman empire) into subjection.'

In these circumstances, easily to be explained from a socio-logical point of view, there is no reason whatever to question a tradition of Davidic descent current in a particular Rekhabite or Qainite tribe of carpenters (ḥarashîm).   That the Jewish itinerant craftsmen of that day should have included ' reduced ' noblemen in their ranks is not surprising, and that these would be the very people to preserve the tradition of their descent is just what one would expect.   Add to this the fact that however doubtful the

---

¹ jarad, hence jōr°dîm, ' déclassés.' Cf. Gen. r., sect. 71, 71a, etc. ; Levy Nhb. Wb., ii. 264a.

² Saying of R. Papa (died in 376), Sanhedrin, 106a.

³ Gen. iv. 17 sqq.

⁴ Gen. r., sect. 23, toward the beginning : 'Irad—this means, "I chase them from the world."'

⁵ Cf. Gen. iv. 12.

⁶ Another form of Qain with the archaic post-positive article.

⁷ Cf. A. J. Sinclair, Journal of the Gypsy Lore Society, new series, i. 203 : 'the Sleb or Nwar are tattooers among the Beduins. They also circumcise and are doctors.'

⁸ Cf. Gen. r., sect. 71, 71a : ' he who has fallen from his fortune,' i.e. ' the man of broken fortunes is like unto a dead man '; further, Levy, Nhb. Wb., s.v. jārad.

⁹ Pesiq. r., Minni Ephraim, 23b.

details of his tragic fate remain, in spite of all researches, Żerubabel, the Davidite, who rebuilt the temple, certainly came to an unfortunate end, and it is natural that his downfall should have involved his relations, or at least a goodly number of them, in misery and obscurity.

Again, we have to note the fact, frequently emphasized since the time of Grotius,[1] that the genealogy of David in Matthew's Gospel expressly names the two notorious harlots Tamar and Rahab, and calls attention to Solomon's being the offspring of David's adulterous marriage with ' her of Uriah.' This can serve but one object, namely, as a retort to the Jewish slander upon Jesus, whom his adversaries called ' the son of the harlot.' [2] For it thus indicated that the opprobrious term must consistently be applied also to the greatest of the Jewish kings.[3] The slander need not in its origin have had any connexion with the story of the miraculous conception. It can be sufficiently explained by the evil reputation of the daughters of the ' wayfaring people,' who, like the itinerant women of the Ṣleb, the Nwar, or other gipsy-like vagabonds of the desert of to-day, were dancers and players and therefore regarded as prostitutes,[4] quite capable of attracting and ' degrading ' men of the highest ancestry.

From a sociological point of view there is thus not the slightest reason to doubt the historicity of the Davidic descent of a particular family of itinerant carpenters. More than the fact that such traditions existed among the relations of Jesus need not be admitted. To investigate what degree of truth there is in the tradition would be idle. But it can hardly be doubted that Paul and James the Just honestly believed it. So it matters little that we have no means of deciding whether the alleged son or grandson of Zerubabel, who ended his life in poverty and left to his children and children's children no more than a pedigree, orally transmitted and becoming more and more confused, was a genuine or a supposed descendant of David, or a mere pretender. At all events, there are certainly more king's children about in the world than appear in the genealogies. Add to this that in the Oriental harems the sons of freeborn wives and those of slave concubines were not always sharply distinguished. It is clear, finally, that had there never been a genuine prince in reduced circumstances among these

---

[1] Cf. the latest contribution to the subject : Clyde Pharr in *Am. Journ. Phil.*, xlviii. (1927), p. 146 *sqq.*

[2] *Pesiq. Rab.*, 21 (100b, 101a).

[3] According to the so-called Lucianic recension of the LXX. text (ed. Lagarde, 1883), King Jeroboam was the son of a harlot (1 *Kings* xi. 26) ; even Melkhisedeq is said by the Jews to have no more illustrious origin, according to Epiphan., *Haeres.*, lv. 7, ed. Holl, ii. 333. The same origin is assigned to Jephtha the judge (*Judg.* xi. 1).

[4] Cf. the example of Ja'el, the famous Qenite heroine of *Judges* v. 24-7, called a harlot in a Baraitha Meg. 15a (Strack-Billerbeck, i. 20, No. 1).

'wayfaring folk,' no one would have attached any credit to the tales of these ' grandees ' living incognito in their midst.[1] What numbers of such adventurers there are among the gipsy-like pedlars and jugglers of the East may be inferred from the jesting names applied by the Arabs to the class as a whole—*banu Sasan*, ..e. ' Sassanidae ' or scions of the old Persian royal house, and ' Barmecides ' or sons of the old Bactrian family of the famous vizir of the Calif Harun al Rashid.

Here, it would seem, as Dr. Schweitzer has ingeniously surmised, is to be found the real key to the understanding of the messianic claims of Jesus the Naṣōraean.   Imagine the situation of that moment, fraught with portentous meaning for the faithful, when Pilate by planting the emperor's standards on the holy mount seemed to have fulfilled the prophecy of Daniel concerning the ' abomination of desolation ' standing in the holy place !   Now, if ever, the measure of the crimes committed by the ' godless government' was complete ; now, if ever, must God's chosen 'son of David' appear.   Yet among the noble Davidides dwelling in their stately home in Jerusalem,[2] perhaps also in part in Bethlehem, the call of the hour produced not the slightest echo.   Their attitude was certainly the same as that of the rest of the nobility, the landowners in the country, the householders,[3] and the high priesthood in the city.   Like all Jewish aristocrats, they were, if not pro-Roman at heart, at least opportunist and conservative, regarding the activist partisans of freedom with coolness or actual hostility. They who had much, nay, everything, to lose by war, were all for peace, almost at any price.   None of the ' sons of David '[4] had ever given the least trouble to the Hasmonaeans, no ' ben David ' had figured among the opponents of that 'Philistine' Herod the Great and the Herodians.   Why should they at this moment plan a rebellion against the Romans ?   Why should people who for centuries after the fall of Zerubabel had never made the least attempt to recover a leading position in the nation, suddenly make common cause with the 'zealots,' 'outsiders,' 'brigands,' or whatever epithet that party might be given by the aristocrats ?   When

---

[1] Cf. the vast literature on the various pretenders who, from the Middle Ages to modern times, have aroused the attention of the credulous masses and often enough even of the authorities.   A good many of them belonged to this very class of itinerant adventurers, and some of them may have had genuine claims, which they could not prove in the face of the illwill and deliberate misrepresentation of persons interested in discrediting the true heirs to a throne or other large estate.

[2] See above, p. 322 n. 1.

[3] Cf. Josephus, *Halōsis*, iv. §§ 207 and 379.

[4] Their political opinion is found in the genuine nucleus of the heavily interpolated so-called *Ecclesiastes*, the real title of which is *Dibhrēj qehillath Ben David* : ' Acts (or Words—as we should say now, ' Minutes ') of the assembly of the son of David,' i.e. the assembly called (as in 1 *Kings* viii. 1) by King Solomon, supposed to have come back from his exile.

Mattathias and his sons had arisen for freedom, when Ḥezeqiah the Galilaean and his son Judas, when Simon and Athrongas, rose against the despots, which of the sons of David had ever moved a finger in those struggles ? Conversely, which of the champions of freedom had ever thought it possible to inspire one of the noble scions of the old royal house to liberate the people from the foreign yoke ? Of the Davidides who had made their peace with this world,[1] none can have desired to promote the coming of the 'future world' by strife and suffering.

Far otherwise was it with those members of the clan who, homeless and without possessions, roamed through the land with the 'wayfaring folk,' supporting themselves with their manual labour as carpenters and craftsmen, even as Hillel the Davidide earned his living as a woodcutter, and of all the splendour and wealth of the old royal house had inherited but the entrancing dreams of world-dominion by the grace of God, and the ancestral tradition of the *kosmokratōr* Solomon,[2] driven into exile and his place taken by the demon Ashmodai. Is it surprising that these people, disinherited by fate, should have cherished as a last con-solation in misery the ancient prophecies of a return of the old splendour, of a restoration of the throne of David and of a return of the exiled King Solomon, the 'son of David' the legendary king of the whole world, said to have ruled first over the hosts of the upper and the lower world, then only over all the inhabitants of the earth, then only over the tribes of Israel, until nothing but his bed and his sceptre and finally only his beggar's staff [3] remained to the great king, turned into a nameless wanderer, who ' had not where to lay his head '—the unfortunate ruler of whom nobody knew whether he was dead or alive, straying incognito through foreign lands, whence he would come back at the end of days ? Is it surprising that in one of these sons of David the blood of the old adventurer and freebooter, victorious in battle and risen to be King of Israel, while yet remaining a *troubadour*,[4] should have stirred up again and driven this poet [5] and dreamer to

---

[1] Even the descendants of the poor Davidide Hillel sided with the high priest-hood. Cf. Josephus, *B.J.*, iv. 3. 9; *Vita*, 38 *sq.*, 44, 60. The great-grandson of Hillel was a member of the embassy sent to Galilee by the high priests and so gently fooled by Josephus (above, p. 185). Cf. Isr. Lévy, *Revue des Études juives*, xxxi. 203.

[2] Esther rabba, s.v. *bajamim hahem*, and parallels, a legend not later than the Seleucid period, since Alexander is named as the latest *kosmokratōr* known.

[3] *Sanhedrin*, 20b.

[4] On the authenticity of some of the songs attributed to David, see my papers in the *M.V.A.G.* (1917), vol. xxii. (1918), and *J.A.O.S.*, 1926, p. 45.

[5] The *Ṣleb* are still famous as poets and minstrels ; cf. Doughty, *Arabia Deserta*, i. 556 ; Frh. v. Oppenheim, *Vom Mittelmeer zum persischen Golf*, i. 220 ; Butler, *Geogr. Journ.*, xxxiii. (1909), p. 524 ; Wetzstein, *Z.D.M.G.*, xxii. 125, 161 *sq.* Thus there is no difficulty in assuming that the author of the entrancing Gospel parables was one of those *qenîm* and *ḥarashîm*, the 'wayfaring tinkers folk' of antiquity.

step forth from the dark life in which he lived, to proclaim in this time of the deepest humiliation of his people a renewal of the ancient glory through a miracle of God immediately impending ?

That a *ben ḥarash*, a ' son of the carpenter folk,' a poor labourer, could indulge in the alluring dreams of kingship, and that he could find followers to believe in the wandering craftsman as the future liberator-king, becomes intelligible only if we take into consideration the idea of the Messiah coming from among the ranks of the *joreḍîm*, the ' déclassés ' sons of Israel,[1] along with the Christological inferences drawn from the prophecy of Zechariah (ii. 3 *sq.*) concerning the four carpenters in the time of deliverance : [2]

'Jahwe showed me four smiths' (*or* carpenters).[3] ' Then said I, "What come these to do?" And he spake saying, "These are the horns which scattered Judah . . . but these are come to affright them, to cast down the horns of the nations." And these are the four carpenters as David has interpreted them : " Gilead is mine," that is Elijah who belonged to the inhabitants of Gilead : " Manasseh is mine," that is the Messiah who will arise from the sons of Manasseh,[4] " Before Ephraim and Benjamin and Manasseh stir up thy might " ; " Ephraim the defence of mine head," that is the Anointed of war ' (elsewhere Messiah b. Joseph or b. Ephraim), ' who will come from Ephraim,[5] " His firstling bullock " (= Ephraim and his posterity) " . . . with them (his horns) shall he push (*or* gore) the peoples" ; "Judah is my sceptre," *that is the great redeemer who shall arise from the descendants of David.' *[6]

The remarkable fact that these expositors of Zechariah refer to the Messiah b. David as a ' smith' may perhaps be compared with the legend attested both in old Arabian pre-Islamic poetry and in the Qoran,[7] that King David of old times had been an armourer.

Zechariah's mysterious night-vision of the four *ḥarashîm* has never been satisfactorily explained. The key to the riddle is probably to be found in the fact that the word *ḥarash* not only, like the Latin *faber*, means any sort of worker in wood, stone, or metal, but also, in virtue of the original magical conception of the smith's and craftsman's art, has the further meaning of 'magician.' If we adopt this latter acceptation, the sense of the passage is clear. Judah and Israel are menaced by four horns, the horns of the peoples of the world, represented as mighty monsters. The seer beholds these overpowering creatures opposed by four *magicians*, who by their magical art ' cast down' the horns. These 'magicians' are then interpreted by the expositors as denoting the various messianic saviours of the last days : the prophet Elijah, the Messiah b. Joseph (who for the purposes of this interpretation

---

[1] See above, p. 323 n. 9.
[2] *Num. r.*, 14 (172b).
[3] LXX. : τέκτονες. M.T. : *ḥarashîm*.
[4] See *Ps.* lxxx. 3 (2).
[5] See *Deut.* xxxiii. 17.
[6] *Num. r.*, 14 (172b) ; Strack-Billerbeck, i. 700, ii. 294 *sq.*
[7] Surat, xxxiv. 10.

appears in two forms, the Messiah b. Ephraim and the Messiah b. Manasseh, the high priests of the last age), and lastly the Messiah b. David. A 'Davidide' who was at once a *ḥarash*, a worker in iron or wood, and a *ḥakham ḥarashîm*,[1] a 'healer,' could not fail to find in this prophecy of Zechariah [2] a Divine confirmation of his mission. If *ḥarashîm* were called to redeem Israel, if the Messiah b. David was destined to be one of these, who could fail to see the hand of God in the dispensation of Providence which had driven a family of the stock of David into the ranks of these homeless and vagrant workmen ? Far from deterring him from his purpose, his humble rank and calling can only have confirmed Jesus in the consciousness of his mission as Israel's liberator. 'Assuming, as he does, a revaluation of values, on the basis of which what is now great will become small and what is now small become great,[3] he had to expect the Messiah of the last days, if he first leads an earthly existence, to belong to the poor and the humble.' [4]

There is another fact which has not, so far as I know, been noticed before, viz. that these itinerant craftsmen, *ḥarashîm* or *naggarîm*, the *Sleb* of those days, also practised the professions of divination and healing. It is not different with the modern *Sleb*, who ' are good joiners and carpenters, who make for their customers wooden frames for the pack-saddles of their beasts of burden,[5] pulleys for their wells, wooden vessels, and the like.' [6] To their medical skill the Carmelite father St. Élie has devoted a whole section of his monograph.[7] 'On their rounds they treat both men and cattle, by surgery, cauterizing, and anointing.' [8] A parallel may be found in the Old Testament,[9] where a genealogy of the Rekhabites expressly mentions *Beth Rᵉfa'*, the ' tribe of the healer,' as a subdivision of these vagrants. These are the persons whom Josephus [10] has in mind when speaking of the γόητες or ' sorcerers,' who excite the people with their miracles and promises, and whom he holds responsible for various insurrections against the Romans. If such a *ḥarash*, in addition to the general reputa-

---

[1] *Isaiah* iii. 3.

[2] This prophecy at the same time contained the prediction of the ' lowly ' one ' riding upon an ass ' (ix. 9). It is to be noted that the *Sleb* of to-day are also experts in the taming of wild asses, whilst the Bedouins have always preferred camel-breeding. It is likely enough that the ' wayfaring folk ' of old also travelled on asses.

[3] *Mark* x. 31 ; *Matt.* xix. 30 ; *Luke* xiii. 30.

[4] Albert Schweitzer, *op. cit.*, p. 393.

[5] According to Justin Martyr, *Dialog. c. Tryph.*, 80, Jesus was a joiner, who made yokes for cattle and similar agricultural implements.

[6] Doughty, *op. cit.*, p. 280.

[7] *Al Mashriq*, i., No. 15, 18g, p. 680.

[8] Cf. *Mark* vi. 13 on Jesus' disciples anointing the sick.

[9] *I Chron.* iv. 12. Cp. my paper on the Qenites in the Swedish review, *Le Monde Oriental*, 1929, p. 107.

[10] *Ant.*, xx. 5. 1, § 97.

tion enjoyed by his people as faith-healers, quack doctors, and exorcists, could further claim to be a descendant of David and of the wise King Solomon, that expert in all magic, obeyed not only by men but also by beasts and demons, so that to all the skill of the veterinary surgeon he united the prerogative of kingship to heal and to cure by touch,[1] sick people would naturally throng around him. Thus a flood of light is thrown on certain New Testament passages relating how crowds of afflicted sufferers clamouring for miracles were cured by Jesus. Those cases, rightly emphasized by Dr. Schweitzer, become intelligible if we recall how on certain occasions Jesus was hailed by them as 'son of David,' a designation which may be used in a general sense as a 'descendant of David,' or in a more limited sense for a ' second Solomon,' lord of demons. But it does not in the least imply that the person so addressed is the Messiah, the divinely chosen liberator-king, any more than when it was applied to the elder Hillel. Jesus can have had no reason to conceal the family tradition of Davidic descent, in which he believed as sincerely as his brother. True, the *ḥarashim* healed with the knife or redhot iron ; but no one looks for miraculous cures by a word or touch from any ordinary member of this tribe of itinerant ' jugglers ' and tinkers. But if the people had heard of a mysterious king's son, a Solomon *redivivus* hidden among the wandering carpenter folk, they might well have credited him with extraordinary powers. When after the cure of the blind and dumb man 'the multitudes were amazed and said, "Is this the son of David?"'[2] this statement is distinguished from the previous instances,[3] as Dr. Schweitzer failed to observe, by the use of the definite article. The ' ben David ' has here clearly a messianic sound. ' Is not this really the son of David ? ' cannot mean merely 'Is this not really *a* son of David,' a descendant of the mighty king of old, a second Solomon ? It might possibly be interpreted as 'the descendant of David of whom rumour says so much.' But the Evangelist certainly did not so understand it, and the wild excitement of the people is only intelligible if they thought they saw before them *the* son of David of whom it was foretold that he would make the blind to see, the lame to walk, the lepers clean, and the dead to rise.[4] If the relations of Jesus on one such occasion thought that he was out of his senses,[5] they doubtless understood that he regarded himself as more than what they were themselves, as more than just a descendant of David—that he meant henceforth to appear as *the* ben David of the last days.

With experiences of this kind begins the typical cycle of such

---

[1] J. G. Frazer, *The Magic Art and the Evolution of Religion*, London, 1911, i. 368 *sqq.* ; Marc Bloch, *Les rois thaumaturges*, Paris, 1924.
[2] *Matt.* xii. 22 *sq.*   [3] *Mark* x. 47-8 ; *Matt.* xv. 22.
[4] *Matt.* xi. 4-6 ; *Luke* vii. 22 f.   [5] *Mark* iii. 21.

phenomena, the reaction upon each other of the person conscious of an extraordinary call and of the people surrounding the man of destiny. Every one who brings his own faith, capable of moving mountains, into contact with the genius who has faith in his own mission, thus further confirms him in his consciousness of Divine election. Jesus works miracles because he regards himself as the ' ben David ' chosen by God, as the ' smith ' of salvation, as the ' carpenter ' or ' builder ' of the world that is to be recreated, and the miracles he works confirm his faith in his election by the grace of God.

THE MESSIANIC SECRET. THE TRIBUTE MONEY AND THE SERVICE OF MAMMON

The external conditions of the life of Jesus discussed above not only furnish a simple and satisfactory explanation of the origin of his consciousness of messiahship, but also at once render intelligible a number of circumstances attendant on his appearance which have long been a mystery. In particular, they explain that apparently restless, one is tempted to say aimless, wandering from place to place which in the Gospels gives an impression that Jesus continually sought to withdraw himself from persecutors and admirers alike. It also solves that much-debated question, the so-called messianic secret.

Dr. Schweitzer had still to admit that ' the question why Jesus made a secret of his expectation of being revealed as the Messiah cannot be fully answered. We can only gather from his attitude that he was most anxious to keep it a secret : his motives are not ascertainable.' It may now be said quite simply that the reasons for his attitude are to be sought in the most obvious motives of worldly wisdom and political precaution. An aspirant to a kingdom, without a following, in search of helpers and confidants, cannot without more ado appear with his claims in the open market. He must speak in innuendoes, indicate his meaning by parabolic actions, such as the messianic miracle of the feeding of the multitudes, refrain from every word which would enable his opponents to convict him of his real plans and intentions, if he is not to be annihilated before having brought even to a small circle of the elect the good news that the longed-for liberation is at hand. As an apt illustration we may adduce the story of the slave Clement, claiming, in the reign of Tiberius, to be the secretly murdered Agrippa Postumus[1] and guardedly traversing the country, everywhere trying to win over adherents. These *secreti eius socii*, as Tacitus calls

---

[1] Agrippa Julius Caesar, grandson and legitimate heir of Augustus. See Gardthausen, in Pauly-Wissowa's *R.E.*, x. 183 ff.

them,[1] correspond exactly to the *noṣᵉrîm,* 'keeping the secret of the
kingdom.' [2] All those who are regarded as 'lost,' as 'God-forsaken,'
all those who have surrendered to the 'lords of this world,'
to the emperor and his race, are not predestined to understand
him; not to prevent these rejected ones from finding an opportunity
for repentance and redemption,[3] but to prevent the opponents of
the Messiah's kingdom, οἱ ἔξω, from hearing and seeing what is in
preparation, lest by a precipitate interference they nip the flower
in the bud.   For these reasons Jesus acted on a passage he found
in the prophet Daniel, immediately before the verset which had
such decisive influence on his public appearance, viz. the apocalyptic calculation of the time of the setting up of the 'abomination
of desolation' in the sanctuary : [4] 'many shall purify themselves
and make themselves white and be refined ; but the wicked shall
do wickedly, and none of the wicked shall understand,[5] but they
that be wise shall understand.'   His secret is no other than that
of the Baptist, no other than that ' kept ' by the Naṣōraeans from
the outset for the most cogent reasons, the secret from which the
noṣᵉrîm took their name.

The most instructive instance of this wise concealment of
doctrines not to be revealed to opponents is the dialogue concerning
the tribute money.[6] The messengers sent to ensnare him ' who
leads the people astray' ask Jesus outright what his attitude is
toward the doctrine of Judas of Galilee and his *Barjonîm* followers,
who ever since the governorship of Coponius (A.D. 6-9) had advocated refusal to pay taxes to the Romans.   A frank reply to this
question would have explained unequivocally his political convictions.   The answer he gave, though failing to deceive the spies,[7]
has effectually deceived the majority of later commentators.   Thus
it happened that Jesus is now commonly supposed to have taught
not merely subjection to the Romans but unconditional recognition
of all worldly authority and of every government, no matter how
rotten.   Says the late Edward Holton James : [8] ' These words
(i.e. ' Give to Caesar,' etc.) have been a stumbling-block to those
who wished to reform or to abolish the wrongs of human society.
They have been a rock of defence for the unjust ruler.   They have
been so interpreted and twisted as to make Jesus the active apologist
for nearly every form of wrong or wickedness which man can

---

[1] *Ann.,* ii. 39 *sq.*: 'tum per idoneos et *secreti eius socios* crebrescit vivere
Agrippam *occultis primum sermonibus, ut vetita solent,* mox vago rumore apud
imperitissimos cuiusque promptas aures aut rursum apud turbidos eoque nova
cupientes.' Cf. 2 *Macc.* viii. 1 : ' Judas the Maccabee and those around him
secretly (λεληθότες) entered the villages,' etc.
[2] See above, p. 233₈.
[3] The terrible words of *Mark* iv. 12b are missing in *Luke* ix. 10.
[4] *Dan.* xii. 10.   [5] Cf. *Isaiah* vi. 10.
[6] *Matt.* xxii. 15 *sqq.*   [7] Cf. *Luke* xxiii. 2.
[8] *The Trial before Pilate,* Concord, Mass., 1909, p. 22.

commit.' Through the conventional interpretation the political attitude taught by Jesus is just identified with that of Paul, which is that of the Essenes of Josephus and of the rabbinical Quietists.[1]

But that is to miss the most essential circumstance in the story. Jesus has not a single *denarius* with him ; he has to have one brought to him by his questioners. How comes that ? Why is the wandering craftsman so completely penniless ? Has he found no work for weeks and spent his last savings, or has he given up working in order to teach, entirely against rabbinic principles and habits ? If so, why is there no word to this effect ? Some explanation is clearly wanted here. The solution of the difficulty is simple : Jesus has no money because he *will* have none of it. This refusal to have anything to do with money at all is not isolated. ' Why,' we read in the Talmud,[2] ' is Naḥum called the holiest of holy [3] (men) ? Because he never in his whole life so much as looked at a coin.' In the corresponding passage in the Babylonian Talmud we read : [4] ' Rabbi Menaḥem bar Simai, a son of the holy. Why is he so called ? Because he never looked at a coin.' This Rabbi Menaḥem was a son of the late Tannaite Simai, and lived in the third century of our era. But the anecdote told in the Palestinian Talmud of a Naḥum of whom no further particulars are given may well have been erroneously transferred to a later Menaḥem.[5]

However that may be, Jesus who carries no money thus acts in this particular respect like the Essenes, among whom 'there is no commerce,[6] but each of them takes what he wants as his own, for it is accumulated by none,' 'and they have no private property whatsoever among them.' [7] He further expressly forbade his disciples to carry any money,[8] and to accept payment from anybody.[9] The only reward [10] for their labour was to be their food, ' for the labourer is worthy of his meat.' [11]

[1] See above, p. 257 nn. 3 and 7.
[2] *T.J. Meg.*, iii. 74a. *Aboda zara*, iii. 42, 43b.   [3] Cf. above, p. 138 n. 1.
[4] *T.B. Pesaḥ*, 104a ; *Aboda zara*, 50a.
[5] *Naḥum* was currently used as an abbreviation of *Menaḥem*. The ' holy (people),' among whom Naḥum or Menaḥem is distinguished for special ' holiness,' are doubtless the Essenes, who were not allowed to carry money with them. The Naḥum or Menaḥem here referred to may be the famous Essene Menaḥem, a contemporary of Herod the Great, and extolled by Josephus, *Ant.*, xv. 371 *sqq.*
[6] This attitude was taken up *in theory* by some of the Christian fathers, notably Tertullian, *De idol.*, 11.
[7] *Ant.*, xv. 373 *sqq.* ; *Halōsis*, ii. 122, 127. Cf. Lucian (*De Peregr. morte*, ch. xiii.), who ranks it as one of the leading innovations of Christianity that they hold all their possessions in common. (Th. Gaster.)
[8] *Mark* vi. 8 ; *Luke* ix. 3.
[9] This rigorous defence of Jesus has been expurgated in the canonic gospels, but it is frequently mentioned by early Christian witnesses (Alfred Resch, *Agrapha* [2], Leipzig, 1906, p. 198, saying, No. 171 : ' Accept nothing from anybody and own nothing on earth ' ; Armenian : ' Do not accumulate money in this world ').
[10] "μισθός," *Luke* x. 7, means ' board and lodging.'
[11] *Matt.* x. 10.

To give a correct idea of this fundamental rule, one must compare what modern travellers have to tell of the itinerant craftsmen of the desert, the Ṣleb, so called because of their bearing the cross-mark (aṣ-ṣalib), the ' sign of Qain,' on their forehead :

> ' One ought to draw a distinction between voluntary and involuntary poverty, the former of which alone is properly called "lack of possession " (Besitzlosigkeit). In this sense the Ṣleb are certainly without possession. Poverty in the desert is the surest protection. Knowing this, they have no ambition to become rich [1] and the owners of numerous camels, horses, etc., the less so because they have practically no competitors in their special callings in Arabia. They appear to work for ridiculously low wages. . . .' [2]

Doughty writes : [3]

> ' The Ṣolubba . . . have corn and dates enough, besides samn and mereesy for their smith's labour. The Solubby has need of a little silver in his metal craft, to buy him solder and iron ; the rest, increased to a bundle of money, he will, they say, bury in the desert sooner than carry it along with him, and return, perhaps after years, to take it up again, having occasion, it may be, to buy him an ass.'

Their lack of possessions is to be explained only by their having absolutely no needs and by their consciousness that, with their known peaceable disposition, riches could be of no use to them. Their goods being few, their existence is proportionately free of care.[4] In contrast to these are the Bedouins, who are in continual fear lest the successful raid of some powerful neighbouring tribe rob them of all their possessions. Hence that careless and naïve serenity [5] reflected in the features of the Ṣleb, as contrasted with the ever-suspicious bedouin. It is quite conceivable that the Ṣleb, if permitted to pass into the social position of their employers, would from their point of view make no profitable bargain. On their vocation as journeymen Huber [6] merely states that at the time of the date-harvest they repair to the oasis of Ṭaima, where in return for their services they accept payment in dates, which, on reaching their home in the Ḥala, they conceal in hiding-places and keep for the summer, when they live on hunting. According to the same author, during the winter months, when the bedouins have brought in their harvest of dates, etc., and in consequence of the revival of vegetation have milk, cheese, fat, and meat in abundance, the Ṣleb

---

[1] Cf. *Matt.* vi. 19 against the accumulation of wealth, and *Luke* xii. 16-21, the parable of the silly rich man (ὁ θησαυρίζων αὐτῷ).

[2] W. Pieper, *op. cit.*, 24 n. 2, 34 *sq.*

[3] *Arabia Deserta*, i. 283.

[4] Cf. *Matt.* vi. 25, *Luke* xii. 22, *Matt.* vi. 34, about not worrying for the coming day—the great ' stone of stumbling ' for the modern economist.

[5] The serenity of the ' children ' in *Matt.* xviii. 3.

[6] *Journal d'un voyage en Arabie* (1883-4), p. 588.

resort to them to do smith's work. These wandering craftsmen do not scorn money on principle, as appears from their breeding of asses and their trade with these animals. But they are still in the primitive economic stage of symbiotic barter and free reciprocal service. The statements reflecting on what Western travellers [1] superciliously call their 'beggarliness' show that they still, without any 'reckoning' [2] of the respective value of what is given and what is taken, gladly and naïvely accept from, or indeed beg of, every one what they need,[3] as willingly as they impart to every one what they in their capacity of skilled workmen and physicians are in a position to give.

Wherever men with these long-inherited and naïve economical ideas are brought into contact with the hardness of a society bent on wealth and given to commerce, and in addition ground down by hard taxation, the moral questionableness of the whole system of grasping covetousness [4] must be painfully brought home to them.

No wonder, then, that Jesus, the wandering carpenter and healer, the Qenite or Rekhabite, rejects money on principle, both for himself and his disciples. He postulates the gratuitous gift of all services to one's neighbour as a free act of love. Thus only the discourse on the tribute money becomes intelligible. The 'lovers of money' [5] who carry about with them and possess the Roman emperor's money,[6] and with it the image of the 'lord of this world,' [7] the enemy of God who claims worship for himself, owe 'his money,' the poll-tax, to that lord. They have fallen away from God and so have irretrievably incurred servitude and the payment of tribute to the emperor. But he who, like Jesus and his disciples, disdains Caesar's money and the whole monetary system of the empire, and who enjoys with his brethren the loving communion of all possessions of the 'saints,' such an one has renounced the service of idols and is no longer indebted to Caesar but merely to God, to whom he owes body, soul, thoughts, words, and works—in short, everything. 'Render unto Caesar the things that are Caesar's' really means : 'Throw Caesar's, i.e. Satan's, money down his throat,[8] so that you may then be free to devote yourselves wholly to the service of God.' 'For no man can serve two masters : for either he will hate the one and love the other, or else he will hold to the one and despise the other. Ye cannot serve God and

---

[1] Doughty, op. cit., i. 284 ; Lady Blunt, op. cit., ii. 110.
[2] In this respect, cf. Matt. xx. 12-15.
[3] Cf. Matt. vii. 7, Luke xi. 9, the naïve confidence of the wandering tinker.
[4] Luke xiii. 15, ' beware of all πλεονεξία ' =Exod. xx. 17.
[5] Luke xvi. 14.
[6] I.e. silver ; the local kinglets could only coin copper.
[7] John xii. 31.
[8] The reader will remember the anecdote about the Parthians pouring molten gold into the throat of Crassus (Cass. Dio., xl. 27. 3 ; Florus, iii. 11. 11).

mammon,' [1] *mammon* being the whole system of money and credit, [2] which, like some rival god [3] and the author of all evil, is the real temporal 'lord of this world.' [4] Far from sanctioning the payment of tribute to Caesar, Jesus is wholly on the side of Judas of Galilee, but goes far beyond him in that he requires his disciples, the citizens of the coming kingdom of God, to renounce not only their service of Caesar, but also, and above all, their service of mammon. He who no longer possesses money, uses money, or wishes to use money, need pay no more taxes to Caesar.   He who continues and wishes to continue in the service of that enemy of God, the demon mammon, must also bear Caesar's yoke ; he is unworthy of the kingdom of freedom, of the new Israel which acknowledges no master but God. [5]

THE HIGHER RIGHTEOUSNESS

There could be no clearer indication of Jesus' attitude toward the law of the Jewish state than the explanation set forth in the preceding chapter of the true meaning of his public pronouncement on the tribute money.

The Baptist, in complete accordance with the scribes and pious men of his time, had taught that the Messiah would not come until the Jews had fulfilled the law in its every detail ; once they had done so he would come forthwith.   The idea that God had imposed the impossible condition that *all* Israel must faithfully ' fulfil all the law,' [6] whereby redemption might be delayed by a single sinner, had been given up once the prophetic utterance had been discovered that God would be content with the ' righteousness ' of the ' elect,' of the small ' remnant ' which would ' inherit the kingdom,' while the rejected are destined either to eternal punishment or to mere annihilation.   None the less, the longed-for

---

[1] *Matt.* vi. 24 ; *Luke* vi. 13.

[2] The derivation of *mammon* from '*aman*, ' to believe,' ' trust,' goes back to the seventeenth century. Cf. my book *Das Geld* (Munich, 1924), p. 165.   Yet there is a possibility that this etymology is, after all, secondary, and that *mammon* is derived from '*aman* II, ' to pile up.'   At all events, it is a common Semitic word, and St. Augustine still knows it as the Punic equivalent of *lucrum*.

[3] Cf. *Didascalia apost.*, ed. Hauler, p. 46 : ' de solo *mammona* cogitant quorum deus est sacculus ' (' whose god is their purse ').   As the companion of Satan himself, *Mamonas* appears in the *Passio Sancti Bartholomaei Apostoli*.

[4] Tertullian, *Adv. Marc.*, iv. 33 : ' iniustitiae enim auctorem et dominatorem totius saeculi nummum scimus omnes.'   Letter of Emperor Hadrian (*Hist. Aug. Vita Saturnini*, 8), ' unus illis deus nummus, hunc Christiani, hunc Judaei, hunc omnes venerantur et gentes.'

[5] Curiously enough, the first to discover the true meaning of Jesus' saying about the tribute-money was Richard Wagner. See the quotation from his unfinished Passion-play *Jesus of Nazareth*, written during the revolution of 1848 (not published until 1887) in Weinel, *Jesus im XIX. Jahrhundert*, Tübingen, 1907, p. 166.

[6] *Matt.* iii. 15.

liberator-king had to this hour delayed his coming. Clearly, then, something more, a higher flight than had yet been attempted, was demanded of the elect if the hour of redemption was to strike. That is the thought announced in the words of Jesus : [1]

> ' For I say unto you, that except your righteousness shall exceed that of the scribes and Pharisees, ye shall in no wise enter into the kingdom of heaven.'

On the other hand, he disclaims any intention of destroying even a tittle of the revealed law or of the prophets : rather he has come to fulfil the law.[2] Even so the scribes and Pharisees had thought to obey the Lord better by surrounding each regulation with a hedge of expositions and securities against unwitting transgression, until in the course of time the yoke of God's dominion had become a grievous burden.

What the people thought of the law appears from the bitter criticism of Moses and Aaron which the *Haggadah* [3] puts into the mouth of the rebel leader Korah, and which the scribes doubtless heard often enough on the lips of the rebel Zealots :

> ' When we were given the ten commandments, each of us learnt them directly from Mount Sinai ; there were only the ten commandments, and we heard no orders about " offering cakes " or " gifts to priests," or " tassels." It was only in order to usurp the dominion for himself and to impart honour to his brother Aaron that Moses added all this.'

The Haggadist, in Korah's name, is particularly caustic about the law on ' gifts to priests ' ; this is what he says :

> ' One day there came a widow and two orphans who owned a field and wished to till it. Then said Moses, " Thou shalt not employ ox and ass together at the plough." When they wished to sow, he said, " Thou shalt not sow thy field with two kinds of seed " ; when they would reap, he said, " You must leave a gleaning " ; when they would make a granary, he said, " Gifts for the priests, first tithe and second tithe, must be given." . . . There was now nothing left for the widow (to do) but to sell the field. She did so and bought two lambs, to turn them to account and clothe herself with their wool. When the lambs had young, Aaron came and made his claim, " The firstlings you must give me as wages, for so has Jahweh commanded : Every firstborn," etc. . . . And when the time came for shearing the lambs, he said, " The best of the shearing of thy sheep must thou give to me." Then the widow could no longer comply with these demands and decided to kill the lambs and consume them. But when she had killed them, Aaron said, " The shoulder, the two cheeks, and the maw must ye give to me." Then the widow protested, " Though I have

---

[1] *Matt.* v. 20.   [2] *Matt.* v. 17 *sq.*
[3] *Talm. Bab., Berakhoth*, 32a; Moses Gaster, *The Chronicles of Jerahmel* (Orient. Transl. Fund, iv.), p. 160, c. lv., and the parallels on p. xcvii.

even killed the lambs, yet I cannot get rid of this man ; the lambs are a votive on behalf of me." Aaron replied, " Then are they wholly mine, for thus saith Jahweh : Every devoted thing shall belong to thee." And he took the lambs and departed, leaving the widow and orphans lamenting. Thus did they treat these poor wretches when they appealed to the Lord.'

If there is only a particle of the truth in this powerful satire on priestly greed, it is not surprising that at least the popular preachers, in their messianic expectations, went so far as to say that ' in the world to come the laws will be abolished, even that relating to forbidden food.' [1] The following doctrine [2] was taught in the name of R. Menaḥem of Galilee, a Tannaite of uncertain date, who from the tenor of his words I am inclined to identify with the celebrated Essene of that name previously mentioned : [3]

' In the future (i.e. in the days of the Messiah) all offerings shall cease ; and likewise all confessions shall cease ; only the confession of thanks shall not cease in all eternity. That is indicated by the passage : [4] " (Again shall be heard) the voice of joy and the voice of gladness, the voice of the bridegroom and the voice of the bride, the voice of them that say, Give thanks to the Lord of hosts, for the Lord is good, for he keepeth his mercy for ever to them that bring thank-offerings into the house of the Lord." '

Horodezky [5] has rightly pointed out that every one of the alleged Messiahs who appeared in Jewry ' sought first to lighten the yoke of the law, as the prophets had done before them.' Of the pseudo-Messiah who about the year 720 (under the caliphate of Omar II.) promised to restore Palestine to the Jews of Arabia, and who had a large following there and in Spain, we are told by the contemporary Gaon R. Natronai :

' many were misled by him and fell into heresy, getting accustomed . . . to partake of forbidden meats and drinks, to use the wine of the heathen, to transact business on the second day of the feast,' etc.

In a similar way, Jesus in the well-known touching words promised the people a drastic alleviation of their burdens : [6]

' Come unto me, all ye that labour and are heavy laden, and I will give you rest. Take my yoke upon you and learn of me, for I am meek and lowly in heart ; and ye shall find rest unto your souls. For my yoke is easy, and my burden is light.'

Such an alleviation would, of course, have been quite impossible had Jesus really intended to take over into the ' kingdom of God '

[1] *Talm. Bab., Nidda*, 61b ; *Midr. Shokher ṭob*, 146.
[2] Cf. Strack-Billerbeck, i. 246.
[3] See above, p. 332 n. 5.   [4] *Jerem.* xxxiii. 11.
[5] *Arch. f. Religions Wiss.*, xv. (1917), p. 121 *sq.*
[6] *Matt.* xi. 28 *sqq.* As to the form, cf. *Isaiah* iv. 1-3.

Y

the burden of the traditional Pharisaic interpretation of Scripture,[1] instead of merely accepting the written law in the spirit and not in the letter, as the Karaites subsequently attempted to do. How an effective alleviation of burdens ($\sigma\epsilon\iota\sigma\acute{\alpha}\chi\theta\epsilon\iota\alpha$ [2]) is to be reconciled with the assurance that not a jot or tittle of the law is to be destroyed becomes intelligible only when it is observed that Jesus intends to fulfil both law *and prophets* ; whereas, on the contrary, many of the scribes show no great love for the prophets, and sometimes imagine that in the messianic age the prophets and hagiographa will lose their validity, the Torah of Moses continuing to be binding even in the world to come.[3]

For the writings of the prophets, Jeremiah in particular, contain all the foundations necessary for the most drastic 'innovation' ($\nu\epsilon\omega\tau\epsilon\rho\iota\sigma\mu\acute{o}s$), to use Josephus' favourite term when he wishes to disparage the Zealots.[4] It is in Jeremiah [5] that we find that antinomian sentence :

'How can ye say, We are wise and the law of the Lord is with us ? But, behold, the false pen of the scribes hath made of it falsehood.'

On the strength of that assertion, Jeremiah, the son of a priest, declares that all the laws of sacrifice are a forgery of the scribes : [6]

'I spake not unto your fathers, nor commanded them in the day that I brought them out of the land of Egypt, concerning burntofferings or sacrifices : but this thing I commanded them saying, Hearken unto my voice.'

On such a basis Jesus could adopt, then, any simplification and modification of the law which seemed justifiable to his conscience, without infringing an iota of the 'genuine' law.[7] From Jeremiah,[8] and from him alone, he drew his 'authority' to declare in a single saying the abolition of the whole food-law : [9]

'Not that which goeth into the mouth but that which cometh out of the mouth defileth the man';

[1] *Matt.* xxiii. 3 : 'all that the scribes tell you, do it.'
[2] As it was called by the Athenian social reformer Solon.
[3] *Jerus. Meg.*, i. 70d, 51 ; Strack-Billerbeck, i. 246.
[4] The idea that the Messiah will 'novellate' the law (*ḥiddush thorah*) is common in Hebrew literature: *Pesaḥ.* xii. 107a ; *Lev. r.s.* xiii. 156d, etc. Cf. *John* xiii. 34 ; *Barn.* ii. 6 ; and Tertullian was perfectly right when he insisted (*De praescr. haer.*, 13) : 'Jesum Christum praedicavisse novam legem.'
[5] viii. 8. Jesus quotes the parallel passage, *Isaiah* xxix. 13, about the ἐντάλματα ἀνθρώπων, 'man-made commandments' (*Mark* vii. 7 ; *Matt.* xv. 9).
[6] vii. 22 *sq.* ; cf. vi. 20.
[7] Strangely enough, this is in principle exactly the 'philological' and 'critical' procedure which, a century and a half later, was practised by Marcion in dealing with the canonical gospels. Similarly, in the Pseudo-Clementines—or rather in their principal source, the 'Preaching of Peter'—the prince of the apostles teaches his hearers that the laws of Moses were not written down till long after Moses, and that it is therefore necessary to find out 'the genuine parts of the scriptures' among the numerous forgeries (Schliemann, *Die Clementinen*, pp. 196 ff.).   [8] viii. 13.   [9] *Mark* vii. 15.

more than that, to allow the seventy messengers, sent to the seventy gentile nations, to eat whatever food will be set before them.[1] In a striking parable, quoted more than sixty times by early Christian witnesses,[2] although ruthlessly expunged from the canonical gospels, Jesus says that like reliable bank-cashiers, who know how to distinguish the genuine from the spurious coins, the students of the law ought to become ' experts in coinage ' ($\delta\acute{o}\kappa\iota\mu o\iota$ $\tau\rho\alpha\pi\epsilon\zeta\hat{\iota}\tau\alpha\iota$),[3] so as to keep the good and to reject the false. He disdained those minor distortions and adaptations of the law in daily use with the scribes, such as Hillel's introduction of the *Prosbul*, intended to do away with the unexpected economical consequences of the well-meant ordinance on the remission of debts in the sabbatical year.

' No man seweth a piece of undressed cloth on an old garment . . . and no man putteth new wine into old wineskins . . . but they put new wine into fresh wineskins.' [4]

A far bolder revolutionary, he thus gives a new law of ' higher righteousness ' in new words and a new revelation : ' it was said to them of old time . . . but I say unto you.' [5] The old writer who collected into a ' sermon on the mount ' [6] the remains of what the Galilaean Messiah had preached to the men in the mountains on the ' renewal of the law,' was guided by a right feeling that Jesus consciously intended to reintegrate the law which Moses had brought down from Sinai. And it was a right feeling that led him to place in the forefront of the new revelation the beatitudes on the poor,[7] the afflicted, the hungry and thirsty, the persecuted, to whom the revelation of the new law brings good news.

The ' kingdom of God ' involves indeed a complete reversal [8] of men's present fate ; it cannot be otherwise if it is to 'fulfil the prophets,' if it is to mean that general reversal by which the manifest injustices prevailing in ' this world' will be righted in the next.

[1] *Luke* x. 8.　　　　[2] Resch, *Agrapha* [2], pp. 112-122, No. 87.
[3] The saying was known to Paul, I *Thess.* v. 21 f., and to the author of *Hebr.* v. 14.　　　　[4] *Mark* ii. 21 *sq.*
[5] *Matt.* v. 21 *sq.*　　　　[6] *Matt.* v. 1: $\mathring{a}v\acute{e}\beta\eta$ $\epsilon\mathring{\iota}s$ $\tau\mathring{o}$ $\mathring{o}\rho os$.
[7] *Luke* vi. 20b : ' Blessed are the poor,' etc., has been misinterpreted owing to the corrupt text of the parallel passage in *Matt.* v. 3. There an old gloss, $\mathring{e}v$ $\pi v\epsilon\acute{u}\mu\alpha\tau\iota$, meaning ' in inspired moments,' made by some reader not wholly convinced of the blessedness of the poor, was early drawn into the text. One cannot imagine a Jew calling blessed the ' poor in spirit,' i.e. the simpletons ' devoid of inspiration.' Lack of inspiration—religious or otherwise—is a curse, a cutting off from contact with God, in Jewish eyes.
[8] *Mark* x. 21 ; *Matt.* xix. 30, xxiii. 12 ; *Luke* xiii. 30, xiv. 11. Cf. *Talm. Baba Bathra*, 10b : ' When Joseph the son of R. Jehoshu'ah b. Levi (*ca.* 256) was ill, he had a vision. His father said to him : " What hast thou seen ? " He answered : " A world turned upside down ('*ōlam hapukh*) I have seen : what is lowest was highest, and what is highest was lowest." His father said : "A better world hast thou seen."'

'If you will not lift up high that which is low among you, and turn down that which is high, and place to the left what is on the right side and shift to the right side that which is on the left, ye cannot enter into my kingdom.'[1]

'Up with the low, down with the high,'[2] had similarly been predicted by the prophets as the message of the time when 'he' should 'come whose right it is, and I will give it to him.'[3] The poor, the persecuted, the hunted of the present are the rightful owners of the future. The rich have already in this world received the fulfilment of the blessings promised to them. They who now suffer shall be elected, they who weep shall rejoice, the hungry and thirsty shall be satisfied, for those reviled by all a rich reward is reserved in heaven. Those who are now full-fed shall hunger, those who laugh here shall mourn and weep.[4] Indeed, it would seem, though the connexion of this thought with the announcement of the 'new law' is not attested by external evidence, that Jesus regards those who in this world are accounted sinners because they have come into conflict with the laws of this world, as better fitted to enter into the future kingdom than those who have punctiliously observed the old law and are on that very account hardly open to the call to a new order of life. 'I came not to call the righteous, but sinners.'[5] According to the *Epistle of Barnabas*[6] he chose his disciples 'among men who had been the worst sinners,' a statement in perfect harmony with Celsus'[7] accusation that Jesus collected his associates among ill-famed publicans and 'the worst sailors.'[8]

What Jesus meant by the 'higher righteousness' is familiar to all, and under the heading 'ethics of the sermon on the mount' has been constantly discussed throughout the ages. It is the principle, thought out and carried through to the last logical consequence, under no circumstances to do wrong to another, not even in self-defence or in retaliation, a requirement which, as Celsus justly urged,[9] had a long time before been consistently preached by the Platonic Socrates.[10]

The new commandment, not to resist evil,[11] if carried to its radical conclusion, forbids, of course, all reprisals for wrongdoing

---

[1] *Acta Philippi* (cod. Oxon.), ch. xxxiv. (Lipsius, *Apokryphe Apostelgesch.*, 1884, ii. 2, p. 19).

[2] Cf. *Luke* xvi. 15 : 'That which is high among men is abominable in the sight of God.'

[3] *Ezek.* xxi. 26 *sq.* (Hebr. text, 31 *sq.*).   [4] *Luke* vi. 33.

[5] *Mark* ii. 17.   [6] v. 9.

[7] Orig., *C. Celsum*, i. 62.   [8] ναύτας πονηροτάτους.

[9] *Ibid.*, vii. 58.   [10] *Crito*, § 10 (i. 59, ed. Stephanus).

[11] *Matt.* v. 39 ; cf. also the neo-Pythagorean parallels, ' better to suffer wrong than to kill,' in Jamblich, *Vita Pyth.*, 155, 179 ; *ibid.*, 51, 'not abuse others nor defend yourself when abused '; Isidore Lévy, *La Légende de Pythagore*, Paris, 1927, p. 316 n. 13.

even by resort to some court of law.   This inference is expressly drawn : [1]

> 'Judge not, and ye shall not be judged ; condemn not, and ye shall not be condemned ; release, and ye shall be released ; give, and it shall be given unto you. . . . For with what measure ye mete, it shall be measured to you again.' [2]

And not merely the punishment of the evildoer, nay, even any censure of human failings, is forbidden.   One whose well(house) [3] is in such disrepair that a whole beam has fallen into the water has no right to object to a splinter floating in his neighbour's spring. Nor does he allow his disciples to resort to a civil court : [4]

> ' If any man would go to law with thee and take away thy coat ' (the most indisputable personal possession), ' let him have thy cloke also.'

The same principle of non-resistance to injustice is inculcated in the case of requisitions (ἀγγαρεία) on the part of the Roman troops. Not only must there be no refusal, but one should volunteer to do more than is required : [5]

> ' Whosoever shall compel thee to go a mile, go with him twain.'

Strangely enough, the fundamental political meaning of these words has not been even remotely apprehended by any commentator known to me.   Their true import was first recognized by a learned Oxford theologian, the late Miss Lily Dougall : [6]

> ' Consider the teaching of Jesus as it struck his first hearers. Who are those who compelled the Galilaean peasant to go a mile ? They were Roman soldiers, acting as armed police, any man of whom had the right to make one of a conquered race carry his traps for a certain distance. . . . Who were those who "used" the people "despitefully" ?   Assuredly the arrogant officials, both high and low, of a dominant race rose before the mind's eye of every member of those Jewish crowds to whom Jesus preached. . . . The Jewish nation, weak and poor, but the prouder for that, was at this time vibrating with suppressed revolution.   Judas of Galilee had headed a rising : Pilate more recently had ruthlessly quelled in blood a riot in the very temple : Theudas was soon to head a rebellion.   If to members of Sinn Fein in the spring of 1921 had been said, " Forgive your enemies, bless them that persecute you, do good to them that

---

[1] The idea that in the golden age mankind may dispense with the judge is equally known to the pagan world (Ovid, *Metam.*, i. 89 ; cf. also Calpurnius, *Eclog.*, i. 71, nor are there tribunals in the ideal state of the Stoic Zeno).

[2] *Luke* vi. 37.

[3] *Ibid.*, 41 *sq.* : there is a confusion of the two meanings of Aramean *'aijna* = (1) ' well,' (2) ' eye ' in the Greek gospels.

[4] *Matt.* v. 40 ; *Luke* vi. 29.   In *Luke* xii. 14, Jesus refuses to arbitrate between brothers quarrelling about an heirloom.

[5] *Matt.* v. 41.

[6] *Hibbert Journal*, xx. (Oct. 1921), p. 114 *sqq.*

despitefully use you," to whom would they have supposed the words to refer but to the English ? Would not such teaching to them seem the suggestion of a national policy?' [1]

This interpretation gains added force from the occurrence of a similar train of thought [2] in the speech of King Agrippa II. to the Jews determined to revolt from Rome : [3]

'" Nothing so checks blows as submission to them, and the resignation of the wronged victim puts the wrongdoer to confusion." Granting that the Roman officials are intolerably harsh, it does not follow that you are wronged by all Romans or by Caesar ; yet it is against them that you are going to war.'

The opening words, which may well be proverbial, strikingly recall the saying of Jesus on turning the other cheek (to the smiter), though the difference is plainly perceptible. At all events, it is clear that this aspect of Jesus' preaching, with its recommendation of patient quietism, cannot have been unwelcome either to the Romans or to those opportunists,[4] the Herodians and the priestly aristocracy in Jerusalem, who worked for tolerable relations with Rome. Similarly, his words on the tribute money, i.e. his injunction to dispense with money altogether or quietly pay the tribute, must have been judged as a relatively harmless extravagance. This sufficiently explains why he was continually watched and spied upon, while otherwise left in peace for a considerable time. So long as he was satisfied to take exception to the Sabbath and the food-laws only, which did not to a great extent injure the interests of the priesthood, all went well ; it was his final attack on the sacrificial system and the banking business in the temple which armed the priestly caste against him. On the other hand, his doctrine of a radical pacifism must have met with some sympathy from Jews of all parties, including the activists, since even the latter were by no means over-confident of a victory in an armed conflict with the Romans. Living as outlaws in the wilderness of the mountains, where Jesus preached to them, they were no less eagerly awaiting a miracle than the quietists in town and country. If these odd ' latter-day saints ' and advocates of ' perfect righteousness' were seeking a new way of abating the

---

[1] The reader will recall the *ahimça*, or 'non-resistance' policy, advocated by Mahatma Gandhi.
[2] St. Augustine, *Ep.* 138$_{10}$ (*C.S.E.L.*, xliv. 134), compares the Roman political principle (Sallust, *Catil.*, ix. 5): 'accepta iniuria ignoscere quam persequi malebant.'
[3] *B.J.*, ii. 351 *sq.* ; cf. Epictet., iii. 12. 10.
[4] Jesus was not at all impervious to considerations of political expediency ; cf. *Luke* xiv. 31. The passage, disconnected in its present context, is evidently a fragment taken from a discussion with the Zealots on the problem of fortifying the country and the chances of raising a sufficiently strong force against the Romans. Contrast this sober reasoning with the vainglorious boast quoted above, p. 198 n. 1, from *Deut.* xxxii. 30.

Lord's anger with his people, whose business was it to hinder them? If a new self-ordained doctor of the law preached to the rich the duty of giving away all their possessions, no one was forced to listen to him, much less to obey; and if he taught the poor that they must serve all men willingly, joyfully, and gratuitously, without anxious care for their livelihood, and that they would easily obtain all the necessaries of life without buying them, in exchange for their labour, by simply begging from good men,—who would feel disturbed by doctrines so comforting to the rich and powerful in all ages, so long as they were accompanied by a recommendation not only of complete non-resistance but of a comprehensive and all-forgiving love of enemies?[1] The oppressors of the people could not but welcome the idea of Jesus bidding the poor, the outcast, and the sinners to extend the law of love of one's neighbour to the Roman enemy,[2] and seeking to induce the Jews to include in their feelings of brotherly affection the conquerors and rulers of the Holy Land.

The obvious sympathy with which the pro-Roman aristocratic priest Josephus speaks of the Essenes as 'ministers of peace'[3] and loyal subjects of all constituted authority cannot have been altogether refused by his party-friends to the wandering carpenter who blesses the peacemakers as the true children of God and promises the meek that, by God's mercy and without any action on their part, they shall inherit the whole earth.[4]

At the same time it is not to be implied that the radical pacifism of the sermon on the mount is in any way derived from Essenism.[5] The roots of this moral attitude are rather to be sought in the peculiar ethics of those wandering tribes of craftsmen, the Qenites and Rekhabites, the Ṣleb or Ṣalubîm of the rabbis,[6] to whom 'the carpenter's son' and his forefathers, by upbringing, if not actually by blood, no doubt belonged. We are told of the modern Ṣleb that it was their extraordinary peaceableness which more than anything else attracted the attention of the European traveller to this tribe. 'It is remarkable that in the desert,

---

[1] The principle is first enjoined in the pre-Christian *Testament of Gad*, vi. 7; cf. R. H. Charles, *Transactions of the Third International Congress for the History of Religions*, Oxford, 1908, i. 32. Cp. also the *Letter of Aristeas*, § 227: 'I am of the opinion that we must bestow our favour by preference upon our adversaries. Thus we shall win them over to their duty and to our profit.'

[2] *Matt.* v. 43; *Luke* vi. 27.   [3] *B.J.*, ii. 135.

[4] τὴν γῆν may mean, more modestly, 'the land,' and not 'the whole earth'; cf. *Deut.* iv. 1; vi. 18; xvi. 20.

[5] See above, p. 23 n. 1; p. 257 n. 4. Nothing could be less certain than that the Essenes *were* pacifists.

[6] *Exod. rabba*, 42 (99a): R. Yaqim (about A.D. 300) has said: 'There are three arrogant races—among animals the dog, among birds the cock, among men the Jew.' Says R. Isaac b. Redipha (about 300): 'Is this a shame for the Jews? No, a glory; either (you are) a Jew, or a Ṣalub' (that is, a meek and undignified Ṣolubi; the usual translation, 'either a Jew or a crucified one,' is absurd).

where in consequence of the natural conditions the life of its inhabitants, whether men or beasts, is a war of all against all, there is still one people which takes no part in this general feud.' [1] According to Wright,[2] during a battle they all repair to the scene as disinterested spectators, to tend the wounded of both sides when the fight is over. Similarly they are wont to entertain both pursued and pursuers with equal hospitality, and not to inform the latter in which direction the other party has gone. Their gentleness and hospitality are unanimously attested by all Europeans. With their unique knowledge of the country which they scour as hunters, they are always ready to act as guides through the desert,[3] to show the right way to strayed and exhausted travellers, or to offer them hospitality in their camps. The *Sleb*, who has made himself indispensable to the Arab by his valuable services, never engages in a quarrel with him, and pays to nearly every tribe a tribute or ' brotherhood tax.' In short, these peculiar ' cross-bearers ' may be described as a most peaceable, meek, amiable, and contented lot. They are extremely polite, and, according to the Carmelite father St. Élie, abhor theft and all forms of deceit. Nothing is more sacred in their eyes than a debt.

From those qualities and from the sign of the cross, the mark of Qain, some writers have rashly concluded that the *Sleb* are of Christian origin, as if the modern Syrians and Copts, Christians though they be, showed the slightest approach to such ethical tenets! I venture to submit, on the contrary, that the well-known pacifist doctrines of the wandering carpenter Jesus are ultimately derived from the special experiences of those nomad craftsmen, who from remote ages, in the midst of the struggle for existence of warring tribes, have successfully fought their way through life by such an attitude of radical pacifism and willing service towards all. To them the thought must have occurred frequently that if only other tribes would learn to act in the Rekhabite manner, they might forthwith find deliverance from the torture of mutual oppression and enter the longed-for reign of everlasting worldwide peace.

' THE KINGDOM OF GOD IS WITHIN YOU '

We have the means of ascertaining much more precisely than is commonly supposed what Jesus thought of the nature of the kingdom of God and of the manner of its coming into being.

---

[1] Pieper, *op. cit.*, p. 10 *sq.*
[2] *An Account of Palmyra*, p. 49.
[3] v. Oppenheim, *op. cit.*, i. 220.

There is the short and disconnected saying in *Luke* xvii. 20 *sq.*:

'And being asked by the Pharisees, when the kingdom of God cometh, he answered them and said, "The kingdom of God cometh not with observation:[1] neither shall they say, Lo, here! or there! for lo, the kingdom of God is ἐντὸς ὑμῶν."'

But this, as is well known, does not furnish a sufficient and convincing answer to the question, because the meaning of ἐντὸς ὑμῶν ('within' or 'in the midst of you') has always been hotly disputed.

It has been overlooked, however, in the discussion of this passage, that the fortunate discovery of a pertinent fragment of the 'Sayings of Jesus,'[2] if correctly restored, offers as complete information on the conception of the 'kingdom' in the preaching of Jesus as one could desire:

'such (are) the words the [saving (words) which]
Jesus the living[3] spake [and taught to Judas who (is called)]
also Thomas, and he said [unto him that every one who-]
soever shall hear these words, [of death]
shall not taste.   [Saith the Lord Jesus :]
Let him not cease who see[keth the kingdom until]
He findeth, and when he findeth [he shall wonder and won-]
dering he shall reign an[d reigning he shall]
rest.   Saith J[esus, who will they be]
who draw us [into the kingdom if]
the kingdom in heav[en is ?   Shall we be drawn by]
the birds of the heav[ens or by any of the beasts that a-]
re under the ear[th, if it shall be there,[4] or shall they be]
the fishes of the se[a that will car-]
ry you over and is it that the king[dom is beyond (the) sea ?]
Within you [i]s it, [and whosoever of you himself]
shall know, shall find i[t with none to guide him].
Yourselves ye shall know [and ye shall know that children]
are ye of the Father who b[egat you in the beginning.]
Ye shall know yourselves in [the fear of your Father]
and then be yourselves the te[rror of your enemies].'[5]

Any one can see at once that this second utterance, restored as above, supplies from the mouth of Jesus himself the long-sought interpretation of the phrase ἐντὸς ὑμῶν in *Luke* xvii. 21.   The passage, in common with others, shows that the traditional 'sayings of Jesus' have often been torn from a richer context and so

[1] More exactly : 'according to (astrological) observation.'
[2] Oxyrhynchus Papyri, iv. 658.
[3] I.e., apparently, 'in his lifetime.'   A protest against visionaries quoting words of Jesus spoken after his resurrection.
[4] The two ideas of 'flying upwards into heaven' and 'descending under the earth into Hades' are contrasted in Plato's *Legg.*, p. 905a, in the Scythian symbolic letter in Herodot., iv. 131 f. ; Eurip., *Medea*, 1296 f. ; *Hekabe*, 1099 ff. (Geffcken, *Arch. f. Rel.-Wiss.*, xxvii., 1929, pp. 347 f.).
[5] For the details of the reconstructed Greek text, see vol. ii. pp. 218 ff. of the German edition.

rendered difficult to understand, especially where the connexion
with the Old Testament scriptures on which the maxims are based
is no longer recognizable. In the present case the lesson that the
kingdom of God is to be sought neither ' here ' nor ' there,' or,
more specifically, neither in heaven above nor beyond the sea nor
beneath the earth, is clearly modelled on that impressive speech of
Moses (of which use is made also in the *Book of Baruch* [1] and by
Paul [2]) in *Deut.* xxx. 11-14 :

> ' For this commandment which I command thee this day is not
> . . . far off. It is not in heaven, that thou shouldst say, Who shall
> go up for us to heaven, and bring it unto us, and make us to hear it,
> that we may do it ? Neither is it beyond the sea, that thou shouldst
> say, Who shall go over the sea for us, and bring it unto us, and make
> us to hear it that we may do it ? But the word is very nigh unto
> thee, in thy mouth and in thy heart, that thou mayest do it.'

That Jesus quotes a passage relating to the understanding and
practice of the *Torah*, to answer the question about the way to the
kingdom of God,[3] perfectly accords with the view of the rabbis [4]
who identified the realization of the dominion of God with man's
fulfilment of his commands. To attain to that kingdom, man has
only to fulfil the commandment, implanted by God in his heart,[5]
of brotherly love to all.

It will be observed that Jesus expressly rejects the idea of a
kingdom of God localized in heaven, an idea familiar, of course, to
Babylonian Polytheism [6] no less than to Mandaean gnosis and to
the pious author of the *Assumption of Moses*.[7] In the same way
he repudiates the Essene doctrine, derived from Orphic and Pythagorean ideas, of an Elysian kingdom beyond the ocean on the isles
of the blessed. He likewise rejects the view, current in the Eleu-
sinian and Osiris mysteries, of Elysian fields in the underworld.[8]
Clearly and explicitly he declares that the ' kingdom of God ' has
nothing whatever to do with these heathen, un-Jewish ideas of a
world beyond. He declares, to use modern phraseology, that the
' kingdom ' is in no way a transcendent sphere lying outside the
world of experience and reality, but is on the contrary a political,
moral, and religious state of people here on earth. ' The heavens

---

[1] iii. 29.   [2] *Rom.* x. 6 *sqq.*
[3] His questioners must have believed the ' kingdom ' which is ' to come ' to
exist somewhere, e.g. in heaven, whence it will come down at the end of days.
[4] Strack-Billerbeck, i. 176 n. 1.
[5] The ' natural law,' as it is called in the ' Apostolic Constitutions ' (Lietzmann,
Kl. Texte, No. 61, p. 13). Only after men have perverted this ' natural law ' has
God given the written one.
[6] *sharrut shamē*, ' kingdom of heaven,' iv. Rawl. ², 5a, 8.
[7] According to these naïve ideas, the righteous were to be wafted up on the
wings of eagles or on clouds (cf. 1 *Thess.* iv. 17). See above, p. 258₉.
[8] Cf. Jos., *Ant.*, xviii. § 14, on the Pharisee doctrine.

belong to God, the earth he has given to men.'[1] Since, on the contrary, owing to Paul's influence, such doctrines have been accepted by the Church, it is clear why the wonderful saying was not included in the Gospels. What Jesus meant was simply this: So soon as men, or the elect, attain to a knowledge of their status as children of God and act accordingly, i.e. treat each other as brothers, they forthwith enter, without a guide, without the aid of any fabulous monsters, into the kingdom of God. To attain this knowledge there is no need to journey to heaven, to cross the ocean, to descend into the underworld. In his heart and conscience every man bears the law by the following of which the kingdom of God can be realized here and now. It lies within every man's power to build that kingdom. No enemy or oppressor can prevent it ; on the contrary, every enemy will tremble before God's children fraternally united in the fear of the Lord.

The peculiar emphasis laid on the moral requirement of self-knowledge is clearly inspired by that passage in Jeremiah so tellingly expressing the thought of the Deuteronomist on the law written in hearts and consciences :[2]

> ' I will put my law in their inward parts, and in their heart will I write it ; and I will be their God and they shall be my people ; and they shall teach no more every man his neighbour, and every man his brother, saying, Know the Lord : for they shall all know me, from the least unto the greatest.'

As to the words ' the kingdom is within you' ($\dot{\epsilon}\nu\tau\grave{o}s$ $\dot{\upsilon}\mu\hat{\omega}\nu$), they are doubtless an echo of *Deut.* xxx. 14, ' The word is very near unto thee, *in thy mouth and in thy heart, that thou mayest do it.'*

The Sending Out of the Seventy in search of a Kingdom. The Appointment of the Twelve Judges of Israel

Notwithstanding the meaning of the phrase ' the kingdom of God is within you,' established in the previous chapter, it would be a great error to regard the kingdom announced by Jesus as a purely spiritual state without any political character whatever. The last words of the *logion* we have been discussing, to the effect that the community of God's children, once they had recognized themselves as such, would be the terror of all the enemies of Israel, are in themselves enough to forbid such a spiritualizing of a very concrete political conception. For the Jews the Law has always been the covenant (*b'rith*), binding every individual to God and

---

[1] Cf. *Baraitha Sukkah*, 5a ; Mekhiltha on *Exod.* xix. 20 (65) ; W. Bacher, *Die Agada der Tannaiten*, i. 185 n. 3 : 'R. Jose b. Ḥalafta says : God did not descend upon Mt. Sinai, Elijah did not ascend to heaven. The heavens belong to God ; the earth he has given to man ' (*Ps.* cxv. 16).

[2] *Jer.* xxxi. 33 *sq.*

thereby uniting the individuals into one people. A *gnōsis*, a knowledge of God or of self, 'redeeming' the individual without liberating the people from exterior oppression and without a renewal of the covenant of Sinai concluded after the release from bondage in Egypt, would have appeared entirely worthless to Jesus and to his hearers.

This message of Jesus is still clearer (if that is possible) in the sentence preceding the one just discussed and which is quoted in the *Gospel according to the Hebrews*.[1] It concerns the seeking and the finding of the kingdom :

'He who seeks his kingdom must never cease until he has found it, and when he has found it he will wonder, and, lost in wonder, he will become a king and as sovereign will finally win (his well-earned) rest.'

This saying is unintelligible so long as the reader does not realize to whom it is addressed. It is surely impossible that a whole kingdom should have been promised to every pious individual, to every son and heir of God's kingdom. It is a negation of the very idea of rulership if in the coming kingdom there are to be no more subjects or simple citizens, no 'last' who were once first ; the kingdom is doubtless thought of as a monarchy, not as an anarchical rule of the many (Homer's πολυκοιρανίη). The enigma is explained by the fact that here again we are dealing with the fragment of a speech—this time of the instructions delivered to the 'seventy '(-two) when sent out on their mission.

We know from the commentaries on the miracle of Pentecost in the *Acts* the Jewish view that the land of Israel was surrounded by seventy(-two) peoples, filling the countries of the world.[2] According to an old legend, the Sanhedrin was a world-ruling corporation of an importance equal to that of the Roman senate, and it was the duty of its members to know the seventy(-two) languages of the world so as to dispense with all interpreters.[3] The number of the seventy(-two) who were sent by Jesus 'into every city and place '[4] (*or* 'country')[5] may be very simply explained by this number of the nations of the world ; they will have received their commission forthwith, as soon as so many disciples had collected around him. Each one of the disciples, who were to start 'by twos' so that they might help each other in any emergency as long as possible, was to journey to one of these nations,

---

[1] Clem. Alex., *Strom.*, ii. 9. 45.

[2] The Seleucide empire was divided into seventy-two provinces (Appian, *Syr.*, 62).

[3] *Talm. Bab. Meg.*, 13b ; *Men.*, 65 ; Strack-Billerbeck on *Acts* ii. 6.

[4] 'Whither he himself would come ' (later).

[5] *Luke* x. 1. These world-embracing plans might seem incompatible with *Matt.* xv. 24 : 'I am not sent but to the lost sheep of the house of Israel.' But at that time was not every corner of the ancient world dotted with settlements of those 'lost sheep ' ? (Philo, *Leg. ad Gaium*, §§ 213 *sqq.*)

to convert it to submission to the will of God and of his Anointed, and then to rule over the kingdom thus established. None was to rest until he had found his destined kingdom ; so soon as he had reached the country allotted to him by God, he would be astonished at the wonderful rapidity with which he would gain his dominion, and as king of the country the ambassador of Jesus (for this is the meaning of ' apostle ')[1] after his toilsome wandering would at last find rest. Hence the words of the author of the *Revelation* : ' Jesus Christ . . . the prince of the kings of the earth . . . hath made us kings and priests,' or ' Thou hast made them . . . kings and priests, and they shall reign over the earth.' [2] The Seventy are thus regarded as the Sanhedrin of the future Israel of God's kingdom. As the Roman senate appeared to foreign ambassadors like an assembly of kings, as it governed the peoples of the world through senatorial proconsuls, so must the members of this new Sanhedrin go forth, each to found for himself a kingdom. As ' king of kings ' the Messiah would rule over the liberated world, surrounded by the twelve ' judges ' appointed in accordance with the Deuteronomic law [3] for the reunited tribes of Israel. Like a Roman emperor, he would in course of time favour each city and district with a personal visit.[4]

Whatever, in these promises of a peaceful victory of the word of God and a dominion of the king's messengers over all the nations of the earth, may appear to a modern reader the utopian dream of a fantastic imagination, is in reality the logical consequence of that firm, mountain-moving, childlike faith in the immediately impending miraculous intervention of God the Father, a faith shown by Jesus himself in every word and constantly enjoined upon his disciples. If man will but do the bidding of God, the Lord will grant success : he who is sent out as a beggar to seek a kingdom will find it, provided, in obedience to God's command, he never desists from the quest.

If one is inclined to regard such schemes of world-dominion as overweening fancies, it must not be forgotten that at the same time a new conception of the ruler's calling is taught to these future kings : [5]

> ' The kings of the Gentiles have lordship over them, and their great ones exercise authority over them, and they that have authority

---

[1] The nearest equivalent to the term *apostoloi* is the office and dignity of the Carlovingian *missi regales*, who are not merely ' king's messengers ' but travelling ministers of the ruler. An *apostolos* is not unlike also to the *legatus* of the Roman *imperator*. In no case should the reader any longer think of the ' apostles ' as simple ' missionaries ' of the Christian faith.

[2] *Rev.* i. 5-6, v. 10, viii. 10.

[3] *Deut.* xvi. 18. Cf. the twelve princes of Israel, *Num.* i. 44 ; *Josh.* iv. 2, 4.

[4] *Luke* x. 1.

[5] *Luke* xxii. 25 ; cf. *Mark* x. 42 *sq.*, *Matt.* xx. 25 *sq.* Luke appears to have preserved the last part of two clauses each containing three members.

over them are called Benefactors (εὐεργέται). But ye shall not be
so. Would one of you be a great one, let him be servant of all :
among you let the oldest be as the youngest, and he that is chief as
he that doth serve.'

In accordance with the counsel of the old sages to David's grandson
Rehoboam,[1] the king is to be the servant of his people ; and the
'Son of Man,' identifying himself with the suffering 'servant' of
deutero-Isaiah, though ' king of kings ' is but the *servus servorum
Dei*.

Through the recovery of the speech delivered to the Seventy on
their departure we can now also explain the wrong impression apt
to be created by the instructions given to the Twelve, especially if
taken out of their proper context. When we read in *Matthew* [2]
that the Twelve who were destined to be princes and judges of the
twelve tribes of Israel were not to go to the nations of the world,
nor even to enter any city of the Samaritans, the passage has the
appearance of a narrow-minded Jewish nationalism. Such an
attitude would be irreconcilable with the promise, excellently
attested by Q,[3] made by Jesus to those who would come from the
east and the west and sit down with the Jewish patriarchs in the
kingdom of God. It would be an inconceivable retrogression from
that universalism of the prophets actively pursued by the Pharisees.[4] Above all, it would be quite unthinkable in a Naṣōraean
who had received the baptism of John and, like the Baptist, would
not recognize as Abraham's children his descendants by blood, but
only those who did the works of Abraham and the will of God.
One who regarded apostate Israel as on a level with the heathen
and in need of the proselyte's baptism could never have wished to
exclude the born heathen, repentant and coming to baptism, from
the kingdom of God.

The very idea of the messianic kingdom, meant to be a world-
wide, a ' catholic ' theocracy, is incompatible with the theory
that Jesus wished to establish a petty Jewish Free State, not em-
bracing even Samaria. The ' Shiloh ' of Jacob's blessing is he
' whom the nations obey, upon whom the nations wait.' [5] The
kingdom of David, which the Messiah b. David was to restore,
could not in the time of Jesus be conceived but as world-embracing,
and only so could he himself picture the kingdom of God. The
commission to the Twelve not to trouble about the Samaritans,
not to take the road to the Gentiles, is therefore intelligible only on
the supposition that at the same time the seventy(-two) were sent
to the seventy(-two) nations, while the Twelve were not to leave
the Land of Promise. The division of labour among the few

[1] 1 *Kings* xii. 6 *sq.*
[2] x. 5.
[3] *Matt.* viii. 11 ; *Luke* xiii. 29.
[4] *Matt.* xxiii. 14.
[5] *Gen.* xlix. 10.

labourers in the Lord's harvest-field was made necessary by the imagined shortness of the interval before the coming of the Anointed One : [1]

> ' verily I say unto you, ye shall not have gone through the cities of Israel, till the Son of Man be come.'

For the rest, I leave open the question how far it may have been true that Jesus had at any time seventy(-two) real and trustworthy disciples ; for even within the Twelve the existence of a still smaller circle of intimate friends, distinguished from the rest, can be clearly noticed. None the less, it would seem that Jesus on occasions was actually surrounded by a sufficiently large audience to be able to dispatch as many as seventy persons on this world-wide errand. That these emissaries did not proceed very far in the execution of their task appears evident from the mention of their early return.[2]

' FISHERS OF MEN '

Beside the lost Jewish sheep in the 'cities of Israel'[3] and the nations of the world, the kingdom must naturally embrace a third group of elect, the Jews in the Dispersion. The sending of messengers to bring these back to the homeland seems to have been Jesus' first care : the carrying out of this task was the aim of the call of the four ' fishers of men.'

Some years ago I pointed out[4] that the words of Jesus calling the fishermen on the shore of the Lake of Galilee, ' Come ye after me and I will make you fishers of men,'[5] isolated as they are, could only be understood in a *bad sense*.[6] To fish men can only mean to ensnare them by violence or deceit, to say nothing of the equivocal slave-hunter's phrase ' catch men alive ' ($\dot{\alpha}\nu\theta\rho\dot{\omega}\pi o\nu\varsigma$ $\zeta\omega\gamma\rho\epsilon\hat{\imath}\nu$) used in this context by Luke.[7] If a boatswain and fisherman, known to have been a *Barjona* or ' extremist,' whilst his companions are described as the worst sinners,[8] were thus mysteriously summoned by an unknown itinerant workman to join him instantly for the ' catching ' or ' fishing ' of men, how else could he have interpreted the words but as a call to some daring enterprise such as kidnapping or highway robbery ? And are not both the silent unquestioning desertion of their boats and nets, and their ready

---

[1] *Matt.* x. 23.   [2] *Luke* x. 17.   [3] *Matt.* x. 23.
[4] *Orpheus the Fisher*, London (Watkins), 1921, p. 86.
[5] *Luke* v. 10 ; cf. *Mark* i. 17, *Matt.* iv. 19.
[6] Cf. *Eccl.* ix. 12 : ' man also knoweth not his time: as the fishes that are taken in an evil net . . . so are the sons of men ensnared in an evil time.' A long list of similar passages in my book (quoted above, note 4) on p. 86 n. 1.
[7] v. 10.
[8] Not only by Celsus, hostile to the Christians, but also in the *Epistle of Barnabas*, on which cf. above, p. 340₆.

response to the mysterious laconic call, most easily intelligible if they so interpreted it ?

A modern Christian reader imports his own ideas into the words of Jesus and assumes a familiarity with the whole symbolism of 'the Fish ' and the fishermen connected with Christian baptism, without considering whether such an assumption is historically possible. I would not altogether exclude the possibility that in this call to be ' fishers of men ' we may have a secret watchword of the Naṣōraeans, since we are told in the Fourth Gospel[1] that Andrew, the brother of Peter, and another disciple of Jesus had been followers of the Baptist, and since the metaphors of the 'fisher of souls' and the ' bad fisher ' in Mandaean literature[2] suggest that the Baptist, in his exposition of Ezekiel's vision of the life-giving stream, may have been accustomed to interpret symbolically the fish and the fishermen there mentioned.[3]

A number of instances have been collected by Dr. I. Scheftelowitz[4] showing that pious, law-abiding Israelites were sometimes compared to fishes in the waters of instruction. It is therefore just conceivable (though of course no more than conceivable) that the Baptist interpreted the fish in that wonderful stream issuing from the sanctuary to mean the Israelites rising regenerate from the waters of Jordan, and regarded his own disciples as 'fishers of men.' If that were so, and if Andrew, before receiving the call from Jesus, really had been a disciple of John, then the fishermen on the Lake of Galilee may have understood the words in a metaphorical, i.e. messianic, sense. But such a theory is in no way convincing and is quite unnecessary, since, as already stated, the instant response to the summons is quite intelligible if the words were understood in their literal meaning. Only, it must then be assumed that Jesus afterward disclosed the true meaning of the metaphor. In any case the traditional account remains somehow insufficient and esoteric.

Of Jesus' real meaning there can be no doubt. He is referring, as ever, to Holy Scripture, and there is but one passage in the Old Testament which can be quoted in illustration of his words. In the prophet Jeremiah[5] he found the following oracle :

> ' Therefore, behold, the days come, saith the Lord, that it shall no more be said, As the Lord liveth, that brought up the children of Israel out of the land of Egypt ; but, As the Lord liveth, that brought up the children of Israel from the land of the north, and from all

[1] i. 40.
[2] *Book of Jahja*, ed. Lidzbarski, ii. 138 *sqq.* The wicked ' fisher of souls ' occurs also in the so-called gospel of Gamaliel, Montague Rhodes James, *The Apocryphal New Testament*, Oxford, 1924, pp. 147 *sqq.*
[3] *Ezek.* xlvii. 9 *sq.*
[4] *Arch. f. Religions-Wiss.*, xiv. (1911), p. 2 *sqq.* ; xvi. (1913), p. 300 *sqq.*
[5] xvi. 14 *sqq.*

the countries whither he had driven them: and I will bring them again into their land that I gave unto their fathers.   Behold, I will send *for many fishers*, saith the Lord, and *they shall fish them*; and afterwards I will send for many hunters, and they shall hunt them from every mountain, and from every hill, and out of the holes of the rocks.'

The sense of the passage is clear : as in so many other promises of future salvation, we have here a promise of the reassembling of the dispersed.   They are to be brought back to the last man.   In the time of Cyrus (538) only a few families, driven by ardent love for the homeland, had found their way back to Palestine.   Even when the temple was rebuilt (529-515) the majority of the exiles were contented with sending an embassy with presents.[1]   Ezra (*ca.* 430) brought back a few thousand 'Zionists,' as we should call them now.   The remainder had found a second home abroad, and in their new surroundings had become rather indifferent to the promises of the prophets.   Even the pious held back, believing that the time of salvation was not yet come, and awaiting a miraculous intervention of God as a signal for the restoration of Israel.   In Jerusalem itself people asked themselves whether they should continue the building of the temple by their own painful toil, or wait for God to work a miracle for his sanctuary.[2] And so the ' gathering of the dispersed ' remained incomplete. But 'on that day,' so dreamed the unknown prophet whose work is preserved in *Jeremiah*, even the last of the hesitating and loiterers, even those who would remain in exile willingly, would be fetched home.   God will raise up a band of ' fishers ' who will 'fish' them out of the sea of the nations and of heathendom ; he will send out a host of ' hunters ' who will ferret them out from the mountains and glens, wherever they may have concealed them-selves, round them up, and bring them home rejoicing.

If it is this passage that is behind Jesus' call to the Galilaean fishermen, it is for this final and complete messianic restoration of the dispersed from the four winds, from the four corners of the earth, to the Holy Land, that he would summon the four 'fishers of men.'   Truly, a discouragingly small force for such a superhuman, world-wide task.   Yea, but had not the Lord promised to send out multitudes of hunters and fishers into all the world to catch the prey ?   Only a beginning had to be made ; the completion would be wrought by the Lord.   ' Put out into the deep,' Jesus calls to the fishermen, ' and let down your nets for a draught.'[3]   ' The kingdom of heaven is like unto a drag-net ($\sigma\alpha\gamma\eta\nu\eta$) that was cast into the sea, and gathered of every kind : which, when it was filled, they drew up on the beach ; and they sat down and gathered the good into vessels, but the bad they cast away.   So shall it be in the end of the world : the angels shall come forth and sever the

---

[1] *Zech.* vi. 9 *sqq.*   [2] *Hagg.* i. 2 *sqq.*   [3] *Luke* v. 4.

Z

wicked from among the righteous.' [1] The work of the few human fishers will be completed by the Father's heavenly messengers, as may be seen in another simile : [2] ' The labourers are few : pray ye therefore the Lord of the harvest that he send forth his labourers into his harvest ': in the fulness of time the ' Son of Man ' will send forth his angel reapers to complete the harvest.

Thus every word of Jesus in these early days breathes that firm, mountain-moving faith in the imminent miraculous intervention of God.   It is no idle waiting, but an active 'storming of the kingdom ' of heaven, that he demands.   Men need but make a beginning : God will give the rest ; man's task is to fulfil the ' higher righteousness,' to help in realizing the predictions of the prophets, banish all worry about the following day, not to question what, as king's messengers, they are to say in each case to move men's hearts. The Spirit will enlighten them, and they will find the kingdom if they seek without resting, until the ' Son of Man ' come.

THE KING'S MESSAGE

The four ' fishers of men,' [3] the twelve future judges of the restored twelve tribes, the new seventy(-two) elders of the polity of Moses as the king's messengers to the seventy(-two) nations of the world, are sent out by this unknown ' son of David,' who in poverty and lowliness wanders through the country as a tramping craftsman and healer. He himself pursues his way, teaching here and there on the Sabbath in the synagogues, at other times on the roads, on the mountain slopes, on the shore of the lake, or in the houses, wherever he turns for work and rest, relieving sufferers and enrolling recruits for his kingdom of God. His repeated successes in curing the ' possessed,' in spite of certain cases of relapse after temporary alleviation, which he freely admits and explains,[4] confirm his confident trust in his election by God and in the immediate coming of the new era.

Before his emissaries could have traversed even the towns and villages of Israel,[5] however great their speed,[6] those 1240 days of Daniel's prophecy, between the setting up of the ' abomination ' in the temple and the final catastrophe, would needs have run their course. And who knows whether God in his infinite mercy might not shorten that term ? But all fell out otherwise. Long before

---

[1] *Matt.* xiii. 47 *sqq.*   The last judgment is effected by the ejection of the wicked from the Land of Promise, in which the elect will blissfully dwell for ever.

[2] *Matt.* ix. 37=*Luke* x. 2 ; cf. also *Matt.* xiii. 39.

[3] One for each of the ' four corners ' of the world.

[4] *Matt.* xii. 43 *sqq.* ; *Luke* xi. 24 *sqq.*   The end of *Matt.* xii. 45—missing in *Luke* xi. 26—is not genuine (Wellhausen).

[5] There were in Galilee alone 204 villages and towns, if we are to believe Josephus, *Vita*, § 235.

[6] On the speed recommended to them, cf. *Luke* x. 4.

the last period had elapsed, the Twelve, the Seventy,[1] or such remnants as were still left of the two groups, returned to the Master.[2] They told him of all they had done and taught ; they had anointed with oil and healed the sick and ' possessed,' and cast out many devils.   Of course, there had been occasional cases of failure.   In reply to their enquiry into the reason for these disappointments, the Master consistently attributes them to their lack of sufficient faith.[3]   But of the outcome of their embassy not a word is said by the disciples, not a word of their having carried out their commission and traversed the cities of Israel.   Nowhere are we told of any concerted meeting after an interval, followed by a resumption of their travels.   On the contrary, the extant records, under an expression of the satisfaction of Jesus and his disciples at the successful conquest of the demons, conceal but ill the fact that the disciples prematurely and finally abandoned their journey and returned to their Master because their preaching had been ineffective and their own faith uncertain—because, once they had left behind the invigorating presence of Jesus, the strength had failed them to carry the message everywhere with that indomitable ardour which later on was shown by Paul.

The expected miracle which Jesus had promised for the immediate future had delayed too long.   The disciples were ' perplexed,' and could not fail to be perplexed.

Jesus had taught the necessity of beginning on a small scale. The ' higher righteousness ' would force its way ; the kingdom of God was already there ; among those who had subjected themselves to God's will and taken their yoke upon them it was in a small measure realized.   As the seed ripens for the harvest without man's agency, as the tiny grain of mustard-seed in one year's time grows into a luxuriant shrub in which the birds of heaven nest, as the tiny morsel of leaven permeates three measures of meal, even so, through a mere handful of trusty messengers of the Lord, the whole world, Jews, Samaritans, and heathen nations, would be peacefully conquered for the kingdom of God.   Nothing was needed but firm faith ; the Lord would do the rest, in his own good time.   The sons of the kingdom may still be few in number, but

' Fear not, little flock, for it is your Father's good pleasure to give you the kingdom.' [4]

In reply to the anxious question, ' When, Lord, when comes the day ? ' he ever rebukes their impatience.   The kingdom ' cometh not with observation.'   No expectation and observing the signs of the heavens will accelerate its coming.   Confidence is needed : ' Shall not God avenge his elect, which cry to him day and night

[1] *Luke* x. 17.
[2] *Mark* vi. 30 ; *Luke* x. 10a.
[3] Cf. *Mark* ix. 28 ; *Matt.* xvii. 19.
[4] *Luke* xii. 32.

should he suffer (this) for a long time over them ? I say unto you that he will avenge them speedily.'[1] Man cannot reckon with God, ' Lord we have done what thou commandedst us : now do thou thy part, now, forthwith, to-day.' For, 'Who is there among you, having a servant ploughing or keeping sheep, that will say unto him, when he is come in from the field, Come straightway and sit down to meat, and will not rather say unto him, Make ready wherewith I may sup, and gird thyself and serve me, till I have eaten and drunken ; and afterward thou shalt eat and drink ? Doth he thank the servant because he did the things that were commanded ? '[2] God is master, who decides at his pleasure when we may sit down to supper in the kingdom : who dares rebel if he still tarries a while ? ' Say,' therefore, 'we are unprofitable servants ; we have done that which it was our duty to do.'[3] Only the wicked servant will ' say in his heart, My lord delayeth his coming.'[4] All these consolations, which to burning, eager hearts may more than once have sounded like poor comfort, are unmistakable answers to importunate questions of disciples who, weak in faith, could not endlessly hope and wait.

Among the names of those who followed the call of the carpenter we find those of Simon the Zealot and Simon *Barjona*. If the gospel of quietism, of non-resistance to evil, could win these hard men of action, it must have been because Jesus had shown them some way of devoted action which would compel the saving intervention of God. The ' conversion ' and ' change of mind ' ($\mu\epsilon\tau\acute{a}\nu o\iota a$) which the envoys were to preach to all the world can have been no mere inward compunction: the king's messengers must have gone out under an exacting charge, hard to fulfil, and have likewise claimed from their hearers hard and great action, and not simply the adoption of a special messianic belief, a special Christology.

What this demand was cannot long remain unknown to any un-biased reader of the Gospels—to wit, to renounce all one's posses-sions,[5] i.e. to sell everything[6] and to distribute the proceeds among one's poorer brethren ; to 'deny oneself,'[7] i.e. to renounce one's name[8] and fame and worldly position, to assume the sign of the cross,[9] the sign of God's elect[10] and the tribal sign of the homeless,

---

[1] *Luke* xviii. 7.　　　　　　　　[2] *Luke* xvii. 7-9.
[3] *Ibid.*　　　　　　　　　　　[4] *Luke* xii. 45 ; *Matt.* xxiv. 48.
[5] *Luke* xiv. 33 ; *Mark* x. 21.　Cp. above, p. 332 n. 9 ; below, p. 362$_{2\text{-}3}$.
[6] This is what the Maccabees did before the final battle (2 *Macc.* viii. 14).
[7] *Mark* viii. 34, and parallels.
[8] As the Baptist had done (above, pp. 252$_2$, 240 l. 25).
[9] *Matt.* x. 38 : $\lambda a\mu\beta\acute{a}\nu\epsilon\iota\nu$ $\sigma\tau a\nu\rho\acute{o}\nu$. The parallels have instead $\beta a\sigma\tau\acute{a}\zeta\epsilon\iota\nu$, ' to lift a heavy weight,' an alteration of the text due to the evangelists thinking of the crucifixion, which Jesus could not have foreseen. Clem. Alex., *Strom.*, i. 12, 80, p. 880, says, in quoting this *logion*: " $\tau\grave{o}$ $\sigma\eta\mu\epsilon\hat{\iota}o\nu$ $\beta a\sigma\tau\acute{a}\sigma a\iota$." The original wording was obviously $\lambda a\mu\beta\acute{a}\nu\epsilon\iota\nu$ $\tau\grave{o}$ $\sigma\eta\mu\epsilon\hat{\iota}o\nu$, and the ' taking of the cross ' had, in the original saying of Jesus, the sense in which the crusaders of a later age under-stood it.　　　　　　　　　[10] *Ezek.* ix. 4, 6 ; *Rev.* vii. 3 *sqq.*

wandering Rekhabites and tramping Qenites, the 'sign of Cain,'[1] and to follow Jesus as leader and king.

There remains only the question to what sort of life Jesus intended to lead his adherents, and this must have been the burning question on the lips of all to whom these demands were addressed. In any case it is not to be believed that the summons to 'the great renunciation' could have been heard by deeply moved contemporaries with the comfortable self-satisfaction and the obtuse lack of understanding which characterize the modern Christian reading it sleepily in his Bible on a Sunday morning, to forget all about it twenty-four hours later. Certainly, not a single follower or opponent of Jesus would have ventured to rob the simple words of their true import, by having recourse to one of those evasions adopted by many ever since Clement of Alexandria wrote his *Quis dives salvetur*. The historian, seeking only to ascertain the actual facts, cannot fail to admit that the yoke of Jesus, easy and light for the poor and miserable, seemed intolerably hard, oppressive, and devoid of any practical sense to the leisurely rich.

Again, one must practically exclude the idea that Jesus himself meant to unite his followers into a religious mendicant order of wayfaring saints passively awaiting with prayer and fasting the end of this world. Nor, with his expectation of the immediately impending Divine redemption of Israel from the yoke of the 'lords of this world,' can he have thought of founding any cenobitic or hermit settlements such as are mentioned by Josephus. Such plans would never have raised hopes of the people's liberation from the Roman yoke, and to us they appear irreconcilable with the portrait of the personality of Jesus as reflected in his extant words. Again, it would surely have been no fulfilment of his wishes and claims that individual believers, abandoning their business, should join his little Rekhabite band of tramping craftsmen and wandering teachers and take to the road with him, sharing his life and work. Lastly, he cannot have thought that it would be a sufficiently strong effort to compel the coming of the kingdom that every believer should continue in his present station in life in unselfish love of his neighbour and perfect submission even to wrong and violence until it would please God to punish the wicked and radically to renovate this lost world. The call of Jesus for definite, liberating action was directed to the people of Israel as a whole.

Not individuals only, but the people as such, or at least the 'remnant' of the true Israel, were to renounce all their possessions and thus accomplish that hardest sacrifice for which the followers of Judas Maccabee [2] had set the example. The Land of Promise,

[1] Cf. my paper in the *Monde Oriental* of 1929, pp. 50 ff.
[2] See above, p. 356 n. 6; below, p. 359₃.

the people's God-given property, had in punishment for their sins been converted into a new house of bondage. Since according to Deuteronomic law [1] they were not allowed to own the Promised Land under the overlordship of foreigners, they were to sell and abandon it. A new exodus into the wilderness under the leadership of a new Moses [2] was inevitable.

The number of possible courses open was indeed strictly limited. Among these few Jesus had to make his choice. Between the alternatives of a passive waiting for God's intervention to liberate his people from the foreign yoke, and an active struggle for the realization of God's kingdom, Jesus had clearly taken his stand on the side of the Zealots, who 'since the days of the Baptist had sought to take the kingdom by storm.' [3] On the question of joining the Zealots in a revolt against Rome and the Jewish authorities dependent on Rome, he had decided in the 'Sermon on the Mount,' the political significance of which has been emphasized above,[4] against active resistance to wrong. If God's commandment 'Thou shalt not kill' and the Golden Rule were to be inviolably observed, an armed rebellion, a war of liberation, could not be agreeable to God. But if, as was taught both by the Baptist and by Judas of Galilee, the subjection to foreign dominion was a grave infraction of the Deuteronomic law of kingship and an apostasy from God, what course remained? Obviously, none but what in Roman history is known as the *secessio plebis*, an exodus, a return to the nomad life of privation but of freedom in the desert, such as Hosea [5] had preached and a particular group of Zealots and *Barjonim* had repeatedly sought to carry into execution. If, as King Agrippa has pointed out in his great speech,[6] the whole inhabited world was Roman and subject to the dominion of the 'prince of this world,' there remained only the uninhabited desert as a place of refuge for the God-fearing.

The period in the desert had been the time of the bridal love of the community of Israel for her Divine bridegroom: [7] the tribes

---

[1] xvii. 14 *sq.*

[2] Therefore Moses and Elijah are seen and heard (below, p. 372 n. 7) talking to Jesus about τὴν ἔξοδον αὐτοῦ ἣν ἔμελλε πληροῦν, 'his *exodus*, which he was to accomplish in Jerusalem' (*Luke* ix. 31). Exactly the same words τὴν ἔξοδον αὐτοῦ are used by Josephus, *B.J.*, vii. p. 439, where he describes the projected exodus of the poor weaver Jonathan of Cyrene, 'who led not a few' of the Jews 'into the desert, promising to show them divine "miracles and manifestations"' (σήματα καὶ φάσματα δείξειν). The commentators, who are wont to explain the word ἔξοδος in *Luke* ix. 31 by comparing 2 *Peter* i. 15, where it means the exit of the soul out of the body, forget that this mystic sense of the word is based on Philo's allegorical explanation of the 'exodus' from Egypt as symbolizing the liberation of the soul from the bondage of matter (*Leg. alleg.*, ii. 77). But this allegory occurs nowhere but in the Hellenistic *Soph. Sal.*, iii. 2; *ibid.*, vii. 6, the word is explained by adding 'life' ('entrance into life and exit out of it'); equally so in Josephus, *Ant.*, iv. 189 (Philo, *de Virt.*, 77), and in Pap. Lond., 77, 57.

[3] See above, p. 259 n. 1. [4] See above, p. 341 f.

[5] ii. 17. [6] *B.J.*, ii. § 388. [7] *Hos.* xi. 1.

had left the fleshpots of Egypt and the 'house of bondage' to serve their Lord and Master. A new exodus into the wilderness under a new Moses could alone blot out Israel's sins, bring her freedom, and make her worthy, under a new Joshu'a ben Nun or Jesus IXΘΥC,[1] to recover from God's hand the Land of Promise, after the heathen nations have annihilated one another[2] in the last messianic war, along with the unredeemed and eternally lost children of Israel.

To understand the stern command of Jesus 'to renounce all and follow him' in its simple original meaning, one has only to read the summons for freedom of that great model of Jewish heroes, Mattathias ben Joḥanan of Modein, in the *First Book of Maccabees* : [3]

> 'And Mattathias cried out in the city with a loud voice, saying, Whosoever is *zealous* for the law and maintaineth the covenant, let him come forth after me. And he and his sons *fled into the mountains* and *forsook all they had in the city.* Then many that sought after justice and judgment *went down into the wilderness* to dwell there, they and their sons and their wives and their cattle . . . they went down into the secret places in the wilderness.'

From the opening words of that fateful summons, 'Whosoever is zealous for the law,' the party of the 'Zealots' in the time of Herod the Great derived their name. Every 'zealot for the law' was required by Mattathias to 'follow him.' His followers, seeking 'justice and judgment,' 'forsook all they had in the city' and 'went down into the desert to live there.' That is what Jesus demands of his followers, to cast off all fettering possessions as chains of slavery, to leave all behind and follow him to liberty. Whenever some one asks his advice and inquires into the whereabouts of his dwelling,[4] he replies :

> 'Come and see.[5] . . . The foxes have holes and the birds of the air have nests ;[6] but the son of man hath not where to lay his head.'[7]

Into the same context belongs, most probably, also the famous saying, 'In my Father's house there are many mansions,'[8] early misunderstood and misinterpreted. God's house is the wide world, and there are many places of rest for the homeless wanderer. Any one leaving his home and his friends like Abraham[9] of old

---

[1] *Ben Nun* simply means 'fish,' and here, I think, is the ultimate root of the symbol IXΘΥC applied to Jesus by the early Church.
[2] This is foretold by *Ezek.* xxxviii. 21, *Zech.* xiv. 13, *Hagg.* ii. 22, *Enoch* lvi. 7 ; cf. *Bar.* lxx. 7.
[3] ii. 27 *sq.*   [4] *John* i. 39.   [5] *Ibid.*
[6] Cf. Plutarch, *Tiberius Gracchus*, ix. 4 : 'The wild beasts of Italy have holes and nests and places of rest, but to those who fight and die for Italy nothing but the light and the air is left ; without house and home they roam about with their wives and children.'
[7] *Matt.* viii. 20 ; *Luke* ix. 59.   [8] *John* xiv. 2.   [9] Cf. *Acts* vii. 3.

will be rewarded a hundredfold.[1] Whoever ceases to cultivate his field and leaves it will be sent into God's harvest-field.[2] Whoever leaves his boats and nets will be made a ' fisher of men.' [3] In short, he advocates complete withdrawal from all economic labour, non-co-operation, and a general flight from the Land of Promise.

If Josephus, in spite of good sources, was not aware that the doctrines of Judas of Galilee were dependent upon the preaching of the Baptist, it is not surprising that he should also have failed to see any connexion between the promises of the 'miracle-worker' crucified by Pilate and those 'jugglers' (γόητες), i.e. Rekhabites, who, under the governorship of Felix, led the people out into the wilderness to show them 'signs of liberty.' [4] But this cannot, of course, prevent the modern historian from seeing such a connexion. In fact, some of the most enigmatical utterances and actions of Jesus find their most simple and luminous explanation in the assumption of such a summons issued by him, though not expressly told in the Gospel tradition.[5] Above all, we have the exhortation which has at all times been the subject of debate : [6]

' Be not anxious for your life, what ye shall eat or what ye shall drink ; nor yet for your body, what ye shall put on. Is not the life more than the food, and the body than the raiment ? Behold the birds of the heaven : they sow not, neither do they reap, nor gather into barns ; and your heavenly Father feedeth them. Are not ye of much more value than they ? . . .[7] And why are ye anxious concerning raiment ? Consider the lilies of the field, how they grow : they toil not, neither do they spin ; yet I say unto you that even Solomon in all his glory was not arrayed like one of these. But if God doth so clothe the grass of the field, which to-day is and to-morrow is cast into the oven, (shall he) not much more (clothe) you, O ye of little faith ! Be not therefore anxious, saying, What shall we eat ? or, What shall we drink ? or, Wherewithal shall we be clothed ? (for after all these things do the Gentiles seek) ; for your heavenly Father knoweth that ye have need of all these things. But seek ye first his kingdom and his righteousness, and all these things shall be added unto you.'

This utterance, which, torn from its context as it is read to-day, would appear as a preposterous condemnation of natural fore-thought in domestic matters, at once becomes significant and justified if it is assumed to have been addressed to reluctant persons of little faith, hankering after the fleshpots of Palestine,

---

[1] *Mark* x. 29 ; *Matt.* xix. 29 ; *Luke* xviii. 29.
[2] *Matt.* ix. 37 *sq.* ; *Luke* x. 2.   [3] See above, p. 353.
[4] *B.J.* and *Halōsis*, ii. § 258 *sqq.* ; *Ant.*, xx. 8. 6, and 10 § 188.
[5] See, however, above, p. 358 n. 2, and below, p. 372₂, on ' the exodus he was to accomplish.'
[6] *Matt.* vi. 25 *sqq.*
[7] The verset about the impossibility of adding an ell to one's stature belongs to some different discourse ; see below, p. 415 n. 7.

who had asked Jesus on what they could live and wherewithal they could be clothed if they followed him into the desert.

Nor can any reader fail to note that the Gospels attribute to Jesus a symbolical repetition of the two great miracles of Moses in the desert, the feeding of the people with bread from heaven[1] and the drawing of water from the rock.[2] Of the miracle of the loaves Dr. Albert Schweitzer writes : ' Weisse pointed out years ago that the miraculous feeding constitutes one of the greatest historical problems, in that the narrative, like that of the transfiguration, is embedded in a definite historical context and therefore imperatively calls for explanation.' The desired historical connexion of this messianic 'acted parable' can still be clearly recognized. Two of the accounts emphatically state that the people ' followed ' Jesus into the desert.[3] The disciples lay stress on the fact that they were in the desert, and expressly ask, ' Whence can we get bread enough *in the desert* to satisfy so many ? '[4] This is the question—the fundamental question, that is, and not a problem arising out of this single occasion. And Jesus replied with an easily intelligible symbolic action, a δρώμενον, that God would supply all their needs to a people obedient and first seeking for the kingdom, adding that man does not live by bread alone in the solitude,[5] but by the word of God : ' Not hunger for bread, nor thirst for water, but a hunger for hearing the words of the Lord '[6] was befitting the believers : ' Blessed are they that hunger and thirst after righteousness, for they shall be filled.'[7] Jesus was therefore the first to do what the *ḥarashîm* (the γόητες of Josephus) did, imitating him, in the time of Felix. He led out a multitude into the desert and there showed and interpreted to them the miracle of the manna and other 'tokens of coming deliverance.' He thought of doing what the rebel Theudas, the ' friend ' or ' acquaintance ' of St. Paul,[8] who passed himself off as a Joshua (=Jesus) *redivivus*,[9] had attempted to do by crossing the Jordan : in God's appointed time he hoped to lead the people back across the Jordan into the Land of Promise, liberated from its enemies by the final messianic war.[10]

For a mountain-moving faith, reading the scriptural story of the exodus from Egypt of a vast multitude (600,000 men)[11] and of their wondrous forty years in the wilderness as a veracious history

---

[1] *John* vi. 31 ; cf. *Z.N.T.W.*, 1925, p. 187.
[2] On the exact parallelism between Moses and the hoped-for Messiah, cf. Strack-Billerbeck, i. 87, ii. 481. Halévy, *Moïse dans l'histoire et dans la légende*, Paris, 1927.
[3] *Luke* ix. 11 ; *John* vi. 2.　　　　　[4] *Mark* viii. 4 ; *Matt.* xv. 33.
[5] See above, p. 285 n. 3.
[6] *Amos* viii. 11 ; *Matt.* v. 6.　　　　　[7] *Ibid.*
[8] Clem. Alex., *Strom.*, vii. 17 : Valentinus (the Gnostic) was 'a hearer of Theudas, who was an acquaintance (γνώριμος) of Paul.'
[9] *Acts* v. 36.　　　　　　　　　[10] Cf. above, p. 359 n. 2.
[11] *Exod.* xii. 37 ; *Num.* i. 46 *sqq.*

of Divine miracles, the idea of leading a people of believers out of enslaved Palestine into the free desert could not appear as anything fantastic or impossible. In the desert lived, in poverty indeed, but free and owning no master but God, the nomad tribes of Ishmael, and above all the Rekhabite fellow-tribesmen of the wandering carpenter's son. Why should it be impossible to lead back the faithful ' remnant ' into the wilderness and to feed them there ? Certainly only a miracle could feed some hundred thousand beyond the region of cultivation, but who knew whether the number of the elect might not after all be as small as the little band leaving Mesopotamia at the bidding of God along with Abraham ? And in the event that thousands followed the call, was there any reason to doubt that God would again feed them by a miracle ?

The idea, then, would not seem unwarranted that Jesus desired to lead his followers back to the Rekhabite life in the desert. If his messengers went through the cities and villages of Israel with the call to ' come back ' (*shubhu !*), they meant by that, after the manner of Hosea, a return to the free desert life of the olden days.

This theory gives the simplest possible explanation of the messengers' lack of success in raising recruits for the kingdom. The small landholders certainly did not show the slightest inclination to give up their farms.[1] The attitude of the wealthy is aptly characterized by the doubtless historical passage on the ' rich youth,' ' owning many lands and goods,'[2] whom 'Jesus loved.' All the recruits that could be reckoned with must therefore have come from the ranks of the destitute, such as those who at a later date were prepared to follow the weaver Jonathan of Cyrene into the African desert.[3] But even among the poor the message of Jesus cannot, for obvious reasons, have met with the hoped-for response. Those who had retreated into the desert with the Maccabees had received arms as the first gift of their leaders ;[4] those who afterwards repaired with the Zealots into the mountains knew that they were embarking on a lusty guerilla warfare in which those who had nothing to lose might possibly gain something. Not without some reason does Josephus invariably speak of them as λησταί, 'robbers.' But what novel sort of champion of liberty was this who would lead his followers to the freedom of the desert but forbid them absolutely to make war or even to resist attack, and would impose upon them an even stricter justice than the one with which they had doubtless more than once come

---

[1] ' multas divitias et agros,' Old Latin, so-called African text of *Mark* x. 22 and of Clement of Alexandria (χρήματα πολλὰ καὶ ἀγρούς).

[2] *Mark* x. 29 ; *Matt.* xix. 29 ; cf. also *Luke* xix. 29, where the word 'lands' has been omitted.

[3] Jos., *B.J.*, vii. 11. 1.   [4] 1 *Macc.* xiv. 32.

in conflict?   What was to be hoped from a new *'abba barjonîm* who would not allow his followers to plunder the surrounding districts, but would have them wander through the desert weaponless and, like the poor and humble *salubîm*, the modern *Sleb*, serve the other tribes by their labour or even beg of them?   Such a prospect could not tempt many even among the *ebhionîm* in Israel, who for all their piety and love of liberty did not care overmuch to become tramps and beggars.   So the envoys must have returned disappointed, having abandoned their recruiting campaign.   Even their Master's own success can never have exceeded very modest limits.   The ' crowds ' attracted by him and his disciples were invalids who came to be healed of diseases, and sometimes also their relatives.   Others pressed around him to hear a great preacher ' instructed unto the kingdom of heaven . . . who bringeth forth out of his treasure things old and new.' [1]   But those who renounced all to follow him in this early period can never have been many more than those four, those twelve, and, finally, those seventy.   At the most there may at one time have been several hundreds.[2] The mission could not be other than a complete failure, could not but end with a shattering of the trustful confidence even of those first converts of the hidden Messiah.   God had not intervened, and the coming of the ' Son of Man ' announced by Jesus did not take place before the return of his delegates.   His call died away unheard.

' I CAME NOT TO SEND PEACE, BUT A SWORD '

The greatest difficulty encountered in every attempt to present the life and work of Jesus according to the evidence of his own words preserved in the sources is the sharp, irreconcilable contradiction between the so-called ' fire and sword' sayings on the one side and the beatitudes on the peacemakers and the meek, the prohibition to kill, to be angry, to resist wrong, and the command to love one's enemy, contained in the sermon on the mount, on the other.

To deny that the 'fire and sword' words were spoken by Jesus and to attribute them to a political group of Zealots within the original community,[3] who foisted upon the Master the expression of their own feelings, expectations, and efforts, seems, without further proof, a sort of special pleading.

Since the Church from the days of Paul consistently followed

---

[1] *Matt.* xiii. 52.
[2] Cf. above, p. 10 n. 1, Sossianus Hierocles on the ' 900 bandits ' of Jesus.
[3] Cf. *Luke* ix. 54, where some Zealots want to draw down by prayer fire from heaven upon the Samaritans.

the path of reconciliation with the empire, those words would certainly have been deleted had it been possible to do so, i.e. had they not been too surely attested as genuine. As a matter of fact, though not suppressed outright and by common consent, they have in the course of time been toned down as much as possible. Where *Matthew* makes the Master say,[1] ' Think not that I came to cast peace [2] on the earth ; I came not to cast peace, but a sword,' *Luke*,[3] in the extant text,[4] weakens the hard word, replacing ' a sword' by 'division.' Conversely, half of the original saying preserved in *Luke*,[5] ' I came to cast fire upon the earth ; and what will I, if it is already kindled ? ' is wanting in *Matthew*, a prudent and not surprising omission if one recalls the charge made against the apostles of wishing to set the temple on fire,[6] and, later on, against the Christians under Nero.[7]

The question must be asked, Which is more probable, that Jesus should have spoken thus of himself as the kindler of the messianic world-conflagration, or that a party in the original community with incendiary tendencies should have put these words into his mouth ? The answer cannot be doubtful. A further point to be borne in mind is the fact that the sharp contradiction in question occurs only in the *Gospel of Matthew*. Only there do we find side by side the saying about the sword, and the beatitudes of the meek and the peacemakers and the prohibition to resist violence.

In *Luke* these blessings are all wanting, as is the fundamental prohibition of resistance to wrongful oppression.[8] The command to love one's enemies, it is true, stands unaltered, but this does not necessarily conflict with a permission to use the sword in an honourable and holy war. Every decent soldier knows that he may engage in a life-and-death struggle for nation and country without a spark of hatred for an opponent whom he respects as a man. The ' hymns of hate ' have at all times been the specialty of the cowardly rabble who in times of war ' keep the home fires burning.'

There is therefore no inconsistency in the Jesus of *Luke*, even though at the close of the work he calls his followers to arms. To the critics who would simply strike out the 'sword' passages as

---

[1] x. 34.

[2] βαλεῖν = heṭil shalom, a Semitism. Nobody casts a sword; but fire is thrown. This proves that Matthew's source contained what *Luke* xii. 4, 9 read about ' casting a fire ' on the earth.

[3] xii. 51.

[4] Certainly not the original text, since *Luke* alone has preserved Jesus' command to buy swords.

[5] xii. 49. [6] Apocryphal *Gospel of Peter*, § 26.

[7] *Ann.*, xv. 44. See above, p. 9 n. 1.

[8] vi. 29 : ' turning the other cheek ' remains ; but the context is merely an exhortation to humility toward one's own people, like *Mark* ix. 50. The armed enemy of one's country does not give blows on the cheek, but strikes with the sword.

an interpolation one might retort with equal justice that the passages about peacemaking and non-resistance in *Matthew* are the interpolations of a group of pacifists, represented by Paul, in the early Church.   For the ' fire and sword ' passages are attested by two Gospels, the sayings about peacemaking by only one.   A third course would be to follow Mark alone, who knows neither the ' sermon on the mount,' with its code of 'higher righteousness,' nor the ' fire and sword ' passages.   But his Jesus, though unencumbered by inconsistencies, is also shorn of his fascinating singularity. Nor will it do to point out the common experience that thorough consistency is a virtue rarely possessed by humans.   For we are not dealing here with the all too familiar contradiction between life and doctrine observable in so many philosophers, but with a clash of two entirely different conceptions of messianic redemption.   The idea of the ' better righteousness,' of self-sacrifice and non-resistance, is irreconcilable with the announcement that the Redeemer brings to mankind the sword of rebellion.   The commentators have of course acquired the habit of interpreting passages such as *Matt.* x. 35, 38, and *Luke* xii. 51 *sq.*, by pointing to the coming disruption of families into Christians and non-Christians.   They fail to answer the question why a brother who remained a Jew should have persecuted a 'Christian,' i.e. a Messianist brother, with such bitterness, the whole difference of opinion turning about the problem whether the expected Messiah was yet to come, or whether he had already revealed himself in the form of the carpenter Jesus. Why should such a relatively unimportant, one might almost say academic, question have divided Israel and the whole world into two hostile camps, and that in face of the fact that the Jews were not unanimous among themselves as to whether a Messiah would come at all, or whether God might not after all prefer to judge the world himself ?   The question must therefore have involved some more deep-seated antagonism of principle, of practical politics, of man's attitude toward the powers that be.   When, after all, have orthodox Jews ever 'delivered' heretics to death on account of their dissenting opinions or sought to exterminate them with fire and sword ?

Insurrection and war between brothers for Jesus' sake could only arise if his faithful followers wished to hurry their brethren into some fateful act, and in so doing naturally met with the bitter opposition of their relatives, whose very life and existence were thereby threatened.   If the faithful wished to follow their Master into the wilderness, they must indeed have been prepared for the most lively opposition, for parents would naturally hold back their children and husbands their wives from a step of such consequence.   Jesus' call must certainly have led to disruption and strife among families, as did the call to the civil war a generation or so later,[1] and as it had done in the period of the Maccabees. Those who accept this interpretation—and I must confess that with A. Schweitzer I do not see any other—will admit that the sayings about the sword and fire may well have been pronounced by the same person who delivered the ' sermon on the mount ' on non-resistance and the peacemakers, but certainly not at the same period of his life.

A simple solution of the seeming inconsistency lies in the natural assumption of a spiritual development on the part of the author. A very good and in many respects a striking parallel is offered by the dilemma faced by more modern pacifists with their well-known and justly discredited phrases of 'the war to end war,' the war which is to be 'the last war,' etc. The hoped-for miracle of Jahweh failing to be forthcoming, the followers of the new Messiah had only two ways open to them—either to wait indefinitely or else to follow the path shown by the Baptist, Judas of Galilee, and the Zealots, i.e. to take the kingdom of God by storm, to seek the way to peace through a holy war.

If Jesus ever put to himself the question whether an exodus without resort to force would be possible, he must have read the clear and unequivocal answer not only in the ruthless measures by which the Romans effectively quenched all attempts at rebellion, but even more in the story of the first exodus in the time of Moses. There we are expressly told that the children of Israel went up ' armed ' out of the land of Egypt.[2] Then there was the story of the pursuit by the Egyptians, requiring another miracle on the part of Jahweh ; and lastly, there were the wars against the tribes in the desert.

Only if the number of the ' elect ' following his call was so small as to escape detection by the Romans could he count upon a peaceful exodus and a subsequent peaceful life in Rekhabite fashion. There may have been a time when Jesus did not expect more followers, though that cannot have been at the time when he sent out the Twelve and the Seventy. Then he evidently wanted his message to reach many, hoping, perhaps, to muster around him two-fifths or even three-fifths of the whole population.[3] If such a crowd could be put in motion and asked to meet for the feast of the Passover, the day of the exodus from Egypt, then there was perhaps a hope of taking the opponents by surprise and breaking away

---

[1] Josephus, B.J., ii. 13. 8, § 264 ff. : ' the jugglers (γόητες) and brigands, banding together, incited numbers to revolt . . . threatening to *kill* anybody who submitted to Roman domination . . . looting the houses of the wealthy, they murdered their owners and *set the villages afire*'—procedures exactly analogous to those practised by the Sinn Feiners against loyalists, not so many years ago.

[2] *Exod.* xiii. 18. The word ' armed ' is intentionally suppressed in the Greek version, because the Jews in Ptolemean Egypt were not allowed to possess arms. For the same apologetic reason, Josephus, *Ant.*, ii. 15. 3, insists upon telling us that the Jews emigrated unarmed and through a miracle of God received the arms, washed on shore, of the drowned Egyptian army.   [3] Cf. *Luke* xii. 52.

into the near-by desert. But the chances were small that he could make such a move without a collision with the Roman garrison or the Herodian troops—nay, with opponents from among his own people. Nor could he very well lead the crowds, unarmed, like sheep for the slaughter, against an attack of pursuers in the more than probable event of a decisive battle. Even if Jesus himself trusted too confidently in the miraculous and seasonable help of God, Simon the Zealot and Simon *Barjona* can have been under no delusion as to the dangers involved. And Jesus himself, when he thought over the situation, must have realized that he was bringing not peace but the sword to those prepared to follow him.

This, then, is the easy solution of the apparently irreconcilable contradictions. From the previous failures of Judas of Galilee and his rivals Jesus had learnt that the 'fulfilment of all righteousness' was not enough to ensure the intervention of God, and that armed revolt was not the 'way of the law' pleasing to God. The 'better righteousness' appeared to him ordained by God; and since the Deuteronomic law of royalty forbade the people of Israel to submit to foreign rulers, there remained only renunciation of ' houses and lands'—in fact, of the Land of Promise itself.

In the early period of his messianic career, the period of the sermon on the mount, Jesus was a thorough quietist. Exactly how he departed from this attitude we do not know. It may be that the Zealots among his disciples, whom he had already won over in spite of his pacifistic doctrines, gradually drove him forward on the fatal road. It may also be that in the face of the impenetrable silence of heaven he decided on his own account to give up waiting, and, in the rôle of the 'prophet like Moses' promised in *Deuteronomy*,[1] to lead the people out of the land of bondage to freedom.

If the sequence in the traditional text could be trusted, the momentous decision may have been taken before he sent out his royal messengers. For the sayings about the fire and the sword occur in the very speech made to those messengers. But two important circumstances militate against such a conclusion. So long as he hoped for the intervention of God he seems to have contemplated but a small circle of 'elect' ones and to have refrained from attempts to rouse the masses. Furthermore, so long as he had to conceal his Messiahship and speak only in parables, his words could have no very far-reaching effect.

Subsequently he appears to have changed his mind. In his instructions to the Twelve we are suddenly told :[2]

'There is nothing covered that shall not be revealed, and hid that shall not be known. What I tell you in the darkness, speak ye in the light : and what ye hear (said) in the ear, proclaim upon the housetops.'

[1] *Deut.* xviii. 15.   [2] *Matt.* x. 26 *sq.*

Allied to this passage [1] are the words :

> ' Is the lamp brought to be put under the bushel or under the bed,
> and not to be put on the stand ?   For there is nothing hid save that
> it should be manifested :   neither was anything made secret but that
> it should come to light.'

This saying could certainly find no more suitable position than in
such an address.   But it is equally certain that the disciples would
have preferred to take any risk rather than shout from the
housetops what was confided to them in the same speech as it now
stands—-to wit, that their Master was to bring to the inhabitants of
the country not peace but the sword and civil war, and that he was
yearning to 'cast fire upon the earth.'

What could have been shouted freely from the housetops can
only have been the good news of Jesus in its original form.   The
proclamation of non-resistance could not have been unacceptable
to the ' lords of this world.'   Messengers carrying such a message
were threatened by no danger from either Romans or Jews.   On
the other hand, we know from the events which took place under
Festus and Catullus that messengers sent to summon people to
leave all their possessions and march into the desert had every
reason to fear persecution of every kind—nay, danger to life
and limb.

The injunction henceforth to proclaim the secret openly from
the housetops can therefore hardly belong to the same parting
speech as the prediction that the messengers must be prepared for
persecution and death for Jesus' sake.   As a matter of fact, Luke [2]
has inserted these words in a totally different context.   The same
conclusion is reached when one reads the messengers' instructions
in *Matthew*—first the avowal of Jesus that he brings not peace but
a sword, and then the command to the disciples to salute and carry
peace into every house.[3]   It is not different with the address to
the Seventy in *Luke*.[4]

Our attempt to draw a distinction between an earlier and a later
mission is not mere conjecture.   Apart from the fact that Luke
gives two distinct messengers' instructions, to the Twelve and the
Seventy respectively,[5] we have the express attestation of such a
distinction from the mouth of Jesus himself in the most remarkable
of all the sayings about the sword : [6]

> ' And he said unto them, When I sent you forth without purse and
> wallet and shoes, lacked ye anything ?   And they said, Nothing. And
> he said unto them, *But now,* he that hath a purse, let him take it, and
> likewise a wallet :   and he that hath none, let him sell his cloke and

---

[1] *Mark* iv. 21 *sq.* ; *Luke* viii. 16 *sq.* ; cf. *Matt.* v. 14 *sqq.*
[2] xii. 2 *sqq.*   [3] *Matt.* x. 11 *sqq.*   [4] x. 5 *sq.*
[5] *Luke* ix. 1 *sqq.* ; x. 1 *sqq.*   [6] *Luke* xxii. 35 *sqq.*

buy a sword. For I say unto you, that this which is written must be fulfilled in me : And he was reckoned with the transgressors; [1] for that which concerneth me hath fulfilment.[2] And they said, Lord, behold, here are two swords. And he said unto them, That is enough.'

Here it is highly significant that the time of the first sending out is distinguished from ' now ' (ἀλλὰ νῦν). By this ' now ' Luke understands that last hour of all which Jesus spent with his disciples. He puts the words among the parting speeches of Jesus after the last supper, clearly because he interprets one phrase to mean ' that which is predicted of me hath now an *end*,' and therefore places it as near as possible to the close of Jesus' life.

This date, however, is highly improbable. For it is inconceivable that at the moment when he knew himself betrayed and lost, Jesus, instead of urging his disciples to instant and secret flight, should have bidden them sell their last dispensable article of clothing to buy weapons quite useless to a single fugitive pursued by soldiers. Moreover, the phrase ' hath an end ' certainly has no reference to the end of his life.[3]

The words therefore belong to another period, of course considerably later than the first mission, when Jesus wished his disciples armed for a longer journey. He assumes that many of them already have a sword; only to those who have not, the most urgent instruction is given to sell even their warm upper garment, their protection in the cold night and against bad weather, and to buy a sword with the proceeds. The disciples, significantly enough, have not waited for this order. They reply that each of them has two swords, and produce them. That Jesus should assume many of his followers to be armed might seem surprising ; but it must not be forgotten that even the Essenes, those ' ministers of peace '—by the grace of Josephus—carried nothing with them on their journeys *except arms*, as a protection ' against brigands.' The μάχαιραι here mentioned are short swords or daggers, which would be carried concealed under the clothes, for the open bearing of arms was naturally not permitted to the population of a Roman province.[4] This practice of secreting two daggers beneath the raiment is familiar from the descriptions in Josephus [5] of the *sicarii* (i.e. knife-men), who took their name from this weapon (*sica*).[6] Josephus certainly would have called the small troop armed to their teeth a ' band of *sicarii*.' It was for a leader of ' dagger-men ' that Paul was taken by a Roman tribune,[7] and

---

[1] Cf. *Isaiah* liii. 12.   [2] Greek ' end.'
[3] Cf. also M. Salomon Reinach, *Cultes, Mythes et Religions*, iv. (Paris, 1912), p. 167 *sqq.*   [4] Cf. App. xix., below, pp. 616 f.
[5] *B.J.* and *Halōsis*, iv. § 563 ; *Ant.*, xx. § 186.
[6] John, already removed from the original tradition, is the only one who mentions a ' sheath ' (xviii. 11). Matthew simply says, ' into its place ' (xxvi. 52).
[7] *Acts* xxi. 38.

2 A

Sossianus Hierocles describes the followers of Jesus as 'nine hundred robbers.'[1] The word 'dagger-men' (*sicarii*) denoted a definite class of criminals (like the American 'gunmen'), against whom special provisions were made by Sulla in the *lex Cornelia de sicariis et veneficis*.[2] Jesus is fully aware of the illegality of this arming of his disciples and of his own direction to purchase a weapon ; none the less, he sees no escape from this bitter necessity. The prediction of the prophet must be fulfilled, according to which the righteous servant of the Lord must be numbered among the lawless transgressors (ἄνομοι).

It must not be supposed that Jesus was thinking of the law of the Roman oppressors. The burden weighing most heavily on his conscience was the tragic necessity of breaking that law of the 'better righteousness,' of non-resistance, which he had himself proclaimed as the will and ordinance of God. Seeing in the writings of the prophets the revelation of that will, he now resigned himself to the realization that the peaceful kingdom of God could only be established through battle.[3] Israel had marched out of Egypt into the desert 'armed' for battle ; the second Moses could not without weapons bring his followers to the promised goal. 'It must needs be that offences (σκάνδαλα) come, but woe to the man through whom the offence cometh.'[4] He who is reckoned among the transgressors of the law, as the Scripture[5] had said, bears the sins of many, whose impenitent violence and hardness of heart had prevented the kingdom from coming by the peaceful path of ready submission to God's will. As a ransom for them he must give his life.

THE PREDICTIONS OF SUFFERING AND DEATH

The arrangement (σύνταξις) of the sayings of Jesus, in the extant Gospels, in chronological order (τάξις) was disputed in very early days in a familiar passage of Papias,[6] and is in fact altogether insufficient to allow of far-reaching conclusions. But the intrinsic probability of the view that Jesus was continually driven on in consequence of the lack of external results commensurate with his high expectations, gives us at least an idea of the historical development of his aims and resolutions. He began by preaching the 'better righteousness,' sent out his first followers as messengers to proclaim that stern rule, and then proceeded to preach the abandonment of houses and lands, which means that from the attitude of 'non-resistance' he progressed to that of 'non-coöpera-

---

[1] See above, p. 10 n. 1 and p. 363 n. 2. Two thousand armed followers surround Jesus on Mount Olivet according to the *Toldoth Jeshu* (p. 16 l. 17, ed. Wagenseil, Alfdorf, 1681), that is, according to a lost passage of *Josippon* (see above, pp. 111 ff.).
[2] Pauly's *Real Encycl.*, iv. 969.　　　[3] *Joel* iv. 9.　　　[4] *Matt.* xviii. 7.
[5] *Isaiah* liii. 12.　　　[6] Euseb., *Hist. eccl.*, iii. 39. 15 *sq.*

tion.' Those who followed his call were to hold themselves in readiness for a *secessio plebis*, for the great exodus from the land of bondage, to take place on the Passover festival, the anniversary of the first exodus. We have just seen how he issued his command to his followers to arm themselves, a command which can have been given only on the eve of the departure of this *militia Christi* on the fatal journey to Jerusalem.

This march of the Galilaeans to the capital was of course no necessary stage in the exodus he was about to accomplish.[1] The shortest route from Galilee into the desert leads not southwards but due east to the region of Trachonitis and Ḥauran, always a favourite haunt of rebels in guerilla warfare against the Romans.[2]

Why, then, did Jesus insist on 'accomplishing his exodus in Jerusalem'?[3] Peter, the Barjona, viewing the situation in the light of human intelligence and not in that of God's designs[4] as they could be guessed from Scripture, was thoroughly opposed to this journey.[5] When he and James and John were afterwards asked why Jesus had offered this challenge to the Roman world-power, an action which to outsiders looked like deliberate suicide, they referred the critic to a vision they once had when half asleep,[6] and in which they had seen and heard no less than the two greatest prophets of old, Moses and Elijah, talking with Jesus[7] about the 'exodus which he was to accomplish in Jerusalem.' Six days[8] after Peter's confession of his belief in the Messiah at Caesarea Philippi, Jesus had taken these three disciples apart on to a high mountain (*or* 'to the mountain'), i.e. to one of the peaks or to the actual summit of the snow-clad Hermon, clearly under the influence of the story of Moses' ascent of the holy Mount Sinai, to be 'nearer' to the divinity.[9] So Jesus and his companions in this momentous hour sought the cloud-wrapt summit of the mountain, sacred ever since the beginnings of history.[10] The disciples, overcome by fatigue, fall into a deep sleep just underneath the mountain top. At sunrise they are awakened not only by the flood of light but also by the words of the Master, addressing his God, not

---

[1] *Luke* ix. 31.　　　　[2] *B.J.*, i. § 398 ; *Ant.*, xv. § 344.

[3] *Luke* ix. 31 : "τὴν ἔξοδον αὐτοῦ . . . πληροῦν ἐν Ἰερουσαλήμ." Cf. above, p. 358 n. 2.

[4] *Mark* viii. 33 ; *Matt.* xvi. 23.　　　　[5] *Matt.* xvi. 22.

[6] *Luke* ix. 32 : "βεβαρημένοι ὕπνῳ" might even be translated 'weighted down with slumber' instead of 'heavy with sleep' (A.V.)

[7] *Mark* ix. 4 : "συνλαλοῦντες τῷ Ἰησοῦ"; cf. *Matt.* xvii. 3.

[8] *Mark* ix. 2 ; *Matt.* xvii. 1 ; *Luke* ix. 28, has 'nine' through a misreading of the Greek numeral sign F for an H. 'Six' is an obvious allusion to the six days in *Exod.* xxiv. 15 *sq.*, passed by Moses on the mountain before the revelation of God was vouchsafed to him.

[9] *Exod.* xxiv. 1, 2, 12.

[10] *2 Peter* i. 18 : "ὄντες ἐν τῷ ὄρει τῷ ἁγίῳ." Ḥermon means 'the sanctuary,' or 'great sanctuary.' Even now the ruins of a sanctuary and a sacred cave are visible on the flat top.

Elijah,[1] in solitary prayer, for enlightenment on the ἔξοδον αὐτοῦ [2] ἣν ἔμελλε πληροῦν, as Moses had once received it on Mt. Horeb,[3] imploring him for the gift of the prophetic spirit promised through Isaiah [4] to the servant of God who would obediently take up his burden. The voice they hear in the midst of the shining morning mist [5] sounds to them like an echo of the voice of God, a *Bath Qōl*.[6] Still half in a dream,[7] they hear the final words of Moses' consolation : [8]

‘ The Lord thy God will raise up unto thee a prophet from the midst of thee, of thy brethren, like unto me ; unto him ye shall hearken,’

and believe they see Moses and Elijah standing beside Jesus in supernatural splendour. When they finally wake up completely they see none but Jesus, surrounded by the rays of the morning sun, and they hear his familiar voice bidding them not to be afraid. Before waking up, and still in a dream, without realizing the full import of his words,[9] Peter had asked him to remain there : [10]

‘ Master, it is good for us to be here, and let us make tents.’

---

[1] Cf. *Mark* xv. 34 ; *Matt.* xxvii. 46, where Jesus' cry, ‘ Eli, Eli ’ (‘ My God, my God ’) is mistaken for an appeal to Elijah.

[2] See above, pp. 358 n. 2, 360 n. 5.

[3] *Exod.* xxxi. 4.   [4] xlii. 1.

[5] On the "νεφέλη φωτεινή, ἣ ἐπεσκίασεν αὐτῳ," cf. 2 *Macc.* ii. 8 : "ὀφθήσεται ἡ δόξα τοῦ κυρίου ὡς ἐπὶ Μωϋσῇ ἐδηλοῦτο."

[6] The ‘ daughter of the voice ’ is explained as an echo of a voice from heaven by the tosaphist to Sanhedr. 11a (Strack-Billerbeck, i. 125) ; cf. 127a on *Matt.* iii. 17 : ‘ if a man deals a blow with all his force and a second tone is heard at a distance, produced by the blow, such a voice was heard, hence it was called the " daughter of the voice." ’ Cf. also *Exod. r.* 29 (89a) ; Midr. to Canticles, i. 3 (85a), etc.

[7] A *Bath Qōl* is heard in a dream by R. Joḥanan b. Zakkai (*ca.* A.D. 70), *Ḥagiga* 146 (in the parallel *j. Ḥag.*, ii. 77a, 57, the dream is omitted, just as in *Mark* and *Matt.* the words "βεβαρημένοι ὕπνῳ· διαγρηγορήσαντες δέ" of *Luke* are missing). Voices overheard or caught by chance were considered as *bath-Qōl*, corresponding to the Greek practice of kledonomancy, especially if they chanced to be quotations from the O.T. ; cf. Strack-Billerbeck, i. 134 K, especially *j. Shabb.*, vi. 8, c. 56. If then, as pointed out above, the disciples hear Biblical quotations in the words of the praying Jesus, on waking up, they have heard, according to Jewish belief, a *bath-Qōl*, an echo of the voice of God. Cf. also *Jebh.*, xvi. 6 (Strack-Billerbeck, i. p. 133, No. 29), where the voice of a man on a mountain-top is considered a *bath-Qōl*, the more readily because the man responsible for it was never found.

[8] *Deut.* xviii. 15.

[9] *Mark* ix. 6 : ‘ For he wist not what to say,’ i.e. what he answered to Jesus' command, containing, evidently, an exhortation to the ἔξοδος ὃν ἔμελλε πληροῦν, since Peter replies with his request to remain there and to pitch a camp. *Luke* ix. 33 has ‘ not knowing what he said,’ i.e. he did not realize that he opposed with his request the decision of God himself.

[10] *Luke* ix. 33 : ‘ it is good for us to be here : and let us make tabernacles *three : one for thee, one for Moses, and one for Elijah.*’ The italicized words are probably an addition dating from the time when the episode had been localized on Mt. Tabor. There were the three *tabernacula salvatoris* still seen by Antoninus of Piacenza and Arculph (*Encycl. Bibl.*, 4884, § 5), and later converted into a church. It is not very credible that Peter, who was, after all, an orthodox Jew, should, even in a dream, have proposed a measure so reminiscent of the old, pagan mountain cults so intensely hated and so frequently denounced by the prophets.

This proposal clearly betrays Peter's opinion on the fateful 'exodus to be realized in Jerusalem.' He regards the march to the capital as both superfluous and fatal. It was good to be here on Hermon ; here one might erect tents and assemble believers, as Barak had once mustered the people on Mt. Tabor for a war of independence,[1] and through the Wadi 'Ajam pass over by the quickest route to the Syrian desert or to the hollows of Trachonitis, the old robber's nest of Zenodoros.

Nowhere was it written how large must be the number of the elect. The more followers gathered round Jesus, the harder was the task of leading such a crowd and providing for them, and the greater the probability of an armed collision with the Romans, at all hazards to be avoided, since on the issue of such a conflict Jesus himself can have had few illusions.

On the other hand, he doubtless believed that he must announce the impending trials of the last days to the whole people, to give an opportunity to all of following God's call and being saved. Moreover, he was clearly forced on to the fatal road by the idea that he must set on foot a movement of hundreds of thousands, the picture of the exodus from Egypt with the fantastic figures given in the Pentateuch. The messianic rising he was to initiate could not be regarded as realized if he left the country with a band of some hundred elect. If he wished, however, to put at least two-fifths of the population [2] in motion, the method of sending out messengers had proved altogether unsatisfactory. He must try the effect upon the masses of his own overpowering eloquence and the spell of his own words in a place where and at a time when he was sure to reach the greatest multitudes of his people. That could only be in Jerusalem at the time of the great pilgrimage at the feast of the Passover.

The desired result could only be obtained, of course, if he openly proclaimed himself to be the Messiah. This he knew full well ; but he knew, no less, that in so doing he would inevitably draw upon himself the hatred of all opponents, both the Jewish hierarchy and the Roman military authorities. That he would be able to withstand their combined hostility he can never have ventured to hope. Indeed, it is doubtless true, as has long been recognized, that he sought martyrdom and went to Jerusalem to die there.[3]

This intention was wholly unexpected by the disciples and quite unintelligible to them : [4] quite naturally so, since the idea of a suffering Messiah and the messianic interpretation of the

---

[1] *Exod.* iv. 6, 12, 14.   [2] See above, p. 366 n. 3.
[3] A great number of early liturgical texts speak of the Saviour's 'voluntary death ' or ' voluntary passion.'
[4] *Mark* ix. 32 ; *Luke* ix. 45.

'servant' songs in *Isaiah* can hardly at that time have been very popular, and were in fact probably confined to those Baptist and Zealot circles which sought to console themselves by such meditations for the fall of men like Ḥizqiah and Judas of Galilee, or, at the most, to those Pharisee schools who explain in various passages of the so-called *Fourth Book of Maccabees*[1] the sufferings of the martyrs under Antiochus Epiphanes as a 'ransom,'[2] an expiatory offering for the sins of the people. Whether Jesus derived from them the application of the 'servant' songs to Israel's future redeemer, or whether the idea had originated with himself, it is certain that with growing conviction he recognized in that righteous sufferer of old the tragic prototype of his own fate.

These remarkable songs of the Lord's servant doubtless did not originally refer to a personification of the suffering people of Israel, but to an individual regarded as historical who, as Sellin has seen, had some essential features 'in common with Israel's first redeemer, Moses.' God's servant[3] was, like Moses, called, for the sake of the covenant between God and Israel, to liberate prisoners from the house of bondage; but, unlike Moses, he was destined to be a martyr to this mission and must give his life as an offering and a ransom to bear the iniquities of many. Among the numerous identifications proposed, the most likely is probably that which sees in him the unhappy Zerubabel, the descendant of David, who led the exiles back to Jerusalem, rebuilt the temple, but was prevailed upon by the prophets of his time to assume the title of King of Israel and to revolt against Cambyses.[4] It can hardly be doubted that he came to grief at the hands of the Persians and was crucified as a rebel by order of Darius I.[5] His martyrdom was interpreted as a redeeming sacrifice to the idea of redemption (ge'ulah, λύτρωσις).[6]

If, then, Jesus felt himself called to liberate his people from

---

[1] i. 11, vi. 29, xvii. 26.   [2] ἀντίψυχον.

[3] Moses is thus called in *Num.* xii. 7 *sqq.*; *Deut.* xxxiv. 5; *Josh.* i. 2, 7; I *Kings* viii. 53, 56; *Mal.* iii. 22; *Ps.* cv. 1.

[4] See vol. ii. pp. 677 ff. of the German edition of this book, on *Ps.* ii.

[5] This was first seen by Sellin, *Serubbabel* (1898); his later theories are no improvement on his first hypothesis. Cf. also H. Winckler, *Die Keilschr. u. d. Alte Testament*, p. 291 *sqq.*

[6] If a man falls into debt and is obliged to sell land or his next-of-kin, the *go'el* is expected to redeem the land or the person. In both cases a price or ransom (λύτρον) has to be paid. If Israel was to be redeemed of slavery, it was natural to suppose such a ransom necessary also in this case. Since such slavery was regarded as a punishment for indebtedness to God, the ransom assumed the character of a sin-offering. The Mosaic narrative of the first redemption of Israel from slavery in Egypt contains no such train of ideas, foreign or repugnant to the mind of the author (*Exod.* xxxii. 32 *sq.*). When, later on, the Pharisees elaborated their theory of the rebirth of the righteous (*Ant.*, xviii. § 14; *B.J.*, iii. § 374; *C. Apionem*, ii. § 218), the mysterious verset of *Isaiah* liii. 10 seems to have been interpreted as referring to the rebirth of Zerubabel, the suffering 'ben David,' as the future victorious Messiah.

the house of bondage and to redeem Israel's inheritance, the Land of Promise, the fate of the unhappy Zerubabel, his reputed ancestor, must have impressed itself upon his consciousness, an omen as it were of his own fate, so that he came to the final conviction that he must pass through the final woes, the messianic war, through suffering and death.

Gloomy forebodings of this inevitable fate must slowly have clouded his vision of the future. If at first he had regarded himself as a second Moses who must lead the people into the wilderness but die before being permitted to conduct his flock into the Land of Promise, his undertaking must have gradually appeared to him more and more desperate. The miracle of God had not yet appeared, the heavens remained silent to his incessant and passionate prayer. With painful clearness there must have dawned upon him the fateful conviction that he was not the new Moses called to victory, but that he must drink instead the cup of suffering of Zerubabel, slain by the enemy, a sin-offering and ransom for his people. ' They that take the sword shall perish with the sword.' [1]

Gradually, also, and with growing clearness, he came to regard the coming of the ' Son of Man ' [2] as his own resurrection from the dead. It was indeed conceivable and possible to expect such a metamorphosis of Jesus into the messianic ' Son of Man ' in his own lifetime as the disciples had imagined had come to pass on the top of the mountain, when his whole figure had been transformed in their eyes, when his robe of skins had been changed into a robe of light as white as snow, his face resplendent with the divine glory ' like unto the sun '—indeed, like the face of Moses on Mt. Sinai after his meeting with Jahveh. For in the curious and too much neglected story of Saul, anointed king by Samuel, the seer promises the monarch : ' The Spirit of the Lord will come upon thee, and thou shalt prophesy with them, and shalt be turned into another man.' [3] The Messiah, like the newly anointed king, was thus expected, on the occasion of his first public appearance, to receive from above the Spirit of God and to be ' transformed into another man.'

Now, this is precisely the centre-piece and basis of the enigmatic story of the metamorphosis of Jesus. There first appear Moses and Elijah—Moses who had anointed the first high priest, and Elijah who had anointed the king Jehu of Israel as well as the prophet Elisha, the very Elijah who, according to Jewish belief,

---

[1] *Matt.* xxvi. 52. He expected to die by the sword like a captive king (1 *Sam.* xv. 33) ; hence the allusions at the last supper to the dismemberment of his body and the outpouring of his blood, as well as the mention of his impending ' baptism of blood ' in the question to the Zebedaids (*Matt.* x. 38 ff. and parallels). [3] Cf. 1 *Sam.* x. 6.
[2] On this figure, cf. below, p. 560 n. 3.

was to come back to reveal the Messiah. Then a cloud over-shadows the three figures, and a voice from heaven is heard to say, ' This is my beloved son,' etc., an episode which was long ago recognized as a close parallel to the story of Jesus' baptism in the Jordan. Through this coming down of the Spirit and the Divine recognition as son of God, Jesus, like King Saul of old, is ' trans-formed into another man.'

The strong emphasis laid in this narrative upon the 'cloud' which overshadows Jesus becomes intelligible if the messianic significance of this feature is recalled. Clearly, we have here that coming of the ' Son of man ' ' with the clouds of heaven ' predicted by Daniel and applied by Jesus to himself, the realization of which the disciples believed that they had witnessed in their vision of the transfiguration. This fleeting dream-vision of Peter and his two companions is, of course, a very modest fulfilment of those pre-dictions which had raised expectations of an overwhelming blaze of light illuminating in one moment, like lightning, everything under heaven from horizon to horizon, at the coming of the Son of man. However, it is possible that Jesus himself [1] conceived of that coming, not as a blinding cosmic display of light, but merely as a spiritual illumination in the hearts of all mankind. Otherwise it is difficult to explain that anxious question, ' Howbeit when the Son of man cometh, shall he find faith on earth ? ' [2]—a question which has no meaning if he expected a coming of the world-king amid legions of angels and a blaze of glory. If it pleased God—and he looked for this mercy to the last—his own glorification and the enlightenment of the elect might be brought about by an ' outpour-ing of the Spirit,' without the necessity of a previous death of him-self and of some chosen believers.[3] But the longer the yearned-for miracle was delayed, the more it became certain that the final ' trial ' ($\pi\epsilon\iota\rho\alpha\sigma\mu\delta\varsigma$) was unavoidable, that the elect heirs of the kingdom must first die and then rise on the third day,[4] and that for himself in particular the promised 'return of the Son of man ' was synonymous with his own resurrection from a martyr's death.

The Foundation-Stone and the Pillars of the New Com-munity. The Keys of the Kingdom and Peter the Viceroy

If Jesus was so perfectly certain of his own death, the question naturally arises, Who was to conduct the planned exodus into the

---

[1] Like Paul, 2 Cor. iv. 6.   [2] Luke xviii. 8.

[3] Mark ix. 1 (and parallels).

[4] Hos. ii. 6 : the resurrection on the third day is the general destiny of the elect, not merely of the Messiah.

desert until such time as he, resuscitated by God's mercy, would again appear at the head of his disciples and himself lead them back into the Land of Promise, by then freed from the enemy ? The answer is supplied by the incident of Caesarea Philippi, which is so closely associated with the predictions of suffering and death— the appointment of a temporary *vicarius* of Jesus in the much-debated speech to Simon *Barjona*. The genuineness of these words has been quite unjustly questioned by critics who had not even understood their literal meaning or known the wealth of Scripture lore underlying them. To the disciple who had been the first to do homage to Jesus as God's Anointed, the future King of Israel replies : [1]

> ' Blessed art thou, Simon *Barjona*, for flesh and blood hath not revealed it unto thee, but the Father which is in heaven. And I also say unto thee that thou art the Rock, and upon this rock I will build [2] the community of my choice,[3] and the gates of the underworld shall not prevail against it. I will give unto thee the keys of the kingdom of heaven, and whatsoever thou shalt bind on earth shall be bound in heaven,[4] and whatsoever thou shalt loose on earth shall be loosed in heaven.' [5]

The whole speech is intelligible only if one is in a position to follow all the wealth of Scriptural allusions which it contains.

The τέκτων, the Rekhabite carpenter and builder, speaks in parables drawn from his craft. The *qehillah* is in reality no edifice built with hands, but designates the new 'house of Israel' (*beth Jisra'el*), as the Arabs call the tribe *ahl*, literally 'tent.' With reference to this figurative expression *beth Jisra'el*, the rabbis [6] were accustomed to speak of persons whom we might call the 'pillars of society' as 'tent-poles' (*jathedoth 'ohalim*). The three great patriarchs, Abraham, Isaac, and Jacob, were called 'tent-poles' of the world,[7] the world as a whole being regarded as a cosmic tent.[7] If the *beth Jisra'el* is thought of as a house of stone, its leading representatives may be fitly described as ' corner-stones of the people ' (*pinnoth ha'am*). Thus we read in *Judges* xx. 2 :

> ' And the corner-stones of all the people, even of all the tribes of Israel, presented themselves in the *assembly* (ἐν ἐκκλησίᾳ) of the people of God.'

---

[1] *Matt.* xvi. 17 *sqq.*
[2] Cf. *Ruth* iv. 11 : ' build the house of Israel.'
[3] μου τὴν ἐκκλησίαν, my *qahal* or *qehillah*, the assembly called by me. It is the *qehillath ben David*, the assembly called by the new *ben David*, the new Solomon, the ' prince of peace,' after the example of the assembly called by Solomon, 1 *Kings* viii. 1.
[4] I.e. by God. The word is not to be understood in a local sense.
[5] *Kelaim*, 14b ; Levy, *Nhb. Wb.*, s.v. *jathed*.
[6] Talm. J. *Ta'an.* iv. 67d, etc.
[7] Cf. my *Weltenmantel und Himmelszelt*, p. 595.

Similarly, in 1 *Sam*. xiv. 38 :

> 'And Saul said, Draw nigh hither, all ye corner-stones of the people.'

In *Zech*. x. 4 we have the two figures in conjunction :

> 'The Lord hath visited his flock the *house* of Judah. . . . From him shall come forth the corner-stone (*pinnah*), from him the tent-pole (*or* " pillar," *jathed*).'

The patriarchs who rank as 'tent-poles of the world' are also called its 'foundation-stone.'[1] In particular, the *Midrash Yelamdenu*[2] affords a striking parallel to the passage in *Matthew*, including the use of the word *petra* :

> 'From the top of the rocks I see him' (*Numb*. xxiii. 9). 'I see those who have come forth from the creation of the world. (It is) like a king who would erect a building. He had the ground dug ever deeper and sought to lay the foundation, but found only bogs, and so in many (other) places. Then he would have them dig in but one more place, and he found in the depth a rock (*petra*). Then said he, Here will I build ; and he laid the foundation and built. Even so God sought to create the world, and he sat and thought on the generation of 'Enosh and the generation of the flood. He said, How can I create the world, seeing that these ungodly people will arise and provoke me ? But when God looked upon Abraham that was to be, he said : See, I here found a rock (*petra*) on which I can build and establish the world. Therefore he called Abraham a rock (*ṣur*), as it is written, "Look unto the rock whence ye were hewn"' (*Isaiah* li. 1).

By the ' king who would erect a building ' is meant David, who wished to erect the temple on Zion, and in sinking the foundations struck upon the ' stone of foundation ' or ' of drinking ' (*'eben shethijah*), which according to the ancient pre-Israelite legend[3] closed the opening to the great abyss (*tehom*), the flood-gates of the underworld, from which the great flood of old broke out, and threatened to break out again when David moved this stone.[4]

As David founded the visible temple of God on the foundation-stone of the world, the holy rock on Mt. Zion, so will the Messiah ben David build a new house of Israel, ' the assembly in the wilderness,'[5] the community of those called by him, on a 'foundation-stone ' against which the gates of the abyss shall not prevail. As the Midrash conceives the foundation-stone on which God has built the true temple, his universe,[6] to be not a dead rock but a ' living stone,' namely the patriarch Abraham, for whose merits the

---

[1] *Exodus rabba*, 16 (76c).   [2] *Jalquṭ*, i. 766.
[3] M. Gaster, *Folklore*, ii. 204.   [4] *Sanhedrin*, x. 29a, and elsewhere.
[5] *Acts* vii. 38.
[6] Cf. τὸ ἅγιον κοσμικόν, *Hebr*. ix. 1, and *B.J.*, v. 458, where the Zealots retort to the Romans that ' the world was a better temple for God than this one.'

world was preserved from destruction and indeed erected, so the just one 'that believeth' in the Lord becomes the true 'foundation-stone' of the house of Israel.[1] As Abraham, who for the sake of his faith fled from his home and country, became the rock on which the house of Israel and the whole creation were built, so now is Simon *Barjona* to become the foundation-stone of the new house of Israel, the new *ecclesia*, the spiritual house of 'living stones'[2] to be erected in the wilderness, because he believed with the firmness of a rock in Jesus as the Messiah. If in the early messianist community Simon Cephas, James, and John rank as the 'pillars of the *qehillah*,'[3] this title was also doubtless derived from a saying of Jesus.[4]

The usual exegesis fails to note that the two metaphors of the living foundation-stone and the living pillars are to be connected with the prophecies of suffering. Pillars in human form, such as Jesus might have seen in the Hellenistic architecture of Herod's palace at Tiberias,[5] were called by the ancients 'Telamons,' i.e. τλήμονες[6] = 'patient sufferers,' and there was a widespread custom of making a living mortal the foundation-stone of a new building, a rite known both to Greeks and Semites.[7] To be elected as foundation-stone is therefore tantamount to being destined as a foundation sacrifice. The weight of the whole edifice rests with all its crushing load upon the foundation-stone, whilst the pillars have at least to support the architrave. These characteristic builders' metaphors thus clearly express the special idea of the ruler as a *servant* of the community.[8]

Again, it is most significant that the conception of the person thus elected having the power over the keys is closely connected with the symbolism of the 'tent-pole' (*jathed*). In *Isaiah* xxii. 20 *sqq.* we read :

'In that day I will call *my servant* . . . and he shall be a father . . . to the house of Judah. And *the key of the house of David* will I lay upon his shoulder ; and he shall open and none shall shut, and he shall shut and none shall open. And I will fasten him as a tent-pole (*jathed*) in a sure place ; and he shall be for a throne of glory[9] to his father's house.'

It is to this obvious Old Testament passage and to no other that allusion is made in the words of Jesus about the keys, which fanciful

---

[1] *Isaiah* xxviii. 16.
[2] I *Peter* ii. 5. Hermas, Vision iii. 5.
[3] *Gal.* ii. 9.
[4] Cf. *Apoc.*, iii. 12.
[5] According to Jos., *Vita*, § 65, the palace of Herod was adorned with representatives of living beings. According to the *Josippon*, these figures represented vanquished nations, a well-known symbolism of Hellenistic architecture.
[6] Vitruvius, *De archit.*, vi. 10. 6.
[7] I *Kings* xvi. 34 ; Tylor, *Primitive Culture*, i. 104 *sqq.*
[8] Cf. above, p. 349 n. 5.
[9] Near the tent-pole, that is, where the tent is highest, there stands the high seat of the head of the family.

commentators [1] have sought to explain by Persian, Babylonian, and Roman ideas on the gatekeeper of hell and heaven.

As for the phrase 'binding and loosing,' the Slavonic Josephus now conclusively proves that the expression indicates the absolute authority of a king or ruler. We read in the *Halōsis* [2] of high priest Hyrcanus as ' having merely the name of ruler, without the power to decide, to bind or to loose, to do good or harm.'

It is thus not doctrinal authority [3] but royal sovereignty that Jesus would confer upon Simon Cephas, a fact completely in accordance with the messianic interpretation of the ' elect foundation-stone ' given in the Targum on *Isaiah* xxviii. 16 :

' Behold, I set in Zion a king, a strong king, mighty and terrible : I will strengthen him and I will confirm him, saith the prophet. But the just who believe these things, when tribulation cometh shall not be moved.'

Naturally, it is not accidental that Jesus, immediately after the appointment of Peter as keeper of the keys and temporary vice-gerent, announces to his disciples his own sufferings and death ; for it is only his premonition of his own impending fate which justifies his consigning the keys to one of his disciples. Peter is not his successor in authority but a deputy-Messiah, a viceroy of God's kingdom on earth during the expected short period of his own absence.

'As a man, travelling to another country, having left his house and given authority to his servants, to each one his work, commanded also the porter to watch ' [4] until ' the master of the house cometh.'

[1] W. Köhler, *Arch. f. Rel. Wiss.*, viii. 214 *sqq.*

[2] i. 242 ; Berendts-Grass, i. p. 99. Cf. *B.J.*, i. § 111.

[3] Prof. von Dobschütz does not hesitate to say (*Z.N.T.W.*, 1928, p. 343 ; *ibid.*, 1929, p. 115 n. 3) that, according to *Matt.* xvi. 17 ff., Peter is appointed by Jesus as ' chief-rabbi ' (*Oberrabbiner*) of the Christian church! As a matter of fact, nothing in any way like a chief-rabbi was known to ancient Judaism until the period of the exilarchs.

[4] *Mark* xiii. 34, 36.

XIV

THE ACCOUNT OF THE WONDER-WORKER ON THE MOUNT OF OLIVES AND HIS CRUCIFIXION, AS GIVEN IN THE 'HALŌSIS' OF JOSEPHUS

THUS far, we have followed the Christian Gospels for our reconstruction of the 'Galilaean' period in the life of Jesus. Neither in the *Antiquities* nor in the *Halōsis* has Josephus a word to say about anything which Jesus did or said in Galilee or elsewhere prior to his coming to Jerusalem immediately before his arrest and crucifixion. This gap, though obviously unwelcome to the modern reader and critic, removes the last doubt as to Josephus' narrative being absolutely independent of the Christian 'missionary' literature. Since the *Antiquities*, as we have seen, were unquestionably tampered with, we cannot be perfectly sure on the point whether after all Josephus might not have thrown out a few hints on Jesus' earlier career ;[1] but in the *Halōsis* the story opens with the appearance of Jesus and his followers on the Mount of Olives before the walls of the capital. This point of view, however natural for a writer born and bred in Jerusalem, is thus completely different from that of the Galilaean authors of the Gospels. If by some mishap the Gospels had been lost, no reader could have formed from Josephus alone the slightest opinion of the character of the hero and his strange previous life. It would be impossible to tell him apart from the long line of rebel leaders upon whom Josephus lays the whole responsibility for the downfall of the Jewish people.

The essential condition for a correct appreciation of his statements by the reader is that he must first set aside entirely such knowledge as he has gained from the Gospels, and secondly adhere strictly to the principle laid down by Théodore Reinach more than thirty years ago for the criticism of the *Testimonium Flavianum* :[2] namely, that the text must be stripped of everything incompatible with the Jewish historian's antipathy to Christianity, as attested by Origen,[3] with his partisanship for the Pharisees, and with his hostility to all 'innovators' (νεωτερίζοντες) so visible throughout his writings. Since from a person like Josephus we cannot look for a fair estimate of the motives of opponents of his own party, the aristocrats (οἱ πρωτεύοντες), the 'better class,' and the Phari-

[1] See above, p. 54 ll. 10 ff.   [2] See above, p. 46 n. 1.   [3] See above, p. 38 n. 2.

sees with their contempt for the crowd, we can lay down a very simple principle of criticism : everything of anti-Christian character, every contemptuous or disparaging allusion to Jesus and his followers, may be regarded offhand as the authentic work of Josephus ; every statement exonerating Jesus and favourable to him and his disciples is to be set aside as an interpolation or correction introduced by a Christian reader or copyist. This, of course, implies nothing for the credibility or lack of such either of individual statements or of the whole picture thus obtained of the first appearance of Jesus and the subsequent events. For, being composed exclusively of hostile and malicious touches, the portrait may be presumed to be tendentiously distorted and hence misleading. But for that very reason it may be extremely instructive and valuable for the modern historian as a set-off to the accounts from the Christian side—always provided, of course, that the division of the two distinct strata running through the traditional text be clear-cut, and that even after the removal of the presumed interpolations it yields a sensible interpretation of the facts.

The procedure indicated must be rigorously followed. The possibility of understanding Josephus as a sort of Nicodemus, and his account of Christian origins as the outcome of a half-hearted inclination toward the messianist movement, has been seriously discussed above, where we have seen that the attempted explanations have convinced no one and have only led to a complete rejection of valuable evidence. This disposes of the wavering and uncertain methods of exegesis still found in Berendts' first work, in Frey, and partly in Goethals.[1] No further advance is possible on that road. The solution of our problem lies solely in a sound separation of the sources—a method, by the way, which had to be applied to all Jewish writings transmitted solely by Christian scribes, works such as the *Book of Enoch*, the *Testaments of the XII Patriarchs*, the *Book of Jubilees*, the *Sibylline Oracles*, and the *Odes of Solomon*, before pronouncing an opinion on their age and origin. Had their authors also been regarded as ' half-Christians,' the history of the religion and the literature of the last pre-Christian centuries would present a somewhat curious appearance.

Indeed, I fail to see why the work of Josephus should not be treated on the same simple and straightforward principle. In his case, however, still another task arises—to wit, the filling of gaps caused by the censor with the help of quotations made at a date when those gaps did not yet exist. As has been shown above,[2] certain old and hitherto unverifiable citations from Josephus could now be identified in the Slavonic text of the *Halōsis* or attributed to the lost second edition of the *Polemos* in twenty-four books. This again is no unheard-of novelty, for the method has always

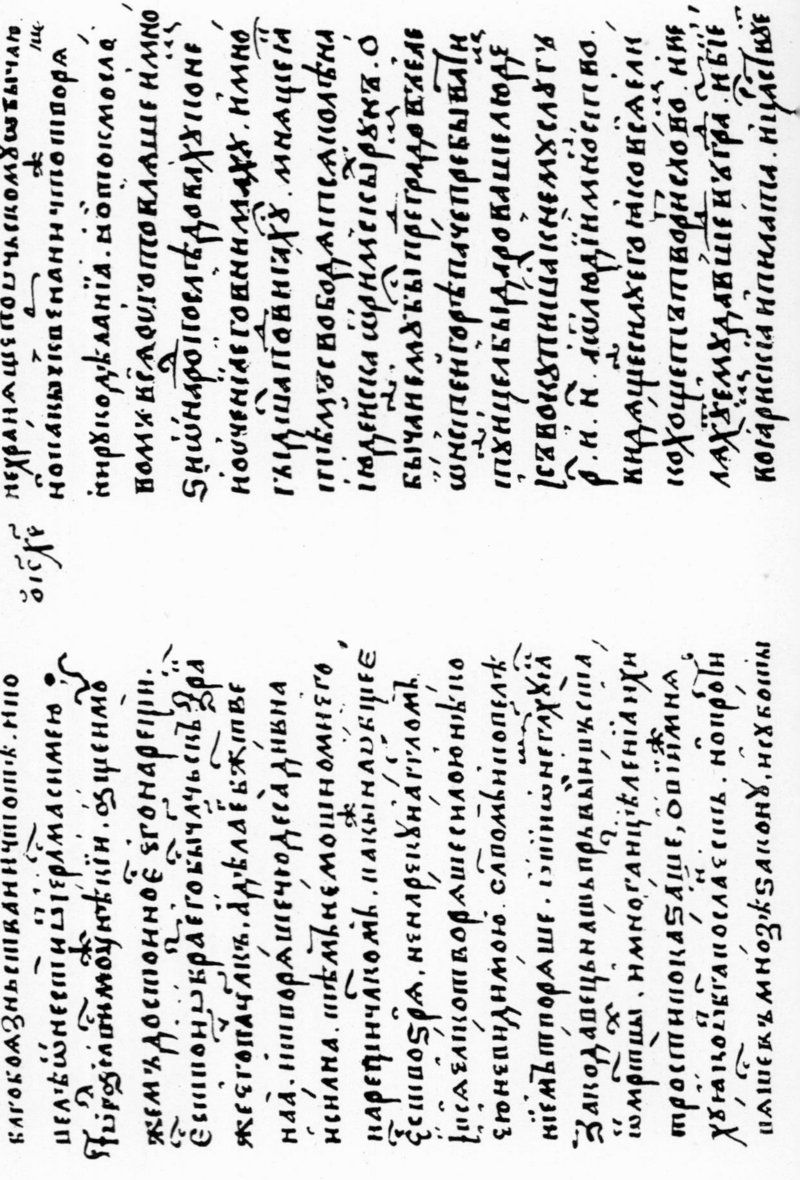

PLATE XXIV

THE SLAVONIC JOSEPHUS ON THE APPEARANCE OF 'THE WONDER-WORKER' ON MOUNT OLIVET, AND HIS DEATH

F° 64 R°—65 V° OF COD KYRILLO-BJELOS. 63/1302, LENINGRAD PUBLIC LIBRARY

(SEE P. 383-4 F.)

been used for the completion of fragmentary papyri. Had the editors of Josephus done their duty, we should find in each edition a short appendix with fragments, i.e. quotations not to be found in the standard text. The well-known collections of *Fragmenta Historicorum Graecorum* of Müller and of Jacobi contain nothing but such fragments preserved only through quotations in later writers. If, then, Andrew of Crete and other Byzantines will be seen to be employed below for the restoration of statements about Jesus in the *Halōsis*, I claim that my method in no way differs from the use of Eusebius, Zonaras, and the excerpts of Constantine Porphyrogenitus for the textual criticism of *Antiquities*, xviii. 3. 3.[1] Lastly, as every scholar knows, writings are often copied or used *without* any mention of the source, and consequently not only direct quotations but borrowings where no source is named can also be used for reconstructing the text, provided that a use of the original document can be inferred with some show of reason.[2] In this way the most serious gap of the *Halōsis* can be filled by an isolated anonymous fragment in John Malalas.[3] Only those unfamiliar with these methods of source analysis—used, for example, for the recovery of long trains of thought of Posidonius or Theophrastus from the writings of Cicero—can regard this procedure as bold and unwarranted.

I begin by presenting an English version of the Slavonic text,[4] as found in the various MSS., with a selection of the essential variant readings, the Greek retroversions of crucial or characteristically Josephan expressions, and the most necessary explanatory notes:

[5] 'At that time [6] there appeared [7] a certain [8] man,[9] if it is meet to call him a man.[10] His [11] nature [12] and form was [13] human,[12] but the

---

[1] See above, p. 59.   [2] On this, cf. below, pp. 396 ff.   [3] Below, pp. 461 ff.

[4] The original, with all essential variants, is printed in the German edition of this book, vol. ii. p. 296. Cf. our Pls. XXIII.-V.

[5] Between ii., §§ 174 and 175, of the Greek *War*. Kas. 444 (in top margin) has : 'Of the Lord, our Redeemer Jesus Christ, the Son of God, and of the divine form of his appearance and of his miracles.' Syn. 991 (bottom margin) : ' Soul-saving narrative of our Lord Jesus Christ, how he did many miracles,' to which is appended in cursive script, ' This more from other books and (*read* than) the Gospel and Apostolos.'

[6] ' also,' Acad.   [7] =τότε δὲ ἐφάνη (togda javi sja).

[8] ἀνήρ τις, muž nékij ; cf. above, p. 46, last *a linea*.

[9] Exactly parallel to *B.J.*, iii. 229 : "ἔνθα καὶ ἀνήρ τις ἐξεφάνη . . . λόγου καὶ μνήμης ἄξιος. Σαμαίου μὲν παῖς ἦν, Ἐλεάζαρος δ' ἐκαλεῖτο . . ."

[10] Cf. above, p. 52, the corresponding phrase of the Greek *Testimonium*.

[11] ' And his,' Acad.

[12] Cf. *Ant.*, xvi. 220 : " ἦν μὲν γὰρ ὁ τῆς Ἀραβίας βασιλεὺς Ὀβάδας ἀπράγμων . . . τὴν φύσιν" ; c. *Apion.*, i. 26 : " θείας φύσεως μετεσχηκέναι."

[13] From the singular form of the verb, Dr. Thackeray (*Josephus*, iii. 648, n. *e*) would conclude that the words ' and form ' are a later addition. Leaving aside all questions of Slavonic syntax, one might with the same show of reason allege that the words ' nature and' were interpolated for apologetic (i.e. anti-docetic) reasons. Anyhow, " φύσις καὶ μορφὴ αὐτοῦ ἀνθρωπίνη ἦν " is perfectly good Greek.

appearance of him [1] more than (that) of a human (being) : [2] yet his works (were) divine, He wrought [3] miracles wonderful and strong.[4] Wherefore it is impossible for me to call him a human (being). But, on the other hand, if I look at (his) ordinary [5] nature,[6] I will not call him an angel.

'And all, whatsoever he wrought through an invisible power he wrought by a word and command.[7] Some said of him, "Our [8] first lawgiver is risen from the dead and hath vouchsafed many cures and artifices." [9] But the others thought that he was sent from God. But in many things he opposed the law and kept not the Sabbath according to the custom of (our) forefathers. Yet, again,[10] he [11] did nothing shameful nor any daring acts,[12] but merely by (his) word did he prepare everything. And many of the multitude followed after him and hearkened to his teaching. And many souls were roused,[13] thinking that thereby the Jewish tribes could free themselves from Roman hands. But it was his custom rather to abide without the city on the Mount of Olives. There also he granted cures to the people. And there gathered to him of helpers [14] 150, but of the mob [15] a multitude. But when they saw his power, that he accomplished by a word whatsoever he would, and when they had made known to him their will, that he should enter the city and cut down the Roman troops [16] and Pilate and rule over us,[17] he did not disdain us.[18] And when thereafter news of it was brought to the Jewish leaders, they assembled together with the high priest and said, " We are powerless and (too) weak [19] to resist the Romans. Since, however, ' the bow is bent,' [20] we will go and communicate to Pilate what we have heard, and we shall be free from trouble, in order that he may not hear (it) from others and [21] we be robbed of (our) goods and ourselves slaughtered and (our) children dispersed.[22] " [23] And they went and

---

[1] ' his appearance,' Kas.　　　　　　[2] ὑπὲρ ἄνθρωπον, see below, p. 389 n. 6.
[3] ' And he wrought,' Kas.　　　　　　[4] ' luminous,' Kas.
[5] or ' common,' ' commonplace.'　　Rum. version : ' human nature.'
[6] " εἰς τὴν κοινὴν φύσιν ἀπιδών"; cf. B.J., iii. § 369 : " τῆς κοινῆς ἁπάντων ζῴων φύσεως."
[7] λόγῳ καὶ προστάγματι. The words ' through an invisible power' are not found in the Rum.
[8] Om. ' our,' Acad.　　　　　　　　[9] Cf. τεχνάζων, Ant., xviii. 85.
[10] ' also,' Acad., Syn.　　　　　　　[11] ' this man,' Syn. 991.
[12] ἐπιχειρήματα, Russ. rukodelania.　[13] ἤρθησαν.
[14] ὑπηρέται.　　　　　　　　　　　　[15] ὄχλου.
[16] ' everything Roman,' Acad.　　　[17] ' them,' Acad.
[18] οὐ κατεφρόνησεν ἡμᾶς, Syn. 182. ' But he did not heed it,' Acad., Syn. 770, 991 ; Kyrillo-Bjelos. 1303 ; Kas. ; see below, p. 458 n. 3.
[19] Dr. Thackeray, loc. cit., iii. p. 649, note c, has acutely observed that this phrase is the Josephan ἀσθηνής cum infinitivo = ' too weak to do something ' (Ant., x. § 215 ; xiv. § 317).
[20] This allusion to Ps. xi. 2 is omitted as unintelligible to the non-Jewish reader in the Rumanian version.　　　　　　　　　　　[21] Om. ' and,' Acad.
[22] Justin Martyr, Apolog., i. 52, p. 87 D, E, quoting an apocryphal book of Zacharia, " τὰ ἐσκορπισμένα τέκνα" (without adding ' of Israel '). Against this, cf. John xi. 52 : " τὰ τέκνα τοῦ θεοῦ τὰ διεσκορπισμένα." Rum., ' and he sells our children as slaves.'
[23] In the lower margin of Syn. 991 : ' Of the bringing of Jesus Christ before Pilate ' ; on the verso, a little lower, there is written in cursive script in the left margin : ' But this is not written in the Gospel.'

reported (it) to Pilate. And he sent and had many of the multitude slain. And he had that wonder-worker brought up, and after he had held an enquiry concerning him, he pronounced (this) judgment: He is [1] [*a benefactor, but* [2] *not*] a malefactor [*nor*] [3] a rebel [*nor*] covetous of king(ship). [4] [*And he let him go, for he had healed his dying wife. And after he had gone to his wonted place, he did his wonted works.* [5] *And when more people again gathered round him, he glorified himself* [6] *by his action(s) more than all. The scribes were stung with envy and gave Pilate thirty talents to kill him. And* [7] *he took (it) and gave them liberty to carry out their will (themselves).*] And they took him [8] and crucified him *contrary* [9] to the law of (their) fathers.' [10]

THE CHRISTIAN INTERPOLATIONS IN THE SECTION ON JESUS IN THE 'HALŌSIS'

The most cursory perusal of the passage just quoted will convince any intelligent reader that we are here facing the same problem as in the case of the famous *Testimonium Flavianum*. At first glance one is struck by expressions intelligible only if coming from a Christian pen. Thus it is inconceivable that Josephus could have put into Pilate's mouth a testimony to the complete innocence of Jesus and actually represented the governor as investing the wonder-worker with the dignity of a public benefactor (εὐεργέτης). Such a sentence as 'he is a *benefactor, not* a malefactor, *nor* a rebel, *nor* thirsting for king(ship) ' cannot possibly have been penned by Josephus. On the other hand, it is easy to recognize that the word 'benefactor' as well as the particles 'not,' ' nor,' ' nor,' which are historically so improbable, are not wanted in the sentence and have been interpolated by an indignant Christian to correct what was to him an intolerable statement. If these words be omitted, we are left with a plausible verdict: 'he is a malefactor, a rebel, a robber, thirsting to be king.'

Equally impossible is it to believe that Josephus could have known, accepted, and recounted the legend of Pilate's acquittal of Jesus, a myth obviously invented to exonerate the Roman authorities and to incriminate the Jews. This historically impossible statement has probably been derived artificially, after the fashion of the *midrashîm*, from Acts iii. 13 (Πειλάτου κρίναντος [11] ἐκείνου

---

[1] ' that he was,' Acad. ; Syn. 770, 991 ; Kas.
[2] Add ' is,' Syn. 770 ; Kas. [3] ' and,' Syn. 991.
[4] Rum., ' [neither] a robber [nor] a malefactor [nor] a rebel [nor] an impostor of kingship.'
[5] Om. ' works,' Kas. [6] Om. ' himself,' Syn. 770, Kas.
[7] Om. ' and,' Kas. [8] Om. ' him,' Syn. 991.
[9] On this word, cf. below, p. 388 ll. 29 ff.
[10] Rum., ' according to the law of the emperors.'
[11] v. l. : κρίνοντος.

ἀπολύειν), the clause having been torn from its context and κρίναντος ('when he was determined' *or* 'about to acquit him') interpreted as 'after he had decided to acquit him.' The following statement, that Jesus was crucified by the Jews, rests on a literal interpretation of isolated sentences such as *Luke* xxxii. 25 : 'but Jesus he delivered up to their will'; *John* xix. 6 : 'Take him yourselves and crucify him'; xix. 16 : 'he delivered him unto them to be crucified'; *Gospel of Peter* iii. *sq.* : 'And he delivered him to the people. . . . And they crucified . . . the Lord.' [1] The same biased account of the events is found in the forged *Acts of Pilate*, especially in the so-called *Rescript of the Emperor Tiberius to Pilate*.[2]

The motive given for the alleged acquittal, namely, the miraculous healing of Pilate's dying wife, still missing in the Rumanian text and hence obviously a quite late interpolation, is another *midrash*, extracted from that lady's words in *Matt.* xxvii. 19 : 'for I have suffered many things this day in a dream because of him,' by placing a comma after 'this day' and appending 'I was healed' at the end. The legend in this form is found in the Latin *Vita beatae Virginis Mariae et Salvatoris Rhythmica*,[3] the introduction to which expressly mentions 'Hegesippus' and Josephus [4] among the sources utilized.

Of quite unmistakable Christian origin is the sentence, 'The doctors of the law were stung with envy,' etc. The word νομοδιδάσκαλος does not occur in Josephus. Moreover, while that author finds fault with the Sadducees for their severity as judges,[5] he never attacks the doctors of the law in general as the Gospels do. Lastly, the whole sentence is merely a paraphrase of *Mark* xv. 10, *Matt.* xxvii. 18, 'for envy they had delivered him up.'

The bribe of thirty talents has long been recognized as a simple multiplication, in keeping with the high rank of the recipient, of the thirty pieces of silver paid by the high priests to the traitor Judas. The venality of Pilate was well known to the Christians, thanks to the work of Philo.[6] For the rest, the story of the governor who accepts a bribe but does nothing himself beyond shutting his eyes to the illegal actions of the donors, is simply an imitation of the

---

[1] Cf. also *Acts* ii. 22 *sq.*, iii. 15 ; 1 *Thess.* ii. 15.

[2] M. R. James, *Apocr. Anecd.*, Texts and Studies, v. 1, p. 78, 1₁; 18₁; 1₁₁; 1₁₁: "τοῦτον παρέδωκας τοῖς παρανόμοις 'Ιουδαίοις" is exactly parallel to the sentence about the Jews crucifying Jesus *against* their ancestral laws, in the Slavonic Josephus.

[3] Ed. by Voegtlin, Tübingen, 1889, p. 162, vv. 4762-73.

[4] Obviously an interpolated Latin MS. of the *War* corresponding to the copy used by the Slavonic translator, maybe of the same type as the one read by Jacobus de Voragine (above, p. 95 n. 1).

[5] See above, p. 225 n. 6.

[6] *De legat. ad Gaium*, § 38 ; the work was the main model—besides 2 *Macc.* 9— for all the consolatory narratives gloating over the miserable death of the persecutors of the pious.

story of Gessius Florus and the Jewish elders of Caesarea,[1] where the governor accepts eight talents from the Jews as the price of his assistance in putting a stop to the vexations of the Hellenized Syrians, and then decamps, 'leaving a free field to sedition, as though he had sold the Jews a licence to fight the matter out themselves.' Our legend is presupposed in the forged *Acts of Pilate* [2] and reappears in the *Vita Rhythmica* already mentioned.[3]

The unhistorical character of the narrative is convincingly shown by the statement that Jesus was *crucified by the Jews*, i.e. put to death in Roman fashion and according to Roman law. Had the Sanhedrin really bribed the Roman governor to be left a free hand against a hated heretic, he would have been *stoned* in the Jewish manner like Stephen and James, and his body subsequently suspended on a stake. What reason could the Jews have had for resorting to a form of execution contrary to the rules of their own penal law?[4] Apart from the historical improbability, not to say impossibility, of the story, it is inconceivable that it could have been penned by Josephus. For who is to believe that a member of an eminent priestly family and an avowed follower of the Pharisee party, always boasting of his scriptural learning, could have laid the blame for what, according to the text of the MSS., was an inexcusable judicial murder, upon the Jewish 'teachers of the law' and their alleged 'envy,' and done so even more strongly than the Christian reporters? How could Josephus have dared to represent the founder of the Christian sect, in such disfavour at the Flavian court [5] and so detested by the Jews, as an innocent victim of the contemptible venality of a Roman governor? What could induce him to offer such an insult at once to the Romans and to his own countrymen and peers?

True, there are cases where the *Antiquities* rectify a contrary and erroneous statement in the *War* or the *Halōsis*. But in general, and particularly in the narrative of other events which occurred in Pilate's administration, the later work is in substantial agreement with the earlier one, so that we may reasonably assume the reports about Jesus in the *Halōsis* and the *Antiquities* to have been originally consistent, at least in their original trend. Flagrant contradictions would then have their origin in Christian interpolations. If we are told, for example, both in the *Antiquities*

---

[1] *B.J.*, ii. 287 *sq.*
[2] *Rescriptum Tiberii*, loc. cit., p. 78, 1_{12}; p. 79, 1_{16}.
[3] Verses 4786 *sqq.*
[4] Josephus, *B.J.*, i. 4. 6, § 97, unequivocally condemns King Alexander Jannai, who had his conquered opponents crucified. In *Ant.*, xiii. 14. 2, § 383, we learn that the king, on account of this inhuman cruelty, was called 'Thrakidas' by the Jews.
[5] Cf. the words of Titus on the destruction of the temple and his desire to destroy root and branch the messianist beliefs, as recorded by Sulpicius Severus after Tacitus, below, p. 552 n. 1.

and in Tacitus that ' on the indictment of the principal men among us Pilate sentenced (Jesus) to the cross,' we may suppose the older record also to have ascribed the indictment—their proper duty— to the Jewish leaders, the sentence and its execution to Pilate.

Neither Berendts nor any of his critics has observed that such a representation of the events, unobjectionable in every respect, is actually to be found in the Slavonic Josephus as soon as the sentences to which exception is taken are simply excluded. In this way we obtain the following text :

> ' And they (the Jewish leaders) went and communicated (it) to Pilate.[1]   And he sent and put many of the multitude to death.   And he had that wonder-worker brought up, and, after he had held an enquiry concerning him, he gave his sentence : [2] He is a malefactor,[3] a robber, a rebel,[4] thirsting to become a king.   And they took him and crucified him.'

The change of subject from ' Pilate ' to an indefinite ' they ' is no objection to such a restoration, this phenomenon being rather frequently met with in the Slavonic Josephus.[5]

As has been mentioned above,[6] Josephus' phrase, 'to sentence to the cross' ($\sigma\tau\alpha\upsilon\rho\hat{\omega}$ $\dot{\epsilon}\pi\iota\tau\iota\mu\hat{\alpha}\nu$), is the equivalent of the Roman legal formula employed by Tacitus, ' supplicio afficere.'   The full technical term for this penalty was ' supplicium more majorum ' ($\dot{\eta}$ $\kappa\alpha\tau\dot{\alpha}$ $\tau\dot{\partial}\nu$ $\pi\dot{\alpha}\tau\rho\iota o\nu$ $\nu\dot{\phi}\mu o\nu$ $\delta\dot{\iota}\kappa\eta$).   Now, since after the deletion of the Christian interpolation the subject of the sentence, 'And they took him and crucified him,' is no longer ' the Jews ' but ' the Romans,' the text of the following words must originally have run, not '*contrary* to the law of their fathers,' but '*according* to the law of their fathers,' answering to the Latin.

The Slavonic *črez*, 'against,' used in the phrase '*črez očeskij zakon*' ='against the law of the ancestors,' $\pi\alpha\rho\dot{\alpha}$ $\tau\dot{\partial}\nu$ $\pi\dot{\alpha}\tau\rho\iota o\nu$ $\nu\dot{\phi}\mu o\nu$,' ' contrary to the law of their fathers,' betrays the hand of the late Christian reviser.   For in the *Halōsis* (i. 209), where the Greek has the almost identical phrase, ' against Jewish law,' $\pi\alpha\rho\dot{\alpha}$ $\tau\dot{\partial}\nu$ $\tau\hat{\omega}\nu$ 'Ιουδαίων $\nu\dot{\phi}\mu o\nu$, the Slavonic equivalent used for the preposition $\pi\alpha\rho\dot{\alpha}$ is not *črez* but *krome*.   Since such small particles are generally admitted to be among the most significant indices of an author's style, we must infer, either that the first book comes from a different translator—which is very improbable—or (and this seems to be the obvious explanation) that the *črez* in the passage under consideration comes not from the Slavonic translator, who found in his copy $\kappa\alpha\tau\dot{\alpha}$ $\tau\dot{\partial}\nu$ $\pi\dot{\alpha}\tau\rho\iota o\nu$ $\nu\dot{\phi}\mu o\nu$, and translated accordingly, but from a later *Russian* reader who, as a member of the Judaizing

---

[1] Cf. the ἔνδειξις in the *Testimonium*, above, p. 61₂₄.
[2] *cognovit.*
[3] κακοῦργος = *maleficus* = *magician*, below, p. 460₃.
[4] στασιαστής = *seditiosus.*
[5] For example, i. 18 (Berendts-Grass, p. 79).
[6] See p. 55 ll. 3 ff.

sect,[1] was sufficiently acquainted with the Jewish law to know that the crucifixion of a living person was not permitted. This correction presupposes, of course, that the Russian reader found in his text the above-criticized interpolation.

The hypothesis that the Greek *Halōsis*, or at least some of its MSS., had κατὰ τὸν πάτριον νόμον, in spite of the interpolation inculpating the Jews, is by no means improbable if we recall the Deuteronomic ordinance[2] according to which the body of a criminal stoned to death should be hanged on a tree, and that in the Talmud[3] the execution of Jesus is actually so represented. In any case it would appear clear that 'contrary to the fathers' law' in place of 'in accordance with' can only have come into the text as a correction, and only after it had been interpolated by a Christian hand. It is nothing but an attempt to smooth over an unevenness created by the interpolations. Exclude this late alteration along with the obvious Christian insertion in favour of a text like 'according to the law of the emperors,'[4] as attested by the Rumanian version, and we are left with a statement which can unhesitatingly be attributed to Josephus himself.

THE CHRISTIAN OMISSIONS AND ADDITIONS IN THE OPENING SENTENCES ON THE NATURE AND FIGURE OF JESUS

The very first sentence of the section on Jesus in the *Halōsis* contains the singular phrase, 'a man, if one may call him a man.' Here the context leaves no doubt that the writer, either in good faith or ironically, proposed to himself and the reader the question whether this wonder-worker may not have been a superhuman being. The possibility, discussed above,[5] that the author may have intended to represent him as a monster is here excluded by what follows : ' his nature and figure were human, but his appearance ὑπὲρ ἄνθρωπον, more than human.' The fundamental importance of the sentence makes it necessary to enquire carefully what precisely is offered us by the Russian translator and what may have stood in his Greek original.

To begin with the last part of the phrase, there can be little doubt that the Russian *pače člk* renders the Greek ὑπὲρ ἄνθρωπον,[6] ' more than a man.' Now, in the *Antiquities* (iii. 318) Josephus speaks of the many qualities possessed by Moses as ' more than human power' (ὑπὲρ ἄνθρωπον δύναμις). Thus, while he actually

[1] See above, pp. 155 ff.   [2] *Deut.* xxi. 22, xvii. 7.
[3] Klausner, *Jesus of Nazareth*, p. 27.
[4] ' emperors ' being a correction for ' fathers ' (*imperatorum* for *patrum*) by a scribe who knew that, at the time of Jesus, laws were made by the emperors and not by the *patres* of the senate.
[5] See p. 52.
[6] Cf. the examples collected in Sreznĕvski's *Dictionary*, ii. 891.

attributes 'superhuman power' to the Hebrew lawgiver,[1] he will only allow the 'appearance' of a superhuman being to Jesus, the *Moses redivivus*,[2] and declines to call him an angel. One has only to peruse the sections in the *Antiquities* dealing with Moses to recover not only the ideas but even the exact Greek words which disclose the meaning of this ambiguous passage in the Slavonic *Halōsis*. The infant Moses may be recognized as divine by his form,[3] his stature and his beauty: his appearance (ὄψις) compelled the passers-by to turn round and gaze at him. One should also compare Philo's description [4] of the messianic return of the dispersed Israelites to the Holy Land, 'conducted by an apparition more divine than is the manner of human nature,[5] invisible to others and manifest only to those who are being saved.' There the mysterious guide can be no other than the superhuman figure of Moses returned in the glorified shape of a spirit or an angel from heaven.

The phraseology of the corresponding passage of the *Halōsis* is in close agreement. The word *zrak* renders the Greek ὄψις in the Russian translation of *Dan.* iii. 19.[6] The word *obraz* renders the Greek μορφή in the Gospel of Ostromir. If therefore the Slavonic text speaks of the divine figure (*obraz*) of Jesus, this corresponds closely to the θεία μορφή of Moses in Josephus' text. The Russian *obraz* may also render a Greek εἰκών.[7] The Russian *estestvo* is the ordinary word for Greek φύσις.[8] The Greek φύσις ἀνθρώπων, 'human nature,' is in Slavonic čelověčeskoe estestvo.[9]

The section in question must then have run as follows in the original Greek, the words enclosed in brackets being interpolations:

'His nature and form were human, but his appearance was more than man [but his works were divine]; (for) he wrought miracles wonderful and powerful: [wherefore it is impossible for me to call him a man]. But again, looking at his commonplace nature, I will not call him an angel.' [10]

It is obvious that only a Christian could say that the works of Jesus were divine. It is indeed a commonplace of the Fathers that

---

[1] Called 'a great angel' in the *Assumptio Mosis*, i. 14.
[2] See above, p. 384₉; below, p. 620, App. XXII.
[3] *Ant.*, ii. 232 : παῖδα μορφῇ θεῖον.
[4] *De exsecrationibus*, § 8 sq., ii. 435 M. : "θειοτέρα ἢ κατ᾽ ἀνθρωπίνην φύσιν ὄψις." Cp. Epiphanius, *Haer.*, xxx. 17, on the Ebionite idea that the Messiah is a man-like figure, invisible to men in general ("τὸν Χριστὸν εἶναί τι ἀνδροείκελον ἐκτύπωμα ἀόρατον ἀνθρώποις").
[5] See below, pp. 395 and 411 n. 4.
[6] Sreznévski, i. 998b.   [7] *Ibid.*, ii. 539.   [8] *Ibid.*, i. 834.
[9] For example, in the Old Russian translation of the Greek saint's lives of the so-called *Paterik Sinajskij* of the eleventh century.
[10] "καὶ φύσις μὲν καὶ μορφὴ αὐτοῦ ἀνθρωπίνη ἦν, ἡ δὲ ὄψις αὐτοῦ ὑπὲρ ἄνθρωπον, [[ἀλλὰ πράξεις αὐτοῦ θεῖαι]] τέρατα δ᾽ ἐποίει παράδοξα [[καὶ δυνατά (or ἐμφανῆ or λαμπρά)]]. [[Διὰ τοῦτο ἀδύνατόν μοί ἐστιν ἄνθρωπον ὀνομάζειν αὐτόν]]. Πάλιν δὲ εἰς τὴν κοινὴν φύσιν (αὐτοῦ) (ἀπιδών, βλέπων or σκοπῶν) οὐδὲ ἄγγελον αὐτὸν καλέσω."

the miracles prove the divine nature of Jesus.[1] Equally inconceivable is it to suppose that Josephus should have said that it was *impossible* for him to call him a man ; for that goes far beyond the hesitating phrase in the opening sentence, ' if one may call him a man,' quite aside from the open contradiction with the phrase ' his nature was human.' To obtain, then, a consistent meaning of this confused paragraph, one must begin by setting aside the bracketed words, no doubt the marginal comments of a Christian reader. What remains is quite in keeping with Josephus' attitude of cool rejection and with the restored text of the opening sentence of the *Testimonium* : [2]

> ' At that time there appeared a man, if one should call him a man. . . . His nature and form were human, for he displayed wonderful signs and feats of power. Again, having regard to the nature he had in common (with all men), I shall not call him an angel.'

Clearly, however, we have not yet recovered the whole text. As in the *Antiquities*, ' if one should call him a man ' remains obscure until one has recourse to the early imitation in the ' Lentulus letter ' [3] and inserts from there the words ' whom his disciples call a Son of God.'

> ' At that time there appeared a man, if one may call him a man ⟨whom his disciples call a Son of God⟩. His nature and form were human,' etc.

That gives a good logical connexion and at once explains the final clause, 'Again . . . *I* will not call him an angel ' ; for else a reader of the present mutilated text might well ask, Who desired Josephus to call Jesus an angel ? [4] But if we supply the words from the ' Lentulus letter,' that is, the words which the forger of that letter still found in his Josephus and utilized, it is at once clear that the Jewish historian is inveighing against the designation of Jesus as a *ben elohîm*. For him, as is shown by his version [5] of the story of the fallen angels in *Gen.* vi., a 'son of God' is simply an angel. His conception of such angelic beings as possessing remarkable stature and beauty appears from his narrative of the Samson story,[6] as well as from other passages.[7]

Under these circumstances it becomes intelligible why Josephus lays such stress on the fact that the wonder-worker who gave him-

---

[1] Cf. Melito of Sardes, frag. vi., ed. Otto, p. 416 ; Orig., *C. Cels.*, ii. 48 ; iii. 28, 33 ; Hippol. on *Ps.* ii., ed. Wendland, i. p. 146 ; Novatian, *De trin.*, 11 (Migne, *P.L.*, iii. 904) ; *Acta Thom.*, xlvii. 143 ; Victorinus Poetoviensis, *De fabr. mundi* (Migne, *P.L.*, v. 313) ; *Acta Andreae et Matth.*, ii. 1. p. 79.
[2] See above, p. 62. [3] See above, p. 52 l. 13 ; below, p. 404₂.
[4] The reader may recall the anecdote of the Spartan king who said to a panegyrist of Herakles : ' But who on earth says anything *against* Herakles ? '
[5] *Ant.*, i. 3. 1 : ' sons of God' become 'angels' (as in the LXX.).
[6] *Ant.*, v. 8. 2 (=*Judges* xiii.).   [7] For example, *Ant.*, xv. § 25.

self the *appearance* of being 'more than a man' can have been only a human figure, nay, an everyday, ordinary creature (κοινὴ φύσις), and therefore no 'angel' or 'Son of God.' But on this point he must have said more than now appears in the text. Any one with the slightest notion of the art of story-telling will recognize that a brief statement like ' his nature and his form were human ' cannot be abruptly flung at the reader and left at that, without further elaboration and a more detailed justification.

A good instance is found in the *Jewish War* : [1]

'Among those serving in the cohorts was one named Sabinus, a native of Syria, who showed himself both in might of hand and in spirit the bravest of men. Yet any one seeing him before that day and judging from his bodily features would not have taken him even for a decent soldier. *His skin was black, his flesh shrunk and hairy* ; but within that slender frame there dwelt an heroic soul.'

This narrative is inconceivable without the italicized words furnishing the necessary details of the unsightly appearance of this distinguished soldier. The loss would at once be felt were these words accidentally omitted or intentionally deleted ; the reader would certainly ask for what reasons this man would not have been taken for a good soldier, and a narrator must have anticipated such a question. In the same way the general assertion of the Slavonic Josephus that the nature and figure of Jesus were purely human inevitably provokes the question how far the historian can make good such an assertion—in particular, how he can speak of this wonder-worker's 'ordinary nature.'

As a matter of fact, I had come to the conclusion that something was missing here, long before I discovered that the deleted clause was not hopelessly lost, but that by a happy accident a description of Jesus had been preserved elsewhere, perfectly filling the supposed gap. I had even published [2] my restoration of the whole section long before I received, through the kindness of the late Konrad Grass, the last sheets of his edition of Berendts' translation, from which I learnt of the till then unedited title of the Jesus chapter in the codex Kasan 444. [3] This marginal title, containing a statement of the contents of the pericope which does not agree with the extant text, strikingly confirmed the correctness of my restoration of the original passage.

[1] *B.J.*, vi. 54 *sq.*

[2] A lecture delivered before the Académie des Inscriptions et Belles-Lettres in Paris, 28th June 1926, printed in the *Revue de l'Histoire des Religions*, xciii. (1926), pp. 1-21.

[3] 'Of our Lord Redeemer Jesus Christ, the Son of God, and of the *divine figure of his appearance* and of his miracles,' Berendts-Grass, i. 268. Note that the extant text does not speak of a 'divine' but only of a ' human ' figure ; that no details are given and no miracles mentioned.

THE THREE EXTANT MSS. WITH BISHOP ANDREW OF CRETE'S QUOTATION FROM JOSEPHUS ON THE BODILY APPEARANCE OF JESUS

Andreas Cretensis, Cod. Paris. Graec. 1630, P. 124. *Schol. ad Joh. Damasc.*
De fide orthod. IV, 16 PARIS. GRAEC. NO. 901 F° 87 R° AND NO. 1119 FOL. 140 V°

(SEE P. 393, NOTE 4)

XV

ECCE HOMO

'. . . and last of all he was seen of me also.'

1 Cor. xv. 8

Josephus on the Bodily Appearance of Jesus

EVERY student of Christian iconography is familiar with Ernst v. Dobschütz's learned collection[1] and critical edition of all extant sources relating to the historical development of the literary portrait of Jesus. Many of our readers will also remember a number of passages in the Church Fathers concerning the plain, nay, ugly appearance of 'Jesus when in the flesh.' If any traces or echoes were preserved anywhere of a description of the carpenter of Nazareth, deleted from Josephus' *Halōsis* because of its offensive ring in the ears of Christians of a later age, they must surely be found in v. Dobschütz's *magnum opus*. A first glance at the index of names shows that we are not mistaken in this expectation. Josephus is, in fact, quoted as a star witness for the genuineness of a detailed description of the human appearance of Jesus, preserved in varying form and extent and repeatedly and reverentially copied by a number of authors. It is not, indeed, found in any one of the numerous passages on the subject in the ante-Nicene Fathers,[2] always quite brief and couched in general terms, but is attested by a well-known and thoroughly trustworthy Byzantine bishop of the eighth century.

Andreas Hierosolymitanus or Cretensis was born at Damascus about 660, removed to Jerusalem in his fifteenth year and was there consecrated by the Patriarch Theodore, sent to Constantinople (695), and at the beginning of the eighth century appointed Archbishop of Crete, in which dignity he died, at Gortyn.[3] This ecclesiastic, who plays an important rôle in the history of Christian church music, says in a remarkable fragment on image worship : [4]

' But moreover the Jew Josephus in like manner narrates that the Lord was seen having connate eyebrows,[5] goodly eyes, long-faced,[6] crooked,[7] well grown.'[8]

---

[1] 'Christusbilder,' in Harnack's *Texte und Untersuchungen*, N.F., iii. (1899).
[2] Collected in Herzog-Hauck, *Protest. Realencycl.*, iii³. 64, 35-54.
[3] See below, App. xxi., p. 618. Ruins of his church are still in existence. See Pl. xxxvii. of the German edition.
[4] Dobschütz, *op. cit.*, p. 189. The three only MSS. of this important text are reproduced on our Pl. xxv.
[5] σύνοφρυς. [6] μακροπρόσωπος. [7] ἐπίκυφος. [8] εὐήλιξ.

The same statement is found in a scholion to John of Damascus [1] in two MSS. in the Bibliothèque Nationale : [2]

' Since moreover Josephus the Jew, as some say, . . . in like manner narrates that the Lord was seen having connate eyebrows, goodly eyes, long-faced,[3] crooked, well grown. . . .'

This scholion must at one time have been found in a somewhat fuller form in numerous MSS. of the above-mentioned work, since it has passed over into the Latin version of John of Damascus produced about 1150 by Burgundio Pisano. Thence [4] it was taken over by Jacobus de Voragine, the famous author of the *Legenda aurea* [5] (1298), and by Vincent of Beauvais [6] (*c.* 1264). The quotation of Bishop Andreas, who has been most frivolously charged with having invented it, is confirmed by various circumstances. In the first place, the *Vita beatae Mariae et Salvatoris rhythmica* —that remarkable thirteenth-century poem, which expressly mentions Josephus among its sources and combines the two stories found in the interpolated Slavonic *Halōsis*, to wit, the healing of Pilate's wife and the bribing of the governor—likewise contains a detailed description of the personal appearance of Jesus and his mother.[7] Secondly, we have a similar description in the *Church History* of Nicephorus Callistou [8] of the ' God-man's figure (θεανδρικῆς μορφῆς) of our saviour Jesus Christ . . . as we received it from ancient writers,' immediately following a transcript of the famous *Testimonium* which ends with the words, ' These things also Josephus (wrote).' [9]

Of the two writers dependent on the scholion of John of Damascus it should be noted that, whereas Vincent of Beauvais uses the full and explicit phrase ' Josephus ut ait historia,' Jacobus de Voragine is content with the more indefinite expression ' in quadam antiqua historia,' by which is obviously meant the *Historia belli Judaici* or *Historia captivitatis Jerusalem*. From

---

[1] *De fide orthod.*, iv. 16.

[2] *Par. Reg.*, 1986 and 2928, now *Graeci*, Nos. 901 and 1119; Dobschütz, 187, 189.

[3] μακροπρόσωπος.

[4] Or directly from a MS. of the Latin Josephus. See above, p. 95 n. 1.

[5] Ed. J. G. Th. Grässe, p. 707 : ' cujus autem imaginis dominus fuerit . . . idem Josephus testatur : fuit enim bene oculatus, bene superciliatus, longum vultum habuit et fuit acclivis, quod est signum maturitatis.'

[6] *Spec. Hist.*, viii. 23 : ' Testimonia Josephi de Johanne Baptista et de domino Hiesu et ejus facie corporali ' : Johannes Damascenus, i. iii° : ' Ipse quoque Josephus, ut ait historia, tradit dominum Jhesum visum fuisse communiter ciliatum, id est conjuncta supercilia habentem, bene oculatum, longum vultum habentem.'

[7] Dobschütz, 307. The details, *capilli, supercilia, nasus*, etc., are here so altered as to give a vague picture of ideal beauty.

[8] Migne, *P.G.*, cxlv. 747.

[9] ' He was full seven spans (high), with beautiful eyes, a long nose, tawny hair, black eyebrows, his neck gently bent so that the carriage of his body was not quite upright and rigid.'

PLATE XXVI

THE 'EPISTLE OF LENTULUS'

WITH THE CLAUSE BORROWED FROM THE 'Halòsis' OF JOSEPHUS 'apparuit homo, si fas est hominem dicere.'
Cod. Paris. Lat. 17730 saec. XV F° 7 V° AND 8 R°

this one may reasonably conclude that when Theodorus Anagnostes, Nicephorus Callistou, Theophanes, and Anastasius Bibliothecarius [1] speak of the personal appearance of Jesus, quoting as their authority ' the historian' (ὁ ἱστορῶν) or ' some of the historians' (τινὲς τῶν ἱστορικῶν), or the like, these writers mean no other than Josephus, who, as appears from phrases used elsewhere by Nicephorus [2] and other Byzantines,[3] was regarded as ' the historian' of the time of Jesus.

The description in question appears, without any mention of its source, in the monk Epiphanius of the Callistratou monastery [4] in Constantinople (before A.D. 780), and in an almost contemporary epistle from the Oriental patriarchs assembled in Jerusalem to the Emperor Theophilus.[5] A Byzantine homily concerning miracle-working images [6] appeals to ' the contemporary eyewitnesses.' [7]

Lastly, mention must be made of an anonymous scholion with the inscription ' concerning the Lord's human form (ἀνθρωπίνη μορφή).' [8] The title ' concerning the Saviour's God-man-like figure' (περὶ τῆς τοῦ σωτῆρος θεανδρικῆς μορφῆς) in the aforesaid Byzantine homily is a very instructive corrective of this, and forms a bridge to the ' divine figure' in the superscription of the Jesus section in codex Kasan 444 of the Slavonic Halōsis.

That rubric, it will be remembered, runs thus : ' Of the Lord our Redeemer Jesus Christ, the Son of God, and of the divine form of his appearance (περὶ τῆς θείας μορφῆς τῆς ὄψεως) and of his wonderful works.' As we have seen above, this heading does not correspond at all to the traditional text, since the latter describes the form of the wonder-worker as purely human, his appearance (ὄψις) only as superhuman, and his works as divine. One has only to compare the superscription to the anonymous scholion, ' concerning the Lord's human form,' to perceive that that is the true and original text of the rubric, and that by progressive stages of correction ἀνθρωπίνη μορφή has been altered first to θεανδρικὴ μορφή and finally to the θεία μορφή represented by the Russian MS. Naturally, the censor intended to introduce a similar correction into the text itself, but a careless reviser has, fortunately, forgotten to alter the word ' human' in the text after having corrected the title according to the directions received by his superior or according to a revised copy. Furthermore, it is evident that no one would have given the title 'concerning the Saviour's form and his wonderful deeds' to a passage actually

[1] The quotations are given in App. XXI., p. 619.
[2] P.G., cxlv. 693 B.   [3] Cedren., Hist. comp., p. 225, ed. Paris.
[4] Dobschütz, p. 302.   [5] Ibid., p. 303.
[6] Dobschütz, p. 246.
[7] The expression is derived from Luke i. 2.   [8] Dobschütz, p. 305.

containing nothing whatever about his personal appearance, nor enumerating his miraculous exploits. In other words, it is impossible to suppose the title to have referred originally to the short clause ' his nature and his form were human ' ; on the contrary, the title confirms the conclusion reached above and actually before this final proof was available to me, viz. that the section of the *Halōsis* under consideration must have contained originally a detailed description of the nameless wonder-worker and some particulars at least about the wonders he was said to have wrought.

The so-called 'Letter of Lentulus' and the Passage on Jesus in the 'Halōsis'

Mention has been made repeatedly, in the course of this study, of the so-called *Epistula Lentuli de effigie Christi*, and we may now be in a position to solve the old enigma presented by this document and to arrive at a plausible explanation of its genesis. It is a highly remarkable and doubtless Christian forgery, preserved in numerous MSS. and old prints. It was re-edited in 1899 by Dr. v. Dobschütz [1] with a full and very welcome *apparatus criticus*. That scholar, however, as he himself admits, failed to reach any satisfactory conclusion concerning its age and the precise form of literature to which it may be said to belong. The inscription found in one MS., ' de forma et operibus Jesu Christi,' closely agrees with the title of the chapter on Jesus in the Slavonic Josephus, ' of Jesus Christ, the Son of God, and of the form of his appearance and of his wonderful works.' Again, there is a striking agreement of the opening sentence of this epistle, 'apparuit temporibus istis,' with the extant Slavonic text of the *Halōsis*, as opposed to the *Testimonium* in *Ant.*, xviii. 53, which reads, ' there lived, *or* there arose at that time . . .' (γίνεται κατὰ τοῦτον τὸν χρόνον . . .). In the Slavonic we have *todga iavi*, ' at that time *appeared* (ἐφάνη) a man,' etc.

This curious agreement becomes still more significant if we transfer to the text—as since the disclosure of the *Halōsis* we are surely justified in doing—the highly instructive reading of the Paris and Munich MSS.,[2] relegated by Dobschütz to his *apparatus criticus*, viz. ' *apparuit temporibus istis* et adhuc est [3] *homo, si fas est hominem dicere*,' etc. For it is clear that this small parenthesis has not been *interpolated* by the writer of the archetype of the two MSS. as an allusion to the famous *Testimonium* (what object could there be in that ?), but conversely that this treacherous echo of Josephus' ironical remark, betraying the forger's source, has been

---

[1] *Op. cit.*, p. 308 *sqq.*   [2] Reproduced on our Pls. xxvi. and xxvii.
[3] On these words, cf. below, p. 405 n. 2.

PLATE XXVII

THE 'EPISTLE OF LENTULUS'

SAME TEXT AS OUR PLATE XXVI FROM COD. MONAC. LAT. 6007 F° 122 V°, R° AND 123 R°

(SEE P. 396, NOTE 2)

deleted from the archetype of the overwhelming majority of MSS. because it was obvious that the forgery would at once be detected if so striking an expression, taken from the *Halōsis*, a book composed during the reign of Vespasian or Titus, or from the *Antiquities*, published under Domitian, were to appear as coming from the pen of one Lentulus, supposed to have written at the time of the first appearance of Jesus under Tiberius.

There can therefore be no doubt that the forger of the 'Lentulus letter' knew the section of the *Halōsis* 'on the human form of Jesus and his wonderful works,' and that he found there a series of statements concerning his personal appearance such as Andrew of Crete and the other authorities already mentioned read in their MSS. of Josephus. The obvious intention of this pious fraud was to replace this description of Jesus, so offensive to the later Christians and hence deleted subsequently in the archetype of the Slavonic text, by another, more edifying pen-portrait. Yet in the polemical writings against the iconoclasts the testimony of Josephus as to the human characteristics of Jesus was used to refute those who maintained that no one could know anything about the physical appearance of Jesus—not, however, without having undergone an editorial revision intended to retouch, as far as that was possible without destroying entirely the individual character of the portrait, the most objectionable features.

At first sight it might be supposed that the simplest way of refuting a malicious description in Josephus of the personal appearance of Jesus would have been to put another and more flattering description into the mouth of the principal official witness, his judge Pontius Pilate, the more so because upon that officer had been foisted a number of spurious 'acta' ($\dot{\upsilon}\pi o\mu\nu\dot{\eta}\mu\alpha\tau\alpha$) of the trial along with various reports to the emperor and to Herod, accompanied by the replies they were supposed to have drawn. As a matter of fact, in a Paris MS.[1] we actually find the remarkable description of Jesus, elsewhere ascribed to one Lentulus, but here entitled 'Pilati ad Romanos de X̄ro,' so that this so-called epistle would without any hesitation have been reckoned with the Pilate apocrypha had this MS. alone survived. Since, however, this superscription stands quite isolated, little weight would attach to it, were it not for the fact that its title closely corresponds to certain ancient traditions, equally in need of explanation and hitherto misunderstood, to the effect that *Pilate* had a 'forma' or an 'image' ($\epsilon\dot{\iota}\kappa\dot{\omega}\nu$), or even several 'images,' of Jesus prepared for himself.[2]

The syncretistic Gnostics, who were apparently the first to

---

[1] Paris. lat., 2962 (saec. xv./xvi.) : cod. f. 2 of Dobschütz; cf. our Pl. xxviii.
[2] Dobschütz, 98 : Iren., *Adv. haer.*, i. 25. 6; Epiph., *Haeres.*, xxvii. 6, and elsewhere. See App. xx., below, pp. 617 f.

make portraits of Jesus, both 'painted and sculptured in various materials,' along with 'statues of the ancient sages Pythagoras, Plato, and Aristotle,' claimed as the historical basis for this portrait, newly introduced among the figures of the great thinkers, that 'forma' or those εἰκόνες made by Pilate of his prisoner. Credulous relic-hunters of the eighth century were shown this legendary likeness (*imago*) on the wall of the so-called *praetorium* of Pilate in Jerusalem, and at that time there might conceivably have been a *painting* in this locality, although the complete absence of any imitations of it (in contrast to the famous Abgarus and Veronica portraits) practically excludes such a possibility. It is also conceivable that people such as Epiphanius should have been ignorant and uncritical enough to believe in the story of the portrait of an interesting prisoner painted by order of his judge. Yet it is highly improbable that cultivated philosophers, eclectic followers of the neo-Platonic and neo-Pythagorean schools, rich and broad-minded enough to erect in their private chapels costly statues of all the sages of the past, were at the same time so naïve as to believe such a fable, much less to put it in circulation.

What these distinguished and tolerant eclectics really said and meant can no longer be unintelligible to any one since the discovery of the numerous papyri which have taught us that in ancient legal and business life the word εἰκών or εἰκονισμός denoted that written description of an individual called 'signalement' in French, ' hue-and-cry ' in archaic English. The device, a man's official personal description by certain marked features,[1] was largely employed in the records of criminal and civil cases or in the official proceedings of the political authorities throughout the Hellenistic and Roman East.

Foolish as it would be to suppose a Roman governor to have called in a portrait-painter or a sculptor to perpetuate the features of an accused malefactor, however remarkable his appearance, it is no less plausible that the writ of indictment (μήνυσις, *libellus*), the records or minutes (ὑπομνήματα), the *acta* of the preliminary enquiry (*cognitio*) and of the trial itself, must needs have contained an εἰκών (*iconismus*) of the accused. From the standpoint of our present-day knowledge of ancient chancellery practice nothing is

---

[1] Cf. E. Rohde, *Der griech. Roman*², Leipzig, 1900, p. 160 n. 1. ; Gradenwitz, *Einführung in die Papyruskunde*, Leipzig, 1900, p. 126 *sqq.* ; J. Fürst, *Die liter. Porträtmanier im Bereich des griech. -röm. Schrifttums*, Philologus, lxi. (1902), p. 377 *sqq.*; Mitteis-Wilcken, *Grundzüge und Chrestomathie der Papyruskunde*, Leipzig, 1912, ii. 75 ; cf. i. 194 and 529 ; J. Hasebroek, *Das Signalement in den Papyrusurkunden*, Berlin, 1921, pp. 79-117 ; Alessandra Caldara, *I connotati personali nei documenti d'Egitto dell' età greca e romana*, Milano, 1924 ; F. Smolka, *De ratione personarum describendarum in papyrorum actis adhibita*, Eos, xxvii. (1924), p. 75 *sqq.*; G. Misener, *Iconistic Portraits*, Classical Philology, vol. xix., April 1924, pp. 97-123. This whole literature was not yet in existence when v. Dobschütz, *op. cit.*, p. 294 *sq.*, dealt with the problem.

PLATE XXVIII

THE ORIGINAL TITLE OF THE SO-CALLED 'EPISTLE OF LENTULUS':
EPISTULA PILATI AD ROMANOS

COD. PARIS LAT. 2962 SAEC. XV/XVI F° 174

(SEE P. 397, NOTE I)

more probable than that Pilate actually had an εἰκών of 'Jesus called Christ' drawn up, and that it had found its proper place in the genuine 'acts' of Pilate recording the trial of Jesus and published by the Emperor Maximinus Daïa in A.D. 311.[1]

Since it is inconceivable that the Gnostics of the age of Alexander Severus (A.D. 222-235) could have appealed to the genuine documents first published by Maximinus (A.D. 311), and since it is equally improbable that before such a publication any one could be in possession of or have knowledge of the old copies of the genuine *iconismus*, we can only suppose that their portraits of Jesus were drawn from some apocryphal εἰκών attributed to Pilate—in other words, that they knew the so-called 'Lentulus letter,' in the shape it has in the Paris MS., under the title 'nota Pilati de effigie Jesu Christi.' This pamphlet need not have circulated as an independent work. Just as the report (ἀναφορά) of Pilate to Tiberius appears in some MSS. as an appendix to the late *Acts of Pilate* of the time of the Emperor Theodosius, so this spurious *iconismus* may have formed a constituent portion of, or an appendix to, those lost older, but likewise forged, *Acts of Pilate* referred to by Justin Martyr[2] and Tertullian.[3] In this form, as a Pilate apocryphon, the piece is then certainly older than the reign of Alexander Severus. Since, like the Pilate forgeries in general, it is clearly directed against Josephus and obviously alludes to his peculiar wording, and since such refutations are as a rule written at a time when the refuted work was still recent, not half a century later, when the excitement over an obnoxious publication had long died down, I should have no hesitation in dating this piece, along with the lost oldest Pilate apocrypha, back into the last decades of the first century.

At this point a further question arises : why has this pamphlet, in all MSS. but one, abandoned the ascription to Pilate, offhand intelligible to every reader, in favour of the highly aristocratic but otherwise rather puzzling 'Lentulus,' a name common in the Roman *gens Cornelia*, but for that very reason very ambiguous and hitherto at least a riddle to the modern scholar? In reality the enigma is not hard to solve. A glance at the *fasti consulares* to which the ancient Church had recourse in all investigations into the date of the crucifixion[4] will show, three years before the year of that event (i.e., according to the usual reckoning of a three-year ministry, in the year when Jesus made his first appearance) and five years before the classical consulate of Rufio and Rubellio (the fifteenth year of Tiberius), the names 'Agrippa II. et Lentulo coss.'

---

[1] See above, p. 16 n. 3.
[2] *Apol.*, 35 (Migne, *P.G.*, xli. 885).   [3] *Apol.*, 21.
[4] Cf. above, p. 296; further, the 'series of consular dates' (εἱρμὸς ὑπατείας) for the alleged thirty-three years of Jesus' life in Epiph., *Haeres.*, li. (*P.G.*, xli. 979 *sqq.*).

given as those of the eponymous consuls of the tenth year of that emperor's reign. The Christian reader who drew all his historical information from such condensed abstracts might well imagine that this Lentulus was the same person as his namesake of whom he read in a similar source : [1] 'Lentulo et Silvano coss. In his temporibus adnuntiavit Elisabeth angelus.' According to the *Chronicon Paschale* [2] the conception and the birth of Jesus took place in the consulate of one Lentulus and one Piso.

The name of Lentulus thus appeared sufficiently closely linked with the cardinal events in the Gospel story to impress a not wholly uneducated forger, who sought in the Christian extracts from the Roman consular *fasti* a name for an imaginary pro-consular official superior in rank to the equestrian officer Pilate, by whose witness that of Pilate might be confuted or 'rectified.' He thus fabricated an alleged report to the emperor such as the im-perial agents really used to send to their august lord. The need for such 'rectification' by an imaginary superior of Pilate cannot, however, have been felt until, in consequence of the publication of the genuine *Acts of Pilate* in 311, it was discovered that the de-scription of Jesus actually drawn up by Pilate's orders *agreed verbatim with the objectionable statement of Josephus*, which it had been sought to invalidate by the spurious evidence of Pilate, the agreement being due to the simple reason that Josephus had in fact obtained these details from no other source than the extracts from the official report of Pilate included in the *commentarii* of Tiberius.

Since, therefore, Pilate had ceased to be an utilizable witness against Josephus in the controversy with Jews and heathens, the forged document was now ascribed to the consular Lentulus. In this final form, which the work cannot have assumed before A.D. 311, it appears to have lived on like other apocrypha in the Greek Church, and reference was made, in support of this retouched portrait of Jesus, not only to Josephus, or to ' the historian ' or ' historians,' but generally to ' the ancients,' or even to ' the original eye-witnesses ' (ἀπ' ἀρχῆς αὐτόπται). Seeing that no canonical or apocryphal gospel ever attempted a description of Jesus—in keeping with the saying of Paul, ' even though we have known Christ after the flesh, yet now know we him no more ' [3]— the ' eye-witnesses ' cannot mean the Apostles, and the expression can only refer to the εἰκόνες, fraudulently attributed to Pilate or to his contemporary Lentulus. In the West, where neither the art nor the literature of the Middle Ages betrays the slightest trace of any acquaintance with such a personal description of Jesus, it is only toward the end of that period, at the earliest in the thir-

---

[1] Euseb., *Chron.*, ed. Schoene, i. 226.
[2] Ed. Bonn, p. 372.   [3] 2 *Cor.* v. 16.

teenth century, that the Latin version of the now lost Greek text makes its appearance.

The MS. of the Lentulus letter, preserved in the Cistercian monastery of Zwettl,[1] bears the note, ' Haec lata sunt de Cistercio,' i.e. ' brought from Citeaux.'   The reader who recalls the leading part played by Arnold, Abbot of Citeaux, in fighting the heretical movement in Southern France,[2] will not reject the hypothesis that the Lentulus' letter which has come down to us in Dr. Gaster's Rumanian MS. 89, along with the *Acts of Pilate* and portions of the *Halōsis* of Josephus, was first brought by those heretical Josephinist ' passagini' mentioned above[3] from the Balkan provinces to Italy and Southern France, there to be translated into Latin.

That the pamphlet originated in the Eastern empire is indicated not only by the fact that the Rumanian version professes to be derived from one of ' Maximos, a monk of the Vatopaedi monastery on Mt. Athos,' but also by the subscription to the lost Jena MS. : [4] ' quae epistula reperta est in armariis Romae. explicit epistula.   Jacob(us) de Columpna [5] A.D. MCCCC XXI reperit eam in libro antiquissimo in capitolio d(e)dic(a)to (a) domino patriarcha Constantinopolitano.'

The presentation of a MS. by the Patriarch of Constantinople to Rome may have occurred in the period before the schism, that is to say, before Photius, since the period of negotiations for reunion before the Council of Florence, in 1429, is excluded by the late date and the adjective *antiquissimus* applied to the codex in question.   We had best regard the MS. as a present from the Byzantine patriarch to a Roman cleric at the time of the Latin empire in Constantinople.   This would again carry us to the thirteenth century, in which the *Halōsis* was translated into Slavonic[6] and was used in the West in the Latin *Vita beatae Mariae et Salvatoris rhythmica*.   It is quite conceivable that in the time of Gregory IX. and Frederick II., in consequence of the heresy threatening the Greek and Roman Churches alike, pertinent documents of use for apologetic purposes were sought and obtained from Byzantium.   In any case, a MS. emanating from the Patriarch of Constantinople can only have been written in Greek.

THE WARRANT FOR THE ARREST OF JESUS

From the account of Josephus,[7] here in complete agreement with the apocryphal *Acta Pilati*,[8] it appears, as indeed one might

[1] Dobschütz, p. 325.

[2] L. J. Newman, *Jewish Influences on the Christian Reform Movements*, New York, 1926, p. 154 *sq.*

[3] See p. 65.   [4] Dobschütz, p. 324.

[5] Jacopo di Niccolò Colonna, Lord of Palestrina, died 1431 (Litta, *Famiglia Colonna*, tav. 5).

[6] See above, p. 148.   [7] See above, p. 385 l. 1.   [8] M. R. James, *op. cit.*, p. 96.

2 C

have assumed, that the Jewish authorities laid their information against Jesus before the Roman governor while the accused was still at liberty ; the Gospels, on the contrary, represent him as being arrested by the Jews and dragged to Pilate, who is totally ignorant of the charge brought against the prisoner. Obviously, the political situation forced the high priests to take this action against one of their own nation and faith, and an exact parallel is found in that chapter of the same historian where he describes how the wealthy members of the Jewish community of Cyrene gave information to the governor Catullus against the weaver Jonathan, guilty of having planned an exodus of the Cyrenean Jews into the Libyan desert.[1] In that case their measure of self-preservation did not help the notables very much, probably because the Roman officials had already detected the affair, though to be sure Josephus denies it. There can be little doubt that Pilate would have held the Jewish hierarchy responsible for the proclamation of Jesus as king of the Jews, had they not betimes decidedly and unambiguously dissociated themselves from the dangerous undertaking. Thus driven into a corner, the high priests could not but inform the Romans as quickly as possible. This information ($\mu\dot\eta\nu\nu\sigma\iota\varsigma$, *libellus*), whether written or oral, must have contained not only the name and the charge [2] ($a\"\iota\tau\iota o\nu$), but also, to facilitate arrest, an *iconismus* of the accused. Name, charge and $\epsilon\dot\iota\kappa\dot\omega\nu$ [3] formed then, along with the offer of a reward, the essential contents of what in modern parlance we should call the writ or warrant of arrest, issued on receipt of the information and publicly posted up in numerous copies. Hence we hear of several $\epsilon\dot\iota\kappa\dot o\nu\epsilon\varsigma$ or $\dot\epsilon\kappa\tau\nu\pi\dot\omega\mu\alpha\tau\alpha$ of Jesus made by order of Pilate.

Curiously enough, nobody seems to have noticed so far that such warrants of arrest against Jesus, issued by the Jewish high priests immediately before the passover of his execution, are clearly mentioned in so many words in the fourth gospel (xi. 55 ff.) :
' And the Jews' passover was nigh at hand. . . . Then sought they for Jesus . . . the high priests [4] had even issued warrants [5]

[1] *B.J.*, vii. 439.   See also *B.J.*, ii. 342.

[2] Thus in the forged ' Acts of Pilate,' James, *op. et loc. cit.*

[3] *Digest*, xi. 4. 1, 8a—measures prescribed for arresting *fugitivi* ($\delta\rho\alpha\pi\epsilon\tau\alpha\dot\iota$): ' eorumque nomina et cuius se quis esse dicat ad magistratus afferantur, ut facilius adgnosci et percipi fugitivi possint. Notae autem et cicatrices verbo contineantur.'

[4] The words following, 'and the Pharisees,' are evidently misplaced. A political party or religious sect is certainly not a body entitled to issue orders or warrants for arresting an offender against the law. These words, ' the Pharisees,' are obviously a marginal gloss referring to v. 55 : ' and they spake among themselves standing in the sanctuary, " What think ye, that he will not come to the feast ? " '

[5] "$\delta\epsilon\delta\dot\omega\kappa\epsilon\iota\sigma\alpha\nu$ $\dot\epsilon\nu\tau o\lambda\dot\alpha\varsigma$"; var. ' *a* warrant,' " $\dot\epsilon\nu\tau o\lambda\dot\eta\nu$," meaning either *the* warrant of arrest or the numerous *copies* of it that were broadcast.

that if any man knew where he were, he should denounce [1] (him) that they might arrest [2] him.'

In ancient as in modern times such public notices contain as full and complete a description as possible of the person 'wanted.' For a good example the reader may compare the following writ,[3] relating to two fugitive Alexandrian slaves accused of theft in the year 145 B.C. : [4]

'On the 25th of *Epiphi* a servant of Aristogenes, (son) of Chrysippus, delegate of Alexandria, has escaped (2nd hand : in Alexandria). His name is Hermon, otherwise Nilus : by race a Syrian of Bambyce : age about eighteen years : of medium height, beardless, straight-legged, with a dimple in the chin, a mole to the left of his nose, a scar above the left angle of his mouth, tattooed on the right wrist with foreign characters. He has with him a string-purse (δέσιν) with three minas of gold, ten cowry-shells,[5] an iron ring on which hangs a flask of oil and bath-scrapers, around the body an overcoat and a girdle. Whoever brings back this fellow shall receive two ta(lents) of brass (2nd hand : 3000 . . .). If he is denounced after having reached the asylum of a sanctuary, one ta(lent) (2000 . . .); if shown to be in the hands of a solvent and responsible person, three ta(lents) (2nd hand : 5000 . . .). Information may be given [6] by any one to the chief magistrate's officers. His companion in flight is Bion, a slave of Callicrates, one of the chief ministers at court : short of stature, broad-shouldered, bow-legged, grey-eyed. He also has gone off with a cloak and a child's jacket and a woman's toilet-case worth six talents and . . . of brass (2nd hand : 5000 . . .). Whosoever brings him back shall receive the same amount as for the above-named. Information to be given concerning him also at the chief magistrate's.'

The small size of the sheet and the writing, far from obtrusive, prove that the papyrus was not intended to be posted up on a wall. Clearly we have here merely the official model for the *albi proscriptio*, the copy written in a public place on a white surface with black and red letters,[7] as well as for the proclamatio (κήρυγμα) by the public town-crier, a convenient procedure for publishing the personal description of fugitive slaves, known from the pages of Petronius [8] and Lucian.[9] Let us now compare with this genuine

---

[1] μηνύσῃ : cp. below, note 6.
[2] πιάσωσιν, the legal term for 'arrest' (see *Papyr. Lond.*, 46. 172, " κλέπτην π." = 'arrest a thief,' and cp. *Acts* xii. 4).
[3] Papyr. Par. 10 (Graec. 2333) in the Louvre, P. M. Meyer, *Jurist. Papyr.*, No. 50.
[4] Cf. Pl. xxix.
[5] πίνας, mother-of-pearl shells, an interesting proof that shell-money was used for small change in Ptolemaic Egypt.
[6] μηνύειν ; cp. μήνυσις, above, pp. 398 l. 33. 402 l. 21, 443 l. 17.
[7] Quint., xii. 3. 11 : ' si ad album et rubricas transtulerunt.'
[8] *Sat.*, 97.
[9] *Fugitivi*, 27.

and certainly typical warrant the following text of the so-called 'Letter of Lentulus':

'There has appeared in these times and still is (at large) **a man, if it is right to call** (him) **a man, of** great[1] **virtue, called Christ whose name is Jesus, who is said by the gentiles to be a prophet of truth,** whom his **disciples call Son of God,**[2] **raising the dead and healing all diseases : a man of stature tall,** medium, i.e. **fifteen palms and a half**[3] and sightly (*statura procerus mediocris et spectabilis*), **having a** venerable **face, which beholders might** love and **dread, having hair** of the colour of an unripe hazel (*nucis avellanae praematurae*) and smooth almost to the ears, but from the ears down corkscrew curls (*circinos crispos*) somewhat darker-coloured (*caeruliores*)[4] and more glistening, waving downwards from the shoulders, **having a parting on the middle of his head after the manner of the Naziraeans,** a brow smooth and most serene, **with a** face without a wrinkle or **spot,** beautified by a (moderately) ruddy colour;[5] **with nose** and mouth there is no fault whatever. **Having a beard** copious but **immature** (*at impuberem*), of the same colour as the hair (and) not long but **parted** (*bifurcatam*) **in the middle. Having a simple and mature aspect,** with blue eyes of varying hue (*variis*) and bright (*claris existentibus*). In rebuke terrible, in admonition bland and amiable. Cheerful, yet preserving gravity : he sometimes wept,[6] but never laughed.[7] In stature of body tall and erect (*propagatus et rectus*) : having hands and arms delectable to the sight. In converse grave, sweet and modest, so that justly according to the prophet was he called beauteous **above the sons of men.**[8]

'**For he is the king of** glory, upon whom angels desire to look, at whose beauty sun and moon marvel, the **saviour of the world,** the author of life : to him be honour and glory for ever, Amen.'

It has long been seen that we have here no letter or official report of a governor to the emperor (even the forger did not so regard it), still less an *epistula ad Romanos*, as one MS. entitles it, since both the address and the closing salutation are wanting, which the forger of the Pilate letters, for instance, was clever enough to insert. The so-called 'letter' is in reality a 'hue-and-cry' notice. Whether the Romans had an expression such as 'epistula requisitoria,' or the like, for such a writ, I do not know :

---

[1] *magnae*, corr. from *magicae* ; cf. below, pp. 410₂, 424₂, and above, p. 52 (first lines), on μάγον changed into μέγαν in Lucian.

[2] Here the old printed edition of the epistle of Lentulus, quoted as *h* by von Dobschütz, adds : '*sed filius eius unigenitus erat.*'

[3] Thus the lost MS. of Goldast.

[4] Lit. 'more bluish.' Evidently the forger had before his eyes a picture in which, by contrast with the light yellow colour of the hair, the shades looked indeed bluish.

[5] See below, p. 425 n. 17.

[6] *flevit . . . risit*. The forger inadvertently lapses into the past tense, though the letter purports to be taken as the description of a person still living !

[7] Cf. the silly statement that Plato never laughed, Diog. Laërt., iii. 26.

[8] *Ps.* xlv. 3. Cp. above, p. 384 n. 2, ὑπὲρ ἄνθρωπον.

PLATE XXIX

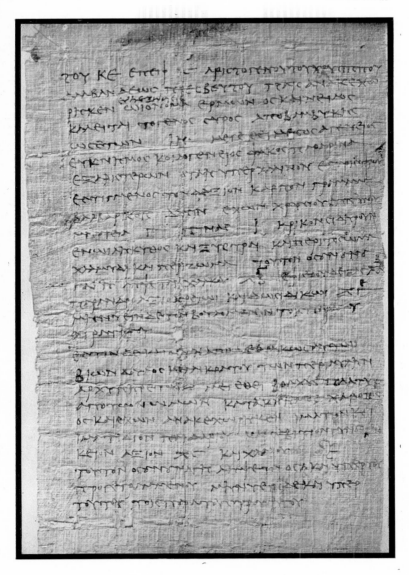

WARRANT FOR THE ARREST OF TWO THIEVES AT LARGE
GIVING THE HUE AND CRY OF THE FUGITIVES

(PAPYRUS IN THE LOUVRE, PARIS NO. 10 GRAEC. 2333)

'nota' or 'nota de forma' is more likely to have been the official phrase.[1] Anyhow, since the Latin translation was only made in the late Middle Ages, no stress can be laid on that point. The *genuine* writ or warrant necessarily bore a precise date, showing the day and month of issue, as in the Alexandrian papyrus quoted above. By the vague introductory ' istis temporibus ' without any previous and more exact statement of time, the document betrays its character as an *extract from an historical narrative*, as indeed it is, since it is of course not the genuine warrant but an extract from Josephus, whose description of Jesus according to the genuine judicial act, or rather the extracts from it in the *commentarii* of Emperor Tiberius, the forger utilized.

None the less, the opening words, 'apparuit temporibus istis et adhuc est,' are very well suited to a public notice,[2] and correspond closely to the opening of the genuine poster above mentioned : ' On the 25th of the month of Epiphi a slave has gone off, named,' etc. This suggests the possibility that Josephus himself made use of the copy of the warrant which he or his collaborators found in the official papers of the imperial archives.

' NOMEN FUGITIVI ET CUJUS SE ESSE DICAT '—BEN PANDARA

Where the papyrus warrant has 'whose name is Hermon, otherwise Neilos,' the Lentulus letter reads, 'whose name is Jesus called the Christ.'[3] On the other hand, the reader of the Slavonic Josephus, in the passage previously quoted,[4] will note with astonishment that the name of Jesus does not occur in it at all. True, Josephus is ignorant of the names of a score of other personages mentioned by him in a similar connexion.[5] But in this particular case the name must have been mentioned, because we find it used without further explanation in the passages to be discussed below[6] on the imprecatory inscription against Jesus in the temple, and—in some of the MSS.—also in the exposition of the Shiloh oracle, to say nothing of its undoubted occurrence in the *Antiquities*.[7] The story in the *Halōsis* is indeed so carelessly put together that in the crudely connected excerpts from the more

---

[1] On the *litterae formatae*, cf. below, pp. 444 f.
[2] ' There has appeared in these (*istis*, not *his*) days and still is (in the neighbourhood) a man,' etc. This interpretation is, of course, nothing more than a conjecture, for there is, naturally, no difference between the narrative style of the historian and that of the police officer, who also begins his document with the story of the fugitive's crime.
[3] Cf. above, p. 404.
[4] Cf. above, pp. 383 f.
[5] E.g. the Samaritan prophet (*Ant.*, xviii. 4. 1) and the Egyptian impostor (*B.J.*, ii. 13. 5).
[6] Cf. p. 548 n. 2.
[7] xx. 200, xviii. 63.

extensive originals the name of a person is not always mentioned on his first introduction, but suddenly makes its appearance later on in the narrative. Thus we read in ii. 169 :

' Now after that there was sent by Tiberius to Judaea a governor who secretly by night brought an image of the emperor into Jerusalem and set it up in the city.'

Then in § 170 we hear, with a change of subject :

' and when it was morning the Jews saw it,' etc.

Only in § 171, after two further changes of subject, is Pilate's name mentioned. It would therefore be practically the same phenomenon on a larger scale if Jesus were not named in this section though his name is introduced without a proper explanation in one of the later books. Had we, then, no further clue, we should perhaps have to be content with this explanation of the certainly remarkable anonymity of the wonder-worker crucified by Pilate.

But, since we have been able to show that the Lentulus letter is so closely dependent upon this section of Josephus, we should no doubt be justified in assuming the name of Jesus to have stood originally in the *Halōsis* itself, as it does in the Greek *Antiquities* and in the Hebrew *Josippon*, the more so because it cannot very well have been missing on a writ of indictment such as has been utilized by Josephus, and because the formula ὁ λεγόμενος Χριστός in *Ant.*, xx. 20, corresponds exactly to the *nominatus* or *vocatus Christus*, or *cui nomen est Christus*, in ' Lentulus.' [1]

Again, the rubric of this section in the *Halōsis*,[2] 'Of our Lord Redeemer *Jesus Christ* the Son of God and of the . . . form of his appearance and of his wonderful works,' closely corresponds to the *nominatus Christus, cui nomen est Jesus . . . quem ejus discipuli vocant filium dei, suscitans mortuos*, etc., with the personal description that follows, in the Lentulus epistle. One need, then, have no hesitation in assuming that in the Slavonic version the details of the human form of Jesus—'omnia terrenae originis signa,' to use the words of Tertullian [3]—have been suppressed together with the clause containing the wonder-worker's name.

There must, of course, have been a good reason for this— possibly a statement in the passage to which Christians took grave objection ; and one would think, perhaps, that the objection lay in the patronymic if, as has often been conjectured, Josephus, like Celsus [4] at a later date, described Jesus as the son of Pandera or Panthera. This supposition would be further supported by the

---

[1] Cf. above, p. 404 l. 4 f.   [2] Cf. above, p. 392 n. 3.
[3] Below, p. 411 the *motto*, and p. 431 l. 24.
[4] More exactly, the Jew quoted by Celsus, Origen, *C. Cels.*, i. 28.

fact that he is called ben Joseph ben Pandera in certain *Josippon* MSS., where 'ben Joseph' may be a late insertion. Yet when one looks more closely into the matter the conjecture becomes rather unlikely. For in that case the deletion of the patronymic would have been perfectly sufficient. In the second place, the statement of Epiphanius [1] to the effect that Jacob, the grandfather of Jesus, bore the surname ' Panther,' shows that Christians found no difficulty in accounting for the name ' bar Panthera,' which in itself conveyed no sinister meaning whatever. Had Josephus actually described Jesus as ' son of Panthera,' it would have been a simple and entirely satisfactory expedient for the Christian editor to make a small insertion, on the authority of Epiphanius, and write 'Jesus son of Joseph the son of Jacob Panthera,' [2] instead of deleting the whole clause. Lastly, there is good reason to doubt that the patronymic ' bar Panthera ' has any historical foundation.

Now, it has indeed been shown by Dr. Deissmann [3] that the name ' Panther' applying to persons of either sex is found quite frequently among Syrians of this period and among these social strata. For example, at Bingerbrück was found the tombstone of an archer named Tiberius Julius Abdes [4] Pantera, born at Sidon in Phoenicia and serving in a Roman cohort transferred to Germany in A.D. 9,[5] and there is a possibility that this was the soldier referred to by Celsus and in Jewish tradition. The old hypothesis that the story of this Pantera as the ' wonder-worker's ' father was the Jewish answer to the Christian myth of the parthenogenesis lacks a sound basis, because the Greek word παρθένος does not appear to exist as an Aramaic loan-word, and thus it would be difficult to explain the assumed corruption of *bar Parthena* > *bar Panthera*. Rather than the myth of the parthenogenesis, the claim of Jesus and his family to be descended from King David may have induced the Jews to insinuate that he was nothing but the bastard son of a Roman, i.e. of an enemy of the Jews. This could be done by some ignorant fanatic through an identification (based on a glaring anachronism) of Jesus' mother Mirjam with the priest's daughter Mirjam barth Bilga, a renegade who had married a soldier of the Seleucid army.[6] It must be admitted that this conjecture does not account for the name *Pantera*, but it could perhaps be argued that such a person was actually known to have been on intimate terms with Jesus' family. Still, I personally

[1] *Haeres*, 78.
[2] Cf. above, p. 99 n. 2, the text of the Hebrew *Josippon*.
[3] *Oriental. Studien.*: *Festsch. f. Th. Nöldeke*, Giessen, 1906, p. 871 *sqq.* ; *Licht vom Osten*, Tübingen, 1923, p. 57 n. 4.
[4] =' Servant of Isis,' an obviously pagan name.
[5] Pl. xxx. The stone is now in the Museum at Kreuznach.
[6] *T. Sukka*, iv. 28 ; *B. Sukka*, 56b ; *J. Sukka*, v. 7.

believe that the true explanation must be sought in a different direction.

It is to be noted that the Jewish sources always use the form *Pandera* (not *Pantera* or *Panthera*) of the name. Now, Pandaros in the *Iliad*[1] is the person who breaks the armistice confirmed by solemn oaths and hurls a lance at Menelaus, in punishment of which crime he was himself hit by a lance in the mouth and his tongue severed at the root. Hence the name for people of his type,[2] just as Judas and Benedict Arnold have become similarly proverbial in designating the traitor class. The expression 'Pandar's voice' occurs in a hitherto unexplained midrash,[3] and may therefore be supposed to have been familiar to the Jews of the period. *Ben Pandara,* ' son of Pandarus,' ' Pandarus *redivivus,*' was then a not unfitting heinous designation of the man who, by his triumphal entrance into Jerusalem, had broken the truce existing between Romans and Jews ever since the end of the war of Varus (4 B.C.), and who had thus revived the Zealot uprisings which, in the eyes of a Josephus and his class, finally led to the destruction of Jerusalem and of the Temple. The late Amoraean R. Ḥisda was at all events the first to regard Pandera as the physical father of Jesus ; but at that time the historical connexions had already disappeared from man's memory. I believe it out of the question, therefore, that Josephus could have known the patronymic *ben Pandara*, and the cause leading to the deletion of the sentence in question must have been quite different.

Thus, to my mind, there remains but one possibility accounting sufficiently for such a deletion, and that is the fact that the whole section would have provoked the censor's wrath because it connected the name of Jesus with an insurrectionary movement. So it was deemed preferable simply to omit the name. If anybody still objected, it was he who suggested such a connexion and who was therefore guilty of blasphemy. The Jewish readers, on the other hand, knew very well who was meant, even with the crucial name omitted.[4] The deletion is then most probably the work of a Jewish owner who thus chose the lesser of two evils as a measure of self-protection.

---

[1] iv. 93 ff.

[2] Dio Chrysostom, 74, § 400 R ; *Schol. Demosth.*, xxiv. 121.

[3] *Gen. r.*, sect. 50, 49d ; Levy, *Neuhebr. Wörterb.*, iv. 305b, s.v. *Qala Pandar* ; Strack-Billerbeck, i. 574, § 1 : there were five judges in Sodom—'Vomiter of Lies,' ' Master of Lies,' ' Master of Wickedness,' ' Perverter of Justice,' ' Pandar's Voice.' The reader will remember that ' pander ' means ' procurer ' in English, hence the pimp Pandarus in the story of Troilus and Cressida (especially characteristic in Chaucer's treatment ; Th. Gaster) ; also *panderism* and the verb ' to pander ' ; all this derived from Boccaccio, who was familiar with the ancient Greek term and uses it in the *Decameron*.

[4] On the deletions of the name of Jesus in the Hebrew *Josippon*, cf. above, p. 94 n. 2.

PLATE XXX

TOMBSTONE OF AN ARCHER, TIB. JUL. ABDES PANTERA

BORN IN SIDON, PHOENICIA, HAVING SERVED IN A COHORT TRANSFERRED FROM SYRIA TO THE RHINE
IN A.D. 9. FOUND NEAR BINGERBRÜCK, NOW IN KREUZNACH, MUNICIPAL MUSEUM

'Qui dicitur a gentibus "Filius Dei"'

The clause which follows in the Lentulus letter after the words 'Jesus nominatus Christus,' to wit, 'qui dicitur a gentibus propheta veritatis, quem ejus discipuli vocant filium Dei,' is clearly akin to the clauses of the *Halōsis* quoted above : [1]

'Some said of him, that our first lawgiver Moses was risen from the dead and was now again displaying many cures and arts,[2] but others thought that he was sent from God.'

The phrase *propheta veritatis* clearly refers to a definite idea characteristic of the Jewish-Christian circle in which the 'Preaching of Peter' used by the author of the pseudo-Clementine writings [3] originated. This idea may be summed up as follows. In every age only one 'true prophet'[4] arises, and Jesus was this true prophet. It is not a heathen but a Jewish-Christian or Jewish-Gnostic idea, to be found among the Samaritans, Elkesaites, Mandaeans, Manichaeans, and finally in Islam ; further, though independently of this group, in Zoroastrianism.[5] On the other hand, it is quite foreign to Western thought in the Middle Ages, a fact which should be noted by those who regard the 'Lentulus letter' as a thirteenth-century forgery. If the word 'veritatis' is wanting in some MSS., it must be a later interpolation, so that Jesus was originally described simply as 'the prophet,' referring either to the well-known belief that he was a reincarnation of one of the prophets of old, or else to the promised prophet of *Deut.* xviii. 15.

The idea in question, I repeat it, is not heathen but thoroughly Jewish, or, rather, characteristic of a primitive Ebionite type of Jewish Christianity. Conversely, the conception that a man of extraordinary eminence, gifted with supernatural powers, must be a son of some god was specially current among the Greeks for whom Josephus' *Polemos* was written. It seems unmistakable, therefore, that the clause as it now stands has arisen through an intentional transposition of the genuine text of Josephus, which must have stated just the reverse, viz. 'who is called by (some) Greeks a "son of God," but whom his disciples call the prophet of truth.'

The first of these two statements, with its highly valuable evidence of the Hellenistic origin of this un-Jewish and mythical idea of a genuine 'son of God'—an idea not to be derived from the familiar adoptionist passage in the Second Psalm—was, in the eyes

[1] Cf. p. 384 ll. 7 ff.
[2] On this notion, cf. App. XXII., below, p. 620.
[3] *Hom.*, viii. 10, iii. 21. 11, xii. 29.
[4] The 'reliable prophet' ($\pi\rho\omega\phi\eta\tau\eta\varsigma\ \pi\iota\sigma\tau\acute{o}\varsigma$) of 1 *Macc.* xiv. 41 ; cf. iv. 46.
[5] Walter Bauer, *Joh. Evang.*[2], p. 31, to *John* i. 21.

of Christians believing this doctrine to be based upon apostolic tradition, as objectionable as the further statement that the disciples, the leading contemporary witnesses, saw in Jesus no more than a prophet, or at most *the* prophet foretold by Moses. Consequently, the whole clause [1] was deleted by the Christian editor of Josephus, whilst the more adroit and less ruthless forger of the Lentulus letter had recourse to a mere transposition, thus producing a thoroughly acceptable and apparently sensible text. For the disciples of a later period reading and appreciating the Fourth Gospel, Jesus *was* the Son of the Father, to be known only through him; and it was then of common knowledge that Hellenism, too, believed in prophets :

' The Hellenistic narrative literature took it for granted that such men could foresee the future, read the thoughts of those whom they met, heal the sick, and even raise the dead for a moment or for longer. In the pagan world the honourable title for them was " prophet," the contemptuous one " sorcerer " (γόης).' [2]

According to the *Assumption of Moses*, an apocalypse of the date of the War of Varus, the prophet predicted in *Deut.* xviii. 15 would be the ' divine prophet for all the world,' that is, for both Jews and Gentiles. In transposing the clauses the forger correctly assumed the idea of the Messiah to be meaningless to heathen in the time of Jesus. In the eyes of Romans like the centurion of Capernaum, the Syrophoenician woman, the Greeks in Jerusalem who ' wanted to see Jesus,' [3] he was a ' son of God,' a hero or demigod like Pythagoras, the son of Apollo and Parthenis, or a god wandering on earth in human form, such as Paul and Barnabas were mistaken for by the people of Lystra. If such conceptions were applied to a political leader they would seem to be a very real danger for the Roman government, not only in Judaea but throughout Syria, and it is therefore perfectly natural that they should be mentioned in the indictment of Jesus and included in the warrant for his arrest.

Even the mention of the most stupendous of miracles attributed to Jesus, ' suscitans mortuos, sanans (omnes) [4] languores,' [5] can without hesitation be imputed to the genuine text of Josephus, provided they are regarded as representing the *opinion of the disciples* [5] concerning the prophet in whom *they* believe. Just as

---

[1] Its authenticity is supported by a passage in the *Testimonium Flavianum* which it serves to explain : ' many of the Jews and many also of the Greek nation he drew away after him.'

[2] Reitzenstein, *Hellenistische Mysterienreligionen*, p. 13 (3rd ed., Leipzig, 1927, p. 26).

[3] *John* xii. 21.   [4] Wanting in many MSS.

[5] This is a Jewish formula : God is called ' healer of the suffering . . . who quickens the dead ones ' in the *Shmon'esre*-Prayer (Th. Gaster).

the resurrection of Jesus is mentioned by Josephus in the *Testimonium* in *oratio indirecta* as the opinion of the disciples,[1] so here, without committing himself, he must have spoken with some detail of these astonishing and mighty wonders of the 'wonder-worker.' Otherwise it would be difficult to understand why the marginal rubric quoted above [2] should entitle this paragraph as we have seen, adding ' and of his miracles.' In the extant text of Lentulus there is a striking incongruity between the accusative 'quem ejus discipuli vocant' and the following nominatives, 'suscitans . . . sanans.' This may naturally be explained as due to a corrector who wished to make Josephus himself attest what the latter merely reports as attested by the disciples, and therefore altered the accusative of an indirect statement into the nominative of a direct one. The genuine archetype of this passage accordingly ran thus :

'who is called by (some) Greeks a son of God, but whom his disciples call the prophet (of truth), a raiser of the dead and healer of all diseases.'

Therewith evidently ends the brief *αἴτιον* prefixed to the warrant, unless the words of the final doxology, ' he is the king of glory . . . the saviour of the world,' [3] be considered as part of the original accusation preserved in the spurious *Acts of Pilate*, to wit, ' *he says he is a king*,' etc.[4] Then follows the *iconismus* proper.

THE GENUINE PEN PORTRAIT OF ' JESUS WHO IS CALLED THE CHRIST.' HIS STATURE

'. . . omnia terrenae originis signa et in Christo fuerunt. Haec sunt quae illum Dei filium celavere non alias tantum modo hominem existimatum, quam ex humana substantia corporis.'   TERTULLIAN, *De Carne Christi*, c. 9, P.L. ii. 772.

The warrant for the arrest of the thievish slave Hermon surnamed Neilos [5] gives the lad's approximate age immediately after the charge. A corresponding statement is wanting in the ' Lentulus letter,' doubtless because the forger knew no more about the age of Jesus than he did of the precise date of the document he interpolated. Josephus himself, and, we may therefore assume,

[1] Above, p. 55.
[2] Cf. p. 392 n. 3.
[3] It should be noted that the term ' saviour of the world ' (*σωτὴρ κόσμου*) is a well-known official title of Hellenistic kings and the Roman emperors (Wilh. Weber, *Untersuchungen z. Gesch. d. Kaisers Hadrian*, Tübingen, 1907, pp. 225 f., 229). The words ' *praeter filios hominum* ' in the quotation from *Ps.* xlv. 3 (above, p. 404 n. 8) are strongly reminiscent of the phrase about Jesus' appearance only being "*ὑπὲρ ἄνθρωπον*." They may well be a clever alteration of that objectionable sentence.
[4] M. R. James, *Apocr. N.T.*, p. 96 l. 20. Cp. above, pp. 402 n. 2, 401 n. 8.
[5] Cf. above, p. 403.

the genuine *Acta,* appear to have been equally in the dark on this subject. As a matter of fact, no one of his contemporaries or of the following generation seems to have had any definite information on this point, and he himself appears, as the Gospels state, to have met most questions with silence.[1] Thus the gap in the warrant is best explained, for in the case of Bion, Hermon's companion in flight, instead of the exact age we find only a statement of the general impression which the informer had obtained as to the criminal's approximate age. A corresponding statement occurs in the Lentulus letter, ' aspectum habens simplicem et maturum,' where *maturum* is to be translated by ' elderly.' Such an impression agrees pretty well with the remark of the Jews to Jesus, ' Thou art not yet fifty years old,' etc.[2]

The clause in question, besides, does not stand in the right place, namely at the head of the *iconismus,* and the same is true of the statement inserted in the middle of the appended character-sketch, ' in statura corporis propagatus et rectus,' which likewise belongs to the beginning, where in fact we find, at the head of the whole description, ' homo quidem statura procerus mediocris.' Such transpositions generally betray the hand of a copyist who erroneously incorporated marginal notes into the text and at the wrong place.

But aside from such transpositions, we are facing, in this text, a number of outright alterations which cannot be the consequence of mere scribal blunders. For example, the incompatibility of ' statura mediocris '[3] (medium height) and ' procerus ' (exceedingly tall) is obvious, though the ignorant scribe may have been naïve enough to interpret the phrase to mean ' mediocriter procerus.' Similar contradictions will have struck the reader in the quotations from the anti-iconoclast polemists quoting from Josephus, and discussed in a previous chapter.[4] Thus Andrew of Crete in the same breath says that Jesus was bent, or even crooked (ἐπίκυφος), and well grown (εὐήλιξ).[5] Evidently he interpreted the phrase to mean that Jesus was by nature well grown but stooping by habit. Similar contradictions occur with regard to Jesus' hair, described both as rich and curly (οὐλόθριξ) and at the same time as scanty (ὀλιγόθριξ).[6] The same type of inconsistency occurs in the Lentulus letter with regard to Jesus' beard, said to have been both ' copiosa ' and ' impuber.'[7] Less striking, though

---

[1] *Luke* xxiii. 12 ; *Mark* xv. 5 ; *John* xix. 9.

[2] *John* viii. 57. The statement that Jesus was forty-six years old is based on a rabbinical interpretation of *John* ii. 20 *sq.* The thirty years in *Luke* (cf. above, p. 293 n. 1) are nothing but the thirty years of David when he became king of Israel, and of Joseph when he became viceroy of Egypt, transferred to the Messiah *ben David* and *ben Joseph.*

[3] Cf. *B.J.*, vi. 169.   [4] Cf. above, pp. 393 ff.   Cf. below, p. 619, App. xxi.

[5] Cf. above, p. 393 nn. 7 and 8.   [6] Cf. below, p. 619 ll. 11, 17, 23.

[7] See above, p. 404 l. 17.

quite unmistakable, is the contradiction between the epithet σύνοφρυς (or 'communiter ciliatus'), i.e. with his eyebrows meeting above the nose, and the following εὐόφθαλμος ('bene oculatus'), that is, with kindly eyes or with a kind glance. For it is to be noted that eyebrows meeting above the nose indicate a vampire in Greece, a werewolf in Scandinavia, an 'evil eye' in many different parts of the world,[1] notably in Palestine.[2]

This circumstance explains the words of the Lentulus letter, 'vultum habens . . . quem possent intuentes formidare,' i.e. a face from which spectators might shrink. No doubt, vultum was followed by 'communiter ciliatum,' according to the description in Vincent of Beauvais, going back to Josephus.[3] Christians naturally took exception to the implication involved, and thus we find, in the Byzantine homily mentioned above,[4] the epithet σύνοφρυς replaced by εὔοφρυς, 'with good' or 'beautiful eyebrows,' whilst the Legenda Aurea has 'bene superciliatus.' Another substitution which easily suggested itself was the epithet εὐόφθαλμος, 'with good eyes,' often added to σύνοφρυς, just as the Legenda Aurea adds the quite superfluous 'bene oculatus' to the already improved 'bene superciliatus.'

Lastly, in the Lentulus letter the 'communiter ciliatum' is omitted altogether, and to the ominous 'quem possent intuentes formidare' there is appended—quite in keeping with the erotic attraction of beautiful eyes darkened by strong and therefore meeting eyebrows [5]—'et diligere.' [6]

It may, then, be regarded as proved that the personal description of Jesus in the Halōsis similarly underwent the usual 'corrections' at the hands of Christian copyists and readers with a view to embellishment. A tentative restoration of the text must therefore clearly start from the principle that the lectio difficilior, i.e. the one which would give offence to believing Christians and to their Hellenistic ideal of male beauty, must be retained.

Following this principle and taking up the significant details one by one, we encounter first the indication regarding his age, 'in appearance elderly,' completely opposed to the traditional thirty years of Luke.[7] Both statements could be harmonized by supposing that Jesus looked much older than he actually was. This detail may therefore be regarded as most probably genuine.

Statura mediocris, found in the 'Lentulus letter,' is, as we have

[1] Seligmann, Zauberkraft des Auges, Hamburg, 1922, p. 260 ; Thorpe, Northern Mythology, ii. 169.
[2] Einszler, Zeitsch. d. Deutsch. Palaest. Vereins, xii. p. 201.
[3] Cf. above, p. 394 n. 6.   [4] Cf. p. 395 n. 6.
[5] Cf. Tennyson's 'charm of married brows.'
[6] The addition may possibly reflect the term ἀγαπήσαντες of the Testimonium; cf. above, p. 69₂₁.
[7] iii. 23.

seen, irreconcilable with *procerus*. Goldast's now lost MS. of the 'Lentulus letter' had '*xv. palmorum et medii*,' which, more or less in harmony with the epithet τρίπηχυς occurring in a letter of certain Oriental bishops [1] to the Emperor Theophilus, as well as in a Byzantine homily in defence of iconolatry,[2] and perfectly in keeping with Josephus' general phraseology,[3] does not at all correspond to the average height of a man, as was the opinion of Prof. v. Dobschütz,[4] but falls far short of it.[5]

Since the ell or cubit in most systems is equivalent to a foot and a half,[6] τρίπηχυς would give us a height of four feet and a half, considerably below average. If, with G. F. Hill,[7] we follow the statements of Julian of Ascalon concerning the measures in use in the Byzantine province of Palestine, and assume that the cubit (πῆχυς) is the 'royal cubit' of the Egyptian system, that is, a little more than nineteen inches, the total would be about fifty-eight inches. If instead we adopt the simple ell, the total will amount to about fifty-four inches, truly a pigmy height. If we adopt the statement of the Goldast MS., fifteen palms and a half will give us a height varying between forty-seven and fifty-two inches. At all events, we now understand the following statement, μικρὸν ἐπικε-κυφώς, 'slightly dwarfed,' certainly not the work of Christian forgers, for the later Church naturally pictured its founder as a man of stately height.[8] The word 'procerus' of the 'Lentulus letter' corresponds to the statements of Nicephorus Callistou [9] representing Jesus as 'seven spans high according to the royal or surveyor's standard' (σπιθάμαι βασιλικαί or γεωμετρικαί), and of Epiphanius Monachus [10] giving him a height of six feet. All this is of course in agreement with the well-known tendency of the Byzantine clerks to depict Jesus as a man of commanding majesty. That Jesus was below medium height is in any case the opinion of Tertullian,[11] Celsus,[12] and the *Acta Johannis Leucii*.[13]

To these documents must be added a number of Syrian testimonies collected and admirably commented upon by Dr. Rendel

---

[1] v. Dobschütz, *op. cit.*, p. 303.

[2] *Ibid.*, p. 246.

[3] Cf. τρίπηχυς, *B.J.*, v. § 193 ; ἐπτάπηχυς, *Ant.*, xviii. § 103, is probably misread for ἑπτάπους, since even a giant cannot be seven ells high.

[4] *Op. cit.*, p. 297, p. 300, where he thinks that three ells are equivalent to six feet. Such large ells exist, indeed, but only in a very late metrical system. Still, this fact may help to explain why the shocking statement escaped correction.

[5] Cf. the *iconismus* of Augustus—who was *statura brevis*, five feet and two inches high—in Sueton., *Aug.*, 79.

[6] Josephus certainly has this usual cubit in view when he gives τρίπηχυς as the height of the balustrade surrounding the inner court of the temple ; cf. *B.J.*, v. § 193.

[7] *Encycl. Bibl.*, s.v. ' weights and measures,' col. 5294.

[8] Cf. above, p. 394 n. 9.   [9] Cf. above, p. 394 n. 8.   [10] Above, p. 395 n. 4.

[11] ' illud corpusculum,' *Adv. Marc.*, iii. 17.

[12] σῶμα . . . μικρὸν καὶ δυσειδές, Orig., *C. Cels.*, 55, 75.

[13] c. 89 *sq.*, ed. Bonnet, ii. 196. The work is not much posterior to Celsus.

Harris.[1] In the first place, there is a statement in the pages of Ephrem Syrus [2] (A.D. 320-79), corresponding to the above-quoted Greek authority about a measurement of ' three ells ' :

> ' God took human form and appeared in a form of three human [3] ells ; he came down to us small of stature.'

In another treatise of Ephrem, extant only in Armenian,[4] we read :

> ' Our Lord came, he appeared unto us as a man small of stature.'

Similarly we are told in the hymn entitled *The King's Manifestation*, by Theodore of Mopsuhestia, preserved only in Syriac : [5]

> ' Thy appearance (=*hezwah*), O Christ, was smaller than that of the children of Jacob,'

i.e. smaller than that of the other Israelites.

The most important piece of evidence, however—which we owe to Dr. Harris—hails from the Syrian *Acts of Thomas*, in which the Apostle Thomas constantly appears as the twin-brother of Jesus and so closely resembling him as to be mistaken for him.   In these circumstances the following paragraph is of the highest importance : [6]

> ' The Apostle lifted up his eyes and saw people raised up one upon another, that they might see him, and going up to lofty places.   And the Apostle saith to them :
> ' " Ye men who are come to the assembly of the Messiah, men who wish to believe in Jesus, take unto yourselves an example from this, that if ye do not raise yourselves up, ye cannot see me, who am little." '

Dr. Harris has rightly observed that the ' double' of Jesus, small of stature, is here thought of as in the same position as Jesus in *Luke* xix. 3, and as giving a spiritual interpretation of the relation between Christ and those who wished to see him.   The author of these Acts must therefore have understood the Lucan passage to mean 'he sought to see Jesus . . . and could not for the crowd, because he (i.e. Jesus, not Zacchaeus) was little of stature.'   The recovered text of Josephus now confirms that interpretation. There is no doubt that the author of the *Acts of Thomas* believed Jesus and his twin-brother Jude to have been both exceedingly small.[7]

---

[1] *Bull. John Rylands Libr.*, x. (1926), pp. 1-15 of the reprint.
[2] *Hymn. de eccl. et virg.*, ed. Lamy, iv. 632.
[3] I.e. expressly ' ordinary ' as opposed to ' royal ' ells.   [4] Ephrem Arm., ii. 278.
[5] *Bull. John Rylands Libr.*, ix. (1925), No. 2, July.   [6] *Acta Thom. Syr.*, p. 178.
[7] This is the reason why Jesus speaks of himself as ' the smallest (μικρότατος) in the kingdom of God ' (*Matt.* xi. 11).   Dr. Rendel Harris has not overlooked either *Matt.* vi. 27 or *Luke* xii. 25 about the impossibility of ' adding an ell to one's stature by worrying.'

Andrew of Crete [1] knows of an image of the mother of Jesus in Lydda, from which he deduces [2] that Mary, too, was no more than three ells high. There must therefore have been a tradition that the whole family of Jesus was extremely short of stature.

Now, it is very significant that modern travellers report the itinerant tribes of craftsmen mentioned before—the Ṣleb, that is, who correspond to the ancient Naṣōraeans and Rekhabites—to be indeed much smaller than the rest of the population, Bedouin and Fellaḥin. They are actually described by Sachau [3] as a pigmy people. There is nothing incredible, then, in the statement that the Rekhabite carpenter Jesus was not taller than three cubits.

In this connexion we must further consider the meaning of the epithet ἐπίκυφος, 'hunchbacked,' for μικρὸν ἐπίκυφος and ὑπόκυφος are obvious Christian modifications of the word, pointing to a fact historically only too probable. Medical science knows well that tragic form of distortion, the cyphosis of feeble adolescents, caused by hard work and long hours, a form particularly common among joiners and carpenters.[4] Immediately a peculiar light is thrown on the curious passage in *Luke* iv. 23. There, after reading from *Isaiah* lxi. 1,

> 'God hath appointed me to carry glad tidings to the *sufferers*. He hath sent me to *heal* those of broken heart, to proclaim . . . recovering of sight to the blind,'

Jesus adds the comment, 'To-day hath this scripture been fulfilled in your ears,' and forestalls an objection which he seems to see on the lips of his audience by saying : 'Doubtless (πάντως, *lit*. 'in any case') ye will say unto me this parable, "Physician, heal thyself."' The impossibility of interpreting this clause by the one following, 'Whatsoever we have heard done at Capernaum, do thou also here in thine own country,' has long been recognized. That clause belongs to the following, not to the preceding, context ; before it there is evidently missing the reply of Jesus to the anticipated objection of incredulous scoffers. Yet the fact that he foresees the retort *as a certainty* ('Doubtless ye will say') presupposes two things : first, that Jesus himself must have had some infirmity which he might mockingly be called upon to heal; and secondly, that this infirmity must have been visible to all, and so striking

---

[1] *De sanct. imag. veneratione*, Migne, *P.G.*, xcvii. 1304.

[2] He does not state how a picture can prove anything as to the size of the original. The explanation is probably to be found in our Pl. xxxi., showing a picture of Jesus drawn to scale, derived from a so-called *crux mensuralis*. Cf. v. Dobschütz, *Christusbilder*, p. 299. The Church was interested in the problem of the bodily resemblance between Jesus and his mother on account of its fight with the Docetic heresy, which denied the human body of Jesus.

[3] *Le Monde Oriental*, xvii., 1923, p. 5 n. 1.

[4] German surgeons are wont to call this kind of spinal distortion 'Schreiner-kyphose' (carpenter's cyphosis), as Prof. Hans von Baeyer kindly tells me.

PLATE XXXI

IMAGE OF JESUS WITH MEASUREMENTS
ACCORDING TO A *CRUX MENSURALIS* OF CONSTANTINOPLE

COD. LAURENT., PL. XXVa, Fº 15 Vº

SEE P. 416 NOTE 2)

that the taunt would rise to the lips of all who looked upon the speaker. Both of these conditions for this interpretation of the remark (which has certainly not been invented but preserved, thanks to the special impression it made on the physician Luke) are best fulfilled by the assumption, based on the testimony of Josephus and the Christian Church down to the eighth century, that Jesus, like Plato,[1] Kant, and Moses Mendelssohn, was ἐπίκυφος.

Nor is Jesus' answer to the scoffers very difficult to guess. Like the later Church fathers when discussing this matter, he probably pointed to the passage in *Isaiah* lii. *sq*., where the Servant of the Lord who 'shall be exalted and lifted up and shall be very high,' and at whom 'kings shall shut their mouths,' is said to have 'no form or comeliness,' crooked and shrivelled like 'a root in a dry ground,' 'a man of sorrow and acquainted with sickness, despised and rejected of men . . . smitten of God and afflicted, yet wounded for their transgressions.'[2]

In the eyes of those Jews who interpreted the songs of the *'Ebed Jahveh* as referring to the Messiah, the crooked form of the sufferer could not very well be quoted as an objection to his election as the Lord's Anointed. Does not a midrash[3] say, 'In the year-week in which the son of David comes they bring iron bars and lay them upon his neck until his form is bowed (*lit.* 'compressed') ; and he cries out and laments and his voice mounts up on high'? Does not a Jewish proverb[4] teach, 'The just must be bowed, so will he stand erect'?

Moreover, the fact that Jesus had to bear the hard fate of a deformed body may go far in helping to understand this remarkable character, which has been said[5] to fuse the most contradictory features into a transcending unity. We know all too well how frequently weak and deformed children have to suffer from the cruelty and neglect of their environment, which cannot but produce a peculiar reaction in their infantile psyche[6] of a far-reaching effect even in later life. This goes far to explain Jesus' indifference toward his parents and brothers.[7] Of a delicate constitution, such persons will suffer from insults far more than others, which throws light on the severe punishment demanded by Jesus for com-

---

[1] Cf. Plutarch, *De adul. et am. discr.*,9: *quom. adul. poet. aud. deb.* 8. Eustathius, *Opp.*, p. 553. 16 : " ὁ Πλάτων ἐπίκυφος (ἦν)."
[2] *Isaiah* lii. **13** *sqq*.   [3] *Pesiqta rabb.*, 36 (162a).   [4] *Shabbath.* **104a**.
[5] Karl Weidel, *Jesu Persönlichkeit*, Halle, 1908, endorsed by A. Schweitzer, *loc. cit.*, p. 580 f. (not trsl. in *The Quest for the Historical Jesus*) : ' King and beggar . . . revolutionary and sage, fighter and prince of peace, ruler and servant, man of action and poet, all in one.'
[6] Cf. Walter v. Baeyer, *Zur Psychologie verkrüppelter Kinder : Zeitsch. f. Kinderforsch.*, xxxiv. (1928).
[7] *John* ii. 3 *sq*. ; *Mark* iii. 33 ; *Matt.* xii. 48. Jesus never refers to his father.

paratively harmless insults such as ‘wight’ ($\dot\rho\acute\alpha\chi a$).[1] or ‘fool’[2] ($\mu\hat\omega\rho\epsilon$).

Under such circumstances it is also explainable how every ‘neighbour’ and next-of-kin, though to the weak naturally an ‘enemy,’[3] came to be included in the sphere of that all-embracing love which is the nucleus of Jesus’ teaching. For the cripple has to face the dilemma either to wrap everything into a powerful, misanthropic hatred,[4] or else to overcome this feeling of revenge by the high moral superiority[5] of a Plato, a Moses Mendelssohn, or a Kant. We know how he chose the latter of the two, and we may well imagine that it was not at Golgotha that he had the first occasion to cry out, ‘ Father, forgive them, for they know not what they do.’

Nor can it be an accident that the proportionately small number of maimed in body has furnished so many of the greatest intellects. Forced by his solitude and isolation into a contemplation of the world of the spirit and of religion, the weak and suffering finds a natural compensation for what he is denied in a conscious and devoted development of his intellectual gifts to the very limits of the powers of which the human soul is capable.[5] In the poor and deformed body of Immanuel Kant there lived thus the indomitable spirit of the greatest of the thinkers of that glorious eighteenth century and at the same time of the greatest of idealists of modern times at all events, whose dream of world-peace, though anything but Utopian, the world is so slow to realize.

In the case of Jesus the whole paradoxical thought of his being the vicarious sin-offering and world-redeemer can be best understood as the solution, proposed in the Deutero-Isaiah, of the question which had occupied Job—to wit, why it is that the innocent must suffer. If the maimed in body refuses to consider himself as forsaken by his God, as a sinner punished for some guilt[6] of which he is unconscious, he cannot but assume that there is such a thing as a vocation to suffering and believe in the inscrutable plan of salvation in which his own life and suffering are called upon

---

[1] *Ta'an*, 20b: ‘ Wight, perhaps all the people of thy city are as ugly as thyself,’ shows that the term was used as a byword for ill-favoured individuals.

[2] *Matt.* v. 22. In *Matt.* xxiii. 17, though, Jesus does not hesitate to use the same term for his opponents.

[3] The biography of the youthful Byron is an excellent case in point. In his late drama ‘ The Deformed Transformed,’ the mother says to her son, ‘ Out hunchback ! ’ As a matter of fact, the poet had never been able to forget that his own irascible mother had once called him ‘ lame-foot.’

[4] Richard III., Alexander Pope the ‘ wicked little wasp of Twickenham,’ and Pietro Aretino are good examples.

[5] The well-known humour of hunchbacks like Aesop, which opened for them their careers as court fools in the time of the Renaissance, is a peculiar manifestation of this superiority.

[6] See *John* ix. 3 about the ‘ man blind from his birth ’: ‘ neither hath this man sinned, nor his parents.’ See also below, p. 509 n. 4.

to play some part. Nothing but this conviction of being thus elected can afford him the desired compensation for his depressed and hampered self-feeling.

To seek such a compensation, a repressed nature of this type will escape from the hard and harsh reality into the realm of fairyland. The glorious day-dreams of the millennium, that time of bliss when all strife and all hate will disappear from earth, when all that is crooked (σκολιά) will be made straight,[1] find their best explanation in this peculiarity. They console the suffering and heavy-laden for the bitter reality which, in the light of the old messianic prophecies, appears only as a nightmare, promptly to be chased away by the dawn of a new day—a new, a perfect era. From just such a depressing feeling of his own bodily imperfections a Plato took over the old Orphic idea of the body as the prison of the soul, to build for himself a realm of ideas so totally different from the rationalism of a Socrates, a realm of perfection, the true home of the soul, from which all was banished that was frail and full of flaws. The 'kingdom of God' in the thought of Jesus was not much different, though less transcendental. It was the lost paradise, the garden of the desert,[2] vanished some time during the early childhood of mankind, which he proposed to bring back. Differing in this from the descendant of the old royal family of Athens,[3] Plato, who spent his whole life in pondering over the best state and tried to realize it in Sicily with the co-operation of a human ruler,[4] the Davidide Jesus, in spite of or rather because of his servile form, feels that he is himself that secret incognito king of that wonderful realm, the monarch whom God some time in the future—nay, right here and before the passing of the present generation—will transform while at the same time 'revealing' his 'kingdom.'

No doubt, the real mystery of such a mental development must be sought and found in the natural and as a rule all-powerful desire of such persons, to whom the ordinary satisfaction is denied, to be great, glorious, to achieve the superhuman, what cannot be accomplished by others, to see themselves in the rôle of the hero, the leader, the liberator—a desire which, if coupled with the inner consciousness of the Divine call, the sure sign of every genius, will

---

[1] *Luke* iii. 5.

[2] *gan 'eden* (*'eden*=Akk. *edinnu*=Sum. E-DIN=steppe, desert). The 'garden of the desert' is the fairyland-like oasis in the East where once upon a time men led the happy life of owners of palm-trees, and whence they were driven forth on account of their sins. Jesus will show the way back to those who trustingly follow him into the desert. A dying man, he still hopes to get there on that same day with the loyal λῃστής. Ideas of this sort are still alive among present-day Bedouins.

[3] According to Thrasyllos in Diog. Laërt., iii. 1, Plato's father, Ariston, was a descendant of the last king of Athens, Kodros.

[4] Cf. Plut., *De stoic. rep.*, 1043C : " κἂν (ὁ σοφὸς) αὐτὸς βασιλεύειν μὴ δύνηται, συμβιώσηται βασιλεῖ."

finally grow to overwhelming proportions. It certainly is not accidental that weak and crippled individuals have so often played a conspicuous part in revolutions.[1]

THE FACE WITHOUT COMELINESS

The description of age, stature, and height is usually followed, in these old police portraits, by a statement of the colour of the skin. This item may be omitted, however, as in the two warrants quoted above.[2] It would therefore not be surprising if the quotations made from Josephus at the time of the anti-iconoclastic controversy did say nothing about it. Fortunately, one of them [3] has preserved the word ' dark-skinned ' ($\mu\epsilon\lambda\acute{a}\gamma\chi\rho o\upsilon\varsigma$), which must be genuine, because it obviously contradicts the statement ' cum facie sine ruga et macula aliqua, *quam rubor venustat*,' which is certainly of Christian origin. The laudatory intention of the word 'venustat' and the implied comparison with King David in the ruddy countenance [4] are obvious. The ' sine macula ' probably does not correspond to a Greek $\ddot{a}\sigma\eta\mu o\varsigma$ of the genuine document ; for the Naṣōraean Jesus must of course have borne the Qenite mark of the cross on his forehead.[5] The word $\mu\alpha\kappa\rho o$-$\pi\rho\acute{o}\sigma\omega\pi o\varsigma$, ' long-faced,' and $\sigma\acute{\upsilon}\nu o\phi\rho\upsilon\varsigma$, drawn from Josephus by Andrew of Crete, are unquestionably genuine. They occur frequently in the papyri and are not of the nature of embellishments, especially in connexion with the phrase in the Lentulus letter, ' quem (*sc.* vultum) possint intuentes formidare,' which, however, as unparalleled in the papyri and unsuited to an official document, should be regarded as a malicious addition of Josephus. Similarly, the word $\dot{\epsilon}\pi\acute{\iota}\rho\rho\iota\nu o\varsigma$, ' long-nosed,' is certainly authentic, since an attempt has been made to alter it to $\epsilon\ddot{\upsilon}\rho\iota\nu o\varsigma$, ' well-nosed,' which is further enhanced in the phrase of Lentulus, ' nasi . . . nulla prorsus reprehensio.' The papyri furnish such parallels as $\dot{o}\xi\acute{\upsilon}\rho\rho\iota\nu(o\varsigma)$, $\pi\alpha\chi\acute{\upsilon}\rho\rho\iota\nu$, etc.

The classification of the nose is generally followed by a description of the hair. The statement of the ' Lentulus letter,' 'capillos habens coloris nucis avellanae prematurae' (of the colour of a half-ripe hazel-nut) 'ab auribus aliquantum ceruliores et fulgentiores' (darker and more glossy), at once betrays itself as an invention of the Christian forger, who has an idealized painted portrait of Christ before him and describes the lighter and darker

---

[1] Wuertz, *Seelenleben des Krüppels*, Leipzig, 1921, p. 24, recalls, among others, Marat. [2] Cf. above, p. 403.

[3] An anonymous scholion, v. Dobschütz, *loc. cit.*, p. 305**.

[4] " $\pi\upsilon\rho\rho\acute{a}\kappa\eta\varsigma$ $\mu\epsilon\tau\grave{a}$ $\kappa\acute{a}\lambda\lambda o\upsilon\varsigma$ " (Baσ. a, xvi. 12).

[5] Cf. above, pp. 234 n. 8, 356 n. 9. " $\ddot{a}\sigma\eta\mu o\varsigma$ " may have replaced a description of the " $o\dot{\upsilon}\lambda\acute{\eta}$."

tints with which the painter had sought to represent fair hair. For the genuine official descriptions of a person never gave the colour of the hair, clearly because in the region in question the population was dark-haired almost to a man ; neither can such a description of colour by means of a would-be poetical simile be attributed to Josephus. One might be tempted to see in this insertion the hand of a Nordic, hence of a mediaeval, forger, desirous of attributing to Jesus the characteristics of his own race ; for the Patriarch Photius [1] knows already of some iconoclasts who made fun of the various Christ portraits, representing him with the racial characters of a Roman, an Indian, a Greek, or an Egyptian. In reality, the fair hair of Jesus is no doubt due to the desire to depict him as like as possible to King David as described by Josephus,[2] where it is to be noted that David in his turn owes his fair hair to the ideal portrait of the 'sun-king' and 'world-saviour' Alexander the Great.[3] For the recovery of the true portrait of Jesus the feature of the fair hair is probably without any value, the less so because it could hardly be harmonized with the 'dark skin' mentioned above, although it must be admitted that nowadays fair hair is sometimes found among the Sleb.[4]

On the contrary, the epithet $\dot{o}\lambda\iota\gamma\dot{o}\theta\rho\iota\xi$,[5] the by no means flattering statement derived by the Byzantine writers from 'the historian,' i.e. from Josephus,[6] to the effect that Jesus was 'scantyhaired,' is certainly no Christian invention and consequently genuine. The attempt was soon made to improve this reading into $o\dot{v}\lambda\dot{o}\theta\rho\iota\xi$, 'curly-haired,' or $o\dot{v}\lambda os$, 'curly.' The scanty hair here attested is quite in keeping with the statement in the 'Lentulus letter,' corrected, it is true, by interpolation, but still preserved, on the undeveloped beard, 'barbam habens impuberem.' The Arabic Carmelite St. Élie [7] expressly notes the fact that the Sleb have only a sparse growth of beard on cheeks and chin. He does not mention the hair on the head, which in fact is concealed largely by the turban (keffîje) worn by these people.

The 'Lentulus letter' furnishes another valuable detail which cannot have been invented by a Greek, much less by a mediaeval Latin forger, for the simple reason that it presupposes a special knowledge of ancient Jewish custom, in the words ' discrimen habens in medio capite *juxta morem Nazaraeorum.*' The glossary gives us the Greek equivalents for 'discrimen,' $\dot{a}\nu\alpha\kappa\tau\dot{\epsilon}\nu\iota\sigma\mu\alpha$ or $\delta\iota\dot{a}\kappa\rho\iota\mu\alpha$, a ' parting.' ' Nazaraean ' is the form exclusively used in Jerome's *Vulgate*, and by the author of the Latin version of

---

[1] *Epistle* 64, v. Dobschütz, p. 107*.
[2] *Antiqq.*, vi. 8. 1 : ' fair . . . with blue eyes.'
[3] Aelian, *Var. Hist.*, xii. 14.
[4] St. Élie, *Al Mashriq*, i. p. 676.
[5] von Dobschütz, p. 107, No. 9a, c, g.
[6] Cf. above, p. 345 l. 4.
[7] *Al Mashriq*, i. 676.

Josephus made for Cassiodorus, to render the Greek Ναϲιραῖοϲ. 'Mos Nazaraeorum,' therefore, refers doubtless to the unshorn hair of the Nazirites, whom Josephus himself mentions as Ναϲιραῖοι .. εὐχὴν πεποιημένοι ... κομῶντεϲ καὶ οἶνον οὐ προϲφερόμενοι,[1] and whose vow in another passage is assumed to be well known.[2]

It appears from the familiar story of Samson and Delilah [3] that the Nazirites were accustomed to divide their long and burden-some crop of hair and twine it in plaits ; Samson has seven such plaits. In the Mishna treatise, *Nedarin*, 9b, mention is made of a Nazirite on a visit to the high priest Simon the Just (310-290 B.C.), who wore his *q^ewuzoth* or bunches of hair arranged like 'high hillocks' ; in *Pesiqta rabbati*, 96, we read of the hairy prophet 'Elijah as a *ba'al q^ewuzoth*, 'the man with the bundles of hair.' That Jesus wore his hair in this Nazirite fashion was also well known to the anonymous writer of the treatise, ' On the Lord's human form,' [4] who describes him as τὴν κόμην μέγαϲ (long-haired) καὶ ϲυνεϲταλμένοϲ θριξί (with plaited hair), οὖλοϲ τοὺϲ βοϲ-τρύχουϲ, ἀκερϲοκόμηϲ (unshorn), ἀϲκεπήϲ, διχῇ πρὸϲ τὸ μέτωπον τοὺϲ πλοκάμουϲ διεϲταλμένοϲ. Here the πλόκαμοι (from πλέκειν, ' plait ') are the ' plaits ' (*mahlepoth*) of the Nazirite, of the ἀκερ-ϲοκόμηϲ who leaves his hair uncut. The strong growth of hair and the curly locks (βόϲτρυχοι) like grape-clusters are introduced by the anonymous author to correct the malicious description given by Josephus, 'with little hair (but) parted in the middle after the manner of the Nazirites,' the people who had too much of it and could not otherwise tie it up. Ἀϲκεπήϲ, 'uncovered,' 'bare-headed,' under the scorching sun of Palestine can only apply to the pos-sessor of an unusually thick covering of hair ; the interpolated word may also perhaps be intended to explain that Jesus' way of wearing his hair could be known, since people generally covered their hair with a turban or the like.

Nicephorus Callistou,[5] or his source, from the statement that Jesus parted his hair ' after the manner of the Nazirites,' drew the inference that he actually observed the Nazirite vow from early youth all his life long ; ' for no razor was ever raised to his head nor hand of man save that of his mother in his infancy.' Yet that Jesus was no Nazirite is clear, although ignorant persons at an early date confused Ναζωραῖοϲ (*nosri*) with Ναϲιραῖοϲ. Men called him a ' wine-bibber ' [6] because they were surprised at a Rekhabite and one of the ' wandering folk' who defied the custom of his tribe by drinking wine, but not because as a Nazirite he had taken a vow to abstain from wine. The fashion of wearing the

---

[1] *Ant.*, iv. 72.
[2] *B.J.*, ii. 313.
[4] v. Dobschütz, *loc. cit.*, p. 305**.
[6] *Matt.* xi. 12 ; *Luke* vii. 34 (Q).

[3] *Judges* xvi. 13 *sq*.
[5] *P.G.*, cxlv. 69.

hair in this way is still that of the modern Ṣleb, who 'plaits his hair as women do,'[1] parting the plaits on either side and keeping them in position with a red band.   The statement of Lentulus that the beard also was 'in mento parum bifurcata' can hardly be genuine. The papyri afford no parallel, and there is no occasion to part a ' barba impuber ' in the middle.   I cannot recall having seen or read of any case of such foppish treatment of the beard by Syrians or Arabs.   This trait probably comes from the imagination of the same forger who described the beauteous locks, the ' capilli plani ad aures ' and the 'circini crispi,' as he saw them in some Byzantine icon ; or it may be due to an erroneous repetition and to the subsequent insertion in the wrong place of the words διάκριμα ἔχων ἐν μέσῳ.[2]

The correctness of the foregoing arguments can best be tested by examining whether the portions of the traditional description of Jesus recognized as genuine, after the exclusion of the words shown to be interpolations and forgeries, hang together and yield a significant and consistent text.   Such is indeed the case, and we have in fact recovered, as the reader will see on the following pages, a vivid and lifelike portrait of Jesus, penned with unmistakable malevolence, but on that account all the more valuable.

---

[1] St. Élie, *Al Mashriq*, p. 677.
[2] See below, p. 426, right column, after the number [46].

The Description of Jesus,

Textus restitutus	*Emendationes Christianorum*

§ 174a

* Τότε δὲ καὶ ἐφάνη ἀνήρ τις [1]

[μ|αγικ|ῆς δυνάμεως [2]] |. . . . . .| [3]　　　| 9 |　　|εγαλ| [2]

εἴγε ἄνδρα λέγειν χρὴ αὐτὸν [4]

[[7] ὃν |Ελληνες| μέν |(τινες)| υἱὸν　　|οἱ| |μαθηταὶ αὐτοῦ| [7]　　[
θεοῦ [5]

καλοῦσιν[, οἱ δὲ |μαθηταὶ αὐτοῦ| [7]　　|ἀλλὰ ἦν θεοῦ　　|Ελληνες| [7] ⎫ 9
λέγουσιν τὸν ἀληθείας προφήτην [7]　　υἱὸς μονογενής ! [6]　　⎭

νεκροὺς ἐγείρα|ντα| καὶ πάσας νόσους　　|ς|
ἰασάμενο[ν [8]].　　　　　　|ς|　　　　　　　　]

§ 174b

Καὶ [9] φύσις καὶ μορφὴ [9] αὐτοῦ
　　　　　|ἀνθρωπίνη| ἦν [10]　　|θεανδρικὴ| [11]　　|θεία| [12]

ἀνὴρ γὰρ [13] ἦν ἁπλοῦς τὴν ἰδέαν [14],

ἡλικίᾳ [15] τέλειος [16], |μελάγχρους| [17]　　|πυρράκης| [17]

---

[1] Above, p. 52 and p. 383₅.₉.　　　　[2] Above, p. 404 n. 1.
[3] On the omission of Jesus' name, cf. above, p. 405₄.₅.
[4] Above, p. 52 and p. 383₁₀. Allusion to the name *bar naša* = υἱὸς ἀνθρώπου for Jesus.
[5] = *bar laha, ben elohim* = ἄγγελος.
[6] Cf. above, p. 404 n. 2.
[7] 'Qui dicitur a gentibus propheta veritatis, quem eius discipuli vocant filium Dei,' above, p. 404₂. On the necessary transposition, cf. above, pp. 409 f.
[8] 'Suscitans mortuos, sanans omnes languores,' above, p. 404 l. 6. Eusebius, *Dem. ev.*, iii. (*P.G.*, xxii. 195-6) : "παντοίοις ἀσθενειῶν εἴδεσι καταπονουμένοις τὴν ἴασιν ἀφθόνως δωρούμενος."
[9] On καί—καί, cf. *Matt.* x. 28 : "καὶ ψυχὴν καὶ σῶμα."

Josephus, *Halōsis*, ii. §§ 174a *et seq.*

Reconstructed Original Text   *Christian Alterations*

§ 174a

At that time also there appeared
a certain [1] man

of |magic| power [2] |. . .| [3] |great| [2] |_____ 9 _____|

— if it is meet to call him a man,[4]

[7] whom |(certain) Greeks| call a son |his disciples| [7]
of (a) god,[5]   but he *was* the only-born
        son of God! [6]

but |his disciples| the true prophet [7] |the Greeks| [7]

who |is supposed to have| raised |_____ 9 _____|
dead persons

and to have cured all diseases.[8]

§ 174b

Both his nature[9] and his form[9] were
|human| : [10] |god-manlike| [11] |divine [12]|

for he was [13] a man of simple
appearance,[14]

mature [16] age,[15] |dark| skin,[17] |ruddy| [17]

---

[10] Above, p. 395 l. 17. It is not altogether impossible that here or after [47]
Josephus may have quoted as his authority the *iconismus* drawn up by order of
Pilate, and that the gnostic references quoted above, p. 398, to the εἰκόνες of Jesus
made for Pilate were in reality aiming directly at this passage in Josephus.

[11] Above, pp. 394 l. 22, 395 l. 19.   [12] Above, p. 392 n. 3, p. 395 l. 25.

[13] On the necessity of this insertion, cf. above, p. 392.

[14] ' *aspectum habens simplicem*,' above, p. 404.

[15] ' *homo quidem statura* . . .,' above, p. 404.

[16] ' *maturum*,' above, pp. 404 and 412 l. 11.

[17] Below, App. xxi. p. 620 l. 3. But '*rubor genarum modestus venustate*' above,
p. 404. Moses is said to have been πυρράκης bei Artapanus (*Fragm. Hist. Graec.*,
iii. 224); the same is said of King David in the Greek version of I *Sam.* xvi. 2.

Textus restitutus   Emendationes Christianorum

⟨⟨βραχύς⟩⟩, ⌈τρίπηχυς⌉ 20 |μέσος| 18 ⌐γα¬ 19   ⌈ἑπτὰ σπιθαμῶν⌉ 21
                                          |ἐξ ποδῶν| 24

||ἐπί|κυφος 22, ⌈μακροπρόσωπος 28, |ὑπὸ| 23   σεμνο 25   ⌊μικρὸν 27
                                          ⌈εὐήλιξ 26

||ἐπί||ῤῥινος 29 ||εὔ|| 30

σύν|οφρυς 29⌊, ὥστε οἱ ἰδόντες αὐτὸν   εὔ| 32 ⌊εὐόφθαλμος 31 |μελαν| 32

⌈φοβεῖσθαι μέλλοιεν 34   ⌈ἀγαπᾶν καὶ 33

|ὀλιγό||θριξ| 35, ⌊διάκριμα ἔχων |οὖλο| 36 ⌐ς¬ 37 ⌊χρώματος
                                  καρύου Ποντικοῦ προώρου 38

ἐν μέσῳ τῆς κεφαλῆς
κατὰ τὸ τῶν Ναζιραίων 39 ἔθος 40,

⌈πώγονι ⌊_ἀνήβῳ⌋⌊ 47.   ⌈μέτωπον λεῖον καὶ εὐδιώτατον, ἄσημον
                                  καὶ ἀῤῥυτίδωτον 41, πυρράκης μετὰ
                                  κάλλους 42, γλαυκὸς τὰ ὄμματα 43,
                                  εὔστομος 44
                                  ⌊περισσῷ 45 καὶ ⌊_θριξὶ ὁμοχρόῳ 45,
                                  διάκριμα ἔχων ἐν μέσῳ, βραχίονες καὶ
                                  χεῖρες ἰδεῖν ἥδισται 46 δακτύλους τῶν
                                  ἀχράντων χειρῶν μακροτέρους συμμέ-
                                  τρως, καὶ ἁπλῶς ὡς τῆς τεκούσης
                                  χαρακτήρ 48

18 ' statura mediocris,' above, p. 404 l. 7 and pp. 413 f.
19 ' statura procerus,' above, p. 404 l. 7 and pp. 413 f.
20 Cf. above, p. 414 nn. 1 and 3.
21 Above, p. 394 n. 9. But ' xv. palmorum et medii,' above, p. 414 l. 2, p. 404 n. 3.
22 Cf. above, pp. 416 ff.
23 Above, p. 416 l. 13 ; below, p. 619 last line.
24 Above, p. 41410.   25 Above, p. 404 l. 9.
26 Above, p. 4125.   27 Above, p. 416 l. 13.
28 Above, p. 394 n. 3.   29 Above, p. 4134.6.
30 Above, p. 395 n. 1.   31 Above, p. 413 l. 3.
32 Above, p. 413 l. 15 ; p. 420 l. 28 ; below, p. 619 l. 38.

Reconstructed Original Text	*Christian Alterations*

short| growth, |three cubits| [20] |medium| [18] |high| [19] |seven spans| [21]
tall |six feet| [24] (high)

hunchbacked,[22] |with a |long| |a little [27] [23] |well-grown,
face,[26] |venerable| [25] |erect |handsome|

a |long| nose,[29] |handsome|

|eyebrows |meeting above the |goodly [32] black [32] | ℈ |
nose| [30] ,| |with a good eye [31]

so that the spectators| could take |could love him and [33]
fright [34]

with |scanty| hair| [35], |(but) having |curly| [38] |of the colour of unripe
                                                    hazel-nuts,[38]

a line in the middle of the head   with a smooth and unruffled, un-
after the fashion [40] of the Nazir-   marked and unwrinkled fore-
aeans,[39]   head,[41] a lovely red, blue eyes,[43]
                                                 beautiful mouth,[44]

and with an undeveloped |beard|.[47] |and copious [45]

                                      |of the same colour as the
                                      hair,[45] |not long, parted in
                                      the middle,[45]
                                      arms and hands full of grace,[46]
                                      the fingers of the unsullied
                                      hands of moderate length, on
                                      the whole of the same type as
                                      his mother.[48]

---

[33] Above, p. 413 n. 6.
[34] 'quem possent intuentes formidare,' cf. p. 404 l. 9.
[35] Above, p. 421₅.
[36] Above, p. 412₆.
[37] οὐλόθριξ, finally οὖλος, cf. p. 421 l. 26.
[38] Above, p. 420 l. 34.
[39] Above, p. 422 ll. 1-3.
[40] Above, p. 404 l. 14, p. 422 l. 1.
[41] Above, p. 420 n. 5.
[42] Above, p. 425 n. 17.
[43] Above, p. 421 n. 2.
[44] 'oris nulla reprehensio,' cf. above, p. 404 ll. 15 f.
[45] 'barbam copiosam capillis concoloratam,' cf. above, p. 404 l. 18 and p. 423₂.
[46] Above, p. 404 l. 24.
[47] Above, p. 404 l. 17.
[48] With these words the old *iconismus Christi* ends; cf. v. Dobschütz, p. 247.

Textus restitutus

§ 174c

ἡ μὲν ὄψις⁴⁹ αὐτοῦ ὑπὲρ ἄνθρωπον⁵⁰,|

θαύματα (γὰρ) ἐποίει παράδοξα
　　　　καὶ δυνατά⁵¹ |

πάλιν δέ, εἰς τὴν κοινὴν φύσιν⁵⁴
　　　　(αὐτοῦ)⁵⁵ ἀπίδων⁵⁶

οὔτε καλέσω (αὐτὸν) ἄγγελον⁵⁷.

Πάντα δὲ ὅσα ἐποίει ⌈τινὶ ἀοράτῳ
　　　　　　　　δυνάμει⁵⁸,⌉

λόγῳ⁵⁹ καὶ προστάγματι⁶⁰ ἐποίει.
　　　　　　[. . . .]⁶¹

Emendationes Christianorum

⌊ἀλλὰ πράξεις αὐτοῦ θεῖαι⁵²,

|διότι ἀδύνατόν ἐστιν ἐμοὶ ἄνθρωπο[ν
καλεῖν⁵³ αὐτὸν

[ϑ]

[ϑ]

§ 174d

Ἄλλοι μὲν ἔλεγον περὶ αὐτοῦ (ὅτι)
πρῶτος ἡμῶν νομοθέτης
ἀνέστη καὶ πολλὰς ἰάσεις καὶ τέχνας⁶²
παρέσχεν,
ἄλλοι δὲ ὅτι ὑπὸ θεοῦ ἀπεσταλμένος
ἐστίν, κτλ.

---

⁴⁹ Above, p. 390 l. 8.
⁵⁰ Above, pp. 384 n. 2, 389 n. 6, 390 n. 10 ; cf. Athen., v. 213b.
⁵¹ Above, pp. 384₄, 390₁₀ ; cf. Eusebius, *Dem. evang.*, iii. 6 (*P.G.*, xxii. 225).
⁵² Above, p. 390 ll. 33 f.　　　　　　⁵³ Above, p. 390 n. 10.
⁵⁴ Above, p. 384 n. 6.　　　　　　　⁵⁵ Above, p. 384 l. 4.
⁵⁶ Above, p. 390 n. 10.　　　　　　　⁵⁷ Above, p. 391.
⁵⁸ Above, p. 384 n. 7.　　　　　　　⁵⁹ Above, p. 384 n. 7.
⁶⁰ On this phrase, cf. Marmorstein, *The Quest*, 1926, p. 154 ; cf. also *Matt.*
viii. 16, and *Ant.*, xx. 5. 1, on Theudas.

Retroversion

Reconstructed Original Text	Christian Alterations

§ 174c

Only his (outer) appearance [49] was super-human] [50]

(for) he wrought surprising and striking feats [51]

Again, however, in view [56] of his [55] commonplace physique [54]

I shall not call him an angel.[57]

But everything he did through some invisible power [58]

he did through his word [59] and a phrase of command [60]

]but his deeds were divine [52]

wherefore I cannot call him a man [53]

[He claimed to be . . .[61]]

§ 174d

Others said that he was our first lawgiver

resuscitated from the dead and accomplishing

many cures and magic tricks.[62]

But others said that he had been sent by God.

But in many things he opposed the law

and did not keep the Sabbath after the manner of our fathers.

He himself did nothing shameful [63] and did not put his hand thereto, but through his word he prepared everything, etc.

---

[61] Here also there may originally have been mentioned the name of the miracle-worker, his genealogy and messianic claims.

[62] Cf. Orig., *C. Cels.*, i. 26, about Moses teaching witchery to the Jews.

[63] Cf. *Luke* xxiii. 41 ; Orig., *C. Cels.*, ii. 59, 'he has neither done *nor said* something wrong.'

As will be seen, this composite text has been obtained by n‹
‘witchery’ whatever, but by simply separating all portion›
favourable to Jesus, and therefore *a priori* to be suspected as o‹
Christian origin, from the text of the *Halōsis*, from the quotation›
from Josephus found in certain Byzantine chroniclers and th›
letter of Lentulus shown to have drawn on the text of Josephus
and by putting together the material thus left.   To believe that ‹
narrative so coherent and logical can be a mere play of accident i›
to believe the impossible.   But quite aside from this, it is well t‹
point out that, far from contradicting the Gospel narrative, thi›
text throws light on a number of hitherto unexplained passages
But if the genuineness of the portrait thus restored needs furthe›
attestation, the appended reproduction of a photograph showin≀
a group of Ṣleb will supply it.   Replace the old flint-stone gun
by hunting spears, bows,[1] and crooked throw-sticks, and, thanks t‹
the ‘immutability’ of the Orient, the picture of these short, lea›
people with their long faces and noses, their scanty beards, an‹
their peculiar dress, can still bring before us to-day the outwar‹
appearance of those Rekhabite itinerant craftsmen to whom Jesus
according to all historical and sociological considerations,[2] mus›
have belonged.

Tertullian on the ‘Marks of Jesus’ Earthly Origin ’

The portrait of Jesus drawn by Josephus as reconstructed i›
the previous chapters does not, of course, in the least correspon‹
to the traditional idealized picture of the Naṣōraean Messiah.   I›
a most striking manner a prophetic remark of Dr. Albert Schweit
zer [3] has come true : ‘ The defenders of the historicity of Jesus ’—
he said—‘ must consider carefully the import of their undertaking
. . . They have to reckon with the possibility that they defen‹
the historical claims of a personality which may turn out to b‹
quite different from what they imagined when embarking on thi›
defence.’   None of the numerous lives of Jesus, none of th‹
numerous novels written about him, none of those wildly fantastic
apocryphal stories of certain ‘ psychic ’ swindlers, in any wa≀
resembles this or can even remotely do so.   Not even the livelies›
imagination could have evoked quite such a figure, and the reade›
will, I hope, take the author’s word for it that he himself had no›
the least idea of this strange and unexpectedly lifelike portrait o›
Jesus before the completion of the patient and minute work o›
sorting out and putting together the many pieces of this puzzle.

[1] The late director of the Berlin Oriental Seminary, Eduard Sachau, sav›
them hunting with bow and arrow in Syria in 1882 (Pieper, *l.c.*, pp. 22 and 32).
[2] See above, pp. 231 ff., 322 ff., 356 n. 9.
[3] *Gesch. d. Leben Jesu Forschung*, Tübingen, 1921, p. 151 (not in the Engl›
trans. of 1911).

Yet, strange and bewildering as is this small, bent, and homely figure when first emerging from behind the veil which pious delusion has managed to weave around it for centuries, every detail agrees with the portrait of Jesus ' after the flesh ' which, though wilfully ignored by Paul,[1] was embraced by Tertullian with almost passionate affection : ' Quodcumque illud corpusculum sit,' he writes,[2] ' quoniam habitum et quoniam conspectum fuit, si *ingloriosus*, si *ignobilis*, si *inhonorabilis*—meus erit Christus.[3] Talis enim habitu et aspectu annuntiabatur : ⟨quemadmodum expavescunt multi super te, sic sine gloria erit ab hominibus forma tua⟩.[4] Sermo vere species et decor ei est.' Then he further quotes *Ps.* xxii. 6, the very psalm the opening words of which had been on Jesus' lips as he expired, and hence regarded in its entirety as a confession of the suffering Christ : ' But I am a worm and no man, a reproach of men (*ignominia hominum*). All they that see me laugh me to scorn.'

In disputes with the Docetae, who would gladly have spiritualized Jesus into an incorporeal and insubstantial being, evidence that he was a man of 'flesh and blood' was to Tertullian invaluable. With an emphasis and a display of a macro- and microcosmic symbolism hardly relished by the modern reader, the impassioned rhetorician insists that Jesus had not only flesh and blood but muscles, sinews, bones, and hair. Then he continues : ' haec omnia terrenae originis signa et in Christo fuerunt. Haec sunt quae eum Dei filium celavere, non alias tantummodo hominem existimatum quam ex humana substantia corporis.' No doubt we have here an allusion to Josephus' enumeration of the ' terrenae originis signa,' those bodily marks regarded as proving the ' human bodily substance' (' humana substantia corporis') of the ' so-called Christ,' and to his express refusal, in view of this ' common nature,' to see in Jesus an angel.

'Aut edite,' he asks in the immediate context, 'aliquid in illo coeleste de Septentrionibus et Vergiliis et Suculis emendicatum ? '[5]

To understand this sentence one has to recall that Marcion's pupil Appelles[6] did teach that Jesus had an angel's body com-

---

[1] 2 *Cor.* v. 16.　　　　　　　　　[2] *Adv. Marc.*, iii. 17.

[3] Tertullian unquestionably knew Josephus (cf. Harnack-Preuschen, *Gesch. d. altchristl. Lit.*, Leipzig, 1893, p. 858). He may also have had before him forged *Acta Pilati* now lost. It is certainly curious that as early as 1628 Nicolas Rigault, in his edition of Tertullian dedicated to Cardinal Richelieu, compared with this the ancient poetical warrant of arrest of Eros (Mosch., i. 3) : '' εἴ τις ἐνὶ τριόδοισι πλανώμενον εἶδεν ἔρωτα—δραπετίδας ἐμός ἐστιν.'' Cf. p. 406 of the second edition (Paris, 1765).

[4] *Isaiah* lii. 14. Cf. above, p. 404, in the ' Lentulus letter': ' quem possent intuentes formidare.' See also p. 426₃₄.

[5] ' Or do you discover in him anything celestial ' (to-day we should say, ' anything astral') ' which he has begged from the Great Bear, the Pleiades, or the Hyades ? '

[6] Tert., *De carm. Christi*, 6 (Migne, *P.L.*, ii. 763) ; *Adv. Marc.*, iii. 11 (*ibid.*, 335).

posed of astral substance ; and, above all, the popular ideas of
Hellenistic star-lore about star-gods descending from heaven and
walking about among men, as attested by the prologue to the
Rudens of Plautus.[1] Tertullian turns to his opponent with the
ironical enquiry whether he can discover any sign of astral origin
in Jesus' lowly, earthly appearance.

As a matter of fact, not all the Church fathers so severely
reject such heathen astral notions.   Two centuries after Tertullian,
Jerome does not hesitate to speak of ' something starry ' in the
countenance and eyes of Jesus : ' nisi enim habuisset et in vultu
quiddam oculisque *sidereum*, nunquam eum statim secuti fuissent
apostoli.' [2]

Tertullian had with real emotion denied that the personal
appearance of Jesus bore any marks of heavenly splendour, nay,
even of human comeliness : ' adeo nec humanae honestatis corpus
fuit, nedum coelestis claritatis.'   In the ardour of battle with the
Docetae he carries his extravagance of language so far as to write :
' The ignominy of the face (of Jesus) would roar (as a witness
against the heretics) if it could.' [3]

To one moved to deny the unsightliness of Jesus he makes an
imploring appeal : ' Quid destruis necessarium dedecus fidei ? ' [4]
It is worth noting that even here copyists and printers have often
altered the word *dedecus* (disgrace), which appeared to them
irreverent, into *decus*—a tampering belonging to the type we have
had ample occasion to discuss in connexion with the *Testimonium
Flavianum.*

A final remark, the correctness of which will be confirmed by
any who have observed the attitude of a Southern crowd towards
an accused and condemned person, is psychologically fine and not
unworthy of the rich legal experience of the learned lawyer
Tertullian : ' No one would have mishandled, much less spat upon,
Jesus, had not the face of the condemned, so to speak, provoked
his tormentors to such brutality.' [5]

On Tertullian's words already quoted, 'nec humanae honestatis corpus,' the Abbé Migne remarks in a note that the Abbé
Rigault, the seventeenth-century editor of our author, actually
concluded from this strong expression that Jesus was in some way
deformed (' deformem Christum putat ').   In fact, Rigault severely

[1] ' The star Arcturus there says that by day he walks among mortals, as do the
other stars, in order that they may note the doings of men and report to the
highest god Jupiter on their conduct, but also that they may interfere in human
affairs here on earth, protecting the innocent, punishing the wicked, etc.'

[2] *Epist.*, 65, *Ad Principiam.*

[3] l. 1-3, li.   Kautsch, *Pseudepigr.*, ii. 430 *sq.* ; Strack-Billerbeck, iii. 474 (so,
too, in the Midrash Gan 'Eden : Th. Gaster).

[4] *Adv. Marc.*, c. 5.

[5] ' An ausus esset aliquis ungue summo perstringere corpus, nedum sputamini-
bus contaminare faciem, nisi merentem,' *ibid.*

censures the theologians [1] who cannot imagine their Christ otherwise than as possessing the most beautiful stature and countenance. ' Quid destruis necessarium dedecus fidei ? Quodcumque Deo indignum est, mihi [2] expedit. Hoc dici potest etiam iis, qui adversus Tertulliani et omnium veterum scriptorum traditionem Christum statura vultuque formosissimum sibi imaginantur.' Obviously, Rigault could not thus have expressed himself had he not been sure of the concurrence of Cardinal Richelieu, to whom his book was dedicated.

No less bold and undaunted is the attitude of the French Oratorian Louis Thomassin [3] (1619-95). On the question which at that time was being hotly debated, [4] whether Jesus was beautiful or ill-favoured, he pronounced himself as follows : ' Christus temporalia omnia aspernari : quod erat institutum ejus non edocuisset, si formae elegantiam magni fecisset.' He adds that the beauty of Christ predicted by the Psalmist [5] lies in his exalted righteousness, and 'vera carnis pulchritudo non nisi immortalitas.' This opinion is quoted, though without exact reference, by E. Michel in Amman's *Dictionnaire de Théologie catholique*. No contradiction or ecclesiastical censure of this thesis ever ensued, and in fact none is conceivable in view of the abundance of patristic sources which could be quoted in its support.

THE ' TRANSFIGURATION ' OF JESUS ON THE HOLY MOUNT

The complete disappearance of the genuine pen-portrait of Jesus is but a proof of the far-reaching Hellenization of the Jewish Messiah, a process which took place in the first centuries of the Church, beginning with Paul and indeed chiefly through Paul. What was forgotten was really, as Paul says, [6] the Christ who appeared ' in the flesh ' and whom he would ' know no more.' What was preached to the heathen was the *glorified* king of kings, as he appeared to the most intimate disciples in the ecstatic vision on the top of Mt. Hermon and as he was now expected to appear at his second coming.

From the days of the dissensions between the schools of Shammai and Hillel, i.e. from the time of Herod the Great, we can trace

---

[1] Some freethinkers, though, would fall under the same censure ; for example, Ernest Renan—cf. *Vie de Jésus*, p. 842 : '(Jésus) sans doute (!) une de ces ravissantes figures qui apparaissent quelquefois dans la race juive . . .'
[2] I.e. to Tertullian or any opponent of the Docetic heresy.
[3] *Dogmat. theolog. de incarn. verbi Dei*, Paris, 1680, lib. vi., chap. vii. : ' De pulchritudine carnis Christi.'
[4] *Loc. cit.*, p. 265 : 'magno contentionis aestu controvertitur . . . quaestio, an pravitate oris vilescere affectarit ' (*scil.* Jesus Christus).
[5] *Ps.* xlv. 3.
[6] 2 *Cor.* v. 16.

2 E

a belief among the Jews [1] to the effect that the bodies of the risen would be refashioned in the future world of the Messianic age, and indeed not necessarily in the same form which they had in the present world. Thus, according to the Syriac *Apocalypse of Baruch*,[2] the dead, in order to remain recognizable, were indeed to rise in their old form, but after the Judgment the aspect, alike of those who are condemned and of those who are justified, is changed. ' The aspect of those who are now godless shall become worse than it (now) is,' whilst as for ' those who have now been justified according to my law, who have had understanding in their life, and who have planted in their heart the root of wisdom, their splendour shall then shine forth in a different form, and the aspect of their faces shall be transformed into . . . dazzling beauty. . . . They shall be transformed, these and those, the latter into the splendour of angels, and the former shall yet more waste away into monstrous spectres and forms strange to behold.' On the other hand, the righteous ' shall be changed into every form that they may desire.' The same expressly applies to those still alive on the Day of Judgment, who have therefore never tasted death.[3]

Although this Apocalypse cannot have been written until after the destruction of Jerusalem, this whole naïve conception is certainly purely Jewish and not dependent on the Pauline doctrine,[4] for the peculiar (Greek) feature in Paul's doctrine of transformation is just the idea of the resurrection body as a 'spiritual (pneumatic) body,' [5] of which the Jewish Apocalypse knows nothing.

We need have no hesitation, then, in postulating such a belief in a transformation or metamorphosis of all entrants to the kingdom for Jesus and his disciples. The vision of the transfiguration, discussed above, shows what importance was attached in this circle to these expectations, which correspond in every particular to the promises quoted above from the Baruch Apocalypse.

The phrase used by Mark (ix. 2) is καὶ μετεμορφώθη ἔμπροσθεν αὐτῶν. In the Luther Bible the verb is rendered by ' verklärte sich ' ('was glorified'). However, that would be in Greek ἐδοξάσθη, a word not employed in the present context, where we have instead μετεμορφώθη, ' his figure (μορφή) was altered.' [6] In *Luke* ix. 29 the miraculous nature of the phenomenon is essentially weakened ; we read merely, ' as he was praying, the appearance of his face was

---

[1] *Genes. rabba*, 14 (10c) ; Strack-Billerbeck, iii. 473 *sq.*, to 1 *Cor.* xv. 35.

[2] l. 1-3, li. Kautsch, *Pseudepigr.*, ii. 430 *sq.* ; Strack-Billerbeck, iii. 474 (so too in the Midrash Gan 'Eden : Th. Gaster). Cp. *Daniel* xii. 3.

[3] xlix. 2. The answer given in chs. l.-li. to the question asked applies to both quick and dead.

[4] 1 *Cor.* xv. 52 : ' we shall all be changed.'

[5] 1 *Cor.* xv. 44. On the considerations leading to this doctrine, cf. above, p. 286 n. 4, p. 287 n. 1. [6] Auth. Vers. : ' he was transfigured.'

altered,' whilst *Matt.* xvii. 2 appears originally to have presented a conflation of the two expressions,

" καὶ μετεμορφώθη ἔμπροσθεν αὐτῶν **καὶ ἔλαμψε ὡς ὁ ἥλιος τὸ** πρόσωπον αὐτῷ,"

unless, as I believe, the words printed in heavy type are a later, though quite apposite, addition to the text.[1] The most original reading is probably that attested by Tatian's *Diatessaron*, the recension of Pamphilus and both Latin versions, 'And Jesus was transformed before them and his face did shine as the sun.'

One gains an impression that the reader was to think that the whole 'alteration' consisted in an effect of light, i.e. an illumination and glorification of the countenance, such as art has sought to express by the halo of Jesus and the glorified saints. On the other hand, Mark and his phrase μετεμορφώθη ὁ Ἰησοῦς quite frankly imply that the whole form of Jesus was altered, as indeed it must have been altered if the hidden Messiah, the secret king of Israel and of the world, was to be made manifest. For what made him unrecognizable were, as Tertullian insists, just those ' terrenae originis signa, quae eum Dei filium esse celaverunt,' those human, all too human, marks of his ' bond-servant's form.' [2]

A messiah like that Simon of Peraea who, though a slave, in the days of the Baptist put himself forward as king, 'relying on his tall and handsome figure,' [3] had no occasion to wait for a divine attestation of his claims through any transfiguration in the sight first of his closest followers and then of all the world. For such a man it sufficed to assume the crown and throw the purple around his shoulders to find as many followers as he could desire. Jesus, on the contrary, could not openly proclaim himself as the Messiah or promise to his disciples the coming of the ' Son of man ' in glory, except on the condition that God at the right moment would by a miracle change, exalt, and irradiate with visible royal majesty his poor bond-servant's frame.[4] Just as the bewitched prince in fairy tales when released from the enchantment recovers his former beauty, or as Athena at the right moment frees from the disguise of his beggar's body the divine Odysseus, unrecognized under his former mask, so will God reveal his Anointed through a transfiguration and glorification, first to the disciples, then to all the people.

David Friedrich Strauss in his first *Life of Jesus* had already raised the question whether Jesus could not have thought of his *parousia* as a transformation occurring within his lifetime.

[1] Cf. *Apoc. Baruch*, loc. cit. : ' they shall be changed into every form they desire . . . into the splendour of glory,' and *Daniel* xii. 3.

[2] *Philipp.* ii. 7.   [3] *B.J.*, ii. 57.

[4] The claims of the king-pretender Alexander are rejected at first sight by Augustus because of his ' slave's body ' ; cf. *B.J.*, ii. § 107 ; *Halōsis*, ibid.

' Friedrich Wilhelm Ghillany (1807-76) treats this possibility as an historical fact.'[1] Lastly, Dr. Schweitzer has adduced cogent reasons in support of this view. After the conclusions now reached there can be no doubt that such is the correct interpretation of the expectation and teaching of Jesus. The disciples' vision of the transformation already realized on Mt. Hermon is not intelligible unless they, and consequently their Master, lived and moved in this belief.

The Varying Aspect of Jesus according to Origen, Augustine, and in Christian Art

The vision of the transfiguration receives some additional light from the analogous narrative of the *Odyssey* just referred to. There Telemachus, through the mercy of Athena, can see and recognize his father in all his splendour and manly beauty, though to the other spectators he continues in the guise of the poor and squalid beggar. In the same manner Peter and the sons of Zebedee might behold Jesus on the mount in the splendour of his divine majesty, though to the other disciples, and of course to all outsiders, his secret remains hidden.

In other words, we are here dealing with ancient popular belief : ' the gods in no wise appear visibly to all.'[2] Just so in Philo, Moses, the re-born Messiah, will be visible only to the redeemed but concealed from the rest.[3] There can be no question of a theological subtlety or Gnostic sophistry (as v. Dobschütz calls it) when Origen[4] records a tradition according to which Jesus appeared in two forms—the poor and ill-favoured form of the bond-servant, visible to all and held up against the Christians by Celsus, and the changed and glorified figure of the holy mount, in which form he is expected by the Church to appear at his return.

In Luke's Gospel[5] the disciples going to Emmaus do not recognize their risen Master by his looks but only through the manner of the breaking of the bread and his blessing. The glorified form of the risen Lord is obviously not supposed to be known only to the three witnesses of the transfiguration on the mount ; but the rest saw only his poor earthly body during his lifetime, and cannot recognize the transfigured Christ. 'Therefore,' says Augustine[6] in unison with Tertullian, ' therefore he appeared ugly (*foedus*) to his persecutors,' and he adds the following explanation :

---

[1] A. Schweitzer, *The Quest of the Historical Jesus*,[2], p. 363 (p. 412 of 3rd German edition).

[2] *Odyssey*, xvi. 160 *sqq.*   [3] *De exsecr.*, §§ 8-9, ii. 435 M.

[4] *Comm. in Matt.*, § 100.

[5] xxiv. 16. Cp. *Ps.-Marc* (i.e. Aristion the presbyter) xvi. 12, 'after that he appeared in another form (ἐν ἑτέρᾳ μορφῇ) to two of them. . . .'

[6] *Enarratio in Ps. cxxvii.*, cap. 8.

' for they had not the eyes wherewith to see the beauty of Christ. To what sort of eyes did Christ appear beautiful ? What eyes did Christ himself seek for when he said to Philip, I have been long with you and have ye not seen me?'[1] Those eyes must be cleansed that they may see that light, and if but lightly touched by the splendour they are fired with love, so that they wish to be healed and become illuminated. ' For that ye may know that Christ when loved is beautiful, the prophet says, "fairer than the children of men,"[2] his beauty surpasses (that of) all men.'

Again, the doctrine that Jesus appeared to every one as each was capable of seeing and could benefit by seeing him is found in the same passage of Origen.[3] Nor was there anything surprising in this, since the creative word of God, the Logos, could naturally assume any form at will. The doctrine has a Docetic ring, but is also quite intelligible from the point of view of that simple popular belief in accordance with which God appears to Abraham in the form of three wanderers, Athena to Telemachus in the form of Mentor and to Odysseus in that of a blue-eyed maiden or a swallow.

A Tertullian and an Augustine, who expressly emphasize the fact that Jesus appeared devoid of any physical charm to his persecutors, could therefore take no offence at finding in Josephus an enumeration of the 'terrenae originis signa' which his enemies noticed to the exclusion of anything else : ' non enim habebant oculos unde Christus pulcher videretur.'

Conversely, the idea that Jesus appears to each man in accordance with his deserts makes it at once intelligible that Paul and his followers had no desire whatever to know more about the mortal frame of the Christ martyred on the cross, and were content to serve in spirit the glorified risen Lord. It is equally intelligible that hardly any painter or sculptor ever regarded himself as so blind, so unworthy to descry and to portray the triumphant beauty and the true nature of Jesus Christ, as to condescend to reproduce the historical appearance of that deformed and puny figure.

The necessarily inadequate conceptions which an artist may form of the glory of the Redeemer are regarded by the Church as purely subjective and devoid of any canonic authority. St. Augustine quite shared this general view :

' It is unavoidable, when we believe certain concrete facts which we have read or heard of but have not seen, that the mind should conceive something having corporeal lineaments and form, such as may occur to its thought, which may be true or not. Even if it is true, which can very rarely happen, it is of no profit that we

---

[1] *John* xiv. 9. [2] *Ps.* xlv. 2.
[3] ' Unicuique apparebat secundum quod fuerit dignus.'

should hold to this as an article of faith, although it may be useful
for something else which is suggested by it. . . . For indeed the
outward appearance of the very flesh of the Lord varies and is
fashioned according to the diversity of the innumerable imaginations
(of men). None the less, this individual appearance was one only,
whatever it may have been. Nor in our faith which we have concerning the Lord Jesus Christ is that salutary which the mind
fashions for itself, which may be very different from the reality, but
that only which we think about (Jesus) the man as belonging to the
species of mankind.'[1]

The words have been and still are the *magna charta* of Christian
art to represent and conceive Christ in such a manner 'as is
possible and therefore profitable to those who see him.'[2] They
would perfectly justify even the bold modern painter or sculptor[3]
who could and would dare to let that fiery spirit shine through the
earthly features of a pitiable and maimed body. Their authority
alike covers those painters, sculptors, and poets who loved to
portray Jesus as a Greek philosopher,[4] as well as those others who
dreamt of him as a King David *redivivus* or a youthful Alexander
the Great—nay, even those who did not shrink from investing
him with the majesty conferred by Greek genius upon the chief
of their gods.[5]

So long as the Church is unprepared and unwilling to return to
that aniconic cult of the Semitic East, she must put up with the
unavoidable imperfections of all subjective imagery; and even
those Christians who have, in old Jewish fashion, renounced all
worshipful contemplation of the work of human hands, should not
forget that even speech—nay, thought—is a hopelessly inadequate
medium for any expression of the Absolute.

THE VARIOUS EPIPHANIES OF THE CHRIST IN THE APOCRYPHAL ACTS, AND THE UNRECONCILED CONTRADICTIONS IN THE FALSIFIED ΕΙΚΩΝ ᾽ΙΗΣΟΥ

The views of Origen and Augustine are not confined to the
theology of the learned, but reappear in the thoroughly popular
narratives of the transfiguration, the so-called apocryphal *Acts of
the Apostles*. Thus in the *Acts of Peter* we read :[6]

'. . . wherefore the Lord, whom neither we nor the Jews can
worthily behold, was induced by his compassion to show himself in

---

[1] *De Trinitate*, viii. 4. 7. [2] Origen, *loc. cit.*

[3] Certain attempts to picture a physically unattractive Jesus could be singled
out in Byzantine, German, Dutch, and Spanish art.

[4] Jesus and Paulus: "καταγεγραμμένοι ὡς ἂν φιλόσοφοι"; Euseb., *Ep. ad.
Constantiam Augustam*; Boivin in *Not. ad Nikeph.*; Gregoras, *Hist. Byz.*, ed. Bonn,
p. 1301. On pictures representing Jesus as a Greek philosopher of the Cynic
school, cf. G. A. Müller, *Die leibliche Gestalt Jesu Chr.*, Wien, 1909, p. 69.

[5] Cf. the Byzantine Texts, v. Dobschütz, p. 107 *sqq.*

[6] *Actus Vercell.*, 20 ; Henneke, *N.T. Apokryphen*, p. 241.

another form and to appear in the image of a man.   For each one of us saw him as it was within his capacity and power to see (him).   But now will I interpret to you what has been read to you ere now.[1]   Our Lord wished to let me see his majesty on the holy mount ;[2] but when I saw his luminous glory along with the sons of Zebedee, I fell down as dead[3] and closed mine eyes and heard his voice in a manner which I cannot describe.   I believed that by his radiance I had been robbed of my eyesight.   And I recovered breath a little and said within myself, Perchance my Lord hath wished to bring me hither in order to deprive me of my eyesight.   And I said, If this is thy will, I do not object, O Lord.   And he gave me his hand and raised me up ; and when I stood on my feet, I saw him again in such wise as I could conceive him.   How then, most beloved brethren, hath the merciful Lord borne our weaknesses and taken our transgressions upon himself, even as the prophet saith,[4] "He bears our sins and hath pain for us ; we believed that he was in pain and afflicted with wounds."   For indeed he is in the Father and the Father in him.[5] . . . He will comfort you, for that ye love him—him who is *great and quite small, comely and ugly*: *small* for the ignorant, *great* to those who know him, *comely* to the understanding and *ugly* to the ignorant, *youthful and aged* . . . *glorious* but amongst us appearing *lowly and ill-favoured.*'

In the following section (21) Jesus appears to a group of blind old women, who gain their sight through the brilliance of the Glorified One :

' To them said Peter, Tell what ye have seen.   They said, We have seen an elderly man[6] of such beauty as we cannot describe ; but others said, We have seen a lad who tenderly touched our eyes ; thus were our eyes opened.   Therefore Peter praised the Lord and said, Thou alone art the Lord God ; to offer thee praise, how many lips should we need, to thank thee in accordance with thy compassion ?   Therefore, my brethren, as I told you but now, the unchangeable God is greater than our thoughts, even as we have heard from the aged widows how they have seen the Lord in varying forms.'[7]

In similar fashion the *Acts of John* reproduces the story of the transfiguration on the mount :[8]

' At another time he taketh me (and) James and Peter into the mountain where his custom was to pray : and we beheld (in) him such a light as it is not possible for a man that useth corruptible speech to tell what it was like.   Again in like manner he leadeth us three up into the mountain, saying, Come ye with me.   And we again went : and we beheld him at a distance praying.   Now therefore I,

---

[1] I.e. the Gospel story of the transfiguration in the canonic Gospels.
[2] 2 *Pet.* i. 18 ; cf. above, p. 434.   [3] *Apoc. Joh.*, i. 17.
[4] *Isaiah* liii. 4.   [5] *John* x. 38, xvii. 21.   [6] Cf. above, p. 425₁₆.
[7] Cf. ' O thou of many forms (πολύμορφος), who art the only begotten son,'
Acts of Thomas, c. 48.
[8] Tr. M. R. James, *Texts and Studies*, v. (1897), p. 7, § 3 *sq.*

because he loved me,[1] drew nigh unto him softly as though he should not see, and stood looking upon his hinder parts.[2] And I beheld him that he was not in any wise clad with garments, but was seen of us naked thereof, and not in any wise as a man : and his feet whiter than any snow, so that the ground there was lighted up by his feet : and *his head reaching unto heaven*;[3] so that I was afraid and cried out, and he turned and appeared as *a man of small stature.*'

In the same document [4] the call of the fishers is curiously fused with the appearance of the risen Lord on the shore of the Lake of Gennesareth narrated in the appendix to the Fourth Gospel :

' For when he had chosen Peter and Andrew, who were brethren, he cometh to me and to my brother James, saying, I have need of you : come unto me. And my brother (hearing) that, said, John, what could this child have, that called to us upon the shore ? And I said, What child ? And he (said) to me again, The one that is beckoning to us. And I answered, Because of our long watch which we have kept at sea thou seest not (aright), my brother James : but seest thou not the man that standeth (there) well-grown and comely and of a cheerful countenance ? But he said to me, Him I see not, brother, but let us go forth, and we shall see what he would have.[5] And so, when we had brought the ship to land, we saw him also helping along with us to settle the ship. And when we departed from the place, wishing to follow him, again he was seen of me as having a head rather bald, but a thick and flowing beard : but to James (he appeared as) a youth whose beard was newly come.[6] We were therefore perplexed, both of us, as to what that should mean which we had seen ; (and) then as we followed him, both of us by little and little became (more) perplexed as we thought upon the matter. Yet unto me there appeared this, which was still more wonderful : for I would try to see him in private, and I never at any time saw his eyes closing,[7] but only open. And oftentimes he appeared to me as a small man and uncomely, and then again as one reaching to heaven.'

Then follow utterances put into the mouth of John on the palpable substance ($\tau\grave{o}$ $\dot{v}\pi o\kappa\epsilon\acute{\iota}\mu\epsilon\nu o\nu$) of the body of Jesus :

' Also there was in him another marvel : when I sat at meal he would take me upon his own breast, and I would consider with myself ;[8] and sometimes his breast was felt of me to be smooth and tender, and sometimes hard, like stones. . . . Sometimes [9] when I

[1] *John* xx. 2. [2] Cf. *Exod.* xxxiii. 23.
[3] Cf. Plutarch, parall. 32, a man seeing his dead father, $\mu\epsilon\acute{\iota}\zeta o\nu\alpha$ $\mu o\rho\phi\grave{\eta}\nu$ $\dot{\alpha}\nu\theta\rho\acute{\omega}\pi\omega\nu$ $\kappa\epsilon\kappa\tau\acute{\eta}\mu\epsilon\nu o\nu$, disappearing at the summit of a mountain.
[4] Tr. James, *op. cit.*, pp. 3-5, § 2.
[5] Or, ' what it meaneth.' [6] Cf. above, p. 427[47].
[7] Cf. *Ps.* cxxi. 4. [But it is to be noted that demons in popular belief are supposed to be sleepless ; cf. *Mod. Lang. Review*, xxiv. 200-4.—Translator's note.]
[8] Or, ' I pressed (him) fast to myself.'
[9] James, *op. cit.*, p. 9, § 7.

would lay hold of him, I met with a material and solid body : and at other times again when I felt him, the substance was immaterial and bodiless and as it were not existing in any wise.'

It would seem evident that these alleged utterances of the beloved disciple John, who lay on the Lord's breast and could therefore rank as a classic witness, are directed against the assertion of Josephus previously quoted [1] that the ' nature ' or ' being ' (φύσις) of Jesus was purely human, the ordinary nature common (κοινή) to all men.

Only by bearing in mind the theological doctrine of the two oppositely constituted forms of Jesus, the earthly and the trans-figured, one can understand the extraordinarily delicate manner in which the text of Josephus has been manipulated and the official description of the Christ falsified. On logical grounds one would expect that the copyist who beside ' bent ' or ' crooked ' (ἐπίκυφος) wrote ' well-grown ' (εὐήλιξ), beside ' long-nosed ' (ἐπίρρινος) ' with a handsome nose ' (εὔρρινος), and so on, would have got rid of the resulting contradiction by cancelling the genuine features which he considered objectionable, whereby the original description would have been irretrievably lost. That this did not happen is easily explained by the necessity of not sacrificing the evidence afforded by the ' terrenae originis signa ' of the body of Christ, evidence which, as shown by the passionate disquisitions of Ter-tullian, was quite indispensable in the contest with the Docetae. Unwelcome as these statements appeared to pious worshippers of the Godhead of Christ, they could not venture to abandon wholly what was so urgently needed to prove the real humanity of Christ, the actual incarnation of the Logos. So in the last resort it is owing to the Docetae, who so vehemently contested the doctrine that God became man, that the most striking evidence of the historicity of the man Jesus was allowed to survive, though under the protective retouchings by pious forgers.

In such a state of affairs one must, of course, be prepared for the conjecture, as obvious as it is easy to refute, that the evidence in question has no genuine nucleus whatever, but is a Christian fiction from beginning to end—in other words, that the contra-dictions discussed above [2] have arisen, not through Christian im-provements of a genuinely anti-Christian text, but through free invention of a portrait of Christ which intentionally and from the outset strove to unite the unsightly features of the first earthly appearance of Jesus with the charm of the glorified form of the vision on the mount and the Christ of the second coming.

A glance at p. 427, presenting separately the flattering state-ments and their opposites, will suffice to show that the origin of

---

[1] Cf. above, pp. 428 f.54-56 ; cp. 424 f.9-10.   [2] Cf. p. 412 f.

so lifelike and inimitable a picture of the 'unsightly' appearance cannot be explained in this way. For while the ' human ' form is described in terms so individual as to exclude altogether the supposition that they could be the product of fanciful invention, the features of beauty are so vague, indefinite, and void of all individuality that their invention is obvious. Every one knows exactly the meaning of σύνοφρυς, but what on earth is εὔοφρυς, ' with beautiful eyebrows ' ? Are weak and delicately pencilled or strong and bushy eyebrows ' goodly ' or ' beautiful ' ? Every one knows all too well what ἐπίκυφος signifies ; but what is one to make of εὐήλιξ, ' well-grown ' ? And if any one wanted to invent a detailed description of a human, all too human, form, why did he select just those unattractive features and not other deformities to be found in real life and in the papyri, and hence no less suited for purposes of caricature ? Why should Jesus have been described precisely as an ἐπίκυφος, and not equally well as an ἀριστερόπηρος, ' lame on the left side,' or a κατάκνημος, ' bow-legged ' ? Would it not have been more effective, if a caricature was meant, to say ἀναφάλακρος, ' bald,' instead of ὀλιγόθριξ, ' scanty-haired ' ? With what object could the parting of the hair in the Nazirite fashion have been invented ? I think that a glance at the re-covered *iconismus* proves that we have here no fictitious caricature, but a description, pitiless indeed and coldly official but as a whole the faithful description, of a real man. Furthermore, we can point to a parallel instance in which the improving alterations of the Christian copyist, in the present case purely hypothetical, are actually indicated by a comparison of the various MSS.

The Official Description of St. Paul

Students of Christian iconography have for some time been familiar with a similarly quite relentlessly realistic portrait of the 'second founder of Christianity,' the apostle Paul.

In the *Acts of Paul and Thekla*, composed, or rather forged, 'out of love for Paul,' by some presbyter of Asia Minor [1] about the year A.D. 170, we read (§ 2) :

' And a man named Onesiphorus, who had heard that Paul was coming to Iconium, went forth with his children Simmias and Zeno and his wife Lektra to meet him (and) to invite him to his house. For Titus had informed him (διηγήσατο) what Paul was like in appearance. For he (Onesiphorus) had not seen him before in the flesh, but only in the spirit. And he proceeded to the royal road that leads to Lystra and stood waiting for him, and he scanned the passers-by with the report of Titus to guide him (κατὰ τὴν μήνυσιν

[1] Tertullian, *De Capt.*, 17.

Τίτου). And he saw Paul coming, a man small in stature, bald-headed, bow-legged, in good form,[1] with meeting eyebrows and a rather prominent nose, full of grace, for at times he looked like a man, and at times he had the face of an angel.'[2]

A brief counterpart to this occurs in the so-called *Passion of Paul*,[3] where we are told how Paul was arrested *en route* by the sentries : ' and he was easily recognizable, having a crooked body (ἔγκυφος ὢν τὸ σῶμα), a black beard, and a bald head.'

Those two pen-portraits of Paul are in more than one respect highly instructive. To begin with, the second passage exemplifies the practice, for which evidence has already been adduced from Petronius and Lucian,[4] of the use of writs by the ancient police. For the sentries naturally recognize Paul from the official description, the μήνυσις in the strict sense, with which they have been furnished betimes.

It is highly significant that the description of Paul transmitted to Onesiphorus by Titus is also called a μήνυσις, since the word, the exact equivalent of the French *signalement*, as a rule denotes ' information laid before the authorities.' Moreover, it is obvious how expedient it was to send previous notice[5] of the coming of an emissary to the communities which he proposed to visit, and for security to attach to this μήνυσις a description (εἰκών) of the person concerned. The Jews must have been quite familiar with this Hellenistic custom, for a midrash to *Ps.* xvii. 7[6] says :

' If the man is on a journey, *iqonija* (= εἰκόνια) of the messengers (or angels) go before him and proclaim, Make way for the image (= τῷ εἰκονίῳ) of the Holy One, blessed be He ' :[7]

which means that God sends out dispatches called *iqonija shel mal' akhîm* before the traveller, with instructions to entertain him well, because he is an 'image' of God.

A description (εἰκών), similar to that contained in the μήνυσις, would be attached to the letters of recommendation[8] which the traveller carried with him as certificates and presented in person. Letters of this type accumulated rapidly in the archives of the Christian communities, and at the time of the Diocletian persecution it was thus possible to deceive the Roman officials by delivering up to them, instead of the holy scriptures, only such old letters of introduction.[9] At the end of the beautiful letter of introduction

---

[1] εὐεκτικός used by Plato, *Laws*, iii. 684c ; Aristotle, *Eth.*, v. 11 ; but of athletic bodies.
[2] Cf. above, p. 429₅₇ : ' I will not call him an angel.'
[3] Lipsius, *Acta Apost. Apocr.*, p. 236 *sqq.*
[4] Cf. above, p. 403 nn. 8 and 9.
[5] *Acts* xviii. 27.
[6] Jalq., ii. 95c ; *Deut. r.*, s. 4, 255d.
[7] *Midrash Tehillim*, in loc.
[8] 2 *Cor.* iii. 1.
[9] *epistulae salutatoriae*, Dom. H. Leclerq, in Cabrol's *Dict. d'archéol. chrét.*, ii. 1, p. 862.

of Aurelius Archelaus to his chief, the military tribune Julius Domitius (second century), now in the Bodleian, the writer says : [1]

24 (LA)-	
25 TOR(IS) T(IBI) MITTO ICO(NIS-MUM) [2]	(I send) t(hee) the pen-por[trait] of the [bea]rer, that
26 ILLUM. UT (SIT) IPSE (LOCO) INTER-	it may itself recommend him (in place)
27 CESSORIS U(T I)LLUM CO(MMEN-DARET)	of a guarantor.
28 ESTOTE FELICISSI(MI DOMINE MUL-)	May ye be blessed with all fort(une, sir, for ma-)
29 TIS ANNIS CUM (VESTRIS OMNI-BUS)	ny years with (all your . . .)
30 BENE AGENTES HANC EPISTULAM ANT'OCULOS HABETO DOMINE PUTATO ME TECUM LOQUI. VALE.	prospering. Hold this letter before thine eyes, sir, imagine that I am talking with thee. Farewell.

Such a letter, provided as it was with the description, the *forma*, of the bearer, was therefore called *litterae formatae*.[3] The word makes its first appearance rather late with reference to the date of the first use of this method. The opinion that these ' canonic' letters of introduction were called *litterae formatae*, because they were drawn up in a secretly fixed form, utilizing ciphers against unauthorized use in case of loss or theft, introduced by the Council of Nicaea (A.D. 325), is erroneous. The particular system of ciphers found on this occasion was rather introduced to protect from misuse the ' epistulae canonicae *quas mos Latinus formatas vocat*' ; [4] the letters themselves were in use long before. The italicized words show that the name was familiar at an earlier date. The directions laid down by the Nicene Council were that such epistles had to begin with certain ciphers, viz. π, υ, a (the first letters of the words $\Pi(a\tau\rho\dot{o}\varsigma)$, $\Upsilon(\acute{\iota}o\hat{\upsilon})$, $\mathrm{A}(\gamma\acute{\iota}o\upsilon\ \pi\nu\epsilon\acute{\upsilon}\mu\alpha\tau o\varsigma)$, followed by the first letter of the name of the sender, the second letter of the name of the addressee, the third letter of the name of the recipient and bearer of the credentials, the fourth letter of the city whence the epistle was dated, and in addition the number of the indiction year, thus precluding the possibility that such credentials could be misapplied by erasure and the insertion of another name or a later date, or delivered to some other address,

---

[1] Grenfell-Hunt, *Oxyrh. Pap.*, ii. 318 *sq.* See our Pl. XXXII.

[2] So I supply, with reference to another military letter, Mitteis-Wilcken, *Chrestom.*, p. 537, No. 453, line 8 : ' nomina eorum et iconismos huic epistolae subieci.'

[3] Ducange, *Gloss. Lat. med. aevi*, s.v.

[4] The error goes back to Fr. v. Wyss, *Mitteilungen der antiquarischen Gesellschaft von Zürich*, 1853, Abh. vii. p. 30 : ' *litterae formatae* are letters used in ecclesiastical matters, using a definite form, i.e. ciphers, by way of credentials.' This erroneous definition was taken over by a number of more recent authors.

PLATE XXXII

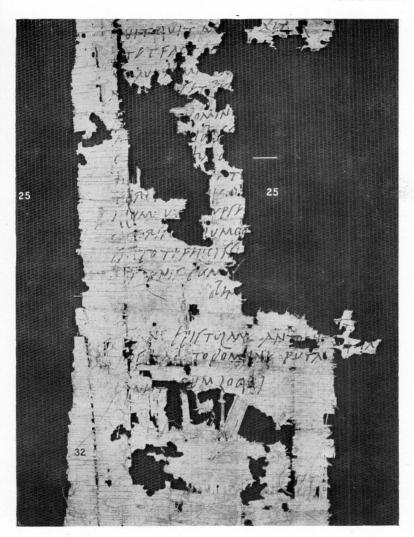

EPISTULA SALUTATORIA OF AURELIUS ARCHELAUS, *BENEFICIARIUS* TO THE
MILITARY TRIBUNE JULIUS DOMITIUS

MENTIONING (IN LINE 25) THE ' ICO(NISMUS LA-)TORIS ' (PEN-PORTRAIT OF BEARER).   THE PAPYRUS,
NOW IN THE BODLEIAN LIBRARY, OXFORD, IS HERE REPRODUCED FOR THE FIRST TIME
(SEE P 444, NOTE I)

without the fraud being detected. This cipher could not, however, prevent an unlawful possessor of the letter from passing himself off as the person named in the letter of introduction. This contingency (just as in the case of a modern passport) could only be prevented or rendered difficult by a description of the person recommended, i.e. by his *forma* being included in the letter. A vague and imperfect description might of course enable an accomplice of somewhat similar appearance to turn to account a document which he had purloined or found ; but without a description the mere insertion of such a secret cipher could be no protection whatever against misuse. *Litterae formatae* means, therefore, not a letter with cipher clauses as prescribed by the Nicene Council, but one furnished with the *forma* of the bearer.

Such *litterae formatae* must frequently have been possessed and exhibited by the earliest envoys of the Church. Where they had been preserved by individual hosts or communities, they would later be held in due honour as dear memorials—nay, worshipped as relics of the first heralds of the Gospel. When Tertullian says [1] that the apostolic Churches still had read to them the genuine letters of their founders ' recalling the sound of their voices [2] and reproducing the face of each one of them,' this last statement is certainly best explained as referring to their *litterae formatae*, those letters of introduction describing the 'facies' of the apostle whose imminent arrival they were meant to announce.

It is therefore in no way surprising to meet in the apocryphal *Acts of the Apostles*—i.e. in the early edifying miracle legends of the ancient Church—with descriptions of Paul producing the impression of being historically true and which may well go back to such a genuine documentary source ; the more so because there are less individual, yet not altogether worthless, parallels to the literary portraits of Paul in the case of Barnabas,[3] Peter,[4] Andrew,[5] and Mark.[6]

---

[1] *De praescr. adv. haeret.*, 36.

[2] It is worth recalling in this connexion the various ancient pen-portraits of celebrated persons describing not only their features but also their voices; according to Timotheos (Diog. Laert., iii. 5, 7), Plato had a thin voice ($\iota\sigma\chi\nu\delta\phi\omega\nu os$). Quoting Aristoxenos' description of Socrates, Cyrill (*c. Julian*, vi. 208) says, ' of this quality was his voice,' etc. Plutarch, Pompeius 2 : " $\tau\dot{\eta}\nu$ $\delta\psi\iota\nu$ $\check{\epsilon}\sigma\chi\epsilon\nu$ . . . $\pi\rho\sigma\tau\upsilon\gamma\chi\acute{a}\nu ov\sigma a\nu$ $\tau\hat{\eta}s$ $\phi\omega\nu\hat{\eta}s$."

[3] Lipsius, *Acta Apost. Apocr.*, ii. 2, p. 299.   [4] Malalas, 330 D.

[5] *Epiphan. mon.*, ed. Dressel, pp. 47, 53 (*P.G.*, lxx. 226 *sq.*).

[6] Lipsius, ii. 335.   According to the Antimarcionite second-century prologues to the canonic gospels (Wordsworth-White, i. p. 171), Mark had ' stumpy fingers.' Such features are still mentioned in passports or writs under the rubric ' special characteristics.'   The objection that it is historically unmethodical to look for documentary bases in what are, after all, ' historical novels ' (for the *Acts of Paul and Thekla* certainly fall largely into this category) is not admissible. Supposing we had no documentary sources throwing light on Louis xi., it would still be perfectly correct to utilize Sir Walter Scott's *Quentin Durward*, seeing that the writer must have known and drawn on trustworthy documentary sources and portraits which, according to this supposition, were afterwards lost.

THE MS. READINGS AND THE ORIGINAL TEXT OF THE
DESCRIPTION OF PAUL

A glance at the personal description of Paul already given shows
at once that the tradition has come down to us in a form exactly
corresponding to the one found in the *iconismus* of Jesus. The first
thing of note is the idea current in the two apocrypha of the changing or double appearance of Jesus ; it is here expressly transferred
to Paul :

> ' at times he looked like a man, and at times he had the face (*or*
> the personality, since πρόσωπον can mean either) of an angel.' [1]

In the description we meet with precisely the same contradictions observed in that of Jesus. Immediately after ' bow-
legged ' (ἄγκυλος ταῖς κνήμαις) stands εὐεκτικός, a word which,
according to Aristotle,[2] denotes the good deportment, the sound
condition of body, which a man obtains through athletic exercises.
Theoretically, it is true, even a man by nature small and bandy-
legged could in this way acquire an athletic figure ; but it is
difficult to believe that such was Paul's case, the more so since
the term is quite out of harmony with the other features of the
description. Moreover, according to the *Passion of Paul*, which
comes down to us as part of the same *corpus* which also contains the
Acts of Paul and Thekla, the sentries actually recognize Paul by
his crooked body (ἐπίκυφον σῶμα). Now, an ἐπίκυφον σῶμα is
just the opposite of an εὐεκτικὸν σῶμα. Lipsius' codex *m*, in fact,
instead of εὐεκτικόν reads προσεκτικόν, ' attentive.' Some one
has therefore first wished to explain the attribute ἐπίκυφος as the
attitude of a man attentively bending over something (e.g. his
books),[3] and εὐεκτικός has only arisen, through a further improvement, out of προσεκτικός. The position, then, is precisely the
same as in the portrait of Jesus, where the Naṣōraean is called in
the same breath ἐπίκυφος and εὐήλιξ, ' hunchbacked ' and ' well-
grown.'

In the description of Paul this position of things is evident if
the *apparatus criticus* of Lipsius is taken into account. Codex *c*
of the Latin version actually calls Paul *subcambaster*, which is the
Vulgar Latin equivalent for μικρὸν ἐπίκυφος, ' somewhat crooked.'
Codex *g*, in place of ἄγκυλον ταῖς κνήμαις, ' bow-legged,' offers us
εὔκνημος, ' with good legs.' The Syriac presents a shamefaced
intermediate stage in the process of improvement : ' his legs were
a little crooked (i.e. μικρὸν ἄγκυλον ταῖς κνήμαις) and his knees
were projecting *or* far apart,' which in Greek can only be ῥαιβός

---

[1] Cf. above, p. 429₅₇ : ' I am not going to call him an angel.'
[2] *Ethics*, v. 11.
[3] Cf. Lucian, *Hermotimos*, c. 2 : " καὶ ὡς τὸ πολὺ ἐς βιβλίον ἐπικεκύφετο."

or ῥαιβοσκέλης. In view of the clearly idealizing tendency of this version it is inconceivable that this further unflattering feature can be a later insertion. Conversely, in an accurate description it is clearly expedient to supplement the general statement ' bow-legged' by the important distinction, whether this applies to x-legs or o-legs ; as will be seen, it is the second alternative which is indicated as correct by the Syriac word 'arqobh, an equivalent of the Greek ῥαιβός.

Where the Greek offers μικρὸν τῷ μεγέθει or μικρομεγέθη, the Latin codex M has not, like c and d, statura brevis, but pusillus, ' diminutive,' ' dwarfish,' just such a word as one might expect from the surname of Saul of Tarsus, Paulus, which corresponds to Greek νάννος or μικρότατος and is in keeping with Chrysostom's description of Paul as a τρίπηχυς ἄνθρωπος.[1] Where the Greek Acts speak of ' bald-headed,' the Latin MSS. M and c only refer to the Apostle's intentionally 'shorn head' (attonso capite), evidently with regard to Acts xxi. 24, where Paul is to have his head shorn along with four Nazirites, as if ever after he had gone about with a close-cropped head.

The phrase ' with meeting eyebrows,' which was found ob-jectionable by many of the copyists of the portrait of Jesus, has been replaced in the Latin codex M by 'with short eyebrows,' brevibus superciliis. The 'meeting eyebrows,' which are generally strong, bushy eyebrows, agree with the profile of Paul in the bronze disc showing Peter and Paul and found in the Domitilla cata-combs.[2] There the Apostle of the Gentiles has uncommonly thick and projecting eyebrows.

The statement regarding the formation of the nose has also been improved, for the Greek μικρῶς ἐπίρρινον does not corre-spond to the naso aquilino found in all the Latin MSS. People with noble aquiline noses are called in Greek γρυποί, and rank as ' high-minded,' so that the motive for the alteration is obvious. In fact, the Greek MS. m has instead of ἐπίρρινον the correction γρυπόν.

The bronze disc reproduced on Pl. XXXIII., with the two profiles alleged to be those of Peter and Paul, gives the Tarsian a pro-nounced and apparently broad but somewhat snub nose, recalling the Socrates type. Such a nose would be termed παχύρρινος or ἔνσιμος or ὑπόσιμος, but hardly ἐπίρρινος. In all other monu-ments of early Christian and Byzantine art [3] Paul is constantly represented with a long, curved nose,[4] ῥέπουσαν τῷ προσώπῳ ῥῖνα,

---

[1] Opp., ed. Montfaucon, viii. 618. Incidentally, this is good evidence that τρίπηχυς cannot mean ' six feet high ' either here or in the description of Jesus.
[2] Cf. our Pl. XXXIII., reproduced from Armellini's publication, Röm. Quart. Schrift, 1888.
[3] Cf. v. Dobschütz, Paulus, vol. ii. (Halle, 1926).
[4] An explanation of this strange discrepancy is suggested below, p. 453. ff. 5-12.

' a nose sloping towards the face,' as Nicephorus Callistou [1] describes it.

Here, then, the MSS. themselves enable us clearly to recognize the gradual revision which the portrait has undergone. It originally described Paul as ' quite small, bald-headed, bow-legged, with knees far apart, with meeting eyebrows, large eyes,[2] a long nose, and a red, florid face.' [3]

It is obvious that the forger of Asia Minor who, according to the evidence of Tertullian,[4] confessed to having concocted the *Acts of Paul* ' out of love for the apostle,' would never have introduced a description of his hero so unflattering that it would be found intolerable by the copyists of the book and quoted by the enemies of Christianity with malicious glee,[5] had it not been recognized at the time of the forgery as historically accurate or attested by unquestionable and unquestioned documents.

THE STIGMATA OF JESUS ON PAUL. THE EARLY TRADITIONS ABOUT A TWIN-BROTHER AND DOUBLE OF JESUS

The author of the *Acts of Paul* must already have been conscious of the similarity of the description of Paul to that of Jesus, for in § 21 he says of Thekla :

' As a lamb spies around in the wilderness, so she sought for Paul. And while she let her glance move over the crowd, she saw the Lord sitting there in the form of Paul.'

This strange motive, which in itself does not necessarily presuppose that the author believed Jesus and Paul to have resembled each other,[6] must be compared with the parallel passages in the *Acts of Thomas*,[7] where time and again Judah Thauma, i.e. ' Judas the twin,' appears as strikingly like his deceased brother Jesus, whose twin he was. Suffice it to mention the story of the princess and her bridegroom who had both been persuaded by Judas Thomas to make a vow of chastity. During the wedding night Jesus himself appears to them in the shape of Thomas, and the bridegroom quite naturally observes : ' But thou hast just left ; how then art thou still here ? ' But the Lord replies to him : ' I am not Judas, I am

---

[1] *P.G.*, cxlv. 853.

[2] From the Syriac text, ed. Wright, *Apocr. Acts of the Apostles*, London, 1871, ii. 117.

[3] *ruborus*, Lat. cod. *c* ; Malalas, p. 332 A.

[4] *De baptismo*, c. 17.

[5] Cf. the Byzantine pseudo-Lucian, *Philopat.*, xii. : ' a bald-headed, long-nosed Galilaean who had ascended to the third heaven.'

[6] Cf. above, p. 437 ll. 16-18, the parallels from Genesis and the *Odyssey*.

[7] Lipsius, *op. cit.*, i. pp. 227, 250, 256, 269 ; Wright, *op. cit.*, pp. 155, 170, 179, 185, 196 ; Rendel Harris, *The Twelve Apostles*, Cambridge, 1927, p. 48 *sq.*

PLATE XXXIII

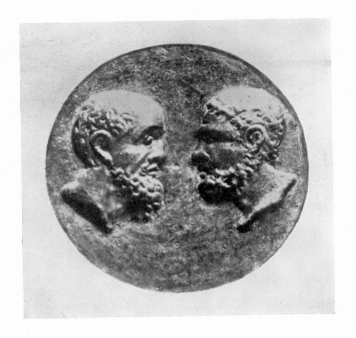

BRONZE DISC WITH SECOND CENTURY PORTRAITS OF
SS. PETER AND PAUL

FOUND IN THE DOMITILLA CATACOMBS. AFTER ARMELLINI'S PUBLICATION
Römische Quartalschrift, 1888, pp. 130-136

the brother of Judas.' [1] He then sits down on the bed and reminds them of what Thomas had told them previously. A donkey upon which Thomas had conferred the boon of human speech forthwith addresses the apostle as ' thou twin-brother of the Messiah.'

Nor does the Greek text [2] differ in the slightest in this respect. The physical likeness of the twin-brothers [3] is emphasized in the speech of a demon driven out of a woman : [4] ' What have we to do with thee, thou ambassador of the Most High . . . why doest thou resemble God thy Lord, who concealed his majesty and appeared in the flesh ? ' [5]

No less ambiguously the girl saved from death [6] says of her saviour Jesus Christ to Thomas : ' and he took me without the place, where there were men ; but he who resembled thee (ὁ σοὶ ὅμοιος) took me, brought me to thee and said . . .'

As will be seen, the aretalogy of Judah Thauma knows no greater item to report in his praise than his resemblance to his twin-brother Jesus, reported to have been so pronounced that he appears as the double of Jesus, just as Jesus is often taken for Thomas.

Dr. Harris has shown furthermore that this strange tradition occurs also in the Latin, where it was found objectionable at a comparatively late period. Priscillian speaks with perfect unconcern about 'Judas apostolus . . . ille didymus [7] domini.' A writer so generally read as Isidore of Seville says of him : ' Thomas apostolus, Christi didymus nominatus et iuxta Latinam linguam Christi geminus [8] ac similis salvatoris. . . .' Yet this explanation of the name did not at all necessitate such an emphasis of the likeness of Thomas and Jesus.   In the Anglo-Saxon Church the same explanation occurs in the Gospel narrative itself,[9] and in the opinion of Dr. Harris the Latin original of the Anglo-Saxon version already had these words.

According to the pseudo-Ignatius letter addressed to John, not Judas but the Ṣaddiq Jaʿaqob was the twin-brother and exact double of Jesus.[10]

There can be no question about the essential fact that a tradition like this does not spring up overnight and without

---

[1] *Ibid.*

[2] *Acta Thomae*, ed. Bonnet, p. 29.

[3] On the alteration of *thauma* to *thehoma* (=*abyssus*), cf. *ibid.*, p. 49.

[4] Wright, p. 185.   [5] Bonnet, c. xli. p. 33, gives the Greek text.

[6] Wright, p. 196.   [7] The Greek loan-word points to a Greek source.

[8] The explanation of Thomas =*geminus* has become almost canonical through the *Onomastica Sacra*, though a number of MSS. and variants have only *abyssus*. From Isidore the sentence was taken over into certain variants of the *Legenda Sanctorum*, and even into the *Breviarium Romanum* (cf. Harris, p. 56).

[9] E.g. in the West Saxon Bible, *John* xx. 24, xxi. 2 ; cf. Harris, p. 56. ' Thomas, an of þm twelfon, þe is gecwedn Didimus, þaet is gelícust, on ure geþeode . . . Thomas, þe is gecwedn gelícust.'

[10] Rendel Harris, *loc. cit.*, p. 57.

2 F

historical foundation of some sort. For what Christian would
have been foolish enough to invent such a legend, seeing that it is
most apt to undermine the very basis of the orthodox tradition
concerning the resuscitation of Jesus? For if Jesus were given such
a double, every adversary of Christianity would immediately jump
to the conclusion that the person appearing to Peter, to the
disciples at Emmaus, to the women, and to the Five Hundred, was
simply the twin-brother of Jesus, call him Judas Thomas or
Ja'aqob the Ṣaddiq. In exactly the same way the incredulous
neighbours in *John* ix. 9 had maintained that the beggar who had
received back his eyesight from Jesus was not the blind-born
beggar at all but another individual closely resembling him ("ἀλλ'
ὅμοιος αὐτῷ ἐστιν"). In other words, the story of the resurrection would have to be judged in the same manner as the appearance
of the dead Alexander, slain by Herod the Great, who deceived the
Jews of Melos and was explained by Augustus as the attempted
imposture on the part of a double, presumably an illegitimate slave
brother of Alexander. The reader will also recall the famous
story of the pseudo-Smerdes, recognized as the genuine brother of
Cambyses even by the latter's sister, the queen Atossa.[1] Similarly,Tacitus mentions the appearance of a false Agrippa Postumus,
whom Tiberius decided to have secretly slain; and Suetonius'
account of a false Nero will also come to mind.[2]

If, in spite of all this, the expected explanation is not found in
the pages of the rabbi Tryphon, the Jewish opponent of Justinus,
or of Celsus as handed down by Origen, this merely proves that
these two polemists did not know the tradition of a twin-brother
of Jesus, and his double. Yet there must have been earlier opponents of Christianity better informed ; for it is certainly significant
that the story in the *Gospel of John* is careful to emphasize that
when Jesus appeared to the disciples while all the doors were
closed, Judas Thomas was not with them. It is most striking to
see how the text of the West Saxon Bible allows this tendency to
appear with a rare clearness—*John* xx. 19 : in the evening, behind
barred doors, from fear of the Jews, the disciples are sitting together, when suddenly Jesus stands among them, calming them
with the greeting, 'Peace be with you.' And the disciples are glad
(ἐχάρησαν) to see the Lord. Without regard for the context there
was added, precisely between the greeting and the expression of
the disciples' joy, a sentence to the effect that Jesus showed them
his wounds, evidently without this frightful sight interfering in the

---

[1] Cf. Prašek, *Der Alte Orient*, xiv. 25. The false Joan of Arc was recognized
by her brothers after the Maid had been burned at Compiègne.

[2] There is no want of more recent examples : cf. the histories of Warbeck,
the false Demetrius, etc. On the latter in particular, cf. Mérimée, *Der falsche
Demetrius*, Leipzig, 1869 ; Pierling, *Rome et Démétrius*, Paris, 1878.

least with the joy of the disciples. The resuscitated Jesus is then recognizable by his wounds, which his double, 'Jude Thomas, *who was so like him*,' would not have been able to show, and this significant phrase was inserted at a later date.

Nor did all this suffice. *John* xx. 24 has thought it wise to state expressly that Thomas the *alter ego* was at that time not with the others, thus precluding the simple explanation that in the twilight the frightened disciples might have taken him for the risen Jesus. The last step was to make Thomas himself express the greatest doubts about the reality of Jesus' appearance and to feel his wounds. Nor is it accidental that in *John* xxi. 2, where Jesus appears on shore to the disciples in a boat, the presence of Thomas among the latter is expressly mentioned.

Lastly, the theory according to which the Ṣaddiq Ja'aqob was the twin-brother [1] of Jesus, and his double, is probably responsible for the emphasis laid in 1 *Cor.* xv. 7 on the appearance of Jesus to this very Ja'aqob.

All this goes far to prove that the tradition about a twin-brother of Jesus resembling him in every detail is very old, and caused no small trouble to the early apologists, precisely because it furnished a most plausible, natural, and altogether satisfactory explanation of the appearances of the supposed risen Jesus. Yet it was impossible to suppress it altogether, because this Thomas was evidently quite proud of his resemblance to Jesus, and had disciples of his own, as shown by the *Acts of Thomas*, who could testify to the fact. So long as there were ' Thomas Christians,' loyal members of the universal Church, such a tradition could not be ruled out. It required the various schisms and the heresy-hunting of the following centuries to establish definitely the dogma of the ' only-begotten [2] son of God.' Only so long as the Oriental Church was proud of still having a striking likeness of its Founder in the person of his twin Thomas, could Paul and his adherents themselves lay any stress on and attribute any value to their own physical likeness to Jesus the Crucified.

This consideration at length leads us to the pathetic request of the apostle, hitherto never satisfactorily explained : [3]

' From henceforth let no man trouble me, for I bear (about with me) on my (own) body the marks of Jesus,'

which means, ' I am a marked man like Jesus, smitten with his *stigmata*.' Not because he can point to old scars from scourgings

---

[1] *Ja'aqob* is explained in *Gen.* xxv. 26 as a fitting name for the second of twins. The tradition has probably no other foundation.

[2] The tradition in question is quite reconcilable with the twinship of Jesus and Thomas ; for in the ancient Dioscuri legends the father of one of the twins is commonly a god, whilst the other has a human father. Yet it is absolutely irreconcilable with the dogma of the permanent virginity of Mary.

[3] *Gal.* vi. 17.

in the past, but because he, like Jesus, is an unfortunate man oppressed and burdened with bodily infirmities,[1] does he ask his
readers to have some consideration for his infirmities and not to
add to his troubles in the future.

This resemblance of Paul to Jesus explains the curious fact,
which long ago struck Erwin Preuschen,[2] that the Coptic *Apocalypse of Elijah* [3] and the Armenian *Apocalypse of Daniel* [4] describe
the Antichrist, i.e. the false messiah who is to appear before the
second coming of Jesus, with all the characteristic features of the
signalement of Paul. The Coptic text depicts him as ' thin-
legged, bald-headed, with a tuft of white hair in front of his head,
with eyebrows reaching to his ears, leprous on his hands, capable
of metamorphosing himself into a child, an old man, etc., but
incapable of changing the appearance of his head.'

This not very flattering description is still supplemented by the
Armenian text, which depicts him as 'with curved knees, crippled,
with handsome eyebrows,[5] with sickle-like claws, with a pointed
head, full of charm. . . .' [6]

Preuschen was the first to see that these descriptions contain
one feature absent from the ordinary *iconismus* of Paul but throwing a peculiar light on the apostle's own words in 2 *Cor.* xii. 7,
where he refers to a ' thorn ' in his flesh. Preuschen concluded
that he must refer to some malady which had left its traces, whilst
the verb κολαφίζειν (lit. ' to box some one's ears ') would indicate
not merely ' fits,' but the disease itself. The *Apocalypse of Elijah*
indeed suggests that Paul suffered from leprosy, called ṣara'ath
(from ṣara') in Hebrew, a word of which the original meaning is ' to
strike ' (*Arab.* ـصرع). The leper is ' stricken by God.' [7] Since the
disease strikes the head more than any other part of the body,
the verb κολαφίζειν is explained by Preuschen as a rather drastic
euphemism for the distemper. More probably κολαφίζῃ is a corruption of κελεφίζῃ, ' (who) gives (me) leprosy.' [8] Anyhow, the ' tuft
of white hair' in the fore part of the head ascribed to the Antichrist
is in complete harmony with this result, since leprosy does indeed

---

[1] *Acts* xiv. 12 cannot be used as an objection to this ; the ancient gods liked
to assume a most humble incognito to test men. The queen of Olympus and
Aphrodite did not hesitate thus to assume the shape of a decrepit old woman.

[2] *Z.N.T.W.*, ii. (1901), p. 187-92.

[3] Ed. Stern, *Zeitsch. f. Egypt. Spr.*, 1886, p. 115 *sqq.*; ed. Steindorff, in
Gebhardt-Harnack, *T.U.*, N.F., ii. 3, Leipzig, 1899.

[4] Kalemkiar, *W.Z. f. K.M.*, vi. (1892), p. 133. 15 *sqq.*; trans. *ibid.*, p. 239.
11 *sqq.* Venice ed. of the *Arm. Apocr. of the Old Testament*, p. 249 ; cf.
Preuschen, *Z.N.T.W.*, ii. (1901), p. 192.

[5] εὔοφρυς, cf. above, p. 426₃₂.   [6] Cf. above, p. 443 l. 3.

[7] *Lev.* xiii. 44, xxii. 4.

[8] On κελεφός = *elephantiacus*, κελεφία = ' leprosy,' Syr. *glāfāna* = ' leprosi,'
gallāfitā = ' scabies,' *glāfā* = 'scall,' see H. H. Schaeder, *Studien der Bibliothek Warburg*, vii. pp. 271 and 272, n. 3.

colour white the hair of the parts of the skin which it attacks. Even the ' sickle-like ' claws have been recognized by Preuschen as a symptom of leprosy, caused by the leprosy knots in the finger-joints. The bushy brows, as indicated by the epithet εὐρύοφρυς, find their explanation in the thickening of the arches of the eyes noticeable in all lepers in a late stage of the disease, the fatal knots so changing the facial features, this and the sunken nose giving a ' satyr-like ' or ' leonine ' expression to the individual, a fact which probably explains the profile of Paul on the bronze disc of St. Agnese,[1] with its satyr-like features reminding some archaeologists of Socrates. Even the indications of Malalas using for Paul the epithets λευκόχρους and ἀνθηροπρόσωπος would hardly mean originally a white and tender skin and a florid complexion, but rather the pale, leaden complexion of those stricken with *lepra albicans* and the exanthema of the face at the bursting of the knots. The baldness of the head may well be connected with this disease, as the Jews knew very well.[2]

Preuschen has further pointed out that the counsel given by James the Ṣaddiq to Paul to have himself cleansed in the temple along with four Nazirites, though he himself had taken no such vow,[3] and the adoption of this counsel as well as the following ' seven days,' are best understood if Paul, as one cured from leprosy, had himself pronounced ' clean ' by the priests.[4]

The descriptions of the Antichrist, of Jewish-Christian origin, clearly show the advantage his opponents took of his distemper to represent him as a man ' stricken by God.' His adherents did not for that reason waver in their allegiance,[5] for according to certain Jewish traditions the Messiah himself was to be a *Ḥiwwara*, that is, a leper.[6]

Nor is it admissible to suppose Josephus and the Jewish Christians simply to have taken the peculiar features of the Antichrist as they found them in the popular Jewish apocalypses and to have attributed them to the two men whom they cordially detested, to wit, Jesus and Paul, the features of that popular Antichrist being altogether different and wholly fantastic.[7]

---

[1] See our Pl. XXXIII.

[2] *Lev.* xiii. 40-44.

[3] *Acts* xxi. 20-27 ; cf. Preuschen, p. 194 *sqq.*

[4] Naturally, there was no real ' cure ' of leprosy. But, as may be seen from *Lev.* xiii. and the Talmudic commentaries, the patient might be pronounced ' clean ' from the purely cultic view-point and admitted to the community. On the other hand, 'scall,' *psoriasis, leukoma, vitiligo,* etc., were not distinguished by the Jewish priests from true *elephantiasis.*

[5] *Gal.* iv. 14 : ' you have not spat out (ἐξεπτύσατε) at the torment in my flesh, but received me as if I were . . . the Messiah.'

[6] Strack-Billerbeck, ii. 286.

[7] Cf. Bousset, *Der Antichrist*, p. 101 *sq.*

An Opponent's Physical Defects in Ancient Political Invective

Now that plain evidence has been found, in the tradition on the portrait of Paul, of a textual development in perfect harmony with the parallel development of the portrait of Jesus, there remains for us to trace the history of pen-portraits in ancient literature.

Von Dobschütz blamed his predecessors for altogether neglecting this problem, and for their failure to draw what seemed to him the obvious conclusion as to the late origin of the portrait of Jesus. When he dealt with this question in 1899, Ivo Brun's excellent book on 'the literary portrait'[1] had escaped his notice, as had the investigations of J. Fürst on the 'personal descriptions in the Diktys story,'[2] whilst detailed studies dealing with the *iconismi* of the papyri were not then available. He could therefore maintain that the literary portrait, as a special development of rhetorical ἔκφρασις, began among the Latins with Suetonius and among the Greeks with Plutarch. He had overlooked Josephus' description of the Syrian soldier Sabinus,[3] evidently derived from the man's military papers,[4] copied in the report about his prowess to general headquarters. Thus it was not merely the fact that the *Halōsis* had not yet been disclosed to the Western world that led v. Dobschütz to the opinion that the references of Byzantine writers, contemporaries of the iconoclast controversy, to older historians, Josephus being one of these, were but a fiction.

The truth is that the literary portrait is as old as Greek literature. When the crafty Odysseus says of his pretended comrade Eurybates,

'And I will tell thee of him too, what manner of man he was : he was round-shouldered, brown-skinned, and curly-haired,'[5]

the scholiast rightly calls this sketch an εἰκονισμός. And who does not know that cruelly scornful description in the *Iliad* of Thersites, that first representative of democratic opposition recorded in history ?—

'ill-favoured beyond all men that came to Ilios, bandy-legged was he, and lame of one foot, and his two shoulders rounded, arched down upon his chest ; and over them his head was warped, and a scanty stubble sprouted on it.'[6]

One can see with what diabolic cunning the Greeks of the Homeric age practised that basest of political arts—emphasizing, that is, the physical defects of an adversary to render him ridicu-

---

[1] *Das literarische Portrait*, Berlin, 1896.
[2] *Philologus*, lxi. (1902), p. 377 *sqq.*
[3] Cf. above, p. 392$_1$.   [4] Cf. above, p. 444$_2$.
[5] *Od.*, xix. 245 *sq.* (Butcher and Lang).
[6] *Il.*, ii. 216 *sqq.* (Lang, Leaf, and Myers).

lous in the eyes of the hearers, the *argumentum ad hominem*
the theory of which was complacently taught by the Roman
Cicero and practised by him, without scruple, with the greatest
effect.[1]   It is quite true that the description of Jesus in Josephus
cannot be compared with the tactful pen-portraits of Plutarch nor
with those of Suetonius or his sources.[2]   Josephus did not have to
look there for models ; he found them rather among those rhe-
toricians who never scrupled to allude with biting scorn to the
bodily infirmities of their opponents, their obscure extraction, or
their humble parentage.[3]

True enough, Josephus has not taken the trouble to present his
readers with a sketch of the human imperfections of any other of
those Zealots or misleaders of the people whom he so cordially
detested.   The reason is simple.   Josephus did not waste his
efforts on persons of little or no importance whatever for the sequel
of events.[4]   With Jesus it was quite different.   His adherents still
lived, even after his death—nay, after the destruction of Jerusalem
—a menace to the peace of the empire as well as to conservative
Pharisaic Judaism.   The poor pseudo-messiahs who had come
forth from obscurity, to have their day, like the kings of the
Saturnalia, and then to be plunged again into everlasting oblivion,
might well be left in their graves.   The Naṣōraean, who after his
death continued to live and to make converts even in the palace
of the Flavian dynasty, was a far more terrible enemy.   To destroy
his memory every means was felt to be good.

THE ROMAN INDICTMENT OF JESUS AS THE SOURCE OF JOSEPHUS

Josephus' statement concerning Jesus, the opening section of
which we have just restored,[5] belongs to the history of Jewish[6] and
heathen polemic against the Messianist or (as after Antiochene and
Hellenistic fashion we should say to-day) the Christian propaganda.[7]

Josephus is quite familiar with the chief points of that propaganda ; he knows that the Messiah called himself ' Son of Man,'
that is, ' Man,' whereas his Hellenistic followers speak of him as

---

[1] *De Oratore*, 68-72 ; *Pro Sestio*, viii. § 18 *sq.*

[2] The portrait of Augustus comes from his freedman and secretary, the Syrian
Julius Marathus.   But Suetonius did not hesitate, on occasion, to use the caricature drawn by an opponent, as in his portrait of Caligula.

[3] Cf., for example, the attack of Demosthenes (*De Corona*, xviii. § 259) on
Aeschines.

[4] Besides, none of the other messianist leaders had been tried before a Roman
court-martial.   Where should Josephus find their *iconismi* ?

[5] Cf. above, pp. 424-29.

[6] On the Jewish measures taken against Paul's propaganda, cf. Justin. Mart.,
Dial., cviii.

[7] It was originally a propaganda for the *Civitas Dei*, the Christian theocracy,
of a perfectly terrestrial form and meaning and opposed to the Roman empire.
Cf. the *Passio Pauli*, ii. (Hennecke, p. 210).

'Son of God,' and his Jewish adherents as an 'angel,' as the 'true prophet,' i.e. Moses *redivivus*, the true wonder-working prophet of the final age.

Whence did he derive this knowledge? It is to be noted, in the first place, that in the *Halōsis* no trace can be found of any utilization of the *Logia* of Matthew, and we may conclude without hesitation that our author came to know these only after the completion of the *Halōsis*, since they are clearly drawn upon in the *Testimonium Flavianum* of the *Antiquities*.[1] This is somewhat surprising, since the Samaritan Thallus had already read and controverted these messianic predictions as early as the middle of the first century.[2]

On proceeding to examine Josephus' statement for other possible sources, one cannot help noting the highly significant 'Some said of him . . . but the others . . .; his disciples call him . . ., but the Greeks . . .,' and so on.

This typical confrontation of various conflicting opinions is obviously based on the record of the statements of witnesses, whether made at the trial or at the preliminary enquiry, and summed up in the writ of indictment (*libellus*). As unmistakable is the playing off of these witnesses against one another so as to expose their mutual contradictions. How can he be a man, a 'Son of God,' and an angel at the same time? How can he be Moses come to life again when in so many points he disregarded the law of Moses—the Sabbath, for example? How can he be a messenger of God if he sets himself up against the commands of God? Certainly there are witnesses to the fact that he himself never did anything disgraceful (ἄτοπον) or high-handed (ἐπιχειρήματα) [3] —that is admitted and recognized; but even so, it is established that by his word he 'prepared' and instigated the whole affair.

Then comes the climax of the attack. Wonderful as his power, displayed on various occasions, seems to be, how can any one be taken for an angel or a messenger of God who shows such a pitiable figure, so ordinary and commonplace a physical nature? And now follows the reading of the detailed personal description of a diminutive man, scarce three cubits high and, alas! of so plain an appearance! It is the merciless *argumentum ad hominem*, according to all the rules of Graeco-Roman rhetoric.

The whole ring of these words is clear and unmistakable. It is the tone of the prosecuting attorney driving the victim into a corner down to the smallest detail; the well-bred, gentlemanly irony of the sceptic, 'si hominem dicere fas est.' Josephus, or his secretary, has done nothing beyond copying the *Acta Pilati*, the governor's report about the judicial procedure against Jesus from the *Commentarii* of Tiberius.

[1] See above, p. 55 ll. 34 ff.　　[2] See above, p. 298.　　[3] Cf. above, p. 384 n. 12.

XVI

THE CRISIS

REBELLION PLANNED OR ACTUALLY ATTEMPTED ?

WE have seen above [1] the text of Josephus relating the arrival of the Galilaean wonder-worker on the Mount of Olives, a text leaving no doubt whatever as to the hostility of the writer towards the hero of this episode. Yet in spite of this the passage culminates in a strangely favourable result for the accused : he can at most be regarded as the spiritual originator of what happened.

This result is the more remarkable in that it is in contradiction to the Gospels—at variance, therefore, with what the Christians themselves were prepared to admit. The counsel for the prosecution, the governor's *comes et adsessor*, then, either knew nothing of the incident with the money-changers in the temple, or else the witnesses had successfully contested it. In contrast to John the Baptist, of whom Josephus or his source informs us that he summoned the Jews to freedom, we are told of Jesus merely that ' many of the multitude followed him and hearkened to his teaching, and many souls were in commotion, thinking that thereby the Jewish tribes might free themselves from Roman hands.'

It is not his preaching, then, which raises these high-flown expectations ; the masses themselves entertain these hopes because they regard the wonder-worker as a Moses *redivivus*. There is no indication of any Christian alteration of the original text in this paragraph. On the contrary, the idea that the multitude expects from Jesus the miracle of the liberation of Israel, while he passively lets himself be driven on by the excitement of the crowd— that idea runs right through the following section :

' Now it was his custom to sojourn upon the Mount of Olives,[2] and there he bestowed his healings upon the people. And there assembled unto him of helpers [3] one hundred and fifty, and a multitude of the populace.[4] Now when they saw his power, that he accomplished whatsoever he would [5] by a (magic) word, they called

---

[1] Cf. above, pp. 383 ff.
[2] This was also the scene of the first appearance of the Egyptian pseudo-messiah ; cf. *B.J.*, ii. § 262 ; A. Marmorstein, *The Quest*, xvii. 153.
[3] Cf. above, p. 384 n. 14.   [4] Slav. *ljudii*=ὄχλοι.
[5] Cf. Egesippus, ii. *c*, 12, ed. Ussani, *C.S.E.L.*, lxvi. p. 163 : ' hic in potestate habebat, ut omnia, quae fieri vellet, imperaret.'

upon him to enter into the city, cut down the Roman [1] troops and Pilate, and to rule over us,[2] and he disdained us not.' [3]

In the traditional text of the *Halōsis* there follows the sentence about the information laid before Pilate by the Jewish leaders when the news reached them, whereupon Pilate forthwith through his soldiers has crowds of people massacred and the wonder-worker arrested, the latter being then condemned as a *maleficus* (i.e. a ' sorcerer '), a rioter, a pretender to the crown, and led off to execution.

According to this version of the story, then, Josephus has depicted Pilate's massacre of the people and the execution of the wonder-worker as purely precautionary measures of intimidation, as an extraordinarily severe and barbarous punishment of a mere plan of the Zealots which had not yet got even so far as an attempt to revolt, and he has represented the condemnation of the wonder-worker as a political act not far removed from judicial murder.

It is, of course, quite conceivable that Josephus, at least in his original *Capture of Jerusalem*, written for his countrymen, should have given a version of events representing the meditated revolt as nipped in the bud through the information laid before Pilate by the Jewish leaders. Josephus has in fact described several abortive attempts at rebellion. Thus in *Ant.*, xviii. 5. 2, Herod Antipas has John arrested and slain before the feared insurrection broke out ; in xx. 5 we are told that Fadus gave Theudas no time to try his messianic exodus, but promptly had him cut down with many of his followers by a cavalry contingent. In xviii. 4. 1 Pilate himself massacres the Samaritans, whose false prophet had promised them to rediscover the ark of the covenant hidden in a hole on Mt. Gerizim, before they could ascend the mountain; and in xx. 8. 6, in the story of the Egyptian sorcerer who proposed to shatter the walls of Jerusalem by blowing the trumpets of Jericho, Felix instantly, on the mere announcement of a gathering on the Mount of Olives, has 400 people butchered.

Were one completely to forgo the temptation to insert after the words ' to rule over us, and he disdained us not,' a sentence corresponding to one of the Gospel accounts of the messianic entry into Jerusalem, the unaltered Slavonic statement would yet present us with a thoroughly plausible narrative and depict a procedure very similar to the story of the Egyptian false prophet. A rabbi is reported as working spectacular cures and preaching on the Mount of Olives : the mob gathers round him and plans a messianic rising in which Jesus is to figure as God's Anointed,

---

[1] Cf. *B.J.*, i. § 172.   [2] *B.J.*, ii. § 262.

[3] I.e. as subjects : ' he did not disdain the kingship over us that was offered to him.'

the liberator-king. When the hierarchy and through them Pilate hear of it, a military attack is made on the crowd on the Mount of Olives, just as was made by Felix a number of years later. But whereas, then, the pseudo-messiah disappeared in the crowd never to be seen again, Jesus is arrested, brought up for judgment, and, the plot having been thus frustrated, crucified for the mere weakness of having consented to that plot, just as Theudas[1] was taken alive and, without trial, beheaded or hewn in pieces.

A story of this type has nothing intrinsically improbable about it, and the tendency to represent Pilate as a brutal butcher of men and an oppressor of the Jews is quite reconcilable with the aims of Josephus in this first edition of his work. He extenuated as far as possible the guilt of the Jews in this matter, emphasizing the frightful harshness of Pilate; and no doubt also, as we may safely suppose, Pilate himself in his report to Tiberius, used by Josephus, had suppressed the significant details recorded in the Gospels of the messianic entry, the proclamation of Jesus as king of the Jews, the events in the temple court, and so on, because it was naturally embarrassing to the governor to have to admit that such things could occur without his having intervened in time to prevent them.

The legal admissibility of the procedure against Jesus as described in the Slavonic version of Josephus cannot well be doubted. To the Roman jurist the mere appearance of illegal intention is sufficient ground for punishment: ' dolus pro facto accipitur,' ' consilium non factum puniendum est.'[2]

Even if Berendts' obsolete rendering, ' but he heeded not,' were right and Jesus had merely failed to pay due attention to the seditious counsels of the people and his associates, i.e. to make every effort to counteract them, there would still be under Roman law a case of ' culpa lata.'[3] Moreover, the procedure of a provincial governor's court was essentially not a ' cognitio,' but a ' coercio,' left to the free discretion of the magistrate, the procedure *extra ordinem* of a court not strictly bound by the law. Where the ' disobedience' to the executive was notorious, there was no need for any ' cognitio ' to establish it ; where such a ' cognitio ' took place, it was not tied to any fixed forms. Instead of the regular ' accusatio' made by a plaintiff, the mere information of a ' delator ' sufficed, and even that was not necessary if the governor through his own military intelligence department (the ' speculatores ') possessed sufficient knowledge of the action or plot.

---

[1] *Ant.*, xx. 5. 1 ; Euseb., *Hist. eccl.*, ii. 11. 1.
[2] *Coll. leg. Mos.*, i. 7. 1 ; Cicero, *Pro mil.*, 19 ; Seneca, *De benef.*, v. 14.
[3] *Dig. L.*, xiv. 2, 13. 2 (Ulpianus) = ' nimia negligentia,' i.e. ' non intellegere, quod omnes intelligunt.'

The punishment for such 'crimina extraordinaria' was left to the governor's discretion. The offence of rebellion, especially when appearing in the form of high treason,[1] fell in imperial times without exception under the category of 'crimina extraordinaria'; the arming of the participants ranked as one of the particularly aggravating circumstances of the crime, as did also the formation of 'coetus nocturni,' such as the nightly assemblies of the followers of Jesus on the Mount of Olives, from the midst of which he was arrested. The author of sedition fell, moreover, under the penalties of Sylla's 'lex Cornelia de sicariis et veneficis' and under the law against acts of violence.[2] The mere gathering together of a crowd might be interpreted as an offence deserving of death. Punishment for revolt was to be inflicted forthwith, no appeal being allowed : even the capital punishment of a Roman citizen was not subject to imperial confirmation. The crime of sorcery, with which Jesus is charged in the Christian *Acts of Pilate* and which occupies the first place in the verdict reported by Josephus, ranked in Roman law as a specially serious offence punishable by death.[3]

Pilate may therefore quite well have proceeded in the manner represented by the Old Russian version of the *Halōsis*, though the planned rebellion had not yet been translated into action.

On the other hand, it is inconceivable that Josephus should originally have spoken of a mere plan of revolt, because the passage immediately following the section dealing with Jesus, and which relates to the disturbances caused by the building of the aqueduct, begins with the words, ' And after that they caused *a second tumult.*' Berendts expressed just surprise at those words, because ' the revolt ' in the case of Jesus ' in our narrative never actually broke out.' The expression ' a second revolt ' cannot hark back to the story of the imperial standards, because, apart from the distance separating the two in the text, ' there was,' in Berendts' words,[4] 'no actual revolt in consequence of the imperial standards being brought into the temple.' Berendts therefore was doubtless right when he said that the archetype of the Slavonic version must have narrated the story of Jesus as the *first revolt*. A supplementary insertion in the restoration of the Josephus' text is therefore unavoidable.

---

[1] Cicero, *Orat. part.*, xxx. 105 : ' (maiestatem) minuit is, qui per vim multitudinis rem ad seditionem vocavit.' The intention is sufficient ; cf. Ulpian, *Dig.*, xlviii. 4. 1 : ' maiestatis crimine tenetur is cuius opera dolo malo consilium initum erit . . . quo coetus conventusve fiat, hominesve ad seditionem convocentur.'

[2] *Dig.*, xlviii. 8. 3, §§ 4 and 6, 3 pr. ; Paulus, 5, 22. 1=*Dig.*, xlviii. 19. 38, § 2 : ' auctores seditionis et tumultus vel concitatores populi . . . in crucem tolluntur.'

[3] Apuleius, *Apol.*, xxvi. 27 ; Paulus, v. 23. 17 ; Mommsen, *Röm. Strafr.*, p. 639 *sqq.*

[4] *Texte und Untersuchungen*, xiv. 1, p. 53.

A Fragment of the ' Halōsis ' in John of Antioch

The conclusion reached in the previous section is fully confirmed by another piece of evidence,[1] likewise noticed by Berendts but not recognized by him as one of the sentences missing in Josephus—indeed, possibly the only sentence deleted there.   Prof. v. Dobschütz it was who suggested to him [2] that a fragment of John of Antioch [3] (a chronicler of uncertain date somewhere about A.D. 620), surviving in a unique MS.[4] of the ' Excerpts ' of the Emperor Constantine Porphyrogenitus and preserved in the Escurial, contains the Christian [5] fable of Pilate's bribery.   Considering that this incident is elsewhere found only in the *Rescriptum Tiberii* [6] and in the *Vita beatae Mariae et Salvatoris rhythmica*,[6] both of which show clear echoes of the *Halōsis*, it is certainly noteworthy that John of Antioch also mentions a revolt of the Jews in Jerusalem at the time of Jesus, and thus again comes to a certain extent into contact with the Slavonic Josephus.

To quote Berendts : [7]

' In the same fragment is found a further feature not to be explained by the Gospels.   We read, "And they were all gathered together in Jerusalem and stirred up insurrection against him, pouring forth blasphemies upon God and Caesar."   Here, too, we may detect in the last resort an echo of our Slavonic statement, though seriously distorted.   The revolt against Caesar is in the Slavonic Josephus indeed only contemplated ; the movement against Jesus is only a consequence of his refusal to participate in that opposition.' [8]

A closer investigation of the fragment [8] permits us to go considerably further.   It runs thus :

' That under Tiberius the king, the Lord Jesus, being thirty-three years of age, was accused by the Jews of destroying their religious doctrine ($\delta \delta \xi a v$) and introducing another new one in its stead. [   ] And they were all gathered together in Jerusalem and stirred up insurrection against him ($\kappa a \tau' a \dot{v} \tau o \hat{v}$), pouring forth blasphemies upon God and Caesar.   Thereupon taking courage ($\dot{\epsilon} \nu \tau \epsilon \hat{v} \theta \epsilon \nu \pi a \rho \rho \eta \sigma i a \nu \lambda a \beta \delta \nu \tau \epsilon s$) they laid hold on him by night and delivered him to Pontius Pilate, the governor, who, whether from cowardly terror of the multitude or because of a promise of money, having found no fault (in him), ordered him to be crucified ; and after he was crucified there was a

---

[1] C. Müller, *Fragm. hist. Graec.*, iv. (Paris, 1851), p. 571, No. 81.
[2] *Texte und Untersuchungen*, xiv. 1, p. 52 *sq.*
[3] Sometimes called John Malalas ' the Rhetorician.'
[4] Cf. the reproduction on p. 446 of vol. ii. of the German edition of this book.
[5] Cf. above, p. 386.   [6] Cf. above, p. 386_{2·3}.
[7] *Op. et loc. cit.*
[8] Berendts' erroneous interpretation is based on the Christian alteration of the words *nas ne nebreze* (above, p. 384 n. 18), the tendentious character of which he did not perceive.

great earthquake and darkness over all the earth. And having tasted of death, he rose from the dead on the third day and was taken up into the heavens. There have been many witnesses who have seen and recorded (this).'

The text as it stands makes an impossible assertion. The words κατ' αὐτοῦ in their present context can only mean ' they rose against Jesus.' But for such a ' revolt *against* Jesus ' the tradition has no place. For, granted that it could have had a practical purpose, it could never have afforded the Jews a pretext for delivering him to Pilate and laying an accusation against him. Furthermore, according to *Mark* xiv. 2 and *Matt.* xxvi. 5 the high priests, as one can well imagine, were anxious above all to avoid a tumult of the people. Why should a Christian chronographer deliberately set aside the statements of the Gospels to the effect that the Jews arrested and brought the innovator Jesus before the Romans for sentence, acting in all this entirely within their legal rights, to substitute for this illuminating and thoroughly plausible account such an unnecessary and nonsensical invention about an ' uproar of the people ' or ' rising against Jesus ' promoted by the Jews themselves and said to have first given them the necessary courage (παρρησίαν) to arrest and deliver him to Pilate ? I can make no sense of the passage unless something like this ' rising ' of the Jews was somehow reported as having happened immediately before the crucifixion of Jesus. In that case the chronographer would simply have distorted something that lay before him—obviously, as Berendts assumed, the narrative of Josephus in the Greek text which was the basis of the Slavonic *Halōsis*.

The solution of the difficulty is simple enough. The sentence which puzzled Berendts, ' and they were all gathered together in Jerusalem and stirred up insurrection against him,' is found also in the ' Report ' (*Anaphora*) of Pontius Pilate, where it is strangely split into two portions. Pilate there says :

' Jerusalem, in which . . . all the multitude of the Jews, being gathered together, have delivered to me a certain man called Jesus, bringing many charges against him . . . and when many stirred up insurrection against *me*, I ordered him to be crucified.'

Obviously, this gives much better sense than the statement in John of Antioch. Here the accusations are laid 'against him,' i.e. against Jesus ; the arrest follows as in the Gospels, but the insurrection is ' against *me*,' i.e. against Pilate. The governor is thus assailed by a rising of the Jewish populace,[1] and thereby driven to take the harsh course of crucifying Jesus.

[1] Cf. also the *Acta Pilati*, 9, and Tertullian, *Apol.*, 21.

The situation is very similar in the Latin 'Letter of Pilate to Tiberius ' :

> ' unless I had feared that a sedition of the people, who were almost seething with indignation, would arise, perchance that man would be living with us still.'

It can be clearly seen that this 'rising' of the Jews against Pilate in these two Christian forgeries represents an attempt to identify the rising of the followers of Jesus against Pilate before the Passion, which is mentioned by Josephus, with the ' tumult ' of the enemies of Jesus mentioned in *Matt.* xxvii. 24 :

> ' when Pilate saw that he prevailed nothing, but rather that a tumult was arising.'

To sever all possible connexion between the στάσις which preceded the Passion and which it was found impossible to blot out entirely even in the Gospel tradition,[1] the Christian forgers of the various records of Pilate could do no better than transpose the rising to the time *after* the arrest of Jesus, and thus to convert it from a rising of his followers into a tumult of his enemies against him.

Turning back, now, from the Greek *Anaphora* and the Latin ' Letter,' to the curious account of John of Antioch, we see without difficulty that the absurd traditional text of the chronographer can at once be brought into harmony with the tolerable though highly biased statement in the two other passages by a simple transposition of the second and third clauses. We thus obtain the following text :

> '₁Under the Emperor Tiberius the Lord Jesus, being thirty-three years of age, was accused by the Jews of destroying their belief and introducing a new one. ₃↑Thereupon they had the daring to lay hold on him by night and to deliver him to the governor, Pontius Pilate.↓ ₂And being all gathered together in Jerusalem, they stirred up an insurrection against him' (i.e. Pilate !), ' giving vent to blasphemies against God and Caesar. ₄And he' (Pilate), 'whether from cowardly terror of the multitude or because of the promise of a bribe, though he found no fault (in him), ordered him to be crucified,' etc.

If, on the other hand, one compares the actual text of John of Antioch with the account in the *Halōsis*, such a comparison at once shows that the source of John, or of his authority as discussed below, was a MS. of Josephus which already contained the Christian interpolation of the bribery of Pilate, but which, at the point indicated by square brackets in the text quoted above on p. 461 l. 30, had suffered a less extensive erasure than the MS. utilized by the Slavonic translator.

If we insert in the gap indicated by the square brackets in the

---

[1] *Mark* xv. 7 ; *Luke* xxiii. 19.

text of the chronographer the peculiar statements of the Slavonic Josephus on the revolt planned by the multitude following Jesus, the narrative, so absurd in its present form, suddenly becomes thoroughly intelligible and clear ; in particular, the words 'against him ' retain their natural reference to Pilate.　We then get the following statement :

> ' Under the Emperor Tiberius, when thirty-three years of age, Jesus was accused by the Jews of destroying their doctrine and introducing a new one, [*and in particular of attacking the traditional consecration of the Sabbath.*[1]　*For he did many miracles and effected many cures, even on the Sabbath*].　[But when the people saw his power, that he could do whatsoever he would by a word, they required him to enter into the city, cut down the Romans and Pilate, and rule over them.]　And having all trooped into Jerusalem, they stirred up an insurrection against him ' (*sc.* Pilate), ' uttering blasphemies against God and Caesar.　And hereupon (the high priests) plucked up courage to seize him by night and to deliver him to Pilate,' etc.

It should be noted that the words κατ' αὐτοῦ only acquire their natural reference to Pilate if the most objectionable sentence, ' But he disdained us not,' had already been deleted, and even then the reference is not entirely clear.　By a further deletion of the equally dubious if not yet more objectionable clause about the plan of revolt, the absurd sentence in John of Antioch about an ' insurrection against Jesus ' can have arisen out of such a perfectly intelligible narrative; whilst the reading of the *Anaphora* and the ' Letter of Pilate,' as shown above, presupposes, in place of this omission, merely a transposition of that one striking sentence. Conversely, the sentence ' and they all gathered together in Jerusalem and stirred up insurrection,' etc., fits excellently into the gap after the words ' But he disdained us not ' in the text of the *Halōsis*, a text which must be at the base of the chronographer in one form or another.

The insertion into the text of the *Halōsis* of this one peculiar sentence perfectly harmonizes with what is logically required by the opening of § 175, ' and thereupon they caused a *second* insurrection.'　If this one sentence really comes from Josephus (and it is impossible to hit upon a more obvious source), that writer depicted the insurrection planned by the Zealots as actually realized, and the opening words of § 175 are then fully justified.

Nor can it be denied that those lines are perfectly in keeping with the statement that the rebels ' uttered blasphemies [2] against God and Caesar,' and with the Gospel story of the triumphal entry

---

[1] For this sentence, cf. the *Anaphora Pilati* and the *Acts of Pilate*, i. p. 502, Thilo.

[2] The word is familiar to Josephus. See *Ant.*, xx. §§ 108 and 110.

of Jesus into Jerusalem. For the cries, ' Blessed be he that cometh
in the name of the Lord,' [1] are in the eyes of Josephus and those of
the Jewish high priests [2] blasphemies against God, and the ex-
clamations, ' King of Israel,' [3] an insult to the emperor.[4]   That is
all that need have been said by Pilate in his official report to
Tiberius, and consequently no more need have stood in Josephus.
There is, then, a very strong probability that through this unique
MS. of the Escurial another easily discernible gap in the narrative
of the Slavonic Josephus can be filled.

John of Antioch probably did not draw directly on the *Halōsis*,
for his chronological statement concerning the age of Jesus agrees
with the traditional Christian chronology but not with the statement of Josephus, who refers to Jesus as a man of 'mature age.' [5]

Berendts [6] noted that the preceding fragment of John (No. 80)
contains a statement on the death of Herod Antipas which goes
beyond what is told in Josephus, to wit, that he was murdered in
his own bedroom, his wife being a partner to the plot.   It is
attributed by the Bodleian MS. of Malalas [7] to the ' very wise
Clement.'   One may therefore conjecture that John drew his
information from a lost chronological work of Clement of Alexandria.   Now, Clement [8] in turn made use of a chronographer who
wrote in the tenth year of Antoninus Pius [9] (A.D. 149), who in his
turn utilized Josephus for his investigation of the year-weeks in
Dan. ix.[10]   As the statement on the age of Jesus cannot have
been missing in a Christian chronographer, the conjecture that our
fragment comes from this older chronographer through the medium
of Clement of Alexandria would not seem too bold.   As both of the
intermediate sources are older than the Christian revision of the
writings of Josephus, which did not take place until after the time
of Origen or perhaps after 312, one need not wonder that in part
they preserved a more perfect text of the much mishandled *History
of the Jewish War.*   As a matter of fact, Dr. Schlatter [11] thinks that
the chronographer Judas, a lineal descendant of the family of
Jesus and the last bishop of the Jewish-Christian Church, mentioned
by Eusebius [12] as writing ' in the tenth year of Severus,' is identical
with Clement's ' chronographer of the tenth year of Antoninus
Pius,' and that Eusebius had erroneously confused Alexander
Severus with Antoninus Pius.   If this fairly plausible hypothesis

---

[1] *Mark* xi. 9 and parallels.   [2] *Mark* xiv. 64 ; *Matt.* xxvi. 65.
[3] *John* xii. 13.
[4] A ' crimen laesae majestatis '; cf. *John* xix. 12.
[5] Cf. above, p. 425₁₅₋₁₆.
[6] *Op. cit.*, p. 53.   [7] Page 239, 18th ed., Bonn.
[8] *Stromat.*, i. 21. 147.
[9] Cf. A. Schlatter, *Zur Topographie und Geschichte Palaestinas*, 1893, p. 403 *sqq.*
Harnack, *Texte und Untersuchungen*, xii. 1 (1894), p. 12.
[10] Schlatter, *op. et loc. cit.*
[11] *Op. et loc. cit.*   [12] *Hist. eccl.*, vi. 7.

be accepted, it would result in the curious fact that we owe it indirectly to a member of Jesus' family that the sentence about the στάσις caused by Jesus has been preserved, in spite of the efforts of later Christian censors.

Thus, contrary to all expectation, it has actually been found possible to recover almost in its entirety from old and newly disclosed sources the section of Josephus' *Halōsis* derived directly from the official report of Pilate, the governor, to the Emperor Tiberius, relating to the personality of Jesus, his appearance on the Mount of Olives, the subsequent insurrection of the people in Jerusalem, his condemnation and crucifixion.

THE COMPLETE STATEMENT OF JOSEPHUS ON PILATE'S GOVERNORSHIP

On the basis of the results obtained above,[1] the complete narrative of the *Halōsis*, ii. 9. 2-4 (§§ 169-77), would read as follows :

'And after that there was sent to Judaea by Tiberius a governor who secretly by night brought to Jerusalem Caesar's image which is called *semaia* ; and he set it up in the city. And when morning came the Jews saw (it) and raised[2] a great uproar ; and they were aghast at the sight, because their Law was trampled under foot, for it forbids the presence of any image in the city. And the people of the surrounding neighbourhood, when they heard what had happened, all rushed in passion to the spot, and hastened to Caesarea and implored Pilate to remove the *semaia* from Jerusalem and permit them to maintain the customs of their fathers. But when Pilate obdurately refused their request, they fell upon their faces and remained motionless for five days and five nights.

'And after that Pilate took his seat on the throne in the great hippodrome and summoned the people, as though he would answer them, and he ordered the soldiers suddenly to surround the Jews, in full armour. And when these beheld the unexpected sight (of) three battalions surrounding them (on all sides), they were sore afraid. And Pilate spake threateningly to them, " I will cut you all down, if you will not receive Caesar's image," and he ordered the soldiers to draw their swords. But the Jews all with one consent fell down and, extending their necks, exclaimed that they were ready as sheep for the slaughter, " rather than that we should transgress the law." And Pilate, marvelling at their Godfearing purity,[3] ordered the *semaia* to be removed from Jerusalem.

'At that time, too, there appeared a certain man ⟨*of magical*[4] *power*⟩, if it is permissible to call him a man, ⟨*whom (certain) Greeks*

---

[1] Cf. pp. 424-29. [2] Lit. ' fell into.'
[3] ' their fear of God and (their) purity ' : Gr. τὸ τῆς δεισιδαιμονίας ἄκρατον, ' their unmitigated superstition.'
[4] Lentulus : ' great.'

call a son of God, but his disciples the true prophet, (said to) raise the dead and heal all diseases⟩. His nature and his form were human ; ⟨*a man of simple appearance, mature age, small stature, three cubits high, hunchbacked, with a long face, long nose, and meeting eyebrows, so that they who see him might be affrighted, with scanty hair (but) with a parting in the middle of his head, after the manner of the Nazirites, and with an undeveloped beard*⟩. Only in semblance was he superhuman, (for) he gave some astonishing and spectacular exhibitions. But again, if I look at his commonplace physique I (for one) cannot call him an angel. And everything whatsoever he wrought through some invisible power, he wrought through some word and a command. Some said of him, "Our first lawgiver is risen again and displays many healings and (magic) arts," others that "he is sent from God." Howbeit in many things he disobeyed the law and kept not the Sabbath according to (our) fathers' custom. Yet he himself did nothing shameful or high-handed, but by (his) word he prepared everything.

'And many of the multitude followed after him and accepted his teaching, and many souls were excited, thinking that thereby the Jewish tribes might be freed from Roman hands. But it was his custom most (of the time) to abide over against the city on the Mount of Olives, and there too he bestowed his healings upon the people. And there assembled unto him of helpers [1] one hundred and fifty and a multitude of the mob.[2]

'Now when they saw his power, how that he accomplished whatsoever he would by a (magic) word, and when they had made known to him their will, that he should enter into the city, cut down the Roman troops and Pilate and rule over us, he disdained us not. ⟨*And having all flocked into Jerusalem, they raised an uproar (against Pilate),*[3] *uttering blasphemies alike against God and against Caesar*⟩. . . .[4]

'And when thereafter knowledge of it came to the Jewish leaders, they assembled together with the high priest and spake : We are powerless and (too) weak to withstand the Romans. But seeing that " the bow is bent," [5] we will go and impart to Pilate what we have heard, and we shall be safe, lest he hear (of it) from others and we be robbed of our substance and ourselves slaughtered and the children (of Israel) dispersed.

[1] ὑπηρέται.   [2] ὄχλος πολύς.
[3] The words in ( ) may or may not have stood in the original text ; cf. above, p. 464.
[4] That something is still missing here will be seen below (pp. 482 ff.), when Suidas' quotation from Josephus about 'Jesus officiating in the temple with the priests' will be discussed.
[5] Cf. *Ps.* xi. 2 : ' For lo, the wicked *bend their bow*, they make ready their arrow upon the string, that they may privily shoot at the upright in heart. If the foundation is destroyed, what can the righteous do ? The Lord is in his holy temple,' etc. ; further, *Zech.* ix. 9 *sqq.* : ' Rejoice greatly, O daughter of Zion ; shout, O daughter of Jerusalem : behold, thy king cometh unto thee : he is just, and having salvation : lowly, and riding upon an ass, and upon a colt, the foal of an ass . . . and his dominion shall be from sea even to sea, and from the river even to the ends of the earth. . . . When I have *bent Judah for me*, filled *the bow* with Ephraim, and raised up thy sons, O Zion, against thy sons, O Greece . . .'

'And they went and imparted (the matter) to Pilate, and he sent and had many of the multitude slain. And he had that wonder-worker brought up, and after instituting an enquiry concerning him, he passed (this) sentence upon him: "He is a malefactor,[1] a rebel, a robber [2] thirsting for the crown."[3] And they took him and crucified him according to the custom of (their) fathers.

'And after that they caused a second uproar. For Pilate had carried off the sacred treasure called Corbonas and spent it upon pipes for an aqueduct, wishing to bring in water from the Jordan from a distance of two hundred furlongs. And when the people cried out against him, he sent and beat them with cudgels; and three thousand were trodden down in the (ensuing) flight, but the rest were quieted. . . .'

The unprejudiced reader of this chapter will in the first place be unable to doubt any longer its Jewish origin. No Christian knew the Old Testament Scriptures sufficiently well to understand that short allusion to the ' bent bow,' much less to be able to invent it and put it into the mouth of the Jewish high priests. Neither Berendts nor any one of the Protestant or Catholic theologians who have hitherto dealt with the Slavonic Josephus has recognized or explained the quotation.

The next thing of note, particularly remarkable in view of the complete ignorance of Roman law displayed, according to Theodor Mommsen, in the forged *Acta Pilati*, is the judicially correct narrative of the legal procedure against Jesus. The narrative is from the outset designed to establish the fact of the three capital crimes, to wit, magic (*maleficium*), rebellion (*seditio* and *latrocinium*), and high treason (*crimen laesae maiestatis*), thereby justifying the result of the magistrate's judicial examination (*cognitio*). In that object, moreover, it is completely successful. The facts—admitted even by the interpolated Christian text—under Roman law permit of no other verdict save the one which is to be read in the critically restored text. An acquittal, such as is substituted by the Christian interpolations, is quite inconceivable, and, from what we know of the Emperor Tiberius, would have cost Pilate his head.

The complaints of the Jews about the violation of their Law, which the witnesses for the prosecution doubtless did not fail to bring up to the Romans, are only quite summarily mentioned, and do not figure at all in the sentence, once it has been established that no illegal or high-handed *act* could be proved against Jesus.

But the most striking and conclusive proof of the authenticity of the narrative is the fact that it contains absolutely nothing of those acts, under Roman law highly incriminating, which the Gospels themselves frankly admit, unaware that thereby they make impossible the Christian contention of the perfect innocence of

---

[1] Or ' sorcerer,' *maleficus*.
[2] Thus the Rumanian version. Cf. above, p. 385 n. 4.
[3] *carižadec*, lit. ' king-thirsty.'

Jesus and the theory of the judicial murder of which he was the victim. According to Roman law,[1] one is guilty of a *crimen laesae maiestatis*, deserving of death, so soon as one openly and without commission assumes powers which are the sole privilege of the government and its officers. The overthrowing of the money-changers' tables in the temple, the expulsion from the sacred precincts of the dealers in cattle for the sacrifices (quite apart from the actual assault with the scourge), the order to carry nothing [2] through the temple—these are so many expressions of an official authority which Jesus assumed unto himself in his own right, and which, according to Roman law, constituted an invasion of the functions of the temple police and their *segan* ($\sigma\tau\rho\alpha\tau\eta\gamma\acute{o}\varsigma$), and consequently a *laesio* or *minutio maiestatis* of the Roman sovereign, a crime deserving of death. The tumultuary proclamation of a ' king of the Jews ' without licence from Caesar is of course in itself high treason, and the words of Jesus requiring the Pharisees to leave his disciples alone are quite sufficient to establish what the Romans call *dolus malus*, if not *culpa lata* : [3] they show, if admitted or proved, the full responsibility of the *auctor seditionis*, thus proclaimed king, for the action of the multitude.

What later Jewish forger who knew the Gospels and wished to represent Jesus as a revolutionary would have let these choice statements of the Christians themselves escape him ? How could he have neglected to repeat the accusations of the Jews [4] to the effect that Jesus had impeded the payment of the tribute to Caesar and called himself an ' anointed king ' ? [5] Why should he not have made use of the summons of Jesus to pull down Herod's temple [6] to represent him and his disciples as ' malefactors wishing to burn' it ? [7]

It is easy to understand why Pilate in his report to the emperor avoided depicting events which he had been unable to prevent, in more vivid colours than were absolutely necessary in his own justification on the measures taken, and in particular the three crucifixions. It is equally natural that Josephus knew nothing of these events, which happened before his time, beyond what he found recorded in the *commentarii* of the imperial chancery. But it would be difficult to understand such a version of the story, at once plainly hostile and yet suppressing the gravest items of the accusation, as emanating from a Jewish interpolator who wrote after the four Gospels had come into existence and been widely disseminated.

---

[1] Cicero, *De inv.*, ii. 13. 56 : ' maiestatem minuere est aliquid de re publica, cum potestatem non haberes, administrare.' Marcianus, *Dig.*, xlviii. 4, 4 : ' qui privatus pro potestate magistratuve quid sciens dolo malo gesserit.'
[2] Or rather, ' no armour,' *Mark.* xi. 16 ; cf. below, p. 488 n. 1.
[3] See above, p. 459₃.   [4] *Luke* xxiii. 2.   [5] $\chi\rho\iota\sigma\tau\grave{o}\varsigma \ \beta\alpha\sigma\iota\lambda\epsilon\acute{u}\varsigma$, *ibid.*
[6] *John* ii. 19 ; cf. below, p. 494.   [7] *Gospel of Peter* 26.

Equally impossible is it to attribute the whole account, without eliminating Christian interpolations, to a Christian apologist of the stamp of the forger of the *Acta Pilati* and similar documents. For such a person would necessarily have made some attempt to explain away or put another interpretation upon facts rashly admitted in the Gospels, instead of suppressing them and mentioning in their place, wholly unnecessarily, seriously incriminating matters such as the hopes associated with the appearance of Jesus for a liberation from the Roman yoke, and the Zealots' subsequent plans of revolt against Pilate, with a massacre of the Roman garrison.

How, moreover, is one to explain in that case the remarkable fact that a Christian or a Jew of the post-apostolic age knows nothing whatever of the Twelve being appointed by Jesus the future judges of the twelve tribes of Israel or of the appointment of the Seventy-two as a Sanhedrin for the future empire,[1] but instead thrusts into the foreground the hundred and fifty ministers (ὑπηρέται), unheard of elsewhere, who cannot be understood but as the new town council of elders for Jerusalem [2] after its occupation ? If it is Josephus (or Pilate) who writes thus, an explanation is at hand, viz. that their authorities—in other words, Judas, the paid agent of the hierarchy, or the Roman *speculatores*—represented the situation thus and no otherwise : the traitor may have had good reasons for sparing the twelve, to whose number he himself belonged. In fact, it has always caused surprise that none of the disciples of the innermost circle shared the fate of Jesus or was even reported to the Romans. Judas may have screened the seventy-two on similar grounds, whilst just these newly appointed hundred and fifty, strangers to the more intimate associates, may have seemed to him deserving of no consideration. It is equally conceivable that the twelve and the seventy-two are included in the hundred and fifty, i.e. that in the last moment before the entry the constitution contemplated for the ' kingdom to come ' was simplified so as to admit of only one great council of elders— a κοινόν—in Jerusalem. It would be idle to speculate on the true explanation of this striking figure. It is enough to know that it

---

[1] See above, p. 348₂.₄.₅.

[2] *Nehemiah* v. 17 declares that he fed the *seganîm*, the elders or leaders of the town (*ziknê ha'ir*), one hundred and fifty men, at his table. This passage, overlooked even by a scholar like Schürer (ii. 1, p. 150, Engl. trsl.), clearly shows that the post-exilic town council of Jerusalem (which may in fact be identical with the ' commons,' τὸ κοινόν of Jerusalem, repeatedly mentioned by Josephus) was composed of one hundred and fifty town councillors. These ' aldermen,' like the Attic ' prytanes,' had the right to be fed at the expense of the town, and Nehemiah says in so many words that he provided for them, so as not to lay a burden upon the taxpayers. The word *seganîm* is not translated in the Greek Bible ; as a consequence, no one not conversant with the Hebrew text could know who the hundred and fifty men fed by Nehemiah were, and what the whole sentence meant.

can be explained very easily from the historical facts, but can in no way be derived from any parallel statements in any Christian or Jewish sources known to us to-day.

All things considered, then, I regard it as undeniable that this account of the appearance and downfall of Jesus is in every respect independent alike of the Gospels and of those curiously distorted yet not wholly worthless Jewish traditions to be found in the Talmud and later Haggadic literature down to the notorious *Toldoth Jeshu.*

It is henceforth possible, therefore, by the comparison of two versions of the story, wholly opposed to each other in their origin and aim, to form a comparatively unbiased picture of the real events which preceded the crucifixion of Jesus.

THE TRIUMPHAL ENTRY

' When he was come into Jerusalem, all the city was stirred.'
MATT. xxi. 10.

Scholars who deny or try to restrict by some special pleading the messianic character of the preaching of Jesus have always taken the strongest objection to the accounts of his triumphal entry into Jerusalem. Wellhausen,[1] with the approval of Dalman [2] and Cheyne,[3] conjectured that the messianic colouring of the narrative is a later addition, as is in fact suggested by the Fourth Gospel : [4] ' these things ' (i.e. the entry on the ass's colt, etc.) ' understood not his disciples at the first : but when Jesus was glorified, then remembered they that these things were written of him, and that they had done these things unto him.' Doubtless, advocates of the widespread view that the Gospel narratives of the *dies palmarum* are an exaggerated picture of commonplace events,[5] which in the bustle of pilgrims crowding to the feast might have remained practically unnoticed, might now appeal with a show of reason to Josephus. Were one to abandon as unnecessary the proposed insertion of the Escurial fragment into the Slavonic text, the Russian *Halōsis* might in fact be cited as evidence to show that neither the Romans nor the Jewish leaders had any knowledge whatever of a public proclamation and of Jesus as the ' king of peace ' riding upon the ass, nor of the tumult in the temple directly connected therewith. The so-called ' cleansing of the

---

[1] *Isr.-Jüd. Gesch.*, p. 381.
[2] *Worte Jesu*, i. 182: cf. *Gramm.*, 198 ; H. Windisch, *Der mess. Krieg*, Tübingen, 1909, p. 49.
[3] *Encycl. Bibl.*, 2118.   [4] *John* xii. 18.
[5] The O.T. inspiration for the scene, or for part of it, was found in 2 *Kings* ix. 13. For, as Dr. Klausner (*Jesus of Nazareth*, London, 1925, p. 310) correctly observed, in that crucial passage the captains of the host ' *took every man his garment, and put it under him*' (Jehu) ' on the top of the stairs, and blew with trumpets, *saying, Jehu is king.*'

temple' might accordingly have been confined to a passionate rhetorical outburst of Jesus, passing unnoticed in the noise of the crowd, a mere squabble of words leading to a scuffle with some of the nearest money-changers and cattle-dealers. In such an environment, accustomed as it was to boisterous commotion, a few light tables might be upset through the vehemence of a quarrel without any need for the temple authorities to take the matter very seriously.

Those who have set their heart upon representing the story of Jesus as though the Founder of the universal church never did anything but indulge in rhetoric,[1] will never be dissuaded from viewing these events through the inverted telescope of their non-political point of view and in this easy way seeing them as a pretty and idyllic miniature.

For the unprejudiced reader of the sources, however, there remains the fact that in the *Halōsis* the collision of the Jews with Pilate over the building of the aqueduct constitutes the ' *second tumult,*' and that Josephus must therefore have regarded the events leading up to the crucifixion of Jesus as the *first* uproar, and must accordingly have described them in words similar to the Escurial fragment of John of Antioch. With the words of the excerpt of Constantine Porphyrogenetus, certainly derived from Josephus, ' and they all gathered together in Jerusalem and raised an uproar' (στάσιν ἐκίνουν), the original Christian tradition is in striking agreement, notwithstanding all subsequent attempts to tone down the originally quite vivid colours.

As has repeatedly been observed before, Mark[2] has not hesitated to describe what took place at the entry into Jerusalem and the temple as ' the insurrection ' (ἡ στάσις). He says of Jesus[3] surnamed Bar Abba, or Bar Rabba, 'And there was one called Barabbas, (lying) bound with them that had made insurrection, men who in *the* insurrection (ἐν τῇ στάσει) had committed manslaughter.' In *Luke*[4] this sentence is completely altered : ' the insurrection,' by which a writer can only allude to a familiar event mentioned shortly before (chapter xi.), here becomes 'a certain riot that happened in the city.'

It may be presumed to be notorious that no commentator could ever explain what was meant by ' *the* insurrection ' and ' *the* rebels ' ;[5] and simply because no one could or would admit that the proclamation of the Davidic kingdom[6] in the existing aristocratic or hierocratic client-republic—an attempt equivalent to

---

[1] This in spite of *Thess.* i. 5 : ' Our gospel came not unto you in word only, but also in power.'   [2] xv. 7.
[3] 'Jesus Barabbas' was the reading found by Origen in some MSS. of *Matt.* xxvii. 16 *sq.*
[4] xxiii. 19: "διὰ στάσιν τινὰ γενομένην ἐν τῇ πόλει."
[5] τῶν στασιαστῶν, *Mark* xv. 7.   [6] *Mark* xi. 10.

proclaiming the Duc de Guise King of France on the Place de la Concorde—could not in the eyes of an author writing in Rome under Vespasian or Titus amount to anything less than a στάσις, a *seditio*. Likely enough, *Mark*—whether the hypothetical proto-Mark or the extant Gospel, in which one may without difficulty postulate considerable deletions of objectionable passages at the hands of ecclesiastical revisers—originally used the word στάσις also at the first mention of these events. If we set the two passages side by side—

Mark xi. 11.	*Matt.* xxi. 10.
And he entered into Jerusalem.	And when he was come into Jerusalem, *all the city was stirred,*[1] saying, Who is this ?—
⌐ 9 ⌐	

and further note the complete and highly significant blank at this point in the corresponding narratives of *Luke* and *John*, we cannot but recognize that in *Mark* a clause must have been struck out answering to the strong phrase ἐσείσθη πᾶσα ἡ πόλις in *Matthew* at the point indicated by the empty square, for a city is not ' shaken ' by the people's question, ' Who is this ? ' and the reply, ' Jesus the prophet.' That creates no ' shock ' (σεισμός), but at the most a ' murmur ' (γογγυσμός). Here again the lack of logical coherence is clearly traceable to an old erasure, dating from the time when careful provision had to be made for the unmolested diffusion of the Gospels throughout the Roman empire.

THE LIBERATION OF BARABBAS

The alteration of '*the* insurrection' into '*a* certain insurrection' is by no means the only change that has been made in Mark's statement about Jesus Barabbas. Mark's phrase, ' bound with the rebels who had committed manslaughter in the insurrection,' in no way implies that Barabbas himself had blood on his hands. He had been arrested along with those who were seized as murderers : Mark never says that he really belonged to their number or had himself been guilty of murder. Only the reading ' with his fellow-rebels,' adopted by Lucian of Antioch,[2] brings Barabbas into any connexion with the insurrectionary murderers : in *Luke*, Barabbas alone is imprisoned for insurrection and murder, no companions being mentioned, whilst *John* merely states that ' Barabbas was a bandit ' (or ' rebel,' λῃστής). Luke, in *Acts* iii. 14, was the first to make him a downright ' murderer.' But the support which he received from the high priests and their mass of

---

[1] " ἐσείσθη πᾶσα ἡ πόλις."

[2] Cf. the Syrian version of *Mark* xv. 7, which adds, ' he was a man seditious and a murderer,' obviously under the influence of *Acts* iii. 14.

followers, on the contrary, strongly suggests that he was a well-known partisan of the hierarchy, the son of an *Abba* (Father) or *Rabba* (Master), both words designating a venerable doctor of the law, connected, not with the rebels, but with their opponents, who in the mêlée had been captured along with them and was now destined to share their punishment. If it was a case of mistake on the part of the Roman guard, such as would often occur in every tumult of this kind, then Pilate, yielding to the voice of the people, might well have liberated him ' for the feast,' i.e. with such dispatch that the innocent man might still take part in the Passover celebration. But to pardon a known and condemned rebel was notoriously beyond the power of a Roman governor,[1] and by doing so he would have been guilty of an invasion of the prerogative of the emperor such as the suspicious Tiberius would have been the last to tolerate. No one, in fact, has hitherto succeeded in discovering an illustration in Jewish or pagan writings [2] of the alleged Jewish custom of obtaining pardon for a prisoner at the Passover (the so-called *gratia paschalis*).

A synopsis of the parallel passages in the Gospels shows clearly how the idea of such a customary right gradually arose :

Mark xv. 6-8.	*Matt.* xxviii. 15 *sq.*	*Luke* xxiii. 17.[3]	*John* xviii. 39.
Now at the feast [4] he released (ἀπέλυε) unto them one prisoner whom they asked of him.[5] And there was one (Jesus) Barabbas, bound along with the rebels who (plur.) had committed manslaughter in the insurrection. And the multitude went up [6] and began to ask, as was the custom,[7] that he release Barabbas unto them.	Now at the feast the governor was wont (εἰώθει) to release unto the multitude one prisoner, whom they would. And they had then a notable prisoner called Barabbas.	Now he must needs release unto them at feast-time one prisoner.	But *ye have a custom* that I should release unto you one at the Passover.

---

[1] Cf. Modestinus, *Dig.*, xlviii. 19. 31, and the words of Diocletian, *Cod.*, ix. 47. 12 : ' vanae voces populi non sunt audiendae . . . quando obnoxium crimine absolvi desideraverint.' There is no evidence whatsoever to the effect that Roman provincial governors ever had the right of pardon such as is vested, for example, in the governor of an American State.

[2] The parallel adduced by K. Kastner, *Jesus vor Pilatus*, Diss., Breslau, 1912, p. 29, and Deissmann, *Licht vom Osten*, Tübingen, 1923, p. 229 *sq.*, is not exact, since there it is a question of a pardon in the course of the *cognitio*, not after the passing of the sentence.   [3] This verset is absent in the best MSS.

[4] κατὰ δὲ τὴν ἑορτήν. Cf. v. Soden, ed. maj., Göttingen, 1913, ii. 225, where this variant—Iᵃ δ₅₅—is unjustly relegated to the third appendix of entirely negligible variants.

[5] ὃν παρῃτοῦντο, var. lect. ὃνπερ ᾐτοῦντο : ' whomsoever they asked for.'

[6] ἀναβάς, var. lect. ἀναβοήσας : ' began to clamour.'

[7] καθὼς ἔθος ἦν. So Tatian and a number of MSS. of the recension of Pamphilos. The rest have: ' . . . to ask him (to do) as he was wont to do ' (καθὼς ἐποίει αὐτοῖς), or ' was always wont to do ' (καθὼς ἀεὶ ἐποίει αὐτοῖς) ' unto them.'

The text of Mark quoted above, as recovered from several witnesses of the Caesarean recension, describes an intelligible and credible procedure, on a single occasion, but in no way presupposing a custom of a Passover pardon. Pilate's reply, in the form of a question, ' Will ye that I release unto you the king of the Jews ? ', becomes intelligible only if we adopt the reading preserved by Origen giving the prisoner's name as 'Jesus Barabbas.' Pilate had heard the cries for Jesus bar Abba (or Rabba) (Jesus the Son of the Father or the Master), and indignantly supposed that he was being asked to liberate the prisoner Jesus, king of the Jews. Not till he discovered that the petitions proceeded from the enemies of the Jewish king, anxious to see the latter crucified as soon as possible, did he, in deference to the loyalist party led by the high priests in their urgent *acclamatio*, release the other Jesus, the Bar Abba of whom he previously knew nothing, against whom therefore there was no charge of any account, and who had merely been arrested along with the rebels and murderers. Such an attitude is quite conceivable, for after the recent crushing of the Zealots' rising he had every reason not to displease the opposite party, which had hitherto assisted him.[1] It is inconceivable that the Roman governor could have liberated a rebel ($\lambda\eta\sigma\tau\acute{\eta}s$) at the instance of the mob ; but it is perfectly natural that he should be prepared to gratify the masses of pro-Roman supporters of the hierarchy, led by the high priests, by releasing to them at the feast one of their own number, the son of a learned rabbi, who had erroneously been arrested by his soldiers in the turmoil of the fray.[2]

In this account of Mark, approximating close to the facts, the first $\tau\grave{\eta}\nu$ in the phrase $\tau\grave{\eta}\nu$ $\acute{e}o\rho\tau\acute{\eta}\nu$ (' the feast ') very early dropped out, probably accidentally through ' homoioteleuton,' with the result that he appeared to speak of something which happened ' at every feast.' The conative imperfect ($\acute{a}\pi\epsilon\lambda\acute{v}\epsilon\iota$), variously used in the New Testament,[3] really meant 'he decided,' or 'proceeded to liberate,' but was interpreted, as in *Matthew*, as indicating a custom. In the interpolated text of *Luke* this has become a binding duty ($\acute{a}\nu\acute{a}\gamma\kappa\eta$). The alteration of $\grave{o}\nu$ $\pi\alpha\rho\eta\tauo\hat{v}\nu\tauo$, ' whom they asked for,' into $\acute{o}\nu\pi\epsilon\rho$ $\mathring{\eta}\tauo\hat{v}\nu\tauo$, and finally into $\grave{o}\nu$ $\mathring{a}\nu$ $\mathring{\eta}\tauo\hat{v}\nu\tauo$, ' whomsoever they asked for,' also shows the inception of the idea of the Passover pardons as a custom.

A correct appreciation of the MS. tradition therefore clearly

---

[1] *John* xviii. 3 ; *Mark* xiv. 43 ; *Matt.* xxvi. 47.

[2] The multitude ($\acute{o}\chi\lambdaos$) here mentioned was a crowd of adherents of the hierarchy, hastily armed with clubs and knives to encircle the Mount of Olives and to prevent an escape of the wonder-worker such as was managed later on by the Egyptian messiah. The Roman cohort was far too small to surround the mount effectively.

[3] Cf. Radermacher, *Neutest. Gramm.*, Tübingen, 1924, p. 154 ; Debrunner-Blass, *Neutest. Gramm.*, p. 188, § 326.

shows how by a purely literary process the legend of the Passover pardon of a criminal has been extracted from the Greek text of Mark's Gospel. The purpose of the evangelists, long since pointed out, in emphasizing the responsibility of the Jews for the death of Jesus by this doubtless true story of a popular demonstration against him and in favour of a man of the same name, son of a rabbi and accidentally arrested together with him, thus leads eventually to the conversion of this *protégé* of the high priests into a rebel robber and murderer, who 'for a certain insurrection in the city lay in prison.' Therewith, of course, all sense of what Mark meant by 'the insurrection' and 'the rebels' was obliterated, and the way opened which finally led to the pious legend of a popular rising of the enemies of Jesus against him and Pilate.

The Messianic Acclamation 'Osanna'

The most instructive and noteworthy passage [1] in the otherwise insignificant and absurd so-called *Acta Pilati* of the fourth century is the curious, inconclusive dispute between the Jewish plaintiffs and the lackey or 'runner' (*cursor*) of Pilate, concerning the true meaning of the people's cry, 'Hosanna,' an altercation which reads almost like a learned controversy of Biblical scholars, but no doubt has a very important historical background.

'The *cursor* says to Pilate: "My Lord Governor, when thou sentest me to Jerusalem to Alexander,[2] I saw Jesus riding upon an ass, and the children of the Hebrews held branches in their hands and cried out, and others spread their garments beneath him,[3] saying, 'Save now ($\sigma\tilde{\omega}\sigma o\nu$ $\delta\acute{\eta}$), thou that art blessed in the highest, that comest in the name of the Lord.'" And the Jews say to the runner, "The children of the Hebrews cried in Hebrew, How then hast thou it in Greek?" The runner answers them, "I did ask one of the Jews and said, What is it that they cry out in Hebrew? and he interpreted it to me." Pilate said unto them: "And how cried they in Hebrew?" The Jews say unto him, "*Hosanna membrome barachama Adonai.*" Pilate saith unto them: "And the *Hosanna* and the rest, how is it interpreted?" The Jews say unto him: "Save now, thou that art blessed in the highest, blessed is he that cometh in the name of the Lord." Then Pilate said unto them: "If you yourselves bear witness to the words which were said of the children, wherein hath the runner erred?" And they held their peace.'

So far as I know, this highly peculiar statement has never been quoted by expositors of the notoriously difficult passage about the

[1] M. R. James, *Apocryph. N.T.*, p. 97.
[2] This name appears, along with others, as that of a Jewish high priest. The writer is probably thinking of the man mentioned in *Acts* iv. 6 as being the son or grandson of Herod who bore this name.
[3] See above, p. 471 n. 5.

Osanna cries in the Gospels,[1] in contradistinction to the far less valuable notice in Jerome,[2] who asserts that in the *Gospel to the Hebrews* for *Hosanna in excelsis* he read *Osanna barrama.*

One sees at a glance that the Hebrew text transcribed in Greek is corrupt, but there is no difficulty in restoring it. Βαραχαμμα (for 'Blessed be he that cometh') must naturally be corrected to βαρουχ ἀββᾶ ; and before 'Αδωναί the word βασεμ (= 'in the name of ') has dropped out.

The words *βαρουχ ἀββᾶ βασεμ ἀδωναι, εὐλογημένος ὁ ἐρχόμενος ἐν ὀνόματι Κυρίου, are simply a few lines from *Ps.* cxviii. 26, in the Hebrew-Greek columns of Origen's *Hexapla.* If they are immediately preceded by ὡσαννα, the writer must of course have intended to represent the *hoshi'ah na* (= σῶσον δή, LXX.) which occurs in the preceding verset of the Psalm. The words ἐν ὑψίστοις (' in the highest'), or, as read in the *Acta Pilati,* ὁ ἐν ὑψίστοις, are, however, notoriously derived, not from this Psalm, but from *Ps.* cxlviii. 1, 'Praise him in the heights,' to which we have a clear allusion in *Luke* xix. 37, 'the whole multitude . . . began to . . . praise God.' But this verset in Greek transliteration runs ἀλληλουια ἀλληλου ἠθ ἀδωναι μην ἀσσαμαιμ ἀλληλουου βαμρομημ. Of course, the μεμβρομη(μ)[3] of the *Acta Pilati* is nothing but the last of these transliterated words (= ἐν ὑψίστοις) with one consonant inserted for the sake of euphony, and, as before, the usual confusion of μ and β.[4]

The author's object in this interrogation of Pilate's Greek runner is perfectly clear. In the first place, the cries with which the multitudes hailed Jesus are to be explained as pious words of prayer, and in particular from the Hallel-*Ps.* xcviii., which was regularly sung at the slaughtering of the Paschal lambs on the eve of the feast. The insertion of the article before ἐν ὑψίστοις is intended to make it quite clear that the words 'Save now, thou (who art enthroned) in the heights' are to be understood as an appeal to God. Furthermore, the cries, according to the runner's evidence, are those of children (παῖδες), not of responsible adults. This version of the story is of course based on *Matt.* xxi. 15 *sq.,* where Jesus, on reaching the temple, is greeted by the παῖδες (which might also mean 'servants,' 'slaves')[5] with the cry of *Hosanna,* and replies to the indignant protest of the high priests and scribes by a reference to *Ps.* viii. 2, 'Did ye never read, Out of the mouth of babes and sucklings thou hast perfected praise?'; whereby the ambiguous παῖδες is clearly restricted to the one

---

[1] *Mark* xi. 9 *sq.* ; *Matt.* xxi. 9 *sq.* ; *Luke* xix. 38.
[2] *Epist.,* 20, ad Damas.
[3] μρ naturally becomes μβρ. Cf. Zimri = Ζάμβρη
[4] Cf. Βέρωδαχ for Μέροδαχ = *Marduk.*
[5] Cf. below, p. 481₄.₈.

meaning, 'children,' and the demonstration converted into innocent 'child's-play.' In the Christian *Acta Pilati* the cries, which in *Mark* xi. 9 are vaguely stated to have been raised by those who went before and those who followed, and in *Luke* xix. 37 come from 'the whole multitude of the disciples,' appear as the cries of children, as though the crowd of disciples consisted of school-children.

This gallant runner entirely suppresses the words of political significance which stand out prominently in *Mark, Luke,* and *John,* 'Blessed be the kingship of David,' 'Blessed be he that cometh, the king,' 'Blessed be the king of Israel'—words which, moreover, have already disappeared in *Matthew.*

Here we have, then, an obvious attempt to brazenly deny that Jesus was really acclaimed king by the people, and in this the Jews[1] were at one with the Christians in disclaiming before the Romans all responsibility for the treasonable cry. This purpose also readily explains the unexpected philological interest of Pilate in the original Hebrew text, and its true meaning.

When looking at the Syriac versions of the Gospels, whether the Peshitto or the Curetonian and Sinaitic texts, one finds that *Hosanna* is without exception rendered אושענא, i.e. אושַׁעְנָא, *'osha'na.* Marx[2] long ago recognized that in the current Aramaic vernacular this simply means 'Free us.'[3] On the other hand, Keim[4] saw that the word *'osha'na* has nothing whatever to do with the *hoshi'ana* of *Ps.* cxviii. 25, and cannot be constructed with the dative, 'to the son of David,' which, however, goes quite well with the *hoshi'ana* of *Ps.* cxviii. 25. Lastly, Cheyne[5] emphasized Nestle's acute observation that the Aramaic *Targum* of *Ps.* viii. 3, the very verset which, according to *Matt.* xxi. 16, is quoted by Jesus in justification of the cry of *Hosanna,* has in place of the Hebrew עז, 'strength' or rather 'courage,' of which the Greek equivalent is αἶνον, 'praise,' the word *'ushna*; this in the transliterated form *οὐσενα closely resembles ὠσάννα, and in combination with τῷ υἱῷ Δαυείδ means 'strength to the son of David!'

It is therefore through no accident or mere ignorance that the most fantastic translations[6] of ὠσάννα are to be found in the Fathers, and not merely through unintentional corruption that

[1] *John* xix. 15, 21.
[2] Ap. Hilgenfeld, *Nov. Test. extra canonic.,* iv. 25.
[3] σῶσον ἡμᾶς, thus actually in the Rumanian *Acts of Pilate.*
[4] *Jesus von Nazareth,* iii. 91.
[5] *Encycl. Bibl.,* col. 2118.
[6] Clement of Alexandria translates ὠσάννα with φῶς καὶ δόξα καὶ αἶνος. Suidas, or rather his patristic source, explains the word with εἰρήνη καὶ δόξα (of course from *Luke* xix. 38), adding that it was erroneous to translate σῶσον δή. According to St. Augustine (*De Doctr. Christ.,* ii. 11, and *Tract. in Joh.,* li. 2), Osanna is a mere interjection expressing glee, etc. etc.

the traditional text of *Mark* xi. 10, *Matt*. xxi. 9, *Luke* xix. 38, and the *Didachē* x. 6, is in such senseless disorder.

'Hosanna in the highest' in *Mark* and *Matthew* is quite impossible, because 'Free us in the heights' has as little meaning as 'Save now in the heights.' Here on earth men have always yearned for freedom and help, not in heaven above. The author of the *Acts of Pilate* accordingly evades the difficulty by inserting the definite article, ὡσάννα ὁ ἐν τοῖς ὑψίστοις, 'Save now (or 'free us') (thou who art) in the heights.'

In *Matt*. xxi. 9, ὡσάννα τῷ υἱῷ Δαυείδ, 'Free us for the son of David,' is equally impossible ; still more absurd is the phrase in the *Didachē*, 'Hosanna to the God of David.' In *Luke* xix. 38, objection has always been taken to the article before βασιλεύς in 'Blessed be he that cometh, the king, in the name of the Lord,' whilst the verset ends with the unmeaning 'peace in heaven and glory in the highest,' as though 'peace in heaven' could be of importance to any one, or as though war had hitherto prevailed among the heavenly hosts. The usual comparison with the beautiful hymn in *Luke* ii. 14, 'Glory to God in the highest, and on earth peace among men of good will,' only brings out more glaringly the absurdity of the traditional text in the last clause of xix. 38.

Yet the restoration of the original text presents no insuperable difficulties. In *Mark* xi. 10, 'in the highest' is nothing but an old marginal gloss,[1] originally intended to explain or supplement the word 'blessed' : 'Blessed (in the heavenly heights) be he that cometh in the name of the Lord : blessed (in the heights) the kingdom of David.' The gloss is intended to exonerate the multitude of the followers of Jesus from the suspicion of having acclaimed the incoming Messiah and the Davidic kingdom : the pious pilgrims merely meant to say, 'Blessed be the Messiah and his kingdom in the heights above.' 'In the highest' must therefore simply be omitted, both here and in Matthew. In *Matt*. xxi. 9 the words 'to the son of David' must be transposed so as to read, 'the companions cried, saying to the son of David, *Osanna*' (i.e. 'Free us'). A striking parallel, one in which the insurrectionary meaning of the cry is perfectly clear, can be found in the Hebrew *Josippon*. When King Agrippa II. enters Jerusalem the crowd salutes him with the outcry, '*hoshi'anu*, serva nos, rex : non amplius subiecti erimus Romanis.'

The displacement of words above analysed arose through a corrector having attached to ὡσάννα ('*osha'na*) the meaning of ὡσιέννα, *hoshi'ana*, in *Ps*. cxviii. 25, and wished to read the clause as a prayer to God, 'Help the son of David !' The senseless '*Hosanna* to the God of David,' followed by 'Maranatha,' in the *Didachē*, which has survived in one MS. only, naturally once ran

---

[1] It is omitted in various MSS. of the Caesarean text.

ὡσάννα (υἱεὶ) Δαυείδ, μαρᾶνα θᾶ, ' Free us, son of David : our Lord, come ! ' : τῷ θεῷ is a marginal gloss purporting to show that *Osanna* (' Free us ') is a prayer addressed directly to God himself. In *Luke* xix. 38, ' Hosanna' disappears entirely, and, to make the correction more effective, the words ' began . . . to praise God ' are inserted in the preceding verset.　The words of the acclamation itself, through the repeated editing of the text, are in utter confusion.　Originally they must have run, ' Blessed (be) the king that cometh in peace and glory ' (ἐν εἰρήνη(ι) καὶ δόξα(ι)). Against the word ' blessed,' with the same object as in *Mark*, there was written in the margin ' in heaven,' ' in the heights ' (is he blessed).　A further improvement was designed to alter the political acclamation, 'Blessed (be) the king who cometh in peace and glory,' of the ' Prince of Peace' upon his ass, into a quotation, as in *Mark* xi. 9, from *Ps.* cxviii. 25.　The text then looked like this :

ἤρξαντο ἄπαν τὸ πλῆθος
τῶν μαθητῶν χαίροντες αἰνεῖν (αὐ)τὸν❡　❡ ΤΟΝ ΘΕΟΝ.
φωνῇ μεγάλῃ περὶ πασῶν ὧν εἶδον
δυναμέων² λέγοντες·
εὐλογημένος ❡ ὁ βασιλεὺς　　　❡ ΕΝ ΟΥΡΑΝΩΙ·
ὁ ἐρχόμενος ❡ ἐν εἰρήνῃ　　　❡ ΕΝ ΟΝΟΜΑΤΙ ΚΥΡΙΟΥ
καὶ δόξᾳ❡　　　　　　　　❡ ΕΝ ΥΨΙΣΤΟΙΣ·

The impossible traditional text has arisen through misplacement of the *obeli* belonging to the glosses.

In conclusion, it now becomes clear that it was only through the artificial alteration of *'osha'na*, ' Free us,' into *hoshi'ana* of the Psalmist that the palm-branches found their way into John's narrative.[1]　The festal bouquets of the Feast of Tabernacles, of which the principal item was a palm-branch, were expressly known as ' Hoshannas.'　At the Passover feast, of course, none of the pilgrims carried ' the palm-branches ' in their hands.　They strewed the road with a carpet of green brought from the borders of the fields,[2] and for a like purpose cut branches from the trees ; but that they bore ' the palm-branches ' in their hands is clearly an invention of later Greek ignorance on Jewish matters.

THE OCCUPATION OF THE TEMPLE

Jesus had set out from Galilee with a small band of secretly armed followers [3] to issue in Jerusalem a summons to freedom, to an exodus into the wilderness.　Since this was to begin on the anniversary of the exodus from Egypt, it is clear that he and his company must have reached the Mount of Olives some days

---

[1] *John* xii. 13.　　[2] στιβάδας, *Mark* xi. 8.　　[3] Cf. above, pp. 368 ff.

earlier. On the road and at this spot a multitude of pilgrims, attracted by the fame of former miracles [1] and the spectacle of others more recent, had joined the band. Around a nucleus of one hundred and fifty closer associates, some hundreds more—perhaps, according to the highest estimate of later tradition, amounting in all to some two thousand people [2]—may have assembled. Over against these there was the Roman garrison of Jerusalem, a cohort of five or six hundred men, with a corresponding number of camp-followers and the usual auxiliary troops, and in addition a Levitical guard in the temple of unknown but probably quite inconsiderable strength. Whether the Roman custom, attested for the first time of the governor Florus, of concentrating in the capital at the feast of the Passover the greater part of the Roman forces in Palestine, under the personal command of the governor, was already in force in the administration of Pilate, or was not rather first introduced in consequence of the events of the Passover of A.D. 21, cannot be decided. In the latter case the prospects of a sudden attack were not actually bad, provided a sufficiently large part of the city population joined in the revolt against the foreign oppressors.

The peculiar tactics of a surprise occupation of the dominating positions of the city were quite familiar to the Zealots. As early as the time of Archelaus they had attempted such a *coup d'état* :

' And when the feast of unleavened bread, called Passover, came round, a time when a multitude of sacrifices is offered to God, count-less numbers of the people from all over the country came to the ceremony, and the insurgents stood in secret in the temple and suddenly sprang up, and there was general confusion.' [3]

By this sudden ' up-springing ' Josephus refers to the sudden drawing of the concealed swords of the so-called *sicarii*.

From the Levitical temple guard under the command of the *segan* (στρατηγός) or captain of the temple not much was to be feared, for it might be hoped that a considerable portion of this national police force would prove amenable to the temptation of the messianic glad tidings and go over to the Davidic liberator-king when he made his triumphal entry. The statement that the παῖδες in the temple, the 'sons of the slaves of Solomon,' [4] the ἱερόδουλοι, νεωκόροι, [5] or *Nethinîm*, [6] or those ' buds of priest-hood ' [7] spoken of in the Mishnah as devoted to certain guard duties, [8] much to the vexation of the high priests and scribes

---

[1] *John* xii. 8.   [2] See above, p. 370 n. 1.

[3] *Halōsis*, ii. 10, Berendts-Grass, p. 234.

[4] *Ezra* ii. 55 ; *Neh.* vii. 57, etc.

[5] Philo, *De praem. sacerd.*, § 6 ; 1 *Esdr.* i. 27.

[6] δεδόμενοι (=*dediticii*) ; cf. 1 *Chron.* ix. 2 (codd, B, A).

[7] *Pirḫē kehunah*, an allusion to the budding staff of Aaron.

[8] Schürer, Engl. trans., Edinburgh, 1910, vol. ii. 1, p. 273 n. 208.

2 H

greeted Jesus with the cry, ' Power to the son of David ! ' makes it probable that these hopes were not illusory.

In this way, finally, a fragment of the *Halōsis*, preserved by Suidas, and which before the discovery of the Slavonic work could not be placed, meets with a satisfactory explanation : [1] ' We find,' says the lexicographer,[2]

> 'Josephus the historian of "The capture of Jerusalem" (of whom Eusebius the son of Pamphilus quotes a good deal in his Ecclesiastical History) saying clearly in the memoirs of his captivity[3] that Jesus officiated in the sanctuary with the priests.[4] Finding that Josephus says this, who was a man of that age (ἄνδρα ἀρχαῖον ὄντα), living not long after the apostles, we have searched for confirmation of this story also in the divinely inspired scriptures.'[5]

There was thus an express statement in Josephus to the effect that 'Jesus did service in the temple with the priests,' which in connexion with the accusation against Jesus as it occurred in the text can only mean that he performed sacred functions to which only the priests were entitled by the Law.[6] Naturally, the simple-minded Suidas did not realize the full meaning of all this. Adducing *Luke* iv. 17, he concluded that Jesus must have been a priest, since he was evidently allowed to read from the Bible in the synagogue, and since also in the Christian Church no layman was allowed such a privilege. However, the fact itself is highly probable, since, according to Jewish notions, the Messiah, like the Hasmonaean kings, was to unite the priestly dignity with the kingly office. It is furthermore extremely probable that Jesus, in presuming to offer incense in the temple as a pure sacrifice, did so with the full consciousness of his divine vocation, without paying much heed to the question how far his genealogy entitled him to such an action. On the other hand, it is more than probable that the isolated statement in *Luke* iii. 24, to the effect that there was a Levite in Jesus' genealogy, was inserted and the relationship of Mary with the mother of the Baptist, a descendant of Aaron, was emphasized for the purpose of justifying Jesus' priestly acts in the temple during its brief occupation by his adherents. Perhaps such a kinship, by no means unusual among Rekhabite families,[7] could indeed be proved, for the accusation brought against Jesus

---

[1] s.v. Ἰησοῦς, ed. Bernhardy, i. 2, p. 971. [2] On the context, cf. App. xxiv.
[3] See above, p. 120, on this original title of Josephus' first draft.
[4] See above, p. 467 n. 4.
[5] " εὕρομεν οὖν Ἰώσηπον τὸν συγγραφέα τῆς Ἁλώσεως Ἱεροσολύμων (οὗ μνήμην πολλὴν Εὐσέβιος ὁ Παμφίλου ἐν τῇ Ἐκκλησιαστικῇ αὐτοῦ Ἱστορίᾳ ποιεῖται), φανερῶς λέγοντα ἐν τοῖς τῆς αἰχμαλωσίας αὐτοῦ ὑπομνήμασιν, ὅτι Ἰησοῦς ἐν τῷ ἱερῷ μετὰ τῶν ἱερέων ἡγίαζε. τοῦτο οὖν εὑρόντες λέγοντα τὸν Ἰώσηπον, ἄνδρα ἀρχαῖον ὄντα καὶ οὐ μετὰ πολὺν χρόνον τῶν ἀποστόλων γενόμενον ἐζητήσαμεν καὶ ἐν τῶν θεοπνευστῶν γραφῶν τὸν τοιοῦτον λόγον βεβαιούμενον," κ.τ.λ.
[6] Cf. what has been said above, p. 469 n. 1, on the crime of *minutio maiestatis* in Roman legislation. [7] See above, p. 245₂.

by the high priests [1] apparently did not mention such an illegal assumption of a sacred office. Yet not much can be made of this *argumentum e silentio*, since we cannot be sure that the document in question, the temple inscription mentioned by Josephus,[1] has come down to us intact and without mutilations on the part of Christian copyists. At all events, Jesus *may* have been justified even according to the letter of the Law when he dared to approach his God in the sanctuary without the mediation of an official priest.

There can certainly be no doubt about the fact that the words of Suidas, μετὰ τῶν ἱερέων ἡγίαζε, fully confirm our supposition that one group of the priests, perhaps the ' bloom of the *kehunah*,' had gone over to the rebels. No doubt, also, the Gospel fragment of Papyr. Oxyrhynchos, No. 840,[2] so often and so hotly discussed, belongs to the same context.

After the final words of some parable directed against the Pharisaic casuists, experts in getting around the letter of the Law,[3] we find the following story :

' And he took them and led them into the ἁγνευτήριον [4] itself, and went about in the sanctuary (ἐν τῷ ἱερῷ περιεπάτει). Then there came a certain Pharisee, a high priest (ἀρχιερεύς) called . . ., encountered them and said to the Saviour (τῷ σωτῆρι) [5] : " Who hath bidden thee enter this sanctuary (ἁγνευτήριον) and to look at these sacred objects (ἅγια σκεύη),[6] without having bathed first (μήτε λουσαμένῳ), and without thy disciples having at least washed their feet (μήτε μὴν τῶν μαθητῶν σου τὰς πόδας βαπτισθέντων) ? [7] Thou hast rather entered this place, which is unsullied, as an impure one (μεμολυ[μένος] ἐπάτησας), whilst ordinarily no one enters there without having washed [8] and changed his clothes,[9] nor dares to look at the

---

[1] See below, pp. 521 f.

[2] Grenfell and Hunt, *A Fragment of an Uncanonical Gospel from Oxyrhynchos*, Oxford, 1908, reprint from *Oxyrh. Papyri*, v. ; H. B. Swete, *Zwei neue Evangelienfragmente*, Lietzmann's *Kl. Texte*, No. 31 ; Preuschen, *Z.N.T.W.*, 1908, p. 1 *sqq.* Cf. further : Deissmann, *Licht vom Osten*, p. 33 n. 1 ; and Hennecke, *Neutestam. Apokr.²*, p. 31, No. 19.

[3] " πρότερον πρὸ τοῦ ἀδικῆσαι πάντα σοφίζεται," etc., about the punishment awaiting evildoers after their resurrection for the Last Judgment.

[4] According to Preuschen, *Z.N.T.W.*, ix. (1908), p. 5, =*qodesh*, ' the holy ' (ἁγνίζειν=*qiddesh*, *Ex.* xix. 10). So also W. Bauer in Preuschen's *Greek-German Dict. to the N.T.²*, referring to Porphyry, *De Abst.*, iv. 5.

[5] Cf. Preuschen, *op. cit.*, p. 9 n. 2, who rightly observes that the expression is foreign to the Synoptics. Yet it occurs in the Gospel of the Infancy in *Luke* ii. 11, coming from a special source. Cf. σωτὴρ τοῦ κόσμου, the well-known title of the emperors, applied to the Messiah in *John* iv. 42. What is meant is the saviour from war and oppression.

[6] The table with the shewbread, the candlestick, and the altar of incense.

[7] Cf. *John* xiii. 10.

[8] Cf. *B.J.*, v. § 227 ; also Joma iii.a, Marmorstein, *Z.N.T.W.*, xv. (1914), p. 336 : ' No one is allowed to enter into the inner court, not even the ritually pure, without having taken a plunge-bath.'

[9] Since the disciples of Jesus, according to *Matt.* x. 10 and *Luke* ix. 3, were not allowed to possess two suits (δύο χιτῶνας), no change of clothes was possible in their case.

holy objects.[1] And immediately the Saviour stopped, with his
disciples, and replied to him : " Thou, then, who art in this
sanctuary, art thou pure ? " And he saith to him : " I am pure.
For I have washed in the pond of David (ἐν τῇ λίμνῃ τοῦ Δαυείδ)[2]
and have descended one flight of stairs[3] and mounted the other,
and I have put on white and pure clothes, and then I came to look
at these holy objects." The Saviour replied and said unto him :
" Woe upon you, O blind, who do not see.[4] Thou hast bathed
in this water poured in (τούτοις τοῖς χεομένοις ὕδασι), in which
by day and by night ' dogs ' and ' swine ' are wallowing (ἐν οἷς
κύνες καὶ χοῖροι βέβληνται νυκτὸς καὶ ἡμέρας) ; thou hast washed
and cleansed thy outer skin,[5] which is also done by whores and
flute-players,[6] who bathe, adorn themselves, and put on artificial
colours to rouse the concupiscence of men, but within they are full
of scorpions and all wickedness. But I and my disciples, of whom
thou sayest that we did not bathe, we plunged into the living waters
coming down from heaven (ἐγὼ δὲ καὶ οἱ [μαθηταί μου] οὓς λέγεις μὴ
βεβα[πτίσθαι βεβάμ]μεθα ἐν ὕδασι ζω[οῖς ἀεννάοις τοῖ]ς[7] ἔλθουσι ἀ[π'
οὐρανοῦ])."'

The words on the χεόμενα ὕδατα, the ' water poured in,' agree
perfectly with the statements of the Mishnah discussed by Brandt
on the *lishkath hag-gullah*, the ' hall of the fountain,' the ' well-
house ' of the temple, ' in which there was the fortified cistern of
the fountain, with the wheel above, and from which the water
was taken to supply the whole court.'

The ' dogs ' and ' swine ' in the purifying bath of the priests
have puzzled the exegetists only because they have failed to
realize the passionate coarseness of the invective. ' Dogs ' in this
context is, of course, only the abusive name well known throughout
antiquity for the παθικός, the temple-slave of the Syrian and
Canaanite *'Asherah*, whilst χοῖροι, 'swine,' denotes simply men
without any sense of cleanliness or decency.[8]

Finally, the forced explanations how the holy implements
could be seen from the court of the non-priestly Israelites are use-

---

[1] I.e. look at them unwashed.
[2] Cf. above, p. 273 l. 37. There must thus have been old cisterns (*shithin*) under
the foundations of the temple, the construction of which was attributed to David.
Herod the Great seems to have converted a number of them into subterranean
regular bathing-ponds.
[3] Cf. Middot, i. 9 ; Tammid, i. 1 ; German translation by Brandt, Suppl. xviii.
of *Z.N.T.W.*, Giessen, 1910, p. 128. If a priest sleeping in the sanctuary became
ceremonially unclean, he went down to the bath-chamber, washed, and came up
again.
[4] Cf. *Matt.* xv. 14 ; xxiii. 16 *sq.*, 19, 24.
[5] Cf. above, p. 249, on the doctrine of John.
[6] On the Syrian flute-girls cf. Mau's article *Ambubaiae* in Pauly-Wissowa,
R.-E., i., 1816.
[7] Cf. above, p. 273 ll. 16 f. and n. 6.
[8] Cf. *Prov.* xi. 22 : ' As a jewel of gold in a swine's snout, so is a fair woman
which is without discretion.' Cf. also the interesting observation of Dr. M. R.
James, *The Apocr. New Testament*, p. 29 n. 2, on the words added to 1 *Kings* xxii.
38 in the Greek version.

less, for the text clearly shows that Jesus must have done something quite unheard of, and it matters little whether the word ἀγνευτήριον designates the outer hall of the *hējkal* or only the court of the priests. The text states that the priest objects to the appearance of non-priests in this holy place. If thus interpreted, the passage allows of two inferences, namely, (1) only priests were allowed to enter this part of the sanctuary, ånd (2) even they only after having first washed their feet and changed their clothing. Both rules were actually in force.[1] The place in question was the ' Holy ' as distinguished from the ' Holy of Holies,' and I believe that the word ἀγνευτήριον denotes the temple building and ἱερόν (=*qodosh*) the place between the altar and the Holy of Holies, precisely where the sacred instruments were found.

It is evident, then, that Jesus did not stand among the crowd of the simple Jews who were shown the golden table and the curtain at a distance on a holiday, for who would have taken notice of him and observed that he had not properly washed to be ceremonially clean ? But he not only entered the temple building, the ' Holy,' called *qodesh* or *hējkal*, but even took his disciples with him. It goes without saying that a simple pilgrim could never have carried out such an unheard-of violation of the priestly rules ; in normal times the guards of the sanctuary would have prevented him most effectively from so doing.

The event described by the fragment presupposes, then, the occupation of the temple by the adherents of Jesus, and the support he found on the part of the παῖδες of the sanctuary. Only as the messianic ruler could he venture to enter the temple itself and view the holy implements, etc., to offer incense on the altar with his own hand. At this juncture a popular high priest, significantly a Pharisee (for the most unpopular Sadducee, Caiaphas, kept out of the way), ventured to voice his objections, and the ensuing dialogue has accidentally been preserved to us on this papyrus fragment, incidentally a proof of the fact that many Gospels must have perished at an early date. The passage also proves that Jesus conceived of the temple, no longer as the mysterious dwelling of a jealous deity, worshipped according to an old-fashioned ritual and in the gloom, but as the meeting-house for all men, the central synagogue of the country, where people would assemble to worship the Omnipresent and Eternal in spirit and in truth. Bold as was this attack of the old prophetic opposition on the cult instituted by Solomon after the model of other

---

[1] Cf. Maimuni, *Beth Habbeḥira*, 7, 21 : ' The temple (*hējkal*) is more sacred than the place between the outer hall ('*ulām*) and the altar ; the priest must not enter the *hējkal* without previous washing of hands and feet (*raḥuṣ jadaîm uraglaîm*).' In the Tosefta (*Kelaim* i. 1, 6) there is a debate on the question whether one may enter the place between the outer hall and the altar without previous washing.

Oriental cults, it must have found a tremendous echo among the partisans of this deeper piety.[1]

THE COLLISION WITH THE ROMANS

The most menacing peril could have come from the Roman garrison in the temple-fortress known since Herod's time as ' Antonia,' *if* this castle (*birah* or $\beta\hat{a}\rho\iota\varsigma$) were then occupied by the Romans. From the statements of Josephus [2] on the custody of the high priest's ceremonial vestments it would seem as if the Roman garrison had always lain in the Antonia. But the contrary is suggested by his statement elsewhere [3] that the governor Gessius Florus, in A.D. 66, with the troops he had brought from Caesarea, sought to force his way through and occupy the temple and the castle, but was prevented by the mob. The Roman garrison, therefore, at the time of Florus lay in the royal palace of Herod on the west of the city, and the Antonia was in the hands of the temple guard under the command of the captain of the castle (*'ish hab-birah*).[4] If the garrison was not strong enough to hold both Herod's palace and the Antonia, the Romans were strategically quite justified in preferring to command the higher western hill, the more so because, as far as we can tell from the sources, the only communications the Antonia had with the temple court were stairways, and consequently in the event of disturbances in the temple its garrison could be easily blockaded and cut off from the city.

At the time of Paul's arrest for having brought Trophimus into the temple in defiance of the purity law, Fort Antonia was certainly occupied by the Romans. When he was being brought into the barracks ($\pi\alpha\rho\epsilon\mu\beta o\lambda\acute{\eta}$), he was, owing to the pressure of the crowd, carried by the soldiers up the steps ($\tauo\grave{\upsilon}\varsigma$ $\dot{\alpha}\nu\alpha\beta\alpha\theta\muo\acute{\upsilon}\varsigma$), from which by the tribune's permission he delivered an address to the people.[5]

If the situation in the time of Pilate was similar, and if, moreover, as in the time of Cumanus,[6] the precaution had already been taken of posting Roman guards at the great festivals on the porticoes surrounding the temple court, ready to nip in the bud any popular disturbances, then it is hardly conceivable that events such as the so-called cleansing of the temple could have taken place. One would have to regard them, with Origen,[7] as a greater miracle than the changing of water into wine at the marriage of Cana, or else to assume a wholly improbable surprise attack on and intimidation of the Roman garrison.

Matters are quite different if these measures were first intro-

---

[1] Cf. above, pp. 336 ff. and p. 8 n. 4, on the currents hostile to the priests, which are so clearly visible in the Agada.

[2] *Ant.*, xv. 11. 4 ; xviii. 4. 3.

[3] *B.J.*, ii. 15. 5, § 328.

[4] *Acts* xxi. 31.

[5] *Acts* xxi. 36-40.

[6] *Ant.*, xx. 5, 3.

[7] In Joann., x. (*P.G.*, xiv. 352).

duced by the Romans in consequence of the events of the Passover week of A.D. 21, and if the statement of Josephus to the effect that the predecessors of Cumanus acted as he did applies to the governors who succeeded Pilate and were warned by his example.

It is quite possible that, just because the march of the cohorts into the Antonia with the *semaia* had roused such a storm of Jewish indignation in A.D. 19, Pilate had been ordered by Tiberius to remove the garrison out of that fortress altogether and to transfer it to Herod's palace. Only if the Roman garrison, whether in the modest dimensions of a *cohors equitata*, or appropriately strengthened, lay in the palace on the west of the city, could a *coup* like the march into the temple, with the subsequent attack on the money-changers and merchants, be attempted and carried into execution. Only in these circumstances is it conceivable that Jesus, having been proclaimed King of Israel, could for several days teach in the temple unassailed,[1] under the protection of his numerous followers,[2] even if he took the precaution of spending the nights outside the city in the village of Bethany.[3]   M. Maurice Goguel [4] doubted the historicity of the account of the triumphal entry into Jerusalem and the ' purification of the temple,' mainly on the ground that the long delay of the Romans in re-establishing law and order appeared inexplicable. ' If,' he wrote, ' the account of the entry of Jesus into Jerusalem must be taken literally, it would furnish a very sufficient motive for Roman intervention. If the entry had provoked the popular enthusiasm which Mark relates, one could not understand how the Roman authorities waited several days to intervene. Waiting under these conditions would give a nascent movement time to grow to a point at which it would become irrepressible.'

These objections, however, will not convince a reader with any experience in such matters. The main thing for the Romans was, of course, to make their own attack forceful and irresistible. That could not be done by precipitation and in the simple way in which Archelaus had cowed a more spontaneous and unpremeditated outbreak in 4 B.C. If the Zealots, reinforced by partisans from the city, were in possession of the strongly fortified temple, the recapture of the sanctuary required the bringing up of reinforcements, of siege engines, and above all a precise exploration of the state of affairs in the open country, in the city, and on the Temple Mount, the establishment of contacts and an understanding with the high priests and the loyalists, the distribution of weapons to the latter, and the like. For all this a few days of only apparent inaction would by no means seem an excessive delay.

---

[1] *Mark* xiv. 49 ; *Matt.* xxviii. 55 ; *Luke* xxii. 53.
[2] *Luke* xix. 48 : ' The people all hung upon him listening.'
[3] *Mark* xi. 11; *Luke* xxi. 37 *sq.*   [4] *Revue de l'histoire des religions,* xlii. 318.

More significant still, the statements of Josephus on the message sent by the high priests to Pilate hardly admit of any other conclusion save that on the day of Jesus' entry the governor was not yet in Jerusalem.   For had he been living in the city, he would naturally have received notice of such proceedings before any one else through his scouts (*speculatores*), and the high priests could not have expected to make much impression with their belated information.   The situation was quite different if the governor was still in his residence at Caesarea and was only expected with his reinforcements on the eve of the Passover, always assuming that the later practice was already in force and the governor was accustomed to come to Jerusalem with a special body of troops for the festivals.   It is quite conceivable that this measure was only the outcome of the events of this year, and that Pilate was enjoying himself quietly in the delights which the relatively civilized Caesarea offered to a gentleman of his class, when the· high priests' message came as an unpleasant surprise. The postponement of the counter-stroke is in any case easy to understand.   But it is indeed impossible to suppose Pilate to have sat still with his cohort in the Antonia above the temple court, allowing events to take their course under his very eyes, a few steps beneath him.

In that case the garrison of the castle would, of course, immediately have made a charge upon the crowd and events would have developed precipitately.   If we assume that Fort Antonia was in Roman hands, we must regard the statements about Jesus remaining for several days in the temple, and about his issuing orders,[1] as unhistorical.   From the statements that at the time of the entry the Hallel-*Ps*. cxviii. was being recited, it is to be inferred that this event took place not before midday of the 'day of preparation,' and was immediately followed by the invasion of the temple, which could not be prevented by the surprised Roman garrison, but might have been checked by a speedy counter-attack and a massacre of the people.   On that theory the events would have followed one another with such giddy speed that on that ground alone one would hesitate to adopt such a view.

On the whole, it would seem more satisfactory to accept the statements of the Synoptists on the duration of Jesus' stay in the temple and Josephus' story on the sending of troops by Pilate, and to find the explanation in the simple hypothesis that in 21, just as later on in 66,[2] the temple and Fort Antonia were held only by a Jewish temple-guard, which, as may well be imagined, showed

---

[1] *Mark* xi. 16: 'and would not suffer that any man should carry armour (σκεῦος) through the temple.'

[2] If it be asked why, with the events of 21 behind him, Florus could, in 66, make the same fatal mistake, the answer can easily be found in the philosopher Hegel's famous essay, *Why man cannot profit by the lessons of history*.

no desire for any strong opposition to the patriots and the scion
of David.

THE ATTACK ON THE TEMPLE BANKS

After what has been said above [1] on Jesus' repugnance to the
service of mammon and to money as something satanic and opposed to God, his procedure against the money-changers or bankers
is at once intelligible.

Like every great shrine in the Orient and the Hellenic world,
the temple at Jerusalem was by nature a great public treasury, or,
as one might say, with certain self-evident reservations, *the* national
bank.   The treasure-chambers of the temple contained, besides
immense stores of wealth belonging to the sanctuary in the archaic
form of 'raiment [2] money' [3] and wrought precious metal, along
with considerable sums of coined currency,[4] also vast deposits made
by individual creditors, and not merely by widows and orphans.[5]
For the rich of that day likewise 'trusted in the holiness of the
place,' [6] and did not hesitate to confide their wealth to the protection of ' Him that gave the law concerning deposits,' [7] so that
Josephus could correctly speak of those chambers as the ' general
repository of Jewish wealth.' [8]   These deposits were by no means
allowed to lie idle, but were all the time profitably employed in the
process of money-transfer inherited by the Jews no less than by
the whole Hellenic world from Babylon, where the bills of exchange, bonds, and personal cheques had long before been invented.
The prohibition of interest in lending and borrowing between Jews
did not prevent the claiming and conceding of shares in the profits
reaped from Jewish commercial undertakings.   This prohibition
did not, either, obtain for dealings with non-Jews, where the
common high rate of interest was exacted by all parties concerned.
Furthermore, there were doubtless ways and means [9] of evading
the prohibition and taking interest even from Jewish borrowers.
At all events, Josephus' account [10] of the burning of the archives
in Jerusalem by the insurgents gives an appalling picture of the
oppressive indebtedness of the poor to the rich, the intention of
the incendiaries being to ' destroy the money-lenders' tallies
($\sigma\nu\mu\beta\delta\lambda\alpha\iota\alpha$) and to prevent the exaction of debts, in order to win

---

[1] Cf. pp. 332 ff.   [2] Cf. *Matt.* vi. 19 (*Luke* xii. 33).
[3] Cf. Eisler, *Das Geld*, München, 1924, p. 122 *sq.*
[4] Cf. 2 *Macc.* iii. 6.   [5] *Ibid.*, iii. 10.
[6] *Ibid.*, iii. 12.   [7] *Ibid.*, iii. 15 ; cf. *Exod.* xxii. 7.
[8] *B.J.*, vi. 282.
[9] The Greek and Roman money-lenders employed as a rule slaves and freedmen to carry on their business, and the Jewish capitalists may similarly have
drawn on the services of non-Jewish middlemen.   The servant who is to trade
with the talents of his master in *Matt.* xxv. 28 must be regarded as such a factor.
Against this circumvention of the Law the rabbis pronounced that ' the hand of
the slave is the hand of the master ' (Strack-Billerbeck, i. 971).
[10] *B.J.*, ii. 427.

over a host of grateful debtors and to rouse the poor against the wealthy with impunity.'

Seeing that the latter left their disbursements and recovery of debts in the hands of the bankers (τραπεζῖται, shulḥanim),[1] and that these also collected the *sheqel*-tax for the temple and distrained upon those unwilling or unable to pay,[2] one can imagine how these persons were hated by the humbler folk in the country, the *'ammē ha'areṣ*, and can only wonder that nothing worse happened to them than what is told by three of the Evangelists.[3]

To understand in what sense Jesus, in words taken from the old prophets, could reproach the money-dealers with having converted God's house from a ' house of prayer for all nations ' into ' a den of burglars,' [4] we must recall the important fact that the money-changers unscrupulously accepted and consigned to the treasury vaults of the temple coins regarded with such abhorrence by the pious because they bore the image of Caesar and heathen gods. For it was permitted to exchange the shekels of taxpayers living at a distance for gold *darics* bearing the image of the Persian king.[5] The medallion with Caesar's image on the *semaia* (Pl. xxii.) is in fact nothing but an ordinary Roman coin; and though usually the size may have been different, the essential character did not change thereby. Thus the very people who had moved heaven and earth because one such medallion had been brought into the holy city and within the temple precincts, thought nothing of piling up thousands of these same idolatrous images on the coins of the realm in the temple court and thus ' violating' the law of God.

It is needless to add that the attack of Jesus was directed not only against this visible and tangible side of the temple tribute, but against the whole system, against the mammonist spirit which had gradually permeated temple service and people alike.

The Expulsion of the Cattle-Dealers

It is a remarkable fact that the cognate narrative of the expulsion of the cattle-dealers is best preserved in the Fourth Gospel, where we read : [6]

'And he found in the temple those that sold oxen and sheep and doves . . . and he made a scourge of cords and drove them all out of the temple along with the sheep and the oxen.'

---

[1] Cf. Mayer-Lambert, ' Les changeurs et la monnaie en Palestine,' *Revue des Études juives*, 1907-8.

[2] Strack-Billerbeck, i. 761 *sq.*

[3] *Luke* xix. 45 omits the attack on the money-changers—no doubt because that episode formed the best basis for the charge that the disciples were ληϲταί; for it is not to be supposed that the scattered money remained lying on the ground.

[4] Or, ' violators of the law,' *me'arat pariṣîm* ; cf. *Jer.* vii. 11.

[5] *Sheq.*, ii. 1 ; Strack-Billerbeck, i. 767a.

[6] *John* ii. 14 *sq.*

In *Mark* xi. 15 and *Matt.* xxi. 12 the oxen and sheep are omitted, as is also the scourge, to mitigate the violence of the procedure and to get rid of the improbability of this naïve picture of a single man driving before him not only entire herds of oxen but their intimidated owners as well.   *Luke* xix. 45 merely writes 'them that sold,' not mentioning the objects for sale.

With this simplified form of the narrative the weakening of the severest words of condemnation into 'Make not my Father's house a house of merchandise ' [1] is quite in keeping.   Since the sellers of doves are mentioned in verset 14 and again in 15 as having been driven out of the temple, verset 16, 'and to those that sold doves he said,' is clearly a late harmonizing.

It is noteworthy that in these omissions it is just the sellers of doves who have been left intact.   For, whereas this is doubtful in the case of the larger sacrificial beasts, it is known beyond any doubt that it was customary to purchase the doves by means of special brass checks from the temple authorities themselves,[2] so that the action of Jesus must have been directed against Levitical and official vendors and not, or at least not exclusively, against any unauthorized dealers strolling about the temple.

The motives for the attack have been almost entirely obliterated by the Christian tradition.   Of the speeches Jesus made on this occasion, only the prophetical catchwords about the conversion of the ' universal house of prayer ' into a ' den of burglars ' have survived.   Any one conversant with the time-honoured tricks of the entrenched middleman will understand the pronounced hostility of the pilgrims from the country against precisely this class.   For whilst to purchasers they raised the price of their beasts to the maximum, to the sellers they would always object one of the many faults which made an animal unfit for sacrificial use, thus manipulating the prices.   This fact, moreover, is expressly attested for the sale of doves.[3]

Yet the attack can hardly have been directed against these abuses alone.   As in the case of the temple bank and the money-changing business, the whole system of this sacred traffic in wine, oil, incense, wood, and animals for sacrifice would be an abomination to Jesus.   Seeing, however, that the abolition of the trade in these things anywhere in the neighbourhood of the altar would have rendered sacrifices impossible for any one not himself a farmer or cattle-breeder, and that such a limitation of the offerings to objects reared by the farmer himself was naturally neither intended nor practicable, the conclusion can hardly be avoided that the attack was aimed against the whole sacrificial system as such, and that the temple was to be converted from a reeking slaughter-house, securing preferential treatment for the rich by

---

[1] *Ibid.*, ii. 16.   [2] *Sheqalim*, vi. 5.   [3] *Ker.*, i. 7.

placating the divinity with lavish gifts of blood and fat, into a pure ' house of prayer ' for all the world.

The invectives of the prophets [1] against the absurd superstition that God must be fed or could be bribed by offerings are familiar to every reader of the Scriptures, and can hardly have failed to make a deep impression on Jesus. There was, moreover, the Jewish expectation, attested by the oldest collection of *mid-rashîm*,[2] that in the messianic age all sacrifices would cease except the thank-offering (*todah*), i.e. what the Church speaks of as εὐχαριστίαι and εὐλογίαι. The Midrash expressly quotes *Ps.* l. 13 :

'Should I eat the flesh of bulls or drink the blood of goats ? Sacrifice unto God thanksgiving, and pay thy vows unto the Most High,'

a verset from one of two songs [3] of those ' pious' ones [4] who ' have made a covenant with God concerning the sacrifice.' [5]

When the sacrifices ceased altogether with the destruction of the temple in A.D. 70, the substitution of prayer for sacrifice was based on a passage from *Hosea* (xiv. 1 *sq.*) :

'O Israel, return unto the Lord thy God. . . . Take with you *words* and return unto the Lord. Say unto him, Take away all iniquity and turn toward kindness : so will we *render the bullocks of our lips.*'

From the same prophet [6] Jesus twice quoted on different occasions [7] the divine words of hostility to the sacrifices:

'I desire mercy and not sacrifice (and the knowledge of God more than burnt-offerings).'

It is most likely that he used the same words when he drove the cattle-dealers out of the temple, and that the saying imputed to him by Epiphanius [8] on the authority of the *Gospel of the Ebionites*, 'I am come to abolish the sacrifices ; and if ye cease not to sacrifice, the wrath will not cease from you,' may at least in substance be genuine.

The ordinary view that Jesus had no objection to the sacrificial cult of his time and country is very poorly supported. The direction given to the healed lepers to make the customary offering [9] is given at the beginning of his ministry, and in no way excludes our assuming that Jesus, who wished to alter and abrogate nothing in

---

[1] E.g. *Hos.* v. 6, viii. 13 ; *Amos* v. 22 *sqq.* ; *Isaiah* i. 11 *sqq.* ; *Jer.* vi. 20.
[2] *Pesikta*, x. 77a, with Salom. Buber's note. Cf. also *Monatsschr. f. Gesch. u. Wiss. d. Judentums*, 1899, p. 153 *sq.*
[3] *Psalms* l. and li. belong together.
[4] *hasidîm*, *Ps.* l. 5. It is the programme of some congregation opposed to sacrifices, as were the Essenes.
[5] *Ps.* l. 5.
[6] *Hos.* vi. 6.
[7] *Matt.* ix. 13, xii. 7 ; cf. *Mark* xii. 2-34.
[8] xxx. 16.
[9] *Mark* i. 44.

the law ' till all things be accomplished,' [1] had nevertheless determined to declare the law of sacrifice abolished at the opening of the new era, i.e. simultaneously with his public self-revelation as Messiah.

It has often been noticed as a remarkable fact that in the account of the last supper, elsewhere so clearly indicated as corresponding to the *Seder* feast, the eating of the paschal lamb is not mentioned. The phrases ' to eat the passover,' ' to prepare the passover,' [2] where preparations for the *Seder* are referred to, may designate the paschal meal as a whole and need not denote the paschal lamb. In the Diaspora, where the prescribed slaughter of the lamb in the temple was impossible, it is known that the meal was eaten without this principal dish.[3] If Jesus had decided to declare the sacrificial law abolished from the moment of his revelation as Messiah, he may have celebrated this last *Seder* with his disciples in this, the manner usual outside Jerusalem and Palestine. At all events, it is striking that the comparison—on which such stress is laid by Paul—of his impending sacrificial death to the slaughter of the paschal lamb is quite alien to his own words and thoughts, and that he symbolizes such ideas only by the rite of breaking the bread and the pouring out of the wine, just as though he were keeping a paschal feast without a lamb, like Jews living at a distance from Jerusalem. At any rate, that was the view of the Ebionite Jewish Christians, the same people who represented Jesus as saying that he was come to abolish the sacrifices, when in their Gospel, in reply to the question, ' Where wilt thou that we prepare for thee to eat the passover ? ' they make the Saviour say, ' Did I then desire to eat this passover as meat ? ' (τοῦτο τὸ πάσχα κρέα φαγεῖν), i.e. to eat the paschal lamb ? [4]

For the further development of events a decision of the moot question, whether Jesus wished to abolish the sacrifices altogether or merely to remove prevailing abuses, is of no decisive importance. For one thing is certain beyond all doubt : the priests must have gained an impression from his proceedings that the most vital sources of revenue of the temple and the very means of subsistence of the priesthood, the *sheqel*-tax and the sacrifices, were most seriously threatened by his attack on the temple banks and the cattle-merchants. Even if they were possibly inclined at first to make common cause with the national rising against the Romans under the leadership of a Davidic king, they could only regard as their deadly enemy a ruler who in this fashion destroyed the economic basis of their class.

---

[1] *Matt.* v. 18.   [2] *Mark* xiv. 12 and parallels.
[3] The Passover papyrus of Elephantine has no mention of the lamb ; cf. Arnold, *Journal of Bibl. Lit.*, 1912, p. 9.
[4] Epiphan., xxx. 22.

' DESTROY THIS TEMPLE '

There is furthermore the utterance of Jesus on the destruction and rebuilding of the temple, and which falls into this fateful period of his career, to which some attention must be given.[1] The same utterance, it will be recalled, is also mockingly repeated to him on the cross by the jeering multitude.[2] The most incriminating version of this saying (which Jesus himself never denied [3]) appears in *John* ii. 19 in connexion with the story of the purification of the temple, in all probability a more original version of the account than the wording preserved in *Mark* xi. (after verset 17) and *Matt.* xxi. (after verset 13).

Even Luke, who in his Gospel has carefully omitted everything which could recall this most revolutionary of all the sayings of Jesus, knew it well. For in *Acts* (vi. 13 *sq.*) he makes witnesses, whom of course he calls ' false witnesses,' come forward who have heard Stephen ' say that this Jesus the Naṣōraean shall destroy this place,' that is, the temple. Jesus is therefore, so Stephen is reported as saying, to fulfil on his second coming what he had promised at his first appearance.

In *John*, through whose statement it is established that the saying was actually uttered, it is rendered innocuous by being addressed, not to an excited multitude but to the Jewish opponents of Jesus, who wished to see a miracle from him. In this context it practically means, '*If* you destroy the temple,' which his opponents neither could nor would, ' I will build it again in three days.' To this the evangelist added, ' But he spake of the temple of his body,' an allegorical interpretation of the speech which would be the more incomprehensible to the Jews in that it presupposes the entirely un-Jewish idea that the Godhead dwelt incarnate in the body of Jesus, as a Greek god in his temple.

Yet another attempt to render the dubious utterance harmless is attested by Codex Bezae and the quotation of Cyprian from the old Latin version of *Mark* xiii. 2. According to this text, Jesus is represented as appending to the prophecy of the fall of the temple, ' Seest thou these great buildings ? There shall not be left here one stone upon another, which shall not be thrown down,' the words ' and in three days another shall arise without hands.' The unknown writer who devised this evasion intended to say that Jesus did not order the destruction of the temple ($\lambda\acute{\upsilon}\sigma\alpha\tau\epsilon$, *John* ii. 19), but prophesied it ($\lambda\acute{\upsilon}\sigma\epsilon\tau\epsilon$), and that the words were not addressed to the Jews but to the Romans, who actually razed the temple to the ground in A.D. 70. After this destruction by the

---

[1] *Mark* xiv. 58 ; *Matt.* xxvi. 61 ; Luke omits this saying.
[2] *Mark* xv. 29 ; *Matt.* xxvii. 39 *sq.*
[3] *Mark* xiv. 61 ; *Matt.* xxvi. 63 : ' but he held his peace.'

enemy, a new temple would arise in three days, 'without action of human hands,' which an interpolator had introduced into *Mark* xiv. 58. What is meant by this is best illustrated by a passage in Tacitus,[1] where one reads, among the signs portending the fall of the temple, of the wonderful appearance of a temple aloft in the clouds, which seemed suddenly to flash out in fire. To the earthly sanctuary corresponds that archetype in the heavens which was shown to Moses [2] when he was called to build the tabernacle, that ' true tabernacle ' [3] not built by hands, in which, according to the Christian view, the glorified Messiah, on his return to his heavenly home, officiates as the true high priest.

It is obvious that these apologetic evasions neutralize each other. If, with the interpolator of *Mark* xiv. 58, the temple that is to be destroyed is ' made with hands,' then Jesus cannot have spoken, as in *John* ii. 21, ' of the temple of his body.' Again, he cannot have offered to show the Jews a miracle with his promise to build a new temple in three days, for a miraculous building, such as Aladdin produces with his magic lamp, is created not in three days but in an instant.

On the other hand, the numerous attempts to give the ' hard saying ' an unobjectionable form prove that, notwithstanding all endeavours to represent as ' false witnesses ' those who had heard it, it was undeniable that Jesus had really said something of the kind. Which of the various traditional versions of the saying is historical can be easily recognized. ' I am able to destroy the temple of God,' as Matthew has it, would be a harmless, vainglorious boast of Jesus, asserting his power to effect such a work of destruction, quite unlike him as we know him. The essential part of the sentence would then lie in its second half, ' and to build it again in three days,' for any Herostratus could destroy the most splendid edifice of this kind by wanton incendiarism, of which indeed the *Gospel of Peter* [4] tells us that the disciples were actually suspected on the strength of this saying of their Master. That Luke was unwilling to repeat the utterance in this form we can now readily understand, having regard to the charge of sorcery. A reader who would not recognize Jesus as a god—and what reason had the Romans for doing so from the little they had heard and seen of him ?—must have regarded the author of such a statement either as a megalomaniac or as a dangerous magician.

Mark's version, ' I will destroy the temple,' is a promise given by Jesus to destroy and re-erect the building. The evangelist may have understood the threat of destruction as an announcement of the God-sent catastrophe of A.D. 70, and have looked for

---

[1] *Hist.*, v. 13. [2] *Exod.* xxv. 6 *sq.*, xxvi. 30.
[3] *Hebr.* viii. 2.
[4] § 26 : ' We were sought for . . . as wishing to burn the temple.'

the restoration at the time of the second coming. But the words
in no wise agree with what Jesus could expect at the time when he
was under the belief that he must shortly die, and had promised
after his resurrection to withdraw at the head of the elect to
Galilee,[1] where a new Jerusalem was to arise,[2] or rather to descend
from heaven.[3] When and why should he have planned to carry
out the demolition of the Herodian temple ?

Clearly, it is John alone who has preserved the genuine text,
'Destroy this temple, and in three days I will raise it up,' words
which, detached from their misleading context, are readily intelligible and thoroughly in keeping with the narrative of the so-
called purification of the temple. To Jesus the temple, which
should be ' a house of prayer for all nations,' now appears only as
'an abode of crime' : ' Destroy this temple ' links on excellently
to ' ye have made it a den of robbers.'

The antipathies against the temple erected by Herod the
Great, which find expression in these words, were shared by many
of the most pious Jews of the period. Built by a ruler whom the
Jews regarded as an alien, an Arab, even a Philistine, it was
adorned with a golden eagle over its principal gateway, considered
by the Zealots as an idol, as the ' abomination of desolation in the
holy place.' They even had once tried, at the risk of their lives,
to remove it, a bold undertaking for which Herod had taken bloody
vengeance on many loyal martyrs.[4] At a later date Josephus [5]
could assert without fear of contradiction that he had been commissioned by the Jerusalem assembly to press for the demolition
of the palace of Herod at Tiberias, because, contrary to the law,
it was adorned with representations of living creatures.

Furthermore, followers of the old prophetical religion dis-
approved of the building of any temple whatever, considering it
disobedience to God's declared will and an imitation of heathen
customs. When David desired to build a temple for Jahveh, God
commissioned the prophet Nathan to say to him : [6]

' Thus saith the Lord, Shalt thou build me an house for me to
dwell in ? Whereas I have not dwelt in any house since the time
that I brought up the children of Israel out of Egypt, even to this
day, but have walked in a tent and in a tabernacle. In all places
wherein I have walked with all the children of Israel, spake I a word
with any of the judges of Israel, whom I commanded to feed my
people Israel, saying, Why have ye not built me a house of cedar ?. . .
Moreover, the Lord telleth thee that the Lord will make thee a house.'

---

[1] *Mark* xiv. 28=*Matt.* xxvi. 33.
[2] According to the Midrash Jalqut to *Deut.* xxxiii. 19, the temple ought to
have been built originally on Mt. Tabor. See A. Schweitzer, *loc. cit.*, pp. 309
and 433₁.   [3] *Rev.* xxi. 2.   [4] *B.J.*, i. 33. 2-4 ; *Ant.*, xvii. §§ 149-58.
[5] *Vita*, xii. § 65.   [6] 2 *Sam.* vii. 5 *sqq.*

God desires nothing better than the holy tabernacle which was brought with his people from the wilderness, which Moses by his command erected according to the heavenly pattern that was shown to him, and which David after its many wanderings established on the top of Mt. Zion.

When Zerubabel wanted to rebuild the destroyed temple, the voice of a prophet [1] was heard against this project :

' So saith the Lord, " The heaven is my throne, and the earth the footstool of my feet : what manner of house would ye build me, and what manner of place that I should rest there ? Did not my hand make all these things ? " '

As Luke, while in his Gospel suppressing the ' I will destroy this temple' of the witness mentioned by Mark, later on alludes to these very words in the trial of Stephen, so do we find in this report of Stephen's speech [2] all the ideas necessary for the understanding of the words of Jesus about pulling down and rebuilding :

' Our fathers had the tabernacle of the testimony in the wilderness, even as He appointed who spake unto Moses, that he should make it according to the pattern he had seen. Which (tabernacle) also our fathers, in their turn, brought in with Joshua when they entered on the possession of the nations, which God thrust out before the face of our fathers, unto the days of David ; who found favour in the sight of God and asked to find a tent-dwelling ($\sigma\kappa\acute{\eta}\nu\omega\mu\alpha$) for the God of Jacob. But Solomon built him a house. Howbeit the Most High dwelleth not in (houses) made with hands ; as saith the prophet,[3] " The heaven is my throne, and the earth the footstool of my feet : what manner of house will ye build me ? saith the Lord, or what is the place of my rest ? Did not my hand make all these things ? " Ye stiff-necked and uncircumcised in heart and ears, ye do always resist the Holy Ghost : as your fathers did, so do ye.'

If the building of Solomon's temple was sinful disobedience to their fathers' God, who, like the Rekhabite tent-dwellers, would live in no fixed abode but only in a tabernacle, then the conclusion is obvious, ' Destroy this temple, and in three days will I build it up,' even as God had promised by the mouth of the prophet Amos : [4]

' In that day will I raise up the tabernacle of David that is fallen.'

What the carpenter Jesus promises to build up ' in three days ' —in the few days remaining until the paschal feast of the exodus to freedom in the wilderness—and what could easily be built up in that time, is a new portable tabernacle of a few wooden poles, a

---

[1] *Isaiah* lxvi. 1 *sqq.* ; cf. A. v. Gall, Βασιλεία Θεοῦ, Heidelberg, 1926, p. 189 n. 4.
[2] *Acts* vii. 44-51.   [3] *Isaiah* lxvi. 1 *sq.*
[4] ix. 11, a passage quoted by James, the brother of Jesus, in *Acts* xv. 16.

2 1

few planks of acacia, a few rugs, coverings, and skins, just like that
sanctuary which the pious-minded fathers had built for themselves with the work of their own hands and decorated with the
ornaments lovingly offered by their wives.

Down with that towering gold and marble temple of the foreign
despots, desecrated by its idol! Up with that empty, simple
hut, the modest image of the world-wide heavenly tabernacle, in
which the God of the wilderness dwells, and which will accompany
the elect on the march to freedom! 'Destroy this temple, and in
three days will I build it up.'

> ' I will raise up the tabernacle of David that is fallen and close up
> the breaches thereof, and I will raise up its ruins and I will build it
> as in the days of old ; that they may conquer the remnant of Edom,[1]
> and all the nations which were called by my name, saith the Lord
> that doeth this. Behold the days come, saith the Lord, that the
> ploughman shall overtake the reaper, and the treader of grapes him
> that soweth seed ; and the mountains shall drop sweet wine, and all
> the hills shall melt. And I will bring back the captivity of my people
> Israel, and they shall build the waste cities and inhabit them, and
> they shall plant vineyards and drink the wine thereof ; they shall
> also make gardens and eat the fruit of them. And I will plant them
> upon their land, and they shall no more be plucked up out of their
> land which I have given them, saith the Lord thy God.' [2]

The idea that God himself or the Messiah would destroy
Herod's temple and replace it by another was not unknown to the
Jews. Toward the end of that remarkable apologetic pageant of
symbolical animals in the *Book of Enoch* [3] we read that the ' Lord
of the sheep '

> ' folded up that old house : they carried off all the pillars . . . and
> laid it in a place in the south of the land. And I looked on until the
> Lord of the sheep brought a new house greater and loftier than that
> first one, and set it up in the place of the first which had been folded
> up : all its pillars were new, and its ornaments were new and larger
> than those of the first, the old one which he had taken away.'

But in this baroque bit of fancy the Jews imagine the temple
of the last times even greater and more magnificent than the
extravagantly splendid building of. Herod. On the other hand,
the dream of the followers of the old Rekhabite religion of the
prophets, that one day the homely tabernacle of the wilderness
period would reappear, was faithfully cherished by the Samaritans.
The Samaritan messiah mentioned by Josephus [4] as one who

---

[1] The usual expression at that time for the Idumaean dynasty of the Herodians
and the Roman empire.

[2] *Amos* ix. 11-15.

[3] xc. 28 *sq*. On this strange document, cf. my *Orphisch-dionysische Mysterien-
gedanken*, p. 212 *sqq*.

[4] *Ant.*, xviii. 4. 1.

'thought little of a lie' and adroitly arranged the whole matter to catch the public ear, is probably no other than Simon Magus, a native of Gitta. Of him Josephus narrates that he undertook to show his countrymen on the top of Mt. Garizim the sacred objects (τὰ ἱερὰ σκεύη) hidden there by Moses. The whole scheme was based on nothing but the old popular belief that at the end of this era of divine wrath and at the beginning of the new age of mercy Joshua ('Ιησοῦς) would ' return ' (ta'eb) and re-establish the tabernacle with the ark of the covenant.[1]

One form of this legend occurred in the lost works of Nehemiah, used by the author of the second book of Maccabees ; [2] here Nehemiah replaced Zerubabel as the builder of the second temple, and the old tabernacle, the ark, and the altar of incense are hidden in a cave on Mt. Nebo. If one reads carefully the passage in Stephen's speech in Acts vii. 46 previously discussed, and asks oneself why it is said of David that he found favour in the sight of God and therefore asked God that he might find a tabernacle (εὑρεῖν σκήνωμα), not that he might build one, in contrast to the disobedient, ambitious Solomon, who, instead of the tabernacle ' found ' through God's mercy by David, presumed to build a new permanent house for God, it is apparent that an Haggadic answer must have been discovered in Ps. cxxxii. 5 to the question whether the tent for the ark mentioned in 2 Sam. vi. 17 was the old tabernacle, and, if so, how David could have ' found ' it. Stephen, or Luke, must have known of a midrash in which it was said that God, in answer to the prayer of King David, had allowed him to find the right place on the top of Mt. Zion, and in the cave thereunder the old tabernacle of the wilderness wondrously concealed. As a matter of fact, in a newly discovered Jeremiah apocryphon [3] the prophet Jeremiah, before the destruction of the temple by the Babylonians, conceals the high-priestly gown of Aaron under the corner-stone of the sanctuary—that is, under the holy rock, the sakhra on Mt. Zion.

Accordingly, the Messiah b. David must also have been expected on his manifestation to renew that sanctuary which God himself had once ordered to be erected, the ' true tabernacle ' in which from henceforth God's Shekinah would graciously take its abode among men. In his words about the destruction of Herod's temple and the building of another sanctuary in three days, Jesus undertook to fulfil this expectation. But as it was utterly alien to the genius of the messianic renovator of the law of God to search in some mouldy underground cavern, or maybe in the unknown

---

[1] Cf. Poznanski, Der Schilo, p. 286 sq. ; A. Merx, Beih. xvii. z. Z.A.T.W., Giessen, 1909, pp. 28 and 43. Moses Gaster, Asatir, London, 1927, p. 91.
[2] ii. 4-6 ; according to verset 13, derived from the ' records of Nehemiah.'
[3] Ed. A. Mingana, Bull. John Rylands Libr., xi. (1927), No. 2.

tomb of the first lawgiver, for the old stone tables of the covenant, instead of engraving the new law upon the tables of the heart of the elect, so was it far from his thought to work a delusive miracle and to rediscover beneath the earth, or in some *genizah* of the temple,[1] the ' remains ' of the old ' fallen tabernacle of David.' The son of the carpenter courageously undertook to build afresh a new tabernacle in three days. A new ' tent of witness ' was to accompany the new Israel into the wilderness on the road to freedom.

The Counterstroke : The Massacre in the Temple

Jesus could be under no delusion as to the fact that his attack on the bankers, the cattle-dealers, and finally on the temple itself, was bound to make the ruling hierocracy his deadly enemies, and that he would have to deal not only with these Jewish opponents but also with the Romans. He was prepared for an armed encounter, and expected himself to be taken prisoner and executed.

Since he had determined neither to flee nor to offer resistance, and must have said to himself that the enemy would concentrate their attack upon him, he could hardly expect any other fate, unless God intervened at the last moment, granting victory to the little band and thus ' letting the cup pass from him.' If he fell into the hands of his Jewish opponents, who did not possess the *ius gladii*, it was to be feared that they would deliver him up to the Romans.[2] Seeing that at the last supper he predicted that his body would be broken like bread, his blood poured out like wine, he cannot, as has rightly been recognized,[3] have expected the shameful death of slaves and criminals on the cross, by which his body would not be divided, nor his blood poured forth in streams. He must clearly have thought that after the engagement he would be beheaded or hewn in pieces by his furious foes.[4] That was precisely the end of the messiah [5] Theudas, who, while attempting to cross the Jordan with his followers, was surprised and taken alive by the cavalry of Fadus—that he was hewn in pieces.[6] In fact, the fate of Agag, the king of the Amalekites, who was defeated by

---

[1] According to *Tosephta Soṭa*, xiii. 1 (W. Bacher, *Encyclop. of Relig. and Ethics*, vol. vi. p. 187a), the sanctuary erected by Moses was 'concealed' at the building of the temple of Solomon.

[2] *Mark* x. 35 *sq.* ; *Luke* xviii. 33 *sq.*

[3] Goetz, *Das Abendmahl*, Leipzig, 1920 (*Unters. zum N.T.*, ed Windisch, viii. 17).

[4] In *Sukkah*, xxxii. 9, the Messiah b. Joseph killed in battle is called שׁנהרג, but הרג means ' to kill with the sword '—in particular, ' to behead ' (see Levy, *Nhb. Wb.*, i. 490b, s.v. *haeraeg* and *harigah*).

[5] Origen was aware that Theudas figured as the Messiah: cf. *In Joann.*, vi. ; *P.G.*, xiv. 217.

[6] *Acts* v. 36 (D*), διελύθη.

Saul, shows that, according to the martial law of primitive Israel, a captured enemy king was 'hewn in pieces before the Lord,'[1] just as the Arabs after a successful battle were accustomed to make an offering, occasionally a human offering, as a *naqiᶜa*, literally (an offering) ' hewn in pieces.'[2] Since the cavalry of the Romans in Palestine, the renowned *ala Sebastenorum*,[3] consisted of Samaritans, Theudas was doubtless not decapitated according to Roman custom,[4] but in the old Israelitish fashion hewn or hacked in pieces.

Jesus was not prepared for the *servile supplicium* of crucifixion, but for the horrible sanguinary fate of kings—to be hewn in pieces before the Lord ; of Roman legislation on the punishment of an *auctor seditionis* he had scarcely thought.

For the rest, he must have hoped that the counterstroke of the Romans would be delayed long enough to leave him time to issue the summons for the new exodus to the Jews now streaming together for the Passover from every quarter of the known world. In order that none of them might lose the opportunity of hearing this decisive proclamation—in order, too, that, as God of old had commanded Moses, the march might begin on the day of the feast— he must have deferred the departure of his followers into the desert, visible, in the near distance, from the camp of his small force on the Mount of Olives. That thereby a possibility of success, a chance of anticipating the Roman attack by hasty flight, was sacrificed, no one will believe who takes into account the superior rapidity of the Roman auxiliary cavalry in comparison with such a slow-moving procession of people mounted at best on asses and mules. As at a later date the governor Catullus easily overtook and cut down the bands of Jonathan, the weaver of Cyrene, on their exodus into the wilderness,[5] so would it probably have fared with this exodus even had the measure been sped up. In the existing condition of things the partisans of Jesus can only have hoped by battles around the temple on the north and around the southern extremity of the city walls, to be mentioned immediately, and finally by a stubborn rearguard action on the Mount of Olives, to hold up the Romans until the rest were in safety ; and even this plan could have a prospect of success only if the numbers of insurgents who joined the Galilaean rebels far exceeded those of the enemy, and if the Romans were not, through treachery, apprised beforehand of all his intentions and the moment fixed for their execution.

---

[1] I *Sam.* xv. 33.
[2] Robertson Smith, *The Religion of the Semites*, p. 491 ; cf. p. 363.
[3] Schürer, i⁴, pp. 460-2 (Engl. trans., vol i. 2, p. 52 n. 51).
[4] In 4 B.C., for example, Varus had beheaded the messiah Simon of Peraea ; cf. above, p. 264 n. 3.
[5] Cf. above, p. 362₃.

The Roman attack came more quickly than the Galilaeans had thought. Indeed, from the brief words of Josephus [1] to the effect that Pilate ' sent and slew many of the multitude,' no inference can be drawn as to the moment and the details of the counterstroke. But from the trustworthy statements of the Synoptists that the arrest of Jesus followed immediately after the paschal supper, held in secret, we may infer with a good deal of probability that the troops had appeared on the scene as early as the afternoon of the ' day of preparation,' at the time when the paschal lambs were ordinarily killed at the great altar in the temple, and forthwith had begun to cut down the multitude.

Pilate himself has not hesitated on another occasion to employ against the Jews [2] the practice of the *sicarii* of concealing weapons beneath civilian garb and then swiftly producing them, a practice by means of which the temple was occupied by the insurgents in the time of Archelaus and probably also on the occasion of Jesus' triumphal entry into Jerusalem. Against a cohort approaching in arms, the huge city doors, or at least the temple gates, could be promptly closed and then the almost impregnable fortifications could be defended for a long time. On the other hand, nothing was easier than to mix the Samaritan auxiliary troops—who of course knew the vernacular, and carried concealed weapons—among the procession of Jewish pilgrims streaming into town, and thus to introduce them in overpowering strength into the temple. Once a sufficiently superior number had forced their way in, the mass of the insurgents could by a sudden and ruthless attack with drawn swords be easily dispersed and ejected from the sanctuary.

These conclusions, derived from purely tactical considerations, are confirmed when we insert in its proper context a conversation of Jesus with his disciples, which in its present position in *Luke* xiii. 1-6 is wholly unintelligible :

' Now there came at this time some who told him of the Galilaeans, whose blood Pilate had mingled with their sacrifices. And he answered and said unto them, Think ye that these Galilaeans were sinners above all the Galilaeans, because they have suffered these things ? I tell you, Nay : but, except ye repent, ye shall all in like manner perish.'

Thereupon the bewildered messengers ask further :

' And what about those eighteen upon whom the tower in Siloam fell and killed them ? '

To which Jesus replies :

' Think ye that they were offenders above all the inhabitants of Jerusalem ? I tell you, Nay : but, except ye repent, ye shall all likewise perish.'

---

[1] Cf. above, p. 385 ll. 1 f.   [2] *B.J.*, ii. 9. 4 ; *Ant.*, xviii. 3. 2.

THE ROMAN COUNTERSTROKE 503

In these words the various commentaries profess to find a mere general theoretical reflection on the connexion between guilt and Divine punishment, or, as it has been expressed, the contribution of Jesus to the problem of Job. There actually appear to be scholars who think that Jesus could have said that all his contemporaries who do not repent (i.e. generally repent of their evil life) will 'likewise perish' (πάντες ὡσαύτως)—in other words, all the unrepentant will sooner or later be struck on the head by a falling tower or slaughtered with the sword by the Romans while in the act of slaying their own sacrifice at the altar. Even if the absurdity of this is mitigated according to certain MSS. by the substitution of ὁμοίως [1] for ὡσαύτως in both sentences, the ordinary interpretation represents Jesus as having explained to his disciples, like some Pharisaic bookkeeper of divine justice, that all catastrophes in nature and history are the normal and necessary retribution for unrepented sin. And all that long after the disillusioned Solomon b. David had seen 'the wicked buried and go (in peace), while they that had done right must depart from the holy place and be forgotten in the city,' [2] and long after he had found 'righteous men unto whom it happeneth according to the work of the wicked,' and also 'wicked men to whom it happeneth according to the work of the righteous'; [3] and again, 'there is a righteous man that perisheth in his righteousness, and there is a wicked man that prolongeth (his life) in his evildoing,' [4] and 'All things come alike to all : there is one event to the righteous and to the wicked, to the clean and to the unclean, to him that sacrificeth and to him that sacrificeth not : as is the good, so is the wicked'; [5] or, as Job complains, 'It is all one ; therefore I say, He destroyeth the perfect and the wicked ; the tents of the robbers prosper and they that provoke God are secure.' [6] At a time when pedantic and misleading books are written and read on 'Jesus as a philosopher,' the ordinary commentator does not shrink from foisting upon him the superficial and contemptible wisdom of the interpolator who wrote between the lines of the above passages from Ecclesiastes, 'Because sentence against an evil work is not executed speedily, because the sinner doeth evil a hundred times and still prolongs his ways, the heart of the sons of men is emboldened in them to do evil.' [7] He does not shrink from attributing to the Master the childish doctrine that it is only a question of time before all sinners are overtaken here upon earth by the so-called punishment of God, although even a poorly instructed scholar could reply from Scripture, 'Ask them that go by, ye will not mistake their tokens,'

---

[1] I.e. 'in a similar way.'
[2] *Eccles.* viii. 10.
[4] *Ibid.*, vii. 15.
[6] *Job* ix. 22, xii. 6.

[3] *Ibid.*, viii. 14.
[5] *Ibid.*, ix. 2.
[7] *Eccles.* viii. 11 *sq.*

(how often it happens) ' that the evil man is spared from the day of calamity; on the day of wrath they are led away.' [1]

And yet no one can be ignorant of the fact that Jesus, like all messianists of his time, expected a totally different adjustment of the manifest injustices of this world through the coming of 'the future world,' in which those who have suffered and struggled here will enjoy the bliss of the kingdom of God, from which the wicked will be excluded and ' cast out '; while that saying of his in the Fourth Gospel on the man born blind [2] palpably proves that his conception of guilt and punishment is completely in line with that of the *Book of Job*. It is therefore imperative to seek for an explanation of the passage in *Luke* which does not drive us to such inconsistencies.

Now, it is an established fact, repeated from the time of Papias [3] down to the latest representatives of the ' *formgeschichtliche Schule*,' that the actions and utterances of Jesus have not been transmitted in their strict historical order.

It is obvious, for instance, that the narrative of the attack on the money-changers and cattle-dealers and of the challenge to destroy the temple has, by the last editor of the Fourth Gospel, been violently torn from its historically significant and true position in connexion with the events which inevitably led to the arrest and condemnation of Jesus,[4] and has been artificially and tendentiously transferred to the opening of his public ministry. The object of this deliberate manipulation of the text is evident. It is intended to render impossible the sort of argument used by those who find the condemnation of Jesus as a rebel who 'stirreth up the people ' [5] amply justified by these proceedings, admitted even by Christians. This was accomplished by giving a version of the story which, while not suppressing or contesting these things (it was far too late for that), maintained that neither the Jews nor the Romans had ever regarded these measures of Jesus as an occasion for any judicial procedure. On the contrary, after these actions he is supposed to have been able to teach and work, quite unmolested, for several years more.

Similarly, we were able to show [6] that Luke omitted in their true place the words of Mark, whose Gospel he knew quite well, ' I will destroy this temple,' and instead introduced some quite inconspicuous words into the ' false ' accusations of the Jews, brought forward against Stephen in the second volume of his historical work.

[1] *Job* xxi. 29 *sq.*
[2] *John* ix. 3: ' Neither did this man sin nor his parents.'
[3] Ap. Euseb., *H.E.*, iii. 39. 15 *sq.*
[4] Cf. Roland Schuetz, *Z.N.T.W.*, viii. (1907), p. 247 *sq.*
[5] *Luke* xxiii. 5.
[6] Cf. above, p. 497.

We are therefore perfectly justified in assuming that there has been a similar displacing in the case of *Luke* xiii. 1-4, and in transposing the two 'Job's messages' which are brought to Jesus to their natural place in the narrative of events, immediately before his arrest.

Berendts[1] has already expressed the opinion, heartily supported by Goethals, that when Josephus tells us that '(Pilate) sent and had many of the people slaughtered,' the same event might be referred to as in *Luke* xiii. 1. This contention is the less to be rejected in that so far no other reasonable explanation has been offered of this story of the massacre of the Galilaeans at their sacrifices in the temple. If it refers to the counter-attack of Pilate on the Galilaeans who had pressed into the temple with Jesus, and who in the time-honoured manner on the afternoon of the ' day of preparation' were busy with the slaughter of the paschal lambs,[2] while Jesus with his companions had already left the temple and was on the way to the house in which the supper had been prepared for him, then the reported words at once become intelligible. Jesus then does not speak in general terms of 'repentance' for a sinful life, but quite simply of a ' return' from the path which had led to this catastrophe, of repentance for the deeds of violence just perpetrated.

He asks the messengers whether they believe that their killed comrades were worse sinners than all the other Galilaeans who had taken part in the revolt, and at once answers his own question in the negative : on the contrary, all who do not ' return,' or, if the Greek word must be kept, 'repent' of what they have done, will in like manner perish. Here we have, not an absurd general statement on sin, punishment, and 'repentance warding off the decree of fate,' but a perfectly sound pronouncement on very definite events thoroughly in keeping with the time and subject-matter. If it is asked what the Galilaeans had to repent of, what they had done contrary to the will of Jesus, one has only to recall the words of *Mark* xv. 7 on the ' rebels who in the insurrection had committed manslaughter.' No one will wish to believe that Jesus, who only after a hard struggle of conscience had decided to allow his followers to bear arms in self-defence, could therefore have also sanctioned the suggestion of the Zealots 'to enter into the city and cut down Pilate and the Romans.' Not even Josephus, to whom we owe this information as to the Zealots' plans—in other words,

---

[1] *Op. cit.*, p. 48 *sq.*

[2] This is no contradiction to Jesus' attitude toward the cattle-dealers and the sacrificial cult. For it does not follow that Jesus wholly rejected the slaughter of beasts after the manner of the Baptist, and it is furthermore extremely likely that in many things his followers did not carry out their Master's injunctions. Possibly he and the Twelve kept a Passover without a paschal lamb, whilst the outer circle kept it in the traditional manner.

not even the Roman prosecutor—had ventured to charge him with giving any sanction whatsoever to this plan of attack. Even the historian who is entirely uninfluenced by any idealizing and apologetic aims may confidently presume, after all that is known with certainty of Jesus and his teaching, that before his entry into Jerusalem he had most strictly enjoined his followers to avoid all bloodshed so far as that was at all possible. On the other hand, every one who knows the hot-headed Jewish Zealots of that time and the Galilaeans, the most combative of them all, cannot but believe that blades once drawn by such fanatics would not be sheathed again before blood had flown.

Any one knowing the world and humanity in general, and Jerusalem, Galilee, and Rome in particular, not through Sunday sermons alone, knows, without having read *Mark* xv., that, if not the attack on the money-changers, at least that on the cattle-dealers must have cost not a few men's lives. In the whole world there is not an ox-driver who would let either his herd or his master be driven from the market by a stranger without drawing his knife and striking and stabbing his opponent. The kingly prophet, of whom even official prosecutors said that he ' did nothing high-handed ' but ' only with a word prepared everything,' must have watched with dismay the excesses to which the unchained passions of his own followers carried them. The horror of the peacemaker, who saw himself drawn into the bloody battles of this world, as soon as the sword which he was to bring was drawn, as soon as the fire which he was to cast was kindled—this dismay quivers yet in the words ' except ye repent (*or* desist) ye shall all in like manner perish.' What he had willed and planned was the exodus into the wilderness, screened, if necessary, by an armed rearguard defence, but no stubborn battle with the Romans for the possession of the temple and city of Jerusalem, which meant nothing to him and, according to his deepest conviction, were doomed to inevitable ruin in the messianic war of the princes of this world.

The Fall of the Tower of Siloam

The best proof of the correctness of this interpretation of *Luke* xiii. 1 lies in the fact that it also at once explains the follow-ing question and answer concerning the fate of the eighteen inhabitants of Jerusalem who were killed by the falling tower of Siloam.

As early as 1920 the director of the Edmond de Rothschild excavations in Jerusalem, the French officer of engineers and pro-fessor of Egyptology at the École Pratique des Hautes Études of the University of Paris, Major Raymond Weill,[1] conjectured that 'the

---

[1] *La cité de David, compte-rendu des fouilles exécutées à Jérusalem sur le site de la ville primitive, campagne de 1913-14*, Paris, 1920, p. 118.

PLATE XXXIV

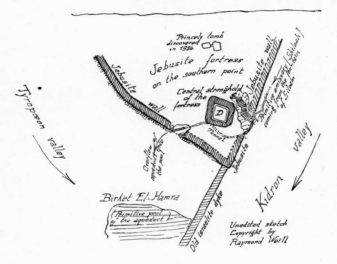

Southern point of the "City of David" (Mount Zion)

Princely tomb discovered in 1924

Jebusite fortress on the southern point

Central stronghold of the fortress

Jebusite wall

Jebusite wall

Primitive emissary (Shiloah) coming from the fountain of Siloah

Tyropoeon valley

Kidron valley

Overflow of aqueduct from the pool

Tunnel

Jebusite dyke

Birket El-Hamra

(Primitive pool of the aqueduct)

Old Israelite dyke

Unedited sketch Copyright by Raymond Weill

THE TOWER OF SILOAM EXCAVATED BY MAJOR RAYMOND WEILL FOR BARON EDMOND DE ROTHSCHILD

THE SOUTHERNMOST TOWER OF THE FORTIFICATIONS OF JERUSALEM BATTERED DOWN DURING THE COUNTER ATTACK OF THE ROMANS AGAINST THE FOLLOWERS OF JESUS, EIGHTEEN OF WHICH WERE CRUSHED UNDER ITS RUINS. (LC. XIII, I-4)

(SEE P. 508, NOTE 2)

tower in Siloam ' mentioned in this passage was one of the towers of the city wall of Jerusalem then rediscovered. In ignorance of the results of these excavations, Dr. Billerbeck,[1] merely on the ground of the statements in Josephus [2] concerning the course of the city wall in the neighbourhood of the pool of Siloam, made the same conjecture, without realizing, however, that this hypothesis is quite incompatible with the ordinary assumption that the fall of this tower was accidental. For who can believe that the *magister fabrorum* of the Roman army of occupation was so remiss in his supervision as to allow fortifications, only recently restored by Herod the Great after Pompey's storming of the city, to fall into such decay that one of the towers could collapse by itself ? Nor can we explain *Luke* xiii. 4 by an earthquake, for the author would certainly not have omitted to mention this dramatic detail in his picture of Divine punishment. Dr. Billerbeck himself quotes the thoroughly trustworthy Rabbinic tradition [3] that there had never been a case of the fall of a building in Jerusalem, a fact adduced as one of the ' ten wonders which were granted to our fathers in the sacred place,' but which finds its natural explanation in the fact that the whole city stood upon solid rock.

If this tower—which must have been a fortress tower, for at the time there can have been neither steeple nor minaret [4]—did not collapse of itself, then it must have been deliberately overthrown by some one with heavy siege machinery. If, moreover, in the connected sentence [5] it is Pilate who has the Galilaeans massacred in the temple, it is surely not too bold to assume that the same Roman governor is responsible for the assault on and overthrow of ' the tower in Siloam.' If, according to the conjecture of Bernhard Weiss, now confirmed and only slightly modified by the *Halōsis* of Josephus, the Galilaeans in question were in revolt against the Romans and therefore fell victims to the Roman sword, then the same will also doubtless be true of the Jerusalemites, who were holding and defending the tower of Siloam. For why else should the Romans have attacked and overthrown with battering-ram and *testudo* a tower of their own garrison town ?

On the basis of these, in my opinion convincing, considerations, I have not hesitated before this [6] to conclude that the Galilaeans,

---

[1] Strack-Billerbeck, ii. 197.   [2] *B.J.*, v. § 145.
[3] *Aboth de R. Nathan*, 35.
[4] Nor can there be any question of this tower having been one of the fortified tower-like houses of the dominating families, a building of the type found in the mediaeval Italian cities and also in the territory of the ancient Axumites or Minaeans and Sabaeans. For, quite aside from the question whether such towers existed in Jerusalem (the πύργος of *Luke* xiv. 28 is clearly a fortress tower), the same would hold true for a tower of this kind. Imagine the Bargello of Florence tumbling down *accidentally* !
[5] *Luke* xiii, 1.   [6] *Klio*, xx. (1926), p. 495.

who at the entry of Jesus broke into the city from the Mount of
Olives, occupied the temple, while the *Barjonîm* of Jerusalem,
who had made common cause with them, surprised the guards and
seized the tower of Siloam, so that Pilate in his counter-attack had
to reconquer both places.

The procedure of the rebels is strategically quite intelligible.
A glance at the map shows that the fortified temple with its fort
Antonia dominates the northern portion of the city. On the other
hand, it appears from Josephus [1] that for any officer making the
round of Jerusalem along the battlements, to assure himself that
the city was quiet and in the hands of the garrison, Siloam formed
the terminal point of his tour of inspection, quite naturally, since
the pool of Siloam lay at the extreme south—more precisely the
south-east— of the city, and at the same time at the southern point
of the old city of David. Any one holding Antonia in the north
and the city tower 'on the Siloah' at the southern extremity, even
though the Roman *cohors equitata* with a squadron of Samaritan
cavalry were still in occupation of Herod's palace on the western
hill, could well consider himself master of Jerusalem. In view of
the comparative weakness of the Roman garrison in Palestine, the
position of Pilate was extremely serious if the country, roused
by the bands of pilgrims streaming back after the feast, joined
in the revolt.

It is thus intelligible that the governor should, before the arrival
of the day of the Passover, bend all his efforts on recovering his
hold on the city and on laying hands on him who had been proclaimed king of the Jews by the insurgents.

As for the ' tower in Siloam,' this singular phrase is now finally
explained by the further excavations of M. Raymond Weill [2] and
the discovery of the southernmost point of the city walls of
Jerusalem. Siloam, in Hebrew *Shiloaḥ*, means literally ' emissary' [3] (from *shalaḥ*, 'send,' 'emit'), i.e. 'aqueduct,' and the whole
valley is called the valley of Shiloaḥ, after the waterworks which
in primaeval times were constructed underground alongside the
walls to carry the water from the spring situated in the north of the
city of David into the reservoir in the little valley of the ' cheese-
makers ' (*Tyropoeon*) to the south of this hill. The ' tower in
Siloam ' is the tower standing upon or above the aqueduct with
the object of defending this important structure.

The peculiar configuration of this valley with its watercourse
may perhaps throw light on a remarkable tradition concerning the
capture of the old Jebusite stronghold of Jerusalem by King

---

[1] *B.J.*, ii. 16. 2, § 340.

[2] *Revue des études Juives*, 1926, lxxxii. pp. 103-110. I am indebted to Major
Weill for his specially prepared sketches, Pls. xxxiv.-v.; and his photograph,
Pl. xxxvi. [3] Thus *John* ix. 7 : ἀπεσταλμένος.

PLATE XXXV

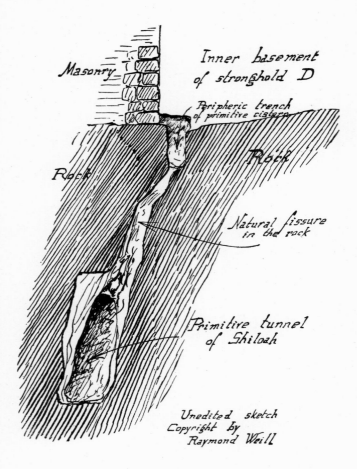

SECTION OF THE TOWER OF SILOAM

SHOWING THE ROCK FISSURE CONNECTING ITS BASEMENT WITH THE WATER-TUNNEL
(SHILOAH)

(SEE P. 508, NOTE 2)

David. Many years ago, in a notice [1] on Parker's excavations on Ophel, I pointed out that the much-debated sentence in 2 *Sam.* v. 8 becomes clear and intelligible if the word *baṣ-ṣinnor,* ' through the watercourse,' be transposed to a previous line, so that the reading is :

v. 6. ' And the king and his men went to Jerusalem against the Jebusites, the inhabitants of the land ; and they spake unto David saying, Thou shalt not come hither, but the blind and the lame shall turn thee away (meaning, David cannot come in hither).[2]

v. 7. ' Nevertheless David took the stronghold of Zion (that is the city of David) [3] through the watercourse.

v. 8. 'And David said on that day, Whosoever smiteth the Jebusites hits also the lame and the blind, that are hated of David's soul. Wherefore they say, Blind and lame come not into the house.' [4]

At that time I believed that the 'watercourse' by which David penetrated into the fortress might be identified with the shaft discovered by Parker. But now it is a far more attractive theory to think of the cleft in the rock found by Major Weill (Pl. xxxvi.) [5] leading from the water-channels right into the basement of the ' tower above Siloam,' that is, into the heart of the fortifications at the southern end of the old Jebusite stronghold.

If in the time of Jesus it was still known, or could be read in better MSS. of the *Books of Samuel* than have come down to us, that King David made his way into Jerusalem at this spot, this may have had some influence on the decision of the Zealots to secure this particular tower.

At all events, the fact that the word *baṣ-ṣinnor,* ' through the watercourse,' now appears in a wrong position proves that it does not belong to the original narrative but is a marginal gloss incorporated into the text by a later copyist and at the wrong place. Verset 7, therefore, originally simply read : ' Nevertheless David took the stronghold of Zion.' The marginal gloss ' through the watercourse ' was added later, at the time when the cleft, now rediscovered, was exposed in the construction of the new aqueduct, and the fable grew up that it was by this fissure that David reached the fortress.

The ' tower above Siloam ' was certainly connected by tradition

---

[1] *Frankfurter Zeitung,* 28th May 1911, p. 147.

[2] An old gloss giving the sense correctly ; the fortress is so strong that a garrison of blind men could repel every enemy.

[3] Gloss.

[4] Proverbial phrase, meaning that such persons, presumably smitten by God, bring ill-luck into the house. The customary phrase for dismissing such beggars at the door is here quaintly carried back to the time of David. Because of the prejudice against blind and crippled beggars, Jesus charitably commands the well-to-do to invite them, and not kinsmen and rich neighbours, to dinner and supper (*Luke* xiv. 13).

[5] See Major Weill's detailed explanation, vol. ii. pp. 518 ff. of the Germ. edition.

with David's capture of Jerusalem. Whether it was the strategic importance of the place that determined their plans, or the desire of the followers of the new Messiah, the 'Son of David,' to link their proceedings to the history of the older King David, may be left an open question. In any case, the execution of their surprise attack was quite independent of its Davidic prototype ; for the rebels were within, not outside, the city, and had therefore no need to reach the tower by the rock chimney. All they had to do was to make an unexpected assault on the gates and overpower the weak garrison, to be in possession of a strong and dominating bastion which could without difficulty be secretly supplied with provisions and water through the fissure in the rock.

The fate of the tower under the violent attack of the Roman artillery shows how gravely Pilate viewed the situation and how successfully he mastered it.

They that were crucified with him ' in the same condemnation.' The Last Supper

With the massacre in the temple and at the tower of Siloam the insurrection might be regarded as quelled, though the real author of the sedition was still at large. At each of the places seized by the rebels one of the insurgents must have been in command, and these two leaders are doubtless the two λῃσταί crucified on the right and left of Jesus, who ' under the same condemnation,' [1] i.e. 'under the same sentence' or on a similar charge, hung with him on the cross. Of these one cries to him, ' Art not thou the Messiah ? save thyself and us '—very natural words if he had taken part in the undertaking of Jesus which had ended so disastrously, but hardly explainable if, according to the usual view, the speaker was a highwayman without the remotest connexion with Jesus and whom the Messiah had not the least reason to save. The words of the other λῃστής, over the historicity or lack of which there is no need to rack one's brains (since it is the intention of the evangelist author that matters), are equally intelligible under the circumstances. He blames the request of his companion as opposed to the will of God, who, according to the teaching of Jesus, requires the death and passion of the Messiah as the ' ransom ' (λύτρον) or for the redemption (ge'ulah, λύτρωσις) of Israel. He himself is prepared loyally to share the ' cup ' with Jesus, his leader, king, and lord, and consequently receives the promise, ' To-day shalt thou be with me in the gan 'eden,' in the ' garden of the wilderness,' [2] in that oasis lost since the day of the

---

[1] " ἐν τῷ αὐτῷ κρίματι," Luke xxiii. 40.
[2] On 'paradise' situated not in heaven but on earth, cf. e.g. Theophil., Ad Autolyc., c. xxiv.

PLATE XXXVI

ENTRANCE INTO THE CREVICE BY THE TOWER OF SILOAM
SECTION ON PLATE XXXV
(SEE P. 509, NOTE 5)

Fall, with the fountain and the fruit-trees beside the four streams, to which Jesus is about to be miraculously transferred, there to abide until his second coming. The confession, ' For we receive the due reward of our deeds : but this man hath done nothing amiss,' [1] just like the words of Jesus discussed above,[2] emphasizes the contrast between the actions of the lawless ones who had boldly undertaken to fight for freedom and the liberator-king and had shed blood in the fight, and Jesus' own command, who had obviously directed them, on entering and occupying the city, to avoid any attack on their opponents, to let them come on quietly and to leave the issue to God.

That Jesus himself and the Twelve were not captured by the Romans on their recovery of the temple and the southern city tower is at once explained by the moment when the surprise attack was made on the temple, namely, at the time of the slaughter of the paschal lambs. By that time Jesus had betaken himself with his disciples to the distant house, where in a closed upper chamber he still found some hours of quiet and composure to keep with his followers that parting meal which was to precede the exodus into the wilderness and the hard rearguard contests he expected. With a tranquillity which has its pale counterpart only in the parting discourses of Socrates with his disciples, Jesus reveals once more to his following his tragic forebodings of death and suffering, while pronouncing the inauguratory blessings of the festal meal, through the simple acted parables[3] of the breaking of the bread and the pouring out of the wine from the cup which he has blessed into the cups of the disciples.[4] Linking his forebodings of death with an exposition of the eightieth Psalm, he reveals to them the mystery of the ' vine ' of David,[5] i.e. of the vine of Israel described in the Psalter, the authorship of which used to be attributed to David : [6] the vine brought by God out of Egypt, planted in the promised land and there made to flourish until its enclosing wall was broken down, so that the beasts of the field, the peoples of the world, could trample it under foot. But a shoot still remains, from which a new vine is sprouting, the Son of man, the Messiah. As this Messianic offshoot of the vine of Israel, Jesus reveals himself in a grand symbolism[7] which must be a stray fragment from this paschal *derashah*, immediately preceding the prediction of the shedding of his blood, the blood of the ' vine of David,' which will

---

[1] Cf. the identical words in Josephus, above, p. 429 n. 64.
[2] Cf. pp. 505 f.
[3] Similar symbolic actions in *Ezek.* xi. 3, xiv. 3, xv. 11 *sqq.* ; *Jerem.* xviii 3, 11.
[4] For what follows, cf. also *Z.N.T.W.*, 1926, pp. 5-37, and *The Quest*, xiv. (1923), p. 322 *sqq.*
[5] Cf. *Didaché*, ix. 1.　　　　　[6] 2 *Macc.* ii. 13.
[7] *John* xv. 1 *sqq.*

be spilled for many even as the vine lets its blood flow in the wine-press. He who is now going to his death will, after the last cup of this paschal meal, partake of wine no more until he returns to drink the new wine, the wine of the next vintage, with his followers. For then the messianic war of the nations will have spent itself, the affliction of the last days will be over, and Jesus, returning from the far-off ' garden of the desert ' to his faithful flock, will lead back the elect from the wilderness into their liberated country, marching before them to Galilee.[1]

After these parting words solemnly devoting the Master to his tragic fate, his companions sing the *Hallel* and repair [2] with him to the accustomed place [3] on the Mount of Olives, where the last remnants of the small band of the followers of the defeated king await him, and where the dispersed fugitives are to assemble from all quarters for the exodus which he is about to accomplish. In this walled piece of garden ground, called after an olive-press *Gathsemanin*, Jesus will pass in prayer his last rest before the decisive hour of the exodus and of the last fight, before the arrival of the pursuers who were being brought up by the traitor, as Jesus for some time must have been aware. Not to be taken by surprise, he posts his three most trusted followers, Peter and the sons of Zebedee, as guards.[4] Returning after an hour, he finds them, tired out from the excitement of the day, asleep at their posts, and warns them once more to watch and to pray that God may spare them the final tribulation.

Up to the last Jesus hopes for a miracle from God, who, if He only would, could save him from torture and death, bring on the king-dom without a $\pi\epsilon\iota\rho\alpha\sigma\mu\acute{o}s$, without those terrible ' birth-pangs ' of the Messiah, and send down legions of heavenly hosts against the enemies of God's suffering servant. But now as before, as in all those years of burning, unconquerable hope and expectation, as in the long centuries that have followed that fearful, fateful night, a pitiless, brazen heaven looms motionless, in impenetrable silence, above the tortured ' Son of man.'

And the hour comes when the sufferer is delivered into the hands of sinners. The traitor approaches at the head of the Roman cohort, reinforced by the emergency constabulary of the high priests, volunteers armed hurriedly with knives and cudgels. The feeble attempt to offer armed resistance, in which one of the

---

[1] See above, pp. 496$_{1-3}$, 510 n. 2, 419 n. 2.

[2] It is difficult to believe that the city gates were unguarded. Either the last supper was kept at a house outside and not, as represented in *Mark* xiv. 13. within the city, or one of the gates, on the east side of the city, was still in the hands of the followers of Jesus on the fatal night.

[3] *Luke* xxii. 39 (only) : ' as his custom was.'

[4] The clear command in *Mark* xiv. 34 : ' Abide ye here and watch,' is already in *Matt.* xxvi. 38, 40 (' watch with me '), paraphrased and divested of its realistic sense.

company of Jesus [1] inflicts a light wound on one of the high priest's party, Jesus himself orders to be abandoned.[2] The prisoner is led away, first to the palace of the high priest's family on the Mount of Olives, where the band accompanying him make a brief halt, while Jesus is maltreated and harassed with threats and questions by the high priests, and while Peter, unrecognized, warms himself at the fire in the courtyard and thrice denies his Master. At length the soldiers again burst in and escort the prisoner before the Roman governor's court-martial which forthwith assembles in the *praetorium*, i.e. in Herod's palace on the west of the city. The passing of sentence upon the *auctor seditionis* taken *in flagranti* and in the midst of armed followers, one of whom had offered violent resistance, certainly detained the court not an instant longer than was necessary. It was then still night [3] when, after further maltreatment and derision, the Roman soldiers with great glee invested the *Saturnalia* king (as they put it) with a mock crown and purple cloak. Whereupon the vanquished liberator was led off to the place of execution. In the bearing of the cross he was aided by a pilgrim just coming to the feast, who was met on the road to the city and pressed into this service. His name was Simon of Cyrene, whose two sons, Alexander and Rufus,[4] afterwards became Christians and at the time when Mark wrote in Rome were well known in the community. He and the Galilaean women, who alone of all his erstwhile followers dared to watch the end from a short distance, heard the last despairing cry of the desolate dying martyr, ' My God, my God, why hast thou forsaken me ? '

---

[1] *Mark* xiv. 47 and parallels. Only *John* xviii. 16 names Peter.

[2] *Matt.* xxvi. 52.

[3] According to the astronomical calculations of M. Daniel Sidersky (*Mém. Acad. Inscr.*, xii. 2, Paris, 1911, p. 38), Passover night of the year 21 A.D. (above, p. 19 l. 24) was the night from the 15th to the 16th of April.

[4] *Mark* xv. 21 ; a Rufus is mentioned in Paul's salutations to the Roman Christians, *Rom.* xvi. 13 ; there is no reason why the two should not be identical.

XVII

The 'Titulus' on the Cross and the Pillory Inscription on the 'Door of Jesus' in the Temple

TO the cross on which Jesus suffered and died there was affixed, according to Roman custom,[1] a ' title ' (titulus),[2] an inscription stating his guilt,[3] more briefly an αἰτία,[4] describing the Naṣōraean as ' king of the Jews.' The wording was probably—

OYTOΣ EΣTIN[5] IHΣOYΣ O NAZΩPAIOΣ
O BAΣIΛEYΣ TΩN IOYΔAIΩN.

THIS IS JESUS THE NAṢŌRAEAN
THE KING OF THE JEWS

According to *John*[6] and a number of MSS. of *Luke*, the inscription was written in Hebrew (or Aramaic), Latin, and Greek, clearly with a view to being understood by the greatest possible number of a polyglot population. The Fourth Gospel[7] alone adds the thoroughly credible statement, for the invention of which no apparent reason can be imagined, that the high priests protested to Pilate against this inscription, saying that he ought not to have written ' the king of the Jews,' but ' *who called himself* king of the Jews ' ; to which Pilate sharply retorted that the text of the inscription must stand as it was.

Both utterances may very well be historical. It is obvious that the designation of a hanged person as ' king of the Jews ' must have been regarded as an insult to the whole Jewish people, as the *servile supplicium* of a true and lawful king of the Jews at the hands of a heathen governor would have been an intolerable national disgrace. The Sanhedrin must therefore inevitably have expostulated to Pilate that he should alter the title indicating the cause of punishment, and the wording of their expostulation is indeed highly instructive for the understanding of the designation of Jesus in Josephus as ' the so-called Christ.'

[1] Sueton., *Domit.*, 10 ; *Calig.*, 32 ; Dio Cass., liv. 8 ; Euseb., *H.E.*, v. 1. 44.
[2] *John* xix. 9.
[3] *Mark* xv. 26 : " ἐπιγραφὴ τῆς αἰτίας αὐτοῦ." ·
[4] *Matt.* xxvii. 37.
[5] *Mark* xv. 26, cod. D, and the Gothic version of Ulfilas.
[6] *John* xix. 20.　　　　　　　　　　[7] *John* xix. 21.

Equally intelligible is the Roman governor's sharp rejection of the petition. In the first place, the question of the disputed legitimacy of this Davidic king was one to which the Roman was supremely indifferent. He would have hanged one of the recognized blue-blooded Davidides of Jerusalem with the same imperturbability with which he executed this wandering carpenter and secret scion of royalty. Again, according to Roman law the *acclamatio* of a king by the assembled people, such as had admittedly been offered to Jesus, was a valid elevation to the throne. It was essential for Pilate, who had to justify in Rome not only the crucifixion of Jesus and the two other "λῃσταί" but the wholesale massacre in the temple and at the tower of Siloam as well, to be able to impute to the Jewish people, as such, complicity in the messianic rising. He could not consider for a moment the idea of reporting that Jesus had merely given himself out to be a king, which in itself would not have constituted a crime. He *had* been proclaimed by the people their ruler and *had* exercised kingly power, if only for a brief period. Lastly, the specification of his 'guilt' was an official extract from the sentence which had been pronounced, and he could not think of altering it on account of the protest of the hierarchs, of whose loyalty he was far from convinced, and of whom he might, not unreasonably, harbour a suspicion that they would probably have sided with the party of independence had the Romans been defeated by the Zealots.

Rejected by Pilate, the high priests, as now appears from the Old Russian translation of the *Halōsis* of Josephus, took the necessary measures on their own ground and were careful to rectify the superscription on the cross, and this on the very spot where Jesus had held short-lived sway as a messianic king.

In the fifth book of the *Jewish War*, as also in the older *Capture of Jerusalem*, we have a detailed description of the temple, drawn from a special source, a sort of 'guidebook' through the sanctuary for the use of pilgrims, a work naturally composed before 70, and resembling the treatise *Middoth* in the Mishnah. In the passage relating to the separation of the outer court from the court of the women we read : [1]

' Proceeding across this (open court) towards the second (court of) the temple, one found it surrounded by a stone balustrade, three cubits high and of exquisite workmanship ; in this at regular intervals stood pillars (στῆλαι) giving warning, some in Greek, others in Latin characters, of the law of purification, to wit, that no foreigner was permitted to enter the holy place, for so the second (enclosure of the) temple was called. It was approached from the (level of the) first (court) by fourteen steps ; the area above was quadrangular and

[1] *B.J.*, v. 193 *sqq.*

screened by a wall of its own . . . and there were two (gates) on the east—necessarily, since in this quarter a special place of worship was walled off for the women.'

Corresponding to that, we have in the Russian, according to Berendts' copy of cod. Mosc. Acad., 651, fol. 154 verso, the following text. The lines permit of easy retranslation into Greek : the Slavonic is given in the usual transliterated form.

Vneiže   stoęchu   stolpi ravni i   na   nich   titly gramotami
'Εν αὐτῷ δ' εἰστήκεσαν στῆλαι ἴσαι καὶ ἐπ' αὐταῖς τίτλοι γράμμασιν
In this   stood   pillars of equal size and on them inscriptions written

ellinskymi   i   rimskymi   i   židovskymi propovĕdajušte   zakonъ
'Ελληνικοῖς καὶ 'Ρωμαϊκοῖς καὶ 'Ιουδαϊκοῖς προσημαίνοντες (τὸν) νόμον
in Greek   and Roman   and Jewish   proclaiming   the   law

čistotĕ   i da ne   preidet vnutrь inoplemennikъ. to   bo   (vto)ro
(τῆς) ἁγνείας μηδένα παριέναι ἐντὸς ἀλλόφυλον.   τὸ γὰρ δεύτερον
of holiness, nobody should enter (who is) of different race. For the second

naricachu svętoe.   di   stepeni prochodimo i   na četyri ugly
ἐκαλεῖτο (τὸ) ἱερόν. τεσσαρεσκαίδεκα βαθμοῖς ἀναβατὸν καὶ εἰς τετράγωνον
(court) was called the holy (place). By 14 steps it is approached and as a square

sъzdanъ   vrъchъ
πεποίηται   ἄνω
it is built   above (the first court)

i   nad   tĕmi titlami   četvertaę titla   visęšte   tĕmi (že)
καὶ ἐπάνω τούτων (τῶν) τίτλων τέταρτος τίτλος ἐκρεμάσθη τοῖς αὐτοῖς μὲν
And above those inscriptions a fourth inscription was hung in the same

gramotamı pokazaa   : *Isusa cĕsarę ne carstvovavša, raspętago ot*
γράμμασιν μηνύων· 'Ιησοῦν βασιλέα οὐ βασιλεύσαντα σταυρωθέντα ὑπὸ
letters   saying :   'Jesus a king who did not reign was crucified by

Ijudei   zane propovĕdaše   razorenie '   grada   i
(τῶν) 'Ιουδαίων διότε ἐπροφήτευσε (τὴν) καθαίρεσιν (τῆς) πόλεως. καὶ
(the) Jews because he foretold (the) destruction of (the) city   and

opustĕnie cerkvi
(τὴν) ἐρήμοσιν (τοῦ) ναοῦ.
the desolation of (the) temple.'

Berendts has seriously obscured the meaning of this passage for himself and for his critics, who pronounced their opinions in ignorance of the Slavonic text, by his unfortunate rendering of the Slavonic *titly* (=τίτλοι, *tituli*) by 'tablets with inscriptions,' although nothing is said about ' tablets,' for which the word πίνακες would be used. The unwarranted introduction of this idea appears to produce an entirely gratuitous contradiction to the statements of the Greek *Polemos* and to archaeological discovery mentioned below. The Old Russian word *stolpi*, which in the first of the lines quoted is reproduced by Greek στῆλαι, means literally ' pillars,' ' posts,' or ' supports.' The word στῆλαι in the Greek *Polemos* must also here mean 'pillars,' and cannot refer to a thin plate with an inscription incised or in relief, such as one thinks of when an archaeologist speaks of a *stele*.

As is well known, in the year 1871 Clermont-Ganneau [1] discovered one of these warning inscriptions built into a garden wall of an abandoned *madrissah* near the *Bab el Atne* in Jerusalem. In later mentions of this object one commonly reads of an inscribed ' tablet,' and Berendts himself has employed this misleading expression.

In reality, the *titulus*, which may now be seen in the Tshinili Kjöshk Museum in Constantinople, and on which marks of axes made, as Mommsen conjectured, by the soldiers of Titus are pointed out to the visitor, stood on a block of limestone 58 centimetres high, 86 centimetres broad, and 37 centimetres deep. An illustration of this block is given on our Pl. XXXVII. ; another, of the inscribed surface only, appears in Deissmann's *Licht vom Osten*.[2] According to Josephus, the elegantly latticed barrier was ' three ells high' (τρίπηχυς), i.e., according as one assumes the simple or the 'royal' ell to be meant, about 158 or 142 centimetres. The pillars (στῆλαι) supporting the lattice-work consisted therefore of at least three such blocks, superimposed the one upon the other. 3 × 58 gives 174 centimetres as the height of a pillar, i.e. a super-elevation above the lattice-work of 16 centimetres, or, including a strong 8-centimetres covering stone slab, of about 24 centimetres, dimensions quite in keeping with what might be assumed for such an architectural arrangement. In these circumstances it is clear that the inscriptions in the three languages stood on the three blocks, one above the other. Since one ascended by five steps to the court thus screened off, the inscription even on the lowest block could be read with ease during the ascent.

The statement of the *Halōsis* that the warning inscriptions were in three languages has more intrinsic justification than that in the *Polemos*, viz. that they were only in Greek and Latin. For there were, of course, Aramaic-speaking peoples, such as the Samaritans, Syrians, Phoenicians, Parthians, and Elamites, to whom the court behind the barrier was as inaccessible as to the Greeks and Romans. In fact, long before the discovery of the Slavonic Josephus the well-known archaeologist W. Jahn had expressed the opinion that there must also have been such inscriptions in Aramaic.

We are told in the Slavonic passage that ' above those three inscriptions there *hung* a fourth.' Accordingly, in this single

---

[1] *Pal. Exploration Fund, Quarterly Statement*, 1871, p. 132 ; cf. Dittenberger, *Orientis Graeci Inscriptiones Selectae*, ii. 598, etc.

[2] Fourth edition, 1923, p. 62 *sq.*

instance (for an inscription such as is here mentioned was of course not affixed to every pillar, like the warning inscription, which was properly repeated everywhere in triplicate) the pillar consisting of three blocks must have been surmounted by a fourth before that fourth inscription could be ' hung ' above the three that were there already. That is to say, in this instance a stone plaque in the manner well known to every epigraphist was affixed with bronze pins to the stone pillar ; that method, in fact, was far more appropriate for an inscription added at a later date than a direct engraving upon a block which may have been, through ornamentation or for other reasons, quite unsuited for the purpose.

Such a heightening of the pillars one might *a priori* expect to find at the entrances, where the steps from the outer court pene-trated the barrier to the ' holy place ' within, since in the case of a work of such richness as is here attested [1] the builders would certainly not have neglected to give special distinction to the pillars right and left of the barrier gates.

When Jesus made his triumphal entry into the temple, he must have reached the holy place through one of these entrances,[2] and no place could therefore have appeared more appropriate for the placing of an inscription to commemorate the downfall of one so hateful to the hierarchy, of the ' king that did not reign' but would have devoted this temple to destruction, than the pillar of the gate through which he was conducted amidst shouts of ' Osanna.'

This conjecture, based purely on the actual nature of the enclosure of the sanctuary, receives a brilliant confirmation from the mention, hitherto wholly enigmatic,[3] of a ' door of Jesus the Crucified' in the temple. It is mentioned in connexion with the murder of James the Just in the memoirs (ὑπομνήματα) of Hege-sippus [4] (*ca.* 180), where we are told that certain malicious 'heretics' were in the habit of vexing the aged Ṣaddiq Ja'aqob, who spent his days in almost continuous prayer in the temple, with the seemingly innocuous question of an ignorant visitor to the sanctuary, 'Which is the door of Jesus ? ', to which he was wont to reply, 'Jesus is the Redeemer.' Immediately before he was hurled from the temple battlements he was again mockingly asked to point out 'which is the door of Jesus the Crucified.' To which question James replied with a loud voice, ' What is this you ask me concerning Jesus, the *bar nasha* ? He sitteth in heaven at the right hand of the Father,[2] and will one day come on the clouds of heaven.' There-

---

[1] Cf. above, p. 515, seventh line from the bottom of the page.
[2] Cf. *Acts of John*, 109 (M. R. James, *Apoc. N.T.*, p. 268) : ' O Lord Jesus . . . we glorify *thine entering of the door*. We glorify the resurrection shown unto us by thee.'
[3] Prof. Kirsopp Lake in his translation of Eusebius (1926) in the Loeb Classical Library, No. 153, p. 173 : ' The *Gate of Jesus* is a puzzle.'
[4] Ap. Euseb., *H.E.*, ii. 23.

PLATE XXXVII

INSCRIBED STONE-BLOCK FROM THE PILLARS OF THE BARRIER SURROUNDING THE INNER
FORECOURT OF THE TEMPLE

THE INSCRIPTION THREATENS CAPITAL PUNISHMENT TO GENTILE TRESPASSERS
(TSHINILI KJOESHK MUSEUM, CONSTANTINOPLE)

(SEE P. 517, NOTE 2)

upon he was thrown from the pinnacle of the temple and, being still alive, was beaten to death with a fuller's club. Only one Rekhabite priest [1]—the fact is significant—vainly endeavours to protect his kinsman, who, praying for his persecutors, gives up the ghost. On the spot where the horrible deed was consummated there might still be seen in the time of Hegesippus an inscribed *stele* [2]—certainly not an inscription on a tomb, for there can of course be no question of a tomb 'beside the temple' ($\pi\alpha\rho\grave{\alpha}$ $\tau\hat{\omega}$ $\nu\alpha\hat{\omega}$), or anywhere within the sanctuary, or indeed within the city: moreover, the Saddiq's tomb was shown at a later date on the Mount of Olives.

There was in the temple, then, a door popularly known as 'the door of Jesus the Crucified,' just as in Gunde Shapur the city gate on which the skin of the prophet Mani, flayed alive, had been nailed was for centuries afterwards called the 'Mani Gate'; [3] there was, moreover, not merely one inscription recalling the downfall of Jesus, but another [4] commemorating the death of his brother, James the Just.

In order to understand these facts epigraphists will recall the Hellenistic custom of $\sigma\tau\eta\lambda\acute{\iota}\tau\epsilon\upsilon\sigma\iota\varsigma$, the *damnatio memoriae* of political criminals and persons guilty of sacrilege by special pillory inscriptions, preferably placed in the sacred precincts, to make the man thus branded into an $\dot{\alpha}\nu\acute{\alpha}\theta\eta\mu\alpha$, to devote his name to the deity for everlasting punishment, or, conversely, to set before the deity a testimony recording the penalty duly inflicted. Thus at Athens there was to be found, on the Akropolis, a brazen pillar on which were blazoned the names of those guilty of high treason and religious outrage (the $\dot{\alpha}\lambda\iota\tau\acute{\eta}\rho\iota\omicron\iota$ $\kappa\alpha\grave{\iota}$ $\pi\rho\omicron\delta\acute{\omicron}\tau\alpha\iota$); [5] and the practice was by no means confined to Athens.[6]

It is therefore in no way surprising to learn from the *Halōsis* of Josephus that the Sadducaean and Boethusaean high-priesthood of the last years of the temple, strongly Hellenized as it was, had set up in conspicuous position in the sacred precincts malevolent inscriptions regarding Jesus and his brother, to commemorate the

---

[1] According to Epiphanius, *Haeres*, lxxviii. 14, it was Simon, son of Klophas.

[2] Cf. Jerome, *De viris illustr.*, 2; the tomb was still shown, *ca.* 530, on the Mount of Olives to Theodosius (*Itin. Hieros.*, ed. Geyer, p. 140).

[3] Bevan, in Hastings' *Encycl. of Relig. and Eth.*, viii. 397a.

[4] Cf. also the excerpt of Hegesippus by Andrew of Crete, *Vita St. Jacobi*, Ἀνάλεκτα Ἱεροσολυμιτικῆς σταχνολογίας, ed. Papadopulos-Kerameus, i. 10. 21: " καὶ λαβόντες αὐτὸν ἔθαψαν (on this error, see above, ll. 7 ff.) ἐν τόπῳ καλουμένῳ καλῷ πλησίον τοῦ ναοῦ τοῦ θεοῦ." Here it is not a question of a τόπος καλός near the temple, but the στήλη, the *titulus* was in a עֲלָא, *qala'*, that is, an *intercolumnium* in the hall of the temple, at the precise place where James had been hurled down. The very use of this word proves that the statement is derived from Hegesippus, of whom Eusebius, *H.E.*, iv. 22. 8, expressly says that he used to quote "ἐκ τοῦ καθ' Ἑβραίους εὐαγγελίου καὶ τοῦ Συριακοῦ καὶ ἰδίως ἐκ τῆς Ἑβραΐδος διαλέκτου."

[5] *Lycurgi oratio in Leocratem*, ed. Blass, Leipzig, 1899, § 117, p. 48.

[6] Cf. the passages cited in Stephanus' *Thesaurus*, s.v. στηλίτευσις.

downfall of these their deadly enemies. If the inscription read by Josephus or his authority was affixed to one of the pillars of the gates in the *soreg* surrounding the sanctuary, then nothing could be more natural than that this particular gate, through which Jesus passed into the temple, should be called in popular speech ' the gate of Jesus the Crucified,' just as we have a so-called ' gate of Jekhoniah,' so called because through it King Jekhoniah was led into captivity,[1] and the like, and that mischievous persons made use of this fact to remind the Ṣaddiq in this cruel way of the fate of his unfortunate brother.

That Josephus in his description of the sanctuary says nothing about the ' titulus notissimus ' of James, which according to Jerome stood 'beside the temple' (*juxta templum*), i.e. in the wall [2] of one of the temple courts, may of course be accidental. But it is much more likely that the passage has suffered from Christian erasures (like the passage, only contained in the Hebrew *Josippon*, and there, too, deleted at an early date, concerning the collision of the followers of ' ben Joseph ' with the Pharisees in the reign of Caligula),[3] and that originally the *Halōsis* or the *Polemos*, like the *Archaeology*, mentioned not only Jesus but also the brother of ' Jesus called the Christ.' In any case, something more may be gathered from the sources concerning the fate of ' the Lord's brother ' [4] and the real reason for his στηλίτευσις in the temple than previous investigators have succeeded in recognizing.[5]

Coming, finally, to the wording of the epigraphic monument quoted by Josephus, we have to note in the first place that the words used of the ' fourth inscription indicating in the same characters that Jesus was a king who did not reign, having been crucified [[by the Jews]] because he prophesied the destruction of the city and the desolation of the temple,' are not a literal reproduction but only a short paraphrase of the document, just as the words 'announcing the law of holiness that no foreigner may pass within' by no means present the far longer exact text of the extant warning inscription. It is quite possible that the polyglot inscription, or rather the three inscriptions, of which two may have stood respectively on either pillar of the gateway and the third on the lintel of the gate, began with a mention of place and date (' This is the door through which on the . . . ') ; it is, moreover, highly probable that the name 'Jesus' was accompanied by a patronymic ' son of Joseph ' or by the designation *Naṣōraean* (*han noṣri*), as on the title on the cross, without which it would be too indefinite.

---

[1] Mishnah *Middoth*, ii. 6; *Sheqalim*, vi. 3; Schürer, *Z.N.T.W.*, vii. (1906), p. 58.
[2] Cf. above, p. 519 n. 4, on the '*qala*.' [3] Cf. above, pp. 96 f.
[4] Lucien Cerfaux, ' Le titre Kyrios et la dignité royale de Jésus,' *Revue des sciences philosophiques*, xii. (1923), p. 140 *sq.*, has pointed out that the title of ἀδελφὸς τοῦ κυρίου usually designates the viceroy or *vazîr*.
[5] Cf. below, pp. 540 ff.

Lastly, it is evident that the bracketed words [[*by the Jews*]] are a Christian interpolation into the text of Josephus, of which the object is to prove conclusively, by a special testimony, graven in stone, that it was the Jews and not the Romans who crucified Jesus. That the expression ' by the Jews ' is inconceivable in an inscription set up by the Jewish high priests needs no argument : they would not even have said ' by us,' but would have used some much more precise definition of the authorities who passed the sentence, e.g. ' by decree of the Sanhedrin under the presidency of,' etc. One might ask whether the words ὑπὸ τῶν Ἰουδαίων may not have taken the place of a ὑπὸ τῶν Ῥωμαίων ; but this is impossible, since an execution by the Romans could not plausibly be presented as having taken place on the basis of a false prophecy. As in the case of all sections of the *Halōsis* previously quoted, the acknowledgment of the authenticity of the passage stands or falls with the rigid exclusion of phrases which may without exception be recognized by their tendency and the impossibility of the statements they contain as downright Christian interpolations.

After the exclusion of this short addition to the text, the remainder is not only above suspicion but a document of the highest importance, because wholly independent of all other sources. It contains a justification of the execution of Jesus entirely different alike from that which may be extracted from the previous account of Josephus himself in the second book of the *Halōsis*, and from all statements advanced by the Gospels. According to Josephus, Jesus was accused on the one hand of sorcery, on the other of inciting to rebellion and high treason. It is with these two or three crimes that Jesus is charged in Josephus' own statement and in the underlying Roman indictment. According to *Luke* xxiii. 2, the Jewish authorities accused Jesus before Pilate of seducing the people to disloyalty (διαστρέφοντα τὸν λαόν), of hindering the payment of the taxes (κωλύοντα φόρους Καίσαρι διδόναι), and of putting himself forward as King of Israel. Before the alleged court of Jewish priests he was charged with blasphemy because he called himself 'Son of God,' and with inciting the mob to destroy the temple.[1] The accusation on the temple inscription is quite independent of all these charges, and refers exclusively to the death ordained in *Deuteronomy*[2] for the false prophet, very significantly, since the indictments under Roman law were untenable according to Jewish legislation and popular feeling. The Sanhedrin might as well have accused the Maccabees of ' high treason ' and the prophets Elijah and Elishah of sorcery. In no case could miraculous cures and the like be actionable crimes under the Jewish laws against witchcraft (*qishuph*).

[1] *Mark* xv. 58 ; *Matt.* xxvi. 36 ; *John* ii. 19.
[2] xviii. 20 *sqq.*

The statement in the present accusation, that the 'king who did not reign' prophesied the destruction of the city and the desolation of the temple, refers to utterances of Jesus such as those in *Matt.* xxiii. 37 *sq.*, *Luke* xiii. 34 *sq.* : ' O Jerusalem, Jerusalem, thou that killest the prophets and stonest them that are sent unto thee . . . behold, your house is left unto you desolate'; and *Luke* xix. 41 *sqq.* : 'when he beheld the city he wept over it, saying . . . that the days shall come upon thee when thine enemies shall encompass thee about with a palisade[1] and close thee in on every side and lay thee even with the ground . . . and shall not leave one stone upon another within thee'—utterances which there is not the least ground for regarding as spurious *vaticinationes ex eventu.* The whole political situation at that time was serious enough, and Jerusalem had seen sieges of the type here referred to, and that not so long before, in the time of Pompey and again of Herod the Great. To the blind leaders whose blindness to all the signs of the times Josephus bemoans at a later period,[2] such predictions appeared to fall under the ruling of the law in *Deut.* xviii. 20 *sqq.* :

> ' But the prophet who shall speak a word presumptuously in my name, which I have not commanded him to speak, or that shall speak in the name of other gods,[3] that same prophet shall die. And if thou say in thy heart, How shall we know the word which the Lord hath not spoken? (know that) when a prophet speaketh in the name of the Lord, if the thing follow not nor come to pass, that is the thing which the Lord hath not spoken : the prophet hath spoken it presumptuously.'

Such a false prophet was put to death for blasphemy, the penalty being stoning, followed by the hanging of the corpse on a stake. The composition of the inscription in question is therefore a diplomatic master-stroke of the Jewish hierarchy. It has contrived to mention that Jesus was proclaimed king and at the same time to emphasize the fact that he never actually ruled over the Jews, i.e. that their leaders never recognized his sovereignty. It mentions the fact that he was hanged upon the stake (ἐσταυρώθη), but passes in silence over the fact, so wounding to national feelings, that the ephemeral king of the Jews was delivered up to the Roman overlords to suffer the shameful death of a slave. The inscription successfully endeavours to represent the fate of Jesus as well deserved according to Jewish law. Without any express statement to that effect, his downfall is represented as a judgment of God, by whomsoever brought about, in accordance with the Divine law against false prophets who slander God and provoke His wrath by falsely claiming a Divine inspiration which they have not

---

[1] Cf. *Jer.* lii. 4.   [2] *B.J.*, vi. 5. 3.
[3] Cf. the accusation levelled against Jesus that he effected his cures through a δύναμις ἀόρατος, i.e. a *Bel-zebul*, a *spiritus familiaris.*

received. He deserved (it is implied) to hang upon the stake, because he predicted the destruction of the city which still flourishes unimpaired, and the desolation of the temple in which the crowds of the faithful daily pass the maledictory inscription on their way to the altar. The document is thus the oldest testimony to that train of thought whereby the rabbis for centuries consoled themselves for the Sanhedrin's loss of power to pronounce sentence of death. Even in exile at Jabneh such sentences were believed to be still passed, the penalty being inflicted by God himself.[1] If the high court condemned any one to stoning, a wall was supposed to collapse and fall upon him ; if the person was condemned to burning, he perished in a conflagration ; and so on.[2]

Of course, this over-subtle diplomatic wording of a testimony visibly exposed did not fail also to produce its evil effects. No one who read the inscription and was imperfectly informed in the matter of the Sanhedrin's power over life and death at that period could extract from the words any other meaning than that which the Christian interpolator expressly introduced into the text of Josephus, namely, that Jesus was put to death *by the Jews* for a religious crime. To be sure, the Christians of the Roman empire for whom Mark and the evangelists dependent upon him wrote would have reached this unhistorical conclusion even without this equivocal evidence of the high priests ; but the remarkable fact that later Jews themselves believed that Jesus was stoned and hanged by their own authorities in accordance with Jewish law [3] may perhaps indicate that this triumphal inscription of the hierarchy on the downfall of Jesus was not without influence on the popular conscience.

But there is another yet more remarkable fact. The influence which can be shown to have been exercised upon the Jews by that inscription, constantly seen by so many pilgrims, readable from the outer court by gentiles, and continually interpreted by guides and sextons for visitors to the world-famed Herodian temple—that influence can be traced among the heathen Syrians of Samosata as early as the middle of the eighth decade of our era, i.e. at the date when the *Halōsis* of Josephus was written. In the Syriac 'Letter of Mara bar Serapion to his son Serapion,' [4] a consolatory epistle quite unaffected by Christian ideas, from a Stoic who had fled from Samosata to Seleucia and was prevented by the Romans from returning to his home, we find the following remarkable passage :

'What more should we say if sages are outrageously treated by tyrants . . . ? For what profit had the Athenians from their murder

---

[1] *Kethub.*, 30a ; Strack-Billerbeck, ii. 197 *sq.*, to *Luke* xiii. 2.
[2] Mishnah *Sanhedrin*, ii. 4 ; cf. *Sifrē* on *Deut.* viii. 10.
[3] *Sanhedrin*, f°. 43a.
[4] In Cureton, *Spicilegium Syr.* (1855), p. 45.

of Socrates, for which they were requited by famine and plague ? [1]
Or the Samians from their burning of Pythagoras, for which their
whole land was in a moment buried by sand ? [2] Or the Jews from
the execution of their wise king, seeing that from that time forward
the kingdom was taken away from them ? For justly did God take
vengeance for those three sages : the Athenians died of hunger, the
Samians were enveloped in the sea, the Jews were destroyed and,
ejected from their kingdom, live everywhere in dispersion. (But)
Socrates is not dead, thanks to Plato, nor Pythagoras, thanks to the
statue of Hera,[3] *nor the wise king, thanks to the new law which he has
given.'*

Ewald [4] and Bickell [5] long ago correctly recognized that this
writing is precisely dated by certain sentences. The author
laments the abduction of a portion of the citizens of Samosata to
Seleucia and their separation from their relatives, but hopes that
the Romans will permit them all to return home, after they have
promised ' to be obedient subjects of the kingdom which fate has
given us.'   This is only intelligible if Mara bar Serapion was one
of the refugees from Samosata when Commagene was seized by
the legions of Caesennius Paetus in the fourth year of Vespasian
(A.D. 73), and its king Antiochus, together, of course, with his
partisans, fled the country.[6]

Shortly after the year 73, therefore—at the utmost some years
after Samosata's day of misfortune, for Mara's exile may have been
prolonged—the Hellenized Syrians knew of Jesus. They did not
call him by that name, nor did they know anything of the Christian
belief in his resurrection, but they had heard of a ' wise king of the
Jews,' whom that people had unjustly put to death, a crime for
which God has punished them by the loss of their national independence and by dispersion among all nations. And just as
gentiles in the age of Severus placed statues of Jesus beside those
of Pythagoras, Plato, and Aristotle,[7] so those Syrians mention the
' wise king ' and lawgiver along with Pythagoras and Socrates.
Just as the assistants of Josephus represented to Graeco-Roman
readers the Jewish politico-religious sects of the Sadducees,
Pharisees, and Essenes, along with the *Barjonîm* of Judas of Galilee,
as four philosophical schools of the Jews, so primitive Christianity
appeared to the Hellenistic world as a new fifth ' philosophy ' of
the Jews, and Jesus as a wandering philosopher and preacher of a

---

[1] The plague of Athens is here represented as a punishment for the death
of Socrates.

[2] A legend unattested elsewhere.

[3] Confusion of Pythagoras the philosopher of Samos with Pythagoras the
sculptor, also of Samos (Diog. Laert., viii. 46). He furthermore mistakes the
statue of the Samian Hera by Smilis for a work of the Samian sculptor Pythagoras.

[4] *Gött. gel. Anz.*, 1856, p. 661.

[5] *Conspectus rei Syrorum litterariae*, p. 17.

[6] *B.J.*, vii. 7. 1-2.   [7] Cf. above, p. 398 ll. 2 f.

new and better manner of life, like another Socrates or, better still, like another Pythagoras, who also led a wandering life, founded a new politico-religious community and became a martyr to his own teaching.

This conception is thoroughly in harmony with that of the oldest bearers of the Christian message. Isidore Lévy,[1] in a most valuable investigation, has recently shown that not only the whole plan of the Gospels but also many significant individual features are (partly through the medium of a Jewish neo-Pythagorean life of Moses) dependent on a widely disseminated legendary life of Pythagoras. Early Christian art loves to portray Jesus and the apostles in the garb of Cynic philosophers. Pictures of Jesus and Paul ' characterized as philosophers ' are mentioned in the letter of Eusebius to the princess Constantia,[2] which, though edited by the anti-iconoclastic school, doubtless has a genuine nucleus.

Accordingly, the heathen Syrians' conception of the ' sage ' who was wickedly murdered by the Jews might well have come from the Christian preaching of the Gospel. But that Jesus should have been known as a ' wise king ' and ' lawgiver,' such as Minos of Crete, Lycurgus of Sparta, Zaleucus of Locris, and Charondas of Catana, can hardly be referred to the scanty traces of such ideas in the Christian apocrypha ;[3] for in that case Mara b. Serapion must have known the story of the resurrection. At this early date we can hardly think of any other source save that inscription on Jesus, 'the king who did not reign,' written in three languages and constantly pointed out to a succession of Jewish and gentile visitors to the temple of Jerusalem—an inscription which until the destruction of the sanctuary kept alive before the eyes of the world, graven in durable stone, that transient *titulus* 'king of the Jews' on the whitened wooden tablet on the cross, a monument which may still be hidden to-day beneath the ruins of the Herodian temple or built into some wall and awaiting its rediscovery.

Merely for the sake of completeness I should like, at the close of this section, to allude to an objection to the authenticity of the Jesus inscription in the Slavonic Josephus which has been raised by Father Hermann Dieckmann, S.J. (Valckenburg).[4] He believes that ' Josephus could hardly have written these words after the fearful fulfilment of the prediction of Jesus against Jerusalem and the temple.' The only remarkable thing about this argument is

[1] *Recherches sur la légende de Pythagore*, Paris, 1926 ; *La légende de Pythagore de Gréce en Palestine*, Paris, 1927.

[2] Boivin in ' Not. ad Nicephor. Gregoras,' *Hist. Byz.*, ed. Bonn, p. 1301 *sqq.* Paul is represented as a philosopher in Chrysostom, *Hom.*,vi.; *Opp.*, ed. Montfaucon, ii. p. 60; *Hymn. de Petro et Paulo*, H. A. Daniel, *Thes. Hymn.*, ii. 376. Cf. above, p. 438 n. 4.

[3] *Didachē*, xiv. 3 ; *Passio Pauli*, 2 ; Clem., *Hom.*, iii. 19 ; *Mart. Polyc.*, ix. 3, xvii. 3.

[4] *Zeitsch. f. kath. Theologie*, Innsbruck, 1926, p. 47.

that no one hitherto has taken the least exception to the story, likewise recounted by Josephus,[1] of that other Jesus, son of Ananus,[2] the rude, illiterate peasant who, at a time 'when the city was enjoying profound peace and prosperity,' plagued its inhabitants with incessant cries of 'Woe to Jerusalem!'; who was therefore chastised by ' some of the leading citizens,' brought by the magistrates before the Roman governor Albinus, by the latter's command lacerated with scourges, yet never ceased his ill-omened cries, ' without cursing those who beat him,' and was finally dismissed by the governor as a maniac. Of him Josephus himself narrates that he witnessed the fulfilment of his predictions against the city before he met his own end during the siege through a stone hurled from a ballista. He expressly emphasizes the fact that the Jewish magistrates ' believed that the man was under some supernatural impulse,' but yet did not take to heart his predictions.

The views of Josephus concerning prevision of the future must be duly considered. According to him it was by no means restricted to selected ' men of God ': a madman like Aristobulus,[3] and a common individual (an 'am ha'areṣ) officially regarded as a lunatic, can occasionally see into the future, because ' the spirit is divine and marks what will be done on the part of God.'[4] Only, men rarely hearken to the ' supernatural impulse,' as Josephus remarks at the close of his narrative : [5]

' Reflecting on these things, one will find that God has a care for men, and by all kinds of premonitory signs shows his people the way of salvation, while they owe their destruction to folly and calamities of their own choosing.'

Accordingly, in addressing the Jews, for whom the *Halōsis* is written, Josephus had not the least reason for denying to Jesus, albeit in his opinion a sophist and magician, the correctness of his premonitions of the future ruin, afterwards so terribly realized. The incident was for him rather another instance of that blindness of his countrymen which he so often laments and which led to their insurrection against Rome. From no legal standpoint need the sentence mentioned in the inscription have appeared to him unjust, so long as he was convinced that Jesus had without inspiration from God, 'by some unseen power,'[6] i.e. through a *Be'el zebul* or 'familiar spirit,'[7] foreseen the future. For, according to the Law,[8] that prophet is guilty of death who without Jahveh's com-

---

[1] *B.J.*, vi. 5. 3, §§ 300-9.
[2] Or, according to other MSS., *Ananias*.
[3] *B.J.*, v. 5. 4.
[4] *Halōsis*, i. § 608; Berendts-Grass, p. 209. Cp. Ps.-Clem., *Hom.* xvii., about impious men having true prophetic visions.
[5] *Ibid.*, vi. 310.
[6] Cf. above, p. 384 n. 7.
[7] *Mark* iii. 22.
[8] *Deut.* xviii. 20.

mission, by the aid of 'other gods,' announces what is to come, even if his prophecy is correct. We know from Origen[1] that the heathen Phlegon of Tralles also credited Jesus with a knowledge of *some* future things. What was right for a pagan in these matters would certainly appear reasonable to the Jew Josephus, so long as he was addressing his co-religionists. On the other hand, that in the edition intended for Vespasian and Titus he had no desire to credit Jesus with prophetic insight into the future, thereby giving the appearance of sympathy with that Christian heresy which brought Flavius Clemens and Flavia Domitilla into the deepest disfavour at court, will surprise no one who has realized, from the other deviations of the Greek edition from the Slavonic *Halōsis*, the extraordinary precaution and servility of this worldly-wise and unscrupulous sycophant.

THE MESSIANIC DISTURBANCES UNDER CALIGULA AND THE 'SERVANTS' OF THE WONDER-WORKER IN THE TIME OF CLAUDIUS

The remark of the *Testimonium Flavianum* to the effect that even after the crucifixion of Jesus his followers 'did not cease (to create disturbance)' has received new light from the discovery of the doubtless genuine sentence contained in the *editio princeps* and in certain MSS. of the Hebrew *Josippon*, stating that in the time of the Emperor Gaius, i.e. in the governorship of the intelligent and honourable Petronius, 'battles' (*milḥamoth*) and 'quarrels' (*qeṭaṭoth*) broke out in Judaea between the Pharisees and the 'bandits among our people who inclined to the son of Joseph'—that is, Jesus. From the following sentence about 'Ele'azar, who 'committed many misdeeds until the Pharisees overpowered him,' we were able to conclude that the leader of this messianist uprising under Caligula was none other than the 'robber chief' 'Ele'azar, son of Deinaeus,[2] who between A.D. 48 and 60 was captured by Felix, and of whom Josephus expressly says that he ravaged the country for twenty years,[3] so that he may very well have given the Pharisees trouble as early as the reign of Caligula (36-41) and have occasionally defeated them. The mention of two priests, one Deineias, variously misspelt Αἰνείας and Phineas, and one Lazarus, among the followers of Simon Peter the Barjona in the pseudo-Clementines,[4] suggests the identity of these two men with this 'Ele'azar b. Dinai and with his father.

On the other hand, the messianic uprising of the 'followers of

---

[1] *C. Cels.*, ii. 14.
[2] *Ant.*, xx. 6. 11 ; *B.J.*, ii. 12. 40 *sq.*, 13. 2.
[3] *B.J.*, ii. 13. 2.
[4] Cf. above, p. 103 n. 1.

the son of Joseph ' under Caligula, headed, according to our restoration of the partly deleted passage of the *Josippon*, by this 'Ele'azar b. Dinai, seems to be identical with the armed uprising of the Jews against Caligula's orders to place his statue in the temple of Jerusalem, which is mentioned by Tacitus.[1]

The explanation why the followers of Jesus should throw in their lot with the Zealots, resolved to resist such a desecration of the chief sanctuary, appears to have been suggested to them by the command of Jesus [2] to take to the mountains as soon as they should see the 'abomination of desolation' placed in the temple. For then would they see the ' Son of man ' come down upon the clouds of heaven at the head of the heavenly hosts. Confiding in these words and expecting the imminent return of their Master, those valiant men of simple faith seem to have dared to offer armed resistance both to the sacrilegious attempt of the mad emperor and to the opportunist policy of the more conservative loyalists.

It is quite credible that their guerilla warfare should have caused heavy casualties on both sides, and that those of the rebels who fell into the hands of the loyalists were in most cases crucified.[3] The leader, 'Ele'azar b. Dinai, held out, until twenty years later his fate overtook him. Whether he was executed in spite of all promises given him by the governor Felix, or whether he was allowed to rot in his prison, the discreet Josephus has wisely neglected to tell us.

On the strength of the many analogies discussed in previous chapters, we are certainly entitled to ascribe the fact that the Old Russian version of the *Halōsis* shows no trace of a messianic uprising in the section dealing with the reign of Caligula to no other reason than the ruthless activity of the Christian censor. Fortunately, the 'false pen of the scribes' has left untouched in the Greek original of the Slavonic version [4] another account of. the earliest followers of Jesus as they appear in the reign of Claudius.[5]

'. . . Claudius again sent his officers to those kingdoms, Cuspius Fadus and Tiberius Alexander, both of whom kept the people in peace, by not allowing any departure in anything from the pure laws.[6] But if notwithstanding any one did deviate from the word of the Law and information was

---

[1] *Hist.*, v. 9 : ' dein iussi a Gaio Caesare effigiem eius in templo locare arma potius sumpsere (Iudaei) ' ; cf. above, p. 65₃.

[2] Cf. above, p. 67 n. 4. [3] Cf. the text above, p. 110 l. 13.

[4] Our Pls. xxxviii. f.

[5] Berendts-Grass, p. 279 *sq*. For the immediately preceding passage, cf. above, pp. 206 f. [6] Cf. the parallel in *B.J.*, ii. 220.

PLATE XXXVIII

THE SLAVONIC JOSEPHUS PASSAGE ABOUT 'THE SERVANTS
OF THE WONDER-WORKER' ON MOUNT OLIVET AT THE
TIME OF EMPEROR CLAUDIUS

COD. KYRILLO-BJELOS. 63/1302, Fᵒ 71 Rᵒ, Vᵒ AND 72 Rᵒ

LENINGRAD PUBLIC LIBRARY

(SEE P. 528, NOTE 5)

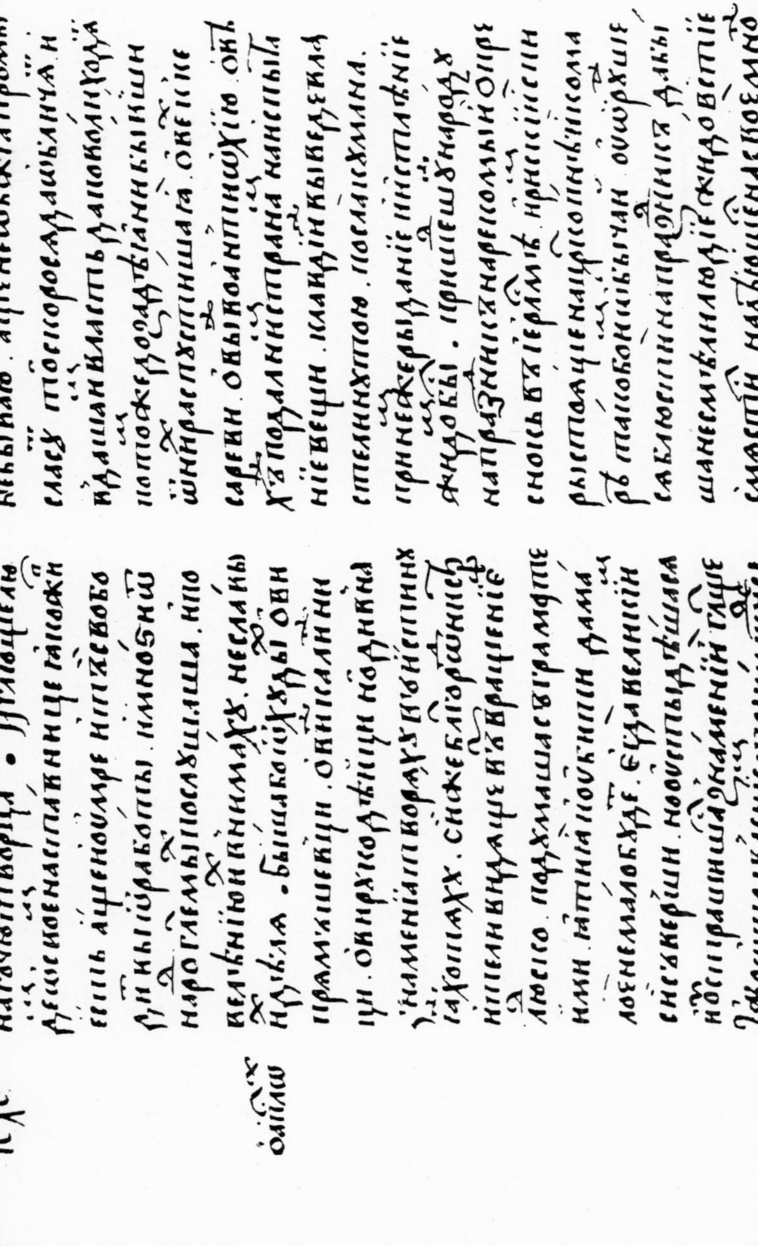

PLATE XXXIX

laid before the teachers of the Law, they punished or banished him, or sent (him) to Caesar.

'And since in the time of him [1] many helpers [2] of the wonder-worker aforementioned had appeared and spoken to the people of their Master, (saying) that he was alive, although he had been dead,[3] and "he will free you [4] from bondage," many of the multitude hearkened to the(ir) preaching and took heed of their directions,⟨ for they were of the humble[5](r sort), some mere tailors,[6] others sandal-makers, (or) other artisans.

'But when these noble governors saw the falling away of the people, they determined, together with the scribes, to seize (them) for fear lest the little might not be little, if it ended in the great.[7]

'But afterwards for the deeds done by them they sent them away, some to Caesar, others to Antioch for a trial of the(ir) cause, others to distant lands.'

Christian additions.

⟨ not on account of their reputation. But wonderful were the signs which they worked, in truth what(ever) they wanted.

and put (them) to death

But they shrank back and were in terror at the signs, saying, "Not through drugs [8] do such wonders come to pass ; but if they do not proceed from the counsel of God, then will they quickly be exposed." [9] And they gave them liberty [10] to go where they would.

---

[1] Cod. Kas., below the text in red : ' of Caesar Claudius.'

[2] *slug=ὑπηρέται.* '*Conservi*' of Peter are mentioned Ps.-Clem., *Rec.* iv. 4 ff.

[3] Cf. the words of Festus in *Acts* xxv. 19 : " περί τινος Ἰησοῦ τεθνηκότος ὃν ἔφασκε ὁ Παῦλος ζῆν."

[4] Kas. ; *Syn.*, 770 : ' us.'

[5] A learned allusion to *Jer.* v. 4 : ' Surely these are humble, they are foolish, for they know not the way of the Lord.' Cp. *Ecclus.* xxxviii. 28 ff. on the impossibility of the artisans acquiring wisdom.

[6] Thus *Syn.*, 182. Other MSS. : ' shoemakers,' which is the same as the following ' sandal-makers,' and hence obviously wrong.

[7] Cf. *Ant.*, ii. § 333 : "τὰ μικρὰ ποιῆσαι μεγάλα."

[8] Kas., Arch., *otravlenijem*=διὰ φαρμακείας.

[9] Imitation of *Acts* v. 38.

[10] Cf. above, p. 385, the Christian interpolation about Jesus being acquitted by Pilate. The transparent purpose of both forgeries is the artificial creation of precedents which could be quoted in order to influence the judicial procedure of Roman magistrates against the Christians. They are therefore certainly anterior to 312 A.D.

2 L

The trained reader of historical documents will need no elaborate argument in support of the exclusion of the Christian interpolations relegated to the margin in the foregoing quotation. Josephus was far from admiring, as ' wonderful signs,' any healings or the like performed by people whom he despises as ' jugglers ' or ' magicians ' (γόητες) ; and, furthermore, in this case he clearly knew nothing of such feats, since he bases the success of the preaching not on the impression created by such miracles, but on the political hopes which the announcement of the resurrection of Jesus must have raised.[1] The sentence about the miracles wrought by the followers of Jesus is clearly nothing but an indignant objection of a Christian reader to the contemptuous words of Josephus about these ' small ' or ' humble ' people, whom various scribes [2] actually identify with the apostles, although the 'many helpers of the Wonder-worker,' of whom Josephus speaks, clearly indicate a wider circle. If we were to believe Josephus to have spoken with such admiration of the acts of the apostles, we might also credit him with the forged *Testimonium Flavianum* as it stands in the *Antiquities*.

The words ' not on account of their reputation,' appended to ' took heed of their directions,' indicate the place where the interpolator had intended to insert his complete note. But since he could not get the whole sentence [3] into the narrow margin, he had to write the rest a little further down, and hence a part of it was introduced into the text by later copyists at the end of the sentence.

Similarly, the words 'and put to death' betray their character as an addition by a Christian scribe who recalled the execution of the sons of Zebedee by Herod Agrippa immediately before the appointment of Fadus, and probably also the unhistorical legends of martyrdom early associated with the names of all the apostles.[4] For if the governors had really determined to sentence these people to death, they would not have been content, as it appears from the final clause that they were, with sentences of banishment.

Unmistakable as another Christian interpolation is, the pious legend telling how the governors at first were induced by the miracles performed by these people to leave them at liberty—indeed, to give them a privilege ' to behave as they would ';[5] an absurdity which could only have been penned by one entirely ignorant of the

---

[1] Cf. *Luke* xxiv. 21 ; *Acts* i. 5.

[2] *Cod. Cyril.-Bjel.*, 63/1302 (see Pls. xxxviii. f.), and *Cod. Acad.*, add in margin in red ink, ' of the Apostles.' *Arch.* adds after the word ' humble,' ' the apostles.'

[3] His note ran : ' not on account of their reputation (i.e. as famous scribes, etc.), but (because) they wrought wonderful signs,' etc.

[4] Heracleon (*ca.* 170), quoted by Clem. Alex., iv. 9. 71, still knows that Matthew, Philip, Thomas, Levi, and other apostles did *not* die as martyrs.

[5] Cp. above, p. 529 n. 10.

customs of the Roman administration. The section, moreover, is dependent upon the interpolation a few lines above stating that the followers of Jesus wrought stupendous miracles.

But most significant of all for the Christian origin of the excluded clauses is the fact noticed by all previous critics, though often very curiously explained, namely, that the famous saying of Gamaliel in *Acts* v. 38 *sq.* is put into the mouths of Fadus and Alexander. It is noteworthy, however, that the saying appears in altered form, designed to afford the Christians official evidence to the effect that their healings were *not* produced by drugs (φάρμακα), and that consequently they cannot be described as sorcerers and poisoners.[1]

The whole section on the release of the followers of Jesus flatly contradicts the final clause on the sentences of banishment imposed; and the text of the MSS.[2] on which Berendts based his translation, questioned by himself, ' But afterwards, being prevailed upon (?) by them, they sent them away,' has simply arisen from a desire to adjust this contradiction and at the same time to get rid of the ominous words, ' the (*mis*-)deeds which were done by them.' Grass's emendation of the text[3] is as simple as it is convincing.

After elimination of these foolish and quite unmistakable interpolations, the remaining statement is intrinsically unobjectionable and historically very instructive. Only ignorance could believe that a decisive argument against the authenticity of this supposed ' addition ' may be derived from the fact that it represents the two governors as holding office simultaneously instead of the one succeeding the other.[4]

Any one who has read Josephus carefully, instead of merely looking up an occasional passage, knows that even the Greek text[5] shows clear traces of a source in which Cuspius Fadus and Tiberius Alexander appear to govern simultaneously. Schürer[6] himself found it surprising that Josephus should assign to the period of these two governors (ἐπὶ τούτοις) the famine which in *Acts* xi. 28-30 is mentioned as happening at about the time of the death of Herod Agrippa (A.D. 44), although he describes Alexander as the successor of Fadus. The epitomizer of the *Antiquities* sought to remove this stumbling-block by correcting ἐπὶ τούτοις to ἐπὶ τούτου, and Niese has placed this misleading reading in his text,

---

[1] Cf. Euseb., *Dem. ev.*, iii. 6 : ' whoever has found out the whole Christian tribe . . . practising witchcraft and using drugs (φαρμακεύον)? "

[2] *dozadéjani*, *Acad.* and *Kas.*; Syn., 991, *do zadéanii*; Syn., 770, same; Syn., 182, *za déjanii*; *Arch.*, *pozadéjani*.

[3] ' The variant of Syn., 182, *zadéjanii byv'še ot nich*, can easily be corrected into *za déjanija byvša ot nich*="for deeds done by them." '

[4] Thus Prof. Paul Schmiedel, *Neue Züricher Zeitung*, 1926, No. 1346.

[5] *Ant.*, xx. 5. 2, § 101 *sq.*   [6] *Op. cit.*, i.

though ἐπὶ τούτοις is supported by Eusebius, the old Latin version (' horum temporibus '), and all the Greek MSS. Although according to Suetonius[1] the reign of Claudius suffered from ' assiduae sterilitates,' it is hardly conceivable that the famine in Judaea extended over the terms of office of two governors and that there were four consecutive years of drought and bad harvests (44-48). Had Josephus intended to speak of so unusually protracted a drought, almost recalling the seven years' famine in Egypt, he would surely have expressed himself more clearly and at least have spoken of a ' long ' and not merely of a ' great ' famine.

What is decisive is the fact that the practice of two governors holding office simultaneously is not such an unheard-of thing as some ignorant people imagine. On the contrary, it is well attested by Tacitus for this same period of the reign of Claudius. In this instance Tacitus and Josephus diverge. Whereas Josephus[2] quite unambiguously represents Cumanus as sole governor of the district of Judaea, and Felix as coming to Palestine as his successor, Tacitus[3] says no less clearly :

' Felix had for some time been in command of Judaea. . . . He had as a rival in the worst crimes Ventidius Cumanus, who held a part of the province, which was so divided that the Galilaeans were subject to Cumanus, the Samaritans to Felix.'

Such a division of powers, with a special administrator for Galilee, a region always inclined to revolt, is by no means inappropriate, and is in keeping with the earlier partition of the province into four kingdoms or ' tetrarchies ' ; indeed, according to Tacitus[4] the governors were sent by Claudius into their provinces after the decease or after the limitation of the authority of ' the kings.' The plural used by Josephus in the Slavonic version,

' Claudius sent his officers to those kingdoms,'

shows precisely the same view of the situation. There is literally nothing to prevent us from believing that, as is implied by Josephus or the older documents utilized in the Halōsis, after the death of Agrippa (44-48) the government of Palestine was really a sort of condominium of Cuspius Fadus and Tiberius Alexander, with a division of jurisdiction similar to that which Tacitus describes for the immediately subsequent periods of Cumanus and Felix.

We can well imagine that Claudius, or his officials, considered it expedient to entrust the delicate task of governing this province to a thoroughly Hellenized Jew like Tiberius Julius Alexander,

---

[1] Vitae, Claudius, 18. [2] Ant., xx. 6. 1-3 ; B.J., ii. 12. 3-7.
[3] Annals, xii. 54.
[4] Hist., v. 9 : ' Claudius, defunctis regibus aut ad modicum redactis, Iudaeam provinciam equitibus Romanis aut libertis permisit.'

nephew of the philosopher Philo,[1] who would naturally be familiar with the idiosyncrasies of his countrymen, so difficult to handle,[2] and through his immense wealth would have no temptation to plunder them, while at the outset not sufficiently trusting him to assign so important a military position to him alone as *procurator sine collega*. After a certain period of probation Alexander may then have taken over the *imperium* of Fadus as well, and so once more united the government of Judaea in his hands, just as Felix took over the office of Cumanus when the latter was deposed by Ummidius Quadratus. In both cases, considering Josephus' working method as described above,[3] it is more than likely that he sometimes quite unintentionally distorted certain details of the case, a feature still noticeable in his work; whereas Tacitus, drawing directly on the documents, is more to be trusted. Yet even one who, with Schürer,[4] thinks it necessary to reject the narrative of the greatest of Roman historians must admit that what is tolerated in Tacitus must be acceptable in the Slavonic Josephus. If no one has ventured to deny the Tacitean authorship of the passage in question because it attests the simultaneous functioning of two governors in the time of Claudius, the gratuitous contention that 'Josephus, who was surely familiar with these matters, cannot possibly have represented two Roman governors as ruling simultaneously' may be safely neglected.

Nor can it be urged that the Slavonic Josephus does not represent the true historical facts because he mentions the sending of Jewish transgressors against the law to Rome, such a procedure being applied only to Roman citizens who appealed to Caesar.[5] But it is to be noted, in view of perfectly clear statements of Josephus himself,[6] that even provincials might be sent by the governor for trial to Rome, if on account of the difficulty of the case he wished to leave the unravelling of it to the emperor.

The governor of Judaea was equally at liberty to send accused persons to Antioch, which Josephus relates was done in the case of some of the 'Wonder-worker's' followers, and to leave the decision

---

[1] *Ant.*, xx. 100.

[2] Cf. the appointment of Sir Herbert Samuel as first British Commissioner of the Palestine Protectorate after the Balfour declaration. The comparison may be extended to the fact that, jointly with this distinguished Jewish statesman, Sir Ronald Storrs, K.C.M.G., C.M.G., C.B.E., Governor and Commander-in-Chief, Cyprus, well known for his pro-Arab sympathies, was appointed deputy-Commissioner as a guarantee of the mandatory Power's goodwill towards the Mahometan majority of the population. In an entirely similar way the Roman Empire could not afford to antagonize the pagan Hellenistic Syrians of the country, who, after all, were the co-religionists of the world-rulers. Just as in the case of Tiberius Alexander, the experiment was never repeated.   [3] Cf. p. 135.

[4] Div. I., vol. ii. p. 173 *sq.*, n. 14, of Macpherson's trans.

[5] Schmiedel, *loc. cit.*

[6] *Ant.*, xvii. § 297, xx. § 131=*B.J.*, ii. 243; *Ant.*, xx. § 161=*B.J.*, ii. 253. *Vita*, iii. § 13.

to the legate of Syria resident in that city. Seeing that the pro-
consular governor of Syria possessed jurisdiction over the provincial governors of the provinces of Judaea, Samaria, and Galilee,[1]
who were either of equestrian rank or, since the time of Claudius,
as now appears, nothing but freedmen of the emperor, it was
certainly highly expedient to leave difficult decisions at the outset
to this superior officer.

It shows mere lack of insight into the political circumstances
of the time if a critic doubts that the Roman governors of this
period, one of whom was himself a born Alexandrian Jew, could
have severely punished transgression of the *Jewish* law.   From a
passage in the Hebrew Josephus previously quoted,[2] and from the
accusations against Jesus, Stephen, and Paul, it is clear that the
followers of Jesus were looked upon by the Jews above all as
transgressors and disparagers of the revealed Law inherited from
their fathers, as lawbreakers, as *conscious* antinomians, or, even
worse, as downright criminals.   Jesus himself is represented as
saying to the Sabbath-breaker that he was cursed and a transgressor of the Law if he did not know what he was doing, but
blessed if he acted with knowledge,[3] i.e. with the saving knowledge
that with the dawn of the messianic era the old ordinance was
abrogated.

For this reason the people who were convinced that the
Messiah had already appeared and the messianic kingdom of
Israel had begun, and who hourly looked for its glorious realization
through the return of the crucified son of David 'with the clouds
of heaven'—in short, the Messianists or Christians—could best be
recognized by their attitude of detachment from the Mosaic Law.
In Judaea, when a man was prepared, like Paul or Peter, to eat
anything, even meat that had been offered to idols, and to sit at
table with heathen, the explanation was quite different from what
it would be in the cultivated and cosmopolitan Alexandria.   There
such conduct merely showed that he had learnt through an all too
'philosophic' and 'enlightened' interpretation of Philo's works
that most commandments were to be taken not literally but alle-
gorically, so that in the end, along with the philosopher's own
nephew the governor Tiberius Alexander, he came to see in the
Roman Jupiter and the Greek Zeus but another aspect of the
'unknowable' God of philosophy,[4] no less venerable and no more
imperfect than the old Jahveh of the Qenites of Mt. Sinai.   Such a
freethinker or 'Epicurean' need scruple no longer to do homage
to the emperor's image with a few grains of incense, while reserving
to himself the full freedom of his philosophic opinions on this most

---

[1] *Ant.*, xviii. 89 ; *B.J.*, ii. 244 ; Tacitus, *Ann.*, xii. 54.
[2] Cf. above, p. 96.   [3] *Luke* vi. 4 (cod. Bezae).
[4] Thus the *Letter of Aristeas*, § 16.

unphilosophical god seated on the imperial throne. In return there stood open to him, if his father had grown wealthy and become a Roman citizen, the whole *cursus honorum* up to the highest position, the throne of the world, ere long to be disgraced by a Syrian of Emesa, and therefore doubtless also within the range of the ambition of an Alexandrian Jew who had broken down or overleapt the ' hedge ' with which the Pharisees had surrounded their people as a protection against the enticements of Hellenism.

Quite different was the position in Palestine when a man awoke to the knowledge that the Sabbath was made for man and not man for the Sabbath, that nothing that goeth into the mouth defileth the man, that every creature of God is pure to the pure, and when he lived accordingly. By such conduct he betrayed himself, not as a disciple of the Epicurean or of that Stoic philosophy so highly esteemed in Rome, but as one of that 'harbour mob'[1] who had acclaimed a poor itinerant carpenter as king of the Jews and now awaited his return as lord of the whole world. Such a lawbreaker would immediately be recognized as one of the fomenters of that 'pest' which threatened not only the rule of the Roman people[2] but the maintenance of that superior and enlightened philosophical contemplation of the world and its follies to which the Hellenized Jew of Alexandria had pledged himself heart and soul.

And so there came about that at first glance strange yet easily comprehensible confederacy between the Hellenized Jew Tiberius Julius Alexander, sent to Palestine by Claudius first as the colleague of Fadus and then as sole governor, on the one hand, and the national *ḥaburah*—nowadays it would be called the 'fascio'—of conservative Jews, the supporters of the hierarchy and opponents of the Hellenization and Romanization of the priest-ruled state, on the other.

If the Jews had based all their former revolts for the realization of the Deuteronomic royalty law,[3] i.e. for political independence, on the ground that the foreign rulership hindered them in the free exercise of their religion—indeed (as in the recent attempt of Caligula), threatened to drive them to apostasy from the beliefs of their fathers—now the nephew of the pious Philo brought them a pledge from Claudius that from henceforth not only should they be free to follow the Law of Moses, but the Roman governor, with and through the teachers of the Law, would ensure that the traditions of their fathers were strictly observed : the Roman lictors would now see to it that, down to 'mint, anise, and cummin,'

---

[1] Cf. above, p. 351 n. 8 ; p. 340 n. 8.
[2] Cf. below, p. 536 n. 2, the letter of Emperor Claudius.
[3] Cf. above, p. 251 ll. 3 ff.

everything was duly tithed for the priests and that due respect was paid to the scribes and their orders by the refractory 'people of the land' ('ammē ha'areṣ). Rome, they were told, had duly recognized that the enemy of the scribes and the priests was also Caesar's enemy, that the Sabbath-breaker and despiser of the food laws was also an enemy of law and order and a danger to public security. Mere notification would suffice to put the governor and his court in motion against the lawless : the Sanhedrin could count on his full support in the maintenance of such peace and order in the country as were essential to ensure the unmolested payment alike of the taxes to Caesar and of the tithes to the hierarchy. The appointment of the Jew Tiberius Alexander, whose father had provided the costly gold and silver plating for the gates of Herod's temple,[1] would show that the emperor in his great mercy was indeed prepared to pay the utmost regard to the Deuteronomic regulations, and to put the Jews, as they had always desired, under the rule of one who was really their countryman of the purest blood, and no mere Idumaean proselyte like Herod Agrippa : all this provided, of course, that henceforth they would keep the peace, which recently again a new would-be Joshua or Jesus, a so-called Theudas or 'God-given' prophet and demagogue, much to the regret of the Roman government and the high priests in Jerusalem, had so grievously disturbed that with the best will under the sun a bloody intervention of the Sebastenian cavalry of the governor's former Roman colleague could not be avoided. The emperor hoped that his clemency would be duly appreciated, for he would otherwise be compelled to abandon this experiment of a liberal and conciliatory policy, to enforce with the greatest severity what is essential to the security of the Roman empire, and 'to show what a well-disposed ruler can do when his mind is turned to righteous wrath.'[2]

On the basis of some such provisional tacit agreement, satisfactory to all the high contracting powers, 'the Roman governors did' actually for a time, what has been thought incredible, 'look after the business of the Jewish teachers of the Law,' while, conversely, on the principle of Roman law, familiar also to Jews, *do ut des*, or *do ut facias*, the Jewish teachers of the Law looked after the political business of the governors and the maintenance of law and order—a covenant such as has often been repeated in history, the state acting as the buttress of orthodoxy, and the orthodox priests and ecclesiastical scribes as guardians of the security of the state. So long as Roman policy adhered to this course—as it did until Tiberius Alexander was superseded by the rapacious Felix,

---

[1] *B.J.*, v. 5. 3, § 205.
[2] The last words are from the letter of Claudius to the Alexandrians. Cf. H. Idris Bell, *Jews and Christians in Egypt*, London, 1924, p. 26.

the brother of Pallas, the powerful freedman of Claudius, and his worthy accomplice Cumanus—the peace of the country seems to have been preserved through a close co-operation of the scribes and the governor. During this time the hated *Minîm*—heterodox antinomian sectaries of every kind, not merely the Naṣōraeans— were, according to the perfectly credible evidence of the Slavonic Josephus, placed under a system of special political vigilance. So soon as through an edict of the governors (such as must be pre- sumed to underlie the opening words of Josephus quoted above)[1] it was publicly announced that it was the emperor's will that all Jews should faithfully observe their ancestral Law, and that con- traventions thereof would be punished, prosecutions for any speeches and conduct in defiance of that Law could be instituted in accordance with the very elastic provisions of the Roman law on high treason, the *crimen laesae maiestatis . . . omnium accusationum complementum*.[2] Roman law [3] prescribed for 'authors of sedition and tumult, or popular agitators,' along with the penalty of cruci- fixion or fighting with beasts in the arena (the choice being left to the judge's discretion and apt to be in accordance with the social standing of the condemned), the further alternative of *deportatio in insulam*, accompanied by confiscation of all property. This last penalty, clearly traceable from the time of Tiberius, was preferably inflicted upon political offenders for *crimen laesae maiestatis*, for *vis publica*, or for *sacrilegium*.

The provincial governor could only propose *deportatio* : the decision of the matter and of the condemned person's future place of abode rested with the emperor.[4]

The banishment was not necessarily confined to an island in the sea : there was also a *deportatio quasi in insulam*, e.g. to a small oasis in the Libyan desert. Moreover, it is to be noted that the Hebrew or Aramaic of the original text of the *Halōsis* possesses one and the same word, *'iyim* or *'iyin*, for ' islands ' and ' distant coasts,' so that the allusion in this passage of Josephus to exile ' to distant lands ' is doubtless intended to cover both *deportatio in insulam* and *deportatio quasi in insulam*.

It is hardly necessary to indicate in detail what an excellent illustration of the provisions of Roman law is afforded by Josephus' account of the proceedings against the followers of Jesus in the time of Claudius. It was clearly politic and in every respect wise on the part of Tiberius Alexander to dispense altogether with public executions such as King Agrippa I. had still ordered in his last years. For they always left ill-will and much excitement behind them, and might well be distasteful to a man of philosophic culture. He was content, then, with simply deporting from the

---

[1] Cf. above, p. 528 ll. 37 ff.
[2] Tacitus, *Ann.*, iii. 38.
[3] Cf. above, p. 460 n. 2.
[4] *Dig.*, xlviii. 22. 6. 1.

country persons reported to him by the Jewish authorities as *parisîm* or *sacrilegi* ; even if they were only deported ' for trial,' they were safely out of the way for years to come. The governor of Syria might, at his pleasure, pardon or conditionally acquit such people, or, if he preferred, send them on to the emperor. The legally prescribed confiscation of property would in the case of such poor fellows at least cover the cost of transportation, and all further responsibility would rest with the emperor. Foreign Jews, who had proved troublesome in Palestine, could simply be deported to their native place.

Obviously, it was this procedure of ' administrative deportation ' which was employed in the governorship of Cuspius Fadus and Tiberius Alexander against the Messianists. The persons concerned—and the fact is highly significant as showing the still persisting purely Rekhabite character of the followers of Jesus—belong exclusively to the class of wandering journeymen : they are tailors and sandal-makers going from house to house to cut and make up into sandals the peasants' household fabrics and the hides of their cattle, or other manual workers, wheelwrights, smiths, carpenters, labourers of all kinds,[1] carrying with them on their rounds the good news of Israel's approaching liberation from the Roman yoke, indeed ' from bondage ' in general, by which many would have understood more than the oppressive dominion of the foreigner.

The strange notion of Berendts, Frey, and other critics that the narrative in question ' generalizes ' the sending of Paul to Rome creates quite needlessly serious chronological difficulties. There is indeed no reason whatever why Josephus' words should refer to the Twelve, of whom only ten were still alive, or to Paul, as if between 44 and 48 there were no more than these eleven Christians in the world.

As a matter of fact, Josephus' statement of the ' helpers ' of Jesus has no perceptible reference to any passage whatever in either the canonical or the apocryphal *Acts of the Apostles*. Like all other statements of our author, it is based on an extract from the reports of the provincial governors to the emperor, and found by him in the *commentarii Claudii*. Neither had he any other source for his information on the insurrectionary movements under Caligula— moreover attested, as we know, by Tacitus.[2]

The clumsy version of the popular preaching in the report of the secretary of a Roman governor, ' there appeared among the people a multitude of the accomplices of the Wonder-worker of

---

[1] Celsus (Orig., *C. Cels.*, iii. 55) mentions 'wool-workers, cobblers (σκυτοτόμους), fullers ' ; cf. also Paul the tentmaker (or leather-worker ? Pesh. in *Acts* xviii. 3), Alexander the coppersmith (2 *Tim.* iv. 14), Hermogenes the coppersmith (*Acts of Paul and Thekla*, 1). The Mishnah expressly mentions the sandal-makers.

[2] *Ann.*, xv. 44 : ' repressaque in praesens exitiabilis superstitio rursum erumpebat.'

Mount Olivet and spoke to the people of their Master, (saying) that
he was alive, although he had been dead, and " he will free you
from your bondage," ' betrays the bewilderment of the Roman to
whom the idea of the resurrection of a dead man is as strange as
later it was to Festus.[1]   It is also important because it has faithfully
retained the *oratio indirecta*, which Josephus must also have employed in the corresponding passage in the *Antiquities*, though
obliterated by a Christian corrector.   (The sudden leap into direct
speech, ' He will free you from your bondage,' is in accordance
with the primitive style shown throughout by the Slavonic translator.)   It is noteworthy that in this instance the Slavonic *Halōsis*
has preserved a passage in indirect quotation which in the falsified
Greek text of the *Antiquities* appears as the author's own statement in direct speech.[2]   For the possibility that the Russian could
on his own initiative have converted into indirect speech what he
found in the direct form of address in his original is excluded by
the otherwise noticeable preference of the Slavonic translator for
the *oratio directa*, exemplified in the above quotation.

This finally clears up a passage in the *Testimonium* discussed
above.[3]   The Greek text in *Ant.*, xviii. § 64, ἐφάνη γὰρ αὐτοῖς
τρίτην ἔχων ἡμέραν (πάλιν) ζῶν, as it stands, is clearly a falsified
statement intended to support the truth of the Gospel story of the
resurrection.   It is of course wanting in the *Halōsis*, which
version has instead an assertion of the ' Wonder-worker's accomplices' bearing on the truth of the resurrection, an assertion which
neither the Roman report nor Josephus himself thought it worth
while to contradict or even to call in question.

One who can still think it possible to-day that this section of
the Slavonic Josephus was interpolated by a Christian—in other
words, that a Christian in all innocence has reproduced the traditional text of the *Antiquities* so awkwardly that the all-important
witness of the Jewish historian to the fundamental article of the
Christian creed has been converted into an unsupported assertion
dismissed by Josephus with a contemptuous shrug of the shoulders—
ought to concern himself with other matters than the investigation
of historical documents.   That the sentence on the resurrection in
the *Antiquities* also originally stood in *oratio indirecta*, and was only
later, by some small omissions, transformed into *oratio recta*, must
now be regarded as definitely proved.

The next important result is the discovery that even the
announcement of the resurrection was originally disseminated
among the people by the Jewish Christians in connexion with a
purely political message and with a distinctly political aim.   The

[1] *Acts* xxv. 19 : ' questions of one Jesus, which was dead, whom Paul affirmed
to be alive.'
[2] Cp. above, p. 60 ll. 5 f.   [3] P. 55 ll. 21 ff.

resurrection of Jesus was originally preached, not to a circle of mystics, like the resurrection of the dying mystery gods or that of the grass and corn spirits rising again from the earth,[1] as an illustration and guarantee of the individual's immortality : ' Be of good cheer, O initiated ones; the god is saved, you too will find salvation from your pains.'[2] No; the Jewish partisans of Jesus preached to the people the certainty of the impending ' liberation from bondage '; nor did they mean, like Paul, liberation from the bondage of sin and wicked spirits, but quite literally liberation from the yoke of their well-known worldly oppressors. Jesus was to return and liberate Israel from bondage [3] in no other sense than King Arthur was believed by the Welsh of the Middle Ages to return to free his people from their Saxon and Norman oppressors.

That is the sole reason for the governors' fear lest this preaching should lead to a ' turning away of the people,' and their hasty intervention, essentially a preventive measure to hinder the ' disease ' from penetrating and extending to the heads of society.

How far-seeing the Roman authorities proved, and how quickly the messianist movement made its way from the servants' quarters and the nursery, abandoned to the slaves,[4] into the ruling ranks, is shown by an incident which took place under the very eyes of Josephus—the conversion of Flavia Domitilla and the consul Flavius Clemens,[5] whose son, Vespasian II., was the destined heir to Domitian's throne. As early as the early part of the second century Pliny the Younger complains [6] ' periclitantium numerum . . . omnis ordinis . . . neque civitates tantum sed vicos etiam atque agros superstitionis istius contagio pervagata est.'

THE END OF JAMES THE JUST, ' THE LORD'S BROTHER '

From certain later sources—which, however, are above suspicion, not only because they are known to utilize genuine old material, but also because the full import of the statements in question was certainly no longer intelligible to the Christians of the post-apostolic period—we gather that James the Just wore the breastplate of the high priest and claimed the right to enter the Holy of Holies ' because he was a Naṣōraean and connected with the priesthood.'[7] Again we read, ' We find that he (i.e. James the

---

[1] I Cor. xv. 35-37 ; John xii. 34.
[2] Firm. Mat., De err. prof. relig., xxii. 1.
[3] Above, p. 529₃₄.   [4] Orig., C. Cels., iii. 55.
[5] Cassius Dio, lvii. 13 (epit. Xiphilini, xlvii. 14. 2). Cf. Pauly-Wissowa, R.E., s.v. Flavius, 62, 166 ; Flavia Domitilla, 227, col. 2733 sqq.; and the articles Clemens (Flavius) and Domitille (Flavie) in Cabrol's Dictionnaire d'archéologie chrétienne, t. iii., ca. 1867-70 ; t. iv., ca. 1402-4.
[6] Ep., xcvi.
[7] " διὰ τὸ Ναζωραῖον ὄντα καὶ μεμίχθαι τῇ ἱερωσύνῃ," Epiphan., Haeres., xxix. 4 (P.G., xli. 396).

Just) . . . was of David's race, being the son of Joseph, and that he was a Naṣōraean, as Joseph's first-born and therefore dedicated (to the Lord), and moreover we have found that he officiated after the manner of the ancient priesthood. Wherefore also he was permitted once a year to enter into the Holy of Holies, as the law commanded the high priests, according to that which is written ; for so many before us have told of him, both Eusebius and Clement and others. Furthermore, he was empowered to wear the high-priestly diadem upon his head, as the aforementioned trustworthy men have attested in their memoirs.' [1]

The reference to Eusebius, Clement of Alexandria, 'and others,' as attesting this curious story in their memoirs, refers to the *Ecclesiastical History* of Eusebius,[2] where one found the ὑποτυπώσεις of Clement and the ὑπομνήματα of Hegesippus quoted as authorities for the martyrdom of James. But the narrative of Epiphanius does not agree with the extract from Hegesippus as given by Eusebius. Differing in this from E. Schwartz, who has suggested another explanation,[3] I venture to think that these inconsistencies can be better explained to-day by the assumption of censorial excisions from the extract on James. The MS. of Eusebius used by Epiphanius was in this passage less abridged than our extant MSS. According to the extant Greek MSS. of the *Ecclesiastical History*, James had the right of entry only to the Holy Place (ἐξῆν εἰς τὰ ἅγια εἰσιέναι), whereas, according to the Syriac and Latin versions of Eusebius, according to Jerome [4] and Andrew of Crete,[5] as well as Epiphanius,[6] he had access to the Holy of Holies (the *debhir*), which was granted only to the high priest on the Day of Atonement. This alleged privilege of the Ṣaddiq cannot, of course, be derived from his being either a Nazirite or a Naṣōraean ascetic abstaining from meat [7] according to the doctrine of the Baptist,[8] two entirely different things obviously confused in the above-quoted Christian sources. More importance attaches to the statement of Epiphanius to the effect that he was ' connected (μεμίχθαι) with the priesthood,' i.e. that his house was related by marriage to Levitical families. That may very well be historically correct ; for, according to rabbinic tradition, Rekhabites or itinerant craftsmen, who had obtained permanent employment in the temple, often married the daughters of priests, so that their grandchildren served in the temple as priests.[9]

This relationship may have justified James in wearing the linen raiment of the priests, to which at that time even the lowest

[1] *Ibid.*, lxxviii. (*P.G.*, xlii. 714).   [2] *H. E.*, ii. 23. 4-6.
[3] *Zeitsch. f. Neutestam. Wissensch.*, iv. (1903), p. 50 *sq.*   [4] *De vir. illustr.*, 2.
[5] *Vita Jacobi*, ed. Papadopulos-Kerameus ; *Anal. Hierosol. stachyolog.*, i. 10. 21.
[6] *Haeres.*, xxix. 4, p. 324, Holl ; cf. lxxviii. 13, p. 1045 ; *P.G.*, xlii. 714.
[7] Euseb., *Hist. eccl.*, ii. 23. 5 (after Hegesipp.).
[8] Cf. above, pp. 235 ff.   [9] See above, p. 245 n. 2.

grades of the hierarchy laid claim.[1] But in no case could a Rekhabite, on the strength of his family's connexion by marriage with the Levites, have made the monstrous claim to enter by right the Holy of Holies. This right and this duty were restricted to one who was actually the high priest or regarded himself as such. Yet Epiphanius, expressly appealing to the memoirs of his authorities, i.e. to the statement of Hegesippus, as retailed in the *Hypotyposeis* of Clement and the *Ecclesiastical History* of Eusebius, declares that James wore the diadem (πέταλον) of the high priest, i.e. regarded himself as the regular high priest of the Jews. Now, it has been shown above,[2] on the evidence of the Greek and Hebrew Josephus, that the Jewish Zealots, the adherents of the Naṣōraean movement for national independence, had refused to recognize as legitimate the Boethusaean and Sadducaean high priests appointed by the Herodians and limited by the Romans to an annual tenure,[3] and proceeded to elect a 'pure and pious' high priest themselves. The first of the Zealots to be chosen high priest in this way seems to have been John the Baptist.[4] After his death in A.D. 36, the diadem appears to have been worn by John the Zebedaid, if we may suppose that the otherwise unreliable epistle of Polycarp to Victor of Rome[5] has taken this particular from good Palestinian tradition, and not invented it or transferred it from John the Baptist to his namesake in order to establish the primacy of the Church of Asia in opposition to the claims of Rome in the dispute on the Passover.[6]

However that may be, it is certain, from the evidence of Papias and the pre-Theodosian festal calendar of Constantinople,[7] that both sons of Zebedee suffered a martyr's death under Agrippa II., in A.D. 44, probably because of John's pretensions to be the legitimate high priest. He consequently cannot come into consideration after that date as a schismatic high priest of the nationalist party. Whether Peter, whom Jesus before his death had appointed his deputy until his second coming, regarded this office as a *worldly* vice-regency and after the death of the Baptist laid no claim to the high priest's diadem, or whether he did wear it, either simultaneously with John or after the latter's death in

---

[1] Josephus, *Ant.*, xx. 9. 6.   [2] Cf. pp. 259 f.
[3] Cf. above, p 18.   [4] Cf. above, p. 260₃.₄.
[5] Euseb., *Hist. eccl.*, iii. 31. 3 = v. 24. 2 *sq.*

[6] It is certainly noteworthy that immediately after the death of the Zebedaid John, the new governor Cuspius Fadus, in 44, requested the Jews to give back the high-priestly robe into the custody of the Romans (*Ant.*, xx. 6).

[7] E. Schwartz, 'Ueber den Tod der Söhne Zebedäi,' *Abh. d. Gött. Ges. d. Wiss.*, N.F., vii. 5; *Nachr.*, 1907, p. 266 *sqq.*; *Z.N.T.W.*, xi. (1910), pp. 89-104; W. Heitmüller, *Z.N.T.W.*, xv. (1914), p. 190. *Ibid.*, p. 214, n. 1, Schwartz has called our attention to the Montanist tradition, Epiphan., li. 33, according to which John was exiled to the island of Patmos under the Emperor Claudius, *i.e.* after 41. He may have been first condemned to *deportatio in insulam* (above, p. 537 ll. 20 f.), and then executed for *reversio illicita.*

44—on all this the records are silent. Considering the great importance which a testimony to the high priesthood of Peter would have
had for the Roman Church, the *argumentum e silentio* is in this
case justifiable, and we may assume that for almost a generation
the Messianists elected no other high priest of their own.

Now, if the extract from Hegesippus quoted by Epiphanius
attests that James the Just, who was slain in the year 62, shortly
before the coming of Albinus, once more assumed the high priest's
diadem, that may appropriately be brought in correlation with
the renewed outbreak of a revolt against the Herodians and Rome
in the time of Festus, as attested by Josephus.[1]   Once again at
that time a seer and wonder-worker, whom Josephus of course calls
a magician (γόης), sought to realize the plan of Jesus of an exodus
into the wilderness, and perished with his followers in the attempt.
In Jerusalem [2] at the same time the high priests were at strife with
the Levites and popular leaders, the former being aided by bands
of ruffians, for whose support they raided the threshing-floors and
carried off the priestly tithes of corn, so that the poorer priests
died of hunger.   Then, if ever, the opponents of this degenerate
clerical nobility, shamelessly scuffling for spoil under the eyes of
the bribed Roman officials, might have chosen as high priest 'the
Lord's brother,' who had once repeated the miracle of Hanan the
Hidden in bringing down rain from a parched sky,[3] and who was
revered by the people for his piety and justice.   On the ground of
such an election he may have felt himself justified in assuming the
diadem of the supreme dignity.   But if he did so, then he not only
had the right but was in duty bound to enter the Holy of Holies
on the Day of Atonement and alone in the presence of his God
to offer the great confession of sins and make atonement for the
people.

If he ventured on such a step, he may, in the confusion of the
times, with the help of a number of priests bitterly opposed to the
Sadducaean despots, have succeeded in secretly reaching the Holy
of Holies and leaving it unmolested.   But the proceeding could
not be kept secret, and the determined old man would doubtless
not have concealed from any one an act which to his opponents
must have appeared the most frightful sacrilege conceivable.
Such an offender could not be allowed to live.   The high priest
Ananus,[4] of whom Josephus himself has not a good word to say,
profited by the interregnum in the Roman governorship after the
death of Festus, when the commander was a mere military tribune,
more easily accessible to a bribe, to summon a meeting of the
Sanhedrin, a thing which he had no right to do without the

---

[1] *Ant.*, xx. 8. 10.   [2] *Ibid.*, xx. 9. 2, § 265 *sqq.*
[3] Epiphan., *Haeres.*, lxxviii. (*P.G.*, xlii. 721).
[4] *Ant.*, xx. 9. 1.

governor's consent. The tribunal itself then summoned James and his companions, put them on trial, and condemned them to be stoned for impiety. It nowhere appears from Josephus, as has been rashly assumed by those who wished to discover an irreconcilable contradiction between his account and that of Hegesippus, that Ananus and his followers were in a position to execute this sentence forthwith. We can well imagine that the Roman military tribune could be moved to connive at the assembling of seventy worthy elders, without taking official cognizance of the fact, since it was evidently a session of a purely academic character. But it is a very far cry from that to the toleration of an arbitrary arrest by the Sadducees of a popular leader with a considerable following even among the loyalists, as appears from the strong protest subsequently made to Albinus, or indeed to the toleration of the lynching of such a man by the excited mob. There is not the least reason to suppose that the deputy-governor would have committed himself so far as that. The execution of the death sentence must accordingly have been brought about by a mischievous ruse, the nature of which the account of Hegesippus permits us clearly to recognize.

We note first that, according to the account of the Christian pilgrim Hegesippus, James at the time of his death was not arrested at all, but was at liberty and so beloved by the people that no one would have ventured to seize him. His opponents could only try to get round him by dissimulation. Josephus speaks of the Sanhedrin ' bringing before it ' (παράγειν) James and some others : but the outcome of such action may have been as humiliating for that body as when on a previous occasion it summoned the youthful Herod to trial.[1]

How under these circumstances the execution of the sentence might be brought about may be easily discovered by a comparison of the account of Hegesippus with certain passages in the Talmud.[2] As late as the third or fourth century it was taught as a Tannaite tradition that a man whom the Sanhedrin condemned to be stoned, without having the power to execute the sentence, ' fell from the roof '—in other words, was punished by God by his meeting with this particular accident. Considering the rare occasions on which the Sanhedrin, at a time when it had lost the power of trying criminal cases, met in solemn session to condemn a trans-

---

[1] B.J., i. 10. 7, § 210 : " ἐκάλει κριθησόμενον."

[2] Keth., 30a (Strack-Billerbeck, ii. 197 sq., on Luke xiii. 2) : '. . . whosoever is guilty of being stoned either falls from the roof or a wild beast tramples him to death. Whosoever is guilty of being burned to death either falls into the fire or is bitten by a snake. Whosoever is guilty of being beheaded is either delivered up to the (pagan) government or assailed by robbers. Whosoever is guilty of being strangled is either drowned or chokes to death.' Cf. Shakespeare, All's Well that Ends Well, iv. 3 : 'Hold your hands ; though I know that his brains are forfeit to the next tile that falls.'

gressor of the Law to death *in contumaciam*, we may with great probability conjecture that in this phrase there is a reminiscence of the fate of James the Just, the more so because a ' fall from the roof ' is not an obvious equivalent for the penalty of stoning. Furthermore, according to an affirmation on oath of R. 'Eli'ezer,[1] the first pupil of R. Johanan b. Zakkai and therefore an inhabitant of Jerusalem contemporary with James the Just, ' even a high priest ' who on entering the sanctuary is guilty of any breach of the purity laws of the precincts must have ' his skull split with a wooden club.' The barbarous punishment here threatened, like the ' fall from the roof ' of the man condemned to be stoned, at once recalls the fate of the ' high priest ' James, who was beaten to death with a wooden club by a man whom the Christians regarded as a ' fuller ' accidentally on the spot. But it is clear that on a day of Passover a workman could not have been strolling in or about the precincts of the temple with the implement of his trade in his hand, and that therefore this person was simply one of the regular club-armed officers of the high priests who ' by chance ' and in plain clothes had remained in readiness in the neighbourhood, to complete the execution of the 'accidentally' fallen victim by 'braining him with a wooden club.'

On the simple assumption that the longer extract from Hegesippus preserved by Epiphanius has been mutilated even more drastically than in Eusebius, it is possible to make quite good sense of the story of the martyrdom of James. The Sanhedrin condemned him to be stoned, not because he preached that the crucified Jesus was the Messiah and would shortly so reappear, for such a doctrine was in no way punishable under Jewish law and did not fall within the meaning of blasphemies deserving of death, but because he, whom the hierarchy could of course never have recognized as a regular high priest, had actually entered the Holy of Holies and immediately in front of it had pronounced the sacrosanct, secret name of God in the prayer of the Day of Atonement. The sentence of stoning passed upon James and his accomplices (i.e. the priests who officiated with him and conducted him to the sanctuary) at an illicit session of the Sanhedrin convened by the high priest Ananus could not be executed forthwith. The fanatics therefore devised the cunning expedient of inviting the old Saddiq to deliver an address from the roof of the temple to the Jewish and heathen pilgrims streaming in for the feast of the Passover. When he consented and once more availed himself of the opportunity to proclaim Jesus to the crowds as ' the Son of Man who was to return on the clouds of heaven,' he was pushed over the parapet and dispatched beneath with the wooden club. The object of the whole plot can only have been to enable his enemies to repre-

---

[1] *Tosephta Kelim*, i. 1. 6 ; *Bab. kam.*, 1 (middle).

2 M

sent to the Romans that the Ṣaddiq had met with an accidental death from a fall through giddiness, just as the Talmudic passages already quoted maintain that the Sanhedrin's solemn death sentences were carried out, so to speak, by the direct avenging intervention of the Deity.

One can well imagine that Josephus passed lightly over the shameful part played in these proceedings by the priesthood, so that he extracted only what was absolutely necessary from the letter of protest sent by the ' most respectable and law-abiding ' Jews to Albinus. On the other hand, the credibility of the account of Hegesippus is guaranteed by the fact that the Christians had not recognized the man with the club, who had to execute the sentence, as an agent of the Sanhedrin, but regarded him as an ordinary fuller fanatically laying about him with his implement. However, it is not improbable that Josephus wrote some lines about the occasion which James had given for the proceedings of Ananus, and did not altogether omit to state the grave provocation which led to the trial by the Sanhedrin. These clauses may have been deleted by a Christian hand with the same object that brought about the mutilation of the Hegesippus passage in Eusebius and Epiphanius, namely, to represent James as a passive victim of his opponents and to conceal his share in the political conflicts of his time. On the other hand, as has been convincingly shown by Dr. Eduard Schwartz,[1] a very clumsy hand interpolated into the Hegesippus story an actual stoning of James, to remove the apparent contradiction to Josephus' words ' delivered them up to be stoned,' quite regardless of the improbability thereby imported into the narrative. For since there were actually no loose stones lying about on the marble floor of the temple courts, the Jews, to carry out their sudden idea, ' Let us stone James the Just,' [2] would have had the difficult task of breaking up the pavement, unless they had brought with them stones concealed in their garments, as the supposed fuller his club. But that would of course have defeated their main object, namely, to represent the affair to the Romans as an accident. The breaking of the skull by the blows of the club could without difficulty be explained as a consequence of the fall, but the bloodshot wounds over the whole body, produced by the stones, would have betrayed the truth all too clearly. Thus, in this last section of Josephus, devoted to a hero of early Christian history, and in the parallel narrative of Hegesippus, the marks of the activity of ' the false pen of the scribes ' are again clearly traceable.

[1] Z.N.T.W., 1903. p. 56.   [2] Euseb., H.E., ii. 23.

XVIII

THE PREDICTED WORLD-RULER—HEROD, JESUS, OR VESPASIAN ?

THE last mention of the crucified Messiah in the *Halōsis* of Josephus occurs in the sixth book at the end of the list of prodigies derived independently by both Josephus and Tacitus from the imperial commentaries, which, according to ancient Roman fashion, conscientiously observed and noted even such things as these.

To this narrative, ending with the pathetic story of the ominous woes pronounced upon Jerusalem by the peasant Jeshu'a b. Ḥanan, Josephus appends an unpleasantly pietist reflection of his own:

B.J., vi. 5. 4, § 310 *sqq.*	Capture of Jerusalem (*Halōsis*).[2]
' Reflecting on these things, one will find that God has a care for men, and by all kinds of premonitory signs shows His people the way of salvation, while they owe their destruction to folly and calamities of their own choosing.	' But if one thinks aright one will find that God gives men all kinds of premonitory signs, foretokening what is for the salvation of our race. We, however, perish through ignorance and evil of our own choosing. For God hath shown signs of wrath, in order that men might recognize the wrath of God, desist from their wickedness, and thereby mollify the Deity. (Although) the Jews had a prophecy that through (being reduced to) a quadrangular form (the) city and the temple would be devastated,
' Thus the Jews, after the demolition of fort Antonia, reduced the temple to a square, although they had it recorded in their oracles [1]	

[1] Probably alluding to some Haggadic interpretation of *Dan.* viii. 22 : ' the four [*horns*] that stood up in place of, or behind, that which was broken ' (the Hebrew word *qᵉrānoth* for ' horns,' which is missing in the present Massoretic text and therefore also in the English A.V., but which both Greek translators read in their exemplar, could be understood, like the Arabian *qurnah*, to mean a projecting ' corner ' of a structure). It is noteworthy that the Arabic Josephus asserts that this and the following prediction on the world-ruler were recorded on inscriptions : ' An inscription on an old stone ran, If the temple is completed and becomes four-square, it will be desolated.' Another inscription was to be found on a stone in the wall of the Holy of Holies : ' If the temple becomes four-square, a king will rule over Israel who will take possession of the whole earth.' The people thought that this was the king of Israel : the wise said that it was the king of Rome (Wellhausen, *Der arabische Josifus*, Berlin, 1897, p. 41). The inscription on the wall of the sanctuary is obviously a legendary distortion of the inscription commemorating the death of James the Just, above, p. 519 nn. 2 and 4.

[2] The Russian text with a Greek interlinear retroversion, showing with what degree of preciseness the original can be recovered, is given as App. xxiv. pp. 622 f.

that the city and the sanctuary would be taken when the temple should become four-square.	they [1] made after (the destruction of Antonia the) sanctuary four-square.

But what more than all else incited them to the war was an ambiguous oracle, likewise found in their sacred scriptures, to the effect that at that time one from their country would become ruler of the inhabited world. This they understood to mean some one of their own race, and many of their wise men went astray in their interpretation of it. The oracle, however, in reality signified the sovereignty of Vespasian, who was proclaimed emperor on Jewish soil. For all that, it is impossible for men to escape their fate, even though they foresee it. Some of these portents, then, the Jews interpreted to please themselves, until the ruin of their country and their own destruction convicted them of their folly.'

What moved (them) to war was an ambiguous announcement found in (the) sacred scriptures that in those times one from (the) Jewish land would become ruler of the inhabited world. Of this (announcement) there were various interpretations. Some believed that Herod (was meant), others again *that crucified Wonderworker Jesus,* [2] others lastly Vespasian. But it is not possible for men to escape judgment, even though they foresee it. Thus the Jews, knowing the portents beforehand, at their pleasure tuned them to their satisfaction ; the rest they calumniated up to their own ruin and that of their country. They were put to shame and shown up as fools.'

A glance at these parallel passages will suffice to show that the words relegated from the second column to footnote [1] are a Christian interpolation. In the first place, they are a superfluous duplication : the Jews disregarded the oracle about the square by the destruction of Fort Antonia ; the prophecy was thereby fulfilled and there was no need for the making of further ' squares ' (=crosses). Secondly, it is clear that the clause has been inserted from a desire to represent the crucifixion of Jesus as the great crime for which the Jews were punished by the destruction of their city and temple. It is highly instructive for the criticism of the Christian interpolations discussed elsewhere,[3] on the crucifixion of Jesus ' by the Jews ' and ' according to the law of their fathers,' that the writer of this clause knew quite well that crucifixion is not a Jewish custom, and that the Jews ' at that time '—a phrase which for this writer means simply in the time of Jesus—first

---

[1] (Christian interpolation) ' began at that time themselves to make crosses for crucifixions, which, as we have said, is a thing of fourfold shape and . . .'

[2] The name was found by Berendts (*op. cit.*, p.12) in Cod. Arch. Mosp., fol. 460 r., col. 1, and in Cod. Acad. It is missing in Cod. Kyr. Bjel., 64/1303, fol. 250 v.; reproduced in vol. ii. Germ. ed., on p. 591. According to this MS. it would seem as though Josephus when writing the *Halōsis* had entirely ignored the name of Jesus. This, however, is so unlikely that I prefer to suppose a deletion of the name in some MSS. Cf. above, p. 405₆.   [3] Cf. above, pp. 387 and 521.

began, in the heathen manner, to make 'crosses themselves for crucifixions.' The plurals, ' crosses ' and ' crucifixions,' although the oracle only required *one* ' four-cornered form,' are an obvious allusion to the three crosses of Golgotha, so familiar to Christian readers of the Gospels. But certain as it is that this clause is a Christian interpolation with transparent purpose, it would be no less certainly erroneous to pass the same judgment on the words referring to Jesus in the account of the interpretation given to the oracle on the world-ruler.

Those words of the *Halōsis*, ' that crucified Wonder-worker (Jesus),' closely correspond to the phrase of Lucian previously quoted,[1] ' that magician . . . who was impaled (ἀνασκολοπι-σθέντα) in Palestine.' Even if the dependence of Lucian on Josephus should be questioned, the supercilious tone common to these two passages is unmistakable. No Christian wrote so. By way of contrast we may note the manner in which the so-called 'Egesippus' paraphrases the sentence which he found in his Greek MS. of Josephus :

> ' id alii ad Vespasianum referendum putaverunt, prudentiores ad Dominum Jesum Christum, qui eorum in terris secundum carnem genitus ex Maria regnum suum per universa terrarum spatia diffudit.'

The Slavonic omits altogether the last sentence in the Greek, to the effect that history has shown the Romanophile interpretation to be correct ; and very significantly, for of course still less than the 'Arab' Herod could the Roman Vespasian be represented by Josephus to his Jewish readers as the true Messiah foretold by God. On the other hand, the allusions to Herod and to Jesus are wanting in the Greek text addressed to Vespasian and Titus. On this Goethals [2] has pertinently remarked :

> ' It would have been the act of a clumsy courtier to recall (to Vespasian) in such a work that this honour was not uncontested, that he had a competitor for the dignity of messiahship in the person of that crucified wonder-worker Jesus.'

The discussion of the Jewish priests on their nation's expectations of a messiah, contained in the *Halōsis*,[3] is in fact omitted in the Greek *Polemos*, in order not to betray how un-Jewish was that interpretation of the passage of Scripture as referring to Vespasian, by which Josephus secured his favoured position at the Flavian court.[4]

Goethals might have added that the allusion to Herod the Great in this passage was not less undiplomatic and must have

---

[1] Cf. p. 11 n. 5 and p. 51 nn. 3 and 4.
[2] *Josèphe témoin de Jésus*, Paris, 1909, p. 14.
[3] Cf. above, pp. 137 f.   [4] *B.J.*, iii. 399 *sqq.*

brought down upon Josephus a reproof from his patron Agrippa II.
For if in this section on the meaning of the 'ambiguous oracle,'
which drove the Jews into revolt, war, and ruin, mention was made
of its interpretation as referring to the person of Herod the Great,
then it must have appeared to readers who happened to light on
this passage as though it was the Herodians [1] who, on the ground
of these old messianic expectations, had pressed for war with
Rome.[2] Agrippa II. and his followers, who had taken up the
directly opposite position and fought throughout the campaign on
the Roman side, would therefore have been perfectly right in
protesting against this clumsiness, and Josephus would have been
compelled to omit the name of Herod at this passage in subsequent
editions of his book.

In this abridged form, with only two alternatives, 'Jesus' or
'Vespasian,' left, the passage was found by 'Egesippus.' The
reverse theory, namely, that a Christian or a Jew was afterwards
impelled to supplement this 'either Jesus or Vespasian' by mentioning a third, old interpretation, that is, Herod, seems to be
utterly improbable. For a Christian who here sought to introduce
his far-fetched learning, derived from Tertullian,[3] Jerome,[4] or
Epiphanius,[5] would certainly, like 'Egesippus,' have so reshaped
the sentence as to show that in his opinion the application to Jesus
alone was correct. Again, a Jew, writing after the time of Josephus, i.e. after the fall of Jerusalem, instead of attending to old
messianic pretensions of Herod quite unknown to rabbinic literature, would rather have had every reason to emphasize the expectation of a future messiah, a hope which remained unshattered by all
the blows of fate.

THE WAR-GUILT OF THE CHRISTIANS IN THE 'HALŌSIS' OF JOSEPHUS

The strangest thing about these words in the *Halōsis* of Josephus is the fact that neither Eusebius nor the Christian author of
the Latin version known as *Egesippus* observed what a monstrous
accusation against the Christians they contained.

[1] It is of course not impossible that there *were* members of the Herodian
party who expected the return in glory of the old Herod the Great, because they
hated and despised as an unworthy scion of the old tiger the opportunist philo-
Roman Agrippa II.

[2] Cf. the similar contention of the Hebrew *Josippon*, above, p. 105 ll. 12 ff.

[3] *De praescr. adv. Haeret.*, 45 : ' Herodiani, qui Herodem Christum esse
credebant.'

[4] *In Matt.* xxii. 15 : ' quidam Latinorum ridicule Herodianos putant, qui
Herodem Christum esse credebant''; id., *Contra Luciferian.*, c. xxii : ' quod
Herodiani Herodem regem suscepere pro Christo.' Philaster, *Haeres.*, xxvii.

[5] *Adv. Haeres.*, xx. ; *P.G.*, xli. 269.

The question of the historical truth or probability of the state-ment can be left out of account altogether.   For the mischievous impression which Josephus, probably unintentionally yet quite clearly, produced by the words in question, viz. that the Herodians, through their belief in the messianic vocation of Herod the Great and his return as world-ruler, had a special share in the outbreak of the revolt from Rome, must clearly have been corrected by himself through the omission of the misleading allusion to this old, and at that time doubtless antiquated, interpretation.   Clearly, therefore, a forger of history who had brought such a manifestly misleading charge against the Herodians may also in this matter have done the Christians indirectly a most serious injustice.

But every reader of the lines in question must see at the first glance that Josephus, by asserting that it was the false application of the prophecy to Jesus—i.e. the expectation of the return of the crucified in glory to enter upon his world-dominion—which above all incited the Jews to war with Rome, shifts the responsibility for the revolt of the year 66 directly on to the followers of Jesus and their announcement of his approaching *parousia*.   In other words, the war-guilt from which the Herodians had justly exonerated themselves is now by the shortened text, as it remained after the deletion of Herod's name and as 'Egesippus' read and translated it, transferred to the Christians.   The passage in this form clearly implies the existence of two interpretations of *Gen.* xlix. 10.   One party expected that the world-ruler, while coming indeed 'from Judah,' would be no Jew but a new emperor called to the throne from Judaea, who would finally deprive the Jews of all independ-ence under a ruler of their own.   This was of course the explana-tion given by a resigned and submissive group, anxious for peace at any price.   The second interpretation—viz. that the world-dominion was destined for a Jew of Judaea—with its reference to the return of the crucified Jesus from heaven as the glorious Christ at the head of legions of heavenly hosts, is clearly the one which could have exercised the bellicose effect emphasized by Josephus.   Thus, quite unambiguously, the Christians, the believers in the messiahship of Jesus, are charged with having driven the Jews into the disastrous war.

That is quite in keeping with the fact already mentioned, that Josephus has dealt with the insurrection of the year 21 much more fully and impressively than with other similar movements, and lets *the anti-Christian tendency of his whole work* plainly appear.   It further explains why the reference to Jesus, which was still read and discreetly paraphrased by Eusebius and 'Egesippus,' after Josephus had himself expunged the name of Herod, was struck out from the extant Christian MSS. of the *Jewish War*.   It is utterly impossible to suppose that these words, which incidentally attribute to the Christians the responsibility for the fall of Jerusalem, could have been inserted by a Christian.

If the reader should ask how far the reproach brought by Josephus against the Christians may contain a grain of truth, the answer must be extracted from two striking facts. In the first place, there is a passage of Sulpicius Severus,[1] which Jacob Bernays [2] and Prof. Weber [3] rightly consider to be derived from a lost portion of the fifth book of the *Histories* of Tacitus, containing an account of the Roman war council at which Titus expresses his opinion that the temple must be destroyed in order that the Christian belief, i.e. the messianic expectation of the return of Jesus, may be radically extirpated. Titus, then, according to this passage, regarded the ' Christians ' who ' took their origin from the Jews,' i.e. the Jewish sect of the messianist followers of Jesus, as the chief promoters of disturbance. The passage has not unnaturally caused great difficulties to modern commentators.[4] But the usual way of evading these, by representing the words as the reflections of the Christian writer or his Christian source, is quite impracticable. For a later Christian must have known that to Christians the destruction of the temple was but the fulfilment of a prediction of Jesus, and could therefore have only given a new impetus to the Christian belief in his return in glory as judge and ruler of the world.

On the other hand, it is clear that objection has been taken to the passage solely because the political importance of the original Jewish-Christian expectation of a messiah has been misunderstood or gravely underrated. The words of Titus contain nothing whatever which a Roman general could not have known or spoken.[5] The antagonism between orthodox Jews and Jewish-Christians must have been, so to speak, officially known ever since the synagogue riots occasioned by Paul throughout the Roman empire, the deportations of the messianists under Claudius—in any case, since the denunciation of the Christians by the Roman Jews at the time of the Neronian persecution. That Titus did not distinguish between the activist messianists, for ever flocking round new leaders, and the followers of Jesus whom Paul had converted into

---

[1] I *Chron.* ii. 30. 6 : ' At contra alii *et Titus ipse euertendum in primis templum censebant,* quo plenius Iudaeorum et Christianorum religio tolleretur : quippe has religiones, licet contrarias sibi, iisdem tamen ab auctoribus profectas : Christianos ex Iudaeis exstitisse : radice sublata stirpem facile perituram.'

[2] *Gesammelte Abhandlungen,* ii. 159-81.

[3] *Josephus und Vespasian,* p. 72 n. 1.

[4] M. M. Valeton, *Verslagen en Mededeelingen d. k. Akad. van Wetenschappen,* Afdeeling Letterkunde, iv. 3, Amsterdam, 1899, pp. 87-116, esp. 105 *sqq.*; Norden, *op. cit.,* p. 653 n. 1 ; Schürer-Macpherson, i. 2, p. 244 *sq.,* n. 115 ; Weynand, in Pauly-Wissowa, *R.E.,* vi. (1909), c. 2703.

[5] Especially after the Christians had been officially accused under Nero of having set Rome afire.

quietists, is in keeping with a speech of Tertullus before Felix, accusing Paul of being ' a mover of insurrections among all the Jews throughout the world and a ringleader of the sect of the Naṣōraeans,' [1] and with the Roman centurion's confusion of the apostle with the Egyptian messiah.[2] Such minor errors are readily intelligible when it appears that the official reports of a Cuspius Fadus and a Tiberius Alexander represented the Christian preaching of the resurrection as a purely political message.

If, indeed, as would appear from the Hebrew Josephus, the arch-brigand 'Ele'azar, son of Deinaeus, was a companion of Peter the *Barjona*, if the rebel Theudas was a friend or acquaintance [3] of Paul, if, indeed, James the Just, as the restored account of Hegesippus informs us, was elected by the opponents of the ruling high priest to take his place, one cannot describe the opinion of Titus as altogether unfounded. The statement [4] that the Christian community at Jerusalem, immediately before the investment of the city and in consequence of a ' Divine warning,' fled to Pella in Transjordania, only proves that the Christians, in accordance with the predictions of Jesus, regarded Jerusalem as irretrievably lost, and by no means that they did not momentarily expect the saving return of their Master and his final victory.

Anyhow, the agreement of the prevailing opinion on the Christians at the Roman headquarters (or, if you prefer, the prejudice against them) with Josephus' outspoken accusation of the messianists is highly remarkable, and forms, in my opinion, a striking argument for the authenticity of the relevant lines in the Old Russian version.

Then there is a further circumstance. It is very striking that in this retrospective survey of the beginnings of the war and the *omina excidii urbis* Josephus never mentions the one man who at the outbreak of the revolt came forward as king of the Jews, to wit, Menaḥem, son of Judas of Galilee.[5] For if the Zealots at the beginning of the revolt set up as king a scion of this old Galilaean rebel dynasty, then it is clear that they regarded this man as the Lord's Anointed and interpreted the oracle in Scripture as referring to him. His name and not that of Jesus or Herod the Great should therefore have been mentioned in this passage. But the omission is satisfactorily explained by the assumption that when Josephus wrote the *Halōsis* he knew nothing of this episode of the proclama-

---

[1] *Acts* xxiv. 5.   [2] *Ibid.*, xxi. 38.
[3] Clem. Alex., *Strom.*, vii. 17 (*P.G.*, ix. 549) : ' Valentine is said to have been a disciple (ἀκηκοέναι) of Theudas, who was a friend (or acquaintance, or disciple : γνώριμος) of Paul.'   [4] Euseb., *H.E.*, iii. 5.
[5] Josephus, *B.J.*, ii. 17. 9, § 442, calls him ' an insufferable tyrant,' but in § 445 tells of his going ' in royal robes ' up to the temple, where the people pelted him with stones from the roof (read ὀροφάς for ὀργάς). He did, therefore, put himself forward as king, i.e. as the messiah, of the last war.

tion of Menaḥem as king and his subsequent martyrdom [1] at the hands of the followers of 'Ele'azar, captain of the temple and son of the high priest, who at the head of the young priests and temple servants had arrogated to himself the leadership of the revolt. Since, according to the narrative of Josephus, neither this 'Ele'azar nor any of the other rebel leaders laid claim to the name or the insignia of a king, it is clear that the strictly messianistic insurgents of the year 66 were the followers of Menaḥem the Galilaean. The rest presumably, in the manner of their Maccabaean forefathers, had their eyes only on the immediate political goal : their leaders would in the event of success have been content with the office of high priest, and would never have dreamed of setting up a messianic, world-wide kingdom. Josephus, therefore, only because at that time he had no information about the appearance of Menaḥem, while he knew well that a section of the rebels stood under the ban of those messianic predictions, along with the antiquated application of that prophecy to Herod mentioned also its supposed reference to Jesus, and thereby threw suspicion on the Christians, the obstinate followers of their crucified Messiah, as the Jewish party more responsible than any for driving the nation to war.

We may well believe Sulpicius Severus, or rather his authority Tacitus, when he implies that this error, momentous for Christians but immaterial for Roman politics and strategy, was shared by Roman headquarters. At any rate, Vespasian, after the destruction of Jerusalem, had all descendants of David rounded up, although there is not the least reason to suppose that this peaceful clan [2] had taken any part whatever in messianistic machinations.

The *Shilo* Prophecy applied to Vespasian. Josephus and Tiberius Alexander

The 'ambiguous prophecy' to which Josephus refers is without doubt [3] the *Shilo* or *Shilu* prophecy of *Gen.* xlix. 10, endlessly discussed by Jews and Christians :

' The sceptre shall not depart from Judah, nor the ruler's staff

---

[1] The in this connexion important §§ 431-4, 440-9 are missing in the Slavonic. According to the *Vita*, § 21, Josephus had hidden in the interior of the temple until a temporary quiet was restored in the city. He probably was then quite unaware of what had been going on outside.

[2] Cf. above, p. 322 n. 1.

[3] That was seen as early as the seventeenth century by Daniel Huet, *Demonstr. evang.*, Paris, 1681, prop. vii., num. xxxii. ; by Natalis Alexander, *Hist. eccl. vet. test.*, Paris, 1677 (1699), diss. xii. p. 250 ; further by O. Gerlach, *Die Weissagungen des Alten Testaments, in den Schriften des Flavius Josephus*, 1863, p. 41, and by Joseph Langen, *Theol. Quartal-Schrift*, Tübingen, 1865, i. 4.

from a son of his loins,[1] until the *Shilu*[2] comes, and [3] he is the expectation of the Gentiles,' *or*, 'and him shall the peoples obey,' [4]

which obviously means, there shall be no interruption in the government of a Jewish dynasty until he comes (from Judah ?) whom all peoples shall obey. This exposition was commonly supported by such predictions as *Micah* v. 1 (2) *sqq.* :

> ' But thou, Bethlehem . . ., albeit but little among the districts [5] of Judah, out of thee shall come forth one that shall be ruler in Israel . . . for now shall he be great unto the ends of the earth,'

and by the other 'messianic' prophecies of Jewish world-dominion. The oracle was ambiguous because, at least to those who no longer understood the meaning of the Babylonian loan-word *shilu*—in other words, all or most readers of the Hellenistic age—it left the question open whether the expected world-ruler would be of Jewish origin or not. The sentence might equally well be taken to mean that the ruling house of Judah would not cease until it had produced the expected world-ruler, or, on the contrary, that it would end only with the subjugation of all peoples, including the Jews, by a foreign, non-Jewish world-ruler.

The high hopes of the Herodians who saw in Herod the Great, the first non-Jewish dynast, the *Shilu* promised to the Jews, have been mentioned in a previous chapter.[6] They were by no means buried with that monarch. On the contrary, there are clear indications which suggest that this party attached such messianic hopes to Agrippa I., the sufferer who had been released from prison by Caligula and exalted to the throne, who had been invested by Claudius with the whole kingdom of his grandfather, and who had allowed himself to be borne in triumph into Alexandria and to be hailed by his countrymen as *maran*, ' our lord ' ; [7] that they regarded the imprisonment which he had undergone in Rome as the 'woes' or 'sufferings' of the Messiah—nay, that in the end they had not shrunk from an apotheosis of this conceited kinglet, who had appeared before the people arrayed in the shining robe of a *roi soleil*.[8] It was probably just these dangerous tendencies which moved the counsellors of Claudius to refuse the youthful Agrippa II. the succession to his father's throne,[9] and to send in his stead Tiberius Alexander, the Hellenized Jew from Alexandria, as imperial governor.

---

[1] R.V., ' from between his feet.'

[2] Bab. loan-word for ' king ' ; cf. my paper in the *Expository Times*, xxxvi. (1925), p. 477, and above, p. 137 note 10.

[3] Following the LXX. : " καὶ αὐτὸς προσδοκία ἐθνῶν."   [5] Or ' clans.'

[4] After Massor. T.

[6] Cf. above, p. 137 ff.

[7] *Ant.*, xviii. 6. 11 ; Philo, *In Flacc.*, § 5 *sq.* (ii. 521 M).

[8] *Ant.*, xix. § 344.   [9] Cf. above, p. 206 l. 20.

The idea that the destroyer of Jerusalem, the conqueror of the Jews, was for that very reason the predicted world-ruler of the final age was by no means confined to the wretched Josephus. Three days before Nero's death, Hillel's pupil, the celebrated R. Johanan b. Zakkai, had predicted Vespasian's elevation to the principate and been richly rewarded for his prophecy;[1] and the *omina imperii* tell of similar oracles of a Syrian priest on Mt. Carmel[2] and of the great heathen mystic Apollonius of Tyana.[3]

When Prof. Wilhelm Weber writes,[4]

' One might almost regard the whole story as a game got up between Josephus and the general staff, who used him for political ends,'

I am now, after the edifying insight afforded by the Old Russian *Halōsis* into the character of Josephus, perfectly convinced that he has hit the nail on the head. Weber rightly pointed out that Vespasian was in Alexandria when he received the oracle of Apollonius, in which he was praised as the βούκολος, as the ' good shepherd,'[5] without whom the human flock must go to ruin. But it was precisely in Alexandria that Vespasian was represented as healing a blind man and another with a crippled hand, who had been directed to him ' by dreams.'[6] If one turns back to the debate of the anti-Herodian priests on the expected messiah, recounted in the *Halōsis* of Josephus,[7] one notes at once that according to Jewish ideas the lame and the blind were destined to be healed under the Lord's Anointed. One further recalls that among the king-makers surrounding Vespasian one of the shrewdest was the then prefect of Egypt, who administered to the Libyan legion the oath of allegiance to Vespasian, and was afterwards chief of the general staff of Titus. I mean, of course, the Romanized Jew, Tiberius Alexander.

The inference is obvious. None but this apostate nephew of the great Philo, with his intimate knowledge of the soul of the Jewish people and their messianic dreams, could have conceived the idea of fetching from among the crowd of beggars who at all times swarmed round the synagogues the alleged blind man and his unfortunate companion with the crippled hand, and instructing them how they must force their way to the general headquarters, and into the very presence of the general himself, with the story

---

[1] *Aboth de R. Nathan*, c. 4, and parallels.
[2] Tacitus, *Hist.*, ii. 78 ; Suet., *Vesp.*, 5-6.
[3] Philostr., *Vita Apoll.*, v. 27-43.   [4] *Josephus and Vespasian*, p. 43 n. 5.
[5] Cf. *Isaiah* xliv. 28 on Cyrus appointed to be the ' shepherd,' and xlv. 1, the ' Anointed ' of God.
[6] Dio Cassius, exc. Xiphilini, lxvi. 8.   [7] Cf. above, p. 137 notes 6 and 7.

of their God-sent dreams of healing, and not rest until the great
man, the saviour of the world, had performed for them the
messianic miracle.

How far Vespasian himself was privy to these plots, how far the
superstition of the Roman, who afterwards took for his counsellor
the intriguing astrologer Seleucus,[1] was utilized by his courtiers to
drive forward the hesitating and distrustful old soldier, can no
longer be made out. Certain it is that heathen and Jews vied
with each other in staging those *omina imperii* so necessary to him.[2]
Yet certainly, too, a Hellenized Jew who had made his peace with
Rome, like Tiberius Alexander, at a time when his countrymen had
been profoundly stirred and stimulated to a desperate war with
Rome by the interpretation of those ancient messianic prophecies
as in course of fulfilment, had the strongest reason to represent to
them, by another interpretation of *Gen.* xlix. 10, the subjection to
a world-power, which every unprejudiced person must have seen
to be inevitable, as not only acceptable but even as willed and
ordained by God.[3] No less must Mucianus, the governor of Syria,
have been concerned to stem the flood of the Jewish messianic
propaganda, to dock those widespread Sibylline broadsides of
their pointed anti-Roman allusions, and to put them, so far as
possible, at the service of Vespasian and his cause. Tiberius
Alexander and Mucianus must have been the two confidential
counsellors of Vespasian who alone with Titus were present at the
theatrical *début* of the captured 'prophet' Josephus,[4] and so super-
intended the performance of a carefully prepared comedy. We
have referred above [5] to the probability that, even before being
taken prisoner, Josephus had been in treasonable communication
with the Roman intelligence officers, in particular with his 'old
acquaintance and friend,' the military tribune Nicanor.[6] Without
such good connexions at headquarters he would never have succeeded in being brought before the commander-in-chief and obtaining credit for his alleged prophetic mission. His whole later
position at the imperial court was built on two facts : on the one
hand, the impossibility of getting rid of a 'seer' who professed to
be inspired by God himself and whose name appeared at the head
of the list of the *omina imperii*, without robbing the most important
of these premonitions of its credibility ; on the other, a desire to
retain the lasting goodwill of one who knew too much about the
dark beginnings of the new dynasty and the methods employed for

[1] Tacitus, *Hist.*, ii. 78.
[2] Cf. Dio Cassius, lxxiv. 3, the official collection of miracles assembled in
order to prove to his credulous contemporaries the divine mission of the usurper
Septimius Severus as emperor by the grace of the gods.
[3] They could refer to prophecies such as *Jer.* xxvii. 1-15, on the necessity of
submitting to Nebuchadnezzar.
[4] *B.J.*, iii. 399.   [5] Cf. p. 195 ll. 34 ff.   *B.J.*, iii. 346.

creating 'a certain authority and majesty for an unlooked-for and new emperor.' [1]

Nothing could be more significant for the Christology, i.e. the messianic ideas current in the period immediately preceding the genesis of the Synoptic Gospels, than the fact that in A.D. 73 Josephus could make his readers believe that in the year of Vespasian's insurrection the Jews built their messianic hopes, not on any living Jew, but partly on Herod the Great, partly on Jesus the crucified wonder-worker and king without a kingdom, partly on the Roman general and enemy of their people, Flavius Vespasianus.

Two of these three saviours of the world, whom Herodians, Christians, and pro-Romans vied with each other in claiming as indicated by the messianic prophecies of the Old Testament, had then been dead for more than a generation. Those who looked for the resurrection of Herod the Great,[2] or his victorious return from heaven at the head of legions of angels, did not stand alone in that credulous age. It had been predicted of the Emperor Nero, shortly before his fall in 68, that he would exchange the dominion of Rome for that of the Orient—according to some, indeed, for dominion over the kingdom of Jerusalem.[3] After the death of this emperor, whom some had pronounced to be the son of Jupiter and Juno,[4] 'there were not wanting persons who for a long time decorated his tomb with spring and summer flowers and exhibited sometimes his images . . . sometimes his edicts as though he were alive and would shortly return.' [5] When, twenty years after his death, during Suetonius' youth, a man of unknown origin gave himself out to be the risen Nero, he found such powerful support in Parthia that with the help of the enemy he was almost 'restored' to the throne of Rome.

It is no longer difficult to explain the origin of the heathen idea of the redemptive return of a dead ruler. Franz Kampers has sought to show that a return of Alexander the Great from the other world was expected very soon after his untimely death.[6]

That may well be so. The easiest explanation of such ideas is the fact that people simply refuse to believe in the death of a great man, distrust the news of his decease, suspect some plot of his enemies, and look for the king's return from temporary imprisonment, from abroad, etc. In the same manner, according to the third century Alexander Romance, the Egyptians still awaited

---

[1] Tacitus, *Hist.*, iv. 81. One can imagine the ironical smile of the historian when he read to his friends the sentence stating that the eye-witnesses (of the *omina imperii*) stuck to their statements even after the extinction of the Flavian dynasty, ' when they could no longer hope for a reward for their lies,' which fact he reports as a proof of the truth of the *omina* in question.

[2] Cf. above, p. 550 nn. 1-5. [3] Sueton., *Nero*, 40.

[4] *Orac. Sib.*, v. 140. [5] Sueton., *Nero*, 57.

[6] *Vom Werdegang der abendländischen Kaisermystik*, Leipzig, 1924, p. 100 n. 1.

King Nectanebus, who had fled from the Persians into the interior of Ethiopia :

> ' This king who has fled will again come to Egypt, not as an old man, but in the strength of youth, and will subjugate our enemies the Persians.'

It is in Egypt, where the idea prevails that the dying king, like the sun, goes in ' to his horizon,'[1] that the thought of his rising again in rejuvenated form must inevitably have developed. Where the dead monarch was shut into the innermost chamber of an artificial mountain of stone, there it must have been thought possible for the mighty man to emerge once more from this dark cave to save his people in their direst need.

In ancient Babylon the roots of the belief in the return of the king in godlike form can be traced still further. According to a remarkable Sumerian poem, enumerating the names of the kings of Isin,[2] the famous primaeval monarchs are implored to return to earth with plaintive cries of ' How long does he rest ? ', recalling the ' How long, O Master, holy and true, dost thou not judge ? ' of the Apocalypse of John.[3]

The belief in Nero's return may be traced, then, to popular ideas of a journey of the deceased emperors to heaven, ideas which arose out of the rites of apotheosis (the eagle flying heavenward out of the funeral pyre) and were easily associated with the Hellenistic belief in the descent from heaven of the god-sent ruler, the saviour-king destined to deliver the world sunk in misery. To the Romans the idea was familiar by the time of Pompey[4] at the latest, and in 40 B.C. it was popularized by the Sibyllines disseminated by Cleopatra's agents in Rome, Alexandria, and Syria, and by Vergil's ' *iam nova progenies caelo demittitur alto*' in the fourth eclogue.

It was in honour of the youthful Emperor Nero that T. Calpurnius Siculus composed fresh eclogues, lavishing upon him in elaborated form the encomiums of Vergil's fourth eclogue. The gods sent down Nero from heaven ; the gods after a time again

---

[1] Cf. A. Erman, *Die Literatur der Aegypter*, p. 29.
[2] Hilprecht, *Babyl. Exped. of Univ. of Pennsylvania*, vol. xx. pt. i. p. 46.
[3] vi. 10.
[4] Cicero, *De imp. Cn. Pomp.*, xli : ' omnes . . . Cn. Pompeium sicut aliquem non ex hac urbe missum sed de caelo delapsum intuentur.' Cf. *ad Quintum fratrem*, i. 1, 17 : ' Graeci sic te . . . intuebuntur, ut quendam . . . de caelo divinum hominem in provinciam delapsum putent.' According to Suetonius (*August.*, 94), Cicero told Julius Caesar that he had seen in a dream a noble youth let down from heaven by means of a golden chain (*demissum caelo catena aurea*) to the summit of the *mons Capitolinus*, where Jupiter handed him a flail. When he saw Octavian he recognized him as the boy of his dream. This seems to be the story against which Lucretius directed the two sceptical lines (*De natura rerum*, ii. 1153 f.) :
> ' *Haud ut opinor, enim mortalia saecla superne,*
> *Aurea de caelo demisit funis in arva.*'

snatched away this precious gift.[1] No wonder, then, that those of his subjects who had admired him, or for one reason or another felt far less happy under the new dynasty, looked for his return from heaven. That such hopes centred on him in particular is readily intelligible. For, inasmuch as all the earlier Julio-Claudian emperors were succeeded by their own or their adopted descendants, the desire to recover from heaven the Caesar who had just been spirited away could not arise among the adherents of this dynasty. When the dynasty itself had died out with Nero, to make room for another, Caesars only in name, matters were quite different.

To the Jews the idea of a saviour-king descending from heaven had long been familiar ; it most probably is of Mesopotamian origin and of considerable age.[2] When Jerome renders *Is.* xlv. 8, ' rorate coeli desuper et nubes plurant justum,' giving the last word a personal meaning ('And let clouds rain down the just one'), i.e. reading *ṣaddiq* instead of *ṣedeq*, 'righteousness,' he was certainly led to do so by the messianic interpretation put upon the passage by his rabbinic advisers. The standard passage is, of course, *Dan.* vii. 13 *sq.*, on the 'Son of Man' coming down 'with the clouds' of heaven, the last of David's line,[3] with whom Jesus identified himself. The Saviour-King comes down from heaven because immediately after his birth 'winds and storms had torn him from the hands of his mother in the royal palace of Bethlehem in Judah.'[4]

Anyhow, the Targum on the passage in *Chronicles* writes :

' 'Anani, that is, *the king, the Messiah*, who will be revealed.'

Similarly the Midrash *Tanchuma* B Toldoth, § 20 (70b), on the same passage :

' Who is 'Anani ? He is the king, the Messiah,'

and here we find an express reference to the coming of the ' Son of

---

[1] Cp. Horace, *Carm.*, i. 2 (to Augustus), ' *serus in caelum rediens diuque laetus intersis populo Quirini.*'

[2] Cf., for example, in the great chronological prism in the Ashmolean Museum at Oxford, No. 444, Weld-Blundell Coll., ed. S. Langdon, in the Oxford ed. of *Cuneiform Texts*, vol. ii. (1923), p. 4 : ' When the kingdom came down from heaven,' etc.

[3] The last and youngest of the descendants of Zerubabel enumerated in 1 *Chron.* iii. 24—in other words, the last descendant of David known to Scripture— is named 'Anani. The name, an abbreviation of '*Anan-jah* ('Jahveh has answered') has nothing remarkable about it, but in popular etymology was derived from '*anan* (' cloud '), and interpreted as ' one from the clouds,' ' a son of the clouds.' According to the LXX. (the Massoretic text is here corrupt) in 1 *Chron.* iii. 19-24, this 'Anani lived eleven generations after Zerubabel, whose coronation is usually dated in the year 519 B.C. If we reckon roughly thirty years to one generation, 'Anani flourished about 190 B.C., so that he may well have seen the persecutions under Antiochus IV., beginning in 175, and been the liberator-king whom the author of *Daniel* vii. urged in vain to lead the messianic rebellion against the Seleucidic dynasty.

[4] Talm. Jerush., *Berakhoth*, 2. 4 (Strack-Billerbeck, i. 83 ; cf. *Rev.* xii. 5).

Man' with the clouds of heaven in *Dan.* vii. 13. With this should be compared the name of the Messiah, *bar-Nephele* ('son of clouds'), attested in Sanhedrin, 96b, which R. Naḥman (died 320), the authority there quoted, interpreted by popular etymology as 'son of the fallen,' and which originally is *nothing but a Greek translation of 'Anani*.

There is nothing surprising, then, in Josephus' statement that some of the Jews expected their liberation and the establishment of a Jewish world-empire from the 'return' of Herod the Great, come back from heaven, whither, according to a particular eschatology, his glorified soul was supposed to have departed. This did not by any means prevent another party from attaching the same sort of hopes to the Naṣōraean carpenter crucified by Pilate.

According to Josephus and his patrons Agrippa ii. and Tiberius Alexander, all such hopes were vain. They had led only to the destruction of Jerusalem and the final dispersion of the Jews, a terrible chastisement of God to those obdurate of heart who could not understand that the expected *shilu*, the world-ruler, was none other than Vespasian, the new Nebuchadnezzar, rising from Judah to the imperial throne of Rome.

XIX

WEST AND EAST—WORLD-EMPIRE AGAINST WORLD-REVOLUTION

FROM 65 B.C., when Scaurus, the lieutenant of Pompey, interfered in the disputes of the last two Hasmonaean princes, down to the fall of Bar Kokh^eba, in the reign of Hadrian (A.D. 135), we behold that desperate struggle, flaming up again and again, between the *Imperium Romanum* and the last resolute fighters who dared, not only to resist the Caesars and their legions—for that was attempted also by other nations with an equally blind obstinacy, though with better success—but to contend with them over the rule of the whole inhabited world. The historical meaning of this struggle, which exalts it high above the wars fought between the Roman Empire and the 'Barbarians' on the Rhine, on the Danube, on the Euphrates, and on the walls of Britain, both then and centuries later, lies in the fact that in this struggle clashed, perhaps not for the first time in history but certainly for the first time with a clear consciousness of the contrasting principles involved, the world-empire of the masters and the world-revolution of the oppressed.

Deep-rooted and age-old conflicts which in our days again darken the consciousness of men as sinister and threatening shadows, rose then for the first time clearly noticed on the horizon of historical experience. Any reader of Josephus' *Jewish War* in its entirety who compares on the one hand the national Roman sources, and on the other the Sibylline prophecies on coming catastrophes, must notice two things—first, the strong consciousness which the ancient world had of the contrast between West and East as it appeared in this very struggle which Josephus, slightly exaggerating, it is true, yet not without a deeper significance, called 'the greatest war of all times'; and secondly, the glowing, irreconcilable hatred displayed in his work against the 'zealots' and the innovators,[1] i.e. the rebels in general,[2] and against the 'tyrants,' the rebel leaders, to whom he ascribes the responsibility for the civil war, for the clash with Rome and hence the ruin of his people.

The constant danger threatening the ancient city-state from

---

[1] νεωτερίζοντες.   [2] τὸ λῃστρικόν.

the Orient, which of necessity and by an innate law strove for
world dominion and ended by forcing its own imperialistic
doctrine upon an unwilling Occident, was the chief cause of the
awakening to political self-consciousness of the Mediterraneans:
'fore ut valesceret Oriens';[1] 'imperium in Asiam revertetur ac
rursus Oriens dominabitur atque Occidens serviet'[2]—these words
express the persistent fear, the constantly recurring nightmare,
haunting the Graeco-Roman statesmen.

Time and again, from the procemium of Herodotus, that peculiar
oldest known discussion of a question of 'war-guilt,' the historico-
philosophical doctrine of ancient historiography is based upon the
conflict of Asia and Europe, Orient and Occident, a contrast first
entering into the consciousness of the Occident through the clash
of the free Greek city-states with the Persian world-monarchy.
The attack of the Persians is regarded as the revenge of the
Asiatics for the destruction of Troy by Agamemnon, and Alexander's expedition is considered in turn as the revenge for the
Persian invasion of Greece. Equally so all the important steps of
the conquest of the Orient by Rome were accompanied by oracles
giving vent to the hatred of the conquered by a threatening
announcement of a future revenge. From the time of the Syrian
and Aetolian War of 191-190 B.C., Phlegon[3] reports such prophecies, transmitted to him by Antisthenes of Rhodes, a contemporary of Polybius: 'There will come far from Asia, from the
Orient, a king, fording the Hellespont with a huge army, and he
will overthrow thee, O Rome, and impose upon thee the yoke of
slavery.' Nor were replies from the Roman side wanting: recourse was had to the foundation legend of Rome, and the Sibyl
had to legitimize the Roman claims of dominion over the Orient
by virtue of the fabled Roman descent from Aeneas of Troy. In
88 B.C. the conquered Orient rose against the Roman rule, under
the leadership of none other than Mithridates; again the Sibyl
spoke and threatened a frightful revenge: the Italians will have
to do slaves' service to Asia, the mad Rome will be trampled into
dust by its mistress.[4]

It seemed as though this struggle was to find its end in the
decisive battle of Actium. There were definitely buried, not so
much the ambitious plans of Mark Antony as the dreams of world
dominion of the Egyptian Queen Cleopatra over a conquered
world-empire for herself and her son Alexander Helios, with
Alexandria for a centre and a capital, uniting the old Persian
empire with the *orbis Romanus*. Vergil,[5] who in his New Year's

---

[1] Tacitus, *Hist.*, v. 13. [2] Lactantius, *Div. inst.*, vii. 5. 11.
[3] *Mirac.*, ch. iii. p. 69 *sqq.* [4] *Orac. Sibyll.*, iii. 350 *sqq.*
[5] See the short summary of my lecture on the fourth eclogue, *Revue des Études Latines*, iv. (1926), p. 82 *sq.*; and H. Jeanmaire, *Le Messianisme de Virgile*, Paris, 1930.

congratulatory poem addressed to Pollio, the consul of 40 B.C., paraphrases the Sibylline verses broadcast from Alexandria pointing out the imminent birth of the future cosmocrator, now turns to sing of the 'good Emperor Octavianus, the noble scion of the Troic dynasty, uniting Europe and Asia again in one peaceful empire.'

The fear of the Asiatic Greeks, after the unfortunate Parthian campaign of Antony, lest the enemy should profit by the destructive civil wars to send again his cavalry to the very shores of the Mediterranean, may be gauged from the exaggerated honours bestowed by them upon the victor Augustus, the 'saviour of mankind,' [1] the restorer of what had been tottering and had seemed to be doomed.[2]

> 'In peace now rest land and sea; the cities flourish through good laws, harmony, and bliss; everything good comes to bloom and bears fruit; men are full of good hope for the future, and of good courage for the present time.' [1]

But in the very midst of these good hopes of the Greeks there loomed up, like a flash of sheet-lightning from the Eastern danger spot, the Jewish rebellion after the death of Herod the Great (4 B.C.).

As early as the time of Hyrcanus (47 B.C.), before the usurpation of the Hasmonaean throne by the Idumaean Herod, made possible through Roman help, Herod had energetically repressed a powerful rising of the Galilaeans, headed by Ḥizqiah, the father of Judas of Galilee and apparently thought by his followers to have been a re-incarnation of the old King Ḥizqiah, the conqueror of the Philistines, whose return in glory R. Joḥanan b. Zakkai still awaited on his death-bed in A.D. 80.[3] The powerless hatred of the Synhedrion against his executioner Herod attests the popularity of the man, as does the μέγιστον στῖφος of his adherents and the participation of the great Pharisee Shammai (Σαμείας) in this case, which proves, moreover, that the ideology of the movement, generally quite unknown to us, had not yet separated so appreciably from the Pharisaean doctrine as it did in after-times when the son of Ḥizqiah, Judas of Gaulan, had become its leader.

So long as the iron fist of Herod was weighing on the country, prohibiting any free assembly on public streets and squares and effectively preventing any planned revolt by a vast net of spies and public informers,[4] the sultry quiet before the breaking of the storm lay brooding over the country. But no sooner had the news of the

---

[1] Inscription of Halicarnassus, *Anc. Greek Inscriptions in the British Museum*, No. 894.

[2] Inscription of Priene, Dittenberger, *Or. Gr. Inscriptiones*, ii. No. 458.

[3] *Berakh.*, 28b, *Aboth di R. Nathan*, 25 (76); Strack-Billerbeck, i. 31. 2.

[4] *Ant.*, xv. 10. 4: "καὶ ἐν τῇ πόλει καὶ ἐν ταῖς ὁδοιπορίαις ἦσαν οἱ τοὺς συνιόντας εἰς ταὐτὸν ἐπισκοποῦντας." This system of a secret police the Romans doubtless took over from Herod, combining it with their own state and military police (*speculatores*).

last grave disease of the old king penetrated among the people than the first act of violence occurred—the destruction of the golden eagle at the temple gate by the disciples of Judah bar Sepphorai and of Mattathia bar Margaluth. The account of Josephus, derived from Nicolaus of Damascus, i.e. indirectly from the official acts utilized by this court historiographer of the king,[1] is remarkable chiefly because it shows clearly that the zealots for the Law were animated by the peculiarly Pharisaean belief in the immortality and everlasting bliss of any one who sacrificed his life in the service of the Divine Law.[2] This faith in the 'kingdom of God' must of necessity have filled the believers with a contempt of death and an exceptional bravery quite on a par with the analogous idea which was to play such an important part in the spread of Islam. According to all probability, this belief—foreign to the ancient Israel and first found in *Dan.* xii. 2, that is, shortly before the rebellion against Antiochus IV.—was one of the chief causes of the Maccabees' victory as well as of the wonderful bravery of the Jewish fighters for freedom in their long struggle against the oppressors, a bravery admitted by the Romans themselves.[3]

By a last pounce of the dying tiger the rebellion was bloodily repressed, only to flame up anew as soon as Herod, called 'the Great' by the Greeks, had been carried to his tomb on the shoulders of his Thracian, Germanic, and Gallic mercenaries. The people, crowded together in the sanctuary, immediately demand of Archelaus, the presumptive heir to the throne, an amnesty for all political prisoners, relief from the unbearable burden of taxation, and, a thing unheard of in the past, the right to choose for themselves a 'pure and pious' high priest in the place of the Hellenized favourites chosen and deposed by Herod according to his own

---

[1] *B.J.*, i. 33, 1-4 ; *Ant.*, xvii. 6, 2-4.

[2] *Halōsis*, Berendts-Grass, p. 221 *sq.* ; cf. *B.J.*, i. § 650 : '. . . for the souls of those who came to such an end attained immortality and an eternally abiding sense of felicity.' It is worth noting that the parallel account in the *Antiquities* has dropped the metaphysical part of this passage, leaving only the brilliant renown attached to such a deed. The reason for this alteration is clear. The good Josephus had realized in the meantime that his description left no doubt about the identity of these ' rebels ' with his own party, the Pharisees ; hence he took care, in his later work, to make his heroes talk as if they had been Sadducees. As for the tenets of this belief, they need not have been of a transcendental nature, alike in this to the originally Hellenistic notions about the isles of the blessed, the heavenly paradise, or the chthonic Elysian fields, adopted by the Pharisees and fought by Jesus (cf. above, p. 346 ll. 22 ff.). The Zealots may well have hoped for a resurrection in a golden age in their own home country, the 'promised land,' even as the followers of the Maccabees.

[3] Dio Cass., lxvi. 6. 3 : ' However small their number against the superiority of the enemy, they were not conquered until a part of the temple burst into flames. Then they rushed voluntarily upon the swords of the Romans, and killed one another, whilst still others slew themselves with their own hands or jumped into the flames. It appeared to all who saw it, but chiefly to themselves, that it was not death, but victory, salvation, and bliss, to perish thus together with the temple.' On the source of this passage, cf. Wilh. Weber, *Josephus und Vespasian*, Berlin, 1921, p. 24.

good will and pleasure. After the refusal of these demands, quite unacceptable to Archelaus, and the slaughter in the temple, the rebels retired into the mountains and the desert.

They chose for their *meshuaḥ milḥamah*—that is, high priest and army chaplain in one—Joḥanan b. Žekharjah, a priestly Rekhabite descended from a famous sept of wonder-workers and rain-charmers, who on the banks of the Jordan in a flaming speech declared renegades and heathen all those who had submitted to the Idumaean and to Rome and thus disregarded the Deuteronomic royalty law. They have to submit to the proselyte's baptism before being counted again as Jews and sons of Abraham. To the rebels, who were perhaps willing to be content with a high priest after the type of the first Hasmonaeans for their head, he promised the coming of a 'stronger one,' the latchet of whose shoes he declared himself unworthy to loose—the coming, that is, of the *shilu*, the universal monarch who would be obeyed by all peoples after the imminent purification of the world by the three floods of the last days, the flood of water, of wind, and of fire.

On this announcement of a coming saviour and liberator-king, anointed by God, there stepped forth, not one but three messiahs, all feeling chosen for this rôle, namely, Judas of Gaulan, the son of Ḥizqiah; the handsome, tall slave Simon of Peraea; and the gigantic shepherd Athronga; of whom the latter two were certainly people of the lowest strata and unknown parentage, a circumstance which, far from being a shortcoming in the eyes of their adherents, was then considered rather as a sure token of the Saviour, Son of God.[1] An enormous following from Judaea, Galilee, Idumaea, Peraea, and from among the larger part of the Herodian troops, made the situation appear very dangerous for the Romans. The three bands of the messiah kings went to Jerusalem, besieging the Roman garrisons in the hippodrome, Herod's palace, and the fort Antonia. In the fierce struggle the beautiful porticoes of the Herodian temple perished in the flames, the first warning token of worse catastrophes which were to come and ruin that marvellous monument.

No doubt the discord arising between these three ill-fated 'tyrants' made it possible for the legions of Varus, for Gratus and the troops of Archelaus, to stifle the rebellion in a flood of blood, even before the year was gone. The handsome Simon was cut down, Athronga was probably crucified with many other captive rebels.[2] Only Judas of Galilee managed to escape with his most

---

[1] Prayer on a cylinder inscription of *patesi* Gudea (A, ii. 28 *sqq.*; iii. 1 *sqq.*): ' I have no father, thou art my father ; I have no mother, thou art my mother ; in a sanctuary thou hast begotten me.' Cf. *Mark* iii. 33, *Matt.* xii. 48, the words of Jesus, ' Who is my mother ? ', etc.

[2] *B.J.*, ii. 4. 3, mentions this fate only as overtaking his four brothers ; but as there were not more than four of them in all, the text seems to be in disorder.

faithful followers into the mountains. Johanan the high priest, who had administered the *sacramentum militare* to the fighters for freedom, continued to live on as an outlaw, a ' hidden one,' Ḥanan ha Neḥeba, 'with the animals' in the bush of the Jordan valley, appearing only now and then, like a bodiless spectre, a *jinn* of the wilderness, a wild man or a satyr, causing consternation with his ever and anon repeated announcement of the coming terror of the last days, now and then baptizing newly won fighters for the last messianic war.

Ten years later, Judas of Galilee ventured upon another stroke, on the occasion of the census of Quirinius (A.D. 6-7), when the humiliated and oppressed people had once more been brought to realize the full extent of its servitude. By a bold stroke on the royal armouries he obtained weapons for his adherents, who flocked to him from everywhere. He was seconded by the Pharisee Ṣaddōq, so that his own views, except in the matter of the Roman tribute, cannot have been markedly different from those of the *Perushîm*. We do not know when and how he perished. Yet his work was continued by his sons, who were henceforth the leaders of the party refusing under all circumstances to pay the Roman tribute money, the party of the *Barjonîm*, the outlaws, the extremists, who lived in the forests and deserts, referred to as 'robbers' by Josephus and the Romans, the valiant zealots for the Law.

From now on, the fires of the rebellion are slowly smouldering beneath the ashes, until sixty years later the flames were to burst forth in a mighty blaze devouring Jerusalem and the temple itself. But long before that there followed again and again serious and bloody revolts. Until A.D. 19, after the suppression of the Galilaean uprising of A.D. 6-7 by Quirinius and Coponius, there reigned quiet in the exhausted country, the consequence of the severe blood-letting. The gradual pacification, aimed at by the moderate wing of the Pharisees as well as by the Sadducaean priestly nobility, was abruptly broken by the folly of the new governor, Pontius Pilate, who, in contrast to the diplomatic attitude of his predecessors, ordered the cohort to enter the castle of the temple with the portrait medallion of the emperor. By this foolhardy action, the consequences of which he hardly realized,[1] he brought to pass the fulfilment of Daniel's prophecy on the ' abomination of desolation,' filling the masses with a conviction that now the coming of the prophesied Messiah, the Davidide ''Anani' the ' Son of man with the clouds' of heaven,[2] must be imminent.

About this time, then, there appeared a man—if it is possible to

---

[1] Cf. the somewhat similar cause of the Sepoy rebellion in India in the naïve ignorance of General Hewett, who could not understand why the Indian soldiers should refuse to use new Enfield-rifle cartridges merely because they had been greased with suet. [2] See above, p. 560 n. 3.

call this royal beggar, glowing with faith in his God and filled with
Divine inspiration, this poor and crippled wandering workman,
whose words have now for almost two millennia resounded through
the world, by the same miserable name which designates also the
fearful sheep of the human herd, as well as the rapacious beasts
eager for power, against whose obtuseness and hardness of heart
this incomparably precious and fragile vessel of the spirit was to
be shattered.

Descended from the progeny of that ill-fated Zerubabel, sunk
into oblivion and misery for centuries, or at least believing himself
to be thus descended,[1] and brought up with the faith and in the
tradition of such fateful lineage, he grew into the consciousness of
having been chosen for a liberator-king, of having been destined
to unheard-of grandeur and unheard-of suffering, to be the
martyred ' servant of God ' and at the same time the future world-
ruler.　The mysterious healing power emanating from the glance
of his kindly dark eye, from his consoling word, and from the light
touch of his skilful hand, convinced the crowds of the sick and the
afflicted, the possessed and the burdened all over the land, of the
saving nearness of the secret king.　He himself is carried, by the
confidence of the cured and the steadily increasing number of the
believers, far above himself and his every-day consciousness.
Filled with admiration for the great herald of the final days who
had initiated the struggle for the kingdom of God and prophesied
the coming of the Messiah for the nearest future, he had formerly
followed the ' Hidden One,' whose sept was akin to his own, either
by birth or by marriage, in order to fulfil all the law and to be
taken into the new community of the regenerated Israel.　Yet
what he himself announces goes far beyond the strict demands of
the old hermit.　If the latter had required the fulfilment of all
righteousness as the condition of the coming of the Anointed,
Jesus taught the ' better righteousness ' of ' non-resistance,' the
hard and quiet heroism of the weak.　Not to do wrong to any one,
ahïmsā, as again in our own time a great spirit, a mahân âtmâ, a
religious genius, is trying to teach in India ; not to resist even the
oppressors, but to conquer their hardness by a victorious kindness ;
not to judge a brother nor to seek justice against him ; not to
strive for gain, but to help every one by giving kindness ; not to
rule over any one, but to serve all, nay, even to love one's enemies.

Along with this superhuman demand of disinterested pacifism
he promises the poor, the oppressed, and the heavy-laden an easier
yoke, a new law of God, a new constitution, a redemption from
the pressure of the hierocratic state become unbearable, redemption also from the pressure of the superimposed hostile world-
empire and of the incarnate arch-enemy of God ruling over it until

---

[1] Cf. above, pp. 321 ff.

the end of this aeon. The people who listened to this preaching
were attracted not so much by the narrow path he pointed out to
them, as by the alluring hope of a golden age in which the first
would be last and the last would be first, when those who
hunger and thirst would be fed, whilst those who are satiated now
would then be hungry; and still more by the dark rumour that
the despised sinners would partake of that kingdom before the
righteous. Here and there one of these wild fellows followed him :
thus Simon the *Barjona*, the outlaw, whom he called Kephas and
Petrus ; Simon and Judas, the Zealots, the Fanatics, former companions of the sons of Judah of Galilee ; further, two or three
adherents of the Baptist.

Having collected a small band, he started on the laying down
of a constitution (οἰκονομία) of his kingdom : twelve are to go
out to call the twelve tribes of Israel; seventy-two ambassadors are
to go to the seventy-two nations of the Gentiles to demand their
submission to the kingdom of God, after the manner of the
Persian great king asking for earth and water. The notion of
pacifying the world by a mere message and an announcement of
peace and the goodwill of the only true God had long before Jesus
driven the Pharisaic missionaries [1] over land and sea, to convert
all peoples ; it is taught here, with a childlike trust in God which
has never again been attained, in these speeches addressed to the
royal messengers.

After the return of those 'of little faith,' who only in the nearness of the mysterious powers of their Master were capable of
sustained enthusiasm, there followed the first falling away of this
pious confidence in the kindness of an all-loving Father in heaven.

The terrible God of the fathers, who according to the teaching
of the prophets rejects the animal offerings of the priestly code,
demands an infinitely harder sacrifice : nothing will satisfy Him
but the decisive deed—to renounce everything dear to man :
fathers, mothers, children, if they refuse to follow the call, to give
up all possessions, houses, fields, the beloved land of promise
itself, to assume the mark of the cross distinguishing the homeless, wandering tribes, to follow after the liberator into the desert,
the land of freedom, to emigrate from the inhabited world which
is subject to the Romans. As the fathers had left Egypt, the house
of bondage, to go into the desert, following the call of God from
Horeb under their leader, so the select are again to follow their
prophetic guide on a new exodus. That is no revolt, but merely a
'breaking out,' an escape from the unbearable oppression, which
seems to him the true path of salvation. After the example of the
adherents of the Maccabee Mattathia, of the Baptist, and of
Judah of Galilee, he will make the solemn announcement to Israel

[1] They are mentioned in *Matt.* xxiii. 15.

on the great pilgrims' assembly at Jerusalem on the Passover, and thence lead his elect, his new *qehillah*, his ἐκκλησία of the new and true Israel, into the desert.

The Zealots and *Barjonîm* among his followers are not afraid of this enterprise ; but they know better than their *śar shalōm*, their ' prince of peace ' who intends to enter Jerusalem mounted on an ass, that even this road into the desert must lead through the prophesied war of the last days. ' Armed for war ' like their fathers in Egypt they expect to leave Palestine. When their leader, with a heavy heart, has realized this stern necessity and not only permits but even commands them to buy swords, each one for himself, they have anticipated him, and each pulls two daggers, the weapons of the *sicarii*, from his bosom.

From the heights of Mt. Hermon, in the north of Galilee, where Simon *Barjona* in wise forethought would have pitched the camp and would have liked to call the elect for an exodus into the desert, the expedition marches to Jerusalem instead, for the last decisive manifestation, headed by their leader, who for some time past has been expecting captivity, suffering, and death, but who is still secretly hoping for a miracle of God, a shortening of the pre-destined time and a passing of the cup. To the most faithful of his inner circle he confides that he is going to his death, as the ' servant of Jahweh,' to take upon himself the guilt of his people, according to the words of the prophet. Not other peoples are to be the scapegoat for Israel's sins ; [1] Israel's own king and chosen high priest must fall as a piacular sacrifice to force from heaven at last the longed-for redemption.

Thanks to the joining of other pilgrims marching to Jerusalem, and of scattered adherents here and there in the country, the little band grows to a size of several hundred men, encamps in front of the city, on the Mount of Olives, among the tents of the other pilgrims, still increasing through the reputation of the wonder-worker which mysteriously clings to Jesus. About a thousand men enter the city, preceding or following the prophet, who rides into the city sitting on his *Ṣlebî's* donkey, and proclaim him Davidic king of Israel. A passionate cry of the multitude, ' *Osanna*,' ' Deliver us,' accompanies the solemn entry. The prophet is carried forward by the ever-increasing pressure of the crowd into the temple, sud-denly occupied by surprise by men carrying hidden arms. The Levitic guard offers no resistance—nay, the priestly youth, the ' buds ' on the staff of Aaron, which, though dry, blooms once again before its definite end, greet the son of David with cries of joy. The temple, with its castle the Antonia, then without a Roman garrison, is in the hands of the Galilaeans, whilst the *Bar-jonîm* of Jerusalem have at the same time seized the tower stand-

---

[1] This had been the nationalist illusion of *Deutero-Isaiah* xliii. 3 *sq.*

ing above the *Shiloaḥ*, the aqueduct through which, according to an old saga, David himself had once entered the old fortress of the Jebusites.

The Roman cohort in the castle of Herod is far too weak to win back these two strong points, the keys of the fortifications in the extreme north and the extreme south. The movement might even then, like the one of a later day started by the *segan* 'Ele'azar b. Ḥananiah (A.D. 66), have carried with it the leading families of the priestly nobility, had not the attack on the temple banks and the expulsion of the dealers in sacrificial animals, as well as the decisive utterances of the newly proclaimed king against the temple itself, shown to the high priests with unmistakable clearness what the present masters would have to expect in the event of the people remaining the victors.

Thus the messengers sent by the military tribunes of Herod's castle vied with those of the high priest in warning the governor in far-off Caesarea of what had taken place, and in clamouring for the speedy dispatch of his legion. Pilate approached in forced marches, and on the preparation day of the Passover the rebellion was well repressed, the temple reconquered in the same manner in which it had been taken—that is, by a band of apparently peaceful pilgrims. The altar and precincts were flooded with the blood of the Galilaeans cut down in vast numbers; the tower of Shiloaḥ, laid low by the Roman machines, was covering the corpses of eighteen of the rebellious Jerusalemites. In the night, a few hours after the sounds of the *Hallel* announcing the end of the Passover meal had vanished, in the stillness a Roman cohort, increased by a guard of loyalists hurriedly armed by the high priests with clubs and daggers, surrounded the Mount of Olives. After a weak attempt at resistance, given up almost immediately by the express command of Jesus, the leader of the revolt, in Roman eyes only the one-day king of belated and bloody *Saturnalia*, was captured, promptly condemned that same night according to martial law, and crucified along with two other 'robbers,' leaders of the revolt.

Whoever among his adherents were not dead or captured made off in all directions; the shepherd was beaten, the herd dispersed. Among the women and the few faithful who had remained near to find out, at the dusk of day or at the early dawn, what had become of the mortal coil of their erstwhile king,[1] none of course discovered

---

[1] The conjecture of Volkmar (*Die Religion Jesu*, Zürich, 1857, pp. 71 *sq.*, 257-9; *Marcus und die Synopse*, 1876, p. 603) and of A. Loisy (*Jésus et la tradition évangélique*, Paris, 1910, p. 107; *Les évangiles synoptiques*, ii., Paris, 1908, p. 700 *sq.*), to the effect that the corpse of the prophet was simply thrown out, has been most brilliantly confirmed by the Ephesian inscription with the decree of the Archbishop Hypatios (*ca.* 536). Cf. R. Heberdey, *Jahreshefte d. österr. arch. Inst.*, viii., 1905, Beibl. Sp., 70 *sq.*; H. Grégoire, *Rec. des inscr. gr. chrét. d'Asie Mineure*, Paris, 1922, p. 35 *sq.*, No. 108; J. N. Bakhuizen, *De oudchristelijke monumenten van Ephesus*, The Hague, 1923, pp. 129-47; *Z.N.T.W.*, xxvi. (1927), p. 213.

the corpse. What they did see, the one here, the other there, was—
at least according to those to whom ' their words seemed as idle
tales ' and who ' believed them not ' [1]—the twin-brother of their
Master, resembling him in every particular ; and that fleeting
glance, together with a few stray words caught in passing and
doubly significant in that emotion in which they found themselves, was the starting-point of the rumour which spread like
wildfire to the effect that he who had been anointed at Bethaniah
was really and truly, according to his own predictions, risen from
the dead. To seek him who had promised to precede the elect to
Galilee, this little band of people, half-consoled, half-hoping, half-
doubting, returned to their northern homes, never quite to find
again their old life.

Others who, according to the Master's warning, were still
holding themselves in readiness, in Jerusalem, to start on the
exodus under his leadership, congregated around Peter, after
his flight around the Ṣaddiq Ja'aqob. In unceasing prayer
they waited for the second coming, confirmed in that mountain-
moving faith which Jesus himself had commanded both by his
example and his teaching, through strange visions and ecstatic
experiences which they interpreted as the miraculous pouring out
of the Spirit upon all sons and daughters of Israel, the fulfilment
of what the prophets had foretold for the day when the end of this
world would dawn. Phenomena unheard of in the lifetime of
Jesus, who was not at all of an ecstatic nature—such as the miracle
of Whitsuntide, on the anniversary of the Sinaitic legislation—were
explained as meaning the immediate coming of the universal kingdom of God. The words of the holy language, then pronounced
by the believers with ' other tongues,' sounded to the Jewish
pilgrims from all over the East, and attracted by the reputation of
the messianist community, like the familiar sounds of their own
language. The world, split into innumerable linguistic families
since the time of the fateful Tower of Babylon, seemed to be united
once more for at least one happy moment ; the golden age of
universal understanding, of universal brotherhood, seemed to have
come back. What the world-conqueror Sargon had boasted of—
to wit, of having unified the languages of the world—the resuscitated
Jesus, now enthroned with his Father in heaven, had done with
the fiery tongues of the word of God, which could be understood by
all men of goodwill. The royal messengers were to speak in those
tongues. If a short while ago the priests had complained of the
disappearance of prophecy in Israel,[2] the Lord, it appeared, had
now awakened a whole community of prophets. How, after
such an experience, could those filled with enthusiasm as with
new wine doubt any longer that the vanished Messiah had filled

---

[1] *Luke* xxiv. 11. See above, pp. 450 f.   [2] Above, p. 137 n. 13.

them with his own powers, strengthening them mysteriously for further waiting until the day should break for his own second coming in glory ?

The little synagogue witness of the Whitsuntide miracle, according to *Acts* i. 15 just one hundred and twenty members, can at first have been no more than a small circle, a conventicle of faithful (*ḥasidîm*), grouping themselves around Peter. They made an attempt at economic communism, the few blessed with possessions gladly submitting to the command of their dead king to renounce fields, houses, and all possessions, in the expectation, of course, of the coming exodus postponed for a time but none the less certain, and of the establishment of the kingdom of God, when a ten- and hundred-fold compensation was sure to be granted.

As in all such attempts known to history, difficulties naturally were not slow in arising ; a few 'of little faith' simply set aside some small amount as a reserve for themselves in the event of the experiment being doomed to failure. A married couple, Ḥananjah and Saphira, paid for such an attempt with their lives, thanks to the grim resolution of the *Barjona* Shime'on, who was inexorable in such matters. And a great fear befell the community and all those who heard of it,[1] a phrase which shows quite unmistakably that at the time when this edifying story was put down on paper the system was still in vogue and doubtful members were frightened by the death penalty, supposed to be executed magically, on those who did not give up all their possessions to the community.

This communistic principle in the original Christian congregation of Jerusalem, a fact on which a good deal of nonsense has been written, has a double root.

In the first place, the tribal constitution of the Rekhabite tradesmen, i.e. the sept of Jesus with the Ṣaddiq Ja'aqob for their head, was based upon family communism, comparable to the Old Russian *artel*. They had, of course, no reason to exchange this system for another one. According to Josephus' *Halōsis*,[2] it is certain that the adherents of Jesus at the time of the Emperor Claudius were still carrying on their various trades, and there is no reason whatever to suppose that this was different in the years immediately following the crucifixion. The *Acts of the Apostles* emphasize the miraculous cures they worked beside their manual trades no less than the Christian interpolations in the text of the *Halōsis*.

That the announcement of the 'good message' itself was utilized as a means of revenue, with which Paul reproaches certain Christians of a later generation,[3] need not be doubted. The de-

---

[1] *Acts* v. 11.   [2] Cf. above, p. 529 n. 6 ; p. 538 n. 1.
[3] " οἱ πολλοὶ καπηλεύοντες τὸν λὸγον τοῦ θεοῦ," 'the many peddlers of the word of God,' the " χριστέμποροι " or 'Christ-salesmen' of the Church fathers.   2 *Cor*. ii. 17.

scription given by Celsus [1] of those wandering prophets announcing to the people of Syria the imminent world catastrophe and holding themselves up as the future judges to appear at the head of the hosts of heaven, to protect their friends but to pour everlasting fire on the towns and villages of the others, may fit as well the first half of the first century. It was hardly the exalted doctrine and the stern demands of a better righteousness of the Master which so rapidly increased the numbers of the messianists.

Whatever was earned through labour, healing, consoling, teaching, and threatening was to be put, according to the Rekhabite custom, in a communal chest, to be redistributed 'to all according to the wants of each.' [2] Rich people who joined the community were supposed, at least in principle, to follow the command of the crucified king and sell all, to renounce all possessions, house, field, etc. They were paid with the tempting promise that on the coming of the kingdom they would obtain hundredfold compensation, so that many a one who had given a small field would then see himself the happy owner of a princely estate. Add to this that in that time of bliss the curse would have disappeared from the earth, and man would have no longer to cultivate the land in the sweat of his brow, but that the earth would yield spontaneously cornstalks and vines reaching to the clouds.[3] In such a genuine *pays de Cucagne* even a Levite like Joseph Barnabas of Cyprus, not used to agriculture, might well desire a considerable estate instead of his small field, without thereby putting upon himself an undue burden of hard work.

In spite of such fine hopes, however, it is to be feared that this Jewish-Christian community cannot have had much approval and many new converts from people rich either in land or in money. The liberal donators actually named were probably the only ones of whom any knowledge was preserved. Even the contributions of the brothers, who naturally kept what each needed for his own maintenance, can hardly have sufficed to provide for the old people and the widows and orphans. The 'saints' of Jerusalem remained poor down to the time of Paul, and the latter had to collect for them among the Jews in the Diaspora, nay, even among the heathen.

Aside from the Rekhabite habits of the family of Jesus, this communism of property has still another powerful root—that is to say, the archaic family communism of tribal tradesmen, increased by new converts from the outside,[4] was strengthened by the communism, the *milḥamah* or 'com-pany' or bread community,[5] of

---

[1] Origen, *C. Cels.*, vii. 9.   [2] *Acts* iv. 35.
[3] Papias, *Ap. Iren.*, v. 33. 3, p. 417 ; cf. Euseb., *Hist eccl.*, iii. 39. 1, p. 286.
[4] On these outsiders among the Rekhabites, cf. above, pp. 323 ff.
[5] Cf. my study in *Z.N.T.W.*, 1925, p. 286.

the *militia Christi*, who even in the enforced truce between the first and the second coming of their leader honestly shared whatever they had. The document discovered by Dr. Schechter among the treasures of the Geniza of Cairo,[1] and bearing on the messianist community of Damascus, testifies to the existence of another such militia of fighting journeymen, organized for mutual support ever since the war of Varus.[2] It consisted of ' just ' disciples of John the Baptist, revering their master as the legislator of the last days, the ' teacher of justice,' of people who actually had carried out an exodus such as had been preached by Jesus, and were now regarding their settlements in a foreign country as the ' camps ' of Israel in the desert. Such a train of thought is quite natural with men who had deliberately left their own tribal group, forming an army of messianist fighters in expectation of the second coming. We have seen how John the Baptist preached such mutual help between brethren as an absolute, a sacred duty. The communal meals of the brothers and the communistic system of the members is derived from the very natural circumstances of the armed expedition from Galilee to Jerusalem, interrupted by the defeat but by no means ended. The care for widows and orphans [3] means naturally the care for the dependants of those who had paid with their lives for the bold enterprises in Jerusalem and the temple—in other words, the fallen soldiers of the holy war. To conclude, the tribal communism of the Rekhabites naturally and easily develops into the army communism of the *militia Christi*.

More than in the time of Jesus, his adherents, now leaderless, formed a secret association of the $nos^e rîm$ (Ναζωραῖοι), of the οἰκόνομοι τῶν μυστηρίων, bound to keep as strictly as possible the secret of the coming things from the uninitiated. For, as the Gospel of Peter attests, they are still sought after, suspected as they are of ' wishing to burn the temple,' doomed by the inexorable prophecy of Jesus himself.

How careful they had to be is shown by the arrest of Peter and John [4] and of their associates,[5] by the stoning of Stephen, no doubt following quite closely upon the crucifixion, because he had engaged in a debate with two opponents in two of the Hellenistic synagogues, and had on that occasion repeated with too great a frankness Jesus' words against the temple. Following upon this

---

[1] *Documents of Jewish Sectaries*, i.; *Fragments of a Zadokite Work*, Cambridge, 1910.

[2] On its date and Baptist character, see App. XVIII. p. 616, and my paper in the *Transactions of the Fifth International Congress for the History of Religion in Lund* (1929), pp. 327 ff.

[3] *Acts* vi. 2.   [4] *Acts* iv. 3-21.

[5] *Ibid.*, v. 17-42 ; it may be historically true that for some time the authorities were content with warnings, and that one group of moderate Pharisees was opposed to any unnecessary persecution.

execution of the first victim (who in reality was far from being the 'first martyr' of the doctrine of Jesus), the *Acts* relate a general persecution of the messianists, compelling a part of them to seek refuge in Samaritan territory.[1]

First Philip, then Peter and John, find there willing listeners for their glad tidings, a statement thoroughly credible, since a closer examination of the Samaritan tradition has actually shown the Samaritans to have been expecting the second coming of the Old Testamental Joshuah, pronounced Ἰησοῦς by the apostles of the Hellenized Samaritans Philip and Andrew, according to the custom of the LXX. It is there that we first encounter a man who had been for some time trying to gain that region for his own gnostic-Hellenistic doctrines, to wit, Simon, a native of the village of Gitta, near Samaria,[2] but having received a Greek education at Alexandria,[3] the son of a Samaritan emigrant with the Roman *praenomen* Antonius, perhaps a freedman of the triumvir, and probably with the Greek name *Sōtadēs*. The *Acts* admit that he had received from Philip baptism, the *sacramentum militare* of John, which the disciples of Jesus henceforth administered 'in the name of Jesus' as the true anointed king; he was therefore originally a genuine member of the primitive community of messianists.

The same individual appears to have been, in the last year of Pilate's term of office (A.D. 35), the cause of a catastrophe in the northern part of the country, quite comparable to that which in A.D. 21 had taken place in Jerusalem. Under that governor's oppressive rule and that of the no less tyrannical Herod Antipas, feeling must for some time have run high indeed. Forty years after his first appearance, the now aged hermit John the Baptist had again emerged from his retreat in the wilderness of the Jordan valley, appeared here and there in the country, everywhere denouncing the unlawful marriage of Antipas and no doubt repeating his old call to freedom, his old dark threats of a coming flood of judgment, his preaching of repentance and the imminent coming of the liberator-king. The 'old fox' Herod caught him, as Archelaus had done before, but this time he had him taken to one of his strongholds on the southern frontier and there beheaded.

This in itself did not appease the brewing storm. The Samaritan, probably no other than Simon 'the magician,'[4] whom Philip had baptized, was determined to convince the people, by a

---

[1] *Acts* viii. 1b.

[2] *Acts* viii. 9, 11 ; cf. Clem., *Hom.*, ii. 22.

[3] He probably came under Philo's direct influence ; cf. Samaritan Chronicles, Adler and Abu'l Fath, p. 157 ; also Montgomery, *The Samaritans*, Philadelphia, 1912, p. 266 n. 39.

[4] The only alternative would be to identify this 'messiah' with Simon's rival and contemporary Dositheos.

miracle, of no less a fact than that he himself was the expected
Joshua or Jesus, the *ta'eb*.[1] His intention was to lead his armed
followers in solemn procession up Mt. Gerizim, and there, in a
hollow on the top, probably the rock-cave still visible to-day, to
exhibit the old tabernacle and its sacred vessels which Joshua was
reputed to have concealed there. According to Josephus and the
Christian account, the man was an impostor 'who did not mind a
lie.' If that is true, he may be supposed, like so many before and
after him, to have laid his plans for a solemn discovery of relics
by previously secreting them on the spot. According to Jewish
tradition, this pretended 'Jesus' the 'son of Sōtadēs' (*ben Stada*),
who had learned magic in Egypt, was 'a fool' who blindly relied on
his supposed superhuman powers. Perhaps he was one of those
tragic figures whose childlike faith made them imagine that by
fasting and prayer they can extort a miracle from God, one of those
seers whose ecstatic visions drove them step by step to the most
desperate actions. There are reasons for believing that he is
identical, too, with the Egyptian 'pseudo-prophet' who later on,
under Felix, wished to overthrow the walls of Jerusalem by the blast
of his Jericho trumpets, a piece of magic which certainly could not
have been engineered by mining operations on a large scale from
the Mount of Olives without attracting the attention of the Roman
garrison. If this identification be correct, he may in both cases
either have had recourse to the mysterious theurgic magic of
Egypt to obtain the hoped-for miracle, or else have trusted in
mountain-moving faith to the old Rock of Israel. At all events,
Pilate was less concerned with the ideology of the leader than with
the political aspect of the matter, the threatening temper of the
masses. Accordingly, in his usual somewhat rude but quite
effective method, he made a rapid attack with his cavalry,
massacring the mob assembled in the village of Tirathana.

The further development of affairs shows that the attempt of
the primitive community at Jerusalem to win the Samaritans over
for the messianic kingdom of Jesus failed through the intervention
of Simon, in spite of his defeat. What lived on in Samaria was
Simonian and Dosithean Gnosis, i.e. Hellenistic mystery-teaching,
grafted on to a Hemerobaptism allied to the doctrines of John the
Baptist and on the whole a fairly close parallel development to
Mandaism as it grew up in Transjordania and later in Mesopotamia.
A number of Simon's doctrines, through the medium of the Fourth
Gospel, derived from the Gospel of the Alexandrian gnostic
Kerinthos,[2] had a far-reaching influence on the development of

---

[1] On this Simon and the 'paraclete' of the Fourth Gospel, cf. now also my
papers, 'The Paraclete Problem : The True Origins of the Fourth Gospel,' and
'The Paraclete Claimant, Simon Magus,' in *The Quest*, January and April 1930.

[2] Cf. my papers in *The Quest*, January, April, and July 1930.

2 O

the absolutely un-Jewish Trinitarian theology in the Christian Church of the second century.

The bloody defeat of the rising of the year 36 eliminated those who had clung most tenaciously to the political hope of an earthly and tangible deliverance from the fetters of the oppressive world-dominion of the Caesars. There remained the Quietists, who, despairing of all forcible political methods and of the strength of their people, submitted outwardly to ' the rulers of this world,' but all the more passionately strove, by Graeco-Egyptian gnosis and theurgy, for the liberation of the spiritual *ego* from the bonds of the body and the constraint of Matter and Necessity in this dark, hopeless, and daemonic world. Instead of the peaceful attitude of the free peasant under his earthly vine and fig-tree, instead of the free Bedouin's hardy life in the desert, the world-weary pilgrims for eternity now sought admission to the heavenly realms of light through magic spells designed to incline toward them the wicked gatekeepers of a fairy-tale paradise. This stage reached, the so-called Samaritans henceforth disappear from the history of political messianism.

Shortly after the Samaritan rising had been nipped in the bud, and a few months before his death in A.D. 37, the Emperor Tiberius had imprisoned Herod Agrippa I., then aged forty-seven and living as a parasite at the Roman court, a boon companion of Caligula. Agrippa had been guilty of a gross breach of decorum by confessing to Caligula, in the presence of a slave, how eagerly he awaited the suspicious old tyrant's death. The sufferings he endured in the squalor of a Roman prison, among the poorest of the poor, appear to have been romantically exaggerated and interpreted by the partisans of the Herodian family in Palestine and in the Diaspora, who still hoped for a messiah of the house of Herod, as the predicted woes of the innocent, suffering servant of God. When Agrippa's friend Caligula ascended the throne and not only set him free but presented him with a golden chain of equal weight with the fetters he had worn in prison, and finally made him king of the Jews, the old *bon-vivant*, suddenly grown pious through misfortune, could not resist the temptation of showing himself in his new glory to the Jews of the second greatest city of the empire, and having himself proclaimed king by them. This childish triumphal journey led to serious trouble for the Alexandrian Jews ; for in consequence of the translation of the Scriptures into Greek the Hellenic population of that city was all too familiar with the Jewish dreams of world-dominion, and jealously watched over the privileges of the Greeks, who naturally claimed the second place in the empire. A poor fool and megalomaniac was in mockery dressed up as a king and hailed as ' our Lord ' (*Maran*). More momentous to the Jews was the complaint of the Greeks before the governor of Egypt requesting that the Jews, like all other subjects of the empire, should be compelled to recognize Caesar as Lord of the world in a religious sense by setting up his statues in their synagogues, a demand which could count upon full approval on the part of the mad emperor. The bloody conflicts in Alexandria found their repercussion in Syria, where the Hellenistic party, in defiance of the Jews, erected altars to the emperor.

As meet punishment for the destruction of such an altar at Jamnia, Gaius promptly required the setting up of his statue in the temple at Jerusalem. Again, as in the year 19, the fulfilment of the famous prophecy of Daniel threatened to lead to a messianic rising. While Petronius, besieged by petitions from the Jewish masses, from Agrippa and his family, and menaced, moreover, by a Jewish agrarian strike, did all he could to defer the execution of the imperial order or to bring about its repeal, the followers of Jesus, in particular the priest 'Ele'azar b. Dinai, who was somehow connected with Simon *Barjona*, regarded the threatened desecration of the temple as an occasion for renewing the call for a general exodus into the desert and the mountains of Judah. Notwithstanding the efforts of the Pharisees to oppose this apocalyptic preaching and to prevent a panic, 'Ele'azar still found certain followers with whom to withdraw into the hills, and for the next twenty years he harassed the country, until, probably in 58, he was at last taken prisoner by Felix and sent to Rome for trial.

The timely death of Caligula (24th January 41) prevented an open rebellion of the Jews at that time, inevitable as it would have been had the statue of the imperial fool been placed in the sanctuary. In Alexandria, too, order was at once restored on the accession of Claudius. The ringleaders of the Greeks, Isidorus and Lampon, were sentenced to death ; on the other hand, the Jews of the city were strictly forbidden to entertain Jewish immigrants from Syria and Upper Egypt if they did not wish to be treated as abettors of 'a pest which threatens the whole world,' an expression which doubtless refers to the messianic movement. The immigrants whom Claudius ordered at all costs to be kept out of Alexandria are, of course, emissaries of the bands of 'Ele'azar waiting in the mountains and in the desert for the expected return of Jesus. It is not at all improbable that immediately following the threats of Caligula a messianic revolt had been fostered in Egypt outside Alexandria by such agitators and refugees, though it is also possible that Claudius merely wished to prevent an influx of unruly Eastern Jews into the country by the two usual overland and oversea routes.

In Palestine, Agrippa i., who had mended his ways and was now settling down as a worthy and dignified monarch, deliberately conciliated the Pharisees, while at the same time he sought to provide for all contingencies by strengthening the fortifications of Jerusalem and by calling a congress of Oriental princes, which was rudely dispersed by the Romans. The outburst of the messianic movement culminating in the exodus of 'Ele'azar had shown the desirability of a sharper attack on the Christians. The two sons of Zebedee, of whom one, according to the evidence of Christian tradition itself,[1] had donned the diadem of the High Priest and thus gone over to the insurgents, fell into the hands of the king's troops and were promptly beheaded ; Peter, who had been arrested, escaped from prison, released, as the Christians said, by an ' angel.' Agrippa, who took a more prosaic view of the matter, attributed the miracle to the untrustworthiness of his soldiers, influenced no doubt by the messianic predictions of the prisoner, and he did not shrink from having the whole guard executed. In the year 44 this ' great and pious king, friend of Caesar and friend of the Romans,' died, and, since the counsellors of Claudius had certain misgivings about his young son, Agrippa II., the government of the country was entrusted to the Hellenized Alexandrian Jew, Tiberius Alexander, along with Cuspius Fadus, who, like Agrippa I., kept on good terms with the Pharisees, seeking to suppress, by arrests and deportations, the messianic agitation of the Naṣōraeans, which still went on, particularly among the poor wandering artisans. The custody of the High Priest's vestments, clearly in consequence of the crowning of John, son of Zebedee, was provisionally again taken over by the Romans. The result of all these measures was but slight, since the persecution of the loyal followers of Jesus cleared the way for other messianic pretenders, particularly as just at that time, owing to a drought which recalled to the Jewish mind the days of Elijah, a series of bad harvests drove the poorer classes to desperation. As formerly in Samaria a new Joshua or ' Jesus ' had promised to erect the tabernacle on Mt. Gerizim, so now there appeared a disciple or ' acquaintance ' of Paul, a certain Theudas,[2] ready to lead his followers dryshod across the Jordan into the desert, in order to prove himself thus a Joshua *redivivus*, a second 'Jesus.' The enterprise was discovered, the crowd caught by the cavalry of Cuspius Fadus in the act of crossing the stream and partly massacred, partly captured, whilst the ill-fated prophet was hewn in pieces.

About the same time two other leaders of revolt, Jacob and Simon, sons of Judas of Galilee, fell into the hands of the Roman troops ; ' Sir ' Tiberius Alexander had them mercilessly crucified.

Under the next governor, Cumanus, the insecurity of the country and the general hostility against the army of occupation had reached such a point that almost beneath the very gates of Jerusalem a certain Stephen, one of the emperor's slaves, i.e. a

[1] Cf. above, p. 542 n. 5.   [2] See above, p. 553 n. 3.

clerk travelling on official business, was set upon and robbed of his baggage ; the act led to sharp Roman reprisals. Under the eyes of the governor, who according to one account of Josephus [1] because he had been bribed, according to another [2] because he had more important business on his hands, had failed to exact due punishment for the murder in a Samaritan village of one of a party of Galilaean Jews on their way to a feast at Jerusalem, the above-mentioned 'Ele'azar with his band and a multitude of Galilaeans and Jews of Jerusalem set out to make formal war upon the Samaritans. This naturally brought up Cumanus and his troops to the latter's aid. Ummidius Quadratus, the governor of Syria, receiving appeals from both Jews and Samaritans, repaired to Samaria, had those caught with weapons in their hands executed, and sent off a number of Jewish and Samaritan notables to Rome for trial by the emperor, along with the governor Cumanus, who was subsequently deprived of his office.

While the greatest disorder thus prevailed in Palestine, in Rome, too, there arose in the ninth year of Claudius another messiah, he too to be identified, with a certain degree of probability, with Simon Magus, who had escaped at the suppression of the Samaritan revolt, and who, in spite of that experience, still gave himself out to be Joshua (or Jesus) *redivivus*. His claims, according to the legend handed down to us by Hegesippus,[3] were contested by the followers of Jesus, especially by Peter, who had fled from Palestine in the year 42.[4] The brawls, whether between the followers of Jesus and those of Simon, or between the Jewish messianists and their opponents, were, it appears, responsible for Claudius' edict expelling the Jewish community once more from the capital.

Palestine, at the request of the high priest Jonathan, whom Quadratus had sent to Rome, received for governor the emperor's freedman, Felix, who was married to Drusilla, the sister of Agrippa II. He succeeded in capturing 'Ele'azar b. Dinai, whom he sent to Rome for trial ; 'countless' numbers of his followers were crucified. But their extermination brought the tormented country no rest : the remaining insurgents mingled with the crowds, seeking by repeated assassinations to intimidate the loyalists. One of their victims was the high priest Jonathan. This monstrous deed appears to have been regarded as another fulfilment of the prophecy of Daniel.[5] Once more some messianist

---

[1] *Ant.*, xx. 119.   [2] *B.J.*, ii. 233.

[3] Cf. above, p. 75 ll. 39 ff.

[4] The presence of Peter in Rome in the ninth year of Claudius would not be incredible ; but the assertion of ' Egesippus ' (iii. 2, p. 183, Ussani) that Paul was also there is chronologically impossible. Paul plays, indeed, no vital part in this section, and the name is presumably interpolated.

[5] ix. 26.

leaders, opposed to violent methods and the murders perpetrated by the *sicarii*, summoned the people to an exodus into the wilderness, in order there to await the God-sent 'tokens of freedom.' That these preachers of a new exodus, described by Josephus, were of the so-called Naṣōraeans and, without any sharp distinction, included people who believed in the promises of the Baptist, holding Jesus to be the Messiah shortly to reappear and to lead them to victory, cannot be doubted. The departing bands were surrounded by the troops of Felix, cavalry and infantry, and dispersed with great loss.

The noteworthy admission of Josephus that the leaders of these bands, whom he yet holds no less responsible for the downfall of the Jewish state than the *sicarii* themselves, had 'purer hands' than the others, is best explained by the fact that he himself, according to his own confession, had been for three years, though to be sure in the time of his youthful innocence, a Zealot [1] under the leadership of a 'Baptist' named Bannus. If one reflects that his autobiography was designed to meet the charges openly brought against him by Justus of Tiberias, and if one recalls the part he had taken in Galilee in inciting to rebellion against Rome, one is tempted to conjecture that as a young man he had also participated in this very exodus into the wilderness, and that the 'Bannus' in question was no mere contemplative hermit,[2] an entirely un-Jewish type at all events, but just one of those believers, described by the historian, who had seen the error of his ways, as 'jugglers' ($\gamma\acute{o}\eta\tau\epsilon\varsigma$) and 'deceivers' ($\pi\lambda\hat{a}\nu o\iota$), who under Felix had led the people into the wilderness, there to await under strict penance and mortifications the coming of the Messiah, one of those preachers of apocalypse among whom Tertullus and Felix reckoned also, perhaps not altogether wrongly, a Paul of Tarsus,[3] whose family had come from Gis-Ḥalab, the town of the rebel leader John of Gis-Ḥalab.

Paul was confused,[4] in particular, with the so-called 'Egyptian,' the messiah who had assembled some thousands of the messianists

---

[1] *Vita*, § 11 : " $\zeta\eta\lambda\acute{\omega}\tau\eta\varsigma$ $\grave{\epsilon}\gamma\epsilon\nu\acute{o}\mu\eta\nu$ $a\grave{v}\tauo\hat{v}$."

[2] Renan compared him and John to the Indian ascetics of the hermit type (*vanaprastha*), though he freely admits that such asceticism has no basis in Jewish religion.

[3] *Acts* xxv. 5. Paul admits that he was a Zealot (*Gal.* i. 14, " $\zeta\eta\lambda\acute{\omega}\tau\eta\varsigma$ $\acute{v}\pi\acute{a}\rho\chi\omega\nu$," cf. 1 *Macc.* ii. 27, " $\pi\hat{a}\varsigma$ $\acute{o}$ $\zeta\eta\lambda\hat{\omega}\nu$ $\nu\acute{o}\mu\psi$ . . . $\grave{\epsilon}\xi\epsilon\lambda\theta\acute{\epsilon}\tau\omega$ $\grave{o}\pi\acute{\iota}\sigma\omega$ μov . . ." ; see above, p. 359 n. 3), and speaks of his withdrawal for two years into the '*Arabah* (*ib.*, i. 17), *not* to 'Arabia' in the modern sense but to the lower Jordan valley, not far from the Dead Sea. If he had been a peaceful hermit or the harmless preacher of a new doctrine of salvation, it would be inexplicable why he incurred—through his activity in the '*Arabah*, that is, in the immediate neighbourhood of Petra—the enmity of the heathen Nabataean king Aretas (2 *Cor.* xi. 32 f.; in *Acts* ix. 24 the Jews are his only foes in Damascus!). That the Zealot Sha'ul persecuted the followers of Jesus does not exclude his having been himself a Messianist. He may have belonged to the followers of the Baptist or to those of the sons of Judas the Galilaean. It must have been during that life in the desert that Theudas, the Messiah, knew him (above, p. 553 n. 3). [4] *Acts* xxi. 38.

dispersed by Felix on their attempted exodus, and had suddenly appeared with them on the Mount of Olives. Since he had promised that the walls of Jerusalem would fall before him, as those of Jericho had once fallen before Joshua, he, too, must have given himself out as the returning 'Jesus.' Felix was again informed in time by his scouts, and with the help of a small force of loyalists surrounded the Mount and cut down most of the crowd. The leader, who again managed to escape with a few followers, may once more have been the omnipresent Simon of Gitta,[1] the 'Jesus' son of Sōtadēs, who was constantly defying fate in this manner, and who at a much later date fell into the hands of the Jews and appears to have been stoned and hanged at Lydda [2] as a false prophet seeking to seduce the people to the worship of foreign gods.

It goes without saying that by all this the country was anything but pacified. The refugees from the Mount of Olives, reinforced by malcontents from among the peasantry, banded together and scoured the country, everywhere harassing the loyalists and looting their property. As the youthful Josephus, in spite of his priestly descent, went over to the Zealots, as 'Ele'azar the priest put himself at the head of the insurgents, so now the lower priestly orders in general appear to have risen against the high priests appointed by the Romans. These and their followers declared formal war upon their priestly opponents, whom they sought to starve into obedience by confiscation of their tithes.[3]

Furthermore, there was discord between the Jews and the Hellenized Syrians in half or wholly heathen cities like Caesarea, apparently turning on questions of local law, but having in reality its roots in the Jewish striving for independence and the stronger inclination of the Syrians for Roman dominion, recalling in many particulars the quarrels between Hindoos and Moslems in British India.

The incompetency and malice of Felix, regarding which the evidence of Tacitus [4] fully corroborates the condemnation of Josephus, no doubt accelerated the course of events; but even the

---

[1] In the Ps.-Clementine *Recognitions*, ii. 9 (Ante-Nicene Christian Library, vol. iii., Edinburgh, 1867, p. 197), this ancient prototype of Harry Houdini is made to say : ' I am able to render myself invisible to those who wish to lay hold of me, and again to be visible when I am willing to be seen. If I wish to flee, I can dig through the mountains and pass through rocks, as if they were clay. If I should throw myself headlong from a lofty mountain (cf. above, p. 287 n. 1), I should be borne unhurt to the earth, as if I were held up ; when bound, I can loose myself ; being shut up in prison, I can make the barriers open of their own accord.'

[2] b. Shabb., fᵒ. 104b ; pal. Shabb., 43d. Travers Herford, *Christianity in Talmud and Midrash*, p. 345. Hence the Moslem belief that in the last days the Antichrist, the great ' Liar ' (*ad dajjāl*), will appear in Lydda and be slain by Jesus (Clermont-Ganneau, *Horus and St. George*, 1877, p. 10).

[3] Cf. above, p. 543 ll. 17 ff.

[4] *Hist.*, v. 9 : ' per omnem saevitiam ac libidinem ius regium servili ingenio exercuit.'

coming of his honest successor Porcius Festus produced no change. The guerilla war of the rebels continued, and the administration of Festus saw a repetition of the exodus into the desert planned by a pseudo-prophet, the inevitable result being, as usual, a wholesale massacre by the pursuing Roman cavalry.[1] Josephus this time does not name the leader ; but it is fairly certain that this new abortive attempt coincided with the election of the aged James the Just as high priest, and with his downfall in the interim between the death of Festus and the arrival of his successor Albinus.

The deplorable economic situation of the country, dependent as it was on agriculture, since all transit commerce could easily be diverted into safer channels, can be imagined. The continuous impoverishment of the people naturally prevented the regular recovery of the taxes, and Josephus accuses the last of the governors of plundering wealthy individuals and finally even the temple treasury, which was deprived of seventeen talents. It is clear, of course, that such actions were simply the exaction of arrears of the country's tribute, for the full remittance of which first the leading citizens and in the end the sacred treasures were held responsible. The governor had of course to deliver to Caesar a definite sum which, quite apart from the profit he was accustomed to make for himself, he was bound to pay, no matter what were the economic conditions of the country. In addition there was the burden of maintaining the garrison, and the sums extorted as a matter of habit by individual officers and soldiers. Oppression, too, through Agrippa II. and his followers, weighed no less heavily upon the province. In the last edition of the *Antiquities*,[2] written after that monarch's death, Josephus actually reckons the king's relatives and protégés, Saul and Costobar, with their troops, among the ' robbers,' although these were obviously forces which on the one hand were fighting the insurgents and on the other were responsible for the collection of the taxes. In no other manner did the Palestinian *fellah* of the time of Turkish misrule lump the government troops, charged to ' protect ' him and to collect the taxes, together with the robbers of the desert harassing the country by their raids. In addition to the various exoduses *en masse* into the wilderness, there was now a constantly increasing migration of the population to regions less wretched than their own.[3]

So long as the wealthy class by tolerable taxation found in the Romans a support against their poorer compatriots, the tributary peasants on the land, the city mob, and the labourers barely kept alive by public works,[4] it put up with the foreign oppressors,

---

[1] *Ant.*, xx. 188.
[2] *Ant.*, xx. 9. 4.
[3] *B.J.*, ii. § 279 ; *Ant.*, xx. § 255. This is the way in which the Damascene community of the ' New Covenant ' (above, p. 575 n. 2) originated.
[4] *Ant.*, xx. § 219.

though often enough only by choking back its inward rage. But so soon as the wealthy themselves were held answerable for the deficit in taxes, after the peasants and small holders had become insolvent, and the Romans began mercilessly to attack the persons even of the privileged notables who had been promoted to the rank of Roman ' knights,' [1] the army of occupation lost its last support in the country, and a united national uprising against Rome could no longer be averted.

The decisive step leading to a breach with Rome was taken by the young captain of the temple guard, 'Ele'azar, son of the high priest, who discontinued the daily offering for the emperor, thereby openly defying the Romans.

What the aristocrats, whose patience was exhausted, completely forgot was their own utter powerlessness and the consequent impossibility of the hitherto ruling class to maintain its traditional position as leaders of a popular war against the foreign foe. Nothing, absolutely nothing, could induce the people—above all, the old fighters who for two generations had grown up in unceasing strife with Rome—to submit any longer to the leadership of persons who had hitherto done their best to support the Romans in their oppression of the lower orders. If the priestly nobility and the scribal bureaucracy imagined that the people still credited them with a special sanctity and dignity of office, they were altogether deceived, for it had been clearly shown long before—indeed, immediately after the death of Herod the Great—that the people scorned the Boethusaean high priests and all the dependants of Herod as unclean and unworthy of obedience. In fact, the high priest Hananiah and the prudent section of his peers and of the scribes made every effort, even at the last moment, to avert fate with the help of the king and his far too weak forces. For, to any one reviewing the situation the fact must have been clear which has long been recognized by such modern historians [2] as are not colour-blind in the matter of politics, namely, that the final outbreak of war with Rome at the same time initiated the total subversion of the existing order of Jewish society.[3]

The control of the movement at once passed out of the hands of the Jewish aristocracy. The Zealots possessed sufficient weapons from the start, having at the first assault secured by a bold stroke the Idumaean frontier fortress of Maṣada, built by Herod the Great as a huge arsenal, and having, moreover, through the defeat of Florus, captured the whole of the baggage trains as well as plenty of arms from the Roman army. The attempt of

---

[1] In the end, Florus, in defiance of all law, had even such persons crucified.

[2] Cf. Ed. Meyer, *Ursprung und Anfänge des Christentums*, ii. 74; W. Weber, *Josephus und Vespasian*, p. 21.

[3] Similar conditions would obtain if to-day India rose in arms against the British *rajj*.

the high priests with the help of the temple treasury to enlist a faithful bodyguard in Galilee and, thus supported, to retain their command of the people in arms, miscarried through the treachery of the young priestly noble Josephus, in whose breast on the hot soil of Galilee the old rebel spirit of the Baptists revived for a time and strove for the mastery with the ingrained worldly wisdom and lack of scruple of this young scapegrace.

The leader of the captors of Maṣada was Menaḥem, the last surviving son of Judah of Galilee, who had led the revolt against the census of Quirinius, and grandson of the Galilaean rebel leader Ḥizqiah, whom Herod the Great as a youth had put to death. At the head of his victorious army, reinforced by recruits from the plain and well equipped with the stores of the armoury of Maṣada, Menaḥem now marched into Jerusalem as Messiah, ' like a veritable king,' says the mocking Josephus.[1] Once more the city saw the triumphal entry of a liberator-king, once more the cries of 'Osanna, from a multitude easily moved and fluctuating between deepest despair of their own liberty and soaring hopes of world-dominion, hailed a leader convinced of his divine vocation as Israel's redeemer. Streams of blood had been offered by his unruly kindred, thirsting for freedom, to the dream of the liberation of the land and the fulfilment of the Deuteronomic royalty law : his grandfather had fallen in Galilee for his people; his father, God knows when and where, in a similar conflict against the country's enemy; his two elder brothers, Jacob and Simon, had been captured and crucified by order of Tiberius Alexander. And now he, the youngest, like David, entered the holy city as king, only to fulfil the tragic destiny of his house.

To 'Ele'azar, the temple captain, the highborn leader of the insurgents within the city, and to his followers, as also to the partner in his views, the historian Josephus, Menaḥem was no more than ' an insufferable tyrant,' [2] an expression which, thanks to the political doctrine of Aristotle,[3] had acquired a very definite content, and for the assistant of Josephus denoted the unlimited monarch come to the throne after the overthrow of an aristocratic or plutocratic government by a popular insurrection, and basing his power on the support of the poor and oppressed.

Our writer, then, represents the partisans of 'Ele'azar as saying to each other that they had not risen against the Romans for liberty, only to sacrifice this freedom to a Jewish hangman who, even were he to abstain from violence, was at all events far below them in rank. Menaḥem is called a ' hangman '($\delta\eta\mu\iota\sigma\varsigma$) [4] because

---

[1] *B.J.*, ii. 17. 8, § 434.
[2] *B.J.*, ii. § 442 ; the corresponding Hebrew word is *shaliṭ* (the Arabic, *sulṭan*).
[3] *Pol.*, v. 8. 2-3.
[4] *B.J.*, ii. § 443 (as read by Destinon ; the MSS. have $\delta\eta\mu\omega$).

'Ele'azar's party accused him of the murder of the high priest Hananiah (the father of 'Ele'azar) and the high priest's brother Hizqiah, whom Menaḥem's Zealots had dragged from their place of hiding in the canal of the palace garden and slain forthwith.

In revenge 'Ele'azar and his party conspired against Menaḥem; and when the latter in royal robes and in the midst of his body-guard entered the sanctuary to pay his devotions, he found the roofs [1] of the halls surrounding the temple court occupied by a hostile crowd, who pelted him and his followers with stones, while 'Ele'azar fell upon him with his temple guard. Menaḥem's people fled; some were caught and massacred, while his relative 'Ele'azar ben Ja'ir escaped with a party to Maṣada. The 'king' himself took refuge ' in the place called Ophlas,' clearly one of the underground passages on the slope of Ophel recently rediscovered by Parker, Macalister, and Weill. He was dragged forth in the same manner in which his adherents had dragged the high priest from hiding, and after ignominious tortures slain—a messiah, this time, really murdered by his Jewish countrymen.

The followers of Jesus, who must have regarded Menaḥem, like Simon of Gitta and Theudas before him, as the Antichrist, appear to have considered his death as an omen of the imminent fall of Jerusalem. They left the city and repaired to Pella, on the east of the Jordan.

The aristocrats reaped little joy from their short-lived victory. None of the leaders appointed by them could maintain his place, and affairs, of necessity, went ever further on the road to final ruin. The General Assembly (τὸ κοινὸν τῶν Ἱεροσολυμιτῶν), now hold-ing unlimited control over the state, carried out the measure demanded by the rebels after the death of Herod the Great, namely, the election of a high priest by popular vote, in complete disregard of the claims of the old privileged high-priestly families,[2] an object the more easily attained because of the disunion in the ranks of the nobility.[3] The popular leaders made it their aim to murder ' the nobility of the metropolis,' [4] clearly because the aristocrats had long repented of their breach with Rome and sought to renew negotia-tions with the country's enemy, a proceeding which the extremists, from their viewpoint quite naturally, regarded as high treason.

It is unnecessary to repeat here the story of the unhappy war and the siege of Jerusalem down to the destruction of the temple and the death of that devoted band who deemed it 'not death, but victory, salvation, and bliss, to perish with the sanctuary.' [5]

---

[1] *B.J.*, ii. § 445; read ὀροφάς for the meaningless ὀργάς of the MSS.
[2] *B.J.*, iv. § 139. [3] *Ibid.*, iv. § 147 *sqq.*
[4] *Ibid.*, iv. § 181; cf. § 365: ' None escaped save those whose humble birth or fortune put them beneath notice.'
[5] Dio Cassius, lxvi.; the words are those of the victorious enemy, who only attained his end with the gravest loss.

Herod's marvellous edifice had to perish in the flames because the lord of the world-empire fondly imagined that, along with this work of men's hands, he would extirpate that ' pest ' which threatened to shake the Roman dominion to its foundations, the belief in the imminent coming of a world-redeemer and of a wondrous kingdom to liberate all the enslaved and oppressed—heeding neither that omen, portrayed in unforgettable words by Tacitus,[1] of the celestial temple glowing in the clouds of the evening sky, nor the proud answer which the champions of liberty flung back to his summons to them to surrender and thus spare the temple, 'that the world was a better temple for God than this one.' [2]

There is weighty evidence to the effect that the leaders of the revolt at Jerusalem counted upon a united rising on a fixed day of the Diaspora throughout the whole of the Roman empire, and thought that the Mesopotamian Jewry and even the Parthians might be induced to make a simultaneous attack on Syria. That pledges were given, stipulations made, money and weapons secretly sent from the East to Jerusalem and Peraea, admits of no doubt.[3] The family of the King of Adiabene certainly did their utmost in this respect. But in general these hopes proved vain. With the Parthians the presence at the Roman court of hostages of royal birth and the danger from the Alani of the northern steppes carried greater weight than the temptation to take advantage of the embarrassment of the empire and the pressure of the Babylonian Jews. In the communities of the Dispersion the influence of the wealthier Jews, privileged by the Romans and therefore more or less committed to their cause, was generally strong enough to prevent the contemplated revolt, or at least to defer it until it was too late to embark on such an enterprise with any prospect of success. It was only the common misery to which these communities were reduced by the pogroms against the Jewish inhabitants, the consequence of the overthrow of the Jewish state in Palestine, and of which the rich were always the first victims, that created conditions favourable to a world-revolution [4] of all Jewry breaking out in the reigns of Trajan and Hadrian.

It is unmistakable that the Romans deliberately set out to exterminate the belief in the might of the one invisible God, whose earthly Jewish vicegerent was destined, according to the widespread prophecies well known to them through itinerant preachers, to hurl the Caesars from their throne and to replace them as ruler of the world. After the temple at Jerusalem had sunk into ruins, the unavoidable aftermath of the Jewish revolt in Egypt and

---

[1] *Hist.*, v. 13 : ' visae per caelum concurrere acies, rutilantia arma et subito nubium igne conlucere templum.'

[2] *B.J.*, v. 11. 2, § 458.　　　　　　[3] Weber, *op. cit.*, p. 19.

[4] Dio Cassius, lxix. 13 : ' the whole world was as it were shaken by this.'

Libya (where the weaver Jonathan summoned the Jews to an exodus into the desert) gave them the welcome opportunity of closing the other Jewish temple of On (Heliopolis), founded by Onias, and of rendering it useless for worship by the removal of all its sacred vessels. To make the fulfilment of the oracle of a Jewish world-ruler of David's line altogether impossible, Vespasian proceeded to have a list made of all discoverable members of the ancient house and, probably, to proscribe them. That measure appears to have led to the arrest and trial, under Domitian, of the last surviving scions of the family of Jesus claiming descent from David.

All these measures (to which must be added the conversion of the old Jewish temple contribution of a didrachm [1] into a poll-tax payable to the treasury of Jupiter Capitolinus) could only increase to the utmost the exasperation of the Jews in the Diaspora. When at last under Trajan there came the conflict between Rome and the Parthians, for which the Jews were yearning, and when the emperor appeared with his picked troops in Mesopotamia, the Babylonian Jews rose in his rear, simultaneously with their compatriots in Libya, Egypt, Cyprus, and Palestine. This fearful insurrection [2]—of which Prof. Zielinski [3] has rightly observed that it was far greater and more dangerous than that under Nero, and only received less attention in history because no Tacitus or Josephus undertook to describe it—was led by a messiah-king, Andrew [4] of Lycia, that is to say, a Jew who, like Paul, belonged to the Diaspora of southern Asia Minor. This Jewish king, too, was held up to ridicule on the stage at Alexandria, a buffoonery looking weird enough against the background of merciless mutual massacre of Jews and Gentiles which was the sequel of this rising in the various countries. The rebellion, put down by Marcius Turbo and Lusus Quietus, had not yet been quite extinguished when Hadrian took over the government and was called to suppress disturbances both in Alexandria and in Palestine.[5]

When this emperor forbade the Jewish covenant-rite of circumcision, and further proceeded to erect a temple of Jupiter Capitolinus on the ruins of the temple of Jahveh, a furious rebellion broke out afresh in Palestine. The leader this time was a man of the village of Kokheba [6] in Batanaea,[7] the village, be it noted, which, according to Christian tradition,[8] was the home of the kinsfolk of Jesus. He was recognized by the famous Rabbi 'Aqiba as

---

[1] I.e. a labourer's pay for two days (*Tobit*, v. 4), that is, two-thirds per cent. of a minimum income. [2] Euseb., *Hist. eccl.*, iv. 2 ; Orosius, vii. 12.
[3] *Revue de l'Université de Bruxelles*, 1926-7, p. 19 *sqq.*
[4] So Dio Cassius, lxviii. 32. To him, and not to Bar Kokheba, Jesus is made to allude in *John* v. 43.
[5] Euseb., *Chron.*, ed. Schoene, ii. 164 (Armenian).
[6] Schürer (Macpherson's trans., vol. i. 2, p. 298 n. 84) is mistaken in his interpretation of the name ; cf. Levy, *Neuhebr. Wörterbuch*, ii. 312b.
[7] Cf. Euseb., *Hist. eccl.*, i. 7. 14 ; Epiphan., *Haeres.*, 30. 2 and 18.   [8] *Ibid.*

the promised son of David.[1] Since it is hardly conceivable that two different families, unrelated to each other and both claiming to be descended from King David, could have lived in so tiny a place, I consider it more than probable that *Bar Kokhᵉba* belonged to that branch of the family of Jesus which the Christians regarded as 'heretical,' and which they accused of having betrayed to the Romans the last members of the other line, the δεσπόσυνοι in the time of Domitian. That would at once explain on the one hand his appearance as the Messiah (the clan of Jesus would in that case, like that of Judah of Galilee, have produced two kings 'anointed of the Lord'), and, on the other, the fact that the Jewish Christians of Transjordania and Palestine rejected him [2] and were bitterly persecuted by him.[3] The guerilla war conducted by him against the Romans until his fall had reduced Palestine to a desert, after causing enormous losses to both Jews and Romans, so much so that Hadrian in reporting the victory to the senate thought fit to omit the usual formula, ' I and the army are well.' [4] The number of Jewish prisoners was so great that they could not all be sold on the spot, although ' a man was given away for the price of a horse.' [5]

Therewith the dreadful tragedy was ended, and the last of the 'men of violence' who, since the days of John the Baptist, had sought to 'take the kingdom of God by force' was gathered to his fathers. The holy city had sunk in ruins; the Romans had drawn the plough over the ashes of the temple; the promised land was lost, its strongholds broken; and of the people which had forfeited its political existence, well-nigh all the warriors and champions of liberty, all the true sons of the old conquerors with the blood of the predatory tribes of the desert in their veins, were now exterminated. The force of unalterable facts had solved the hard problem which the supposed command of God had presented to the pious in the Deuteronomic royalty law: 'when thou . . . shalt possess and shalt dwell in the land which the Lord thy God giveth thee . . . thou shalt not put a foreigner over thee who is not thy brother.' Now that Israel had lost to the foreigner the land which the Lord had given and was homeless again upon the earth, even the most pious must bow their necks to every foreign yoke until the end of the appointed days.

Those who had taken the sword have perished by the sword and been buried in blood and fire beneath the ruins of the temple fortress, beneath the demolished walls of the rock-castles of Maṣada and Beth-Har, the survivors being deported to harder bondage than their forefathers had ever known.

---

[1] Talm. Jer., *Ta'anith*, iv., fol. 68d (ed. Cracov.).
[2] Cf. Jerome, *Adv. Ruf.*, iii. 31.   [3] Justin Martyr, *Apol.*, i. 31.
[4] Dio Cassius, lxix. 14.   [5] Jerome on *Zech.* xi. 5 and *Jerem.* xxxi. 15.

APPENDICES

APPENDIX I

The Official Records of the Roman Bureaucracy [1]

In Roman times it was the custom that each official, including the imperial governor, should keep a diary of his official acts, entering day by day the important data. In all probability this was already the case under the Ptolemies, although so far the papyri give no information on the subject. We possess the fragment of such an official diary in the Paris papyrus 69,[2] which constitutes seven columns of a roll, originally far longer, containing the diary entries of the στρατηγός of the districts of Omboi and Elephantine in Upper Egypt, dating from A.D. 232. I shall give here an excerpt taken from the first days of the month of Thoth. The stops indicate gaps in the papyrus.

'1st Thoth. The στρατηγός at nightfall went into the gymnasium together with Aurelius. . . . He created, by coronation with a wreath, Aurelius Pelaias, son of Harpaesis, grandson of Hierax, gymnasiarch, and sacrificed on this occasion both at the Caesareum and at the Gymnasium, where he also made libations and uttered vows. Then he went into his second district, that of Omboi, where the customary sacrifices to the god took place . . . and the στρατηγός attended the procession made in honour of this god.'

There follows, in a different handwriting—that is, the hand of the στρατηγός himself—the annotation: 'Read.' Written by a third hand there follows the annotation : ' I, official clerk, Aurelius Artemidorus, have publicly exposed this act and then incorporated it into the official acts. Year 12, on the 2nd of Thoth.' There follows a new page, that is, a new leaf, which, when first written upon at the office of the official, was an independent leaf and was later incorporated into the acts by the clerk, who, after exposing it in public, pasted it on to the previous leaf. This procedure was followed until the roll was fairly thick. Day by day the official examined the entry and signed ' Read,' and every time, after the lapse of several days, a leaf or two having been filled, they were exposed in public, and then incorporated into the acts with the testimony of the official clerk. Having thus been incorporated,

---

[1] Cf. F. Preisigke, *Antikes Leben nach den ägyptischen Papyri*, Leipzig, 1916, p. 63 sq.
[2] See our Pl. I. The Greek text is printed in the *Notices et Extraits des MSS. de la Bibliothèque Nationale*, tome xviii. 2, No. 69. U. Wilcken, *Chrestomathie*, No. 41.

the leaf constitutes a new page in the roll and is duly numbered. The page quoted above is thus No. 4. The public exhibition of the leaf here lasts only a day, for the incorporation into the acts took place on the 2nd of Thoth. The purpose of the exhibition was to render account to the public of the official activity of the office-holder. This stands in open contrast to the modern conception of an official who is responsible only to his superior authorities, not to the public, and even that superior authority is accountable only to Parliament, not to the masses.

APPENDIX II

RABBINICAL TRADITIONS CONCERNING NAMESAKES OF JESUS

The Talmud b. Sanhedrin, 107b,[1] mentions a certain Jeshu,[2] a pupil of R. Jehoshu'ah b. Peraḥjah, who accompanied his master on his flight from the king Alexander Jannai to Egypt, returned with him, but was excommunicated by him because on the journey home he is said to have paid too much attention to the fair face of an innkeeper's wife.[3] In despair he fell away from the Law and worshipped the moon (*lebhonah*).[4] This renegade pupil of a rabbi has in common with the Naṣōraean Messias Jesus only his name, but on account of his flight to Egypt [5] he was at an early period confused with Jesus the son of Sōtadēs, the fool (*shotēh*), ' who had brought witchcraft with him from Egypt,' and who is probably none other than the Egyptian messias who promised to make the walls of Jerusalem crumble by the sound of trumpets,[6] i.e. probably Simon Magus, who passed himself off as the resuscitated Jesus.[7] As a consequence of these confusions and mistakes, there arose in the Babylonian Gemara another anonymous tradition, ' A rabbi has said : Jeshu *han-noṣri* has been guilty of witchcraft and seduced and deceived Israel,' and was attached to the anecdote just

[1] Aufhauser, *Antike Jesuszeugnisse* (Lietzmann, *Kl. Texte*, No. 126, p. 40 *sq.*, where the older literature is given). Cf. also R. Travers Herford, *Christianity in Talmud and Midrash*, London, 1903, pp. 50, 52, 54 n. 1, 40.

[2] In the parallel passage, j. Ḥag., ii. 2, the name is not given, which may be due to an early censorship.

[3] The announcement of the excommunication by four hundred trumpeters is of course a grotesque exaggeration, due to the confusion of this otherwise unknown rabbi's pupil with the famous Egyptian demagogue. See below, n. 6.

[4] MSS. a ' brick ' (*libnah*). I think this is due to a twisting of the original meaning, which was referring to astrological cult practices. There exists, of course, a cult of ' bricks ' made by men, cf. F. C. Conybeare, *Transact. Third Internat. Congr. for the Hist. of Relig.*, vol. ii., 1908, p. 181 : ' I have often seen a Hindu pick up an old brickbat, set it up on end, draw a circle round it, and proceed to say his prayers to it '; but the tendency of this exaggeration is clearly visible.

[5] Travers Herford, *op. cit.*, p. 53, recalls the legendary flight of Jesus to Egypt (*Matt.* ii. 13).

[6] The four hundred trumpeters announcing his excommunication may have been intended as a fitting answer to this foolishness.

[7] This Simon Magus was accused of having instituted a cult to his mistress Helena as Selene. The moon cult referred to above may aim at this particular episode of Simon's biography.

referred to. In a number of MSS., finally, the name *han-noṣri*, referring to the Naṣōraean, became attached to the rabbi Jehoshu'ah b. Peraḥjah's pupil. This mare's-nest of confusions led my old friend Mr. G. R. S. Mead, many years ago, to a discussion of the question, ' Did Jesus live in 180 B.C. ? '

APPENDIX III

A GENUINE RABBINICAL TESTIMONY ABOUT JESUS

Jesus himself has given an interpretation of *Deut.* xxiii. 19, with a quotation from *Micah* i. 7 : [1]

' R. 'Eli'ezer said to R. 'Aqiba : " I once went on the upper street of Sepphoris ; there I met one of the disciples of Jesus the Naṣōraean named Ja'aqob of Kephar Sekhanjah, who said to me : ' In your law (*Deut.* xxiii. 19) there is written : Thou shalt not bring a whore's hire into the house of thy God. Is it permissible to use such hire to make therewith a privy for the high priest ? ' I did not know what to answer him. Then he said to me : ' This is what Jesus the Naṣōraean taught me : She gathered it as the hire of an harlot, and they shall return it to the hire of an harlot (*Micah* i. 7) : it has come from dirt, and to the place of dirt it shall go.' " ' [2]

This dictum of Jesus has hitherto been neither adequately defined nor correctly interpreted. The scurrilous puzzle whether a harlot's hire when given as an offering might be used for the building of a privy for the high priest, and thus utilized in some measure for the treasury of the temple, is put by the heretic antinomian and anti-Pharisaic disciple of Jesus to R. 'Eli'ezer b. Hyrkanos, the teacher of R. 'Aqiba, for no other purpose than to make fun of the efforts of the scribes to interpret *Deut.* xxiii. 19 in a manner profitable to the temple treasure.

The prohibition in question wanted to prevent or abolish the Syrian custom of sacred prostitution. Yet on account of its too general tenor it exempted all prostitutes from payment of the *Sheqel* or temple tax. This again appeared to put a reward on a trade generally considered as shameful. On the other hand, men and women of doubtful repute ran a risk of seeing themselves publicly put to shame by the priests' refusal to accept their offering. The ' problem ' seemed a fertile field for the casuists, and the disciple of Jesus Ja'aqob of Kephar Sekhanjah proposed on his own responsibility a way out of the difficulty, naturally with a view to ridiculing the casuists. Jesus is not quoted but for the last three lines reproduced in this anecdote.

The quotation from Jesus can in no wise refer to the so-called ' throne-house ' of the high priest, but is evidently an independent remark hostile to the priests, made probably on an occasion when in his presence the offering of a woman of doubtful repute was refused on

[1] *'Aboda zara*, 16b–17a.
[2] Laible, *Jesus Christus im Talmud*, Leipzig, 1900, p. 59 ; R. Travers Herford, *Christianity in Talmud and Midrash*, London, 1903, pp. 148 *sq.*, 412 *sq.* ; Klausner-Danby, *Jesus of Nazareth*, London, 1925, p. 37.

2 P

the ground of the Deuteronomic passage. Jesus then quoted the verset from Micah. On consulting it, one will find that in that passage what is meant by harlotry is simply the idolatry of the northern kingdom of Samaria, and that Jesus merely designates the Boethusaean priesthood of Jerusalem as a harlot enticing the people away from the service of Jahveh.[1] The temple desecrated by it appears to him but as a place of impurity. Hence, in his view, the venal priesthood should not refuse the offering of a venal woman.

APPENDIX IV

CHRISTIAN CENSORSHIP

The Codex Justinianus[2] contains the following order of the Emperors Theodosius and Valentinian, dating from the year A.D 449, to burn all writings hostile to Christianity composed by Porphyry 'or any other person' in his blindness, lest they cause God's anger and scandalize the pious. The order applied with equal force to books privately owned, to those of the synagogues and the public libraries of the cities.

"Αὐτοκράτορες Θεοδόσιος καὶ Οὐαλεντινιανὸς A A 'Ορμίσδᾳ ἐπάρχῳ πραιτωρίων· Θεσπίζομεν πάντα ὅσα Πορφύριος ὑπὸ τῆς ἑαυτοῦ μανίας ἐλαυνόμενος ἢ ἕτερός τις κατὰ τῆς εὐσεβοῦς τῶν Χριστιανῶν θρησκείας συνέγραψε παρ' οἱῳδήποτε εὑρισκόμενα πυρὶ παραδίδοσθαι. πάντα γὰρ τὰ κινοῦντα τὸν θεὸν εἰς ὀργὴν συγγράμματα καὶ τὰς ψυχὰς ἀδικοῦντα οὐδὲ εἰς ἀκοὰς ἀνθρώπων ἐλθεῖν βουλόμεθα."

(Follows an edict about the burning of Nestorian books.) The rhythm and construction of the sentence quoted leave no doubt about the fact that the words ἢ ἕτερός τις have been put in at a later date, no doubt for the purpose of extending the measure adopted against the writings of Porphyry (publicly burned as early as 431, at the Council of Ephesus) to *all* books the destruction of which was desired because the fanatics of the new religion did not feel capable any longer of fighting them with purely spiritual weapons. Since a law against the books of Porphyry is well attested for the reign of Constantine,[3] it is to be supposed that the order of Theodosius and Valentinian merely renewed a law of Constantine made ineffective by the reaction under Julian. It is clear, of course, that the writings of Josephus with their sections so hostile to John the Baptist and the Naṣōraean messiah came under this law, as did the Acts of Pilate published by Maximinus Daïa. Yet while the latter could be ruthlessly burned, matters stood differently with Josephus, who for the Christians had become well-nigh canonical.

[1] Cf. also my interpretation of the episode of the adulterous woman, Z.N.T.W., xxii. (1923), p. 305.

[2] Recognovit Paulus Krueger, Berlin, 1877, i. 1, 3 ; cf. also the order of Theodosius and Valentinian (Nov. 42, c. 1 § 2 ; lib. 3, 1, *De Summa Trinitate*) on the burning of the writings of Arius, possession of which was threatened with death.

[3] Cf. the letters in Gelasios of Kyzikos, *Comm. Act. Concil. Nic.* ; Mansi, ii. 919. At the same time the burning of the writings of Arius is ordered and the hiding of books by Porphyry or Arius threatened with the death penalty ; cf. Sozom., ii. 38 ; Socrates, i. 9, 31 (Migne, *P.G.*, lxvii. 88).

This law was the counter-stroke of the Christians to the edict of Diocletian commanding the burning of all Christian MSS.,[1] probably on the basis of the same legal principle that books of mag'c contents (*libri improbatae lectionis*) were to be destroyed.

APPENDIX V

Ignatius on the Jews demanding Documentary Evidence about Jesus from the Christians

According to a variant of the letter of Ignatius to the Philadelphians, the Jews told the Christians that they would not believe the contents of the Gospels unless they could find the statements in question also in the archives (ἀρχείοις) :

" ἐπεὶ ἤκουσά τινων λεγόντων, ὅτι ἐὰν μὴ ἐν τοῖς ἀρχείοις ‟εὔρω, ἐν τῷ εὐαγγελίῳ οὐ πιστεύω. καὶ λέγοντός μου αὐτοῖς, ὅτι " Γέγραπται," ἀπεκρίθησάν μοι· " Πρόκειται" ; ἐμοὶ δὲ ἀρχειά ἐστιν Ἰησοῦς Χριστός, τὰ ἄθικτα ἀρχεῖα ὁ σταυρὸς αὐτοῦ καὶ ἡ πίστις ἡ δι' αὐτοῦ ἐν οἷς θέλω ἐν τῇ προσευχῇ ὑμῶν δικαιωθῆναι. καλοὶ καὶ οἱ ἱερεῖς, κρείσσων δὲ ὁ ἀρχιερεὺς ὁ πεπιστευμένος τὰ ἅγια τῶν ἁγίων ὃς μόνος πεπίστευται τὰ κρυπτὰ τοῦ θεοῦ. αὐτὸς ὢν θύρα τοῦ πατρός, δι' ἧς εἰσέρχονται Ἀβραὰμ καὶ Ἰσαὰκ καὶ Ἰακὼβ καὶ οἱ προφῆται καὶ οἱ ἀπόστολοι καὶ ἡ ἐκκλησία. Ἐξαίρετον δέ τι ἔχει τὸ εὐαγγέλιον, τὴν παρουσίαν τοῦ Κυρίου ἡμῶν Ἰησοῦ Χριστοῦ, τὸ πάθος αὐτοῦ καὶ τὴν ἀνάστασιν. οἱ γὰρ ἀγαπητοὶ προφῆται κατήγγειλαν εἰς αὐτόν, τὸ δὲ εὐαγγέλιον ἀπάρτισμά ἐστιν ἀφθαρσίας."

The original variant, it is true, had ἀρχαίοις, and meant by that the messianic references in the ancient prophets, as is clearly shown by St. Augustinus, Sermo 340, 4 (*P.L.*, xxxviii.-xxxix., 1457) :

' Nonnulli enim paganorum, ut noverint Christum ante prophetatum, quando eis de Scripturis clara proferimus, suspecti ne forte a Christianis ista conficta sint, malunt credere codicibus Judaeorum.'

Which simply means that the Gentiles desired to verify the passages in question in the Hebrew MSS. of the Jews, a desire natural enough, seeing that certain ones, among others the famous Ναζωραῖος κληθήσεται, have not yet been located in Scripture, whilst others come from ' scriptures ' posterior to Jesus.[2] Yet all this does not contradict the fact that the variant reading quoted above may be very old. At all events, it can have arisen only under the impression that the Jews did demand documentary evidence taken from official archives.

APPENDIX VI

Official Acts copied and circulated by Christian Scribes

According to the introduction to the doubtless genuine *Acta SS. Tarachi, Probi et Andronici* (Ruinart, p. 457), a number of Christians

---

[1] Euseb., *Hist. eccl.*, viii. 11.   [2] See above, p. 311.

of Iconium actually named paid 200 denarii to one of the *speculatores* of Sebaste for the materials in question. A similar statement occurs in the *Vita et Passio St. Pontii*, 25 ; Baluze, *Miscell.*, i. 33 ; Leclerq, *op. cit.*, p. 384 n. 22. On the *speculatores*, cf. O. Hirschfeld, *Die Sicherheitspolizei im römischen Kaiserreich*, Kl. Schr., p. 610 ; Lammert in Pauly-Kroll, *Realencyclop.*, iii.A, 2, 1583-86. The statement of the *Passio St. Vincentis* (ed. Ruinart, *Acta Sincera*, i. 389), to the effect that the governor expressly prohibited the taking down of a protocol, is clearly a subterfuge meant to justify the want of documentary bases. The same puerile invention is found in the *Passio Victoris Mauri* (*Acta SS.*, *May 8th*), where the president of the tribunal with the consent of the emperor has all the acts of the trial ' burnt,' not, however, without having obliged all the *excerptores* to declare under oath that they had not put aside any item connected with the affair.

APPENDIX VII

The Dating of the Death of James the Just

Chapter iii. of the fifth book of the *Polemos* contains a vehement accusation by Josephus of John of Gischala and his Zealots because during the siege they did not shrink from using the sacred wine and oil of the temple, and the chapter ends with a vicious attack by the pious author on that ' sinful ' generation. This must have induced a Christian interpolator to introduce the two still greater crimes of the Jews, the crucifixion of Jesus and the murder of James. The re-worker of Eusebius,[1] utilized by the *Chronicon Paschale*, then read in his interpolated copy of the *Halōsis* the following passage (v. 13. 6, § 566) :

" οἶμαι, Ῥωμαίων βραδυνόντων ἐπὶ τοὺς ἀλιτηρίους ἢ καταποθῆναι ὑπὸ χάσματος ἢ κατακλυσθῆναι τὴν πόλιν ἢ τοὺς τῆς Σοδομήνης μεταλαβεῖν κεραύνους· πολὺ γὰρ τῶν ταῦτα παθόντων ἤνεγκε γενεὰν ἀθεωτέραν. Τῇ γοῦν τούτων ἀπονοίᾳ πᾶς ὁ λαὸς συναπώλετο· [ἔτους τρίτου Οὐεσπασιανοῦ ἡ ἅλωσις τῶν Ἰουδαίων γέγονε, ὡς μετὰ ἔτη τῆς αὐτῶν τόλμης κατὰ τοῦ Ἰησοῦ. ἐν ᾧ χρόνῳ καὶ Ἰάκωβον τὸν ἀδελφὸν τοῦ Κυρίου κρεμνισθῆναι καὶ ὑπ' αὐτῶν λιθοβοληθέντα ἀναιρεθῆναι]."

This interpolation of the story of James *immediately before the fall of the city* explains the dating of his death by Hegesippus [2] and in Eusebius,[3] while Josephus himself puts the stoning of James correctly before the beginning of Albinus' term of office, i.e. A.D. 62. The dating of the fall of Jerusalem in the *third* year of Vespasian, against, be it noted, the chronologically exact statement of Josephus himself (*B.J.*, vi. 4. 8, 10. 1, ' *second* year '), clearly shows that the interpolator put the crucifixion of Jesus, which took place forty years previously, in the

---

[1] Cf. E. Schwartz, in his article ' Chronicon Paschale,' Pauly-Wissowa, *R.-E.*, iii. 2475, 15 *sq.*
[2] Euseb., *H.E.*, ii. 23. 18.   [3] *H.E.*, iii. 11. 1.

year 31, and did not recognize the date A.D. 21 indirectly indicated by Josephus (above, p. 17 ff.).

Since St. James is not mentioned at all in the *Halōsis*, it follows that the passage in the *Polemos* is an interpolation, though a very ancient one, since Hegesippus, who wrote about A.D. 180, knew it already. On the other hand, it cannot have been introduced into all MSS. at the time of Origen (born A.D. 185), for had the latter known it he would have added to his criticism of the *Antiquities* something like this : * 'In the *Polemos* Josephus rightly attributes the fall of Jerusalem to the τολμή of the Jews against Jesus.'

APPENDIX VIII

THE RUMANIAN JOSEPHUS FRAGMENTS

The fragments in question are contained in the Cod. Gaster, No. 89, saec. xvii./xviii., in which are found a compilation of the Gospel of Nicodemus and the so-called *Acta Pilati*, the story of the Crucifixion with the *Descensus ad Inferos*, the *Anaphora Pilati*, the *Death of Annas and Caiafas*, and the so-called Letter of Lentulus, with the description of Jesus.[1] The Cod. Gaster, No. 172, is an incomplete copy of the same original, which in the missing part probably contained also the Josephus fragments. This is important because the two codices are linguistically quite different, No. 89 being written in the Valachian, No. 172 in the Moldavian dialect. I owe this important and interesting material to the kindness of Dr. Moses Gaster, who has also most kindly furnished a transcript of the Cyrillic MS. into Latin letters and a German translation of the following texts.[2] I have revised it from the photographs, with the kind assistance of Prof. Mario Roques of the École des langues Orientales vivantes in Paris. The following is a table of contents of the whole MS. The genuine text of Josephus is quoted verbatim and printed in italics.

1. The Birth of our Lord and Saviour Jesus Christ

Account of the birth of Jesus following the *Gospel of Luke* and a Vision of St. Brigit (of Sweden).[3] The latter circumstance proves that a Roman Catholic medium must be supposed—in this case a Polish version.

2. The Adoration of the Magi

The prophecy of the star of the Messiah, said to have originated with an ancient philosopher and prophet called Balaam and then to have been transmitted in the families of the magi from generation to generation.

---

[1] Cf. Gaster, *Literatura populara Romana*, Bucharest, 1883, p. 351.

[2] The German translation of the whole composite Apocryphon is printed in the German edition, vol. i. pp. 430-61.

[3] St. Brigit was born *ca.* 1302, died in 1373, was canonized in 1391.

3. The Arrival of the 'Philosophers' at his Birth

The account follows in the main the Gospel narrative and the Protevangel of St. James the Minor. For the facts relating to the Baptist, the Emesan *Life of John*, published in vol. iv. of the *Patrologia Orientalis*, was drawn upon.

4. The Flight to Egypt

Gospel narrative mixed with the apocryphal legend of the robbers, identified as usual with the λῃσταί on the crosses, a legend found in several apocrypha. The priests in Egypt want to paint the picture of the Saviour, but do not succeed in this.[1] There is added : '*The Emperor Augustus reigned in Rome fifty-seven years, and grew to be eighty-seven years old.*'[2]

5. The Third Principate of Tiberius

After Augustus, Tiberius, who was a mild but avaricious man, assumed the rule. When he appointed some one or gave him a province in charge, he rarely changed the officials ;[3] *for he said : ' If some one has wounds on his feet, he should not drive off the flies nestling on them, for others would come, still hungrier, and cause him still greater pain.'*[4] *When he learned that some one had collected more taxes than he had been asked to impose, he punished him very severely, for he said that it was unwise to shear the sheep down to the flesh,*[5] *and he maintained that taxes must be collected with discretion. Everybody had free access to him. He caused his brother to be killed by a third person,*[6] *and ordered that gold and silver were to be disdained.*[7]

6. The Story of Pilate

Pilate was by birth a Galilaean of the city of Levdania,[8] *and was appointed ' Chief Vojvod ' because he had conquered many provinces,*

---

[1] Curious allusion to certain recently rediscovered Coptic pictures representing Isis with the babe Harpocrates, which were mistaken for pictures of the Madonna with the babe Jesus in her arms. The Byzantine author, then, knew this type of picture, which would fix his source as necessarily prior to the Moslem conquest of Egypt. The mention of early pictures of Jesus shows the anti-iconoclastic tendencies of the compiler.

[2] This chronological item is not found either in the *Halōsis* or in the *Polemos*, but in the *Antiquities* (xviii. 2. 2, § 32 *sq.*). With this line begins the *italicized* text of Josephus, derived from the second edition of the *War*, discussed above, p. 83.

[3] *Ant.*, xviii. 6. 5, § 170.

[4] Cp. *Ant.*, xviii. 6. 5, § 174. Cf. Aristotle, *Rhet.*, ii. 20.

[5] Sueton., *Tib.*, xxxii. 2 ; Dio Cassius, lvii. 10. 5 : ' praesidibus onerandas tributo provincias suadentibus rescripsit : boni pastoris esse tondere pecus, non deglubere.'

[6] The brother meant is Agrippa Postumus, the grandson of Augustus, adopted by the latter and hence in a way a brother of Tiberius.

[7] Cf. Dio Cassius, lvii. 15. 1, on the prohibition of Tiberius against the use of precious metals for the manufacture of table ware—an economic measure designed, together with the prohibition of the import of Chinese silk, to prevent the utilization of precious metals for other purposes than coinage, or their exportation to the countries of the Orient.

[8] Galilaean ' is evidently a mistake for 'Gallian.' Pilate was often considered a Gaul, a native either of Vienne or of Lyons. [Cf. Arturo Graf, *Miti, leggende e superstizioni del medio evo*, Torino, 1892-3, ii. 144. Translator's note.]

wherefore he was sent to Jerusalem as a governor, in the place of Valerius, who was deposed because he had accepted bribes from Ishmael, whom he had named high priest in the place of Simeon, removed by him. He was followed by Eliazar, who was succeeded by Enos and Caiafa, who are Anna and Caiafa. *Pilate brought to Jerusalem the image of the Emperor Tiberius* and demanded for it divine honours. *The Jews refused to* admit the image and to sacrifice to Caesar. *Then Pilate brought a huge Roman army to Jerusalem and killed many of the Jews. Ever since that time Pilate was a governor feared by the Jews.*

7. The Baptism of the Precursor John

Very brief account of John's work, taken from the Emesan *Vita.*

8. The Story of 'Joseph Matathie' on John

About that time, so he told, *there was a man going about among the Jews who wore an odd dress. He had pasted the hair of animals on his body wherever it was not covered with his own natural hair. His face looked savage. In his appearance he looked like a ghost rather than like an human being, so peculiar it was. He also led a very curious mode of life. He ate no bread, and not even on the Passover did he touch of the unleavened bread, saying that this was meant only to remind us of the God who relieved us from bondage. He did not allow wine or other strong drink to come near him. He detested all flesh of animals and abhorred all injustice. He only lived on the buds of trees. He came to the Jews and taught them thus : ' God hath sent me to show you the new path by which you may be freed from your many tyrants, so that not even death* [1] *will have any power over you, but only the Lord above.' When hearing these words, the people followed him ;* [2] *but all he did to them was to plunge them into the water of the Jordan and to tell them to avoid all evil thenceforth.* [3] *Yet the* Pharisees *prohibited him from going on with his teaching and from addressing the masses. However, he replied to them : ' You had better give up your evil deeds.' Simeon the scribe, who was an Essene, rose and said : ' We study the divine laws day after day, whilst thou, like unto a wild animal, hast come forth from the woods, and yet thou darest teach us ? Thou seducest the people with thine impure teaching.' And they wanted to rush upon him like wild animals to kill him. Yet he went over to the other side of the Jordan and continued his teaching.*

9. John the Precursor explains the Dream of Philip

When Philip was still reigning he dreamt that an eagle was about to pick out both his eyes. He called the wise men, but they were unable to interpret his dream, the one giving this, the other a different explanation. But that man of whom we have written before, the one who, dressed in animals' hair, was cleansing the people in the Jordan, called John, arrived without being called from the desert—in fact, quite unexpectedly—and said :

[1] Spiritualizing correction of ' no mortal ' (man).
[2] Correction for ' were excited.'
[3] Cf. the Russian text above, p. 225.

' Listen to the word of the Lord : The dream which thou hast seen foreshadows thy death, for that eagle is a bird of prey and has picked out thine eyes.' [1] *And after he had said this, Philip died the same evening.*

10. An Episode from the Life of the Baptist

Taken from the Emesan *Vita* (*P.Q.*, iv. p. 529).

11. Jesus' Baptism

Said to have happened at the ' seventh hour of night.' [2]

12. Beginning of his Public Career

The first miracle was the conversion of water into wine at the wedding of Cana. The name of the bridegroom was Simon the Canaanite,[3] who lived only two years with his wife, since she then died.

13. Cure of the Woman diseased with an Issue of Blood. The Statue of Jesus in Paneas

From Malalas. Cf. my lecture, *La prétendue statue de Jésus et de l'Hémoroisse de Panéade*, in *Comptes rendus de l'Académie des Inscriptions et Belles-Lettres*, 3rd June 1929; *Transactions of the Fifth Internat. Congr. for the History of Religions*, Lund, 1930, pp. 305 ff. ; in full in *Revue Archéologique*, 1930, pp. 18-27. The story is clearly introduced for the purpose of anti-iconoclastic polemics.

14. Description of Jesus

' He has a very beautiful face,' as the prophet says : ' more beautiful in shape than all children of men.' In growth and stature he was full seven feet high ; his hair was blond and *not very richly developed* ; he had beautiful *eyebrows*, not very curved ; his eyes were brown and clear (gay), just as it is written that his ancestor David was *dark*, with beautiful eyes, with large nostrils, a reddish beard and long hair, for from the time of his infancy, when his mother had clipped his hair, no razor had touched his head. His head was a *little bending*, since his body was tall ; his hair light blond. His face was round, like that of his mother, kindly, mild, and entirely without anger, in all resembling his mother.

This description is the work of Maxim, a Greek monk of the monastery of Vatopeza on Mt. Athos.[4]

15. Josephus on John's Reproval of Herod

Shortly after, Antipas took to wife the wife of his brother,[5] *a cause of*

[1] The reflections on the character of Herod Philippus are deleted.

[2] This corresponds to the continually repeated statement in the Mandaean ' book of John ' that he used to preach at nightfall and during the night.

[3] ' Canaanite ' for Καναναῖος, evidently a very early mistranslation, to conceal the true character of the Καναναῖος = Zealot apostle.

[4] The Rumanian text of this *iconismus* is printed in Dr. Gaster's book quoted above, p. 597 n. 1.

[5] No name is given her in this version ! See above, p. 229 n. 8.

scandal to the scribes. Then a certain man, called John the Savage, came in great rage saying : ' Infamous one, why hast thou married the wife of thy brother ? He hath died an evil death, so wilt thou be cut down by the divine scythe without pity and come to misery in a foreign country and perish there, because thou wilt not leave the first seed to thy brother but only indulge your passions and commit adultery.' Herod in rage ordered him to be beaten and driven off. John, however, did not cease with his reproaches wherever he found him, in public, until Herod had him put in fetters and thrown into prison.

16. John in Prison

From the Emesan *Vita.*

17. The Beheading of the Baptist

From the same source.

18–29. Josephus on Jesus

At that time there appeared a certain man, if it is permissible to call him a man, for his appearance and shape were human, only his looks were more than human and his actions were divine, *for he did many miracles and accomplished powerful deeds.* For this reason it is impossible to call him a man. *But in view of his* human [1] *nature I shall not call him an angel either. He wrought everything by word of mouth. Some said that he was our first lawgiver risen from the dead, others that he had been sent by God. In many points, however, he acted contrary to the Law, for he did not observe the Sabbath according to our custom. He did nothing wrong, neither was he guilty of anything shameful. Many of the people followed after him, listening to his teaching, since they believed that he would free the tribes of the Jews from the hands of the Romans. It was his custom, most of the time, to stay without the city on the Mount of Olives, and there gathered one hundred and fifty pupils and many of the lower classes. Those who had seen his power, how he accomplished anything he wished with a mere word, told him to enter the city and to kill the Roman garrison together with Pilate. He was to be lord in their stead.* Yet his own mind was not turned to these things. *When the chief of the priests of the Jews heard this, they met, saying : ' We cannot accomplish anything against the Romans, so we had better inform Pilate and be without care, for if he hears of it from others he will deprive us of our goods and will kill us and sell our children as slaves. They then went and informed Pilate. He sent for the wonderworker* (*i.e.* Jesus) *and questioned him and recognized that he was a* benefactor and neither a *robber* nor a *malefactor,* nor even a *rebel* or an *impostor eager for rule. He therefore let him go free again, and Jesus returned to his accustomed place, continuing with his calling.*

19. *When still more people flocked to him, the scribes grew even more envious. . . .* There follows the account of Judas' treason and Jesus' capture. *'They therefore took him prisoner and brought him to the*

---

[1] Correction for ' common.'

governor Pilate.' Then follows Pilate's bribery, his enquiry into the
Osanna cries, the episode of Pilate's wife, the trial proper (according to
the Gospels, but much enlarged by apocryphal material). Nicodemus
is made to report to Pilate : ' I say to the scribes, high priests, and
levites : "What do you want to do with *this man who had performed so
many signs and miracles which no one else can do ?*[1] Leave this man in
peace and do not counsel evil against him, for if these signs are from
God they will endure; if not, they will perish."'[2] . . . Pilate then is
made to address the Jews : ' His people are the Jews, who say that he
is *eager for dominion*, therefore I have *pronounced the death sentence
on him.'* And he added : ' First you must bind him *according to
Caesar's law* and whip him, after which he is *to be hanged on the cross.'*

30. The Number of the Talents

' It is written that one talent equals 500 rubels ; according to this
count the sum-total was 15,000 rubels.
' The sum-total of the shekels. It is written that one shekel equals
12 lire, that is, altogether 360 lire ; 1 lira is supposed to equal 60
rubels, which makes, for 360 lire, 21,600 rubels. The measure of the
shekels was 86 quarters (*ferdele* or *merte*), as they were then in currency,
and 16 pounds; but according to our Russian count each pound was the
equivalent of 4 rubels, 22 *altine*, and $4\frac{1}{2}$ *denghiuri* ; 360 lire are then
1685 rubels, 25 *altine*, and 2 *denghiuri*. The measure was $6\frac{3}{4}$ *merte*.
But even according to this count it was very much.'

31. The Crucifixion

According to Malalas.

32. Josephus the Jew on the Temple Curtain

' *Within the temple the gates were all made of gold, fifty-five ells high
and sixteen wide. In front of them there was a curtain of the same height
and width as the gates, of fine Oriental linen, studded with jewels, of byssus,
red silk, and purple, wonderful to behold, for it was done with great art.
The red silk represented the fire, the byssus the earth, the jewels the air, and
the purple the sea, thus corresponding to the four elements. There was
painted upon it the whole sky and its order.* So long as the people
believed, the curtain was whole, but now it is in a sorry state, since all
of a sudden it was rent asunder from top to bottom, at the time when
that benefactor was condemned to death.'[3]

33. The Descensus ad Inferos

', Taken from Polish books.' The whole text is contained in both of
Dr. Gaster's MSS.

---

[1] Cf. above, p. 61 n. 11, and p. 62.   [2] Cf. above, p. 529₉.
[3] Cf. above p. 250 n. 1.

APPENDIX IX

EDITIONS OF TRANSLATIONS OF JOSEPHUS

The first Latin Josephus, at Augsburg, Johann Schüssler, in 1470, was reprinted a ' countless number of times ' [1] previous to the publication of the *editio princeps* of the Greek original.

The best of these editions is that of Basle, 1524. In the same city the Protestant theologian Sebastian Chateillon included Josephus in his Latin edition of the Bible (1551).

From the Latin are derived the following translations : —

German : Caspar Hedion (Strassburg, 1531); the second edition of 1561, revised after the Greek text ; Feyerabend and Rab (Frankfurt, 1571) ; Lautenbach (Strassburg, 1597).[2]

Flemish : Symon Cock (Antwerp, 1552-3).

Spanish : M. Nucio (Antwerp, 1554), prohibited by the censor's *Index Expurgatorius* in 1559, although it contains nothing but the Canonic Testimonium Flavianum.

French : François Bourgoing (Lyons, 1562) ; Jean le Frère de Laval (Paris, 1569) ; Archbishop Gille Genébrard (Paris, 1578) ; Antoine de la Faye (Paris, 1597) ; d'Andilly (Paris, 1668) ; Arnauld Gollet (Paris, 1756), the later ones with due regard for the Greek original.

Italian : Andrea Berna (Venice, 1620) ; Pietro Lauro (Venice, 1638), likewise with consideration of the Greek text.

Dutch : S. de Vries (Amsterdam, 1698), both after the Latin and the Greek.

APPENDIX X

EDITIONS OF THE GREEK TEXT OF JOSEPHUS

The Greek original was carried to the Occident by fugitive Greeks, naturally in the shape it had received in the time of Emperor Alexios Komnenos.[3]

Editio princeps, Basle, Frobenius and Episcopius, 1544 ; edited by Arnold Peraxylos Arlen,[4] pirated in Geneva, 1611 and 1634.

Learned editions : Ittig (Leipzig, 1691), Bernard (Oxford, 1700), Hudson (Oxford, 1720), Havercamp (Amsterdam, Leyden, Utrecht, 1726).

[1] Schürer-Macpherson, *op. cit.*, vol. i. 1, p. 102.
[2] For a full bibliography, cf. Fabricius-Harles, *Bibl. Gr.*, v. 31, 38, 48 ; Fürst, *Bibl. Jud.*, ii. 121-3; and Schürer-Macpherson, vol. i. 1, p. 106.
[3] See above, p. 168.
[4] Born in Brabant, died in Basle in 1561 ; cf. Christian Gottlieb Jöcher, *Allgem. Gelehrtenlexikon*, iii. (Leipzig, 1751), col. 1375. [Translator's note.]

APPENDIX XI

English Translations of the Greek Josephus

Thomas Lodge (London, 1640), Roger Le Strange (London, 1716) ; both excelled by that of the Unitarian William Whiston (Dublin, 1736-41), who in 1710 had lost his university chair at Cambridge on account of his religious tenets. Reprinted many times, and exceedingly popular because commonly read by the young folk on the Puritanical Sundays when more ' secular ' readings were prohibited ;[1] there is a reprint from 1889-90, revised by the Rev. A. R. Shilleto and General Sir C. W. Wilson, another by Prof. D. S. Margoliouth. Thompson and Price, London, 1777-8 ; John Henry Maynard, New York, 1792. The stylistically excellent translation by the Rev. Dr. R. Traill (with annotations by Isaac Taylor, London, 1862) remained incomplete owing to the premature death of the translator. The most recent and reliable translation by Dr. H. St. J. Thackeray, with an edition of the Greek original after Niese, is at present appearing as part of the Loeb Classical Library. The new French translation, undertaken by the late Théodore Reinach in 1900, has just been completed by his brother, M. Salomon Reinach.

APPENDIX XII

Origen's Josephus Text

Origen did not yet know the *Testimonium Flavianum* in its extant form, but in one quite different in tone and contents and leaving no doubt about Josephus' hostility to Jesus and his claims.

Orig., *Ad Matt.* x. 17, ed. Lommatzsch, iii. 46 (on *Matt.* xiii. 55, mention of James, the brother of Jesus) :

" ἐπὶ τοσοῦτον δὲ διέλαμψεν οὗτος ὁ Ἰάκωβος ἐν τῷ λαῷ ἐπὶ δικαιοσύνῃ, ὡς Φλάβιον Ἰώσηπον, ἀναγράψαντα ἐν εἴκοσι βιβλίοις τὴν Ἰουδαϊκὴν ἀρχαιολογίαν, τὴν αἰτίαν παραστῆσαι βουλόμενον τοῦ τοσαῦτα πεπονθέναι τὸν λάον, ὡς καὶ τὸν ναὸν κατασκαφῆναι, εἰρηκέναι κατὰ τὴν μῆνιν θεοῦ ταῦτα αὐτοῖς ἀπηντηκέναι, διὰ τὰ εἰς Ἰάκωβον τὸν ἀδελφὸν Ἰησοῦ τοῦ λεγομένου Χριστοῦ ὑπὸ τούτων τετολμημένα. Καὶ τὸ θαυμαστόν ἐστιν, ὅτι τὸν Ἰησοῦν ἡμῶν οὐ καταδεξάμενος εἶναι Χριστόν, οὐδὲν ἧττον Ἰακώβῳ δικαιοσύνην ἐμαρτύρησε τοσαύτην. Λέγει δὲ ὅτι καὶ ὁ λαὸς ταῦτο ἐνόμιζε διὰ τὸν Ἰάκωβον πεπονθέναι·" c. Cels., ii. 13, ed. Lommatzsch, xviii. 161 : . . . " οὗ (Οὐεσπασιανοῦ) ὁ υἱὸς Τίτος καθεῖλε τὴν Ἱερουσαλήμ, ὡς μὲν Ἰώσηπος γράφει, διὰ Ἰάκωβον, τὸν δίκαιον, τὸν ἀδελφὸν Ἰησοῦ τοῦ λεγομένου Χριστοῦ, ὡς δὲ ἀλήθεια παρίστησι, διὰ Ἰησοῦν τὸν Χριστόν, τὸν υἱὸν θεοῦ." c. Cels., i. 47, Lomm., xviii. 87 : " ἐν γὰρ τῷ ὀκτωκαιδεκάτῳ τῆς Ἰουδαϊκῆς ἀρχαιολογίας ὁ Ἰώσηπος μαρτυρεῖ τῷ Ἰωάννῃ ὡς βαπτιστῇ γεγενημένῳ. . . . Ὁ δ' αὐτὸς καίτοι γε ἀπιστῶν τῷ Ἰησοῦ ὡς Χριστῷ, ζητῶν τὴν αἰτίαν τῆς Ἱερουσολύμων πτώσεως καὶ τῆς ναοῦ καθαιρέσεως· δέον δ' αὐτὸν εἰπεῖν, ὅτι ἡ

---

[1] Cf., for example, Arnold Bennett's novel *Clayhanger* (1911).

κατὰ τοῦ Ἰησοῦ ἐπιβουλὴ τούτων αἰτία γέγονε τῷ λαῷ, ἐπεὶ ἀπέκτειναν τὸν προφητευόμενον Χριστόν· ὁ δὲ καὶ ὥσπερ ἄκων οὐ μακρὰν τῆς ἀληθείας γενόμενος, φησὶ ταῦτα συμβεβηκέναι τοῖς Ἰουδαίοις κατ᾽ ἐκδίκησιν Ἰακώβου τοῦ δικαίου, ὃς ἦν ἀδελφὸς Ἰησοῦ τοῦ λεγομένου Χριστοῦ ἐπειδήπερ δικαιότατον αὐτὸν ὄντα ἀπέκτειναν."

APPENDIX XIII

IMPORTANT CHRISTIAN MARGINAL GLOSSES IN JOSEPHUS MSS.

B. Niese pointed out the existence of very curious glosses occurring in a number of Josephus MSS. (*Hist. Zeitsch.*, lxxvi., 1896, p. 216 n. 2). Thus, for example, several codices bear on the margin the words παραλείπεις, Ἰώσηπε, τὴν μοσχοποιΐαν αἰδοῖ τῶν προγόνων, at the place where in the *Antiquities* Josephus discreetly omits the making of the golden calf (*Ex.* xxxii). In the Cod. Urbinus Vatic., 84 membr. (saec. xi.), the cool remark of Josephus on the prophecy of Micah (*Bell.*, vi. 5. 4, § 312, Niese) is criticized by the following lines, written on the lower margin :

"οὐκ ἀμφίβ(ο)λος ὁ χρησμὸς ἀ(υ)τὸς, ὦ σὺ τεράτ(ουρ)γε Ἰώσηπε. ἀλ(λ)ὰ δῆλον καὶ σαφὲς περὶ τοῦ ἐμοῦ δεσπότου καὶ θεοῦ, τοῦ Χριστοῦ ὃν σὺ παρεξηγούμενος Οὐεσπασιανὸν ἐπεισάγεις τῇ προφητείᾳ ἀλλὰ γὰρ ὁ Χριστὸς μόνος τηνικαῦτα καὶ τῆς Ἰουδαίας ὡρμήθη καὶ τῆς οἰκουμένης ἦρξε. Καὶ ἔτι νῦν ἄρχει. βασιλεὺς βασιλέων αἰώνιος καὶ ὢν καὶ λεγόμενος. Καὶ ὑπὸ πάσης σχεδὸν πνοῆς προσκυνούμ(ενος) καὶ σεβόμενος. Οὐεσπασιανός δὲ ὁ παρὰ σοῦ κολακευόμενος τέφρα καὶ κόνις ὢν διερρύη καὶ ὤχετο." Codex Paris. Bibl. Nat., gr. 1425 s.x-xi., and Codex Ambrosianus D, add to this sentence in margin : " σῆ· ἐν τούτῳ καὶ ὁ μέγας αὐτῷ Ἰω(άνης) Χρ(υσόστομος) συμφώνει."

The Codex Marcianus observes on *B.J.*, iv. 8. 4 (containing the story of Sodom and Gomorrha), where Josephus refers to the story of the divine chastisement of the godless cities as μυθευόμενα, " σῆ(μεῖον). ἄπιστος ἄνθρωπος οὐδὲ Ἑβραῖός ἐστι," 'the unbeliever is not even a Jew"!, which clearly betrays the indignation of the scribe.

At the mention of the Emperor Titus and the praise bestowed upon him by Josephus, the scribe exclaims : " ὦ τῆς κολακείας τοῦ συγγραφέως "!

The following marginal gloss to *B.J.*, v. 13. 6, is found in Codex Berolinensis, 223 (Niese praef. to vol. vi. p. xi) :

" νῦν ἄκων, ἀσεβέστατε καὶ τῆς ἀληθείας ἐχθρέ, τῆς ἀληθείας (sic !) εἴρηκας ὑπ᾽ αὐτῆς ἐκείνης τῆς ὄντως ἀληθείας ἐλαυνόμενος· μήτε γενεὰν ἄλλην κακίας γονιμωτέραν γενέσθαι. μήτε μὴν τηλικαῦτα κακὰ πεπονθέναι τινὰ ἄλλην, καὶ γὰρ ἄλων πολλῶν ἀγαθῶν τε καὶ κακῶν γεγονότων Ἑβραίων ὑμεῖς μόνοι τὴν ὑπερβολικὴν καὶ πασῶν κακιῶν ἐσχάτην κακίαν καὶ ἀδελίαν εἰργάσασθε· τὸν κύριον ἡμῶν Ἰησοῦν Χριστὸν καὶ σωτῆρα τοῦ κόσμου παντὸς σταυρῷ προσηλώσαντες· καὶ διὰ τοῦτο μόνοι ὑμεῖς τοῦ ἀληθεστάτου καὶ ἀψευδοῦς ἐκείνου στόματος τῆς σκυθρωπῆς ἀποφάσεως τὴν δικαίαν ποινὴν ὑφίστασθε· ὡς ἐκεῖνος που φησὶν· ἔσται θλῖψις ἐν τῇ ἁλώσει ὑμῶν οἷα οὐ γέγονεν ἀπὸ καταβολῆς κόσμου οὔτε μὴν ἀλλαχοῦ γενήσεται."

It goes without saying that glosses of this type, precisely because of their personal nature, were not included in the text proper.

THE SOURCES OF THE GENEALOGIES OF JESUS IN
MATTHEW AND LUKE

Cod. Laurentian. plut., lxix. 20 f⁰. 164 v⁰. in marg. ad *Ant.*, xiv.
§ 121, offers the following highly instructive gloss (photograph on
Pl. xiii. of the German edition) :

"περὶ τούτου (scil. Ἡρώδου) καὶ ὁ θεάδελφος Ἰάκωβος ἀπεφήνατο· «οὐκ
ἐκλείψει» λέγων «ἄρχων ἐξ Ἰουδὰ καὶ ἡγούμενος ἐκ μήρων αὐτοῦ ἕως ἂν ἔλθῃ
ὁ ἀπόκειται καὶ αὐτὸς προσδοκία ἐθνῶν.» καὶ γὰρ οὕτως ἔχει· τοῦ γὰρ σωτῆρος
ἡμῶν Ἰησοῦ Χριστοῦ τοῦ ἀληθινοῦ θεοῦ σαρκὶ φανερωθέντος πέπαυται ἡ τῶν
Ἰουδαίων ἡγεμονία καὶ ἀλλόφυλος ὢν Ἡρῴδης Ἀσκαλωνίτης ὁ τοῦ Ἀντιπάτρου
ἐπικρατεῖν τῶν Ἰουδαίων ἦρξατο."

This quotation from James cannot very well be separated from the
statements on the Ascalonite descent of Herod as given by Eusebius [1]
from a letter of Julius Africanus addressed to Aristeides.[2] These
statements evidently go back to the δεσπόσυνοι, i.e. the κατὰ σάρκα
συγγενεῖς of Jesus.[3] In practically all the Christian writers [4] giving
this descent of Herod, with details such as Antipater's office of a temple-
slave at the sanctuary of Apollo at Ascalon, his being carried to Idumaea
by ' robbers,' etc., we also find the anti-Herodian interpretation of *Gen.*
xlix. 10, often even connected, as in the priests' dialogue in the Slavonic
Josephus, with speculations and calculations about the famous seventy
or seventy-two year-weeks of Daniel.

In the above-quoted letter of Julius Africanus we furthermore
find the statement that the aforementioned relatives of Jesus, migrating
through the world from the villages of Nazareth and Kokhᵃba, used to
show a genealogy which, as they said, had somehow escaped the fabled
burning of the Jewish *Toldoth* or genealogies by Herod.[5] For Herod,
being the son of Antipater of Ascalon, etc. etc., and hence a Philistine,[6]
was accused in this document of having burned the genealogies of the
Jewish nobles in order to make it impossible for his political opponents
to refute his claims to a noble Jewish descent.[7]

---

[1] *Hist. eccl.*, i. 6. 2-3 ; i. 7. 11, 13-15. Cf. *Chron. bipart.*, ed. Schoene, 130 ;
ii. 134, 138. German trans. from the Armenian by J. Karst, *G.C.S.*, xx. 209.

[2] Euseb., *H.E.*, i. 7. 11. Special ed. by W. Reichardt in Harnack-Schmidt,
T.U., xxxiv. 3 (1909), p. 1163.

[3] Euseb., *loc cit.* : "τοῦ γοῦν Σωτῆρος οἱ κατὰ σάρκα συγγενεῖς εἴτ' οὖν φανητιῶντες
(=boasting) εἴθ' ἁπλῶς ἐκδιδάσκοντες πάντως δὲ ἀληθεύοντες, παρέδοσαν καὶ ταῦτα ὡς
Ἰδουμαῖοι λῃσταί κτλ . . . ταῦτα μὲν κοινὰ καὶ τοῖς Ἑλλήνων ἱστορίαις."

[4] Justin., *Dial. c. Tryph.*, c. 52 (*P.G.*, vi. 590). Cf. Poznanski, *Schiloh*, p. 506,
Epiph., p. 348 ; Georg. Syncell., *chronogr.*, p. 586, ed. Bonn, where Eusebius'
chapter περὶ τέλους τῆς Ἰουδαίων βασιλείας καὶ Ἡρώδου ἀλλοφύλου is given as a source ;
Chron. Pasch., i. 349 and 361, ed. Bonn ; Sulpicius Severus, ii. 27.

[5] In reality these archives, with their documents, genealogical and other, were
destroyed in the rebellion of A.D. 66.

[6] The term ἀλλόφυλος, constantly applied to Herod, is regularly employed in the
Greek Old Testament for the Philistines, though not in the Hexateuch, where we
find instead the word Φυλιστιείμ. Cf. Stark, *Gaza*, p. 67 *sqq.* ; Reland, *Palaest.*,
p. 75 *sq.* ; G. F. Moore, *Encycl. Bibl.*, 3713. The names Antipater and Herod are
well attested for Ascalon, one of the capitals of the Philistine country, and Herod
may very well have been a descendant of these old Illyrian pirates.

[7] Cf. the corresponding statement of Herod's court historiographer, Nicolaus
of Damascus, Josephus, *Ant.*, xiv. 1, 3.

It seems to be clear that the writing mentioned in the above-quoted Florentine gloss to Josephus as coming from James the brother of Jesus, and containing the anti-Herodian interpretation of the Shiloh passage, cannot be anything else than the genealogy of the clan of Jesus known to Sextus Julius Africanus.[1] It would appear natural enough that these poor descendants of Jesus' family, still existing in the time of Domitian,[2] called such a genealogy the work of their illustrious grand-uncle James the Just, with whose name the apocryphal Gospel of the Childhood of Jesus was in much the same way connected. No doubt the same book is meant in Origen in *Ev. Matt.*, x. 17 (iii. p. 45, Lommatzsch), where the learned father says that the brothers and sisters of Jesus are the children of an earlier marriage of Joseph, and continues with these words :

"(τοῦτο) φασί τινες . . ἐκ παραδόσεως ὁρμῶντες τοῦ ἐπιγεγραμμένου κατὰ Πέτρον εὐαγγελίου ἢ τῆς βίβλος Ἰακώβου,"

since the extant *Protevangel of James* does not contain anything of the sort.

Since the description of this pedigree, 'culled from memory and from the books of *Chronicles*,' seems to fit exactly the βίβλος γενέσεως Ἰησοῦ Χριστοῦ υἱοῦ Δαβὶδ υἱοῦ Ἀβραάμ [3] now prefixed to the *Gospel of Matthew* ; and since a genealogy of Jesus is necessarily also one of his kindred, it is surely legitimate to conjecture that this well-known family tree (and probably also the subsequent story of the children massacred by the same tyrant who is accused by our genealogist of having ruthlessly destroyed the Jewish archives) is copied from the anti-Herodian *Toldoth Jeshu*, compiled by the family of Jesus and known both to Origen and to the Florentine gloss discussed above as a work of James the Just.

Naturally, this genealogy must have concluded, as in the Cod. Syr. Sinaiticus, with the words, 'Josephus, however, begat Jesus, who was

[1] Euseb., *H.E.*, i. 7. 13 *sq.* : "'Ἀναγράπτων δὲ εἰς τότε ἐν τοῖς ἀρχείοις ὄντων τῶν Ἑβραϊκῶνγ ἐνῶν καὶ τῶν ἄχρι προσηλύτων ἀναφερομένων, ὡς Ἀχίωρ τοῦ Ἀμμανίτου καὶ Ῥοὺθ τῆς Μοαβίτιδος τῶν τε ἀπ' Αἰγύπτου συνεκπεσόντων ἐπιμικτῶν Ἡρῴδης οὐδέν τι συμβαλλομένου τοῦ τῶν Ἰσραηλιτῶν γένους αὐτῷ καὶ τῷ συνειδότι τῆς δυσγενείας κρουομένους ἐνέπρησεν αὐτῶν τὰς ἀναγραφὰς τῶν γενῶν, οἰόμενος εὐγενὴς ἀναφανεῖσθαι τῷ μηδὲ ἄλλον ἔχειν ἐκ δημοσίου συγγραφῆς τὸ γένος ἀνάγειν ἐπὶ τοὺς πατριάρχας ἢ προσηλύτους τούς τε καλουμένους γειώρας τοὺς ἐπιμίκτους. Ὀλίγοι δὲ τῶν ἐπιμελῶν ἰδιωτικὰς ἑαυτοῖς ἀπογραφὰς ἢ μνημονεύσαντες τῶν ὀνομάτων ἢ ἄλλως ἔχοντες ἐξ ἀντιγράφων ἐναβρύνονται σωζομένης τῆς μνήμης τῆς εὐγένειας· ὧν ἐτύγχανον οἱ προειρημένοι καλούμενοι. . ἀπο τε Ναζάρων καὶ Κωχαβὰ κωμῶν Ἰουδαϊκῶν τῇ λοιπῇ γῇ ἐπιφοιτήσαντες καὶ τὴν προειρημένην γενεαλογίαν ἐκ μνήμης ἐκ τε τῆς βίβλου τῶν Ἡμερῶν εἰς ὅσον ἐξικνοῦντο ἐξηγησάμενοι. εἴτ' οὖν οὕτως εἴτ' ἄλλως ἔχει σαφεστέραν ἐξήγησιν οὐκ ἂν ἔχοι τις ἄλλος ἐξευρεῖν. . καὶ ἐν τέλει δὲ τῆς αὐτῆς ἐπιστολῆς προστίθησιν ταῦτα . ."

[2] Euseb., *H.E.*, iii. 20, 1-6. They were called Zoker (=Μνήμων or Μνάσων or the like) and Jacob (Philippos Sidetes, ap. de Boor, *Texte u. Untersuch.*, v. 2, p. 169). The last of the family, Conon by name, was put to death in 253 A.D. ; the 'martyrium Cononis ' has been edited by Papadopoulos Kerameus from a MS. of Mount Athos.

[3] The tracing back to Abraham of the genealogy of Jesus is meant to connect him with the prophecy in *Gen.* xxii. 18 : ' through thy seed all the nations of the earth will receive blessing.' This oracle was in turn used as an explanation of *Gen.* xlix. : ' for whom the nations are waiting,' because through him will they receive the blessing foretold.

called the Christ.' It was observed long ago that in this original form the sentence is incompatible with *Matt.* i. 18-ii. 5. The initial words of *Matt.* i. 18, "τοῦ δὲ Ἰησοῦ Χριστοῦ ἡ γένεσις οὕτως ἦν," prove that this sentence is likewise derived from some *Toldoth Jeshu* roll, probably the one used by Luke. The original source obviously continued, immediately after the enumeration of Jesus' brothers and sisters,[1] with *Matt.* ii. 1-23. The story of the three magi fits very well into this context, since it is quoted as a fulfilment of the oracle about the 'expectation of the Gentiles' in *Gen.* xlix. 10, which is the starting-point of this little propaganda tract. As soon as the series of the Hasmonaean rulers, descended 'from Judah' (the Maccabee), or, more generally, the series of Judaean (i.e. Jewish) kings, is brought to an end or interrupted by Herod the Great, 'to whom the sceptre did not belong' (*she lo*),[2] the Gentiles expect the arrival of the 'coming one,' ᾧ ἀπόκειται (to whom it belongs by right). His 'star, rising from out of Jacob,' they have seen. Simultaneously, the ἀλλόφυλος Herod, acting in the rôle of the Antichrist, takes his precautions against the predicted advent of the legitimate Messiah-king; he consults the prophets, and, on their pointing out Bethlehem as the place of the nativity, has all the children of that place massacred. Yet the infant Christ escapes to Egypt and comes back to Galilee after the death of Herod. That is how the lost anti-Herodian *Toldoth Jeshu*, finally utilized by the *Gospel of Matthew*, must have hung together.

Luke, as is well known, has used another genealogy, which purposely omits the names of the ill-famed women Thamar, Rahab, and Bathsheba, carrying back the family tree to ' 'Enosh, son of Sheth, son of Adam, son of God.' In this way it explains the title 'son of God,' together with the other title 'son of man' (*bar 'Enash, bar nasha*), in a most archaic and unorthodox fashion. This genealogy may be traced back to the other branch of Davidides,[3] whom Hegesippus[4] calls 'heretics,' and accuses of having denounced the grandchildren of Jesus' brother Jude to the Emperor Domitian. These *Toldoth Jeshu* knew nothing of the three magi, the slaughter of the innocents, and the flight to Egypt, but gave instead the story of the shepherds, the circumcision of Jesus, his presentation in the temple, the witness of Simeon and Hannah, and the anecdote of Jesus' precocious learning as exhibited in the temple.

---

[1] Cf. the quotation by Origen, above, p. 607 ll. 10 ff.

[2] Euseb., *Chron.*, p. 209 (Karst) : ' Herod, son of Antipater the Ascalonite, and of Kipris the Arab woman, *to whom the kingdom of the Jews did not belong,* obtained the rule through the Romans. In his reign, at the arrival of the Christ, the hereditary high-priesthood and the hereditary dynasty of the Jews were extinct, by which was fulfilled the Mosaic prophecy, "The sceptre shall not depart from Judah," ' etc. (*Gen.* xlix. 10). Also Daniel prophesies the same event, 'And after threescore and two weeks,' etc. (*Dan.* ix. 26). The designation of Herod as ἀλλόφυλος, ' to whom the kingdom does not belong,' is obtained by a pun on the word *shilo*, interpreted as ' she lo '=' to whom *not*,' a pun occurring also in *Ezra* iv. 5-6. Such puns on words are typically Jewish and Rabbinical. Eusebius can hardly have understood such things ; he certainly cannot have invented them. The interpretation of the Daniel text just referred to agrees with the version of Daniel of the Ebionite Theodotion (A.D. 180-92 ; cf. Suidas, s.v. κνίζων, and S. Nili, *Epist.*, i. 63). There the passage is applied, not to the killing of the Messiah, but to the abolition of the high-priestly unction.

[3] Euseb., *H.E.*, iii. 3. 22. [4] In Euseb., *op. et loc. cit.*

Quite recently Prof. Joachim Jeremias [1] concluded from the numerous obvious Hebraisms in *Luke* i.-ii. 40 that this part of the Gospel goes back to a Hebrew source emanating from a circle of the Baptist's disciples [2] and much older than the Greek Gospels. The same Hebraisms have been noticed by G. Kuhn [3] in the genealogies of Jesus themselves. This is in perfect harmony with the statement of Clement of Alexandria [4] to the effect that according to the ' ancients ' (παράδοσις τῶν ἀνέκαθεν πρεσβυτέρων) ' those parts of the Gospels which contain the genealogies ' (τῶν εὐαγγελίων τὰ περιέχοντα τὰς γενεαλογίας) were the first to be committed to writing.

I think that we may consider it an established fact that the two rival septs of Jesus' clan circulated two different Hebrew versions of their royal ancestor's genealogy, birth, and early childhood, which have not been preserved because they taught an adoptionist Christology and contradicted the legend of the virgin birth, but have been utilized in part by Matthew and Luke. These stories were known as *Toldoth Jeshu*, and the anti-Christian *Toldoth Jeshu* [5] are the Jewish reply to these little tracts.

APPENDIX XIV

MORE CHRISTIAN INTERPOLATIONS IN THE JOSEPHUS TEXT

Niese as well as E. Norden [6] pointed out an interpolation in *Ant.*, x. 11. 7, § 276, found in all Greek MSS. but still missing in the second Latin translation at the time of Cassiodorus :

"ταῦτα ἡμῶν συνέβη παθεῖν τῷ ἔθνει ὑπὸ 'Αντιόχου τοῦ 'Επιφανοῦς, καθὼς εἶδεν ὁ Δανίηλος καὶ πολλοῖς ἔτεσιν ἔμπροσθεν ἀνέγραψε τὰ γενησόμενα. [τὸν αὐτὸν δὲ τρόπον ὁ Δανίηλος καὶ περὶ τῆς 'Ρωμαίων ἡγεμονίας ἀνέγραψε καὶ ὅτι ὑπ' αὐτῶν (αἱρεθήσεται τὰ 'Ιεροσόλυμα καὶ ὁ ναὸς [6]) ἐρημωθήσεται.]"

Offhand one might admit the possibility of this being a Jewish interpolation ; but the lateness of the period would pretty well preclude such an hypothesis.

A similar interpolation was pointed out by Ussani [7] in *Ant.*, x. 5. 1, § 78, where the standard text reads as follows :

"'Ιερεμίας δὲ ὁ προφήτης . . . καὶ τὰ μέλλοντα τῇ πόλει δεῖν προεκήρυξε, ἐν γράμμασι καταλιπὼν καὶ [τὴν νῦν ἐφ' ἡμῶν γενομένην ἅλωσιν] τήν τε Βαβυλωνίων αἵρεσιν."

The context shows that Josephus could refer the prophecy of Jeremiah only to the Babylonian captivity, for even in his own speech in *B.J.*, v. 9 (§§ 391-3), where he had the best possible occasion to apply such prophecies to the circumstances of his own time, he did not dream of so doing. To the priest's son those prophecies had evidently been fulfilled, and he would have thought it absurd to expect a second fulfilment. In the context of the *Antiquities* there follows the account of the Babylonian exile, and it would have appeared to him a gross anachronism to men-

---

[1] *Z.N.T.W.*, xxviii. (1929), p. 15 *sq.*
[2] Cf. above, p. 226 ll. 36 f.
[3] *Ibid.*, xxii. (1923), p. 206 *sqq.*
[4] Euseb., *H.E.*, vi. 14. 5-7.
[5] Cf. above, p. 111 and p. 107 n. 1.
[6] *Op. cit.*, p. 648 n. 2.
[7] *Rivista di Filologia*, xlii. (1914), p. 419.

tion there the destruction of Jerusalem by the Romans. There can therefore be no doubt that the words put in brackets were originally marginal glosses by a Jewish or Jewish-Christian reader and included later on in the text.

Another example, though differently interpreted by Ussani,[1] occurs in *Ant.*, vii. 3. 2, § 67 :

" Δαυίδης τοὺς Ἰεβουσαίους ἐξ Ἱεροσολύμων ἐκβαλὼν ἀφ᾽ ἑαυτοῦ προσηγόρευσε τὴν πόλιν. ἐπὶ γὰρ Ἀβράμου τοῦ προγόνου ἡμῶν Σόλυμα ἐκαλεῖτο. Μετὰ ταῦτα δὲ αὐτὴν [φασί τινες ὅτι καὶ Ὅμηρος ταῦτα] ὠνόμασεν Σόλυμα. τὸ γὰρ ἱερὸν τὰ Σόλυμα κατὰ τὴν Ἑβραίων ὠνόμασε γλῶσσαν, ὅ ἐστιν ἀσφάλεια."

The bracketed words were put in by a reader who did not wish to miss in his Josephus copy the Jewish-Hellenistic theory, also taken over by Tacitus,[2] according to which the Solymoi mentioned by Homer were the inhabitants of the Old Testamental Salem.

One might be tempted to consider this interpolator to have been a Jew ; however, the whole ninth book of the *Praeparatio Evangelica* of Eusebius is devoted to no other task than that of showing that the Greeks knew of the existence of the Hebrews and that their historians agree with the Old Testament. From this it would follow that even a Christian might be sufficiently interested in these antiquarian details to add a gloss of this content.

An interpolation not noticed heretofore is found in *B.J.*, v. 5. 7, immediately after the (likewise interpolated) description of the temple curtain, where the breastplate of the high priest is described as follows :

" τιάρα . . κατέστεπτο δ᾽ ὑακίνθῳ· περὶ ἣν χρυσοῦς ἄλλος ἦν στέφανος, ἐκτύπωμα φέρων τὰ ἱερὰ γράμματα [ταῦτα δ᾽ἐστὶ φωνήεντα τέσσαρα]."

It is noteworthy that the bracketed clause is in the present tense, while the rest of the phrase is in the imperfect. One might think, at first sight, that the present tense has its reason in the fact that when the passage was written down the breastplate was still in existence. For Josephus says himself : [3]

" ἡ δὲ στεφάνη εἰς ἣν Μωυσῆς τὸν θεὸν ἔγραψε μία ἦν καὶ διέμεινε ἄχρι τῆσδε τῆς ἡμέρας."

But in that case the whole description should be in the present tense, for the mitre was likewise still existing, though now in the Templum Pacis of Rome. More important still, the text given contains the holy name of God, and the priest's son Josephus would assuredly have been the last to divulge this name to a heathen public. Furthermore, Josephus could not designate יהוה as four vowels, for the Hebrew script of his time used only three vowel characters, א, י, ו, for *a*, *i*, and *u*. There can be little doubt about the fact that the interpolation comes from a Christian hand, from some reader who was anxious to make a show of his antiquarian lore. For this there is documentary evidence. Niese's Cod. C in the Vatican, and Cod. Paris Graec., No. 1428, show in the margin by the side of the words φέρων τὰ ἱερὰ γράμματα a coarse design representing the Hebrew Tetragramm. It is obvious that the bracketed words ταῦτα δ᾽ ἐστὶ φωνήεντα τέσσαρα were originally meant to explain that marginal illustration, and were drawn into the text by a scribe's inadvertence.

[1] *Op. cit.*, p. 397.   [2] *Hist.*, v. 2.   [3] *Ant.*, viii. 3. 8.

APPENDIX XV

THE MUNDUS AND PAULINA EPISODE

The shocking analogy between Paulina's adventure and the corresponding chapter in the Gospel of the Infancy in *Luke* is much more patent in the Latin version of the Christian *Egesippus* than in the standard text of Josephus. I give the passage in question in parallel columns :

Ant., xviii. 3. 4.

[1] About the same time another serious trouble agitated the Jews,[1] [2] and there happened in Rome, in connexion with the temple of Isis, facts which did not fail to cause scandal. I shall mention first the audacious act of the worshippers of Isis, and shall then pass over to the matter of the Jews.[2] There lived in Rome a certain Paulina, noble by her descent and her personal zeal for virtue. She was powerful by reason of her wealth, of great beauty, and, at the age when women are most addicted to coquetry, of great virtue. She was married to one Saturninus, who vied with her in these qualities. Decius Mundus, a knight of the greatest merit, fell in love with her. Since he was aware that she was of too high a rank to be seduced by presents (for she had disdained those which he had sent her in great quantity), he became more and more inflamed, and finally offered her 200,000 Attic drachms for a single night. Since she did not yield even for such a price, the knight, unable any longer to bear his unhappy passion, thought of putting an end to his days by starving. He was thus decided to die, and got ready. Now there was a freedwoman of his father's called Ide, who was an expert in all kinds of crime. Regretting very much the young man's fateful resolution (for it was obvious that he was approaching his end), she went to him

Egesippus, ii. 3, 4.

Under his rule (i.e. that of Tiberius) the well-known joke upon Paulina, a Roman lady of a most noble family, took place. Since she had a great reputation of chastity with all, and was moreover adorned with extraordinary modesty and winning charm, and was therefore inaccessible to the temptation of a certain Mundus, a man of the equestrian order and military leader, she fell into error only through her fault of extraordinary bigotry. For he bribed the priests of Isis, who sent her a message as coming from the god Anubis, inviting her to the temple, since he was delighted with her zeal and modesty and wished to have her one night in order to impart to her something in private. Having received this message, she communicated it with great joy to her husband, saying that the god was listening to her devotions, that he requested her presence, and that she could not but show obedience. Following her own desire and with her husband's consent, she went to the temple of Isis. She passed the night in solitude, ready to receive the divine mystery, and lay down on her beddings thinking that the god would appear to her in her dreams and thus point out to her his will. In the middle of the night, the more easily to deceive the somnolent woman, Mundus in the guise and dress of the god Anubis came, took off his clothes, and began to embrace

[1-1] This was originally the introductory clause of the following chapter on Flavia. It has supplanted the genuine sentence connecting the chapter on Jesus with this one.   [2-2] Not genuine either.

and promised him that he would enjoy the embraces of Paulina. Seeing that he listened to her, she told him that she needed only 50,000 drachms to get for him that woman. Having thus kindled hope in the young man and received the money, she followed a different path from her predecessors, knowing full well that Paulina could not be seduced with money. Knowing that the latter was addicted to the cult of Isis, Ide hit upon the following stratagem. After some negotiations with some of the priests, with a profusion of promises and bribes, 20,000 drachms in cash, and as many to come once the matter was carried through, she told them about the love of the young man, and asked their co-operation to conquer that woman. Won over by the greatness of the sum, they gave her the promise. The oldest of them rushed to Paulina, obtained an interview and requested to speak to her in private. Then he told her that he came from Anubis, for the god, conquered by love for her, invited her to come to him. She received these words with glee, boasted to her friends of the distinction granted to her by the god, and told her husband that she was offered a meal and a night with Anubis. The husband granted her request, since he was convinced of his wife's virtue. She goes to the temple, and after the repast, when the hour of sleep arrived, the temple gates were shut by the priest doing service in the interior and the lights were put out. Then Mundus, who had hidden, did not fail to join her, and she gave herself up to him the whole night, believing that he was the god. He left before the priests, who were privy to his enterprise, began their morning's work, and Paulina, after her return to her husband in the morning, told him about the apparition of Anubis and boasted about it to her friends. Some refused to believe this, others considered the thing a miracle, having no reason for doubt in view of the virtue and good fame of the

her. To the awakened woman he said that he was Anubis. She believed him to be the god, and esteemed herself happy to have been found worthy of the visit of the lord her god. She did not refuse his embraces, questioning only whether a god and a mortal may mix. He quoted the examples of Jupiter, the father of gods, and Alcmena, of Leda and several others who gave birth to gods, adding that she, too, would be the mother of a god through intercourse with him. She returns to her husband full of glee, telling him that she had intercourse with a god and would, according to his promise, give birth to a god. The joy of the husband over the seduction of his wife was great. Afterwards Mundus met the woman and said : ' Paulina, blessed with intercourse with a divinity, the great god Anubis whose mysteries thou receivedst. But learn that thou shouldst not refuse thyself to men any more than to gods, as thou didst, for they do not disdain to give us their shape and their name. The god Anubis called thee to the sanctuary, and Mundus, to join thee there to him. Of what advantage was thy hardness of heart, except that it deprived thee of 20,000 drachms which I had offered thee ? It is easier to imitate the gods, who grant to us what I could not obtain from thee for a great price. Since the name of a human offended thee, it pleased me to call myself Anubis, and thanks to that name I obtained my desire.' At this speech the woman understood that she had been deceived, and in dismay over the insult done to her modesty told her husband about the fraud. Having no reason to get angry at the woman, since he had permitted her to go to sleep in the temple, and convinced moreover of his wife's chastity, he referred the affair to the emperor. The latter, moved to great anger by the outrage on a noble and the atrocity of the crime, had the priests taken from the temple, tortured, and, after their lady. But on the third day after the event, Mundus, meeting her, said : ' Paulina, thou hast saved me 200,000 drachms which thou mightst have added to thy fortune, and yet thou didst not fail to grant to me what I asked of thee. It is of little moment that thou hast tried to insult Mundus ; since I worry little about names but only about the reality of the pleasure, I have given myself the name of Anubis.' Then he left her. She, realizing for the first time that there was foul play, tore her dress and informed her husband of the greatness of the outrage, requesting him to neglect nothing to avenge her. He denounced the matter to the emperor. When Tiberius had learned the exact details of the affair by a judicial inquest against the priests, he had them as well as Ide crucified, caused the temple to be razed and the statue of Isis to be thrown into the Tiber. Mundus he condemned to exile, thinking that he could not inflict upon him a more severe punishment, because passion had made him commit that crime. . . .

confession, executed, whilst he had the statue of Isis thrown into the Tiber. Mundus was granted the liberty of leaving Rome, a heavy fine being considered sufficient in view of the fact that he had acted under the influence of the passion of love.

APPENDIX XVI

THE UTILIZATION OF DOCUMENTARY MATERIAL BY ANCIENT HISTORIANS

On the *tabularium principis*, cf. Hirschfeld, *V.-G.*, i. 206 *sq.*, 3 ; Premerstein, Pauly-Wissowa, *R.-E.*, iv. 756, 20-50.

On the provincial archives, cf. H. Peter, *Gesch. Litt.*, i. 240 ; Mommsen, *Strafrecht*, p. 519, 2, 3 ; O. Seeck, *Zeitsch. d. Savigny Stiftung*, x. ; *Röm. Abt.*, 6 *sqq.* A δημόσιον ἀρχεῖον of the Province of Asia is referred to in Eusebius, *H.E.* (*P.G.*, xx. 476 *sq.*) ; H. Leclerq, *op. cit.*, col. 382, n. 14 *sq.* An *instrumentum provinciae* is found in Apul. Florid., I, ix. ; an *archivum proconsulis* with the diaries of the governors and proconsular officials in Augustin, *C. Crescon.* (*P.L.*, xliii. 359).

A letter of the younger Pliny addressed to Cn. Octavius Titinius Capito, probably in the reign of Domitian, reads as follows :

'C. Plinius Titinio Capito suo : (1) " Suades ut historiam scribam et suades non solus " . . . (7) " Dices : potes simul et rescribere actiones et componere historiam." (12) " tu iam nunc cogita, quae potissimum tempora aggrediar. Vetera et scripta aliis ? parata inquisitio, sed

onerosa collatio. Intacta et nova ? Graves offensae, levis gratia " . . .
(14) "Sed haec me non retardant ; . . . Illud peto, praesternas, ad quod
hortaris, eligasque materiam, ne mihi iam scribere parato alia rursus
cunctationis et morae iusta ratio nascatur. Vale." '

This Octavius Titinius Capito was, according to *C.I.L.*, vi. 789, the
prefect of a cohort, then a distinguished military tribune, *procurator ab
epistulis* under Domitian, *ex senatus consulto* under Nerva, who bestowed
upon him the praetorian decorations, *procurator ab epistulis* under
Trajan, and himself a writer (Pliny, *Ep.*, viii. 12).

APPENDIX XVII

THE VEGETARIAN DIET OF THE BAPTIST

Certain fragments of a commentary on *Matthew*, ascribed to Athan-
asius,[1] interpret the ἀκρίς as an herb (βοτάνη τις), on the ground that
in *Eccl.* xii. 5 it is mentioned along with the almond-tree. Isidore of
Pelusium (died *ca.* 440) in one of his letters [2] says :

'What are the ἀκρίδες . . . on which John the Baptist fed ? They
are not creatures like beetles, as some ignorantly suppose (God forbid !),
but twigs (ἀκρέμονες) of herbs or plants.'

In another letter [3] he remarks that the monks, in emulation of John
the Baptist, ought, if possible, to feed only on cabbage-tops and leaves.
Pantaleon,[4] the deacon of Hagia Sophia (ninth century ?), in an
Epiphany sermon says that John lived on the points or shoots of plants
(τοῖς τῶν βοτάνων ἀκρίσμασιν). But the best and most illuminating of
all these conjectures (for, of course, they are nothing more) is met in the
commentary on *Matthew* by Theophylact of Achrida : [5]

'Some say that the *akrides* were herbs . . . others that they were
fruits or *wild fruits* (ἀκρόδρυα ἤτοι ὀπώρας).'

The reading of the Ebionite Gospel,[6] which for ἀκρίδες substitutes
ἐγκρίδες, 'dough-nuts' baked in oil, is probably based on a recollection
of 'Elijah and the barrel of flour and cruse of oil which failed not during
his stay with the widow of Ṣarephath.[7] The reading ἀχράδες, 'wild
pears,' recommended even by Beza,[8] merits more consideration. The
Ethiopic Bible renders ἀκρίδες by *anvota*, 'grass-tops' ; [9] the Syriac
Gospel has *kamse*, which may mean not only ' locust,' ' ant,' ' snail,' but
also a certain wild vegetable. In the monophysite ' Revelation on the
food of John the Baptist,' the doubtful expression is interpreted as

---

[1] Migne, *P.G.*, xxvii. 1365.   [2] i. 132.
[3] No. 5, addressed to Nilus.   [4] Migne, *P.G.*, xcviii. c. 1245.
[5] Migne, *P.G.*, cxxix. 137 *sq.*
[6] Epiphan., *Haeres.*, xxx. 13, i. p. 350, Holl.
[7] 1 *Kings* xvii. 16.
[8] *Acta SS.*, June iv. 692.   [9] Cf. above, p. 236₈.

referring to certain desert roots ;[1] this work was designed to put an end to monastic conflicts between the βοσκοί or 'grazers,' i.e. vegetarians, and the ἀκριδοφάγοι or 'locust-eaters.'

The reading ἀκρόδρυα, 'tree-fruits,' proposed by Theophylact of Achrida in place of ἀκρίδες, receives special support from a passage in Lucian,[2] which so far as I know had been overlooked hitherto in this connection. The Chaldaean Mithrobarzanes, to prepare Menippus for his journey on the other side of the river, is there represented as first washing himself daily for a whole month at dawn in the Euphrates, while addressing a long prayer to the rising sun.[3] Says Menippus :

'And I came and consorted with one of the Chaldaeans, a wise man and gifted with divine art : he had hoary hair and a venerable flowing beard, and his name was Mithrobarzanes. . . . And the man took me, and first of all, for nine and twenty days, . . . beginning with the (new) moon, washed me, bringing me down at dawn to the Euphrates, while he recited a long oration to the rising sun. . . . And for food we had tree-fruits (ἀκρόδρυα), and for drink milk and honey and the water of the Choaspes, and our bed was on the grass under the open sky.'[4]

As early as the second century of our era there must then have existed καταλουστικοί, mughtasila, Sabaeans, Masbothaeans, Baptists, or Hemerobaptists on the banks of the Euphrates, practising the Mandaic rite of the soul's ' ascent ' to the beyond (masseqta), so delightfully ridiculed by the scoffer of Samosata. These people evidently restricted their food to ἀκρόδρυα, milk, honey, and water, because that was regarded as the fare of the blessed in Paradise. There is thus a strong probability that the original tradition about the Baptist spoke of tree-fruits and young vegetable shoots, and not of the repulsive locusts, which there could have been no religious inducement to consume. On the other hand, it seems to me no less improbable that this is a case of an ordinary lapsus calami or of the unfortunate choice of an erroneous or ambiguous expression. For it is inconceivable that any one wishing to speak of grass or twigs or of an herb called ἀκρίς could have expressed himself so obscurely that an unlearned reader must have understood him to mean a locust. Equally improbable, in my opinion, is the view that the ' locust ' (ἀκρίς) could have arisen out of ' tree-fruit ' (ἀκρόδρυα, or, as Prof. Alexander Pallis [5] of Liverpool supposes, out of a Vulg. Greek ἐκ ῥίζας, ' of roots ') through a mere clerical error. T. K. Cheyne [6] thought of a misreading ḥagabim (' locusts ') for ḥarubim (St. John's bread=carob-pods) in the translation of the Gospel of the Hebrews ; but that would not explain how the ἀκρίδες got into Mark's Gospel. See above, p. 236 n. 16, for a new hypothesis of Mr. Th. Gaster.

[1] Even the ' wild honey ' (μέλι ἄγριον) is replaced by μελεαγρέων ῥίζαι in a poem of Sophronios (P.G., lxxxvii., p. 3756 ; cf. p. 3729 sq.). See the μελάγριαι growing in the desert where St. Cyriacus lives ; Acta SS., Sept. viii. 151, and Suidas, s.v. μελεάγρι : "καὶ ῥίζαις μελεαγρίων καὶ καρδίαις καλάμων αὐτοὺς ἐδεξιοῦτο," a quotation from some Byzantine hermit's life.

[2] Necyom., 6 sq. Cp. Clem. Alex., Paedag., ii. 1. 16, about the apostle Matthew living on seeds, ἀκρόδρυα and vegetables, without meat.

[3] Cf. the similar rite of the Essenes in B.J., ii. § 128.

[4] That is to say, they avoided dwelling in a house ; cf. above, p. 235₃, on the Mandaean priests living under tents in the period preceding their consecration.

[5] A Few Notes on the Gospels, Liverpool, 1903, p. 3.

[6] Encycl. Bibl., col. 2135, art. 'Husks.'

APPENDIX XVIII

JOHN THE BAPTIST, SIMON MAGUS, DOSITHEUS, AND THE MANDAEANS

The first authors of the gnosticizing development of the primitive Naṣōraean doctrine were no doubt the Samaritans Simon Magus and Dositheus. According to the pseudo-Clementine *Homil.*, ii. 23 (*P.G.*, ii. 92), Simon was πρῶτος καὶ δοκιμώτατος among the thirty chosen disciples of the Baptist. After the downfall of the Master, Dositheus became the leader of the disciples, ' because Simon was then in Egypt to practise magic ' (ἀποδημοῦντος γὰρ αὐτοῦ εἰς Αἴγυπτον ἐπὶ τὴν τῆς μαγείας ἐπάσκησιν), and because Dositheus circulated the rumour that he had died there. Yet after his return Simon is said to have again taken the leadership. After this Dositheus, who is called by Epiphanius (*Haeres.*, 13) a learned Jew, who became a Samaritan, and who was fabled not to have died but to have disappeared in a cavern, is said to have been the chief of the Baptists (Σεβουαῖοι, Epiphan., i. pp. 166, 204, 227, Holl=Aram. צבוע, the 'washed ones'; Brandt, Suppl. to *Z.N.T.W.*, xviii. 113, or Μασβώθεοι, Eusebius, *H.E.*, iv. 22. 5, 7; *Constit. apost.*, vi. 6, etc., from *maṣbûta*='baptism'; Brandt, *ibid.*), later on called *Dosithaeans*. Theodore bar Kevani (Pognon, *Inscr. mandaites*, p. 224 *sq.*; W. Bousset, *Hauptprobleme der Gnosis*, p. 383 ; E. Peterson, *Z.N.T.W.*, xxvii. (1928), pp. 65 n. 2, 95 n. 7) says, ' The *Dostai* are called in Maisan Mandaeans, in Beth-Aramajē Naṣōraeans (*Naṣrāiā*).' The 'Cantaeans,' quoted by Theodore as the precursors of the Mandaeans, who derive their doctrine from Abel (*Hibil*), and the Ṣabaeans ('Baptists') mentioned by Albiruni, c. 8, who trace themselves to '*Enosh* (Peterson, pp. 92 and 67 n. 2), are simply the Qenites, usually referred to as Καινῖται, Καιανοί, etc., by the haeresiologists, who are called in the LXX. KENAIOI, KINAIOI, KAINAIOI, etc. *Bar Kevani* (=Saturninos, Σατόρνινος), who writes the word with *k* instead of with *q*, must therefore have drawn on a Greek source. The cosmogonic-mythological speculations of the Mandaeans can be easily derived from people of the type of Dositheus and of Simon, who was educated in Alexandria and who is brought into connexion with Philo by the Samaritan Chronicles.[1]

APPENDIX XIX

THE LAW AGAINST CARRYING ARMS

By accident we have evidence for this early period so far only as Egypt is concerned. From Philo, *in Flacc.*, § 11 (M. ii. 530), it has sometimes been concluded that only the Egyptian Jews were forbidden to carry arms. Yet a papyrus (Wilcken, *Grundzüge*, ii., No. 13 ; cf. J. Nicole, 'Avillius Flaccus préfet d'Égypte et Philon d'Alexandrie d'après

---

[1] Abu'l Fath, p. 157 ; Chron. Adler, 67 ; J. A. Montgomery, *The Samaritans*, Philadelphia, 1912, p. 626 n. 39.

un papyrus inédit,' in *Revue de philologie*, xxii. (1898), pp. 18-27 ; Jean Juster, *Les Juifs dans l'empire romain*, ii., Paris, 1914, pp. 219 n. 6, 220) with an order of Flaccus dating from the twenty-first year of Tiberius—i.e. 33-34, the year following the Palestinian tumults caused by the Egyptian messiah, probably Simon Magus—and renewing the law, in existence as early as the period of the Ptolemies, leaves no doubt about the fact that this law applied to all provincials. According to Mommsen, *Römisches Strafrecht*, p. 658 n. 2, Roman citizens were exempted from this law, which appears to me doubtful, since even in Rome itself no one was permitted to carry arms. Cf. Mommsen-Marquard-Girard, *Droit public romain*, vi. 1, p. 243 n. 1. It is indeed quite natural that ordinary citizens should not have been allowed to possess arms without special authorization. The fact that, according to Dio Cassius, lxix. 12. 2, the Palestinian Jews at the beginning of the second century were allowed to manufacture arms (Krauss, *Talmud. Archaeologie*, i. 205, ii. 310 *sq*.) does not prove that ordinary citizens were permitted to own arms, let alone carry them, as Juster, *op. cit.*, p. 220 n. 2, seems inclined to think. Even to-day the manufacture of arms is in most states a free profession and a private industry, and the sale of arms is usually unrestricted. In spite of this, most states punish the unauthorized possession or the carrying of arms by ordinary citizens. Juster's inference that at the time when the Jews were not allowed to carry arms (Jerome in *Is.* iii. 3 ; *P.L.*, xxiv. 59, written between 408 and 410 : ' apud Judaeos omnis perierit dignitas bellatorum, cum . . . arma portandi non habeant potestatem ') they were surely also forbidden to manufacture arms is therefore far from justified. The prohibition of Cod. Theodosian, xv. 15. 1 (364), ' Nulli prorsus nobis insciis atque inconsultis quorumlibet armorum movendorum copia tribuatur,' is surely no innovation. Cf. Synesius, ep. 107 (Hercher, *Epistologr. gr.*, Paris, 1873, p. 707 : οὐκ ἐξὸν ἰδιώταις ἀνθρώποις ὁπλοφορεῖν).

From the theoretical discussions of the rabbis on the carrying of arms on a Sabbath (Mishna shabb., 6, 14 ; Strack-Billerbeck, i. 996, ii. 827) nothing can be inferred, since it is known that from the purely Jewish point of view private citizens were at all times allowed to carry arms.

APPENDIX XX

PILATE'S ' ICONISMUS ' OF JESUS

Cf. v. Dobschütz, *loc. cit.*, p. 98* ; Iren., *Adv. haer.*, i. 25. 6 (ed. Stieren, i. 253) : ' Gnosticos se autem vocant et imagines quasdam depictas, quasdam autem de reliqua materia fabricatas habent, dicentes formam Christi factam a Pilato illo tempore, quo fuit Jesus cum hominibus ; et proponunt eas cum imaginibus mundi philosophorum, videlicet cum imagine Pythagorae et Platonis et Aristotelis et reliquorum et reliquam observationem circa eas similiter ut gentes faciunt.' Epiphan., *Haer.*, xxvii. 6, p. 310 ; xx. 13 *sqq.*, Holl :

" καὶ ἔνθεν γέγονεν (ἡ) ἀρχὴ Γνωστικῶν τῶν καλουμένων ἔχουσι δὲ εἰκόνας ἐνζωγράφους διὰ χρωμάτων, τινὲς δὲ ἐκ χρυσοῦ καὶ ἀργύρου καὶ λοιπῆς ὕλης,

ἅτινα ἐκτυπώματά φασιν εἶναι τοῦ Ἰησοῦ. καὶ ταῦτα ὑπὸ Ποντίου Πιλάτου γεγε-
νῆσθαι τουτέστι τὰ ἐκτυπώματα τοῦ (αὐτοῦ) Ἰησοῦ, ὅτε ἐνεδήμει τῷ τῶν ἀνθρώπων
γένει. κρύβδην δὲ τὰς τοιαύτας ἔχουσιν εἰκόνας, ἀλλὰ καὶ φιλοσόφων τινῶν,
Πυθαγόρου καὶ Πλάτωνος καὶ Ἀριστοτέλους καὶ λοιπῶν" . . . κτλ.

A free quotation of this Epiphanius passage is found in Nicephor., *Patr.
antirhet.*, c. Euseb. et Epiph. (Pitra, *Spicil. Solesm.*, iv. 297) ; Hippolyt.,
Ref., vii. 32, p. 220 ; xx. 10 *sq.*, Wendland :

"καὶ εἰκόνας δὲ κατασκευάζουσιν τοῦ Χριστοῦ λέγοντες ὑπὸ Πιλάτου τῷ καιρῷ
ἐκείνῳ γενέσθαι."

Antonius Placentinus, *Itin.* (*ca.* 970), c. 23, ed. Gildemeister, Berlin,
1889, p. 17 *sq.*=ed. Geyer, *C.S.E.L.*, xxxix. p. 175 : ' oravimus in
praetorio, ubi auditus est dominus, ubimodo est basilica sanctae Sophiae
ante ruinas templi Salomonis sub platea, quae decurrit ad Siloam fontem
secus porticum Salomonis. In ipsa basilica est sedis, ubi Pilatus sedit,
quando Dominum audivit. Petra autem quadrangulis, quae stabat, in
medio praeturio, in quam levabatur reus, qui audiebatur, ut ab omni
populo audiretur et videretur, in qua levatus est dominus, quando
auditus est a Pilato, ubi etiam vestigia illius remanserunt. Pedem
pulchrum modicum subtilem, nam et staturam communem (= κοινὴ φύσις,
cf. above, p. 384₅₋₆) faciem pulchram, capillos subanellatos, manum for-
mosam, digita longa (quantum) imago designat, quae illo vivente picta
sunt (!), quae posita est in ipso praeturio. Nam de petra illa, ubi stetit,
fiunt virtutes multae ; tollentes de ipsa vestigia pedum mensuram,
ligantes pro singulis languoribus et sanatur. Et ipsa petra ornata est
ex auro et argento.' On statues of Jesus beside that of Homer, cf.
August., *De haeres. liber*, c. 7 ; Oehler, *Cod. haeresiol.*, i. p. 198 ;
Praedestinatus, lib. i., cap. 7 ; Oehler, i. p. 234 : ' The Carpocratian
woman Marcellina had put up in her *lararium* "imagines Jesu et Pauli
et Homeri et Pythagorae."' It is also well to remember the Cologne
philosophers' mosaic unearthed in 1844 and dating from the time of
the Severi (*Zeitsch. f. christl. Kunst*, i., Berlin, 1918, p. 316, and Lersch,
Progr., Bonn, 1845).

APPENDIX XXI

THE ORIGINAL TEXTS CONCERNING THE PHYSICAL APPEARANCE
OF JESUS

Andreas Hierosolymitanus vel Cretensis, ed. Boissonade, Anecd.
Graeca e. Cod. Reg., iv., 1832, pp. 471-4. Cf. Dobschütz, *loc. cit.*,
p. 186* (7) : "ἀλλὰ καὶ ὁ Ἰουδαῖος Ἰώσηπος τὸν αὐτὸν τρόπον ἱστορεῖ
ὁραθῆναι τὸν Κύριον σύνοφρυν (εὐόφθαλμον) μακροπρόσωπον, ἐπίκυφον,
εὐήλικα."

Scholion to Johannes Damascenus, *De fide orthod.*, iv. 16¹, in two
MSS. of the Paris National Library : [1] "ἐπεὶ καὶ Ἰώσηπος ὁ Ἰουδαῖος,

---

[1] Cod. Paris, 1335 (s. xiii.), Combefis, manip. 114. Le Quien, Joh. Damasc,
opp. i. 631a ; Cod. Paris. Coisl. 296, saec. xii. fᵒ. 69 ; Tischendorf, *Anecd. sacra
et profana*, 129 ; v. Dobschütz, p. 303**.

ὥς τινές φασι .. τὸν αὐτὸν ἱστορεῖ τρόπον τὸν κύριον ὁραθῆναι σύνοφρυν, εὐόφθαλμον, μακρόψιν, ἐπικυφῇ τε καὶ εὐήλικα."

Nikephoros Kallistou, Migne, *P.G.*, 145, 747 : "... ἑπτὰ σπιθάμων ἦν τελείων, εὐόφθαλμος καὶ ἐπίρρινος, ἐπίξανθον ἔχων τὴν τρίχα, μέλαινας ὀφρῦς, ἤρεμα ἐπικλινὴς τὸν αὐχένα, ὡς μηδὲ πάνυ ὄρθιον καὶ ἐντεταμένην ἔχειν τὴν ἡλικίαν τοῦ σώματος ..."

Theodoros Anagnostes, Dobschütz, p. 107*, 9a : *Hist. eccl.*, i. 15, ed. Valesius-Reading, Cambridge, 1720, iii. p. 566₂₃₋₂₈ : " ἐπὶ Γενναδίου ἡ χεὶρ τοῦ ζωγράφου ἐξηράνθη τοῦ ἐν τάξει Διὸς τὸν σωτῆρα γράψαι τολμήσαντος. ὃν δι' εὐχῆς ἰάσατο (ὁ) Γεννάδιος· φησὶ δὲ ὁ ἱστορῶν, ὅτι τὸ ἄλλο σχῆμα τοῦ σωτῆρος τὸ οὖλον καὶ ὀλιγόθριχον ὑπάρχει."

Nikephoros Kallistou, *Hist. eccl.*, xv. 23, ed. Fronto Ducaeus, 1639, ii. 623 c ; v. Dobschütz, a. a. O., p. 108* f. : " τούτου δὲ τοῦ Γενναδίου ἱεραρχοῦντος καί τις ζώγραφος ἐπὶ σχήματος Διὸς τὸν σωτῆρα γράψαι τολμήσας ἀντιμισθίαν τῆς πράξεως τὸ ξηρὰν αὐχῆσαι τὴν χεῖρα ἐκτήσατο. ὃν τὸ ἔγκλημα παρρησίᾳ ὁμολογήσαντα εὐχῇ Γεννάδιος ἐξιᾶτο. χρεὼν μέντοι εἰδέναι ὅτι ἐπὶ τοῦ σωτῆρος τὸ οὖλον μᾶλλον καὶ ὀλιγότριχον ἀληθέστερόν ἐστιν, ὡς ἐκ τῶν ἱστορούντων διέγνωμεν."

Theophanes, ed. de Boor, i. 112₂₉₋₃₂, ad anni mundi 5955, Leon a. vi. =463 n. Chr., v. Dobschütz, p. 107* 9 c : "τῷ δ' αὐτῷ ἔτει ζωγράφου τινὸς τὸν σωτῆρα γράψαι τολμήσαντος καθ' ὁμοιότητα τοῦ Διὸς ἐξηράνθη ἡ χείρ, ὃν ἐξαγορεύσαντα δι' εὐχῆς ἰάσατο Γεννάδιος. φασὶ δέ τινες τῶν ἱστορικῶν, ὅτι τὸ οὖλον καὶ ὀλιγότριχον σχῆμα ἐπὶ τοῦ σωτῆρος οἰκειότερόν ἐστιν."

Anastasius Bibliothecarius, Chronogr. tripart., Theophanes, ed. de Boor, ii. 111₁₈₋₂₂, v. Dobschütz, p. 107* g : ' sequenti anno cum pictor quidam pingere salvatorem secundum similitudinem Jovis praesumpsisset, arefacta est manus eius, quem peccatum suum confessum, sanavit Gennadius, aiunt enim quidam historicorum, quod crispis et raris capillis schema in salvatore magis vernaculum sit.'

Epiphanius Monacus Constantinopolit., Dobschütz, p. 302** : " οὕτω καὶ αὐτὸς ἦν εὐόφθαλμος ἐπίρρινος" κτλ.

Dobschütz, a. a. O., p. 303**. Epist. syn. orient. ad. Theophyl. imp., c. 7 : " εὐήλικα, τρίπηχυν, σύνοφρυν, εὐόφθαλμον, ἐπίρρινον, οὐλότριχα, ἐπίκυφον, ἀνεξίκακον."

Anonymous Byzantine homily defending iconolatry, Dobschütz, *l.c.*, p. 246** : "παρέδωκαν οἱ ἀπ' ἀρχῆς αὐτόπται τὸ θεανδρικὸν σχῆμα τρίπηχυ, μικρόν, ἐπικεκυφός ... εὔοφρυ καὶ τοῦτο συνδεμένον, εὐόφθαλμον, εὔρινον, σιτόχροον, οὐλότριχον τὴν κεφαλὴν καὶ ξανθὴν ὀλίγον." " ἀπ' ἀρχῆς αὐτόπται" is derived from *Luke* i. 2.

Anonymous Scholion : "περὶ τῆς τοῦ Κυρίου ἀνθρωπίνης μορφῆς." Dobschütz, p. 305** : " Ἡ καθ' ἡμῶν τοῦ θεανθρώπου μορφή, ὡς παρειλήφαμεν ὑπὸ τῶν αὐτοῦ αὐτόπτων καὶ ἀποστόλων. ἦν τὸ μὲν τῆς ἡλικίας μέγεθος τέλειος ἀνήρ, οὔτε τὸ μέτρον ὑπερβαίνων οὔτε πρὸς τοὐναντίον κατασπώμενος, ἀπέριττος ταῖς σαρξίν, ὑπόκυφος, τὴν κόμην μέγας καὶ συνεσταλμένος θριξί, οὖλος τοὺς βοστρύχους, ἀκερσοκόμης, ἀκούρευτος, ἀσκεπής, διχῇ πρὸς τὸ μέτωπον τοὺς πλοκάμους διεσταλμένος, ἐπίρρινος, ὑποξανθίζων τὰς κόρας τῶν ὀφθαλμῶν, μελάγχρους, μακροτράχηλος, μέτριος τὴν ὑπήνην, οὔτε τανότητι τῶν τριχῶν ταύτην ἐπεσπασμένος, ἀλλὰ συστροφῇ κοσμιότητος σεμνυνόμενος.'

APPENDIX XXII

THE MESSIAH AS A MOSES REDIVIVUS

By the healings of Moses is meant the healing through prayer of Mirjam's leprous hand and the healing of those bitten by snakes ; by the ' arts ' the author evidently means the water supply from a rock, the miracle of the manna, the sweetening of the bitter water, etc. The ἀληθείας προφήτης of the pseudo-Clementines is likewise regarded as the reborn Moses. The peculiar circumlocution ' the first lawgiver ' for Jesus-Moses occurs also in Lucian, *Peregr. Prot.*, 13 : " ὁ νομοθέτης ὁ πρῶτος ἔπεισεν αὐτοὺς ὡς ἀδελφοὶ εἶεν ἀλλήλων," which is hardly a matter of accident, since the words ἄνθρωπος σοφιστής and μάγος ἐκεῖνος ὁ ἀνασκολοπισθείς, likewise found in that passage, leave no doubt about the dependence of the rhetorician of Samosata upon Josephus.

On the miracle of the multiplication of food by Jesus (*John* vi. 31 *sq.*), cf. also my essay in *Z.N.T.W.*, 1925, p. 187.

Nor do the Jewish commentaries leave any doubt about the parallelism of the expected Messiah with Moses ; cf. Midr. Qoh., i. 9 (9b) ; Shir r. 2, 9 *sq.* (100a) ; Num. r., ii. (162b) ; Strack-Billerbeck, i. 87 and ii.481. R.Berekhia (*ca.* 340) said in the name of R. Jishaq (*ca.* 300): 'Just as the first redeemer (i.e. Moses), so the last redeemer (i.e. the Messiah). . . . Just as the first redeemer brought manna down from heaven (*Ex.* xvi. 4), " Behold, I will rain bread from heaven for you," so the last redeemer will bring down the manna (cf. *Ps.* lxxii. 16, " There shall be an handful of corn in the earth "); so the Midr.). Just as the first redeemer let the fountain well up, so also the last redeemer will make the waters to rise (cf. *Joel* iii. 18 : "A fountain shall come forth of the house of the Lord," etc.).'

APPENDIX XXIII

SUIDAS ON JESUS OFFICIATING AS A PRIEST IN THE TEMPLE

The context in which the Josephus fragment is found in the work of the Byzantine lexicographer is not without interest. Under the heading, Ἰησοῦς ὁ Χριστὸς καὶ θεὸς ἡμῶν, Suidas [1] relates the following absurdities :

' In the reign of Justinian there lived in Constantinople a Jewish elder

[1] Ed. Bernhardy, p. 954 *sqq.* The story exists separately in one Parisian and in two Viennese MSS. (Lambeccius, *Bibl. Vindob.*, iv. pp. 158 and 175, viii. p. 367). Cf. Walter, Codex in *Suida mendax de Jesu*, Lips., 1724.

(ἀρχηγός) named Theodosios, a personage well known to many Christians and also to the Emperor. He was urged to convert himself by a Christian called Philippos, an agent of the imperial mint (ἀργυροπράτης), but declined, for purely secular reasons. He confessed, though, that he was convinced of the truth of the Christian persuasion, because, like many other leading Jews, he knew the following secret. There were (at the time of Jesus) twenty-two [1] priests attached to the temple of Jerusalem, and their names were found in a certain list which the author, with a gross anachronism, calls a κῶδιξ, together with their genealogies. Whenever one of the twenty-two departed this life, the Synhedrion chose another. On such an occasion the name of Jesus was proposed by a priest : some said of him that he was not of the tribe of Levi, but of the tribe of Juda, and therefore, since he was apparently not of Levitic lineage, they would not have him become a priest. To which the first priest replies : He is of mixed genealogy. In ancient times there was an intermarriage between the two tribes,[2] and that is where Joseph is descended. To find out the genealogy of Jesus, the assembly cites the parents, but finds out that Joseph has died. However, Mary duly appears and testifies under oath the supernatural conception of Jesus and the virgin birth. Since the worthy fathers still entertain some doubts (not unnaturally under the circumstances), they also have the midwife appear before them, who, fortunately still alive, is not slow in confirming the statements of Mary in every particular. Thereupon Jesus is forthwith appointed priest, and his genealogy, both the celestial and the terrestrial, is duly entered into the κῶδιξ, which at the destruction of the temple was carried to Tiberias and is still kept there under Jewish guard. The good Philippos wants to inform Justinian of these highly interesting facts, but is persuaded by Theodosios of the uselessness of such a step : " a great war would be the consequence and murder would follow," a phrase which lets the cat out of the bag, putting the story in a period posterior to 640, when Palestine was in the hands of the Saracens and a crusade would have been required to fetch the mysterious κῶδιξ. Whilst Justinian is thus deprived of this entertaining story, Philippos cannot help communicating it at least to many of his acquaintances and friends. From them our author got it. Anxious to find out whether this Jew has spoken the truth, he opens his *Josephus* and there finds the statement that "Jesus did (indeed) officiate as a priest in the temple of Jerusalem."'

From this context it follows clearly that the absurd tale was invented to refute two things, namely (1), the Jewish assertion that Jesus was a bastard,[3] and (2), that he illegally assumed to himself priestly rights and privileges. For, quite naturally, the son of Jahveh and a woman of Levitic descent,[4] the foster-son of a presumed half-Levite, was fully entitled to the priestly service in Jerusalem ! The tale was therefore made up in a period when the Byzantine orthodoxy had to combat the Josephinists who used Josephus' historical works to find arguments against the orthodox Christology.

---

[1] A confusion with the twenty-two members of the local *synhedria* (Josephus, *Ant.*, iv. 8. 14 ; *B.J.*, ii. 20. 5).
[2] Cf. *Luke* iii. 24 : the ' son of Levi ' in Jesus' genealogy.
[3] *Jebhamoth*, iv. 13, fol. 49a ; cf. 49b, Dalman in App., p. 7, to H. Laible, *Jesus Christus im Talmud*, Leipzig, 1900, p. 31.
[4] Cf. *Luke* i. 5.

APPENDIX XXIV

Josephus on the Interpretation of the *Shilo* Oracle,
Gen. xlix. 10.

Polemos vi. 5, 4.	Slavonic *Halōsis.*[1]

"Ταῦτά τις ἐννοῶν εὑρήσει τὸν μὲν θεὸν ἀνθρώπων κηδόμενον, καὶ παντοίως προσημαίνοντα τῷ σφετέρῳ γένει τά σωτήρια· τοὺς δ' ὑπ' ἀνοίας καὶ κακῶν αὐθαιρέτων ἀπολλυμένους.

καὶ εἴ τις εὖ ἐννοεῖ, τότε
и аще кто добрѣ разумѣетъ то
εὑρήσει θεὸν προσημαίνοντα ἀνθρώπῳ
обрящеть бᾶ промышляюща за чᾶка.
καὶ παντὶ τρόπῳ προμηνύοντα γένει
и всѣмъ нравомъ проявляющу родоу
ἡμετέρῳ ὅτι πρὸς σωτηρίαν. (καὶ)
нашему, аже на спасение. и
ἡμεῖς δὲ ἀνοίᾳ και κακουργίᾳ
мы[ж] несомыслиемъ. и злодѣйство[м]
αὐθερέτῳ ἀπολλνόμεθα. Θεὸς γὰρ
самоволънымъ погыбае[м]. бᾶ бо
σημεῖα ὀργῆς ἐμήνυσεν, ὥστε γνῶ-
знамениа гнѣвнаа показа. да быша
ναι ἀνθρώπους θείαν ὀργὴν καί
разумѣли люде бᾶжии гнѣвъ. и
παύσασθαι ἀπὸ σφετέρας κακίας καί
престануть от своея злобы и
διὰ τοῦτο κάμψαι θεόν.
тᾱ[м] оумолять бᾶ.

"Ὅπου γε Ἰουδαῖοι καὶ τὸ ἱερὸν μετὰ τὴν καθαίρεσιν τῆς Ἀντωνίας τετράγωνον ἐποιήσαντο, ἀναγεγραμμένον ἐν τοῖς λογίοις ἔχοντες, ἁλώσεσθαι τὴν πόλιν καὶ τὸν ναόν, ἐπειδὰν τὸ ἱερὸν γένηται τετράγωνον.

οὔσης (δ') ἐν Ἰουδαίοις προφητείας
сущу[ж] во июдеихъ прᾱрочьство.
ὅτι τετραγώνῳ σχήματι ἐρημω-
яко четверооуголънымъ образомъ опу-
θήσεται (ἡ) πόλις καὶ (τὸ) ἱερόν.
стѣеть граᾹ и цᾱркы.
[[τότε αὐτοὶ ἤρξαντο σταυροὺς
то сами наᶜша крᶜты
ποιεῖν εἰς σταύρωσιν, ὅ ἐστιν,
дѣлати. на распятие. еже есть
ὡς ἔφαμεν, τετρασχήματόν (τι).]]
яко[ж] рекохо[м]. четверообразныи и.

[1] Edited by Mr. Boris Unbegaun after the photostat of Cod. Kyr.-Bjelos, 64/1303, fol. 250 r⁰. and v⁰. (fig. xlv. p. 591 of the Germ. edition of this book).

Τὸ δὲ ἐπάραν αὐτοὺς μάλιστα πρὸς
τὸν πόλεμον ἦν χρησμὸς ἀμφίβολος
ὁμοίως ἐν τοῖς ἱεροῖς εὑρημένος
γράμμασιν, ὡς κατὰ τὸν καιρὸν
ἐκεῖνον ἀπὸ τῆς χώρας τις αὐτῶν
ἄρξει τῆς οἰκουμένης.

Τοῦτο οἱ μὲν ὡς οἰκεῖον ἐξέλαβον,
καὶ πολλοὶ τῶν σοφῶν ἐπλανήθησαν
περὶ τὴν κρίσιν.

Ἐδήλου δ᾽ἄρα περὶ τὴν Οὐεσπασιανοῦ τὸ λόγιον ἡγεμονίαν, ἀπο-
δειχθέντος ἐπὶ Ἰουδαίας αὐτοκράτορος. Ἀλλὰ γὰρ οὐ δυνατὸν ἀνθρώποις τὸ χρεὼν διαφυγεῖν, οὐδὲ προορωμένοις.

Οἱ δὲ καὶ τῶν σημείων

ἃ μὲν ἔκριναν πρὸς ἡδονήν, ἃ δὲ
ἐξουθένισαν, μέχρις οὗ τῇ τε ἁλώσει

τῆς πατρίδος, καὶ τῷ σφῶν αὐτῶν

ὀλέθρῳ διηλέγχθησαν τὴν ἄνοιαν.

καὶ μετὰ (τὴν) καθαίρεσιν (τῆς)
и по разорении
Ἀντωνίας τὸ ἱερὸν τετράγωνον
анътонии. цр҃ковь четверооугленую
ἐποίησαν. εἰς (τὸν) πόλεμον ἐκίνησε
сотвориша. на ра҃ᵀ. же подвижеᶜ.
κηρύγματα ἀμφίβολα ἐν
проповѣданіа. дво҃ᴴ разумнаа во
ἁγίοις βίβλοις εὑρημένα, λέγοντα
ст҃ыˣ кнїгаˣ обрѣтаемыя глющь ;
ὡς κατ᾽ ἐκείνους καιρούς τις ἐκ
ꙗко в та времена нѣкто от
Ἰουδαϊκῆς γῆς ἔσται ἄρχων δι᾽
июдеискы земля. будеть цр҃ьствоуя наᴰ
ὅλης (τῆς) οἰκουμένης. περὶ τούτου
всею вселеною. о немъ
διάφοροι ἑρμηνεῖαι εἰσίν. οἱ μὲν
разноличнаа сказанна суть. ови бо
ἐνόμισαν (τὸν) Ἡρώδη, οἱ δὲ ἐκεῖνον τὸν
мнѣша. ірода. овиᵂ оного
σταυρωθέντα θαυματοῦργον, οἱ δὲ
распятаго чюдотворъца овиᵂ
Οὐεσπασιανόν. ἀλλὰ γὰρ οὐ
оуеспасиана. но обаче не
δυνατὸν ἀνθρώποις (τὴν) κρίσιν
воᶻможно чл҃коᴹ суда
διαφυγεῖν οὐδὲ καὶ προορωμένοις.
оубѣжати. аще и промыслять.
Ἰουδαῖοι μέν τοι (τὰ) σημεῖα
іюдеи же и [и] знаменна
προνοοῦντες, ὡς δὲ ἤθελον τρέψαντες
судиша. яко же хотѣша. вратящеᶜ
πρὸς ἡδονὴν τὰ ἄλλα δὲ
на свою сладость. другаа же
ἐβλασφήμουν μέχρι (τὸ) ἀπολέσθαι
похоулиша. дондеже погоубивъше
καὶ ἑαυτοὺς καὶ (τὴν) πατρίδα.
и себе и очьство.
ἠλέγχθησαν καὶ ᾐσχύνθησαν καὶ
обличишаᶜ и постыдѣшаᶜ. и
ἐφάνθησαν ἄφρονες.
авишаᶜ безямнии.

APPENDIX XXV

SELECT BIBLIOGRAPHY OF THE SLAVONIC JOSEPHUS PROBLEM

Andrej N. Popov,[1] *A Survey of the Chronographers, compiled in Russian*, Moscow, 1866, pp. 130, 134, 139 (Russ. title above, p. 113 n. 3).

Ismail Ivanovic Sreznĕvski,[2] *Reports and Remarks concerning little-known or unknown Literary Texts*, Supplement to vol. xx. part iv. of the *Memoirs of the St. Petersburg Academy of Sciences*, St. Petersburg, 1879, p. 143 ff. (Russ. title above, p. 113 n. 4).

Michaïl Prince Obolenski, *Annals of the Moscow Society for the History and Antiquities of Russia*, vol. ix., Moscow, 1851 (Russ.).

Gorski and Nevostrujev, *Lectures delivered before the Imperial Society for the History and Antiquities of Russia*, Moscow, 1886, vol. i. pp. 111-114.

N. Bonwetsch in Harnack-Preuschen, *Geschichte der altchristlichen Literatur bis Eusebius*, vol. i., Leipzig, 1893, p. 917.

C. Destinon, *praefatio* to the *Bell. Jud.* in Niese's Josephus, *ed. maior*, vol. vi., Berlin, 1894, p. xxii, quoting from a letter of E. G. Gleye. Cf. Gleye's essay 'Zum Slav. Malalas,' *Arch. f. slav. Philologie*, xvi., 1894, p. 579.

Alexander Berendts,[3] *Die Zeugnisse vom Christentum in slavischen 'De Bello Judaico' des Josephus*, in O. v. Gebhard and A. v. Harnack, *Texte und Untersuchungen*, vol. xiv. part i., Leipzig, 1906.

Berendts' book was reviewed by :—

Emil Schürer, *Theolog. Literaturzeitung*, xxxi., 1906, p. 262 ff.

Abbé Lejay, *Revue critique d'Histoire et de Littérature*, ii., 1906, p. 147.

Jean Réville, *Revue de l'Histoire des Religions*, liv., 1906, p. 151.

Father Adhémar d'Alès, 'Etudes,' *Revue des Pères de la Compagnie de Jésus*, vol. cxii., p. 553.

Reinhold Seeberg, *Reformation*, 1906, No. 19 f.[4]

O. Holtzmann, *Deutsche Literaturzeitung*, 1907, col. 588.

W. Bousset, *Theolog. Rundschau*, x., 1907, p. 297.

H. Jordan, *Theolog. Literaturblatt*, 1907, col. 511.

G. Hoennicke, *Deutsche Literaturzeitung*, 1907, col. 1037.

Adolph von Harnack, the editor of Berendts' publication, has preserved absolute silence about the whole problem ever since 1906.

---

[1] The discoverer of the Slavonic Book of Enoch, assistant-professor at the Lazarev Institute of Oriental Languages in Moscow, born 27th October 1841 in the county of Tambov, died 30th May 1881 during a journey to the Crimea. See his portrait on our Pl. xva.

[2] Compiler of a famous three-volume dictionary of the Old Russian versions of Early Christian authors. On the basis of his collections of Greco-Russian equivalents, a retroversion of the Slavonic Josephus into Greek can be successfully attempted wherever it seems necessary in order to ascertain the genuine words of the lost original. Sreznĕvski was born on 1st June (old style) 1812 in Jaroslavl; died 9th February 1880, as a Fellow of the Russian Academy of Science. See his portrait on our Pl. xvb.   [3] See his portrait on our Pl. xvia.

[4] Reprinted in *Von Christus und dem Christentum*, Gr.-Lichterfelde—Berlin, 1908.

Alexander Berendts, 'Analecta zum slavischen Josephus,' *Zeitschrift für neutestamentliche Wissenschaft*, 1908, pp. 47-70.

Alexander Berendts, 'Die ältesten ausser-christlichen Nachrichten über die Entstehung des Christentums,' *Mitteilungen und Nachrichten für die evang. Kirche in Russland, Theologisch-Pastorales, Beihefte*, vol. lxiii., Nov. 1910, pp. 157-73.

Alexander Berendts, 'Spuren des slav. Josephus in der altkirchlichen Literatur,' in the same periodical, vol. lxiv., Sept.-Nov. 1911, pp. 127-70.

Johannes Frey, *Die Probleme der Leidensgeschichte Jesu*, part i., Leipzig, 1907, p. 35 ff. Reviewed by W. Bousset, *Theolog. Rundschau*, 1907, p. 297.

Johannes Frey, *Der slavische Josephusbericht über die urchristliche Geschichte nebst seinen Parallelen kritisch untersucht*, Dorpat, 1908, extracted from *Acta et Commentationes Universitatis Jurjewiensis-Dorpatensis*, 1908. Reviewed by A. Steinmann, *Theologische Revue*, x., 1910, p. 510.

W. Bousset, *Theolog. Rundschau*, xiii., 1910, p. 438; *Theologie und Glaube*, ii., 1910, p. 414 f. ; *Revue Internationale de Théologie*, xvii., 1910.

Vincente Ussani, 'Questioni Flaviane,' *Rivista di Filologia*, xxxviii., 1910, p. 1 ff. (see also above, p. 62 n. 1).

Berendts' translations have been reprinted by Erich Klostermann in Lietzmann's *Kleinen Texten*, No. 11, Bonn a. Rh., 1911.

Augustin Goethals, *Mélanges d'Histoire du Christianisme* :—

    I. *Josèphe témoin de Jésus*, Paris (Fischbacher), 1909 ; reviewed by W. Soltau, *Berliner philol. Wochenschrift*, xxvii., 1910, No. 24, pp. 662 ff.

    II. *Jean, précurseur de Jésus*, ibid., 1911 ; reviewed by Eberh. Nestle, *Berliner philol. Wochenschrift*, 1912.

    III. *Jésus à Jérusalem*, ibid., 1912.

    IV. *Le Pseudo-Josèphe*, ibid., 1914.

Shirley Jackson Case, *The Historicity of Jesus*, Chicago, 1915, p. 259.

1914-1918

Inter arma silent musae

H. St. J. Thackeray, *Selections from Josephus*, London and New York, 1919, pp. 189 ff.

Vasilij N. Istrin, Essays presented to Lapunov, Učenje Zapiski of the Municipal University of Odessa, Sect. Sc. hum. et soc., vol. ii., 1921, pp. 27-40 (Russ.).

Following a hint of Dr. Moses Gaster, G. R. S. Mead published in *The Quest*, vol. xv., July 1924, pp. 457-79, an article,' 'The Slavonic Josephus Account of the Baptist and Jesus,' reprinted on pp. 97-119 of his book, *The Gnostic John the Baptizer*, London (Watkins), 1924. While preparing this article, my old friend had asked me to look up for him the German literature published since Berendts and Frey. The exceedingly disappointing result of the bibliographical research which I then undertook at Mr. Mead's request caused me to take up the problem myself. I had previously quoted the Slavonic Josephus in an essay on John the Baptist (reprinted, *Orpheus the Fisher*, London, 1921, p. 133₂), following Martin Dibelius, *Die urchristl. Ueberlieferung über Johannes d. Täufer*, Göttingen, 1911, pp. 126₁ and 127₂, ₃-129, without having made an independent investigation of the subject.

The first attempt of my own to grapple with the problem was a lecture before the Anglo-Palestinian Club in Jews' College, London, in the beginning of December 1924. This paper is in the main identical with my essay—

Robert Eisler, ' The Newly Rediscovered Witness of Josephus to Jesus,' *The Quest*, vol. xvi., No. 1, Oct. 1925, pp. 1-15. On page 16 of the same number begins an article on another subject by ' D.D., Th.D.' Vacher Burch, who in his subsequent publications claimed and still claims to have discovered and to have prepared the publication of an early South-Slavonic (that is, Bulgarian) Josephus MS., unknown to the Slavonic scholars of the whole world.

My essay was criticized by A. Marmorstein, ' Some Remarks on the Slavonic Josephus,' *The Quest*, vol. xvii., 1926.

In September 1925 followed Robert Eisler, ' Das wiederentdeckte echte Josephuszeugnis über Jesus,' lecture at the 55th Assembly of German Philologists and Teachers, Erlangen, 29th Sept. 1925. (See *Transactions* of this Congress, published by Teubner, Leipzig, 1925, p. 58.) An analytic and comparative tabulation of the various texts was printed and distributed among the audience. Cf. Klio, *Beiträge z. alt. Geschichte*, xx. 4, 1926, pp. 494 ff.

This lecture was reported and analysed by :—

Franz Kampers, Sunday Suppl. to *Münchner neueste Nachrichten*, Jg. vi., 14th Oct. 1925 ; *Histor. Jahrbuch d. Görresgesellschaft*, vol. xlv. 4, pp. 558-65.

C. F. Lehmann-Haupt, *Frankfurter Zeitung*, 1925, second morning edition of the 13th, 15th, and 17th of December. (French transl. by Salomon Reinach, *Revue Archéol.*, 1926, pp. 322-8.) Cf. Salomon Reinach, *Revue critique d'Histoire et de Littérature*, 15th Dec. 1925, pp. 434 ff.

Dietlef Nielsen, ' Nyt Oldtidsdokument om Jesus,' *Politiken*, 21st Dec. 1925.

L. Wohleb, ' Das älteste nichtchristliche Zeugnis über Jesus, der slavische Josephusbericht,' in the Catholic daily paper *Germania*, 3rd March 1926.

Edgar Salin, *Civitas Dei*, Tübingen, 1926, p. 224 (very important).

Father Hermann Dieckmann, *Zeitschrift f. kathol. Theologie*, Innsbruck, 1926, p. 463-75.

My paper in *The Quest* of 1925 provoked what I am tempted to call the

Strange Interlude

Vacher Burch, ' A Remarkable Discovery concerning Jesus Christ,' *Diocese of Liverpool Review*, No. 1, April 1926. Reviewed by Canon Prof. G. A. Box, *The Observer*, London, 11th April 1926.

Mr. Vacher Burch gave an interview on the subject to *The Times*, London, 13th April 1926, and a letter (14th April 1926) to the editor of that paper.

The readers were immediately reminded by Father Herbert Thurston, S.J., in a letter to the editor of *The Times*, 14th April 1926, of the famous discovery of the Livy MSS. in Naples; see also Salomon Reinach, letter to the editor of *The Times*, 17th April 1926, and Robert Eisler, letter to the editor of *The Times*, 17th April 1926.

An excellent *résumé* was given by Father Herbert Thurston, S.J., 'The Testimony of Josephus to Christ,' in the *Eccles. Review*, vol. lxx. pp. 6-16, Philadelphia, July 1926. Nevertheless, another article of Mr. Vacher Burch appeared in the *Diocese of Liverpool Review*, No. 2, June 1926, announcing the impending publication of his book.

Vacher Burch, *Jesus Christ and his Revelation : Fresh Evidence from Christian Sources and Josephus*, London, 1927, p. 153 ff.

On all these publications see vol. i. pp. 196 ff. of the German edition of this book.

Then followed my lectures on the 13th of January 1926 in the Société des Études Juives in Paris ; on the 17th of January 1926 in the Société Ernest Renan ; on the 28th of June 1926 in the Paris Académie des Inscriptions et Belles Lettres, printed in the *Revue de l'Histoire des Religions*, 1926, pp. 1-21. Robert Eisler, *Jésus d'après la version Slave de Flavius Josèphe* (in German, *Neue Freie Presse*, Vienna, 20th May, 16th and 17th June 1926). Cf. Robert Eisler, 'Wie hat Jesus ausgesehen ? ', *Frankfurter Zeitung*, 1st July 1926.

Reviewed by Hans Lietzmann, 'Wie hat Jesus ausgesehen ? ', *Deutsche Allgemeine Zeitung*, 18th July 1926.

Paul Schmiedel, 'Ein neuer Beweis für die geschichtliche Existenz Jesu ? ', *Neue Züricher Zeitung*, 1926, 22nd Aug. 1926.

Robert Eisler, 'Nochmals das Josephuszeugnis über Jesus,' *ibid.*, 16th Sept. 1926. Reply by Schmiedel, *ibid.*

J. P. Arendzen, 'The Russian Josephus,' *Dublin Review*, July-August-September 1926, pp. 86-106.

H. v. Soden, *Christliche Welt*, 21st Oct. 1926, cols. 1031 f.

Monseign. Pierre Battifol, 'Un prétendu texte nouveau de Josèphe sur Jésus,' *Vie Catholique* (suppl. 'Vie scientifique '), 30th Oct. 1926.

Biblica, 1926, pp, 230 ff. *Verbum Domini*, 1926, p. 191.

Abbé G. Bardy, 'Le témoignage de Josèphe Slave,' *Revue Apologétique*, t. xliii. pp. 344-53.

L. Wohleb, 'Zum literarischen Portrait Jesu,' *Frankfurter Zeitung*, 29th July 1926. 'Zum slavischen *Bellum Judaicum* des Flavius Josephus,' *Philologische Wochenschrift*, 18th Dec. 1926, cols. 1401-3.

Objections by Paul-Louis Couchoud, 'Les textes relatifs à Jésus dans la version Slave de Josèphe,' and by Prof. Maurice Goguel, 'Le témoignage de la version Slave de la *Guerre Juive*,' appeared in the *Revue de l'Histoire des Religions*, 1926, pp. 22-34 and 44-64. My detailed answer to these objections is printed in vol. i. pp. 165-95 of the German edition of this book.

In the course of 1926-7 appeared the great posthumous work of

Alexander Berendts, *Flavius Josephus vom jüdischen Krieg*, Buch i.-iv., nach der slavischen Uebersetzung deutsch herausgegeben, und mit dem griechischen Text verglichen von *Mag. Theol.* Konrad Grass († 25th Nov. 1927), Dorpat, 1924 (printed in instalments until the end of Nov. 1927). It was first utilized by Martin Dibelius, *Urchristliche Geschichte und Weltgeschichte, Theologische Blätter*, Aug. 1927, cols. 220-4.

Hugh Schonfield, ' Jottings on the Slavonic Josephus,' *The Quest*, vol. xviii., 1927, pp. 133-9.

On the 21st and 22nd April 1927 I delivered two lectures, ' L'état présent de la question du Josèphe Slave,' and ' Les origines de la traduction Slave de Flavius Josèphe et l'hérésie joséphiniste,' to the Congrès d'Histoire du Christianisme (Jubilé Alfred Loisy), and to the first Congrès Français des Sciences historiques. They are printed in French, vol. i. of the *Annales d'Histoire du Christianisme*, Paris (Rieder) and Amsterdam (van Holkema and Warendorf's), 1927, pp. 99-113, and *Revue des Études Slaves*, vol. vii. 1/2, 1927, pp. 63-74 ; in English in *The Quest*, vol. xix., Oct. 1928, pp. 1-19, and vol. xx., Jan. 1929, pp. 148-60.

1927 saw the publication of Dr. H. St. J. Thackeray's Introduction to the *Jewish War* in vol. ii. of his Josephus edition and translation in the Loeb Classical Library. The author has honoured me by quoting and incorporating some of my main results in his account of ' the Old Russian Version ' (p. x ff.). Vol. iii., 1928, gives on pp. 635-58, in English, ' the principal additional passages in the Slavonic Version,' with valuable explanatory notes and a list of ' omissions in the Slavonic Version,' books i. and iv., on p. 659 f.

All these publications were ignored by Solomon Zeitlin, ' The Christ Passage in Josephus,' *Jewish Quarterly Review*, vol. xviii., Jan. 1928. He still criticized—two years after I had modified and even abandoned it—an earlier hypothesis of mine concerning an Aramean exemplar of the Russian text.

A rectification of the numerous misstatements of facts in both this paper and the following one (Solomon Zeitlin, ' The Slavonic Josephus and its relation to Josippon and Hegesippus,' *Jewish Quarterly Review*, July 1929, pp. 1-50, reproducing lectures read before the 17th International Congress of Orientalists in Oxford, 29th August 1928, and before the Biblical Society, New York, 27th December 1928) will be found in my article, ' Flavius Josephus on Jesus called the Christ,' in the *Jewish Quarterly Review*, July 1930.

A paper dated November 1928, ' Josephus and Christian Origins,' was published by Dr. Joshua Bloch in the *Journal of the Society Oriental Research*, vol. xiii. No. 3, July 1929, pp. 130-54. Pp. 143 ff. are devoted to ' The Slavonic Josephus.' I shall reply in the same periodical.

In 1928-9 appeared, in instalments, the German edition of this book, ΙΗΣΟΥΣ ΒΑΣΙΛΕΥΣ ΟΥ ΒΑΣΙΛΕΥΣΑΣ, *Die Messianische Unabhängig-keitsbewegung vom Auftreten Johannes des Täufers bis zum Untergang Jakob des Gerechten. Nach der neuerschlossenen Eroberung von Jeru-salem des Flavius Josephus und den christlichen Quellen*, etc., Winter, Heidelberg. It has been reviewed, so far, by :—

Ernesto Buonaiuti, ' La Rivoluzione di Gesu,' *Ricerche Religiose,* 1928, No. 5, pp. 442-5.

Hans Windisch, *Theologische Rundschau,* Neue Folge i., Heft 4, pp. 275 f., 280-7.

Maurice Goguel, *Revue d'Histoire et de Philosophie Religieuse,* viii., No. 4, Strasbourg, July-August 1928, pp. 374 ff. Cp. Maurice Goguel, ' Un nouveau témoignage non-chrétien sur la tradition évangelique selon M. Eisler,' *Revue d'Histoire des Religions,* xcviii., July-Decembre 1928, pp. 1-42.

W. Emery Barnes, *Journal of Theological Studies,* Oct. 1928, pp. 66-8.

L. Wohleb, *Römische Quartalschrift,* 1929, pp. 179 f.

Abbé Gustave Bardy, ' M. Eisler et le témoignage de Josèphe sur Jésus,' *La Vie Intellectuelle,* ii., 15th April 1929.

Reply, *ibid.,* 15th June 1929, pp. 1163-71 : Robert Eisler, ' M. l'Abbé Gustave Bardy et les recherches récentes concernant le témoignage de Josèphe sur Jésus.'

Walter Windfuhr, *Philologische Wochenschrift,* 1929, No. 7/8, pp. 207 ff. ; 1930, No. 47, cols. 1421-1427.

Robert Stahl et P. L. Couchoud, *Mercure de France,* iv., 1929, pp. 194 f.

Aimé Puech, *Revue de Philologie,* 1929, pp. 217 ff. and 426 ff.

G. R. S. Mead, ' A New Quest of the Jesus of History,' *The Quest,* vol. xxi., Oct. 1929, pp. 13-34.

Salomon Reinach, ' Jean Baptiste et Jésus suivant Josèphe,' *Revue des Études Juives,* 1929, pp. 113-36.

Father M.-J. Lagrange, ' Jean-Baptiste et Jésus d'après le texte slave du livre de la Guerre des Juifs de Josèphe,' *Revue Biblique,* xxxix., 1930, pp. 29-46. I shall reply in the same quarterly.

A. D. Nock, *The Classical Review,* Dec. 1929, pp. 223 ff.

G. A. van den Bergh van Eysinga, *Nieuw Theologisch Tijdschrift,* 1929, afl. 4, pp. 360 ff.

Burton Scott Easton, *Anglican Theological Review,* 1930, pp. 325-328.

L'Ami du Clergé, 1929, xlvi. No. 27, p. 420, pretends that I ' have been obliged to admit having been mystified, as Berendts had been before me ' ! I am not aware of having said or written anything to that effect ; still—*sciendum in sacris simulata pro veris accipi* (Servius, *ad Aen.,* ii. 116).

Maurice Goguel, ' Jésus et le Messianisme Politique, Examen de la théorie de M. Robert Eisler,' *Revue Historique,* t. clxii., 1929, Paris, 1930, pp. 1-53. A detailed reply will appear in the same volume. Maurice Goguel, ' Les Théories de M. Robert Eisler,' *Revue d'Histoire et de Philosophie Religieuse,* x., 1930, Strasbourg, pp. 177-90. My reply in the same volume.

Hans Lewy, *Deutsche Litteraturzeitung,* 3rd ser. vol. i. No. 11, 15th March 1930, cols. 481-94. A detailed reply will appear in French in the *Revue Archéologique,* and in German in Prof. Miloš Weingart's review, *Byzantino-Slavica,* 1930.

Georg Wunderle, *Litterarischer Handweiser,* published by Herder & Co., Freiburg i. B., 1929-30, pp. 650-54.

Dr. Moses Gaster is preparing an extensive review for the *Monatsschrift für Geschichte und Wissenschaft des Judentums.*
Walter Bauer, *Theologische Litteraturzeitung,* 1930, No. 24, 22nd Nov., cols. 556-563.

A paper of mine, ' La chronologie de Jean Baptiste et de Jésus dans Matthieu, dans Luc, et dans Flavius Josèphe,' about *Matt.* ii. 22, iii. 1, placing the appearance of John the Baptist under Archelaus, even as the Slavonic Josephus, will appear in the next number of the *Revue Archéologique.* Another one in *Byzantino-Slavica,* Oct. 1930.

INDEX

(1) Authorities

(2) SUBJECTS

Printed in Great Britain
by T. and A. CONSTABLE LTD.
at the University Press
Edinburgh

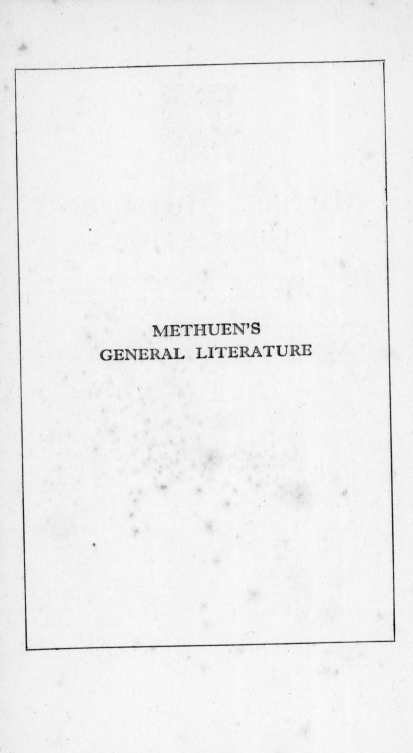

METHUEN'S
GENERAL LITERATURE

A SELECTION OF
MESSRS. METHUEN'S
PUBLICATIONS

This Catalogue contains only a selection of the more important books published by Messrs. Methuen. A complete catalogue of their publications may be obtained on application.

ARMSTRONG (Anthony) ('A. A.' of Punch)
WARRIORS AT EASE
WARRIORS STILL AT EASE
PERCIVAL AND I
PERCIVAL AT PLAY
ME AND FRANCES
HOW TO DO IT
    Each 3s. 6d. net.
LIVESTOCK IN BARRACKS
Illustrated by E. H. SHEPARD.
    6s. net.
TWO LEGS AND FOUR
Illustrated by RENÉ BULL.
    5s. net.

BAIN (F. W.)
A DIGIT OF THE MOON
THE DESCENT OF THE SUN
A HEIFER OF THE DAWN
IN THE GREAT GOD'S HAIR
A DRAUGHT OF THE BLUE
AN ESSENCE OF THE DUSK
AN INCARNATION OF THE SNOW
A MINE OF FAULTS
THE ASHES OF A GOD
BUBBLES OF THE FOAM
A SYRUP OF THE BEES
THE LIVERY OF EVE
THE SUBSTANCE OF A DREAM
    Each 3s. 6d. net.
AN ECHO OF THE SPHERES
    10s. 6d. net.

BALFOUR (Sir Graham)
THE LIFE OF ROBERT LOUIS STEVENSON
Twentieth Edition. 7s. 6d. net.

BARKER (Ernest)
NATIONAL CHARACTER
    10s. 6d. net.
GREEK POLITICAL THEORY
    14s. net.
CHURCH, STATE AND STUDY
    10s. 6d. net.

BELLOC (Hilaire)
PARIS   8s. 6d. net.
THE PYRENEES   8s. 6d. net.
MARIE ANTOINETTE   18s. net.
A HISTORY OF ENGLAND
In 5 Vols. Vols. I, II and III
    Each 15s. net.
ON NOTHING
HILLS AND THE SEA
ON SOMETHING
THIS AND THAT AND THE OTHER
ON
FIRST AND LAST
ON EVERYTHING
ON ANYTHING
EMMANUEL BURDEN
A PICKED COMPANY
    Each 3s. 6d. net.

BIRMINGHAM (George A.)
A WAYFARER IN HUNGARY
Illustrated. 8s. 6d. net.
SPILLIKINS : ESSAYS. 3s. 6d. net.
SHIPS AND SEALING-WAX : ESSAYS
3s. 6d. net.

BLEEK (Dorothea F.)
ROCK PAINTINGS IN SOUTH AFRICA
Illustrated. £2 2s. net.

BUDGE (Sir E. A. Wallis)
A HISTORY OF ETHIOPIA: NUBIA
AND ABYSSINIA
Illustrated. 2 vols. £3 13s. 6d. net.

CHESTERTON (G. K.)
COME TO THINK OF IT . . .
6s. net.
G.K.C. AS M.C. 7s. 6d. net.
THE BALLAD OF THE WHITE HORSE
3s. 6d. net.
Also Illustrated by ROBERT
AUSTIN. 12s. 6d. net.
CHARLES DICKENS
GENERALLY SPEAKING
ALL THINGS CONSIDERED
TREMENDOUS TRIFLES
FANCIES VERSUS FADS
ALARMS AND DISCURSIONS
A MISCELLANY OF MEN
THE USES OF DIVERSITY
THE OUTLINE OF SANITY
THE FLYING INN
Each 3s. 6d. net.
A GLEAMING COHORT 2s. 6d. net.
WINE, WATER AND SONG
1s. 6d. net.

CLUTTON-BROCK (A.)
WHAT IS THE KINGDOM OF HEAVEN ?
ESSAYS ON ART
SHAKESPEARE'S HAMLET
Each 5s. net.
ESSAYS ON BOOKS 3s. 6d. net.
MORE ESSAYS ON BOOKS
ESSAYS ON LIFE
ESSAYS ON RELIGION
ESSAYS ON LITERATURE AND LIFE
MORE ESSAYS ON RELIGION
Each 6s. net.
SHELLEY, THE MAN AND THE POET
7s. 6d. net.

CRAWLEY (Ernest)
THE MYSTIC ROSE
Revised and Enlarged by THEODORE
BESTERMAN. 2 vols. £1 10s. net.
STUDIES OF SAVAGES AND SEX
Edited by THEODORE BESTERMAN.
10s. 6d. net.

DAVIS (H. W. C.)
EUROPE FROM 800–1789
8s. 6d. net.

DERWENT (Lord)
GOYA. Illustrated. 10s. 6d. net.

DUGDALE (E. T. S.)
GERMAN DIPLOMATIC DOCUMENTS,
1871–1914
Selected from the Documents published by the German Foreign
Office. In 4 vols. Vol. I, 1871–
90. Vol. II, 1891–8. Vol. III,
1898–1910.
Each £1 1s. net.

EDWARDES (Tickner)
THE LORE OF THE HONEY-BEE
Illustrated. 7s. 6d. and 3s. 6d. net.
BEEKEEPING FOR ALL
Illustrated. 3s. 6d. net.
THE BEE-MASTER OF WARRILOW
Illustrated. 7s. 6d. net.
BEE-KEEPING DO'S AND DONT'S
2s. 6d. net.

EINSTEIN (Albert)
RELATIVITY : THE SPECIAL AND
GENERAL THEORY 5s. net.
SIDELIGHTS ON RELATIVITY
3s. 6d. net.
THE MEANING OF RELATIVITY
5s. net.
THE BROWNIAN MOVEMENT
5s. net.

EISLER (Robert)
THE MESSIAH JESUS AND JOHN THE
BAPTIST : according to Flavius
Josephus' hitherto neglected
'Capture of Jerusalem' and
other Jewish and Christian
sources. Translated by A. HAG-
GERTY KRAPPE.
Illustrated. Demy 8vo. £2 2s. net

FIELD (G. C.)
MORAL THEORY 6s. net.
PLATO AND HIS CONTEMPORARIES
12s. 6d. net.

FYLEMAN (Rose)
FAIRIES AND CHIMNEYS
THE FAIRY GREEN
THE FAIRY FLUTE
THE RAINBOW CAT
EIGHT LITTLE PLAYS FOR CHILDREN
FORTY GOOD-NIGHT TALES
FAIRIES AND FRIENDS
THE ADVENTURE CLUB
FORTY GOOD-MORNING TALES
SEVEN LITTLE PLAYS FOR CHILDREN

FYLEMAN (Rose)—*continued*
TWENTY TEA-TIME TALES
Each 3s. 6d. net.
THE DOLLS' HOUSE
Illustrated by MARGARET TEMPEST.
5s. net.
GAY GO UP
Illustrated by DECIE MERWIN.
5s. net.
THE ROSE FYLEMAN FAIRY BOOK
Illustrated by HILDA MILLER.
10s. 6d. net.
A GARLAND OF ROSE'S : COLLECTED
POEMS
Illustrated by RENÉ BULL.
8s 6d. net.

GIBBON (Edward)
THE DECLINE AND FALL OF THE
ROMAN EMPIRE
With Notes, Appendixes and Maps,
by J. B. BURY. Illustrated. 7 vols.
Demy 8vo. 15s. net each volume.
Also, unillustrated. *Crown 8vo.*
7s. 6d. net each volume.

GLADSTONE (Mary) (Mrs. Drew)
HER DIARIES AND LETTERS
Illustrated. £1 1s. net.

GLOVER (T. R.)
VIRGIL
THE CONFLICT OF RELIGIONS IN THE
EARLY ROMAN EMPIRE
POETS AND PURITANS
Each 10s. 6d. net.
FROM PERICLES TO PHILIP
12s. 6d. net.

GRAHAM (Harry)
THE WORLD WE LAUGH IN : More
Deportmental Ditties
Illustrated by ' FISH '. *Seventh
Edition.* 5s. net.
STRAINED RELATIONS
Illustrated by H. STUART MENZIES
and HENDY 6s. net.
THE WORLD'S WORKERS
Illustrated by ' FOUGASSE '.
5s. net.
ADAM'S APPLES
Illustrated by JOHN REYNOLDS.
5s. net.

GRAHAME (Kenneth)
THE WIND IN THE WILLOWS
Nineteenth Edition. 7s. 6d. net.
Also illustrated by WYNDHAM
PAYNE. 7s. 6d. net.
Also unillustrated. 3s. 6d. net.
See also Milne (A. A.)

HADFIELD (J. A.)
PSYCHOLOGY AND MORALS
Eighth Edition. Crown 8vo. 6s. net.

HALL (H. R.)
THE ANCIENT HISTORY OF THE
NEAR EAST
Illustrated. £1 1s. net.
THE CIVILIZATION OF GREECE IN
THE BRONZE AGE
Illustrated. £1 10s. net.
A SEASON'S WORK AT UR OF THE
CHALDEES. Illustrated. £1 5s. net.

HERBERT (A. P.)
HONEYBUBBLE & CO. 6s. net.
MISLEADING CASES IN THE COMMON
LAW. With an Introduction by
LORD HEWART. 5s. net.
MORE MISLEADING CASES. 5s. net
LIGHT ARTICLES ONLY
Illustrated by GEORGE MORROW.
6s. net.
WISDOM FOR THE WISE
Illustrated by GEORGE MORROW.
5s. net.
THE WHEREFORE AND THE WHY
Illustrated by GEORGE MORROW.
3s. 6d. net.
THE BOMBER GIPSY 3s. 6d. net.
THE SECRET BATTLE 3s. 6d. net.

HOLDSWORTH (Sir W. S.)
A HISTORY OF ENGLISH LAW
Nine Volumes. £1 5s. net each.

HUDSON (W. H.)
A SHEPHERD'S LIFE
Illustrated. 10s. 6d. net.
Also unillustrated. 3s. 6d. net.

HUTTON (Edward)
CITIES OF SICILY
Illustrated. 10s. 6d. net.
MILAN AND LOMBARDY
THE CITIES OF ROMAGNA AND THE
MARCHES
SIENA AND SOUTHERN TUSCANY
NAPLES AND SOUTHERN ITALY
Illustrated. *Each 8s. 6d. net.*
A WAYFARER IN UNKNOWN TUS-
CANY
THE CITIES OF SPAIN
THE CITIES OF UMBRIA
COUNTRY WALKS ABOUT FLORENCE
ROME
FLORENCE AND NORTHERN TUSCANY
VENICE AND VENETIA
Illustrated. Each 7s. 6d. net.

**INGE (W. R.), D.D., Dean of St.
Paul's**
CHRISTIAN MYSTICISM
(The Bampton Lectures of 1899).
Sixth Edition. 7s. 6d. net.

KIPLING (Rudyard)
BARRACK-ROOM BALLADS
255th *Thousand.*
THE SEVEN SEAS
186th *Thousand.*
THE FIVE NATIONS
143rd *Thousand.*
DEPARTMENTAL DITTIES
116th *Thousand.*
THE YEARS BETWEEN
95th *Thousand.*
Four Editions of these famous
volumes of poems are now pub-
lished, viz. :—
Crown 8vo. Buckram, 7s. 6d. *net.*
Fcap. 8vo.   *Cloth,* 6s. *net.*
Leather   7s. 6d. *net.*
Service Edition. Two volumes
each book. *Square Fcap. 8vo.*
   3s. *net each volume.*
TWENTY POEMS FROM RUDYARD
KIPLING
482nd *Thousand.*   1s. *net.*
A CHOICE OF SONGS
Second Edition.   2s. *net.*

LAMB (Charles and Mary)
THE COMPLETE WORKS
Edited by E. V. LUCAS. Six
Volumes. With Frontispieces.
   6s. *net each.*
SELECTED LETTERS
Edited by G. T. CLAPTON.
   3s. 6d. *net.*
THE CHARLES LAMB DAY BOOK
Compiled by E. V. LUCAS.
   6s. *net.*

LANKESTER (Sir Ray)
SCIENCE FROM AN EASY CHAIR
SCIENCE FROM AN EASY CHAIR:
Second Series
DIVERSIONS OF A NATURALIST
GREAT AND SMALL THINGS
Illustrated. *Each* 7s. 6d. *net.*
SECRETS OF EARTH AND SEA
Illustrated. 8s. 6d. *net.*

LINDRUM (Walter)
BILLIARDS.   Illustrated. 6s. *net.*

LODGE (Sir Oliver)
MAN AND THE UNIVERSE
   7s. 6d. *net* and 3s. 6d. *net.*
THE SURVIVAL OF MAN
   7s. 6d. *net.*
RAYMOND   10s. 6d. *net.*
RAYMOND REVISED   6s. *net.*
MODERN PROBLEMS   3s. 6d. *net.*
REASON AND BELIEF   3s. 6d. *net.*
THE SUBSTANCE OF FAITH
   2s. *net.*

RELATIVITY   1s. *net.*
CONVICTION OF SURVIVAL   2s. *net.*

LUCAS (E. V.)
THE LIFE OF CHARLES LAMB
2 Vols.   £1 1s. *net.*
THE COLVINS AND THEIR FRIENDS
   £1 1s. *net.*
VERMEER THE MAGICAL   5s. *net.*
A WANDERER IN ROME
A WANDERER IN HOLLAND
A WANDERER IN LONDON
LONDON REVISITED (Revised)
A WANDERER IN PARIS
A WANDERER IN FLORENCE
A WANDERER IN VENICE
   Each 10s. 6d. *net.*
A WANDERER AMONG PICTURES
   8s. 6d. *net.*
E. V. LUCAS'S LONDON   £1 *net.*
INTRODUCING LONDON
INTRODUCING PARIS
   Each 2s. 6d. *net.*
THE OPEN ROAD   6s. *net.*
Also, illustrated by CLAUDE A.
SHEPPERSON, A.R.W.S.
   10s. 6d. *net.*
Also, India Paper.
   Leather, 7s. 6d. *net.*
THE JOY OF LIFE
6s. *net. Leather Edition,* 7s. 6d. *net.*
Also, India Paper.
   Leather, 7s. 6d. *net.*
THE GENTLEST ART   6s. 6d. *net.*
And THE SECOND POST   6s. *net.*
Also together in one volume.
   7s. 6d. *net.*
FIRESIDE AND SUNSHINE
CHARACTER AND COMEDY
GOOD COMPANY
ONE DAY AND ANOTHER
OLD LAMPS FOR NEW
LOITERER'S HARVEST
LUCK OF THE YEAR
EVENTS AND EMBROIDERIES
A FRONDED ISLE
A ROVER I WOULD BE
GIVING AND RECEIVING
HER INFINITE VARIETY
ENCOUNTERS AND DIVERSIONS
   Each 3s. 6d. *net.*
CLOUD AND SILVER
A BOSWELL OF BAGHDAD
'TWIXT EAGLE AND DOVE
THE PHANTOM JOURNAL
ZIGZAGS IN FRANCE
TURNING THINGS OVER
TRAVELLER'S LUCK
   Each 6s. *net.*

LUCAS (E. V.)—*continued*
ROVING EAST AND ROVING WEST
5s. net.
Mr. Punch's COUNTY SONGS
Illustrated by E. H. SHEPARD.
10s. 6d. net.
' THE MORE I SEE OF MEN . . .'
OUT OF A CLEAR SKY
IF DOGS COULD WRITE
' . . . AND SUCH SMALL DEER '
Each 3s. 6d. net.
THE PEKINESE NATIONAL ANTHEM
Illustrated by PERSIS KIRMSE.
1s. net.
See also **Lamb (Charles).**

LYND (Robert)
IT'S A FINE WORLD   5s. net.
THE GREEN MAN
THE PLEASURES OF IGNORANCE
THE GOLDFISH
THE LITTLE ANGEL
THE BLUE LION
THE PEAL OF BELLS
THE MONEY-BOX
THE ORANGE TREE
Each 3s. 6d. net.

McDOUGALL (William)
AN INTRODUCTION TO SOCIAL
PSYCHOLOGY   10s. 6d. net.
NATIONAL WELFARE AND NATIONAL
DECAY   6s. net.
AN OUTLINE OF PSYCHOLOGY
10s. 6d. net.
AN OUTLINE OF ABNORMAL PSYCHO-
LOGY   15s. net.
BODY AND MIND   12s. 6d. net.
CHARACTER AND THE CONDUCT OF
LIFE   10s. 6d. net.
MODERN MATERIALISM AND EMERG-
ENT EVOLUTION   7s. 6d. net.
ETHICS AND SOME MODERN WORLD
PROBLEMS   7s. 6d. net.

MALLET (Sir C. E.)
A HISTORY OF THE UNIVERSITY OF
OXFORD
In 3 vols.   Each £1 1s. net.

MAETERLINCK (Maurice)
THE BLUE BIRD   6s. net.
Also, illustrated by F. CAYLEY
ROBINSON.   10s. 6d. net.
OUR ETERNITY   6s. net.
THE UNKNOWN GUEST   6s. net.
POEMS   5s. net.
THE WRACK OF THE STORM
6s. net.
THE BURGOMASTER OF STILEMONDE
5s. net.
THE BETROTHAL   6s. net.

MOUNTAIN PATHS   6s. net.
THE GREAT SECRET   7s. 6d. net.
THE CLOUD THAT LIFTED and THE
POWER OF THE DEAD
7s. 6d. net.
MARY MAGDALENE   2s. net.

MARLOWE (Christopher)
THE WORKS. In 6 volumes.
General Editor, R. H. Case.
THE LIFE OF MARLOWE, by C. F.
TUCKER BROOKE, and DIDO.
Edited by the Same. 8s. 6d. net.
TAMBURLAINE, I AND II. Edited by
U. M. Ellis-Fermor.
10s. 6d. net.

MASEFIELD (John)
ON THE SPANISH MAIN
8s. 6d. net.
A SAILOR'S GARLAND 3s. 6d. net.
SEA LIFE IN NELSON'S TIME
7s. 6d. net.

METHUEN (Sir A.)
AN ANTHOLOGY OF MODERN VERSE
195th Thousand.
SHAKESPEARE TO HARDY: An
Anthology of English Lyrics
26th Thousand.
Each, Cloth, 6s. net.
Leather, 7s. 6d. net.

MILNE (A. A.)
BY WAY OF INTRODUCTION
6s. net.
TOAD OF TOAD HALL
A Play founded on Kenneth
Grahame's ' The Wind in the
Willows.'   5s. net.
THOSE WERE THE DAYS: Collected
Stories   7s. 6d. net.
NOT THAT IT MATTERS
IF I MAY
THE SUNNY SIDE
THE RED HOUSE MYSTERY
ONCE A WEEK
THE HOLIDAY ROUND
THE DAY'S PLAY
MR. PIM PASSES BY
Each 3s. 6d. net.
WHEN WE WERE VERY YOUNG
Twentieth Edition. 206th Thousand.
WINNIE-THE-POOH
Tenth Edition. 118th Thousand.
NOW WE ARE SIX
Fifth Edition. 119th Thousand.
THE HOUSE AT POOH CORNER
Third Edition. 105th Thousand.
Each illustrated by E. H. SHEPARD.
7s. 6d. net.
Leather, 10s. 6d net.

MILNE (A. A.)—*continued*

THE CHRISTOPHER ROBIN STORY BOOK. *Second Edition.*
Illustrated by E. H. SHEPARD.
5s. net.
THE CHRISTOPHER ROBIN BIRTHDAY BOOK
Illustrated by E. H. SHEPARD.
3s. 6d. net.

MILNE (A. A.) and FRASER-SIMSON (H.)

FOURTEEN SONGS FROM 'WHEN WE WERE VERY YOUNG'
Twelfth Edition. 7s. 6d. net.
TEDDY BEAR AND OTHER SONGS FROM 'WHEN WE WERE VERY YOUNG' 7s. 6d. net.
THE KING'S BREAKFAST
Third Edition. 3s. 6d. net.
SONGS FROM 'NOW WE ARE SIX'
Second Edition. 7s. 6d. net.
MORE 'VERY YOUNG' SONGS
7s. 6d. net.
THE HUMS OF POOH 7s. 6d. net.
Words by A. A. MILNE.
Music by H. FRASER-SIMSON.
Decorations by E. H. SHEPARD.

MORTON (H. V.)

THE HEART OF LONDON 3s. 6d. net.
Also with Scissor Cuts by L. HUMMEL. 7s. 6d. net.
THE SPELL OF LONDON
THE NIGHTS OF LONDON
Each 3s. 6d. net.
IN SEARCH OF ENGLAND
THE CALL OF ENGLAND
IN SEARCH OF SCOTLAND
IN SEARCH OF IRELAND
Each illustrated. 7s. 6d. net.
THE SOUL OF SCOTLAND 1s. net.

NEUBURGER (Albert)

THE TECHNICAL ARTS AND SCIENCES OF THE ANCIENTS.
Translated by H. L. BROSE.
Illustrated. £2 2s. net.

OMAN (Sir Charles)

A HISTORY OF THE ART OF WAR IN THE MIDDLE AGES, A.D. 378–1485
2 vols. Illustrated. £1 16s. net.
STUDIES IN THE NAPOLEONIC WARS
8s. 6d. net.

PERRY (W. J.)

THE ORIGIN OF MAGIC AND RELIGION
THE GROWTH OF CIVILIZATION
Each 6s. net.
THE CHILDREN OF THE SUN
£1 1s. net.

PETRIE (Sir Flinders)

A HISTORY OF EGYPT
In 6 Volumes.
Vol. I. FROM THE 1ST TO THE XVITH DYNASTY.
Eleventh Edition, Revised.
12s. net.
Vol. II. THE XVIITH AND XVIIITH DYNASTIES.
Seventh Edition, Revised. 9s. net.
Vol. III. XIXTH TO XXXTH DYNASTIES
Third Edition. 12s. net.
Vol. IV. EGYPT UNDER THE PTOLEMAIC DYNASTY
By EDWYN BEVAN. 15s. net.
Vol. V. EGYPT UNDER ROMAN RULE
By J. G. MILNE.
Third Edition, Revised. 12s. net.
Vol. VI. EGYPT IN THE MIDDLE AGES
By STANLEY LANE POOLE.
Fourth Edition. 10s. net.

PONSONBY OF SHULBREDE (Lord)

ENGLISH DIARIES £1 1s. net.
MORE ENGLISH DIARIES
12s. 6d. net.
SCOTTISH AND IRISH DIARIES
10s. 6d. net.

RUTTER (Frank)

EL GRECO
Illustrated. £1 16s. net.

STEVENSON (R. L.)

THE LETTERS
Edited by Sir SIDNEY COLVIN. 4 Vols. *Each 6s. net.*

SURTEES (R. S.)

HANDLEY CROSS
MR. SPONGE'S SPORTING TOUR
ASK MAMMA
MR. FACEY ROMFORD'S HOUNDS
PLAIN OR RINGLETS?
HILLINGDON HALL
Each illustrated. 7s. 6d. net.
JORROCKS'S JAUNTS AND JOLLITIES
HAWBUCK GRANGE
Each illustrated. 6s. net.

TAYLOR (A. E.)

PLATO : THE MAN AND HIS WORK
£1 1s. net.
PLATO : TIMÆUS AND CRITIAS
6s. net.
ELEMENTS OF METAPHYSICS
12s. 6d. net.

TILDEN (William T.)
THE ART OF LAWN TENNIS
Revised Edition
SINGLES AND DOUBLES
Each illustrated. *6s. net.*
THE COMMON SENSE OF LAWN
TENNIS
MATCH PLAY AND THE SPIN OF THE
BALL
Each illustrated. *5s. net.*

TILESTON (Mary W.)
DAILY STRENGTH FOR DAILY NEEDS
Thirty-fourth Edition. 3s. 6d. net.
India Paper. *Leather, 6s. net.*

TRAPP (Oswald Graf)
THE ARMOURY OF THE CASTLE OF
CHURBURG
Translated by J. G. MANN.
Richly illustrated.
Limited to 400 copies.
£4 14s. 6d. net.

UNDERHILL (Evelyn)
MYSTICISM. *Revised Edition.* 15*s. net.*
THE LIFE OF THE SPIRIT AND THE
LIFE OF TO-DAY *7s. 6d. net.*
MAN AND THE SUPERNATURAL
7s. 6d. net.
CONCERNING THE INNER LIFE
2s. net.
THE HOUSE OF THE SOUL *2s. net.*

VARDON (Harry)
HOW TO PLAY GOLF
Illustrated. *Nineteenth Edition.*
5s. net.

WAND (J. W. C.)
THE DEVELOPMENT OF SACRA-
MENTALISM *6s. net,*
A HISTORY OF THE MODERN CHURCH
8s. 6d. net.

WILDE (Oscar)
THE WORKS
In 16 Vols. *Each 6s. 6d. net.*
I. LORD ARTHUR SAVILE'S CRIME
AND THE PORTRAIT OF MR. W. H.
II. THE DUCHESS OF PADUA
III. POEMS
IV. LADY WINDERMERE'S FAN
V. A WOMAN OF NO IMPORTANCE
VI. AN IDEAL HUSBAND
VII. THE IMPORTANCE OF BEING
EARNEST
VIII. A HOUSE OF POMEGRANATES
IX. INTENTIONS
X. DE PROFUNDIS AND PRISON
LETTERS
XI. ESSAYS
XII. SALOME, A FLORENTINE
TRAGEDY, and LA SAINTE
COURTISANE
XIV. SELECTED PROSE OF OSCAR
WILDE
XV. ART AND DECORATION
XVI. FOR LOVE OF THE KING
5s. net.
XVII. VERA, OR THE NIHILISTS

WILLIAMSON (G. C.)
THE BOOK OF FAMILLE ROSE
Richly Illustrated. *£8 8s. net.*

Methuen & Co. Ltd., 36 Essex Street, London, W.C.2

930